D1612675

THE VICTORIA HISTORY OF THE COUNTIES OF ENGLAND

A HISTORY OF CAMBRIDGESHIRE AND THE ISLE OF ELY

VOLUME VI

THE VICTORIA HISTORY OF THE COUNTIES OF ENGLAND

EDITED BY C. R. ELRINGTON

THE UNIVERSITY OF LONDON
INSTITUTE OF
HISTORICAL RESEARCH

Oxford University Press

OXFORD LONDON GLASGOW
NEW YORK TORONTO MELBOURNE WELLINGTON
IBADAN NAIROBI DAR ES SALAAM LUSAKA CAPE TOWN
KUALA LUMPUR SINGAPORE JAKARTA HONG KONG TOKYO
DELHI BOMBAY CALCUTTA MADRAS KARACHI

ISBN 0 19 722746 5

Printed in Great Britain
at the University Press, Oxford
by Vivian Ridler
Printer to the University

INSCRIBED TO THE

MEMORY OF HER LATE MAJESTY

QUEEN VICTORIA

WHO GRACIOUSLY GAVE THE TITLE TO

AND ACCEPTED THE DEDICATION

OF THIS HISTORY

Whittlesford Church from the south

A HISTORY OF THE COUNTY OF CAMBRIDGE AND THE ISLE OF ELY

EDITED BY A. P. M. WRIGHT

VOLUME VI

PUBLISHED FOR
THE INSTITUTE OF HISTORICAL RESEARCH
BY
OXFORD UNIVERSITY PRESS
1978

Distributed by Oxford University Press until 1 January 1981
thereafter by Dawsons of Pall Mall

CONTENTS OF VOLUME SIX

LIST OF ILLUSTRATIONS

Grateful acknowledgement is made to the Cambridge Antiquarian Society, Mrs. R. Taylor, and Mr. Marcus Marsh for permission to reproduce photographs, prints, and drawings in their possession; and to the Royal Commission on Historical Monuments (England), Country Life Ltd., the Royal Institute of British Architects, the Courtauld Institute of Art, CIBA-GEIGY (U.K.) Ltd., and Tube Investments Research Ltd. for permission to reproduce photographs which are their copyright. Photographs dated 1975 and 1977 are by A. P. Baggs.

LIST OF ILLUSTRATIONS

LIST OF MAPS AND PLANS

The maps and plans, except for Baker's map and the plans of churches, were drawn by K. J. Wass from drafts by Susan M. Keeling and A. P. M. Wright; those of the hundreds and of the parishes in Radfield hundred are based on the Ordnance Survey with the sanction of the Controller of H.M. Stationery Office, Crown Copyright reserved. The plans of Linton and Sawston churches were drawn by A. P. Baggs and are based on surveys by the Royal Commission on Historical Monuments (England).

EDITORIAL NOTE

VOLUME SIX of the Cambridgeshire History has been edited and almost entirely written by the central staff of the *Victoria History*. Help given to the writers by many people and institutions is gratefully acknowledged and is mostly recorded in appropriate footnotes, but it is necessary to mention here those whose assistance was not confined to particular passages: the Librarian, Mr. E. B. Ceadel, and the staff of the University Library, Cambridge; the Archivist, Mr. J. M. P. Farrar, and the staff of the Cambridgeshire Record Office; the Ely Diocesan Archivist, Mrs. A. E. B. Owen; the Royal Commission on Historical Monuments (England); the Master of the Charterhouse; and, among college librarians and bursars who gave access to college records, those of Gonville and Caius, Jesus, King's, Pembroke, Peterhouse, Queens', St. John's, and Trinity Colleges, Cambridge.

The *General Introduction* to the *History* (1970) outlines the structure and aims of the series as a whole. The names of counties by which places outside Cambridgeshire are identified in the text below are those of the counties as existing on 31 March 1974.

LIST OF CLASSES OF DOCUMENTS IN THE PUBLIC RECORD OFFICE

USED IN THIS VOLUME WITH THEIR CLASS NUMBERS

Chancery	
	Proceedings
C 1	Early
C 2	Series I
C 3	Series II
	Six Clerks Series
C 5	Bridges
C 6	Collins
C 47	Miscellanea
C 54	Close Rolls
C 60	Fine Rolls
C 66	Patent Rolls
C 78	Decree Rolls
C 93	Proceedings of Commissioners for Charitable Uses, Inquisitions, and Decrees
	Masters' Exhibits
C 110	Horne
C 114	Unknown
C 131	Extents for Debts
	Inquisitions post mortem
C 132	Series I, Hen. III
C 133	Edw. I
C 134	Edw. II
C 135	Edw. III
C 136	Ric. II
C 137	Hen. IV
C 138	Hen. V
C 139	Hen. VI
C 140	Edw. IV and V
C 141	Ric. III
C 142	Series II
C 143	Inquisitions ad quod damnum
C 145	Miscellaneous Inquisitions
C 146	Ancient Deeds, Series C
	Chancery Files
C 258	Tower Series, Cercioriari
C 260	Tower and Rolls Chapel, Recorda
Court of Common Pleas	
	Feet of Fines
C.P. 25(1)	Series I
C.P. 25(2)	Series II
C.P. 40	De Banco Rolls
C.P. 43	Recovery Rolls
Duchy of Lancaster	
D.L. 30	Court Rolls
Exchequer, Treasury of the Receipt	
	Ancient Deeds
E 40	Series A
E 42	Series AS
Exchequer, King's Remembrancer	
E 112	Bills, Answers, etc.
E 117	Church Goods
E 126	Decrees and Orders, Entry Books, Series IV
E 134	Depositions taken by Commission
E 150	Inquisitions post mortem, Series II
E 164	Miscellaneous Books, Series I
E 178	Special Commissions of Inquiry
E 179	Subsidy Rolls, etc.
Exchequer, Augmentation Office	
E 310	Particulars for Leases
E 315	Miscellaneous Books
E 318	Particulars for Grants
E 321	Proceedings of Court of Augmentations
Exchequer, Pipe Office	
E 358	Enrolled Accounts, Miscellaneous Accounts
Ministry of Education	
Ed. 7	Public Elementary Schools, Preliminary Statements
Ed. 49	Endowment Files, Elementary Education
Home Office	
H.O. 67	Acreage Returns
	Various, Censuses
H.O. 107	Population Returns
H.O. 129	Ecclesiastical Returns
Inland Revenue	
I.R. 18	Tithe Files
Justices Itinerant, Assize and Gaol Delivery Justices, etc.	
J.I. 1	Eyre Rolls, Assize Rolls, etc.
Court of King's Bench (Crown Side)	
K.B. 26	Curia Regis Rolls
K.B. 27	Coram Rege Rolls
Exchequer, Office of the Auditors of Land Revenue	
L.R. 2	Miscellaneous Books
Probate	
Prob. 6	Act Books: Administrations
Prob. 11	Registered Copies of Wills proved in P.C.C.
General Register Office	
R.G. 9	Census Returns, 1861
R.G. 10	Census Returns, 1871
Court of Requests	
Req. 2	Proceedings
Special Collections	
S.C. 2	Court Rolls
S.C. 5	Hundred Rolls
S.C. 6	Ministers' Accounts
	Ancient Petitions
S.C. 8	Rentals and Surveys
S.C. 11	Rolls
State Paper Office	
S.P. 23	State Papers Domestic, Interregnum, Committee for Compounding with Delinquents
Court of Star Chamber	
	Proceedings
Sta. Cha. 2	Hen. VIII
Sta. Cha. 8	Jas. I
War Office	
W.O. 30	Miscellanea
Court of Wards and Liveries	
Wards 7	Inquisitions post mortem
Wards 9	Miscellaneous Books

NOTE ON ABBREVIATIONS

Among the abbreviations and short titles used the following may require elucidation:

Assizes at Camb. 1260	W. M. Palmer, *The Assizes held at Cambridge, A.D. 1260* (Linton, 1930)
Black, *Cambs. Educ. Rec.*	*Guide to Education Records in the County Record Office, Cambridge*, comp. A. Black (Camb. 1972)
Blomefield, *Collect. Cantab.*	F. Blomefield, *Collectanea Cantabrigiensia* (Norwich, 1750)
Blomefield, *Norf.*	F. Blomefield and C. Parkin, *An Essay towards a Topographical History of the County of Norfolk* (11 vols., Lond. 1805–10)
C.A.S.	Cambridge Antiquarian Society, Publications (including 8vo series, 4to series, and 4to new series)
C.R.O.	Cambridgeshire Record Office (including Quarter Sessions records, references to which begin with the letter Q)
C.U.L.	Cambridge University Library
Caius Coll. Libr.	Gonville and Caius College, Cambridge, Library
Caius Coll. Mun.	Gonville and Caius College, Cambridge, Muniments
Camb. Chron.	*Cambridge Chronicle* (1744–1934)
Camb. Ind. Press	*Cambridge Independent Press* (1807–1934), and (from 1934) *Cambridge Independent Press and Chronicle*
Camb. Region (1938)	*The Cambridge Region*, ed. H. C. Darby (Camb. 1938)
Camb. Region, 1965	*The Cambridge Region, 1965*, ed. J. A. Steers (Camb. 1965), published for the British Association for the Advancement of Science
Camb. Univ. Doc. (1852)	*Documents relating to the University and Colleges of Cambridge* (3 vols., H.M.S.O. 1852)
Cambs. Agric. Returns, 1905	Board of Agriculture Returns for Cambridgeshire 1905, copy *penes V.C.H.*
Cambs. Ch. Goods, temp. Edw. VI	*Inventories of Cambridgeshire Church Goods, temp. Edward VI*, ed. J. J. Muskett (reprinted from *East Anglian*, N.S. vols. vi–x [1895–1904])
Cambs. Episc. Visit. 1638–65, ed. Palmer	W. M. Palmer, *Episcopal Visitation Returns for Cambridgeshire, 1638–65* (Camb. 1930)
Cambs. Lay Subsidy, 1327	*Cambridgeshire and Isle of Ely, Lay Subsidy for the Year 1327*, ed. C. H. Evelyn White (reprinted from *East Anglian*, N.S. vols. x–xii [1903–8])
Cambs. Local Hist. Counc. Bull.	*Cambridgeshire Local History Council, Bulletin*
Cambs. Village Doc.	*Documents relating to Cambridgeshire Villages*, ed. W. M. Palmer and H. W. Saunders, parts i–vi (Camb. n.d.)
Cassey's Dir. Cambs.	*History, Topography and Directory of Buckinghamshire, Cambridgeshire and Hertfordshire*, publ. R. Cassey (Lond. [1864])
Char. Digest Cambs. 1863–4	*General Digest of Endowed Charities*, H.C. 433 (1867–8), lii (II)
Char. Don.	*Abstract of Returns relative to Charitable Donations for the Benefit of Poor Persons*, H.C. 511 (1816), xvi
Charterho. Mun.	Muniments of the Charterhouse, Charterhouse Square, London
Church School Inquiry, 1846–7	*Returns to the General Inquiry made by the National Society into . . . Schools . . ., 1846–7 . . .* (Lond. 1849)
Clare Coll. Mun.	Clare College, Cambridge, Muniments
Compton Census	Bishop Compton's Census, 1676, William Salt Library, Stafford
Copinger, *Suffolk Manors*	W. A. Copinger, *The Manors of Suffolk: notes on their history and devolution* (7 vols., Lond. 1905–11)
E.D.R.	*Ely Diocesan Remembrancer* (1886–1916)
E. Suff. R.O.	East Suffolk Record Office, Ipswich
Eccl. Top. Eng.	J. H. Parker, *The Ecclesiastical and Architectural Topography of England* (7 vols., Oxf. and Lond. 1848–55)
Educ. Enquiry Abstract	*Education Enquiry Abstract*, H.C. 62 (1835), xli
Educ. of Poor Digest	*Digest of Returns to the Select Committee on Education of the Poor*, H.C. 224 (1819), ix (I)
Essex R.O.	Essex Record Office, Chelmsford
Farrer, *Feud. Cambs.*	W. Farrer, *Feudal Cambridgeshire* (Camb. 1920)

NOTE ON ABBREVIATIONS

Fox, *Arch. Camb Region*	C. F. Fox, *Archaeology of the Cambridge Region* (Camb. 1923)
Gardner's Dir. Cambs. (1851)	*History, Gazeteer, and Directory of Cambridgeshire*, publ. Rob. Gardner (Peterborough, 1851)
Gibbons, *Ely Episc. Rec.*	A. Gibbons, *Ely Episcopal Records* (Lincoln, 1891)
Gooch, *Agric. of Cambs.*	W. Gooch, *General View of the Agriculture of the County of Cambridge* (Bd. of Agric., Lond. 1813)
H.L.R.O.	House of Lords Record Office
Hampson, *Poverty in Cambs.*	E. M. Hampson, *The Treatment of Poverty in Cambridgeshire, 1597–1834* (Camb. 1934)
Jesus Coll. Mun.	Jesus College, Cambridge, Muniments
King's Coll. Mun.	King's College, Cambridge, Muniments
Liber de Bernewelle	*Liber Memorandorum Ecclesie de Bernewelle*, ed. J. W. Clark (Camb. 1907)
Lysons, *Cambs.*	D. and S. Lysons, *Magna Britannia*, vol. ii, part i: *Cambridgeshire* (Lond. 1808)
M.H.L.G. List	Ministry of Housing and Local Government: Provisional List of Buildings of Architectural or Historic Interest
Mon. Inscr. Cambs.	*Monumental Inscriptions and Coats of Arms from Cambridgeshire*, ed. W. M. Palmer (Camb. 1932)
Morant, *Essex*	P. Morant, *The History and Antiquities of the County of Essex* (2 vols., Lond. 1768)
P.N. Cambs. (E.P.N.S.)	P. H. Reaney, *The Place-Names of Cambridgeshire and the Isle of Ely* (English Place-Name Society, vol. xix, Camb. 1943)
Palmer, *Cambs. in 16th cent.*	W. M. Palmer, *Cambridgeshire in the 16th Century* (a fragment) (Camb. 1935)
Palmer, *Wm. Cole*	W. M. Palmer, *William Cole of Milton* (Camb. 1935)
Pemb. Coll. Mun.	Pembroke College, Cambridge, Muniments
Peterhouse Mun.	Peterhouse, Cambridge, Muniments
Pevsner, *Cambs.*	N. Pevsner, *The Buildings of England: Cambridgeshire* (2nd edn., Lond. 1970)
Poor Law Abstract, 1804	*Abstract of Returns Relative to the Expense and Maintenance of the Poor* (printed by order of the House of Commons, 1804)
Poor Law Abstract, 1818	*Abstract of Returns to Orders of the House of Commons Relative to Assessments for Relief of the Poor*, H.C. 82 (1818), xix
Poor Law Com. 1st Rep.	*First Report of the Poor Law Commission*, H.C. 500 (1835), xxxv
Poor Rate Returns, 1816–21; 1822–4; 1825–9; 1830–4	*Poor Rate Returns, 1816–21*, H.C. 556 App. (1822), v; *1822–4*, H.C. 334, Suppl. App. (1825), iv; *1825–9*, H.C. 83 (1830–1), xi; *1830–4*, H.C. 444 (1835), xlvii
Porter, *Cambs. Customs*	E. Porter, *Cambridgeshire Customs and Folklore* (Lond. 1969)
Proc. C.A.S.	*Proceedings of the Cambridge Antiquarian Society* (from 1859) (including vols. i–vi (1859–88), styled *Cambridge Antiquarian Communications*)
Queens' Coll. Mun.	Queens' College, Cambridge, Muniments, deposited in Cambridge University Library
31st Rep. Com. Char.	*Thirty-first Report of the Commissioners Appointed to Enquire Concerning Charities* (the Brougham Commission), H.C. 103 (1837–8), xxiv
Rep. Com. Eccl. Revenues	*Report of the Commissioners Appointed to Inquire into the Ecclesiastical Revenues of England and Wales* [67], H.C. (1835), xxii
1st Rep. Com. Employment in Agric.	*First Report of the Commissioners on the Employment of Children, Young Persons, and Women in Agriculture* [4068], H.C. (1867–8), xvii
St. John's Mun.	St. John's College, Cambridge, Muniments
Teversham, *Hist. Sawston*	T. F. Teversham, *A History of the Village of Sawston* (2 vols., Sawston, 1942–7)
Trans. C.H.A.S.	*Transactions of the Cambridgeshire and Huntingdonshire Archaeological Society* (1900–50)
Trin. Coll. Mun.	Trinity College, Cambridge, Muniments
Vancouver, *Agric. in Cambs.*	C. Vancouver, *General View of the Agriculture in the County of Cambridge* (Bd. of Agric., Lond. 1794)
V.C.H. Cambs.	*Victoria History of the County of Cambridge*

CHILFORD HUNDRED

CHILFORD hundred occupies the south-east corner of Cambridgeshire, stretching 12 miles along the valley of the Bourne, between the Suffolk border and the river Cam or Granta. All its constituent parts except West Wickham lie south of Wool Street. That road marks a prehistoric trackway between Haverhill (Suff.) and Cambridge, of which the part west of Horseheath was overlaid by a Roman road.[1] It was known locally in the 13th century as Wulves Street and to 19th-century antiquaries as the Via Devana.[2] In 1066 the area, assessed at 54½ hides, was divided among eleven vills, Little Abington, Hildersham, Barham, Camps, Horseheath, and West Wickham each being assessed at 5 hides, Pampisford at 5¼, Great Abington at 6, Great and Little Linton together at 6¼, and Babraham at seven.[3] The vills underwent some rearrangement to form the modern parishes. While Great and Little Abington, separated by the river Bourne and each with its own church, remained distinct and Hildersham, despite an agrarian and manorial division along the river, remained a single parish, the vills or manors of Great Linton, Little Linton, and Barham, having after 1300 only one place of worship, were gradually combined to make Linton parish, although Barham remained partially distinct until the 18th century. Further east the area called in 1086 Camps was from the 12th century divided between Great and Little, later Castle and Shudy, Camps. Olmstead, at the south-eastern tip of Castle Camps, although lying until after 1835 ecclesiastically in Helions Bumpstead (Essex), remained attached to Castle Camps for tenurial and civil purposes. Bartlow, however, at the north-western corner of Castle Camps, was from the 12th century a distinct though small parish. Its field-land south of the river, called Bartlow End, was reckoned to belong to Essex. Nosterfield hamlet, connected by tenure and jurisdiction with Castle Camps, was after the 13th century incorporated into Shudy Camps parish. The hamlet of Streetly and the ancient manor of Enhale were included in West Wickham.

The hundred court probably met originally at the centrally placed 'Cildeford', just downstream from Linton village. By 1279 it had given its name to a neighbouring field.[4] Chilford hundred remained throughout the Middle Ages in the king's hands.[5] In the late 13th century it was being farmed and administered with Whittlesford hundred by a single bailiff.[6] The lords of at least one manor in each vill, and of three at Babraham, claimed to hold view of frankpledge, usually with the assize of bread and of ale. Barham had a separate view, and the bishop of Ely had the view at Streetly. The men of Nosterfield and Olmstead owed suit to courts attached to Castle Camps manor, whose lord also had the view at Bartlow.[7] The fees held of the honor of Richmond still sent suitors in the early 14th century to a general tourn for the honor's dependencies throughout the hundred.[8] In the 17th century Chilford hundred was linked administratively with Radfield and Whittlesford hundreds.[9]

The hundred lies mainly upon the chalk, overlaid on the higher ground by glacial clays,[10] once heavily wooded. In the western part, along the Bourne valley, men have lived since the Middle Ages in nucleated villages close to the river, with village streets

1 *Proc. C.A.S.* lvi–lvii. 42–60.
2 *P.N. Cambs.* (E.P.N.S.), 30–2.
3 *V.C.H. Cambs.* i. 408–10.
4 *P.N. Cambs.* (E.P.N.S.), 99, 110; cf. W. M. Palmer, *Antiquities of Linton* (1913), 2.
5 e.g. *Feud. Aids*, i. 154.
6 e.g. J.I. 1/83 rot. 37; J.I. 1/86 rot. 56.
7 *Rot. Hund.* (Rec. Com.), i. 52; ii. 413–30, 568; *Plac. de Quo Warr.* (Rec. Com.), 99, 104–7.
8 S.C. 2/155/71 mm. 1–2.
9 e.g. *Cal. S.P. Dom.* 1634–5, p. 442.
10 Geol. Surv. Map 1", drift, sheet 205 (1932 edn.).

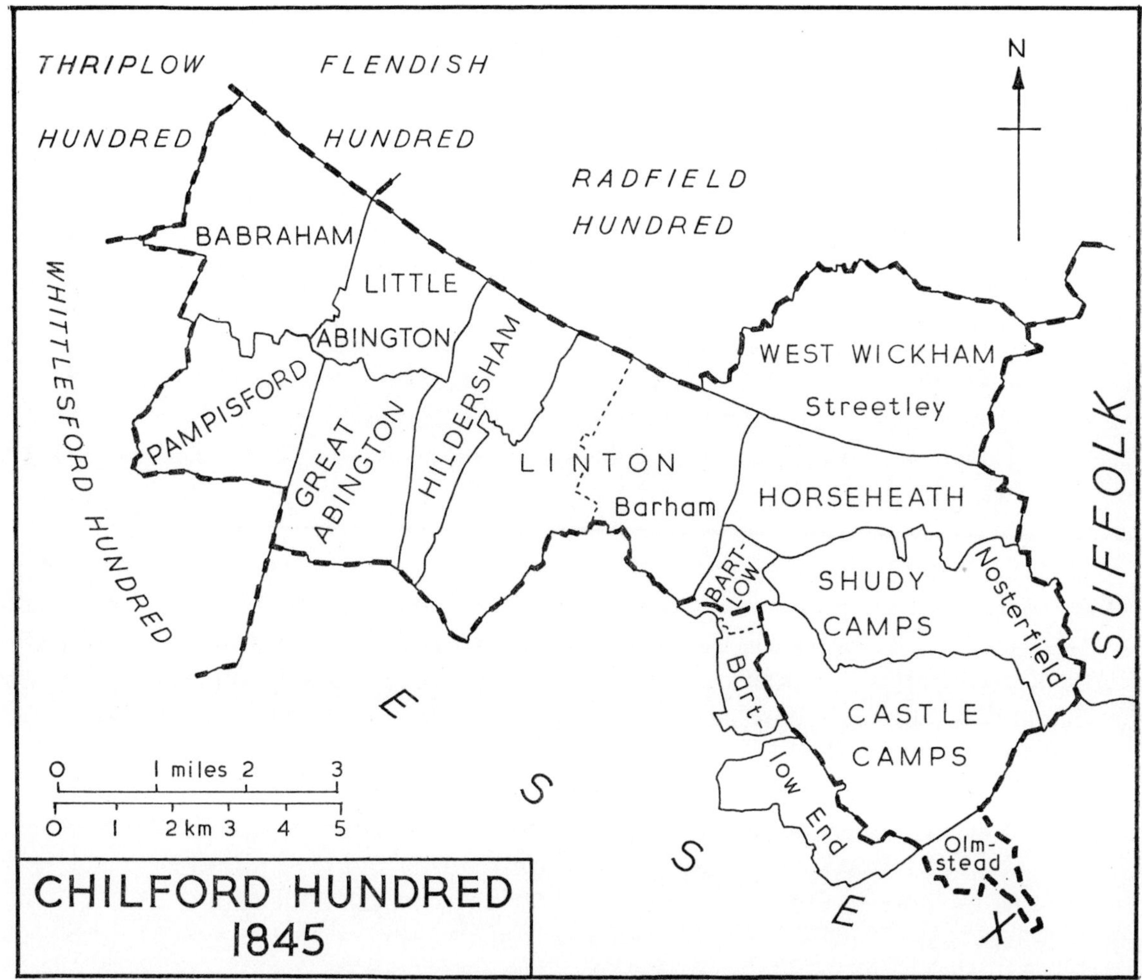

often leading across it. In the eastern part settlement is more scattered, with small village streets, outlying hamlets, and isolated farmsteads. The two parts of the hundred also differed agriculturally. In the Bourne valley open fields covered most of the area outside the village closes. On the eastern uplands only the western parts lay in open fields, while to the east lay extensive ancient inclosures, probably produced by assarting, mostly held in demesne, and sometimes formed into parks; the larger settlements, with the churches, lay near where the fields and closes met. Most of the settlements in the hundred, and particularly the eastern ones, had rather more than three fields, grouped by the 18th century, and probably earlier, for cultivation in a triennial rotation which was also usual on the inclosed arable. Large demesne sheep-flocks were kept; smaller owners, especially in the east, preferred to keep cattle. Saffron was grown in the area from the late 15th century to the mid 17th, and in the 17th century root crops were introduced at Linton and water-meadows were established at Babraham. The open fields were inclosed by parliamentary awards, mostly between 1799 and 1863. Babraham and Horseheath, each being virtually in a single ownership by 1800, were inclosed without awards. The inclosure of Hildersham in 1889 was the latest in the whole county. Thereafter the land was mostly devoted to mixed farming.

Linton, a market-town with two fairs from the 13th century to the 19th, had the only notable industrial activity in the hundred, but there as elsewhere population declined from a peak in the mid 19th century. In the west part of the hundred, nearer to Cambridge, it recovered after the 1940s, while in the east the shrunken settlements were barely more populous in 1970 than in 1800.

GREAT AND LITTLE ABINGTON

THE TWO parishes of Great and Little Abington,[1] 7 miles south-east of Cambridge, are divided by the river Granta. Although their history is recorded here in a single article, they were distinct parishes and remain so. Great Abington, to the south, covers 1,588 a., Little Abington, to the north, 1,309 a.[2] The southern boundary of Great Abington is also the county boundary; the northern boundary of Little Abington runs along the ancient Wool Street. To the west both parishes are bounded by a branch of the Icknield Way. The boundary between them follows the river, diverging near the centre along a former channel south of the main surviving stream. The intermediate area was formerly Little Abington's Midsummer Meadow.[3] A modern channel, south of the parish boundary, may have been made or straightened *c.* 1710 to form a canal in the grounds of Abington Hall.[4] Further west a channel north of the boundary was made in the 1650s to draw off water for the Babraham water-meadows.[5]

The soil of both parishes lies mainly upon chalk, overlaid upon the high ground near the county boundary with boulder clay, and in the north part of Little Abington with glacial gravels. Along the river runs a broad strip of alluvium and gravel. The ground there is predominantly level at about 100 ft. Further south it swells gradually and then more rapidly to a down of over 300 ft. The Brent Ditch[6] runs from Pampisford diagonally across the south-western corner of Great Abington. To the north the ground rises to a plateau of over 200 ft. covering much of the north part of Little Abington. Both parishes have been predominantly agrarian. Their open fields were inclosed under Acts of 1801.

Great Abington parish is comparatively well wooded. In 1086 it had woodland for 20 pigs.[7] By the southern boundary lay until after 1700 a demesne wood of the earls of Oxford, perhaps once part of a continuous belt of woodland along the ridge, and called by 1200 Abington grove.[8] It was said to cover 28 a. in 1263[9] and *c.* 53 a. about 1600.[10] It suffered much in the Middle Ages from tenants seeking fire-wood and building materials there,[11] who claimed a right to gather rods to thatch their tenements.[12] Lessees of the demesne also often neglected to keep it adequately fenced, or overcropped the timber.[13] In 1716 the enclosure in which the wood lay contained 66 a.,[14] but it was probably cleared soon after, for *c.* 1726 it was spoken of as partly pasture.[15] By 1801 only 10½ a. of wood, called Bush Park, survived at its north-western corner, the remainder, called the Great Park, being under grass.[16] By the late 19th century there was a smaller wood of 13 a. further north, called South grove. The park around Abington Hall, *c.* 87 a. in 1929, was and remains well stocked with trees.[17] Little Abington, although containing woodland for 20 pigs in 1086,[18] was later less wooded; after inclosure small plantations, amounting by 1929 to *c.* 35 a., were made.[19]

The population of Great Abington has generally been larger than that of Little Abington, although in 1086 there were 16 peasants and 4 bondmen in Little Abington and only 14 peasants in Great Abington.[20] In 1279, however, Great Abington included *c.* 48 tenants, Little Abington only *c.* 35.[21] In 1327 the former contained 37 taxpayers, the latter 27.[22] Later Little Abington's population was for some time only half that of Great Abington, where there were 96 adults in 1377 and 19 people taxed in 1524. Great Abington had 32 families in 1563 and 205 inhabitants in 1686. In contrast Little Abington contained 45 adults in 1377, 7 taxpayers in 1524, and only 15 families in 1563.[23] By the late 17th century its population was about two-thirds of Great Abington's. Thus in 1676 there were 53 adults there, compared with 82 at Great Abington.[24] In 1728 Great Abington had 47 families with 222 members, Little Abington 32 with 168 members.[25] Great Abington's population rose from 274 in 1811 to 382 by 1831, but thereafter fell almost continuously to 331 in 1851, 279 in 1881, and 219 in 1921. Little Abington's increased from 168 in 1811 to 307 by 1851 and in 1871 at 339 exceeded Great Abington's, but fell by 1881 to 264 and had declined to 188 in 1931. Following new building, numbers at Great Abington more than doubled to 503 in 1951 and 690 in 1971, when those at Little Abington were 341.[26]

Until modern times most of the dwellings in the two villages of Great and Little Abington lay along a street that runs south from the main Cambridge–Linton road north of the river.[27] A hump-backed bridge, probably late-19th-century and bombed in 1940,[28] used to carry the street across the river. In Great Abington many timber-framed and thatched cottages survive along the street. In each village the church stands west of the street, and in Little Abington the original settlement turned along a lane leading towards the church.[29] In 1666 Little Abington contained *c.* 20 houses, and there were 48 in Great Abington in 1686.[30] Except for the Hall and the inns at Bourn Bridge, where the Icknield Way

[1] This account was written in 1973.
[2] *Census*, 1961.
[3] B.L. Maps 1690(1); cf. C.R.O., 124/P 1–2 (draft incl. map).
[4] C.R.O., 619/E 20, m. 5.
[5] Ibid. E 14–20.
[6] See p. 105.
[7] *V.C.H. Cambs.* i. 390.
[8] King's Coll. Mun., G 67, deed *c.* 1200.
[9] C 132/3/1 no. 7.
[10] C.R.O., 619/M 66.
[11] e.g. ibid. M 3, ct. roll 8 Hen. IV; M 5, ct. roll 8 Hen. V.
[12] Ibid. M 25.
[13] e.g. ibid. M 6, ct. roll 4, 10 Hen. VI.
[14] B.L. Maps 1640(15).
[15] C.R.O., 619/T 22.
[16] C.R.O., R 60/24/2/30 (incl. map); C.U.L., Maps bb. 53(1)/93/73–4.
[17] O.S. Map 6″, Cambs. LV. SW. (1891 edn.); C.R.O., SP 1/8.
[18] *V.C.H. Cambs.* i. 374.
[19] O.S. Map 6″, Cambs. LIV. NW. (1891 edn.); C.R.O., SP 1/8.
[20] *V.C.H. Cambs.* i. 408–9.
[21] *Rot. Hund.* (Rec. Com.), ii. 422–4.
[22] *Cambs. Lay Subsidy, 1327*, 22–3.
[23] *East Anglian*, N.S. xii. 238; E 179/81/134 m. 2d.; B.L. Harl. MS. 594, f. 199v.; C.R.O., 619/Z 1.
[24] Compton Census.
[25] B.L. Add. MS. 5828, f. 83.
[26] *Census*, 1811–1971.
[27] C.R.O., 124/P 1–2.
[28] Ibid. R 57/17/1, f. 42; cf. O.S. Map 6″, Cambs. LV. SW. (1891 edn.).
[29] C.R.O., 124/P 1–2.
[30] E 179/242/22 f. 113; C.R.O., 619/Z 1.

crosses the Granta, there were no dwellings far from either village until farmsteads were built in the fields after inclosure. About 1800, when the villages were very overcrowded, many cottages being doubly and trebly tenanted,[31] there were 34 houses in Little Abington and 47 in Great Abington. The number of inhabited houses in Great Abington remained constant between 1821 and 1921 at between 60 and 70. At Little Abington it had risen from 47 in 1821 to 70 by 1871, but fell to 55 in 1931.[32] Thereafter both villages expanded. In Great Abington from the 1930s the Land Settlement Association built *c.* 45 houses to a standard design along roads laid out across the middle of the parish.[33] After 1950 several housing estates, partly council built, partly speculative, were built around closes east of the high street, raising the number of dwellings from 137 in 1951 to 203 in 1971. In Little Abington *c.* 45 more expensive houses in large gardens were laid out along the Cambridge road and, in the 1960s, along Bournbridge Road, north-east of the church. The village had 85 houses in 1951, 130 in 1971.[34] Many timber-framed, thatched cottages at the heart of the village, sold from the Hall estate in 1930, were bought in 1954 and renovated by the Cambridgeshire Cottage Improvement Society.[35] Two were converted into a studio pottery.[36]

The Three Tuns in Great Abington village, a 17th-century building, was open, possibly in 1687,[37] certainly by 1756.[38] From 1922 until after 1937 it was run by the People's Refreshment House Association, a temperance organization.[39] It was still open in 1973, as was the Crown in Little Abington, where the Bricklayers' Arms, open in 1861, was sold in 1912,[40] and the Princess (later Prince) of Wales, open by 1896, was closed *c.* 1963.[41]

The principal link with the outside world was once the Cambridge–Linton road, north of the river, called until the 18th century the Portway.[42] In Little Abington three fieldways ran north towards Woolstreet Way.[43] From Great Abington the Broadway ran south from the village street towards the wood and village common, and Sawston and Whittlesford ways ran across the parish.[44] The road through the villages towards Hildersham and Linton was turnpiked in 1765,[45] several tollgates being put up on the outskirts,[46] and was disturnpiked in 1876.[47] A bypass running north-east of the villages[48] was opened in 1969.[49] The main road along the western boundary, between Stump Cross and Newmarket, was a turnpike from 1724[50] until 1870.[51]

On that road at Bourn Bridge, which existed by 1279,[52] an inn had been established north of the bridge by 1687, when it had 9 beds and stabling for 22.[53] The King's Arms, as it was called after 1700, was kept from *c.* 1703 to 1720 by William Cole, father of the antiquary William Cole, who was born there in 1714. After 1720 the inn was rebuilt in brick on a larger scale to serve as a posting house. County balls and assemblies were held there, J.P.s and turnpike trustees convened there, fox-hounds and beagles met there. For some time after *c.* 1750 the inn was eclipsed by the White Hart, south of the bridge, which had gradually been enlarged from a toll cottage by its tenants Robert Lagden (d. 1777) and his wife Emma (d. 1781), who although a Quaker was noted for her gallantries. Smuggled tea hidden there may have given her son Jeremiah Lagden, a substantial Little Abington landowner, a local reputation as a highwayman. The White Hart was closed after 1797.[54] The King's Arms was closed shortly before 1850 because of the advent of the railway. Only its stables, converted into five cottages, survived in 1973.[55] The Cambridge–Haverhill railway line, opened in 1865 across Great Abington parish a little south of the village, was closed in 1967.[56]

In 1299 the earl of Oxford claimed free warren in Great Abington under a charter of 1251.[57] His game included hares, rabbits, and partridges, which his tenants and even the vicar regularly poached.[58] In the late 17th century John Bennet, then lord, tried to establish a decoy pond.[59] His successors, the Westerns, had put up a new dovecot by 1720, and reserved in their leases all sporting rights, sometimes let, as in the 1770s to Lord Grosvenor.[60] In the 1920s the parishes were said to produce up to 2,000 partridges in a season, up to 1,000 pheasants, and hares.[61]

The village feast was held in the 19th century on 29–30 May, enlivened by the visits of travelling gipsy showmen.[62] Ancient harvest customs maintained in the 1860s included adorning the last load of corn reaped with branches and flowers and the traditional horkeys or harvest suppers.[63] Cricket flourished at Abington from that period, encouraged by the squire, E. J. Mortlock, whose daughter, Mrs.

31 Vancouver, *Agric. in Cambs.* 58.
32 *Census*, 1801–1931.
33 Cf. C.R.O., R 57/17/1, f. 66.
34 *Census*, 1951–71; cf. C.R.O., SP 1/1, 3–4.
35 *Cambs. Local Hist. Counc. Bull.* xxv. 19–20.
36 Ibid. 19; cf. *Camb. Ind. Press*, 3 May 1968.
37 W. M. Palmer, *Neighbourhood of Hildersham* (Camb. 1924), 29.
38 C.R.O., 619/M 20, p. 1.
39 *Kelly's Dir. Cambs.* (1922–37); local information.
40 R.G. 9/1029; C.U.L., Maps 53(1)/91/65.
41 *Kelly's Dir. Cambs.* (1896–1937); C.R.O., SP 2/1.
42 Cf. C.R.O., 619/T 2; Jesus Coll. Mun., terrier 1768.
43 e.g. ibid.; B.L. Maps 1690(1).
44 C.U.L., MS. Plan 614; cf. C.R.O., 619/M 66; King's Coll. Mun., G 76.
45 Haverhill and Red Cross Road Act, 6 Geo. III c. 84.
46 Cf. C.U.L., MS. Plan 627.
47 Annual Turnpike Acts Continuance Act, 1876, 39–40 Vic. c. 39.
48 Cf. *Camb. News*, 17, 22, 30 June 1965.
49 Ex inf. the County Surveyor.
50 Stump Cross Roads Turnpike Act, 10 Geo. I, c. 12; cf. *C.J.* xx. 287, 289.
51 Annual Turnpike Acts Continuance Act, 1870, 33 and 34 Vic. c. 73.
52 *Rot. Hund.* (Rec. Com.), ii. 423: called Abington bridge.
53 W.O. 30/48; cf. C.U.L., MS. Plan 614.
54 B.L. Add. MS. 5823, f. 212v.; Horace Walpole, *Letters*, ed. W. S. Lewis, i. 363–4; *Trans. C.H.A.S.* iv. 17–29; cf. Porter, *Cambs. Customs*, 202–3.
55 *Trans. C.H.A.S.* iv. 24; *Gardner's Dir. Cambs.* (1851); cf. *Camb. Evening News*, 22 June 1972.
56 *V.C.H. Cambs.* ii. 132–3; ex inf. Brit. Rail Hist. Research Dept.
57 *Plac. de Quo Warr.* (Rec. Com.), 104; *Cal. Chart. R.* 1226–57, 472; cf. *Rot. Hund.* (Rec. Com.), ii. 423.
58 e.g. C.R.O., 619/M 1, ct. roll 11 Edw. II; M 2, ct. roll 19 Ric. II; M 4, ct. roll 4 Hen. IV; M 5, ct. roll 3 Hen. V.
59 Ibid. 619/E 20 m. 27.
60 Ibid. 619/T 22, 28; B.L. Add. MS. 5823, ff. 218v.–219.
61 Ibid. SP 1/8.
62 *Eng. Topog.* (Gent. Mag. Libr.), ii. 12; *Cambs. Local Hist. Counc. Bull.* xviii. 15–20.
63 *Cambs. Local Hist. Counc. Bull.* xx. 31; xxi. 26–7.

Mortlock, bought the customary cricket ground north of the school for the village after 1930.[64] Great Abington had a Working Men's Institute by 1896. J. J. Emerson, owner of the Hall estate, built in 1909 a village institute,[65] which was used by the local Working Men's Club until its dissolution in 1925[66] and was bought for the villages in 1954.[67] By 1907 Abington had a Rifle Association which was still flourishing in the 1930s.[68] The picturesque quality of Great Abington's main street was recognized in 1972 by putting all electrical cables underground.[69]

MANORS AND OTHER ESTATES. Before the Conquest King Edward's thegn, Wulfwin son of Alfwin, held 6 hides at Great Abington, whose reversion he had promised to Ramsey abbey. The Conqueror, however, granted all Wulfwin's lands to Aubrey de Vere, who in 1086 held the whole township,[70] which descended to his heirs male, later earls of Oxford,[71] as the manor of *GREAT ABINGTON*. Aubrey had also before 1086 seized ½ yardland previously held by Almar, a sokeman of King Edward, but Picot the sheriff recovered it from him, and held it on the king's behalf in 1086.[72] Half a yardland was farmed from the Crown in 1166 by the sheriff,[73] and from 1176 until after 1216 by Simon the clerk.[74] By 1230 it had been incorporated in the principal manor.[75]

The earls of Oxford retained that manor with few interruptions until the late 16th century.[76] The whole manor was frequently assigned to dowagers, who often held it for long periods. Thus Alice, widow of Earl Aubrey (d. 1214), had it until after 1244;[77] Alice, widow of Earl Robert (d. 1296), until 1312;[78] and Maud, widow of Earl Thomas (d. 1371), until 1413.[79] The dowagers are said to have used the manor-house as a dower-house.[80] The reversion of the manor, forfeited in 1388 by the condemnation of Earl Robert, Richard II's favourite, was restored to Robert's cousin and heir Richard in 1406.[81] Richard's son John, a Lancastrian, was executed in 1462, and the manor was granted to Richard, duke of Gloucester.[82] John's son John, a minor, was restored in 1463,[83] but forfeited his lands in 1471, whereupon Great Abington was again given to Gloucester,[84] who as Richard III granted it in 1484 to Sir Robert Percy.[85] Earl John was restored by Henry VII in 1485.[86] On his death in 1513 the manor, always previously considered to be held in chief,[87] was erroneously stated to be held of the honor of Boulogne,[88] a mistake that persisted.[89] John's nephew and heir John died in 1526, and from then to 1559 his wife Anne held Great Abington in dower.[90] The heir male Edward, earl of Oxford, who came of age in 1571, had sold Great Abington manor by 1578 to Robert Taylor of Babraham,[91] who in 1590 also purchased Little Abington,[92] the two manors afterwards descending together.

Robert Taylor died probably in 1596.[93] In 1599 his successor Robert Taylor sold both manors to Sir John Spencer[94] (d. 1610), the London financier whose daughter and heir Elizabeth married William, Lord Compton, created earl of Northampton in 1618. The earl died in 1630[95] and his wife in 1632. Their son Spencer, the royalist earl, was killed in battle in 1643. His son Earl James,[96] fined as a royalist in 1651,[97] in 1652 sold the Abington manors, then occupied by his mother Mary,[98] to John Bennet,[99] a cousin of the owners of Babraham.[1] Bennet died in 1663, leaving Little Abington to his young son John and Great Abington for life to his wife Elizabeth, who released her interest to her son in 1678. The younger John died in a debtors' prison in 1712, leaving one son, John, who was dead without issue by 1720. His father had in 1690 mortgaged most of the Abington estate to Thomas Western,[2] a wealthy London ironmonger, who took possession in 1697. At his death in 1707 Western left his interest to his third son Maximilian,[3] who foreclosed in 1709[4] and died in 1720.[5] After the estate had been many years in Chancery[6] Maximilian's son Thomas bought out the rights of Bennet's heirs-at-law in those properties at Abington mortgaged to others.[7] Thomas Western died in 1754, leaving both manors

64 Ibid. xix. 14, 19; C.R.O., R 57/17/1, f. 52v.; cf. SP 1/8, 9. Mrs. Mortlock used her father's rather than her husband's surname.
65 *Kelly's Dir. Cambs.* (1896–1922, 1925).
66 C.R.O., 331/Z 2, 1909, Dec., p. lxxxix; Z 6, 1925, Feb., p. 497.
67 Char. Com. files.
68 C.R.O., 331/Z 2–8, *passim.*
69 *Camb. Evening News*, 20 May 1972.
70 *Ramsey Chron.* (Rolls Ser.), 152–3; *V.C.H. Cambs.* i. 390, 408.
71 For their descent see *Complete Peerage*, x. 193–254.
72 *V.C.H. Cambs.* i. 362, 408.
73 *Pipe R.* 1166 (P.R.S. ix), 85.
74 Ibid. 1176 (P.R.S. xxv), 71; 17 John (P.R.S. N.S. xxxvii), 67.
75 Ibid. 1230 (P.R.S. N.S. iv), 56.
76 e.g. *Liber de Bernewelle*, 254; *Rot. Hund.* (Rec. Com.), ii. 422–3; *Cal. Inq. p.m.* i, p. 185; iii, pp. 229–30; vii, p. 271; viii, p. 515; xiii, p. 95.
77 *Cur. Reg. R.* vii. 312; *Close R.* 1242–7, 260.
78 *Plac. de Quo Warr.* (Rec. Com.), 104.
79 *Cal. Close*, 1369–74, 272–3; 1408–13, 389.
80 Palmer, *Neighbourhood of Hildersham*, 15.
81 C 137/90/17 no. 12.
82 *Cal. Pat.* 1461–7, 197.
83 Ibid. 287; cf. *Hatton's Bk. of Seals*, p. 175.
84 *Cal. Pat.* 1467–77, 287, 560; cf. *Rot. Parl.* vi. 144–8.
85 *Cal. Pat.* 1476–85, 434.
86 *Rot. Parl.* vi. 281–2.
87 e.g. *Bk. of Fees*, ii. 921; C 138/25/53 no. 31.
88 C 142/28 no. 123.
89 e.g. Wards 7/34 no. 132; C 142/490 no. 189.
90 C.R.O., 619/M 9–10, *passim.*
91 C.P. 25(2)/93/842/20 Eliz. I Hil. no. 10; the court was held in Taylor's name from 1574: C.R.O., 619/M 11, ct. roll 16 Eliz. I.
92 See p. 7.
93 Beaven, *Aldermen of London*, i. 192; ii. 44.
94 C.P. 25(2)/93/863/41 Eliz. I East. no. 10; cf. *D.N.B.*
95 Wards 7/134 no. 132; cf. *Complete Peerage*, ix. 677–9; *Hist. Today*, xi. 48–55.
96 C 142/490 no. 189; *Complete Peerage*, ix. 679–83.
97 *Cal. Cttee. for Compounding*, ii, pp. 1246–50.
98 S.P. 23/218 pp. 1, 138; cf. C.R.O., 619/M 13, *passim.*
99 C.P. 25(2)/538/1652 Hil. no. 17.
1 C.R.O., 619/E 20, m. 1. Bennet's father John (d. 1631) was son of Sir Thos. Bennet (d. 1627), uncle of Thos. Bennet whose widow bought Babraham: cf. Beaven, *Aldermen of London*, ii. 45, 175, 177; Prob. 11/151 (P.C.C. 21 Skynner); Prob. 11/159 (P.C.C. 54 St. John); C 110/175 Morell v. Paske no. 1.
2 C.R.O., 619/E 20–1, *passim*; C 78/1365 no. 1.
3 C.R.O., 619/M 43; Prob. 11/493 (P.C.C. 49 Poley); cf. Burke, *Extinct Peerage* (1883), 579–80.
4 C.R.O., 619/E 20, m. 6.
5 Ibid. E 23–4.
6 Cf. C 110/175 Morell v. Paske, *passim.*
7 C.R.O., 619/E 7; 619/T 23; cf. C 78/1365 no. 1.

to his eldest son Thomas[8] (d. 1781).[9] Thomas's son and heir, the Revd. Charles Western, sold the estate, apparently in 1784, to James Pierson,[10] a London merchant, who resold it in 1800 to John Mortlock,[11] the Cambridge banker and boroughmonger.[12]

Mortlock died in 1816, leaving the estate to his second and fourth sons, Thomas and Frederick Cheetham Mortlock.[13] Frederick resigned his interest *c.* 1820 and died in 1838. His son John Frederick asserted that his uncles had cheated him out of his inheritance, pursued them with lawsuits and pamphlets, and was transported in 1843 for shooting at his uncle E. D. Mortlock, vicar of Great Abington.[14] Thomas Mortlock died in 1859, leaving his property to his nephew Edmund John Mortlock[15] (d. 1902), who sold the estate in 1901 to John James Emerson (d. 1918).[16] Emerson later bought the lay rectory and vicarage lands, so uniting almost the whole of both parishes in a single ownership. When his son James John Emerson sold the estate in 1929 several of the farms were acquired by their tenants, including H. W. Cowell, who bought most of the Great Abington property, *c.* 1,240 a. In 1936 he sold 690 a. of it to the Land Settlement Association, the owner in 1973. About 490 a. in Little Abington were bought in 1929 by James Binney of Pampisford Hall. Abington Hall and the Hall farm, with the lordship of the manor, were acquired by Julius Bertram,[17] a London solicitor (d. 1944);[18] the Hall and 24 a. were sold in 1946 to the British Welding Research Association, the owner in 1973.[19]

Abington Hall stands a little west of Great Abington village and presumably on the site of the medieval manor-house of the earls of Oxford, which *c.* 1350 included a hall and possibly a chapel.[20] In 1417 the dowager countess Alice had a hall and two solars demolished;[21] a house called the knight-chamber, ruinous through its neglect by the earl's farmers, was repaired *c.* 1432.[22] The Bennets had a substantial house there, with 24 hearths in 1664[23] and consisting *c.* 1716 of five bays. About 1712 Maximilian Western did much rebuilding, put up the stables, and began to lay out an ornamental canal.[24]

The house was incorporated, probably in the late 18th century, in a three-storey building of nine bays, in red brick with stone dressings. It has a north porch with Roman Doric columns, and a pedimented south front with an iron verandah at ground level. Inside much late-18th-century decorative work survived in 1951, including doorheads and fireplaces. The hall had a screen with Tuscan columns, the former dining room a similar screen. The Westerns and their successors usually let the house from *c.* 1770 to after 1900,[25] the tenants including Sir Sampson Gideon, Bt., in the 1770s,[26] the earl of Chatham up to 1820, and Lord Maryborough, the duke of Wellington's brother, *c.* 1822.[27] The Emersons lived at the Hall, but it was empty in 1937.[28] The British Welding Research Association converted the Hall into flats and offices and the stables into workshops, and in the 1950s built two laboratories there.[29]

The Mortlocks usually lived at Abington Lodge, which stands just south of the bridge. It was built or rebuilt by Capt. Roger Sizer (d. 1724), tenant of the largest farm, and bought *c.* 1730 by Col. Vachell, who enlarged it substantially.[30] The interior contains a large, earlier fireplace. The house stands in landscaped grounds, once covering 22 a. From 1775 to 1780 Lord Grosvenor used it as a shooting-box.[31] It was bought in 1812 from Frances, widow of Thomas Holt (d. by 1800), by John Mortlock,[32] whose grandson E. J. Mortlock lived there and left it at his death in 1902 to his daughter Alice Mortlock (d. 1950).[33]

Five hides at Little Abington held by Eddeva the fair before the Conquest had by 1086 been granted with her other lands to Count Alan, lord of Richmond,[34] with which honor the overlordship subsequently descended.[35] Another hide, held of Eddeva by a priest who could not withdraw himself without leave, had been seized by 1086 by Aubrey de Vere, although Count Alan maintained his claim.[36] By the mid 12th century *LITTLE ABINGTON* manor was held of the earls of Richmond by Alan son of Emery, among whose heirs it was later disputed.[37] About 1195 Simon le Bret, who had inherited land from Alan at Ainderby (Yorks. N.R.), sued Hamon and William, sons of another Alan and apparently grandsons of Alan son of Emery, and John de Lanvaley, probably their cousin, in the Richmond honorial court for 5 hides at Little Abington, of which John held 1¼ hide. Hamon and William lost their shares by default.[38] After they had released

[8] Prob. 11/808 (P.C.C. 156 Penfold); *Mon. Inscr. Cambs.* 2.
[9] Palmer, *Wm. Cole*, 78–9; Prob. 11/1080 (P.C.C. 371 Webster).
[10] C.R.O., 619/M 20, pp. 16–25; cf. C.P. 43/795 (2nd nos.) rot. 43.
[11] Lysons, *Cambs.* 78, where Pierson's purchase is dated 1775; C.R.O., 619/M 20, pp. 27, 40.
[12] For Mortlock's career, see *Proc. C.A.S.* xl. 1–12; *Camb. Hist. Jnl.* viii. 145–65; P. W. Matthews and A. W. Tuke, *Hist. Barclays Bank* (1926), 181–6.
[13] Prob. 11/1584 (P.C.C. 489 Wynne).
[14] J. F. Mortlock, *Experiences of a Convict* (Sydney, 1968), pp. ix–xx, and *passim.*
[15] Ibid. 231–2; cf. *Alum. Cantab. 1752–1900*, iv. 477–8.
[16] C.R.O., SP 1/8; ibid. 331/Z 5, 1918, May.
[17] C.R.O., SP 1/8; R 57/17/1, f. 55v.
[18] *Who was Who, 1941–50*, 94.
[19] C.R.O., R 57/17/1, f. 16; ex inf. the Secretary; sale plan, 1946, *penes* the Association.
[20] C 134/28/17 no. 8; C.R.O., 619/M 40–1; cf. Palmer, *Neighbourhood of Hildersham*, 15–16.
[21] C.R.O., 619/M 6, ct. roll 2 Hen. VI.
[22] Ibid. 10 Hen. VI.
[23] E 179/84/437 rot. 58.
[24] B.L. Maps 1640(5); C.R.O., 619/T 22; 619/E 20, m. 5; 619/E 25; *Cambs. Local Hist. Counc. Bull.* iv. 8.
[25] Cf. *Camb. Chron.* 15 Oct. 1791; *Kelly's Dir. Cambs.* (1858–1900).
[26] Palmer, *Wm. Cole*, 78–9; cf. *V.C.H. Cambs.* ii. 413–15.
[27] *Eng. Topog.* (Gent. Mag. Libr.), ii. 13; C.R.O., P 1/11/1.
[28] *Kelly's Dir. Cambs.* (1904–37).
[29] C.R.O., R 57/17/1, ff. 16, 66.
[30] B.L. Add. MS. 5823, ff. 215, 219; cf. C.R.O., 619/M 43–4.
[31] B.L. Add. MS. 5823, ff. 218v.–219.
[32] Lysons, *Cambs.* 78–9; C.R.O., P 1/11/1; C.R.O., SP 1/11.
[33] *Kelly's Dir. Cambs.* (1864–1900); Burke, *Land. Gent.* (1906), 1198; C.R.O., R 57/17/1, ff. 52v., 53v.
[34] *V.C.H. Cambs.* i. 374.
[35] e.g. *Liber de Bernewelle*, 254–5; *Rot. Hund.* (Rec. Com.), ii. 423; *Cal. Inq. p.m. Hen. VII*, ii, p. 67; C 142/490 no. 189.
[36] *V.C.H. Cambs.* i. 390.
[37] *Cur. Reg. R.* i. 72; cf. *Red Bk. Exch.* (Rolls Ser.), ii. 588; *Early Yorks. Chart.* v (Y.A.S. extra ser. ii), 239–40.
[38] *Cur. Reg. R.* Ric. I (Pipe R. Soc. xxiv), 239–40; cf. *Mem. R.* 1208 (Pipe R. Soc. N.S. xxxi), 87–8. For the descent, see *Cur. Reg. R.* i. 72, where Hamon is called John's 'nepos', son of his uncle.

their interests to John, he sued Simon in 1199 for the 5 hides of the manor, which Simon later claimed to hold in pledge.[39] In 1201 Simon agreed to release the half of the manor which he then held as ½ knight's fee to John's kinsman William de Lanvaley[40] (d. 1204).[41] The same year William, or his son and heir William, entailed the other half, to be held of him as ½ knight's fee, upon John,[42] who died without issue after 1214. John's wife Christine probably retained a life-interest[43] until *c.* 1229, when the manor had reverted to Hawise, daughter and heir of the younger William de Lanvaley (d. 1217), whom her guardian the justiciar Hubert de Burgh had married by 1227 to his son John.[44] By 1236 John de Burgh had subinfeudated the manor to his follower Hugh de Vaux.[45] John died in 1274 and his son and heir John,[46] implied as overlord in 1279,[47] died in 1280, whereupon his lands were divided between two daughters as coheirs.[48] None of their descendants, however, is recorded to have had any rights over Little Abington. In 1248 Hugh de Vaux settled the reversion of his estate on his nephew William de Vaux[49] (d. by 1251).[50] William's heir was his brother John,[51] described as mesne lord in 1279.[52] On John's death in 1287 only the advowson of Little Abington was included in the partition of his lands among his daughters and coheirs.[53] In 1309 the manor was said to be held of his elder daughter Parnel of Narford by a nominal service.[54] Thereafter the rights of the Vauxes, as of the Burgh coheirs, were forgotten, and the manor was often stated to be held directly of the honor of Richmond.[55]

Before 1276 John de Vaux had further subinfeudated Little Abington to Robert Tuddenham of Ereswell (Suff.), who held it in demesne as 1 knight's fee in 1279.[56] Robert died in 1309, leaving his lands to his elder son Robert[57] (d. *c.* 1336), whose heir was his brother Thomas's son Robert, then a minor.[58] That Robert died in 1361 and was succeeded by his son John.[59] Sir John Tuddenham died in 1392 and his son and heir Robert[60] late in 1405.[61] Little Abington was probably thereupon included in the dower of Robert's wife Margaret, for her second husband, Thomas Misterton (d. 1434),[62] was said to be lord in 1428.[63] On Margaret's death the manor passed to Robert's eldest surviving son Thomas.[64] Sir Thomas Tuddenham, a prominent Lancastrian, was beheaded for conspiracy in 1462.[65] His lands, including Little Abington, were restored in 1465 to his sister and heir Margaret, widow of Edmund Bedingfield.[66] After her death in 1476 they descended to her grandson Edmund Bedingfield,[67] who died holding the manor in 1496.[68] Under his will the manor passed on his widow Margaret's death in 1514 to his second son Robert,[69] who died as rector of Oxburgh (Norf.) in 1539,[70] whereupon it went to a third son, Sir Edmund Bedingfield[71] (d. 1554),[72] who settled it on his fifth son Edmund. Edmund died in 1565, leaving it to his wife Grace[73] who with her second husband, James Taverner, sold two-thirds in 1568 to George Fuller,[74] rector of Hildersham (d. 1591).[75] In 1582 Edmund's son Christopher released the remaining third to Fuller.[76] In 1590 Fuller sold the manor to Robert Taylor, already lord of Great Abington, who also acquired *c.* 140 a. in Little Abington and elsewhere in 1591 from Fuller's brother John and from Francis Robinson.[77] His manors and other acquisitions afterwards descended together. No evidence has been found giving the site of Little Abington manor-house.

Two fees in Little Abington were separated from the chief manor in the 13th century. One, perhaps that held *c.* 1236 by Hervey Fitz Pain,[78] whom Simon son of Simon le Bret had unsuccessfully sued for a carucate there in 1214 and 1235,[79] was said in 1279 to be held of the heirs of Hugh of Windsor, tenants under John de Burgh, by John Gerunde who occupied 100 a. in demesne.[80] John was succeeded between 1284 and 1302 by Richard Gerunde.[81] Richard or a namesake and his wife Alice had 114 a. settled on them in 1335,[82] which Richard held in 1346. He died after 1363.[83] The Gerunde fee may

39 *Rot. Cur. Reg.* (Rec. Com.), i. 240, 451; *Cur. Reg. R.* i. 72, 93; iii. 262; cf. *Cal. Inq. Misc.* i, p. 170, showing that John and Simon at some time each occupied half the manor.

40 *Pipe R.* 1200 (P.R.S. N.S. xii), 47; *Feet of Fines* (Rec. Com.), 288.

41 *Pipe R.* 1204 (P.R.S. N.S. xviii), 23–41. For the Lanvaley descent see Farrer, *Honors and Knights Fees*, iii. 287–91.

42 *Cur. Reg. R.* iii. 74, 218.

43 B.L. Cott. MS. Tib. C. ix, ff. 128–9; *Cart. Mon. St. John Colchester* (Roxburghe Club, 1897), i. 202, 205.

44 *Rot. Litt. Claus.* (Rec. Com.), i. 231, 324, 328, 341; cf. *Bracton's Notebk.* ii, p. 40; *Bk. of Fees*, ii. 1351; *Cur. Reg. R.* xiii, p. 309.

45 *Liber de Bernewelle*, 254–5; cf. *Bk. of Fees*, i. 492–3; *Pat. R.* 1225–32, 361; C.P. 25(1)/24/19 no. 1.

46 *Cal. Fine R.* 1272–1307, 36, 41; *Cal. Inq. p.m.* ii, pp. 91–2.

47 *Rot. Hund.* (Rec. Com.), ii. 423.

48 *Cal. Inq. p.m.* ii, p. 198; *Cal. Close*, 1279–88, 136.

49 C.P. 25(1)/24/25 no. 1. For the Vaux pedigree see Dugdale, *Mon.* vi. 70; Dugdale, *Baronage*, i. 526–7.

50 *Cal. Pat.* 1247–51, 366, 440.

51 *Ex. e Rot. Fin.* (Rec. Com.), ii. 160–1.

52 *Rot. Hund.* (Rec. Com.), ii. 423.

53 *Cal. Inq. p.m.* ii, pp. 402–4; *Cal. Close*, 1279–88, 530.

54 *Cal. Inq. p.m.* v, p. 47.

55 e.g. C 140/53/38 no. 3; Wards 7/34 no. 132.

56 *Rot. Hund.* (Rec. Com.), i. 52; ii. 151, 423.

57 *Cal. Fine R.* 1307–19, 40; *Cal. Inq. p.m.* v, p. 47.

58 *Cal. Fine R.* 1327–37, 505; *Cal. Inq. p.m.* vii, pp. 42, 194–5.

59 *Cal. Inq. p.m.* xi, p. 181.

60 C 136/78 no. 30.

61 C 137/52 no. 18.

62 Blomefield, *Norf.* vi. 174; *Wills proved in Consist. Ct. Norwich, 1370–1550*, ii (Norf. Rec. Soc. xvi), 260.

63 *Feud. Aids*, i. 182.

64 C 138/27 no. 42; *Cal. Close*, 1422–9, 27.

65 Wedgwood, *Hist. Parl. 1439–1509, Biog.* 880–1; cf. *Cal. Pat.* 1461–7, 186, 195.

66 C 140/18 no. 34; *Cal. Fine R.* 1461–71, 163–6; cf. C 1/33 no. 348.

67 C 140/53 no. 38; *Cal. Pat.* 1467–77, 595.

68 *Cal. Inq. p.m. Hen. VII*, ii, pp. 8–12, 67.

69 Prob. 11/11 (P.C.C. 7–8 Horne); cf. Blomefield, *Norf.* vi. 176–9.

70 Emden, *Biog. Reg. Univ. Camb.* 50; Blomefield, *Norf.* vi. 92.

71 E 150/639 nos. 9–10.

72 E 150/649 no. 15.

73 C 142/144 no. 179.

74 Blomefield, *Norf.* ix. 206–7; C.P. 25(2)/93/835/10 Eliz. I Hil. no. 4; cf. C 2/Eliz. I/T 2/28.

75 *Alum. Cantab. to 1751*, ii. 184.

76 *Cal. Pat.* 1563–6, 483; C.P. 25(2)/93/846/24 Eliz. I Trin. no. 5.

77 C.P. 25(2)/94/854/32–3 Eliz. I Mich. nos. 10, 15; C.P. 25(2)/95/855/33–4 Eliz. I Mich. no. 5.

78 *Liber de Bernewelle*, 254–5.

79 *Cur. Reg. R.* vii. 256, 263; *Close R.* 1234–7, 194, 378.

80 *Rot. Hund.* (Rec. Com.), ii. 424.

81 *Feud. Aids*, i. 140, 145.

82 C.P. 25(1)/28/68 no. 70.

83 *Feud. Aids*, i. 163; *Cal. Close*, 1361–4, 350; *Cal. Fine R.* 1356–68, 242.

eventually have come to the Bustelers and Paryses, successively lords of Hildersham,[84] of whom land at Little Abington, formerly of Richard Gerunde, was held in 1512.[85] William le Busteler (d. by 1336) had in 1309 been leasing Little Abington manor from Robert Tuddenham, and was named as its lord in 1316.[86] His son Robert owned land there, over which he was granted free warren in 1336.[87] Land at Great and Little Abington was included in the estate which passed from the Busteler coheirs to Robert Parys[88] and his descendants. In the early 16th century the Paryses owned a substantial estate there called Westleys,[89] of which Sir Philip Parys sold 160 a., probably the demesne, to John Chapman in 1554.[90] By 1600 Westleys, then *c.* 120 a., belonged to Edward Lucas of Thriplow (d. 1603), who was succeeded by his wife.[91] In 1722 120 a., perhaps the same estate, belonged to Richard Lucas.[92] The Paryses and their successors, however, retained after 1554 lordship over much freehold and copyhold land in Little Abington, usually held to be attached to their manor at Hildersham, which was therefore styled Hildersham with Little Abington manor.[93] From 1801 to 1811 it was briefly owned by John Mortlock, lord of the Abingtons.[94]

Another part of Little Abington continued, after the lawsuit of *c.* 1200, to be held of Simon le Bret's heirs. One William of Wissant then held of the chief fee over 30 a. which his wife Helewise later, probably after 1227, gave in marriage with their daughter Maud to Robert Butler. Maud in her widowhood granted the land to St. Radegund's nunnery, Cambridge, which held 60 a. in demesne in 1279.[95] The nunnery retained the property until its suppression in 1496, when its estates passed to the newly founded Jesus College,[96] which held *c.* 80 a. at Little Abington in the 17th century and *c.* 63 a. in the 18th,[97] for which 49 a. were allotted at inclosure in 1801.[98] In 1813 the estate was exchanged for land at West Wratting with J. C. Perne, impropriator of Little Abington rectory,[99] with which the Jesus estate thereafter passed.

In 1279 Waltham abbey (Essex) held of Robert Tuddenham *c.* 90 a. in Little Abington, including 60 a. in demesne and half a mill.[1] The land had been given by various tenants of the manor, including Ralph son of Ernald who *c.* 1200 gave 30 a. that he had held of William of Wissant.[2] The abbey apparently retained some land in the early 16th century, which in the 18th was said to belong to Jeremiah Lagden[3] (d. 1804). The 94 a. allotted for Lagden's lands at inclosure[4] had by 1821 been combined with Little Abington rectory estate.[5] Sawtry abbey (Hunts.) in 1279 held *c.* 18 a. of Robert Tuddenham,[6] which had been sold by 1556 to George Gill.[7]

In 1279 Roger son of John and Richard of Bassingbourn held half a mill each and 85 a. and 53 a. respectively in Great Abington, apparently following the division of a larger estate, and in Little Abington, as parceners, *c.* 155 a.[8] In 1324 240 a. in the Abingtons and Hildersham and half a mill were settled on Roger of Abington with remainder to his son Edmund[9] (d. before 1393). John Abington succeeded his father John in 1398[10] and died in 1431, when he held 80 a. in Great Abington.[11] In 1448 his son John Abington sold that land to King's College, Cambridge,[12] which *c.* 1640 owned *c.* 70 a. in Great Abington and *c.* 67 a. in Little Abington.[13] At inclosure the college was allotted 56 a. in Great Abington and 34 a. in Little Abington,[14] which it sold to Thomas Mortlock in 1859.[15] Clare College also had an estate in Little Abington, derived from John Bolton's lands conveyed to feoffees for the college in 1524.[16] The college was allotted *c.* 50 a. at inclosure,[17] and in 1873 owned 55 a., then on lease to E. J. Mortlock, who had bought the freehold by 1900.[18]

Most of 1 hide at Little Abington, held in 1279 of Robert Tuddenham by Robert Christian,[19] had by 1500 come to William son of John Mars, who held two-thirds of it of the honor of Richmond, together with other holdings called Leverers, amounting in 1540 to 170 a., and Willinghams, both held of John Parys. Mars died in 1511 and his daughter and heir Margaret[20] married Nicholas Smith (d. after 1538).[21] Leverers belonged by 1602 to Sir John Spencer, lord of the manor.[22] Willinghams, *c.* 80 a., was sold in 1563 by Margaret Smith to Robert Chapman,[23] who soon after sold it to Thomas Amy (d. 1583). Amy's daughter and heir Joan (d. 1617) married Robert Higham (d. 1609). Her son and heir James Higham[24] (d. 1658) left his land to his daughter Amy

84 See pp. 61–2, 84–5.
85 E 150/65 no. 3.
86 *Cal. Inq. p.m.* v, p. 47; *Feud. Aids*, i. 155.
87 *Cal. Chart. R.* 1327–41, 378.
88 e.g. *Cal. Close*, 1377–81, 476; *East Anglian*, N.S. vi. 246; C 137/72 no. 32; C 139/29 no. 48.
89 C.R.O., 619/M 9, ct. roll 25–6 Hen. VIII; *Cat. Anct. D.* i, C 374.
90 C.P. 25(2)/68/558 no. 7.
91 C.R.O., 619/M 12, ct. roll 3 Jas. I; S.P. 14/23 no. 15.
92 C.R.O., 619/M 59.
93 C 142/116 no. 7; C 142/263 no. 35; C.R.O., R 51/25/35, p. 163 and *passim.*
94 C.R.O., R 51/25/35, pp. 216, 250.
95 *Rot. Hund.* (Rec. Com.), ii. 424; *Pleas before King's Justices*, ii (Selden Soc. lxviii), pp. 16–17; B.L. Cott. MS. Tib. C. ix, f. 123; *Cal. Chart. R.* 1300–27, 223; Jesus Coll. Mun., deeds 1, 2; *Pat. R.* 1225–32, 155.
96 Gray, *Priory of St. Radegund* (C.A.S. 8vo ser. xxxi), 146, 162; *V.C.H. Cambs.* iii. 421.
97 Jesus Coll. Mun., terriers 1635, 1768.
98 C.R.O., Q/RDz 5, p. 81.
99 Jesus Coll. Mun., Memorabilia Bk. p. 181.
1 *Rot. Hund.* (Rec. Com.), ii. 423.
2 B.L. Cott. MS. Tib. C. ix, ff. 127, 128v., 228.
3 C.R.O., 619/E 2; Jesus Coll. Mun., terriers, 16th cent., 1768.
4 Jesus Coll. Mun., Memorabilia Bk. p. 181; C.R.O., Q/RDz 5, pp. 80–1.
5 C.R.O., 334/02.
6 *Rot. Hund.* (Rec. Com.), ii. 423; *Tax. Eccl.* (Rec. Com.), 269.
7 *Cal. Pat.* 1555–7, 148.
8 *Rot. Hund.* (Rec. Com.), ii. 222–4; cf. King's Coll. Mun., G 67 *passim.*
9 C.P. 25(1)/28/72 no. 5.
10 King's Coll. Mun., G 67, no. 16; C.R.O., 619/M 2, ct. roll 21 Ric. II.
11 C.R.O., 619/M 6, ct. roll 10 Hen. VI.
12 King's Coll. Mun., G 68–73; cf. C.R.O., 619/M 9, ct. roll 19 Hen. VIII.
13 King's Coll. Mun., G 76, 79.
14 C.R.O., Q/RDz 5, pp. 80, 89.
15 Ex inf. Mr. John Saltmarsh, of King's Coll.
16 *31st Rep. Com. Char.* 104; *Camb. Univ. Doc.* (1852), i. 267.
17 C.R.O., Q/RDz 5, p. 80.
18 *Rep. Com. Univ. Income* [C. 856–II], p. 73, H.C. (1873), xxxvii (3).
19 *Rot. Hund.* (Rec. Com.), ii. 423.
20 E 150/65 no. 3; cf. C.R.O., 619/E 2.
21 C 1/857 nos. 1–2; C.P. 25(2)/68/560 no. 9.
22 B.L. Maps 1690(1).
23 C.P. 25(2)/93/833/5 Eliz. I Hil. no. 1.
24 C.R.O., 619/T 12; *Mon. Inscr. Cambs.* 2; Wards 7/60 no. 62.

Smee whose son John Smee in 1688 sold part of it to John Bennet the younger.[25] In 1730 certain trustees sold 120 a. of Smee's estate, including Willinghams, to Thomas Western.[26] By the mid 18th century only one other large property still belonged to a locally resident family, that of the Wards. John Ward, who succeeded his father in 1760, left *c.* 90 a. on his death in 1762 to his cousin Mary, wife of William Fairchild;[27] she and her son Joseph were dead by 1804. Their lands, for which *c.* 125 a. were allotted at inclosure, were conveyed in 1805 to Benjamin Keene and in 1808 to William Sanxter.[28] By 1811 they had been annexed to the Mortlock estate.[29]

The impropriate rectories of Great and Little Abington were sold in 1540 to Sir Philip Parys,[30] after whose death in 1558 they passed in turn to his grandson Robert (d.s.p. 1572) and his younger son Ferdinand.[31] The latter sold them *c.* 1576 to Thomas Dalton of Hildersham, already perhaps lessee of Little Abington rectory.[32] On Dalton's death in 1602 Great Abington rectory passed to his youngest son Thomas[33] (d. before 1619). His successor was his eldest brother Michael's second son Thomas, who died in 1639, leaving it to his son Michael, a minor.[34] Michael was dead by 1656; his brother and heir Richard Dalton[35] sold Great Abington rectory in 1679 to John Bennet, lord of the manors,[36] with which it descended thereafter. At inclosure *c.* 230 a. were allotted for the rectorial tithes in Great Abington.[37]

Thomas Dalton (d. 1602) was succeeded in Little Abington rectory by his eldest son Michael,[38] who, having survived his eldest son Oliver (d. 1619), settled it in 1639 on the marriage of Oliver's son Michael to Susan Tyrell.[39] The younger Michael was succeeded between 1647 and 1661 by his son Tyrell Dalton[40] (d. 1682).[41] Tyrell's son Tyrell (d. 1730)[42] sold the rectory with 50 a. in 1701 to John Perne[43] (d. 1715). Perne's estate probably passed to his son Chester Perne, who lived at Little Abington and on his death in 1753 left his estates to the children of his brothers John (d. 1770) and Andrew (d. 1772), both clergymen.[44] Andrew's son Andrew, to whom 175 a. were allotted for rectorial tithes at inclosure, was succeeded in 1807[45] by his second son, John Chester Perne (d. 1823). The next owner, Andrew's widow Susan, said to hold the impropriation *c.* 1830, died in 1836.[46] By 1841 the Perne lands belonged to F. P. Newcome.[47] In 1850 the rectory estate, with the former Jesus College and Lagden lands, was sold to Benjamin and Joseph Kent.[48] Benjamin owned the whole farm by his death in 1863. His successor, Alfred Oslar Kent, died *c.* 1900, whereupon it was sold to J. A. Wootten of Cambridge and resold in 1909 to J. J. Emerson, lord of the manors.[49] When the manorial estate was broken up in 1929, Lay Rectory farm, *c.* 370 a., was bought by S. E. Franklin.[50]

Little Abington rectory house may have stood just north of the bridge on the site of the Old House, a timber-framed building probably of the 17th century, its front rendered in 18th-century style. It was apparently occupied in the late 18th century by Jeremiah Lagden, and was styled the rectory house in 1850.[51] About 1951 it was bought by the marquess of Cambridge, who lived there in 1973.[52]

ECONOMIC HISTORY. The 6 hides at Great Abington in 1086 included demesne land for 3 plough-teams, and there were 9 *villani* with land for 5 plough-teams, and 5 bordars. The value of the manor, apparently at farm, had been raised from £6 to £8 since 1066. Of the 5 hides at Little Abington half was in demesne, with 3 plough-teams and 5 *servi*, while 11 *villani* had 5 teams; the manor was worth £10, as much as in 1066.[53]

At Great Abington the arable was probably being extended up to the early 13th century when assarts were recorded near Abington grove and Hildersham wood.[54] In 1279 of *c.* 1,080 a. of arable recorded, the demesne comprised *c.* 500 a. In 1263 it had been said to come to 241 a. 'on one side' and 455 a. 'on the other', but in 1296 included only 520 a. Free tenants in 1279 held *c.* 250 a., of which 130 a. were shared by Roger son of John and Richard Bassingbourn, one man had 44 a. and two others 1 yardland each. Fourteen lesser freeholders had only 36 a. between them, mostly in one-acre lots, for which rents of 2*s.* an acre were usually charged. About 300 a. were held in villeinage, including 16 half-yardlands of 16 a. Their holders were liable to do 2 week-works throughout the year, and 5 a week in harvest, besides 2 harvest-boons and averages. The 5 tenants of quarter-yardlands, each of 8 a., owed the same services, except that they and the 5 cottars did only 1 week-work. Each half-yardlander had also to plough 7 a. a year for the lord. By 1279 week-works could be commuted at ½*d.* each, or 1½*d.* in harvest, and ploughing at 4*d.* an acre. The

25 C.R.O., 619/T 12, 15; 619/M 17, p. 16.
26 *East Anglian*, N.S. xiii. 268.
27 C.R.O., R 51/25/35, pp. 39–46, 60–2.
28 Ibid. pp. 215–16; R 59/5/10/1; Q/RDz 5, p. 79.
29 C.R.O., 334/02.
30 *L. & P. Hen. VIII*, xv, p. 467; E 318/7 no. 842.
31 C 142/116 no. 7; C 142/60 no. 17.
32 C.R.O., 619/E 1; cf. Req. 2/196/6.
33 Prob. 11/100 (P.C.C. 64 Montague); Wards 7/26 no. 242.
34 Prob. 11/182 (P.C.C. 15 Coventry); C 142/604, no. 117; cf. *Visit. Cambs.* (Harl. Soc. xli), 41–2.
35 *Lincoln's Inn Admission Reg.* i. 273; cf. *Visit. Essex 1664–8*, ed. J. J. Howard (London, 1888), 28.
36 C.P. 25(2)/634/31 Chas. II Mich. no. 12.
37 C.R.O., Q/RDz 5, p. 87.
38 Wards 7/26 no. 242; C 142/254 no. 71; cf. *D.N.B.*
39 C.R.O., 619/E 1; L 66/15.
40 Prob. 11/203 (P.C.C. 26 Essex, will of Joan Tyrell); *Lincoln's Inn Admission Reg.* i. 286.
41 *Mon. Inscr. Cambs.* 57.
42 *Alum. Cantab. to 1751*, ii. 6; cf. Lysons, *Cambs.* 197.
43 C.P. 43/472 rot. 108.
44 *Alum. Cantab. to 1751*, iii. 348; cf. B.L. Add. MS. 5808, ff. 46v.–47; Add. MS. 5823, f. 214.
45 Prob. 11/1481 (P.C.C. 507 Ely); *Alum. Cantab. 1752–1900*, iv. 94–5; C.R.O., Q/RDz 5, p. 77.
46 Mon. in Lit. Abington ch.; *Rep. Com. Eccl. Revenues*, pp. 344–5.
47 C.R.O., 334/02.
48 C.U.L., Maps bb. 53/85/5.
49 *Kelly's Dir. Cambs.* (1858–1900); C.R.O., 296/SP 992, 1057.
50 C.R.O., SP 1/8.
51 Palmer, *Neighbourhood of Hildersham*, 41; C.U.L., Maps bb. 53/85/5.
52 C.R.O., R 57/17/1, f. 51; cf. Burke, *Peerage* (1959), 378–9; *Who's Who* (1972).
53 *V.C.H. Cambs.* i. 362, 374, 390, 408–9. On pp. 390, 408, a possibly imaginary tenant of Aubrey called Firmat has been introduced.
54 King's Coll. Mun., G 67, nos. 14, 25.

reeve was excused his services during his year of office. The lord could tallage his tenants at will.[55]

At Little Abington there was much more free land. Robert Tuddenham's demesne included only 240 a. in 1279 (210 a. in 1309), and John Gerunde's only 100 a., out of *c.* 1,130 a. of arable. Neither Gerunde nor St. Radegund's had any villeins, and Tuddenham had only 4 half-yardlanders, with 60 a. between them, and 1 cottar. Those tenants owed 2 week-works throughout the year and 3 by 1309, except in harvest when they had to reap 10 a. each and render a harvest-boon; they had also to plough 10 a. a year. The freeholders ranged from Robert Christian, with 157 a. altogether, through 4 others with over 120 a. between them, to 25 small tenants sharing 180 a. A few freeholders had land in both parishes. Most free tenants in Little Abington owed scutage, sheriff's aid, and castle-ward pence to Richmond castle.[56]

Great Abington manor's yield of £30 in 1263 included £12 from rents.[57] The demesne was estimated at 300 a. in 1331.[58] In 1371 it probably amounted to 540 a., of which *c.* 360 a. were under cultivation in any one year.[59] In 1350 94 a. out of 371 a. in the sown fields were left unsown, and in 1366 78 a. of 362 a., on account of 'debility'. In the mid 14th century the lord received only a small cash profit from his demesne farming, only £5 in 1349–50, compared with £10 arising from rents and commutations. Little corn was sold, what was not needed for seed going in liveries to farm servants, who included 6 ploughmen, a carter, and a shepherd. The village smith held his smithy by making the lord's ploughshares. Wheat, pigs, and poultry were delivered to the lord's household when he was living near by. Most profit probably came from the demesne flock: in 1366 287 fleeces fetched £10. Timber was sold from time to time: in 1350 16 a. of the wood were sold for £28, perhaps to offset a decline in other receipts caused by the Black Death, which had struck the village severely. Five of 15 half-yardlands and 2 of 4 nine-acre 'warelands' had been thrown into the lord's hands. Only 2 were soon re-let at rents. Some holdings were still held on customary terms in 1366, their works being used mainly for threshing and thatching, and only a seventh of the works they owed were commuted. Their harvest-boons were exacted in full. Ten half-yardlands, however, and all four smaller holdings were rendering no works, being nominally in the lord's hands, and in practice soon let for rents.[60] From the 1360s to the 1420s most customary half-yardlands were usually let for terms of 3–10 years; thereafter some prospective tenants expected grants for terms of life.[61] The lord found 8 vacant tenements falling into ruin in 1418.[62] Some neifs left the manor. A whole family fled *c.* 1393, allegedly to escape maltreatment by the lord's farmer, and in 1413 eleven neifs were known to be absent.[63] From the 16th century copyholds were regularly, as previously in practice, inherited by the youngest son, or by daughters jointly; on transfer, through death or otherwise, the lord received a fine that was nominally arbitrary but usually of 1½ year's rent.[64] The demesne had been put to farm by 1368 and remained at farm thereafter,[65] except between 1407 and 1411, when the bailiff cheated the lord, sowing the lord's seed and using the lord's ploughs on his own land.[66]

By the 14th century Great Abington was being cultivated on a triennial rotation,[67] but it is unclear how the various small furlongs and doles whose names survive[68] were grouped together. About 1350 the demesne arable under cultivation was said to lie in Hildersham field, Stocking, and Canonsdown, of which the first and second were sown both with winter crops (wheat, rye, and dredge) and with barley, while spring corn (barley and oats) was sown in the second and third. Similarly in 1366 barley and dredge were sown in both winter and spring.[69] About 1575 it was said that the ancient custom was three sowings, for wheat and rye, for barley, and for oats.[70] About 1600 the arable was apparently divided into three large fields, West, Stumping Cross, and Ditch fields, the last perhaps lying south of the Brent Ditch.[71] In the late 16th century some men possessed inclosed crofts within the common fields, and were ordered not to sow them independently, but to remove their fences and let beasts common there when the field lay fallow.[72] The principal peasant crop was usually barley:[73] *c.* 1620 one farmer had sown 52 a. of barley and oats but only 12 a. of wheat and rye.[74] From the early 16th century saffron was also grown in the fields, and required protection from commoning beasts.[75] Great Abington's meadows along the river were liable to flooding.[76] A permanent common, amounting *c.* 1600 to 60 a., lay next to Abington grove and was partly intercommonable with Hildersham.[77]

Great Abington usually supported many sheep. In 1086 Aubrey de Vere had a flock of 120, and his men were said to have driven away 380 sheep from a half-yardland which he had usurped.[78] In 1347 the village rendered 70 stone to a levy of wool, of which 44 stone came from 15 villagers charged with over 1 stone each, 15 stone from 38 others, and 11 stone from the demesne,[79] on which *c.* 1350 there were

[55] *Rot. Hund.* (Rec. Com.), ii. 422–3; C 132/31/1 no. 7; C 133/76/7 no. 8; C.R.O., 619/M 41.
[56] *Rot. Hund.* ii. 423–4; C 134/8 no. 11.
[57] C 132/31/1 no. 7.
[58] C 135/28/17 no. 8.
[59] C 135/222 no. 15.
[60] C.R.O., 619/M 40–1; cf. 619/M 1, ct. roll 16 Edw. II.
[61] Ibid. M 1–6, *passim.*
[62] Ibid. M 5, ct. roll 6 Hen. V; cf. M 6, ct. roll 4 Hen. VI.
[63] e.g. ibid. M 1, ct. roll 48 Edw. III; M 2, ct. roll 16 Ric. II; M 3, ct. roll 10 Hen. IV; M 4, ct. roll 4 Hen. IV; M 5, ct. roll 1 Hen. V.
[64] Ibid. M 19, pp. 21–3.
[65] Ibid. M 1, ct. roll 48 Edw. III; M 2, ct. roll 16 Ric. II; M 3, ct. roll 8 Hen. IV; M 5, ct. rolls 5–6 Hen. V.
[66] Ibid. M 3, ct. roll 10 Hen. IV; M 4, ct. rolls 12–13 Hen. IV.
[67] e.g. C 135/222 no. 15.
[68] e.g. King's Coll. Mun., G 67, 76; C.R.O., 619/M 9, ct. roll 36 Hen. VIII.
[69] C.R.O., 619/M 40–1.
[70] Ibid. M 11, ct. rolls 15, 20 Eliz. I.
[71] Ibid. M 66; cf. B.L. Maps, 1640(15).
[72] C.R.O., 619/M 9, ct. roll 25 Hen. VIII.
[73] e.g. B.L. Add. MS. 5861, ff. 87v., 104.
[74] Palmer, *Neighbourhood of Hildersham*, 27.
[75] C.R.O., 619/M 11, ct. roll 20 Eliz. I; cf. B.L. Add. MS. 5861, ff. 20v.–21.
[76] B.L. Add. MS. 5823, ff. 212–13; cf. C.R.O., 619/E 20, *passim.*
[77] C.R.O., 619/M 66; cf. Gt. Abington Incl. Act, 41 Geo. III, c. 61 (Private, not printed), p. 1.
[78] *V.C.H. Cambs.* i. 408.
[79] E 179/242/8 m. 8.

from 260 to 320 sheep. Sometimes sheep were brought from the lord's other manors to feed at Great Abington after harvest.[80] In 1575 the lord was said to have a right to fold 500 sheep,[81] and in 1606 Sir John Spencer directed his lessee to keep a sheep for every acre of his farm.[82] In the 15th century some villagers were keeping 100 or 120 sheep, and *c.* 1433 a shepherd in charge of 600 trespassed in the lord's wood.[83] Ancient rights of common and foldage began to be reduced in the early 16th century: the King's College fold, claimed for 300 sheep, was reduced in 1535 to 80 sheep, while Westleys was restricted to 140 sheep-commons and the other tenants to 200 altogether. The college's and Parys's farmers were ordered not to take in strangers' sheep while villagers were willing to make up numbers in their folds from their own sheep.[84] Cattle were stinted in 1560 at 6 for each plough kept, and in 1591 commoners were forbidden to take in outsiders' cattle.[85] By 1679 copyholders were permitted to keep only one sheep in the lord's fold for every 2 a. they owned. The lord was still being requested to provide a parish bull and boar in 1737.[86]

The fields of Little Abington were also divided into relatively small blocks, some of which were called fields.[87] By 1600 they were grouped into three, Mill, Middle, and West fields.[88] The usual three-field rotation was followed, barley, the principal crop, being apparently sown in both the winter and spring fields. By 1700 clover and sainfoin, and by 1748 vetches and lentils, had been added to the traditional crops.[89] Saffron was probably grown on the Jesus College estate from the late 15th century,[90] and the vicar William Bolton (d. 1500) had saffron gardens by the boundary with Babraham.[91] There was little if any permanent common pasture. As at Great Abington extensive rights of common were attached to some ancient tenements: Willinghams with 80 a. might pasture 80 sheep.[92] The village raised 71½ stone of wool for the levy of 1347, mostly from villagers.[93]

In the early 16th century most of the land in Great Abington outside the demesne was divided among *c.* 17 copyholders, one or two of whom by combining several half-yardlands occupied 50 a. or more.[94] The largest free tenement, then owned by King's College, was often leased to the lords of the manor.[95] Few villagers were prosperous. Of 19 taxpayers in 1524 only John Martin, farmer of Westleys, was taxed at £5, the others being taxed at £2 or less, and 16 at £1.[96] Among the more prominent yeoman families were those of Bilduck, Beteyn, and Amy, which flourished, the last in several branches, in both parishes until the late 17th century.[97] Robert Amy was lessee of Great Abington rectory when he died in 1588.[98] About 1600, out of *c.* 370 a. of copyhold, three Amys held *c.* 80 a., Robert Higham, successor by marriage to another Amy, held 53 a., Robert Beteyn held 73 a., and the remainder was divided among 21 men, of whom 5 had over 20 a. each. Some 37 a. was held of the lord by tenants at will or on lease. The demesne, besides 30 a. of inclosed meadow, included 457 a. in the fields.[99] In the early 17th century it included several middle-sized farms, one of 123 a. near the wood, another of *c.* 160 a. Sir John Spencer apparently kept the latter, which included the land around the hall, in hand for a time, converting a 40-a. close from tillage to pasture.[1]

Little Abington, though less populous than its neighbour, was perhaps more prosperous. Seven people taxed there in 1524 had between them goods worth £33, compared with £25 altogether at Great Abington,[2] and under Charles II there were proportionately more dwellings with more than two hearths at Little than at Great Abington.[3] By 1600, however, Little Abington also was dominated by the demesne land, then called Cardinals, which comprised *c.* 466 a., including 430 a. of arable, divided into two farms. By then the lord also owned Leverers farm, *c.* 178 a., and thus controlled almost half the parish. Sir John Spencer agreed *c.* 1600 to sell the land he owned west of the Newmarket road to Sir Horatio Palavicino,[4] into whose Babraham estate it was thereafter incorporated. From 1663 to *c.* 1765 the Bennets of Babraham and their successors held the lease of the Jesus College estate in Little Abington with other land amounting to 140 a.[5] The number of substantial independent landholders in the parish declined from about 10 in the early 16th century[6] to about 7 by the 17th[7] and only 3 in the mid 18th century, as successive lords bought up more property.[8]

In 1653 the manorial estate included one substantial farm, perhaps in Little Abington, and six smaller holdings. Some land in Great Abington may have been in hand, for John Bennet the elder bought farming equipment with the estate.[9] From the late 17th century the area in Great Abington under independent yeoman owners diminished as the manorial estate was enlarged. John Bennet the younger began from 1683 to buy copyholds amounting to *c.* 100 a., including land of the Smee, Amy, and Beteyn families.[10] He consolidated his demesne, presumably by exchange and agreement, into large inclosed fields

80 C.R.O., 619/M 40–1.
81 C.P. 25(2)/93/842/20 Eliz. I Hil. no. 10.
82 *East Anglian*, N.S. xiii. 232.
83 C.R.O., 619/M 4, ct. roll 4 Hen. IV; M 6, ct. roll 11 Hen. VI.
84 Ibid. M 9, ct. rolls 25, 27 Hen. VIII.
85 Ibid. M 11, ct. rolls 2, 33 Eliz. I.
86 Ibid. M 25, 27.
87 e.g. C.R.O., 619/E 2; Jesus Coll. Mun., terrier 16th cent.
88 C.R.O., 619/M 66.
89 e.g. King's Coll. Mun., G 82; B.L. Add. MS. 5861, f. 86v.; Add. MS. 5823, f. 212.
90 Jesus Coll. Mun., leases 1473, 1508.
91 Prob. 11/12 (P.C.C. 11 Moore).
92 C 78/32 no. 33 m. 35.
93 E 179/242/8 mm. 7d.–8.
94 C.R.O., 619/M 50–5.
95 e.g. King's Coll. Mun., G 92.
96 E 179/81/134 mm. 2d.–3; cf. C.R.O., 619/M 9, ct. roll 27 Hen. VIII.
97 e.g. S.P. 14/23 no. 15; C.R.O., 619/M 50–6; 619/M 11, ct. rolls 2–6 Eliz. I; cf. B.L. Add. MS. 5861, ff. 20v.–21, 83.
98 Prob. 11/73 (P.C.C. 44 Leicester).
99 C.R.O., 619/M 66.
1 *East Anglian*, N.S. xiii. 232–3, 267–8.
2 E 179/81/134 mm. 2d.–3.
3 See pp. 278–80.
4 B.L. Maps, 1690(1).
5 Jesus Coll. Mun., Memorabilia Bk. p. 177; cf. Bodl. MS. Gough Camb. 103(7), p. 3.
6 e.g. C.R.O., 619/E 2; Jesus Coll. Mun., terrier 16th cent.
7 C.R.O., 619/M 66; King's Coll. Mun., G 79.
8 e.g. King's Coll. Mun., G 81; Jesus Coll. Mun., terrier 1768.
9 C.R.O., 619/M 42.
10 Ibid. E 11; T 2–8.

covering most of the eastern half and southern end of the parish. The western side and a few blocks along the eastern edge were left divided in the traditional fashion into strips, shared among 13 owners. The copyholders released their rights of common over the newly inclosed fields in 1686, and the process had probably been completed by 1687.[11] In the upshot, of a manorial estate amounting in 1716 to 636 a., *c.* 465 a. lay in the new inclosures and only 11 a. in the uninclosed fields to the west. There were also *c.* 70 a. of ancient closes around the Hall.[12] John Bennet sowed sainfoin on *c.* 35 a. which he had kept in hand.[13] He also installed engines *c.* 1690 to water the grounds round the Hall and a 100-a. plot, but his underground pipes broke.[14] His enterprises were imprudently financed,[15] and he became bankrupt in 1697. The Great Abington estate included *c.* 1726 a great farm of 444 a. comprising most of the new inclosures and farmed from New House farm, built south-east of the Hall by 1716, another farm including *c.* 55 a. of pasture closes near the Hall and *c.* 35 a. of arable run from the old farmstead east of the Hall, and *c.* 60 a. of small holdings. The smaller farm, called Hall farm, covered 200 a. by 1771.[16] Thomas Western (d. 1754) went on buying out the copyholders,[17] and by 1800 the Hall estate included most of the parish.

At Little Abington the land was still being farmed in the customary open fields *c.* 1794,[18] and even at Great Abington traditional methods probably continued on the uninclosed lands, over which rights of common were being regulated in 1737.[19] In 1801 Great Abington produced 176 a. of wheat, 92 a. of rye, 245 a. of barley, and 127 a. of oats; 20 a. of turnips were also grown.[20] In that year, shortly after John Mortlock had bought the manors, inclosure Acts were procured for both parishes, unopposed except by Mortlock's principal tenant. The Act for Little Abington provided for most of the land west of the turnpike to be allotted to the Adeane estate in Babraham.[21] The land of each parish was probably divided the same year, and the Great Abington award was executed in 1804, that for Little Abington not until 1807.[22] At Great Abington, where the earlier inclosures were included in the award, almost the whole parish was allotted to John Mortlock who emerged with 1,131 a. out of 1,532 a., besides his ancient closes. The vicar received *c.* 79 a. and King's College 56 a. along the eastern boundary. Seven men who were allotted 13 a. between them for common rights had been bought out by Mortlock before 1818.[23] At Little Abington, where 1,166 a. were allotted, Mortlock received 585 a. in the west part of the parish, and Andrew Perne, the impropriator, *c.* 224 a. in the east. The centre was divided between the vicar with 71 a. and Jesus, King's, and Clare colleges with *c.* 135 a. together. The Lagden estate received *c.* 94 a. by the eastern edge, and the Fairchild devisees 126 a. Two other allottees had just over 3 a.[24] During the next 110 years virtually the whole of both parishes was gradually incorporated into the Abington Hall estate.

By 1818 Great Abington, apart from the glebe, had been divided into three large farms, an arrangement that survived until the 1930s. The Hall farm, covering in 1929 229 a., included the land nearest the village. South of the main east–west road lay New House farm, comprising 657 a. in 1818, 634 a. in 1929. The southern third of the parish, including the 60 a. of former woodland called Great Park, formed Abington Park farm, covering 543 a. in 1818, 539 a. in 1929. A new farm-house north of the Park had been built by 1818. In Little Abington the Mortlock land south of the Cambridge road, probably farmed until the 1830s with Hall farm, later became Bancroft farm, of 119 a. in 1929. Its ancient timber-framed farm-house was burnt down in a family feud in the 1860s. North of the road was Grange farm, 475 a. in 1929, for which a new farmstead was built out in the fields. Similarly the consolidated Lay Rectory farm of *c.* 360 a. had a large farm-house built just outside the village, and by 1871 an extra farmstead in the fields, called New Barns. Between 1850 and 1900 it was farmed by its owners, the Kents. The smaller glebe and college properties in the middle of the parish were consolidated after their absorption into the Hall estate as College Field farm, covering in 1929 156 a.[25]

In both parishes most of the land was arable. In 1818 only 78 a. of 1,215 a. on the larger farms in Great Abington were under permanent grass. New House farm was then being cultivated on a four-year rotation.[26] John Mortlock had earlier kept a considerable flock of Southdown sheep, fed partly on hay and turnips,[27] and the two parishes together provided employment for up to 12 shepherds in the mid 19th century.[28] Lay Rectory farm was described as an excellent turnip farm in 1850.[29] In 1929 there were still only 85 a. of permanent grass in Great Abington and 120 a. in Little Abington.[30]

Most of the working population throughout the 19th century were farm labourers. In each parish in 1831 44 families were dependent on agriculture, and only 7 on crafts and trade.[31] In 1851 69 men and boys were employed on the farms at Great Abington; in 1871 41 men and 23 boys worked at Great, and 27 men and 16 boys at Little, Abington.[32] In 1873 it was estimated that *c.* 250 out of 300 inhabitants at Great Abington were of the labouring class. At Little Abington *c.* 1877 the proportion was two-thirds.[33] In the early 20th century 4 a. of the Hall estate were let as allotments for them.[34] Fourteen people in 1871 were attached to the households at the Hall and Lodge as gardeners, grooms, and game-

[11] C.R.O., 619/M 14, ct. roll 1686; C.U.L., MS. Plan 614.
[12] B.L. Maps, 1690(1).
[13] C.R.O., 619/M 43–4.
[14] Ibid. E 20, m. 27.
[15] Cf. C 78/1365 no. 1.
[16] C.R.O., 619/M 43–4; 619/T 22–3.
[17] e.g. C.P. 43/295 (2nd nos.) rott. 43–6.
[18] Vancouver, *Agric. in Cambs.* 56–8.
[19] C.R.O., 619/M 27.
[20] H.O. 67/9.
[21] *C.J.* lvi. 19–20, 293; *L.J.* xliii. 313, 488; Gt. Abington Incl. Act, 41 Geo. III, c. 61 (Private, not printed); Lit. Abington Incl. Act, 41 Geo. III, c. 123 (Private not printed).
[22] Cf. C.R.O., Q/RDz 5, pp. 84, 92.
[23] Ibid. pp. 85–92; cf. C.U.L., Maps 53(1)/93/73–4.
[24] C.R.O., Q/RDz 5, pp. 73–84.
[25] C.U.L., Maps 53(1)/93/73–4; MS. Plan 614; C.R.O., SP 1/8; *Kelly's Dir. Cambs.* (1858–1937); *Cambs. Local Hist. Counc. Bull.* xxi. 29–31; R.G. 10/1592.
[26] C.U.L., Maps 53(1)/93/73–4.
[27] Gooch, *Agric. of Cambs.* 49–50, 272–4.
[28] e.g. R.G. 9/1029; R.G. 10/1592.
[29] C.U.L., Maps bb 53/85/5.
[30] C.R.O., SP 1/8.
[31] *Census*, 1831.
[32] H.O. 107/1761; R.G. 10/1592.
[33] C.U.L., E.D.R., C 3/25–6.
[34] C.R.O., SP 1/8.

keepers.[35] From 1843 to *c.* 1922 John Rickett and his son J. J. Rickett kept a stonemason's and builder's business.[36] Otherwise neither parish usually had more than two or three craftsmen such as carpenters, blacksmiths, wheelwrights, shoemakers, and tailors.[37] After 1900 even those few disappeared.[38] A new element entered parish life when in 1936 the Land Settlement Association bought New House farm to divide it into 10-a. smallholdings for people from areas such as South Wales and County Durham for market-gardening and pig- and poultry-rearing. By 1962 46 such holdings had been established. From *c.* 1950 the produce included tomatoes and lettuces, and glass-houses covered 9 a. of the estate by 1968.[39] The Welding Research Association at Abington Hall employed a staff that increased from 40 in 1946 to 125 in 1958.[40] From the 1950s the village began to have a large proportion of middle-class residents, who mostly worked in Cambridge and large neighbouring villages.[41]

By a charter of 1257 the earl of Oxford was granted a weekly market at Great Abington on Fridays and a three-day fair at the feast of St. Lawrence.[42] Neither is recorded later.

Aubrey de Vere had a water-mill at Great Abington in 1086.[43] By 1279 it was apparently attached to the free tenement divided between Richard Bassingbourn and Roger son of John.[44] Roger's half had come by 1342 to Roger Abington, with whose lands it was conveyed to King's College in 1448.[45] In 1318 the miller was accused of forbidding the earl's customary tenants to grind their own grain,[46] and a successor in 1405 was not keeping his dams in repair.[47] The mill was not recorded after 1500. Little Abington manor also included a mill in 1086.[48] About 1200 John de Lanvaley and later his widow Christine released a mill, with the customary yardland of Ralph Sexmere, to Waltham abbey,[49] of which Walter Sexmere held it in 1279.[50] By 1395 Sexmere mill belonged to Robert Parys, who had lately moved its floodgates to a new place, causing flooding in Great Abington's meadows.[51] His widow Catherine and brother Nicholas continued the nuisance between 1409 and 1416.[52] Half a mill included in a conveyance of 1554 by Sir Philip Parys to John Chapman[53] is not recorded later. The site of neither mill has been traced. A windmill may have stood on or near Windmill hill in Little Abington by 1600,[54] but there was no mill in either parish by the 19th century.[55]

LOCAL GOVERNMENT. Under Edward I the earl of Oxford had at Great Abington view of frankpledge, which he claimed in 1299 by prescription, with the assize of bread and of ale and a gallows and tumbrel.[56] By custom 4*s.* of the court issues were paid twice yearly to the bailiff of the hundred.[57] In 1376 the goods found on a thief who escaped were seized for the lord.[58] In the 14th and 15th centuries a court leet was usually held annually at Trinity, and one or more courts baron in spring or autumn. After 1500 a single session for all purposes was held once a year, and later at longer intervals.[59] In 1403 two men were fined for revealing the counsels of the leet and opposing its decisions in open court.[60] By ancient custom the reeve was to be elected by the villeins out of court,[61] but the court regularly chose two ale-tasters,[62] one or two constables or under-constables,[63] and haywards.[64] After 1530 it sometimes appointed two men to oversee the fields.[65] The court undertook the usual leet jurisdiction down to the early 17th century. As late as 1653 it was forbidding inhabitants to harbour strange inmates, or to build cottages on the waste without the assent of the township.[66] In 1681 eleven such inmates were being sheltered and three non-commonable dwellings had been built.[67] It also enforced regulations and customs concerning agriculture,[68] a practice continued at intervals until 1737 or later by verdicts of the jury;[69] after 1663[70] the verdicts ceased to be recorded on the rolls, which were thereafter solely a record of copyholds. Court rolls survive for 1318, 1321–2, and, with gaps, for 1354–1435, 1450–1, 1485–99, 1527–48, and 1558–1694, and court books for 1711–1841.[71]

It was said in 1276 that the bailiff of the honor of Richmond had made himself steward to Robert Tuddenham and usurped view of frankpledge and the assize of bread and of ale at Little Abington, also withdrawing the Gerunde and St. Radegund fees from the sheriff's tourn.[72] In 1334 the reeve and four men from Little Abington did suit to the honor court at Linton, at which the assize of ale was enforced for their township;[73] although Tuddenham was said to have view of frankpledge in 1279, in

35 R.G. 10/1592.
36 *Cambs. Local Hist. Counc. Bull.* xvii. 25; *Kelly's Dir. Cambs.* (1858–1922).
37 e.g. H.O. 107/66; R.G. 9/1029; *Cambs. Local Hist. Counc. Bull.* xxi. 27–9.
38 *Kelly's Dir. Cambs.* (1900, 1937).
39 C.R.O., R 57/17/1, ff. 55v.–56; *Camb. Ind. Press*, 11 Nov. 1961; 3 May 1968.
40 C.R.O., R 57/17/1, f. 66.
41 *Camb. Ind. Press*, 11 Nov. 1961.
42 *Cal. Chart. R.* 1226–57, 475.
43 *V.C.H. Cambs.* i. 390.
44 *Rot. Hund.* (Rec. Com.), ii. 422.
45 King's Coll. Mun., G 67–73.
46 C.R.O., 619/M 1, ct. roll 11 Edw. II.
47 Ibid. M 3, ct. roll 6 Hen. IV.
48 *V.C.H. Cambs.* i. 374.
49 B.L. Cott. MS. Tib. C. ix, f. 128v.
50 Ibid. f. 228; *Rot. Hund.* ii. 423.
51 C.R.O., 619/M 2, ct. rolls 18–19 Ric. II.
52 Ibid. M 3, ct. roll 10 Hen. IV; M 5, ct. roll 4 Hen. V.
53 C.P. 25(2)/68/558 no. 7.
54 C.R.O., 619/M 66.
55 *Cambs. Local Hist. Counc. Bull.* xx. 28–9.
56 *Rot. Hund.* (Rec. Com.), i. 52; ii. 422; *Plac. de Quo Warr.* (Rec. Com.), 104.
57 e.g. C.R.O., 619/M 1, ct. roll 11 Edw. II; M 3, ct. roll 7 Hen. IV.
58 Ibid. M 1, ct. roll 50 Edw. III.
59 Ibid. M 1–12, *passim.*
60 Ibid. M 4, ct. roll 4 Hen. IV.
61 Ibid.
62 e.g. ibid. M 1, ct. roll 48 Edw. III; M 2, ct. roll 6 Ric. II.
63 e.g. ibid. M 2, ct. rolls 10, 18 Ric. II; M 7, ct. roll 18 Edw. IV; M 11, ct. roll 1 Eliz. I.
64 e.g. ibid. M 12, ct. roll 15 Jas. I.
65 e.g. ibid. M 9, ct. roll 22 Hen. VIII.
66 Ibid. M 13, ct. roll 1653.
67 Ibid. M 26.
68 Ibid. M 9, ct. roll 25 Hen. VIII; M 9–13, *passim.*
69 Ibid. M 22–27.
70 Ibid. M 13, ct. roll 14 Chas. II.
71 C.R.O., 619/M 1–20.
72 *Rot. Hund.* (Rec. Com.), i. 52.
73 S.C. 2/155/71 mm. 1–2.

1309 his tenants were said not to render suit of court.[74] Leet jurisdiction at Little Abington may therefore have been absorbed by the Richmond court. No evidence has been found after 1279 for the existence of a separate court for Little Abington manor. In the early 18th century the Great Abington court occasionally appointed one constable for each parish.[75] In the 18th and 19th centuries, perhaps owing to the absence of a court for Little Abington, the transfer of some copyholds there was made in the court of Hildersham with Little Abington manor;[76] that court was also appointing a constable and a pinder for Little Abington in the 1720s.[77]

In the early 19th century Great Abington was apparently administered by a small vestry, comprising a churchwarden, two overseers, and two or three of the wealthier parishioners.[78] Expenditure on the poor had increased from *c.* £60 in 1776 to £96 by 1783–5 and £166 in 1803 when 22 people were on permanent relief.[79] Those regularly supported from the rates still numbered between 22 and 28 from 1813 to 1815. The cost between 1813[80] and 1834 was usually over £300, and sometimes exceeded £350.[81] About 1830 the farmers were expected to find work for the able poor in proportion to the size of their farms, and large families had an allowance from the rates.[82] In practice over two-thirds of the money spent in the early 1830s apparently went to widows and the aged.[83]

At Little Abington the amount spent on the poor and the numbers relieved were smaller. The cost rose from £6 in 1776 to £38 in 1783–5 and £80 by 1803 when 9 persons were permanently supported. In 1814 13 persons were on permanent relief, and the total cost was £156.[84] About 1830 large families were assisted from the rates, and of the then normal expenditure of *c.* £160 about half usually went to the aged, mostly widows, and less than a quarter on casual relief, given mostly to large families and the sick. Men working for the parish seldom took over £10 a year, and might be employed on the road or, as in 1830–2, on repairing the parish houses.[85] Those houses, three cottages occupied in 1836 by paupers rent-free, were sold in 1837 to help meet the cost of building Linton workhouse.[86]

Both parishes were from 1835 part of the Linton poor-law union,[87] were incorporated with the Linton R.D. in 1934 into the South Cambridgeshire R.D.,[88] and were included in South Cambridgeshire in 1974.

CHURCHES. The church of Little Abington includes fabric which may be of *c.* 1100; demesne tithes there were granted *c.* 1130, and the advowson was recorded *c.* 1200. Great Abington had its own church by 1217:[89] the advowson was attached until the early 14th century to the manor of the earls of Oxford,[90] who sometimes presented relatives, such as Earl Robert's son Gilbert de Vere, rector while still a minor *c.* 1289.[91] Before 1217 the earls had granted two-thirds of their demesne tithes to Hatfield Broadoak priory (Essex), to which the rector was ordered to pay 17*s.* 4*d.* a year. Earl Hugh (d. 1263) granted the priory a site for a barn to store its tithes,[92] which were worth 5 marks in 1254 and 1291.[93] In 1329 the earl was licensed to grant the rectory itself to the priory for appropriation,[94] which had been accomplished by 1344. A vicarage was ordained, of which the advowson remained with Hatfield priory until its dissolution in 1536.[95] In 1538 two yeomen presented under a grant for that turn made by the priory.[96] In 1540 the advowson was granted to Philip Parys with the impropriate rectory,[97] with which it descended in the Parys and Dalton families until bought by John Bennet in 1679, after which it passed with the manors until 1929.[98]

At Little Abington the advowson was attached to the manor by *c.* 1200, when Simon le Bret granted half the advowson to Waltham abbey (Essex). Simon, however, failed in warranting the grant in 1204, when William de Lanvaley the younger, to whom he had meanwhile released the manor, recovered the advowson.[99] William's successor John de Burgh granted it in 1239 to Hugh de Vaux,[1] whose heir John de Vaux did not subinfeudate it with the manor to Robert Tuddenham, but retained it until his death in 1287, whereupon it was included in the purparty of his elder daughter Parnel, wife of William of Narford[2] (d. 1302).[3] In 1316 Parnel granted the advowson, said erroneously to be held of Robert Tuddenham, to Pentney priory (Norf.). The priory had appropriated the rectory by 1341,[4] and retained it until its dissolution in 1537,[5] but the advowson of the vicarage was reserved to the bishop of Ely, who continued to collate to it until the 16th century.[6] Being in the bishop's patronage the vicarage was exempted from the archdeacon of Ely's jurisdiction until the 18th century.[7] The Crown occasionally presented during vacancies of the see.[8] In 1540 the grant of Little Abington rectory to Philip Parys purported

[74] *Rot. Hund.* ii. 423; C 134/8 no. 11.
[75] C.R.O., 619/M 19, pp. 8, 13, 15–16.
[76] Ibid. R 51/25/35, especially pp. 39–46, 60–2, 147–8, 155–61.
[77] e.g. Hildersham ct. bk. 1706–44, ff. 27, 38, *penes* Mr. H. B. Binney.
[78] C.R.O., P 1/11/1.
[79] *Poor Law Abstract, 1804*, 34–5.
[80] Ibid. *1818*, 28–9.
[81] *Poor Rate Returns, 1816–21*, 10; *1822–4*, 37; *1825–9*, 15–16; *1830–4*, 15.
[82] *Rep. H. L. Cttee. on Poor Laws*, H.C. 227, pp. 326–7 (1831), viii.
[83] e.g. C.R.O., P 2/12/9.
[84] *Poor Law Abstract, 1804*, 34–5; *1818*, 28–9.
[85] *Rep. H.L. Cttee. on Poor Laws*, pp. 346–7; C.R.O., P 2/1/1–10.
[86] C.R.O., P 2/19/1; P 2/1/2, at end.
[87] *Poor Law Com. 1st Rep.* 249.
[88] *Census*, 1931.
[89] See below.
[90] e.g. *Rot. Hund.* (Rec. Com.), ii. 422.
[91] *Cal. Papal Reg.* i. 501.
[92] Essex R.O., D/D 6A T 1/2; B.L. Add. Ch. 28397.
[93] *Val. of Norwich*, ed. Lunt, 276; *Tax. Eccl.* (Rec. Com.), 267.
[94] C 143/205 no. 15; *Cal. Pat.* 1327–30, 397.
[95] *E.D.R.* (1890), 461; (1909), 48; Dugdale, *Mon.* iv. 435; *V.C.H. Essex*, ii. 109.
[96] *E.D.R.* (1912), 19.
[97] *L. & P. Hen. VIII*, xv, p. 467.
[98] *E.D.R.* (1914), 361; C.U.L., E.D.R., B 2/18, f. 216.
[99] B.L. Cott. MS. Tib. C. ix, ff. 101v., 104v.; *Cur. Reg. R.* iii. 218, 262.
[1] C.P. 25(2)/24/19 no. 1.
[2] *Rot. Hund.* (Rec. Com.), ii. 423; *Cal. Inq. p.m.* ii, p. 404.
[3] *Cal. Inq. p.m.* iv, p. 76.
[4] C 143/115 no. 9; *Cal. Pat.* 1313–17, 435; *E.D.R.* (1890), 416.
[5] Dugdale, *Mon.* vi. 70; *V.C.H. Norf.* ii. 390.
[6] e.g. *E.D.R.* (1893), 57; (1911), 69.
[7] B.L. Add. MS. 5823, f. 213v.; cf. Add. MS. 5842, ff. 14v.–15; Bentham, *Hist. Ely*, 269.
[8] e.g. *Cal. Pat.* 1399–1401, 364; 1429–36, 491.

to include the advowson of the vicarage,[9] so Parys's successor Michael Dalton claimed to present upon a vacancy in 1604. Bishop Heton conceded his claim in 1608, but the bishop's nominee retained the living,[10] and the bishops continued to collate vicars until the mid 18th century.[11] By the 1730s, when for 70 years it had been the practice for both benefices to be held by the same man, the bishop had agreed with the Westerns, as patrons of Great Abington, that since the two livings were separately too poor to attract clergymen, the two patrons should nominate to both alternately. In 1736 the bishop collated to Little Abington independently, but within two months his nominee resigned in favour of the man presented to Great Abington by Thomas Western. Thereafter the bishop apparently no longer exercised the patronage,[12] and was last recorded as patron *c.* 1792;[13] Little Abington vicarage was served by the vicars or sequestrators who held Great Abington. In 1802 the Crown presented to Little Abington, for reasons unknown, the man who had already held Great Abington for 10 years.[14] Andrew Perne, the impropriator, was said to be patron of Little Abington in 1800, and his widow in 1836,[15] probably in error. Thomas Mortlock was styled patron in 1851[16] and E. J. Mortlock from 1877. The patronage of both livings passed with the manors to the Emersons,[17] and was sold in 1930 to the Martyrs' Memorial Trust to which it still belonged in 1973.[18] In 1947 the two benefices were formally united, the ecclesiastical parishes remaining distinct.[19]

About 1130 Count Stephen, lord of Richmond, granted demesne tithes at Little Abington to St. Mary's Abbey, York,[20] to whose dependent priory at Rumburgh (Suff.) they were being paid by 1291, when they were worth 4 marks.[21] In 1326 Alan, abbot of St. Mary's, leased them to Pentney priory, which retained them until 1463 when after 10 years' non-payment the abbey took possession again.[22] Rumburgh's properties were annexed in 1528 to Wolsey's proposed college at Ipswich and were sold by the Crown in 1531.[23]

In the early 13th century the two rectories, after deducting monastic portions, were of almost equal value, Great Abington being taxed at 10 marks in 1217 and 1254, Little Abington at 9 marks. In 1276, however, they were worth respectively 30 and 13 marks, but in 1291 16 and 12 marks.[24]

The glebe of Great Abington rectory, 30 a. in 1279,[25] was included in the appropriation to Hatfield priory. The vicar had only 1¼ rood near his vicarage. Besides the small tithes, levied *c.* 1700 according to an ancient modus, he received from the rectory a cash pension of £2 a year and 6 qr. of corn, and from 10 copyhold messuages 245 eggs and 14 bu. of barley.[26] At inclosure in 1801 the vicar was allotted *c.* 78 a. for his glebe and tithes.[27] The pension, charged in 1929 on Abington Hall, was redeemed *c.* 1958.[28]

Of Little Abington's rectorial glebe, 40 a. in 1279,[29] 12½ a. were assigned to the vicar,[30] who had also the small tithes, levied by a modus by 1700, and tithes of hay. A pension due to him from the rectory, 33*s.* 4*d.* *c.* 1700,[31] had been increased by 1877 to £5 a year, which in 1929 was charged on Lay Rectory farm.[32] At inclosure the vicar was allotted *c.* 71 a. for his glebe and tithes.[33] The glebe of both vicarages was sold in 1907 to J. J. Emerson.[34] Following appropriation the two vicarages were almost equally poor, Great Abington being worth £7 16*s.* 2*d.* in 1535, Little Abington £7 6*s.* 4*d.*[35] In 1650 Great Abington yielded only £18 a year, while the vicar of Little Abington, having received in 1649 a substantial augmentation, was supposed to have £30 a year.[36] About 1728 their respective incomes were £22 and £20.[37] Following an augmentation by lot of £200 from Queen Anne's Bounty in 1778[38] the value of Great Abington had risen to *c.* £80 by 1830 and £160 gross in 1877. That of Little Abington stood at £87 in the early 19th century, and in 1877 included *c.* £105 from the glebe.[39]

Great Abington vicarage house, ruinous in 1615, was burnt down probably in the 1660s and not rebuilt.[40] Its site has not been traced. Resident vicars later lived in Little Abington vicarage house,[41] which stood a little east of the church, close to the river.[42] It was reconstructed *c.* 1810 by the then vicar, and *c.* 1830 Queen Anne's Bounty lent £327 for similar rebuilding.[43] When during the 19th century Great Abington again had vicars of its own, they sometimes lived at Ivy Lodge,[44] a Georgian house on the Hildersham road. Little Abington vicarage was sold in 1961,[45] and a new house built at the north end of its grounds.

In 1521 Great Abington contained a guild of St. Anne,[46] and in 1524 possibly also a guild of All

9 *L. & P. Hen. VIII*, xv, p. 467.
10 C.U.L., E.D.R., G 1/7, f. 206 and v.; cf. ibid. B 2/32, f. 4.
11 P.R.O., Inst. Bks. ser. A, iii, p. 31; ser. B, i, p. 60; iv, p. 133.
12 Ibid. ser. C, i, f. 438v.; B.L. Add. MS. 5823, f. 216.
13 C.U.L., E.D.R., B 8/4.
14 P.R.O., Inst. Bks. ser. C, i, f. 445v.; and see below.
15 Lysons, *Cambs.* 79; C.U.L., E.D.R., C 3/21.
16 *Gardner's Dir. Cambs.* (1851).
17 C.U.L., E.D.R., C 3/26; *Kelly's Dir. Cambs.* (1864–1929).
18 Ex inf. the Deputy Secretary, Church Pastoral Aid Society.
19 *Lond. Gaz.* 31 Oct. 1947, p. 5139.
20 *Early Yorks. Chart.* iv (Y.A.S. extra ser. i), pp. 8–10.
21 *Tax. Eccl.* (Rec. Com.), 267; cf. E 40/14291–2.
22 C 1/33 no. 38.
23 *V.C.H. Suff.* ii. 78.
24 *Val. of Norwich*, ed. Lunt, 226, 536, 558; *Tax. Eccl.* (Rec. Com.), 267.
25 *Rot. Hund.* (Rec. Com.), ii. 422.
26 C.U.L., E.D.R., H 1/1, terriers 1615, 1639; B.L. Add. MS. 5823, ff. 212, 273v.; C.R.O., SP 1/8.
27 C.R.O., Q/RDz 5, p. 87.
28 Ibid. SP 1/8; *Camb. Ind. Press*, 13 Jan. 1970.
29 *Rot. Hund.* (Rec. Com.), ii. 423.
30 C.U.L., E.D.R., H 1/1, terriers 1615, 1635, 1663.
31 B.L. Add. MS. 5823, f. 212.
32 C.U.L., E.D.R., C 3/26; C.R.O., SP 1/8.
33 C.R.O., Q/RDz 5, pp. 76–7.
34 Ex inf. the Church Com.
35 *Valor Eccl.* (Rec. Com.), iii. 393.
36 Lamb. Pal. MS. 904, ff. 274, 277; cf. W. A. Shaw, *Hist. Eng. Ch. 1640–60*, ii. 524.
37 C.U.L., E.D.R., B 8/1.
38 Hodgson, *Queen Anne's Bounty*, 310; cf. *Eng. Topog.* (Gent. Mag. Libr.), ii. 16.
39 *Rep. Com. Eccl. Revenues*, pp. 344–5; C.U.L., E.D.R., C 3/26.
40 C.U.L., E.D.R., H 1/1, terrier 1615; B 8/1.
41 Ibid. B 7/1; C 1/6; cf. B.L. Add. MS. 5823, f. 215.
42 C.R.O., 124/P 1–2.
43 *Eng. Topog.* ii. 17; *Rep. Com. Eccl. Revenues*, pp. 344–5; C.U.L., E.D.R., C 3/21.
44 C.R.O., R 57/17/1, f. 42.
45 Ex inf. the Church Com.
46 B.L. Add. MS. 5861, f. 84v.

Saints.[47] In 1561 the earl of Oxford granted the guildhall or church house to John Amy as copyhold.[48] It may have been the long timber-framed building by the path to the church. Land in the two parishes left for lights and obits was sold by the Crown in 1548, 1568, and 1571.[49] Under John Bolton's will proved 1509 each church received 3*s*. a year for repairs and 4*d*. for the curate, and there was a provision for masses. When Bolton's lands were settled on Clare College in 1524 it was agreed that a fellow of Clare should preach in Little Abington church on the first Sunday in Lent.[50] The sermons probably continued in the early 18th century;[51] the churchwardens of each parish still received 3*s*. 4*d*. for repairs in the 20th century.[52]

Little Abington saw a rapid turnover of seven vicars through exchanges between 1389 and 1402.[53] John Drury, vicar from 1435, was bound over in 1448 not to molest the duke of Somerset's tenants, and was deprived in 1465.[54] Early-16th-century vicars of each parish were usually resident,[55] and some, such as Henry Amy, at Little Abington *c*. 1532–*c*. 1552, and Robert Thurger, at Great Abington *c*. 1538–*c*. 1552,[56] were probably from local families.[57] After 1560 the two livings were sometimes held jointly. Thomas Chamber was vicar of Great and curate of Little Abington in 1564 when he was alleged not to catechize or read the homilies.[58] Thomas Goodman, vicar of Little Abington by 1567, was then curate and sequestrator of Great Abington to which he was presented in 1573.[59] He used to serve both churches on the same day. The parishioners complained in 1578 that he attended more diligently to his husbandry than to his pastoral duties, in 1590 that he did not preach regularly, and in 1594 that he was found in the alehouse while they awaited him in church.[60] After his death in 1604[61] the livings were again separated. Roger Wincoll retained Little Abington from 1635 until his death in 1655 despite his poverty, company-keeping, and (by 1650) imbecility.[62] Henry Taverner at Great Abington also retained his living in 1650, although he frequented alehouses and opposed parliament.[63] Before 1660, however, he had had two successors, one probably a Presbyterian.[64]

From 1661 to 1828 the two cures were again held jointly, Great Abington being probably sometimes held by sequestration. John Boughton, vicar 1666–93, combined them with a fellowship at St. John's. His successor, Thomas Colbatch (1693–1732), an Oxford man,[65] was conscientious but eccentric.[66] In 1728 he was holding two Sunday services alternately at each church, with communion at the three principal feasts, a practice continued until the 1830s.[67] William Benning, vicar 1753–92,[68] lived in Essex in 1775 and employed a curate who held services twice on Sundays, probably alternately at each church,[69] as was done in 1825 when the same congregation was said to have long attended both.[70] In the late 18th century it was proposed to demolish Great Abington church because of its damp situation and unite the two parishes.[71] George Barlow, vicar 1792–1828, was resident in 1825 but employed a curate, being himself curate at Saffron Walden. There were then *c*. 40 communicants.[72] After his death the livings were separated.

The next vicar of Great Abington also held Newmarket St. Mary and Woodditton.[73] In 1835 Thomas Mortlock presented his own brother, Edmund Davy Mortlock, a fellow of Christ's College, where he lived, staying when in Great Abington at Thomas's cottage in the village. He introduced a second Sunday service, preached every Sunday, and had in 1836 *c*. 70 communicants. His contemporary at Little Abington, Charles Townley (1828–70), also held two Sunday services, and claimed 45 communicants and in 1851 an afternoon congregation of 140. E. D. Mortlock resigned in 1845.[74] Of his successors, Robert Goodwin (1845–88) also held Hildersham, and J. A. H. Law (1890–3) Babraham,[75] and they usually lived at their other benefices. The successive vicars of Little Abington lived in their own parish.[76] Goodwin, who employed two curates and held two Sunday services at Great Abington, claimed in 1873 that 250 out of his 300 parishioners came to church, and an average of 18 out of 50 communicants attended monthly communions. E. L. Pearson, who held similar services at Little Abington, had in 1877 a congregation of up to 150, including 57 communicants.[77] A. W. Smyth, who held both livings from 1893,[78] began to celebrate communion every Sunday and introduced special services for Lent and saints' days. In 1897 there were 82 communicants.[79] The two vicarages were afterwards always held by the same man.[80] From the 1920s the vicar complained of very poor attendance at church.[81] In 1973 the two churches were still used alternately, on Sunday mornings and evenings, by a congregation drawn from both villages.[82]

47 E 179/81/134 m. 3.
48 C.R.O., 619/M 11, ct. roll 4 Eliz. I; cf. *Trans. C.H.A.S.* i. 351.
49 *Cal. Pat.* 1548–9, 48; 1566–9, p. 163; 1569–72, p. 404.
50 C.U.L., consist. ct. wills, 1st ser. reg. E, ff. 58v.–59; *31st Rep. Com. Char.* 99, 104.
51 B.L. Add. MS. 5802, f. 8.
52 C.U.L., E.D.R., C 1/6; C 3/17; *Char. Digest Cambs. 1863–4*, 372–3; Char. Com. files.
53 *E.D.R.* (1890), 134, 173; (1898), 90, 108, 126.
54 *Cal. Pat.* 1429–36, 491; *Cal. Close*, 1447–54, 55, 57; *E.D.R.* (1902), 220; (1905), 128.
55 e.g. B.L. Add. MS. 5861, ff. 71, 76, 83, 87.
56 Ibid. f. 116; *E.D.R.* (1912), 19; *Cambs. Ch. Goods, temp. Edw. VI*, 60–1.
57 Cf. C.R.O., 619/M 8–11, *passim*.
58 C.U.L., E.D.R., B 2/4, ff. 21, 116–17.
59 Ibid. B 2/6, 8; *E.D.R.* (1914), 361.
60 *East Anglian*, N.S. xiii. 162; C.U.L., E.D.R., B 2/11, 13.
61 B.L. Add. MS. 5823, f. 218.
62 C.U.L., E.D.R., B 2/47A; Lamb. Pal. MS. 904, f. 249; B.L. Add. MS. 5823, f. 218.
63 Lamb. Pal. MS. 904, f. 274.
64 B.L. Add. MS. 5823, f. 217; *Bury Classis*, ii (Chetham Soc. N.S. xli), 189.
65 C.U.L., E.D.R., B 2/58, 67; A 6/3; *Alum. Cantab. to 1751*, i. 186; *Alum. Oxon. 1500–1714*, 299.
66 Palmer, *Wm. Cole*, 79; cf. B.L. Add. MS. 5823, f. 212.
67 C.U.L., E.D.R., B 8/1; C 1/6.
68 *Alum. Cantab. to 1751*, i. 135.
69 C.U.L., E.D.R., C 1/1.
70 Ibid. C 1/6.
71 Ibid. B 7/1, p. 114.
72 Ibid. C 1/6.
73 *Rep. Com. Eccl. Revenues*, pp. 344–5.
74 C.U.L., E.D.R., C 3/21; *Alum. Cantab. 1752–1900*, iv. 477; vi. 215; H.O. 129/188/2/1/1.
75 *Alum. Cantab. 1752–1900*, iii. 87; iv. 108.
76 Cf. C.U.L., E.D.R., B 1/16, 39.
77 Ibid. C 3/25–6.
78 *Alum. Cantab. 1752–1900*, v. 577.
79 C.U.L., E.D.R., C 3/36.
80 *Crockford* (1896 and later edns.).
81 C.R.O., 331/Z 6–8, *passim*.
82 Ex inf. the vicar, the Revd. R. Coates.

The church of *ST. MARY*, so called in 1518,[83] at Great Abington comprises a chancel, nave with south aisle and porch, and west tower. It is built of field stones with ashlar dressings. The fabric of the nave and chancel is early-13th-century at latest. Several lancets remain, including some small ones in the north wall of the chancel set in deep round-headed embrasures, perhaps of an earlier period. The two-storey west tower, surmounted by a short leaded spire, is also 13th-century, having no buttresses. Its west window consists of three lancets under a continuous moulding. Its arch is probably of the early 14th century, when also the south aisle with its four-bay arcade of quatrefoil piers was added. In the 15th century new windows were inserted in the nave and south aisle, and a three-light east window replaced three lancets in the chancel. A little medieval glass survived until 1816.[84] The south porch is 14th-century, and the south door probably medieval, but the doorway mouldings have been renewed. A similar north doorway was blocked and a modern window inserted there. The nave was still thatched in 1783, and the chancel as late as 1816.[85] There is no chancel arch, and a continuous waggon-roof, panelled and probably put up after 1605, extends as in 1742 over nave and chancel.[86] The font is early, with a plain round top on an octagonal base. In the south wall of the chancel is a double piscina. Stairs in the north wall of the nave, under a small window high up, probably led to the rood-screen which was still in place in 1742. The pulpit had formerly a sounding board of 1634.[87] Against the north wall of the chancel stands the monument of Sir William Halton (d. 1639), with his armoured figure recumbent on its side; as lessee of the manor, he probably lived at Abington Hall.[88] In 1644 William Dowsing destroyed 2 crosses and 40 superstitious pictures.[89] The south side of the church needed repair in 1665, and the whole was in bad condition in 1685.[90] It was found to be very dirty in 1783, the windows in decay and partly stopped with plaster.[91] In 1816 the east end of the aisle was used as a manorial pew, and a singing gallery stood by the tower.[92] The church had 250 sittings, 169 of them free, in 1873, when the children sat in the chancel.[93] The tower was repaired by 1897, and the whole church was restored between 1895 and 1900,[94] when the interior walls were left stripped of their plaster, and the fittings entirely renewed. A lightly painted organ in the chancel was brought from Pampisford church, probably between 1891 and 1897.[95] The churchyard was closed in 1885 because it was liable to flooding.[96]

The church had one chalice *c.* 1278, and two in 1552 with a silver cross.[97] Sir William Halton left it a communion cup worth £10,[98] presumably the silver cup and paten dated 1638 which the church still possessed in 1973, with an almsdish of 1727 and a plated flagon of 1876.[99] There were two bells in 1552 and three in 1742.[1] Of the five bells in 1783 three were broken.[2] In 1816 there were two bells, one of 1663 by Miles Gray, and recast in 1817 by Thomas Mears, the other recast in 1789.[3] Both survived in 1973. The registers are virtually complete from 1664; a register beginning in 1538 had been lost by 1783.[4]

The church of *ST. MARY*, so called in 1520,[5] at Little Abington, consists of a chancel, nave with north chapel and south porch, and west tower. It is built of field stones with ashlar dressings and was formerly much patched with brick.[6] The fabric of the nave may be of *c.* 1100. Its surviving doorways have round arches and heavy stonework. The blocked north doorway has rough chip-carving on its abacus. The chancel was rebuilt in the 13th century, of which period are its arch and the lancets in the north wall. The three stepped lancets, originally in the east wall, reinstated at the restoration of 1885, had been replaced by a three-light Perpendicular window, which retained until after 1742 some fragments of glass with donors' figures, dated 1526.[7] The three-storey tower is probably 14th-century, having a renewed Decorated west window and substantial buttresses. The belfry windows are cusped. In the south wall of the tower is a medieval tomb-recess. Bequests for leading the steeple were made in 1508 and 1520.[8] The tower arch and the western windows of the nave are probably also 14th-century. The eastern windows in the south wall of the nave are rectangular and were probably inserted in the late 15th century. The date of the small north chapel, which stands beyond an arch, is uncertain, for its windows were redesigned in the 19th century.[9] The south porch, though medieval, was much repaired in brick.[10] The chancel contains an early piscina with dog-tooth carving. The font, also early, has a massive square basin set on five columns.

The church was said to be badly covered *c.* 1300,[11] but was probably tiled by 1619.[12] The timbers of the roof were replaced in the 19th century, except for

[83] B.L. Add. MS. 5861, f. 63. See below, plate facing p. 257.
[84] *Eng. Topog.* (Gent. Mag. Libr.), ii. 14–15.
[85] Ibid. 13; Palmer, *Wm. Cole*, 78; C.U.L., E.D.R., B 7/1, p. 114.
[86] Palmer, *Wm. Cole*, 78; C.U.L., E.D.R., B 2/59, p. 37.
[87] Palmer, *Wm. Cole*, 78.
[88] C.R.O., 619/M 13, ct. roll 1653.
[89] *Trans. C.H.A.S.* iii. 89.
[90] C.U.L., E.D.R., B 2/59, p. 37; B 2/59A, f. 23.
[91] Ibid. B 7/1, p. 114.
[92] *Eng. Topog.* ii. 14–15.
[93] C.U.L., E.D.R., C 3/25.
[94] *E.D.R.* (1898), 68; (1899), 152; C.U.L., E.D.R., C 3/36; *Kelly's Dir. Cambs.* (1900).
[95] C.R.O., 331/Z 6, 1929, July, p. 56.
[96] C.R.O., P 1/6/1.
[97] *Vetus Liber Arch. Elien.* (C.A.S. 8vo ser. xlviii), 64; *Cambs. Ch. Goods, temp. Edw. VI*, 59.
[98] Prob. 11/181 (P.C.C. 191 Harvey).
[99] List of Cambs. ch. plate, *penes V.C.H.*

[1] *Cambs. Ch. Goods, temp. Edw. VI*, 60; Palmer, *Wm. Cole*, 78.
[2] C.U.L., E.D.R., B 7/1, p. 114.
[3] *Eng. Topog.* (Gent. Mag. Libr.), ii. 13; *Cambs. Bells* (C.A.S. 8vo ser. xviii), 117; *Kelly's Dir. Cambs.* (1858–1937).
[4] B.L. Add. MS. 5823, f. 217; C.U.L., E.D.R., B 7/1, p. 114; C.R.O., P 1/1/1–9.
[5] B.L. Add. MS. 5861, f. 71. See below, plate facing p. 257.
[6] *Eng. Topog.* ii. 18.
[7] Ibid. 19; B.L. Add. MS. 5802, f. 6v.
[8] C.U.L., consist. ct. wills, 1st ser. reg. E, ff. 58v.–59; B.L. Add. MS. 5861, f. 71.
[9] They were changed after 1742: B.L. Add. MS. 5802, f. 6v.
[10] Cf. C.U.L., E.D.R., B 2/59A, f. 22.
[11] *Vetus Liber Arch. Elien.* (C.A.S. 8vo ser. xlviii), 64–5.
[12] C.U.L., E.D.R., B 2/37, f. 36; cf. *Eng. Topog.* ii. 18.

a few of the principal beams. A block of late medieval seating, surviving in the nave, was copied for the Victorian seating. Of the rood-screen, for which William Bolton (d. 1500) left £2 and which survived in 1742,[13] only fragments remain, made up in a modern framework on a thick stone base. The three-decker pulpit, with a sounding board dated 1675, was removed, along with the high pews, in 1873.[14] The chancel contains a wall-monument, with miniature obelisks and caryatids, to Oliver Dalton (d. 1619) and tablets to members of the Perne and Fasset families.

The chancel was in great decay in the 1560s, through the fault of the tenant of the rectory,[15] and needed plastering and whitewashing in 1665 and 1685.[16] In 1816 the tower arch was still blocked with plaster and a singing gallery.[17] The church had 226 sittings, 140 free, in 1877.[18] It was thoroughly restored in 1885 at the expense of A. H. D. Hutton, then vicar, with J. P. St. Aubyn as architect,[19] but box-pews on the south side of the chancel were not removed until 1916. An organ, replacing a barrel-organ, was given in 1897 and fills the north chapel.[20] The church had a silver-gilt chalice *c.* 1278, and two, with a silver cross, in 1552.[21] In 1973 it had a paten of 1728 and a cup and paten of 1828.[22] There were three bells in 1552 and 1742,[23] but only one, dated 1620 and possibly by Brian Eldridge, survived in 1973.[24] The surviving registers begin in 1687, and are virtually complete.[25]

NONCONFORMITY. In 1675 six people were presented for not coming to church at Great Abington,[26] and there were six dissenters there in 1676, but none at Little Abington.[27] A Quaker member of the Amy family was imprisoned in 1678 for refusing to pay tithe on wild pigeons.[28] In 1728 Great Abington was said to have five dissenting families, and Little Abington six dissenters;[29] in 1783 Little Abington alone had a dissenting family.[30] Although a house there was registered for dissenting worship in 1798,[31] the parish still included only two dissenting families, both of long standing, in 1825, when at Great Abington the only recorded dissenter was one labourer.[32] In 1826, however, two men registered their houses for such worship, as did a preacher from Linton in 1833.[33] Neither parish had any permanent nonconformist congregation until after the 1870s,[34] when the Congregationalists from Sawston began mission work at Little Abington,[35] having a preaching station there from *c.* 1888.[36] The vicar believed their main audience to be drawn from immigrant labourers.[37] Although the meeting-house had 60 sittings in 1899 there were only seven full members in 1905 and 10 in 1916. Numbers varied thereafter between five and eight.[38] The chapel was still in use in 1973, being affiliated to the United Reformed Church.

EDUCATION. Although there was said to be a schoolmaster at Little Abington *c.* 1607,[39] neither village had a regular school in the 18th century.[40] Shortly before 1818 a school on Dr. Bell's system, with up to 55 pupils, was set up for both parishes. Being supported mainly by the wealthy tenants of the Hall, it collapsed when the Hall became vacant in the 1820s.[41] From then until 1870 the Abingtons were served mainly by dame schools and Sunday schools. Day and Sunday schools, supported by the new vicars, began in 1829 at Little Abington and in 1832 or 1833 at Great Abington, but appear to have been short-lived. In 1833 two other schools had *c.* 40 pupils, partly paid for by their parents. A new tenant of the Hall probably supported a school for 30 girls. Two Sunday-school teachers also taught adults to read on winter evenings.[42] About 1846 two dame schools had together 40 paying pupils, mostly girls.[43] The vicar of Little Abington usually paid for at least the eldest child in each family to be made literate.[44] In 1877, after the establishment of a board school, the vicar still maintained an evening school for adults at Little Abington.[45]

In 1873, at the suggestion of the squire, E. J. Mortlock, a school board was formed for the two parishes, with the support of the two vicars. Mortlock provided the site in Great Abington at a nominal rent, and paid for building the school, which was opened in 1874.[46] In 1897 the vicar was teaching in the school before normal lessons began.[47] Average attendance was 68 in 1876, 83 in 1896,[48] 71 in 1919, and 79 in 1936.[49] The building belonged to the lord of the manor until 1930 when the county

[13] Prob. 11/12 (P.C.C. 11 Moone); Palmer, *Wm. Cole*, 79.
[14] Palmer, *Wm. Cole*, 79; C.R.O., P 2/1/2, at end.
[15] C.U.L., E.D.R., B 2/3, p. 147; B 2/4, p. 117.
[16] Ibid. B 2/59, p. 36; B 2/59A, f. 22.
[17] *Eng. Topog.* ii. 18.
[18] C.U.L., E.D.R., C 3/26.
[19] *Kelly's Dir. Cambs.* (1888); C.R.O., P 2/1/2, at end; *E.D.R.* (1887), 52.
[20] C.R.O., R 57/17/1, f. 11; *E.D.R.* (1899), 66; *Cambs. Local Hist. Counc. Bull.* xvii. 23.
[21] *Vetus Liber Arch. Elien.* 64; *Cambs. Ch. Goods, temp. Edw. VI*, 61.
[22] List of Cambs. ch. plate, *penes V.C.H.*
[23] *Cambs. Ch. Goods, temp. Edw. VI*, 61; Palmer, *Wm. Cole*, 79.
[24] *Kelly's Dir. Cambs.* (1858–1937); *Cambs. Bells* (C.A.S. 8vo ser. xviii), 117.
[25] C.R.O., P 2/1/1–8.
[26] C.U.L., E.D.R., B 2/62, f. 35v.
[27] Compton Census.
[28] Palmer, *Neighbourhood of Hildersham*, 27.
[29] B.L. Add. MS. 5828, f. 83.
[30] C.U.L., E.D.R., B 7/1, f. 113.
[31] G.R.O. Worship Returns, Ely dioc. no. 158.
[32] C.U.L., E.D.R., C 1/6.
[33] G.R.O. Worship Returns, Ely dioc. nos. 506, 509, 575.
[34] Cf. C.U.L., E.D.R., C 3/26.
[35] R. Ball, *Hist. Sawston Cong. Ch.* 11, 15–16.
[36] *Cong. Yr. Bk.* (1888).
[37] C.U.L., E.D.R., C 3/36. He thought they were Methodists.
[38] *Cong. Yr. Bk.* (1899 and later edns.).
[39] C.U.L., E.D.R., B 2/33, f. 40.
[40] Ibid. B 7/1, pp. 110–14; B 8/1.
[41] *Educ. of Poor Digest*, 55; C.U.L., E.D.R., C 1/6; cf. C.R.O., P 1/11/1.
[42] C.U.L., E.D.R., C 3/21; *Educ. Enquiry Abstract*, 50.
[43] *Church School Inquiry, 1846–7*, 2–3.
[44] *Cambs. Local Hist. Counc. Bull.* xvii. 22–3; C.R.O., R 57/17/1, f. 41.
[45] Ed. 7/5; C.U.L., E.D.R., C 3/26.
[46] *Lond. Gaz.* 31 Oct. 1873, p. 4777; *Cambs. Local Hist. Counc. Bull.* xix. 15; C.R.O., R 60/8/1/2, pp. 1–3.
[47] C.U.L., E.D.R., C 3/36.
[48] *Rep. of Educ. Cttee. of Council, 1876–7* [C. 1780–1], p. 739, H.C. (1877), xxix; *Schs. in receipt of Parl. Grants, 1896–7* [C. 8546], p. 14, H.C. (1897), lxix.
[49] *Bd. of Educ., List 21, 1919* (H.M.S.O.), 15; *1936*, 17.

council bought it.[50] In 1908 J. J. Emerson built a new house for the master, elaborately thatched and timbered, south of the school.[51] By 1905 the school had a separate infants department.[52] In 1937 the older children were transferred to Linton village college, and Abington school, partly rebuilt, was reorganized in junior mixed and infants departments.[53] It was again enlarged in 1962,[54] and was still open in 1973.

CHARITIES FOR THE POOR. John Bolton, by will proved 1509, left a contingent reversion of all his lands to pay 3*s.* 4*d.* a year each to the churches of Great and Little Abington and Hildersham, the residue going to pay the taxes falling on the poor folk of the three parishes, and any surplus being for masses and preaching.[55] In 1524 the land was settled on Clare College, subject to its finding a fellow in orders to preach and say mass in accordance with the will and paying 6*s.* 8*d.* to each parish, of which 3*s.* was for church repairs, 4*d.* for the curate, and 3*s.* 4*d.* for the poor, sums which the college was paying in 1546.[56] Little Abington was still receiving 3*s.* 4*d.* for its poor in 1786; Great Abington's share had then been unpaid for many years,[57] but payment was resumed in 1788. In 1837, of the 6*s.* 8*d.* received by each parish, half was given at Little Abington to the aged and widows, and at Great Abington half had until lately been distributed among the poor.[58] In 1863 also the money went to the poor.[59] In 1929 the payment was charged upon the Hall,[60] whose owners redeemed it in 1966 for £10 paid to 'John a Bolton's' charity in each parish.[61]

John Jefferies by will dated 1674 charged his land in Little Abington with rendering yearly a comb of barley or its price, to be divided among the poor there. Payment had ceased long before 1786.[62] Alice Margaret Foakes, formerly resident at the Old House, Little Abington,[63] by will proved 1927, left £100 for the poor of both parishes. A Scheme of 1936 governed the use of the income. Little had been spent before 1944.[64]

BABRAHAM

BABRAHAM, the most northerly parish in Chilford hundred, lies across the river Granta 6 miles southeast of Cambridge.[1] Its boundaries, enclosing an area of 2,387 a., are formed on the north and east by ancient roads: on the north is the road called Worsted or Wool Street,[2] which was scheduled as a site of special scientific interest in 1951 when it was a grassy track;[3] on the east is a branch of the Icknield Way running from Stump Cross to Newmarket. The southern and western boundaries follow the river Granta and field boundaries. The parish is traversed by the Cambridge–Linton road, south of which the land is low-lying, mostly below 100 ft., on either side of the river. North of the road it rises more steeply, reaching 200 ft. at Fox's Burrow, Signal Hill, and Copley Hill which is surmounted by a barrow. Severe floods affected Babraham in 1655 and 1749.[4]

The course of the river Granta as it runs through the parish has frequently been changed. An encroachment on the river bank had been made by 1260,[5] and between 1330 and 1361 a water-mill was made valueless when the river changed its course.[6] A watercourse north of the main river, diverging from it in Little Abington, was made in the 1650s by Thomas Bennet of Babraham to irrigate his meadows.[7] Although sporadic use of the watercourse continued in the 18th and 19th centuries, it fell out of use in the early 20th century[8] and was a dry ditch in 1973. Before 1735 the stretch of the main river close to Babraham Hall was straightened to form an ornamental canal: the original course was still visible in 1973.[9]

Most of the parish lies over the Lower Chalk, overlapping the Middle Chalk in the north-east corner. The soil on the northern slopes of Babraham is thin, dry, and chalky, and there was a chalkpit and limekiln just north of the main road.[10] The subsoil in the southern half of the parish is gravel.[11] Babraham is wholly agricultural; its open fields were mostly inclosed in the early 19th century by the single landowner without a formal award.

The 38 tenants recorded in 1086 had increased to more than 60 by 1279,[12] and Babraham's population probably reached its highest point in the mid 14th century when 121 people were taxed.[13] Only 40

[50] C.R.O., SP 1/8–9.
[51] *Kelly's Dir. Cambs.* (1925).
[52] *Public Elem. Schs. 1907* [Cd. 3901], p. 27, H.C. (1908), lxxxiv.
[53] Black, *Cambs. Educ. Rec.* 39; *Bd. of Educ., List 21, 1938* (H.M.S.O.), 19; cf. C.R.O., 331/Z 8, 1938, Sept. p. 73; Oct. p. 81.
[54] *Camb. Ind. Press*, 3 May 1968.
[55] C.U.L., consist. ct. wills, 1st ser. reg. E, ff. 58v.–59.
[56] *31st Rep. Com. Char.* 104; *Camb. Univ. Doc.* (1852), i. 267.
[57] *Char. Don.* i. 89.
[58] *31st Rep. Com. Char.* 99.
[59] *Char. Digest Cambs. 1863–4*, 372–3.
[60] C.R.O., SP 1/8.
[61] Char. Com. files.
[62] *Char. Don.* i. 89; *31st Rep. Com. Char.* 99.
[63] *Kelly's Dir. Cambs.* (1912).
[64] Char. Com. files.

[1] This account was written in 1973.
[2] C.U.L., Maps bb. 53(1)/95/58–63.
[3] *Nature Reserves and Sites of Special Scientific Interest* (Cambs. and Isle of Ely Planning Dept. 1965), p. 72.
[4] Carter, *Hist. Cambs.* 117–19; B.L. Add. MS. 9412, f. 264 and v.
[5] *Assizes at Camb. 1260*, 13.
[6] *Cal. Inq. p.m.* vii, p. 205; xi, p. 171.
[7] See p. 25.
[8] D. W. Butcher, *Short Hist. of Babraham Hall and Estate* (1954), 8.
[9] B.L. Add. MS. 5819, f. 157; C.R.O., air photographs 1949.
[10] C.U.L., Maps bb. 53(1)/95/58–63.
[11] Gooch, *Agric. of Cambs.* 12; I.R. 18/13515 p. 6.
[12] *V.C.H. Cambs.* i. 409–10; *Rot. Hund.* (Rec. Com.), ii. 413–14.
[13] E 179/242/8 m. 9.

people were assessed in 1524,[14] and there were 36 households in 1563.[15] Twenty-eight houses paid the hearth tax in 1665, and there were 70 communicants in 1676 and 149 people in 32 families in 1728.[16] By 1801 the population had reached 196, and it continued to grow until a peak of 304 was reached in 1861. After a slight fall it recovered to 308 in 1901, declining to 200 in 1931 and 226 in 1951, since when new building in the village has caused an increase to 327 in 1971.[17]

Traces of a Roman building, probably a villa, were found in 1952 on the parish boundary between Babraham and Stapleford.[18] The building stood well away from the village, however, which is said to owe its name to a Saxon woman, Beaduburh.[19] The position of the church, ¼ mile from the village and close to Babraham Hall, has prompted suggestions that the village has been moved from its original site;[20] no evidence for such a removal has come to light, although medieval itineraries show that a branch of the Icknield Way passed through Babraham,[21] and it is possible that the road from Pampisford once continued due north, passing close to Babraham church and Copley Hill and joining the Ashwell or Street way. Alternatively the present village street has been represented as a part of the Icknield Way.[22] The village was wealthy in the Middle Ages: it paid more tax than any other in Chilford hundred *c.* 1250,[23] and its assessment was second only to that of Linton in 1327 and as late as 1571.[24] As the land was gradually collected into one large estate during the 16th century, however, so the wealth of the parish was concentrated into fewer hands. Babraham in the later 17th century had only two substantial farm-houses, each with 9 hearths, besides the Hall with 40 hearths, and more than a third of the village houses had only one hearth.[25]

The acquisition of the manor and virtually all the land in Babraham in 1632 by the Bennet family, succeeded by the Adeanes, gave the parish resident squires for most of the 17th, 18th, and 19th centuries. The Hall was occasionally leased, as for example to George, Earl Cadogan, between 1875 and 1888,[26] but the Bennets and Adeanes usually lived there themselves. The two families dominated every aspect of parish life, as founders of the charity which provided education and alms-houses, landlords who dictated agricultural methods, and patrons and benefactors of the church. Babraham was recommended in the 19th century as an example of a well-managed parish.[27] New cottages were built by the Adeanes *c.* 1870 on the farms outside the village,[28] and in 1871 there were more dwellings scattered around the parish than in the village.[29] The village itself has remained small, along a single street; it includes the George inn, probably a 17th-century farm-house, the alms-houses and old school of 1730, and Chalk Farm and Home Farm, both of the 17th century. A row of cottages was built along the street in the 19th century, and C. R. W. Adeane built the Madeline Hall, named after his wife, for the village in 1903.[30] A new school south of the village was built in 1959, and a group of council houses more recently at the north end of the village street. An estate of *c.* 60 houses was built *c.* 1950 by the Agricultural Research Council for the staff of the Institute of Animal Physiology established at Babraham Hall, but it was inside the park and was physically and socially distinct from the old village.[31] Most of the parish belonged in 1973 to a trust set up by Sir Robert Adeane, and new building was strictly controlled.

The Cambridge–Linton road was a turnpike from 1766 to 1876,[32] and the road forming the parish's eastern boundary from 1724 to 1870.[33] Babraham is connected by minor roads with Pampisford and Sawston. The railway line from Great Chesterford (Essex) to Six Mile Bottom, opened in 1848 but closed three years later,[34] ran just inside the eastern boundary and its course was still visible in 1973. The Cambridge–Haverhill line, open from 1865 to 1967, just crosses the parish in the south.

Inns at Babraham mentioned from the 13th century were probably on the main road from Stump Cross to Newmarket, at Bourn Bridge.[35] The Angel, recorded as an inn in 1490, was still standing in 1600;[36] the Swan, open in 1543 and 1565, survived in 1600;[37] other named messuages which were perhaps inns in 1600 were the Chequer and the Griffin.[38] Three ale-house licences were granted for Babraham in 1682.[39] The George, perhaps an inn, had some land attached to it in 1488–9, and the new George was recorded in 1600;[40] though perhaps on a different site it was open as a public house in 1778,[41] and survived in 1973.

A feast was held on Whit Sunday in the 18th century, on the green outside the George inn.[42] Babraham amusement fair was held on 1 May, also in front of the George, until *c.* 1930.[43] Plough Monday was observed in the village until 1929,[44] and the

[14] E 179/81/134 m. 2.
[15] B.L. Harl. MS. 594, f. 199v.
[16] E 179/84/437 rot. 58; Compton Census; C.U.L., E.D.R., B 8/1.
[17] *Census*, 1801–1971.
[18] O.S. Map 1/25,000, TL 45 (1956 edn.); Butcher, *Babraham Hall*, 18.
[19] *P.N. Cambs.* (E.P.N.S.), 100.
[20] *Proc. C.A.S.* xxxvii. 19.
[21] Fox, *Arch. Camb. Region*, 145.
[22] *Proc. C.A.S.* lvi–lvii. 43.
[23] *East Anglian*, N.S. vi. 266.
[24] *Cambs. Lay Subsidy, 1327*, 21–2; *Proc. C.A.S.* ix. 130–1.
[25] E 179/244/23 rot. 55.
[26] *Kelly's Dir. Cambs.* (1875 and later edns.); C.R.O., R 52/1/1.
[27] *Jnl. Royal Agric. Soc.* vii. 60; C.U.L., E.D.R., C 3/36.
[28] *1st Rep. Com. Employment in Agric.* 358.
[29] R.G. 10/1591.
[30] [C. R. W. Adeane], *Babraham* (Sawston, n.d.), 28.
[31] Char. Com. files.
[32] Haverhill–Redcross Road Turnpike Act, 6 Geo. III, c. 84; Annual Turnpike Acts Continuance Act, 1876, 39 & 40 Vic. c. 39.
[33] Stump Cross Roads Turnpike Act, 10 Geo. I, c. 12; Annual Turnpike Acts Continuance Act, 1870, 33 & 34 Vic. c. 73.
[34] *V.C.H. Cambs.* ii. 133.
[35] C.U.L., Palmer MS. B 17, p. 18; *E.D.R.* (1900), 178, 217; (1904), 107.
[36] Gibbons, *Ely Episc. Rec.* 414; B.L. Add. Ch. 39052.
[37] *Cambs. Fines*, 1485–1603, ed. Palmer, 48; C 3/137/56; B.L. Add. Ch. 39052.
[38] B.L. Add. Ch. 39052.
[39] *Proc. C.A.S.* xvii. 97 n.
[40] C.U.L., Queens' Coll. Mun. 13/4, f. 34; B.L. Add. Ch. 39052.
[41] *Mon. Inscr. Cambs.* 277.
[42] Carter, *Hist. Cambs.* 119; [Adeane], *Babraham*, 24.
[43] *V.C.H. Cambs.* ii. 87 n.; [Adeane], *Babraham*, 6.
[44] [Adeane], *Babraham*, 24–5.

annual Horkey supper was given in January or February by C. R. W. Adeane for his employees until at least 1914.[45] Adeane was running coal, clothing, and benefit clubs in 1897.[46]

The antiquary William Cole spent his boyhood at Babraham, where his father was the Bennets' steward.[47]

MANORS AND OTHER ESTATES. About half of Babraham was held before the Conquest by Eddeva the fair, whose land there was given to Count Alan of Brittany.[48] Count Alan's successors became earls of Richmond, and the main manors of Babraham were described until the 15th century as being held of the honor of Richmond.[49] In 1086 the tenant of Count Alan's larger estate, comprising 2½ hides and 24 a., was Brian de Scalers.[50] Geoffrey de Scalers, son and heir of Geoffrey de Scalers, gave Babraham church to Waltham abbey in the 1180s.[51] He had been succeeded by 1202 by another Geoffrey,[52] who held the manor, later called *BRUISYARDS*, *c.* 1235.[53] John de Scalers was lord of Babraham by 1249 and probably went on crusade in 1271.[54] His estate there was held in 1279 by Sir Warin of Hereford (d. after 1290).[55] In 1310 the manor was settled on Warin's son John of Hereford,[56] who was succeeded between 1316 and 1346 by Sir Thomas of Hereford (d. after 1361),[57] although Thomas of Lavenham was described as lord of the vill in 1347.[58] In 1388 the manor was held for life by Roger Ferrour by demise from Sir Robert Carbonell and others, who were then licensed to grant the reversion to Bruisyard abbey (Suff.) in exchange for property in Norfolk.[59] Ferrour released his rights in 1390,[60] when the abbey presumably took possession.

Bruisyard abbey surrendered its property in 1539 to the Crown, which immediately granted the manor to Nicholas Hare.[61] A year later Hare conveyed it to Alan Chapman, whose kinsman Thomas Chapman had leased it from the abbey in 1535,[62] and on Alan's death in 1553 it passed to his widow Margaret and then to their eldest son John.[63] John Chapman had by 1558 conveyed most of the manor to Henry Veysey and others.[64] In 1558 Chapman was convicted of counterfeiting money, and although he was pardoned the same year, Bruisyards was granted by the Crown as forfeit in 1563 to John Roynon, a yeoman of the wardrobe,[65] who was still claiming the manor unsuccessfully in 1565.[66] John Chapman's son Alan, who had succeeded his father by 1570, granted a long lease of all his Babraham property *c.* 1572 to Robert Taylor, a teller of the Exchequer,[67] and in 1576 Taylor purchased the estate outright and bought out all the other claimants.[68]

Robert Taylor's fortune, with which he built a new house and greatly extended his lands at Babraham, was lost in 1588 when one of his servants embezzled £7,500 of government money for which Taylor was held accountable.[69] In 1589 Taylor sold the estate to Sir Horatio Palavicino, the English government's financial agent abroad.[70] He settled at Babraham *c.* 1592[71] and made further additions to the manorial estate, leaving more than 2,500 a. in Cambridgeshire to his son Henry on his death in 1600.[72] Sir Henry Palavicino (kt. 1611) had livery of the lands in 1614, but died without issue in 1615. His successor, his brother Tobias, rapidly dissipated the family fortune, and obtained an Act of Parliament in 1624 to enable him to sell his lands.[73]

Tobias sold his whole Babraham estate in 1632 to Richard and Thomas Bennet, sons of a London alderman,[74] and their mother-in-law Elizabeth Lamott.[75] Thomas Bennet's estate was sequestered in 1651 for his support of Charles I, and in 1660 he was created a baronet.[76] His son Sir Levinus Bennet succeeded him in 1667, and sat as M.P. for Cambridgeshire from 1679 until his death in 1693,[77] when the manor passed to his son Richard.

Sir Richard's heir on his death in 1701 was his daughter Judith, who died a minor in 1713 leaving as heirs her five aunts, the daughters of Sir Levinus Bennet.[78] Of them, Judith (d. unmarried 1724) devised her fifth share to Bennet Alexander, son of her sister Levina (d. 1732); Mary (d. 1725), wife of James Bush, was predeceased by her son Levinus (d. 1723), who had devised his reversion of one-fifth of the manor to Judith Bennet, with whose own share it passed to Bennet Alexander; and Jane, wife of James Mitchell, left her fifth to her son William.[79] The share of the last surviving aunt, Dorothy Page (d. 1735),[80] was presumably divided between Bennet Alexander and William Mitchell, for in 1765

45 C.R.O., 331/Z 1, Feb. 1905, p. xii; 331/Z 4, Apr. 1914.
46 C.U.L., E.D.R., C 3/36.
47 Palmer, *Wm. Cole*, 7.
48 *V.C.H. Cambs.* i. 374.
49 S.C. 6/944/13.
50 *V.C.H. Cambs.* i. 374.
51 *Proc. C.A.S.* lix. 121–2; *Papsturkunden in England*, ed. Holtzmann, i, p. 620.
52 *Cur. Reg. R.* ii. 291–2.
53 *Liber de Bernewelle*, 255.
54 *Proc. C.A.S.* lix. 121 n. 2; *Cal. Pat.* 1266–72, 588. For further discussion of the Scalers descent see *Proc. C.A.S.* lix. 117–21.
55 *Rot. Hund.* (Rec. Com.), ii. 413; *Cal. Close*, 1288–96, 96, 119.
56 C.P. 25 (1)/285/28 no. 40.
57 *Feud. Aids*, i. 155, 163; *Cal. Inq. p.m.* xi, p. 202.
58 E 179/242/8 m. 6d.
59 *Cal. Pat.* 1377–81, 170; 1385–9, 527; cf. *V.C.H. Suff.* ii. 131–2.
60 C.P. 25(1)/29/89 no. 22.
61 *L. & P. Hen. VIII*, xiv(1), pp. 122, 254.
62 Ibid. xv, p. 53; *Valor Eccl.* (Rec. Com.), iii. 443.
63 C 142/107 no. 6; C 3/47/39.
64 *Cambs. Fines*, 1485–1603, ed. Palmer, 59–62.
65 *Cal. Pat.* 1557–8, 379–80; 1558–60, 216; 1560–3, 475.
66 C 3/155/29.
67 C 2/Eliz. I/T 4/40.
68 Ibid.; *Cambs. Fines*, 1485–1603, ed. Palmer, 80, 82.
69 L. Stone, *An Elizabethan: Sir Horatio Palavicino*, 272.
70 Ibid. 1–5, 272; *Cambs. Fines*, 1485–1603, ed. Palmer, 102.
71 *Cal. S.P. Dom.* 1591–4, 286.
72 B.L. Add. Ch. 39052.
73 Stone, *Palavicino*, 297, 309–11, 313; 21 Jas. I, c. 22 (Priv. Act).
74 C.P. 25(2)/400/8 Chas. I Mich. no. 28; C 3/412/5. Their father Thos. d. 1620: cf. Beaven, *Aldermen of Lond.* ii. 53, 177; G.E.C. *Baronetage*, iii. 130, both dating the sale too early; *D.N.B.*
75 Ric. and Thos. married sisters. Ric. was described in 1638 as son of Eliz. Lamott: C 3/412/5; his own mother was Dorothy: *Visit. London*, i (Harl. Soc. xv), 64. His wife's mother Eliz., widow of Levinus Monke, presumably married secondly John Lamott: Prob. 11/325 (P.C.C. 144 Carr, will of Sir Thos. Bennet).
76 *Cal. Cttee. for Money*, iii. 1299–1300; G.E.C. *Baronetage*, iii. 130.
77 G.E.C. *Baronetage*, iii. 130–1.
78 *Eng. Topog.* (Gent. Mag. Libr.), ii. 23 n.; *Mon. Inscr. Cambs.* 6.
79 B.L. Add. MS. 5822, ff. 30v.–31, 195–201; B.L. Add. MS. 5823, f. 20.
80 Palmer, *Wm. Cole*, 82; B.L. Add. MS. 5823, f. 20.

Alexander's son and son-in-law held 3½ fifths between them and Mitchell held 1½.[81] Bennet Alexander assumed the surname of Bennet by Act of Parliament in 1742, and was succeeded in 1745 by his son Richard Henry Alexander Bennet.[82] The whole estate, consisting of the lordship, rectory, and 1,670 a. in Babraham besides land in the surrounding parishes, was offered for sale in 1765,[83] when William Mitchell apparently bought out Bennet and his brother-in-law John Luther.[84] Another sale was postponed in 1767,[85] and Babraham was eventually bought in 1770 by Robert Jones, an East India Company director.[86] Jones's only child Anne married Col. James Whorwood Adeane, and to their son, Robert Jones Adeane, Jones devised Babraham on his death in 1774.[87]

On the death of Robert Jones Adeane in 1823 the estate descended to his son Henry John Adeane,[88] who in 1845 was owner or lessee of all the land in the parish.[89] From him the lordship descended in 1847 to his son Robert Jones Adeane (d. unmarried 1853), to Robert's brother Henry John Adeane (d. 1870), to Henry's son Charles Robert Whorwood Adeane (d. 1943), and to Charles's son Col. Sir Robert Philip Wyndham Adeane, the lord in 1973.[90]

The Scalers family was resident at Babraham in the 13th century and there was a chief messuage attached to Bruisyards manor in 1279 and 1388.[91] In the 16th century there was a manor-house surrounded by a moat 40 or 50 ft. wide, perhaps on the moated site on the south bank of the river.[92] Robert Taylor built a new house called Babraham Place on the north bank *c.* 1580.[93] The house, described by Cole as one of the noblest Gothic houses in the county, was of brick with stone dressings and was built round a courtyard with the main front facing the road to Cambridge.[94] Tobias Palavicino embellished the great hall with a marble mantelpiece bearing his arms;[95] the house was taxed on 40 hearths in the 1660s,[96] and was surrounded by a park of 14 a. in 1765.[97] Babraham Place was demolished in 1766–7 and the materials were sold, some being used to repair Chesterton sluice.[98]

Robert Jones, the purchaser in 1770, built a 'neat small seat' on the same site,[99] which was pulled down in 1832–3 to make way for Babraham Hall, built in 1833–7 to the design of Philip Hardwick.[1] The house was originally a tall symmetrical block in brick with stone dressings, of interest as an early example of the revival of the Jacobean style. The symmetry was disguised, though the style was to a large extent retained, when the house was considerably enlarged and internally remodelled in 1864. At the same date the gardens were laid out according to a 16th-century plan.[2] Further alterations, including a billiard room, were probably made later in the 19th century. The Hall and 450 a. were sold by Col. Adeane in 1948 to the Agricultural Research Council, which established the Institute of Animal Physiology there; in 1952–3 the old kitchens, servants' quarters, and outhouses were pulled down, and several blocks of laboratories have since been built.[3]

Count Alan of Brittany's second estate in Babraham in 1086 comprising 3 or 3½ yardlands, had previously been held by Alric the priest from Eddeva the fair, and was held in 1086 by Ralph.[4] No record of the land in the 12th century has been found, but in 1279, 1282, and *c.* 1285 50 a. were held of the honor of Richmond as ¼ knight's fee by Sir Roger Walsham.[5]

The king's land in Babraham in 1086 comprised 2½ yardlands, in the keeping of Picot the sheriff, and formerly held by Wulfwin under Earl Alfgar.[6] The land was in the sheriff's hand as a purpresture, rendering £1 a year in 1165,[7] and was granted in 1166 to Hamelin of Babraham, paying the same yearly sum.[8] Hamelin died *c.* 1190 and was succeeded by his son Walter.[9] Thomas Hamelin succeeded his father William in 1235.[10] After 1260 Thomas became a monk, and his estate of 123 a. was delivered to his son John in 1285. It was then held in chief by the serjeanty of keeping a goshawk and paying the king 20*s.* for mewing it, later reckoned to be a fee-farm.[11] John conveyed to his son Walter Hamelin in 1316 *c.* 66 a.,[12] which on Walter's death in 1350 descended to his son John.[13] The heirs of John Hamelin (d. 1361) were his sisters Alice, wife of Richard Gerunde, and Marion, who settled the estate in 1363 on Maud, Richard's daughter, and her husband Simon Bokenham.[14] On Simon's death in 1393 it passed to his brother Roger, who in 1394 enfeoffed Simon's widow Christine.[15]

By 1401 the former Hamelin estate had come to Thomas Mounpellers, probably by marriage with Christine.[16] It may therefore be identified with the manor later known as *MOMPELLERS*. That estate, called Hameletts, was granted for life by the Crown to William Denton with 190 a. in 1488, after

[81] C.R.O., L 52/1–4.
[82] Burke, *Ext. & Dorm. Baronetcies* (1838), 57; B.L. Add. MS. 5819, f. 177.
[83] Bodl. MS. Gough Camb. 103 (7), p. 5.
[84] C.R.O., L 52/1–4.
[85] B.L. Add. MS. 5819, f. 42v.
[86] *Hist. Parl., Commons*, 1754–90, ii. 691–2; B.L. Add. MS. 5822, p. 208.
[87] *Hist. Parl., Commons*, 1754–90, ii. 13, 692; cf. *V.C.H. Cambs.* ii. 73–4.
[88] *31st Rep. Com. Char.* 101.
[89] I.R. 18/13515 p. 15.
[90] Burke, *Land. Gent.* (1952), 11–12.
[91] *Rot. Hund.* (Rec. Com.), ii. 413; *Cal. Pat.* 1385–9, 527.
[92] C 3/202/30; C.U.L., Maps bb. 53(1)/95/58–63.
[93] B.L. Add. MS. 5802, f. 37v.; B.L. Add. MS. 5819, f. 171.
[94] B.L. Add. MS. 5819, ff. 176v.–177v.
[95] *Mon. Inscr. Cambs.* 4.
[96] See pp. 279–80.
[97] Bodl. MS. Gough Camb. 103(7), p. 5.
[98] B.L. Add. MS. 5819, f. 176v.; Palmer, *Wm. Cole*, 83.
[99] B.L. Add. MS. 5823, f. 19v.
[1] Butcher, *Babraham Hall*, 10–11; *D.N.B.*; see above, plate facing p. 128.
[2] Butcher, *Babraham Hall*, 11–12.
[3] Cf. ibid. 11, 14; *Inst. of Animal Physiology, Annual Rep. 1960–1*, 10; *1968–9*, 21.
[4] *V.C.H. Cambs.* i. 374, 409.
[5] *Rot. Hund.* (Rec. Com.), ii. 414; *Cal. Inq. p.m.* ii, p. 220; *Feud. Aids*, i. 140, giving Balsham for Walsham.
[6] *V.C.H. Cambs.* i. 362, 410.
[7] *Pipe R.* 1165 (P.R.S. viii), 62.
[8] Ibid. 1166 (P.R.S. ix), 85.
[9] Ibid. 1190 (P.R.S. N.S. i), 116.
[10] *Ex. e Rot. Fin.* (Rec. Com.), i. 282.
[11] *Assizes at Camb. 1260*, 13; *Cal. Inq. p.m.* ii, p. 347; *Feud. Aids*, i. 176.
[12] *Cal. Pat.* 1313–17, 518.
[13] *Cal. Inq. p.m.* ix, p. 375.
[14] Ibid. xi, p. 202; *Cal. Pat.* 1361–4, 350.
[15] *Cal. Fine R.* 1391–9, 106; *Cal. Pat.* 1391–6, 447–8.
[16] *Feud. Aids*, i. 176; C.P. 25(1)/30/93 no. 1.

the outlawry for felony of its former owner, Edmund Church,[17] against whom lands in Babraham were probably recovered in 1499.[18] When William Denton died in 1506 Mompellers, said to be held of Bruisyard abbey, passed to his widow Mary (d. after 1514) and then to his kinsman Thomas Denton of Henley (Oxon.).[19] In 1536 Thomas conveyed the manor to the lessee Alan Chapman, to whom Thomas Denton of Denton (Cumb.) released it in 1549.[20] Alan's son John conveyed parts of the manor to Edward Wood and many others,[21] but in 1576 John's son Alan Chapman sold Mompellers to Robert Taylor with Bruisyards manor, with which Mompellers descended thereafter.

The Hamelin estate had a chief messuage in 1285, 1350 (when it was ruinous), and 1362.[22] William Denton (d. 1506) lived in the manor-house of Mompellers, which stood on a moated site.[23] Edward Wood was accused of removing glass, wainscot, ceilings, and tiles from the house, and later of pulling down part of its wall.[24]

In 1086 1½ yardland, which had been held of Earl Gurth T.R.E. by his man Lemmar, was held by Countess Judith.[25] That estate has not been traced further. Robert Fafiton held in 1086 1¼ hide which had been held of Earl Alfgar by Godeva.[26] Robert's land in Trumpington had by 1212 become part of the estates of Mortimer of Wigmore.[27] By *c.* 1235 ¼ fee at Babraham belonging to the 'honor of Fafiton', held by the Mortimers, was held under the earl of Winchester as mesne lord by Tristram of the Ash.[28] In 1242 that ¼ fee was held of Ralph Mortimer, perhaps by marriage to a widow, by John of Cottenham, under whose name it was entered among the fees held of the Mortimers until 1425.[29] Robert Tristram died in 1289 leaving 140 a. at Babraham, held from Sir Edmund Hemgrave (d. 1334) under the earl of Lincoln, to his son John, aged two.[30] By 1311 Robert atte Ash held that fee.[31] A John Tristram was resident at Babraham in 1328.[32] By 1346 Robert Tristram and his parceners were said to hold the ¼ fee, as were John Wilford and others in 1428.[33] It may have been the land in dispute between Wilford's heirs, including his son John, and his feoffees in the 1460s,[34] but its later fate is not known.

Hardwin de Scalers in 1086 held 2 yardlands of the king's fee, formerly held by four sokemen from King Edward, and 1 or ½ yardland of the abbot of Ely's fee, formerly held by two sokemen. The land was held from Hardwin by Durand.[35] About 1235 Herbert de Alençon, probably as mesne lord, held lands of Hardwin's fee in Cambridgeshire,[36] which had passed by 1269 to William de Criketot.[37] William's son William (d. 1299) was overlord in 1279, with Roger Barbedor as his mesne tenant,[38] and in 1308 William Barbedor was the last mesne lord recorded.[39] The Babraham estate was held *c.* 1235 by John of Sawston,[40] and in 1279 by his son William (d. 1308) under the Barbedors.[41] It descended in the Sawston family, with Dale manor in Sawston,[42] from William to John, recorded at Babraham in 1350,[43] and was held in 1428 by Ralph Sawston,[44] but has not been traced further.

In 1086 Pirot held from Eudes the steward 1½ yardland formerly held freely by Alfric Campe from King Edward.[45] Before 1162 Ralph Pirot became a monk at Colchester abbey (Essex), to which he gave ½ hide at Babraham, confirmed by his son Ralph. Between 1152 and 1162 Colchester granted a perpetual lease of the land to Sawtry abbey (Hunts.),[46] to which the pope confirmed Coplow Grange in Babraham, perhaps part of the same grant, in 1164.[47] By 1228 other grants or purchases had enlarged Sawtry's Babraham estate to over 180 a.[48] On its dissolution in 1537, the site and lands of the abbey were granted to Sir Richard Williams *alias* Cromwell, who sold Coplow Grange to George Gill.[49] In 1556 Gill sold it to John and Thomas Amy,[50] and John settled it in 1591 on his son Nicholas (d. *v.p.* 1596, leaving a minor son Erasmus).[51] Coplow Grange was apparently purchased between 1612 and 1614 by Sir Henry Palavicino, and descended with the manorial estate after his death.[52]

The remainder of Ralph Pirot's estate, whose lordship presumably descended in his family with Pyratts manor in Sawston,[53] was held in 1302 by Thomas of Pampisford[54] and was later known as *RUMBOLDS* manor. Ralph of Coggeshall held it in 1346, and William Rumbold in 1428.[55] By 1497 it was apparently held by Edith Green of Little Leighs (Essex), whose sons-in-law and executors, Sir William Fynderne and Sir Henry Tey, defended their right to it in 1499;[56] under Edith's will, they granted the income from it to Queens' College, Cambridge, in 1502, to maintain a priest for 60 years.[57]

17 *Cal. Pat.* 1485–94, 259.
18 C.P. 40/949 rot. 355.
19 C 142/29 no. 68.
20 *Cambs. Fines*, 1485–1603, ed. Palmer, 42, 55; E 315/123 f. 185v.
21 C 3/6/20; Sta. Cha. 2/24/171; C 2/Eliz. I/T 4/40; C 3/184/4.
22 *Cal. Inq. p.m.* ii, p. 347; ix, p. 375; xi, p. 202.
23 E 315/123 f. 185.
24 Sta. Cha. 2/22/143; C 3/47/39.
25 *V.C.H. Cambs.* i. 398, 410.
26 Ibid. 397, 410.
27 *Red Bk. Exch.* (Rolls Ser.), ii. 527; cf. Farrer, *Feud. Cambs.* 219.
28 *Liber de Bernewelle*, 255; cf. *V.C.H. Cambs.* v. 201.
29 *Bk. of Fees*, ii. 922; *Cal. Inq. p.m.* (Rec. Com.), iii. 236; iv. 87.
30 *Cal. Inq. p.m.* ii, pp. 436–7; vii, p. 415; cf. *Feud. Aids*, i. 145; *Knights of Edw. I*, ii (Harl. Soc. lxxxi), 218.
31 *Cal. Inq. p.m.* v, p. 154.
32 *Cambs. Lay Subsidy, 1327*, 21.
33 *Feud. Aids*, i. 163, 182.
34 C 1/28 no. 389; C 1/69 no. 353; C 1/27 no. 185.
35 *V.C.H. Cambs.* i. 365, 385, 389, 410.
36 *Liber de Bernewelle*, 262–3.
37 *Cal. Inq. p.m.* i, p. 223.
38 *Rot. Hund.* (Rec. Com.), ii. 414; *Knights of Edw. I*, i (Harl. Soc. lxxx), 251–2.
39 *Cal. Inq. p.m.* v, pp. 48–9.
40 *Liber de Bernewelle*, 255.
41 *Rot. Hund.* (Rec. Com.), ii. 414; *Cal. Inq. p.m.* v, pp. 48–9.
42 See p. 251.
43 *Cal. Inq. p.m.* ix, p. 375.
44 *Feud. Aids*, i. 182.
45 *V.C.H. Cambs.* i. 383–4, 410.
46 *Cart. Mon. St. John Colchester* (Roxburghe Club), i. 179; ii. 527; cf. *Complete Peerage*, x. 474 n.
47 *Papsturkunden*, ed. Holtzmann, i, pp. 366–7, 409–11.
48 B.L. Cott. MS. Tib. C. ix, f. 153.
49 *L. & P. Hen. VIII*, xii (2), pp. 468–9; E 321/14/28.
50 *Cal. Pat.* 1555–7, 148.
51 C 142/326 no. 49.
52 C 142/349 no. 159.
53 See p. 249.
54 *Feud. Aids*, i. 145.
55 Ibid. 163, 182.
56 C.P. 40/947 rot. 319; *Visit. Essex*, i (Harl. Soc. xiii), 58.
57 C.U.L., Queens' Coll. Mun. 17/15.

In 1562 Rumbolds was sold by William Brian to Clare Hall, Cambridge.[58] The manor was probably part of the college estate claimed and apparently won by Sir Horatio Palavicino in 1599,[59] for it was not mentioned thereafter as a distinct estate. Clare Hall had acquired another estate in Babraham before 1540; what it did not lose to Sir Horatio in 1599 it gave to Tobias Palavicino in 1631 in exchange for land at Dullingham.[60]

The manor called *CIFREWASTS* was in 1302 probably part of the estate of Thomas of Pampisford, who had married Elizabeth, widow of Richard Cifrewast (d. before 1274).[61] Thomas was alive in 1316, but by 1324 Richard Cifrewast, grandson of Richard and Elizabeth, was in possession.[62] On Richard's death in 1330 his estate, held from John Kirkby, passed to his son Roger,[63] who was succeeded in 1361, when it was held of the honor of Richmond, by his son John Cifrewast.[64] Sir John died in 1394 and his widow Catherine in 1403,[65] and their son John (d. 1441) obtained orders for livery of her dower in 1406 and 1421.[66] In 1499 Sibyl, one of John's three daughters, and her fifth husband, Thomas Danvers, warranted Cifrewasts with Rumbolds to Sir William Fynderne and Sir Henry Tey;[67] those manors descended together after that date.

Before 1502 Queens' College held land in Babraham amounting to 76½ a. by 1489;[68] it was given more by John Ottwar *c.* 1529[69] and exchanged some land in Bartlow for 30 a. in Babraham in 1527.[70] Apart from its rights over Cifrewasts and Rumbolds the college estate covered *c.* 200 a., which was granted on a perpetual lease to Sir Horatio Palavicino and his children in 1598 and became part of the manorial estate.[71]

The lands called *BEVERECH* and *TAKELYS*, which descended with *WILLINGHAMS* and *BLUNTS*, may have derived their names from the Babraham families of Beverech (fl. 1327–1429) and Takely (fl. 1327–1411).[72] In 1543 Robert Lockton of Sawston (d. 1550) settled the four estates held from Alan Chapman on his wife Elizabeth;[73] John Chapman sold the property, covering 330 a., to Thomas Altham in 1556,[74] and it was part of Sir Horatio Palavicino's estate in 1600.[75]

The reputed manor of *DEPENHAMS* was probably the estate of Thomas Depenham (fl. 1434), whose father John had held land in Babraham.[76] It was conveyed in 1573 by Robert Twyford to John Machell, who apparently gave it to his father-in-law Sir Francis Hinde in 1581,[77] though it was probably the estate sold by Machell to Sir Horatio Palavicino in 1595.[78]

William I gave ½ yardland, held before the Conquest of the thegn Wulfwin by his man Godwin or Godric, to Aubrey de Vere.[79] Aubrey's son of the same name, who founded Hatfield Broadoak priory (Essex) *c.* 1135, gave it among other lands 1 knight's fee at Babraham.[80] In 1256 the priory was taxed on the estate,[81] which was not mentioned later and may have been absorbed into its larger estate in Great Abington.[82]

Waltham abbey (Essex), to which Geoffrey de Scalers (d. by 1202) gave Babraham church and 17 a.,[83] was granted free warren there in 1253.[84] By 1279 the rectory estate consisted of 100 a. and a messuage.[85] The abbey was dissolved in 1540,[86] and in 1560 the rectory was granted to Richard Baker and Sir Richard Sackville.[87] Robert Taylor acquired it before 1589 when he conveyed it with the manors to Sir Horatio Palavicino,[88] and Tobias Palavicino held it in 1625, though it had been farmed since 1601 by Sir Oliver Cromwell; Cromwell had married Sir Horatio's widow and his daughters and son had married Sir Horatio's three children.[89] From 1632 the rectory descended with the Babraham manor. The great tithes of the non-manorial land were commuted in 1845 for a rent-charge of £28 10*s.*[90]

A small estate in Babraham and other parishes was given in 1347 to St. John's hospital, Cambridge,[91] and was transferred with the hospital's other lands to St. John's College in 1511.[92] The rectory estate owed £13 6*s.* 8*d.* a year to the college in 1560.[93] In 1765 the college's estate was held on lease by the lord of the manor,[94] and the college exchanged land with H. J. Adeane in 1844,[95] after which it owned 103 a.[96] The land was sold in 1878.[97] A rent-charge of £13 6*s.* 8*d.* a year, due to Jesus College, Cambridge, from the rectory estate in 1545,[98] 1765, and 1873,[99] was in 1948 apportioned between the Agricultural Research Council and Sir Robert Adeane.[1] Emmanuel College received a rent-charge from the manor of Babraham in 1734 and 1765.[2]

58 *Cambs. Fines*, 1485–1603, ed. Palmer, 67; *Camb. Univ. Doc.* (1852), i. 271.
59 Stone, *Palavicino*, 278.
60 *Clare Coll., 1326–1926*, ed. M. D. Forbes, 76.
61 *Feud. Aids*, i. 145; *V.C.H. Berks.* iii. 72–3.
62 *V.C.H. Berks.* iii. 72–3; *Cal. Close*, 1323–7, 157.
63 *Cal. Inq. p.m.* vii, p. 205; *Cal. Close*, 1330–3, 75.
64 *Cal. Inq. p.m.* xi, p. 171.
65 *V.C.H. Berks.* iii. 73; *Cal. Inq. p.m.* (Rec. Com.), iii. 305.
66 *Cal. Close*, 1405–9, 160; 1419–22, 102.
67 C.P. 40/947 rot. 319; *V.C.H. Berks.* iii. 73.
68 C.U.L., Queens' Coll. Mun. 13/4, ff. 33–34v.
69 B.L. Add. MS. 5802, f. 38v.
70 C.U.L., Queens' Coll. Mun. 13/4, f. 35v.
71 Stone, *Palavicino*, 273.
72 *Cambs. Lay Subsidy, 1327*, 21–2; *Cal. Close*, 1409–13, 235; *Cal. Pat.* 1422–9, 511.
73 E 150/97 no. 1.
74 C 3/6/20.
75 B.L. Add. Ch. 39052.
76 *Cal. Close*, 1429–35, 299.
77 C.P. 25(2)/93/838/15 Eliz. I East. no. 6; *Cambs. Fines*, 1485–1603, ed. Palmer, 86.
78 C.P. 25(2)/94/859/37 Eliz. I East. no. 6.
79 *V.C.H. Cambs.* i. 390, 410; *Complete Peerage*, x. 193.
80 *V.C.H. Essex*, ii. 107.
81 *Liber de Bernewelle*, 197.
82 See p. 14.
83 *Proc. C.A.S.* lix. 113, 117.
84 *Cal. Chart. R.* 1226–57, 427.
85 *Rot. Hund.* (Rec. Com.), ii. 413.
86 *V.C.H. Essex*, ii. 170.
87 *Cal. Pat.* 1558–60, 305–7.
88 C.P. 25(2)/94/853/31 Eliz. I Trin. no. 5.
89 C.U.L., E.D.R., B 2/32, f. 96v.; B 2/18, f. 76v.; Stone, *Palavicino*, 305.
90 I.R. 18/13515 pp. 1–18.
91 *Cal. Pat.* 1345–8, 352.
92 *V.C.H. Cambs.* iii. 445.
93 E 318/Box 44/2400 m. 2; *Cal. Pat.* 1558–60, 307.
94 Bodl. MS. Gough Camb. 103(7), p. 5.
95 C.R.O., 124/P 4.
96 Ibid. 152/P 1; *Rep. Com. Univ. Income* [C. 856–II], p. 364, H.C. (1873), xxxvii (3).
97 *V.C.H. Cambs.* iii. 445.
98 *Camb. Univ. Doc.* (1852), i. 132.
99 Bodl. MS. Gough Camb. 103(7), p. 6; *Rep. Com. Univ. Income* [C. 856–II], p. 281, H.C. (1873), xxxvii(3).
1 Char. Com. files.
2 B.L. Add. MS. 5837, f. 118v.; Bodl. MS. Gough Camb. 103(7), p. 6.

The Benedictine nunnery of Swaffham Bulbeck held *c.* 30 a. at Babraham which by 1248 was held at farm of it by William son of John,[3] and probably in 1270 by William Kirkby,[4] whose son John had succeeded him by 1286,[5] and bought 60 a. there in 1300.[6] In 1332 another John Kirkby sold the reversion of 140 a., mostly at Babraham, to John Breton and others.[7] The land has not been traced later.

ECONOMIC HISTORY. Babraham in 1086 comprised almost 7 hides, of which about one-quarter was in demesne; the land was worked by 26 *villani*, 12 bordars, and 1 *servus*. The parish contained land for 8 plough-teams, and 7 were there, 3½ of them owned by the *villani*. All the estates had maintained their value since 1066, except Robert Fafiton's.[8]

The description of Babraham in 1279 is incomplete, omitting the estates of the Hamelin and Tristram families and that of Sawtry abbey, each covering more than 100 a. Sir Warin of Hereford had 220 a. in demesne, besides 112 a. of grass, Sir Roger Walsham 50 a., and William of Sawston 53 a. Their tenants included *c.* 9 freeholders of 10–40 a. and up to 60 small tenants with between ¼ a. and 10 a. Rents were paid almost entirely in money and no customary tenants were recorded.[9] Later medieval inquisitions mention only one estate where works were owed, that of Robert Tristram in 1289,[10] and the absence of references to copyhold at Babraham in any period suggests that customary tenure disappeared very early.

Between four and six open fields were mentioned in the late 15th century, in the 16th and 17th,[11] and *c.* 1800.[12] Their names changed, but Cambridge, Burgoyne or Burgin, Sawston, and Bournbridge fields were often among them. About 1800 Sawston and Burgin fields partly overlapped the boundary with Sawston, while Chalkpit and Farm fields lay north of the Cambridge–Linton road.

The only grain crop recorded in the 16th century was barley.[13] In 1513 William Cowper, a Babraham farmer, dealt in grain on a large scale,[14] and William Thurgar of Babraham was ordered in 1597 to supply grain to local markets.[15] Saffron was grown in small plots and gardens, some of them leased from Sawtry abbey, in the early 16th century.[16] Robert Tristram (d. 1289) had a dovecot,[17] and the parish was said in the 18th century to be remarkable for its honey.[18]

In 1488–9 there were *c.* 10 substantial landholders in Babraham.[19] During the 16th century the whole parish was consolidated into one estate. About 1800 the land was divided between five farms ranging from 85 a. to 552 a. and a number of smallholdings.[20] The concentration of land in single ownership made possible agricultural improvements which required a large outlay of capital. The irrigation of the meadows in Babraham was undertaken in 1653 or 1654 by Thomas Bennet, the lord of the manor,[21] although later attributed to Sir Horatio Palavicino.[22] At a cost of £10,000 a new watercourse was constructed, diverging from the river in Little Abington, where it was controlled by a three-sluice dam and running north of Babraham Hall. It was extended in 1659. The work was supervised by Thomas Bennet's cousin Hugh May,[23] later a well-known architect,[24] assisted by a Mr. Cromwell. The purpose was later referred to as watering or overflowing the adjacent land, and there is no evidence of true floating as in Wiltshire,[25] but *c.* 200 a. inclosed from the common fields increased in value fivefold or more after watering.

Pastoral farming was always prominent at Babraham; in 1086 205 sheep were recorded.[26] In 1347 Babraham's assessment at 109 stone of wool was higher than that of neighbouring parishes.[27] There were butchers there in the 15th century.[28] The lessee of Coplow farm employed a shepherd in 1536,[29] and the lords of Bruisyards and Mompellers manors had liberty of foldage.[30] John Machell sold his sheep-pastures at Babraham to Sir Horatio Palavicino in 1595,[31] and a farm was leased with 600 sheep in 1637.[32] William Cole's father in the early 18th century leased part of his Babraham farm, probably the open land in the north part of the parish, to the earl of Godolphin's steward for the earl's race-horses.[33] There were over 550 a. of heath in Babraham *c.* 1800, and another 125 a. were intercommonable with Sawston and Pampisford.[34]

In 1794 *c.* 1,350 a. were still in open fields, cultivated in common. On the inclosed arable land a three- or four-year rotation was practised.[35] Less than 700 a. had been inclosed by *c.* 1800,[36] and there were open fields at Babraham in 1806,[37] but by 1829 apparently no common arable land remained. In 1829 the main farm-houses were Cot (later Copley Hill), Reed Barn (or Slough, later Reed), Chalk, Home, and New Barn (later Church) farms. Church Farm, north-west of the village street, was later demolished.[38] Rollypooly Barn was extended after 1829 and by 1901 was Rowley Farm.[39] Home farm

[3] C.P. 25(1)/24/24 no. 3; cf. Dugdale, *Mon.* iv. 457.
[4] C.P. 25(1)/25/32 no. 14.
[5] C.P. 25(1)/26/41 no. 4.
[6] C.P. 25(1)/26/48 no. 1.
[7] C.P. 25(1)/28/68 no. 10.
[8] *V.C.H. Cambs.* i. 409–10.
[9] *Rot. Hund.* (Rec. Com.), ii. 413–14.
[10] C 133/53 no. 5.
[11] C.U.L., Queens' Coll. Mun. 13/4, f. 33 (1488–9); C 3/6/20 (1560); B.L. Add. Ch. 39052 (1601); C.U.L., E.D.R., H 1/1 (1615).
[12] C.U.L., S 696.c.95.38.
[13] B.L. Add. MS. 5861, pp. 29, 67.
[14] *L. & P. Hen. VIII*, Addenda, i, p. 154; iv (1), p. 619.
[15] *Acts of P.C.* 1597, 72–3.
[16] C.U.L., Queens' Coll. Mun. 13/4, f. 35; B.L. Add. MS. 5861, p. 135; Palmer, *Cambs. in 16th cent.* 23, 25.
[17] C 133/53 no. 5.
[18] B.L. Add. MS. 5861, p. 231.
[19] C.U.L., Queens' Coll. Mun. 13/4, f. 33.
[20] C.U.L., S 696. c. 95. 38.
[21] This account of the water-meadows in the 17th cent. is based on C.R.O., 619/E 14–24.
[22] A. Young, *Annals of Agric.* xvi. 177.
[23] *Visit. Sussex*, 1634 (Harl. Soc. liii), 105.
[24] Colvin, *Biog. Dict. Eng. Architects*, 382–4.
[25] *Wilts. Arch. Mag.* lv. 105–17, esp. n. 25.
[26] *V.C.H. Cambs.* i. 409–10.
[27] E 179/242/8 m. 6d.
[28] *Cal. Pat.* 1429–36, 13; 1446–52, 351.
[29] Palmer, *Cambs. in 16th cent.* 23.
[30] *Cal. Close*, 1409–13, 235; *Cal. Pat.* 1553–4, 368.
[31] Stone, *Palavicino*, 274–6.
[32] *Cal. Cttee. for Compounding*, iv. 2752.
[33] B.L. Add. MS. 5819, ff. 175–6.
[34] C.U.L., S 696.c.95.38.
[35] Vancouver, *Agric. in Cambs.* 55.
[36] C.U.L., S 696.c.95.38.
[37] Gooch, *Agric. of Cambs.* 12.
[38] C.U.L., Maps bb. 53(1)/95/58–63.
[39] Ibid.; O.S. Map 6″, Cambs. LIV. NE. (1903 edn.).

was the smallest holding with 348 a. in 1871; the other farms had between 400 and 580 a. each.[40] The six farms survived in 1973.

Improved farming methods at Babraham were encouraged by H. J. Adeane, lord of the manor 1823–47, and the increased production from previously uncultivated land was attributed in 1845 to the judicious application of capital and to the spirited manner in which the land was farmed.[41] By 1825 a four-course rotation was stipulated for Adeane's tenants: the principal crops in the 19th century were wheat and barley, with large quantities of turnips grown for feed.[42] Flax lands and parsley beds were mentioned in 1765,[43] and there was a potato field in 1829.[44] Three-quarters of the land in the parish (1,751 a.) was under crops in 1845.[45]

The 17th-century watercourse was used throughout the 18th and earlier 19th century for occasional irrigation of the water-meadows, which covered *c.* 165 a. in 1794.[46] Experts were critical, however, of the use made of the system: the water was distributed unevenly, for only seven weeks in the early summer and autumn, and the meadows were mown only once a year.[47] Although no one at Babraham realized the potential use of irrigation, and in spite of the restricted period of watering, the land watered rose two or three times in value in the 19th century. R. J. Adeane rebuilt his sluice in 1820, and his son guarded his access to the sluices in Little Abington.[48] The watercourse apparently fell out of use in the later 19th century, was repaired in 1890, and was decayed by the early 20th century.[49] In 1845 it was the only one of its kind in southern Cambridgeshire.[50]

In 1794 there were *c.* 1,000 sheep in the parish,[51] and 419 a. were under pasture in 1845.[52] Jonas Webb, the well-known breeder of Southdown sheep, was tenant of Church farm in Babraham from *c.* 1820 until his death in 1862.[53] Although a few Cambridgeshire farmers had already tried Southdowns,[54] Webb imported stock from Sussex breeders and increased the amount of mutton on each animal in his flock of 2,400 sheep, which won many prizes; his rams were leased to breeders in America and Europe. The flock, reduced to 969 sheep, was sold in 1862 to breeders from North and South America, Australia, and all parts of Europe. Jonas Webb's brother Samuel, tenant of Reed Barn farm until *c.* 1879,[55] also bred Southdowns, and Samuel's successor Henry Lambert bred Hampshire Down sheep.[56]

Jonas Webb was also a successful breeder of Shorthorn cattle, which had been introduced at Babraham *c.* 1830 by H. J. Adeane from Lord Spencer's herd in Northamptonshire.[57] One Babraham farmer in 1806 found dairy cows more profitable than sheep.[58] R. J. Adeane (d. 1823) bought cattle in London for fattening,[59] and C. R. W. Adeane, lord of the manor 1870–1943, was a notable breeder of Shorthorns and served as president of the Royal Agricultural Society.[60] By 1905 the area of permanent pasture in the parish had increased to 553 a.;[61] rising feedstuff costs and low meat prices in the earlier 20th century gradually cleared Babraham of most of its stock,[62] and the common was ploughed for the first time in 1953.[63] Babraham farms were mainly arable in 1973, growing barley, wheat, sugar-beet, potatoes, and oats.

The Institute of Animal Physiology was established by the Agricultural Research Council in 1948 at Babraham Hall, to study the fundamental physiology of farm animals.[64] About 320 a. of the 450 a. purchased in 1948 were farmed, including *c.* 250 a. reclaimed from derelict scrub. Besides providing animals for experiments, the farm was designed to be commercially self-supporting; its stock in 1971 included over 700 sheep, 430 pigs, a herd of cattle, and poultry, and its manager had bred prize-winning sheep and Jersey cattle.[65]

Humphrey Darnton (d. 1803), a Babraham farmer, kept his labourers' wages down when prices were high by allowing them cheap pork, cheese, and rice.[66] Forty-six of the 51 families at Babraham were dependent on agriculture in 1811,[67] and in 1841 62 of the 114 males were agricultural labourers.[68] Nonetheless, there was in 1867 a great shortage of labour, which had to be imported from neighbouring parishes.[69] No industry or other employment developed in Babraham, which remained small and entirely agricultural. The Institute of Animal Physiology employed 136 staff in 1971,[70] many of whom lived on the housing estate inside the park.

The smaller Richmond estate had a water-mill in 1086 and 1279; Bruisyards had one in 1279 which was not recorded later.[71] A water-mill belonging to Mompellers manor was recorded between 1316 and 1401,[72] and was perhaps extant in 1499.[73] Cifrewasts had a mill between 1330 and 1421,[74] and there was

40 H.O. 107/1761; R.G. 9/1028; R.G. 10/1591.
41 *Jnl. Royal Agric. Soc.* vii. 60; I.R. 18/13515 p. 15.
42 C.U.L., Doc. 668, nos. 12, 14; I.R. 18/13515 pp. 6, 18; Gooch, *Agric. of Cambs.* 103.
43 Bodl. MS. Gough Camb. 103(7), p. 7.
44 C.U.L., Maps bb. 53(1)/95/58–63.
45 C.R.O., 152/P 1.
46 Bodl. MS. Gough Camb. 103(7), p. 5; Vancouver, *Agric. in Cambs.* 55.
47 A. Young, *Annals of Agric.* xvi. 179–80; W. Smith, *Observations . . . on Water Meadows* (Norwich, 1806), 116–17.
48 C.U.L., Doc. 668, nos. 1–16.
49 Butcher, *Babraham Hall*, 8.
50 *Jnl. Royal Agric. Soc.* vii. 60.
51 Vancouver, *Agric. in Cambs.* 56.
52 C.R.O., 152/P 1.
53 C.U.L., Doc. 668 (12, 14). For Webb's achievements see *D.N.B.*; R. Trow-Smith, *Hist. Brit. Livestock Husbandry 1700–1900*, 276 n., 277; E. Burritt, *Walk from Lond. to John O'Groats* (Lond. 1864), 93, 98–9, 103; *E. Anglian Mag.* 1955, 275–7; Camb. Public Libr., 'Catalogue of Sheep and Cattle Sold 1862'.
54 Gooch, *Agric. of Cambs.* 272.
55 *Kelly's Dir. Cambs.* (1847–79).
56 [Adeane], *Babraham*, 22–3.
57 Ibid. 22; *D.N.B.*
58 Gooch, *Agric. of Cambs.* 267.
59 Ibid. 271.
60 [Adeane], *Babraham*, 23; tomb in chyd.
61 Camb. Agric. Returns, 1905.
62 [Adeane], *Babraham*, 23; local information.
63 Butcher, *Babraham Hall*, 17.
64 *Camb. Region, 1965*, 240–1.
65 *Inst. of Animal Physiology, Annual Rep. 1960–1*, 11; *1970–1*, 22.
66 Gooch, *Agric. of Cambs.* 288.
67 *Census*, 1811.
68 H.O. 107/66.
69 *1st Rep. Com. Employment in Agric.* 358.
70 Ex inf. the Librarian, Inst. of Animal Physiology.
71 *V.C.H. Cambs.* i. 409; *Rot. Hund.* (Rec. Com.), ii. 413–14.
72 *Cal. Pat.* 1313–17, 518; 1361–4, 350; *Feud. Aids*, i. 176.
73 C.P. 40/949 rot. 355.
74 *Cal. Inq. p.m.* vii, p. 205; *Cal. Close*, 1405–9, 160; 1419–22, 102.

a road called Mill way in the 15th century.[75] There was a miller in 1581,[76] but apparently no mill at Babraham in 1601,[77] and none was recorded thereafter. A local tradition that a windmill once stood in the meadows is probably unfounded.[78]

John of Brittany, earl of Richmond, was granted a weekly Monday market at Babraham in 1335, confirmed in 1344,[79] but no evidence of its existence has been found.

LOCAL GOVERNMENT. The honor of Richmond held a court at Babraham from the 13th to the 15th century, to which other Cambridgeshire manors held of the honor owed suit, being sometimes said to be held as of the manor of Babraham.[80] A sentence given in the honorial court in the late 13th century was later reversed by the king's court.[81] The Richmond court met at least once a month in 1356 and 1426,[82] and twice yearly or more in 1486;[83] a court roll survives for 1334.[84]

The holders of the Richmond manors also held view of frankpledge at Babraham *c.* 1235, in 1279 and 1282,[85] and in the 15th century.[86] The abbot of Waltham in 1299 claimed view of frankpledge and the assize of bread and of ale by prescription,[87] and court rolls exist for various dates in the 15th century and 1540.[88] The Waltham court had profits valued at 1*s.* 5½*d.* in 1540,[89] but it probably lapsed at the Dissolution.

Although conveyances of the amalgamated manors in the 16th century and later always included the right to hold a court leet, there is no record of courts actually being held. Babraham had two constables and a town herdsman in the 1550s.[90] A parish rate for recasting a bell in 1599 was made by Sir Horatio Palavicino at his house with his servant and the two churchwardens, though parishioners protested at the lack of public discussion.[91]

Expenditure on poor-relief rose sharply to £208 in 1803, when 16 people received permanent relief.[92] By 1813 it had reached a peak of £486 when 26 people were on permanent relief,[93] but it gradually fell to £117 in 1828 and £130 in 1834.[94] No one in Babraham was permanently unemployed in 1829.[95] The parish was included in the Linton poor-law union in 1835 and was transferred to the South Cambridgeshire R.D. in 1934,[96] remaining in South Cambridgeshire in 1974.

CHURCH. The record of a priest, Alric, in 1066 suggests that there was then a church in Babraham.[97] The church was given by Geoffrey de Scalers to Waltham abbey, probably in the 1180s; it was also claimed, however, by Sawtry abbey, which already held land in Babraham and to which Geoffrey's father had withdrawn as a Cistercian monk. Both houses obtained papal confirmation of their claims between 1191 and 1195, but by 1198 Sawtry had abandoned to Waltham all its claims in the church, except to certain tithes on its own lands. By a further settlement of 1228 Sawtry gave the church 23 a. in return for freedom from tithe on *c.* 180 a. of its land in Babraham.[98] Coplow Grange, Sawtry's farm, was still accounted free from great tithes in the 16th century.[99]

Waltham abbey appropriated the church in the 13th century, probably between 1228 and 1253 when it was granted free warren in Babraham. A vicarage was ordained before *c.* 1278.[1] All the known presentations to the benefice before 1540 were made by Waltham abbey, except in 1476 when the abbot granted a turn to John Elrington, treasurer of the royal household.[2] From the Dissolution the Crown retained the advowson[3] until 1728[4] or later. Bennet Alexander Bennet was said to be patron before his death in 1745,[5] and the advowson descended with the manor thereafter, though the Crown presented by lapse in 1798.[6] The patron in 1973 was Sir Robert Adeane.[7]

The vicarage of Babraham was exempted from taxation through its poverty in 1445;[8] in 1535 it was worth only £6 5*s.* 9*d.* and was the poorest living in Camps deanery.[9] In 1650 it was valued at £20 a year,[10] but its yield had risen to £31 15*s.* 6*d.* by 1728.[11] The vicar's income had once come from small tithes, which he was receiving in the 16th century,[12] and from 14½ a. glebe, which he held in 1615.[13] By 1748, however, the lord of the manor was paying a fixed sum of £30, charged on the manorial estate in 1765, in place of tithes and glebe.[14] From 1839 the Adeanes paid the vicar 100 guineas a year,[15] raised by 1877 to £125,[16] the rent-charge fixed when the small tithes were formally extinguished in 1845.[17]

[75] *P.N. Cambs.* (E.P.N.S.), 100.
[76] *East Anglian*, ii. 218.
[77] B.L. Add. Ch. 39052.
[78] [Adeane], *Babraham*, 24.
[79] *Cal. Chart. R.* 1327–41, 350; 1341–1417, 32.
[80] e.g. *Cal. Inq. p.m.* ii, pp. 219–20; *Cal. Inq. p.m. Hen. VII*, i, p. 400.
[81] *Liber de Bernewelle*, 140.
[82] *Cal. Inq. p.m.* x, p. 227; *Cal. Close*, 1422–9, 234–5.
[83] *Cal. Inq. p.m. Hen. VII*, i, p. 23.
[84] S.C. 2/155/71.
[85] *Liber de Bernewelle*, 276; *Rot. Hund.* (Rec. Com.), ii. 413–14; *Cal. Inq. p.m.* ii, p. 220.
[86] *Cal. Inq. p.m.* (Rec. Com.), iv. 105, 169, 275.
[87] *Plac. de Quo Warr.* (Rec. Com.), 106–7.
[88] S.C. 2/155/45; S.C. 2/173/31–8; Essex R.O., D/DP M 1154.
[89] Dugdale, *Mon.* vi. 68.
[90] Sta. Cha. 2/22/143.
[91] *Trans. C.H.A.S.* vi. 22–3.
[92] *Poor Law Abstract, 1804*, 34–5.
[93] Ibid. *1818*, 28–9.
[94] *Poor Rate Returns, 1825–9*, 15–16; *1830–4*, 15.
[95] *Rep. H.L. Cttee. on Poor Laws*, H.C. 227, pp. 326–7 (1831), viii.
[96] *Poor Law Com. 1st Rep.* 249; *Census*, 1931 (pt. ii).
[97] *V.C.H. Cambs.* i. 374, 409.
[98] *Proc. C.A.S.* lix. 113–17, 121–3.
[99] Palmer, *Cambs. in 16th cent.* 23–5; E 321/18/60; E 321/14/28.
[1] *Vetus Liber Arch. Elien.* (C.A.S. 8vo ser. xlviii), 66.
[2] *E.D.R.* (1906), 125.
[3] Cf. Gibbons, *Ely Episc. Rec.* 453, 456.
[4] C.U.L., E.D.R., B 8/1.
[5] B.L. Add. MS. 5802, f. 40.
[6] C.U.L., E.D.R., B 8/4, f. 3.
[7] *Ely Dioc. Dir.* 1972–3.
[8] *E.D.R.* (1902), 122.
[9] *Valor Eccl.* (Rec. Com.), iii. 504.
[10] Lamb. Pal. MS. 904, f. 271.
[11] C.U.L., E.D.R., B 8/1.
[12] Palmer, *Cambs. in 16th cent.* 25.
[13] C.U.L., E.D.R., H 1/1.
[14] B.L. Add. MS. 5823, f. 18; Bodl. MS. Gough Camb. 103(7), p. 6.
[15] I.R. 18/13515 p. 9.
[16] C.U.L., E.D.R., C 3/26.
[17] I.R. 18/13515 pp. 9, 13, 18; C.R.O., 152/P 1.

There were 3 a. of vicarial glebe in 1877.[18] No vicarage house is recorded until the 19th century, though some 16th-century incumbents were resident.[19] There was no house in 1615,[20] and in 1836 the curate lived in a house belonging to H. J. Adeane.[21] A new house was built between then and 1841, probably by H. J. Adeane on the institution of Joseph Singleton in 1839.[22]

John de Scalers (fl. 1246–71) founded a chantry in the chapel of St. Mary in Babraham church, apparently in the 1260s, endowing it with 2 messuages, 40 a., 15*s*. rent, and pasture for 4 cattle; if the founder and his heirs failed to present, a priest was to be appointed by the prior of Anglesey.[23] The chantry-priest of St. Mary was taxed in 1347,[24] and there was a priest in 1406.[25] Anglesey presented in 1439, but in 1479 and 1491 the abbess of Bruisyard presented.[26] The foundation, not mentioned as a chantry after 1492,[27] may have been connected with the guild of St. Mary in Babraham church recorded in 1504.[28] The 18 a. of chantry and obit lands sold by the Crown to Sir John Butler and Thomas Chaworth in 1553 may have been part of the chantry's endowment.[29]

Robert Wistowe, vicar in 1363, was then at Avignon trying to secure another living.[30] In 1504 Margaret, countess of Richmond, provided for a Cambridge university preacher to give sermons every year in a number of churches including Babraham. The sermons were abolished in 1679.[31] John Hullier, vicar from 1549 until *c.* 1555, was burned to death for heresy at Cambridge in 1556.[32] The parish was without a vicar and was served by a curate 1561–7,[33] and was sequestrated in 1569.[34] The vicar from 1617, Thomas Thornton, was ejected from his college fellowship in 1644 but retained the living of Babraham until his death in 1651.[35]

From the 1660s the cure was served by a succession of curates and sequestrators.[36] In the 18th century incumbents were usually non-resident fellows of Cambridge colleges; they included William Geekie, vicar in 1725, a fellow of Queens' College,[37] Stephen Whisson, vicar from 1746 to *c.* 1766, university librarian 1751–83, who also held a living in Norfolk,[38] and Henry Lloyd, vicar 1798–1831, who was Regius Professor of Hebrew at Cambridge and lived at Edinburgh.[39] The long incumbency of Joseph Singleton, vicar 1839–89, and the provision of a vicarage house set new standards of pastoral care at Babraham. The curate who preceded Singleton had raised the number of communion services each year from three to four,[40] and by 1877 there were six.[41] In 1851 the average attendances were 90 people at the morning service and 190 in the afternoon.[42] The Adeane family took a close interest in maintaining the church throughout the 19th century.[43] In modern times Babraham has often been held with neighbouring parishes, such as Great Abington 1890–3 and Hildersham 1919–21 and 1960–2.[44] Since 1947 Babraham has been held in plurality with the vicarage of Pampisford by dispensation, the vicar living since 1958 at Babraham.[45]

The church of *ST. PETER*, so called since the 12th century,[46] is of field stones and rubble with dressings of freestone, and has a chancel, an aisled and clerestoried nave with north and south porches, and a west tower. The chancel and lower parts of the tower surviving from the mid 13th century show that the church was then a building larger than average for the area, and a 12th-century capital re-used as rubble in the chancel may be evidence of an earlier church. The chancel, already well lit, was provided with more windows and a south doorway in the 14th century. The nave was completely rebuilt with aisles and arcades of four tall bays early in the 15th century, and the south porch and upper stages of the tower are of about the same date. Later in the 15th century the church was furnished with a pulpit, font cover, rood-screen, and seating. After the Reformation the church was apparently kept in good repair; the north porch and clerestory were probably not added until the later 16th century. The altar-rails were destroyed in the 17th century, perhaps by William Dowsing in 1644, and a new set was made in 1665, about which time the east face of the tower was strengthened with brickwork. Other additions of the period were associated with the Bennet family: a large monument of 1667 to Sir Thomas and Richard Bennet in the south aisle, the reredos of 1700, and a monument to Judith Bennet (d. 1713). Many early fittings, including the screen, were removed during an extensive restoration of 1770–4 by Robert Jones, when the chancel roof was slated and the nave roof completely rebuilt.[47] The chancel was again repaired shortly before 1836, and the church was thoroughly restored between 1890 and 1910.[48] Many monuments to members of the Adeane family were installed in the 19th and 20th centuries, including the east window of stained glass designed by John Piper in 1966.

In 1552 the church had four bells and a sanctus bell.[49] In 1599 the sanctus bell was in the house of Sir Horatio Palavicino, and neither he nor the parishioners were willing to pay for it to be rehung.[50]

18 C.U.L., E.D.R., C 3/26.
19 e.g. Bodl. MS. Gough Eccl. Top. 3, f. 49.
20 C.U.L., E.D.R., H 1/1.
21 Ibid. C 3/21.
22 H.O. 107/66; I.R. 18/13515 pp. 7, 9.
23 *Vetus Liber Arch. Elien.* (C.A.S. 8vo ser. xlviii), 4–6; *Proc. C.A.S.* i. 205–6.
24 E 179/242/8 m. 9.
25 *E.D.R.* (1899), 158.
26 C.U.L., E.D.R., L 3/1, ff. 17v., 47; B.L. Add. MS. 5823, f. 18v.
27 C.U.L., E.D.R., L 3/1, f. 48.
28 *Trans. C.H.A.S.* i. 384.
29 *Cal. Pat.* 1553, 290–1.
30 Emden, *Biog. Reg. Univ. Camb.* 643; *Cal. Papal Pets.* i. 415.
31 Cooper, *Annals of Camb.* i. 273–4 and n.
32 Ibid. ii. 103–4.
33 C.U.L., E.D.R., B 2/3, p. 99; B 2/4, p. 20; B 2/6.
34 Gibbons, *Ely Episc. Rec.* 163.
35 *Alum. Cantab. to 1751*, iv. 233.
36 C.U.L., E.D.R., B 2/67 *passim*; B 7/72.
37 B.L. Add. MS. 5823, f. 20; *Alum. Cantab. to 1751*, ii. 205.
38 *Alum. Cantab. to 1751*, iv. 383.
39 Ibid. *1752–1900*, iv. 189; C.U.L., E.D.R., C 1/4.
40 C.U.L., E.D.R., B 8/1; C 1/4; C 3/21.
41 Ibid. C 3/26.
42 H.O. 129/188/1/1/1.
43 e.g. C.U.L., E.D.R., C 3/21; C 3/36; mons. in ch.
44 *Crockford* (1896), s.v. J. H. A. Law; (1926), s.v. P. R. Phillips; (1961–2), s.v. F. R. Powney.
45 Ibid. (1947 and later edns.); *Ely Dioc. Dir.* 1972–3.
46 *Proc. C.A.S.* lix. 121–2.
47 Palmer, *Wm. Cole*, 10, 83; *Proc. C.A.S.* xxxv. 68.
48 C.U.L., E.D.R., C 3/21, 36; *E.D.R.* (1903), 154; (1904), 254; (1905), 58.
49 *Cambs. Ch. Goods, temp. Edw. VI*, 65.
50 *Trans. C.H.A.S.* vi. 11–12.

Four of an original peal of five bells remained in 1882, though one was broken; two (formerly three) were by John Draper of Thetford, 1615, given by Sir Henry Palavicino,[51] and survived in 1973, although one was cracked.[52] The church plate *c.* 1278 included two chalices, as in 1552, when one was taken.[53] Patens were given to the church by Elizabeth Lamott in 1633 and Dorothy Page in 1735, and a flagon by George Thorpe, curate, in 1685.[54] The parish registers begin in 1651, and are virtually complete.

NONCONFORMITY. In 1797 a house in Babraham was registered for nonconformist worship.[55] In 1807 there were one papist and a few Protestants, perhaps Methodists, who occasionally attended another church.[56] Four people in 1877 attended a chapel in Sawston, and in the 1880s members of the Congregational chapel there held Sunday evening services in a house at Babraham.[57] Only two or three families were thought to be nonconformists in 1897.[58]

EDUCATION. A schoolmaster was mentioned in 1607.[59] In 1730, under the will of Judith Bennet,[60] a charity school was established at which all the children of the parish were to be taught free, except those whose parents held land worth £50 a year, and the schoolmaster, a member of the Church of England, was to teach the catechism.[61] The children were also taught spelling and arithmetic.[62] In 1818 20–30 pupils aged 7–14 attended the school, and an evening school was occasionally held in the winter for the older children.[63] In 1837 *c.* 30 children whose parents were settled parishioners were taught free; all the pupils learnt reading, writing, and arithmetic, and H. J. Adeane paid the master's wife £5 a year to teach the girls 'plain work'.[64] Additions were made to the school, which stood in the middle of the row of alms-houses, in 1861 and 1869, and a new room for infants was added in 1902 when the number of pupils reached 70.[65] A night school was poorly attended in 1867 and had been abandoned by 1877 for lack of support,[66] but the schoolmaster held technical classes on winter evenings in 1897 and 1900 and there was then a parochial library.[67] In 1872 most of the children were withdrawn from the school in protest at the imposition of fees, and although by 1878 Babraham children were again educated free, fees being paid only by pupils from other parishes, strong opposition was aroused by a Scheme giving the trustees powers to charge if necessary.[68] Attendance had fallen to 31 by 1922, and senior pupils were transferred to schools at Great Abington and Sawston in 1925 and to Sawston village college in 1930.[69] A new primary school was opened in 1959 on a site in Babraham bought from the Agricultural Research Council and conveyed in 1961 to the trustees of the educational charity.[70]

CHARITIES FOR THE POOR. By will proved 1723 Levinus Bush devised the reversion of one-fifth of the manor of Babraham, after the death of his father James (d. 1726), to his aunt Judith Bennet, on condition that she leave £1,000 to charitable uses. Judith (d. 1724) gave £500 to build a free school and alms-houses for six women in Babraham, and for the other £500 charged her lands with £25 a year for apprenticing former pupils. In expectation of another legacy of £1,000, under James Bush's will dated 1723, Judith also charged her lands with £100 a year for the schoolmaster, almspeople, and apprentices. After Judith's death, however, James transferred the legacy to his daughter-in-law Sarah Bush, and a Chancery decree of 1734 reduced the rent-charges to £50 a year for the school and alms-houses and £25 a year for the apprentices.[71]

Although the school and alms-houses were built in 1730, the rent-charges were not regularly paid: suits for payment and arrears were brought in 1734, 1757, 1762, and 1793.[72] In 1765 £1,353 stock was purchased, increased to £2,195 by 1863, but reduced to £1,256 by 1963. The charity's income in addition to the £75 rent-charge was £59 in 1837 and £66 in 1863.[73] A Scheme of 1878 provided that the whole net income, apart from the alms-house stipends and upkeep and the apprentices' fund, should be devoted to the school, and in 1908 Bush and Bennet's charity was divided into an alms-house charity, and an educational foundation. The income of the alms-house charity was £108 in 1961, and £256 in 1965. The six almswomen each received 3*s.* a week in 1806[74] and 1877, with gifts of coal and clothing at Christmas. In 1959 the almswomen received 6*s.* a week, but after the modernization of their house a Scheme of 1963 allowed the trustees to charge small rents. The alms-houses, three red-brick one-storey dwellings on each side of a central two-storey block used for the school until 1959, were modernized in 1959–60 when the six one-room houses were converted to four.

In the 1830s boys from the largest and most deserving families were apprenticed outside the parish.[75] In 1877 it was difficult to find either apprentices or tradesmen to take them. The

[51] *Cambs. Bells* (C.A.S. 8vo ser. xviii), 118; Palmer, *Wm. Cole,* 82; *Eng. Topog.* (Gent. Mag. Libr.), ii. 22.
[52] Ex inf. the vicar, the Revd. R. A. Spalding.
[53] *Vetus Liber Arch. Elien.* (C.A.S. 8vo ser. xlviii), 66; *Cambs. Ch. Goods, temp. Edw. VI,* 64.
[54] Palmer, *Wm. Cole,* 82.
[55] G.R.O. Worship Returns, Ely archdeac. no. 2.
[56] C.U.L., E.D.R., C 1/4.
[57] Ibid. C 3/26; R. Ball, *Hist. Sawston Cong. Ch.* 11.
[58] C.U.L., E.D.R., C 3/36.
[59] Ibid. B 2/23, f. 40v.
[60] The foundation of the charity is described in detail below.
[61] B.L. Add. MS. 5822, pp. 199–200.
[62] Bodl. MS. Gough Camb. 103 (23).
[63] *Educ. of Poor Digest,* 55.
[64] *31st Rep. Com. Char.* 103.
[65] Ed. 7/5; Char. Com. files; see below, plate facing p. 176.
[66] *1st Rep. Com. Employment in Agric.* 358; C.U.L., E.D.R., C 3/26.
[67] C.U.L., E.D.R., C 3/36; *E.D.R.* (1900), 51.
[68] Char. Com. files.
[69] *Bd. of Educ., List 21, 1922* (H.M.S.O.), 15; Black, *Cambs. Educ. Rec.* 39.
[70] Char. Com. files.
[71] B.L. Add. MS. 5822, pp. 196–207; Add. MS. 9412, f. 258 and v.
[72] B.L. Add. MS. 5822, p. 206; Lysons, *Cambs.* 84.
[73] Except where otherwise stated this account is based on Char. Com. files; *31st Rep. Com. Char.* 100–3; *Char. Digest Cambs. 1863–4,* 2.
[74] B.L. Add. MS. 9412, f. 260v.
[75] C.U.L., Doc. 849; Doc. 1633.

proposed diversion of the money to the almswomen or the school in years when no-one applied for apprenticeship was fiercely opposed by the labourers, and never formally adopted, but after 1913 when applications ceased completely the money was usually divided between the almswomen.

BARTLOW

BARTLOW is one of the smallest parishes in Cambridgeshire.[1] It covered 377 a. until 1965 when 7 ha. were transferred from Ashdon (Essex). In 1971 it covered 156 ha. (385 a.).[2] It lies 12 miles south-east of Cambridge, 5½ miles north-east of Saffron Walden (Essex), and 5½ miles west of Haverhill (Suff.). The parish boundary follows on the west the road from Ashdon to West Wratting, on the north a bank called Bartlow Broad Balk, on the east in part an old field-path stopped up at inclosure,[3] and on the south a stream and an irregular line which was straightened after the construction of the railway in 1865.[4] The south-west corner of the parish is at the point where the river Bourne from the south, a stream flowing through Bartlow from the east, and a stream from the north join to form the river Granta. The stream flowing through Bartlow was diverted and straightened before 1837,[5] but in 1974 it had been dry for several years.

Pieces of land within Ashdon parish, adjoining the county boundary with Castle Camps and together covering 1,072 a., formed what was known as Bartlow End, Stevington End, or Bartlow hamlet,[6] formerly part of Bartlow parish although they were in Essex. In an area that was heavily wooded as late as the 14th century[7] county boundaries were perhaps established early but approximately, according to geographical features such as the ridge between Ashdon and Castle Camps, whereas tenurial boundaries, and following them parish boundaries, were at a later date given precision as settlement slowly extended. In 1086 Bartlow was probably part of the estate of Aubrey de Vere, based on Castle Camps, as was part of Stevington;[8] the geographical position of Overhall, Winsey Farm, Bourne, and perhaps Newnham Hall, all part of Bartlow End[9] and all settlements separate from Ashdon in the 13th century,[10] suggests that they were colonized westwards from Castle Camps rather than eastwards from Ashdon. The name of Westoe, close to Bartlow, suggests that it too was settled westwards from Castle Camps, and Bartlow was hidated in Castle Camps *c.* 1235.[11] Inhabitants of Bartlow End attended Bartlow church and paid church-rates to it until the 20th century, but in 1801 agriculture in the hamlet was integrated with that in Ashdon.[12] The hamlet relieved its poor separately from Bartlow,[13] and therefore was accounted a separate civil parish in the 19th century, lying in the Linton poor-law union, but it was united with Ashdon civil parish in 1946.[14]

The highest point in the parish, at its north-east corner, lies just under 300 ft., but the village and the land by the stream are below 200 ft. Bartlow lies on the Upper Chalk, and its soil is chalky, with some gravel and clay. The parish is entirely agricultural, and was cultivated in open fields until inclosure in 1863.[15]

The Bartlow Hills, said to be the finest Romano-British burial mounds in Britain,[16] stand south of and close to Bartlow village, though only one of the four surviving mounds stands inside the parish boundary. Although they were long believed to cover the bodies of those slain at the battle of Ashingdon (Assandun) in 1016,[17] excavation showed them to be the graves of a wealthy family of A.D. 80–140. A small Roman villa north of the mounds, occupied into the later 4th century, was excavated in 1852.[18]

Bartlow, first mentioned in 1232[19] though the church is of the late 11th or early 12th century, appears to have originated as a subsidiary settlement to Castle Camps, as suggested above. A lost 'Brining', recorded in 1207,[20] may have been close to Bartlow or held with it. Bartlow had 32 tenants in 1279 and 32 people paid the poll tax in 1377.[21] There were 20 households in Bartlow in 1563, though only 11 were taxed in 1674.[22] The village contained 15 families in 1728,[23] and the rector counted 88 inhabitants in 1782.[24] Apart from a fall to 56 people in 1811, the population of Bartlow village fluctuated between 82 and 123 from 1801 until 1921, after which there was a slow decline. The population in 1971 was 70.[25]

Bartlow village lies in the south-west corner of the parish, in the south-east angle of the cross-roads formed by the road from Linton to Castle Camps and Shudy Camps and the road from Ashdon to West Wratting. It is a small, compact settlement, bounded on the east by the grounds of Bartlow Park,

1 This account was written in 1974.
2 *Census*, 1961–71.
3 C.U.L., Maps bb. 53(1)/01/4; C.R.O., Q/RDc 80.
4 C.R.O., 296/SP 918.
5 C.U.L., E.D.R., H 1/7, terrier 1837.
6 Most aspects of the history of Bartlow End are reserved for treatment under Essex.
7 C 133/76/7 no. 8; C 135/222 no. 15.
8 *V.C.H. Cambs.* i. 408; *V.C.H. Essex*, i. 536.
9 C.R.O., 296/SP 1060.
10 *Trans. Essex Arch. Soc.* N.S., xix. 29; *Rot. Hund.* (Rec. Com.), i. 145.
11 *Liber de Bernewelle*, 254.
12 H.O. 61/9.
13 C.U.L., E.D.R., C 1/4.
14 *Census*, 1891, 1951.
15 Vancouver, *Agric. in Cambs.* 59–60; C.R.O., Q/RDc 80.
16 Pevsner, *Cambs.* 232; see also *V.C.H. Essex*, i. 311; iii. 39–44; Fox, *Arch. Camb. Region*, 191, 193, 226.
17 B.L. Add. MS. 5802, f. 25.
18 *Arch. Jnl.* x. 17–21; Fox, *Arch. Camb. Region*, 185, 193.
19 *P.N. Cambs.* (E.P.N.S.), 101.
20 *Cur. Reg. R.* v. 5.
21 *Rot. Hund.* (Rec. Com.), ii. 426; *Cambs. Village Doc.* 101.
22 B.L. Harl. MS. 594, f. 200; see below p. 280.
23 C.U.L., E.D.R., B 8/1.
24 C.R.O., par. reg.
25 *Census*, 1801–1971.

originally belonging to Bartlow House. Bartlow Hall and the rectory were the only large houses in the village in the later 17th century;[26] a row of 16th-century cottages, called Maltings Cottages, stands east of the road to Ashdon, and the Three Hills is a 17th-century cottage with 18th-century and later extensions. North of the Linton–Camps road are the Dower House, built in the early 19th century as Bartlow Cottage,[27] and Chetwynd House, formerly the school. The village has not expanded in the 20th century and Bartlow Park is the only new building there. At the point where the stream crosses the Ashdon road there was a ford and footbridge until 1931, when a brick bridge was built.[28]

There were two alehouses in Bartlow in 1682.[29] Inn-keepers were buried in 1736 and 1790,[30] and the Three Hills was a public house in 1847[31] and 1974.

The railway from Shelford to Haverhill (Suff.), which runs across the southern edge of the parish south of the river, was opened in 1865,[32] and an extension to Saffron Walden, diverging at Bartlow, in 1866. Bartlow station, at the railway bridge over the Ashdon road, was closed in 1967 with the line to Haverhill,[33] and was converted into a private house called Booking Hall.

Benefit clubs for rent, coal, clothing, and shoes were run in Bartlow village and hamlet in the early 20th century.[34] The Bartlow feast was held on 2 June in 1753.[35]

MANOR. Bartlow was not among the estates of Count Alan of Richmond before 1086,[36] and it was therefore probably part of the 2½-hide estate at Castle Camps of Aubrey de Vere, held T.R.E. by the thegn Wulfwin.[37] By *c.* 1235, however, the manor of *BARTLOW*, or *BARTLOW HALL*, was held under the earl of Oxford as of the honor of Richmond,[38] and it was said to be part of that honor until the 16th century.[39] Alice of Ashdon held land in 'Brining' before 1207,[40] and Ralph of Ashdon and Maurice of Bartlow *c.* 1235 held 1 knight's fee in Bartlow, hidated in Castle Camps with land in Finchingfield (Essex).[41] In 1269 the manor was granted to William of Chishill by Robert Gikel,[42] whose family held a fee at Finchingfield.[43] Sir William held the lordship as ¼ fee of Gikel's heirs in 1279[44] and 1282,[45] and John of Chishill held it of another Robert Gikel before 1299[46] and in 1316[47] and 1325.[48] In 1331 John granted the reversion after his death to John Hotham, bishop of Ely (d. 1337),[49] whose probable heir Sir John Hotham (d. 1351) vindicated his right to the advowson against John son of William of Chishill in 1349.[50] The manor was subsequently acquired by William of Clopton, perhaps the eldest son of Sir William of Clopton who in 1347 bought Newnham manor, Ashdon.[51] In 1374 William's widow Avice quitclaimed Bartlow to Isabel, probably his daughter and heir, and her husband John Mohaut of Kingston,[52] also called John Kingston,[53] dead by 1392, when she had married William Clipston.[54] Clipston was murdered in 1406,[55] and the manor passed under an entail to Robert Kingston, a son of John and Isabel.[56] Robert lived at Bartlow in 1434 and held the manor in 1440.[57] Before 1459, however, the lordship had passed to John Tiptoft, earl of Worcester,[58] and descended to his son Edward in 1470. When Edward died unmarried in 1485[59] Bartlow was assigned to his father's sister Joan, widow of Sir Edmund Ingoldisthorpe,[60] and on her death in 1494 passed to her granddaughter Isabel, wife of William Huddleston and later of Sir William Smith.[61] Isabel's heir in 1516 was her son John Huddleston of Sawston (d. 1530), to whose widow Elizabeth, who married secondly Sir Thomas Butler, Bartlow was awarded in dower.[62] Her son John Huddleston was lord of Bartlow before his death in 1557, and was succeeded by his son Sir Edmund (d. 1606).[63] Edmund's son Henry held Bartlow in 1624,[64] but later sold the manor and advowson to Jon Baker, rector of Bartlow (d. 1639).[65] Baker's son Jon (d. 1645)[66] left three daughters as coheirs and the manor was divided between them. Blaise Pratt, husband of the eldest daughter Anne (d. 1668), improved the Hall and estate despite opposition from Anthony Bettenham, reputed husband of the second daughter Elizabeth (d. 1696);[67] Pratt presented to the rectory in 1667,[68] apparently lived in the Hall in 1672,[69] and was buried at Bartlow in 1689.[70] Elizabeth Mapletoft (d. 1717)

26 E 179/84/437 rot. 58.
27 H.O. 107/66.
28 C.R.O., 331/Z 6, Oct. 1931, p. 81.
29 *Proc. C.A.S.* xvii. 97.
30 C.R.O., par. reg.
31 *Kelly's Dir. Cambs.* (1847).
32 *V.C.H. Cambs.* ii. 133.
33 C.R.O., Q/RUm 50; *Camb. News*, 13 July 1967.
34 C.R.O., 331/Z 1, Dec. 1904; 6, Dec. 1930, p. 94; 7, Dec. 1936, p. 94.
35 Carter, *Hist. Cambs.* 123.
36 *V.C.H. Cambs.* ii. 315.
37 Ibid. i. 390, 408.
38 *Liber de Bernewelle*, 254.
39 S.C. 2/155/71; C 142/52 no. 5.
40 *Cur. Reg. R.* v. 5.
41 *Liber de Bernewelle*, 254.
42 C.P. 25(1)/25/32 no. 7.
43 Morant, *Essex*, ii. 364; *Trans. Essex Arch. Soc.* (3rd ser.), i. 185–7.
44 *Rot. Hund.* (Rec. Com.), ii. 426.
45 *Cal. Inq. p.m.* ii, p. 220.
46 Pemb. Coll. Mun., Barham, S 1, f. 19.
47 *Feud. Aids*, i. 155.
48 C.P. 25(1)/27/63 no. 12.
49 *Essex Feet of Fines* (Essex Arch. Soc.), iii. 15.
50 *E.D.R.* (1893), 95; cf. *Cal. Inq. p.m.* ix, pp. 429–30; *Cal. Close*, 1333–7, 686; *Cal. Pat.* 1350–4, 299.
51 Morant, *Essex*, ii. 321, 540; cf. *Essex Feet of Fines*, iii. 81, 86.
52 *Cal. Close*, 1374–7, 76.
53 Ibid.; C.P. 25(1)/29/86 no. 10.
54 C.P. 25(1)/289/56 no. 239; C.P. 40/549 rot. 211.
55 *Cal. Pat.* 1408–13, 70.
56 Pemb. Coll. Mun., Barham, S 1, f. 23. Possibly not the eldest son: cf. *Cal. Close*, 1422–9, 315.
57 *Cal. Pat.* 1429–36, 385; *Essex Feet of Fines* (Essex Arch. Soc.), iv. 30.
58 Bodl. MS. Rawl. B. 319, f. 112; *Cal. Pat.* 1452–61, 519; *E.D.R.* (1905), 234.
59 *Complete Peerage*, xii (2), 846.
60 *Cal. Inq. p.m. Hen. VII*, i, pp. 10, 463.
61 Ibid.; C 142/32 no. 69.
62 C 142/52 no. 5; C 1/1105 no. 49.
63 C 142/111 no. 15.
64 C 2/Jas. I/R 9/7.
65 *Trans. C.H.A.S.* vi. 25 n.; C 3/433/17. The forename of Baker and his son was spelt Jon, or occasionally Jonah, but not John.
66 *Walker Revised*, ed. Matthews, 77–8.
67 C 3/433/17.
68 P.R.O. Inst. Bk. ser. B, i, f. 61.
69 E 179/244/23 rot. 55.
70 C.R.O., par. reg.

inherited a third of the advowson, and presumably of the manor, and purchased the other two-thirds.[71] By 1750 the lordship was held by Edmund Mapletoft, rector of Bartlow 1711–50, whose widow and son Edmund sold it in 1751 to Francis Dayrell of Shudy Camps.[72] The manor descended in the Dayrell family until the late 19th century.[73] The Revd. Thomas Dayrell was awarded 178 a. in Bartlow at inclosure in 1862.[74] The manor was offered for sale with the estate in 1891 after the death of C. L. Dayrell,[75] and was apparently bought with the Dayrells' Shudy Camps estate in 1898 by Arthur Gee (d. 1903).[76] Bartlow Hall farm was sold again in 1903, presumably with the lordship, to the Revd. C. H. Brocklebank, a prominent landowner and farmer who had bought Bartlow House in 1899.[77] On his departure from the village in 1927 the lordship passed to his son C. G. Brocklebank,[78] who sold the estate in 1936 to Lord De Ramsey, lord lieutenant of Huntingdonshire.[79] In 1962 it was purchased from him by Lt.-Col. (later Brig.) A. N. Breitmeyer,[80] the owner in 1974.

There was a manor-house at Bartlow in 1279,[81] and in 1397 William Clipston's manor-house was attacked by his enemies.[82] The manor was known as Bartlow Hall in the mid 15th century;[83] Lady Butler in 1540 leased the 'hall or chief farm place' of Bartlow,[84] and the hall served as the farm-house for the Bartlow estate from the later 15th century when the lords of the manor no longer lived in the parish. The present house, known as the Old Hall, stands south-west of the church by the river and dates from the later 16th century; it was ruinous in the 1650s, was extensively repaired by Blaise Pratt,[85] and had 9 taxable hearths in 1665 and 1672.[86] Minor additions were made to the south in the 18th century and there was much restoration in the 19th.

Bartlow House was mentioned in 1768 when it was in separate ownership from the manor.[87] Thomas Barnard, the occupant since at least 1824,[88] sold the house in 1846 to Mrs. Maria Cotton,[89] whose kinsman Richard Archer Houblon lived there from *c.* 1858 to *c.* 1892 and added to the park.[90] His heir Col. G. B. Archer Houblon sold it in 1899 to the Revd. C. H. Brocklebank, and Bartlow House became the residence of the lords of the manor. The house, which stood north of the churchyard on the Linton–Camps road and had over 20 a. of park in 1899, burned down in 1947, leaving its stables and out-buildings which were converted into accommodation for employees of the estate.[91] Brig. Breitmeyer built a large new house called Bartlow Park, east of the site of Bartlow House, after 1962.

Ickworth priory (Suff.) was said in 1254 and 1341 to hold property in Bartlow,[92] but had no estate there in the 16th century.[93]

ECONOMIC HISTORY. In 1279 William of Chishill, lord of Bartlow, held 66 a. of arable, 5 a. of meadow, and 2 a. of pasture in demesne, but had only three tenants, who owned no arable. Some 30 other free tenants held directly of the earl of Oxford or of his tenants, and occupied *c.* 53 a. Three owned together 26 a., no others over 4 a. Almost all paid only small money-rents; three each had to send one man to 3 boon-works in harvest for the earl.[94] Bartlow was mainly arable, and the parish assessment for tax in 1341 was reduced because 200 a. had gone out of cultivation.[95] The lord of the manor's property in 1397 included 40 qr. of barley, 24 qr. of wheat, 6 qr. of oats, 3 qr. of peas, some malt, and a haystack.[96] Nonetheless, Bartlow contributed 21½ stone of wool to the tax in 1347, of which 9 stone came from Elizabeth, widow of Nicholas de Beauchamp.[97]

The main crops mentioned in the 16th and 17th centuries were wheat and rye,[98] and the rector also collected tithes on cows, pigs, wool and lambs, eggs, cheese, honey, wax, apples, and wood.[99] Bartlow Hall farm was almost all arable in 1550;[1] in the 1650s Blaise Pratt improved the farm and sowed wheat and rye, but Anthony Bettenham contended that the land should lie fallow for seven years, and refused to till the fields.[2] The Hall farm was the only one in Bartlow, although parts of the parish were farmed from Horseheath;[3] as a result no group of yeomen developed in the parish, and there were only two substantial taxpayers in 1524.[4] The common fields of the parish, mentioned in the 17th century and later, were Bartlow field, which included all the land north of the Linton–Camps road, and Church-meadow field south of the stream.[5] Stocking, Long-meadow, Deane, and Hadstock fields were probably just outside the parish boundary in neighbouring parishes, for the Hall farm and rectorial glebe both included land outside Bartlow:[6] in 1792 the Hall farm covered 157 a., of which 20 a. were in Essex.[7]

In the 18th century a threefold rotation was practised, and the principal crop was wheat; barley, oats, turnips, clover, and trefoil were also grown.[8] Wool and lambs formed a considerable part of the tithes,

[71] C.U.L., MS. Mm. 1. 39, p. 159.
[72] C.R.O., R 52/9/2A.
[73] See p. 51.
[74] C.R.O., Q/RDc 80.
[75] Ibid. 296/SP 918.
[76] C.U.L., Maps bb. 53(1)/89/34.
[77] Ibid.; C.R.O., 296/SP 1024; *Alum. Cantab. 1752–1900*, i. 387.
[78] C.R.O., 331/Z 6, Apr. 1927, p. 26.
[79] *Camb. Ind. Press*, 17 Aug. 1962.
[80] Ibid.; local information.
[81] *Rot. Hund.* (Rec. Com.), ii. 426.
[82] *Cal. Inq. Misc.* vi, p. 90.
[83] Bodl. MS. Rawl. B. 319, f. 112.
[84] C 1/1105 no. 49; C 1/1202 no. 28.
[85] C 3/433/17.
[86] E 179/84/437 rot. 58; E 179/244/23 rot. 55.
[87] Palmer, *Wm. Cole*, 21.
[88] C.R.O., par. reg.
[89] C.U.L., Maps bb. 53(1)/89/34.
[90] Ibid.; *Kelly's Dir. Cambs.* (1858, 1892).
[91] *Camb. Ind. Press*, 16 Feb. 1962.
[92] *Val. of Norwich*, ed. Lunt, 227; *Inq. Non.* (Rec. Com.), 213.
[93] S.C. 6/Hen. VIII/3408.
[94] *Rot. Hund.* (Rec. Com.), ii. 426.
[95] *Inq. Non.* (Rec. Com.), 213.
[96] *Cal. Inq. Misc.* vi, p. 90.
[97] E 179/242/8 m. 8; *Cal. Close*, 1341–3, 122.
[98] B.L. Add. MS. 5861, p. 175; C 3/433/17.
[99] C.R.O., par. rec., tithe receipt bks.
[1] C 1/1202 no. 28.
[2] C 3/433/17.
[3] C.U.L., MS. Plan 679, pp. 6, 21.
[4] E 179/81/134 m. 4.
[5] C.U.L., E.D.R., H 1/1, terrier 1663; C.R.O., Q/RDc 80.
[6] C.U.L., E.D.R., H 1/1, terriers 1615, 1663; Essex R.O., D/P 18/30/87–8.
[7] C.R.O., par. rec.
[8] Vancouver, *Agric. in Cambs.* 59–60; Essex R.O., D/P 18/3/87.

and Thomas Hayward, tenant of Bartlow Hall farm 1762–95, kept *c.* 200 sheep.[9] The farm was leased with a right of sheep-fold in 1540,[10] and there were shepherds in Bartlow from the 17th to the 19th century.[11] Three flocks had rights of sheepwalk in Bartlow and the hamlet, most of the suitable land being shared between them, though the Hall farm had exclusive rights over 37 a.[12] In 1801 just over half the arable in the parish was under barley, with 33 a. of wheat and smaller amounts of oats, rye, peas, and turnips or rape.[13] Sainfoin was tried in 1806.[14]

About 86 a. had been inclosed by 1753,[15] but many holdings were still in strips in 1837 and 1848.[16] Bartlow was inclosed with Shudy and Castle Camps in 1862, under the Second Annual Inclosure Act, 1858.[17] Land was exchanged between estates in the three parishes; the Revd. Thomas Dayrell, as lord of Bartlow manor, received 178 a. in Bartlow, the rector 32½ a., and Stanlake Batson of Horseheath 78 a. The trustees of Linton meeting-house with 13 a. and Henry, Viscount Maynard with 4 a. were the only others to receive land in Bartlow.[18] The Hall farm was said to comprise 340 a. in 1851,[19] and 396 a. in 1891 of which 193 a. lay in Bartlow.[20]

Bartlow House and the Dower House both had farm buildings,[21] but the Hall farm was the only establishment large enough to employ many labourers and provided most of the work in the parish.[22] The Revd. C. H. Brocklebank of Bartlow in the early 20th century owned and farmed *c.* 1,250 a. in Cambridgeshire and Essex; he kept a well known flock of Hampshire Down sheep, and a herd of pedigree Shorthorns, and served as president of the Cambridgeshire Agricultural Society 1918–19 and the Dairy Shorthorn Society 1930–1.[23] Bartlow has remained largely arable since inclosure,[24] and the main crops are wheat and barley, with oats, beans, and sugar-beet.[25] Almost all the inhabitants are employed by the local landowner on the estate, and no other form of employment has arisen in Bartlow.[26]

The malting trade expanded in the parish in the 18th century,[27] there was a malting-house in 1819,[28] and brewers and maltsters were recorded in the 1840s and 1850s,[29] but later disappeared.

LOCAL GOVERNMENT. In 1279 the earl of Oxford was said to hold view of frankpledge and the assizes of bread and of ale in Bartlow;[30] no evidence of the holding of manorial courts, or of copyhold tenure, has been found in the parish. There were two constables in 1377,[31] and one in the 1750s. Bartlow hamlet had its own churchwarden in 1749.[32] There were separate overseers of the poor for the village and hamlet, and poor-relief in the two settlements was administered separately; more people were usually relieved in the hamlet than in the village, and it had higher poor-rates in the 18th century.[33] Annual expenditure on the poor in Bartlow fluctuated sharply in the late 18th and early 19th century, reaching peaks of £115 in 1813 and £112 in 1833, although it could be as low as £40 or £50.[34] The parish became part of the Linton poor-law union in 1835, and part of the South Cambridgeshire R.D. in 1934,[35] remaining in South Cambridgeshire in 1974. Bartlow hamlet was also included in the Linton poor-law union in 1835, but by 1911 was part of the Saffron Walden R.D., in which it remained after amalgamation with Ashdon civil parish in 1946,[36] becoming part of the Uttlesford district in 1974.

CHURCH. In spite of the belief that Bartlow church was built by King Cnut near the site of the battle of Ashingdon (Assandun) in the early 11th century,[37] no documentary references to the church have been found earlier than the 13th century, and the building dates from the late 11th or early 12th. The advowson belonged to Sir William of Chishill in 1279,[38] and descended with the lordship until *c.* 1751. The advowson was conveyed to feoffees in 1393,[39] and in 1399 granted for life to John Sleaford, rector of Balsham,[40] who presented in 1400.[41] Robert Kingston, lord of the manor, presented in 1437.[42] When the next vacancy occurred, in 1469, three different rectors were presented by Thomas Westley, John, earl of Worcester, and John, earl of Oxford; the earl of Worcester's right was upheld in 1470,[43] and his son's guardian and stepfather, Sir William Stanley, presented in 1472 and 1480.[44] The bishop collated by lapse *c.* 1500,[45] but all subsequent 16th-century incumbents were presented by members of the Huddleston family, lords of the manor, although Margery Blodwell attempted to present in 1526.[46] Jon Baker, the rector, bought the advowson

[9] Essex R.O., D/P 18/3/82, 88.
[10] C 1/1202 no. 28.
[11] C.U.L., Doc. 850; Essex R.O., D/P 18/3/87; D/P 18/3/89, p. 77; H.O. 107/1761.
[12] Essex R.O., D/P 18/3/80, 82, 87.
[13] H.O. 67/9.
[14] Gooch, *Agric. of Cambs.* 151–2.
[15] Essex R.O., D/P 18/3/80A, p. 23.
[16] C.U.L., E.D.R., H 1/7, terrier 1837; ibid. Maps bb. 53(1)/01/4.
[17] 21 & 22 Vic. c. 61.
[18] C.R.O., Q/RDc 80.
[19] H.O. 107/1761.
[20] C.R.O., 296/SP 918.
[21] Ibid.; C.U.L. Maps bb. 53(1)/89/34.
[22] H.O. 107/1761.
[23] *Who's Who in Cambs.* (1912); *Alum. Cantab. 1752–1900*, i. 387.
[24] Cambs. Agric. Returns, 1905.
[25] *Kelly's Dir. Cambs.* (1937).
[26] *Camb. Ind. Press*, 16 Feb. 1962.
[27] Vancouver, *Agric. in Cambs.* 60.
[28] C.R.O., par. rec.
[29] H.O. 107/66; H.O. 107/1761; *Kelly's Dir. Cambs.* (1847).
[30] *Rot. Hund.* (Rec. Com.), ii. 426.
[31] *East Anglian*, N.S. xii. 239.
[32] C.R.O., par. rec., chwdns.' accts.
[33] Ibid. par. reg.; Vancouver, *Agric. in Cambs.* 60–1; C.U.L., E.D.R., C 1/4.
[34] *Poor Law Abstract, 1818*, 28–9; *Poor Rate Returns, 1825–9*, 15–16; *1830–4*, 15.
[35] *Poor Law Com. 1st Rep.* 249; *Census*, 1931 (pt. ii).
[36] *Census*, 1851, 1911, 1951.
[37] B.L. Add. MS. 5802, f. 25.
[38] *Rot. Hund.* (Rec. Com.), ii. 426; cf. C.P. 25(1)/25/32 no. 7.
[39] *Cat. Anct. D.* i, C 492.
[40] Pemb. Coll. Mun., Barham, S 1, f. 23; Blomefield, *Collect. Cantab.* 201.
[41] *E.D.R.* (1898), 90.
[42] C.U.L., E.D.R., L 3/1, f. 15.
[43] *E.D.R.* (1905), 213, 234, 254.
[44] Ibid. (1906), 77; C.U.L., E.D.R., L 3/1, f. 33.
[45] C.U.L., E.D.R., L 3/1, f. 49.
[46] C.P. 40/965 rot. 420; *E.D.R.* (1911), 101.

with the manor after 1624, his son presented in 1639,[47] and the patron in 1667 was Blaise Pratt, husband of one of the younger Baker's three coheirs. Elizabeth Mapletoft, widow, perhaps of Edmund Mapletoft, inherited a third of the advowson and purchased the other two-thirds.[48] She presented to the living in 1704 and 1711, William Mapletoft in 1750, each naming a relative, and Edmund Mapletoft, son of the late rector, in 1772, being subsequently presented himself by Robert Fiske in 1775.[49] In 1782 William Hall presented Joseph Hall, probably his son.[50] His successor John Bullen, rector 1828–63, may have been presented by a descendant of William Hall's daughter, Elizabeth Bullen, and himself owned the advowson in 1836.[51] Robert Watkins was said to be patron by 1858, and held the rectory himself 1866–72.[52] The Revd. H. S. Patterson apparently presented himself to the living in 1872,[53] and H. and F. Bullard presented in 1877.[54] In 1894 Lt.-Col. W. C. Western nominated his son W. T. Western, and his executors were patrons in 1904.[55] The advowson of Bartlow thereafter belonged to the Revd. C. H. Brocklebank until 1927, and then to his son C. G. Brocklebank, and later to his executors.[56] In 1972 the patronage was exercised by Brig. A. N. Breitmeyer.[57]

The rectory was taxed at 100*s.* in 1254 and 16 marks in 1291.[58] It was exempted from taxation for poverty in 1487,[59] but in 1535 was worth £19 16*s.* 8*d.*, being the fourth richest living in the deanery.[60] It was worth £100 a year in 1650 and 1728,[61] and £259 net *c.* 1830.[62] After commutation of tithes its value rose to £347 in 1851 and £460 in 1877.[63]

In addition to the great and small tithes from Bartlow, rectors received tithes from small plots in West Wickham and Horseheath and from Bartlow hamlet in Ashdon.[64] Individual farmers made agreements for the composition of their tithes in the 1720s, and when corn tithes in the hamlet were offered in kind in 1776 it was thought inconvenient.[65] In 1767 Edmund Mapletoft successfully sued the tenant of Bartlow Hall farm and the rector of Ashdon concerning tithes of wool and lambs, which he claimed in kind.[66] The tithes were commuted in 1848,[67] and the rent-charge yielded £281 10*s.* in 1851.[68]

The church was endowed with 30½ a. in 1279,[69] and the glebe comprised 64½ a. in 1663.[70] On the inclosure of West Wickham in 1813 1½ a. were allotted to the rector of Bartlow in place of tithes.[71] There were 66 a. of glebe in 1851;[72] the rector of Bartlow received 23 a. in Ashdon that year at inclosure,[73] and 32½ a. at the inclosure of Bartlow in 1863.[74] The rector still had 55 a. in 1900,[75] but by 1933 only 2 a. lying in Horseheath remained.[76]

There was a rectory house in 1279[77] and in 1355.[78] Jon Baker was accused of letting the house lie desolate in 1643,[79] but in 1663 it had 18 rooms, 2 barns, and extensive out-buildings,[80] and was taxed on 6 hearths in the 1660s.[81] Rectors of Bartlow lived in the house, which stood on the south side of the churchyard, from the 16th century to the 19th. Considerable additions and repairs were made to the house *c.* 1835 by John Bullen, the incumbent.[82] In 1928 the rectory was pulled down, and C. G. Brocklebank gave Crossways House as a rectory.[83] From 1946 Bartlow was held with other livings, incumbents were no longer resident, and Crossways House was sold in 1950.[84]

An anchorite at Bartlow in 1279 owned 1½ a.[85] There was a chaplain there in 1366, 1406,[86] and 1468.[87] John Fesant, rector in 1399, was licensed to study in Cambridge for three years, as was his successor Richard Hert in 1402 and 1405.[88] Arthur Dudley, rector 1526–77, held two other livings, in Staffordshire and Cheshire, and lived at Lichfield where he was a prebendary;[89] Bartlow was served by curates, paid for in the 1540s by Lady Butler, the patron.[90] Religious conservatism may have prompted a parishioner who tried to save a pax in 1552,[91] and the holy-water stoup remained intact in 1562.[92] Jon Baker, rector 1599–1639, was presented in 1599 for not holding services on many holy days or on certain weekdays.[93] His son Jon, rector from 1643, was ejected from the living in April 1644; he was a staunch Royalist and had refused the Covenant, had threatened parishioners who attended

[47] C 3/433/17; P.R.O. Inst. Bk. ser. A, iii, p. 99. In 1639 the king presented Rob. Mapletoft because of the outlawry of Henry Huddleston: Rymer, *Foedera* (1737–45 edn.), ix (1), 256; cf. *D.N.B.*; but Mapletoft was evidently not instituted.

[48] C.U.L., MS. Mm. 1. 39, p. 159.

[49] P.R.O. Inst. Bks. ser. B, iv, p. 134; ser. C, i, ff. 439v.–440.

[50] Ibid. ser. C, i, f. 440; *Alum. Cantab. 1752–1900*, iii. 202.

[51] Inscr. in ch.; C.U.L., E.D.R., C 3/21.

[52] *Kelly's Dir. Cambs.* (1858); *Alum. Cantab. 1752–1900*, vi. 366.

[53] *Kelly's Dir. Cambs.* (1869); *Crockford* (1896).

[54] C.U.L., E.D.R., C 3/26; *Clergy List* (1892).

[55] *Kelly's Dir. Cambs.* (1896); *Alum. Cantab. 1752–1900*, vi. 412; *Crockford* (1907).

[56] *Kelly's Dir. Cambs.* (1904, 1922); C.R.O., 331/Z 6, Oct. 1927, p. 75; 331/Z 8, Feb. 1939, p. 631.

[57] *Ely Dioc. Dir.* (1973–4).

[58] *Val. of Norwich*, ed. Lunt, 227, 536.

[59] *E.D.R.* (1909), 106.

[60] *Valor Eccl.* (Rec. Com.), iii. 504.

[61] Lamb. Pal. MS. 904, f. 270; C.U.L., E.D.R., B 8/1.

[62] *Rep. Com. Eccl. Revenues*, pp. 344–5.

[63] H.O. 129/188/2/6/6; C.U.L., E.D.R., C 3/26.

[64] C.U.L., E.D.R., H 1/1, terrier 1615.

[65] C.R.O., par. rec.

[66] Essex R.O., D/P 18/30/82, 87–90.

[67] I.R. 18/13518.

[68] H.O. 129/188/2/6/6.

[69] *Rot. Hund.* (Rec. Com.), ii. 426.

[70] C.U.L., E.D.R., H 1/1, terrier 1663.

[71] Ibid. H 1/7, terrier 1837.

[72] *Gardner's Dir. Cambs.* (1851).

[73] Essex R.O., Q/RDc 39A.

[74] C.R.O., Q/RDc 80.

[75] *Kelly's Dir. Cambs.* (1900).

[76] E. E. Phillips and J. J. Rickett, *Hist. St. Mary's Ch. Bartlow* (Cambridge, 1933), 49.

[77] *Rot. Hund.* (Rec. Com.), ii. 426.

[78] Phillips and Rickett, *Bartlow Ch.* 38.

[79] *Walker Revised*, ed. Matthews, 77–8.

[80] C.U.L., E.D.R., H 1/1, terrier 1663.

[81] E 179/84/437 rot. 58; E 179/244/23 rot. 55.

[82] C.U.L., E.D.R., C 3/21; Ed. 7/5.

[83] Phillips and Rickett, *Bartlow Ch.* 49; C.R.O., par. rec.

[84] C.U.L., Maps 53(1)/95/8.

[85] *Rot. Hund.* (Rec. Com.), ii. 426.

[86] *Cal. Pat.* 1364–7, 259; *E.D.R.* (1899), 158.

[87] *E.D.R.* (1907), 136.

[88] Ibid. (1900), 141, 178; (1901), 20.

[89] *Faculty Off. Reg.* 1534–49, ed. Chambers, 117; B.L. Add. MS. 5813, f. 65; *Cal. Pat.* 1563–6, 112.

[90] *E.D.R.* (1912), 184, 224; C.U.L., E.D.R., B 2/6; B 2/8.

[91] *Cambs. Ch. Goods, temp. Edw. VI*, 61.

[92] *V.C.H. Cambs.* ii. 176.

[93] *Trans. C.H.A.S.* vi. 25.

services elsewhere, and was accused of drinking, swearing, and scandalous conduct.[94] Richard Wells (or Weller), 1646–51, was described in 1650 as 'a very able man';[95] Adiel Baynard, 1651–67, also held livings in Essex and Wiltshire from 1662.[96] William Kilborne, rector 1704–11, and master of Saffron Walden school, resigned to be succeeded by his pupil Edmund Mapletoft, rector 1711–49. From Mapletoft the living was inherited by his son Edmund, rector 1750–72, and grandson Edmund, rector 1775–82.[97] The first Edmund was resident in 1728, also employing a curate, as did his absentee successor in 1775.[98] During his long incumbency 1782–1828, Joseph Hall lived almost continuously at Bartlow; in 1806 he was involved in a dispute with the tenant of the Hall. He and John Bullen both held two Sunday services and thrice yearly communions.[99] On Census Sunday in 1851 58 people attended the morning service and 86 the afternoon one.[1] By 1877 there were also 12 communions a year, and 3 or 4 a month in 1897. Most inhabitants of the village, 150 in 1877, were church-goers.[2] Bartlow was held in plurality with Shudy Camps 1939–45, and with Horseheath 1946–72 when incumbents lived at Horseheath.[3] The rector from 1972 was instituted to Bartlow and Linton in plurality under a pastoral scheme, and lived at Linton.[4]

Bartlow hamlet in Ashdon long retained its connexion with Bartlow church. Robert Walton, lord of Waltons manor in Ashdon, gave cloth and a book to the church in the 14th century,[5] and six inhabitants of the hamlet were ordered in 1599 to receive communion at Bartlow, though they might attend Ashdon church at other times and participate in civil parish affairs there.[6] Inhabitants of the hamlet were commonly baptized, married, and buried at Bartlow: sons of the earl and countess of Lincoln, living at Waltons, were baptized at Bartlow in 1785 and 1786.[7] Inhabitants of the hamlet also paid church-rates to Bartlow in the 19th century. The portion of Bartlow parish lying in Essex, in the archdeaconry of Ely, was transferred in 1914 from the diocese of Chelmsford to that of Ely.[8] Bartlow also served people living at Westoe, in Castle Camps parish, who were far from their own church.

The church of *ST. MARY*, so called by 1521,[9] is of field stones and rubble with dressings of freestone, and has a chancel, nave with north porch, and circular west tower, one of the two such towers in Cambridgeshire. The tower is apparently all that survives of the late-11th- or early-12th-century church, the west window being inserted in the earlier 14th century at about the same date that the whole of the nave and chancel were rebuilt. Alterations to the structure in the 15th century included a new east window, the north and south doorways and north porch, and the buttresses on the south wall. Fragments of glass and wall-paintings survive from the 15th century, including depictions of a St. Christopher, painted over one of St. Michael weighing souls, and on the north wall St. George's dragon.[10] The rood-loft, mentioned as new in 1506,[11] was backed by a board filling the upper part of the chancel arch. Apart from a new communion table and rails installed in 1756,[12] and occasional repairs, little work was carried out on the church in the 17th and 18th centuries. There was a general restoration under the direction of R. R. Rowe in 1879, when most of the window tracery was renewed,[13] and there were extensive repairs to the roof in 1897.[14]

The three bells, which survived in 1974, were made in London *c.* 1460, perhaps by William Chamberlayne.[15] The church had one chalice *c.* 1278,[16] perhaps the same silver chalice and paten as in 1552.[17] A silver cup and paten belonged to Bartlow in 1837,[18] and with two more patens and two flagons given in the 19th and 20th centuries, were still there *c.* 1960.[19] The parish registers begin in 1573 and are virtually complete.[20]

NONCONFORMITY. Joan Willowes, a widow, was frequently presented as a recusant between 1579 and 1599, although there was some doubt whether she lived in Bartlow or in Essex.[21] Another Bartlow woman was presented with her in 1599.[22] Though there were five families of Independents in 1728,[23] they may have lived in the hamlet, and in 1783 there was only one nonconformist family, who attended the meeting-house at Linton.[24] There were no dissenters in Bartlow village in 1807,[25] and only one family in 1825;[26] none were known in 1836 or 1897.[27]

EDUCATION. There was a small school at Bartlow for poor children by 1807,[28] though the only establishment besides the Sunday school in 1825 was for teaching girls needlework, both schools being supported by the rector.[29] Children from Bartlow village attended schools in Bartlow End hamlet in 1833.[30] The rector supported a day-school in the village in 1836, apparently held in the rectory which

94 *Walker Revised*, ed. Matthews, 77–8; B.L. Add. MS. 5802, f. 25v.
95 Lamb. Pal. MS. 904, f. 249.
96 *Alum. Cantab. to 1751*, i. 113.
97 Ibid. ii. 15, 138; *1752–1900*, iv. 316; C.R.O., par. reg.
98 C.U.L., E.D.R., B 8/1; C 1/1.
99 Ibid. C 1/4; C 1/6; C 3/21; C.R.O., par. reg.; B.L. Add. MS. 9413, f. 39.
1 H.O. 129/188/2/6/6.
2 C.U.L., E.D.R., C 3/26; C 3/36.
3 *Crockford* (1940 and later edns.).
4 *Ely Dioc. Dir.* (1973–4).
5 *Vetus Liber Arch. Elien.* (C.A.S. 8vo ser. xlviii), 56.
6 *Trans. C.H.A.S.* vi. 25.
7 C.R.O., par. reg.; *Complete Peerage*, ix. 534.
8 C.U.L., E.D.R., G 3/23A, p. 238.
9 B.L. Add. MS. 5861, p. 175; see below, plate facing p. 257.
10 *Proc. C.A.S.* xxviii. 80; C.R.O., 331/Z 6, Apr. 1928, p. 29; May 1928, p. 37.
11 *Trans. C.H.A.S.* i. 384.
12 Phillips and Rickett, *Bartlow Ch.* 31.
13 Ibid. 20; *Kelly's Dir. Cambs.* (1879).
14 C.U.L., E.D.R., C 3/36.
15 MS. notes by H. B. Walters (1936), *penes V.C.H.* The inscriptions are given in full in *Cambs. Bells* (C.A.S. 8vo ser. xviii), 121.
16 *Vetus Liber Arch. Elien.* (C.A.S. 8vo ser. xlviii), 56.
17 *Cambs. Ch. Goods, temp. Edw. VI*, 60–1.
18 C.U.L., E.D.R., H 1/7, terrier 1837.
19 List of ch. plate, *penes V.C.H.*
20 Deposited in C.R.O.
21 Palmer, *Cambs. in 16th cent.* 2–3; *Cath. Rec. Soc.* liii. 3; Bodl. MS. Gough Eccl. Top. 3, f. 4.
22 *Trans. C.H.A.S.* vi. 24–5.
23 C.U.L., E.D.R., B 8/1.
24 Ibid. B 7/1, p. 118.
25 Ibid. C 1/4.
26 Ibid. C 1/6.
27 Ibid. C 3/21; C 3/36.
28 Ibid. C 1/4.
29 Ibid. C 1/6; *Poor Law Abstract, 1804*, 34–5.
30 *Educ. Enquiry Abstract*, 50.

he had recently extended,[31] and it had 17 pupils in 1846.[32] From 1872 the parish guaranteed £70 a year towards the school.[33] A National school was built at Bartlow in 1875, north of the Linton–Camps road;[34] it was attended by 27 boys and 17 girls in 1877, and reached its highest average attendance of 47 in 1889.[35] Attendance declined slowly thereafter, to 40 in 1896, 27 in 1906, and 15 in 1922.[36] The senior pupils were transferred to Linton village college in 1937, and when in 1939 the number of children attending Bartlow school fell to 9 it was closed, the junior pupils being transferred to schools in Linton.[37]

CHARITY FOR THE POOR. Thomas Carter D.D., rector of Debden (Essex), by will proved 1697 gave a rent-charge of £4 on the tithes of Debden for woollen cloth for four poor people, three from Debden and one from Bartlow, after 10*s.* had been deducted for an annual sermon.[38] The cloth was given regularly from 1702. By 1775 it was customary to give it, sometimes in the form of a coat, to a member of the church congregation who was impoverished but not receiving parish relief,[39] a qualification which sometimes made a recipient hard to find. Two rectors of Bartlow, Joseph Hall 1782–1828, and John Bullen 1828–63, gave an extra coat of their own gift with Carter's charity.[40] The rector of Debden from the 1860s to the 1890s objected to paying £4 each year from his income and occasionally refused, but the trustees' claim was upheld by the Charity Commissioners. By a Scheme of 1891 Bartlow received a quarter of the income after the payment of 10*s.* to the rector of Debden for a sermon. The rent-charge was redeemed by the Church Commissioners in 1956 for £160 stock; the charity was regulated by a scheme in 1970, and 17*s.* 6*d.* a year was paid to the rector of Bartlow to be spent on a coat.

CASTLE CAMPS

CASTLE Camps lies 15 miles south-east of Cambridge, at the south-eastern extremity of the county.[1] It is basically triangular, and its south-western and eastern sides form the county boundary. That to the south-west probably follows a line traced from point to point through the ancient woodlands which formerly separated Cambridgeshire from Essex.[2] The straighter eastern side along the watershed may follow the pale of the former Camps park. The northern boundary with Shudy Camps, based on divisions between fields and inclosures, was and is much overlapped in terms of land-holding and cultivation, and at its western end follows a tributary of the river Bourne. The ancient hamlet of Olmstead at the south-eastern corner of the parish was sometimes reckoned by the 18th century to belong to Helions Bumpstead parish (Essex) upon which it depended ecclesiastically, and to which its tithes were still paid in 1840,[3] although it was earlier treated for feudal and jurisdictional purposes as part of Castle Camps and Cambridgeshire. In the 19th century, having been included in Risbridge poor-law union in Essex, it was sometimes described as part of Helions Bumpstead in Cambridgeshire.[4] In 1885 it was officially transferred for all civil purposes to Castle Camps.[5] Before that change the ancient parish of Castle Camps covered over 2,700 a., while Olmstead contained 429 a.,[6] and from 1891 the enlarged parish measured 3,184 a.[7] In 1965 an area at the southern tip of Olmstead was transferred to Essex, and the county and parish boundary elsewhere was straightened, so that in 1971 Castle Camps, enlarged by *c.* 73 a. taken from the Essex parishes of Ashdon, Hempstead, and Helions Bumpstead, covered 3,198 a. (1,294 ha.).[8] The history here printed deals with the ancient parish, including Olmstead.

The soil of Castle Camps lies mainly upon boulder clay, itself lying over chalk which is near the surface where the ground is lowest to the north-west. Along the east side of the parish runs a flat-topped ridge at over 400 ft., from which the ground falls away south-eastwards towards Olmstead, while two arms of high ground, each of over 350 ft., extend westward from the ridge. Down the narrow valley between them run three water-courses, one rising near ponds formerly feeding the castle moat, which meet south-east of Camps Hall farm to form a small brook which runs north-westward down the valley through Bartlow into the Bourne.[9]

The high ground along the south-western boundary was once heavily wooded. The name of Camps, probably dating from the early English period, presumably referred to small fields originally inclosed from that woodland. In 1086 it still covered the whole area later divided between Castle and Shudy Camps, sometimes distinguished until the 14th century as Great and Little Camps.[10] In 1086 there

[31] C.U.L., E.D.R., C 3/21; Ed. 7/5.
[32] *Church School Inquiry, 1846–7*, 2–3.
[33] Ed. 7/5.
[34] *Kelly's Dir. Cambs.* (1875).
[35] C.U.L., E.D.R., C 3/26; *Rep. of Educ. Cttee. of Council, 1888–9* [C. 5804-I], p. 530, H.C. (1889), xxix.
[36] *Schs. in receipt of Parl. Grants, 1896–7* [Cd. 8546], p. 14, H.C. (1897), lxix; *Public Elem. Schs. 1907* [Cd. 3901], p. 27, H.C. (1908), lxxxiv; *Bd. of Educ., List 21, 1922* (H.M.S.O.), 15.
[37] Black, *Cambs. Educ. Rec.* 40; *Bd. of Educ., List 21, 1938* (H.M.S.O.), 19.
[38] *32nd Rep. Com. Char.* H.C. 108, p. 744 (1837–8), xxv. Unless otherwise stated this section is based on Char. Com. files; C.R.O., par. rec.
[39] C.U.L., E.D.R., C 1/1.
[40] *31st Rep. Com. Char.* 103–4.
[1] This account was written in 1975.
[2] Cf. W. M. Palmer and C. Fox, *Shudy Camps, Castle Camps, and Ashdon* (1924), 27.
[3] C.U.L., E.D.R., C 1/4; Essex R.O., D/CT 58 A.
[4] e.g. Prob. 11/816 (P.C.C. 172 Paul, will of Judith Reynolds). Olmstead was excluded when the parish bounds were beaten in 1761: C.R.O., par. reg. TS.
[5] *Census*, 1851–91.
[6] C.U.L., E.D.R., tithe award 1840; Essex R.O., D/CT 58 A; *Census*, 1881.
[7] *Census*, 1861–1961.
[8] *Census*, 1971; Cambs. & Isle of Ely Order, 1964 no. 366 (H.L.G. 14603).
[9] O.S. Maps 1/2,500, TL 54, 64 (1953 edn.).
[10] *P.N. Cambs.* (E.P.N.S.), 102.

was woodland here for 500 pigs.[11] In 1263 the manor included small woods of oak and thorn and in 1279 40 a. of groves.[12] In 1296 there were *c.* 210 a. of foreign woodland.[13] To the west the former Westoe Lodge was once surrounded by woodland of which 7 a. survived *c.* 1840.[14] South-east of it lay ancient inclosures, covering 120 a. *c.* 1586, whose name, Stocking, and curved edge suggest that they were assarts from former woodland. Further south-east lay Langley (formerly Langeney) wood, then of *c.* 75 a., and Willesey (once Williottshey) wood of *c.* 30 a.,[15] both demesne woods whose lessees in the 17th century were required to plant new timber there.[16] In 1840 Langley wood covered 72 a. and Willesey wood 23 a.[17] The latter had by 1863 been cleared and converted to arable.[18] Further east again lay inclosures around a farmstead called Charlwood by 1450;[19] in 1567 on Olmstead Hall farm Queens' College sold for clearance the timber on a 19-acre field later called Stocking. Waverley wood there, further east, had been stubbed up by 1822.[20] The areas cleared of woodland were, like the rest of the parish, mainly devoted to arable farming on a triennial rotation, although pasturage was also important on the large demesne farms. Much of the parish was, perhaps from its beginnings, inclosed as several, not much open-field land existing in the 16th century. The few remaining common fields were inclosed in 1862. In the 20th century the parish economy was entirely based on farming.[21]

It has been suggested that such parishes along the county's eastern edge were originally settled by men moving westward through the forest from Essex and Suffolk.[22] In early modern times Castle Camps had apparently closer links, economically and socially, with places to the east such as Haverhill and Helions Bumpstead than with the villages further down the Bourne valley.[23] In 1086 21 peasants and 6 *servi* were recorded on Aubrey de Vere's manor,[24] on which there were *c.* 60 tenants in 1279, when *c.* 25 others held of Olmstead manor, where there were *c.* 20 messuages, and 2 or 3 more of Westoe fee.[25] In 1327 28 men beside the lord paid tax at Castle Camps and 14 possibly at Olmstead.[26] In 1377 113 adults paid the poll tax[27] and in 1524 33 people paid the subsidy.[28] There were 37 householders in the ecclesiastical parish in 1563,[29] and the manor had *c.* 35 resident tenants in the 1560s and 41 by 1584.[30] The population may have grown to over 300 by 1640, but declined thereafter.[31] There were 185 adults in 1676[32] and *c.* 400 parishioners in 80 families in 1728.[33] From the late 18th century numbers increased rapidly, reaching 550 by 1811, 734 by 1831, and 949 by 1851.[34] In the 1860s the population was swollen by 30 families of labourers deriving from and working in Shudy Camps where there was a shortage of cottages.[35] Thereafter the population declined slowly, partly through emigration, to 891 in 1871 and 713 in 1901, and fell in the 20th century to 505 in 1931 and, after a brief recovery in 1961, to 442 in 1971.[36]

As in other once heavily wooded areas settlement in Castle Camps consisted of scattered hamlets and farmsteads rather than one nucleated village. In the Middle Ages a group of houses stood in a field north-west of the castle, where one or two buildings survived in 1618[37] and earthworks still mark the site.[38] The hamlet of Olmstead lay by the three-acre green recorded in 1279,[39] and several tenants of the earl of Oxford still dwelt around it *c.* 1450 and perhaps *c.* 1536.[40] After 1600 only Olmstead Green and Olmstead Hall farms and one or two dependent cottages survived.[41] In 1885 the place contained only four dwellings with 20 inhabitants.[42] Westoe, where the demesne lay in one block, had probably never contained more than the manor-house, to which a separate farmstead was added by 1800.[43] The main settlements in the parish were probably already in the 15th century, as in the 20th, at Camps Green and Camps End, lying off roads from Cambridge which forked to run north and south of the earl of Oxford's park.[44] East and west of each hamlet lay the small, mostly inclosed, fields of the villagers, and between them a belt of several demesne ⅔ mile wide. At Camps Green the houses lay along a wide green running north from the northern road called Broad street. Those east of the green were squeezed against the park pale, and the street was called Park Street by 1450. There were then 21 messuages and 23 cottages held of the manor, while the sites of 6 messuages and 5 cottages lay empty. In 1586 Camps Green probably contained *c.* 14 houses and 8 cottages, and in 1618 35 buildings. The lord occasionally granted plots of waste there for building cottages, and in the early 17th century other cottages were put up there without the land required by law.[45]

[11] *V.C.H. Cambs.* i. 390.
[12] C 132/31/1 no. 6; *Rot. Hund.* (Rec. Com.), ii. 424.
[13] C 133/76/7 no. 8.
[14] C.U.L., E.D.R., tithe award 1840.
[15] Charterho. Mun., MR 2/587, pp. 334–5; cf. ibid. MR 2/557A pt. ii, pp. 6–8; MR 2/572, 577; map 1618; cf. Langeney field, mentioned *c.* 1360: B.L. Add. MS. 5805, f. 97v.
[16] e.g. Charterho. Mun. D 2/117, 122.
[17] C.U.L., E.D.R., tithe award 1840.
[18] Charterho. Mun., AR 5/25; cf. C.R.O., Q/RDc 80, incl. award & map, 1863.
[19] Charterho. Mun., MR 2/557A pt. ii, pp. 10–11.
[20] C.U.L., Queens' Coll. Mun., box 13, no. 62; cf. box 66, surveys, 1799, 1822.
[21] See pp. 42–4.
[22] C. Taylor, *Cambs. Landscape* (1974), 85–90.
[23] Of Castle Camps wills examined touching on other parishes between 1500 and 1700, only one refers to any village to the west, but nine to places to the east or south-east.
[24] *V.C.H. Cambs.* i. 390.
[25] *Rot. Hund.* (Rec. Com.), ii. 424–6. Some belonged to other vills.
[26] *Cambs. Lay Subsidy, 1327*, 25.
[27] *East Anglian*, N.S. xii. 239.
[28] E 179/81/134 m. 4.
[29] B.L. Harl. MS. 594, f. 199v.
[30] Charterho. Mun., MR 2/217, ct. rolls 1, 6, 26 Eliz. I.
[31] Cf. C.R.O., par. reg. TS.
[32] Compton Census.
[33] C.U.L., E.D.R., B 8/1.
[34] *Census*, 1801–51.
[35] *1st Rep. Com. Employment in Agric.* 360.
[36] *Census*, 1871–1971.
[37] Charterho. Mun., map 1618.
[38] *Proc. C.A.S.* lxiv. 41–3.
[39] *Rot. Hund.* (Rec. Com.), ii. 426.
[40] Charterho. Mun., MR 2/557A pt. ii, pp. 5, 25.
[41] Ibid. map 1618; MR 2/588A; Essex R.O., D/D Q 1/1.
[42] *Census*, 1891.
[43] C.U.L., E.D.R., tithe map 1840.
[44] The following account is based on Charterho. Mun., MR 2/557A pt. ii, pp. 5–19 (rental 28 Hen. VI); MR 2/587 (survey of manor 1586); MR 2/572, 577 (demesne surveys, 1613, 1618); map 1618.
[45] e.g. ibid. MR 2/217, ct. rolls 21, 24 Eliz. I; MR 2/218, ct. roll 7 Jas. I; MR 2/221, ct. roll 21 Jas. I; cf. MR 2/587, pp. 179–81.

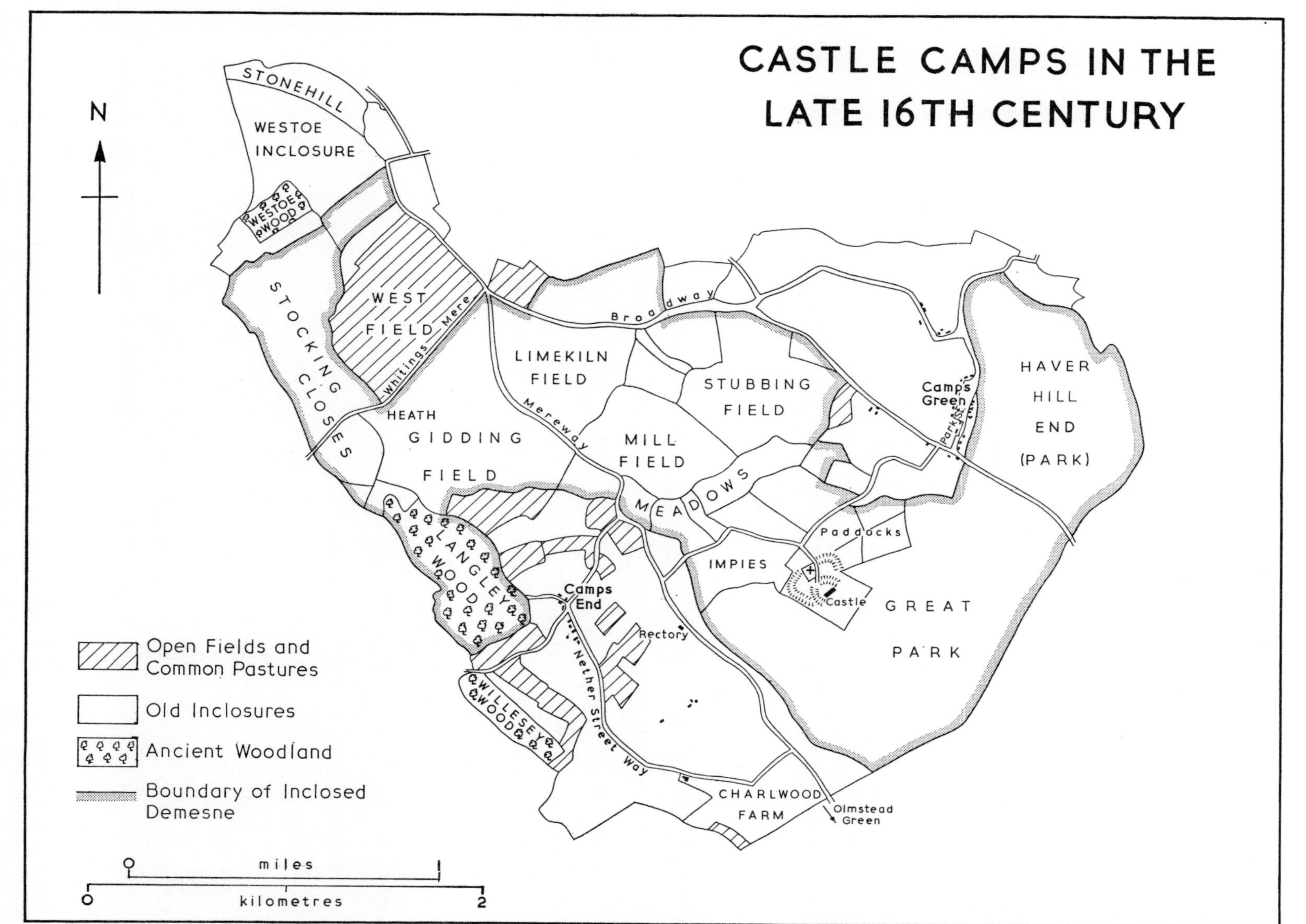
CASTLE CAMPS IN THE
LATE 16TH CENTURY
N
STONEHILL
WESTOE INCLOSURE
WESTOE WOOD
STOCKING CLOSES
WEST FIELD
Whitings Mere
HEATH
GIDDING FIELD
LIMEKILN FIELD
Mereway
Broadway
STUBBING FIELD
MILL FIELD
MEADOWS
Camps Green
Park St
HAVER HILL END (PARK)
Paddocks
IMPIES
Castle
GREAT PARK
LANGLEY WOOD
Camps End
Rectory
Nether Street Way
WILLESEY WOOD
CHARLWOOD FARM
Olmstead Green
Open Fields and Common Pastures
Old Inclosures
Ancient Woodland
Boundary of Inclosed Demesne
0
miles
1
0
kilometres
2

The smaller settlement called Camps End lay by a cross-roads east of Langley wood and along the road running east from it called by 1586 the Netherstreet way. There were 6 messuages and 3 cottages there in 1586, and 13 buildings in 1618. Further east stood single farmsteads, such as Parkin's and Browning's farms, the latter mentioned in 1586,[46] where traditional timber-framed farm-houses, probably 17th-century, survived in 1975. There were *c.* 70 dwellings in the parish under Charles II[47] and 74 houses in 1801, when 2 or 3 families were sometimes crowded into each.[48] A few houses of the 18th century or earlier survive at Camps Green, including one 17th-century one east of the school with a central gable, but there are many one-storey cottages of *c.* 1800, timber-framed and plastered, and some still thatched. Several were built on encroachments made since the 16th century on the green, of which only two fragments survived in 1975. Of 207 dwellings in the parish in 1851 only *c.* 45 stood at Camps End, and almost 140 at Camps Green.[49] By 1881 35 houses stood empty, and there were only 155 inhabited houses by 1931, and 187 in 1961.[50] The mid 20th century saw little new building in the parish except for a few council houses built before 1956, mostly at Camps Green.[51]

Two alehouses were licensed at Castle Camps in 1682.[52] About 1800 there were 2 public houses, the George, closed *c.* 1910, and the Cock, which with the New Inn, opened by 1871, survived in 1975.[53] There was a parish lending library by 1887.[54] In 1970 the village had, besides long-established football and bowls clubs, a men's club occupying since 1951 the former Baptist chapel. A building was acquired for a village hall in 1952.[55]

On the plateau south-east of the castle an R.A.F. fighter airfield was located in 1941, which remained in active use until 1945 and was closed early in 1946. The land was sold between 1963 and 1966.[56]

MANORS AND OTHER ESTATES. In 1066 King Edward's thegn Wulfwin held 2½ hides at Camps which by 1086 had with Wulfwin's other lands been assigned to Aubrey de Vere[57] (d. *c.* 1112). The manor of *GREAT CAMPS*, later *CASTLE CAMPS*, descended until the late 16th century in the male line of the Vere earls of Oxford, who held it in chief for 3½ fees as parcel of their barony, and retained it continuously in demesne.[58] In 1388 it was briefly forfeited by the attainder of Earl Robert,[59] but was restored in 1393 to his uncle and heir Earl Aubrey.[60] When Aubrey's grandson Earl John was executed in 1462 the manor was granted to Richard, duke of Gloucester,[61] but was restored in 1463 to John's minor son and heir John.[62] Following the latter's attainder in 1471 Castle Camps was again granted to Gloucester[63] who, as Richard III, granted it in 1484 to Sir Robert Percy.[64] Earl John was again restored in 1485,[65] and was succeeded in 1513 by his nephew Earl John[66] (d. 1526), whose widow Anne received the manor and castle as part of her jointure. The new earl, John (d. 1540), a second cousin, seized Camps castle in 1526.[67] Anne had got possession by 1534[68] and retained the estate until her death in 1559[69] when it passed to the next earl, also John (d. 1562).[70]

John's son and heir, the extravagant Earl Edward, in 1580 mortgaged and in 1584 sold the estate to the London merchant Thomas Skinner. Skinner died as lord mayor in 1596.[71] In 1598 his eldest son and heir John, knighted in 1604,[72] assigned the manor as security for his debts[73] to his father-in-law Thomas Markham and Markham's son Sir Griffin.[74] Upon Griffin's condemnation for conspiracy in 1603 the king granted his interest in Castle Camps to his kinsman and creditor Sir John Harington,[75] at whose instance the manor was sold in 1607 by trustees to pay Skinner's debts.[76] The purchaser, the rich money-lender Thomas Sutton,[77] took possession in 1608,[78] and settled Castle Camps manor shortly before his death in 1611 upon his foundation at the Charterhouse, London.[79] In 1919 the governors of the Charterhouse sold, mostly to their tenant-farmers, all of the estate except Castle farm and the lordship of the manor,[80] which they retained in 1975.[81]

Probably before 1100 a castle was built on the north-west slope of the eastern ridge. A two-acre motte, surrounded by a wet moat 25 ft. deep, had to the north-west a small bailey, across whose banks the church was later erected. A new and larger bailey was made perhaps in the late 13th century. Little remains of the fortifications.[82] The earls' chief messuage recorded in 1331 and 1371[83] presumably stood within the motte. Probably in the late 15th

46 Charterho. Mun., MR 2/587, p. 63.
47 See below, pp. 279–80.
48 *Census*, 1801; Vancouver, *Agric. in Cambs.* 63.
49 H.O. 107/1761.
50 *Census*, 1881, 1931, 1961.
51 *Camb. Evening News*, 31 May 1974.
52 *Proc. C.A.S.* xvii. 97.
53 C.R.O., P 34/3/7; R.G. 10/1592; *Kelly's Dir. Cambs.* (1869–1937); *Camb. Ind. Press*, 13 May 1960.
54 C.R.O., P 34/1/4.
55 *Camb. Ind. Press*, 13 May 1960; *Camb. Evening News*, 5 Oct. 1970; Char. Com. files.
56 Ex inf. the Air Historical Branch (R.A.F.).
57 *V.C.H. Cambs.* i. 390.
58 *Complete Peerage*, x. 193–254; *Liber de Bernewelle*, 253; *Rot. Hund.* (Rec. Com.), ii. 424; *Feud. Aids*, i. 145, 154, 167, 181; *Cal. Inq. p.m.* i, p. 185; iii, p. 229; vii, p. 271; viii, p. 515; xiii, p. 95.
59 *Cal. Fine R.* 1383–91, 242.
60 *Cal. Inq. Misc.* vi, p. 15; *Cal. Close*, 1392–6, 42–3.
61 *Cal. Pat.* 1461–7, 197.
62 Ibid. 287.
63 Ibid. 1467–77, 297, 560; cf. C 145/327 no. 1.
64 *Cal. Pat.* 1476–85, 434.
65 *Rot. Parl.* vi. 281–2.
66 Cf. C 142/28 no. 123.
67 *L. & P. Hen. VIII*, iv, pp. 41–2, 1086, 2000.
68 Cf. ibid. vii, p. 220.
69 Cf. *Cal Pat.* 1547–8, 380.
70 E 178/3618; cf. C 3/176/6.
71 Charterho. Mun., D 2/48–9, 53–4; Beaven, *Aldermen of London*, ii. 43.
72 C 142/254 no. 79; Nicholls, *Progresses of Jas. I*, i. 214.
73 For details see N. Shipley, *Bull. Inst. Hist. Res.* xlviii. 162–81.
74 Ibid. 166–9; cf. Charterho. Mun., D 2/64, 66; C 2/Jas. I/H 13/47; C 2/Jas. I/H 2/68.
75 S. Gardiner, *Hist. England, 1603–42*, i. 107–13, 138–9; *D.N.B.* s.v. Harington; Hist. MSS. Com. 9, *Salisbury*, xv, pp. 98, 130, 212; *Cal. S.P. Dom.* 1603–10, p. 125; Charterho. Mun., D 2/67–78.
76 Charterho. Mun., D 2/82, 102.
77 Ibid. D 2/89, 96; cf. [R. Smythe], *Hist. Acct. of Charterhouse* (1808), 135–52.
78 *Bull. Inst. Hist. Res.* xlviii. 177–9.
79 *D.N.B.*; P. Bearcroft, *Hist. Acct. of Thos. Sutton and Charterhouse* (1737), 34–109.
80 C.R.O., SP 34/4; cf. *Kelly's Dir. Cambs.* (1922, 1937).
81 Ex inf. the Registrar.
82 *V.C.H. Cambs.* ii. 21 (plan and description wrongly oriented, N. being given for S.); *Proc. C.A.S.* lxiv. 38–41.
83 C 135/28/17 no. 8; C 135/222 no. 15.

century a four-storey brick tower was built,[84] attached to which was a large house where Countess Anne (d. 1559) dwelt in her widowhood.[85] The house, apart from the tower, was rebuilt, probably by Thomas Skinner, in the late 16th century.[86] It stood within a rectangular brick-walled inclosure, much of which survives, with a semi-classical gateway, and had a four-bay gabled front, probably facing north-west.[87] Thomas Sutton lived there from 1608 to 1611;[88] it was leased from 1616 to James Weston, baron of the Exchequer (d. 1634).[89] In 1639 the lessee was Sir James Reynolds of Olmstead Green, and in 1646 his son John Reynolds[90] (d. 1658), a Cromwellian general.[91] By 1666 the castle was inhabited by Sir Thomas Dayrell (d. 1669), and next by his eldest son Sir Francis Dayrell (d. 1675);[92] the Dayrells afterwards removed to Shudy Camps and the castle was occupied by tenant farmers.[93] The great house largely fell down *c.* 1738, whereupon the Charterhouse constructed a smaller farm-house[94] facing north, incorporating a fragment of the earlier building in a back wing. A farm-house for the main demesne farm, built near the middle of the parish between 1586 and 1597,[95] was by the late 17th century often called Camps Hall,[96] its name in 1975. The house was rebuilt in the 19th century.

In the 13th century the manor included a park, said in 1263 to be 4 leagues round,[97] which by 1269 probably covered all the high ground east of the castle between the two roads as far as the parish boundary.[98] In 1331 the park was reckoned to include 200 a.[99] In 1586 it comprised the great park of 400 a. between the roads and an extension east of Camps Green, called the little park or Haverhill End, of 202 a.[1] In 1330 Earl Robert (d. 1331) was granted free warren at Castle Camps.[2] The deer in the park were frequently poached from the 13th century[3] to the 16th.[4] Deer were still kept there in the 1560s,[5] but after 1586 it was divided up and converted to pasturage, probably by 1596.[6]

The manor of *WESTOE*, in the west end of the parish, passed *c.* 1199 from Ralph son of Hugh to his son Hugh of Westoe.[7] In 1272 Roger of Westoe sold 100 a. there, held as ½ knight's fee of the earl of Oxford, to John of Sawston (d. after 1275), whose widow Catherine held 121 a. there of Roger in 1279.[8] John's son and heir William[9] (d. 1308) was succeeded by his son John, aged 19,[10] who still held Westoe in 1360.[11] Elizabeth Sawston, probably his daughter, was tenant by 1372,[12] and with her husband Austin Keeling conveyed the estate, held for life by John's widow Margery, to John Kingston of Bartlow and others in 1385.[13] In 1426 Ralph, son of Thomas Sawston of Sawston, released Westoe manor to Margaret, daughter and heir of John Kingston's son Richard.[14] About 1450 the estate belonged to John Oldale.[15] In 1465 John Gent, groom of the king's chamber, released it to Richard Vere (d. 1476) of Great Addington (Northants.).[16] Vere's son and heir Henry (d. 1493) left three daughters,[17] of whom Elizabeth and Amy released their estates in Castle Camps in 1526 and 1538 respectively to the third sister Audrey and her husband John Brown.[18] In 1555 Audrey and her son George Brown sold their whole property there to Richard Tyrell[19] (d. 1566), whose son Edward[20] held it of Thomas Skinner in 1586.[21] Edward's son Sir Robert Tyrell had succeeded by 1613[22] and sold Westoe in 1632 to William, Lord Maynard[23] (d. 1640). William's son William (d. 1699)[24] and William Neville of Holt (Leics.) mortgaged Westoe Lodge and 26 a. around it in 1667.[25] In 1671 Neville sold the property to Clement Neville (d. 1683) who enlarged his Westoe estate and left it to his nephew Sir Thomas Neville of Holt, Bt.[26] In 1711 Sir Thomas sold it to Elizabeth Wenyeve, under whose will it passed in 1722 to William and Edward Wenyeve. They sold it *c.* 1737 to Thomas Carter and he in 1748 to Richard Crop,[27] who owned the Lodge, *c.* 32 a. of surrounding park, and 27 a. near by[28] and died in 1796. He was succeeded first by his widow, then by his great-nephew Charles Long. Benjamin Keene, owner of Linton, held Westoe on lease by 1806 and made the Lodge his main seat;[29] he had bought the freehold by 1825, when he owned *c.* 145 a. at Westoe.[30] He died in 1837, and his son C. E. Keene[31] had sold

84 Cf. print by S. and N. Buck (1730–1), reproduced below, facing p. 256.
85 Cf. *L. & P. Hen. VIII*, Addenda, p. 355.
86 Cf. print by Buck; Charterho. Mun., MR 2/571.
87 Charterho. Mun., drawing of house in map 1618; print by Buck.
88 Cf. Charterho. Mun., D 2/577.
89 Ibid. MR 2/572; D 2/117, 122; Foss, *Judges of Eng.* vi. 373–4.
90 Charterho. Mun., D 2/142, 146, 149, 156.
91 *D.N.B.*
92 Charterho. Mun., D 2/163; *Mon. Inscr. Cambs.* 80–2; Prob. 11/329 (P.C.C. 53 Coke); Prob. 11/348 (P.C.C. 64 Dykes).
93 Cf. Charterho. Mun., D 2/167 sqq.
94 Palmer, *Wm. Cole*, 90, stating that the tower had fallen by 1744; Lysons, *Cambs.* 157 says that it survived until 1779.
95 Mentioned in Charterho. Mun., D 2/61, but not in ibid. MR 2/587, pp. 337–8.
96 Ibid. D 2/168, 171.
97 C 132/31/1 no. 6.
98 Cf. C.U.L., Queens' Coll. Mun., box 64, 17/12.
99 C 135/28/17 no. 8.
1 Charterho. Mun., MR 2/587, pp. 139–41, 327–8.
2 *Cal. Chart. R.* 1327–41, 190–1.
3 e.g. *Cal. Pat.* 1287–92, 97; 1313–17, 63.
4 *L. & P. Hen. VIII*, xiv (2), pp. 178–9; *Trans. C.H.A.S.* iii. 7–22.
5 *Remains of Edm. Grindal* (Parker Soc.), 266, 289.
6 Cf. Charterho. Mun., D 2/86, 91, 95.
7 *Rot. Cur. Reg.* (Rec. Com.), i. 287, 406–8; cf. *Cart. Mon. St. John Colchester* (Roxburghe Club, 1897), i. 238–9.
8 C.P. 25(1)/15/33 no. 19; *Abbrev. Plac.* (Rec. Com.), 263; *Rot. Hund.* (Rec. Com.), ii. 424.
9 C.P. 25(1)/26/42 no. 7.
10 *Cal. Inq. p.m.* v, pp. 48–9.
11 Ibid. x, p. 520.
12 Ibid. xiii, p. 100.
13 C.P. 25(1)/29/88 no. 14.
14 *Cal. Close*, 1422–9, 315.
15 Charterho. Mun., MR 2/557A pt. ii, p. 5.
16 *Cal. Close*, 1461–8, 262–3.
17 *Cal. Fine R.* 1471–85, 105; 1485–1509, 185; *Cal. Inq. p.m. Hen. VII*, iii, pp. 478, 510; cf. *V.C.H. Cambs.* v. 178.
18 *Essex Feet of Fines* (Essex Arch. Soc.), iv. 162, 219, 232.
19 C.P. 25(2)/83/711 no. 2.
20 Charterho. Mun., MR 2/217 ct. roll 8 Eliz. I; cf. Morant, *Essex*, ii. 541.
21 Charterho. Mun., MR 2/587, p. 353.
22 Ibid. MR 2/106.
23 C.P. 25(2)/527/8 Chas. I Trin. no. 6.
24 *Complete Peerage*, viii. 599–601.
25 C.R.O., R 59/5/11/1A; cf. E 179/84/437 rot. 4.
26 C.R.O., R 59/5/11/2–7; cf. G.E.C. *Baronetage*, iii. 203.
27 C.R.O., R 59/5/11/8–9; cf. ibid. par. reg. TS. *sub* 1767; B.L. Add. MS. 5808, f. 57.
28 C.R.O., R 59/5/11/10–11.
29 B.L. Add. MS. 9412, f. 297v.
30 C.R.O., R 59/5/11/15.
31 Prob. 11/1889 (P.C.C. 33–4 Nicholl).

171 a. around Westoe Lodge[32] by 1863 to Thomas Chalk[33] (d. 1901). In 1903 Chalk's executor sold 180 a. in Castle Camps to the Revd. C. H. Brocklebank of Bartlow House, with whose estate they afterwards passed,[34] belonging in 1974 to Brig. A. N. Breitmeyer.[35]

The manor-house, occasionally recorded in the Middle Ages,[36] had 10 or more hearths *c.* 1660 and contained a library of 220 books.[37] Westoe Lodge, standing in 1840,[38] was demolished probably between 1851 and 1861,[39] only a farm-house further north remaining.

The manor later styled *OLMSTEAD* or *HOLMSTEAD HALL* was held in 1259 by Maurice, son of John, of Olmstead.[40] Maurice died shortly before 1269, when his son William, who had been among the rebels in the Isle of Ely, was required to redeem his property at Olmstead.[41] By 1279 the manor, comprising 160 a. and held as ½ knight's fee of the earl of Oxford under the honor of Richmond, had passed to William's infant son John.[42] Simon of Horncastle and his wife Lucy, perhaps William's widow, held that ½ fee *c.* 1302.[43] John still held Olmstead in 1348,[44] when he settled 240 a. on his eldest son Robert.[45] In 1367 Robert settled the manor on John Bek and Robert Nailinghurst,[46] and in 1373 Thomas Nailinghurst released it to Sir Aubrey de Vere.[47] In 1376 John Wombe of Hempstead (Essex) conveyed the manor to William Bateman and others, probably feoffees.[48]

In 1400 Olmstead Hall was conveyed to other feoffees probably to the use of William Skrene, serjeant-at-law,[49] to whom William Olmstead, butcher, released the manor in 1417.[50] Skrene died after 1424,[51] and Olmstead passed to his son Thomas (d.s.p. 1466). Thomas's heir was the minor John Skrene, later knighted, son of John (d. 1452), son of Thomas's brother William (d. 1431).[52] Sir John Skrene died in 1474, leaving no close kinsmen; the various mesne lords claimed his lands as escheats,[53] and in 1475 Richard, duke of Gloucester, as lord of Castle Camps, granted Olmstead to Sir Robert Chamberlain, his servant and Sir John's executor.[54] Three claimants alleging descent from sisters of Serjeant Skrene released their interest in 1475 and 1477 to Chamberlain and others,[55] as did Sir John Skrene's widow Elizabeth in 1478,[56] and in 1477 the manor was conveyed to feoffees for Queens' College, Cambridge;[57] it was vested in fellows of the college in 1482.[58] From 1500 the college held it under the Veres and their successors at Castle Camps,[59] and retained Olmstead Hall farm, amounting *c.* 1800 to 270 a.,[60] until its sale in 1920 to W. S. Kiddy.[61]

The farm-house once owned by Queens', surviving within a moat close to the parish boundary, may occupy the site of the manor-house; an alternative site is the moat beside the road at Olmstead Green.[62]

Another estate at Olmstead was amassed by the Reynolds family.[63] James Reynolds held tenements at Olmstead Green by 1586[64] and by 1609 had built a large house there.[65] Reynolds, knighted in 1618, held on lease 300 a. of adjacent pasture in the former park from 1614 and the main demesne farms *c.* 1640.[66] When he died aged 80 in 1650 his Olmstead Green farm passed to his son James (d. 1662) whose son and heir James died in 1690 and was presumably succeeded by his eldest son, Capt. Robert Reynolds.[67] About 1726 the farm descended to Robert's son, Sir James Reynolds,[68] chief justice of the Common Pleas in Ireland 1727–40 and later a baron of the English Exchequer.[69] Sir James built at Olmstead an elegant summer residence, called the Green House,[70] which in 1755 contained a substantial library. At his death in 1747 he left the estate to his unmarried sister Judith (d. 1755) with remainder to his nephew James Hatley,[71] who *c.* 1767 apparently offered the house and *c.* 250 a. in Castle Camps for sale.[72] The estate was later acquired by the executors of William Prior Johnson (d. 1776), whose son-in-law Thomas Richardson[73] occupied it in 1780.[74] Thomas's son William, who took the surname Prior Johnson, held

32 C.U.L., E.D.R., tithe award 1840.
33 Ibid. reapportionment 1879; cf. C.R.O., Q/RDc 80.
34 Charterho. Mun., MR 2/387B; cf. *Kelly's Dir. Cambs.* (1937).
35 Ex inf. Brig. Breitmeyer.
36 e.g. C.P. 25(1)/25/33 no. 19; C.P. 25(1)/29/88 no. 14.
37 E 179/84/437 rot. 4; cf. B.L. Add. Roll 42699.
38 C.U.L., E.D.R., tithe award.
39 Mentioned in H.O. 107/1761, but not in R.G. 9/1029, nor in C.R.O., Q/RDc 80, map.
40 *Essex Feet of Fines* (Essex Arch. Soc.), i. 231.
41 J.I. 1/83 rot. 2 and d.
42 *Rot. Hund.* (Rec. Com.), ii. 125.
43 *Feud. Aids*, i. 145; cf. *Essex Feet of Fines*, ii. 133.
44 *Feud. Aids*, i. 154, 162. The John of Olmstead who died in 1312 leaving 29 a. there, held of a namesake, to his son William (*Cal. Inq. p.m.* v, p. 185; *Cal. Fine R.* 1307–19, 133) was perhaps a younger son of Maurice: cf. *Cal. Close*, 1272–9, 431; *Cat. Anct. D.* v, A 11885.
45 C.P. 25(1)/28/75 no. 14.
46 C.P. 25(1)/29/82 no. 24.
47 *Cal. Close*, 1369–74, 589.
48 Ibid. 1374–7, 450.
49 C.P. 25(1)/30/92 no. 4; cf. *Cal. Pat.* 1392–6, 486; 1396–9, 28; *Cal. Close*, 1409–13, 67.
50 *Cal. Close*, 1413–19, 438; cf. ibid. 1419–22, 54–5.
51 *Cat. Anct. D.* iii, D. 899.
52 C 140/20/25 no. 5; cf. C 139/145 nos. 5, 6; *Cal. Fine R.* 1461–71, 186; 1471–85, 83.
53 Prob. 11/6 (P.C.C. 19 Wattys); C 140/50/42 nos. 1–10.
54 C.U.L., Queens' Coll. Mun., box 66, 13/70, 85.
55 Ibid. 13/69; *Cal. Pat.* 1477–85, 58; *Cal. Close*, 1476–85, 89–90.
56 C.P. 25(1)/294/77 no. 121.
57 C.U.L., Queens' Coll. Mun., box 66, 13/71–5.
58 Ibid. 13/76.
59 Ibid. 13/77–80; cf. Charterho. Mun., MR 2/557A; 565C; 587, p. 309.
60 C.U.L., Queens' Coll. Mun., box 66, surveys 1799, 1822.
61 Ex inf. the Domestic Bursar; cf. *Kelly's Dir. Cambs.* (1916–22).
62 C.U.L., Queens' Coll. Mun., box 66, survey 1799 shows the farm on its present site. The moat by the green then belonged to W. P. Johnson, but the farm-house of his farm already in 1618 stood north of the road; cf. Charterho. Mun., map 1618; MR 2/588A; Essex R.O., D/DHc P 27.
63 Cf. Req. 2/26/217; Charterho. Mun., MR 2/217, ct. roll 21 Eliz. I.
64 Charterho. Mun., MR 2/557A pt. ii, pp. 5, 25; MR 2/587, p. 309.
65 Ibid. MR 2/218, ct. rolls 7, 9 Jas. I; MR 2/219, ct. roll 3 Chas. I; cf. Sta. Cha. 8/253/23.
66 Nicholls, *Progresses of Jas. I*, iii. 480; Charterho. Mun., D 2/115, 150; MR 2/572.
67 *Trans. Essex Arch. Soc.* N.S. viii. 57–60; C.R.O., par. reg. TS.; Prob. 11/399 (P.C.C. 79 Dykes).
68 Charterho. Mun., MR 6/14, pp. 272, 335–7.
69 Foss, *Judges of Eng.* viii. 163–4: to be distinguished from his uncle Jas., also a judge (d. 1739), who acquired the lease of Olmstead Hall farm *c.* 1723: *D.N.B.*; Morant, *Essex*, ii. 532; Charterho. Mun., MR 6/12, f. 18 and v; MR 6/13, pp. 325, 430–2.
70 B.L. Add. MS. 5805, p. 100; Charterho. Mun., MR 2/588A.
71 Prob. 11/755 (P.C.C. 160 Potter); Prob. 11/816 (P.C.C. 122 Paul).
72 Charterho. Mun., MR 2/588A.
73 Prob. 11/1023 (P.C.C. 391 Bellas).
74 Essex R.O., Q/RPc, land tax return 1780.

the Olmstead land from 1793 until the 1830s.[75] About 1840 the owner was James W. Prior Johnson,[76] from 1866 the Revd. J. W. Carver, and in 1882 Carver's widow. By 1886 the estate had been acquired by Daniel Gurteen of Haverhill (Suff.) (d. 1894), and in 1908 belonged to W. B. Gurteen.[77] By 1922 Henry Ruse, whose family had been tenants there since the 1860s, had bought it.[78] The Green House, standing in 1767,[79] was presumably identical with Greenhouse Farm a symmetrical timber-framed house of the early 18th century, refronted in brick in the 19th, which was pulled down in 1969.

ECONOMIC HISTORY. Of the 2½ hides at Camps held by Aubrey de Vere in 1086 half was in demesne, and there were six *servi* and four plough-teams to cultivate it. Seventeen *villani*, who with 4 bordars occupied the rest, could provide another 7 plough-teams. The income from the manor had increased from £12 to £15. Another ½ hide held by an under-tenant had one team to work it.[80] By 1279 when the cultivated area had been greatly enlarged, probably at the expense of the woodland, the Vere demesne, *c.* 740 a. in 1263, comprised half of the 1,400 a. of arable in the chief manor. The Westoe demesne in 1279 was 121 a., while its 3 free tenants had only 31 a. Of *c.* 290 a. of arable in Olmstead the demesne covered 160 a. The tenants there, all freeholders, were 5 with 12 a. or more occupying 77 a., 12 with 5 a. or less occupying 34 a., and 8 with only their messuages and fractions of an acre.[81] In 1348, perhaps after further assarting, the Olmstead demesne included 336 a. of arable and 32 a. of meadow and pasture.[82] In 1279, apart from the 100-acre glebe, only 160 a. were held freely of the Vere manor, including 2 free tenements of 48 a. and 46 a. The 7 other freeholders held less than 20 a. each. Of the customary land *c.* 100 a. called mol-land, including 4 half-yardlands and 6 quarter-yardlands, was held mainly by rent, though also owing harvest-boons. The blacksmith held ½ yardland by supplying ploughshares. Eighteen half-yardlanders with 16 a. each owed 2 works a week between Michaelmas and Whitsun and 4 between Whitsun and Michaelmas, ploughing 9 a., and carrying hay. Nineteen cottars occupied 16 cottages and *c.* 12 a. of smallholdings, some owing harvest-boons like the molmen. The earl might tallage all his villeins at will.[83]

The area of demesne arable regularly ploughed possibly shrank from *c.* 600 a. in 1331 to 540 a. in 1371, when there was a triennial rotation. Another 180 a., not the regular fallow, were uncultivated.[84] In 1340 the yield of corn from the parish was said to have fallen by two-thirds since 1291,[85] and in 1347 the earl's tenants' tax was reduced from 10 marks to 5½.[86] The value of the manor allegedly declined from 100 marks *c.* 1315 to just over £15 by 1371, when the demesne was partly at farm.[87] By 1432 the whole demesne was on lease to William Petyt, whose descendants still occupied it in 1525.[88] Under Elizabeth beneficial lessees paid large entry fines and could sublet land for double the rent which they paid.[89]

Copyhold remained predominant. By 1371 all but 80 of the works due had been permanently commuted.[90] In 1618 the 40 copyholders, paying £48 a year, held *c.* 727 a. of copyhold,[91] and *c.* 1800 the Charterhouse manor included only 138½ a. of freehold compared with *c.* 725 a. of copyhold.[92] By 1450 the standard holdings had been broken up and recombined; out of 36 holdings, totalling *c.* 605 a., 6 of over 30 a. covered *c.* 265 a. and another 6 of over 20 a. covered 140 a.[93] Of 33 inhabitants taxed altogether at £224 in 1524, 22 worth £2 each or less had only £30 between them, while 6 people with £10 or more shared £155.[94] By 1586 out of 624 a. held of the manor 12 men with 20 to 60 a. occupied 380 a., including 180 a. held by 4 men with over 30 a. each, while 33 lesser tenants had only 168 a. The largest single landholder, John Bryant of Shudy Camps, owned *c.* 75 a. overlapping the border of that parish.[95] In 1618 his heir Edward Bryant owned 202 a. in the two parishes, including 72 a. in Castle Camps.[96]

By the 16th century, and probably by 1450, relatively little open-field land remained, most of the demesne and tenants' land lying in severalty.[97] In 1586 the tenants' several land, apart from 257 a. in closes and crofts, still lay in sections styled furlongs, and their portions of such furlongs, though hedged round, were mainly strip-shaped. In 1450 the *c.* 253 a. of open arable was divided among 12 named fields, 9 of which were still recorded in 1586. They were mostly small; only five exceeded 20 a.; four of those, including Tangley, Ereslade (later Yestley), and Lowtishay (later Lowsell), totalled 81 a. The largest, the West field, *c.* 85 a. in 1450 and 87½ a. in 1586, lay at the western end of the parish. It was also called Westoe field, but was distinct from the inclosed Westoe estate, measured in 1618 as 60 a., which lay further west. To the east the parish fell into three portions. The largest was the enclosed demesne, stretching across the centre of the parish to the castle and park: in 1586, when only 16 a. of demesne lay in the common fields, it contained *c.* 143 a. of meadow and pasture, mostly just west of the castle, and 607 a. of arable, including from east to west Stubbing field (*c.* 93 a.), Mill field (70 or 66 a.), Limekiln field (*c.* 75 or 84 a.), and Gidding

75 Charterho. Mun., MR 2/513, pp. 276–82; Essex R.O., Q/RPc, returns 1790–1830.
76 Essex R.O., D/CT 58 A.
77 *Kelly's Dir. Essex* (1866–1914), s.v. Helions Bumpstead.
78 Ibid.; *Kelly's Dir. Cambs.* (1922).
79 Cf. Charterho. Mun., MR 2/588A.
80 *V.C.H. Cambs.* i. 390.
81 C 132/31/1 no. 6; *Rot. Hund.* (Rec. Com.), ii. 424–6.
82 C.P. 25(1)/28/75 no. 4.
83 C 132/31/1 no. 6; *Rot. Hund.* ii. 424–6; C 132/76/7 no. 8.
84 C 135/28/17 no. 8; C 135/222 no. 15.
85 *Inq. Non.* (Rec. Com.), 213.
86 *Cal. Inq. Misc.* ii, p. 507; *Cal. Pat.* 1345–8, 399.
87 C 143/118 no. 4; C 135/222 no. 15.
88 Essex R.O., D/D Pr 137–9; B.L. Add. MS. 5861, f. 91v.
89 C 2/Eliz. I/M 5/14.
90 C 135/222 no. 15.
91 Charterho. Mun., map 1618; MR 2/511, 574A. The figures include land in Shudy Camps.
92 Ibid. map *c.* 1800.
93 Ibid. MR 2/557A pt. ii, pp. 5–19.
94 E 179/81/134 m. 4.
95 Charterho. Mun., MR 2/587, pp. 353–61, 376–451.
96 Ibid. map 1618.
97 This account is based on Charterho. Mun., MR 2/557A pt. ii, pp. 5–19 (rental 28 Hen. VI); MR 2/587 (survey 1586); D 2/61, 100 (leases 1597, 1609); MR 2/577, 572 (demesne surveys *c.* 1612, 1617); map 1618; C.U.L., E.D.R., tithe award and map 1840.

field (*c.* 116 or 154 a.). The tenants held small blocks of inclosed strips in the corners of two of them, and in 1597 the lord was said to have sheep-walk over his own fields, suggesting that the demesne arable had been formed from common fields. The area to the south included *c.* 385 a. held in severalty by the tenants and *c.* 65 a. of small open fields of which *c.* 42 a. lay near Langley wood. The several land there, although consolidated into blocks, some of 10 or 20 a., had once been held in strips of 2 a. or less. North of the demesne was another area held in severalty, where no open-field land survived in 1618, but many holdings still lay in narrow strips.

Although little commonable land remained, the traditional triennial rotation persisted even on the demesne where in 1597 240 a. was to be cultivated in three seasons.[98] In 1609 its lessee was required to summer-till his land after every two years according to the custom of the country,[99] and in 1671 another lessee needed special permission to sow 100 a. with corn for three years running.[1] During the 18th century the forecrop and aftercrop were regularly distinguished on the demesne and other farms.[2] In 1801 there were 198 a. of wheat, 253 a. of barley, and 245 a. of oats, besides 78 a. of peas and beans; there were only 12 a. of turnips and 2 a. of potatoes, partly because of the heavy water-logged soil.[3] Sainfoin had been grown on Westoe farm by 1766,[4] and by the 1790s a system of one crop followed by a fallow was beginning to replace the customary rotation.[5]

The courts occasionally regulated rights of common in the 16th century, forbidding cattle to be put in the corn field before the rector had declared harvesting finished.[6] Custom allowed a tenant 2 sheep on Camps Green for each penny which he contributed to the common fine of 6*s.* 8*d.* and 2 sheep on the common fields for each acre which he owned in them.[7] Because of shortage of common-field land smaller farmers often kept cattle rather than sheep, and had much of their several land under permanent grass. One farm in 1714 included 11 a. of mowing ground and 24 a. of feeding ground for its cattle, and had only 27 a. under the plough.[8] Tithe of milk was the subject of a prolonged lawsuit in the 1710s.[9] The only large flock of sheep belonged to the demesne farms:[10] in 1607 the manor was said to include a sheep-course for five or six hundred sheep.[11] Including the park the demesne comprised in 1618 787 a. of grass and 721 a. of arable.[12] The lessee of Camps Hall farm *c.* 1770 had a flock of 240 sheep.[13] About 1795 *c.* 500 Norfolk sheep were kept in the parish. Old inclosures, long partly hollow-drained, yielded a rich herbage, but much pasture remained unimproved.[14] Some grassland was later ploughed and in 1840 the parish contained 760 a. of permanent grass compared with *c.* 1,750 a. of arable.[15]

The demesne farms were gradually reorganized from the 1580s. By 1607 the park had been divided by hedges, the 202 a. of Haverhill End being shared among 5 men.[16] The main demesne farm, 360 a. of arable and 84 a. of grass, was let as one unit in 1597 with a newly built farm-house.[17] Under Sir John Skinner the demesne holdings were subdivided, one farm of 150 a. having 10 occupants,[18] but Thomas Sutton reconstituted the large farm, giving it 437 a. of arable and *c.* 56 a. of grass.[19] In 1613–14 the Charterhouse relet the demesne as 12 farms: only four of the lessees, occupying 164 a. out of 1,597 a., came from Castle Camps.[20] From 1626 Sheepcoteley farm, the large western farm of 566 a., was let to the tenant of the castle, and from *c.* 1640 to Sir James Reynolds, already lessee of *c.* 290 a. of pasture in the park, and his son John.[21] The land was divided anew after *c.* 1665: on the west Camps Hall farm amounted to 587 a. by 1722,[22] and Castle farm to the east covered *c.* 365 a. in 1671[23] and gradually between 1646 and 1719 absorbed *c.* 210 a. of smaller leaseholds to the north.[24] The Charterhouse apparently granted beneficial leases, the large farms going to outsiders until the 18th century.[25] In the 1740s Castle farm was divided, *c.* 283 a. being farmed from the rebuilt farm-house at the castle, and 248 a. further north from the newly built Moat Farm.[26] By 1800 consolidation had produced two other large farms, Hill (later Whitens Mere) farm of 183 a., and one of 155 a. that was later added to Moat farm.[27] Those large farms remained long in the same families: Camps Hall farm of 605 a. was occupied by the Colliers from 1744 to *c.* 1860, and Moat farm by the Frenches from 1747 to the 1820s and then by the Leonards until *c.* 1900.[28]

Outside the demesne consolidation had by *c.* 1760 produced copyholds of 124 a. and 66 a.,[29] and soon afterwards there were only 13 farmers in the parish.[30] Olmstead lay in two large farms, both entirely inclosed: the southern one, Olmstead Hall farm, covered *c.* 270 a. in 1799,[31] and Greenhouse farm, mostly north of the road and sometimes let with adjoining farms in Helions Bumpstead, comprised in 1794 *c.* 196 a., of which *c.* 80 a. lay outside the parish. There was also Charlwood farm of 70 a. just west of the old parish boundary.[32] About 1800 the rest

98 Charterho. Mun., D 2/61.
99 Ibid. D 2/100A.
1 Ibid. D 2/163.
2 e.g. C.R.O., P 34/3/1.
3 H.O. 67/9.
4 C.R.O., R 59/5/11/10.
5 Vancouver, *Agric. in Cambs.* 63.
6 Charterho. Mun., MR 2/217, ct. roll 8 Eliz. I.
7 Ibid. MR 2/219, ct. rolls 6, 13 Jas. I.
8 C.R.O., P 34/3/1.
9 E 134/5 Geo. I Hil./5.
10 Charterho. Mun., D 2/61.
11 Ibid. MR 2/571.
12 Ibid. MR 2/572.
13 C.R.O., P 34/3/2.
14 Vancouver, *Agric. in Cambs.* 63.
15 C.U.L., E.D.R., tithe award 1840.
16 Charterho. Mun., D 2/86, 91.
17 Ibid. D 2/61.
18 E 178/3635; Charterho. Mun., D 2/108.
19 Charterho. Mun., D 2/62, 100.
20 Ibid. MR 2/571–2; D 2/104–15.
21 Ibid. D 2/125, 142, 149.
22 Ibid. D 2/160, 162, 171, 186.
23 Ibid. D 2/163.
24 Ibid. D 2/119, 143–4, 150, 153, 185.
25 Ibid. D 2/104–190.
26 Ibid. D 2/191, 194; cf. MR 2/581–2.
27 Ibid. map *c.* 1800; D 2/190; MR 2/583–4; AR 5/25; cf. C.U.L., E.D.R., tithe award 1840.
28 Charterho. Mun., D 2/189, 192; AR 5/7, 9, 16, 23, 25; *Kelly's Dir. Cambs.* (1858–1900).
29 Charterho. Mun., MR 2/565C.
30 C.R.O., P 34/3/2–7.
31 C.U.L., Queens' Coll. Mun., box 66, survey 1799; cf. Essex R.O., D/CT 58 A.
32 Charterho. Mun., MR 2/588A; D 2/48, 54; cf. MR 2/587, pp. 10–11; Essex R.O., D/DHC P 27.

of Castle Camps, apart from the Charterhouse and Westoe estates, amounted to *c.* 945 a., and belonged to 25 landowners of whom three with over 100 a. each had 354 a., while 17 with 50 a. or less owned *c.* 320 a. The Dayrells of Shudy Camps, who then owned *c.* 83 a.,[33] later acquired more land, buying 70 a., mostly in the smaller open fields, in 1825.[34] About 1840 the Charterhouse owned over half the parish, 1,541 a., divided into four farms; the Dayrells owned 276 a., farmed by six men; the Westoe estate comprised 171 a., William Carter of Shudy Camps owned 193 a., W. P. Johnson had Charlwood farm of 62 a., two local men had farms of 95 a., and 10 other landowners altogether 103 a. In all, six large farms of 150 a. or more accounted for 1,741 a. out of 2,490 a. of farmland in the parish.[35]

Only 205 a. of open field remained in 1840 of which 105 a. lay in the large western field, called by 1723 Camps Rows, and *c.* 15 a. in the adjacent Stonehill and Westoe Garden. The other 85 a. lay as before mostly around Langley wood.[36] In 1858 an order was obtained for inclosing Castle Camps simultaneously with Shudy Camps and Bartlow.[37] The common fields had been divided by 1862. The area allotted, including 109 a. of old inclosures, was 315 a., of which the Charterhouse received 116 a., including an allotment for sheep-walk, the Dayrell estate *c.* 62 a., Rebecca Carter 56½ a., and Thomas Chalk 54 a. Ten others, none with over 7 a., shared *c.* 26 a.; the great west field was divided between Westoe and Whitens Mere farms and Rebecca Carter.[38] In 1879 the Charterhouse consequently owned 1,649 a., the Dayrells 265 a., William Carter 208 a., Thomas Chalk 173 a., James Leonard 142 a., the rector 72 a., and four others 74 a.[39]

The three large Charterhouse farms in the centre of the parish were sold to their tenants in 1919.[40] South of them the land west of Olmstead was shared by three partly intermingled farms and the rectory glebe.[41] The ancient inclosures west of Camps Green were divided among four small farms of 60 a. or less, mostly belonging to estates in Shudy Camps.[42] Of the 21 farmers recorded at Castle Camps in 1851, seven, each working over 100 a., occupied 1,870 a., while 12 with under 50 a. occupied only 243 a.[43] By 1871 there were only 16 farmers.[44] After the break-up of the Charterhouse and Dayrell estates between 1900 and 1920, the 12 substantial farms in the parish were mostly owned by the men who farmed them, which was still so *c.* 1970. Much land was occupied by the Haylock family. Thomas Haylock owned Hill farm by 1922, and Moat farm by 1933, and held Castle farm on lease; in 1960 he occupied the largest single farm in the parish.[45]

Pastoral farming may have declined slightly in the later 19th century. In 1905 there were 2,075 a. of arable and 654 a. of grass in the parish,[46] and on the Charterhouse estate, where in 1840 there had been 387 a. of grass, there were only 240 a. in 1919.[47] In the 1930s parts of the heavy clay land, apparently on the east side of the parish, were beginning to revert to scrub.[48] In 1960 crops included wheat, potatoes, and sugar-beet, and 80 a. south-west of Camps Green had been planted with fruit trees.[49]

In 1821 109 out of 138 families were supported by agriculture,[50] and *c.* 1830 there were 86 adult farm labourers and another 56 aged between 10 and 20.[51] Not all could find work in the parish. In 1861 when there were *c.* 190 labourers the farmers provided work for only 83 men and 36 boys.[52] Wages remained among the lowest in the county, 9*s.* for married and 7*s.* for single men *c.* 1830 and 10*s.* a week in the 1860s.[53] By 1830 the Charterhouse provided one-rood allotments: in 1840 it was letting 11 a. of Moat farm for that purpose,[54] and in 1919 its estate included 21 a. of allotments.[55] Many women and girls did 'slop-work', making cheap clothes for a manufacturer at Haverhill.[56] By 1851 there were 46 slopmakers beside 14 needlewomen and dress-makers, and in 1861 106 women were thus employed.[57] In 1897 many people were emigrating to Tottenham Hale (Mdx.).[58]

Other kinds of opportunities for employment in the parish had diminished. Limekiln field was so named in 1586 from a kiln standing apparently in its south-west angle,[59] where a chalkpit survives overgrown with trees. A meadow north-west of that field was between 1618 and 1755 renamed Brick-kiln meadow.[60] There were still bricklayers in the parish in 1841, when there were also 5 carpenters, 4 blacksmiths, 5 thatchers, 7 shoemakers, and 3 tailors.[61] In 1871 9 boot- and shoemakers, 7 carpenters, and 3 wheelwrights remained.[62] By 1879 there was only one shoemaker's workshop, not recorded after 1929, and the wheelwrights and tailors had disappeared by 1916, although a forge was still working in 1933. There were two shops in 1937 and 1975.[63] In 1960 most of the men still worked on the farms, while many women were employed in factories at Haverhill.[64]

The earl of Oxford's manor by 1263 had a windmill, which presumably stood in Mill field, where

[33] Charterho. Mun., map *c.* 1800.
[34] Ibid. MR 2/378.
[35] C.U.L., E.D.R., tithe award 1840; C.R.O., R 59/5/11/13–15.
[36] C.U.L., E.D.R., tithe award 1840; cf. Charterho. Mun., MR 2/583.
[37] Second Annual Incl. Act, 1858, 21–2 Vic. c. 61; *Special Rep. of Incl. Com.* H.C. 2409, pp. 171–3 (1857–8), xxiv.
[38] C.R.O., Q/RDc 80, and map.
[39] C.U.L., E.D.R., tithe reapportionment 1879.
[40] C.R.O., SP 34/4.
[41] Ibid. 296/SP 1060; C.U.L., Maps 53(1)/91/169; cf. C.U.L., E.D.R., tithe map 1840.
[42] C.R.O., 296/SP 918, 1024.
[43] H.O. 107/1761.
[44] R.G. 10/1592.
[45] Cf. *Kelly's Dir. Cambs.* (1900–1937); *Camb. Ind. Press*, 13 May 1960.
[46] Cambs. Agric. Returns, 1905.
[47] C.R.O., SP 34/4; C.U.L., E.D.R., tithe award 1840.
[48] *V.C.H. Cambs.* i. 308.
[49] *Camb. Ind. Press*, 13 May 1960.
[50] *Census*, 1821.
[51] *Rep. H.L. Cttee. on Poor Laws*, H.C. 227, pp. 326–7 (1831), viii.
[52] R.G. 9/1029.
[53] *Rep. H.L. Cttee. on Poor Laws*, pp. 326–7; *1st Rep. Com. Employment in Agric.* 359–60.
[54] *Rep. H.L. Cttee. on Poor Laws*, pp. 326–7; Charterho. Mun., AR 5/23, p. 95; C.U.L., E.D.R., tithe award 1840.
[55] C.R.O., SP 34/4.
[56] *1st Rep. Com. Employment in Agric.*, 360.
[57] H.O. 107/1761; R.G. 9/1029.
[58] C.U.L., E.D.R., C 3/36.
[59] Charterho. Mun., MR 2/587, p. 335; map 1618; cf. ibid. MR 2/579.
[60] Ibid. MR 2/584.
[61] H.O. 107/66.
[62] R.G. 10/1592.
[63] *Kelly's Dir. Cambs.* (1879–1937).
[64] *Camb. Ind. Press*, 13 May 1960.

a pond was called the mill pond in 1597.[65] That mill was ruinous by 1371.[66] Between 1586 and 1618 a new windmill was built further west, on the brow of the hill.[67] After reconstruction in 1635 it was regularly let with the surrounding Camps Hall farm until the 1720s.[68] It was possibly still in use in 1861,[69] and was pulled down in 1910.[70]

LOCAL GOVERNMENT. In 1279 the earl of Oxford, besides holding view of frankpledge and the assize of bread and of ale, was entitled to keep a tumbrel and gallows.[71] A plot near Langley wood was later called Hangman's acre.[72] In the late 16th century the earls' court still had leet jurisdiction.[73] It had forbidden parishioners to take in inmates without the consent of the chief men of the leet by 1609, and was allotting fines half to the lord, half to the poor. In 1650 those receiving strangers were ordered to safeguard the parish.[74] In 1559 and later the court elected two constables and occasionally an ale-taster.[75] In the 1640s it appointed a hayward[76] and sometimes fined men for refusing the constable's office. Leet proceedings had become purely formal, although regulation of common rights continued until the 1650s.[77] After 1700 the registration of copyholds became the court's sole business. Court rolls survive for 1557–1739,[78] and court books for 1620–1935.[79]

Jurisdiction over Olmstead, which in 1285 was fined for not being represented before the royal justices as a separate vill,[80] was ambiguous. In 1279 its lord owed suit both to the earl of Oxford's court at Castle Camps and to the honor of Richmond's tourn in south-east Cambridgeshire,[81] to which it sent four men in 1334.[82] The men of Castle Camps did not invariably recognize Olmstead as part of their township. About 1545 men apparently living at Olmstead were excluded from benefit under the bequest of Lewis Blodwell (d. *c.* 1521), to relieve Castle Camps township from tax, on the grounds that they belonged to Helions Bumpstead.[83] Under Elizabeth I the lords of Castle Camps held a nominally separate view of frankpledge for Olmstead.[84] Its proceedings sometimes went unrecorded,[85] and soon became purely formal. By *c.* 1630 even the exaction of a common fine, the last relic of jurisdiction over Olmstead, had ceased.[86]

The expense of poor-relief rose from £187 in 1776 to £264 by *c.* 1785 and £513 by 1803, when 53 people obtained regular relief. By 1813 expenditure had again more than doubled to £1,313 and *c.* 50 people were on regular relief.[87] Expenditure seldom fell below £1,000 a year until *c.* 1830,[88] when large families were receiving allowances and 15 unemployed labourers were working for the parish.[89] The parish became part of the Linton poor-law union in 1835,[90] was incorporated with the rest of Linton R.D. into the South Cambridgeshire R.D. in 1934,[91] and was included in South Cambridgeshire in 1974.

CHURCH. Castle Camps had a church before 1111, which in that year Aubrey de Vere (d. *c.* 1112) granted to Abingdon abbey (Berks.) when endowing his priory at Earl's Colne (Essex), newly founded from that abbey.[92] Aubrey's son Aubrey (d. 1141) agreed that the priory might annex the church at the next vacancy,[93] but in and after 1217 the church was still an unappropriated rectory.[94] The advowson belonged in 1263 to the earl of Oxford as lord of the manor, with which it afterwards descended.[95] Earl Edward (d. 1604) sold turns exercised by John Bendyshe of Steeple Bumpstead (Essex), who in 1579 presented his kinsman Robert Bendyshe,[96] and by John Persfield in 1586.[97] From 1611 the advowson belonged to the Charterhouse, which in accordance with its statutes normally presented former masters or pupils of Charterhouse school.[98] It still owned the advowson in 1974. From 1945 the rectory was held jointly with Shudy Camps vicarage.[99]

Whereas the rector did not receive the tithes of Olmstead, he was entitled to tithes from beyond the northern and western boundaries of Castle Camps. Until after 1291 Hatfield priory's estate at Nosterfield, in Shudy Camps, was apparently reckoned as part of Great Camps in respect of a tithe portion arising from it.[1] The rights of the priory and the rector of Castle Camps to tithe from land apparently lying in the western fields of Shudy Camps, held of Westoe fee by Horseheath men, were upheld at arbitration *c.* 1313 against the rector of Horseheath.[2] In the 17th century the rector of Castle Camps was entitled to great and small tithes from 32 a. in Shudy Camps, 20½ a. in Bartlow, and 4 a. in Horseheath.[3]

65 C 132/31/1 no. 5; Charterho. Mun., D 2/61.
66 C 135/222 no. 15.
67 Charterho. Mun., MR 2/577; D 2/116; map 1618.
68 e.g. ibid. D 2/146, 151, 186.
69 R.G. 9/1029.
70 Palmer and Fox, *Shudy Camps*, 26.
71 *Rot. Hund.* (Rec. Com.), i. 52; ii. 424.
72 Charterho. Mun., MR 2/217, ct. roll 6 Eliz. I.
73 Ibid. MR 2/217–9, *passim*.
74 Ibid. MR 2/219, ct. roll 7 Jas. I; MR 2/222, ct. roll 1650.
75 e.g. ibid. MR 2/217, ct. rolls 1, 4, 7 Eliz. I.
76 Ibid. MR 2/222, ct. rolls 17, 21 Chas. I, 1649.
77 Ibid. MR 2/221–2, *passim*, especially ct. roll 20 Chas. I.
78 Ibid. MR 2/217–240.
79 Ibid. MR 6/11–21 (1620–1786); MR 6/517–21 (1786–1833); MR 6/241–3 (1839–1935). The proceedings before 1839 are recorded in books covering all the Charterhouse manors in the locality.
80 *Assizes at Camb. 1260*, 46.
81 *Rot. Hund.* (Rec. Com.), ii. 425.
82 S.C. 2/155/71 mm. 1–2.
83 Prob. 11/20 (P.C.C. 20 Maynwaring); C 1/1141 nos. 6–8.
84 e.g. Charterho. Mun., MR 2/217, ct. roll 4 Eliz. I.
85 e.g. ibid. 24–34 Eliz. I.
86 e.g. ibid. MR 2/219–22, *passim*; last mentioned in ct. roll 6 Chas. I.
87 *Poor Law Abstract, 1804*, 34–5; *1818*, 28–9.
88 *Poor Rate Returns, 1816–21*, 10; *1822–4*, 37; *1825–9*, 15–16.
89 *Rep. H.L. Cttee. on Poor Laws*, H.C. 227, pp. 326–7 (1831), viii.
90 *Poor Law Com. 1st Rep.* 249.
91 *Census*, 1931 (pt. ii).
92 *Colne Priory Cart.* (Essex Arch. Soc., occ. ser. i), 1–2, 6.
93 Ibid. 17–18.
94 *Val. of Norwich*, ed. Lunt, 536; cf. *Vetus Liber Arch. Elien.* (C.A.S. 8vo ser. xlviii), 56.
95 *Cal. Inq. p.m.* i, p. 185; *Rot. Hund.* (Rec. Com.), ii. 424; Charterho. Mun., D 2/54, 89.
96 *E.D.R.* (1904), 379.
97 Gibbons, *Ely Episc. Rec.* 441.
98 Cf. *Alum. Cantab. to 1751*, *1752–1900*, under rectors' names.
99 *Crockford* (1947 and later edns.).
1 *Val. of Norwich*, ed. Lunt, 227; *Tax. Eccl.* (Rec. Com.), 267, 270.
2 B.L. Add. Ch. 28553.
3 C.U.L., E.D.R., H 1/2, doc. with terriers; Shudy Camps tithe award 1841.

The glebe was reckoned at 104 a. in 1279,[4] and in 1615 and 1638 at *c.* 89 a. by local measure, lying mostly in the south part of the parish. In 1779 there were said to be 97 a. of glebe,[5] but when accurately measured in 1840 it came to only 70 a.,[6] of which *c.* 14 a. were sold in 1904, and other portions later,[7] leaving 36 a. in 1975.[8] By the early 18th century both great and small tithes were regularly taken by composition, which was occasionally revised.[9] John Watson, rector 1703–24, caused some resentment *c.* 1715 by demanding, according to ancient custom and the practice of neighbouring parishes, payment of tithe milk at the church porch the whole year round and not only in summer.[10] The tithes were commuted under an agreement of 1838 for a rent-charge of £650 of which £20 was laid on the glebe.[11]

The rectory was taxed at 12 marks in 1217 and 1254 and at 22 marks in 1291.[12] In 1535 it was worth £15 4*s.* 2*d.*,[13] by 1650 £160,[14] and in 1728 £200.[15] About 1830 it was valued at £570,[16] and after increasing in value until the 1870s had declined by 1896 to £407 net.[17]

The rectory house stood by 1615 amid 16 a. of inclosed pasture south of the road to Olmstead, almost ½ mile south-west of the church.[18] In 1638 it included a parlour, hall, and kitchen.[19] John Watson (d. 1724) rebuilt it as a handsome seven-bay brick-fronted house, partly with materials from the decaying mansion at the castle.[20] It was kept in good repair throughout the 18th and 19th centuries.[21] In 1952 it was sold to Col. A. G. B. Stewart and renamed Berghane House.[22] The rector thereafter lived at Shudy Camps.[23]

A rector in 1337 obtained leave of absence at the countess of Salisbury's instance.[24] His successor in 1349 was only in minor orders, and in 1350 was given leave of absence to study.[25] Another in 1353 was required to hire a priest to instruct him in his duties.[26] In the late 14th century and early 15th a parish chaplain was employed,[27] and a chantrist was recorded in 1437.[28] In 1471 the duke of Gloucester presented his clerk Thomas Barrow, later Master of the Rolls.[29] In 1543 the countess of Oxford was paying, besides her own chaplain at the castle, a curate who became rector in 1547.[30]

In 1524 a guild at Castle Camps had a stock worth £7.[31] Its guildhall was confiscated, and in 1549 sold,[32] as was also a close of 2 a. left by Robert Allen in 1519 to maintain a sepulchre light.[33]

Geoffrey Astley, rector from 1557, although not a graduate and a poor preacher, was resident in 1561,[34] but by 1563 had departed, leaving the parish to a curate who failed to catechize the children and the rectory to a farmer.[35] Later Elizabethan rectors frequently employed curates, sometimes unlicensed, and were often themselves pluralists, as was William Hutchinson, rector 1590–1605 and archdeacon of St. Albans.[36] Thomas Sutton's presentee, Abraham Bedell, rector 1611–30, apparently served in person.[37] His successor, Dr. Nicholas Grey, was successively headmaster of Charterhouse, Merchant Taylors, Eton, and Tonbridge schools.[38] He employed curates in his parishes of Castle Camps and Saffron Walden, but persecuted his more puritan parishioners for not receiving communion at the altar rails. In 1638 his curate was directed to report those not communicating thrice a year. Grey forbade one yeoman to bring in a 'godly' minister to preach a funeral sermon at Castle Camps, and his curates there preached in favour of ceremonies and read the services in the chancel facing east. During the civil war they read out royal but not parliamentary declarations and orders.[39] Grey was formally ejected in 1644 and replaced by Nahum Kenitie, a puritan schoolmaster from Linton,[40] whose successor, Faithful Theate, was described in 1650 as orthodox and godly.[41] Martin Francis, ordained by the Cambridge presbytery in 1658,[42] escaped displacement in 1660, having been re-ordained, because Grey died before he could be reinstated.[43]

The next rector, Thomas Hall, being a non-juror, resigned in 1691 in favour of his son-in-law.[44] John Peter Allix, rector 1724–60, son of a Huguenot refugee, was also dean of Ely and, until 1733, vicar of Swaffham Bulbeck,[45] but often resided at the new rectory and in his absence employed a curate. In 1728 services were held twice on Sundays, and *c.* 30 people attended the thrice-yearly communions.[46] In 1775 and 1807 services were held twice on Sundays in summer and communions four times a year, and

[4] *Rot. Hund.* (Rec. Com.), ii. 424.
[5] C.U.L., E.D.R., H 1/2, terriers 1615, 1638, [1666], 1779.
[6] Ibid. Castle Camps tithe award 1840.
[7] C.R.O., P 34/1/4; P 34/3/8.
[8] Ex inf. Mr. F. Harwood, the sequestrator.
[9] e.g. C.R.O., P 34/3/1, 2, 7.
[10] E 134/5 Geo. I Hil./5.
[11] C.U.L., E.D.R., tithe award 1840.
[12] *Val. of Norwich*, ed. Lunt, 227, 536; *Tax. Eccl.* (Rec. Com.), 267.
[13] *Valor Eccl.* (Rec. Com.), iii. 504.
[14] Lamb. Pal. MS. 904, f. 272.
[15] C.U.L., E.D.R., B 8/1.
[16] *Rep. Com. Eccl. Revenues*, pp. 346–7.
[17] *Kelly's Dir. Cambs.* (1869–83); C.U.L., E.D.R., C 3/36.
[18] C.U.L., E.D.R., H 1/2, terrier 1615; cf. Charterho. Mun., map 1618.
[19] C.U.L., E.D.R., H 1/2, terrier 1638.
[20] B.L. Add. MS. 5805, f. 99.
[21] e.g. C.U.L., E.D.R., C 1/1, 4; C 3/21.
[22] C.R.O., P 34/1/4.
[23] e.g. *Crockford* (1955–6; 1971–2).
[24] *E.D.R.* (1892), 344.
[25] Ibid. (1893), 95, 107, 135.
[26] Ibid. 151.
[27] e.g. B.L. Add. MS. 5842, f. 33v.; *E.D.R.* (1898), 158.
[28] *E.D.R.* (1909), 178.
[29] Ibid. (1906), 16; Emden, *Biog. Reg. Univ. Camb.* 40–1.
[30] *E.D.R.* (1912), 184; (1913), 42–3.
[31] E 179/81/134 m. 4.
[32] *Cal. Pat.* 1549–51, 275–6.
[33] Ibid. 1548–9, 326; B.L. Add. MS. 5861, f. 68; cf. Charterho. Mun., MR 2/557A pt. ii, p. 22.
[34] B.L. Add. MS. 5847, f. 158v.; Add. MS. 5813, f. 66.
[35] C.U.L., E.D.R., D 2/5, f. 30; B 2/4, pp. 119, 124; Charterho. Mun., MR 2/217, ct. roll 9 Eliz. I.
[36] e.g. C.U.L., E.D.R., D 2/5, f. 159; B 2/23, f. 15v.; Bodl. MS. Gough Eccl. Top. 3, f. 11; *Alum. Cantab. to 1751*, ii. 441.
[37] Cf. C.U.L., E.D.R., B 2/32, p. 5; B 2/40A, f. 5v.; P.R.O. Composition Bks. 3rd ser. i.
[38] *D.N.B.*
[39] *Cambs. Village Doc.* 59; B.L. Add. MS. 15672, ff. 7v.–9, 59.
[40] *Walker Revised*, ed. Matthews, 81.
[41] Lamb. Pal. MS. 904, f. 272.
[42] *Bury Classis*, ii (Chetham Soc. N.S. xli), 189.
[43] P.R.O. Inst. Bks. ser. B, i, p. 62; Hist. MSS. Com. 6, *7th Rep.*, p. 106.
[44] B.L. Add. MS. 5842, f. 160; *Alum. Cantab. to 1751*, ii. 289.
[45] *Alum. Cantab. to 1751*, i. 22; B.L. Add. MS. 5805, f. 98v.; *Mon. Inscr. Cambs.* 22.
[46] C.U.L., E.D.R., B 8/1.

the rector was resident.[47] George Pearson, rector 1825–60, continued those practices, preaching at Sunday evensong; in 1836 he had 40 communicants,[48] and in 1851 an average attendance of 170, besides 100 Sunday-school pupils.[49] J. E. Bode, rector 1860–74, had some reputation as a preacher and hymn-writer.[50] His successor introduced monthly communions, but found that few attended.[51] George Pearson's son E. L. Pearson, rector 1879–1911,[52] held weekly communions and special services, introduced cottage lectures, and in winter, because the church was remote, held services in the schoolroom. He had 56 communicants in 1897, but reckoned that only a third of the population went to church.[53] Only two later rectors remained more than seven years.[54] R. E. Royse, rector 1948–52, had High Church leanings, and in 1950 introduced a robed choir.[55]

The church of *ALL SAINTS*, so called in 1470,[56] stands north-west of the castle motte, is built of flint with stone dressings, and comprises a chancel, nave with south porch, and west tower. Before extensive 19th-century remodelling the fabric was mostly of the 15th or early 16th centuries, although the lower part of the chancel walls, including the south door and a piscina, are possibly 14th-century. The chancel received new windows, including a four-light east window, in the 15th century, and the nave of three bays was then rebuilt, making it much higher and wider than the chancel. The tall two-light nave windows partly retain their original Perpendicular tracery. The tower was of three storeys, buttressed and embattled, and looked short beside the nave. The nave roof, originally of *c.* 1500, has kingposts upon tie-beams. The octagonal 15th-century font was largely recut *c.* 1850.[57] Some 14th-century glass surviving in the nave's south windows was reset in 1923.[58] In 1744 some medieval tomb-slabs with insets for brasses survived. The chancel formerly contained slabs to various members of the Dayrell, Neville, and Reynolds families, and on its north wall a marble monument, with a short sarcophagus before a pyramid, to Sir James Reynolds (d. 1747). They were mostly removed into the nave when choir stalls were inserted in 1883.[59]

The church was said to be in decay in 1549, the rector having neglected to repair the chancel.[60] In 1644 William Dowsing broke many windows and ordered the altar-steps to be levelled.[61] Altar-rails with turned balusters had been reinstated probably in the 1660s and a chimney inserted in the chancel by 1665. In 1744 the chancel screen survived.[62] Its base alone remained in 1851,[63] as in 1975. The church was said to be in decent repair throughout the 18th century,[64] but in the early 19th century the chancel received a new ceiling and an east window with cast-iron tracery,[65] perhaps *c.* 1818, when the rector obtained leave to replace the lead roof with slates, themselves replaced in 1883.[66] The old tower collapsed in July 1850. A new one in the Decorated style, standing on concrete, was completed in 1851 with W. G. E. Pritchett as architect. George Pearson rebuilt the 15th-century south porch in 1855 and inserted new windows in the chancel, heightening its walls, in 1856.[67] In 1882–3 the whole church was thoroughly restored by J. P. St. Aubyn. Stone tracery replaced cast-iron in the east window, the west gallery was removed, and the internal woodwork entirely renewed. The nave's north windows were renewed in 1908 and its roof-timbers mostly replaced in 1913.[68]

The plate in 1552 included two silver-gilt chalices and patens.[69] In 1960 there were a silver paten of 1684, acquired in 1686, a cup of 1777–8, and a silver plated paten, flagon, and plate given by George Pearson in 1846.[70] The tower contained four bells in 1552, of which one was riven in 1596,[71] and four in 1744.[72] By 1826 two bells were split, and in 1828 the four were recast by William Dobson of Downham as five. One, broken when the tower fell, was recast in 1852 by John Taylor of Loughborough.[73] The registers begin in 1563 and are virtually complete.[74]

NONCONFORMITY. After the Restoration some puritans refused to attend church.[75] By 1669 there was a conventicle in the parish,[76] and there were five nonconformists in 1676.[77] The two dissenting families in 1783 commonly went to Linton Independent chapel, having no meeting-house of their own.[78] In 1813 a building was registered for dissenting worship, as was another, by different persons, in 1822.[79] The second was probably for the congregation of Baptists, said in 1851 to have been established in 1818; their chapel was built in 1822 at Camps Green. In 1851 it seated 170 with standing room for 60 more, and had an average attendence of 200, besides 68 Sunday-school pupils. The minister, himself an Independent, described his congregation as Independents and Baptists.[80] It survived as a Particular Baptist chapel in 1871,[81] but had disappeared by

[47] Ibid. C 1/1, 4.
[48] Ibid. C 1/6; C 3/21.
[49] H.O. 129/188/2/8/7.
[50] *D.N.B.*
[51] C.U.L., E.D.R., C 3/26.
[52] *Alum. Cantab. 1752–1900*, v. 65.
[53] C.U.L., E.D.R., C 3/36.
[54] *Crockford* (1912 and later edns.).
[55] C.R.O., P 34/1/4.
[56] Prob. 11/5 (P.C.C. 31 Godyn, will of Wm. Petyt).
[57] Descriptions of the church before restoration are in B.L. Add. MS. 5805, ff. 97v.–98, 99 (1744); *Eccl. Top. Eng.* vi, no. 151 (1851).
[58] C.R.O., P 34/1/4.
[59] *Mon. Inscr. Cambs.* 21–2, 248.
[60] C.U.L., E.D.R., B 2/3, pp. 29, 78.
[61] *Trans. C.H.A.S.* iii. 89; cf. C.R.O., P 34/1/4.
[62] C.U.L., E.D.R., B 2/59, p. 40; Palmer, *Wm. Cole*, 90.
[63] *Eccl. Top. Eng.* vi, no. 151.
[64] C.U.L., E.D.R., B 8/1; C 1/1, 6.
[65] *Eccl. Top. Eng.* vi, no. 151.
[66] *Proc. C.A.S.* xxxv. 20.
[67] C.R.O., P 34/1/4; *Kelly's Dir. Cambs.* (1869); *Eccl. Top. Eng.* vi, no. 151.
[68] C.R.O., P 34/1/4; *Kelly's Dir. Cambs.* (1883); *E.D.R.* (1913), 229, 263.
[69] *Cambs. Ch. Goods, temp. Edw. VI*, 63.
[70] C.R.O., P 34/1/4; MS. list of ch. plate *penes V.C.H.*
[71] *Cambs. Ch. Goods, temp. Edw. VI*, 63; C.U.L., E.D.R., B 2/13, f. 168v.
[72] Palmer, *Wm. Cole*, 90.
[73] C.R.O., P 34/1/4.
[74] Ibid. P 34/1/1–14.
[75] e.g. C.U.L., E.D.R., B 2/54; B 2/59A, f. 87v.
[76] *Orig. Rec. of Early Nonconf.* ed. Turner, i. 40.
[77] Compton Census.
[78] C.U.L., E.D.R., B 7/1, p. 119; C 1/4.
[79] G.R.O. Worship Returns, Ely dioc. nos. 271, 439; cf. C.U.L., E.D.R., C 1/6.
[80] *Gardner's Dir. Cambs.* (1851); H.O. 129/188/2/8/15; *Educ. Enquiry Abstract*, 52.
[81] R.G. 10/1592.

1877. It was perhaps amalgamated with the Independent chapel at Camps Green, which seems to have been founded in 1852 and built in 1856,[82] but later traced its origins to 1812 or 1817.[83] A house was given for the minister *c.* 1880. In 1897 a third of the population were said to be dissenters.[84] In 1916 the chapel had 350 sittings. Its adult membership had by then declined from 56 in 1899 to 31, and from the 1930s fluctuated around 30.[85] It was still open in 1974, when it was attached to the United Reformed Church.[86]

EDUCATION. There was an unlicensed schoolmaster at Castle Camps in 1579,[87] but no regular school was recorded before the 19th century, although 30 children were being taught in 1728.[88] A Sunday school held at the church by 1807[89] had 70 pupils in 1818. Benjamin Keene's wife Mary (d. 1823) in 1818 and Keene himself in 1836 supported a school for *c.* 26 girls, while the rector in 1818 maintained another girls' school which by 1833 also took paying pupils. A third school, started after 1825, was attended in 1833 by 28 boys.[90] Benjamin Keene by will proved 1838 left £300, which later yielded £9 a year, to maintain the church Sunday school.[91] In the 1960s an annual £7 10*s.* was still being paid to that Sunday school,[92] which had expired by 1974. In 1846 there were two day-schools supported by subscriptions and school-pence. A master taught one with *c.* 38 pupils, which had a £25 grant from the National Society, a mistress the other with *c.* 21 pupils. They probably combined to form a Sunday school with 120 pupils, attached to the National Society, and held in a building in the churchyard. In 1851 the day-school's average attendance was 60.[93] The pupils were mostly very young, for most parents sent their children to work at seven years old, and in the 1860s few adult parishioners of the labouring class could sign their names.[94] The rector was still financing the school in 1858.[95] In 1863 W. M. Collier of Camps Hall farm gave *c.* £50 to endow the day-school, which still received £1 a year from that source in the 1960s.[96]

In 1865 the school was reorganized as a Church of England mixed school, including an infants' department. With a building grant and gifts from the Charterhouse, a new schoolroom in Gothic style was completed at Camps Green in 1866, the old one being left for the Sunday school. There were then 96 pupils paying school-pence on the books,[97] and in 1877 120.[98] The average attendance, 73 in 1872, rose to 124 by 1888 and 153 by 1906.[99] The schoolroom was enlarged in 1876, and again in 1886 to accommodate 160 pupils, and a master's house was built in 1892.[1] In 1897 the school received a voluntary school-rate.[2] Attendance declined from 107 in 1914 to 75 by the 1930s.[3] In 1937 the older pupils were transferred to Linton village college, leaving 34 juniors.[4] The surviving junior day-school was taken over by the county council in 1960, and enlarged to take also the younger children from Shudy Camps.[5]

CHARITIES FOR THE POOR. Bartholomew Stavers by will dated 1784 left £100, the interest, £4 10*s.*, after maintaining his tomb, to be given to the poor in bread on 27 December. In 1837 it was all being distributed indiscriminately in small sums.[6] In 1895 an eighth of the capital was severed to form a distinct charity for repairing the tomb, and the remainder was managed, under a Scheme of 1936, with the other parish charities.

Sophia Elizabeth Keene by will proved 1856 left £100 for the rector, George Pearson, to distribute among 30 poor persons. He invested it to provide coal for the poor at Christmas, and added £100 of other benefactions for the same purpose. When Pearson died in 1860 he left for the poor £100, invested with £41 given anonymously. In 1890 it was ruled that Olmstead Green was not included in the area entitled to enjoy those charities. In 1918, owing to the scarcity and high price of coal, cash doles were given instead. In the 1960s the income, just over £11, was normally used to provide credit at local foodshops for old-age pensioners, but occasionally given in cash. The number of beneficiaries was reduced from 30 in 1965 to 16 after 1970.[7]

In 1954 Thomas Haylock of Moat farm settled on trustees a plot just east of Camps Green on which he built four bungalows, to be called Haylock's alms-houses, for disabled poor long resident or born at Castle Camps.[8]

[82] C.U.L., E.D.R., C 3/26; R.G. 9/1029; G.R.O. Worship Reg. nos. 9422, 23927; *Kelly's Dir. Cambs.* (1929); *Camb. Ind. Press*, 13 May 1960.
[83] e.g. *Cong. Yr. Bk.* (1875).
[84] C.U.L., E.D.R., C 3/36.
[85] *Cong. Yr. Bk.* (1899 and later edns.).
[86] Cf. G.R.O. Worship Reg. no. 23927.
[87] C.U.L., E.D.R., D 2/5, f. 159.
[88] Ibid. B 8/1.
[89] Ibid. C 1/4.
[90] *Educ. of Poor Digest*, 56; *Educ. Enquiry Abstract*, 52; C.U.L., E.D.R., C 1/6; C 3/21; cf. Burke, *Land. Gent.* (1933), 1275.
[91] Prob. 11/1889 (P.C.C. 33–4 Nicholl).
[92] *Char. Digest Cambs. 1863–4*, 12–13; Char. Com. files.
[93] *Church School Inquiry, 1846–7*, 2–3; cf. *Gardner's Dir. Cambs.* (1851); H.O. 107/1761.
[94] Cf. *1st Rep. Com. Employment in Agric.* 359–60.
[95] *Kelly's Dir. Cambs.* (1858–64).
[96] *Char. Digest Cambs. 1863–4*, 12–13; Char. Com. files.
[97] Ed. 7/5; C.R.O. 391/P 17.
[98] C.U.L., E.D.R., C 3/26.
[99] *Rep. Educ. Cttee. of Council, 1872–3*, [C. 812], p. 385, H.C. (1873), xxiv; ibid. *1888–9* [C. 5804-I], p. 531, H.C. (1889), xxix; *Pub. Elem. Schs. 1907* [Cd. 3901], p. 26, H.C. (1908), lxxxiv.
[1] *Kelly's Dir. Cambs.* (1879, 1888); *E.D.R.* (1892), 800.
[2] C.U.L., E.D.R., C 3/36.
[3] *Bd. of Educ., List 21, 1914* (H.M.S.O.), 26; *1922*, 15; *1932*, 16.
[4] Ibid. *1936*, 16; Black, *Cambs. Educ. Rec.*, 51.
[5] C.R.O., P 34/1/4; *Camb. Ind. Press*, 13 May 1960.
[6] *Char. Don.* i. 88–90; C.U.L., E.D.R., C 1/4; *31st Rep. Com. Char.* 104.
[7] *Char. Digest Cambs. 1863–4*, 12–13; Char. Com. files.
[8] Char. Com. files; *Camb. Ind. Press*, 13 May 1960.

SHUDY CAMPS

THE PARISH of Shudy Camps,[1] covering 2,362 a.,[2] lies 12 miles south-east of Cambridge. At its western end its southern boundary partly follows a brook and its northern one an ancient track leading towards Horseheath, but otherwise the boundaries mainly follow ancient field boundaries. The parish includes on the east the ancient hamlet of Nosterfield, which was originally more closely connected feudally and ecclesiastically with Castle Camps. The ground rises gradually from *c.* 225 ft. by the western stream to over 375 ft. at Mill Green, and after sinking to 325 ft. in a shallow depression, down which a watercourse flows from Nosterfield End into Horseheath, again reaches 375 ft. at the eastern boundary. The soil lies mainly upon boulder clay, overlying chalk, which is exposed at the western end. The heavy clay was once well wooded. In 1086 one manor included woodland for 12 pigs.[3] In the 13th century two woods nearly touching, Frakenho wood, held *c.* 1219 of Ely priory, and Northey wood, lay among the fields west of the village.[4] Part of Frakenho wood survived in 1586,[5] and Northey wood still covered *c.* 26 a. in 1841, when the parish contained *c.* 56 a. of woodland.[6] The Dayrells, lords of the manor, later felled much of Northey wood, and by 1936 only 10½ a. remained.[7] At Nosterfield Hatfield priory owned in 1279 38 a. of wood, called *c.* 1230 Goodwood,[8] standing in the south-eastern corner of the parish. It was still wooded in 1618 and covered 31½ a. in 1793,[9] but had probably been cleared by 1799.[10]

An Anglo-Saxon cemetery discovered in 1933, south-west of the village near the Castle Camps border, was probably of the early Christian period. It contained 148 burials, including 33 children, in two groups.[11] In 1086 there were 16 peasants and 6 *servi* on Robert Gernon's manor,[12] and in 1279 *c.* 40 men probably resident held land of the fees in Shudy Camps, and another 45 of the Nosterfield fees.[13] In 1327 28 people paid the subsidy,[14] and in 1377 141 adults were assessed to the poll tax.[15] There were 26 taxpayers in 1524,[16] and 30 households in the parish in 1563.[17] The population rose fairly quickly until *c.* 1600 and more slowly until 1700.[18] In 1676 there were 141 adults occupying *c.* 43 houses,[19] and in 1728 after a decline 200 people in 42 households.[20] The population rose again from *c.* 1750 and by 1801 there were 349 inhabitants in 59 families. After reaching a peak of 418 in 1831 numbers declined again, more sharply after 1851 because of emigration, to 322 in 1871. They recovered to 379 in 1891, but fell to 261 in 1921 and 240 in 1951. By 1971 the population had increased slightly to 283.[21]

Settlement in the parish probably originated in clearings in the woodland. The largest group of dwellings, surrounded by open fields which survived until inclosure *c.* 1862, lies along the village street towards the centre of the parish, and may not have been the oldest. In 1586 that road was called Newton, and in 1664 Nether, Street.[22] At its eastern end the houses stand almost entirely on the south side, and at its western end on the north. A smaller settlement, called in 1586 Rowhedge hamlet, apparently stood by Church field[23] close to the church and Lordship Farm near the southern boundary of the parish, and was probably identical with that later called Church End, where three or four houses survived east of the church in 1841.[24] The hamlet of Northo to the north-west probably existed by *c.* 1200,[25] and nominally survived *c.* 1800,[26] but by 1841 what was then called Northway had only two houses, one a gamekeeper's.[27] No buildings remained by 1950. A settlement by the Horseheath road at Mill Street, by 1664 renamed Mill Green, was recorded by 1493 and styled a hamlet in 1793.[28] The hamlet of Nosterfield was recorded indirectly in 1086, and directly by *c.* 1130.[29] The road there was called the new street in the early 13th century.[30] For many years the number of dwellings in the parish scarcely increased from *c.* 40 in the 1660s[31] being still only 41 in 1811.[32] The Dayrells are said to have removed several cottages when laying out Shudy Camps park after 1700.[33] New building brought the number of houses to 73 by 1831, and thenceforth it remained almost constant, varying between 68 and 77, until the 1950s.[34] In the mid 19th century there were *c.* 25 houses by the village street. Mill Green had 8 in 1841 and 10 by 1871, and Nosterfield End *c.* 10 in 1841 and 1871, besides farmsteads in the adjoining fields. There were also 6 dwellings, with up to 50 inhabitants, at Cardinals

1 This account was written in 1975. Neither the name of the parish, once called Little Camps by contrast with Great Camps to the south, nor that of Nosterfield hamlet have been fully explained: *P.N. Cambs.* (E.P.N.S.), 103–7.
2 *Census*, 1961.
3 *V.C.H. Cambs.* i. 381.
4 Cf. C.P. 25(1)/23/9 no. 22.
5 Charterho. Mun., MR 2/587, p. 238.
6 C.U.L., E.D.R., tithe award 1841.
7 Palmer and Fox, *Shudy Camps*, 27; C.R.O., R 57/16/1.
8 *Rot. Hund.* (Rec. Com.), ii. 428; B.L. Add. Ch. 28443.
9 Charterho. Mun., map of Castle Camps 1618; MR 2/419.
10 B.L. Maps, O.S.D. 146 (ii); cf. C.U.L., E.D.R., tithe award 1841.
11 *Proc. C.A.S.* 4to ser. N.S. v. 1–30.
12 *V.C.H. Cambs.* i. 381.
13 *Rot. Hund.* (Rec. Com.), ii. 427–9.
14 *Cambs. Lay Subsidy, 1327*, 25–6.
15 *East Anglian*, N.S. xii. 256.
16 E 179/81/134 m. 5.
17 B.L. Harl. MS. 594, f. 199v.
18 Cf. C.R.O., par. reg. TS.
19 Compton Census; cf. below, p. 280.
20 C.U.L., E.D.R., B 8/1.
21 *Census*, 1801–1971.
22 Charterho. Mun., MR 2/587, p. 365; MR 2/419; C.R.O., Nosterfield Priors ct. bk. 1656–1886, p. 9.
23 Charterho. Mun., MR 2/587, p. 456.
24 H.O. 107/66.
25 Cf. C.P. 25(1)/23/9 no. 22; *Rot. Hund.* (Rec. Com.), ii. 428.
26 Lysons, *Cambs.* 158–9.
27 H.O. 107/66.
28 B.L. Add. Ch. 25868; C.R.O., Nosterfield Priors ct. bk. 1656–1886, p. 9; Charterho. Mun., MR 2/419.
29 *V.C.H. Cambs.* i. 408; *Reg. Regum Anglo-Norm.* ii, p. 284.
30 B.L. Add. Ch. 28470.
31 See below, p. 279.
32 *Census*, 1811.
33 B.L. Add. MS. 5836, f. 222; cf. Charterho. Mun., MR 2/419.
34 *Census*, 1831–1951.

Green immediately adjoining Horseheath.[35] The land around the village was then, as in 1975, cultivated mainly from three farm-houses standing by the street and Lordship Farm near the church; further east the farm-houses, probably since the Middle Ages, have stood independently of the larger settlements, within their blocks of ancient inclosures.[36] Several timber-framed farm-houses such as Carter's Farm, are probably of 17th- or 18th-century origin. Some, such as Mill Green Farm, have been refaced, and have sash windows and classical doorcases. The cottages are mostly 19th-century. Even after the 1950s there was little new building, except for a few council houses and a group of more expensive houses called Parkway, built in 1972 in the south-west corner of the park.[37]

The village lay away from main roads, being linked to its neighbours by lanes winding through the fields. Its main street is said to have continued eastward towards Nosterfield until it was diverted north and south when the park was made.[38] The Cambridge–Haverhill railway line, opened in 1865 and entirely closed in 1967, ran across the centre of the parish.[39] The main village inn, the Three Horseshoes, established by 1793 in premises previously occupied for brewing,[40] was closed in 1969.[41] At Cardinals Green the Chequers inn was recorded from 1841 to *c.* 1910.[42] In 1960 the village had no clubs or societies, nor even a recreation ground.[43]

Some round, flat-topped mounds, up to 15 ft. high, resembling those at Bartlow, survived just south of Shudy Camps Park in the 1870s, but had been removed by 1900.[44]

MANORS AND OTHER ESTATES. In 1086 2 hides at Camps which Lepsi had held in 1066 under Earl Harold were held by Turstin of Robert Gernon.[45] The overlordship of that estate, later the main Shudy Camps manor, passed with Gernon's other lands after 1118 to William de Munfitchet, with whose barony it descended in the male line until his great-grandson Richard de Munfitchet died in 1267.[46] When Richard's estates were divided among his coheirs in 1274 the lordship over Shudy Camps was assigned to his sister Margery's granddaughter Alice Bolbec and her husband Walter of Huntercombe (d. 1313).[47] By *c.* 1300, however, it had been transferred to the descendants of Richard's other sister Philippa, who had married Hugh de Plaiz (d. 1244).[48] Joan, widow of Philippa's grandson Giles de Plaiz, received it as part of her dower in 1302.[49] In 1346 the manor was held of Giles's grandson Richard[50] (d. 1360), whose son John's daughter and heir Margaret (d. 1391) married Sir John Howard (d. 1438). Their granddaughter and eventual heir Elizabeth Howard married John, earl of Oxford (d. 1462),[51] and the overlordship thereafter descended with Castle Camps manor, to which the owners of Hanchetts manor and other estates in Shudy Camps owed quit-rents from the 15th century to the 18th.[52]

By 1166 the manor was held under the Munfitchets by Geoffrey of Camps,[53] who with his son William claimed Nosterfield manor in 1179 and died, probably after 1182.[54] His other son Geoffrey died under Richard I,[55] whereupon the estate mostly passed to Gillian, the elder Geoffrey's daughter.[56] Gillian married William of Knapwell, by whom she had a son Samson,[57] commonly called Samson Burre (fl. 1202–20).[58] In 1220 Gillian and Samson were sued for $\frac{1}{2}$ fee at Shudy Camps by Thomas de Capeles, who claimed as grandson of Gillian's sister Margery,[59] and possibly obtained a partition, for in 1236 and 1242 the fee was said to be held by William Burre, son of Samson, and his parceners.[60] William was probably alive in 1257[61] but dead by 1263 when the manor was held by Walter son of Samson Burre and Henry Hanchach,[62] who had succeeded his father Thomas in 1250,[63] and perhaps held the Capeles share.

By 1279 Henry Hanchach (d. after 1286) held the bulk of the manor, including 160 a. of demesne, as 1 knight's fee, while Walter Burre held $\frac{1}{2}$ knight's fee with only 40 a. in demesne under Henry.[64] Walter was probably dead by 1300. Of his land part went to Waltham abbey,[65] the rest being split among villagers. In 1346 fractions of a fee were held of Richard de Plaiz by four groups of people.[66] Henry Hanchach's son William held the main manor, later called *HANCHETTS*, in 1302 and owned Walter's 40 a. at his death in 1310. His son and heir Thomas, then aged 15,[67] held Hanchetts in 1316 and 1346,[68] and in 1365 settled land there then held by Agnes, widow of John Hanchach.[69] The descent of Hanchetts then becomes uncertain. In

[35] H.O. 107/66; R.G. 10/1592; cf. B.L. Maps, O.S.D. 146 (ii).
[36] Cf. C.U.L., E.D.R., tithe award 1841.
[37] *Camb. Evening News*, 7 Mar., 8 Dec. 1972.
[38] *Proc. C.A.S.* 4to ser. N.S. v. 34; cf. Palmer and Fox, *Shudy Camps*, 10.
[39] See p. 83.
[40] Charterho. Mun., MR 2/419.
[41] *Camb. Ind. Press*, 20 Nov. 1969.
[42] H.O. 107/66; *Kelly's Dir. Cambs.* (1904–8).
[43] *Camb. Ind. Press*, 13 May 1960.
[44] *Proc. C.A.S.* 4to ser. N.S. v. 35.
[45] *V.C.H. Cambs.* i. 381.
[46] For the descent, see ibid. v. 148; cf. *Red Bk. Exch.* (Rolls Ser.), i. 350; *Liber de Bernewelle*, 253.
[47] *Cal. Close*, 1272–9, 82; cf. *V.C.H. Cambs.* v. 148–9.
[48] For the Plaiz descent, see *Complete Peerage*, x. 535–41.
[49] *Cal. Inq. p.m.* v, p. 140.
[50] *Feud. Aids*, i. 162.
[51] *Complete Peerage*, x. 541–2.
[52] e.g. Charterho. Mun., MR 2/369A, 557A, 565C.
[53] *Red Bk. Exch.* (Rolls Ser.), i. 350.
[54] *Pipe R.* 1179 (P.R.S. xxviii), 34; 1182 (P.R.S. xxxi), 75.
[55] Cf. *Cur. Reg. R.* ix. 172.
[56] e.g. B.L. Cott. MS. Tib. C. ix, f. 130 and v.; cf. *Cur. Reg. R.* i. 1.
[57] e.g. B.L. Cott. MS. Tib. C. ix, f. 130v. To be distinguished from the Wm. of Knapwell, married to a Sarah, who released the advowson in 1219 in return for land at Camps and died by 1242: C.P. 25(1)/23/9 no. 6; *Liber de Bernewelle*, 253; C.P. 25(1)/24/15 no. 11; *Bk. of Fees*, ii. 919.
[58] Cf. *Cur. Reg. R.* ii. 134; iv. 26, 184, 236; viii. 51, 235.
[59] Ibid. viii. 378; ix. 372.
[60] *Liber de Bernewelle*, 253; *Bk. of Fees*, ii. 925; cf. B.L. Cott. MS. Tib. C. ix, f. 131v.
[61] *Cal. Pat.* 1247–58, 657.
[62] C 132/31/1 no. 6.
[63] *Ex. e Rot. Fin.* (Rec. Com.), ii. 225.
[64] *Rot. Hund.* (Rec. Com.), ii. 427; B.L. Add. MS. 5823, f. 230v.
[65] Cf. B.L. Cott. MS. Tib. C. ix, f. 131v.; *Cal. Pat.* 1292–1301, 557.
[66] *Feud. Aids*, i. 162.
[67] Ibid. i. 145; *Cal. Inq. p.m.* v, p. 140; *Cal. Fine R.* 1307–19, 79.
[68] *Feud. Aids*, i. 155, 162.
[69] C.P. 25(1)/29/82 no. 11. Apparently therefore distinct from the Thos. Hanchach killed at Castle Camps earlier in 1365: *Cambs. Village Doc.* 94; see also *Cal. Close*, 1377–81, 476; *East Anglian*, N.S. vi. 245–6.

1396 John Dowesdale was said to hold it,[70] and John Hanchach held ¼ fee in 1428[71] and 1450.[72] In 1514 James, son and heir of John Hanchach, released the estate to feoffees,[73] perhaps for Sir Richard Cholmeley, who held Hanchetts at his death in 1522. He entailed it on his brother Roger,[74] a Yorkshire landowner, knighted in 1535,[75] who died in 1538. Sir Roger's son and heir Richard, knighted in 1544,[76] sold Hanchetts in 1546 to John Bentley, of a local yeoman family,[77] who died in 1594.[78] His son John was succeeded in 1597 by his eldest son George[79] (d. 1635). George's son and heir George[80] died *c.* 1665[81] and in 1666 his son John Bentley and widow Mary were dealing with the estate.[82] John may have held part in 1684.[83] By 1700 Hanchetts was owned by Sir Marmaduke Dayrell,[84] whose elder brother Sir Francis (d. 1675) had devised an interest in Shudy Camps manor to him.[85] Sir Marmaduke was succeeded in 1730 by his son Francis[86] (d. 1760). Passing over his eldest son Brownlow (d. 1773), who became insane, Francis left his Shudy Camps estate to his son Marmaduke[87] (d. 1790), in whose time and that of his son Marmaduke (d. 1821)[88] the manorial rights of the other surviving manors were bought in. The last Marmaduke's eldest son Capt. Francis Dayrell died without issue in 1845 and was succeeded by his brother the Revd. Thomas Dayrell[89] (d. 1866). Of Thomas's sons the two eldest, Marmaduke Francis and Charles Lionel, died without issue in 1877 and 1890 respectively. Their next brother, the Revd. Richard Dayrell,[90] offered the debt-burdened estate for sale in 1898. It was bought by Arthur Gee, who took the name of Maitland[91] and died in 1903, whereupon it was again sold.[92] In 1904 Canon F. F. S. M. Thornton bought over 300 a. including the house and park, which after his death in 1938 were sold again in 1939, when the estate was broken up.[93] About 1905 another 160 a. of former Dayrell land had been acquired by G. F. Thornton, who sold them with *c.* 420 a. of other land in 1936.[94]

The site of the chief messuage of Hanchetts manor, recorded in 1279,[95] was empty in 1310.[96] It apparently lay in 1586 near Holm Mead field,[97] perhaps where the modern Lordship Farm stands. An inclosure further east, named Eldbury and by 1891 Elbrow,[98] may represent an earlier site. Shudy Camps Park, the seat of the Dayrells, was built by Sir Marmaduke Dayrell *c.* 1702,[99] and consists of a long narrow front range, later remodelled and heightened, and an irregular block at the back, reconstructed in the mid 19th century in Tudor style, with offices and stables to the south. By 1800 it was surrounded by a park covering in 1841 102 a.,[1] whose creation during the 18th century had led to many lawsuits with other landowners.[2] From the late 1860s the Dayrells usually let the house or left it empty.[3] The house and park were requisitioned during the Second World War and bought in 1949 by Mr. D. T. Wellstead,[4] who still owned them in 1975.

The estate of Waltham abbey (Essex), later *SHARDELOWES* manor, was mainly derived from the Camps family's manor. In 1226 the abbey appropriated the church, given it by Gillian of Camps, and held the 20 a. of glebe in 1279.[5] Gillian's son Moses, a clerk, gave the abbey 20 a. given him by his mother,[6] and by 1300 the abbey also had 11 a. owned *c.* 1290 by Walter Burre.[7] In 1279 it held 107 a., including 30 a. held of Henry Hanchach, 16 a. held of Sir William Mortimer, and 34 a. given by Walter Burre and his father.[8] The abbey in 1346 held fractions of the Hanchach fee,[9] which it exchanged in 1350 for two Essex manors with Sir John Shardelowe.[10] When Sir John died in 1359 his heir was his elder brother Edmund's son John, but he had already in 1354 conveyed his Shudy Camps lands to feoffees including his brother Sir Thomas,[11] who was still dealing with them in 1373 but had died by 1383.[12] The younger John died, having survived his son Thomas, in 1391,[13] whereupon his feoffees conveyed that estate in 1392 to his family foundation, St. Martin's college in Thompson church (Norf.).[14] The college retained the estate until its surrender to the Crown in 1540.[15] In 1541 its former lands were granted to Sir Edmund Knyvett,[16] who

70 C 143/413 no. 26.
71 *Feud. Aids*, i. 181.
72 Charterho. Mun., MR 2/557A, pt. ii, p. 4.
73 C.P. 25(2)/4/18 no. 19.
74 Prob. 11/20 (P.C.C. 22 Maynwaryng); C 142/38 no. 23.
75 *L. & P. Hen. VIII*, iii, p. 1114; viii, pp. 52, 84. To be distinguished from Sir Ric.'s illegitimate son, the judge Sir Roger Cholmeley (d. 1565): *D.N.B.*
76 *L. & P. Hen. VIII*, xiii (1), p. 347; xiv (1), p. 253; xix (1), p. 378.
77 C.P. 25(2)/4/22 no. 65.
78 Prob. 11/84 (P.C.C. 70 Dixy).
79 Wards 7/60 no. 65.
80 C 142/545 no. 84.
81 C.R.O., Nosterfield Priors ct. bk. 1656–1886, pp. 3, 8, 11.
82 C.P. 25(2)/633/18 Chas. II East. no. 3.
83 Charterho. Mun., MR 2/369A.
84 B.L. Add. MS. 5836, f. 221v.; Add. MS. 9412, f. 101v.; cf. Charterho. Mun., MR 2/419.
85 Prob. 11/348 (P.C.C. 64 Dykes).
86 Prob. 11/636 (P.C.C. 91 Auber).
87 Prob. 11/861 (P.C.C. 461 Lynch); cf. B.L. Add. MS. 5842, f. 195 and v.; mon. in ch.
88 C.R.O., par. reg. TS.; *Alum. Cantab. to 1751*, ii. 24–5; *1752–1900*, ii. 261.
89 Burke, *Land. Gent.* (1858), 288; cf. Charterho. Mun., MR 2/378; C.R.O., Shardelowes Alingtons ct. bk. 1727–1884, pp. 61–7; *Gardner's Dir. Cambs.* (1851).
90 Burke, *Land. Gent.* (1906), 444; *Kelly's Dir. Cambs.* 1858–88).
91 C.R.O., 296/SP 918, 1024; *Kelly's Dir. Cambs.* (1900).
92 *E.D.R.* (1903), 174; C.R.O., 296/SP 1024.
93 *Kelly's Dir. Cambs.* (1904–37); C.R.O., 515/SP 1673.
94 C.R.O., R 57/16/1.
95 *Rot. Hund.* (Rec. Com.), ii. 427.
96 *Cal. Inq. p.m.* v, p. 140.
97 Charterho. Mun., MR 2/587, pp. 232–3.
98 e.g. B.L. Cott. MS. Tib. C. ix, f. 131v.; C.R.O., 296/SP 918.
99 Inscr. on bldg.
1 C.U.L., E.D.R., tithe award 1841; cf. B.L. Maps, O.S.D. 146 (ii).
2 Palmer and Fox, *Shudy Camps*, 10.
3 e.g. *Kelly's Dir. Cambs.* (1869–88); cf. C.R.O., 296/SP 918.
4 *Camb. Ind. Press*, 13 May 1960; ex inf. Mr. Wellstead.
5 B.L. Cott. MS. Tib. C. ix, ff. 155–6; *Rot. Hund.* (Rec. Com.), ii. 427.
6 B.L. Cott. MS. Tib. C. ix, ff. 130–131v.
7 Ibid. f. 131v.; *Cal. Pat.* 1292–1301, 537.
8 *Rot. Hund.* (Rec. Com.), ii. 427–9.
9 *Feud. Aids*, i. 162.
10 B.L. Harl. MS. 3739, ff. 146–52v.; C 143/298 no. 1.
11 *Cal. Inq. p.m.* x, pp. 441–2; cf. ibid. viii, pp. 365–6.
12 E 42/70, 105, 153; *Cal. Pat.* 1381–5, 379.
13 Prob. 11/1 (P.C.C. 8 Rous); cf. *Cal. Pat.* 1385–9, 379.
14 C 143/413 no. 26; *Cal. Pat.* 1391–6, 109; cf. Blomefield, *Norf.* i. 458; ii. 366–8.
15 *L. & P. Hen. VIII*, xv, p. 413.
16 Ibid. xvi, p. 381.

immediately sold Shardelowes, said to include 300 a. of arable in Shudy Camps and Horseheath, to John Aleyn.[17]

In 1547 Aleyn sold the estate to the brothers John and Barnaby Mynott, half to each.[18] Barnaby settled his half, subsequently called *SHARDELOWES MYNOTTS*, on his son Edward in 1584 and died in 1599.[19] Edward (d. 1602) was succeeded by his son John, aged 11,[20] who died in 1630. His heir was his son Barnaby, but John's and Edward's widows held five-ninths of the estate as dower.[21] Barnaby probably died in 1680.[22] By 1682 his half had come to James Mynott,[23] who in 1702 released that and 90 a. more to Bridget, widow of James Reynolds (d. 1690).[24] Later it was acquired by Robert Bridge of Nosterfield End farm, who had continual lawsuits with the Dayrells, especially over sporting rights.[25] Bridge died in 1756, leaving that estate to his younger son Robert (d. 1770), who devised his lands to his daughter Elizabeth Sarah. In 1778 she married Edward Hussey,[26] whereupon the manor was settled on them.[27] In 1791 they sold it to one Rich, who resold it in 1801 to Marmaduke Dayrell (d. 1821).[28]

The other half, later called *SHARDELOWES ALINGTONS*, passed with *c.* 240 a., from John Mynott (d. 1589) to his son William,[29] who sold it in 1592 to John Disbrowe.[30] The latter died in 1610, having settled it on his second son Joseph,[31] who sold it after *c.* 1618 to Ambrose Andrews of Horseheath (d. 1625). Andrews's son and heir Ambrose[32] with Barnaby Mynott (d. 1680) released it in 1640 to William, later Lord Alington (d. 1648),[33] with whose Horseheath estate it descended for a time. In 1722 it passed, under a settlement of 1692, to Charles Seymour, duke of Somerset[34] (d. 1748), whose father had married Lord Alington's daughter Elizabeth.[35] The duke settled those Cambridgeshire lands in 1732 upon his daughters, and Shardelowes was assigned in 1762 to Charlotte (d. 1805), wife of Heneage Finch, earl of Aylesford (d. 1777).[36] Their son Heneage arranged to sell the estate in 1812, and 145 a. with the manorial rights were bought by Marmaduke Dayrell (d. 1821).[37] Shardelowes farmhouse, belonging to that half-manor, is timber-framed and plastered, with two gables facing south and a bulky central chimney-stack, and may date from before 1600.

By 1279, and perhaps by 1219, the prior of Ely held a manor at the hamlet called Northo, said to have been given long before by the eponymous, but probably legendary, lady Shudda.[38] By 1279 the whole fee, *c.* 90 a., had been granted at rent to sixteen free tenants.[39] The nominal manor was transferred in 1541 to the newly founded dean and chapter of Ely,[40] of whom John Bentley held a 34-acre farm in free socage in 1590.[41] Another part was by 1762 attached to Shardelowes Alingtons, with which 40 a. were sold in 1812.[42]

Much land between Northo and Shardelowes farm, amounting to 282 a. in 1841, belonged to Carbonells manor, later Cardinals farm, whose manor-house stood in a tongue of Horseheath projecting into Shudy Camps, and which from *c.* 1500 was included in the Horseheath estate. At inclosure in 1862 68 a. were allotted for its Shudy Camps open-field land to Stanlake Batson.[43]

The land of the estates treated above lay in the west and centre of the parish. Nosterfield to the east had probably lain outside Robert Gernon's manor. In 1086 Norman of Nosterfield held ½ hide at Camps of Aubrey de Vere (d. *c.* 1112),[44] and from the 12th century the Nosterfield fees were held of the earls of Oxford as mesne lords under the honor of Richmond.[45] Between 1128 and 1135 Henry I granted to Aubrey de Vere (d. 1141) land at Nosterfield formerly held by Geoffrey son of Alan under Richard Fitz Wimar, steward of that honor,[46] to which the Veres still in 1371 owed a £2 quit-rent.[47] The Vere lands there were gradually alienated. Probably in the 1190s the earl of Oxford gave a manor there to his sister Alice on her marriage *c.* 1195 to Geoffrey de Say.[48] On Geoffrey's death in 1214 that manor passed to their son, another Geoffrey, born by 1197,[49] who died between 1265 and 1271.[50] He had previously granted it in marriage to his daughter Maud, wife of Geoffrey de Crek, with whom Maud held 1 carucate there in 1272.[51] In 1279 as a widow she held 190 a. there in demesne.[52] By 1282 the estate has passed to Geoffrey's younger son, Robert de Say,

[17] C.P. 25(2)/4/21 no. 41.
[18] *Cal. Pat.* 1547–8, 49; cf. B.L. Add. MS. 5861, f. 25v.
[19] C 142/258 no. 54.
[20] Wards 7/38 no. 92.
[21] C 142/491 no. 15.
[22] C.R.O., par. reg. TS.
[23] C.P. 25(2)/634/33–4 Chas. II Hil. no. 7.
[24] C.P. 25(2)/910/1 Anne Mich. no. 13.
[25] Palmer, *Wm. Cole*, 111; cf. B.L. Add. MS. 5808, f. 53; Add. MS. 9412, f. 101 and v.
[26] Essex R.O., D/DO T 671; Charterho. Mun., MR 6/17, pp. 102, 169–71; MR 2/513A, B.
[27] C.P. 25(2)/1476/18 Geo. III Trin. no. 15.
[28] B.L. Add. MS. 9412, f. 103v.; cf. *Camb. Chron.* 19 Nov. 1791; C.R.O., Nosterfield Priors ct. bk. 1656–1886, pp. 94–5.
[29] C 142/220 no. 59.
[30] C.P. 25(2)/94/856/34 Eliz. I Hil. no. 2.
[31] Wards 7/34 no. 128.
[32] C.R.O., par. reg. TS.; Prob. 11/146 (P.C.C. 97 Clarke).
[33] C.P. 25(2)/401/16 Chas. I Mich. no. 7.
[34] C.R.O., Shardelowes Alingtons ct. bk. 1666–1718, ff. 6v.–10; 1727–1884, ff. 1–8; C.P. 25(2)/898/4 Wm. & Mary Trin. no. 11.
[35] *Complete Peerage*, i. 106–9; xii (1), 365–6.
[36] Ibid. i. 364–6; C.R.O., R 70/48, abstract of title, 1812; cf. C.P. 43/760 rott. 381–2.
[37] C.R.O., L 92/121; 346/T 18; cf. ibid. 297/SP 918.
[38] *Rot. Hund.* (Rec. Com.), ii. 428; cf. C.P. 25(1)/23/9 no. 22; probably acquired after 1154, since not mentioned in the *Liber Eliensis*.
[39] *Rot. Hund.* ii. 428.
[40] *L. & P. Hen. VIII*, xvi, p. 575.
[41] Wards 7/60 no. 65.
[42] B.L. Add. MS. 9412, f. 103; cf. C.R.O., 346/T 18.
[43] C.U.L., E.D.R., tithe award 1841; C.R.O., Q/RDc 80.
[44] *V.C.H. Cambs.* i. 408.
[45] Cf. *Rot. Hund.* (Rec. Com.), ii. 428–9.
[46] *Reg. Regum Anglo-Norm.* ii. p. 284; cf. *Early Yorks. Chart.* v (Y.A.S. extra ser. ii), 18–21.
[47] C 135/222 no. 15.
[48] *Rot. Hund.* (Rec. Com.), ii. 428, ascribing the gift anachronistically to Earl Robert, succ. 1214; cf. *Complete Peerage*, xi. 467–8; *Pleas before King's Justices*, iv (Selden Soc. lxxxiv), 132.
[49] *Cat. Anct. D.* ii, C 2287; iii, C 3188; *Rot. de Ob. et Fin.* (Rec. Com.), 527; *Rot. Litt. Claus.* (Rec. Com.), i. 124, 323; to be distinguished from his elder brother Geof. (d. 1230), lord of Linton; cf. Dugdale, *Mon.* iv. 151.
[50] *Cal. Chart. R.* 1257–1300, 52; cf. *Cal. Pat.* 1266–72, 545; *Rot. Hund.* (Rec. Com.), ii. 196.
[51] C.P. 25(1)/25/35 no. 57.
[52] *Rot. Hund.* ii. 428.

a clerk (d. after 1302), who in 1288 granted the reversion of 1 carucate there to Robert de Tiptoft for the latter's younger son Pain,[53] killed in 1314. Pain's minor son John held land at Nosterfield in 1325 and possibly in 1347.[54] In 1451 Thomas Tulyet conveyed *SAYSBEREWICK* manor, perhaps the same estate, with 112 a. partly in Castle and Shudy Camps, to Richard Bonyfaunt.[55] In 1511 Nicholas, son of Roger Bonyfaunt (d. 1494), sold that manor to Sir Richard Cholmeley,[56] whose nephew Sir Richard in 1546 sold a manor called *JAKS*, including a close called Says and held of the honor of Richmond, with 270 a. to Thomas Higham (d. 1561). Higham left Jaks with 180 a. of arable[57] to his widow Alice for life, with remainder to his son Robert, who eventually obtained Jaks, despite disputes with Alice's second husband Robert Baker between 1579 and 1593.[58] Jaks was sold in 1678 to Richard Reynolds, who owned it with 153 a. in 1702 and possibly in 1721.[59] Later it was absorbed into the farm belonging to the Bridge family, which had held land south of Nosterfield End of Castle Camps manor since the 16th century.[60] Robert Bridge (d. 1756) left it to his younger son Robert (d. 1770).[61] By 1806 it belonged to Thomas Bridge Little (d. 1835), son of Robert's elder brother John. In 1841 Thomas's nephew John Bridge owned the whole, as Nosterfield End farm of 220 a.[62] He died *c.* 1864 and his brother Capt. R. O. Bridge sold the land in 1874.[63] By 1891 it belonged to Daniel Gurteen of Haverhill.[64]

Another part of the former Say fee, *c.* 90 a., there and at West Wickham, was sold in 1296 by Robert de Say to William of Berardshay.[65] In 1279 William already held 53 a. at Nosterfield, including 24 a. held of Hatfield priory which had acquired that land from the prior of Ely, and 12 a. which Alice de Say had *c.* 1220 given to the nuns of Castle Hedingham (Essex) for their clothing.[66] About 1375 Geoffrey Hunden settled on Joan, widow of Adam Gatesbury, for her life 110 a. at Shudy Camps and West Wickham,[67] probably the estate called Barsy's, held *c.* 1450 of the Veres by the heirs of Richard Gatesbury (fl. 1347).[68] In 1534 Richard Braughing sold, perhaps to Philip Parys, manors there called *BERARDSHEYS* and *TUYS* with *c.* 220 a.,[69] from which presumably derived the Barsey farm covering *c.* 170 a. in the north-east corner of the parish owned in 1721 by James Reynolds,[70] serjeant-at-law, later chief baron of the Exchequer (d. 1739).[71] Reynolds devised the reversion to his nephew, also a judge, Sir James Reynolds of Olmstead Green[72] (d. 1747), who left the farm in reversion to his sister Isabella's son James Hatley.[73] James was presumably succeeded after *c.* 1770 by John Hatley (d. *c.* 1791)[74] and his Shudy Camps lands belonged in the 1820s to Capt. John Hatley who was succeeded *c.* 1830 by George Frere and James Hatley Frere (d. 1866), grandsons of James Hatley's sister Susanna.[75] In 1841 J. H. Frere owned Barsey farm of *c.* 130 a., while George had *c.* 170 a. further west, later Lower House farm.[76] George died in 1854. His son Bartle John Laurie Frere (d. 1893)[77] owned his part *c.* 1862, and had also bought Grange farm, *c.* 57 a.[78] By 1888 he also possessed Barsey farm.[79] Much of his property was acquired by Daniel Gurteen (d. 1894), a Haverhill clothing manufacturer. By 1891 Gurteen had also acquired Priory farm from the Dayrells, besides Nosterfield End farm and Carter's farm, *c.* 160 a. in the west part of the parish owned in 1841 and 1863 by Rebecca Carter. By 1900 the western part of his property belonged to Jabez Gurteen (d. 1924) of Halstead, while the eastern part, including Priory farm, was owned between 1903 and 1916 by W. B. Gurteen and in 1945 by D. M. Gurteen.[80] Mill Green farm had apparently belonged in 1721 to Richard Reynolds,[81] who had succeeded his father Richard in 1702 and died *c.* 1763 leaving his lands to his nephew James Raymond (d. *c.* 1785). The latter's son and successor, the Revd. John Raymond, had died by 1840, and John's son Henry A. Raymond by 1845. Henry's widow Anna[82] occupied the 250 a. estate in 1862. James Raymond (d. 1876) left it to Raymond Inglis.[83] By 1879 it belonged to Lt.-Gen. William Inglis (d. 1888), whose widow owned it until the 1910s.[84]

The other substantial estate at Nosterfield, later *NOSTERFIELD PRIORS*, derived from the gift of 1 carucate there, apparently by Robert de Vere (d. 1221), to Hatfield Broadoak priory (Essex).[85] His

53 *Cal. Inq. p.m.* ii, p. 220; C.P. 25(1)/26/43 no. 15; cf. *Cat. Anct.* D. iii, C 2447; B.L. Cott. MS. Tib. C. ix, f. 131v.

54 *Complete Peerage*, xii (2), 94–6; cf. *Cal. Pat.* 1324–7, 96; E 179/242/8 m. 10.

55 C.P. 25(1)/30/99 no. 5.

56 *Cal. Inq. p.m. Hen. VII*, i, pp. 421, 540; *Cambs. Fines*, 1485–1603, ed. Palmer, 27.

57 C.P. 25(2)/4/22 no. 67; C 142/134 no. 177; C 2/Eliz. I/H 6/53; cf. B.L. Add. Ch. 25865.

58 C 2/Eliz. I/H 6/53; Charterho. Mun., MR 2/587, p. 366; cf. C.P. 25(2)/94/858/36 Eliz. I Trin. no. 15; C 2/Jas. I/B 36/41.

59 Essex R.O., D/DB 946; C.R.O., L 86/85.

60 Cf. Charterho. Mun., MR 2/587, pp. 311–20, 367; ibid. map 1618.

61 See above; also Charterho. Mun., MR 2/565C.

62 *Camb. Chron.* 22 Feb. 1806; C.R.O., Nosterfield Priors ct. bk. 1656–1886, pp. 49, 67–8, 129–35; C.U.L., E.D.R., tithe award 1841.

63 C.R.O., Nosterfield Priors ct. bk. 1656–1886, pp. 196–9, 217–19; C.U.L., Maps 53(1)/87/50, 54, 57.

64 C.R.O., 296/SP 918.

65 C.P. 25(1)/26/43 no. 31; cf. B.L. Add. MS. 5823, f. 252.

66 *Rot. Hund.* (Rec. Com.), ii. 428–9; cf. B.L. Add. Ch. 28517.

67 C.P. 25(1)/788/50 no. 762.

68 Charterho. Mun., MR 2/557A pt. ii, p. 4; cf. E 179/242/8 m. 10.

69 C.P. 25(2)/51/270 no. 2; cf. Essex R.O., T/A 432, nos. 221–4.

70 C.R.O., L 86/85.

71 *D.N.B.*; Foss, *Judges of Eng.* viii. 160–2.

72 Prob. 11/695 (P.C.C. 89 Henchman).

73 Prob. 11/755 (P.C.C. 160 Potter); cf. *Trans. Essex Arch. Soc.* N.S. viii. 59.

74 C.U.L., MS. Plan 679; C.R.O., Shardelowes Alingtons ct. bk., 1727–1884, f. 29.

75 *31st Rep. Com. Char.* 107–8; cf. Burke, *Land. Gent.* (1871), 472–3; *D.N.B.* vii. 707–10.

76 C.U.L., E.D.R., tithe award 1841.

77 Burke, *Land. Gent.* (1952), 929–32.

78 C.R.O., Q/RDc 80; L 92/122–3; cf. 296/SP 918.

79 Cf. *Kelly's Dir. Cambs.* (1888–92).

80 C.R.O., 296/SP 918, 1024; 515/SP 1927; Nosterfield Priors ct. bk. 1895–1925, pp. 23–4; *Kelly's Dir. Cambs.* (1888–1937); cf. *Kelly's Dir. Suff.* (1900), 157, 159.

81 Cf. C 93/50/31; C.R.O., L 86/85.

82 C.U.L., MS. Plan 679; C.R.O., Nosterfield Priors ct. bk. 1656–1886, pp. 27, 45, 47, 72–4, 144–5, 170–1; ibid. R 70/48, 1 Mar. 1809; C.R.O., 346/T 18.

83 C.U.L., E.D.R., tithe award 1841; *Kelly's Dir. Cambs.* (1858); C.R.O., Q/RDc 80; ibid. Nosterfield Priors ct. bk., pp. 231–6.

84 *Kelly's Dir. Cambs.* (1879–1916); cf. *D.N.B.* s.v. Inglis, Sir Wm.

85 *Rot. Hund.* (Rec. Com.), ii. 428.

son and heir Hugh attempted to recover the land *c.* 1232, but confirmed it in free alms to the priory in 1235.[86] Having acquired over 35 a. from other donors,[87] the priory had in 1279 198 a., half the Nosterfield demesne.[88] Upon its surrender in 1536[89] the king granted the estate in 1538 to Charles Brandon, duke of Suffolk, who within a month had sold it to the London goldsmith Robert Trapps and his son Nicholas[90] (d. 1544). After Robert's death in 1560[91] the lands were divided in 1565 between Nicholas's daughters and coheirs, Nosterfield Priors being assigned to Mary (b. 1542) who married Giles Paulet, a younger son of William, marquess of Winchester.[92] Giles (d. 1579) was succeeded by his son William then aged 15,[93] who died in 1638, having settled that manor on his younger son Giles, who still held it in 1656.[94] It probably reverted to Giles's elder brother William or William's son Bernard (d. *c.* 1700)[95] for in 1704 it was settled on Edward Leigh, later Lord Leigh (d. 1738), and his wife Mary, whose mother Elizabeth Holbeach was Bernard's daughter and heir. It descended in turn to the Leighs' son Thomas, Lord Leigh (d. 1749), and grandson Edward, Lord Leigh,[96] who still owned it in 1764.[97] From 1767 the priory farm was briefly included in Lord Montfort's Horseheath estate,[98] and by 1779 had been sold to Marmaduke Dayrell (d. 1790).[99]

In 1166 William de Miniac held ⅛ knight's fee of the earl of Oxford.[1] Geoffrey de Miniac, who held it by 1209,[2] gave 9 a. *c.* 1220 to the Hospitallers of Shingay. Geoffrey's son William (fl. 1247) gave other land to Waltham abbey. William's son John held 107 a. in Nosterfield of the Veres in 1279, and died after *c.* 1300.[3] It may have been that fee which was held of the Veres by William le Harper of Horseheath *c.* 1333, by Thomas at Fen in 1346, by William Walkelate as ⅛ fee in 1360, by Thomas Messager in 1371, and John Hunt in 1401.[4] Between 1279 and 1429 20 a. in Shudy Camps and Horseheath held in chief by rent belonged successively to the Pantfield, Coleman, and Warner families.[5] Land east of Nosterfield End amounting to 63 a. in 1841 was then included in Queens' College's estate at Helions Bumpstead.[6] It had been sold by 1920.[7]

ECONOMIC HISTORY. On Turstin's 2 hides at Shudy Camps land for 2 plough-teams was kept in demesne in 1086, and there were 6 *servi* to help work it. The 8 *villani* had 4 teams between them, and there were 8 bordars. The value of the estate had doubled to £4 since 1066.[8] By 1279, on the manors representing that estate, *c.* 575 a. altogether, the lords' demesnes covered 212 a., including 200 a. of arable; Waltham abbey had 107 a., and the earl of Oxford 40 a. in demesne. Another 36 free tenements on the Hanchach and Burre fees, including only one over 11 a., amounted together to only 113 a., and 16 freeholders held the 90 a. of Northo hamlet. Apart from 4 cottagers owing harvest-boons, Henry Hanchach had only 2 customary tenants, one owing 9 harvest-boons for 3 a., the other 32 for 8 a., besides rents in kind. Walter Burre's 1 villein with 3½ a. owed 11 such boons, as did 3 cottagers. The Nosterfield fees had larger demesnes and slightly more customary land. Of 930 a. there the Say demesne accounted for 202 a., Hatfield priory's for 198 a., and John de Miniac's for 107 a. Maud de Crek's 2 half-yardlanders with 15 a. each had formerly rendered 1 work a week from Michaelmas to Whitsun and 2 thenceforth to Lammas, besides ploughing 4½ a. and reaping 8 a. in harvest. On the priory manor 3 half-yardlands of 16 a. owed exactly double those works. Compared with 94 a. in Nosterfield held in villeinage *c.* 275 a. were held freely. Six freeholders with over 25 a. each held together 240 a. out of 415 a. of freehold in the whole parish.[9]

By the 13th century the open-field land in the west part of the parish was different in character from Nosterfield, where land brought under cultivation by assarting ancient woodland was in modern times divided among inclosures held in severalty.[10] The 500 a. of open field, which showed in the 1790s no sign of ridge and furrow,[11] lay in three main blocks of 208 a., 125 a., and 188 a. Furthest west was Stanefield, recorded *c.* 1200,[12] and divided by 1586[13] into Further Stone field, of *c.* 115 a. in 1841, and Hither Stone field of 84 a. to the south. The latter adjoined to the east Manages (originally Manhedge), used as pasture by 1586.[14] The land of Northo hamlet, north-east of those fields and Northey wood, covering *c.* 145 a. in 1841, was probably inclosed early, being at least partly several in 1303.[15] Great Northway close of 20 a. was copyhold of Nosterfield manor in 1661.[16] By 1722 the area was

[86] *Close R.* 1231–4, 40; *Essex Feet of Fines* (Essex Arch. Soc.), i. 108.
[87] B.L. Add. Ch. 25876, 28373, 28443, 28445, 28450, 28455–6, 28470; C.P. 25(1)/24/14 no. 11; cf. *Close R.* 1231–4, 309.
[88] *Rot. Hund.* (Rec. Com.), ii. 428; cf. *Feud. Aids,* i. 140.
[89] Cf. S.C. 6/Hen. VIII/952 rot. 8.
[90] *L. & P. Hen. VIII,* xiii (2), p. 492; xiv (1), p. 75; cf. ibid. xv, p. 445.
[91] Prob. 11/30 (P.C.C. 15 Pynning); *Cal. Pat.* 1563–6, 403.
[92] C 142/71 no. 97; *Cal. Pat.* 1563–6, pp. 2, 192.
[93] C 142/189 no. 50; cf. C 146/10954.
[94] C 142/772 no. 132; C.R.O., Nosterfield Priors ct. bk. 1656–1886, p. 2.
[95] Cf. *Wilts. Visit. Pedigrees, 1623* (Harl. Soc. cv–cvi), 147–8; *V.C.H. Warws.* iv. 141.
[96] C.P. 25(2)/988/7 Anne Trin. no. 2; *Complete Peerage,* vii. 566–9.
[97] C.P. 43/724 rot. 395.
[98] C.R.O., Nosterfield Priors ct. bk. 1656–1886, pp. 55–66; cf. C.U.L., MS. Plan 679.
[99] Essex R.O., D/Db 1/T 5; C.P. 43/841 rott. 362–3; B.L. Add. MS. 9412, f. 103v.
[1] *Red Bk. Exch.* (Rolls Ser.), i. 353.
[2] Cf. *Pipe R.* 1209 (P.R.S. N.S. xxiv), 188.
[3] *Rot. Hund.* (Rec. Com.), ii. 428; B.L. Add. MS. 5823, ff. 225v., 245, 256v.
[4] C.P. 25(1)/28/67 no. 21; C.P. 25(1)/28/75 nos. 16, 24A; *Cal. Inq. p.m.* x, p. 513; xiii, p. 100; *Cal. Close,* 1399–1402, 252.
[5] *Rot. Hund.* (Rec. Com.), ii. 428; *Cal. Pat.* 1307–13, 159; C 143/75 no. 12; *Cal. Inq. p.m.* viii, pp. 242–3; xv, pp. 106–7; C 137/34 no. 2; C 139/37 no. 4.
[6] C.U.L., E.D.R., tithe award 1841; *Rep. Com. Univ. Income* [C. 856-II], p. 236, H.C. (1873), xxxvii (3).
[7] C.U.L., Maps 53(1)/92/38.
[8] *V.C.H. Cambs.* i. 381.
[9] *Rot. Hund.* (Rec. Com.), ii. 427–9; C 132/31/1 no. 6.
[10] The account of the layout is based on C.U.L., E.D.R., tithe award and map, 1841; cf. C.R.O., 124/P 37 (*c.* 1770); ibid. Q/RDc 80 (1863).
[11] Vancouver, *Agric. in Cambs.* 62.
[12] B.L. Cott. MS. Tib. C. ix, f. 130v.
[13] Cf. Charterho. Mun., MR 2/587, pp. 251–65.
[14] C.P. 25(1)/23/9 no. 22; Charterho. Mun., MR 2/587, p. 265; cf. *31st Rep. Com. Char.* 107–8.
[15] B.L. Cott. MS. Tib. C. ix, f. 131v.
[16] C.R.O., Nosterfield Priors ct. bk. 1656–1886, p. 8.

entirely inclosed, and *c.* 1770 was mostly included in Carbonells farm based in Horseheath.[17] Land called Stockings *c.* 1200 lay north-east of the common, suggesting that woodland had recently been cleared there.[18] From the 17th century the land there, covering in 1841 100 a., was called Carnells,[19] later Carnolds, field. Of Burnard,[20] later Burne, field to the east, still a common field in 1699,[21] only 25 a., entirely in severalty, were left by 1770. Further south across the village street three smaller fields surrounded a block of ancient inclosures called since 1200 Frakenho,[22] where some demesne wood of Hanchetts manor remained in 1586 and 1618.[23] In 1841 that block covered 36 a. Around it lay Frakenho field[24] (later Plumtree shot), Whitehill field, and Townsend field,[25] (together 60 a.) and further east Holm Mead,[26] later Home Meadow, field (45 a. in 1841) and Church field, so named by 1219[27] (61 a.). Among the open fields lay several permanent inclosures, such as Withy croft near Northey wood, and in 1841 *c.* 27 a. of the fields themselves were permanently under grass. The strip south of the later park, *c.* 50 a. in 1841, was probably already kept in severalty in the 13th century.[28] The northern part of the park had by 1770 absorbed Mill field, still a common field in 1664.[29]

From Shardelowes farm and Mill Green eastwards the land was, probably from the 13th century, permanently inclosed into small fields. A 5-a. plot near Nosterfield End was granted *c.* 1210 with all its hedges and ditches. Some closes there, however, were apparently divided in ownership.[30] About 1586 hedged crofts and closes, some of 5 a. or more, lay around Nosterfield End. One field to the north-east, Dunsey field,[31] was divided among different owners *c.* 1590 and in 1657.[32] Further north Barsey farm's 150 a. in the parish was likewise entirely inclosed in 1721.[33] In 1841 *c.* 1,130 a. in the east part of the parish were mostly divided among six farms: Shardelowes (98 a.), Grange (35 a.), and Mill Green farms (220 a.) lay along the road to Horseheath; further east, around Nosterfield End, lay Priory farm (240 a.) and John Bridge's farm (223 a.), and to the north Barsey farm (131 a.).[34]

About 200 a. of the parish were said to lie uncultivated in 1340.[35] On both the open fields and the inclosed farms the traditional triennial rotation, including a fallow, was still observed in the 1790s.[36] One man was growing saffron in 1545.[37] Later, wheat was probably grown in increasing quantities. In 1801 of 787 a. out of 1,100 a. of arable cultivated, 230 a. were sown with wheat, 225 a. with barley, 210 a. with rye, and 112 a. with peas and beans. Potatoes were grown on 1 a., turnips and rape seeds on 8 a.[38] In 1531 John Grant left his widow 6 milk-cattle and had cows going with herds in neighbouring parishes;[39] in 1560 John Wakefield left 36 sheep, besides lambs, and 3 cattle.[40] In 1347 Shudy Camps had contributed 46½ stone to a levy of wool, 14 stone of which came from the owners of five manors, while 40 other contributions ranged from 4 lb. to 2 stone.[41] In the 16th century the sheep-owners paid the shepherd of the common flock in proportion to the number they sent to it.[42] Hanchetts manor then included the right to keep 200 sheep on the common fields.[43] Shardelowes also enjoyed free common and chase throughout the vill, excluding the lord's several closes and meadows; the right was granted in 1303, when Waltham abbey had a sheep-fold for the rectory and another for the land once Walter Burre's.[44] At inclosure the Dayrells were entitled to 4 sheep-walks for 40 sheep each.[45] In 1794 there were 460 Norfolk sheep in the parish,[46] which in 1841 contained, besides the 102-a. park, *c.* 550 a. of grass, including *c.* 275 a. in the inclosed eastern part, compared with 1,699 a. of arable.[47]

By the 16th century the parish was already dominated by a few prosperous yeomen. Of the property assessed for tax in 1524 9 men had £99 between them, while 17 others had only £18. The three wealthiest inhabitants, Robert Higham, William Mynott, and John Grant or Bryant, had together £65.[48] Grant (d. 1531) left £160 in legacies and land in four parishes,[49] and in 1586 his grandson John Bryant (d. 1605) held *c.* 60 a. copyhold of Castle Camps manor in Shudy Camps.[50] In that year one Nosterfield property included 62 a. of closes.[51] In the early 18th century the Dayrells bought much land from such local families as the Bryants, Mynotts, Challises, and Lindsells,[52] and emerged as the largest landowners in the parish, owning in 1841 *c.* 820 a. besides the park. Their land was divided among three substantial tenants. The Horseheath estate had 275 a., the Raymonds 251 a., John Bridge 243 a., George Frere 171 a., J. H. Frere 131 a., and Rebecca Carter 162 a. Of 124 a. owned by ten others, three men had together 102 a. Some 512 a. then remained in open fields.[53] Inclosure was effected, as at Castle Camps and Bartlow, under an order of 1858. Of 588 a. allotted in Shudy Camps,

17 Ibid. P 34/3/3; C.U.L., MS. Plan 679.
18 B.L. Cott. MS. Tib. C. ix, f. 130; cf. C 93/50/31.
19 e.g. C.U.L., E.D.R., H 1/2, list of Castle Camps tithes, 17th cent.
20 C 93/50/31.
21 Ibid.
22 B.L. Cott. MS. Tib. C. ix, ff. 130, 131v.
23 Charterho. Mun., MR 2/587, pp. 235–50, especially p. 238; map of Castle Camps 1618.
24 Ibid. MR 2/587, pp. 464–5.
25 Ibid. pp. 266–7.
26 B.L. Cott. MS. Tib. C. ix, f. 130.
27 C.P. 25(1)/23/9 no. 22.
28 B.L. Cott. MS. Tib. C. ix, f. 131 and v.
29 C.R.O., Nosterfield Priors ct. bk. 1656–1886, pp. 9–10; ibid. 124/P 37.
30 e.g. B.L. Add. Ch. 25876, 28373, 28443.
31 Charterho. Mun., MR 2/587, pp. 311–21; cf. C.U.L., Maps 53(1)/87/50.
32 C 2/Eliz. I/H 6/53; C.R.O., Nosterfield Priors ct. bk. 1656–1886, pp. 4–7.
33 C.R.O., L 86/85.
34 C.U.L., E.D.R., tithe award 1841: areas given here exclude open-field land.
35 *Inq. Non.* (Rec. Com.), 215.
36 Vancouver, *Agric. in Cambs.* 61.
37 B.L. Add. MS. 5861, f. 25v.
38 H.O. 67/9.
39 Prob. 11/24 (P.C.C. 13 Thower).
40 Prob. 11/43 (P.C.C. 11 Mellershe).
41 E 179/242/8 m. 10.
42 Prob. 11/84 (P.C.C. 70 Dixy, will of John Bentley).
43 Wards 7/60 no. 65.
44 B.L. Cott. MS. Tib. C. ix, f. 131v.
45 C.R.O., Q/RDc 80.
46 Vancouver, *Agric. in Cambs.* 62.
47 C.U.L., E.D.R., tithe award 1841.
48 E 179/81/134 m. 5; cf. *L. & P. Hen. VIII*, iii, p. 1118.
49 Prob. 11/24 (P.C.C. 13 Thower).
50 Charterho. Mun., MR 2/587, pp. 459–66; cf. Prob. 11/106 (P.C.C. 7 Hayes).
51 Charterho. Mun., MR 2/587, pp. 315–20.
52 Ibid. MR 2/419.
53 C.U.L., E.D.R., tithe award 1841.

including 75 a. of old inclosures, Thomas Dayrell received 322 a., B. J. L. Frere 167 a., and four others between 4 a. and 88 a. No allotments were made to any smallholders.[54] The sale of Shardelowes and Priory farms *c.* 1891 reduced the Dayrell estate to *c.* 530 a.[55] and further sales had cut it to 145 a. besides the park by 1939.[56] By the 1890s most of the other farms belonged to the Gurteens of Haverhill,[57] although Street, Carter's, and Lower House farms were acquired by G. F. Thornton.[58] Except on the Dayrell estate, most properties had been let to single tenants; in 1841 there were 11 farms of over 100 a., covering 1,486 a., and in 1871 8, covering 1,190 a.[59] There were still 4 substantial farms in the west part of the parish, 4 in the centre, and 3 at the east end in the 20th century, when some were owned by their occupiers.[60] In 1905 there were 1,843 a. of arable and 450 a. of grass.[61]

Emigration reduced the number of farm-labourers living in the parish from 103 *c.* 1830 to *c.* 70 in 1851, about the number for whom there was employment.[62] In the 1860s the women did 'slop-work', making up garments for the Gurteen clothing-works at Haverhill.[63] About 1900 4½ a. of the Shudy Camps estate were let as allotments.[64] There was little non-agricultural work. In 1831 67 families depended on farming and only 7 on crafts and trade,[65] and from *c.* 1850 the only artisans recorded were two shoemakers, a carpenter, and a blacksmith.[66] Of two or three village shops only one was open in 1975. A chicken-hatchery was started after 1949 in buildings in the park, employing 20 people and producing ¾ million chicks a year. It closed after 1969.[67]

Thurstan's mill at Nosterfield, recorded *c.* 1220, was probably still there in 1324.[68] In 1279 a windmill had lately been built on Samson of Frakenho's land, held of the Hanchach fee.[69] Another mill gave its name to Mill field and Mill Street, later Mill Green.[70] The Dayrell estate included a windmill, in use until after 1880, standing just west of Lordship farm-house, with which it was usually let.[71] By 1903 a post-mill and steam-mill, temporarily let separately from the farm, were working there, as was the steam-mill from 1908 to *c.* 1920.[72] The stump of the post-mill survived in 1939.[73]

LOCAL GOVERNMENT. In 1235 the prior of Hatfield agreed that his tenants at Nosterfield should attend the earl of Oxford's view of frankpledge at Castle Camps once a year, although the prior was to take any penalties laid on them.[74] After 1558 men from Nosterfield were still attending a view of frankpledge held for their hamlet by the Veres and their successors,[75] mainly concerned with drains and watercourses.[76] By 1592 business other than tenurial had become purely formal, and only the payment of a common fine, itself ceasing by 1625, remained as a relic of the former dependence.[77]

In 1299 the abbot of Waltham successfully alleged that he and his predecessors had enjoyed view of frankpledge with the assize of bread and of ale at Shudy Camps as at Babraham.[78] In 18th-century conveyances view of frankpledge and other royalties were occasionally ascribed to Nosterfield Priors manor,[79] but the court was described as a court baron,[80] as was that held *c.* 1590 for Shardelowes Alingtons.[81] Court books almost entirely concerned with copyhold transfers survive for Nosterfield for 1656–1925 and Shardelowes Alingtons for 1666–1885,[82] as did some for Shardelowes Mynotts in 1808.[83] A parish constable was mentioned in 1620;[84] pinders were still appointed in 1795 and 1824.[85]

Between 1776 and *c.* 1785 the cost of poor-relief doubled from £71 to £152. In 1803 23 people[86] and *c.* 1813 over 30 were on permanent relief. Expenditure on the poor fell from £652 *c.* 1813[87] to between £350 and £475 in the years up to 1830,[88] after which it again rose to over £500.[89] Unemployed labourers were then being apportioned among the farmers, while special allowances were given for large families.[90] In 1835 the parish was incorporated into the Linton poor-law union,[91] was transferred with the Linton R.D. in 1934 to the South Cambridgeshire R.D.,[92] and in 1974 was included in South Cambridgeshire.

CHURCH. Shudy Camps had a church by *c.* 1200, but the rights to tithe of its incumbent did not cover the whole parish. When the earls of Oxford gave a carucate at Nosterfield to Hatfield priory they also apparently gave the tithe due from it, for the priory enjoyed a portion worth 8 marks in 1254 and 1291.[93] In 1259 it bought out a claim to 1 mark a year from those tithes which the Veres had previously granted

[54] Second Annual Incl. Act, 1858, 21–2 Vic. c. 61; *Special Rep. of Incl. Com.* H.C. 2049, pp. 171–3 (1857–8), xxiv; C.R.O., Q/RDc 80.
[55] C.R.O., 296/SP 918, 1024.
[56] Ibid. 515/SP 1673.
[57] See p. 53.
[58] C.R.O., R 57/16/1.
[59] C.U.L., E.D.R., tithe award 1841; R.G. 10/1592.
[60] *Kelly's Dir. Cambs.* (1859–1937); cf. C.R.O., 515/SP 1375, 1884, 1927, 2434.
[61] Cambs. Agric. Returns, 1905.
[62] *Rep. H.L. Cttee. on Poor Laws*, H.C. 227, pp. 326–7 (1831), viii; H.O. 107/1761; R.G. 10/1592.
[63] *1st Rep. Com. Employment in Agric.* 359; cf. *White's Dir. Suff.* (1864), 492–3.
[64] C.R.O. 296/SP 1024.
[65] *Census*, 1831.
[66] *Kelly's Dir. Cambs.* (1858–1937).
[67] *Camb. Ind. Press*, 13 May 1960; 20 Nov. 1969; ex inf. Mr. D. T. Wellstead.
[68] B.L. Add. Ch. 28393; Hist. MSS. Com. 6, *7th Rep.* p. 581.
[69] *Rot. Hund.* (Rec. Com.), ii. 427.
[70] Cf. B.L. Add. Ch. 25868; and see above.
[71] *Kelly's Dir. Cambs.* (1858–83).
[72] Ibid. (1904); C.R.O., 296/SP 1024; *Kelly's Dir. Cambs.* (1908–22).
[73] *Proc. C.A.S.* xxxi. 27; C.R.O., 515/SP 1673.
[74] *Essex Feet of Fines* (Essex Arch. Soc.), i. 108.
[75] Charterho. Mun., MR 2/217, ct. rolls 1–4 Eliz. I and later.
[76] e.g. ibid. ct. rolls 15, 17, 27 Eliz. I.
[77] Ibid. ct. roll 34 Eliz. I; MR 2/219, ct. roll 13 Jas. I; MR 2/221, ct. roll 1 Chas. I.
[78] *Plac. de Quo Warr.* (Rec. Com.), 106–7.
[79] e.g. C.P. 25(2)/988/7 Anne Trin. no. 2; C.P. 43/724 rot. 395.
[80] Essex R.O., D/Db 1/T 5.
[81] Req. 2/33/122.
[82] In C.R.O., uncatalogued.
[83] B.L. Add. MS. 9412, f. 103.
[84] Sta. Cha. 8/286/4.
[85] C.R.O., Nosterfield Priors ct. bk. 1656–1886, pp. 93, 113.
[86] *Poor Law Abstract, 1804*, 34–5.
[87] Ibid. *1818*, 28–9.
[88] *Poor Rate Returns, 1816–21*, 10; *1822–4*, 37; *1825–9*, 15–16.
[89] Ibid. *1830–4*, 15.
[90] *Rep. H.L. Cttee. on Poor Laws*, H.C. 227, pp. 326–7 (1831), viii.
[91] *Poor Law Com. 1st Rep.* 249.
[92] *Census*, 1931 (pt. ii).
[93] *Val. of Norwich*, ed. Lunt, 227; cf. *Tax. Eccl.* (Rec. Com.), 267, 270.

to St. Nicholas's abbey, Angers (Maine-et-Loire).[94] The priors and their successors at Nosterfield Priors took for themselves the tithes not only of their demesne but also of the copyholds held of them.[95] The rectors of Castle Camps and Horseheath received tithe from land in Shudy Camps, in 1841 from *c.* 30 a. each, while 15 a. on the boundary tithed to Withersfield (Suff.).[96] By the 18th century Barsey farm's 142 a., also in Nosterfield, was exempt from tithes by prescription.[97] Shudy Camps church may originally have received tithe mainly from the land of its founders and patrons. About 1215 their heiress, Gillian of Camps, gave the church to Waltham abbey.[98] In 1219, after William of Knapwell, probably Gillian's stepson, had claimed to present, she bought out his claims for the abbey,[99] which in 1225 appropriated the church. The bishop ordained a vicarage, to which the abbey was to present.[1] Waltham abbey retained the rectory, with the glebe, tithes of corn and hay, and advowson, until its dissolution in 1540.[2] In 1534 it had granted one turn to present, exercised in 1538, to its lessee Sir Giles Alington,[3] who in 1543 purchased the rectory and advowson from two men who had just acquired them from the Crown.[4] In 1546 Alington sold them to Sir Thomas Darcy, who returned them to the Crown, to be included the same year in the endowment of Trinity College, Cambridge.[5] The college retained the impropriate rectory, with a glebe of 5 a. in 1663 and 4 a. in 1841,[6] until 1912. It sold the advowson then to Canon F. F. M. S. Thornton, and the glebe soon after.[7] Canon Thornton died in 1938, leaving the advowson to the bishop of Ely, patron in 1975.[8]

Under the ordination of 1225 the vicar was to have the offerings and small tithes, a suitable house, and the crops grown on 4 a. of the glebe, half wheat, half oats.[9] He retained those rights in the 17th century. By 1740 his crops had been commuted for £4 a year from the rectory. He also claimed two pensions of 5*s.* a year from Priory and Shardelowes Mynotts farms, in lieu of all tithes.[10] His only glebe was a 1-acre close surrounding his house, south of the church.[11] About 1780 the tithes were mostly taken by composition but *c.* 1795 were mostly collected in kind.[12] They were commuted in 1841. Of 2,472 a. in the parish only 1,936 a. were tithable by the impropriator and vicar, to whom £295 8*s.* and £175 12*s.* respectively of tithe-rent-charge were allotted.[13] In 1887 the vicar had 2 a. of glebe by his house.[14] The house, in decay in 1600[15] and supposedly rebuilt by John Sparrow, vicar 1601–49,[16] had only three hearths in the 1660s,[17] and in 1783 was reckoned a mere cottage.[18] About 1836 it was repaired so as to be habitable for a bachelor.[19] Later, probably by 1873, it was rebuilt in grey brick with a grant from Queen Anne's Bounty.[20] It was sold in 1969 to the Quakers, who renamed it Glebe House and used it as a training centre for adolescents. A new and smaller vicarage-house was built north of the church.[21]

The rectory was worth 20 marks in 1217.[22] The vicar had only £9 gross in 1535[23] and £25 in 1650.[24] By 1728 his income was £70, but *c.* 1778 only £63.[25] It stood at £146 *c.* 1830,[26] and had not apparently risen by 1851,[27] despite the tithe commutation and a gift of £200 from Queen Anne's Bounty in 1838 to match £600 given by the Revd. Charles and Mrs. Perry, relatives of the then vicar.[28] It rose to £170 net in 1873.[29]

About 1230 Sir William of Knapwell with the consent of the diocesan and the abbot of Waltham established a chapel in the parish, probably at his house.[30] By 1486 there was a guild of St. Catherine,[31] whose probable guildhall was sold for the Crown in 1571.[32]

In 1264 the rebels from the Isle of Ely captured the vicar and made him pay £2 ransom.[33] In 1462 the bishop rejected Waltham abbey's nominee and appointed Mr. John Petyt, who held the cure until 1497,[34] but had three successors within two years.[35] In the early 16th century the vicars occasionally employed curates.[36] John Sturges, vicar from 1538, ran after his parishioners' wives, and failed in 1550 to preach more than twice a year. His successor in 1561 was equally remiss in preaching.[37]

In 1578 Trinity College began to name its past fellows or students to the living, but few would stay there long, seven successive vicars resigning between 1578 and 1590.[38] John Sparrow, presented in 1601, was in 1638 using a catechism of which Bishop Wren

[94] B.L. Add. Ch. 28416.
[95] e.g. C.P. 25(2)/988/7 Anne Trin. no. 2; Charterho. Mun., MR 2/419; C.U.L., E.D.R., tithe award 1841.
[96] C.U.L., E.D.R., tithe award 1841.
[97] Ibid.; cf. B.L. Add. MS. 5863, f. 221v.
[98] B.L. Cott. MS. Tib. C. ix, f. 154v.
[99] C.P. 25(1)/23/9 no. 6.
[1] B.L. Cott. MS. Tib. C. ix, f. 155.
[2] Cf. Dugdale, *Mon.* vi. 68.
[3] *E.D.R.* (1912), 20; S.C. 6/Hen. VIII/964 rot. 126.
[4] *L. & P. Hen. VIII*, xviii (1), pp. 132, 135–6.
[5] Ibid. xxi (1), pp. 489, 764; xxi (2), p. 342.
[6] C.U.L., E.D.R., H 1/2, terriers 1638, 1663; tithe award 1841.
[7] Ex inf. Miss P. Bradford, college archive cataloguer.
[8] C.U.L., E.D.R., G 3/23B, pp. 116–17; *Crockford* (1973–4).
[9] B.L. Cott. MS. Tib. C. ix, f. 155.
[10] C.U.L., E.D.R., H 1/2, terrier 1740; cf. B.L. Add. MS. 5836, f. 221.
[11] C.U.L., E.D.R., H 1/2, terriers 1638, 1663.
[12] B.L. Add. MS. 5836, f. 222v.; Vancouver, *Agric. in Cambs.* 62.
[13] C.U.L., E.D.R., tithe award 1841.
[14] *Glebe Returns*, H.C. 307, p. 41 (1887), lxiv.
[15] C.U.L., E.D.R., B 2/18, f. 21v.
[16] Palmer, *Wm. Cole*, 110.
[17] E 179/244/22 ff. 115v.–116.
[18] C.U.L., E.D.R., B 7/1, p. 120.
[19] Ibid. C 3/21.
[20] Ibid. C 3/25.
[21] *Camb. Ind. Press*, 20 Nov. 1969; ex inf. Mr. F. Harwood, sequestrator.
[22] *Val. of Norwich*, ed. Lunt, 536.
[23] *Valor Eccl.* (Rec. Com.), iii. 504.
[24] Lamb. Pal. MS. 904, f. 272.
[25] C.U.L., E.D.R., B 8/1; B.L. Add. MS. 5836, f. 222.
[26] *Rep. Com. Eccl. Revenues*, pp. 352–3.
[27] H.O. 129/188/2/9/8.
[28] Hodgson, *Queen Anne's Bounty* (1863), pp. ccxxiv, cclxxviii.
[29] C.U.L., E.D.R., C 3/25.
[30] B.L. Cott. MS. Tib. C. ix, f. 155.
[31] *Trans. C.H.A.S.* i. 397; cf. Prob. 11/11 (P.C.C. 1 Horne, will of John Claydon).
[32] *Cal. Pat.* 1569–72, 404.
[33] J.I. 1/83 rot. 32.
[34] *E.D.R.* (1905), 62; (1909), 61; Emden, *Biog. Reg. Univ. Camb.* 452.
[35] *E.D.R.* (1909), 61, 74.
[36] e.g. B.L. Add. MS. 5861, ff. 20, 99.
[37] C.U.L., E.D.R., B 2/3, p. 80; B.L. Add. MS. 5813, f. 86; *E.D.R.* (1912), 19.
[38] *E.D.R.* (1914), 378–9; Gibbons, *Ely Episc. Rec.* 436, 440, 444, 446.

disapproved,[39] and retained the cure until his death in 1649, assisted in his old age by a curate.[40] His successor, John Wignold or Martin, not a Trinity man, was described as a preaching minister in 1650,[41] but retained the vicarage, having been ordained in 1661, until he died in 1685.[42] Thereafter it was again occupied by Trinity men, and from 1742 by ex-fellows.[43] Abraham Okes, vicar 1711–42, held it in plurality with Haverhill from 1718 to 1723 and thereafter with Withersfield rectory,[44] where he lived. In 1728 he employed a neighbouring vicar as his curate. There was then only one Sunday service, and communions, with *c.* 15 attending regularly, were held four times a year.[45] Between 1752 and 1792 there were eleven changes of incumbent. Some vicars lived at Cambridge and employed curates,[46] as did John Hailstone, vicar 1798–1818, and Woodwardian Professor of Geology (d. 1847). Adam Sidgwick, the next professor, also succeeded him as vicar in 1824.[47] The curates between 1776 and 1825 usually held only one Sunday service, alternately in the morning and afternoon, and communion thrice yearly. Only 8 or 9 attended communion in 1807, *c.* 25 in 1825.[48] The next vicar John Hailstone (d. 1871) came to reside in 1834, started a Sunday school, and held two Sunday services,[49] as did his successor George Perry, vicar 1838–58. In 1851 Perry had an average attendance of 140, besides 60 Sunday-school children,[50] and although resident employed a curate.[51] William Joy, vicar 1863–98, had 282 church-goers including 34 communicants in 1873, when he held monthly communions.[52] By 1897 church-going was declining.[53] After Joy died, aged 80, in 1898, clergymen became reluctant to hold the living, mainly because it was poor. They resigned after three or four years, or withdrew even before induction.[54] The vicarage was vacant from 1911 to 1913,[55] the next vicar resigned in 1916, and in 1919 Canon Thornton, the patron, himself had to take on the incumbency.[56] After his death the living was held from 1939 by the rector of Bartlow, who retained it after moving to Castle Camps rectory, with which Shudy Camps vicarage was held from 1945, the parishes remaining separate.[57]

The church of *ST. MARY*, so called from *c.* 1200,[58] consists of a chancel, nave with south porch, and west tower, and is built of field stones with ashlar dressings, much patched in brick and covered with ivy and peeling 19th-century cement. Fragments of 12th-century carvings have been re-used in the walls, and the south doorway of the chancel is probably 13th-century. That of the nave, perhaps 14th-century, retains the original door under modern boarding, and the porch has medieval roof-beams. The three-storey tower, its upper portion mostly rebuilt in brick though including the earlier belfry windows, has a 14th-century west window, in whose spandrels are carved much-worn figures of the Virgin and Child and of a knight. The nave was apparently widened to the south in the 15th century, leaving the chancel off-centre. Its three-light windows, the western pair renewed, have complicated tracery. The chancel and chancel arch date from later in that century, as do the three-light windows under depressed arches. The plain nave roof is probably of *c.* 1500. In 1496 money was left for building 'the new house of the church'.[59]

William Dowsing destroyed 7 superstitious pictures in 1644.[60] The impropriators and their farmers usually neglected to repair the chancel from the 16th century,[61] and by 1665 its south windows were blocked up, no window being visible there in 1742 or later.[62] In 1703 Sir Marmaduke Dayrell renewed the interior of the chancel, installing a new partition, pulpit, and desk and repairing its ceiling.[63] Then or later its exterior walling was mostly renewed, except for the ashlar, in brick. About 1774 Marmaduke Dayrell installed in the chancel elaborate monuments by Thomas Carter, with urns, obelisks, pilasters, cherubs, and garlands, to his parents Francis and Elizabeth, and a tablet to his brother Brownlow.[64] From that period the church was usually in decent repair.[65] In the 19th century Mrs. Dayrell removed the screen without consulting the vicar or parishioners.[66] A gallery at the west end was still there in 1873,[67] but restoration began in 1870 and, after ceasing for lack of funds in 1879, was completed in 1895 with Pertwee and Hast as architects.[68]

The plate included two chalices *c.* 1275,[69] and two, one silver, one double gilt, in 1552.[70] Dr. James Johnson, chancellor of Ely, gave in 1713 a silver cup and cover,[71] which the church still possessed in 1960.[72]

In 1531 John Grant left £20 to make a new bell.[73] The tower contained four bells in 1552,[74] five in 1742 and later:[75] they are one each of 1621 and 1699, two of 1719 by John Thornton of Sudbury, and one of 1840 by Thomas Mears of London.[76] In 1975

[39] *Alum. Cantab. to 1751*, iv. 128; *Cambs. Village Doc.* 71.
[40] Prob. 11/210 (P.C.C. 155 Fairfax).
[41] *Alum. Cantab. to 1751*, iv. 404; Lamb. Pal. MS. 904, f. 272.
[42] C.U.L., E.D.R., B 2/58, 67.
[43] Cf. *Alum. Cantab. to 1751*, i. 18.
[44] Ibid. iii. 273.
[45] C.U.L., E.D.R., B 8/1.
[46] *Alum. Cantab. to 1751*, *1752–1900*; cf. C.U.L., E.D.R., C 1/1; B 8/4.
[47] *Alum. Cantab. 1752–1900*, iii. 190; v. 456; *D.N.B.*
[48] C.U.L., E.D.R., C 1/1, 4, 6.
[49] Ibid. C 3/21.
[50] *Alum. Cantab. 1752–1900*, v. 97; H.O. 129/188/2/9/8.
[51] C.U.L., E.D.R., B 1/16.
[52] Ibid. C 3/21, 25.
[53] Ibid. C 3/36.
[54] *E.D.R.* (1898), 111; (1901), 127, 183, 205; (1902), 185, 223; (1905), 230.
[55] Ibid. (1911), 34–5, 117; (1912), 52, 72, 110; *Alum. Cantab. 1752–1900*, v. 97.
[56] *Clergy List* (1915); *Crockford* (1926).
[57] *Crockford* (1940 and later edns.).
[58] B.L. Cott. MS. Tib. C. ix, f. 154v.
[59] Prob. 11/11 (P.C.C. 1 Horne, will of John Claydon).
[60] *Trans. C.H.A.S.* iii. 89.
[61] e.g. C.U.L., E.D.R., B 2/3, p. 81 (1550); B 2/11, ff. 168v., 185v. (1591); B 2/59A, f. 19 (1685).
[62] Ibid. B 2/59, f. 14; B.L. Add. MS. 5803, f. 7v.
[63] B.L. Add. MS. 5803, f. 137v.
[64] *Mon. Inscr. Cambs.* 149–50.
[65] e.g. C.U.L., E.D.R., B 7/1, p. 120; C 1/6.
[66] Palmer and Fox, *Shudy Camps*, 14.
[67] C.U.L., E.D.R., C 3/25.
[68] *E.D.R.* (1895), 190.
[69] *Vetus Liber Arch. Elien.* (C.A.S. 8vo ser. xlviii), 54–5.
[70] *Cambs. Ch. Goods, temp. Edw. VI*, 62.
[71] B.L. Add. MS. 5803, f. 137v.
[72] List of Cambs. ch. plate, *penes V.C.H.*
[73] Prob. 11/24 (P.C.C. 13 Thower).
[74] *Cambs. Ch. Goods, temp. Edw. VI*, 62.
[75] Palmer, *Wm. Cole*, 110; *Kelly's Dir. Cambs.* (1858 and later edns.).
[76] *Cambs. Bells* (C.A.S. 8vo ser. xviii), 133.

they were unfit to be rung. The registers are continuous from 1558, but between 1681 and 1767 many entries are missing.[77]

NONCONFORMITY. In 1581 a yeoman who did not come to church was believed to adhere to the heretical Family of Love, then established at Balsham.[78] One family was said to include three Quakers in 1669,[79] and there were eleven nonconformists in 1676.[80] In 1679 ten people were presented for not coming to church.[81] In 1706 John Scotcher was licensed to keep a Quaker meeting-house at Shardelowes manor, his home.[82] By 1728 the only dissenting family was of Presbyterians.[83] One such family worshipped at Linton in 1783,[84] for there was not, then or later, any meeting-house in the parish, and the 40 or so dissenters recorded in the late 19th century attended chapels elsewhere.[85]

EDUCATION. John Wignold, vicar 1649–85, is said to have taught a school,[86] but there was none in the parish in the 18th century.[87] In 1818 a parish school had 20–25 pupils and a Sunday school was held fortnightly. The poor were willing to have their children taught, but usually then as in the 1860s sent them out to work. Both schools had ceased by 1825,[88] but in 1826 the vicar and principal inhabitants started a new Sunday school, in a building west of the church, which by 1833 had *c.* 66 pupils.[89] By 1846 it was linked with the National Society, and a day-school had over 50 pupils. The cost, £40 a year, was met by subscriptions.[90] In 1867 the average attendance was *c.* 20. The vicar had lately started a night-school for adults, but dropped it owing to low attendances.[91] In 1871 there were 35 pupils paying school-pence on the books of the National school, then managed by the vicar, and in 1877 44 older children and 32 infants.[92] A Government building grant in 1876[93] was used to rebuild the schoolroom to accommodate 64. Attendance gradually declined from 60 in the 1880s[94] to 39 by 1901. By 1907 there was also accommodation for 27 infants.[95] Numbers fell further from 40 in 1914 to 20 in 1927 following re-organization in 1921 into junior mixed and infants' sections and the removal of the older children to Castle Camps school; by 1930 attendance was 15.[96] In 1960 there were only 15 pupils, and in 1962 the school was closed and the building demolished.[97]

CHARITIES FOR THE POOR. An alms-house mentioned in 1666[98] has not been traced later. In 1699 it was found that 9 a. had been held since time immemorial for the poor,[99] of which 1 a., called the king's acre and owned by the township in 1586,[1] had perhaps originally been meant to help pay royal taxes. The rest, 8 a. of pasture called the Manages, had according to local tradition been given by a lady.[2] An order of 1699 directed that the rents were to be spent on the poor and the Manages were to remain permanently under grass.[3] In 1728 the land yielded £4 10*s.* for the poor, in 1783 £4.[4] In 1822 the local sheep-owners would no longer occupy the Manages at the old rent, £8, and it was let as fenced allotments to poor persons, 21 of whom occupied it in 1828. In 1830, after lawsuits over rights of way provoked by the occupiers against a neighbouring landowner, a Chancery decree approved the change to arable, and directed that the income from rents be divided among the poor in doles not exceeding 10*s.* each, any surplus being used for coal, food, or clothing. In 1837 the money was given out indiscriminately to 112 persons.[5] In 1863 the rent was £19 a year.[6] The Manages, with adjoining land allotted at inclosure for the king's acre, were let for £10 in 1917 and £16 in 1964 to local farmers. About 1970 the income was given in food vouchers. In 1972 the land was sold to its occupant for £1,870, which was invested to yield £93 a year, distributed in 1974 to five married couples and five single or widowed people.[7]

HILDERSHAM

THE PARISH of Hildersham,[1] covering 1,511 a.,[2] lies 9 miles south-east of Cambridge, and extends from the line of the ancient Wool Street in the north to the Essex county boundary. The river Granta, flowing from south-east to north-west across the centre of the parish, divides it into two unequal

[77] C.R.O., par. reg. TS.
[78] *Cath. Rec. Soc.* liii. 1–2.
[79] *Orig. Rec. of Early Nonconf.* ed. Turner, i. 40.
[80] Compton Census.
[81] C.U.L., E.D.R., B 2/62A, f. 9v.
[82] C.R.O., Q/S 03, p. 69.
[83] C.U.L., E.D.R., B 8/1.
[84] Ibid. B 7/1, p. 120; C 1/4.
[85] Ibid. C 3/25, 27, 39.
[86] Palmer, *Wm. Cole*, 110.
[87] Cf. C.U.L., E.D.R., C 1/4.
[88] *Educ. of Poor Digest*, 64; C.U.L., E.D.R., C 1/6.
[89] *Educ. Enquiry Abstract*, 60; cf. *Gardner's Dir. Cambs.* (1851).
[90] *Church School Inquiry, 1846–7*, 6–7.
[91] *1st Rep. Com. Employment in Agric.* 359; cf. C.U.L., E.D.R., C 3/25.
[92] Ed. 7/5; C.U.L., E.D.R., C 3/27.
[93] *Rep. of Educ. Cttee. of Council, 1876–7*, [C 1780-I], p. 740, H.C. (1877), xxix.
[94] Ibid. *1880–1*, [C. 2948-I], p. 544, H.C. (1881), xxxii; *1892–3*, [C. 7089-I], p. 688, H.C. (1893–4), xxvi.
[95] *Schs. in receipt of Parl. Grants, 1900–1* [Cd. 703], p. 15, H.C. (1901), lv; *Public Elem. Schs. 1907* [Cd. 3901], p. 28, H.C. (1908), lxxxiv.
[96] *Bd. of Educ., List 21, 1914* (H.M.S.O.), 28; *1922*, 16; *1927*, 16; *1938*, 20.
[97] Black, *Cambs. Educ. Rec.* 51; *Camb. Ind. Press*, 13 May 1960.
[98] E 179/244/22 ff. 115v.–116.
[99] C 93/50/31.
[1] Charterho. Mun., MR 2/557A, pt. ii, p. 23; MR 2/587, p. 366.
[2] Cf. *Eccl. Top. Eng.* vi, no. 162.
[3] C 93/50/31.
[4] C.U.L., E.D.R., B 8/1; B 7/1, p. 120.
[5] *31st Rep. Com. Char.* 107–8; cf. *Poor Law Abstract, 1818*, 28–9; Char. Com. files.
[6] *Char. Digest. Cambs. 1863–4*, 32–3.
[7] Char. Com. files; C.R.O., Q/RDc 80.
[1] This account was written in 1973.
[2] *Census*, 1961.

parts. That to the south narrows towards its southern extremity. The river follows a winding course, except that where it passes through the village it was straightened *c.* 1889 after inclosure.[3] East of the village a tongue of Linton parish penetrates between two channels of the river to include the former Hildersham mill. To the west minor branches of the river meander through meadows, one formerly called Sluice meadow.[4] Except for the strip of alluvium and gravel along the river, Hildersham lies mostly upon chalk, overlaid on parts of the higher ground to north and south by boulder clay and glacial gravels. To the south the ground rises from a level area below 200 ft. to over 325 ft. at the county boundary. North of the river a shallow valley runs north-east between slopes rising to over 250 ft. The open fields of the parish, which has been devoted mainly to arable farming, were not formally divided until 1889, under the last inclosure award for the county. Even thereafter, since the bulk of the land was allotted to a single owner, few hedges were planted.

In 1086 Hildersham contained woodland for 20 pigs.[5] Hildersham wood by the Essex boundary was probably much reduced by assarting, as the curved shapes of ancient closes lying north of it suggest.[6] In 1279 it was said to cover 20 a.,[7] in 1308 30 a.[8] In 1777 its estimated area was 21 a.,[9] in 1849 and 1922 18½ a.[10] The extensive plantations in the park around Hildersham Hall, amounting by 1849 to 18 a., were laid out only in the 1810s on former old inclosures.[11] A wooded area just north of the river, called the Alder Carr, which covered only 3 a. in 1799,[12] had by *c.* 1850 been extended over former water-meadows to cover *c.* 15 a.[13]

Hildersham was among the least populous parishes in the Granta valley. In 1086 20 people were enumerated,[14] in 1327 there were 32 tax-payers,[15] and in 1377 47 adults.[16] In 1429 there were said to be only 6 resident householders.[17] In 1524 23 people were assessed to the subsidy,[18] and in 1563 there were only 17 households.[19] The population probably declined even further in the early 17th century, but had recovered by the 1660s.[20] In 1676 there were 72 adults,[21] and in 1728 32 families included 152 people.[22] The population began to grow again in the 1770s,[23] and rose slowly from 170 in 1801 to 248 by 1851; despite a temporary reduction in 1861, ascribed to emigration, it still stood at 245 in 1881. A gradual decline thereafter accelerated, numbers falling from 201 to 146 between 1911 and 1916, and after recovering to 181 by 1931 the population grew only slowly from 148 in 1951 to 177 in 1971.[24]

The village lies along a street which joins the two roads between Linton and the Abingtons that run along the valley on opposite sides of the river. Hildersham church and one manor-house stand north of the river, the other manor-house, later Hildersham Hall, south of the river. Before the 1880s the river was crossed by a ford, and when the water was high the two halves of the village were virtually cut off from one another.[25] The first bridge was built of iron in 1886 at the expense of the rector's sister, Elizabeth Hemington.[26] North of the river the street widened between the church and manor-house into the town green, of *c.* 4 a. in 1777.[27] Another smaller green lay close to the southern manor-house. On it there stood by 1682 the village forge,[28] in use until the 1930s and demolished in 1946.[29]

Apart from the manor-houses and rectory the village contained in the 1660s two or three farmhouses with 7 hearths. The other 20 or so dwellings were mostly cottages, only 4 having even 3 hearths.[30] The 26 houses recorded in 1801 were mostly divided, for they accommodated 45 families.[31] In 1807 there were said to be 4 farm-houses and *c.* 30 cottages.[32] The latter lay along the street in two groups, close to each manor-house, and separated by the area most liable to flooding. The farmsteads, which stood back from the street,[33] included Burford's Farm, named after an 18th-century village family,[34] which is an L-shaped, timber-framed, brick-fronted house of the late 17th or early 18th century.[35] The most ancient house surviving in Hildersham is Withleigh, a long, two-storeyed, timber-framed building of the 16th century, perhaps originally a guildhall; it has an overhang, and an early fireplace.[36] A few other timber-framed, thatched cottages survive, but most of the older buildings are Victorian cottages, of brick and flint or plastered, with slate roofs. The number of houses grew slowly from 29 in 1821 to 56 in 1871 and then fell.[37] In 1883 the rector thought most of the cottages damp and unwholesome because they lay too close to the river.[38] New building, mainly council houses opposite Hildersham Hall, enlarged the village from 42 to 55 houses between 1921 and 1931, but there were still only 59 in 1961[39] and no expansion was planned;[40] there was some in-filling, mainly with bungalows, in the 1960s.

Of the two roads along the valley that south of the

[3] O.S. Map 6", Cambs. LV. SW. (1891, 1950 edns.).
[4] C.R.O., R 56/16/23.
[5] *V.C.H. Cambs.* i. 390.
[6] e.g. C.R.O., 124/P 55.
[7] *Rot. Hund.* (Rec. Com.), ii. 416.
[8] C.P. 40/173 rot. 75.
[9] C.U.L., Doc. 3965.
[10] C.R.O., L 4/41; R 49/8/36.
[11] C.U.L., Maps 53/84/13; C.R.O., L 42/3.
[12] C.R.O., R 51/25/46.
[13] Ibid. 124/P 57.
[14] *V.C.H. Cambs.* i. 390.
[15] *Cambs. Lay Subsidy, 1327*, 23–4.
[16] *East Anglian*, N.S. xii. 240.
[17] *Feud. Aids*, i. 192.
[18] E 179/81/134 m. 3.
[19] B.L. Harl. MS. 594, f. 200.
[20] Cf. C.R.O., par. reg. TS.
[21] Compton Census.
[22] C.U.L., E.D.R., B 8/1.
[23] C.R.O., par. reg. TS.
[24] *Census*, 1801–1971; C.R.O., 331/Z 4, 1914, Oct.; 331/Z 5, 1916, Feb.
[25] *Rep. Sel. Cttee. on Commons*, H.C. 186, pp. 4, 6, 8 (1883), xiii.
[26] Inscr. on bridge; *E.D.R.* (1890), 454.
[27] C.U.L., Doc. 3965.
[28] C.R.O., L 1/10, p. 23.
[29] *Kelly's Dir. Cambs.* (1937); *Camb. Ind. Press*, 1 Aug. 1969.
[30] E 179/84/437 rot. 58; E 179/244/23 rot. 55.
[31] *Census*, 1801.
[32] C.U.L., E.D.R., C 1/4.
[33] C.R.O., R 56/8/23.
[34] Cf. ibid. R 57/25/39.
[35] M.H.L.G. list.
[36] Ibid.
[37] *Census*, 1821–1901.
[38] *Rep. Sel. Cttee. on Commons* (1883), 6.
[39] *Census*, 1921–61.
[40] Cf. *Camb. News*, 24 Sept. 1964.

river was turnpiked in 1765 and disturnpiked in 1876.[41] About 1969 it was widened, and diverted at its western end, when the Abington by-pass was built.[42] Two fieldways, called in the 19th century Pen road and Wood road, led south from the village, and were crossed by Pampisford and Sawston ways. The road leading north from Hildersham forked into Newmarket way and Balsham way.[43] South of the river the Cambridge–Haverhill line was opened in 1865 and closed in 1967.[44]

The village feast expired in the 1890s, but the horkeys or harvest-suppers and the May-day celebrations survived until *c.* 1914, and men were still going round on Plough Monday, cracking whips and collecting money, in the 1930s.[45] Until inclosure the villagers had used Night common, where the street crossed the river, for cricket and other sports after the hay was cut. The inclosure award allotted 8 a. of the adjacent Midsummer meadow for a recreation ground.[46] The rector had set up a parish library by 1897[47] and a cottage was hired in 1906 as a reading-room.[48] A village hut was built in 1920.[49]

A conical Roman burial-mound, 190 ft. round, and resembling those opposite Bartlow, survived in Dovehouse close west of the church until 1852. It had once been used as the site for the maypole.[50]

MANORS AND OTHER ESTATES. The manor of *HILDERSHAM*, held before the Conquest by King Edward's thegn Wulfwin, had been granted by 1086 to Aubrey de Vere,[51] whose descendants probably held it in demesne until the mid 12th century.[52] Their overlordship was formally recorded until the early 17th century.[53] By 1166 Hildersham was held under Aubrey de Vere, earl of Oxford, by Richard de Camville,[54] who divided the manor, settling half upon his daughter Maud's marriage to William de Ros.[55] The result was a distinction, which lasted until the early 14th century, between the two moieties or manors, later called Overhall (or Upperhall) and Netherhall manors,[56] which apparently remained *c.* 1300 a single unit of jurisdiction.[57]

The *NETHERHALL* estate, which *c.* 1800 lay south of the river,[58] was evidently that which passed to Richard de Camville's son, whose successor *c.* 1279 had 20 a. of wood, presumably Hildersham wood.[59] Richard de Camville died in 1176.[60] His son and heir Gerard[61] was disputing the advowson of Hildersham with Maud de Ros in 1210,[62] and died *c.* 1214. Gerard's son and heir Richard[63] died probably in 1217, leaving as heir his daughter Idony. Idony's wardship was granted to William Longspee, earl of Salisbury, who by 1226 had married her to his son William[64] (d. 1250).[65] The moiety or manor, over which the mesne lordship of the Longspees' heirs was recorded up to 1285,[66] was subinfeudated, probably by 1228, to a follower of the Longspees, John le Daneys,[67] whose wife Philippa was said to hold it *c.* 1236.[68] John died in 1241, leaving as heirs two daughters under age, Joan (d. s.p. 1245) and Ela, whose guardian Nicholas de Boleville had married her to his son William by 1254 when she and William were granted free warren at Hildersham.[69] Ela apparently died without surviving issue for by 1269 the moiety or manor had come to Isabel,[70] daughter of Robert Grimbald and John le Daneys's sister Maud,[71] and formerly wife of Richard Pauncefoot (d. after 1262).[72] Isabel held the manor in 1274 and died after 1277.[73] By 1279 her son Grimbald Pauncefoot held that moiety.[74] He was granted free warren there in 1281[75] and died in 1287. His son and heir Grimbald[76] had by 1288 granted his part for life to the judge Ralph Hengham (d. 1311).[77] In 1308 Grimbald's title was challenged by Brice le Daneys of Tickencote (Rut.), as male heir of the Daneys family.[78] Before his death in 1314 Grimbald had apparently sold his Hildersham estate to William le Busteler, who by 1316 had bought out the claims of Grimbald's brother and heir Emery, named as lord in that year.[79] William's ancestors, William le Busteler (d. *c.* 1250) and Robert (killed *c.* 1266), had held a small estate at Hildersham.[80] Busteler was succeeded *c.* 1334 by his son Robert,[81] who had held the other moiety of the manor since 1316[82] and thus reunited the two.

[41] Haverhill and Red Cross Road Act, 6 Geo. III, c. 84; Annual Turnpike Acts Continuance Act, 1876, 39–40 Vic. c. 39.

[42] Ex inf. the County Surveyor.

[43] C.R.O., R 56/16/3; R 51/28/37N, no. 9.

[44] *V.C.H. Cambs.* ii. 132–3; ex inf. Brit. Rail Hist. Research Dept.

[45] C.R.O., 331/Z 6, 1930, Feb., p. 10; 331/Z 8, 1939, Feb., pp. 12–13; cf. Porter, *Cambs. Customs*, 112.

[46] *Rep. Sel. Cttee. on Commons* (1883), 2–3; *Land Com. Special Rep. on Incl. of . . . Hildersham*, H.C. 52, p. 3 (1883), xxi; cf. *Camb. Ind. Press*, 5 May 1961.

[47] C.U.L., E.D.R., C 3/37.

[48] C.R.O., 331/Z 1, 1906, Oct., p. lxxx; Nov., p. xci.

[49] Cf. *Camb. Evening News*, 28 July 1972.

[50] W. M. Palmer, *Neighbourhood of Hildersham*, 12; Fox, *Arch. Camb. Region*, 95–6.

[51] *V.C.H. Cambs.* i. 390.

[52] When they apparently granted tithe from the demesne to Hatfield priory: see p. 67.

[53] e.g. C 142/116 no. 7; Wards 7/53 no. 276.

[54] *Red Bk. Exch.* (Rolls Ser.), i. 353.

[55] *Rot. de Dom.* (Pipe R. Soc. xxxv), 84.

[56] e.g. Lysons, *Cambs.* 211.

[57] *Plac. de Quo Warr.* (Rec. Com.), 105; cf. *Rot. Hund.* (Rec. Com.), i. 52.

[58] C.R.O., R 51/25/46.

[59] *Rot. Hund.* (Rec. Com.), ii. 416.

[60] *Pipe R.* 1175 (P.R.S. xxii), 39; Dugdale, *Mon.* v. 584.

[61] *Pipe R.* 1176 (P.R.S. xxv), 48, 200.

[62] *Cur. Reg. R.* vi. 87, 105.

[63] *Rot. Litt. Claus.* (Rec. Com.), i. 159, 200; *Rot. Litt. Pat.* (Rec. Com.), i. 127.

[64] *Rot. Litt. Pat.* i. 178; *Rot. Litt. Claus.* i. 295–6, 299; ii. 110.

[65] *Complete Peerage*, xi. 382–3.

[66] *Feud. Aids*, i. 140.

[67] Cf. *Close R.* 1227–31, 65; *Rot. Litt. Claus.* i. 356; *Hatton's Bk. of Seals*, pp. 43–4.

[68] *Liber de Bernewelle*, 254: 'Philippus' is presumably an error of transcription; cf. *Close R.* 1237–42, 321; *Bk. of Fees*, ii. 923.

[69] *Ex. e Rot. Fin.* (Rec. Com.), i. 346, 365; *Close R.* 1242–7, 260, 308; *Cal. Pat.* 1232–47, 243; 1247–58, 379.

[70] J.I. 1/83 rott. 32, 33d.

[71] Brydges, *Northants.* ii. 368; cf. *V.C.H. Hunts.* ii. 323 (not entirely accurate).

[72] *Hunts. Fines, 1194–1603*, ed. G. J. Turner (C.A.S. 8vo ser. xxxvii), 32–3.

[73] S.C. 5/Cambs., Chap. ho. ser. no. 1 rot. 1d.; *Cal. Close*, 1272–9, 401.

[74] *Rot. Hund.* (Rec. Com.), ii. 416; cf. *Feud. Aids*, i. 140.

[75] *Cal. Chart. R.* 1257–1300, 248.

[76] *Cal. Close*, 1279–88, 260, 418, 443; 1296–1302, 467–8.

[77] *Plac. de Quo Warr.* (Rec. Com.), 105; *Cal. Close*, 1279–88, 534; *D.N.B.*

[78] C.P. 40/173 rot. 75; cf. *V.C.H. Rut.* ii. 276.

[79] *Cal. Inq. p.m.* v, p. 270; *Feud. Aids*, i. 155; *Cal. Close*, 1313–18, 339.

[80] *Ex. e Rot. Fin.* (Rec. Com.), ii. 224–5; *Cal. Pat.* 1266–72, 110; J.I. 1/83 rot. 32d.

[81] Cf. *Cal. Close*, 1330–4, 448.

[82] *Feud. Aids*, i. 155.

What was evidently the *OVERHALL* or *UPPERHALL* estate, north of the river,[83] was held from before 1185 to after 1210 by Maud de Ros, who survived her husband, William de Ros (d. by 1185)[84] of Horton (Kent), and her son William (d. probably *c.* 1190).[85] She was eventually succeeded by her grandson William de Ros, who was of age by 1210 and died in 1223.[86] His eldest son William held that moiety *c.* 1236[87] and had died without issue by 1243, leaving a widow Godehold, who had brought her dower land there to her second husband Hugh of Windsor by 1250. William's heir, his brother Richard,[88] was dead by January 1246, whereupon his lands were divided between his sisters and heirs, Maud, whom in that year Henry III married to Geoffrey de Percy, a member of his household, and Lora, who the same year married Gilbert Kirkby (d. by 1258).[89] In 1249 Geoffrey and Maud granted 1 carucate at Hildersham, with the reversion of Godehold's dower, to Roger de Ros,[90] Henry III's tailor, who was granted free warren there in 1251[91] and died in 1257.[92] By 1262 his sisters and heirs Thomasine and Emmeline had granted that estate to Henry le Fleming,[93] who complained in 1268 that Percy had disseised him of land at Hildersham during the recent civil war.[94] Maud died, apparently without issue, in 1273,[95] whereupon her interest passed to the Kirkbys. In 1248 Gilbert Kirkby and Lora had granted ¼ knight's fee at Hildersham to Alan Kirkby,[96] to whom Geoffrey de Percy released his share of the manor in 1270,[97] and who died soon after. Possession of Alan's manor was thereupon disputed between Isabel Pauncefoot and the earl of Oxford, its overlord.[98] By 1274 the Kirkby manor was held of Lora de Ros under the earl by Gilbert Kirkby,[99] perhaps the justice of that name who died in 1294.[1] By 1297 the manor had come to Walter Kirkby,[2] whose daughter and heir Margaret was said to hold half the vill in 1299.[3] She was probably dead by 1310, when Roger Kirkby (d. 1313), son by John Kirkby of Margaret, daughter and eventual heir of Lora de Ros, had succeeded to her Kentish lands.[4] By 1316 the Ros moiety of Hildersham had passed to Robert le Busteler,[5] who *c.* 1334 succeeded his father William in the other moiety, as mentioned above, and died in 1366.[6]

Four of Robert's five coheirs sold four-fifths of his lands to Robert Parys[7] (d. *c.* 1377),[8] who was succeeded in them by his younger son Robert. The younger Robert died holding those four-fifths in 1408, leaving as heir Catherine, the infant daughter of his eldest son Robert.[9] She was said to hold Overhall manor in 1412,[10] but probably died soon after[11] and was succeeded by her uncle Henry (d. 1427), who also acquired the other fifth from his uncle Nicholas's executors *c.* 1425.[12] From Henry Parys Hildersham manor descended with the Bustelers manors in Linton and Duxford in the male line of the Paryses until the 1670s.[13] From 1523 to 1542 it was occupied as part of her jointure by Margaret, widow of John Parys (d. 1517),[14] and in 1544 by Elizabeth, daughter-in-law of Sir Philip Parys (d. 1558), and her second husband Sir William Cavendish.[15] When Philip Parys died in 1672, Hildersham was not sold with his other lands, but under his will passed for life to his mother Anne, widow of John Parys (d. 1667), who had married secondly Sir Joseph Colston (d. 1675).[16] She held Hildersham until her death in 1706.[17] The heirs-at-law were then the grandchildren of John Parys's five sisters. One of them, Sir Francis Andrews, Bt. (d. 1759), descended from two of the sisters,[18] bought out the other coheirs in 1706.[19]

In 1747, his son William being insane, Sir Francis settled Hildersham upon his daughter Bridget's marriage to Philip Southcote[20] (d. 1758).[21] Bridget died in 1783, having settled the manor upon her kinsman Robert Edward Petre, Lord Petre[22] (d. 1801).[23] In 1798 or 1799 Lord Petre sold Hildersham to the Cambridge banker John Mortlock,[24] who resold it *c.* 1811 to Thomas Fassett,[25] upon whose death it was again sold in 1820[26] to Col. J. P. Hamilton. He owned it until *c.* 1828, when it was acquired by James Barker, vicar of Great Abington

[83] It was held immediately of the earls of Oxford *c.* 1409: C.R.O., 619/M 3, ct. roll 10 Hen. IV.
[84] *Rot. de Dom.* (Pipe R. Soc. xxxv), 84; *Cur. Reg. R.* vi. 105.
[85] *Clerkenwell Cart.* (Camd. 3rd ser. lxxi), 20–2; cf. *Pipe R.* 1190 (P.R.S. N.S. i), 142, 151. The family was distinct from those of Ros of Helmsley (Yorks. N.R.) and Ros of Lullingstone (Kent); cf. *Cur. Reg. R.* i. 187; vi. 134–5; xiii, pp. 450–1.
[86] *Rot. Lib.* (Rec. Com.), 219; *Ex. e Rot. Fin.* (Rec. Com.), i. 106.
[87] *Liber de Bernewelle*, 254; *Cur. Reg. R.* xiii, pp. 405, 494; xiv, pp. 181–2, 336–7.
[88] C.P. 25(1)/24/21 no. 8; *Cat. Anct. D.* i, C 438.
[89] *Cal. Pat.* 1232–47, 473; *Ex. e Rot. Fin.* (Rec. Com.), i. 447; *Kent Fines* (Kent Arch. Soc., Rec. Branch xv), 407–8, 413–14.
[90] C.P. 25(1)/24/25 no. 7.
[91] *Cal. Chart. R.* 1226–57, 255, 366.
[92] *Cal. Close*, 1256–8, 84, 89–90.
[93] *Cal. Chart. R.* 1257–1300, 44.
[94] *Abbrev. Plac.* (Rec. Com.), 176.
[95] F. R. H. Du Boulay, *Lordship of Canterbury* (1966), 107.
[96] C.P. 25(1)/24/24 no. 9.
[97] *Close R.* 1268–72, 267.
[98] S.C. 5/Cambs. Chap. ho. ser. no. 1 rot. 1d.
[99] *Rot. Hund.* (Rec. Com.), i. 52; ii. 416. Lora was still living in 1286: *Cat. Anct. D.* vi. C 6361.
[1] *Cal. Pat.* 1292–1301, 112, 115; cf. Foss, *Judges of Eng.* iii. 110.
[2] *Coram Rege Roll, 1297* (Index Libr. xix), 148.
[3] *Plac. de Quo Warr.* (Rec. Com.), 105.
[4] Ibid. 310; *Reg. Pecham* (Rolls Ser.), iii. 999; *Cal. Fine R.* 1307–19, 167; cf. Copinger, *Suff. Manors*, iii. 164.
[5] *Feud. Aids*, i. 155.
[6] Ibid. 163; *Cal. Inq. p.m.* xiii, p. 8.
[7] *Cal. Inq. p.m.* xiii, p. 100; *Collect. Topog. & Gen.* i. 262.
[8] *Cal. Close*, 1377–81, 93.
[9] C 137/72 no. 32.
[10] *Feud. Aids*, vi. 407.
[11] Not mentioned in C.R.O., 619/M 4, after ct. roll 13 Hen. IV.
[12] C 139/29 no. 48; Prob. 11/3 (P.C.C. 2 Luffenam).
[13] See p. 85; cf. C 142/116 no. 7; C 142/60 no. 17; C 142/265 no. 35; Wards 7/53 no. 276.
[14] B.L. Add. MS. 5860, ff. 103–105v.
[15] C.R.O., R 51/25/37Q 1, no. 1; cf. *Misc. Gen. & Herald.* 5th ser. ii. 123–6.
[16] Prob. 11/342 (P.C.C. 53 Pye).
[17] C 6/378/76; Prob. 11/492 (P.C.C. 5–6 Poley).
[18] Blomefield, *Norf.* vii. 116–17; G.E.C. *Baronetage*, ii. 146–7; cf. C.R.O., R 55/10/3, nos. 2–4.
[19] C.P. 25(2)/987/5 Anne Trin. no. 12.
[20] Blomefield, *Norf.* vii. 117; C.P. 40/655 rot. 8.
[21] Prob. 11/841 (P.C.C. 310 Hutton).
[22] Prob. 11/1110 (P.C.C. 586 Cornwallis).
[23] G.E.C. *Baronetage*, ii. 146–7; *Complete Peerage*, x. 509–11.
[24] C.R.O., R 51/25/46; R 51/25/35, pp. 216–49.
[25] Ibid. R 51/25/35, pp. 250–83; cf. ibid. R 51/25/47.
[26] Ibid. L 42/3.

1829–35.[27] In 1839 Barker sold it to Lt. Alexander Cotton, R.N., who sold it in 1849.[28] It was bought by 1850 by Edward Huddleston (d. 1852), whose son and heir Ferdinand[29] by acquiring the Stutfield estate[30] came to own virtually the whole parish, which descended with his Sawston estate[31] until 1922 when it was sold[32] to James Binney. Hildersham descended with Binney's Pampisford estate,[33] and in 1973 belonged to Mr. H. B. Binney.[34]

Hildersham Hall stands approximately on the site of the former Netherhall farm-house,[35] which probably survives as a two-storeyed range behind the main block of the Hall. The Hall, built *c.* 1807 to designs by Edward Lapidge, is a stuccoed villa, five bays by three, of two storeys with an attic. It has a porch at the south-east corner, a portico facing west towards a lake, and a central staircase-hall lit by a glass lantern.[36] Thomas Fassett probably laid out, on ground still divided *c.* 1810 into closes,[37] the park of 72 a., which includes an artificial lake and several plantations. Under the Huddlestons the Hall was usually let,[38] and in 1879 the Hall and park were sold to J. K. Thornton (d. *c.* 1904), whose widow occupied them until 1922.[39] They were then sold to Lady E. F. Miller, who lived there until *c.* 1930,[40] and in 1931 to F. W. Rhodes (d. 1938), a nephew of Cecil Rhodes.[41] About 1939 the Hall passed to the Rhodes Trust, which still owned it in 1973, when it was occupied by Miss G. M. Rhodes.[42]

The farm-house belonging to the Upperhall estate, north of the river, which was sometimes called Hildersham Hall in the 18th century[43] but later Manor Farm, includes a timber-framed, L-shaped, two-storey range, probably of *c.* 1600. Its north wing has a gabled overhang. An eastwards extension in brick probably dates from the early 18th century, and a brick wing north of the last was added in the early 19th. It was disused by 1973 and was sold soon after.[44] The name of Dovehouse close across the road[45] suggests the former manorial status of the house.

By 1546 King's College owned an estate at Hildersham, held of the Paryses' manor,[46] which it had probably acquired with its lands at Abington *c.* 1450. In 1583 the college had *c.* 50 a. at Hildersham, *c.* 1840 53 a.,[47] which were sold in 1859 to Robert Goodwin, rector of Hildersham.[48] After his death in 1899 his sisters and heirs Sarah (d. 1909) and Frances (d. 1910)[49] vested the property in 1901 in trustees for the benefit of the church, who sold it in 1918.[50]

By 1800 virtually all the copyhold land in the parish had come into a single ownership. Its largest component derived originally from the Hildersham land acquired by Thomas Dalton[51] (d. 1602), who left his estate to his third son George[52] (d. 1638).[53] In 1649 George's sons Thomas and John sold it to Thomas Puckering,[54] whose land was sold in 1672 after his death to William Eedes, rector of Horseheath (d. 1709).[55] Eedes's son Francis sold *c.* 85 a. in 1709 to Thomas Rickard[56] (d. 1733), whose brother and heir John[57] sold them in 1739 to the unorthodox divine Conyers Middleton. When Dr. Middleton died at Hildersham in 1750 he left over 230 a. to his widow Anne; Anne sold them in 1751 to Thomas Hanway and Hanway in 1753 to Thomas Rumbold Hall.[58] Hall, who owned *c.* 313 a. by 1795, besides leasing the King's College estate,[59] died in 1799. His son Thomas sold his estate, probably in 1800, to John Burgoyne,[60] who had inherited from his father John (d. 1786) *c.* 90 a., bought in 1776 from William and Mary Fairchild,[61] and had himself acquired in 1795 *c.* 95 a., formerly owned by the Offord family,[62] and in 1798 the land of John, son of William Burgoyne (d. 1793).[63] At his death in 1827 John Burgoyne owned *c.* 550 a., which he left to his daughter Mary, who in 1829 married William Stutfield,[64] a London wine-merchant. In 1865 Stutfield and his wife sold their property to Ferdinand Huddleston.[65]

The substantial house attached to the Burgoyne estate in a close just north of the river was probably on the site of the seven-hearth house occupied in 1664 by Thomas Puckering.[66] It was rebuilt or enlarged by Conyers Middleton *c.* 1750,[67] and in the mid 19th century, when it was called the Rookery, comprised two blocks, with a five-bay Georgian front to the garden. It was demolished in 1868.[68] The site was later occupied by a large red-brick house, built after 1900 by Sarah and Frances Goodwin.[69]

ECONOMIC HISTORY. In 1086 Hildersham

27 Hildersham ct. bk. 1784–1828, p. 163, *penes* Mr. H. B. Binney of Pampisford Hall; cf. *Army List*, 1820; *Alum. Cantab. 1752–1900*, i. 152.
28 C.R.O., L 92/20–1; 334/010; L 4/41.
29 C.U.L., Maps 53/84/13; Hildersham ct. bk. 1834–75, p. 73, *penes* Mr. Binney; cf. Burke, *Land. Gent.* (1952), 1307.
30 See below.
31 See p. 250.
32 C.R.O., R 49/8/36.
33 *Kelly's Dir. Cambs.* (1925, 1937).
34 Ex inf. Mr. Binney.
35 C.R.O., R 51/25/46; cf. ibid. R 51/25/42, no. 1.
36 C.R.O., L 42/3; Colvin, *Biog. Dict. Eng. Architects, 1660–1840*, 356.
37 B.L. Maps, O.S.D. 235.
38 e.g. *Gardner's Dir. Cambs.* (1851); R.G. 10/1592.
39 C.R.O., 515/SP 587; 334/010.
40 *Kelly's Dir. Cambs.* (1925, 1929).
41 Ibid. (1933, 1937); C.R.O., 331/Z 8, 1938, Aug., p. 66.
42 Ex inf. the Warden, Rhodes House, Oxford.
43 e.g. Petre Estate Act, 37 Geo. III, c. 130 (Priv. Act); cf. C.U.L., Maps 53/84/13.
44 *Camb. Ind. Press*, 14 June 1973.
45 e.g. C.U.L., Doc. 3965; C.R.O., R 56/16/23.
46 *Camb. Univ. Doc.* (1852), i. 260.
47 King's Coll. Mun., G 83, 89.
48 Ex inf. Mr. J. Saltmarsh of King's Coll.
49 C.R.O., par. reg. TS.
50 C.U.L., Maps 53(1)/91/156.
51 e.g. C.P. 25(2)/94/854/32 Eliz. I East. no. 13; *31st Rep. Com. Char.* 104.
52 Prob. 11/100 (P.C.C. 64 Montague); Wards 7/26 no. 242.
53 Gibbons, *Ely Episc. Rec.* 316.
54 C.R.O., R 51/25/41, no. 3.
55 Ibid. no. 6; *Alum. Cantab. to 1751*, ii. 84.
56 C.R.O., R 51/25/42, no. 2.
57 Ibid. R 51/25/37Q 2, nos. 3–7; *Mon. Inscr. Cambs.* 80.
58 C.R.O., R 51/25/43, nos. 1–8; R 51/25/39A–C; R 51/25/35, pp. 12–19. For Middleton see *D.N.B.*
59 C.U.L., MS. Plan 662.
60 *Camb. Chron.* 20 July 1799; C.R.O., R 51/25/35, pp. 195–201, 230–8; R 51/25/46.
61 C.R.O., R 51/25/35, pp. 116–27, 164–71.
62 Ibid. pp. 105–115, 128–31, 172–7, 191–4; R 51/25/37P, nos. 2–3, 8, 12; ibid. Q 2, nos. 8, 73.
63 Ibid. R 51/25/35, pp. 178–81, 203–8.
64 Ibid. R 51/25/40A, B; par. reg. TS.
65 Hildersham ct. bk. 1834–75, pp. 188–96.
66 E 179/84/437 rot. 58.
67 C.R.O., R 51/25/45, no. 4.
68 Palmer, *Neighbourhood of Hildersham*, 9–10. See below, plate facing p. 81.
69 Cf. C.R.O., 515/SP 453.

contained 11 plough-lands, of which the demesne, assessed at 2½ out of 5 hides in the vill, probably comprised half, and had 4 *servi* and 4 plough-teams of its own to work them. Sixteen *villani* with 7 teams between them occupied the other 2½ hides. The yearly value had been raised from £8 to £10 since Aubrey de Vere received the manor.[70] In 1279 Grimbald Pauncefoot's demesne included 240 a. of arable and 10 a. of meadow and pasture. The tenants included some substantial freeholders, with under-tenants of their own, such as Richard le Breton who had 30 a., and Roger Doget[71] who left 76 a. held of both moieties of the manor to his son Roger in 1295.[72] Most of the parish was probably held in villeinage by tenants, some of whom, probably half-yardlanders, owed week-work and had each to plough for the lord 24 days a year and carry 15 a. of his corn.[73] In the 16th century the standard copyhold tenement, presumably derived from the half-yardland, amounted to *c.* 18 a.[74] In later times, of *c.* 590 a. in the parish not included in the demesne farms, the glebe, and the King's College estate, only *c.* 65 a. were freehold, the rest copyhold.[75] In the 16th century the custom was that copyholds descended to the youngest son,[76] but by the mid 17th they were regularly inherited by the eldest.[77]

By the 16th century there was considerable concentration of ownership among the villagers. Thus the Snarston family, prominent in Hildersham from the 1460s,[78] held over 60 a. *c.* 1540.[79] One copyholder had 110 a. in 1545, another 155 a. in 1590.[80] Of 23 people taxed in 1524 only three were charged on goods worth over £2, including Simon Beteyn,[81] who with two relatives was thought to be worth £85 in 1522.[82] The prosperous Hamond family flourished at Hildersham from the 1520s to the 1690s.[83] Henry Hamond (d. 1660) left 98 a. there besides legacies amounting to £200. He was also, as his ancestors had been since the 1580s, lessee to King's College,[84] which until after 1800 regularly let its Hildersham estate to yeoman families there on beneficial leases at rents in kind fixed since the 16th century.[85] About 1700 there were 14 copyhold tenants, not all living in the parish,[86] and in 1786 ten.[87] In 1777 six of them, occupying respectively 323 a., 89 a., 89 a., 47 a., 40½ a., and 32 a., occupied virtually the whole parish excluding the demesnes and glebe, the others having only 17 a. between them. The manorial estate in 1777 included *c.* 740 a. out of 1,500 a.[88] By the late 19th century, having absorbed the Burgoyne estate, it covered almost the whole parish.[89]

By the 16th century the demesne had been divided into two large farms, probably corresponding to the land of the former moieties and lying respectively north and south of the river. One of them covered *c.* 300 a. about 1580.[90] From the 1660s Francis Westhorp[91] (d. 1689) occupied one of them at a rent below the full value because he also served Lady Colston as bailiff and agent, and was succeeded in turn by his son Francis and son-in-law.[92] About 1800 Overhall farm, north of the river, covered *c.* 320 a., and Netherhall farm, to the south, *c.* 400 a., later reduced to *c.* 320 a. when the park was made.[93] Much demesne land lay in ancient inclosures, which on Netherhall farm included *c.* 1800 some 100 a. north of the road from Linton to Great Abington and *c.* 75 a. near Hildersham wood, perhaps derived from medieval assarting. In the open fields the bulk of the demesne arable was concentrated in large blocks of 10 a. or more. Thus *c.* 270 a. of Overhall farm covered a virtually continuous area along both sides of the road from Linton to Little Abington.[94] The copyholders' land remained until inclosure in the narrow strips typical of open-field cultivation.[95]

About 1800 Hildersham, apart from over 250 a. of old inclosures around the village,[96] was considered as being divided by the river into a north field of *c.* 660 a. and a south field of *c.* 340 a.[97] In earlier periods the arable had been divided into smaller blocks, still called fields in the 18th century,[98] and themselves composed of furlongs or shots varying in size from almost 40 a. to 2 or 3 a.[99] The only permanent common pasture was the 12 a. of St. Margaret's Green, so named by 1590, north-east of the village, where a stream ran down a narrow valley. It was grazed from May to St. Thomas's day by certain cottagers, as well as by the lord and his farmers.[1] The village meadows, such as Broadmeadow, which was intercommonable with Little Abington *c.* 1730, and Midsummer meadow, lay along the river.[2]

How the arable was divided for the customary rotation of crops is unclear. In 1801 864 a., two-thirds of the arable area including closes, were under cultivation, suggesting a triennial rotation.[3] In 1798, however, only half of the 400 a. on Netherhall farm had been cropped.[4] Moreover, the manorial farms each had land on only one side of the river, while the glebe and the King's College estate lay entirely on the north side.[5] In the 16th century a copyholder might devise his lands north and south of the river to different sons,[6] suggesting that even then

[70] *V.C.H. Cambs.* i. 390.
[71] *Rot. Hund.* (Rec. Com.), ii. 416–17.
[72] *Cal. Inq. p.m.* iii, pp. 212–13.
[73] *Rot. Hund.* ii. 416–17.
[74] e.g. C 2/Eliz. I/P 2/22; Req. 2/73/6.
[75] C.R.O., R 51/25/40; C.U.L., Doc. 3965.
[76] B.L. Add. MS. 5861, f. 22v.
[77] C.R.O., L 1/102, p. 38; cf. ibid. R 51/25/35 *passim.*
[78] e.g. *Cal. Fine R.* 1461–71, 252; *Cal. Close,* 1485–1500, pp. 102–3.
[79] C.P. 25(2)/41/19 no. 44.
[80] C.R.O., R 51/25/37N, no. 10; 37 Q 1, no. 1.
[81] E 179/81/134 m. 3.
[82] *L. & P. Hen. VIII,* iii, p. 1118.
[83] C.R.O., R 51/25/37N, nos. 1–9; 37 Q 1, nos. 7, 17, 19–20; E 179/81/134 m. 3.
[84] C.R.O., R 51/25/45; King's Coll. Mun., G 83–8.
[85] C.R.O., R 51/25/44.
[86] Ibid. 619/M 68.
[87] Ibid. R 51/25/36.
[88] C.U.L., Doc. 3965.
[89] See above.
[90] C 2/Jas. I/W 10/43.
[91] E 179/84/437 rot. 58.
[92] C 6/328/76.
[93] C.R.O., R 51/25/46; ibid. L 42/3.
[94] Ibid. L 4/41; ibid. 124/P 57.
[95] Ibid. 124/P 55.
[96] C.U.L., Doc. 3965.
[97] C.R.O., L 4/41; C.U.L., MS. Plan 662; C.U.L., Maps 53/84/13.
[98] e.g. C.U.L., E.D.R., H 1/4, terriers 1625, 1665; C.R.O., R 51/25/37N, no. 9; R 51/25/35, pp. 14–17.
[99] C.U.L., Doc. 3965.
[1] C.R.O., R 51/25/37N, no. 10; *31st Rep. Com. Char.* 104; *Rep. Sel. Cttee. on Commons* (1883), 4.
[2] C.R.O., R 51/25/38; Hildersham ct. bk. 1706–44, f. 46v., *penes* Mr. Binney.
[3] H.O. 67/9.
[4] C.R.O., R 51/25/42, no. 10.
[5] C.U.L., Doc. 3965; cf. C.U.L., E.D.R., H 1/4, terrier 1625; C.R.O., L 4/41; King's Coll. Mun., G 83, 89.
[6] B.L. Add. MS. 5861, f. 32.

Design for a grotto by William Kent

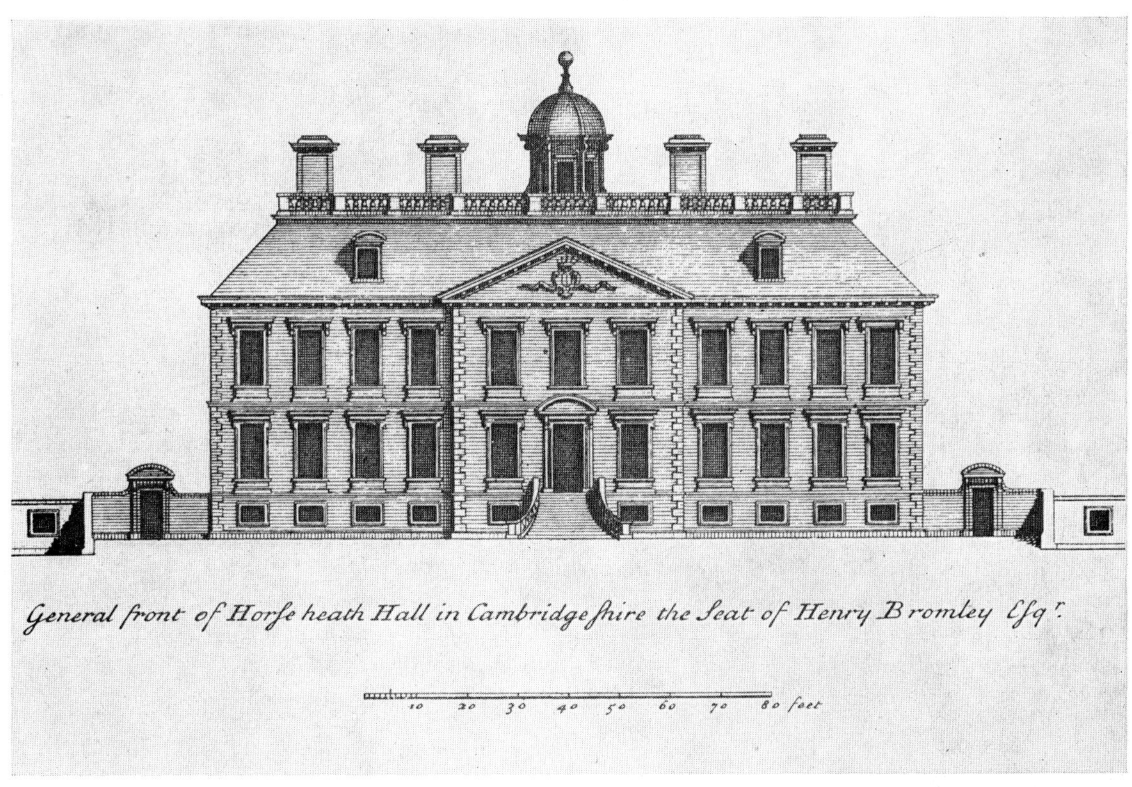

The main front by Sir Roger Pratt

HORSEHEATH HALL

Stetchworth Church: monument to Henry Gorges (d. 1674)

Horseheath Church: monument to Sir Giles Alington (d. 1638) and his wife Dorothy

a separate rotation may have been observed on each side. In the late 19th century it was said that according to tradition only one-sixth of the parish lay fallow each year, after five crops had been taken from it.[7]

The principal crop, as elsewhere in the neighbourhood, was barley. One man in 1527 left his wife 40 a. of barley and only 1 a. each of wheat and rye. Saffron was also grown at Hildersham from the early 16th century.[8] In 1801 319 a. of barley were sown, and 150 a. of wheat, but other grains had become more prominent, including oats at 138 a., and rye at 82½ a., and a variety of roots and grasses had been introduced.[9] Such innovations were probably less difficult on the demesne farms, where large closes and arable blocks could more easily be severed from the customary rotation. About 1690 a lessee of one such farm laid down several parcels of arable with sainfoin to convert them into pasture.[10] In 1796 the tenant of Netherhall farm was required to lay down land after every two crops with clover or grass for two years.[11] His planting of coleseed and turnips[12] probably accounted for most of the 100 a. of those crops recorded in 1801.[13]

The turnips were intended partly to feed a flock of *c.* 280 sheep and lambs.[14] In 1086 there had been 90 sheep at Hildersham,[15] which in 1347 provided almost 26 stone for a levy of wool, including 10 stone from Robert le Busteler's demesne.[16] In the 16th century copyholders were keeping flocks of 20–40 sheep.[17] In the early 18th century the flocks of Upperhall and Netherhall farms were allowed sheep-walk over the common fields only after the villagers' cattle had fed over the stubble for 24 days on the north side of the river and 9 days on the south. The demesne flocks also fed over the meadows and St. Margaret's Green, following the village herd, in the winter. Tenants were still in 1724 forbidden to hire their rights of common for cattle to outsiders or to exercise them unless resident.[18] About 1795 there were *c.* 540 Norfolk sheep in the parish, probably mostly in the demesne farm flocks, one of which included *c.* 260 grown sheep in 1816.[19] It was asserted in 1812 that no right of sheepgate was attached to copyholds,[20] although at inclosure some allotments were made for copyhold rights of common.[21] The lord still claimed in the 19th century to exercise right of sheep-walk over the one-sixth of the fields lying fallow, so preventing other occupiers from introducing more modern farming methods.[22]

About 1800 John Mortlock proposed the inclosure of Hildersham under the same Act as Great Abington but was obstructed by the aged rector, Thomas Salt,[23] who preferred to take his tithes in kind and did not wish the poorer villagers to lose common of pasture for their cows and pigs.[24] In 1812–13 the lord and other landowners exchanged rights of pasture over Broadmeadow,[25] and the disadvantages of open-field cultivation were partly mitigated because soon after 1800 almost the whole parish was concentrated into a few large farms. On the manorial estate Overhall farm was occupied from *c.* 1750 to 1817 by the Mabbutt family; at Netherhall farm William Burgoyne, tenant from 1759, was succeeded in 1793 by his son John (d. 1814),[26] whose bankruptcy compelled him in 1798 to surrender his lease to his kinsman and creditor John Burgoyne (d. 1827),[27] who also farmed in person most of his accumulated copyholds. From *c.* 1820 the manorial land was again for a time divided in two.[28] Old or Manor farm covered *c.* 350 a. north of the river. The glebe and tithes were let with it from 1830. To the south lay New farm of *c.* 343 a.: when Hildersham Hall replaced the former Netherhall farm-house, a new farmstead was built first at Cook's Pen, an old sheep-pen south-east of the village, and then at Pen Farm, established by 1849 in the centre of the south field. Thomas Webb (d. 1876) leased the northern farm from 1830 and Pen farm also from *c.* 1848. His son and partner Thomas eventually succeeded him as tenant after 1865 of virtually the whole parish.[29] The use of labour was intensive. The elder Webb was in 1851 employing 56 men, while William Stutfield, then farming *c.* 420 a., had 24. Only *c.* 35 labourers actually lived in the parish,[30] but men walked over daily to work from more populous villages such as Linton and Balsham. Both landlord and tenant found importing labour more convenient than building new cottages.[31] Webb was evidently disliked by some villagers. Attempts were made to burn down two of his farmsteads. He induced a diviner to 'identify' the suspected culprit, whom he forced to leave the village.[32]

The farm-labourers who then comprised most of Hildersham's inhabitants[33] were poor. Average wages barely rose from 9*s.* a week *c.* 1830 to 10*s.* or 11*s.* in the 1860s,[34] and few cottages had gardens. The cottagers gained little from the survival of the open fields, for by the early 1880s there were only two cows outside the farmer's herd. In 1849 the rector, Robert Goodwin, bought *c.* 6 a. near the church as allotments,[35] replaced at inclosure in the 1880s by 12 a. near the river.[36] In 1970 the land had for some time been let in one lot to the tenant of Manor farm.[37]

The death in 1881 of Thomas Webb the younger

7 *Rep. Sel. Cttee. on Commons* (1883), 6.
8 B.L. Add. MS. 5861, f. 32; 5860, f. 104.
9 H.O. 67/9.
10 C 6/328/76.
11 C.R.O., R 51/25/42, no. 8.
12 Ibid. no. 10.
13 H.O. 67/9.
14 Vancouver, *Agric. in Cambs.* 59; C.R.O., R 51/25/42, no. 10.
15 *V.C.H. Cambs.* i. 408.
16 E 179/242/8 m. 7d.
17 B.L. Add. MS. 5861, ff. 73v., 102.
18 Hildersham ct. bk. 1706–44, ff. 29v.–30, 33v.–34, 46 and v.
19 Vancouver, *Agric. in Cambs.* 59; *Camb. Chron.* 29 Mar. 1816.
20 C.R.O., R 51/25/35, p. 257.
21 Ibid. Q/RDc 82.
22 *Rep. Sel. Cttee. on Commons* (1883), 6–7.
23 C.R.O., R 51/25/41, no. 15; R 51/25/49; *C.J.* lvi. 19–20.
24 H.O. 67/9.
25 C.R.O., R 51/25/38.
26 Ibid. 334/010; ibid. R 51/25/46; ibid. par. reg. TS.
27 Ibid. R 51/25/42, nos. 8, 10.
28 Ibid. 334/010; ibid. L 42/3.
29 Ibid. L 92/20; ibid. 334/010; ibid. par. reg. TS.; C.U.L., Maps 53/84/13.
30 H.O. 107/1761.
31 *1st Rep. Com. Employment in Agric.* 355; *Rep. Sel. Cttee. on Commons* (1883), 6–9.
32 *Camb. Ind. Press*, 5 May 1961.
33 Cf. C.U.L., E.D.R., C 3/26, 37.
34 *Rep. H.L. Cttee. on Poor Laws*, H.C. 227, pp. 326–7 (1831), viii; *1st Rep. Com. Employment in Agric.* 355.
35 *Rep. Sel. Cttee. on Commons* (1883), 4–6, 8; C.U.L., Doc. 3964.
36 C.R.O., Q/RDc 82.
37 *Camb. Ind. Press*, 17 Dec. 1970.

and the expected division of his farm into two or three holdings threatened to revive the disadvantages of open-field cultivation,[38] and a provisional inclosure order was obtained in 1883[39] and confirmed by an Act the same year.[40] The land was divided in 1885, and the award executed in 1889. It allotted *c.* 55 a. for the rectorial glebe, 45 a. for the rector's private estate, *c.* 25 a. for the town land and other public purposes, and *c.* 9 a. to 5 people for rights of common. All the rest of the land involved, 945 a. including 93 a. for the right of sheep-walk, went to the Huddleston estate.[41] By 1895 that estate had been divided into four farms. One, Manor farm of *c.* 890 a. north of the village, was for some time kept in hand. After 1922 part of it was sometimes let separately as Green farm, for which a new farmstead was built north-east of the village. Another Huddleston farm north of the river was often held with the rectory farm, for which a homestead had been built out in the fields by 1912. South of the river were Cook's Pen, of 133 a., and beyond the railway line Pen farm of 373 a., sometimes, as from 1922, let together.[42]

In the 19th century there was little work available in Hildersham except on the farms. In 1831 32 families were engaged in agriculture, only 7 in crafts or trade.[43] The population in 1851 included a shoemaker and a coal-dealer.[44] The village retained its own blacksmith's shop until *c.* 1940, and a carpenter's business, employing 3 men in 1871, developed into a small building firm, which constructed the village bridge in 1886 and survived until *c.* 1925.[45] By 1960 the village shops had all closed, and except for those few employed on the farms the inhabitants worked in Linton, Cambridge, or Haverhill.[46]

In 1254 the Crown granted William de Boleville and his wife Ela a weekly market on Fridays with an annual fair on 19–21 July,[47] but no evidence survives that either was actually established.

Aubrey de Vere owned a mill at Hildersham yielding 10*s.* a year in 1086,[48] presumably that attached *c.* 1190 and later to the Ros moiety of the manor.[49] When the Parys estates were broken up *c.* 1675 Hildersham mill was sold with the Linton estate to Sir Thomas Sclater,[50] who had it rebuilt *c.* 1680.[51] It remained with his successors until after the 1770s,[52] but had been sold by 1800.[53] In the early 19th century the mill belonged to the Reeve family who occupied it until *c.* 1850;[54] it remained in business under various owners until *c.* 1915. The water-mill, which also used steam from the 1890s,[55] stands on a cut some way east of Hildersham village, and straddles the parish boundary with Linton. Its buildings, converted by 1925 into a private house,[56] comprised in 1973 a central mill-block, partly timber-built, spanning the former mill-race, with a brick house to the east, in Linton, and a tall grey-brick block to the west. A windmill, in the same ownership, built by 1837 in a field south of the water-mill,[57] was rebuilt in brick in 1863[58] and survived in 1973 without its sails. Its outbuildings, after use for an agricultural engineer's business, were sold in 1958[59] and were used in 1973 for selling antiques.

LOCAL GOVERNMENT. In 1275 Isabel Pauncefoot and Gilbert Kirkby were said to have view of frankpledge and the assize of bread and of ale at Hildersham.[60] In 1299 Isabel's grandson Grimbald claimed to hold the view jointly with the Kirkby heir, presumably in a single court leet for the whole vill.[61] The manor court was still occasionally styled a court leet and baron in the 1650s,[62] when it was presenting encroachments on the waste and electing haywards.[63] It was still making regulations about common rights 'for the peace and quiet of the tenants' in the 1720s,[64] when purely formal leet sittings were still held and constables and pinders appointed.[65] In the 1790s and in 1836 it formally appointed pinders,[66] and in 1812, under a new lord, began again to declare rules on commoning and to present copyholders for letting cottages decay.[67] A draft court book survives for 1651–9, and there are court rolls for 1672–1732 and court books for 1706–1897. They are principally concerned with copyhold transfers.[68]

In 1564 the churchwardens were said not to be making proper collections for the poor.[69] From the 1680s to *c.* 1835, probably because substantial inhabitants were few, only one churchwarden was usually elected, normally the principal farmer in the parish, who held office continuously for many years.[70] Poor relief was not expensive until the 1780s. In 1776 £14 was spent, a quarter of it on house-rent, *c.* 1785 £55, and in 1803 £87. Fourteen people, besides children, were then permanently supported.[71] In 1814 18 were permanently relieved at a cost totalling £232.[72] In 1829 two men were occasionally employed on roadwork; coal and clothing were distributed to the poor, and the roundsman system may

38 Cf. C.R.O., par. reg. TS.; *Rep. Sel. Cttee. on Commons* (1883), 1–2, 7.
39 *Land Com. Rep. on Hildersham Incl.* H.C. 52, pp. 1–3 (1883), xxi.
40 Inclosure (Hildersham) Prov. Order Conf. Act, 1883, 46 & 47 Vic. c. 84 (Local and Personal).
41 C.R.O., Q/RDc 82; cf. ibid. 334/010.
42 Ibid. R 56/12/24; R 49/8/36; ibid. 334/010; *Kelly's Dir. Cambs.* (1892–1937).
43 *Census*, 1831.
44 H.O. 107/1761.
45 *Gardner's Dir. Cambs.* (1851); *Kelly's Dir. Cambs.* (1858–1937); C.R.O., 331/Z 8, 1939, Sept. p. 79.
46 *Camb. Ind. Press*, 5 May 1961.
47 *Cal. Pat.* 1247–58, 379. No market at Hildersham was recorded in 1279.
48 *V.C.H. Cambs.* i. 390.
49 *Clerkenwell Cart.* (Camd. 3rd ser. lxxi), 20–1; cf. C.P. 25(1)/24/21 no. 8.
50 Cf. C.P. 25(2)/633/26 Chas. II Mich. no. 16.
51 C.R.O., R 59/5/3/1, pp. 76, 79–80.
52 Ibid. R 59/5/3/2, f. 41v.; R 59/5/4/3.
53 Not recorded in surveys of Linton estate after 1800.
54 e.g. C.R.O., Q/RDc 53, p. 154; cf. H.O. 107/66.
55 *Kelly's Dir. Cambs.* (1858–1916).
56 Ibid. (1925).
57 C.U.L., Doc. 3966; cf. *Proc. C.A.S.* xxxi. 27.
58 Inscr. on bldg.
59 C.R.O., 296/SP 1212.
60 *Rot. Hund.* (Rec. Com.), i. 52.
61 *Plac. de Quo Warr.* (Rec. Com.), 105.
62 C.R.O., L 1/102, pp. 11, 68.
63 Ibid. pp. 14, 23, 40.
64 Hildersham ct. bk. 1706–44, ff. 29v.–30, 33v.–34, 46 and v.
65 Ibid. ff. 21, 27, 33, 37, 49, 57v.
66 C.R.O., R 51/25/35, p. 183.
67 Ibid. pp. 257–8, 282–3.
68 Ibid. L 1/102; N.R.A., manorial index; ct. bks. A–E, *penes* Mr. H. B. Binney, of Pampisford Hall; C.R.O., R 51/25/35 (duplicate ct. bk. 1748–1817).
69 C.U.L., E.D.R., B 2/4, p. 119.
70 Ibid. Add. MS. 7208, pt. i, f. 31; C.R.O., R 55/38/1.
71 *Poor Law Abstract, 1804*, 34–5.
72 Ibid. *1818*, 28–9.

have been in force.[73] In 1832 £93 of £133 expended went to the aged, sick, and widows.[74] Hildersham became part of the Linton poor-law union in 1835,[75] was incorporated with the Linton R.D. into the South Cambridgeshire R.D. in 1934,[76] and was included in South Cambridgeshire in 1974.

CHURCH. Hildersham church had probably been established by *c.* 1150 and belonged originally to the Veres, since Hatfield Broadoak priory (Essex), founded by the Veres *c.* 1135, received a portion of tithes at Hildersham, worth 5 marks in 1291.[77] In 1210 the advowson of the rectory was in dispute between Gerard de Camville and his sister Maud,[78] each holding half the manor, and by 1279 was held by Gerard's successors, from whom it passed to the Bustelers.[79] In 1347 Grimbald Pauncefoot's widow Clemence recovered her third turn to present in right of dower against Robert le Busteler.[80] Busteler's successors, the Paryses, retained the advowson,[81] and after the Elizabethan settlement, as papists, were importuned by bishops and such staunch protestants as Sir Francis Walsingham to accept recommendations for the living.[82] In 1638 Charles Parys sold the advowson to Isaac Appleton, who in 1649 sold it to Henry Smith (d. 1702), rector since 1642.[83]

Smith resigned the living in 1684 and presented his son Henry, upon whose marriage in 1685 the advowson was entailed. The younger Smith sold it in 1714 to James Salt, and died in 1736,[84] whereupon Salt had himself presented. He died in 1758 having settled the advowson successively on his sons James (d.s.p. 1797) and Thomas (d. 1806), who each in turn presented himself to the living.[85] In 1801 Thomas Salt sold the advowson to James Goodwin, who presented his son Charles in 1806 and died the same year.[86] Charles, who died in 1847, left the advowson to his second son Robert,[87] who held the rectory upon his own presentation[88] until his death in 1899. In 1901 his sisters and heirs Sarah and Frances vested the advowson in trustees, including the new rector, P. R. Phillips, for the benefit of the church. When Phillips resigned in 1947 presentation was suspended and the cure was thereafter served by neighbouring incumbents or retired clergymen.[89]

The rectorial glebe consisted of *c.* 50 a. of arable in 1279,[90] 62 a. in the 17th century,[91] and 67½ a., including closes, in 1777.[92] The 55 a. allotted for glebe at inclosure in 1889[93] was sold in 1919.[94] In 1951 the church retained 9 a. of glebe.[95] The tithes, still being taken in kind in 1800,[96] were commuted in 1840 for a tithe-rent-charge of £423 15*s.*[97] The rectory house stood *c.* 1560 in a copyhold close opposite the church, held by successive rectors until its enfranchisement in 1848.[98] The house had seven hearths in 1664[99] and was said to be large and in good repair in 1783.[1] A large brick house built in Tudor style *c.* 1851[2] had been sold by 1961.[3]

The benefice was taxed at £12 in 1217, and at 20 marks in 1291,[4] but only at £15 in 1535.[5] By 1650 it was worth £80 a year and in 1728 £100.[6] The rector's gross income was £320 *c.* 1830,[7] and £450 in 1877.[8]

About 1300 a rector gave the church 3 a. in free alms.[9] By the mid 18th century the rent of 3 a. called the town land, yielding 10*s.* a year in the 18th century and £3 5*s.* in the 19th, was by custom devoted to church repairs and expenses.[10] From 1524 3*s.* 4*d.* a year for church repairs was also received from John Bolton's charity.[11] The endowment of the church by Sarah and Frances Goodwin in 1901 is mentioned above.[12]

In the early 14th century the patrons sometimes chose their kinsmen or dependents as rectors. Ralph Hengham presented his clerk John Hengham, rector 1311–21, and William le Busteler in 1321 presented his younger son William, still rector in 1332.[13] William's successor, William Gryselegh, *c.* 1338 until 1342, was frequently absent in the service of the countess of Norfolk or the earl of Suffolk.[14] In 1379 the rector had two chaplains to assist him.[15] In the late 15th and early 16th centuries Hildersham had a guild of the Assumption.[16] Margaret, wife of John Parys (d. 1517), whose dower included the advowson, presented in 1518 William Burgoyne, master of Peterhouse (d. 1523), and then his brother Thomas, rector 1523–50, who held Hildersham in

73 *Rep. H.L. Cttee. on Poor Laws*, H.C. 227, pp. 326–7 (1831), viii.
74 *Rep. Com. Poor Laws* [44], p. 257, H.C. (1834), xxviii.
75 *Poor Law Com. 1st Rep.* 249.
76 *Census*, 1931 (pt. ii).
77 *Tax, Eccl.* (Rec. Com.), 267; cf. *V.C.H. Essex*, ii. 107.
78 *Cur. Reg. R.* vi. 87, 105.
79 *Rot. Hund.* (Rec. Com.), ii. 416. A papal provision to Hildersham made in 1321 (*Cal. Papal Reg.* ii. 215) was apparently ineffective.
80 C.P. 40/352 rot. 344; *E.D.R.* (1892), 827.
81 e.g. *E.D.R.* (1895), 91.
82 Hist. MSS. Com. 4, *5th Rep.* pp. 485–6.
83 C.R.O., R 56/16/1–4; *Alum. Cantab. to 1751*, iv. 99. Incumbents after 1338 are listed in *E.D.R.* (1897), 77.
84 C.R.O., R 56/16/5–8.
85 Ibid. 9–10; Prob. 11/838 (P.C.C. 167 Hutton).
86 C.R.O., R 56/16/12–13, 18; *Alum. Cantab. 1752–1900*, i. 317, s.v. Bones, Chas.
87 Prob. 11/2054 (P.C.C. 319, 1847); C.R.O., par. reg. TS.
88 C.R.O., R 56/16/20–1.
89 Ibid. par. reg. TS.; ibid. 331/Z 5, 1920, Nov. p. lxxxiii; *Crockford* (1951–2, 1961–2, 1971–2); ex inf. the Church Com. and the Revd. E. C. Pearson.
90 *Rot. Hund.* (Rec. Com.), ii. 416.
91 C.U.L., E.D.R., H 1/4, terriers 1625, 1665.
92 Ibid. Doc. 3965.
93 C.R.O., Q/RDc 82.
94 Ex inf. the Church Com.; C.U.L., Maps 53(1)/91/157.
95 *Crockford* (1951–2).
96 C.R.O., R 56/16/14.
97 C.U.L., Doc. 3966.
98 C.R.O., R 56/16/27–9; C.U.L., Doc. 3964; cf. ibid. E.D.R., H 1/4, terriers 1625, 1665.
99 E 179/84/437 rot. 58.
1 C.U.L., E.D.R., B 7/1, p. 124.
2 C.R.O., R 55/38/1.
3 *Crockford* (1951–2, 1961–2); *Camb. Ind. Press*, 5 Apr. 1961.
4 *Val. of Norwich*, ed. Lunt, 227, 536; *Tax. Eccl.* (Rec. Com.), 267.
5 *Valor Eccl.* (Rec. Com.), iii. 504.
6 Lamb. Pal. MS. 904, f. 272; C.U.L., E.D.R., B 8/1.
7 *Rep. Com. Eccl. Revenues*, pp. 348–9.
8 C.U.L., E.D.R., C 3/26, 37.
9 *Vetus Liber Arch. Elien.* (C.A.S. 8vo ser. xlviii), 63.
10 C.U.L., E.D.R., B 8/1; *Char. Don.* i. 88–9; *31st Rep. Com. Char.* 104; C.R.O., R 55/38/1; *Char. Digest Cambs. 1863–4*, 21.
11 See p. 19.
12 See p. 63.
13 C.P. 40/352 rot. 344; *Cal. Papal Reg.* ii. 89; *Cal. Fine R.* 1327–37, 324.
14 *E.D.R.* (1889), 357; (1890), 426, 449.
15 *East Anglian*, N.S. xiii. 191.
16 *Trans. C.H.A.S.* i. 397; cf. Prob. 11/20 (P.C.C. 27 Maynwaring, will of Rob. Bygrave).

plurality with Sandy (Beds.) from 1526.[17] Both were probably non-resident, employing curates.[18]

John Reston, rector 1550–1, was master of Jesus College, Cambridge.[19] His successor Dr. Thomas Heskyns, also usually non-resident, had abandoned the cure by 1561 to go overseas, where he became a Catholic controversialist.[20] George Fuller, rector 1561–91, usually resided at Hildersham, and built up an estate in the neighbourhood,[21] but regularly employed curates,[22] the first recorded being apparently a convinced protestant.[23] Fuller's successor John Smith held Hildersham with Fen Ditton until his death in 1614. In 1593 his curate was said to be failing to catechize the children.[24] Thomas Murriell, rector 1614–29, held two livings and was archdeacon of Norfolk.[25] Henry Smith, master of Magdalene College, Cambridge, was succeeded at Hildersham when he died in 1642 by his son Henry,[26] who held the living throughout the Interregnum, being described in 1650 as an orthodox and godly divine.[27] Through his purchase of the advowson in 1649 the rectory became a family living, held by three successive clerical dynasties until 1900.[28]

The third Henry Smith was resident in 1728, when he was holding communion seven times a year and two services every Sunday. He claimed up to 18 communicants.[29] James Salt was likewise resident in 1775 and conducted services in person,[30] but his brother Thomas, already vicar of Nazeing (Essex), employed the Revd. Andrew Perne of Little Abington as curate.[31] In 1807 the newly presented Charles Goodwin had few communicants[32] and only *c.* 20 in 1825, although he held services twice each Sunday and communion four times a year.[33] He was normally resident, as was his son Robert, who also held Great Abington from 1845, but both usually employed curates, including in 1877 the master of Saffron Walden grammar school. Robert then claimed that almost all the parishioners came to church and up to 47 people attended the monthly communion.[34] By 1897 he was also holding services on weekdays in Lent and on many saints' days, and by 1894 had instituted a surpliced choir.[35] There were 49 communicants in 1905,[36] 43 in 1939, when most of the congregation of 90 went to church every other Sunday.[37]

The church of the *HOLY TRINITY*, so called by 1521,[38] stands west of the street and north of the river. It is built of field stones with ashlar dressings, and consists of a chancel with a south chapel and north sacristy, aisled nave of two bays with a south porch, and west tower. The oldest portions, the vaulted sacristy and the west tower, are of the early 13th century. The tower, unbuttressed and surmounted by a small spike, has simple lancets to the two lower stages and double lancets under restored plate tracery to the third, and inside is divided from the nave by two low arches. The tall nave, rebuilt in the late 13th century, but probably retaining its earlier proportions, has one quatrefoil pier on each side; the clerestory has cusped windows in square frames, possibly restored. The aisle windows have simple Decorated tracery, and may be contemporary with the south chapel built by William le Busteler, rector 1321–32,[39] perhaps as a chantry for his parents. The chancel arch was rebuilt probably *c.* 1400.[40] In the 15th century the chancel was given new windows which still survived *c.* 1850,[41] and a new door to the sacristy.

The octagonal 13th-century font rests on five columns and has trefoiled canopies on each face. Screens between the chancel and the south chapel and nave survived in 1742[42] but were swept away at the Victorian restoration, when the roof also was entirely renewed.[43] Despite William Dowsing's efforts in 1644[44] much medieval glass survived in 1742, and a few fragments that remained *c.* 1880 were then reset.[45] Among notable monuments in the church are the effigies, carved in oak, of a cross-legged knight and a lady, perhaps commemorating William le Busteler (d. *c.* 1334) and his wife.[46] The chancel contains brasses with effigies ascribed to Robert Parys (d. *c.* 1377) and his wife Eleanor, to Henry Parys (d. 1427) and his wife Margery, and to Henry Parys (d. 1466).[47] A tomb-slab carved with a cross lies under an ogee-headed recess in the north wall of the chancel, where Robert Parys's brass once lay.

In 1601 the church windows were found to be much broken and the chancel not whitewashed,[48] and in 1638 the aisles were blocked by two large pews.[49] Both chapel and aisles were out of repair in 1665,[50] and in 1742 the chapel was unfloored.[51] In 1803 the churchwardens sold the lead off the roof and pulled down the south chapel.[52] Between 1853 and 1890 the church was heavily restored by the rector Robert Goodwin, latterly with C. A. Buckler as architect.[53] The chancel and north aisle were

[17] *E.D.R.* (1911), 20, 70; Emden, *Biog. Reg. Univ. Camb.* 108–9.
[18] e.g. B.L. Add. MS. 5861, ff. 73v., 91v., 102; *E.D.R.* (1913), 41.
[19] *Alum. Cantab. to 1751*, ii. 412.
[20] Ibid. ii. 360; Cooper, *Athen. Cantab.* i. 419; B.L. Add. MS. 5813, f. 66.
[21] See p. 7.
[22] Prob. 11/78 (P.C.C. 62 Sainberbe); cf. C.U.L., E.D.R., B 2/11.
[23] See his books listed in B.L. Add. MS. 5861, f. 48.
[24] *Alum. Cantab. to 1751*, iv. 100; C.U.L., E.D.R., B 2/13, f. 3v.; B 2/30A, f. 6v.
[25] *Alum. Cantab. to 1751*, iii. 228.
[26] Ibid. iv. 99.
[27] Lamb. Pal. MS. 904, f. 271.
[28] See above.
[29] C.U.L., E.D.R., B 8/1.
[30] Ibid. C 1/1.
[31] Ibid. B 8/4; cf. ibid. Add. MS. 7208, vol. i, insert: licence, 1797.
[32] Ibid. E.D.R., C 1/4.
[33] Ibid. C 1/6.
[34] Ibid. C 3/17, 26; B 1/16, 39.
[35] Ibid. C 3/37; C.R.O., 331/Z 6, 1932, June, p. 50.
[36] C.R.O., 331/Z 1, 1905, May, p. xi.
[37] Ibid. 331/Z 8, 1939, Jan., p. 4.
[38] B.L. Add. MS. 5861, f. 73v.
[39] *Mon. Inscr. Cambs.* 79.
[40] B.L. Add. MS. 36443, no. 881.
[41] Cf. *Eccl. Top. Eng.* vi, no. 155; *Trans. C.H.A.S.* iv. 64.
[42] Palmer, *Wm. Cole*, 96.
[43] A. G. Hill, *Churches of Cambs.* (1880), 195; cf. *Trans. C.H.A.S.* iv. 63–4; *Kelly's Dir. Cambs.* (1888).
[44] *Trans. C.H.A.S.* iii. 89.
[45] Palmer, *Wm. Cole*, 96; *Churches of Cambs.* 196.
[46] *Mon. Inscr. Cambs.* 79, 253; cf. B.L. Add. MS. 6730, ff. 27–9; C.R.O., 331/Z 5, 1919, Sept., p. lviii.
[47] *Mon. Inscr. Cambs.* 79. Only the third was identified by an inscription.
[48] C.U.L., E.D.R., B 2/18, f. 77v.
[49] *Cambs. Village Doc.* 65.
[50] C.U.L., E.D.R., B 2/59, p. 38.
[51] Palmer, *Wm. Cole*, 96.
[52] *Trans. C.H.A.S.* iv. 62–3, 65.
[53] Cf. B.L. Add. MS. 36426, f. 38; Add. MS. 36433, no. 881; *Churches of Cambs.* 194.

remodelled by 1855 and the south chapel rebuilt soon after. The chancel arch was refashioned, the walls were thoroughly scraped, and at Goodwin's insistence the Perpendicular tracery in the chancel windows was then replaced with reticulated tracery. The tower was raised 13 ft. and the roof replaced and slated in 1878. The chancel was entirely covered *c.* 1890 with paintings[54] which were restored in 1973.[55] Stained glass, including an east window by Clayton and Bell,[56] greatly darkened the church, and an alabaster reredos was installed in memory of James Raymond, tenant at the Hall in 1851 and 1871.[57] When work was completed in 1890[58] the interior appeared, as in 1973, almost entirely Victorian.

In 1542 Margaret Parys bequeathed to the church an organ standing in it.[59] In the early 19th century music was supplied from a singing gallery at the west end erected since 1742. After its demolition *c.* 1870 several players never set foot in the church again. A new organ, given by Robert Goodwin, was installed in 1900.[60] In 1552 the church had three bells.[61] Three new bells were cast in 1581, two of which were sold in 1803. The third and lightest was used in 1880 by John Taylor & Co. of Loughborough in making three new bells,[62] which survived in 1973. A silver cup and paten by Thomas Buttell were acquired in 1569.[63] The parish registers are complete from 1559.[64]

NONCONFORMITY. In 1582 Thomas Dalton and his wife were said to have failed to come to church for a year.[65] Although the manor was owned until 1800 by papists there is no evidence of Catholic recusancy in Hildersham, nor of protestant dissent before 1783, when two families were said to attend a meeting at Linton.[66] In 1825 the number of dissenters was said to be increasing.[67] A house was registered for dissenting worship in 1828, and a building in 1837, the latter by Thomas Hopkins,[68] Independent minister at Linton.[69] Perhaps the same building was the out-station of the Linton chapel, lately adapted for worship, where the Linton minister, G. J. Hall, held Saturday evening services in 1851 with an average attendance of 100.[70] It had closed by 1877, and in 1897 all the inhabitants were said to be nominally church people.[71]

EDUCATION. In 1524 money was left for four boys to go to school,[72] and Hildersham had unlicensed school masters in 1579 and 1601.[73] In 1818 the parish clerk kept a school for 30 boys and his wife taught girls to read and sew, while an evening school was held for young men.[74] In 1833 there was only one day-school with 10 pupils, for whom their parents paid.[75] By 1851 a day-school and Sunday school had been set up in a building south-east of the church.[76] The parochial school was supported in 1864 by contributions from parishioners and in 1879 by the rector and school-pence. It was rebuilt in 1879–80[77] for up to 111 children. Attendance between 1893 and 1914 fluctuated around 40.[78] The school had separate mixed and infants departments in 1914.[79] By 1919 attendance had declined to *c.* 20.[80] Many children went to Abington school, and in 1928, when it had only 7 pupils, Hildersham school was closed.[81]

CHARITIES FOR THE POOR. From 1524 Hildersham received 6*s.* 8*d.* a year under the will, proved 1509, of John Bolton of Little Abington, half for its church, half for its poor. The money was still being paid in 1965. Since 1929 it had been a rent-charge on Abington Hall whose owner redeemed it for £10 in 1966.[82] In 1573 the parish bought with its town stock the 4-a. Bodney's close north of the church, the income to be distributed twice a year to the poor. In 1590 one of the feoffees, Thomas Dalton (d. 1602), acquired the close subject to a rent-charge of £1,[83] which was still received in 1965. By the 18th century the churchwardens were distributing the two charities together, usually at Christmas, in doles of 6*d.* to 1*s.* 6*d.* In 1766 there were 22 recipients including 8 widows, in 1834 14.[84] In the early 20th century the income was saved for several years and then distributed in coal.[85] The cottagers' right to common over St. Margaret's Green, reputed a charity in 1837,[86] was replaced at inclosure in 1889 by allotments.[87]

54 C.R.O., R 58/38/1; *Trans. C.H.A.S.* iv. 62, 64–5; cf. *Kelly's Dir. Cambs.* (1879, 1888); *Camb. National Trust Centre Mag.* Jan. 1974, 13–17.
55 *Camb. Evening News*, 6 Dec. 1972; 3 Aug. 1973.
56 C.R.O., 331/Z 3, 1912, Jan., pp. vi, xii–xiii; *Churches of Cambs.* 194.
57 Cf. H.O. 107/1761; R.G. 10/1592.
58 *E.D.R.* (1890), 454.
59 B.L. Add. MS. 5860, f. 104v.
60 C.R.O., 331/Z 4, 1914, Apr.
61 *Cambs. Ch. Goods, temp. Edw. VI*, 63.
62 *Trans. C.H.A.S.* iv. 62–3; *Cambs. Bells* (C.A.S. 8vo ser. xviii), 150.
63 List of ch. plate *penes V.C.H.*; cf. *Kelly's Dir. Cambs.* (1879, 1888).
64 C.R.O., P 91/1/1–7.
65 *Cath. Rec. Soc.* liii. 2.
66 C.U.L., E.D.R., B 7/1, p. 124.
67 Ibid. C 1/6.
68 G.R.O. Worship Returns, Ely dioc. nos. 523, 619.
69 See p. 103.
70 H.O. 129/188/2/3/12.
71 C.U.L., E.D.R., C 3/26, 37.

72 B.L. Add. MS. 5861, f. 91v.
73 C.U.L., E.D.R., D 2/10, f. 160; B 2/18, f. 77v.
74 *Educ. of Poor Digest*, 60.
75 *Educ. Enquiry Abstract*, 57.
76 *Gardner's Dir. Cambs.* (1851); O.S. Map 6″, Cambs. LV. SW. (1891 edn.).
77 *Kelly's Dir. Cambs.* (1864, 1879, 1888).
78 *Rep. Educ. Cttee. of Council, 1892–3* [C. 7089-I], p. 688, H.C. (1893–4), xxvi; *Bd. of Educ., List 21, 1914* (H.M.S.O.), 27.
79 *Bd. of Educ., List 21, 1914* (H.M.S.O.), 27.
80 Ibid. *1919*, 16.
81 Ibid. *1932*, 17; C.R.O., 331/Z 6, 1928, May, p. 40; June, p. 48.
82 *31st Rep. Com. Char.* 104; Char. Com. files; and see above, p. 19.
83 C.R.O., P 91/1/1, f. 1 and v., and insert; R 51/25/41, no. 5.
84 Ibid. R 55/38/1.
85 e.g. C.R.O., 331/Z 1, 1905, Dec., p. xcii; 331/Z 3, 1911, Jan., p. iii.
86 *31st Rep. Com. Char.* 104.
87 C.R.O., Q/RDc 82.

HORSEHEATH

THE PARISH of Horseheath, covering 1,922 a., lies at the eastern end of Chilford hundred, and its eastern edge forms part of the county boundary with Suffolk.[1] The village, centrally placed, is 14 miles south-east of Cambridge and 5 miles west of Haverhill (Suff.). The northern boundary of the parish runs along the straight ancient road known as Wool Street.[2] The western boundary follows the road from Bartlow to West Wratting along a valley, and the eastern and southern boundaries follow field boundaries, with a detour to the south to include in Horseheath the moated site of Cardinal's Farm.

Horseheath lies on the Upper Chalk where it juts into Cambridgeshire from Essex and Suffolk. The soil at the western end of the parish, where the ground rises from 200 to 300 ft., is chalky, becoming heavier and wetter towards the east, where it lies mostly on boulder clay. Horseheath is the highest parish in the county, lying mostly between 300 and 350 ft. It was once well wooded: there was woodland for 90 pigs in 1086, and 27 a. of demesne woodland were recorded in 1279. Several smaller woods, such as Bower grove and Goodreds wood, survived in the 15th century,[3] but had mostly been cleared by the 18th.[4] In 1973 small blocks of woodland, mostly 19th-century plantations, remained around Horseheath Lodge and at Crow (formerly Coat) croft.[5] Horseheath has been entirely agricultural. Soon after 1800 all its open-field land was in one hand,[6] so that no formal inclosure award was required.

Traces of Roman occupation have been found near the northern boundary and close to the village.[7] By 1086 there were 26 tenants and 3 *servi* at Horseheath.[8] In 1279 there were 64 messuages and 2 cottages, inhabited by *c.* 80 tenants.[9] In 1327 26 people paid the subsidy, and in 1377 121 adults paid the poll tax.[10] There were only 35 taxpayers in 1524,[11] and 34 households in 1563.[12] In 1728 there were 71 families containing 346 people.[13] In the 19th century the population rose from 342 in 1801 to 508 in 1851, fell slightly, and then increased to a peak of 578 in 1871. After a steady decline it reached the low point of 328 in 1951, and then increased to 376 in 1971.[14]

The village presumably stood on its modern site by the 14th century when the parish church was built. The church stands 350 yd. north of the Cambridge–Haverhill road, on a winding village street which runs on to Streetley End in West Wickham. East of the village the main road was apparently diverted round the southern edge of Horseheath park, created by the Alington family in the 15th and 16th centuries, and possibly in the village the road once lay further north close to the church. The names Church street, recorded in 1416,[15] and Netherstreet, of 1449,[16] probably both referred to the village street. The positions of the surviving 16th- and 17th-century houses suggest that buildings were then concentrated along that street, where 18th-century buildings such as Church Farm are also sited. A fragment of the former village green survives at its south end. There were *c.* 48 houses under Charles II[17] and still only 50 dwellings in 1801.[18] In 1839 there were, besides the farmsteads, two or three houses and 31 cottages, into which 53 households were crowded.[19] At Sherwood Green, called in 1629 Sherwood End,[20] eastwards along the main road, several rows of cottages were built in the mid 19th century, one row of five in flint being dated 1838. There were said to be 100 inhabited dwellings in 1851 and 126 in 1871, but by 1901 there were only 93, while 24 stood empty.[21] In 1913 14 houses had lately been demolished, and of 50 remaining 27 were at Sherwood Green.[22] In the mid 20th century an influx of residents, caused partly by the expansion of light industry at Haverhill, was made possible by the building of many new houses, mostly detached, in the spaces between the scattered older dwellings. In 1950–1 twelve new council houses were put up at the southern end of the street.[23]

In 1768 there was a village alehouse called the Bell.[24] By 1839 there were two public houses, the Red Lion and, eastwards along the main road, the Montfort Arms.[25] The Batson Arms at Sherwood Green was opened before 1899.[26] The Montfort Arms, closed after 1915 and sold in 1923, had by 1929 become a café.[27] The Batson Arms closed between 1961 and 1971, when the Red Lion became a restaurant.[28]

The village feast was customarily held on 5–7 June.[29] In 1904 a parish room, styled the Guildhall, was opened, and included a library by 1910.[30] It was closed in 1969.[31] A parish coal and clothing club started *c.* 1900 was probably the benefit club disbanded in 1912.[32] Stanlake Batson (d. 1857)

1 This account was written in 1975.
2 *Proc. C.A.S.* lvi–lvii. 52–8.
3 *V.C.H. Cambs.* i. 408; *Rot. Hund.* (Rec. Com.), ii. 420–2; B.L. Add. MS. 5823, ff. 219v., 242, 249v.
4 Catherine E. Parsons, *All Saints' Church, Horseheath* (1911), 63.
5 Cf. C.U.L., E.D.R., tithe map 1839.
6 See p. 76.
7 Fox, *Arch. Camb. Region*, 226, 231; *Proc. C.A.S.* xiv. 162 n.; xxxi. 99–102; lvi–lvii. 52; lxiv. 28–9.
8 *V.C.H. Cambs.* i. 408.
9 *Rot. Hund.* (Rec. Com.), ii. 420–2.
10 *Cambs. Lay Subsidy, 1327*, 26; *East Anglian*, N.S. xii. 240.
11 E 179/81/134 m. 4d.
12 B.L. Harl. MS. 594, f. 199v.
13 C.U.L., E.D.R., B 8/1.
14 *Census*, 1801–1971.
15 *Cal. Pat.* 1416–22, 32.
16 B.L. Add. MS. 5823, f. 247v.
17 See pp. 279–80.
18 *Census*, 1801.
19 C.U.L., E.D.R., tithe award 1839.
20 C.R.O., R 70/48, 20 Jan. 4 Chas. I.
21 *Census*, 1851–1901.
22 C.U.L., MS. Plan 682.
23 Ibid. Doc. 3980, box ii, 'Village Annals', p. 61.
24 C.R.O., R 70/48, 15 July 1768.
25 C.U.L., E.D.R., tithe award 1839; cf. *Gardner's Dir. Cambs.* (1851).
26 *E.D.R.* (1899), 67.
27 *Kelly's Dir. Cambs.* (1916–37); C.R.O., 515/SP 698.
28 *Camb. Ind. Press*, 3 Mar. 1961; 24 June 1971.
29 H.O. 107/66.
30 C.R.O., 331/Z 1, 1904, Dec., p. lxxxix; Z 3, 1910 Nov., p. lxxxii.
31 *Camb. Ind. Press*, 18 Apr. 1969.
32 C.R.O., 331/Z 1, 1904, Nov., p. lxxix; Z 3/1912, Sept., p. lxvii.

trained race-horses, including the Derby winner of 1834, at Horseheath Lodge by the western boundary.[33] In 1972 part of the old race-course there was reopened for point-to-point races.[34]

MANORS. The principal manor at Horseheath in 1086 comprised 2½ hides held in demesne by Count Alan as successor since 1066 to Eddeva the fair and two of her sokemen. The count's man Alwin had acquired a yardland held in 1066 by Eddeva's man Godwin.[35] From the late 12th century the whole estate was held of Alan's honor of Richmond by the Veres, earls of Oxford,[36] who in turn subinfeudated it.[37] The Veres retained the overlordship until *c.* 1600,[38] and in 1611 it passed as parcel of Castle Camps manor to the Charterhouse, which was still expecting quit-rents from manors in Horseheath in the 18th century.[39]

The largest Richmond fee, later *HORSEHEATH HALL* manor, was probably held in 1199 by Walter de Capeles, who had succeeded his father Aubrey in lands granted by Earl Aubrey de Vere (d. 1194).[40] Walter, whose Cambridgeshire lands were restored to him in 1217 after his rebellion,[41] held ½ fee at Horseheath *c.* 1236.[42] By 1247 Sir Peter of Melling held that manor, apparently in right of his wife Joan.[43] In 1249 Peter and Joan sold the reversion of 2 carucates there after their deaths to Sir James de Audley,[44] who had possession by 1259[45] and possibly by 1252 when he was granted free warren at Horseheath.[46] Audley died in 1272 and was succeeded in turn by his sons James[47] (d. 1273), Henry (d. 1276), and William (d. 1282).[48] Alice, widow of Robert de Beauchamp of Somerset (d. 1263), claimed that James the father had granted Horseheath to her, probably *c.* 1263, and in 1278 William released the manor to her and her son James.[49] Alice, who held *c.* 400 a. in demesne there in 1279, died after 1282,[50] and her son James in or before 1286.[51] He had apparently taken the name of Audley, and left as heir an infant son James.[52] In 1302 and 1305 the manor was occupied by Hugh de Audley, youngest son of James (d. 1272),[53] but by 1313 had reverted to Alice's grandson James,[54] who held it until his death *c.* 1335.[55] James's widow Margaret held it between 1336 and *c.* 1362.[56] His son and heir William Audley died, probably in 1365, without issue, and William's brother and heir Thomas[57] in 1372, leaving a son James,[58] who died young. Horseheath passed, probably in 1378, to Thomas's daughter Elizabeth, who in 1384 entered upon it with her husband John Rose[59] and in 1387 agreed to its settlement for life on her former guardian John Sibill (d. 1392) and his wife Joan.[60] By 1395 it was occupied by Sir Philip Sinclair, claiming as great-grandson of James Audley (d. *c.* 1335)[61] and in 1397 it was bought for William Alington.[62] Alington's descendants retained it until 1700, and had acquired the other manors in Horseheath by 1550. After 1600 they were therefore said to possess the manors of Horseheath Hall, Carbonells, Bowerhall, Limburys, Jacobs, and Goodredges.[63]

William Alington, Speaker in 1429,[64] died in 1446. His eldest son William[65] was succeeded in 1459 by his son John[66] (d. 1480). John's son and heir William[67] was killed at Bosworth in 1485, leaving a son Giles aged two, during whose minority his mother Elizabeth and her second husband William Cheyne held the estates as lessees.[68] Giles, knighted by 1513, died in 1521, and was succeeded by his son Giles,[69] knighted by 1541.[70] Sir Giles was succeeded in 1586 by his great-grandson Giles Alington.[71] Sir Giles, knighted in 1603, died in 1638, when his heir was his eldest surviving son William,[72] who received an Irish barony in 1642 and died in 1648. Lord Alington's elder son Giles died under age in 1660, when his heir was his younger brother William, created an English baron in 1682.[73] William died in 1685 and Giles, his only son, died under age and without issue in 1691. In 1700, following a long Chancery suit, a 500-year term in the Horseheath estate, which had been entailed on William's brother Hildebrand, Lord Alington (d.s.p. 1722),[74] was sold to meet the large portions bequeathed by William to his daughters Juliana, Diana, and Katherine, who between 1700 and 1705 released their reversionary interests to the purchaser John Bromley,[75] a Barbados sugar-planter.

33 *Proc. C.A.S.* xli. 49.
34 *Camb. Evening News*, 16 June 1971; 22 Feb. 1972.
35 *V.C.H. Cambs.* i. 374.
36 Cf. R. Gale, *Reg. Hon. Richmond* (1722), 26.
37 e.g. *Liber de Bernewelle*, 253; *Rot. Hund.* (Rec. Com.), ii. 420–2.
38 e.g. C 140/76 no. 58; C 142/36 no. 16; C 142/592 no. 90.
39 Charterho. Mun., MR 2/557A pt. ii, pp. 3, 23; MR 2/565C.
40 Cf. *Rot. Cur. Reg.* (Rec. Com.), i. 407; ii. 105–6.
41 *Rot. Litt. Claus.* (Rec. Com.), i. 375.
42 *Liber de Bernewelle*, 253.
43 C.P. 25(1)/24/22 no. 21.
44 C.P. 25 (1)/24/25 no. 8.
45 *Close R.* 1259–61, 454.
46 *Cal. Chart. R.* 1226–57, 406.
47 *Cal. Inq. p.m.* i, p. 261; *Ex. e Rot. Fin.* (Rec. Com.), ii. 574.
48 *Cal. Inq. p.m.* ii, pp. 67–9, 121–2, 286–7.
49 *Cal. Close*, 1272–9, 235; *Abbrev. Plac.* (Rec. Com.), 269; cf. *Cal. Pat.* 1258–66, 292, 317; Sanders, *Eng. Baronies*, 51.
50 *Rot. Hund.* (Rec. Com.), ii. 420; *Cal. Pat.* 1281–92, 44.
51 B.L. Add. MS. 39373, f. 86; cf. *V.C.H. Suss.* ix. 176; *Cal. Fine R.* 1337–47, 238.
52 C.P. 40/331 rot. 51; *Cal. Inq. p.m.* iv, p. 272.
53 *Feud. Aids*, i. 145; *Hatton's Bk. of Seals*, p. 293; cf. *Complete Peerage*, i. 347–8.
54 B.L. Add. MS. 5823, f. 248; *Feud. Aids*, i. 155; cf. *Hist. Coll. Staffs.* ix. 258.
55 *Cal. Pat.* 1334–8, 200.
56 *Feud. Aids*, i. 162; *Cal. Pat.* 1358–61, 582; cf. B.L. Add. MS. 5823, ff. 225v., 249.
57 *Cal. Inq. p.m.* xii, pp. 1–2; ibid. xvi, p. 126, dates William's death 1367.
58 Ibid. xiii, p. 127.
59 Ibid. xv, pp. 277–8; *Cal. Fine R.* 1377–83, 125; *Cal. Pat.* 1381–5, 459.
60 C.P. 25(1)/29/89 no. 10; *Cal. Close*, 1399–1402, 561; *Cal. Fine R.* 1391–9, 102.
61 B.L. Add. MS. 5823, ff. 245 and v., 252v.–253; *Cal. Pat.* 1391–6, 592, 614; cf. *Proc. C.A.S.* xxxii. 19, 22.
62 B.L. Add. MS. 5823, ff. 80, 253.
63 e.g. C 142/592 no. 90; C.R.O., R 70/48, 19 June 1664.
64 *Proc. C.A.S.* lii. 32–40; cf. ibid. 30–55; xli. 1–26.
65 C.U.L., MS. Mm. i. 42, p. 259.
66 C 139/177 no. 42.
67 C 140/76 no. 58.
68 *Cal. Inq. p.m. Hen. VII*, i, pp. 13–14, 426.
69 C 142/36 no. 16; Prob. 11/22 (P.C.C. 14 Porch).
70 *L. & P. Hen. VIII*, xvi, p. 502.
71 C 142/211 no. 163.
72 Nicholls, *Progresses of Jas. I*, i. 114; C 142/592 no. 90.
73 *Complete Peerage*, i. 106–8.
74 Prob. 11/380 (P.C.C. 102 Cann); Gibbons, *Ely Episc. Rec.* 322.
75 C.R.O., R 70/48, 25 July 1699, 17 Apr. 1700, 14 June 1705. Hildebrand would not release his own rights: ibid. 9 July 1709.

Bromley died in 1707, having settled Horseheath on his son John. Father and son were both M.P.s for the county.[76] The younger John died in 1718. His son and heir Henry,[77] then under age, was M.P. for Cambridgeshire from 1727 to 1741, when he was created Lord Montfort, and on his suicide in 1755 was succeeded by his son Thomas. The extravagance of Henry and Thomas[78] caused the sale of the estate,[79] which was bought in 1777 by Stanlake Batson.[80] Batson died in 1812, and was succeeded by his son and namesake[81] (d. 1857), whose son Stanlake Ricketts Batson died in 1871. The latter's eldest son Stanlake Henry Batson in 1884, while still under age, alienated his life-interest in order to pay his debts.[82] He withdrew to New Zealand and died in 1921. In 1925 his son S. P. R. Batson sold the whole estate to T. Wayman Parsons, a long-established local farmer.[83] Parsons sold off much land the same year, and after his death in 1942 his executors sold more.[84] His sons A. C. and H. W. Parsons died in 1950 and 1969 respectively.[85] The largest fragment of the estate belonged in 1975 to Mr. T. Cornish of Horseheath Park.[86]

The original manor-house of the Audley manor probably stood east of the village, near the Hall or Hallgate field recorded in the 14th and 15th centuries.[87] Elizabeth I stayed there in 1578.[88] Horseheath Hall was rebuilt between 1663 and 1665 by William, Lord Alington, to a design by Sir Roger Pratt.[89] The new house, of red brick, faced east and west on the highest ground in the park. The main block, of two storeys on a basement, had ten bays including a three-bay pediment to the west. The balustraded roof was surmounted by an octagonal cupola, topped by a gilded ball brought back from the siege of Boulogne in 1544. Single-storey ranges to north and south contained the stables and offices, forming a 500-ft. frontage. John Bromley (d. 1718) began alterations to the house and garden,[90] and his son Henry spent lavishly, employing William Kent on the interior and the gardens. Henry's son Thomas added an orangery in 1762. The furniture and paintings were sold in 1775, and all the remaining contents in 1777.[91] The empty shell was mostly demolished in 1792,[92] and no visible trace remained in 1940, except for an overgrown ornamental pond north of the site. Wrought-iron gates of *c.* 1670 from the Hall survive at Trinity and St. John's colleges, Cambridge, and at Cheveley rectory.[93] Bricks from the Hall were used in neighbouring houses, including the foundations of Horseheath Lodge, on the former heath at the western edge of the parish, which Stanlake Batson (d. 1857) built as his local residence between 1816 and 1825.[94] The Lodge was sold in 1948 to Sir Arthur Marshall, who owned it in 1975.[95] By 1851 a farm-house called Horseheath Park had been built south-east of the site of the Hall.[96]

In 1448 William Alington (d. 1459) was licensed to impark 320 a. at Horseheath.[97] In 1550 Sir Giles Alington obtained leave to convert into a deer-park another 400 a. of enclosed grass and woodland in Horseheath, West Wickham, and Withersfield (Suff.),[98] which was later known as the great park in contrast to the old park.[99] About 1770 the whole park covered 740 a., of which half was in Horseheath parish.[1] It was disparked after the Hall had been demolished.[2]

In 1279 much land in Horseheath depended on 2 fees held of the earl of Oxford under the honor of Richmond in West Wickham parish, *c.* 80 a. being held of Sir Emery Pecche's manor, later Bernhams, and *c.* 270 a. of Stephen de la Haye's, later Layes.[3] Both fees eventually passed to the Alingtons.[4] By 1279 the la Haye land in Horseheath was divided into three estates, the largest being the later *BOWERHALL* manor. Probably before 1200 Mauger son of Reyner held of Stephen de la Haye land at Wickham and Horseheath[5] which Stephen's son Walter granted to Mauger's son Reyner[6] (d. after 1245).[7] Reyner's eldest son Geoffrey of Horseheath (fl. 1257)[8] or Geoffrey's son Geoffrey (fl. from 1280)[9] held over 160 a. in demesne under Stephen de la Haye in 1279.[10] The younger Geoffrey was in possession in 1307.[11] His son and successor Geoffrey, in possession in 1343, had died by 1348, having settled the estate on his wife Joan for life, then on their daughter Elizabeth, wife of John atte Boure of West Wickham.[12] John (fl. 1331–49)[13] was succeeded by Thomas atte Boure (fl. 1352–96)[14] and Thomas by his son and heir Robert atte Boure (fl. 1390–1410).[15] Robert's successor, Thomas atte

[76] Ibid. 15 July 1704; Prob. 11/496 (P.C.C. 18 Poley); *Hist. Parl., Commons,* 1715–54, i. 492–3.
[77] Prob. 11/566 (P.C.C. 231 Tenison).
[78] *Complete Peerage,* ix. 132–4; Horace Walpole, *Letters,* ed. W. S. Lewis, xxxv. 20–2; *Proc. C.A.S.* xli. 33–6; C.R.O., R 70/48, 14 Mar. 1757, 7 Jan. 1767, 15 July 1768.
[79] Lord Montfort's Estate Act, 16 Geo. III, c. 111 (Priv. Act); B.L. Add. MS. 36229, ff. 197–203.
[80] B.L. Add. MS. 36229, ff. 306–17; C.R.O., R 70/48, 29–30 May 1783.
[81] e.g. C.R.O., R 70/48, 27 Aug. 1816.
[82] *Proc. C.A.S.* xli. 48–50; Charterho. Mun., MR 2/390.
[83] C.R.O., Nosterfield Priors ct. bk. 1895–1925, pp. 15–22; C.U.L., Doc. 3980, box ii, 'Village Annals', pp. 17–19.
[84] C.R.O., SP 95/2; 515/SP 107.
[85] Mon. in chyd.
[86] Ex inf. Sir Arthur Marshall of Horseheath Lodge.
[87] B.L. Add. MS. 5823, ff. 219v., 256v.
[88] Nicholls, *Progresses of Q. Eliz.* ii. 221.
[89] *Architecture of Sir Roger Pratt,* ed. R. T. Gunther (1928), 117–31. The following description is based on *Proc. C.A.S.* xli. 14–16, 37–41, and plate iv (from *Vitruvius Britannicus,* iii); B.L. Add. MS. 5808, ff. 227–9. See above, plate facing p. 64.
[90] Prob. 11/566 (P.C.C. 231 Tenison).
[91] B.L. Add. MS. 5808, ff. 227–8; *Proc. C.A.S.* xli. 31–4, 42–7. See above, plate facing p. 64.
[92] *Camb. Chron.* 23 Aug., 17 Nov. 1792; cf. Vancouver, *Agric. in Cambs.* 64.
[93] *Proc. C.A.S.* xli. 34; xlv. 28–9; Pevsner, *Cambs.* 128, 148, 250, 331 n.
[94] *Proc. C.A.S.* xli. 47–9; C.R.O., R 70/48, 27 Aug. 1816, 20–1 June 1825.
[95] Ex inf. Sir Arthur Marshall.
[96] *Gardner's Dir. Cambs.* (1851).
[97] B.L. Add. MS. 5834, f. 1.
[98] *Cal. Pat.* 1549–51, 402.
[99] B.L. Add. MS. 5823, f. 251.
[1] C.U.L., MS. Plan 679.
[2] Lysons, *Cambs.* 217.
[3] *Rot. Hund.* (Rec. Com.), ii. 421–2.
[4] See p. 115.
[5] B.L. Harl. MS. 3697, f. 225v.
[6] B.L. Add. MS. 5823, f. 220v.
[7] *Close R.* 1241–7, 295.
[8] B.L. Add. MS. 5823, ff. 252, 255; also called Geof. son of Reyner: ibid. ff. 223v., 225.
[9] Ibid. ff. 222v., 257v.
[10] *Rot. Hund.* ii. 421.
[11] C.P. 25(1)/26/52 no. 2.
[12] B.L. Add. MS. 5823, ff. 220, 242v., 250 and v.; C.P. 25(1)/28/73 no. 3.
[13] B.L. Add. MS. 5823, ff. 220, 254.
[14] Ibid. ff. 248, 252v.
[15] Ibid. ff. 99v., 102v.; *Cal. Close,* 1409–13, 97.

Boure (fl. 1425–46), was dead by 1457,[16] leaving as coheirs two daughters, Margaret, wife of John Wimbold, and Joan, wife of Richard Methwold (d. 1485). By 1470 the manor was in two moieties.[17] In 1499, after Margaret's death, Wimbold released the reversion of her moiety to Joan's son Richard[18] (d. 1512), whose son and heir William Methwold[19] sold his manor of Bowerhall with 200 a. of arable in 1529 to Sir Giles Alington[20] (d. 1586), with whose estate it thenceforth passed.

Another 112 a., including 76 a. depending on the la Haye fee and held under Alice de Beauchamp, belonged in 1279 to Nicholas,[21] son of Adam Mersey.[22] Nicholas (d. by 1294) was succeeded by his son Nicholas (fl. 1348);[23] *c.* 1405 Robert Segyn released the Horseheath lands of his uncle John Mersey to feoffees, perhaps for William Goodred. New feoffees in 1425 included William Alington (d. 1459), to whom the estate was released in 1447.[24]

About 1200 Stephen and Walter de la Haye and others gave *c.* 20 a. to Walden abbey (Essex). In 1279 the abbey held 12 a. of the la Haye fee, and *c.* 1375 18 a., all let for quit-rents by 1279.[25]

Besides the land which they held of the honor of Richmond the Veres inherited 1½ hide, owned in 1066 by the thegn Wulfwin, which Aubrey de Vere (d. *c.* 1112) had held in chief at Horseheath in 1086, and Norman of Nosterfield under him.[26] Probably by 1200 it had been subinfeudated and divided. One part was probably held *c.* 1235 by William Barbedor,[27] who after 1263 granted it in survivorship to Sir James de Audley (d. 1272) and Alice de Beauchamp and their heirs.[28] After James's death Alice granted it for life to Robert de Plessy, who held 80 a. of her in demesne in 1279.[29] Robert died in 1294.[30] William Befold, who had by 1289 acquired *c.* 50 a. of the land, later granted them to Alan Osmond, whose daughter and heir Alice married William le Harper.[31] In 1310 Harper acquired the quit-rents arising from the Bernham fee in Horseheath[32] and in 1311 held over 115 a. His son John,[33] who was holding *BARBEDORS* for life in 1336, died before his father, who died *c.* 1347 having entailed *c.* 130 a. on Richard son of Henry of Wykes.[34] In 1355 Wykes's feoffees released 55 a. of Barbedors to William Audley, who had claimed it as Alice de Beauchamp's heir in 1342.[35] The other Harper lands perhaps passed to Peter Carbonel of Cambridge (fl. 1346–71),[36] who owned land at Horseheath in 1359.[37] In 1434 Thomas Carbonel sold his manor of *CARBONELLS* there to Bartholomew and John Breanson[38] or Bremsham. About 1450 John Bremsham held of the earl of Oxford land at Horseheath once William le Harper's.[39] In 1486 William Bremsham released 200 a. called Carbonells and Stysteds to Richard Gardiner, alderman of London,[40] who in 1489 left 210 a. to his infant daughter Mary. Mary married Giles Alington (d. 1521), her father's former ward,[41] and Carbonells, usually styled a manor, descended with the Alington estate, its demesne arable remaining distinct in 1615.[42] After 1700 the name was corrupted to Cardinals. About 1770 Cardinals farm covered 207 a., of which all but 12 a. lay in Shudy Camps parish. The farm-house, between two ancient moats in a tongue of land reaching into that parish, was a substantial 17th-century, timber-framed house; it was derelict by 1924 and had been demolished by 1975.[43]

About 1200 Hubert le Poor held 1 fee at Horseheath, possibly of the Veres,[44] and Henry le Poor was suing for 1 carucate and a mill there in 1226.[45] In 1279 Baldwin le Poor held 1 fee as mesne lord under the earl of Oxford.[46] About 1210 Stephen of Oxford, apparently a vassal of the Veres, held land worth £2 a year, probably by order of King John,[47] who in 1215 transferred its possession to Bevis de Knoville.[48] Bevis, who held 1 carucate at Horseheath in 1229,[49] was a knight of the earls Marshal, and had his Cambridgeshire land restored in 1234 after Earl Richard's revolt.[50] Later he probably granted it to the earl Marshal, who subinfeudated it to Ralph de Vautort.[51] In 1245 Vautort granted to William of Horseheath (d. after 1260) 80 a. and a mill there,[52] which William's son John held in 1279, with four mesne lords between himself and the earl of Oxford,[53] and sold in and after 1280 to Alice de Beauchamp.[54]

A third Vere fee was *LIMBURYS* manor, originally held by service of holding the earl of Oxford's

[16] B.L. Add. MS. 5823, ff. 249v., 257v.; Pemb. Coll. Mun., A 8.
[17] B.L. Add. MS. 5823, ff. 222v., 223v.; *Cal. Inq. p.m. Hen. VII*, i, pp. 41–2.
[18] B.L. Add. MS. 5823, f. 250.
[19] E 150/615 no. 7.
[20] B.L. Add. MS. 5823, ff. 222v., 223v.; C.P. 25(2)/4/19 no. 34.
[21] *Rot. Hund.* (Rec. Com.), ii. 420–2.
[22] B.L. Add. MS. 5823, f. 243v.; cf. ibid. ff. 80v., 225, 245.
[23] Ibid. ff. 221v., 226v., 255.
[24] Ibid. ff. 249, 254; cf. *Cal. Pat.* 1416–22, 32; Charterho. Mun., MR 2/557A pt. ii, p. 3.
[25] B.L. Harl. MS. 3697, ff. 225–7; *Rot. Hund.* ii. 422.
[26] *V.C.H. Cambs.* i. 390, 408.
[27] *Liber de Bernewelle*, 254.
[28] B.L. Add. MS. 5823, f. 249.
[29] *Rot. Hund.* ii. 422; cf. *Complete Peerage*, x. 548 n.
[30] *Cal. Fine R.* 1272–1307, 336; a namesake d. 1301: ibid. 444–5; cf. B.L. Add. MS. 5823, ff. 255v.–256.
[31] *Sel. Cases in K.B.* iv (Selden Soc. lxxiv), pp. 19–22; B.L. Add. MS. 5823, f. 250.
[32] B.L. Add. MS. 5823, f. 244.
[33] C.P. 25(1)/27/54 nos. 7, 11.
[34] B.L. Add. MS. 5823, ff. 222v., 226v., 254, 257; C.P. 25(1)/28/67 no. 21; E 179/242/8 m. 5.
[35] B.L. Add. MS. 5823, f. 257; C.P. 40/331 rot. 51.
[36] *Cal. Pat.* 1345–8, 105; B.L. Harl. MS. 3697, f. 226.
[37] B.L. Add. MS. 5823, f. 242v.
[38] C.P. 25(1)/30/97 no. 19.
[39] Charterho. Mun., MR 2/557A pt. ii, p. 3.
[40] B.L. Add. MS. 5823, f. 33v.; C.P. 25(1)/30/101 no. 4.
[41] *Cal. Inq. p.m. Hen. VII*, i, pp. 235–6; cf. Hist. MSS. Com. 55, *Var. Coll.* ii. 297.
[42] C.U.L., E.D.R., H 1/4, glebe terrier 1615.
[43] Ibid. MS. Plan 679; photograph in C.A.S. collection.
[44] B.L. Harl. MS. 3697, f. 225; B.L. Add. MS. 5823, ff. 220v., 243.
[45] *Cur. Reg. R.* xii, p. 519; cf. ibid. xiv, p. 521.
[46] *Rot. Hund.* (Rec. Com.), ii. 421 (giving 'Pouere' as 'Senere').
[47] *Red Bk. Exch.* (Rolls Ser.), ii. 531; cf. *Rot. Litt. Claus.* (Rec. Com.), i. 269.
[48] *Rot. Litt. Claus.* i. 187.
[49] *Close R.* 1227–31, 252.
[50] *Rot. Litt. Claus.* i. 604; *Cal. Pat.* 1232–47, 84; *Close R.* 1231–4, 259, 436.
[51] Cf. *Rot. Hund.* (Rec. Com.), ii. 421; Sanders, *Eng. Baronies*, 90–1.
[52] C.P. 25(1)/24/26 no. 1; B.L. Add. MS. 5823, f. 252; *Assizes at Camb. 1260*, 11.
[53] *Rot. Hund.* ii. 421.
[54] B.L. Add. MS. 5823, ff. 225v.–226, 257.

stirrup when he mounted his palfrey.[55] It probably belonged to Walter Limbury (fl. 1240–63), whose widow Elizabeth[56] held 60 a. in demesne in 1279 and 1282 as ½ fee.[57] By 1298 it had descended to Walter's son John,[58] and he or a John Limbury the younger (fl. from 1312)[59] held it until he died *c.* 1336.[60] John's heir, Sir Philip Limbury, held the manor in 1346,[61] and in 1367 died on pilgrimage, leaving as heir a son Philip[62] who died under age. Sir Philip's widow Joan held the manor for life with her second husband Sir John Clinton.[63] When she died in 1388 80 a. of demesne descended to Sir Philip's daughter Elizabeth, wife of Sir Thomas Trivet.[64] Trivet died the same year[65] and Elizabeth in 1433, when she had no traceable heirs.[66] The manor came into the hands of her executor, the Chancery clerk Nicholas Wimbish,[67] who sold it in 1453 to William Alington (d. 1459).[68] Its lands lay around an ancient moated site at Limberhurst Farm at the east end of the parish.[69]

The largest manor not held of the Veres was derived from ½ hide occupied in 1086 by 5 *villani* of Hardwin de Scalers.[70] Its overlordship passed to Hardwin's son Richard with the half-barony of Shelford,[71] and in 1282 it was held of Richard's heir Richard de Freville.[72] The tenants in demesne were the Scalers family of Babraham.[73] Geoffrey de Scalers (d. by 1202) left as heir his son Geoffrey[74] (d. by 1249) whose eldest son Alexander[75] granted the manor by 1250 to Waltham abbey (Essex). The abbey was granted free warren there in 1253 and held 220 a. in demesne in 1279.[76] In 1350 it granted the manor to Sir John Shardelowe,[77] with whose manor in Shudy Camps the land was given in 1392 to Thompson college (Norf.). Half of the college's estate was eventually bought in 1640 by William, later Lord Alington, and under the name of *SHARDELOWES ALINGTONS* passed by marriage through the Seymours to the Finches, earls of Aylesford.[78] On the death of Heneage Finch, earl of Aylesford, in 1812, his trustees sold the Horseheath land, *c.* 57 a., to Stanlake Batson.[79]

In 1086 Ulveva held ½ yardland of Richard son of Gilbert,[80] of whose descendants the Clares, later earls of Gloucester, a fee at Horseheath was held until the 14th century.[81] When the Clare barony was divided after 1314, the Horseheath fee was assigned to Margaret, wife of Hugh Audley (d. 1347), whose daughter and heir Margaret brought the overlordship to the earls of Stafford.[82] About 1200 the fee was held by Geoffrey son of Richard,[83] (d. by 1236),[84] who was probably succeeded by Henry son of Geoffrey (fl. 1247–70).[85] In 1279 William son of Henry held of the earl of Gloucester 80 a. in demesne,[86] which by 1284 had passed to his brother Michael, tenant in 1302.[87] Michael's son Richard of Horseheath had the estate between 1307 and 1343,[88] and Richard's son William held it as ½ knight's fee in 1346, dying after 1361.[89] It later passed to the Goodred family. William Goodred the elder (fl. 1384–1418 or 1424)[90] was succeeded by William Goodred the younger (fl. 1410–47)[91] who held it in 1428.[92] Part of his lands belonged by 1457 to Hugh Jacob (fl. 1448–77),[93] whose son and heir William (d. 1508) left his Horseheath lands to his youngest son Robert (d. 1518).[94] In 1544 Richard Jacob sold *GOODREDS* manor to Sir Giles Alington with his ancestral lands,[95] themselves by 1640 described as *JACOBS* manor.[96]

Land at Horseheath and West Wickham belonging to John Eyre (fl. 1446–76) passed to his son William. In 1505 William sold *c.* 100 a. there to certain fellows of Pembroke College, Cambridge, who conveyed the land to the college in 1510.[97] Pembroke retained 117 a., including 29 a. in Shudy Camps and 24 a. in West Wickham,[98] until 1877 when it sold 66 a. in Horseheath to S. R. Batson's executors.[99] Its farm-house may have stood within a moat east of the road to West Wickham. By 1610 a new farm-house, timber-framed and thatched, had been built west of the road.[1] It had been demolished by 1975.

ECONOMIC HISTORY. Of the ten plough-lands

55 *Cal. Inq. p.m.* xii, pp. 128–9.
56 *Ex. e Rot. Fin.* (Rec. Com.), ii. 62, 397.
57 *Rot. Hund.* (Rec. Com.), ii. 421 (giving 'Limbery' as 'Bunbery' and 'iii^xx' as 'm^xx'); *Cal. Inq. p.m.* ii, p. 220.
58 B.L. Add. MS. 5823, f. 244v.; *Cal. Close,* 1302–7, 322; *Feud. Aids,* i. 145.
59 B.L. Add. MS. 5823, f. 33v.
60 *Cal. Pat.* 1321–4, 124; *Cal. Fine R.* 1327–37, 315, 441–2.
61 *Feud. Aids,* i. 162.
62 *Cal. Inq. p.m.* xii, pp. 128–9.
63 Ibid. xiii, p. 100; *Cal. Close,* 1364–8, 350; *Complete Peerage,* iii. 314.
64 *Cal. Inq. p.m.* xvi, pp. 205–6; *D.N.B.*
65 *Cal. Inq. p.m.* xvi, pp. 297–9.
66 C 139/64 no. 35.
67 *Reg. Chichele* (Cant. & York Soc.), ii. 495–7; cf. Emden, *Biog. Reg. Univ. Oxon.* iii. 2120–1.
68 B.L. Add. MS. 5823, ff. 244, 245v., 252.
69 C.U.L., MS. Plan 679.
70 *V.C.H. Cambs.* i. 385.
71 Cf. ibid. v. 27–8.
72 *Cal. Inq. p.m.* ii, p. 220.
73 Cf. *Proc. C.A.S.* lix. 120–2.
74 *Pleas before King's Justices,* i (Selden Soc. lxvii), pp. 286, 288–9; *Feet of Fines* (Rec. Com.), 308–9.
75 *Proc. C.A.S.* lix. 120.
76 *Rot. Hund.* (Rec. Com.), ii. 421; *Cal. Chart. R.* 1226–57, 427.
77 B.L. Harl. MS. 3739, ff. 146–152v.
78 See pp. 51–2; see also C.R.O., R 70/48, abstract of title, 1812.
79 C.R.O., R 70/48, 15–16 Mar. 1813.
80 *V.C.H. Cambs.* i. 381.
81 e.g. *Liber de Bernewelle,* 254; *Cal. Inq. p.m.* v, p. 347.
82 e.g. *Cal. Inq. p.m.* xiii, p. 182; cf. *Complete Peerage,* i. 346–7.
83 *Pleas before King's Justices,* i (Selden Soc. lxvii), pp. 266, 377.
84 Cf. *Liber de Bernewelle,* 254.
85 B.L. Add. MS. 5823, ff. 245, 252; *Cal. Pat.* 1266–72, 480.
86 *Rot. Hund.* (Rec. Com.), ii. 422.
87 B.L. Add. MS. 5823, f. 242v.; *Feud. Aids,* i. 140, 145.
88 B.L. Add. MS. 5823, ff. 102v., 221v., 231v.; *Cal. Inq. p.m.* xiii, p. 182.
89 *Feud. Aids,* i. 162; B.L. Add. MS. 5823, ff. 113v., 255; C.U.L., Queens' Coll. Mun. 52/49.
90 *Cal. Fine R.* 1383–91, 68; *Cal. Close,* 1409–13, 97; 1419–22, 18–19; 1422–9, 183.
91 *Cal. Close,* 1409–13, 97; 1447–54, 310; B.L. Add. MS. 5823, f. 249v.; he was perhaps the justice: Foss, *Judges of Eng.* iv. 320–1.
92 *Feud. Aids,* i. 181.
93 Pemb. Coll. Mun., A 8; B.L. Add. MS. 5823, ff. 124, 224v.
94 B.L. Add. MS. 5823, ff. 224v., 243v.; B.L. Add. MS. 5861, f. 65; Prob. 11/13 (P.C.C. 34 Adeane).
95 B.L. Add. MS. 5823, ff. 33v., 79v.
96 e.g. C 142/592 no. 90.
97 Pemb. Coll. Mun., A 2–29; B 1–10, 15–17.
98 Ibid. C 9, 15; C.R.O., 124/P 62.
99 Pemb. Coll. Mun., catalogue, vol. ii, p. 21.
1 Ibid. C 1; C.U.L., E.D.R., tithe award 1839; cf. M.H.L.G. list.

at Horseheath in 1086 five belonged to Count Alan's manor and three to Aubrey de Vere's. There were more than 15 *villani* and 9 bordars, besides 3 *servi* on Aubrey's estate. The values set on the manors had, at £9 10*s*., been restored to those of 1066.[2] In 1279 *c*. 1,085 a. out of 1,755 a. recorded belonged to the demesnes of seven manors. The largest were those of Alice de Beauchamp, occupying 401 a., Waltham abbey with 234 a., and Geoffrey of Horseheath with 172 a. No other lord had over 80 a. of arable. Seven freeholders with 20 a. or more held *c*. 267 a., another 28 with 10 a. or less had *c*. 100 a., and 15 others only their messuages. All but one of the villeins were on Alice de Beauchamp's manor, where three held 20 a. and eleven 10 a., besides three cottagers owing harvest-boons and reaping-works only. Most villeins had once owed 36 works between Michaelmas and Midsummer, and 22 from Midsummer to Michaelmas, while those with 20 a. had also to plough 4½ a., and those with 10 a. had carried 2 cartloads of wheat from the outer fields during harvest. By 1279, however, some customary services had been reduced and some released.[3] In 1348 the Audley manor included only *c*. 115 a. of freeholdings, divided among 36 tenants, only 3 with over 10 a., compared with 548 a. of demesne and customary land.[4] The Alingtons and Bromleys, by buying up their tenants' land, eventually reduced the amount of copyhold to 8½ a. in 1770.[5]

In 1279 there were *c*. 1,700 a. of arable, 19 a. of meadow, 14 a. of pasture, and 27 a. of wood.[6] In 1340 200 a. of arable were said to lie uncultivated.[7] Saffron was being grown at Horseheath *c*. 1525.[8] By 1600 the arable land was being cultivated in three seasons, the forecrop, aftercrop, and fallow.[9] There were more than three fields, however, Barchestrefield, Thorendune, Maplederndene, and Moriland, of uncertain location, being recorded *c*. 1200.[10] By the 16th century the land west of the village was divided into seven open fields.[11] Along the northern edge of the parish lay Bokedale,[12] later Bowdale field or valley,[13] renamed by 1770 Valley field, and west of it Elmdon, later Emden valley or field,[14] covering together 228 a. Southwards across the turnpike road lay Wormwood field,[15] (66 a.), and west of it the Mill field[16] (124 a.), occasionally called Horseheath field.[17] Stone field[18] (179 a.) stretched south-west from Mill field to the Bartlow boundary. East of it, by the southern boundary, were Chalksley field[19] (89 a.), perhaps the Chalk field recorded in 1313,[20] and Toppesbroc,[21] later Tosbrook,[22] field (52 a.). Along the western edge of the parish lay the eponymous horse heath, of which 92 a. remained in 1769 and *c*. 75 a. in 1839. North of it were sheep-pens covering 22 a.[23]

The higher ground east of the village may even before it was imparked in the mid 15th century have been mainly demesne land lying in severalty. Names such as Limbury's field[24] and Boure field[25] suggest the property of a single landowner. An arable strip in the Hall field *c*. 1325 had demesne land on both sides,[26] and William Alington (d. 1459), who was buying arable in Hallgate field in 1449,[27] had lately annexed various crofts to his park.[28] Thomas atte Boure's Longcroft, including woodland, which adjoined a demesne field in 1443,[29] had similarly by 1484 been included in the park.[30] In 1770 the land which had escaped imparking, lying south of the road, was entirely in severalty with no trace of open fields. Its eastern end had since 1450 at least[31] been occupied by the wholly inclosed Limburys manor farm, covering 160 a. in 1726.[32]

In 1086 two flocks at Horseheath contained 136 sheep.[33] In 1347 the village supplied 85½ stone of wool to the Crown, of which 32 stone came from six manorial flocks.[34] William le Harper recovered in 1341 a fold-course, apparently belonging to Barbedors fee.[35] Bowerhall manor, for which 300 sheep were kept in the 15th century,[36] also enjoyed rights of fold-course in 1530.[37] Later the largest flocks were on the Alington estate farms. In 1558 a lessee left his wife 80 wethers.[38] William, Lord Alington (d. 1684), kept flocks of ewes and wethers.[39] Later the Bromleys sometimes kept the right of sheep-walk in hand.[40] In 1783 Manor farm was said to include an unstinted right of sheep-walk.[41]

The Alingtons and their successors dominated the parish economically from the early 16th century. In 1524 Giles Alington was taxed on £88 out of the £170 then assessed upon it, only two others having goods taxed even at £10, while 21 out of 35 taxpayers paid only on £1.[42] Of 52 houses taxed in 1664 only five apart from the Hall and rectory had more than 4 hearths, and 24 had only one.[43] During the 17th century the Alingtons, owning all the manors but one, added to their demesnes by buying up the remaining freehold and copyhold properties. Of 105 strips bordering Pembroke College land the

2 *V.C.H. Cambs*. i. 408.
3 *Rot. Hund*. (Rec. Com.), ii. 420–2.
4 B.L. Add. MS. 5823, f. 150v.
5 C.U.L., MS. Plan 679.
6 *Rot. Hund*. ii. 420–2.
7 *Inq. Non*. (Rec. Com.), 213.
8 B.L. Add. MS. 5861, f. 92.
9 C.U.L., E.D.R., H 1/4, glebe terrier 1615.
10 B.L. Harl. MS. 3697, ff. 225–6.
11 The account of the layout, areas, and modern names is based on C.U.L., MS. Plan 679 (1769–70); C.U.L., E.D.R., tithe award 1839. Areas given as in 1839.
12 B.L. Harl. MS. 3697, f. 225v. (*c*. 1200).
13 C.U.L., E.D.R., H 1/4, terrier 1574.
14 B.L. Add. Ch. 28553 (1313); C.U.L., E.D.R., H 1/4, terrier 1615.
15 C.U.L., Add MS. 6920, f. 37v. (1606).
16 B.L. Add. MS. 5823, ff. 250v., 257v. (1313, 1341).
17 e.g. Pemb. Coll. Mun., C 1 (1610).
18 B.L. Add. Ch. 28553 (1313).
19 C.U.L., E.D.R., H 1/4, terrier 1615.
20 B.L. Add. Ch. 28553.
21 *Feet of Fines* (Rec. Com.), 308–9.
22 e.g. C.U.L., E.D.R., H 1/4, terrier 1574.
23 Cf. C.R.O., R 70/48, 27 Aug. 1816; Pemb. Coll. Mun., C 1.
24 B.L. Add. MS. 5823, f. 256 (*c*. 1300).
25 Ibid. f. 257v. (1446).
26 Ibid. f. 256v.
27 Ibid. f. 219v.
28 Ibid. f. 247v.
29 Ibid. ff. 242, 257v.
30 Ibid. f. 249v.
31 Ibid. f. 225.
32 C.R.O., R 70/48, 19 Jan. 1726.
33 *V.C.H. Cambs*. i. 408.
34 E 179/242/8 m. 5.
35 B.L. Add. MS. 5823, f. 257.
36 Ibid. f. 256v.
37 C.P. 25(2)/4/19 no. 34.
38 Prob. 11/41 (P.C.C. 57 Noodes, will of John Webb).
39 Prob. 11/380 (P.C.C. 102 Cann).
40 e.g. C.R.O., R 70/48, 14 June 1705, 15 July 1768.
41 Ibid. 29–30 May 1783.
42 E 179/81/134 m. 4d.
43 E 179/84/437 rot. 60d.

Alington estate included 61 in 1610, 80 in 1703, and *c.* 90 in 1788; 10 of the remainder belonged to Shardelowes Alingtons and the rectory.[44] By 1770 Lord Montfort possessed all but 37 strips in the open fields, the Bromleys having held the Pembroke property on lease since the 1730s. Indeed, his estate comprised all the farm-land in the parish except 126 a., of which 59 a. belonged to Shardelowes and 22 a. were glebe; eight owners shared the rest.[45] By 1839, having bought Shardelowes in 1813 and acquired the rector's open-field land by exchange in 1829,[46] Stanlake Batson owned all the open fields except for Pembroke's strips, which were leased to him, and possessed all but 33 a. of *c.* 1,800 a. then recorded in the parish. Consequently there was no need for a formal inclosure award or agreement for the remaining 700 a. of nominally open fields,[47] where Batson's farmers had already ploughed away most of the balks by the 1820s.[48]

In 1726 the Horseheath Hall estate included, besides the park, 1,000 a. of farm-land in the parish, divided among five farms of over 150 a.[49] In 1770 Limberhurst farm lying south of the park covered 275 a., besides 53 a. in Shudy Camps, and included near the main road 40 a. of meadow, whose name, Broad Green, suggests that it may once have been a common pasture.[50] In 1610 Pembroke College had been entitled to mow 12 a. of meadow, later part of that farm, but the right to pasture over them belonged to the Alingtons.[51] The open fields to the west were in 1770 divided into three farms by old field-boundaries and were farmed from three farmsteads: Church Farm, opposite the church, had 255 a., including the two northern fields; Manor Farm just south of the village had *c.* 430 a., including Wormwood, Mill, and Stone fields, together 326 a.; and Lower Cardinals farm, by the Shudy Camps road, covered 268 a., including the 128 a. of Tosbrook and Chalksley fields and 53 a. in Shudy Camps parish. Those farms also had between them *c.* 190 a. of inclosed pastures around the village. Heath farm at the western end of Horseheath had *c.* 245 a., including 44 a. in Bartlow, some inclosed arable, and the 92 a. of heath later converted into the grounds of Horseheath Lodge. Altogether the estate then included *c.* 310 a. of grass, *c.* 250 a. of inclosed arable, and *c.* 700 a. of open-field arable.[52] From 1776 the park was let out for grazing cattle.[53] Later its western third was added to Church farm and ploughed up, while the remainder, mostly left under grass, became Park farm.[54]

In 1801 Horseheath still grew mainly the traditional crops, apparently preserving a triennial rotation. Of 767 a. then cultivated there were 190 a. of wheat, 240 a. of barley, 156 a. of oats, and 136 a. of pease and beans, but only 45 a. of turnips and potatoes.[55] In 1806 sainfoin was being grown on the fallow.[56] By 1839 the parish followed a four-course rotation. Of 1,250 a. of arable 300 a. each were under wheat, clover and beans, barley, and turnips. There were also 503 a. of permanent grass and 29 a. of wood and waste.[57] The area under grass later decreased. In 1905 there were said to be only 262 a. of it compared with 1,875 a. of arable.[58] Of 700 a. offered for sale from the Horseheath estate in 1925 195 a., including 115 a. of Park farm, were under grass.[59] Considerable sheep flocks were still kept: there were 4 shepherds in 1851 and 7 in 1871,[60] and Manor farm had 700 sheep in 1894.[61]

Horseheath continued to be divided among the same five or six large farms until the Batsons' estate was sold in 1925. In 1871 five substantial farmers together occupied well over 3,100 a., including land outside the parish. William Purkis, tenant by 1861 of Sherwood Green farm, alone farmed 1,280 a.[62] Christopher Parsons occupied Manor farm (350 a.) from *c.* 1869 until his death in 1905. His son T. W. Parsons was farming Church farm (470 a.) by 1892 and Park farm (440 a. in 1925) by 1904, and eventually bought the estate.[63] In 1937 he occupied two out of the six farms in the parish.[64] Much land that had been put under grass, including most of the park, was reconverted to arable during the Second World War.[65]

Horseheath seldom had many craftsmen. In 1279 the villagers included two smiths and a carpenter.[66] A lime-pit was recorded in 1313, and a lime-kiln in 1608,[67] which in 1615 probably stood in the area at the north-west corner of the parish called in 1773 Limekiln field.[68] One of two tanners recorded in the 1630s had property of *c.* 20 a. and over £165.[69] In 1705 the estate included a smithy,[70] probably one of two standing by the village green in 1839.[71] In 1811 72 families depended on agriculture and only 10 on crafts and trades; in 1831 the corresponding figures were 62 and 35.[72] There were then 49 adult farm-labourers and 18 more under 20, all in employment. In 1830 they demonstrated for higher wages than their 10*s.* a week.[73] The farms employed 116 men and boys in 1851, and 164 in 1871, when William Purkis had 52 labourers and Park farm 53, but many of them lived outside the parish, where only *c.* 70 dwelt in the mid 19th century.[74] In the 1860s many girls also worked at home on 'slop-work' from Haverhill (Suff.).[75] The village in 1861 had 3 smiths, 2 carpenters, 2 wheelwrights,

[44] Pemb. Coll. Mun., C 1, 3, 9.
[45] Ibid. D 14–16; C.U.L. MS. Plan 679.
[46] C.R.O., R 70/48, 15–16 Mar. 1813, 3 Aug. 1829.
[47] C.U.L., E.D.R., tithe award 1839.
[48] Pemb. Coll. Mun., C 11, report 1827.
[49] C.R.O., R 70/48, 19 Jan. 1726.
[50] C.U.L., MS. Plan 679.
[51] Pemb. Coll. Mun., C 1.
[52] C.U.L., MS. Plan 679.
[53] *Proc. C.A.S.* xli. 44.
[54] C.U.L., E.D.R., tithe award 1839.
[55] H.O. 67/9.
[56] Gooch, *Agric. of Cambs.* 151–2.
[57] I.R. 18/13492; cf. C.R.O., R 70/48, lease 12 Mar. 1879; Pemb. Coll. Mun., D 7.
[58] Cambs. Agric. Returns, 1905: probably including land in adjacent parishes farmed from Horseheath.
[59] C.R.O., SP 45/2.
[60] H.O. 107/1761; R.G. 10/1593.
[61] *Jnl. Royal Agric. Soc.* 3rd ser. v. 505–6.
[62] R.G. 9/1030; R.G. 10/1593.
[63] *Kelly's Dir. Cambs.* (1869–1925); cf. R.G. 10/1593; C.R.O., R 70/48, leases 1864, 1869; C.R.O., SP 45/2.
[64] *Kelly's Dir. Cambs.* (1937).
[65] *Proc. C.A.S.* xli. 57; cf. C.R.O., 515/SP 107.
[66] *Rot. Hund.* (Rec. Com.), ii. 420–2.
[67] B.L. Add. Ch. 28553; *Proc. C.A.S.* xli. 10.
[68] C.U.L., E.D.R., H 1/4, terrier 1615; Pemb. Coll. Mun., C 6.
[69] Prob. 11/166 (P.C.C. 88 Seager, will of Thos. Pettit).
[70] C.R.O., R 70/48, 14 June 1705.
[71] C.U.L., E.D.R., tithe award 1839.
[72] *Census*, 1811, 1831.
[73] *Rep. H.L. Cttee. on Poor Laws*, H.C. 227, pp. 326–7 (1831), viii; *Camb. Chron.* 10 Dec. 1830.
[74] H.O. 107/1761; R.G. 10/1593.
[75] *1st Rep. Com. Employment in Agric.* 359.

and 3 tailors,[76] but most of them had disappeared by 1900; one smithy was still working in 1937, when there was also a builder's firm.[77] Owing to the isolation of the village, local employment remained almost entirely in farming until the 1960s. Some residents by then worked at Haverhill or Linton, or even Cambridge.[78] Of three village shops recorded *c.* 1870, only one remained by 1937.[79]

By 1226 there was a windmill at Horseheath,[80] probably the one acquired *c.* 1280 by Alice de Beauchamp,[81] who already owned another in 1279, when there were three millers there.[82] Perhaps by 1295 a windmill stood ½ mile west of the village just north of the way dividing Bokedale from Mill field.[83] It was apparently that acquired from Geoffrey of Horseheath by Sir James Audley in 1332,[84] which remained attached to the principal estate until the 20th century.[85] It remained in use for grinding corn throughout the 19th century, being managed successively by the Turner and Hymus families. Probably disused from soon after 1900,[86] it was demolished *c.* 1924.[87]

LOCAL GOVERNMENT. In 1279 Alice de Beauchamp had view of frankpledge.[88] Under James I Sir Giles Alington held a view of frankpledge and court baron at intervals of two years, which dealt with road maintenance and encroachments by ploughing on ways and balks, handled transfers of copyhold, and elected constables. Minutes survive for 1606, 1608, and 1610.[89]

A building by the green rented from the Horseheath estate as a poorhouse had been demolished by 1839.[90] The cost of poor-relief rose fivefold from £82 in 1776 to £428 in 1813; 27 people were permanently supported by the parish in 1803, and 15 in 1813.[91] From a peak of £456 in 1819 expenditure was reduced to £188 in 1834.[92] In 1830 large families were receiving allowances from the rates.[93] The parish became part of the Linton poor-law union in 1835,[94] was incorporated in 1934 into the South Cambridgeshire R.D.,[95] and was included in 1974 in South Cambridgeshire.

CHURCH. There is architectural evidence of a church at Horseheath in the 12th century. Rectors are recorded from 1234.[96] In 1279 the advowson of the rectory belonged to the earl of Oxford.[97] In 1371 Elizabeth, widow of John, eldest son of Earl John (d. 1360), released a life-interest in the advowson, settled on her in 1342, to John's younger son Aubrey, later 10th earl.[98] The patronage remained with the Veres until after 1600;[99] during the forfeiture of Earl John between 1471 and 1485 it was exercised by Richard, duke of Gloucester, grantee of the earl's Cambridgeshire lands.[1] In 1589 Philip Mynott's executors presented for one turn,[2] probably by grant of Earl Edward (d. 1604). The advowson was attributed to Edward's heir male, Robert, earl of Oxford, at his death in 1632.[3] Between 1669 and 1694 and in 1815 it was formally conveyed, apparently with the former Vere manor of Swaffham Bulbeck, in the Marsh and Parker Hamond families, owners of Pampisford,[4] who never attempted, however, to present to Horseheath. Thomas Wakefield, rector 1589–1626, had in 1626 devised the advowson to a kinsman who was to present Thomas's son Thomas,[5] rector 1626–69. The advowson belonged in 1669 to the Charterhouse, whose governors presented all rectors thenceforth[6] and were patrons in 1973.[7]

In 1268 Waltham abbey claimed the tithes of its demesne in Horseheath,[8] later Shardelowes manor. The tithes apparently passed with the abbey's rectory of Shudy Camps in 1546 to Trinity College, Cambridge, which until 1839 received rectorial tithes from 66 a., once part of Shardelowes, the small tithes going to the vicar of Shudy Camps.[9] In 1313 the rector of Horseheath unsuccessfully claimed tithes from Westoe fee in Castle and Shudy Camps.[10]

The rectory was taxed at *c.* 15 marks in 1254 and 1291,[11] and at 20 marks in 1535.[12] In 1650 it was worth £100 a year, and in 1728 £130.[13] The rector's income was £347 net *c.* 1830 before tithe commutation, and £410 in 1877.[14] Tithes in 1692 had mostly been payable in kind; fixed sums were due from the windmill and the old park.[15] In 1782 part of the park was covered by a modus of £5 13*s.* 4*d.*, but 356 a. were found to owe tithes in kind valued at 2*s.* an acre.[16] The tithes were worth £125 in 1758 and £381 in 1826.[17] They were commuted in 1839 for

76 R.G. 9/1030.
77 *Kelly's Dir. Cambs.* (1900–37).
78 *Camb. Ind. Press*, 3 Mar. 1961.
79 *Kelly's Dir. Cambs.* (1869, 1937).
80 *Cur. Reg. R.* xii, p. 519; cf. ibid. xiv, pp. 513–14.
81 B.L. Add. MS. 5823, ff. 255v., 257.
82 *Rot. Hund.* (Rec. Com.), ii. 420.
83 B.L. Add. MS. 5823, f. 255v.; cf. C.U.L., MS. Plan 679.
84 B.L. Add. MS. 5823, f. 250v.
85 e.g. C.R.O., R 70/48, 14 June 1705.
86 *Gardner's Dir. Cambs.* (1851); *Kelly's Dir. Cambs.* (1858–1904).
87 C.U.L., Doc. 3980, box ii, 'Village Annals', p. 13.
88 *Rot. Hund.* (Rec. Com.), ii. 420.
89 C.U.L., Add. MS. 6920, ff. 37 and v., 74v.–75v., 100v.–104v.
90 Ibid. E.D.R., tithe award 1839.
91 *Poor Law Abstract, 1804*, 34–5; *1818*, 28–9.
92 *Poor Rate Returns, 1816–21*, 10; *1830–4*, 15.
93 *Rep. H.L. Cttee. on Poor Laws*, H.C. 227, pp. 326–7 (1831), viii.
94 *Poor Law Com. 1st Rep.* 249.
95 *Census*, 1931 (pt. ii).
96 Parsons, *Horseheath Ch.* 66–7, listing the rectors.
97 *Rot. Hund.* (Rec. Com.), ii. 420.
98 C.P. 25(1)/288/29 no. 472; cf. *Complete Peerage*, x. 225.
99 Cf. Parsons, *Horseheath Ch.* 66–7.
1 *E.D.R.* (1906), 112; (1908), 57.
2 Gibbons, *Ely Episc. Rec.* 445.
3 C 142/508 no. 15.
4 C.P. 25(2)/633/21 Chas. II Mich. no. 12; C.P. 25(2)/898/6 Wm. & Mary East. no. 8; C.P. 43/930 rot. 254.
5 Prob. 11/150 (P.C.C. 148 Hele).
6 P.R.O., Inst. Bks. ser. B, i, pp. 68, 140; Parsons, *Horseheath Ch.* 66–7.
7 *Crockford* (1973–4).
8 *Val. of Norwich*, ed. Lunt, 550.
9 C.U.L., E.D.R., tithe award 1839.
10 B.L. Add. Ch. 28553.
11 *Val. of Norwich*, ed. Lunt, 227; *Tax. Eccl.* (Rec. Com.) 267.
12 *Valor Eccl.* (Rec. Com.), iii. 504.
13 Lamb. Pal. MS. 904, f. 213; C.U.L., E.D.R., B 8/1.
14 *Rep. Com. Eccl. Revenues*, pp. 348–9; C.U.L., E.D.R., C 3/26.
15 C.U.L., E.D.R., H 1/4, terrier 1692.
16 B.L. Add. MS. 36229, ff. 306–7, 313v.
17 Parsons, *Horseheath Ch.* 63–4.

a tithe-rent-charge of £452 18*s*., including £14 15*s*. assigned to Trinity College and the incumbents of Castle and Shudy Camps.[18] The tithe barn standing north of the churchyard was demolished in 1881.[19]

The church was endowed with a messuage and 26 a. in 1279,[20] and had *c.* 22 a. of glebe in 1574, 1662, and 1770.[21] In 1829 the rector exchanged his 19 a. of open-field land for 11 a. of closes north of the rectory house,[22] where he still owned 15 a. in 1911 and 1973.[23] In 1416 William Goodred gave 3 roods so that the rectory home close could be enlarged.[24] The parsonage house, standing by the churchyard, was regularly recorded between 1615 and 1692.[25] Edward Basset, rector 1709–32, built on the old site an 'exceeding good' rectorial house.[26] It is of three wide bays, timber-framed and plastered, with sash windows and a hipped tiled roof with dormers. It was extensively repaired *c.* 1830, and *c.* 1850 a drawing room was added.[27]

A guild was recorded at Horseheath in 1527.[28] The guildhall had been pulled down by Sir Giles Alington by 1571 when the Crown sold the site.[29]

Rectors presented in 1349 and 1386 obtained licences for non-residence in 1352 and 1390 respectively.[30] A chaplain, probably parochial, and two clerks were recorded at Horseheath in 1378,[31] and another chaplain in 1487.[32] In 1542 Sir Giles Alington was employing and paying a stipendiary priest.[33] William Masterson, rector 1518–*c.* 1556, had regularly resided until the 1540s,[34] but his successor Thomas White, 1557–89, lived with his patron the earl of Oxford in 1561,[35] and later served the living through curates.[36]

The Wakefields, father and son, incumbents between 1589 and 1668, both lived in the parish. They possibly had puritan tendencies: each was presented, in 1591 and 1638 respectively, for not wearing the surplice. The younger Thomas, who had a puritan as curate, was also said to have failed to observe some holy days, and to publish the king's book of sports.[37] In 1650 he was commended as an orthodox and godly divine.[38] From 1669 the Charterhouse, in accordance with its statutes, normally presented former scholars of its foundation.[39] The 18th-century rectors were all well educated, and, holding no other livings, were mostly resident, although Thomas Rowell, 1732–7, lived mainly in London[40] and John Maule, 1776–1825, spent half of every year at Greenwich Hospital where he was a chaplain.[41] There were only seven incumbents in the 18th century and six in the 19th.[42] In 1728 the rector held services not only twice every Sunday but on holy days and on weekdays in Lent;[43] by 1775 there was only one Sunday service.[44] Only *c.* 8 people attended communion in 1807, but 20–30 in 1825, when there were again two Sunday services, and 35–40 by 1836. Although all 300 sittings were free in 1836, disputed pews were allotted to those who paid the largest rates.[45] In 1851 the average Sunday attendance at church was 64.[46] In 1877, although there were said to be 250 church-goers, only *c.* 25 regularly attended the monthly communions; some men went instead to Shudy Camps.[47] The smallness and isolation of the parish made the living less attractive after 1900, and there were ten rectors between 1910 and 1973. From 1918 to 1923 Horseheath was held with Castle Camps, from 1946 to 1973 with Bartlow, and from 1973 with West Wickham.[48]

The church of *ALL SAINTS*, so called in 1508,[49] comprises a chancel, aisleless nave with north and south porches, and west tower, and is built of field stones with ashlar dressings. It was substantially rebuilt in the 14th century and later, although the lowest storey of the tower has thick walling, possibly of the 13th century, and the external walls incorporate pieces of Barnack stone carved with chevrons indicative of a 12th-century building. The 14th-century work includes the west window with Decorated tracery, the upper storeys of the tower with set back buttresses, the triple-chamfered tower arch, the chancel arch, whose responds were possibly recut later, and the two-bay chancel, whose two-light side-windows have curvilinear tracery. The three-light east window may have replaced a group of three lancets. The four-bay nave was remodelled in the late 15th or early 16th century, the walls being heightened to accommodate tall three-light windows. The windows once contained armorial glass recording the Alingtons' marriage alliances between 1430 and 1500,[50] and money was left for the 'battlement' of the church in 1524.[51] The nave has a blocked north doorway to the rood stair with floral carving in its spandrels. The south porch is 15th-century. The north porch, built of brick in the 16th century, had been converted by 1742 to a vestry.[52] The octagonal font is Perpendicular. The 15th-century rood-screen, of five bays with panelled tracery, was repaired in 1721.[53] The 15th-century nave roof, which has moulded beams and some bosses, was repaired in 1764.[54]

In the chancel a brass of a knight in 14th-century

[18] C.U.L., E.D.R., tithe award 1839.
[19] Parsons, *Horseheath Ch.* 65.
[20] *Rot. Hund.* (Rec. Com.), ii. 420.
[21] C.U.L., E.D.R., H 1/4, terriers 1574, 1662; ibid. MS. Plan 679.
[22] C.R.O., R 70/48, 3 Aug. 1829.
[23] Parsons, *Horseheath Ch.* 65; ex inf. the rector, the Revd. P. W. Wills.
[24] *Cal. Pat.* 1416–22, 32.
[25] C.U.L., E.D.R., H 1/4, terriers 1615, 1638, 1662, 1692.
[26] B.L. Add. MS. 5808, f. 173.
[27] Parsons, *Horseheath Ch.* 94–5; C.U.L., E.D.R., C 3/26.
[28] B.L. Add. MS. 5861, f. 99.
[29] *Cal. Pat.* 1569–72, 228.
[30] *E.D.R.* (1893), 136; (1897), 117.
[31] *East Anglian*, N.S. xiii. 191.
[32] *E.D.R.* (1909), 128.
[33] Ibid. (1912), 184; cf. B.L. Add. MS. 5861, f. 13.
[34] e.g. B.L. Add. MS. 5861, ff. 13, 65–6, 91, 99v.
[35] B.L. Add. MS. 5813, f. 66.
[36] e.g. C.U.L., E.D.R., B 2/3, pp. 100, 199; B 2/6; B 2/8.
[37] Ibid. B 2/11, f. 127; *Cambs. Village Doc.* 66.
[38] Lamb. Pal. MS. 904, f. 213.
[39] Cf. *Alumni Carthusiani*, ed. B. Marsh and F. A. Crisp (priv. print. 1913), p. xi.
[40] Parsons, *Horseheath Ch.* 90.
[41] C.U.L., E.D.R., C 1/4; *Alum. Carthus.* 290.
[42] Cf. Parsons, *Horseheath Ch.* 66–7.
[43] C.U.L., E.D.R., B 8/1.
[44] Ibid. C 1/1.
[45] Ibid. C 1/4, 6; C 3/21.
[46] H.O. 129/188/3/1/1.
[47] C.U.L., E.D.R., C 3/26, 37.
[48] *Crockford* (1900 and later edns.); *Ely Dioc. Dir.* (1973–4).
[49] Prob. 11/15 (P.C.C. 34 Adeane, will of Wm. Jacob).
[50] B.L. Add. MS. 5823, ff. 11–12.
[51] B.L. Add. MS. 5861, f. 91.
[52] B.L. Add. MS. 5823, f. 9.
[53] Ibid. f. 11.
[54] Inscr. on beam.

armour may be that of William Audley (d. 1365) whose family arms were once in a chancel window, and in the floor were formerly various brasses to members of the Alington family, dated between 1429 and 1552.[55] Against the south wall is the monument erected by Sir Giles Alington (d. 1586) to himself and his father Sir Giles (d. 1521), of two tiers, each with an effigy, supported by bulbous columns. The upper canopy was removed after 1742.[56] Against the north wall the recumbent effigies of Sir Giles Alington (d. 1638) and his wife Dorothy (d. 1613) lie on a tomb-chest surrounded by their twelve children;[57] the work is ascribed to Nicholas Stone.

The church was usually kept in decent repair between the 16th century and the 18th.[58] In 1644 William Dowsing broke 8 figures of Christ and the prophets, and destroyed over 40 pictured windows, although a little figured glass survived in the nave in 1742.[59] A new pulpit, against the north wall, was put up between 1728 and 1742, by which time a west gallery, blocking the tower arch, had been built for the singers. The whole interior was then painted with scriptural texts and garlands supported by angels, and the chancel ceiling plastered with floral decorations.[60] The church was extensively repaired in the 1820s.[61] A thorough restoration was initiated in 1875, with R. R. Rowe as architect.[62] Between 1880 and 1883 the south wall and ceiling of the chancel were rebuilt. By 1891 the old pulpit, pews, and gallery had been cleared from the nave. The south porch was remodelled in 1894,[63] the stonework of the nave windows renewed in 1912, and the tower repaired in 1925.[64] An organ, bought from a Cambridge church, was installed in 1876, and a clock placed in the tower in 1897.[65]

In 1552 there were three bells in the tower.[66] A tenor bell given in 1606 by Sir Giles Alington was recast and two others were newly cast in 1699 and 1700 by Richard Keene of Royston.[67] There were five bells by 1742. Two were recast as one by Thomas Safford of Cambridge in 1825, and there were four bells in 1974.[68] The church acquired three chalices during the later Middle Ages,[69] and had two of silver in 1552.[70] About 1960 the plate included a silver cup and paten of 1666 and a flagon of 1715.[71] The extant registers begin in 1558 and are complete except for the Interregnum.[72]

NONCONFORMITY. Three people were presented in 1582[73] and one in 1587, 1591, and 1601, for refusing to attend church.[74] At least 13 Quakers at Horseheath, some of whom attended meetings at Linton, were presented in the 1650s and 1660s for refusing to contribute to church repairs and burying their dead in private gardens.[75] In 1663 6 men and 5 women did not attend church.[76] In 1669 meetings attended by 50 or 60 people were held in a private house,[77] and 8 nonconformists at Horseheath were recorded in 1676.[78]

By 1728 there were 20 dissenters, described as Independents or Presbyterians,[79] and houses were registered for Independent worship in 1742 and 1749.[80] Six or seven dissenting families from Horseheath attended the chapel at Linton in 1783.[81] By 1807 there was a small Presbyterian meeting-house at Horseheath with monthly meetings, and by 1825 the congregation had grown to *c.* 100, including two of the principal farmers.[82] The meeting evidently did not survive in 1851.[83] Rooms were registered for worship in 1809 and 1835,[84] and by 1852 a small Primitive Methodist chapel of red brick had been built on the village street.[85] The rector in 1877 thought that not more than six people attended it, but in 1897 its congregation was estimated at a quarter of the population.[86] The chapel was still open in 1973.

EDUCATION. Schoolmasters were licensed at Horseheath in 1609, 1610, and 1613,[87] and in 1663 the parish clerk served as schoolmaster.[88] In 1728 the lord of the manor supported a school for 30 children,[89] probably that which was reported in 1730 to be in association with the S.P.C.K.[90] The parish clerk in 1779 taught *c.* 10 children,[91] but there was no school at Horseheath in 1807.[92]

By 1818 a day-school with *c.* 25 pupils had been established,[93] and in 1833 there were three day-schools, besides a Sunday school started in 1821; 15 girls were taught at the rector's expense, and parents paid for 24 boys and 25 girls to be taught in two other schools.[94] T. C. Percival, rector 1825–48, built a brick and flint National school in the churchyard for boys and girls,[95] and *c.* 1850 there were five other small schools, including one supported by Stanlake Batson to teach 12 girls.[96] The

55 B.L. Add. MS. 5823, f. 11.
56 Ibid. ff. 9–10.
57 Ibid. Two children's figures were missing in 1974. See above, plate facing p. 65.
58 e.g. C.U.L., E.D.R., B 2/59, p. 43; B 8/1; B 7/1, p. 126.
59 *Trans. C.H.A.S.* iii. 84; B.L. Add. MS. 5823, f. 11.
60 C.U.L., E.D.R., B 8/1; B.L. Add. MS. 5823, ff. 11–12.
61 Parsons, *Horseheath Ch.* 15, 17; C.U.L., E.D.R., C 1/6.
62 *Proc. C.A.S.* xxxv. 71, 84.
63 Parsons, *Horseheath Ch.* 19–21; *Kelly's Dir. Cambs.* (1883–1900).
64 C.R.O., 331/Z 3, 1912, Dec., p. ciii; 331/Z 6, 1925, Sept., p. 551.
65 Parsons, *Horseheath Ch.* 35.
66 *Cambs. Ch. Goods, temp. Edw. VI*, 64.
67 *Cambs. Bells* (C.A.S. 8vo ser. xviii), 152; H. B. Walters, MS. list *penes V.C.H.*
68 B.L. Add. MS. 5823, f. 9; Parsons, *Horseheath Ch.* 16.
69 *Vetus Liber Arch. Elien.* (C.A.S. 8vo ser. xlviii), 54–5.
70 *Cambs. Ch. Goods, temp. Edw. VI*, 64.
71 List of ch. plate *penes V.C.H.*
72 Gibbons, *Ely Episc. Rec.* 231.
73 *Cath. Rec. Soc.* liii. i.
74 Gibbons, *Ely Episc. Rec.* 49; C.U.L., E.D.R., B 2/11, f. 168v.; B 2/18, f. 7.
75 *Proc. C.A.S.* lxi. 93; Parsons, *Horseheath Ch.* 85; *Cambs. Episc. Visit. 1638–65*, ed. Palmer, 110–11.
76 C.U.L., E.D.R., B 2/54, f. 24.
77 *Orig. Rec. of Early Nonconf.* ed. Turner, i. 40.
78 Compton Census.
79 C.U.L., E.D.R., B 8/1.
80 G.R.O. Worship Returns, Ely dioc. nos. 81, 109.
81 C.U.L., E.D.R., B 7/1, p. 126.
82 Ibid. C 1/4; C 1/6.
83 Not mentioned in H.O. 129/188/3.
84 G.R.O. Worship Returns, Ely dioc. nos. 222, 595.
85 Ibid. Worship Reg. no. 9178.
86 C.U.L., E.D.R., C 3/26; C 3/37.
87 *Proc. C.A.S.* xxii. 112; C.U.L., E.D.R., B 2/30A, f. 6v.; B 2/32, f. 5v.
88 *Proc. C.A.S.* xxii. 112.
89 C.U.L., E.D.R., B 8/1.
90 *V.C.H. Cambs.* ii. 343.
91 *Proc. C.A.S.* xxii. 116.
92 C.U.L., E.D.R., C 1/4.
93 *Educ. of Poor Digest*, 61.
94 *Educ. Enquiry Abstract*, 57; C.U.L., E.D.R., C 3/21.
95 Parsons, *Horseheath Ch.* 94.
96 *Church School Inquiry, 1846–7*, 6–7; *Proc. C.A.S.* xxii. 119; H.O. 129/188/3/1/1; cf. R.G. 9/1030.

curate in 1867 also taught a night-school in winter, attended by *c.* 25 people.[97] A new National school was built in 1874–5 by the main road,[98] and in 1876 the old school in the churchyard was demolished.[99] The National school in 1875 had *c.* 70 pupils, none paying over 1*d.* a week because of the poverty of the district.[1] There was also a private school with *c.* 30 pupils in 1877.[2] Attendance at the National school rose to *c.* 80 by 1907, but fell to 55 by 1936.[3] Senior pupils were transferred to Linton village college in 1937.[4] Horseheath junior school retained the old National school building in 1973.

CHARITIES FOR THE POOR. Thomas Wakefield, rector 1589–1626, by will proved 1626 left £50 to buy land, the rent to be paid to the poor of the parish.[5] By 1630 9 a. had been purchased, and £2 10*s.* rent was received in 1668.[6] By 1783 rent was received from 5 a. in Balsham,[7] perhaps a separate benefaction but usually identified as Wakefield's charity. In 1837 the income of £6 was distributed to the poor at Christmas. A Scheme of 1936 amalgamated Wakefield's charity and the Balsham land with the Town Green charity. The income from the land in Balsham was to be used for the general benefit of poor parishioners.

Dorothy, widow of William, Lord Alington (d. 1685), by will proved 1702 gave £60 to buy land, the rent to provide bread each Sunday for the twelve poorest churchgoers in Horseheath.[8] The money so used in 1728[9] may have come from 6 a. in Linton which was owned by trustees in 1783.[10] The income from the Linton land, £5 in 1837, was distributed in bread to the poor in 1863,[11] and provided weekly doles of bread to five poor widows in 1911.[12] In 1921 the Linton land was sold and £179 stock was added to the Wakefield charity.

The Town Green charity originated in a rent-charge of £5 which the lord of the manor gave in compensation for householders' common rights in 6 a. of the town green inclosed in his park. The income was given with that from the Balsham land in 1837, and in 1905 was divided among 90 householders.[13] In 1936 it was directed that the Town Green charity should be used for poor householders. The income of the three parochial charities in 1965 was £31.

John Offord at an unknown date gave £10, the interest to go to the poor, and in 1783 10*s.* a year was given to five poor widows.[14] The charity was lost in 1828 when a churchwarden absconded with the money. William Eedes, rector 1669–1709, left £10 to provide an income for the aged poor,[15] and in 1728 the interest on £30 was given annually to the poor;[16] no later evidence of either charity has been found.

LINTON

THE PARISH of Linton,[1] which includes the former market town and Barham hamlet, lies 9 miles south-east of Cambridge. In 1961 it covered 3,817 a.[2] and comprised a rectangular area, 2¼ by 1½ miles, between the line of the ancient Wool Street on the north and the river Granta, with a tongue of land, 1¼ by 1 mile, stretching south-west to the watershed. The southern boundary was also the county boundary with Essex. In 1965 the area between the river and the disused Cambridge–Haverhill railway (54 ha.) was transferred to Linton from Hadstock (Essex), and 3 ha. elsewhere were transferred from Linton to Hadstock, leaving Linton with an area of 3,946 a. (1,597 ha.).[3]

The greater part of Linton has long been devoted to arable farming, the common fields which survived until inclosure in 1838 being interspersed with pasture closes. From the 13th century to the 19th Linton had a market and fairs, and was still in the 20th a local centre for retail trade. Until the 19th century there was activity in trades using locally grown timber, both in building and in processing and using leather, and by the mid 20th there was some light industry. From the 13th century Linton contained two religious houses. Linton priory, a cell of a Benedictine abbey in Brittany, was suppressed after 1400. A convent of the Crutched Friars at Barham survived until the Reformation.[4]

Linton lies mainly on the chalk, overlaid by narrow beds of alluvium and valley gravels along the river and on much of the higher ground by boulder clay or, as at Rivey Hill, by glacial gravels. South of the river the ground rises gradually from 125 ft. near the river to 340 ft. North of the village Rivey Hill, called until after 1840 Ballydon or Ballingdon Hill,[5] rises relatively sharply to over 350 ft.; the ground then sinks to a plateau, mostly over 225 ft., and to the east is a ridge of over 300 ft. crowned by Borley wood.

The Granta follows a winding course, occasionally

97 *1st Rep. Com. Employment in Agric.* 359.
98 Ed. 7/5.
99 Parsons, *Horseheath Ch.* 65.
1 Ed. 7/5.
2 C.U.L., E.D.R., C 3/26.
3 *Public Elem. Schs. 1907* [Cd. 3901], p. 27, H.C. (1908), lxxxiv; *Bd. of Educ., List 21, 1936* (H.M.S.O.), 17.
4 Black, *Cambs. Educ. Rec.* 62.
5 Prob. 11/150 (P.C.C. 148 Hele). Unless otherwise stated, this section is based on *31st Rep. Com. Char.* 104–5; Char. Com. files.
6 Parsons, *Horseheath Ch.* 99–100.
7 C.U.L., E.D.R., B 7/1, p. 126.
8 Parsons, *Horseheath Ch.* 101.
9 C.U.L., E.D.R., B 8/1.
10 Ibid. B 7/1, p. 126.
11 *Char. Digest Cambs. 1863–4*, 24–5.
12 Parsons, *Horseheath Ch.* 98.
13 C.R.O., 331/Z 1, 1906, Jan., p. vi.
14 C.U.L., E.D.R., B 7/1, p. 126. A John Offord leased the Pembroke College farm in 1705 and 1719, and a namesake in 1726: Pemb. Coll. Mun., D 12–14.
15 C.U.L., E.D.R., B 7/1, p. 88.
16 Ibid. B 8/1.
1 This account was written in 1974.
2 *Census*, 1961.
3 Cambs. & Isle of Ely Order, 1964 no. 366 (H.L.G. 14603); *Census*, 1971.
4 *V.C.H. Cambs.* ii. 291–2, 314–15.
5 e.g. Pemb. Coll. Mun., Barham, B 6A (1523); C.U.L., Doc. 643 no. 81 (1838).

ICKLETON: the view northwards from Coploe Hill. The hillside in the foreground is terraced with lynchets

LINTON HIGH STREET in the early 20th century

LINTON: Barham Hall in the early 19th century

WEST WRATTING: Wratting Park from the north-west

BURROUGH GREEN HALL from the east

HILDERSHAM: the Rookery in the mid 19th century

dividing into two branches, notably downstream near Hildersham mill. Until the 19th century it was crossed in Linton only by footbridges, one, called c. 1570 the great bridge, on the village high street, others upstream near the church and Linton mill.[6] An iron road-bridge was built in 1868.[7] The land along the river was liable to flooding, one neighbouring field being called in 1779 Noah's Flood field;[8] after 1968 the embankment of the new by-pass, acting as a dam, aggravated the danger[9] and necessitated a flood control scheme.[10]

The parish represents the territories of three adjacent settlements. The two Lintons, later distinguished as Great and Little Linton, were recorded in 1008,[11] and Barham in 1066.[12] After their combination into a single ecclesiastical parish their earlier distinction was still marked by boundaries between their respective manors and common fields. Little Linton occupied most of the south-western tongue of land, extending in 1279 from Catley northwards to Pinnings ditch, south of the modern Little Linton Farm. Great Linton lay mostly north of the river and west of Barham cross, which stood where the Horseheath and Bartlow roads divide, but in 1279 it also included a narrow strip between Little Linton and Hadstock, containing the former Linton wood and touching Burton wood in Great Chesterford (Essex).[13] When the inhabitants of Linton fee beat their bounds in 1680, they included both Great and Little Linton but left out Barham to the east.[14] Barham fee, which in 1786 covered c. 1,940 a., half the parish, was then reckoned by its lords to include all the field-land east of the old Linton–Balsham road, over the top of Rivey Hill, and a narrow belt of land west of that road.[15]

In the 18th century there were disputes about jurisdiction between the lords of Linton and Barham because freehold, copyhold, and demesne lands belonging to both manors were intermingled throughout the centre of the northern part of the parish. Much land of Michaelotts manor, an offshoot of Barham manor but belonging since 1400 to the lords of Linton, lay in the debated zone. The main issue was the right to shoot and fish, which the owners of Linton had enjoyed or usurped over the whole parish since the early 18th century.[16] Both manors included rights of free warren, under charters of 1246 for Great Linton[17] and 1280 for Barham.[18] About 1460 the lord of Barham built a lodge near Borley wood for his rabbit-keeper. The rabbits were exterminated c. 1520 at the request of the tenants.[19] Rabbits were still being preserved in a warren in Linton wood c. 1580.[20]

The heavy clay at the south-western end of the parish was well wooded in early medieval times. The name Catley implies a clearing,[21] and in 1086 Great and Little Linton had enough woodland to feed 50 pigs.[22] Linton wood, which in 1272 covered c. 60 a.,[23] lay beside the Hadstock boundary. In 1674 it covered 106 a.[24] In the 18th century 10 a. were usually felled each year.[25] At inclosure in 1838 Linton wood amounted to 89 a.[26] Soon afterwards it was cleared and the land converted to tillage.[27] Catley grove, 13 a. in 1950, was established only after inclosure.[28] Rivey wood, north of the village, covering 21 a. c. 1840,[29] lay in an ancient pasture close, first planted c. 1780 as a game preserve.[30] The woodland on the high ground north-east of the village is represented by the modern Borley wood; the former Oaks pasture[31] east of the wood was perhaps named from trees once growing there. In 1279 Barham manor had 130 a. of woodland,[32] later divided into Borley wood to the west, covering c. 95 a. in 1786, and Shortwood to the south-east, then containing 37 a.[33]

Linton was probably settled before Roman times. Early Iron Age remains were found near the Hadstock road in 1948,[34] and a Roman villa lay just across the river from Barham Hall.[35] At a large pagan Saxon cemetery on Barham heath near the Horseheath road 104 burials were inserted into a Romano-British barrow.[36] In 1086 Great Linton contained 21 peasants and 6 *servi*, Little Linton 10 and 4, and Barham 18 and 2.[37] By 1279 there were about 80 tenants, including 35 burgage-holders, resident on Great Linton fee, and 72 on Barham fee, but only 20 on Little Linton fee.[38] In 1327 the whole village contained c. 45 resident taxpayers.[39] In 1377 155 adults paid the poll tax;[40] in 1524 88 people paid the subsidy;[41] and there were 92 households in 1563.[42] The birth-rate increased from c. 19 a year in the 1560s to c. 28 a year in the 1640s;[43] there were only 457 adults in 1676,[44] living in c. 180 houses.[45] The number of households remained stable during the 18th century, standing in 1728 at 252, with 976 inhabitants,[46] and in 1783 at 240.[47] In 1801 246 families included 1,157 people. Thereafter the population increased steadily until 1851 when it numbered 1,858. A subsequent decline, ascribed partly to emigration in 1861, when there were 33 empty

6 C.R.O., L 95/14, ff. iv.–3v., 10; Pemb. Coll. Mun., Barham, T.i.c. (map of Barham fee, 1600).
7 C.R.O., L 95/47; *Camb. Ind. Press*, 15 Jan. 1960.
8 C.R.O., R 59/5/6/7.
9 e.g. *Camb. News*, 8 Oct., 4 Nov. 1968.
10 *Camb. Evening News*, 12 Sept. 1969.
11 *Liber Elien.* (Camd. 3rd ser. xcii), 145–6.
12 *V.C.H. Cambs.* i. 341.
13 *Rot. Hund.* (Rec. Com.), ii. 416, 418; cf. C.R.O., 124/P 64; C.R.O., R 59/14/11/11CC.
14 C.R.O., R 59/5/6/3/1, pp. 120–1.
15 Pemb. Coll. Mun., Barham, S 14; S 16; T.i.c.
16 e.g. C.R.O., R 59/14/11/11C, F, G, P.
17 *Cal. Chart. R.* 1226–57, 294.
18 Ibid. 1257–1300, 262.
19 Pemb. Coll. Mun., Barham, BB 2, ct. roll 17 Hen. VIII.
20 C.R.O. R 59/14/11/7C, ct. roll 22–3 Eliz. I.
21 *P.N. Cambs.* (E.P.N.S.), 110.
22 *V.C.H. Cambs.* i. 341.
23 C 132/42 no. 6.
24 C.R.O., R 59/5/3/1, pp. 392–4.
25 Ibid. R 59/5/4/3.
26 Ibid. Q/RDc 53, map; ibid. R 59/5/6/12.
27 Cf. ibid. 296/SP 1009.
28 Cf. ibid. 152/P 13; ibid. SP 107/7.
29 Ibid. R 59/5/6/12; ibid. SP 107/6.
30 Ibid. R 59/5/6/3A; R 59/14/11/11P.
31 e.g. Pemb. Coll. Mun., Barham, T.i.c.
32 *Rot. Hund.* (Rec. Com.), ii. 418.
33 Pemb. Coll. Mun., Barham, S 16.
34 *Proc. C.A.S.* xlii. 129; xlvi. 31–42.
35 *V.C.H. Essex*, iii. 135–6.
36 *Arch. Jnl.* xi. 95–115; Fox, *Arch. Camb. Region*, 196–7, 260.
37 *V.C.H. Cambs.* i. 341.
38 *Rot. Hund.* (Rec. Com.), ii. 416–20.
39 *Cambs. Lay Subsidy, 1327*, 24.
40 *East Anglian*, N.S. xii. 219.
41 E 179/81/134 m. 3.
42 B.L. Harl. MS. 594, f. 99v.
43 C.R.O., par. reg. TS.
44 Compton Census.
45 See pp. 279–80.
46 C.U.L., E.D.R., B 8/1.
47 Ibid. B 7/1, p. 129.

houses, had by 1901 reduced numbers to 1,455 and by 1931 to 1,316. Post-war expansion raised it again to 1,813 by 1961 and 2,627 by 1971.[48]

The village stands where two low chalk ridges come close together at a crossing of the Granta, from which one part of the village high street runs east and another south[49] to meet the Hildersham road and to turn east along a stretch called Stony Street before bending south again into the Hadstock road. North of the river a minor road from Hildersham divided into Union Lane, which runs into the high street, and a back lane formerly called Cambridge or London Cross way leading to the site of Barham cross, from which Haverhill or Horseheath and Bartlow ways ran east. The road to Balsham ran straight up Rivey Hill until inclosure, when it was diverted along a curving field-way further east.[50]

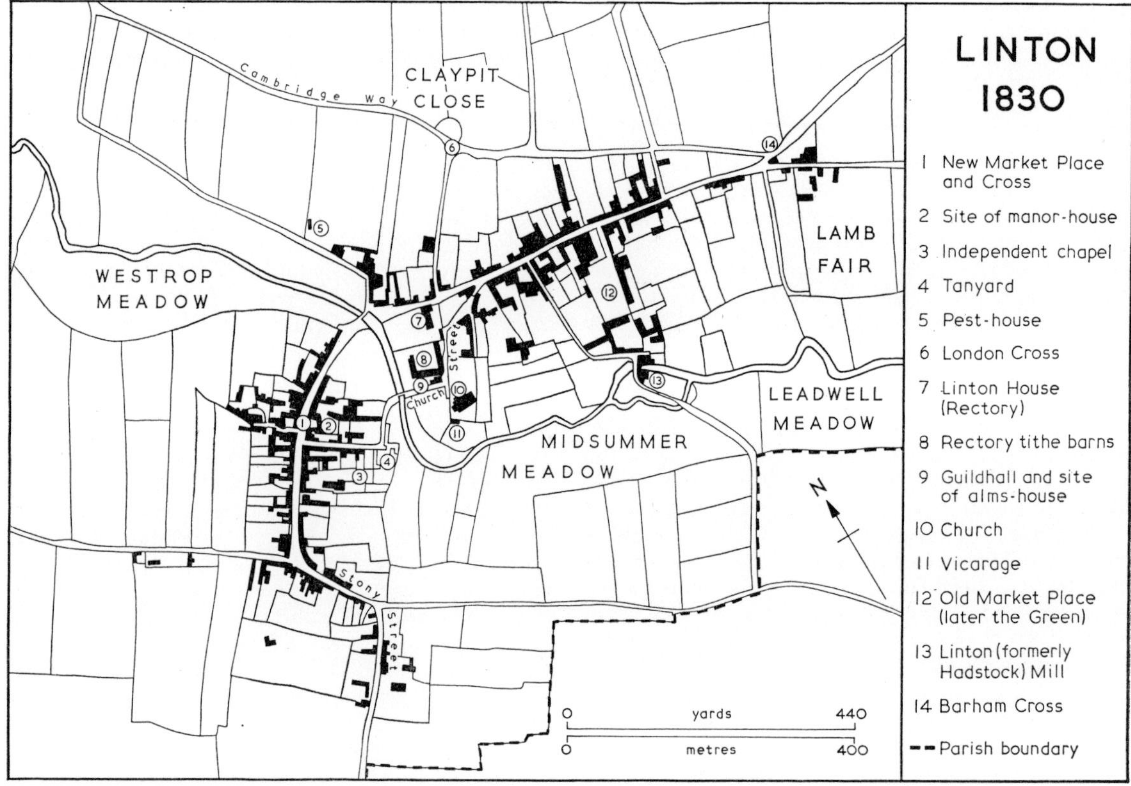

No evidence has been found suggesting that around the sites of Little Linton and Barham manor-houses there were settlements detached from the surviving village. Perhaps the name Little Linton once applied to the area along the high street south of the river. Certainly from the later Middle Ages messuages held of Linton and Barham manors lay intermingled north of the river, the largest block of Barham tenements lying south of the street.[51]

Within the village the larger houses and the workshops, stalls, and shops lay along the high street of which the southern section widened near the middle into the market place. Many poorer dwellings lay along lanes running off the high street. Linton retains many timber-framed, plastered houses, some still thatched, dating from the 17th and 18th centuries, and one or two, such as Chandlers, from the 15th. There are also along the high street larger houses, built of brick or given brick fronts in the 18th century, including the Old Manor House, Cambridge House, Bull House, Clare House, Queen's House of 1731, and Ram House.[52]

The village grew little until after 1801, when there were still only 183 houses in the parish. It was then grossly overcrowded. In 1831 315 households were crammed into 214 houses.[53] Early-19th-century building within the old village limits raised the number of dwellings to 387 by 1851, when *c.* 220 lay along the high street, and *c.* 170 on the lanes, yards, and courts leading off it.[54] Except at Little Linton and Barham manor-houses and the later Catley Park, there was virtually no building away from the village until after inclosure when farmsteads were erected in the fields *c.* 1839 for Heath and Greenditch farms.[55] Chilford Hall Farm, built apparently by 1841[56] north-west of Rivey Hill, has no connection with the supposed manor of Chilford, nor with the original 'Cildeford', presumably on the river, where the hundred court is said to have met.[57] The 20th century saw much new building. Between 1921 and 1951 *c.* 120 new houses were

[48] *Census*, 1801–1971. The figures given exclude the occupants of the workhouse.

[49] For the layout and names of the pre-inclosure roads see Pemb. Coll. Mun., Barham, T.i.c. (1600); ibid. S 6, 9, 18; C.R.O., 152/P 13 (draft inclosure map, 1837); C.R.O., R 59/5/3/1, pp. 99–131; R 59/5/6/3A–B.

[50] C.U.L., Doc. 643 no. 81; C.R.O., Q/RDc 53, p. 31.

[51] Pemb. Coll. Mun., Barham, T.i.c.; cf. C.R.O., R 59/14/11/11A.

[52] For detailed descriptions see M.H.L.G. List. See also above, plate facing p. 80.

[53] *Census*, 1801, 1831.

[54] H.O. 107/1761.

[55] C.R.O., Q/RDc 53, map.

[56] H.O. 107/66.

[57] Cf. *P.N. Cambs.* (E.P.N.S.), 110; Palmer, *Neighbourhood of Hildersham*, 5.

built, another 140 by 1961 and almost 300 more by 1971.[58] Apart from scattered buildings along the Bartlow road the main developments were immediately north and west of the village. By 1950 new streets had been laid out south of the river westwards towards the village college, and north of the river along Union Lane and the back lane as far as the workhouse.[59] New housing estates, including many council houses, were laid out later at the south end of the Balsham road and on the slopes north and east of the village.[60]

The main road from Cambridge to Haverhill (Suff.) and beyond formerly ran along Linton high street. It was turnpiked under an Act of 1765,[61] and coaches ran along it from the late 18th century.[62] The road was disturnpiked in 1876.[63] In 1865 the Cambridge–Haverhill railway line, crossing the parish south of the river, was opened,[64] with a station near the Hildersham road. The line was completely closed in 1967.[65]

By the 17th century Linton had several inns and alehouses. In 1682 8 alehouses were licensed there,[66] and in 1686 there were beds for 29 and stabling for 56 horses.[67] The older inns included the Griffin, recorded from 1575, to which the manor-courts were adjourning in the 1670s;[68] renamed the Crown by 1777 and probably later moved to a new site,[69] it was styled a hotel by 1888 and survived in 1974.[70] The Unicorn, named from the Parys coat of arms, probably existed by 1599.[71] As the Red Lion, so called by 1725, it remained open as a posting-house and inn until the 1850s.[72] The Black Bull, recorded by 1694,[73] was still open in the 1760s, but was soon after converted to a school-house.[74] Other 18th-century inns included the Swan, recorded from 1725 and still open in 1974, in a six-bay whitewashed brick Georgian building on the high street, the White Hart, closed *c.* 1908, the Dolphin, recorded by 1776 and closed after 1937, and the Bell, a five-bay timber-framed 16th-century house, converted by 1974 to a restaurant.[75] By 1700 Linton had a coffee-house near the market-place, probably still open *c.* 1767.[76]

By 1800 there was a friendly society meeting at the White Hart,[77] probably that which had 39 members in 1803 and 70 *c.* 1813.[78] The same or a similar society, instituted under new rules at the Swan in 1825, was confined to tradesmen and artisans earning over 12*s.* a week. Its membership rose from 45 in 1831 to 67 by 1840, then fell by 1869 to 22.[79] By that year a lodge of the Oddfellows, Manchester Unity, was meeting at the market-house, lent by the lord of the manor. It had *c.* 120 members *c.* 1905.[80] After 1870 a branch of the Ancient Order of Shepherds was also established.[81] A new Shepherds' Hall, built for it on Market Lane and opened in 1922, was also used for public meetings and those of the parish council, and was enlarged in 1934 to provide rooms for a social club.[82] In 1968 work began on an elaborate new social centre for the village.[83]

The village maypole was recorded in 1534.[84] Various cultural activities were recorded from the late 18th century. A book club met monthly at the Crown in 1793.[85] A book society, subscribing to Mudie's, flourished from before 1859 to 1867,[86] and was followed by a Literary Institute established *c.* 1873 which usually met at the old market-cross.[87] The Linton society of singers was mentioned in 1790.[88] In the 1960s the village music society ran a miniature festival every summer.[89] The Linton cricket club was formed in 1852,[90] a football club in 1901.[91] In 1969 a small zoo, covering 10 a., was established at Linton.[92]

The parish had a resident barber-surgeon in 1739,[93] besides the apothecary John Disbrowe.[94] In the late 18th century there were usually two apothecaries practising at Linton,[95] and from the mid 19th a pair of surgeons worked there, often in partnership.[96]

In 1381 John Hanchach, who held $\frac{1}{5}$ of the Busteler estates at Linton and elsewhere, was a leader of the Peasants' Revolt in Cambridgeshire, and was beheaded and attainted. His band contained five men from Linton. They did no damage at their native village.[97] During the Great Rebellion both the families owning manors at Linton were royalists. John Millicent of Barham (d. 1686) fled from Linton in 1643 rather than take the Covenant, and was fined in 1647,[98] as was John Appleyard, the Paryses' chief tenant.[99] In 1648 the Cambridgeshire Cavaliers,

[58] *Census*, 1921–71.
[59] O.S. Map 6″, Cambs. LV. SW., SE. (1950 edn.).
[60] O.S. Map 1/2,500, TL 54 (1969 edn.).
[61] Haverhill and Red Cross Road Act, 6 Geo. III, c. 84.
[62] W. M. Palmer, *Antiquities of Linton* (Camb. 1913), 3–5.
[63] Annual Turnpike Acts Continuance Act, 1876, 39–40 Vic. c. 39.
[64] *V.C.H. Cambs.* ii. 132–3.
[65] Ex inf. British Rail Hist. Research Dept.
[66] *Proc. C.A.S.* xvii. 97.
[67] W.O. 30/48.
[68] C.R.O., R 59/14/11/3, no. 1; R 59/5/3/1, p. 27.
[69] *Camb. Chron.* 27 Dec. 1777; 27 Apr. 1793; 24 Apr. 1812; cf. Palmer, *Antiquities of Linton*, 2.
[70] *Kelly's Dir. Cambs.* (1888, 1937).
[71] Palmer, *Antiquities of Linton*, 5; C.R.O., R 59/14/11/3, nos. 2–3.
[72] C.R.O., R 59/14/11/10C; *Camb. Chron.* 28 June 1788; *Gardner's Dir. Cambs.* (1851).
[73] E 134/7 Wm. III Mich./2, pt. 3; C.R.O., R 59/5/3/2, f. 5v.
[74] C.R.O., R 59/5/4/3; *Camb. Chron.* 28 June 1777.
[75] C.R.O., R 59/14/11/10C–F; Pemb. Coll. Mun., Barham, R 3, pp. 56–74; *Kelly's Dir. Cambs.* (1858–1937).
[76] B.L. Eg. MS. 2719, f. 195; C.R.O., R 59/14/11/10C; Palmer, *Antiquities of Linton*, 5.
[77] C.R.O., L 95/37.
[78] *Poor Law Abstract, 1804*, 35; *1818*, 29.
[79] C.R.O., L 95/10.
[80] Ibid. R 59/5/9/8 E 2; ibid. L 95/15A, accts. 1903–5; L 95/50; *Kelly's Dir. Cambs.* (1896–1937).
[81] C.R.O., L 95/31A, notice, 1927; R 54/30/1, pp. 399 sqq.
[82] *Kelly's Dir. Cambs.* (1925, 1937).
[83] *Camb. News*, 24 Jan. 1964; 27 Sept. 1968; Char. Com. files.
[84] C.R.O., R 59/14/11/7A, ct. roll 26 Hen. VIII.
[85] *Camb. Chron.* 27 Apr. 1793.
[86] C.R.O., L 95/13.
[87] Ibid. L 95/15A, rep. 1903; *Kelly's Dir. Cambs.* (1879–1937); cf. C.U.L., Maps 53(1)/91/134.
[88] *Camb. Chron.* 5 June 1790.
[89] e.g. *Camb. News*, 28 June 1965; 22 Dec. 1966.
[90] *Camb. Ind. Press*, 15 Jan. 1960.
[91] C.R.O., L 95/15A, booklet 1911–12.
[92] *Camb. Ind. Press*, 25, 30 July 1969; 15 Jan., 9 Aug. 1972.
[93] E 134/10 Geo. II Mich./3 pt. 5.
[94] Palmer, *Wm. Cole*, 104.
[95] e.g. *Camb. Chron.* 17 Feb. 1781; 12 Sept. 1789; 27 Nov. 1792.
[96] *Kelly's Dir. Cambs.* (1858–1937).
[97] *Rot. Parl.* iii. 111, 175; *Cambs. Village Doc.* 98–101, 137, 168, 244; *East Anglian*, N.S. vi. 245–6.
[98] B.L. Add. MS. 15672, f. 23; *C.J.* v. 204; S.P. 23/198 pp. 729–37.
[99] C.R.O., L 58/5; *Cal. Cttee. for Compounding*, ii, p. 1567.

seeking to relieve the besieged Royalist garrison of Colchester, chose Linton as their rallying point, but were defeated and dispersed by Fairfax's cavalry on 16 June.[1]

The Hebrew scholar and translator of the Authorized Version, Dr. John Richardson, was born at Linton *c.* 1564 of a prosperous yeoman family. He was master of Peterhouse 1609–15, and of Trinity College, Cambridge, 1615–25.[2] Dr. William Mortlock Palmer, the Cambridgeshire antiquary, practised as a physician at Linton from 1900 to 1925 and died there in 1939.[3]

MANORS AND OTHER ESTATES. In the early 970s one Wulfhun granted land at Linton to Ramsey abbey upon becoming a monk there. Between 985 and 992 the abbey exchanged that estate with its patron ealdorman Ethelwine, for property at Toft.[4] In 1008 King Ethelred sold 7 hides, probably comprising both Great and Little Linton, to Ely abbey.[5] The abbey probably lost the estate well before *c.* 1040,[6] and by 1066 Great and Little Linton and Barham, almost 11 hides, all belonged to Eddeva the fair.[7] Then, and in 1086, Ely retained lordship only over one sokeman, holding ¼ yardland in Barhad,[8] from whose holding were probably derived the 60 a. which Alfred Mautein held in 1279 of the heirs of William FitzMartin of Bottisham under the bishop of Ely.[9]

By 1086 the Linton and Barham manors had passed with Eddeva's other lands to Count Alan of Brittany,[10] with whose honor of Richmond the tenancy-in-chief descended after subinfeudation.[11] The Richmond overlordship of Great and Little Linton was recorded until the 17th century,[12] and the owner of Barham was still paying a quit-rent of £3 10*s.* a year, doubled since the 14th century, to the feodary of the honor in 1805.[13] Barham had already been subinfeudated by 1086, but both the Lintons, 6½ hides, were then in Count Alan's hands, apart from 1 yardland still occupied by a sokeman, formerly Alsi Squitrebel's man.[14] When Constance, heir of Count Conan (d. 1171), was taken into Henry II's wardship, her lands included an estate at Linton, yielding rent and corn for sale,[15] and as countess of Brittany she still had demesne land there *c.* 1200.[16]

By 1174, however, *GREAT LINTON* manor, *c.* 4 hides in 1086, was held under the honor of Richmond by William de Mandeville, earl of Essex.[17] When William died in 1189 it was apparently assigned as dower to his widow Hawise, countess of Aumale (d. 1214),[18] whose third husband Baldwin de Béthune granted 45 a. at Linton to 'Suntingfield' hospital *c.* 1203.[19] Great Linton did not pass with the bulk of the Mandeville inheritance, but was probably assigned, on Hawise's death, to Geoffrey de Say (d. 1230), heir male of Earl William's aunt Beatrice (d. 1197).[20] Geoffrey's son William held Great Linton by *c.* 1236,[21] and died in 1272, when he was said to hold it of the earl of Hereford, Beatrice's heir general. William's son and heir William[22] (d. 1295) released his claim to the Mandeville lands to Humphrey de Bohun, earl of Hereford, in 1284 in return for an assurance of Great Linton, to be held of the earl and his heirs.[23] That tenure was occasionally recorded until 1572.[24]

In 1290 William de Say granted Great Linton to John Northwood, a Kent landowner, for life with remainder to Northwood's son John (d. by 1318) and the latter's issue by his wife Mary, possibly Say's daughter. John Northwood, presumably the elder, held Great Linton in 1316,[25] but not apparently when he died in 1319.[26] The manor had been divided, possibly between two daughters and coheirs of Mary.[27] One moiety passed to Elizabeth, wife of Sir John Joce.[28] In 1320 the Joces granted it to William le Busteler of Hildersham,[29] who died *c.* 1334.[30] In 1346 his son Robert was said to hold a quarter and a fortieth of the Great Linton fee, Henry Reresby and his wife Maud an eighth, Hugh Huntingfield a twentieth, and John Martin and William Clopton a fortieth each, presumably the constituent fractions of that moiety.[31] The other had probably passed by 1327 to Bevis de Knoville,[32] who died holding property at Linton of the earl of Hereford in 1338. Bevis's son and heir John[33] (d. 1349×1355)[34] and his wife Margaret settled their half in 1343 for life upon Thomas Sewale,[35] who held ½ fee there in 1346.[36] In 1355 Margaret and her second husband Sir Thomas Moigne released her life-interest to Sewale,[37] who may still have held ½ fee there *c.* 1365.[38] Robert le Busteler was said, however, to hold the whole manor when he died without surviving issue in 1366. His coheirs

[1] Hist. MSS. Com. 38, *14th Rep. IX*, pp. 284–5; *Cal. Cttee. for Compounding*, iv, pp. 2502, 2750, 2900; *Suffolk in Gt. Rebellion* (Suff. Rec. Soc. iii), 94 sqq.; C.R.O., par. reg. TS., 16 June 1648.
[2] *D.N.B.*; cf. C.R.O., R 59/5/9/47.
[3] *Proc. C.A.S.* xxxix. 1–4.
[4] *Ramsey Chron.* (Rolls Ser.), 54.
[5] *Liber Elien.* (Camd. 3rd ser. xcii), pp. 145–6; cf. Robertson, *A.-S. Charters*, 255.
[6] Not included in lists of Ely estates in *Liber Elien.* pp. 153, 162.
[7] *V.C.H. Cambs.* i. 341.
[8] Ibid. 365.
[9] *Rot. Hund.* (Rec. Com.), ii. 420.
[10] *V.C.H. Cambs.* i. 341.
[11] e.g. *Rot. Hund.* ii. 416, 418; *Feud. Aids*, i. 162–3.
[12] e.g. C 142/265 no. 35; Wards 7/53 no. 276.
[13] *Cal. Inq. p.m.* v, p. 247; Pemb. Coll. Mun., Barham, AA 1, acct. 36–8 Hen. VI; S 18A.
[14] *V.C.H. Cambs.* i. 409.
[15] *Pipe R.* 1175 (P.R.S. xxii), 5–6; cf. *Early Yorks. Chart.* iv (Y.A.S. extra ser. i), 108–9.
[16] *Pipe R.* 1200 (P.R.S. N.S. xii), 88.
[17] Ibid. 1174 (P.R.S. xxi), 65; 1176 (P.R.S. xxv), 72.
[18] Cf. *Complete Peerage*, v. 116–17, 119–20.
[19] *Rot. Chart.* (Rec. Com.), 118; cf. *Red Bk. Exch.* (Rolls Ser.), ii. 531. The hospital has not been identified.
[20] See *Complete Peerage*, v. 113–31; xi. 464–75.
[21] *Liber de Bernewelle*, 154.
[22] *Cal. Inq. p.m.* i, pp. 281–2.
[23] C.P. 25(1)/284/22 no. 136.
[24] e.g. *Cal. Inq. p.m.* xiii, p. 137; *Cal. Close*, 1402–5, 227; C 142/60 no. 17.
[25] C.P. 25(1)/26/43 no. 27; *Feud. Aids*, i. 155; cf. *Cal. Pat.* 1318–21, 207.
[26] *Cal. Inq. p.m.* vi, pp. 108–9.
[27] Cf. C.R.O., 331/Z 1, 1905, p. lxxv.
[28] Cf. *Cal. Fine R.* 1307–19, 348.
[29] *Cal. Close*, 1318–23, 230.
[30] Last recorded as living in 1333: *Cal. Close*, 1333–4, 61.
[31] *Feud. Aids*, i. 162.
[32] Cf. *Cambs. Lay Subsidy, 1327*, 21: forename misread as Hugo.
[33] *Cal. Inq. p.m.* viii, p. 108.
[34] *Complete Peerage*, vii. 349–50.
[35] *Cal. Close*, 1343–6, 280; cf. *Cambs. Fines*, 1196–1485 (C.A.S. 8vo ser. xxvi), 108.
[36] *Feud. Aids*, i. 162.
[37] C.P. 25(1)/28/78 no. 11; cf. *Cal. Inq. p.m.* xi, p. 283.
[38] *Cal. Inq. p.m.* xiii, p. 137.

were the descendants of his five sisters. Four of them, Thomas Payn, John Mersey, Henry Helion, and Walter of Linton shortly transferred their interests to Robert Parys of a Cheshire family. The fifth coheir, John Hanchach, then a minor,[39] received possession of his share in 1380.[40] On his attainder it became forfeit to the Crown and was granted in 1383 to a king's yeoman,[41] but had been reunited by 1425 to the other $\frac{4}{5}$ in the Paryses' hands.[42]

When Robert Parys died *c.* 1377[43] his Linton land passed to his elder son Nicholas who held it in 1397 and 1412 and died without issue in 1425,[44] when his lands passed to his brother Robert's son Henry (d. 1427). Henry's son and heir Henry, aged 3 in 1427,[45] died in 1466 when his son and heir Robert was a minor.[46] Robert was succeeded in 1504 by his son John[47] (d. 1517). John's son and heir Philip,[48] treasurer to Bishop Gardiner in the 1530s[49] and receiver-general of the Court of Augmentations 1540–4,[50] was knighted in 1553[51] and died in 1558. His grandson and heir, Robert Parys,[52] died under age in 1572, when Linton passed to Sir Philip's younger son Ferdinand[53] (d. 1601). Ferdinand's son and heir Philip Parys[54] (d. 1617) was succeeded by his eldest son Charles, a minor,[55] who died without issue in 1658. His brother and heir John,[56] like Charles heavily fined as a papist and royalist, had mortgaged Linton by 1659 to two Londoners, Robert Tempest and John Carter, who were named as lords.[57] John Parys died in 1667. His son and heir Philip,[58] the last male of the family, died without issue in 1672, leaving his lands to be sold to pay the accumulated debts.[59] In 1674 they were bought by Sir Thomas Sclater, a wealthy royalist physician.[60] John Parys's widow Anne and her second husband Sir Joseph Colston (d. 1674) retained Michaelotts manor, which was not sold to Sclater until 1677.[61]

Sir Thomas Sclater died without surviving issue in 1684, having settled his lands, called the Catley Park estate, on his nephew Edward Sclater's son Thomas.[62] Thomas assumed *c.* 1715 the surname Bacon, that of his rich wife Elizabeth (d. 1726).[63] When he died in 1736 he left his estates for life to Sarah, wife of his coachman Edward King, with remainder to her sons.[64] Sarah died *c.* 1738. Of her sons Robert King[65] died without issue in 1749 and Thomas Sclater King, having run through his fortune, in 1777, both disreputably.[66] The Catley Park estate had been sold in 1764 to pay Thomas's debts. Thomas Bromley, Lord Montfort, the purchaser,[67] resold it in 1772 to Edmund Keene, bishop of Ely.[68] By 1779 the bishop had transferred it to his son Benjamin, who was succeeded in 1837[69] by his son, the Revd. Charles Edmund Ruck-Keene (d. 1880), whose son Edmund died in 1888. The latter's son, Capt. Charles Edmund Ruck-Keene,[70] sold the Catley Park estate in 1904 to Sir Walter Henry Wilkin,[71] retaining the lordship of the manor, which passed on his death in 1919 to his daughter Olive, who married in 1936 Lt. N. Nightingale.[72] Wilkin was succeeded in 1922 by his son E. V. Wilkin,[73] whose executors sold the estate in 1950.[74]

Great Linton's manor-close of 2 a. was recorded in 1272.[75] In 1558 Sir Philip Parys had a house near Linton market, on what was marked in 1600 as the site of the manor.[76] In the 18th century courts were still held in a gabled house near the market-place, called the manor-house. It was pulled down *c.* 1880.[77] From the 1560s the Paryses had usually lived at Pudding Norton (Norf.), and when in Linton at Little Linton manor-house or at Catley Park, which later became the lord's usual seat. That house, recorded by 1622 if not earlier,[78] was probably built *c.* 1600. It stood on the brow of the hill at the south-west corner of the parish, and had a lower storey of brick possibly surmounted by timber-framing, with a two-storey porch and brick turrets at each corner. Inside were a panelled hall and great parlour, and over them several chambers and a gallery.[79] Thomas Bacon decorated the interior handsomely, installing there a 'most voluminous' library, and rebuilt or enlarged the brick turrets. In 1732 he laid out a park of 100 a. round the house.[80] After 1772 Bishop Keene removed marble fireplaces and sumptuous panelling to refit the bishop's palace at Ely, and demolished the house, leaving only a brick-built fragment for use as a farm-house.[81]

39 Ibid. pp. 7–9; *Collect. Topog. & Gen.* i. 262; cf. *Cal. Close*, 1396–9, 183; *Feud. Aids*, i. 181.
40 *Cal. Close*, 1377–81, 476.
41 *Rot. Parl.* iii. 175; *East Anglian*, N.S. vi. 245–6; *Cal. Pat.* 1381–5, 317.
42 See p. 207.
43 Cf. *Cal. Close*, 1377–81, 93.
44 *Feud. Aids*, vi. 407; *Cal. Close*, 1396–9, 183; *Cal. Pat.* 1429–36, 131; *Mon. Inscr. Cambs.* 231.
45 Prob. 11/3 (P.C.C. 2 Luffenam); C 139/29 no. 48.
46 Prob. 11/5 (P.C.C. 14 Godyn).
47 Prob. 11/14 (P.C.C. 24 Holgrave).
48 Prob. 11/18 (P.C.C. 27 Holder).
49 e.g. *L. & P. Hen. VIII*, vi, p. 415; xiii (1), p. 496.
50 Ibid. xv, p. 180; xix (1), p. 170.
51 *Cal. Pat.* 1553–4, 17.
52 C 142/116 no. 7.
53 C 142/60 no. 17.
54 C 142/265 no. 35; C.R.O., par. reg. TS.
55 Wards 7/53 no. 276.
56 C.R.O., par. reg. TS.; R 55/10/3D.
57 C.R.O., R 59/5/4/1; ibid. L 1/102, pp. 71 sqq.; cf. *Cal. Cttee. for Compounding*, i, p. 702; iv, p. 2744.
58 Prob. 11/325 (P.C.C. 119 Carr).
59 Prob. 11/342 (P.C.C. 53 Pye).
60 C.R.O., R 59/5/9/102; cf. *Proc. C.A.S.* xvii. 124–7.
61 C.R.O., R 59/5/9/105A–B; R 59/5/9/109–10.
62 Ibid. R 59/10/7A; Prob. 11/379 (P.C.C. 11 Cann).
63 Hist. MSS. Com. 29, *Portland VI*, p. 148; cf. *V.C.H. Hunts.* ii. 333, 349.
64 Prob. 11/679 (P.C.C. 194 Derby). Local legend *c.* 1800 alleged that Sarah had been Bacon's mistress: B.L. Add. MS. 9412, f. 146. His will, made in his wife's lifetime, calls her his kinswoman. Cole imputes no illicit connection: B.L. Add. MS. 5808, ff. 56v.–57.
65 C.R.O., L 1/103, ff. 52v.–57v.
66 B.L. Add. MS. 5808, f. 56v.; Prob. 11/769 (P.C.C. 112 Lisle); cf. C.R.O., R 59/5/9/157–64.
67 C.R.O., R 59/5/4/2–6.
68 C.R.O., R 59/5/9/166–8; *D.N.B.*
69 Cf. C.R.O., R 59/5/6/7; *Alum. Cantab. 1752–1900*, iv. 7.
70 Burke, *Land. Gent.* (1937), 1275; C.R.O., L 1/107–10, *passim.*
71 C.R.O., 296/SP 1009; SP 107/6.
72 Ibid. L 1/110–11, *passim*; Burke, *Land. Gent.* (1952), 1408–9.
73 *Who was Who, 1916–28*; *Kelly's Dir. Cambs.* (1908–37).
74 C.R.O., SP 107/7.
75 C 132/42 no. 6.
76 Prob. 11/42A (P.C.C. 26 Welles); Pemb. Coll. Mun., Barham, T.i.c.
77 Palmer, *Antiquities of Linton*, 4; cf. C.R.O., L 1/106, f. 216 (1791); *Proc. C.A.S.* xxx. 62.
78 C.R.O., R 55/10/3A; possibly by 1600: B.L. Add. MS. 5842, f. 190v.
79 C.R.O., R 59/5/3/1, pp. 57–8, 65.
80 Hist. MSS. Com. 29, *Portland VI*, pp. 148–9; B.L. Add. MS. 5808, f. 59; Pemb. Coll. Mun., Linton, D 4–5.
81 B.L. Add. MS. 5842, f. 190v.; Add. MS. 9412, f. 146.

LITTLE LINTON manor, held as 2½ hides by Count Alan in 1086,[82] had been subinfeudated from the honor of Richmond by the 1190s, when it was divided between Ralph Follifoot and Robert de Belhus.[83] Follifoot, a Yorkshireman, was killed *c.* 1198,[84] and succeeded by Alan Follifoot (fl. 1195–1242), who held two-thirds of Ralph's estate at Linton *c.* 1235.[85] Probably by 1236 he had settled the two-thirds on his daughter Alice and her husband Alexander de Scalers (d. by *c.* 1248).[86] In 1266 Alice and her second husband, John of Edgecliffe, sold that part of the manor with *c.* 150 a. to Roger of Leicester.[87] The other third of Ralph Follifoot's manor had passed to Alan's other daughter Joan, married before 1269 to Henry son of Richard.[88] Henry and Joan sold 120 a. at Linton *c.* 1272 to Alexander son of Thomas, who resold the land in 1275 to Roger of Leicester.[89] The ½ knight's fee held by Robert de Belhus (d. by 1204)[90] probably passed later to Richard de Belhus (d. after 1257), who had land in Cambridgeshire in 1253.[91] In 1265 Richard's son Alexander sold 120 a. at Little Linton to Roger of Leicester,[92] who thus held the whole reunited manor in 1279.[93]

Roger, a justice of the common pleas from 1276 to 1289 when he was imprisoned on charges of corruption,[94] had his lands seized for the Crown,[95] but may have recovered some by 1297 and probably still held Little Linton *c.* 1302.[96] Soon afterwards the manor was acquired by Sir Walter Huntingfield of Kent, who in 1316 entailed it upon his younger son John.[97] Sir Walter was granted free warren there in 1318,[98] and was dead by 1340.[99] Sir John Huntingfield held Little Linton in 1346 and died *c.* 1362.[1] His widow Beatrice was life tenant in 1369 when John's son Thomas sold the reversion to John Sleaford, rector of Balsham[2] (d. 1401).[3] Little Linton was later acquired by the Paryses, whose feoffees held it in 1428 with Great Linton manor,[4] with which it thereafter descended.[5]

The site of Little Linton manor-house, where Roger of Leicester had a chief messuage in 1279,[6] was probably then as later at a rectangular moated site close to the river, north-west of the village.[7] The Paryses frequently lived there from the late 15th to the early 17th century. In 1517 the hall, parlour, and chapel were mentioned.[8] The house was normally used as a farm-house from the mid 17th century,[9] the probable date of the oldest parts of the existing house south-west of the moat.[10] It was enlarged and partly rebuilt in the 19th century. The concentric rectangular moats north-west of the medieval one are probably 18th-century fishponds.[11]

In 1086 *BARHAM* manor was divided between Anketil de Furneaux who held 2⅞ hides and Morin who held 1½ hide, both of Count Alan.[12] Morin's portion was probably absorbed into the manor held by Anketil's descendants, whose Barham land was reckoned *c.* 1236 at 4 hides,[13] held of the honor of Richmond for 3 knights' fees *c.* 1300.[14] Anketil (fl. to *c.* 1100)[15] was succeeded by Robert de Furneaux (fl. 1130–5)[16] and Robert by Geoffrey de Furneaux (fl. 1140–92),[17] who held land in Cambridgeshire in 1185.[18] By 1196 his lands had passed to Robert de Furneaux,[19] who had died by 1206 leaving as heir a son Michael under age.[20] Michael still held Barham in 1251.[21] By 1268 the manor had passed to Simon de Furneaux,[22] probably his son, who held it in 1279, and may have died in 1288.[23] Simon's son and heir Robert held Barham *c.* 1302[24] and died in 1313. His son and heir John,[25] a knight by 1320, entailed the manor successively on his sons Robert and John,[26] and died after 1341. It was probably his son John who, having succeeded him, died in 1361,[27] leaving as heir a minor son, John. In 1379 Barham was settled upon that John and his wife Amy in tail, with remainder to his sister Elizabeth. John was dead by 1384, when Amy and her second husband Sir Robert Denny held his lands.[28] Denny became involved *c.* 1397 in a feud with William Clipston, lord of Bartlow, then lessee of Michaelotts, and each despoiled the other's manor-house.[29] In 1396 and 1399 Denny and Amy granted their life-interest to John Fordham, bishop of Ely,[30]

82 *V.C.H. Cambs.* i. 341.
83 *Red Bk. Exch.* (Rolls Ser.), ii. 531; cf. ibid. 528.
84 *Cur. Reg. R.* vii. 340.
85 *Pipe R.* 1195 (P.R.S. N.S. vi), 94; 1242 (ed. H. L. Cannon), 42; cf. C.P. 25(1)/24/17 nos. 2, 4. Another third was probably held then and *c.* 1236 by Alan de Mounay (fl. 1225–53: *Cur. Reg. R.* xii, p. 207; *Cal. Pat.* 1247–58, 176), perhaps in right of his wife Mary as her dower: *Liber de Bernewelle*, 254.
86 *Liber de Bernewelle*, 254; *Yorks. Fines, 1246–72* (Y.A.S. rec. ser. lxxxii), 3; *Proc. C.A.S.* lix. 120.
87 *Yorks. Fines, 1246–72*, 167; C.P. 25(1)/25/31 no. 28; cf. *Close R.* 1264–8, 226.
88 *Yorks. Fines, 1246–72*, 173.
89 C.P. 25(1)/25/36 nos. 8, 19.
90 *Cur. Reg. R.* iii. 241.
91 Cf. *Close R.* 1251–4, 405; *Cal. Pat.* 1247–58, 578.
92 C.P. 25(1)/25/31 no. 24.
93 *Rot. Hund.* (Rec. Com.), ii. 418.
94 Foss, *Judges of Eng.* iii. 116–17.
95 *Cal. Fine R.* 1272–1307, 268–9.
96 *Cal. Chanc. R. Var.* 18; *Feud. Aids*, i. 145.
97 *Feud. Aids*, i. 162; C.P. 25(1)/27/58 no. 2; cf. *Complete Peerage*, vii. 672–3.
98 *Cal. Chart. R.* 1300–26, 376.
99 *Cal. Close*, 1341–3, 103.
1 *Feud. Aids*, i. 163; *Cal. Pat.* 1361–4, 187.
2 *Cal. Inq. p.m.* xiii, p. 86.
3 *Mon. Inscr. Cambs.* 6.
4 *Feud. Aids*, i. 181; cf. C 137/72 no. 32.
5 e.g. Prob. 11/18 (P.C.C. 21 Holder); C 142/265 no. 35; Wards 7/53 no. 276.
6 *Rot. Hund.* (Rec. Com.), ii. 415.
7 *V.C.H. Cambs.* ii. 35.
8 Prob. 11/18 (P.C.C. 21 Holder).
9 e.g. C.R.O., R 59/5/3/1, pp. 33, 412.
10 Palmer, *Neighbourhood of Hildersham*, 7.
11 *V.C.H. Cambs.* ii. 35; cf. C.R.O., R 59/5/9/166–8.
12 *V.C.H. Cambs.* i. 341.
13 *Liber de Bernewelle*, 254.
14 *Feud. Aids*, i. 140; cf. Blomefield, *Norf.* i. 313–15.
15 *Early Yorks. Chart.* iv (Y.A.S. extra ser. i), 2, 5.
16 Ibid. 12–14; *Pipe R.* 1130 (H.M.S.O. facsimile), 27.
17 *Early Yorks. Chart.* iv. 28; *Pipe R.* 1191 & 92 (P.R.S. N.S. ii) 72, 217.
18 *Pipe R.* 1185 (P.R.S. xxxiv), 60.
19 *Chanc. R.* 1196 (P.R.S. N.S. vii), 177.
20 *Rot. Chart.* (Rec. Com.), i. 165; *Cur. Reg. R.* xiii, pp. 49–50.
21 *Yorks. Fines, 1246–72* (Y.A.S. rec. ser. lxxxii), 33–4. In *Liber de Bernewelle*, 254, his name is misread as Nicholas.
22 *Yorks. Fines, 1246–72*, 155, 180.
23 *Rot. Hund.* (Rec. Com.), ii. 418; T. Martin, *Hist. Thetford* (1779), 177.
24 *Feud. Aids*, i. 145.
25 *Cal. Inq. p.m.* v, p. 247; *Feud. Aids*, i. 155.
26 *Cal. Close*, 1318–23, 230; C.P. 25(1)/27/59 no. 17.
27 Cf. *Cal. Close*, 1341–3, 129, 370; *Cal. Pat.* 1354–8, 390; *Cal. Fine R.* 1356–68, 122, 134.
28 Blomefield, *Norf.* i. 314–15; Pemb. Coll. Mun., Barham, S 1, f. 11; cf. *Genealogist*, N.S. xxxviii. 17.
29 *Cal. Inq. Misc.* vi, pp. 103–4; C 258/33/27; S.C. 8/263/13011; S.C. 8/264/13170; S.C. 8/266/13255, 13281.
30 C.P. 25(1)/30/92 no. 3; the bishop was taking homage from the tenants in 1397: Pemb. Coll. Mun., Barham, S 1, f. 15v.

to whom Elizabeth and her husband Thomas Crabb released their remainder in 1400.[31]

The bishop held Barham[32] until in 1424 it was transferred to William Alington and others, possibly as feoffees for Nicholas Parys.[33] Alington was in possession in 1428[34] in his own right, and released Barham in 1440 to his second son Robert, on whose wife Margaret it had been settled in reversion.[35] Robert remained in possession until he died after 1475,[36] and Margaret died in 1480.[37] Thereupon Barham descended to Robert's two daughters or their representatives, as co-parceners.[38] Joan, the elder daughter, had married John Barney (d. 1471) of Witchingham (Norf.),[39] whose elder son Robert died without issue in 1487 and was succeeded by his brother Ralph, then a minor.[40] On Ralph's death in 1544 his son Sir Robert Barney sold his half-share to John Millicent, the lessee with his father Thomas since 1538.[41] The other half-share had passed in 1480 to Robert Alington's younger daughter Ellen, wife of Walter Lockton[42] (d. *c.* 1505).[43] Walter's son and heir Geoffrey died in 1512, leaving a son Robert, then aged 10,[44] who leased his half-share to John Millicent in 1542[45] and died in 1550. Robert's son and heir John Lockton[46] sold his half to Millicent in 1565.[47]

John Millicent, whose ancestors had been prosperous yeomen at Linton since the early 15th century,[48] was a vehement protestant and served Thomas Cromwell,[49] narrowly escaping lynching during the Lincolnshire revolt of 1536.[50] He was succeeded in 1577 by his son Robert[51] (d. 1609). Robert's son and heir Roger was knighted in 1607[52] and died in 1621. His son and heir Robert[53] charged Barham manor in 1628 with a rent of £100, half the yearly value, to Sir Giles Alington.[54] The rent-charge descended[55] to the duke of Somerset, to whom it was due *c.* 1740,[56] and the earls of Aylesford, who were receiving it *c.* 1785–1800.[57] Robert Millicent died in 1631, leaving a son John aged 10,[58] who could not enter upon the estate until the 1650s because it was wholly absorbed by the jointures of Sir Roger's second wife Amphelise and Robert's widow Douglas (d. 1655).[59] John died in 1686 and his only son John,[60] a typical Tory squire,[61] in 1716, after which the heavily mortgaged Barham estate passed in turn to the latter's three sons,[62] each of whom died without issue, Charles in 1729,[63] John in 1734,[64] and Robert, at his death trading in London as an apothecary, in 1741. Barham was sold under Robert's will to pay accumulated debts,[65] and was bought in 1748–9 by Robert's widow Sarah,[66] who immediately married Christopher Lonsdale, vicar of Linton 1740–5.[67] Lonsdale died in 1783,[68] and following his wishes Sarah (d. 1807) devised the manor to Pembroke College, Cambridge,[69] which remained the owner in 1974.[70]

The estate included the former lands of the house of Crutched Friars established at Barham by Robert de Furneaux and endowed *c.* 1293 with the lands which his ancestors had given to St. Margaret's chapel, Barham, amounting in 1279 to 32 a.[71] In 1323 John de Furneaux was licensed to add another 52 a. with the right to fold 120 sheep on the friars' land.[72] The convent, later styled Barham priory, owned *c.* 1532 some 55 a.,[73] although its sheepfold had fallen into desuetude; the lords of Barham opposed its revival and claimed that the priory land was copyhold.[74] The house had been suppressed by 1539 and in 1540 its property was granted to Philip Parys,[75] who sold it in 1553 to John Millicent,[76] with whose estate it thereafter descended.[77]

The conventual buildings furnished a site and materials to build the Millicents' manor-house, hence often called Barham Priory.[78] The original chief messuage of Barham manor, recorded in 1279 and 1313,[79] near which the friary had been built, had probably become ruinous while owned by absentees. Some medieval walling with an arched doorway remains from the priory.[80] The priory house

[31] C.P. 25(1)/30/91 no. 10; *Cal. Close*, 1399–1402, 210.
[32] *Feud. Aids*, vi. 408; cf. Pemb. Coll. Mun., Barham, A 1–4.
[33] C 1/6 no. 176; Pemb. Coll. Mun., Barham, A 5–6; *Cal. Close*, 1422–9, 337.
[34] *Feud. Aids*, i. 181.
[35] Pemb. Coll. Mun., Barham, A 9–11; cf. *Cal. Close*, 1429–36, 139; *Proc. C.A.S.* xli. 2–3.
[36] Pemb. Coll. Mun., Barham, A 12; cf. ibid. BB 1, ct. roll 10 Hen. VII.
[37] *Cal. Fine R.* 1471–85, 177, 201.
[38] C.R.O., R 61/11/1, f. 12; Pemb. Coll. Mun., Barham, AA 2–3; BB 1–2, *passim*.
[39] *Paston Letters & Papers*, ed. Davis, i. 351; cf. Blomefield, *Norf.* vii. 306; xi. 126–7; Wedgwood, *Hist. Parl., Biog. 1439–1509*, 70–1.
[40] *Cal. Inq. p.m. Hen. VII*, iii, p. 504; *Cal. Pat.* 1485–94, 228.
[41] Pemb. Coll. Mun., Barham, BB 2, ct. roll 36 Hen. VIII; B 1, 3.
[42] *Cal. Inq. p.m. Hen. VII*, i, p. 60.
[43] *Cal. Fine R.* 1485–1509, p. 357.
[44] C 142/27 no. 36.
[45] Pemb. Coll. Mun., Barham, B 2.
[46] E 150/97 no. 1.
[47] Pemb. Coll. Mun., Barham B 8–10.
[48] Cf. ibid. L 4–20; M 1B–C; for their pedigree since 1400, C.R.O., R 61/11/1, ff. 22v.–23.
[49] e.g. *L. & P. Hen. VIII*, x, p. 164; xi, p. 56; xii (1), p. 325; xii (2), pp. 387, 418; xiii (1), p. 212; xiv (2), pp. 318, 337.
[50] Ibid. xi, pp. 225, 306–7, 343; xii (1), pp. 175, 177.
[51] Prob. 11/59 (P.C.C. 25 Daughtry).
[52] Wards 7/45 no. 85; Nicholls, *Progresses of Jas. I*, ii. 122.
[53] Wards 7/67 no. 86.
[54] Pemb. Coll. Mun., Barham, E 8–9, 11; cf. B.L. Add. MS. 5848, f. 220.
[55] *Complete Peerage*, i. 106–9, 365–6; xii (1), 77–82.
[56] e.g. Pemb. Coll. Mun., Barham, H 13.
[57] Ibid. R 3, pp. 125–30.
[58] Wards 7/82 no. 38.
[59] S.P. 23/G 198 pp. 729, 732, 737; cf. Pemb. Coll. Mun., Barham, D 4; E 3, 5; F 2, 3, 7; *Mon. Inscr. Cambs.* 108.
[60] Prob. 11/386 (P.C.C. 26 Foot).
[61] B.L. Eg. MSS. 2718–21, *passim*.
[62] Pemb. Coll. Mun., Barham, H 1; cf. ibid. G 7, 9.
[63] Prob. 11/629 (P.C.C. 110 Abbott).
[64] Pemb. Coll. Mun., Barham, H 10.
[65] Prob. 11/707 (P.C.C. 17 Spurway).
[66] Pemb. Coll. Mun., Barham, I 4, 10; cf. ibid. H 7, 8, 13.
[67] Ibid. I 14; *Alum. Cantab. to 1751*, iii. 104.
[68] Prob. 11/705 (P.C.C. 306 Cornwallis).
[69] Pemb. Coll. Mun., W 2, 6; Prob. 11/1457 (P.C.C. 209 Lushington); B.L. Add. MS. 15664, f. 20v.
[70] Ex inf. the Bursary.
[71] C 143/19 no. 14; *Rot. Hund.* (Rec. Com.), ii. 419.
[72] *Cal. Pat.* 1321–4, 262.
[73] Pemb. Coll. Mun., Barham, B 6A; S 15.
[74] C 1/744 nos. 7–9; C 1/1492 no. 37.
[75] S.C. 6/Hen. VIII/7286 rot. 17; *L. & P. Hen. VIII*, xv, p. 467.
[76] *Cal. Pat.* 1550–3, 434.
[77] e.g. Wards 7/45 no. 85; Wards 7/82 no. 38.
[78] Cf. Camden, *Britannia* (1806), ii. 227.
[79] *Rot. Hund.* (Rec. Com.), ii. 418; C 134/32 no. 11.
[80] M.H.L.G. List.

was largely rebuilt in two storeys in the mid 16th century, probably by John Millicent (d. 1577).[81] In 1600 it lay around two courts, called the cloister yard and kitchen yard.[82] In 1621 the house contained a hall, great and little parlours, and gallery, besides chambers, offices, a yeomen's hall, and a coach-house.[83] The house was partially remodelled in the late 17th century, the front receiving some mullion and transom windows and a central pediment, but the Tudor first-floor windows survived unaltered.[84] From *c.* 1717 the Millicents and their successors used only part of the house, the rest being occupied by the tenant of their principal farm.[85] Mrs. Lonsdale's will directed that the master of Pembroke might use the Hall as a country retreat, but must never sub-let it.[86] The then master already had two official residences, and the empty house gradually passed beyond repair. It was mostly demolished between 1832 and 1838.[87] One range of five bays, refronted in brick, with a short 16th-century back-wing, was preserved as a house for the college's tenant.[88]

MICHAELOTTS manor was created from Barham manor by Sir Simon de Furneaux, who granted 60 a. of his demesne and *c.* 50 a. previously held by tenants to his younger son Michael[89] (fl. *c.* 1267 to 1297),[90] who already held 80 a. in 1279.[91] It was to be held as 1 knight's fee, rendering a pair of gilt spurs yearly to the lords of Barham.[92] Michael later granted the land to his nephew Simon, son of Thomas de St. Omer. Simon conveyed it, probably in 1315, to his brother Ralph, who returned it to him the same year.[93] By 1397 Michaelotts belonged to Nicholas Parys,[94] and descended with the Linton manors.[95] The Paryses regularly rendered the spurs, or 12*d.* in lieu,[96] and still paid reliefs for Michaelotts in the early 16th century.[97] Michaelotts contained *c.* 1675 some 185 a., besides the 15-acre Michaelotts wood,[98] which in 1775 was bought by Christopher Lonsdale and reunited with Barham manor.[99]

By 1600 the Paryses' combined manors were formally styled the manors of Great and Little Linton with Chilford and Michaelotts.[1] Robert Parys (d. 1504) owned property called Chilfords,[2] and in 1547 land belonging to *CHILFORD* manor was mentioned,[3] but no evidence has been found of an independent manor of that name.

The church of Linton had been granted by the earls of Richmond before 1163, probably while they still held Linton in demesne, to the Breton abbey of St. Jacut-de-la-Mer (Cotes-du-Nord).[4] By 1279 the abbey had appropriated the church and, besides the great tithes, owned glebe of 20 a. in Great Linton, 23 a. in Little Linton, and 32 a. in Barham.[5] From before 1227 the abbey appointed a prior of Linton to manage the estate,[6] and the land remained almost continuously under the control of priors until after 1400,[7] although during periods of war with France they were required to pay the surplus revenues to the Crown.[8] The last prior, Nicholas Menfrey, held the land at farm of the Crown, singly or more often jointly with English farmers, from *c.* 1370 to *c.* 1410.[9] After the alien priories were suppressed in 1414 Linton priory was occupied under the Crown by farmers, including Nicholas Parys between 1413 and 1421.[10] In 1440 Henry VI granted the reversion to Pembroke College, Cambridge,[11] and in 1450 the bishop approved the appropriation of the rectory to the college.[12] The rectorial glebe was reckoned at *c.* 85 a. in 1523, *c.* 68 a. in 1652, and 60 a. in 1775, besides 5 a. in Hadstock.[13]

By 1466 the college was letting the rectory to Richard Millicent, and by 1523 to his kinsman Thomas Millicent (d. 1549), father of John Millicent, lord of Barham.[14] John Millicent's son-in-law William Bawtry held the lease in 1572 and was succeeded in 1599[15] by his son Thomas, who in 1611 resigned the lease, held on very advantageous terms, to Robert Millicent's second son, Sir John[16] (d. 1641).[17] By 1667 the lessee was Dr. Nathaniel Hardy, dean of Rochester (d. 1670), whose widow Elizabeth and her next husband Sir Francis Clark held it by 1675[18] and sold it in 1694 to John Lone, a Whig lawyer (d. 1700).[19] The lease was sold in 1706 to Thomas Sclater, later Bacon,[20] and remained with the Catley Park estate[21] until in 1761 Thomas Sclater King sold it to Richard Trott[22] (d. 1788). Trott left it to his son-in-law, Edmund Fisher (d. 1819), vicar of Linton 1789–1800,[23] whose son Edmund, already vicar there, retained the rectorial glebe until his death in

[81] Prob. 11/59 (P.C.C. 25 Daughtry).
[82] Pemb. Coll. Mun., Barham, T.i.c.
[83] Ibid. D 2; E 2.
[84] C.A.S. Coll., Relhan drawing no. 337; see also above, plate facing p. 81.
[85] Pemb. Coll. Mun., Barham, Y 13–14, 24–5, 29.
[86] Prob. 11/1457 (P.C.C. 209 Lushington).
[87] Pemb. Coll. Mun., Barham, W 7, 10, 14; house not shown on incl. map.
[88] Cf. Pemb. Coll. Mun., W 18; M.H.L.G. List.
[89] Pemb. Coll. Mun., Barham, S 1, insert, nos. 1, 3, 5.
[90] *Cal. Pat.* 1266–72, 76; 1292–1301, 69, 226.
[91] *Rot. Hund.* (Rec. Com.), ii. 418.
[92] e.g. Pemb. Coll. Mun., Barham, AA 1, rentals *c.* 1360, *c.* 1430.
[93] Ibid. S 1, insert, nos. 2, 4, 6.
[94] *Cal. Inq. Misc.* vi, p. 90.
[95] e.g. C 139/29 no. 48; Wards 7/53 no. 276.
[96] e.g. Pemb. Coll. Mun., AA 1, rental 7 Hen. VI; acct. 2 Edw. IV; S 7; cf. C.R.O., R 61/11/1, ff. 7, 8v.
[97] Pemb. Coll. Mun., Barham, BB 1, ct. roll 16 Hen. VII.
[98] C.R.O., R 59/5/3/1, pp. 114, 366–7.
[99] Pemb. Coll. Mun., Barham, K 19; Prob. 11/1105 (P.C.C. 306 Cornwallis).
[1] e.g. C.R.O., R 59/14/11/7D–S; L 1/103–111, *passim*.
[2] Prob. 11/14 (P.C.C. 24 Holgrave).
[3] C.R.O., R 59/14/11/7B, ct. roll 1 Edw. VI.
[4] *V.C.H. Cambs.* ii. 314; cf. *Rot. Hund.* (Rec. Com.), ii. 504.
[5] *Rot. Hund.* ii. 416, 418–19.
[6] *Rot. Litt. Claus.* (Rec. Com.), ii. 212; *Year Bk. 6 Edw. II* (Selden Soc. xxxiv), 68–70; *E.D.R.* (1894), 197.
[7] e.g. *E.D.R.* (1890), 416; (1894), 212.
[8] e.g. *Cal. Fine R.* 1337–47, 402; *Cal. Pat.* 1345–8, 274; *Cal. Close*, 1346–9, 484.
[9] *E.D.R.* (1893), 151; *Cal. Fine R.* 1369–77, 402; 1377–83, 24, 76, 285; 1399–1405, 191–2, 308; S.C. 6/1093/1 rot. 10.
[10] *Cal. Fine R.* 1413–22, 57, 373; *Cal. Close*, 1413–19, 378–9; S.C. 6/1125/3.
[11] *Cal. Pat.* 1436–41, 377; Pemb. Coll. Mun., Linton, B 1–4.
[12] Pemb. Coll. Mun., Linton, B 6–7.
[13] Ibid. E 4, 10; Barham, V 10.
[14] Ibid. Barham X 1–3; Linton, G 4, L 1.
[15] C.R.O., par. reg. TS.
[16] Prob. 11/94 (P.C.C. 63 Kidd); Pemb. Coll. Mun., Linton, L 2, 3A–B; cf. Barham, X 11, 14, 16.
[17] C.R.O., par. reg. TS.
[18] Pemb. Coll. Mun., Linton, L 6–7; *Alum. Cantab. to 1751*, ii. 304.
[19] Pemb. Coll. Mun., Linton, L 10–11; C 16; *Mon. Inscr. Cambs.* 105.
[20] C.R.O., R 55/10/6; Pemb. Coll. Mun., Barham, P 21.
[21] Pemb. Coll. Mun., Linton, L 13–20; C.R.O., R 59/5/3/2, ff. 30v., 45v., 57v., 102.
[22] Pemb. Coll. Mun., Linton, D 5.
[23] Ibid. L 21–6.

1851.[24] Thereafter it was let directly to working farmers.[25] The rectorial land, for which 78 a. were allotted at inclosure in 1838,[26] still belonged to Pembroke in 1974,[27] except for the closes around the site of Linton priory, which had been sold by 1956.[28] The rectorial tithes were commuted in 1839 for a tithe-rent-charge of £776.[29]

The priory buildings probably stood in the area, between the church and the river, later occupied by Linton House. The buildings had disappeared by 1600, but a large tithe barn, 68 by 27 ft., survived until *c.* 1912.[30] Linton House, called *c.* 1700 the Great House, was built of brick by John Lone in the 1690s, and was occupied by the two Fishers from *c.* 1772 to 1852. After standing empty for 30 years it was bought in 1882 and restored by Barney Ficklin.[31] It has a symmetrical main front to the garden with a recessed centre and short wings. The central doorway has a shell hood. Additions were made to the north in the 18th century.

Other religious houses with land in Linton included Warden abbey (Beds.) and the Austin canons of Thetford (Suff.). Before 1199 members of the Furneaux family granted land in Barham fee, amounting in 1279 to 32 a. held in demesne, to Warden, which acquired other land *c.* 1200. Geoffrey de Furneaux (d. *c.* 1197) granted to the canons of the Holy Sepulchre of Thetford land amounting in 1279 to 3 a. and the right to the ninth sheaf from 36 a. held by Warden. In 1199 the ninth sheaf was commuted for 12*d.* a year.[32] Thetford priory apparently had no land in Barham at its dissolution,[33] and Warden sold its Linton property *c.* 1390.[34] Walden abbey (Essex), to which William de Say granted a rent in 1265, and Westminster abbey were said to have had properties in Linton, parcel of estates elsewhere, which were granted in 1538 and 1541 to Thomas, Lord Audley.[35]

In the 17th and 18th centuries the largest non-manorial estate was that accumulated by the lawyer Robert Flack (1626–1705).[36] In 1663 he bought *c.* 90 a. from the coheirs of the Richardsons, a prosperous yeoman family,[37] in 1672 *c.* 22 a. of demesne from Philip Parys,[38] in 1674 *c.* 74 a. of Michaelotts from the Colstons,[39] and in 1683 over 40 a. from the daughters and coheirs of Adam Lawrence, another Linton yeoman.[40] He left his estate to his grandson Barrington Flack,[41] who died in 1749 having settled his lands for life upon his wife Susannah (d. by 1780) with remainder to his brother-in-law, FitzWilliams Barrington.[42] In 1783 Sir FitzWilliams sold the land, *c.* 265 a., to Benjamin Keene,[43] with whose manors it afterwards passed.

Of the Lawrence family's lands, amounting to 212 a. *c.* 1675, another 65 a. was bought in 1683 by Robert Moore, a Linton grocer.[44] By 1705 he owned *c.* 134 a., which by will of 1711 he left to his son Thomas, who in 1763 devised his lands to his brother Samuel's son Thomas.[45] The latter sold *c.* 122 a. to Benjamin Keene in 1778.[46]

In 1675 David Appleyard's charity for the poor of Balsham held 14 a. in Chilford and Linton fields under Linton manor.[47] At inclosure 21 a. near Borley wood were allotted to the churchwardens of Balsham.[48] Part of the land was sold in 1872.[49]

ECONOMIC HISTORY. AGRICULTURE. In 1086 2 hides out of 3¾ in Great Linton were held in demesne, employing 6 *servi* and 3 of the vill's 8 plough-teams, while 16 *villani* had 5 teams. In Little Linton the demesne included 1½ of the 2½ hides, and the lord had 4 *servi* and 2 plough-teams, while his 8 *villani* had 3 teams. On the two Barham manors there were 3 demesne teams, while the 12 *villani* possessed 3½ between them. There were 5 bordars in Great Linton, 2 in Little Linton, and 6 in Barham. Since Count Alan had obtained the manors the value of Great Linton had been raised from £7 to £12, that of Little Linton from £5 to £7, but at Barham the combined yield had remained stable at £17.[50]

In 1279,[51] besides *c.* 233 a. of demesne pasture and woodland and *c.* 123 a. of common land, the recorded arable in the parish amounted to *c.* 2,810 a., of which *c.* 1,075 a. belonged to Great Linton, *c.* 685 a. to Little Linton, and *c.* 1,050 a. to Barham. The three manors' demesnes came respectively to 360 a., 428 a., and 393 a., thus comprising as in 1086 almost half the village. The smaller lay fees, including Michaelotts, covered 120 a., and religious houses held *c.* 145 a., including the rectory. Of the remainder *c.* 733 a. was freehold, and *c.* 704 a. belonged to customary tenants. The freeholds varied greatly in size. Eleven prosperous freeholders, including Gilbert Kirkby, lord of Hildersham, with 60 a., Robert of Linton with 64 a., and four with full yardlands of 32 a., had 394 a. between them, but *c.* 70 lesser men had altogether only *c.* 107 a.

On Great Linton manor the villein tenants all occupied regular-sized holdings, one a full yardland, 5 three-quarter-yardlands, and 11 half-yardlands. A yardland owed 20 works between Midsummer and Lammas, and 64 from Lammas to Michaelmas, and the ploughing of 22 a. a year. Two cottagers had to do 32 works between Michaelmas and

[24] Ibid. L 27–30.
[25] Ibid. L 31–2.
[26] C.R.O., Q/RDc 53, pp. 37–9.
[27] Ex inf. the Bursary.
[28] *V.C.H. Cambs.* iii. 347.
[29] C.U.L., Doc. 643 nos. 227–8.
[30] Palmer, *Antiquities of Linton*, 14.
[31] Ibid. 14–15; cf. C.U.L., Palmer MS. A 58.
[32] *Cart. Old Wardon* (Beds. Hist. Rec. Soc. xiii), pp. 173–5; *Rot. Hund.* (Rec. Com.), ii. 419.
[33] S.C. 6/Hen. VIII/2621 rot. 26.
[34] *Cal. Close*, 1389–92, 157.
[35] B.L., Harl. MS. 3697, f. 228; *L. & P. Hen. VIII*, xiii (2), p. 192; xvi, p. 378.
[36] *Genealogist*, iii. 296–7; C.R.O., par. reg. TS.; cf. B.L. Add. MS. 2719, ff. 371, 380.
[37] C.R.O., R 59/5/9/47.
[38] Ibid. R 59/5/9/52–3.
[39] Ibid. R 59/5/3/1, pp. 373–4; R 59/5/9/102.
[40] Ibid. R 59/5/9/69–70.
[41] *Mon. Inscr. Cambs.* 103–4; C.R.O., R 59/24/14A no. 2.
[42] C.R.O., R 59/24/14A no. 3; C.U.L., Palmer MS. C 9.
[43] C.R.O., R 59/5/9/94–5, 233, 235, 237.
[44] Ibid. R 59/5/3/1, p. 384; R 59/5/9/118–21.
[45] Pemb. Coll. Mun., Linton, C 15, m. 4; C.R.O., R 59/5/9/135, 156.
[46] C.R.O., R 59/5/9/172–4, 178–9.
[47] C.R.O., R 59/14/11/3 no. 2, rental 1675; cf. R 59/14/11/10C, 10F; Pemb. Coll. Mun., Barham, BB 4, ct. roll 23 Eliz. I.
[48] C.R.O., Q/RDc 53; C.U.L., Add. MS. 6052, f. 6v.; ibid. Doc. 643 no. 81.
[49] C.U.L., Maps 53(1)/88/15.
[50] *V.C.H. Cambs.* i. 341.
[51] The next two paragraphs are based on *Rot. Hund.* (Rec. Com.), ii. 416–20; C 132/42 no. 6; C 134/32 no. 11.

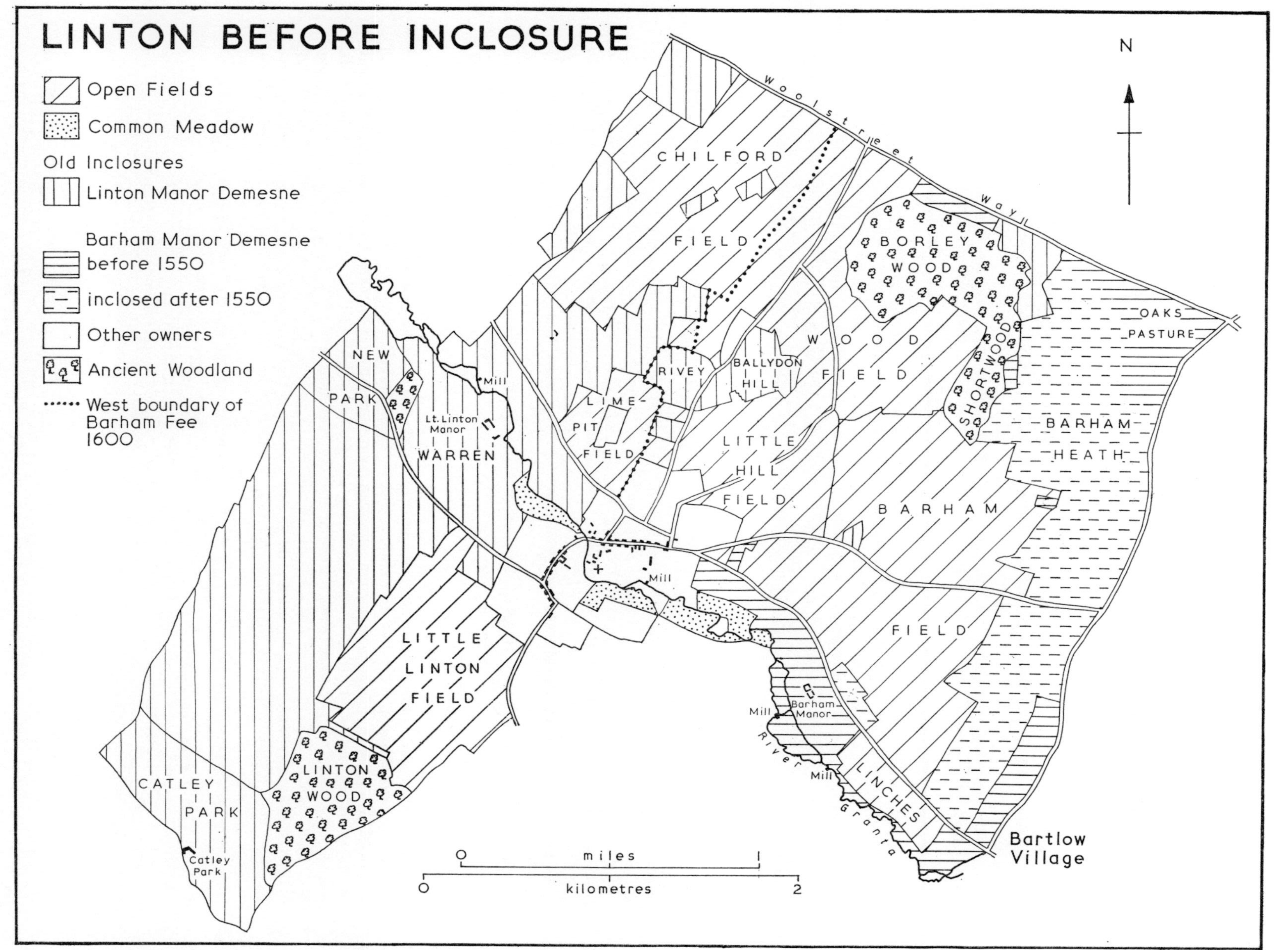
LINTON BEFORE INCLOSURE
Open Fields
Common Meadow
Old Inclosures
Linton Manor Demesne
Barham Manor Demesne
before 1550
inclosed after 1550
Other owners
Ancient Woodland
West boundary of
Barham Fee
1600
N
Woolstreet Way
CHILFORD FIELD
BORLEY WOOD
SHORTWOOD
OAKS PASTURE
WOOD FIELD
BALLYDON HILL
RIVEY
LIME-PIT FIELD
LITTLE HILL FIELD
BARHAM HEATH
BARHAM FIELD
NEW PARK
Mill
Lt. Linton Manor
WARREN
Mill
LITTLE LINTON FIELD
Barham Manor
Mill
River Granta
Mill
LINCHES
Bartlow Village
CATLEY PARK
LINTON WOOD
Catley Park
0
miles
1
0
kilometres
2

Lammas and each reap 7½ a. Little Linton's 4 half-yardlanders and 1 quarter-yardlander were more heavily burdened. Each half-yardlander owed 69 works between Michaelmas and Lammas, and 34 more in harvest, besides mowing for 3 days and sending two beasts every Monday to plough the demesne. On Barham manor there were 5 yardlanders, 2 half-yardlanders, and 5 quarter-yardlanders. Each yardland provided 154 works between Michaelmas and Lammas for ploughing and so on, and 36 more in harvest to reap, thresh, and carry the corn. Eleven men held 1 a. each by doing 50 works between Michaelmas and Lammas, each reaping 4 a., and performing 4 harvest-boons, which 3 cottagers also owed.

The area held of the Linton manors steadily diminished from the 16th century, when the copyholds were all held by rent. In 1575 it comprised approximately 145 a. of freehold arable and 285 a. of copyhold,[52] by 1675 122 a. and 227 a. respectively,[53] and by 1793, after the lord had purchased the Flack and Moore estates, 246 a. altogether.[54] At inclosure *c.* 185 a. were allotted for copyhold of those manors,[55] and were mostly enfranchised between 1860 and 1900.[56] On Barham manor, however, the successors of 11 free tenants, who paid rents *c.* 1350,[57] were later, perhaps because they owed scutage, reckoned to hold by knight-service. In 1397 they did homage and paid reliefs to Bishop Fordham for fractions of a knight's fee.[58] The lords of Barham carefully listed the land so held in the late 15th and early 16th centuries,[59] for most of their tenants, through possessing fragments of that land, became liable to the consequent exactions. The tenants were sometimes recalcitrant.[60] When Robert Millicent (d. 1609), who was especially diligent in asserting his feudal rights,[61] tried to procure the wardship of the minor heir of Thomas Fulwell (d. 1584), a prosperous freeholder, the majority of the homage refused to present that any of Fulwell's land was held by knight-service.[62]

As for copyhold, only two customary tenants remained on Barham manor by *c.* 1380, when tenure in villeinage had apparently been replaced by tenure at farm of supposedly demesne land.[63] About 1430 23 men, including 2 with 30 a. each, occupied *c.* 150 a. on such terms.[64] In 1465 Robert Alington converted those tenures into rent-paying copyholds. A new book of customs which he compiled forbade them to sub-let for more than one year or cut timber without licence. Fines on alienation or death were to be arbitrary.[65] Robert Millicent proved as vexatious to his copyholders as to his freeholders, exacting fines for the redemption not only of land actually sub-let, according to previous practice,[66] but of a copyholder's whole tenement, claiming the whole to be forfeit through the unlicensed sub-letting of part.[67] In 1575 there were *c.* 17 copyholders,[68] whose lands in 1598 covered *c.* 206 a.[69] At inclosure in 1838 202 a. copyhold of Barham manor remained, of which 60 a. were enfranchised to the lord of Linton.[70]

Although the parish was from the Middle Ages largely devoted to arable farming, the common fields covered barely half of it, because much that was not pasture or woodland lay in severalty.[71] In Little Linton the land between the river and the Hildersham road, *c.* 160 a. in 1672, belonged mostly to that manor's warren and new park. South of the road lay an open field called Little Linton, Linton,[72] or Little, field. At inclosure it contained *c.* 200 a. In 1279 Little Linton had 13 a. of common pasture called Museholt,[73] probably near the river. When in 1328 the lord planted willows there, the tenants cut them down to vindicate their right to common.[74] West of that open field the remainder of Little Linton was by 1672, and probably long before, held in severalty as demesne land of that manor. Of the 475 a. it covered in 1672 up to 180 a. was ley ground.[75] North of the river and beyond the road lay the common fields of Great Linton. Of Limekiln field, nearest the village and so named by 1580,[76] only 56 a. remained at inclosure. It was divided from the larger Chilford field to the north, which in 1838 covered *c.* 360 a.,[77] by a belt of closes then amounting to *c.* 100 a. The arable area had been further reduced by piecemeal inclosure. The lord had *c.* 70 a. inclosed as sheep-pens by 1838. In 1551 the Linton court had ordered those with crofts near the highway to leave them open from 1 December to Candlemas.[78]

The fields and pastures of Barham to the east were reckoned to cover *c.* 1,600 a. in 1580, excluding heath and woodland, and *c.* 1,700 a. in 1786, including 410 a. of ancient closes and 975 a. of open fields.[79] In the 13th century the area was divided among many fields, some of which bore the names of later furlongs. About 1275 Michaelotts had land in 7 fields.[80] The area west and south of Borley wood, probably called in the 16th century West and

52 C.R.O., R 59/14/11/3 no. 1, rental 1575.
53 Ibid. no. 2, rental *c.* 1675.
54 Ibid. R 59/14/11/10C, 10F.
55 Ibid. Q/RDc 53.
56 Ibid. L 1/109–11, *passim.*
57 Pemb. Coll. Mun., Barham, AA 1, rental *temp.* John de Furneaux.
58 Ibid. S 1, ff. 15v., 16v.
59 e.g. ibid. BB 1, ct. rolls 12, 20 Hen. VII; BB 2, ct. rolls 9, 16, 26 Hen. VIII.
60 Ibid. BB 2, ct. roll 27 Hen. VIII.
61 Cf. ibid. BB 5, ct. rolls 20, 23 Eliz. I.
62 Ibid. 26, 31 Eliz. I.
63 Ibid. AA 1, rental *temp.* John de Furneaux.
64 Ibid. rental 7 Hen. VI; cf. accts. 36–8 Hen. VI, 2 Edw. IV.
65 Ibid. BB 1, ct. rolls 14, 22 Hen. VII; cf. AA 1, rentals 5–21 Hen. VII; C.U.L., Palmer MS. C 7, ff. 3–18, *passim.*
66 e.g. Pemb. Coll. Mun., Barham, BB 2, ct. roll 8 Hen. VIII.
67 Ibid. BB 2, ct. rolls 26–7 Eliz. I; C 2/Eliz. I/F 6/41.
68 Pemb. Coll. Mun., Barham, S 7.
69 Ibid. AA 4, rental 1598–9.
70 C.R.O., Q/RDc 53.
71 For the layout of the fields see Pemb. Coll. Mun., Barham, T.i.c. (map of Barham fee, 1600); C.R.O., 124/P 64 (Catley Pk. estate map, 1779); 152/P 13 (draft incl. map, *c.* 1837); and for their names and acreages Pemb. Coll. Mun., Barham S 6, 9, 16 (Barham field bks., 1580, 1589, 1786); C.R.O., R 59/5/3/1, pp. 99–131, 412–18 (Linton estate surveys, *c.* 1672–5); Q/RDc 53 (incl. award and map, 1838).
72 C.R.O., R 59/5/6/2 (1573); C.U.L., Palmer MS. C 9 (survey 1731–2).
73 *Rot. Hund.* (Rec. Com.), ii. 418.
74 *East Anglian*, N.S. xiii. 347–8.
75 C.R.O., R 59/5/6/9.
76 e.g. ibid. R 59/14/11/7C, ct. roll 22 Eliz. I.
77 Including up to 100 a. claimed in 1580 as part of Barham fields: Pemb. Coll. Mun., Barham, S 9, pp. 3–9.
78 C.R.O., R 59/14/11/7B, ct. roll 5 Edw. VI.
79 Excluding the land west of the Balsham road.
80 Pemb. Coll. Mun., Barham, S 1, insert, no. 5.

Wood fields,[81] was a single field called Wood field in 1779,[82] but in 1838 it was divided from north to south into Brick-kiln, White Eye, and Little Hill fields, covering together *c.* 270 a. Ballydon hill-top to the south-west was left as pasture or heath. In 1582 Robert Millicent ceded the 40 a. there to Linton manor in exchange for land further east.[83] To the south-east lay Barham field, in 1838 covering *c.* 450 a. The land south of the Bartlow road was mostly ancient closes of Barham manor demesne, *c.* 125 a. by local measure in 1580.

In Barham, as in Linton, the open fields were reduced by the inclosure of single strips, even in the 13th century.[84] After 1465 copyholders were permitted to inclose land accessible from the highway until 1 November, but had to leave it open every third year for the lord's flock to common there.[85] Many such closes had become permanent by 1600, and survived until the general inclosure.[86] Moreover, the lords of Barham gradually enlarged their several holdings adjoining the east part of Barham field. There the land had probably never been under the plough. The north end had been inclosed as demesne pasture well before 1500, and probably belonged to the grange recorded in 1327 and to Bellasyes grange which in 1412 included a sheepfold. By 1500 it was styled the lord's grange called the Oaks, and in 1564, after recent hedging by John Millicent, covered *c.* 87 a.[87] Further south lay Barham heath, presumably derived from 80 a. of heath recorded in 1279, of which the Frith heath lay common from Lammas to Candlemas.[88] By 1550 it was called the lords' heath ground,[89] and was apparently in their sole ownership, for in 1564 they planned to break up parts of it for conversion to arable.[90] By the 1590s Robert Millicent was leasing *c.* 128 a. of arable, lately heath,[91] and by 1600 *c.* 366 a. of the area east of Barham field was divided into blocks called the lord's land, late heath.[92] Cultivation later receded, and *c.* 1735 the Barham estate included 300 a. of ley or barren heath, of which small plots were occasionally ploughed and sown for a year or two.[93] On the eve of inclosure, out of the 2,960 a. of arable in Linton, ancient closes accounted for 1,523 a. and the common fields for 1,436 a.; there were also 265 a. of wood and 420 a. of permanent pasture.[94]

The open fields of Great Linton were under a triennial rotation in 1272,[95] as probably were those of Barham in 1286.[96] In 1581 the latter were divided between the fallow field, the 'tilland' field, and the bullymong field.[97] The early 14th century saw some recession of cultivation, for in 1340 300 a. once yielding corn was lying waste through the tenants' insufficiency.[98] The principal crop was barley. In 1420 the great tithes yielded 60 qr. of barley, 20 of wheat, 4 of pease, and 3 of oats.[99] Even on Barham demesne only 32½ a. of wheat were sown in 1439 compared with 103 a. of barley.[1] By the 16th century rye was also grown.[2] By the 1470s saffron was being cultivated,[3] eventually even in the open fields,[4] and in 1592 24 a. of the fallow field were kept inclosed mainly for saffron.[5]

In 1086 11 cattle and 135 sheep were recorded at the Lintons, and 8 cattle and 137 sheep at Barham.[6] All inhabitants had *c.* 1515 to keep their cattle in the common herd from Midsummer at latest until Christmas,[7] and from 1536 butchers were forbidden to put their fattening calves in the Linton herd.[8] On the fallow fields in the 16th century horses were allowed in first, then cows 6 days later, and sheep after 4 more days.[9] By the 18th century rights of common after harvest were combined for both fees. The joint herd of cows and horses moved a week ahead of the sheep from the fallow field across the stubble of successive fields, spending a week on each.[10]

On Barham manor two men were fined in 1408 for keeping 10 sheep more than their stint.[11] In 1556 the tenants there were stinted to 2 or 3 cows each and forbidden to take in outsiders' cattle.[12] No fresh reductions of stints were recorded in the 16th century or later. Some villagers had flocks of their own, one man leaving 44 sheep in 1517,[13] but the main flocks belonged to the demesnes. In 1613 and 1650 the lords of Linton reserved in leases the right to fold up to 300 sheep, including 30 belonging to their shepherd, his traditional perquisite.[14] In the 18th century Little Linton and Michaelotts farms each enjoyed sheep-walk for 280 sheep.[15] Barham manor had in 1547 included folds for 200 sheep, besides the suppressed priory's lately revived fold for 120.[16] In 1567 John Millicent leased out, with a large farm, the right to fold 220 sheep over Barham's open fields.[17] His son Robert had set up his own flock by 1578,[18] and later charged his tenants rent for putting their own sheep with it. About 1600 it included *c.* 230 sheep belonging to 12 tenants.[19] In 1595 he

[81] Ibid. BB 1, ct. roll 21 Hen. VII.
[82] C.R.O., R 59/5/6/7.
[83] Pemb. Coll. Mun., Barham, P 8.
[84] e.g. C.U.L., Palmer MS. A 56 (from J.I. 1/86).
[85] Pemb. Coll. Mun., Barham, BB 1, ct. roll 14 Hen. VII; cf. BB 2, ct. rolls 14–15 Hen. VIII.
[86] Ibid. T.i.c.; C.R.O., 152/P 13.
[87] *Cambs. Lay Subsidy, 1327*, 24; Pemb. Coll. Mun., Barham, A 2; BB 1, ct. rolls 15, 20 Hen. VII; BB 3, ct. roll 1 Edw. VI; B 7.
[88] *Rot. Hund.* (Rec. Com.), ii. 420.
[89] Pemb. Coll. Mun., Barham, BB 4, ct. roll 1 & 2 Phil. & Mary.
[90] Ibid. B 6; cf. ibid. P 6.
[91] Ibid. AA 4, rental 1593–4.
[92] Ibid. T.i.c.; D 4.
[93] E 112/1084/36 2nd answer.
[94] C.U.L., Doc. 643 nos. 21, 360.
[95] C 132/42 no. 6.
[96] Cf. C.U.L., Palmer MS. A 56 (from J.I. 1/86).
[97] C.R.O., L 95/21A; cf. Pemb. Coll. Mun., Barham, S 9.
[98] *Inq. Non.* (Rec. Com.), 213.
[99] S.C. 6/1125/3.

[1] Pemb. Coll. Mun., Barham, AA 1, acct. 16–17 Hen. VI.
[2] e.g. Prob. 11/69 (P.C.C. 5 Windsor, will of John Cole).
[3] Pemb. Coll. Mun., Linton, C 3; cf. B.L. Add. MS. 5861, ff. 21v.–22, 95v., 116v.
[4] e.g. Pemb. Coll. Mun., Barham, BB 2, ct. rolls 5, 8, 21 Hen. VIII.
[5] Ibid. BB 5, ct. roll 34 Eliz. I.
[6] *V.C.H. Cambs.* i. 341.
[7] C.R.O., R 59/14/11/7A, ct. roll 6 Hen. VIII.
[8] Ibid. 27 Hen. VIII.
[9] Pemb. Coll. Mun., Barham, BB 1, ct. roll 19 Hen. VII; BB 3, 3 Edw. VI.
[10] Ibid. S 17, at end.
[11] Ibid. AA 1, ct. roll 9 Hen. IV.
[12] Ibid. BB 4, ct. roll 3 & 4 Phil. & Mary.
[13] B.L., Add. MS. 5861, f. 65.
[14] C.R.O., R 59/5/3/1, pp. 35, 43.
[15] Ibid. R 59/5/4/3.
[16] C 1/1143 no. 46; cf. C 1/744 nos. 7–9.
[17] Pemb. Coll. Mun., Barham, Y 2.
[18] Ibid. V 4.
[19] Ibid. AA 4, rental 1602–3.

again leased out his sheep-walk, including the right to pasture in the Oaks and the closes round Barham Hall. The lessee was to keep 60 of Robert's sheep with his own, and to manure Robert's land from 1 April to 16 November.[20]

The lords of Linton claimed, as tenants of Michaelotts manor, to feed their flock over Barham fee also, and in 1553 John Millicent recognized their right to sheep-walk there for 300 sheep.[21] In 1581, however, Robert Millicent and Ferdinand Parys agreed to distinguish their rights of sheep-walk territorially. Parys was to have sheep-walk over the western third of Barham as far as Shortwood and along the north side of Borley wood, Millicent retaining the rest.[22] Three separate folds were established, two for Linton manor and one for Barham, which at inclosure had rights respectively over 720 a., 416 a., and 500 a. of the parish.[23]

The Linton demesne consisted by the 17th century of two portions, an inclosed farm, mainly cultivated from Little Linton farm-house and covering in the 1670s *c.* 660 a., and open-field land probably derived from the Great Linton and Michaelotts demesnes, then amounting to *c.* 260 a., besides 63 a. of meadow and pasture.[24] The Paryses probably kept part of Little Linton in hand. Robert Parys (d. 1504) left money to his ploughmen, and his grandson Sir Philip had corn and cattle to be sold at his death.[25] Their open-field land was probably let. Michaelotts, *c.* 117 a. in 1577, was yielding £4 6*s.* 8*d.* rent in 1575, when 17 men held another 117 a. by indenture, much probably on 89- to 98-year leases made *c.* 1553.[26]

Although Barham demesne was still in hand in 1438,[27] it had been transferred to a farmer by 1460.[28] After 1480 the demesne was apparently divided among four men, each paying 33*s.* 4*d.* as farm and as much again in lieu of renders of beer.[29] In 1564 it comprised, besides 31 a. of ancient closes and 87 a. of the Oaks, *c.* 305 a. of arable.[30] In the 1560s John Millicent leased 162 a. to his son-in-law William Bawtry for 40 years, and by 1577 had let out over 120 a.[31] John's son Robert let out even more land, raising his receipts from that source from £80 a year for 330 a. in 1578 to £142 by 1599.[32] In 1593–4, besides the 136 a. of Bawtry's farm, *c.* 360 a. of arable were on lease.[33] In 1603–4 of 55 lessees 15 occupying over 10 a. accounted for 346 a. of the 417 a. then leased. One had 76 a., two others 39 a. and 33 a.[34]

Sometimes the Barham demesne was 'let to halves', a practice already in use among the tenants there *c.* 1500. In 1501 they were forbidden to let copyholds to halves to evade the need for a licence to underlet,[35] and in 1591 a tenant agreed with another to have his land manured, ploughed, and sown in return for half the crop.[36] In 1598–9 Robert Millicent let 257 a. to three men to halves,[37] and in 1611 Sir Roger Millicent let most of the demesne to four men on like terms. Each party found half the seed, the lessee undertook the cultivation, the lessor provided manure from his sheepfold and stables, and had first choice of half the area of corn grown.[38] Philip Parys let Little Linton on similar terms in 1613. The farmer was to be allowed half the seed, and to divide the crop equally before harvest.[39] The farm was still being let in that way in the 1640s.[40]

Most of the land outside the demesnes belonged to a small group of prosperous yeomen. In 1524 9 people taxed at £5 or more owned altogether £85 in goods. The wealthiest, Stephen Fulwell,[41] owned over 60 a. By *c.* 1570 his heir Joan and her husband Henry Lawrence held *c.* 146 a. altogether,[42] of which *c.* 132 a. was divided among coheirs *c.* 1660.[43] Of about 430 a. held as freehold and copyhold of the Linton manors in 1575, 18 persons with 10 a. or more accounted for *c.* 385 a.[44] On Barham manor *c.* 360 a. were held in 1599 by some 40 people, of whom 7 owning 20 a. or more occupied *c.* 280 a.[45] Many men therefore had only a croft or a few open-field acres: of 95 tenements held in Linton in 1575 30 consisted only of messuages or shops and 15 more were of 3 a. or less.[46] Some probably belonged to village craftsmen,[47] and as the population increased many inhabitants came to have no holdings. In 1524 59 men were taxed on goods worth only £1, and 7 on their wages, while 5 had no taxable wealth at all.[48]

The township became increasingly concerned with controlling and maintaining such people. In 1568 the villagers were forbidden to let any but their wives, children, or servants dwell in their houses without the lord's special leave.[49] In 1581 it was ordered that none should take in married couples as under-tenants without giving surety to the parish.[50] In 1577 the right to glean was confined to those with less than 4 a., and in 1583 45 people were reported to have gone gleaning prematurely.[51] Substantial legacies for the poor were made in the 1520s. In 1528 there were thought to be 40 poor householders in the parish.[52] In 1664 25 out of 160 householders were too poor to be rated,[53] and in 1666 only 31 out of 185 had more than 3 hearths, while 43 had 2, and 87 only one.[54]

[20] Ibid. Y 4.
[21] Ibid. B 6.
[22] Ibid. P 6.
[23] C.U.L., Doc. 643 no. 21; cf. ibid. Add. MS. 6052, ff. 42, 55v.
[24] C.R.O., R 59/5/3/1, pp. 366–7, 414.
[25] Prob. 11/14 (P.C.C. 24 Holgrave); Prob. 11/42A (P.C.C. 26 Welles).
[26] C.R.O., L 95/19A; R 59/14/11/3 no. 1, rental 1575; R 59/14/11/7C, ct. rolls 29, 32, 34 Eliz. I.
[27] Pemb. Coll. Mun., Barham, AA 1, acct. 16–17 Hen. VI.
[28] Ibid. acct. 36–8 Hen. VI.
[29] Ibid. AA 2–3, rentals 5 Hen. VII–22 Hen. VIII; cf. BB 1, ct. roll 9 Hen. VII.
[30] Ibid. B 7.
[31] Ibid. Y 2; S 7, f. 3.
[32] Ibid. S 7, ff. 3v.–17; AA 4, rental 1598–9.
[33] Ibid. AA 4, rental 1593–4.
[34] Ibid. AA 5, rental 1603–4.
[35] Ibid. BB 1, ct. roll 16 Hen. VII.
[36] Ibid. BB 5, ct. rolls 33–4 Eliz. I.
[37] Ibid. S 9.
[38] Ibid. Y 6; cf. D 4.
[39] C.R.O., R 59/5/3/1, pp. 45–6.
[40] Ibid. pp. 35–6.
[41] E 179/81/134 mm. 3–4.
[42] *Proc. C.A.S.* xxxi. 9–11; C.R.O., R 59/14/11/3 no. 1, rental, 1575; R 61/11/1, ff. 4v.–5.
[43] C.R.O., R 59/5/6/3A, 3B.
[44] Ibid. R 59/14/11/3 no. 1, rental 1575.
[45] Pemb. Coll. Mun., Barham, AA 4, rental 1598–9.
[46] C.R.O., R 59/14/11/3, no. 1, rental 1575.
[47] e.g. Prob. 11/159 (P.C.C. 50 St. John, will of Thos. Huppup); Prob. 11/166 (P.C.C. 93 Seager, will of John Knowles).
[48] E 179/81/134 mm. 3v.–4.
[49] Pemb. Coll. Mun., Barham, BB 5, ct. roll 10 Eliz. I.
[50] C.R.O., R 59/14/11/7C, ct. roll 23 Eliz. I.
[51] Pemb. Coll. Mun., Barham, BB 5, ct. rolls 19, 25 Eliz. I.
[52] B.L. Add. MS. 5861, ff. 100v., 105v.–106.
[53] E 179/84/437 rott. 59–60.
[54] See p. 279.

By the late 17th century the two demesnes were being consolidated into a few large farms. The inclosed lands of Linton manor were divided in 1672 into Little Linton farm, *c.* 563 a., and the Catley House farm, *c.* 95 a.[55] used mainly for dairy-farming.[56] Little Linton farm comprised in 1764 306 a. of arable, 112 a. of meadow and pasture, and 100 a. of heath. In 1779 its 575 a. included 190 a. of pasture and ley. Not being subject to rights of common it was more valuable than the open-field land.[57] About 1825 it covered *c.* 650 a. Catley Park farm came to *c.* 132 a. in 1779 and *c.* 191 a. in 1825. From 1704 Michaelotts farm and the estate's other open-field land were combined into one unit, covering in 1764 340 a., besides 70 a. of heath. By 1825 as Chilford farm it amounted to *c.* 590 a.

On the Barham estate most of the demesne arable and heath was let out as one farm after 1633.[58] In 1733 it comprised 220 a. of arable, 60 a. of meadow and pasture, and 300 a. of heath,[59] and after 1775 a total of *c.* 757 a. There were also two or three smaller farms, in all some 245 a. in 1786, of which three-quarters was open-field land,[60] to whose tenants the lessee of the main farm had to allow so many nights' folding of the manor flock.[61] After 1800 that estate was reorganized, eventually into two large farms, one of 450 a. in 1814, increased by 1830 to 660 a., based on Barham Hall, the other of 280 a., farmed from Little Barham Hall.[62]

In 1786 the Barham estate comprised 1,187 a., and the Keenes' land there *c.* 346 a. Of the remaining 360 a. of Barham *c.* 220 a. belonged to 7 men with 15 a. or more each.[63] By the 1820s, of some 3,660 a. in the whole parish, comprising 2,880 a. of arable, 510 a. of meadow and pasture, and 263 a. of woodland, eight large farms of over 100 a. covered 2,815 a. Five, totalling 1,680 a., belonged to the Linton estate, two, 960 a., to the Barham estate, and Robert Taylor occupied 197 a. Nine smaller farmers, mostly owner-occupiers, had 375 a. between them, and 25 other occupiers shared 205 a.[64]

There had been some agricultural innovations at Linton in the 17th century, when root crops were introduced. In the 1630s a gardener began to plant carrots and peas in his closes, and his neighbours observed and imitated his success. Turnips soon followed, and by the 1640s they were being grown in the fields also. In the 1650s up to 80 a. of them were planted there, and in 1694 60 a. of turnips and 80 a. of green peas. Normally, after two crops had been taken, peas were sown and cropped before Midsummer, followed by turnips, usually cultivated with the hoe or spade, and picked before Christmas. The intensive digging involved and the rotting compost were thought greatly to improve the soil for the ensuing barley crop.[65] With their increased cultivation elsewhere, peas and turnips were grown less at Linton,[66] where there were 75 a. of turnips in 1760 and only 6 a. of peas; turnips accounted in 1775 for 55 a. and in 1815 for less than 40 a.[67]

Most of the parish remained subject to the traditional three-course rotation, which was also followed on the inclosed arable of the Barham farms.[68] About 1780, on two open-field farms of the Linton estate, 70 a. of wheat and 48 a. of barley were sown as the first crop, and 47 a. of barley and 40 a. of oats as the second, while 124 a. was left as summer land, including 40 a. planted with turnips.[69] Similarly on Barham Hall farm there were in 1787 45 a. of wheat, 90 a. of barley, and 80 a. of oats and pease, besides 100 a. of fallow.[70] Clover, rye-grass, cinquefoil, and trefoil had also been introduced by the 1790s, when a rotation in force included wheat or barley one year, and oats or pease the next followed after a winter's fallowing by turnips in preparation for a succeeding barley crop.[71] Turnips and coleseed were still grown on the fallow in the 1830s and potatoes had been introduced by 1820.[72] The manorial estates still had the largest flocks. Of 850 tithable lambs in 1761, 800 were from three flocks on the Linton estate.[73] Barham Hall farm had a flock of 300 sheep in 1733, and one of 480 in 1787.[74] In 1814 its farmer sold his flock of 380 Norfolk sheep.[75] Cattle were more widely owned. Of 100 cows in Linton in the 1760s and 1770s, 40 were on the Linton estate, the others belonging to over 20 people.[76] Barham Hall farm had a herd of 15 milking cows in 1733.[77]

The Revd. C. E. Ruck-Keene proposed inclosure in 1837.[78] An Act, obtained by June 1838,[79] appointed a single commissioner who had finished dividing the fields by October,[80] although the award was executed only in 1840.[81] Of *c.* 110 landholders in Linton in 1838 only 25 owned more than 5 a. of open-field land, the rest possessing simply smallholdings or crofts, for which they might claim common rights.[82] Of the estimated 3,776 a. in the parish the land allotted comprised 1,495 a. of land to be inclosed and 153 a. of old inclosures entirely surrounded by open fields. Keene received 676½ a. in addition to his 1,090 a. of old inclosures and 90 a. of wood. Pembroke College received 454 a., and 78 a. for the rectorial glebe, in addition to its 606 a. of old inclosures and 146 a. of wood. Smaller allotments were of 95 a. and 62 a., five of 10–50 a.

55 This paragraph is based mainly on C.R.O., R 59/5/3/1, pp. 412–18 (1672); R 59/5/3/2 (rentals 1704–15); R 59/5/4/3 (1763); R 59/5/6/8–11 (1779); Pemb. Coll. Mun., Linton, E 12 (*c.* 1825).
56 Pemb. Coll. Mun., Linton, D 5.
57 C.R.O., R 59/5/3/1, p. 34; R 59/5/6/9.
58 Pemb. Coll. Mun., Barham, Y 7.
59 Ibid. Y 14; E 112/1084/36 bill and 2nd answer.
60 Pemb. Coll. Mun., Barham, S 16, 19; Y 15–36.
61 e.g. ibid. Y 15, 17, 24.
62 Ibid. S 21, 23; Z 1–4.
63 Ibid. S 16.
64 Ibid. Linton, E 12.
65 E 112/623/54; E 134/7 Wm. III Mich./2 *passim*; E 126/16 f. 326 and v.; Pemb. Coll. Mun., Barham, T 5 no. 17; cf. C.R.O., R 59/5/3/1, pp. 34–5, 41, 331; E 134/10 Geo. II Mich./3, pt. 5.
66 C.U.L., Doc. 643 no. 16.
67 C.R.O., P 107/3/1–2; L 95/39.
68 Cf. Pemb. Coll. Mun., Barham, S 19, 21; Y 29.
69 C.R.O., R 59/5/6/7.
70 Pemb. Coll. Mun., Barham, Y 31; cf. Y 1–14.
71 Vancouver, *Agric. in Cambs.* 59–60; cf. C.R.O., P 107/3/1.
72 C.U.L., Doc. 643 no. 81; C.R.O., L 95/39.
73 C.R.O., P 107/3/1–2.
74 E 112/1084/36 answer; Pemb. Coll. Mun., Barham, Y 31.
75 *Camb. Chron.* 30 Sept. 1814.
76 C.R.O., P 107/3/1–2.
77 E 112/1084/36 answer; C.R.O., P 107/3/2.
78 C.U.L., Doc. 643 nos. 2–4.
79 Linton Incl. Act, 1 Vic. c. 7 (Private, not printed) C.U.L., Doc. 643 no. 25; *C.J.* xciii. 71, 315, 597.
80 C.U.L., Doc. 643 no. 81.
81 C.R.O., Q/RDc 53.
82 C.U.L., Add. MS. 6052, *passim.*

totalling *c.* 105 a., and fifteen of under 10 a. amounting to 87 a.; 67 allotments, 19 a. altogether, were made for rights of common only.[83]

Most of Linton continued to be divided into a few large farms.[84] South of the river were Catley Park farm, 130 a. *c.* 1840, but 303 a. by 1871 and in 1902, and Little Linton farm, 601 a. *c.* 1840[85] and 618 a. in 1902. The two farms, totalling 918 a., were run as one in 1950. Chilford farm, north of the river, covered 494 a. and Little Chilford 212 a. *c.* 1840. Together they came to 498 a. in 1902, and 502 a. in 1950. Chilford farm was sometimes, as in 1902, let with Rivey farm, then comprising *c.* 220 a. on the slope south of Rivey Hill, of which 150 a. were sold in 1926,[86] and the Grip farm, whose 260 a. south of the village included much land in Hadstock. The Pembroke estate was still divided into Barham Hall farm, covering 682 a. in 1841, and Little Barham farm of 289 a.; they had been combined by 1871, but were again separate by the 1910s.[87] About 1851 there were still also 10 smaller farmers, of whom Robert Adcock had 100 a. and William Livermore 60 a. Those two farms were later combined into Greenditch farm of *c.* 160 a. In 1879 there were eight farmers in Linton, in 1908 seven, in 1937 six.[88]

In the early 19th century *c.* 120 families usually depended on farming for their employment.[89] In 1830 there were 169 labourers over and 170 under 20; wages were 9*s.* a week, and married men were allowed ½ rood each for growing potatoes, their main food. Their cottages were almost all rented from local farmers and tradesmen.[90] In the mid 19th century the farmers usually employed *c.* 150 men and up to 90 boys,[91] the remaining labourers finding work in neighbouring parishes.[92] The number employed in agriculture gradually declined until by the 1970s it was less than 5 per cent of the population.[93]

Sheep-farming remained important after inclosure. There were 7 shepherds at Linton in 1861, 11 in 1871.[94] In 1902 there were 1,735 a. of arable and only 150 a. of permanent grass on the Keene estate.[95] In 1905 the whole parish contained 3,156 a. of arable, 316 a. of grass, and 194 a. of wood.[96] In 1950 the Linton estate farms were devoted mainly to cereals and root-crops, and contained 200 a. of grass out of 1,630 a.[97] Sugar-beet was being grown by the 1950s. One farm had a flock of pedigree Suffolk sheep, from which stock was exported. A seed-testing station had been established by 1954,[98] and apparently closed *c.* 1970. By 1970 there was an abattoir, principally for pigs.[99]

Mills. In 1086 two water-mills belonged to Great Linton manor and one to Little Linton.[1] In 1272 and 1279 William de Say owned two water-mills of which no later evidence has been found. Little Linton mill, recorded in 1279,[2] stood just downstream from the manor-house. It was at farm in 1516,[3] and still belonged to the estate in the 1670s.[4] In the 18th century it was leased with a windmill,[5] and both were let to the lessee of Little Linton farm in 1805. A new wheel was provided for the water-mill in 1810.[6] It remained in use until *c.* 1875, and was briefly reopened in the 1890s.[7] The timber-framed, thatched mill-house, empty from 1900, was demolished in 1903.[8]

By 1279 Barham manor had two water-mills and a windmill.[9] Windmill shot was recorded in 1468, near the Haverhill road.[10] One water-mill stood a little west of Barham Hall, the other further upstream.[11] One was let as a fulling-mill *c.* 1460, the other remaining a corn-mill.[12] Both the greater and the lesser mills were still in use *c.* 1600, being sometimes in the same hands,[13] but only one survived in 1657, and that too probably closed soon after 1712.[14] The windmill was let separately in 1713.[15] The Barham estate included no mill in 1740.[16]

Linton mill, south of the village, originally belonged to the bishop of Ely's manor of Hadstock in Essex, and was possibly reckoned as part of Hadstock parish until the 19th century.[17] The bishop had a water-mill probably near there *c.* 1270.[18] In the 14th century Walter de Furneaux, brother of John, lord of Barham, granted John, bishop of Ely, 2 a. of waste for building a water-mill, with an 18-ft. way across the meadow from Hadstock.[19] The tithe of the mill was disputed between Linton and Hadstock in the 1370s; then, as in 1580, it was on lease to Linton men.[20] About 1850 it belonged to John Reeve,[21] and in 1884 was sold to F. S. Nicholls,[22] whose family worked it until its sale in 1908[23] to the newly started Linton Milling and Corn Co., which owned and ran it in 1972. After 1954 it produced animal feedstuffs.[24] The building dates

[83] C.R.O., Q/RDc 53.
[84] For details see C.R.O., R 59/5/6/12 (*c.* 1840); 296/SP 1009 (1902); SP 107/7 (1950); *Gardner's Dir. Cambs.* (1851); *Kelly's Dir. Cambs.* (1864–1937); H.O. 107/66, 1761; R.G. 9/1029; R.G. 10/1592.
[85] C.R.O., R 59/5/9/229.
[86] Ibid. SP 107/6.
[87] Cf. Pemb. Coll. Mun., Barham, Z 9–10; *Rep. Com. Univ. Income* [C. 856-II], p. 101, H.C. (1873), xxxvii (3).
[88] H.O. 107/1761; C.U.L., Maps 53(1)/88/73; C.R.O., SP 107/10; 515/SP 1451.
[89] *Census*, 1811–31.
[90] *Rep. H.L. Cttee. on Poor Laws*, H.C. 227, pp. 326–7 (1831), viii; *Rep. Com. Poor Laws* [44], p. 58, H.C. (1834), xxx–xxxii.
[91] e.g. H.O. 107/1761; R.G. 10/1592.
[92] Cf. *1st Rep. Com. Employment in Agric.* 355.
[93] Cambs. Coll. of Arts and Tech., Village Survey, 1972.
[94] R.G. 9/1029; R.G. 10/1592.
[95] C.R.O., 296/SP 1009.
[96] Cambs. Agric. Returns, 1905.
[97] C.R.O., SP 107/7.
[98] H. Nockolds, *Linton* (1954), 5–6, 20; *Camb. Ind. Press*, 15 Jan. 1960.
[99] Cf. *Camb. Evening News*, 1 Oct. 1971; 1 June, 1973.
[1] *V.C.H. Cambs.* i. 341.
[2] *Rot. Hund.* (Rec. Com.), ii. 416, 418; C 132/42 no. 6.
[3] Prob. 11/18 (P.C.C. 27 Holder, will of John Parys).
[4] C.R.O., R 59/5/3/1, p. 53.
[5] Ibid. R 59/5/4/3; R 55/10/27A.
[6] Ibid. R 59/5/9/8, E 2.
[7] *Kelly's Dir. Cambs.* (1864, 1879, 1892–6).
[8] Palmer, *Neighbourhood of Hildersham*, 7.
[9] *Rot. Hund.* (Rec. Com.), ii. 418.
[10] Pemb. Coll. Mun., Barham, O 13; cf. S 15; S 9, 16.
[11] Ibid. T.i.c.
[12] Ibid. AA 1, acct. 36–8 Hen. VI.
[13] Ibid. AA 4, rentals 27, 45 Eliz. I.
[14] Ibid. Y 8–10.
[15] Ibid. Y 12.
[16] C.R.O., R 59/5/6/4.
[17] e.g. Pemb. Coll. Mun., Barham, T.i.c.; C.U.L., Maps 53(1)/88/32.
[18] Pemb. Coll. Mun., Barham, M 1A.
[19] Ibid. S 1, f. 6 (copied 1396).
[20] B.L. Add. MS. 5842, f. 24v.; Req. 2/41/91.
[21] H.O. 107/1761; *Gardner's Dir. Cambs.* (1851).
[22] *Kelly's Dir. Cambs.* (1864–79); C.U.L., Maps 53(1)/88/32.
[23] *Kelly's Dir. Cambs.* (1888–1908); C.U.L., Maps 53(1)/90/11.
[24] *Kelly's Dir. Cambs.* (1912–37); Nockolds, *Linton*, 13; *Camb. Ind. Press*, 15 Jan. 1960; 3 Sept. 1970.

from *c.* 1725;[25] the brick-and-flint miller's house was sold in 1962.[26]

MARKETS AND FAIRS. In 1246 William de Say was granted a weekly market on Tuesdays at Great Linton and a three-day fair at St. Lawrence's feast (9–11 August).[27] In 1282 Simon de Furneaux of Barham was granted a weekly market on Fridays and a three-day fair at St. Margaret's feast (19–21 July).[28] Both fairs endured, but only the Great Linton market. The original site of the market, an open space between the high street and the Hadstock manor mill, had possibly passed out of use by 1363, when it was styled the old market.[29] The new market-place lay halfway along the street south of the river, where it widened to the east into an open space; to the west stood a double row of permanent stalls.[30] In 1528 money was left for building a market-house, which by 1600 stood at the east end of the stalls.[31] Its first importance was as a provision market, regulated by the Linton manor court.[32] From 1528 the court sometimes appointed two men to oversee the sale of meat and fish.[33] In 1536 seven bakers and six butchers were selling at Linton, some of them outsiders.[34] In 1533 men were fined for regrating barley and herrings in the market.[35] By *c.* 1578 one row of stalls was named Butchery Row, another Middle Row.[36] By 1630 there were rows named for the woollen and linen drapers,[37] and stalls were kept by tanners, shoemakers, and glovers.[38] By 1604 two searchers of leather were being appointed,[39] and from 1622 two clerks of the market.[40] Under Charles II besides a clerk and crier there were searchers of flesh, fish, and leather and weighers of bread and butter.[41] Their duties gradually became nominal, and by 1720 all those offices were held by one man.[42]

From *c.* 1640 until the early 19th century Linton market was held on Thursdays. It was still an important corn market in the late 18th century, and by the mid 19th was the only market in the county outside Cambridge.[43] Its stalls were still yielding tolls to the lord in 1807,[44] but by 1850 it was decaying, despite changing the market day, and had expired by 1864. The market-house, a building partly of brick with its lower storey open,[45] became ruinous and was demolished *c.* 1950.[46]

Linton fair, owned by Benjamin Keene in 1807, was probably that held on Ascension day, which was partly a hiring fair, partly for selling pedlary.[47] It lingered into the 1870s, but by 1883 had been superseded by the village flower-show.[48] Barham fair was not recorded in the 15th or 16th centuries, and may have been revived after John Millicent had the charter for it exemplified in 1664.[49] It was mainly for selling sheep and lambs, and was held in an area called Lamb Fair south of Barham cross.[50] About 1806 it was held on 30 July, and in 1867 yielded £15 to Pembroke College.[51] It was formally abolished in 1878.[52]

Linton remained an important centre for local shopping. From the late 18th century to the 1930s it had its own firm of auctioneers and land surveyors.[53] In the late 19th century and early 20th there were usually 4 to 6 bakers, 3 or 4 butchers, 4 or 5 grocers, and 1 or 2 tailors, besides chemists and hairdressers from 1841, and by 1904 a branch of the Sawston Co-operative Society. The largest shop was a general stores, said to have been started in 1739, and taken over in the 1860s by Richard Holttum whose name it still bore in 1937.[54] Its site covered much of the area once occupied by the market stalls.[55] It was later acquired by the International Stores, and had been closed by 1974.

TRADE AND INDUSTRY. William de Say exploited his charter for a market by granting out plots in the village, some sited round the old market-place, in free burgage. By 1279 there were 48 such shops, whose owners included 4 mercers, 2 bakers, 2 potters, a smith, a skinner, a barker, a barber, a tailor, and Adam Caiaphas, perhaps a Jewish money-lender.[56] Burgage tenure is not recorded later, but many shops were held of Linton manor by quit-rents, while others were copyholds.[57] Men from neighbouring towns acquired shops at Linton, a Saffron Walden man owning one *c.* 1549,[58] and two others *c.* 1584.[59] Among craftsmen and traders recorded in the 17th century, besides those usual in villages, were a glazier, a cutler, a rope-maker, a weaver, and a clothier.[60] Others in 1694 included a glover, a locksmith, and a wheelwright, and in 1757 a periwig-maker.[61]

The most important trades were those based on

[25] *Camb. Evening News*, 4 Sept. 1973.
[26] C.R.O., SP 107/3.
[27] *Cal. Chart. R.* 1226–57, 294.
[28] Ibid. 1257–1300, 262.
[29] Pemb. Coll. Mun., Barham, M 2A.
[30] Ibid. T.i.c.
[31] Ibid.; B.L. Add. MS. 5861, f. 106.
[32] e.g. C.R.O., R 59/14/11/7A, ct. rolls 1, 5 Hen. VIII.
[33] Ibid. ct. roll 19 Hen. VIII.
[34] Ibid. ct. roll 27 Hen. VIII.
[35] Ibid. ct. roll 24 Hen. VIII.
[36] Ibid. ct. rolls 20, 24, 35 Eliz. I.
[37] C.U.L., Palmer MS. A 30, rental 1630, ff. 11, 20.
[38] e.g. ibid. ff. 9, 10, 14.
[39] C.R.O., R 59/14/11/7E, ct. rolls 2, 8 Jas. I.
[40] Ibid. 7F, ct. roll 20 Jas. I.
[41] Ibid. R 59/5/3/1, p. 1; R 59/14/11/7K, ct. roll 1662.
[42] Ibid. L 1/103, f. 1.
[43] B.L. Add. MS. 15672, f. 23; Lysons, *Cambs.* 228; cf. *Camb. Chron.* 15 Dec. 1796; *V.C.H. Cambs.* ii. 89.
[44] B.L. Add. MS. 15664, f. 20.
[45] Palmer, *Antiquities of Linton*, 3; *Kelly's Dir. Cambs.* (1864).
[46] Nockolds, *Linton*, 6.
[47] B.L. Add. MS. 15664, f. 20; Lysons, *Cambs.* 228.
[48] *Kelly's Dir. Cambs.* (1864, 1879, 1888); cf. C.R.O., 331/Z 2, 1905, p. lxx; photograph (1883) in C.A.S. colln.
[49] Pemb. Coll. Mun., Barham, F 12.
[50] Ibid. S 16; C.R.O., R 59/5/6/4.
[51] Lysons, *Cambs.* 228; *Rep. Com. Univ. Income* [C. 856-II], p. 108, H.C. (1873), xxxvii (3).
[52] *Lond. Gaz.* 8 Feb. 1878, p. 640.
[53] *Camb. Chron.* 23 May 1789; 7, 28 Aug. 1812; *Kelly's Dir. Cambs.* (1883–1933).
[54] H.O. 107/66, 1761; *Kelly's Dir. Cambs.* (1864–1937); Nockolds, *Linton*, 17.
[55] Palmer, *Antiquities of Linton*, 2; cf. *Proc. C.A.S.* xvii. 97; xxx. 60.
[56] *Rot. Hund.* (Rec. Com.), ii. 417; Pemb. Coll. Mun., Barham, M 1A.
[57] C.R.O., R 59/14/11/3 no. 1, rental 1575; no. 2, rental *c.* 1675.
[58] Ibid. R 59/14/11/7B, ct. roll 5 Edw. VI.
[59] Prob. 11/67 (P.C.C. 43 Watson, will of Mark Dowling); Prob. 11/68 (P.C.C. 1 Brudenell, will of Jas. Goding).
[60] Prob. 11/166 (P.C.C. 93 Seager, will of John Knowles); Prob. 11/260 (P.C.C. 426 Berkeley, will of Phil. Brown); Prob. 11/294 (P.C.C. 424 Peel, will of Thos. Thurger); Prob. 11/283 (P.C.C. 586 Wootton, will of Thos. Tofts); Prob. 11/402 (P.C.C. 194–5 Dyke, will of Ric. Wakefield).
[61] E 134/7 Wm. III Mich./2 pts. 5, 7 (deposns. 18–22); C.R.O., L 1/105, f. 23.

the timber supplied by the manorial woods. Wood-sales yielded much of the profit of Barham manor, both in the 15th century[62] and the 18th.[63] It was mainly local men who bought the wood *c.* 1600.[64] The timber in Linton wood was valued at £1,717 *c.* 1680.[65] About 1795 it was being cut every 10 to 12 years.[66] A sawpit was dug on the old market-place in 1756.[67]

The bark from the timber was used for tanning. There was a tanner at Linton in 1327,[68] and two of the Millicents were active as 'barkers' in the 15th century.[69] A tanner left his son his vats and bark in 1559.[70] About 1725 Thomas Malying owned a tan-yard, probably near the old market-place, with the right to lay his bark on the green there.[71] Edmund Taylor (d. 1804) acquired the yard *c.* 1776, and his heirs probably carried on business until the 1830s.[72] Another tannery stood west of the river near the Independent chapel. Although partly burnt down in 1819,[73] it was still working *c.* 1838.[74] Tanning had ceased at Linton by 1851,[75] but leather-working persisted. Craftsmen in 1736 had included a saddler and a cordwainer.[76] In 1851 there were a currier, 14 shoemakers and cordwainers, and 4 harness-makers, in 1871 12 shoemakers and 3 harness-makers.[77] Of two saddlers' businesses recorded in 1851 that belonging to the Maris family was active from *c.* 1750 to after 1937. From the 1870s to the 1910s there were usually 4 or 5 boot- and shoe-makers.[78]

Building materials were dug and made at Linton from the Middle Ages. A tile-kiln was rented from Barham manor *c.* 1460.[79] By the 16th century a field was named after a lime-kiln,[80] perhaps that held of Linton manor with lime-pits in 1575.[81] In the 1670s a local brick-kiln produced bricks for work on Catley House, until the brick-earth in the pasture there gave out *c.* 1681.[82] The Barham brick-kiln in Woodhole by Borley wood was in production in 1738, as was a lime-kiln on Barham heath in 1745, when both were let to a Cambridge builder.[83] A lime-kiln newly built on the same site *c.* 1774 was still in use in 1814.[84] In 1851 the building trades were represented by 22 bricklayers, 3 thatchers, and a plumber, and in 1871 there were also 4 painters and a glazier. D. P. Day's building firm, employing in 1851 10 carpenters, 8 bricklayers, 2 sawyers, and 10 labourers, survived until 1888. In 1841 there were 16 carpenters at Linton, 14 in 1871. Other woodworkers included wheelwrights, 6 in 1871, coopers, hurdle-makers, a lath-render, and from 1888 a cabinet-maker. The Starling family ran a wheelwright's and coachmaker's business from before 1851 to after 1937.[85]

In 1737 Robert Millicent (d. 1741) was induced to prospect for coal north of Borley wood, where the name Coal Hole Lane survived in 1838. A shaft over 225 ft. deep was sunk,[86] and *c.* 1745 it was alleged that a large vein of good coal had been found,[87] but by 1755 the owners of Barham Hall were having coal carried from Cambridge.[88]

Some new manufactures were introduced in the 19th century. A small hemp factory opened in 1832 to provide employment[89] was not recorded later. By 1851 Henry Prior had a substantial brewery off Stony Street, which closed shortly before 1919.[90] In the 1860s Prior began to produce whiting with materials from a neighbouring chalkpit. There were two whiting-makers in 1871.[91] About 1880 the business was taken over by the Whiffen family, and from 1922 by the Linton Chalk and Whiting Co., whose works, in use until 1937 or later, stood by the Hadstock road.[92] Ten blacksmiths were working at Linton in 1841 and 7 in 1871, but only 3 forges survived by 1900, of which the last ceased working after 1922.[93] A small printing firm set up by 1904 had been succeeded by 1925 by the Eagle Printing Works, still open in 1937.[94] Light industry in Linton in the 1960s included the Crofton Engineering Works, started in 1952, making builders' metal-work, Cathodeon Crystals Ltd., opened in 1953, producing quartz crystals for telecommunications equipment, and a fertilizer-maker.[95]

LOCAL GOVERNMENT. In 1279 the lords both of Great Linton and of Barham exercised view of frankpledge and the assize of bread and of ale, and were entitled to a gallows and tumbrel.[96] Little Linton manor had no such jurisdiction. In 1334 it was instead represented by a reeve and four men at a tourn held there for the honor of Richmond.[97] The Great Linton court sometimes overstrained its authority: in 1272 its members were amerced for hanging a shepherd on his own confession without due process.[98] In the 17th century the lord of Linton

62 Pemb. Coll. Mun., Barham, AA 2–3, *passim.*
63 Ibid. R 4.
64 Ibid. R 1.
65 C.R.O., R 59/5/3/1, pp. 340–61; cf. pp. 291–6, 300–4.
66 Vancouver, *Agric. in Cambs.* 60.
67 C.R.O., L 1/106, f. 185; see also ibid. R 55/10/19B, 19D; *Camb. Chron.* 12 Apr. 1784.
68 *Cambs. Lay Subsidy, 1327*, 24.
69 Pemb. Coll. Mun., Barham, O 13; X 4.
70 B.L. Add. MS. 5861, f. 44.
71 C.R.O., R 59/14/11/10C, 10F; L 1/103, f. 39; cf. Palmer, *Antiquities of Linton*, 9.
72 C.R.O., R 55/10/19C, 19D; R 59/19/21F; R 55/10/22A; cf. L 1/106, f. 190v.; L 1/108, pp. 249–52, 289; *Camb. Chron.* 7 July 1804.
73 C.R.O., L 1/108, pp. 94, 314; C.U.L., Palmer MS. B 29, pp. 75–7.
74 C.U.L., Add. MS. 6052, f. 22v.
75 *Gardner's Dir. Cambs.* (1851).
76 E 134/10 Geo. II Mich./2, pt. 5.
77 H.O. 107/1761; R.G. 10/1592.
78 *Gardner's Dir. Cambs.* (1851); *Kelly's Dir. Cambs.* (1864–1937).
79 Pemb. Coll. Mun., Barham, AA 1, acct. 36–8 Hen. VI.
80 C.R.O., R 59/14/11/7C, ct. roll 22 Eliz. I.
81 Ibid. R 59/14/11/3 no. 1, rental 1575.
82 Ibid. R 59/5/3/1, p. 376.
83 Pemb. Coll. Mun., Barham, Y 16, 19.
84 Ibid. Y 22C, 22G; R 3; S 21.
85 H.O. 107/66, 1761; R.G. 9/1029; R.G. 10/1592; *Kelly's Dir. Cambs.* (1864–1937).
86 *East Anglian*, N.S. xiii. 115–16; cf. C.R.O., Q/RDc 53, p. 24.
87 C.R.O., R 59/5/6/4; cf. *Universal Mag.* Dec. 1747, p. 294.
88 Pemb. Coll. Mun., Barham, Y 20, 24. No geological evidence of coal deposits at Linton has been traced.
89 *Rep. Com. Poor Laws* [44], p. 58, H.C. (1834), xxx.
90 *Gardner's Dir. Cambs* (1851); *Kelly's Dir. Cambs.* (1864–1916); C.U.L., Maps 53(1)/91/134.
91 *Kelly's Dir. Cambs.* (1864–79); R.G. 10/1592; cf. C.R.O., 515/SP 994.
92 *Kelly's Dir. Cambs.* (1883–1937).
93 H.O. 107/66; R.G. 10/1592; *Kelly's Dir. Cambs.* (1900–25).
94 *Kelly's Dir. Cambs.* (1904–1937).
95 Ex inf. the companies; *Camb. Ind. Press*, 15 Jan. 1960; *Camb. Evening News*, 20 May, 19 Oct., 25 Nov. 1972.
96 *Rot. Hund.* (Rec. Com.), i. 52; ii. 416, 418.
97 S.C. 2/155/71 m. 2.
98 C.R.O., 331/Z 1, pp. lxii–lxiii.

claimed felons' chattels, a right actually exercised in 1631, deodands, and waifs and strays.[99]

For Linton manor court rolls survive for 1509–1716 and court books for 1720–1946,[1] and for Barham there are court rolls almost continuously from 1493 to 1596 and rolls and books from 1604 to 1831.[2]

From 1509 the Linton court met twice yearly in spring and, for leet business, in autumn, except between 1528 and 1547 when it met yearly in January or February. After *c.* 1620 it met once a year. In 1513 two Linton tenants were presented for suing a third for debt outside the lord's court.[3] The Barham court met annually, before 1535 at Lammas. From 1577 Robert Millicent held up to four courts a year, probably to control more strictly his tenants' transfers of property. In the same period the record of leet jurisdiction became cursory. The two courts occasionally co-operated formally, as in authorizing in 1549 the diversion of the highway near Barham Hall.[4] Under Henry VIII each court was choosing a constable, one or two ale-tasters, and a hayward or field-reeve of its own, as was still done in the 1630s.[5] The 18th century saw disputes between the two lords over control of the village. The chief farmers of the two estates had been sharing offices, but *c.* 1745 the Millicents' successors questioned Robert King's right to name constables for the whole parish at his Linton court leet.[6]

By the 1570s the churchwardens and constables, with collectors for the poor regularly appointed from 1577, were transacting much business independently of the courts, and accounting to 6 or 8 of the elders of the parish.[7] They managed the former guildhall which Pembroke College had leased in 1564 to feoffees at a nominal rent. The profits were to help to maintain the church, the causeway to it, and Linton's great bridge.[8] The hall was hired for wedding festivities, visiting players sometimes performed there, and rooms in it were let to widows.[9] Although again leased to village trustees for 40 years in 1656,[10] it passed from their hands in 1697 and became a private house.[11] The township owned another town-house or task-house, used partly to accommodate the poor.[12] In the 1580s money for the poor came mainly from legacies.[13] By 1591 fines levied in the Linton court went half to the lord, half to the poor.[14] Charitable gifts needed increasingly to be supplemented by rates by the 1630s.[15]

From the late 17th century the parish was managed by a vestry of 5–10 substantial inhabitants, who met monthly by the 1750s to check the overseers' accounts. Each overseer acted for half a year.[16] General town meetings were sometimes attended by over 20 people, and smaller groups were chosen for special purposes.[17] In the early 19th century the vestry was nominally open, but the churchwardens and overseers apparently settled the rates.[18] The vestry bought a fire engine *c.* 1733 and kept it in the church.[19] In 1748 a pest-house for those with smallpox was built.[20] In 1697 a house was probably bought for a parish alms-house,[21] presumably the same as the four alms-houses where 20 poor people lived in 1783.[22] In 1837 it comprised eight single-room dwellings, next to the old parish workhouse.[23]

By the 1670s there were a dozen people listed as entitled to weekly poor-relief, by 1685 over 20, costing up to 1*s.* a week each.[24] In 1697 the vestry forbade those on relief to beg from door to door, and in 1710 and 1712 restricted the giving of relief to a regular time after Sunday evensong.[25] The expense of relieving *c.* 30 people yearly rose from £60 a year in the 1690s to £130 by 1731, of which a third went on casual relief.[26] In 1737 the parish built a workhouse, near the east end of the high street, to be run by a salaried master and dame.[27] Until the 1770s it usually had between 12 and 22 inmates, who occasionally did such work as spinning and were allowed a liberal diet. By 1748 out-relief, mainly for women, had been resumed. Between 1740 and 1765 expenditure on poor-relief fluctuated between £150 and £170, and from the late 1760s regularly exceeded £200.[28] It increased to over £300 *c.* 1784, of which less than £5 was spent on setting the poor to work.[29] By 1803 it was £579; the workhouse, with 16 inmates under a contractor who took their earnings, cost £101, while 50 people received permanent outdoor relief.[30] Expenditure on the poor rose to £1,850 in 1813, to support 12 people in the workhouse, 52 on permanent out-relief, and 150 relieved casually.[31] It usually exceeded £1,600 until 1822, and fluctuated until 1830 around £1,400.[32] In 1830 41 out of 169 adult labourers were employed on road-work.[33] In 1832 the rates, at 16*s.* in the £, were the highest in the county. Of £2,320 spent on the poor, £793 went to the aged, sick, and widows, £527 to paupers employed by the parish, and £689 on casual relief, apparently including making up wages. Only 9 people, all old or unfit, were in the workhouse in 1833, but 125 obtained out-relief, at 1*s.* a week over the county bread-scale. They were described as the best-fed and most comfortable and thriving paupers in Cambridgeshire, being mostly artisans earning

99 Ibid. R 59/5/3/1, p. 24; R 59/14/11/7H, ct. roll 1631.
1 Ibid. R 59/14/11/7A–S; L 1/103–11.
2 Pemb. Coll. Mun., Barham, BB 1–14; S 11–12.
3 C.R.O., R 59/14/11/7A, ct. roll 5 Hen. VIII.
4 Pemb. Coll. Mun., Barham, BB 3, ct. roll 3 Edw. VI.
5 e.g. C.R.O., R 59/14/11/7A, ct. rolls 2, 3, 9 Hen. VIII; Pemb. Coll. Mun., Barham, BB 1, ct. roll 8 Hen. VIII; BB 7, ct. roll 7 Chas. I.
6 Pemb. Coll. Mun., Barham, T 8 m. 10 and *passim.*
7 C.R.O., L 95/14, ff. 4, 9v., 18v., 21, and *passim.*
8 Ibid. ff. 1v.–3v.
9 e.g. ibid. ff. 4, 5, 7, 12v.
10 Pemb. Coll. Mun., Barham, H 2.
11 Ibid. H 3–18.
12 C.R.O., R 59/14/11/3; C.U.L., Palmer MS. A 30, rental 1630, f. 31.
13 C.R.O., L 95/14, e.g. ff. 7, 10v.–11, 20v.
14 Ibid. R 59/14/11/7C, ct. roll 33 Eliz. I.
15 Ibid. L 95/14, ff. 21–37, and p. 161 (at end).
16 Ibid. L 95/4–5, *passim.*
17 Hampson, *Poverty in Cambs.* 240–1.
18 Ibid. 241; cf. *Rep. Com. Poor Laws*, [44], p. 58, H.C. (1834), xxxii.
19 Palmer, *Wm. Cole*, 104.
20 C.U.L., E.D.R., B 7/1, p. 130; cf. *31st Rep. Com. Char.* 105.
21 C.U.L., Palmer MS. A 20; cf. ibid. E.D.R., B 8/1.
22 Ibid. E.D.R., B 7/1, p. 130.
23 *31st Rep. Com. Char.* 105.
24 C.R.O., L 95/1, *passim.*
25 Hampson, *Poverty in Cambs.* 178–81.
26 Ibid. 180–1.
27 Ibid. 93–4; Palmer, *Antiquities of Linton*, 9.
28 C.R.O., L 95/4–5, *passim.*
29 *Poor Rate Returns, 1787*, Parl. Papers, 1st ser. vol. ix, pp. 307, 561.
30 *Poor Law Abstract, 1804*, 34–5.
31 Ibid. *1818*, 28–9.
32 *Poor Rate Returns, 1816–21*, 10; *1822–4*, 37; *1825–9*, 15–16.
33 *Rep. H.L. Cttee. on Poor Laws*, H.C. 227, pp. 326–7 (1831), viii.

double a farm-worker's wages, who let themselves fall on the rates in winter and intimidated the parish officers. In 1829 a vestryman's corn stacks were fired, and in 1833 two J.P.s narrowly escaped alive from a riot at Linton.[34]

In 1835 Linton became part of the Linton poor-law union,[35] was incorporated with the Linton R.D. into the South Cambridgeshire R.D. in 1934,[36] and was included in South Cambridgeshire in 1974. In 1836, after the guardians had sold the old workhouse, a large new one was built for up to 230 people.[37] It then stood outside the village on the Cambridge road, built of brick with two courtyards.[38] By 1960 and in 1974 it was being used as an old people's home.[39]

An association with 32 members for prosecuting criminals, started at Linton in 1818, organized nightly patrols, hiring a constable for the duty in 1821, but dealt with little except occasional thefts of hay, turnips, or potatoes.[40] Linton had a resident policeman by 1841,[41] and a police station, serving the whole district, by 1861.[42] The parish council, set up in 1894, provided some services for what was becoming a small town, including in the 1890s some winter street-lighting by oil-lamps[43] and a fire-engine manned by volunteers.[44] The council also managed *c.* 25 a. of allotments leased since the 1870s from the Catley Park estate,[45] and *c.* 1906 took over the village recreation ground allotted at inclosure.[46] In 1922 it bought out the lord of the manor's residual rights there, and steadily improved it as a village sports-ground.[47]

CHURCH. The church of Linton was given before 1163 by an earl of Richmond to the abbey of St. Jacut-de-la-Mer,[48] which had appropriated the glebe and great tithes by 1279.[49] Vicars were recorded by *c.* 1275.[50] In 1312 the right to appoint them was in dispute between the bishop of Ely and the prior of the abbey's cell at Linton, who claimed that his predecessor had presented under Edward I.[51] The bishop regularly collated to the vicarage from 1338,[52] and, when appropriating the rectory to Pembroke College in 1450, reserved the collation to himself and his successors.[53] The patronage still belonged to the bishop in 1972.[54]

Tithe portions belonged to certain religious houses. About 1088 Count Alan granted tithe from his lands at Barham to the abbey of St. Sergius and St. Bacchus, Angers (Maine et Loire), whose dependent priory at Swavesey was receiving 18*s.* a year in 1256 and 1325.[55] About 1130 Count Stephen of Richmond granted tithe at Linton to St. Mary's Abbey, York,[56] whose cell of Rumburgh (Suff.) received 3 marks in 1254 and 4 in 1291.[57] In 1302 it let the portion for £5 to the lord of Little Linton, from whose fee the tithe arose.[58] In 1553 Philip Parys, who owned the 60 a. paying the tithe, bought the portion, and Parys's heirs claimed to hold that land tithe-free.[59] Between *c.* 1730 and the 1770s Thomas Bacon and his heirs tried to stretch the exemption, for both great and small tithes, to cover the newly inclosed Catley park, but they failed to exclude the vicar's right to a modus of 5 guineas for small tithes.[60] When the tithes were commuted in 1839 only the original 60 a. were considered tithe-free.[61]

Of the former Barham friary lands *c.* 79 a. were claimed as tithe-free in 1775, and 41 a. in 1807.[62] At the commutation at least 66 a. were allowed exemption.[63] About 1475, in return for a grant of land, Pembroke College released its right to tithe from the Barham demesne woods.[64] Barham heath, never having been under the plough, was not thought liable to pay great tithes, and in 1839 only 3,200 a. out of 3,820 a. in the parish were charged with them.[65]

The vicar had in 1279 only 1½ a. of glebe, in Barham fee, given by the Furneaux family.[66] Pembroke College gave more land in 1473,[67] so that in 1615 he had 9½ a., and *c.* 1730 10½ a.,[68] for which 8 a., still owned by the vicar in 1972, were allotted at inclosure.[69] He had also all the small tithes, a pension of 12*s.* a year from Barham manor, and the tithe of 20 a. of barley and 10 a. each of wheat and oats in Barham fee. About 1470 the tithe of saffron was disputed between the college and the vicar. The college agreed in 1473 that the vicar should have tithe of the saffron grown in named closes, covering *c.* 5 a., and 3*s.* 4*d.* a year for tithe of saffron grown elsewhere.[70] A similar dispute followed the introduction *c.* 1650 of turnips and peas as field-crops. At first the vicar took tithes on them at a fixed rate, but after 1668 John Curtis, under-tenant of the rectory, obliged Thomas Punter, vicar 1663–84, who was heavily in his debt, to relinquish those tithes. In 1694 a new vicar, William Stephens, sought to recover those tithes, and in 1697 the House of Lords confirmed an Exchequer judgement that the vicar was entitled to tithe of turnips, carrots, and peas,

34 *Rep. Com. Poor Laws* [44], pp. 246–7, H.C. (1834), xxviii; ibid. pp. 58*a–d* (1834), xxx–xxxiii.
35 *Poor Law Com. 1st Rep.* 249.
36 *Census*, 1931 (pt. ii).
37 Palmer, *Antiquities of Linton*, 9.
38 C.R.O., Q/RDc 53, map.
39 *Camb. Ind. Press*, 15 Jan. 1960.
40 C.R.O., L 95/18A–D.
41 H.O. 107/66.
42 R.G. 9/1029; *Kelly's Dir. Cambs.* (1864).
43 C.R.O., R 54/30/1, pp. 6, 29–34, 73, and *passim*.
44 e.g. ibid. pp. 48, 267, 287, 290.
45 Ibid. pp. 8–10, 13–14, 253; cf. ibid. R 59/5/7/8; 296/SP 1009.
46 Ibid. R 54/30/1, pp. 216–17, 239.
47 Ibid. pp. 358, 391–2, 400–3; cf. ibid. L 1/11, p. 114.
48 *V.C.H. Cambs.* ii. 314.
49 *Rot. Hund.* (Rec. Com.), ii. 416, 418.
50 *Vetus Liber Arch. Elien.* (C.A.S. 8vo ser. xlviii), 62.
51 *Year Bk. 6 Edw. II* (Selden Soc. xxxiv), 68–70.
52 e.g. *E.D.R.* (1889), 357; (1895), 109; (1898), 19, 159, 177.
53 Pemb. Coll. Mun., Linton, B 6.
54 *Crockford* (1971–2).
55 *Early Yorks. Chart.* iv (Y.A.S. extra ser. i), 1; *Val. of Norwich*, ed. Lunt, 227; *Trans. C.H.A.S.* i. 45; cf. *V.C.H. Cambs.* ii. 317.
56 *Early Yorks Chart.* iv. 10.
57 *Val. of Norwich*, ed. Lunt, 223; *Tax. Eccl.* (Rec. Com.), 267.
58 E 40/14290.
59 *Cal. Pat.* 1553, 153; C.R.O., R 59/5/3, p. 423.
60 Pemb. Coll. Mun., Linton, D 1–2, 4–5.
61 C.U.L., Doc. 643 nos. 225, 357.
62 Pemb. Coll. Mun., Linton, E 11; Barham, S 19, 23.
63 C.U.L., Doc. 643 nos. 225, 357.
64 Pemb. Coll. Mun., Barham, BB 1, ct. roll 10 Hen. VII.
65 C.U.L., Doc. 643 no. 360.
66 *Rot. Hund.* (Rec. Com.), ii. 419.
67 Pemb. Coll. Mun., Linton, C 3.
68 C.U.L., E.D.R., H 1/4, terrier 1615; Pemb. Coll. Mun, Barham, T 7.
69 C.R.O., Q/RDc 53.
70 Pemb. Coll. Mun., Linton, C 3.

cultivated with hoe or spade, both in closes and in common fields.[71] The vicars also faced claims to exemption from the Barham estate, to whose lords they had since 1566 let the small tithes therefrom for a rent[72] which the tenant of Barham Hall farm claimed after 1700 to be a modus.[73]

By the early 18th century the great tithes, though sometimes taken in kind, were frequently compounded for at 20*d*. an acre.[74] The small tithes, from the 17th century, were also mostly taken at fixed rates. In the 1760s they yielded £55–70 a year.[75] The vicar's gross receipts were increased from £120 a year *c*. 1800 to £175 by the 1820s.[76] The tithes were commuted in 1839, immediately after inclosure,[77] and the vicar received a tithe-rent-charge of £267 10*s*.[78]

The church of Linton was worth 30 marks in 1217 and £30 in 1276.[79] In 1291 the rectory was taxed at £20 and the vicarage at £5.[80] In 1535 the latter was worth £10 13*s*. 4*d*.[81] In 1650 it was thought to yield £30 a year,[82] and *c*. 1680 £28, without the disputed tithes. The vicar then thought the parish herdsman's place worth more than his living.[83] The net income rose from £50 a year in 1728[84] to just over £100 in the 1760s and 1770s,[85] and to *c*. £120 in the early 1820*s*.[86] About 1830 it was given as £204 net and in 1851 as £196.[87] It had risen to £260 net by 1877.[88]

About 1280 Geoffrey, then vicar, built a small house at the east end of the high street.[89] The house was inconveniently distant from the church, and in 1473 the vicar exchanged it with Pembroke College for a messuage south of the church.[90] The new vicarage probably remained in use until the early 18th century.[91] It had only four hearths in 1664,[92] and by 1783 was reckoned a mere cottage, while the vicar lived elsewhere.[93] In 1861 the vicar received permission to demolish it.[94] There was no glebe house in 1877,[95] and a 17th-century house north of the church was bought *c*. 1897.[96] It was replaced by a newly built house on the vicarage close *c*. 1965.

In the 13th century a chapel of St. Margaret was established at Barham, and the abbot of St. Jacut held his 32 a. there in 1279 partly by service of keeping it thatched. About 1250 Michael de Furneaux endowed it with 32 a.,[97] which was diverted to found the friary in 1293,[98] and the chapel was probably reserved for the friars. After the Reformation the small building was used until the late 18th century as a private chapel for Barham Hall, and eventually demolished with it.[99]

In 1308 Sir Walter Huntingfield was licensed to grant 60 a. to endow a chantry for his family in St. James's chapel, Linton.[1] It is uncertain whether it was in Linton church or at Little Linton. In 1466 Thomas Millicent and Henry Parys left money to guilds of St. Lawrence and the Trinity.[2] The latter survived until after 1523.[3] In 1507 Nicholas Wickham, then parish priest, left 10 marks to its aldermen and churchwardens as a stock to support an obit, and 2 marks towards making a new guildhall.[4] In 1508 Pembroke College leased out a plot of rectory land by the causeway running north-west from the church as a site for the hall, which was nearly completed in 1523.[5] Since it stood on leasehold ground it escaped confiscation when the guilds were suppressed, and was later converted to parish uses.[6] The building, which survived in 1974, is timber-framed, with a jettied upper storey on two sides and an original arched doorway with carved spandrels on the south. Inside are some original moulded ceiling beams. A guild of Our Lady was recorded in 1484.[7]

The medieval vicars usually resided, but especially in the late 14th century resigned the cure for others at frequent intervals.[8] One vicar fled the parish in 1437, pursued by charges of assault, robbery, rape, and attempted murder.[9] The vicars had usually one or more priests to assist them.[10] The first known pluralist vicar, James Hutton, D.C.L., vicar 1487–90, was chancellor and official to his patron the bishop of Ely.[11] His successor, Ralph Heton, 1490–1532, also held Duxford St. Peter and in the 1520s left Linton to his curates.[12] Some of the most valuable church plate, including a 5-lb. silver cross and silver censers, was sold shortly before the royal commissioners' visit in 1552.[13] Edward Lockton, vicar from *c*. 1546, was deprived for marriage in 1554 but restored by 1561 when he was living on a Somerset benefice.[14]

By the early 17th century Linton was coming under strong puritan influence. Thomas Newcomen, vicar 1582–8, a Crown nominee, rejected the Prayer Book and refused to wear his clerical headgear.[15] In 1605 Thomas Carmbrooke, then vicar, was presented

[71] Pemb. Coll. Mun., Linton, C 16; Barham, T 3, 5; E 112/623/54; E 126/16 f. 326 and v.; E 134/7 Wm. III Mich./2.
[72] Pemb. Coll. Mun., Barham, T 7 no. 9.
[73] Ibid. T 7, *passim*; E 112/1084/36; E 134/10 Geo. II Mich./3.
[74] Pemb. Coll. Mun., Linton, C 14, 15.
[75] C.R.O., P 107/3/1–2; L 95/4D.
[76] Ibid. P 107/1/5; L 95/39.
[77] C.U.L., Doc. 643 nos. 3, 14, 19, 24, 40, 50, 58–9.
[78] Ibid. Doc. 643 nos. 227–8, 231–3, 244, 250, 252.
[79] *Val. of Norwich*, ed. Lunt, 536, 555.
[80] *Tax. Eccl.* (Rec. Com.), 267.
[81] *Valor Eccl.* (Rec. Com.), iii. 504.
[82] Lamb. Pal. MS. 904, f. 269.
[83] E 134/7 Wm. III Mich./2 pts. 4–5.
[84] C.U.L., E.D.R., B 8/1.
[85] C.R.O., P 107/3/1–2.
[86] Ibid. L 95/39.
[87] *Rep. Com. Eccl. Revenues*, pp. 350–1; H.O. 129/188/2/4/4.
[88] C.U.L., E.D.R., C 3/27.
[89] Ibid. Palmer MS. A 56 (from J.I. 1/86).
[90] Pemb. Coll. Mun., Linton, C 3.
[91] e.g. C.U.L., E.D.R., B 8/1.
[92] E 179/244/22 f. 119.
[93] C.U.L., E.D.R., B 7/1.
[94] C.U.L., Palmer MS. A 58.
[95] C.U.L., E.D.R., C 3/27; B 1/39; cf. *E.D.R.* (1891), 588.
[96] C.U.L., E.D.R., C 3/38.
[97] *Rot. Hund.* (Rec. Com.), ii. 419.
[98] C 143/19 no. 14.
[99] Cf. B.L. Add. MS. 5848, ff. 148, 221.
[1] C 143/27 no. 23.
[2] Prob. 11/5 (P.C.C. 13, 14 Godyn).
[3] B.L. Add. MS. 5861, f. 100v.
[4] Prob. 11/16 (P.C.C. 7 Bennett).
[5] Pemb. Coll. Mun., Linton, H 1; B.L. Add. MS. 5861, 100v.
[6] See p. 98.
[7] *Trans. C.H.A.S.* i. 392.
[8] e.g. *E.D.R.* (1895), 109, 125; (1898), 19, 159, 177.
[9] Pemb. Coll. Mun., Barham, S 13, ct. roll 15 Hen. VI; cf. *Cal. Pat.* 1436–41, 178.
[10] e.g. *East Anglian*, N.S. xiii. 191; *E.D.R.* (1906), 188; (1907), 136.
[11] Emden, *Biog. Reg. Univ. Camb.* 323.
[12] Ibid. 216; cf. B.L. Add. MS. 5861, ff. 78, 106, 116v., 118.
[13] *Cambs. Ch. Goods, temp. Edw. VI*, 59.
[14] *E.D.R.* (1913), 41, 63, 210; B.L. Add. MS. 5813, f. 86; C.U.L., E.D.R., B 2/3, 4, 6.
[15] Gibbons, *Ely Episc. Rec.* 82, 436, 444.

for giving communion to the sick at home,[16] and by the 1630s there was a vigorous puritan party, which by 1635 had imported a Scottish schoolmaster.[17] Its members chafed at Carmbrooke's acceptance of Bishop Wren's 'superstitious' innovations and at his bringing Laudian fellows from Pembroke College to preach. In 1641 that party started a lecture at the weekly Thursday markets, and when Carmbrooke died in 1642 they petitioned for Parliament to empower them to elect 'a godly preaching minister'. Wren, however, had granted the patronage for the next turn to Pembroke College, which shortly presented a fellow, Roger Ashton. He obstructed the Thursday lectures, substituting Laudian preachers, and being himself non-resident appointed a like-minded curate.[18] Ashton fled in 1643. The living was sequestrated in 1644, and given to a succession of puritan ministers.[19] By 1649 it was held by Thomas Punter, who, although expelled from his Hadstock curacy in 1644,[20] was styled an 'orthodox and godly divine' in 1650 and had links with the Cambridge presbytery in 1658.[21] Two High-Church vicars were successively nominated in 1661–2,[22] but by 1663 Punter had conformed and was formally reinstated, retaining Linton until his death in 1684.[23]

William Stephens, vicar 1694–1720, also held Hadstock from 1696.[24] His successor, John Bernard, was resident, in lodgings, in 1728, holding two services on Sundays and on fast- and feast-days, and claiming that *c.* 40 people attended communions held every other month.[25] Later the vicarage was held by Edmund Fisher (d. 1819) from 1789 to 1800 and his son Edmund (d. 1851) from 1800 to 1844.[26] The younger Fisher had started a Sunday school by 1807, preached every Sunday, and raised the number of communicants to over 60.[27] In 1836 he held communion seven times a year.[28] In 1851 up to 550 people, besides 130 Sunday-school pupils, attended Sunday afternoon services.[29] In 1877 the vicar held two or three services, besides communions, every Sunday, and claimed up to 50 communicants weekly.[30] In 1897 the vicar employed district visitors to serve his growing congregation, which he reckoned at 1,200 church people, including 240 communicants. Besides three Sunday services he held others on weekdays.[31] He also held services in the workhouse chapel, to which the vicars had acted as chaplains for many years.[32] In the 1890s the church choir numbered 20,[33] and 40 or more in the 1960s.[34] By 1959 the congregation had declined to *c.* 11, but was revived by an energetic High-Church vicar.[35]

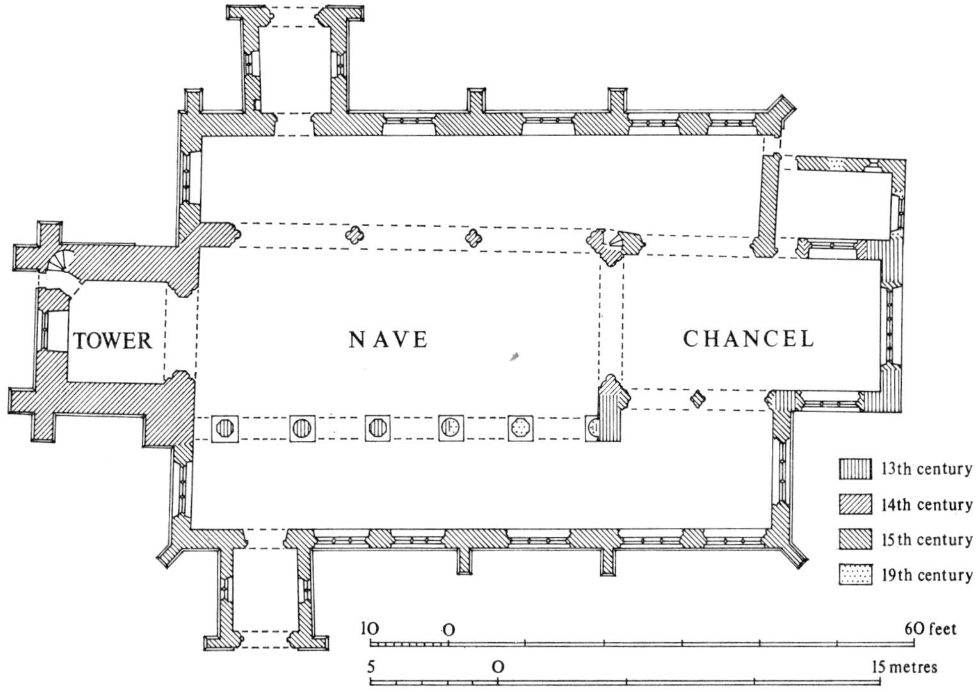

THE CHURCH OF ST. MARY, LINTON

[16] C.U.L., E.D.R., B 2/25, f. 9v.; cf. Hooker, *Works* (1890), ii. 104–5.
[17] C.U.L., E.D.R., B 2/47A, f. 4; Prob. 11/168 (P.C.C. 79 Sadler, will of Rog. Fulwell).
[18] B.L. Add. MS. 15672, ff. 22v.–23.
[19] *Walker Revised*, ed. Matthews, 77, 86; cf. E 134/7 Wm. III Mich./2 pts. 3, 5.
[20] Shaw, *Hist. Eng. Ch. 1640–60*, ii. 524; *Walker Revised*, ed. Matthews, 161–2.
[21] Lamb. Pal. MS. 904, f. 269; *Bury Classis*, ii (Chetham Soc. xli), 201.
[22] P.R.O., Inst. Bks. ser. B, i, p. 71.
[23] C.R.O., par. reg. TS., note *sub* 1663; *Alum. Cantab. to 1751*, iii. 407.
[24] *Alum. Cantab. to 1751*, iv. 157.
[25] C.U.L., E.D.R., B 8/1.
[26] *Alum. Cantab. to 1751*, ii. 142; *1752–1900*, ii. 500.
[27] C.U.L., E.D.R., C 1/4.
[28] Ibid. C 3/17, 21.
[29] H.O. 129/188/2/4/4.
[30] C.U.L., E.D.R., C 3/27; cf. B 1/16, 39.
[31] Ibid. C 3/38.
[32] *Kelly's Dir. Cambs.* (1900).
[33] C.U.L., E.D.R., C 3/38; *E.D.R.* (1893), 69–70.
[34] *Camb. News*, 11 Dec. 1964; *Camb. Ind. Press*, 16 June 1967.
[35] *Camb. Ind. Press*, 25 Jan. 1960; *Camb. Evening News*, 27 Mar. 1971.

The church of *ST. MARY*, so called in 1486,[36] is built of flint with ashlar dressings, and consists of a chancel with north vestry and north and south chapels, an aisled and clerestoried nave with north and south porches, and a west tower.[37] The earliest part of the surviving structure is the six-bay south arcade of *c.* 1200 with alternate circular and octagonal piers and pointed arches. Its clerestory, reopened in the 19th century, has alternate circular and quatrefoil windows. The chancel was rebuilt in the late 13th century and the north aisle of three bays added probably soon after 1300. Later in the 14th century the two eastern bays of the south arcade were combined into a single wide opening, matching the first bay of the north arcade,[38] and providing access to a transeptal chapel, and the chancel arch was rebuilt. The three-stage west tower was built at about that time; it lies partly within the western bay of the nave. The south chapel was probably built in the early 15th century, Nicholas Parys being buried there in 1425,[39] and the north chapel in the late 15th century. St. Lawrence's guild was enlarging the church to the north *c.* 1466.[40] Perhaps *c.* 1500 the aisles were rebuilt, and the nave walls were raised to support a low-pitched roof above a new clerestory, which was probably glazed in the early 16th century: it once contained armorial glass recalling the service of William Parys (d. 1520) to the archbishops of Canterbury.[41] The north and south porches, the vestry, and most of the lower windows are also of that period.

In 1644 William Dowsing destroyed the altar-rails and three crosses, defaced inscriptions, and broke some 80 windows.[42] The church needed much glazing under Charles II,[43] and what little medieval glass, mostly armorial, survived in 1742[44] later disappeared. About 1660 the interior was whitewashed and the piers marbled in black.[45] In the great storm of 1703 the spire of unknown date was blown down through the roof. Repairs were completed in 1705,[46] and the steeple was raised 10 ft. in 1797.[47] A singing gallery had been erected at the west end by 1742,[48] and further galleries were added in 1790 and 1831.[49] In 1870–1 the vicar, E. W. Wilkinson, swept away pews, galleries, and pulpit, and replaced the wide arch in the south arcade with two intended to match the earlier arches further west.[50] About 1879 Pembroke College repaired the chancel and north chapel.[51] The church was restored between 1887 and 1891, and again repaired in 1910.[52] The south chapel, latterly used for storage, was repaired and rededicated in 1964.[53]

On the chancel north wall are fragments of a former Jacobean screen, inserted after 1600, which once bore Bishop Heton's arms.[54] The south chapel, the Parys family's burial place, once contained, besides the brass for Nicholas Parys of an armoured man, which survived without its inscription in 1974, more than ten monuments of 1504–1673 to members of the Parys family.[55] The Millicents took over the north chapel, perhaps remodelling it, for the north doorway bore the date 1587.[56] Against the east wall is a large monument, with effigies, to John Millicent (d. 1686), his wife Alice (d. 1699), and his mother Douglas (d. 1655). Below was a brass to John Millicent (d. 1577).[57] The Millicents had their family pew in the chapel and objected when in 1702 the arch to the chancel was filled with a brick wall bearing a tablet to John Lone, lessee of the rectory, having a provocative epitaph; the wall was later demolished.[58] The two chapels remained attached respectively to the Catley and Barham estates, which were responsible for repairing them in 1783 and 1836.[59] Monuments in the chancel included mural ones to Robert Flack (d. 1705) and several of his children.[60] The large monument to Elizabeth (d. 1726) wife of Thomas Bacon, with an urn and obelisk between life-size statues of Hope and Faith, was carved by Joseph Wilton in 1782 under a bequest from her half-brother Peter Standly (d. 1780), whose bust appears on the obelisk, and who had left £1,000 for making it.[61]

A John Millicent left money to buy an organ in 1511,[62] but after the Reformation there was none until one was placed in the west gallery in 1847.[63] In 1552 there were four bells.[64] In 1557 two new ones were made.[65] The later set of five[66] comprised two by John Draper, dated 1617 and 1630, two by Miles and Christopher Gray, dated 1664 and 1665, and one of 1754 by Thomas Lester and Thomas Peck of London.[67] A small medieval bell was used between 1810 and 1900 as a clock bell in the tower,[68] where there had been a clock since 1610.[69]

There were three chalices *c.* 1350.[70] The parishioners succeeded in retaining both their silver-gilt chalices in 1552,[71] but by 1610 had replaced them with a silver cup and cover.[72] In 1791 Mrs. Lonsdale gave

36 Pemb. Coll. Mun., Barham, L 16.

37 Cf. W. M. Palmer, *Linton Church* (1909); below, plate facing p. 257.

38 Palmer, *Wm. Cole*, 103.

39 *Mon. Inscr. Cambs.* 231.

40 Prob. 11/5 (P.C.C. 13 Godyn, will of Thos. Milsent).

41 *Mon. Inscr. Cambs.* 107, 232; Prob. 11/19 (P.C.C. 31 Ayloffe).

42 *Trans. C.H.A.S.* iii. 84.

43 Palmer, *Linton Ch.* 39.

44 *Mon. Inscr. Cambs.* 105–7.

45 *Cambs. Episc. Visit. 1638–85*, ed. Palmer, 178.

46 C.U.L., Palmer MS. A 58; B.L. Add. MS. 5846, f. 48; Palmer, *Wm. Cole*, 103.

47 *Eng. Topog.* (Gent. Mag. Libr.), ii. 61.

48 *Proc. C.A.S.* xxxv. 79; Palmer, *Wm. Cole*, 103.

49 *Camb. Chron.* 5 June 1790; C.R.O., P 107/1/5, at end.

50 C.U.L., Palmer MS. A 56, letter 1935; A 58, faculty 1870.

51 *Kelly's Dir. Cambs.* (1879).

52 Ibid. (1888, 1896); cf. *E.D.R.* (1888), 173–4; (1911), 16; *Proc. C.A.S.* vii. 15–16.

53 *Camb. Evening News*, 27 Mar. 1971; *Camb. News*, 10 Jan., 17 Apr. 1964.

54 Palmer, *Wm. Cole*, 103.

55 *Mon. Inscr. Cambs.* 105–7, 231–2.

56 Palmer, *Linton Ch.* 12.

57 *Mon. Inscr. Cambs.* 108.

58 Ibid. 105; Pemb. Coll. Mun., Barham, T 6; C.U.L., Palmer MS. A 58.

59 C.U.L., E.D.R., B 7/1, p. 129; C 3/21.

60 *Mon. Inscr. Cambs.* 103–4.

61 B.L. Add. MS. 5808, ff. 59v.–60, 69v.–70v.

62 C.R.O., 331/Z 2, p. lxxxiv.

63 C.U.L., Palmer MS. B 61, corr. 1847; Palmer, *Linton Ch.* 34.

64 *Cambs. Ch. Goods, temp. Edw. VI*, 59.

65 Palmer, *Linton Ch.* 24, 31.

66 Cf. Palmer, *Wm. Cole*, 103; *Kelly's Dir. Cambs.* (1864–1937).

67 *Cambs. Bells* (C.A.S. 8vo ser. xviii), 156.

68 Ibid.; cf. Palmer, *Wm. Cole*, 103.

69 C.U.L., Palmer MS. A 20.

70 *Vetus Liber Arch. Elien.* (C.A.S. 8vo ser. xlviii), 62.

71 *Cambs. Ch. Goods, temp. Edw. VI*, 58–9.

72 C.U.L., Palmer MS. A 20 (from par. recs.).

a flagon, cup and paten, and two almsdishes, all of silver,[73] which the church still possessed *c.* 1960.

The older part of the churchyard was ordered to be closed in 1882,[74] but part remained in use[75] until a new cemetery, managed by the parish council, was opened in 1905.[76] The parish registers begin in 1559 and are virtually complete.[77]

ROMAN CATHOLICISM. The descendants of Sir Philip Parys, who had assisted in and profited from the Dissolution[78] but in 1558 left £10 a year for masses,[79] became recusants, and formed a small nucleus for Catholicism at Linton. Ferdinand Parys's wife Frances and her daughter Elizabeth were regularly presented for recusancy from the 1590s,[80] when Richard Carlton, gentleman, and two other Linton men were fined for recusancy.[81] After Philip Parys's death in 1617 the family normally lived in Norfolk, and only one papist was recorded at Linton in 1676.[82] By 1973 a small congregation of Catholics, usually worshipping at the village college, had its own priest-in-charge.[83]

PROTESTANT NONCONFORMITY. In 1662 6 men and 11 women refused to go to church,[84] and 17 people were presented for absence from church in 1675, 24 in 1678.[85] In 1676 there were 78 nonconformists compared with 428 conformists.[86] At first Quakers were most prominent, and by 1669 30 people, mostly women, were attending weekly meetings conducted by John Harvey, a Quaker grocer.[87] About 1672 there were six Quaker families,[88] and by 1690 they had a burial ground.[89] In 1706 a grocer was licensed to teach at a Quaker meeting-house.[90] There were 15 Quakers in 1728 but they seldom assembled,[91] and the sect had disappeared by the 1780s. Their meeting-house had been sold by 1793, and was demolished in 1921.[92]

By the 1690s there were also many Independents, mostly poor, who had their own minister and met every other Sunday.[93] A barn was licensed for their worship *c.* 1690,[94] and a chapel built in 1698 off Horn Lane west of the river. Inside, a large pulpit faced a singers' gallery over the door, and two other galleries were built in 1703–4. The congregation, including people from other parishes, numbered 83 adults in 1703, 147 in 1728.[95] In the mid 18th century there were *c.* 60 members. There were five ministers between 1698 and 1783, three of whom had eventually to remove elsewhere following disagreements with the congregation. About 1783 there were 27 dissenting families in Linton itself, who sometimes attended the parish church when their minister was absent.[96]

After 1783 the congregation had several temporary ministers, who nearly led it into Socinianism. In the 1790s there was a sharp division over a new minister. Attendance declined to *c.* 100 and there were only 17 full members, including 7 active ones from Linton itself, by 1797 when the larger faction called to be minister Thomas Hopkins, whose energy revived the chapel. In 1799 he started a Sunday school. He set up out-stations in neighbouring parishes, and induced the congregation to admit to communion all protestants professing Trinitarianism. The congregation was then divided into an inner circle of full members, of whom 140 were admitted during Hopkins's ministry, 1798–1839, and a larger group of subscribers, who attended services and shared in electing the minister and managing finances, but not in the chapel's discipline. In 1817 the old meeting-house was pulled down, and a new one on the same site was opened in 1818. An organ was installed in 1827. There were 46 full members in 1820, 74 in 1841, and 94 in 1848. In 1851 attendance averaged 280–350, besides 50 Sunday-school pupils.[97] By 1850 the chapel owned a manse near the Red Lion. Membership declined again to 74 by 1857 and 50 by 1879, but after the chapel had joined the Congregational Union in 1881 it recovered by 1905 to 105. In 1897 there were *c.* 300 dissenters in the parish. Thereafter membership fell steadily to 89 in 1935 and 44 in 1967.[98] By 1972 the chapel was affiliated to the United Reformed Church.[99] William Davey by will proved 1887 left £100, the interest to help repair the chapel.[1]

About 1840 the Primitive Methodists from Saffron Walden established a preaching station at Linton. In 1851 180 to 220 people were said to attend afternoon and evening services.[2] The Saffron Walden minister registered a building in Market Lane for their worship in 1852, and a Linton tailor registered another in 1853 and a third in the High Street, called the Zion chapel, in 1870.[3] The sect was still active in 1883, but by 1888 that chapel had been taken over as a hall by the Salvation Army,[4] which was still working at Linton in the 1970s.[5]

73 C.R.O., P 107/1/4, at end; list of ch. plate *penes V.C.H.*
74 *Lond. Gaz.* 5 May 1882, p. 2066.
75 C.U.L., E.D.R., C 3/38.
76 *E.D.R.* (1905), 49; cf. C.R.O., R 54/30/1, pp. 131, 173–6, 199, 202.
77 C.R.O., P 107/1/1–22.
78 e.g. *L. & P. Hen. VIII*, xiii (2), pp. 66, 92, 102; xv, p. 467.
79 Prob. 11/42A (P.C.C. 26 Welles).
80 e.g. C.U.L., E.D.R., B 2/13, f. 7; Bodl. MS. Gough Eccl. Top. 3, ff. 18–19.
81 *Recusants' Roll, 1592–3* (Cath. Rec. Soc. xviii), 13–15.
82 Compton Census.
83 *Camb. Evening News*, 12 Dec. 1973.
84 C.U.L., E.D.R., B 2/54, ff. 8v.–9v.
85 Ibid. B 2/63A, f. 14 and v.; B 2/62, ff. 36–7.
86 Compton Census.
87 *Orig. Rec. of Early Nonconf.* ed. Turner, i. 40.
88 *Proc. C.A.S.* lxi. 93.
89 Cf. C.U.L., Palmer MSS. A 20, 58.
90 C.R.O., Q/S 03, p. 69.
91 C.U.L., E.D.R., B 8/1.
92 Cf. C.R.O., R 59/14/11/10C, 10F, rentals 1725, 1793.
93 *Freedom after Ejection*, ed. Gordon, 11–12.
94 The following narrative until *c.* 1880 is based, unless otherwise stated, on C.U.L., Palmer MS. B 28, TS. of Ind. chapel accts. 1703–91; B 29, TS. copy of Hist. of Cong. chapel by Thos. Hopkins and others; cf. *Proc. C.A.S.* lxi. 82–3. For chapel life in the 18th century see also *Jnl. United Reformed Ch. Hist. Soc.* i. 174–8, which misdates the rebuilding of 1818.
95 C.U.L., E.D.R., B 8/1.
96 Ibid. B 7/1, p. 130.
97 H.O. 129/188/2/4/11.
98 C.U.L., E.D.R., C 3/38; *Cong. Yr. Bk.* (1905, 1935, 1967–8); *Kelly's Dir. Cambs.* (1908).
99 *Camb. Evening News*, 30 Nov. 1972.
1 *Char. Digest Cambs. 1863–4*, 10–11.
2 H.O. 129/188/2/4/9.
3 G.R.O. Worship Reg. nos. 448, 1374, 19561.
4 Ibid. no. 31082; C.U.L., E.D.R., C 3/27; cf. *Kelly's Dir. Cambs.* (1864–88).
5 *Kelly's Dir. Cambs.* (1900 and later edns.); *Camb. Ind. Press*, 30 Aug. 1973.

EDUCATION. John Lord, curate of Hildersham[6] (d. *c.* 1556), left £100 to Sir Philip Parys to establish a school at Linton. By his will of 1558 Parys directed that £10 a year be paid for 10 years to teach Linton children singing and simple grammar.[7] Linton from the 1570s to the 1630s had usually a resident schoolmaster, often a graduate,[8] and by 1600 a school-house stood in the north-west corner of the churchyard.[9] The churchwardens were maintaining it *c.* 1625.[10] The vicar was licensed to keep a school in 1696,[11] and a charity school had 20 pupils in 1724.[12] No parish school was recorded in the late 18th century,[13] but there were several private ones. The antiquary William Cole attended one kept by a dissenter in the 1720s.[14] Private boarding-schools flourished at Linton from the late 18th century to the mid 19th. One, transferred from Westley Waterless, was opened at the former Bull inn in 1777. Its pupils were taught languages, mathematics, surveying, and accounting.[15] In 1799 the school had 40 boarders and was called the Linton Academy,[16] and it continued until after 1814.[17] A rival boarding-school, started in 1804, lasted at least until 1813.[18] In the 1840s a similar school, called the Collegiate Academy, was kept in Horn Lane. It had 32 boarders in 1851,[19] and had closed by 1861.[20] A girls' boarding-school was kept at Linton from 1871 to 1896.[21]

For the poorer classes there were in 1818 6 or 8 dame-schools, which had *c.* 205 pupils, and the church and chapel Sunday schools, started by 1807 and in 1799, each with *c.* 60.[22] In 1833 the church Sunday school had *c.* 80 pupils, the dissenters *c.* 150, and in 15 day-schools, 14 opened since 1818, *c.* 240 children whose parents could pay for them were taught.[23] A National school was started in 1840. The lord of the manor gave the site, with a barn to be converted for the girls' schoolroom; a brick schoolroom for the boys, with a master's house, was built next to the barn. The school was supported by subscriptions and school-pence, and taught by a master and mistress, often husband and wife. In 1846 there were *c.* 80 pupils.[24] In 1851 there was said to be a British school with 130 pupils, later perhaps merged with the chapel Sunday school.[25]

Average attendance at the National school rose from 138 in 1851[26] to *c.* 250 between 1876 and 1893 and almost 300 by 1900. By 1877 it was divided into a mixed school for *c.* 200 children and an infants' department under the mistress with *c.* 120.[27] A night-school was started *c.* 1875, but attendance soon fell from 94 to 23.[28] The old National schoolhouse in Horn Lane, already twice enlarged, was rebuilt in 1896.[29] Attendance in both departments gradually declined until 1927, but by 1936 had risen again to 192.[30] After Linton village college was opened in 1931 the older children went there and the Church of England school became a junior mixed and infants' school with *c.* 100 children.[31] In 1960 there were *c.* 200.[32] In 1971 the county council decided to open a new primary school in the Hadstock road for children between 7 and 11, leaving the old buildings for the under-sevens.[33]

CHARITIES FOR THE POOR. William Millicent by will proved 1528 provided that within 3 years an alms-house should be built for four poor men and women upon a plot belonging to the Trinity guild just west of its guildhall. The rent of a granary to be built over the dwellings was to pay for their repair. The alms-folk were to be ejected if not contented. The management was to be shared with his heirs,[34] and the alms-house was reckoned a family foundation. His son Thomas (d. 1549) left it 33*s.* 4*d.* for 20 years,[35] and in 1561 Thomas's son John (d. 1577) took a 99-year lease from Pembroke College at a nominal rent of the two cottages used as alms-houses for two poor men and their wives.[36] When in 1697 the college let the plot to John Lone it gave him leave to remove and re-erect the alms-houses,[37] but they were apparently not demolished until 1794.[38]

William Thurgood by will dated 1551 left a £1 rent-charge for the poor. It was duly distributed until 1598 when the partition of the lands charged made it difficult to collect the money. In 1620 a commission of inquiry settled what proportion should be charged on each fraction of land,[39] and the amounts due were re-assessed six times between 1637 and 1803. In 1697 the parish agreed that the money should be distributed in bread every Sunday.[40] By 1783 the £1 was saved up and distributed every 6 or 7 years.[41] Because of the difficulty of tracing ownership collection was abandoned in 1831.[42]

Stephen Fulwell, a Linton-born London grocer, by will proved 1590 left £10 as a stock for the poor, which was received in 1618 and used as a loan

[6] Cf. *E.D.R.* (1912), 184.
[7] Prob. 11/42A (P.C.C. 26 Welles).
[8] e.g. Gibbons, *Ely Episc. Rec.* 175, 180, 183; C.U.L., E.D.R., B 2/11; B 2/32, f. 6; B 2/47A, f. 4.
[9] Pemb. Coll. Mun., Barham, T.i.c.
[10] C.U.L., Palmer MS. A 20 (from acct. 1625).
[11] B.L. Add. MS. 5846, f. 7v.
[12] Mary G. Jones, *Char. Sch. Movement*, 365.
[13] Cf. C.U.L., E.D.R., B 7/1; C 1/4.
[14] Palmer, *Wm. Cole*, 7; cf. B.L. Add. MS. 5812, f. 205.
[15] *Camb. Chron.* 28 June 1777.
[16] Ibid. 29 Oct., 31 Dec. 1796; 12 Oct., 23 Nov. 1799.
[17] Ibid. 19 July 1800; 26 Mar., 23 Apr. 1803; 10 June 1814.
[18] Ibid. 25 May, 7 Dec. 1805; 9 Apr. 1813.
[19] H.O. 107/66; H.O. 107/1761; *Gardner's Dir. Cambs.* (1851).
[20] R.G. 9/1029.
[21] R.G. 10/1592; *Kelly's Dir. Cambs.* (1879–96).
[22] *Educ. of Poor Digest*, 61.
[23] *Educ. Enquiry Abstract*, 58.
[24] Ed. 7/5; *Church School Inquiry, 1846–7*, 6–7; cf. C.R.O., R 59/5/8B, nos. 2–3.
[25] *Gardner's Dir. Cambs.* (1851); cf. *E.D.R.* (1885), 73–4; (1889), 353; *Camb. Ind. Press*, 15 Jan. 1960.
[26] *Mins. of Educ. Cttee. of Council, 1852–3* [1623], p. 319, H.C. (1852–3), lxxix.
[27] *Rep. of Educ. Cttee. of Council, 1876–7* [C. 1780-I], p. 740, H.C. (1877), xxix; *1892–3* [C. 7089-I], p. 688, H.C. (1893–4), xxvi; *Schs. in receipt of Parl. Grants, 1900–1*, [Cd. 703], p. 15, H.C. (1901), lv; C.R.O., R 59/5/8B, no. 4; *Kelly's Dir. Cambs.* (1879).
[28] C.U.L., E.D.R., C 3/27.
[29] *E.D.R.* (1892), 700; *Kelly's Dir. Cambs.* (1888, 1904).
[30] *Bd. of Educ., List 21, 1900* (H.M.S.O.), 24; *1919*, 16; *1927*, 16; *1936*, 17.
[31] Ibid. *1938*, 20.
[32] *Camb. Ind. Press*, 15 Jan. 1960.
[33] *Camb. Evening News*, 3 Dec. 1971; 7 Jan. 1972.
[34] B.L. Add. MS. 5861, f. 100v.
[35] Pemb. Coll. Mun., Barham, B 5.
[36] Ibid. Y 6.
[37] Ibid. Linton, H 3.
[38] Palmer, *Linton Ch.* opp. pl. 2.
[39] C 93/8/9; cf. C.U.L., E.D.R., B 2/25, f. 9v.
[40] C.R.O., P 107/25/1; cf. C.U.L., E.D.R., B 8/1.
[41] C.U.L., E.D.R., B 7/1, p. 130.
[42] *31st Rep. Com. Char.* 105.

charity.[43] Record of it has not been found after the 17th century.

Elizabeth Harrison (d. *c.* 1800) left £100, paid by 1809, the interest to be distributed to the poor. The income, £6 *c.* 1815, was being given in bread in 1837, in proportion to the size of the recipients' families.[44] In 1924 124 loaves were given out. By the 1940s the poor were reluctant to collect their loaves publicly; credit was given at a baker's instead, but since few claimants came forward distribution lapsed. Later the money was distributed in kind in other ways. In 1961 the charity income was £2 10*s*.[45]

Sarah Jane Butt by will proved 1924 left £70 a year in reversion, which bequest took full effect in 1961, to buy coal for the poor of Linton. The income, £40 a year from 1924, £70 from 1961, was used to buy coal in 1964.[46]

J. Brinckmann left £500 *c.* 1918 to the parish council for coal and other goods for the poor. Distribution had begun by 1922.[47] The parish council presumably retained the endowment in 1974.

PAMPISFORD

PAMPISFORD, known until the 17th century as 'Pampesworth', is a small parish 7 miles south-east of Cambridge.[1] Its eastern boundary follows the Roman road that runs north from Stump Cross, and sections of the western and northern boundaries coincide with the river Cam or Granta and the river Granta respectively, while for the rest the edges of the parish follow irregular field boundaries. In 1801 an ancient cross stood at the south-east corner of the parish.[2] Pampisford covers 1,607 a. Its western half is all below 100 ft., but in the east the land rises from 100 to 175 ft. on the edge of the Essex uplands. The soil is light, lying over the Middle Chalk.[3] Unlike the adjoining parish of Sawston, Pampisford has remained predominantly agricultural throughout its recorded history. The land was farmed in open fields until inclosure in 1801.

The parish contains the western half of the Brent ditch, the most southerly of a series of five ancient earthworks. The ditch was known locally from the Middle Ages as the green ditch.[4] Its original purpose was probably defensive: excavation in 1968 revealed the remains of a bank on the north side of the ditch.[5] The ditch has been filled at the point where the Icknield Way crosses it.

About 25 inhabitants were at Pampisford in 1086.[6] By 1279 there were at least 64 tenants there, and in 1377 109 people paid the poll tax.[7] In 1524, however, there were only 39 taxpayers, and 31 households were recorded in 1563.[8] Population had probably changed little by the 1660s, when there were *c.* 35 households.[9] Eighty-nine adults were enumerated at Pampisford in 1676.[10] There were 40 families by 1728,[11] and 46 in 1801 comprising 202 people. The population rose gradually to a peak of 359 in 1851, but as in other Cambridgeshire villages it declined thereafter, reaching its lowest point in 1931 with 237 people. The growth of the village since then has increased its population to 340 in 1951 and 370 in 1971.[12]

Three main roads run through the parish. The Royston–Newmarket road bisects it from south-west to north-east: several 16th-century testators left loads of stones to repair it.[13] It was a turnpike from 1769 to 1874.[14] The road from Stump Cross to Newmarket and the road from Saffron Walden to Cambridge, which crosses the south-west corner, were both turnpiked under an Act of 1724 and disturnpiked in 1870.[15] The Sawston bypass, opened in 1968, diverges from the main road in Pampisford parish.[16] The railway line from Chesterford to Six Mile Bottom, opened in 1848 and closed only three years later, ran close to the eastern boundary of the parish, where the embankment survived in 1973.[17] A station was built near Bourn Bridge on the site later occupied by the Railway Inn.[18] The line from Great Shelford to Haverhill, opened in 1865, ran across the northern part of the parish, and Pampisford station was built close to the former Bourn Bridge station. The line was closed in 1967,[19] and by 1973 the tracks had been removed and the station was derelict.

The half of the parish south-east of the Royston–Newmarket road was uninhabited until Pampisford Hall was built there in the 19th century, when much of the surrounding land became gardens and parkland. The village had grown up *c.* 400 yd. north-west of the road along a single street, with Manor Farm and the old vicarage at each end of the street and the church in the middle. Settlement has always been fairly dispersed, however, and other houses stand along the minor roads linking the village with the main road and with Sawston. Throughout its recorded history the village has been small and poor.

43 C.R.O., L 95/14, f. 21.
44 Ibid.; *Poor Law Abstract, 1818*, 28–9.
45 Char. Com. files; C.R.O., R 54/30/1, p. 396.
46 Char. Com. files.
47 C.R.O., R 54/30/1, pp. 335–6, 361.
1 This account was written in 1973.
2 C.R.O., Q/RDz 6, p. 135.
3 Vancouver, *Agric. in Cambs.* 66.
4 C.U.L., Queens' Coll. Mun. 17/30.
5 *Proc. C.A.S.* lxii. 30–1; cf. Fox, *Arch. Camb. Region*, 126; *V.C.H. Cambs.* ii. 10–11.
6 *V.C.H. Cambs.* i. 365, 374; cf. ibid. 410.
7 *Rot. Hund.* (Rec. Com.), ii. 414–16; E 179/149/41.
8 E 179/81/134 m. 2; B.L. Harl. MS. 594, f. 200.
9 See p. 279.
10 Compton Census.
11 C.U.L., E.D.R., A 4/2; B 8/1.
12 *Census*, 1801–1971.
13 B.L. Add. MS. 5861, pp. 179, 189.
14 Bourn Bridge Road Turnpike Act, 8 & 9 Geo. III, c. 86; Annual Turnpike Acts Continuance Act 1873, 36 & 37 Vic. c. 90.
15 Stump Cross Roads Turnpike Act, 10 Geo. I, c. 12; Annual Turnpike Acts Continuance Act 1870, 33 & 34 Vic. c. 73.
16 *Camb. News*, 22 Sept. 1967.
17 *V.C.H. Cambs.* ii. 133.
18 *Proc. C.A.S.* xxxi. 1.
19 *V.C.H. Cambs.* ii. 133; Clinker and Firth, *Reg. of Closed Stns.*

The church, which underwent substantial alterations and additions in the 12th, 13th, and 14th centuries, is the only surviving medieval building, and Rectory Farm, the old vicarage, and the Chequers are all that remain of a number of 16th- and 17th-century farm-houses. Some cottages in Brewery Road and Beech Lane date from the 17th and 18th centuries.

The population in 1851 was 'almost entirely composed of poor people',[20] but the Parker Hamonds, the first lords of the manor to live in the parish since the 15th century, brought improvements by supporting the school, the church, a Workmen's Institute, and other institutions.[21] The establishment of a brewery, and the growth of industry nearby at Sawston, provided more employment, but Pampisford remained poor and the vicar in 1877 reported some emigration.[22] Part of Sawston's leather industry spread into the parish of Pampisford, when the Eastern Counties Leather Co. Ltd. was established in 1879 at Langford Arch.[23] From *c.* 1880 houses began to spread eastwards along Brewery Road from Sawston. A few council houses have been built in the 20th century in Brewery Road and Church Lane, but most recent building in Pampisford has been by infilling near the centre of the village, particularly in Hamond Close and Glebe Crescent, two new roads created by developers.[24]

The Chequers, a 16th-century building in the centre of the village, was probably open as an inn by 1792.[25] Its thatched roof was destroyed in a fire in 1973.[26] The White Horse, at the junction of Brewery Road and the road from Cambridge to Saffron Walden, was open by 1841[27] and survived in 1973, as did the Railway Inn, opposite Pampisford station, opened *c.* 1900.[28] The Ploughboy, open in 1871, closed *c.* 1965.[29]

The village feast was held in the 1880s on the first Monday in July.[30] On Plough Monday farm workers used to pull a plough down the main street to Manor and Home Farms.[31]

John Webb of Pampisford, a leader of the Peasants' Revolt in Cambridgeshire, was prominent in the attack on Steeple Morden manor and the sale of its goods. He was beheaded at Royston on 6 July 1381.[32]

MANORS AND OTHER ESTATES. A large estate in Pampisford was given to the abbey of Ely by the ealdorman Beorhtnoth from his death in 991.[33] In 1086 the estate comprised 2¾ hides, and another 10 a. were held from the abbot by Hardwin de Scalers, and under him as in 1066 by Snellinc.[34] The Ely lands, known as the manor of *PAMPISFORD*, were granted by Bishop Hervey by 1127 to his nephew William, archdeacon of Ely, for 1 knight's service. Bishop Niel recovered the manor in 1135, but by or after 1166 it was granted away again as 1 knight's fee to Walter of Pampisford.[35] Walter of Ely held the land *c.* 1212 and in 1224.[36] By 1271 it was in the possession of Henry son of Aucher, who had married Ela, heir to the estate, and in 1272 was granted free warren at Pampisford.[37] On Henry's death in 1303 the manor passed to his son Aucher,[38] who was still alive in 1331.[39] His widow Joan married Sir John Shardelowe, who held the manor in 1346.[40] They released it in 1353 to John Cloville whose wife Christine is said to have been Aucher's daughter and heir.[41] The manor passed after 1374 to John's son William; he or his eldest son William (d.s.p.) owned it in 1412.[42] Catherine Cloville, probably the widow of the elder or younger William, held both the Pampisford manors in 1428.[43]

Walter Cloville, brother of William the younger, had succeeded her by 1434. On his death in 1444 or 1445 the manor passed to his younger brother Henry (d. 1453).[44] Henry's son John died in 1489, having enfeoffed his son Henry of his manors.[45] Henry Cloville (d. 1514) was succeeded by his son William (d. 1526);[46] William's widow Mary held Pampisford in 1547 and was followed by their son Francis (d. 1562) and Francis's son Eustace.[47] In 1584 Eustace Cloville sold his estate to Thomas Marsh (d. 1587), a Star Chamber notary, whose son Thomas, sheriff of Cambridgeshire in 1594, held it until his death in 1624 and was succeeded by his son Thomas, sheriff in 1648.[48] The third Thomas died in 1657, leaving the manor to his grandson Thomas who was knighted in 1661 and died in 1677. Sir Thomas's son Edward died without issue in 1701, having devised Pampisford to his wife Grace for life with remainder to William Parker, her eldest son by a previous marriage.[49]

William Parker (d. 1728) was lord of the manor by 1711,[50] having probably succeeded his mother in 1706.[51] William's widow Elizabeth still held the lordship in 1751.[52] Their only son William had succeeded her by 1756 and died without issue in 1776,[53] and his estates were divided between his sisters Grace and Elizabeth. Grace died in 1781, having

[20] H.O. 129/188/1/2/2.
[21] *E.D.R.* (1892), 841.
[22] C.U.L., E.D.R., C 3/27.
[23] See p. 256.
[24] C.R.O., 515/SP 2426.
[25] Ibid. L 57/20.
[26] *Camb. Evening News,* 12 May 1973.
[27] H.O. 107/66.
[28] *Kelly's Dir. Cambs.* (1904).
[29] R.G. 10/1591.
[30] *Proc. C.A.S.* vi. 385.
[31] Porter, *Cambs. Customs,* 98.
[32] *Cambs. Village Doc.* 31.
[33] *V.C.H. Cambs.* ii. 200; *Liber Elien.* (Camd. 3rd ser. xcii), pp. 135–6.
[34] *V.C.H. Cambs.* i. 365, 410.
[35] E. Miller, *Abbey and Bishopric of Ely,* 168, 280; *Liber Elien.* pp. 287–8; *Red Bk. Exch.* (Rolls Ser.), i. 364.
[36] *Red Bk. Exch.* ii. 525; *Cur. Reg. R.* xi, p. 331.
[37] *Cal. Pat.* 1266–72, 518; *Cal. Chart. R.* 1257–1300, 184; cf. Farrer, *Honors and Kts.' Fees,* ii. 290–1.
[38] *Cal. Inq. p.m.* iv, p. 112.
[39] *Cal. Pat.* 1330–4, 186.
[40] *Feud. Aids,* i. 163; cf. Morant, *Essex,* i. 48, 140.
[41] C.P. 25(1)/28/77 no. 16; Morant, *Essex,* ii. 37.
[42] *Cal. Inq. p.m.* xiv, p. 29; *Feud. Aids,* vi. 408; *Visit. Essex,* i (Harl. Soc. xiii), 180–1.
[43] *Feud. Aids,* i. 182.
[44] *Cal. Pat.* 1429–36, 385; Prob. 11/3 (P.C.C. 30 Luffenam); Lamb. Pal. Reg. Stafford and Kemp, f. 293v.
[45] *Cal. Inq. p.m. Hen. VII,* i, p. 205.
[46] Morant, *Essex,* ii. 37; C 142/78 no. 131; C 142/45 no. 91.
[47] C 1/1181 nos. 40–2; Morant, *Essex,* ii. 37.
[48] *Cambs. Fines,* 1485–1603, ed. Palmer, 91; C 142/214 no. 218; C 142/408 no. 118.
[49] F. C. Cass, *South Mimms* (1877), 53–4, 56 (pedigree).
[50] Ct. bk. *penes* Mr. H. B. Binney, Pampisford Hall.
[51] He is said to have bought the manor in 1706: C.U.L., proof copy of E. Hailstone, unpubl. hist. Swaffham Bulbeck, p. 75.
[52] Ct. bk. *penes* Mr. Binney.
[53] Ibid.; Palmer, *Wm. Cole,* 106.

devised her moiety to her sister, the widow of William Hamond (d. 1777). The whole manor descended on Elizabeth's death in 1789 to her son William Parker Hamond,[54] who died in 1812. The estate descended to his son William Parker Hamond (d. 1873) and grandson of the same name (d. 1884). On the death of the third William Parker Hamond the estate passed to his cousin, Col. R. T. Hamond, who sold the lordship and most of his Pampisford lands in 1893 to James Binney.[55] Binney was succeeded in 1935 by his son, R. C. C. J. Binney, who died in 1966 when the estate passed to his brother Mr. H. B. Binney.

The manor held of Ely probably had a manor-house in 1303, perhaps on one of the two moated sites north-east of the village.[56] Manor Farm, also called Lordship Farm, was called a manor-house in 1806,[57] but the lords of the manor were non-resident from the mid 15th to the mid 19th century. Pampisford Hall was built by William Parker Hamond *c.* 1830 on former farm land. The house was apparently a moderate-sized villa with the principal rooms along the south-east front. The service wing was probably rebuilt and the roofs altered in the mid 19th century. Shortly after the sale of the family estate at Croydon (Surr.) in the 1860s[58] Parker Hamond enlarged Pampisford Hall and put in a new grand staircase and dining-room from designs by George Goldie. All the principal rooms were redecorated in the Italian and French Renaissance styles in 1875, when William Parker Hamond (d. 1884) succeeded to the property, and they have been little altered since that time.[59] In 1912 a ball-room was built on the northern end of the house, replacing the servants' hall, and a new west wing was added. The park, which covered 164 a. in the 1860s, was already notable for its trees by the mid 19th century.[60] The formal gardens were designed by G. Marnock. The park contains a fine collection of conifers including over 1,000 foreign species specially imported by the Parker Hamond and Binney families.[61]

The land which became the second manor of *PAMPISFORD* was held before 1066 by Almar from Eddeva the fair, and covered over 1¼ hide. At the Conquest it was given to Count Alan of Brittany, from whom it was held in 1086 by two knights, Ralph de Banks and Ralph Brito. Its overlordship descended thenceforth with the honor of Richmond.[62] Ralph de Banks was lord of the manor in 1224, and *c.* 1235.[63] By 1271 Sir Hugh de Brok held it in right of his wife Isabel,[64] with whom in 1281 he granted it to Robert Ludham for life. Ludham still held it when, after Hugh's death *c.* 1290, Isabel granted the reversion in 1293 to John, parson of Long Itchington (Warws.),[65] from whom it passed to Sir Richard of Wells. By 1302 Wells had granted it to Richard le Breton and his wife Joan for her life, and in 1306 granted his reversionary interest to William Goldington.[66] In 1309 Goldington granted the reversion, from the death of Joan, then remarried to Sir John de Crek, lord in 1316, to John Hinton. In 1319 Hinton conveyed it to Aucher son of Henry, who in 1321 bought out Crek's and Joan's life-interest.[67] The two manors subsequently descended together.[68]

In 1086 there were also several smaller estates. Picot the sheriff had ¾ hide, held from him by Ralph de Banks, and formerly held freely by Edric, the man of Alfric Child; Hardwin de Scalers held, besides his 10 a. of Ely land, 15 a. held in 1066 by two sokemen from King Edward. Eudes the steward's 5 a. were probably attached to his Sawston estate, being held from him by Pirot, and formerly by Burro from Alfric Campe.[69] None of those estates has been traced after 1086.

Two small estates in Pampisford were attached to Hinxton manor. About 1235 William Ferrard and Robert Saffrey (d. by 1242) had held ½ hide of the honor of Richmond.[70] In 1279 John Martin held 30 a. and Robert Saffrey 60 a. of John de Camoys, lord of Hinxton.[71] John Martin still held his land in 1302–3, and a namesake held it in 1346, but by 1428 that fee had passed to Catherine Cloville.[72] William Saffrey, or Reed, held in 1286 from John Stourton, lord of Hinxton, two-thirds of the 100 a. which he held at his death in 1325.[73] His son Brian Saffrey, then aged 14, died in 1349, leaving as heir his daughter Alice.[74] Adam Cove (d. after 1412)[75] owned Brian's lands by 1395. The estate, known as Saffreys in 1402, had by 1519 been acquired by Queens' College, Cambridge.[76] The college then held 187 a. in Pampisford, which had increased by 1524 to 232 a., probably by the addition of an estate called Cockfarnams.[77] The two estates were always leased separately by the college; Saffreys in 1768 covered 170 a., and Cockfarnams, or Cock farm, 50 a.[78] The college owned 200 a. after inclosure in 1801, but held no land in the parish by 1873, and in 1893 College farm with 258½ a., the former Queens' estate, was sold with the Hamond lands.[79] William Saffrey had a capital messuage in 1325.[80] There was a tenement with Saffreys in 1530, which in 1571 stood next to Saffreys grove which was surrounded by a hedge and ditch, suggesting a former moated

54 Parker Hamond Estates Act, 42 Geo. III, c. 53 (Private and Personal, not printed).
55 Burke, *Land. Gent.* (1906), i. 763–4; C.U.L., Maps bb. 53(1)/89/14.
56 *Cal. Inq. p.m.* iv, p. 112; *V.C.H. Cambs.* ii. 37.
57 C.R.O., L 70/34.
58 *V.C.H. Surr.* iv. 222.
59 *Kelly's Dir. Cambs.* (1879); see below, plate facing p. 113.
60 *Kelly's Dir. Cambs.* (1879); ex inf. Mr. Binney.
61 C.U.L., Maps bb. 53(1)/89/14.
62 *V.C.H. Cambs.* i. 374, 410; *Rot. Hund.* (Rec. Com.), ii. 414.
63 *Cur. Reg. R.* xi, pp. 331, 517; *Liber de Bernewelle*, 255.
64 *Cal. Pat.* 1266–72, 518; *Rot. Hund.* (Rec. Com.), ii. 414.
65 C.P. 25(1)/25/39 no. 6; *Cal. Pat.* 1281–92, 375; C.P. 25(1)/26/44 no. 19.
66 *Cal. Close*, 1296–1302, 589–90; C.P. 25(1)/26/50 no. 15.
67 C.P. 25(1)/26/52 no. 28; *Feud. Aids*, i. 155; C.P. 25(1)/27/59 no. 16; C.P. 25(1)/27/60 no. 23.
68 Cf. *Feud. Aids*, i. 163.
69 *V.C.H. Cambs.* i. 384–5, 392, 410.
70 *Liber de Bernewelle*, 255; *Cambs. Fines*, 1196–1485 (C.A.S. 8vo ser. xxvi), 24–5.
71 *Rot. Hund.* (Rec. Com.), ii. 415–16.
72 *Feud. Aids*, i. 145, 163, 182.
73 *Cal. Pat.* 1281–92, 238; *Cal. Inq. p.m.* vi, p. 362. For William's name and identity, see *V.C.H. Wilts.* viii. 37.
74 *Cal. Inq. p.m.* ix, pp. 258–9.
75 C.P. 25(1)/30/94 no. 21.
76 C.U.L., Queens' Coll. Mun. 17/27–8; 13/5, ff. 49–52v.
77 Ibid. 13/5, ff. 52, 60v.
78 Ibid. 17/41.
79 C.R.O., Q/RDz 6; *Rep. Com. Univ. Income* [C. 856-II], H.C. (1873), xxxvii (3); C.U.L., Maps bb. 53(1)/89/14.
80 *Cal. Inq. p.m.* vi, p. 362.

site.[81] In the later 17th century the college's lessees occupied the largest house in the village, taxed on 9 hearths.[82]

The rectory of Pampisford, valued at £11 5*s.* in 1535,[83] had been appropriated to Blackborough priory (Norf.) in 1377.[84] The priory was dissolved in 1536, and the rectory was sold by the Crown in 1553 to Thomas Wren and Edward Slegge.[85] In 1561 Charles Huddleston, younger son of John Huddleston (d. 1530), conveyed it to John Lockton.[86] Edward Wood of Fulbourn owned the rectory in 1579, and died in 1599. His son John sold it in 1600 to James Alington[87] (d. 1626). James devised it to his nephew Sir Giles Alington of Horseheath, who was succeeded in 1638 by his son William.[88] By 1641 the owner was Theophilus Tyrrell of Bartlow.[89] He or a namesake held the advowson until his death in 1707. The rectory passed then to Elizabeth Tyrrell, widow, perhaps his daughter-in-law, who presented to the vicarage until her death in 1767.[90] Pampisford rectory was bought before 1799 by John Mortlock, the Cambridge banker, whose family had been settled at Pampisford since the 15th century. At inclosure in 1801 he was awarded 110 a. for the rectorial glebe and 235½ a. for the great tithes.[91] On John's death in 1816 the land and advowson descended to his second son Thomas (d. 1859), and then to Thomas's nephew E. J. Mortlock[92] who had sold Rectory farm by 1892. It belonged in that year to H. J. W. Asplen; the owner in 1925 was A. E. Fordham (d. 1949).[93]

ECONOMIC HISTORY. Of the 5 hides in Pampisford in 1086, the abbot of Ely held a quarter in demesne. There were 3 *servi* on his estate, and the Ely and Richmond demesnes were cultivated by 3 of the 9 plough-teams. The rest of the land was worked by 14 *villani* and 10 or 7 bordars. Apart from the Richmond estate, which had temporarily fallen in value at the Conquest, all the estates were worth the same in 1086 as in 1066.[94]

In 1279 Sir Hugh de Brok held 160 a. of arable in demesne, Robert Saffrey 60 a., and John Martin 30 a.; each estate had some free and some customary tenants. Holdings of more than 5 a. were rare, except that of the recorded 15 villeins of Henry son of Aucher 7 held 9 a. each. All the villeins on his manor owed services, including up to 4 harvest-boons, and in at least three cases the obligation to appear at the eyre with the reeve and 4 men. Three tenants on the Hinxton fees owed 1 or 2 boon-works, the others rendering only rents.[95] In 1303 Henry son of Aucher had 20 free tenants, besides 24 customary tenants who paid rents of assize and worked on one day a week between Easter and Michaelmas only.[96] Some of William Saffrey's tenants owed works in 1299, but by 1395 all the services on the estate had been commuted.[97]

The pattern of the open fields was settled by the 15th century, when Branditch, Middle, Mill, and Down or Dean fields were recorded.[98] The same field-names were used from then until inclosure,[99] though Dean field may have been small or only occasionally cultivated, for there were only three open fields in 1794 and a note of the fields' acreage in 1799 omitted Dean field altogether. On the eve of inclosure Middle field covered 301½ a., Branditch field 493½ a., and Mill field 353 a.[1]

Sheep were recorded in 1086,[2] and sheep-farming was widely practised in the 14th century, although there were no very large flocks; in 1347 John Shardelowe contributed 9½ stone of wool, and his shepherd Nicholas another 4 stone, to the parish's total of 53 stone paid for a levy of wool, the rest of the assessment coming from 32 others.[3] Livestock remained less important than arable farming: in 1794 there were *c.* 400 sheep at Pampisford; their numbers were expected to fall as a result of inclosure.[4] The only liberty of foldage recorded belonged to Queens' College in 1652 and 1689.[5]

The main crops mentioned in the 16th century were barley, some of which was malted, and rye.[6] Saffron was grown by 1527, and until the early 18th century.[7] Turnips were grown in the 18th century,[8] and there were over 100 a. of wheat in 1806. Arable production was expected to rise by one-sixth as a consequence of inclosure.[9]

Ownership of land in the parish was already concentrated in a few hands by the 16th century. The non-resident lords of the manor owned a large estate, which they often leased to yeomen from neighbouring parishes.[10] Leases of the Queens' College farms were also sometimes held by outsiders,[11] and the group of yeoman farmers in Pampisford was a small one. The Mortlock and Turtylby

[81] C.U.L., Queens' Coll. Mun. 55, lease 21 Hen. VIII; 17/35.
[82] E 179/84/436 rot. 27; E 179/84/437 rot. 58; E 179/244/23 rot. 55.
[83] *Valor Eccl.* (Rec. Com.), iii. 395.
[84] *E.D.R.* (1895), 91.
[85] *V.C.H. Norf.* ii. 351; *Cal. Pat.* 1553, 218, 221.
[86] C.P. 25(2)/93/832/3 Eliz. I Hil. no. 4; Wards 9/129 f. 137v.
[87] C.U.L., E.D.R., D 2/10, f. 155; C 142/262 no. 104; C.P. 25(2)/94/864/42 Eliz. I Mich. no. 22.
[88] C 142/434 no. 85; Gibbons, *Ely Episc. Rec.* 321; P.R.O. Inst. Bks. ser. A, iii, p. 32.
[89] C 3/435/32; P.R.O. Inst. Bks. loc. cit.
[90] P.R.O. Inst. Bks. ser. B, iv, p. 147; ser. C, i, f. 447v.; *Mon. Inscr. Cambs.* 9. The Theophilus named as patron in 1694–7 was distinguished as the elder.
[91] Pampisford Incl. Act, 39 Geo. III, c. 120 (Private and Personal, not printed); *Proc. C.A.S.* xl. 2, 6; C.R.O., Q/RDz 6.
[92] *E.D.R.* (1898), 199; *Kelly's Dir. Cambs.* (1904).
[93] *Kelly's Dir. Cambs.* (1892, 1925).
[94] *V.C.H. Cambs.* i. 365, 374, 392, 410.
[95] *Rot. Hund.* (Rec. Com.), ii. 414–16. The document is defective for the manors of Sir Hugh de Brok and Henry son of Aucher.
[96] C 133/110 no. 9.
[97] C.U.L., Queens' Coll. Mun. 17/26–7.
[98] Ibid. 17/30.
[99] e.g. ibid. 17/35 (1571); 17/41 (18th cent.); C.U.L., E.D.R., H 1/5, terriers 1615, 1639.
[1] Vancouver, *Agric. in Cambs.* 66; C.U.L., Add. MS. 7312 (back).
[2] *V.C.H. Cambs.* i. 410.
[3] E 179/242/8 m. 5.
[4] Vancouver, *Agric. in Cambs.* 67; Gooch, *Agric. of Cambs.* 61.
[5] C.U.L., Queens' Coll. Mun. 55, lease 1652; 17/42.
[6] B.L. Add. MS. 5861, pp. 23, 179, 189, 198.
[7] Ibid. pp. 189, 198; C.U.L., E.D.R., H 1/5, terrier 1639; ibid. A 4/2; Prob. 11/306 (P.C.C. 179 May, will of Frances Jeapes).
[8] C.U.L., Queens' Coll. Mun. 17/40; Vancouver, *Agric. in Cambs.* 66.
[9] Gooch, *Agric. of Cambs.* 61.
[10] e.g. Arthur Holt of Sawston in 1598: C 2/Eliz. I/M 14/25.
[11] e.g. the Twyne family of Hinxton, lessees of Cock farm in the late 16th and early 17th century: C.U.L., Queens' Coll. Mun. 55, lease 1568; 17/36; 17/39.

families were both prominent: John Mortlock owned 72 a. at his death in 1613.[12] By the 18th century only Queens' College and the lords of the manor held estates of any size.

The parish contained a 'moor' or common of *c.* 150 a. by the 16th century, on which cows and horses were pastured in summer and sheep in winter.[13] Of the 155 a. called the Hay 51 a. were intercommonable with Sawston, and in 1675 there was also an intercommon in Branditch field, probably shared with Great Abington.[14] About 20 a. of meadow by the river Cam or Granta were intercommonable with Whittlesford from the end of the hay harvest until Lady Day (25 March), with a bite on Easter Sunday which destroyed most of the hay crop when Easter fell late.[15]

The parts of the parish unsuitable for tillage were used for pasture and meadow: old inclosures half belonging to the lord covered 180 a. in 1801.[16] There were closes in the Brent ditch and at least 27 crofts in the parish ranging in size from ½ a. to 28 a. in the later 16th century.[17] An Act for inclosing the whole parish was obtained in 1799,[18] and the award was made in 1801. There were then *c.* 1,250 a. of open fields and commons. The allotments confirmed the dominance of the few large proprietors; William Parker Hamond thereafter owned 535 a., about a third of the parish, John Mortlock had 365 a. for the rectory, Queens' College 200 a., and its lessee, Alexander Ross, 65 a. R. J. Adeane was allotted 95 a., which he immediately exchanged for land in his own parish of Babraham. No other proprietor possessed more than 50 a.; four, besides the vicar and the charity, had between 10 and 50 a., 158 a. altogether, and 15 others with 6 a. or less had only 47 a. between them.[19]

A large area in the north-east corner of the parish was taken out of cultivation to create the park around Pampisford Hall in the earlier 19th century, and the Parker Hamonds also acquired the Queens' College land before 1893. The number of large farms therefore remained much the same; Rectory, College, Mill, and Manor farm-houses were all standing by 1799; Home farm, as in 1973, had some cottages and farm-buildings but no farm-house.[20] By 1872 the 600 a. of Manor farm were divided, the farmstead and some of the land being leased with Home farm, and part added to Mill farm.[21] Rectory farm, with 400 a., was the only large farm in the parish not sold in 1893 with the Parker Hamond estate, which passed undivided to the Binney family apart from Mill farm, bought by the Eastern Counties Leather Co. Ltd. and sold by them in 1926.[22] Rectory and College farms were working in 1973; Manor Farm was used as a guest-house, and its land was farmed from Sawston.

Although some sheep-farming was practised on the large farms and there were three shepherds in the parish in 1851,[23] agriculture in Pampisford has remained largely arable. Home farm and College farm, each with *c.* 250 a. land in 1893, had only 32 a. and 36 a. of pasture respectively.[24] By 1905 there were 1,053 a. of arable in the parish compared with 177 a. of permanent grass and 101 a. of woods and plantations.[25] The main crops grown were wheat and barley, with a little oats. Farms with land by the two rivers also maintained small dairy-herds, and several farms had dairymaids in 1871.[26]

A water-mill worth 20*s.* on the river Cam or Granta belonged to the Ely manor in 1086.[27] It was recorded in 1303, 1571,[28] 1639, and 1707.[29] John Waldock, the miller, went bankrupt in 1876,[30] but the mill continued to be used for grinding corn and seeds for oil. It was bought with Mill farm from Col. Hamond in 1893 by the Eastern Counties Leather Co. Ltd., which sold the mill in 1941.[31] Pampisford mill was disused by 1960,[32] and by 1973 had been converted to residential use.

Most of the adult males in the parish were agricultural labourers in 1841 and 1851, and it was only with the growth of Sawston's leather and paper industries in the 1850s that any alternative employment became available. The factory of the Eastern Counties Leather Co., built in 1879 at Langford Arch in Pampisford, brought the leather industry closer to the village, and some of the 100 people employed in 1973 making gloves and chamois leather were from Pampisford.[33] Brewing was the only other local industry providing employment from the late 19th century. Apart from those employed on the farms, most inhabitants of Pampisford in 1973 worked at Sawston or in the Langford Arch factory, or in Cambridge.

Brewing was carried on at Pampisford in the mid 19th century by members of the Scruby family, who were also tenants of Rectory farm. William Scruby in the 1840s and Charles Scruby in the next three decades worked a brewery and malt-house,[34] at a site north of the road to Sawston (later Brewery Road) chosen for the purity of a well there.[35] Their business was bought *c.* 1880 by Bathe & Co., who in 1882 built a new brewery close to the old one.[36] By 1891 it belonged to P. L. Hudson, who considerably enlarged the brewery and its business; beer was supplied to his own 22 public houses as well as free houses, three malt-houses were needed to produce enough malt, and the brewery employed 50 people.[37] Hudson died in 1914 and his family sold the brewery

[12] C.U.L., Add. MS. 7312; C 142/645 no. 42.
[13] C.U.L., Queens' Coll. Mun. 13/5, f. 49; Vancouver, *Agric. in Cambs.* 66.
[14] C.U.L., Add. MS. 7312 (back); ibid. Queens' Coll. Mun. 17/38.
[15] Vancouver, *Agric. in Cambs.* 67.
[16] C.R.O., Q/RDz 6.
[17] C.U.L., Add. MS. 7312; ibid. Queens' Coll. Mun. 13/5.
[18] Pampisford Incl. Act, 39 Geo. III, c. 120 (Private and Personal, not printed).
[19] C.R.O., Q/RDz 6.
[20] Ibid. Q/RDc 2.
[21] Electoral reg., 1872 (P.R.O. Census Room); C.U.L., Maps bb. 53(1)/89/14.
[22] C.R.O., R 58/5/10, p. 194; C.U.L., Maps 53/92/11.
[23] H.O. 107/1761.
[24] C.U.L., Maps bb. 53(1)/89/14.
[25] Cambs. Agric. Returns, 1905.
[26] R.G. 10/1591.
[27] *V.C.H. Cambs.* i. 410.
[28] *Cal. Inq. p.m.* iv, p. 112; C.U.L., Queens' Coll. Mun. 13/5, f. 51v.
[29] C.U.L., E.D.R., H 1/5, terrier 1639; A 4/2.
[30] C.R.O., R 58/5/10, p. 195.
[31] Ibid. p. 194; ibid. 515/SP 1713.
[32] O.S. Map 6", TL 44 NE. (1960 edn.).
[33] *Camb. Ind. Press*, 26 Aug. 1960; see below, pp. 256–7.
[34] H.O. 107/66; H.O. 107/1761; R.G. 10/1591.
[35] A. Barnard, *Noted Breweries of Gt. Britain and Irel.* (1891), iv. 484–5.
[36] *Kelly's Dir. Cambs.* (1883); see below, plate facing p. 193.
[37] Barnard, *Breweries*, iv. 484–5, 491; *Cambs. and Peterborough Life*, v. 25.

in 1932 when they left Pampisford.[38] It was later reopened as a malt vinegar brewery, with several changes of ownership.[39] The Pampisford brewery closed *c.* 1950, and its buildings gradually became derelict. In 1965 Mr. Bernard Dixon, whose family had owned it, started a new company called Sealmaster on the same site, to manufacture door seals and draught excluders; most of the old buildings were demolished in 1972, although the engine-house was preserved, and in 1973 a new factory was under construction there.[40]

LOCAL GOVERNMENT. Although view of frankpledge for Pampisford was held *c.* 1235 by the lord of the Richmond manor,[41] in 1299, 1303, and 1325 a court with view of frankpledge belonged to the Ely manor.[42] Henry son of Aucher claimed the assize of bread and of ale as well as view of frankpledge in 1299.[43] William Saffrey had a court baron for his tenants in 1299.[44] There are court books for 1678–1867 and 1869–91. In the 18th century courts were held every two or three years, mainly for transfers of copyholds, although a few agricultural orders were occasionally made. Most copyhold tenements were enfranchised in the mid and later 19th century.[45] There were two constables in 1316 and in 1753,[46] and the court appointed two pinders in the 18th century.[47]

Parish resources were adequate to deal with poverty until the late 18th century, when the poor-rate suddenly increased.[48] Nonetheless, only 12 people were on permanent relief in 1803.[49] Expenditure on poor-relief reached its highest point at £298 in 1822, but conditions improved gradually over the next 10 years and very few people were unable to find work in 1831.[50] Pampisford was incorporated in the Linton poor-law union in 1835; with the rest of Linton R.D. it became part of the South Cambridgeshire R.D. in 1934,[51] and of South Cambridgeshire in 1974.

CHURCH. A half-yardland in Pampisford was held from Countess Judith in 1086 by a priest,[52] whose presence suggests that there was then already a church, though the earliest part of the existing parish church dates from the mid 12th century. The benefice was a rectory until 1377, when the church was appropriated to the Benedictine nunnery of Blackborough (Norf.) and a vicarage was ordained.[53]

The right of presentation to the rectory was in dispute in 1224 and 1271 between the tenants of the two manors,[54] but by 1279 the conflict had been resolved in favour of Sir Hugh de Brok, lord of the Richmond manor.[55] The advowson was included in the grants to Robert Ludham for life, and to John, parson of Long Itchington, but not in that to Joan Breton and her successive husbands. Passing instead with the reversion of the manor, it was acquired from John Hinton in 1319 by Aucher son of Henry.[56] In 1328, however, Hinton sold it to William Lalleford, rector of Rivenhall (Essex), who was licensed in 1329 to assign it to Blackborough priory (Norf.), founded by Roger de Scales, ancestor of Isabel de Scales, of whom Lalleford was said to hold it.[57] The priory presented to the vicarage from 1388 until its dissolution; under a grant made by the prioress in 1527 Robert and William Turtylby and John Hodgkin presented in 1539.[58] The advowson passed with the rectory thereafter, with only a few exceptions: Henry Calton presented in 1571, James Robinett who farmed the rectory presented in 1615, Theophilus Tyrrell was granted one turn by William Alington for 1638, and either the Crown or the bishop of Ely presented by lapse in 1806.[59] The advowson was retained by E. J. Mortlock when he sold the rectory estate before 1892. On his death in 1902 the advowson passed to J. J. Emerson, who had also purchased most of the Mortlocks' Abington lands.[60] When Emerson died in 1918 it was bought by James Binney,[61] and passed with the manor to his heirs.

Picot the sheriff in 1092 granted two-thirds of the tithes from his demesne in Pampisford to his foundation at Barnwell; the grant was later commuted to an annual pension, worth 22*s.* in 1254 and 20*s.* in 1535.[62] Bishop Niel also, in the 12th century, assigned to the scriptorium of Ely two-thirds of the demesne tithes of the Ely estate in Pampisford, taxed at 50*s.* in 1254 and commuted for a pension of 66*s.* 8*d.* by 1535.[63] After those outgoings, the rectory, which was endowed with 32 a. by 1279,[64] was taxed at 12 marks in 1254 and 26 marks in 1291.[65]

Pampisford vicarage was one of the poorest livings in the deanery. In 1535 it was valued at only £8, and in 1650 was said to be worth £24.[66] It was let for £20 in 1707, but the vicar's expenses in travelling to Pampisford and his Sunday dinners reduced the income to less than £15.[67] The vicarage

38 C.R.O., 331/Z 4, May 1914; 331/Z 6, Apr. 1931, p. 33; 515/SP 1161.
39 *Cambs. and Peterborough Life*, v. 25; *Kelly's Dir. Cambs.* (1937).
40 Ex inf. Mr. B. Dixon.
41 *Liber de Bernewelle*, 255, 276.
42 *Plac. de Quo Warr.* (Rec. Com.), 99; *Cal. Inq. p.m.* iv, p. 112; vi, p. 362.
43 *Plac. de Quo Warr.* (Rec. Com.), 99.
44 C.U.L., Queens' Coll. Mun. 17/26.
45 Ct. bks. *penes* Mr. H. B. Binney, Pampisford Hall.
46 *Cambs. Village Doc.* 9; Carter, *Hist. Cambs.* 241.
47 Ct. bks. *penes* Mr. Binney.
48 Vancouver, *Agric. in Cambs.* 68.
49 *Poor Law Abstract, 1804*, 34–5.
50 *Poor Rate Returns, 1822–4*, 37; *Rep. H.L. Cttee. on Poor Laws*, H.C. 227, pp. 326–7 (1831), viii.
51 *Poor Law Com. 1st Rep.* 249; *Census*, 1931 (pt. ii).
52 *V.C.H. Cambs.* i. 398, 410.
53 *E.D.R.* (1895), 91; *Proc. C.A.S.* vi. 391–2.
54 *Cur. Reg. R.* xi, p. 331; *Cal. Pat.* 1266–72, 518.
55 *Rot. Hund.* (Rec. Com.), ii. 414.
56 *Cambs. Fines*, 1196–1485 (C.A.S. 8vo ser. xxvi), 52, 60–1, 72; C.P. 25(1)/26/52 no. 28; C.P. 25(1)/27/59 no. 16.
57 C 143/259 no. 7; *Proc. C.A.S.* vi. 390–1; *Cal. Pat.* 1327–30, 400; *V.C.H. Norf.* ii. 350.
58 *E.D.R.* (1912), 35.
59 Ibid. (1898), 178, 199; P.R.O. Inst. Bks. ser. A, iii, p. 32; C, i, p. 448.
60 *E.D.R.* (1898), 199; *Kelly's Dir. Cambs.* (1904).
61 C.R.O., 331/Z 5, May 1918; Dec. 1919, p. lxxi.
62 *Liber de Bernewelle*, 40; *Val. of Norwich*, ed. Lunt, 226; *Proc. C.A.S.* vi. 392; *Valor Eccl.* (Rec. Com.), iii. 395.
63 *V.C.H. Cambs.* ii. 206; *Val. of Norwich*, ed. Lunt, 226; *Valor Eccl.* (Rec. Com.), iii. 395.
64 *Rot. Hund.* (Rec. Com.), ii. 414.
65 *Val. of Norwich*, ed. Lunt, 536.
66 *Valor Eccl.* (Rec. Com.), iii. 504; Lamb. Pal. MS. 904, f. 270.
67 C.U.L., E.D.R., A 4/2.

was augmented with £200 from Queen Anne's Bounty in 1777, but was still worth only £75 in 1810 and £78 in 1873.[68]

Before the Reformation Blackborough priory paid the vicar 40*s.* a year, 2 qr. of wheat, and 4 qr. of barley.[69] The rectory was sold subject to that charge in 1553,[70] and the payment was still being made in 1707.[71] The vicar also received the small tithes. By 1639 money payments were made for cows, as well as 10*s.* from Pampisford mill and 2*s.* 6*d.* from a dovecot, and by 1707 the vicar had a composition for most other tithes.[72] The vicarage was allotted 37 a. for tithes and the corn-rent due from the impropriator at inclosure in 1801.[73]

A little glebe was attached to the living by 1615, amounting to 9 a. in 1707,[74] and 10 a. were awarded at inclosure for glebe, making the total allotment 47 a.[75] It had been sold by 1973.[76] There was a vicarage house by 1604, probably the small early-16th-century building, the cross-wing of a house, used as a post office in 1973.[77] The vicar was admonished for its decay in 1638, but the incumbent was resident there in 1665.[78] Few incumbents lived in Pampisford after the 17th century, partly because of the smallness and poor condition of the house; in 1783 it was inhabited by a poor family, and the curate in 1836 described it as a cottage not more than 16 ft. square.[79] A new large house, of brick with gabled roofs, was built next to the church between 1841 and 1857.[80] In the 20th century it proved too large and expensive for such a poor living; one incumbent resigned in 1919 after only a year, because he could not afford to keep up so large a house and garden, and the vicar in 1936 moved into a flat converted from the stables to avoid high rates, and resigned the following year when the vicarage was used to house Basque refugee children without any payment to him.[81] Since 1960 incumbents have lived outside the parish, and the vicarage house was sold in 1961.[82]

A guild in the parish church in 1389 had recently been founded for the repair of the roof.[83] Money was left in 1517 to the wardens of the guild of St. Peter and St. Paul, whose stock was taxed in 1524.[84] Small sums and pieces of land, including 7 a. in 1527, were given for obits and anniversaries in the earlier 16th century and as late as 1547.[85]

Chaplains, perhaps of a chantry, were mentioned in the 14th and 15th centuries.[86] Two members of the Cloville family were buried in St. Mary's chapel in the church,[87] and in 1527 there was an image of Our Lady.[88]

The first known rector of Pampisford, Richard of Ludham, accompanied Edward I's representative to Rome in 1298,[89] but later medieval incumbents appear in rentals and as witnesses to wills and were probably resident.[90] The vicar 1472–1500 was Robert Turtylby, a Benedictine monk from York and prior of the Benedictine students at Cambridge, whose institution suggests that incumbents for such a poor benefice were hard to find.[91] Another vicar of the same name, 1518–39, farmed the rectory in 1523 from Blackborough priory.[92] Curates served the living from 1539, paid either by the vicar or by the farmer of the rectory.[93] Robert Baker, vicar 1560–71, also held the vicarage of Sawston, where he lived, and did not preach.[94] His successor, Anthony Fletcher, 1571–85, also held Sawston until forced to resign his second benefice.[95] Michael Crudd, vicar of Pampisford 1585–9, was master of Linton school, and William Wadye who succeeded him was also vicar of St. Andrew's, Cambridge.[96] In 1605 the vicar was presented for not using the cross in baptism and refusing to wear a surplice, and the reading desk was ordered to be removed from the central aisle in 1638, signs of puritan feeling in the parish.[97] The church still lacked books of Canons and of Homilies and needed a new Prayer Book and a Bible in the latest translation in 1665; a parishioner gave copies of Erasmus's and Jewel's works in 1692.[98]

After the Restoration incumbencies became shorter: fourteen men held the living between 1663 and 1718, and six between 1772 and 1788. The benefice was mainly attractive to fellows of colleges, who usually lived in Cambridge and exchanged the living for a richer one as soon as possible. John Bartow, vicar 1697–1706, was a missionary for the S.P.G. in New York for the last four years of his incumbency.[99] In 1728 and 1775 communion was held only three times a year.[1] Matthew Mapletoft, nephew of Elizabeth Tyrrell, the patron,[2] was vicar 1718–44, and was succeeded by his brother Edmund Mapletoft 1745–72, who like his predecessor lived in Bartlow where he was rector. Edmund's son Edmund was briefly vicar of Pampisford from 1772 to 1776.[3] The only other long ministry in the period was that of Thomas Cautley, sequestrator of Pampisford 1788–1806, and also vicar of Sawston.

Until the new vicarage was built *c.* 1850 incumbents of Pampisford were rarely resident; in 1836

68 Ibid.; C. Hodgson, *Queen Anne's Bounty*, 311; C.U.L., E.D.R., C 3/25.
69 S.C. 6/Hen. VIII/2621 rot. 32.
70 *Cal. Pat.* 1553, 218, 221.
71 C.U.L., E.D.R., A 4/2.
72 Ibid.; H 1/5, terrier 1639.
73 C.R.O., Q/RDz 6.
74 C.U.L., E.D.R., H 1/5, terrier 1615; A 4/2.
75 C.R.O., Q/RDz 6.
76 Ex inf. the vicar, the Revd. R. A. Spalding.
77 C.R.O. 346/T 1; *Camb. Ind. Press*, 26 Aug. 1960.
78 *Cambs. Village Doc.* 69; E 179/84/437 rot. 58.
79 C.U.L., E.D.R., B 7/1; C 3/21.
80 Ibid. H 1/8, terrier 1841; B 1/16.
81 C.R.O., 331/Z 5, Sept. 1919, p. liv; 331/Z 7, July 1936, p. 57; July 1937, p. 53; Oct. 1937, p. 77.
82 Ibid. SP 130/2A.
83 C 47/38/28; *Trans. C.H.A.S.* i. 359–60.
84 B.L. Add. MS. 5861, p. 123; E 179/81/134 m. 2.
85 B.L. Add. MS. 5861, pp. 57, 160, 189–90, 198.
86 *Cal. Mem. R.* 1326–7, p. 203; C.U.L., Queens' Coll. Mun. 17/27.
87 Lamb. Pal. Reg. Stafford and Kemp, f. 293v.; Prob. 11/3 (P.C.C. 30 Luffenam, will of Wal. Cloville).
88 B.L. Add. MS. 5861, p. 198.
89 *Cal. Pat.* 1292–1301, 334.
90 e.g. C.U.L., Queens' Coll. Mun. 17/27.
91 Emden, *Biog. Reg. Univ. Camb.* 587.
92 S.C. 6/Hen. VIII/2621 rot. 32.
93 *E.D.R.* (1912), 184; (1913), 41.
94 B.L. Add. MS. 5813, f. 67; C.U.L., E.D.R., B 2/4, p. 132.
95 C.U.L., E.D.R., D 2/10, f. 153v.
96 *Alum. Cantab. to 1751*, i. 433; iv. 309.
97 C.U.L., E.D.R., B 2/25, f. 10; *Cambs. Village Doc.* 69.
98 C.U.L., E.D.R., B 2/59, p. 29; Prob. 11/412 (P.C.C. 218 Fane, will of Hen. Beeton).
99 *Alum. Cantab. to 1751*, i. 101.
1 C.U.L., E.D.R., B 8/1; C 1/1.
2 Palmer, *Wm. Cole*, 106; B.L. Add. MS. 5843, pp. 235, 237.
3 *Alum. Cantab. to 1751*, iii. 138–9; *1752–1900*, iv. 316.

the vicar lived in Devon, and the parish was served by a curate who was also responsible for Stapleford.[4] In 1807 the congregation attended Sawston church when there was no service at Pampisford.[5] Adult attendance at the morning service in 1851 was 54, and in the afternoon 97, and the vicar reported in 1877 that he had given up weekly communions because of small attendance.[6] The small income and the size of the vicarage made it difficult for incumbents without private means to remain at Pampisford for long, and fourteen vicars held the living between 1911 and 1967. Since 1947 Pampisford has been held in plurality with Babraham by dispensation.[7]

The income from Pampisford's charity estate was intended to be used for church repairs, any surplus being devoted to poor-relief.[8] The church-rate was paid from the charity in 1728.[9] Money from the charity was used for major church repairs *c.* 1820, when the fund was £68 in debt, in 1854–5 for restoration, and in 1889 for repairing the north arcade.[10] The charity's net income was divided into two by a Scheme of 1905, one half being devoted to the maintenance of the church.[11]

The church of *ST. JOHN THE BAPTIST*, bearing that dedication by 1753 but named from St. Peter and St. Paul in the 15th century,[12] is built of field stones with dressings of ashlar and has a chancel with north vestry, nave with north aisle and south porch, and west tower with small lead-covered spire. The nave is mid-12th-century and retains its original south doorway with a carved tympanum. A north aisle was added *c.* 1200, when the arcade of four bays was cut through the old wall, and the chancel must have been rebuilt at about the same time. The west tower, which is similar in design to that at Sawston, was added in the earlier 14th century when new windows were also put into the nave and chancel. Minor alterations, including the rebuilding of the chancel arch and the insertion of a rood screen, were made in the 15th century and a porch was added *c.* 1527.[13]

During the later 16th century the chancel was frequently in need of repair,[14] but its condition may have been better in the 18th century.[15] In the 1850s there was an extensive restoration under P. C. Hardwick. The nave was re-roofed and retiled, the north aisle was rebuilt to a greater width, two new windows were put in, most of the other stonework was renewed, and a new south porch put up.[16] Another major restoration was carried out in the 1890s under the direction of Sir Arthur Blomfield. The vestry was added, apparently on the foundations of a medieval chapel which was decayed in the late 16th century, and the chancel was re-roofed and refurnished.[17]

There were three bells and a sanctus bell in 1552.[18] A new fourth bell was cast by J. Eayre in 1743, and the other three are by Thomas Mears and C. and G. Mears of London, 1841 and 1848, replacing bells of 1615 and 1617 by John Draper.[19] One of two chalices with silver patens was confiscated in 1552.[20] There was a silver chalice and a pewter flagon and plate in 1837, and *c.* 1960 the plate included a cup of 1569.[21] The parish registers begin in 1565, and are virtually complete.

NONCONFORMITY. Robert Turtylby, a yeoman of Pampisford, a suspected member of the Family of Love in 1582, had left the parish,[22] and no nonconformists were reported there until the late 18th century. Two houses were licensed for worship in 1797 and 1798, and in 1807 the vicar reported that the number of Calvinist dissenters had recently increased, although there was no meeting-house.[23] In 1825 the curate thought that most inhabitants attended dissenting chapels in neighbouring parishes because only one service a week was held in the parish church and there was no resident Anglican minister.[24] A building in Pampisford was registered for nonconformist worship in 1833;[25] since there was no chapel in the parish, however, numbers of dissenters remained low, being estimated at 20 to 30 in 1873, 3 Independents and 3 Baptists in 1877, and 3 households in 1897.[26]

EDUCATION. No school or schoolmaster was mentioned in the parish until 1807, when there was a Sunday school.[27] Two small schools taught *c.* 30 children in 1818.[28] A day-school for small children was kept by a dissenter in 1825, and by 1833 there were an infants' school with *c.* 20 pupils and a day-school with *c.* 16 girls paid for by a lady resident in the parish.[29]

Shortly before 1847 a school was built opposite the church by William Parker Hamond; supported by subscriptions and payments, it was used as a day-school and a Sunday school, and had 56 pupils in 1847.[30] Between 40 and 45 children attended it in 1873, and there was also an evening school for adults, although the vicar in 1877 refused to hold a night-school, saying that it would do more harm than good.[31] A school board was formed for Pampisford in 1875, and used the school at a nominal rent.[32]

[4] C.U.L., E.D.R., C 3/21. [5] Ibid. C 1/4.
[6] Ibid. C 3/27; H.O. 129/188/1/2/2.
[7] *Crockford* (1947 and later edns.); *Ely Dioc. Dir.* (1972–3).
[8] *31st Rep. Com. Char.* 106; see below, p. 113.
[9] C.U.L., E.D.R., B 8/1.
[10] *31st Rep. Com. Char.* 106; Char. Com. files.
[11] Char. Com. files.
[12] Lamb. Pal. Reg. Stafford and Kemp, f. 293v.; Prob. 11/3 (P.C.C. 30 Luffenam, will of Wal. Cloville); Carter, *Hist. Cambs.* 241.
[13] B.L. Add. MS. 5861, p. 197.
[14] e.g. C.U.L., E.D.R., D 2/10, f. 155; B 2/36, f. 14.
[15] e.g. ibid. B 8/1; B 7/1, p. 131.
[16] Char. Com. files.
[17] C.U.L., E.D.R., B 2/13, f. 184; C 3/38; *E.D.R.* (1890), 470; (1897), 230–1.
[18] *Cambs. Ch. Goods, temp. Edw. VI*, 3.
[19] *Eng. Topog.* (Gent. Mag. Libr.), ii. 62; *Cambs. Bells* (C.A.S. 8vo ser. xviii), 162.
[20] *Cambs. Ch. Goods, temp. Edw. VI*, 3.
[21] C.U.L., E.D.R., H 1/8, terrier 1837; list of ch. plate *penes V.C.H.*
[22] *Cath. Rec. Soc.* liii. 2.
[23] G.R.O. Worship Returns, Ely dioc. nos. 157–8; C.U.L., E.D.R., C 1/4.
[24] C.U.L., E.D.R., C 1/6.
[25] G.R.O. Worship Returns, Ely dioc. no. 574.
[26] C.U.L., E.D.R., C 3/25; C 3/27; C 3/38.
[27] Ibid. C 1/4.
[28] *Educ. of Poor Digest*, 63.
[29] C.U.L., E.D.R., C 1/6; *Educ. Enquiry Abstract*, 59.
[30] *Kelly's Dir. Cambs.* (1847); *Church School Inquiry, 1846–7*, 6–7.
[31] C.U.L., E.D.R., C 3/25, 27.
[32] *Lond. Gaz.* 21 May 1875, p. 2725; Ed. 7/5.

Duxford: St. John's Church showing the base of the tower and the north aisle

Balsham Church showing the rood-screen and chancel stalls

Pampisford Hall: decoration of 1875 in the drawing room

Hinxton Hall: early-19th-century murals in the former drawing room

The school was closed for nearly two years in 1876–7 while the buildings were extended, and Col. R. T. Hamond further enlarged the school in 1887.[33] Average attendance was 58 in 1888, and 48 in 1897.[34]

A new school and teacher's house were built beside the old school in 1899 by James Binney. Attendance fell from 43 in 1900 to 40 in 1908 and 29 in 1912.[35] Senior pupils were transferred to schools at Sawston in 1922, and to the village college there in 1930. The Pampisford school was closed in 1963, the younger children also going to Sawston,[36] and the building in Church Lane became the village hall.

CHARITIES FOR THE POOR. The property later known as the Church and Poor estate was given in or before 1604 by an unknown donor, the income to be used for church repairs and any surplus to be devoted to poor-relief.[37] The feoffees possessed 20½ a. after inclosure in 1801, and in 1837 also owned 3 cottages,[38] and 6 in 1864 and 1905.[39] Small plots were sold in 1921 and 1936, and in 1959 the three remaining cottages, all derelict, were sold, leaving *c.* 15 a. to the charity, some of it used as allotments.[40]

Expenditure on the church left only £9 a year for the poor from 1822 to 1827, and payments in coal to the poor fell even lower and ceased altogether from 1832 to 1835. Two cottages, divided into seven dwellings, were occupied rent-free by the aged poor. In 1864 the whole income of £60 was applied to the church.[41] A Scheme of 1905 divided the net income equally between the church and the poor of Pampisford, but the amount given to the poor fell from £20 in 1905 to £6 in 1907 because of the costs of obtaining the Scheme.[42] The charity's income was £65 in 1952, *c.* £160 in 1962, and £94 in 1971. Until 1959 part of the income was devoted to maintaining the cottages, but since then expenditure has been on fuel and Christmas presents for widows and old-age pensioners.[43]

By will proved 1636 John Jefferie of Sawston charged his property in Pampisford and Babraham with 4 bushels of barley each Christmas for the poor of Pampisford.[44] The corn was given in 1786 and 1816, but had been lost by 1835.[45]

WEST WICKHAM

THE PARISH of West Wickham,[1] lying 10 miles south-east of Cambridge, covers 2,931 a.[2] and is nearly rectangular. The straight southern boundary follows the ancient Wool Street, called in the Middle Ages Wulves street,[3] while on the west and north field boundaries delimit the parish. On the east is the county boundary with Suffolk. In 1814 *c.* 66 a. by the southern part of the eastern boundary and belonging to West Wickham landowners were alleged to be extra-parochial, never having paid tithes, rates, or taxes in any parish. Shortly before, however, the rector of Withersfield (Suff.) had them perambulated and assessed as part of his parish,[4] in which they were subsequently included.[5] West Wickham lies mainly upon boulder clay, overlying chalk, which is exposed at the western corner, lying at *c.* 250 ft. There a water-course runs west down a narrow valley before turning south into Horseheath. From there the ground rises sharply eastward to over 300 ft., and then gradually but steadily to over 400 ft.

The parish was once well wooded, especially on the higher ground to the east and north. In 1086 the woodland could feed 152 pigs.[6] In 1279 three manors had woods covering 74 a.,[7] and in 1770 there were over 3,200 oaks.[8] Mill wood (19 a.) and Yen Hall wood (18 a.) by the northern border were cleared after 1813.[9] Leys wood (18 a.) belonged in 1394 to La Hayes manor. An adjacent close, then called Stocking, recalled earlier clearances.[10] By the eastern border lay Cadges wood (12 a.) and Over wood (53 a.), belonging by 1395 to Streetly manor,[11] which had 40 a. of demesne wood in 1300.[12] Hare wood (43 a.) by the southern boundary, probably called Cow Pasture wood *c.* 1614,[13] lay for a time within Horseheath park.[14]

The parish has long been mainly agrarian. The land to the east, consisting mainly of closes held in severalty, was possibly brought under cultivation later than the western two-thirds, where open fields survived until inclosure in 1813.[15]

The Cambridgeshire Wickham was regularly

[33] Ed. 7/5; *Kelly's Dir. Cambs.* (1888).

[34] *Kelly's Dir. Cambs.* (1888); C.U.L., E.D.R., C 3/38.

[35] *Kelly's Dir. Cambs.* (1900, 1908, 1912).

[36] Black, *Cambs. Educ. Rec.* 70.

[37] Except where otherwise stated, this section is based on *31st Rep. Com. Char.* 106; Char. Com. files.

[38] C.R.O., Q/RDz 6; C.U.L., E.D.R., H 1/8, terrier 1837.

[39] *Char. Digest Cambs. 1863–4,* 32–3.

[40] C.R.O., 515/SP 2298; *Pampisford Guide* (Pampisford Par. Council, 1972), 6.

[41] *Char. Digest. Cambs. 1863–4,* 32–3.

[42] C.R.O., 331/Z 2, June 1907, p. xlix.

[43] *Camb. Ind. Press,* 30 Mar. 1972; *Pampisford Guide,* 6.

[44] Prob. 11/148 (P.C.C. 13 Hele).

[45] *Char. Don.* i. 88–9; *31st Rep. Com. Char.* 107.

[1] This account was written in 1975.

[2] *Census,* 1961.

[3] e.g. B.L. Add. MS. 5823, f. 233 (*c.* 1250). Not, as suggested in *Proc. C.A.S.* lvi–lvii. 56, named after Wolves manor, which the Wolf family owned only after 1360: see below, pp. 116–17.

[4] C.U.L., Doc. 660 no. 71.

[5] e.g. O.S. Map 1″, sheet 51 (1836 edn.), showing the area in Suffolk.

[6] *V.C.H. Cambs.* i. 365, 374, 380.

[7] *Rot. Hund.* (Rec. Com.), ii. 429–30, 568.

[8] B.L. Add. MS. 36229, f. 195.

[9] For the woods see B.L. Add. MS. 36229, ff. 205 and v., 279–81 (*c.* 1776–80); C.R.O., Q/RDc 9, pp. 428–90 (1822) (especially pp. 478–83); Q/RDc 39 (1813).

[10] B.L. Add. MS. 5823, f. 232v.

[11] Ibid. f. 99.

[12] C 133/94 no. 5.

[13] B.L. Add. MS. 5823, f. 95v.

[14] *Proc. C.A.S.* xli. 33–4, and pl. iii.

[15] C.R.O., Q/RDc 9, pp. 428–90.

distinguished as West Wickham only after 1330,[16] presumably with reference to the Wickhams in Suffolk. By 1066 there were three settlements, of which Wickham itself at the centre of the parish and Enhale (later Yen Hall) by the northern boundary were already recorded in 974.[17] In 1086 Enhale had 10 tenants, all bordars, while Streetly by the southern boundary had 10 tenants and *servi* and Wickham thirteen.[18] Enhale later declined in population relatively to the other settlements: few men are described as belonging to it,[19] whereas men of Streetly occur frequently from the early 13th century.[20] In 1279 only three free tenants, out of *c.* 50 in the parish, held solely of Enhale manor.[21] The parish contained 50 taxpayers in 1327;[22] numbers afterwards fell sharply. Only 25 people were taxed in 1524,[23] and there were only 33 households in 1563.[24] In 1676 there were 178 adults.[25] From 332 in 1801 the population rose rapidly to 517 in 1821 and a peak of 572 in 1841, declining after 1851 to 522 in 1871.[26] In 1851 and 1871 *c.* 100 people lived at Streetly End.[27] From 455 in 1881 numbers fell steadily to 336 in 1911, and thereafter remained nearly constant.[28]

In West Wickham village the houses lie in two groups. The larger forms a street running north-east from the Horseheath–Balsham road, with the church and Manor (formerly Parsonage) Farm close to the junction. Further along the street, after a wide gap, is Burton End. Residents and messuages at 'Bovetoun' were recorded from the 1340s,[29] and in 1381 it was called 'Bovetounstreet' hamlet.[30] Streetly End lies ½ mile south of the church, on the road to Horseheath; from that hamlet another road formerly ran to Balsham, but at inclosure it was stopped where it crossed the road which runs across the western half of the parish from Bartlow to West Wratting. Streetly had a village green in 1452, and some crofts there had dwellings newly built on them in the 1460s.[31] At Yen Hall only the farm-house survived in the 18th century.[32]

Some prosperous peasants in the 14th century had fairly elaborate homesteads. In 1322 John Sewale granted his sister a little solar joined to his hall with a granary, a stable, and the use of his bakery.[33] Seven 17th-century timber-framed and thatched cottages, mostly single-storeyed, survive at Burton End, and there are eight others, mostly 18th-century, at Streetly End, also single-storeyed with dormers and central chimney-stacks. About 1974 the second group, after restoration, was declared a conservation area.[34] Larger houses include White Hall in the main village, where a 17th-century timber-framed house received a four-bay brick Georgian front and classical doorcase, and the Mill House at Streetly End, where an early-17th-century T-plan house has a doorcase with ornate carved brackets. Next-door the Red House, built in 1779 probably by Daniel Taylor,[35] had a three-bay red-brick front with a classical doorcase, and contained woodwork possibly from Horseheath Hall.[36] It was demolished *c.* 1945.[37]

In 1851 about half the houses in the parish stood along the main village street, and most of the remainder were divided equally between Streetly End and Burton End.[38] Between 1945 and 1960 *c.* 30 council houses were built north of Streetly End and between the village and Burton End.[39] Each settlement had its own public house, the White Hart at Burton End, probably mentioned in 1768[40] and closed by 1933,[41] and the White Horse on the street and the Chequers at Streetly End, both probably existing in 1813[42] and open in 1975. The village had little organized social life in the mid 20th century, the villagers mostly resorting to West Wratting. A village hall was being built in 1974.[43] High, flat ground north-east of Burton End was included between 1943 and 1952 in the R.A.F. airfield on Wratting Common.[44] Two hangars surviving in 1975 had been converted to warehouses.[45]

MANORS AND OTHER ESTATES. In 1086 Count Alan, lord of Richmond, held in demesne at Wickham 2 hides, which in 1066 had belonged to Eddeva the fair and two sokemen of hers.[46] Before 1133 Alan's heir Count Stephen had granted the manor to Aubrey de Vere[47] (d. 1141), whose descendants the earls of Oxford subsequently held, as 3 or 4 knights' fees, the mesne lordship of Wickham under the honor of Richmond.[48]

Probably *c.* 1150 Earl Aubrey (d. 1194) divided the manor, granting half, later *LA HAYES* or *LEYES* manor, reckoned as 2 knights' fees, to Stephen de la Haye.[49] Stephen was succeeded in 1176 or 1177 by his son Walter,[50] whose lands in Cambridgeshire, confiscated in 1215, were restored to him in 1216.[51] He was succeeded between 1226[52]

[16] C.U.L., Queens' Coll. Mun., 52/23 sqq. (1329 and later). All documents cited from that source for W. Wickham were in 1975 in box 57.
[17] *Cart. Sax.* ed. Birch, iii, pp. 628–31.
[18] *V.C.H. Cambs.* i. 409.
[19] Only references traced: B.L. Add. MS. 5823, ff. 84v. (1344), 231v. (*c.* 1307).
[20] e.g. C.U.L., Queens' Coll. Mun., 52/1 and *passim.*
[21] *Rot. Hund.* (Rec. Com.), ii. 429–30, 568–9.
[22] *Cambs. Lay Subsidy, 1327*, 27.
[23] E 179/81/134 m. 4.
[24] B.L. Harl. MS. 594, f. 199v.
[25] Compton Census.
[26] *Census*, 1801–71.
[27] H.O. 107/1761; R.G. 10/1593.
[28] *Census*, 1881–1971.
[29] B.L. Add. MS. 5823, f. 103; C.U.L., Queens' Coll. Mun., 52/34.
[30] B.L. Add. MS. 5823, f. 95.
[31] Pemb. Coll. Mun., Horseheath, A 3, 12, 13.
[32] Cf. C.R.O., Q/RDc 39.
[33] B.L. Add. MS. 5823, f. 230v.
[34] *Camb. Evening News*, 15 June 1973; *Camb. Ind. Press*, 24 Jan. 1974.
[35] M.H.L.G. List.
[36] *Proc. C.A.S.* xli. 47.
[37] Ex inf. Mr. J. D. Webb.
[38] H.O. 107/1761.
[39] *Camb. Ind. Press*, 9 Sept. 1960.
[40] C.R.O., R 70/48, 15 July 1768.
[41] *Kelly's Dir. Cambs.* (1929–33).
[42] C.R.O., Q/RDc 9, pp. 467, 485.
[43] *Camb. Ind. Press*, 9 Sept. 1960; *Camb. Evening News* 24 Jan., 2 Sept. 1974.
[44] C.R.O., 515/SP 2185.
[45] Cf. *Camb. Evening News*, 9 Aug. 1973.
[46] *V.C.H. Cambs.* i. 374.
[47] *Reg. Regum Anglo-Norm.* ii, p. 266.
[48] e.g. *Cal. Inq. Misc.* i, p. 170; *Liber de Bernewelle*, 253; *Rot. Hund.* (Rec. Com.), ii. 568; *Cal. Inq. p.m.* ii, p. 220; xii, p. 64.
[49] *Cur. Reg. R.* xiv, pp. 503–4.
[50] *Pipe R.* 1165 (P.R.S. viii), 24; 1176 (P.R.S. xxv), 22; 1177 (P.R.S. xxvi), 153; 1191 & 92 (P.R.S. N.S. ii), 203; B.L. Harl. MS. 3697, f. 225v.
[51] *Rot. Litt. Claus.* (Rec. Com.), i. 239, 241, 270.
[52] Ibid. ii. 162.

and 1232 by Stephen de la Haye, who held the manor *c.* 1236[53] and died probably in 1258. His son and heir, another Stephen,[54] redeemed his lands as a rebel in the 1260s[55] and held the manor in 1279.[56] In 1287 he ceded it to his son John,[57] who held it in 1302 and died after 1306.[58] John's son and successor Thomas de la Haye[59] survived his son Simon (d. after 1349)[60] and at his death *c.* 1362 his heir was his brother Robert, a clerk. By 1363 Robert had released his inheritance to Thomas's widow Agnes, who by 1366 had married Alan Ayete.[61] Ayete held Leyes in 1394 and 1406,[62] and died probably between 1413 and 1418. Perhaps in 1415 he or his daughter and heir Margery, who married William Purefoy, sold it to William Alington of Horseheath, the owner by 1428.[63]

Alington already held Streetly manor, and the other manors in the parish were later added to his family's estates, Bernhams in 1476, Yen Hall in 1548, Wolves in 1626. The West Wickham estates descended with Horseheath Hall,[64] with which they were sold in 1700 to John Bromley. In 1777, when the lands of Bromley's great-grandson Thomas, Lord Montfort, were sold,[65] Philip Yorke, earl of Hardwicke (d. 1790), agreed to buy West Wickham, but the conveyance was not completed or possession transferred until 1785,[66] and *c.* 215 a. by the southern boundary remained with the Horseheath estate.[67] The Hardwickes retained West Wickham until the 1890s.[68] In 1899 A. H. Irvine, having foreclosed upon a mortgage, sold the estate to the Revd. John Hodgson, lord until after 1902.[69] By 1904 West Wickham belonged to P. A. S. Hickey[70] who sold most of the farms to their tenants *c.* 1912,[71] and was dead by 1915. In 1916 his executors sold the remaining manorial rights,[72] which by 1922 belonged to H. F. Beales, owner of Manor farm, and were again sold after his death in 1927.[73] Until 1937 manor courts were held in the names of Maggie M. Skarsey and Ella Slater.[74]

Earl Aubrey, having for a time retained half his estate, later *BERNHAMS* manor, later enfeoffed Gerald the marshal with it.[75] From Gerald it apparently passed to Iseult, daughter of his son Roger (d. by 1180) and wife by 1199 of William Russell,[76] who still held the manor *c.* 1236[77] and was possibly living in 1249.[78] Russell's son William, although appealed of murder in 1244,[79] apparently still held the estate *c.* 1255.[80] His son Roger Russell,[81] having fought for the rebels at Lewes and Ely in the 1260s, probably forfeited it,[82] although his sisters Alice and Philippa in 1279 had 55 a. at West Wickham and later granted part to Roger's son John (d. after 1298).[83] The manor had been occupied, probably in 1265, by the royalist Sir Drew Barentyn (d. 1265).[84] Drew's son Sir William[85] sold it in 1274 to another royal retainer, Sir Emery Pecche (d. 1288),[86] who held it in 1279.[87] In 1285 Pecche granted the manor with 2 carucates to Sir Walter Bernham. Sir Walter's son John, tenant from the 1280s,[88] was succeeded between 1304 and 1307 by his son, another John,[89] tenant in 1316,[90] who probably died soon after 1331.[91] His widow Agnes held land at Wickham in 1345. Walter Bernham (fl. 1352) was succeeded by 1364 by his son Roger,[92] who in 1369 sold his lands there to William Wolf of Easton Maudit (Northants.)[93] who died after 1372.[94] By 1381 the lands belonged to William Wolf of Bottisham, who held Bernhams in 1397[95] and died in 1401.[96] After being held for a time by feoffees, possibly for John Wolf of Bottisham,[97] Bernhams belonged by 1428 to John Bury[98] (fl. 1418–48),[99] who in 1442 granted it to his son John (d. after 1468). The younger John's feoffees conveyed Bernhams in 1476 to John Alington (d. 1480) and his son William.[1] Despite William's will of 1485[2] the manor remained with the main Alington estate.

The sites of La Hayes and Bernhams manor-houses are uncertain. The latter apparently stood in 1293 by other messuages, perhaps on the village

[53] *Cur. Reg. R.* xiv, pp. 503–4; *Liber de Bernewelle*, 253.
[54] *Ex. e Rot. Fin.* (Rec. Com.), ii. 282; cf. *Cur. Reg. R.* xv, p. 400; *Abbrev. Plac.* (Rec. Com.), 148.
[55] *Close R.* 1268–72, 260.
[56] *Rot. Hund.* (Rec. Com.), ii. 568.
[57] B.L. Add. MS. 5823, f. 53.
[58] Ibid. f. 57v.; *Feud. Aids*, i. 143.
[59] *Feud. Aids*, i. 155, 163; cf. *Cal. Inq. p.m.* vii, p. 359.
[60] C.U.L., Queens' Coll. Mun., 52/47; cf. *Cal. Close*, 1346–9, 165.
[61] B.L. Add. MS. 5823, ff. 52v., 53, 57v.; C.P. 25(1)/288/49 no. 718.
[62] B.L. Add. MS. 5823, ff. 53, 232v.
[63] *V.C.H. Bucks.* iv. 224; *Feud. Aids*, i. 182; B.L. Add. MS. 5823, f. 53.
[64] Cf. C 140/76 no. 58; C 142/36 no. 16; C 142/592 no. 90.
[65] C.R.O., R 70/48, 17 Apr. 1700; and see above p. 72.
[66] B.L. Add. MS. 36229, ff. 197v., 209–304, especially f. 291.
[67] C.U.L., Doc. 660 nos. 105–6; ibid. MS. Plan 337.
[68] C.R.O., W. Wickham ct. bk. 1856–1937, pp. 1–124; cf. *Complete Peerage*, vi. 305–10.
[69] C.R.O., SP 173/3; ct. bk., pp. 128–48; cf. *Kelly's Dir. Cambs.* (1900).
[70] *Kelly's Dir. Cambs.* (1904); C.R.O., ct. bk., pp. 149–73.
[71] e.g. C.U.L., Maps 53(1)/92/102; C.R.O., 296/SP 1087; 515/SP 2185; cf. *Kelly's Dir. Cambs.* (1912).
[72] C.R.O., ct. bk., p. 174; C.U.L., Maps bb. 53(1)/91/7.
[73] C.R.O., ct. bk., pp. 203–8; SP 173/4.
[74] Ibid. ct. bk., pp. 211–20. *Kelly's Dir. Cambs.* (1929–37) names Sidney A. Taylor as lord.
[75] *Cur. Reg. R.* xiv, pp. 503–4; cf. B.L. Add. MS. 5823, f. 58.
[76] *Pipe R.* 1176 (P.R.S. xxv), 74; 1180 (P.R.S. xxix), 37; *Rot. Cur. Reg.* (Rec. Com.), ii. 138; *Cur. Reg. R.* i. 228; vi. 85, 213–14.
[77] *Liber de Bernewelle*, 253.
[78] *Close R.* 1247–51, 150; cf. *Cal. Pat.* 1247–58, 25.
[79] *Cal. Pat.* 1242–7, 202, 295.
[80] *Close R.* 1254–6, 171; B.L. Add. MS. 5823, f. 242.
[81] B.L. Add. MS. 5823, f. 232v.
[82] *Rot. Selecti* (Rec. Com.), 240.
[83] *Rot. Hund.* (Rec. Com.), ii. 568–9, giving 'Philippa' as 'Philippus'; B.L. Add. MS. 5823, ff. 53, 94v., 103, 228.
[84] J.I. 1/83 rot. 32d.; *Cal. Pat.* 1258–66, 415, 506.
[85] *Cal. Pat.* 1258–66, 324.
[86] B.L. Add. MS. 5823, f. 84v.; *Cal. Inq. p.m.* ii, p. 407.
[87] *Rot. Hund.* (Rec. Com.), ii. 568.
[88] B.L. Add. MS. 5823, f. 84v.; C.P. 25(1)/26/42 no. 23.
[89] B.L. Add. MS. 5823, ff. 58, 94v., 230.
[90] *Feud. Aids*, i. 155.
[91] Last recorded in C.U.L., Queens' Coll. Mun. 52/23A.
[92] B.L. Add. MS. 5823, ff. 102, 228, 230, 232.
[93] Ibid. ff. 57v., 84v.; cf. *V.C.H. Northants.* iv. 13.
[94] *Cal. Inq. p.m.* xiii, p. 127.
[95] B.L. Add. MS. 5823, ff. 57v., 102v.–103; cf. C.U.L., Queens' Coll. Mun., 52/68–9.
[96] C 138/1 no. 16.
[97] B.L. Add. MS. 5823, ff. 85, 103; cf. *Cal. Close*, 1408–13, 97.
[98] B.L. Add. MS. 5823, f. 85; *Feud. Aids*, i. 182.
[99] C.U.L., Queens' Coll. Mun., 52/115–19; *Cal. Close*, 1413–19, 507.
[1] B.L. Add. MS. 5823, ff. 57v., 84v.
[2] Prob. 11/8 (P.C.C. 3 Milles).

street.[3] The former may have been within the moat at Hill Farm, ½ mile east of the main village, between Leys wood and Hall field, so named by 1608.[4] The modern Manor Farm, a timber-framed 17th-century house with an eastern cross-wing, containing panelling of *c.* 1700,[5] was perhaps derived from the parsonage mansion house mentioned *c.* 1546.[6] Until the 1850s it was also called Parsonage Farm, and the tithes were let with it.[7]

Part of William Wolf's land remained separate from Bernhams, probably passing by 1412 to Sir John Tiptoft, later Lord Tiptoft,[8] steward of Bottisham manor since 1405,[9] who held land called *WOLVES* at West Wickham at his death in 1443. Tiptoft's son and heir John, later earl of Worcester,[10] executed in 1470, left Wolves manor, held of John Alington, to his infant son Edward[11] (d.s.p. 1485). Edward's heirs were his aunts, including the aged Philippa, widow of Thomas, Lord Ros (d. 1464).[12] In 1488 she conveyed the reversion of Wolves manor, then held for life by Earl John's widow Elizabeth (d. 1498) and her husband Sir William Stanley, to John Ward, grocer, of London (d. 1501).[13] The estate was later recovered from Ward or his heirs by Henry VII's minister Sir Thomas Lovell (d. 1524), third husband of Philippa's daughter Isabel.[14] Lovell devised Wolves to his brother Sir Gregory's younger son John for life, with remainder to John's elder brother Francis Lovell,[15] who probably held Wolves at his death in 1552. His son and heir Sir Thomas died in 1567 having settled it on his younger brother Gregory,[16] who, after serving for many years in Elizabeth I's household,[17] died in 1597.[18] His son Sir Robert Lovell sold Wolves with 200 a. of arable in 1598 to James,[19] a younger brother of Giles Alington (d. 1573). James died in 1626, leaving his land to Giles's son, Sir Giles Alington (d. 1638).[20]

By 1066 the abbot of Ely had at *STREETLY* a manor of 1½ hide, which although retained in 1086[21] was possibly later subinfeudated since Bishop Niel recovered it before 1135 for the see of Ely.[22] Probably after 1166 it was granted to Jordan of Sandford, a Wiltshire landowner[23] (fl. 1155–74), succeeded in 1175 by his son Thomas.[24] In 1194 Thomas held Streetly as ½ knight's fee of the bishop of Ely,[25] whose successors remained overlords[26] and were compensated with a rent-charge of 2 marks when the manor was granted in mortmain in 1370.[27] That rent was paid to the Charterhouse, their successors as lords of Balsham, until redeemed in 1906.[28] Thomas of Sandford, who had served King John as keeper of Devizes castle 1199–1216,[29] joined the Knights Templars *c.* 1217,[30] and his lands passed to his son Richard[31] (d.s.p. 1221), whose brother and heir Warner[32] died on pilgrimage in 1222 and was succeeded by his next brother Hugh[33] (d.s.p. 1229). Hugh's heir, his brother Thomas,[34] held the manor *c.* 1236[35] and died *c.* 1241. Under a settlement of 1230 Streetly passed in turn to the three sons of Thomas's younger sister Cecily by Hugh Peverel (d. 1229) of Sampford Peverel (Devon),[36] William (d. on crusade 1241), Thomas (d. 1242), and Hugh[37] (d. 1296). It then descended to Sir Hugh's grandson Thomas Peverel, aged 18, who died in 1300 leaving as heirs his sisters Margery, who soon died, Joan, and Denise.[38]

Joan (d. by 1331) and her husband Sir John Wroxall[39] leased their moiety in 1328 to Denise,[40] married by 1302 to John de la Rivere of Tormarton (Glos.),[41] who was granted free warren at Streetly in 1304.[42] Rivere died in 1314, leaving a son John, aged 2,[43] but Denise retained Streetly in her own right.[44] In 1337 or 1343 she obtained a release of Wroxall's rights by the curtesy,[45] and died in 1347 having settled the manor for life on her daughter Lavine, who apparently lived at Ickleton priory. Denise's son and heir Sir John de la Rivere[46] sold his reversionary interest in Streetly in 1350 to Sir

[3] B.L. Add. MS. 5823, f. 230.
[4] C.U.L., Add. MS. 6920, f. 78v.
[5] M.H.L.G. List.
[6] C 3/3/58.
[7] e.g. C.R.O., R 70/48, 15 July 1768; B.L. Add. MS. 36229, ff. 205, 279; H.O. 107/1761.
[8] *Feud. Aids*, vi. 406.
[9] *Cal. Pat.* 1405–8, 101.
[10] C.U.L., Queens' Coll. Mun., 52/109–10; cf. *Cal. Fine R.* 1437–45, 232; *Complete Peerage*, xii (1), 747–9; xii (2), 842–6.
[11] C 140/34 no. 53.
[12] *Cal. Inq. p.m. Hen. VII*, i, p. 10; *Complete Peerage* xi. 105–6.
[13] C.P. 25(2)/30/101 no. 6; cf. *V.C.H. Cambs.* v. 163.
[14] *Complete Peerage*, xi. 106–7; *Cal. Inq. p.m. Hen. VII*, iii, p. 462; cf. Nicolas, *Test. Vetusta*, ii. 528–9; *L. & P. Hen. VIII*, iv (1), pp. 153, 155; *D.N.B.*
[15] C 142/42 no. 163; for the Lovell pedigree, see Blomefield, *Norf.* i. 323–5; vii. 271–3.
[16] C 142/96 no. 41; C.P. 25(2)/83/710 no. 19.
[17] e.g. *Cal. Pat.* 1566–9, p. 318; *Cal. S.P. Dom. Addenda* 1580–1625, pp. 128, 250.
[18] Prob. 11/89 (P.C.C. 20 Cobham).
[19] B.L. Add. MS. 5823, f. 95; C.P. 25(2)/94/862/40 Eliz. I Trin. no. 6.
[20] Prob. 11/150 (P.C.C. 121 Hele); C 142/434 no. 85.
[21] *V.C.H. Cambs.* i. 365. In 1008 the abbey bought 'Strethle' near Hadstock and Linton: *Liber Elien.* (Camd. 3rd ser. xcii), 145–6; that estate was probably Strethall Green (Essex): cf. *Liber Elien.* 129–30, 162, 417 n.; *P.N. Essex* (E.P.N.S.), 530.
[22] *Liber Elien.* 287.
[23] *Red Bk. Exch.* (Rolls Ser.), i. 364; cf. *V.C.H. Wilts.* iv. 403.
[24] *Pipe R.* 1156–8 (Rec. Com.), 57; 1174 (P.R.S. xxi), 29; 1175 (P.R.S. xxii), 99.
[25] *Rot. Cur. Reg.* (Rec. Com.), i. 113; *Feet of Fines* (Rec. Com.), 296; *Red Bk. Exch.* ii. 525. Jordan and Thos. of Sandford should be distinguished from Jordan, a younger son of Gerald the marshal, and his son Thos.: cf. B.L. Add. MS. 5823, f. 58; B.L. Harl. MS. 3697, f. 225; *Feet of Fines*, 315–16; *Cur. Reg. R.* i. 228; ii. 73; iv. 36, 64–5, 167.
[26] e.g. *Liber de Bernewelle*, 253; *Rot. Hund.* (Rec. Com.), ii. 429; C 140/76 no. 58; C 142/36 no. 16.
[27] *Cal. Pat.* 1367–70, 415.
[28] C.R.O., W. Wickham ct. bk. 1856–1937, p. 171; Charterho. Mun., MR 2/168D, 194A, 194D.
[29] *V.C.H. Wilts.* x. 239.
[30] *Pat. R.* 1216–25, 67; *Rot. Litt. Claus.* i. 349.
[31] *Pipe R.* 1218 (P.R.S. N.S. xxxix), 6.
[32] *Rot. Litt. Claus.* i. 453, 479; *Ex. e Rot. Fin.* (Rec. Com.), i. 63.
[33] *Pat. R.* 1216–25, 329; *Ex. e Rot. Fin.* i. 91.
[34] *Close R.* 1227–31, 258. Hugh had an uncle Hugh (d. 1233): *Ex. e Rot. Fin.* i. 253; cf. *Bracton's Notebk.* ii, p. 149.
[35] *Liber de Bernewelle*, 253.
[36] *Close R.* 1237–42, 340; *Cur. Reg. R.* xiv, pp. 71–2; B.L. Add. MS. 5823, f. 124; cf. *Close R.* 1227–31, 155.
[37] *Ex. e Rot. Fin.* (Rec. Com.), i. 182, 361, 384; B.L. Cott. MS. Claud. C. xi, f. 121v.; *Rot. Hund.* (Rec. Com.), ii. 429.
[38] *Cal. Inq. p.m.* iii, pp. 207–8, 450–1.
[39] *Cal. Inq. Misc.* iii, p. 300; cf. *Cal. Pat.* 1307–13, 305.
[40] B.L. Add. MS. 5823, f. 63v.
[41] *Feud. Aids*, i. 145; ii. 249.
[42] *Cal. Chart. R.* 1300–26, 40.
[43] *Cal. Inq. p.m.* v, p. 281.
[44] e.g. *Feud. Aids*, i. 155; *Cal. Close*, 1323–7, 521.
[45] B.L. Add. MS. 5823, f. 52v.
[46] Ibid. f. 63v.; B.L. Add. MS. 5842, f. 136v.; C.P. 25(1)/28/73 no. 4; *Cal. Inq. p.m.*, ix, p. 4.

Walter Manny, K.G. (d. 1372), who in 1363 procured a release from Joan Wroxall's coheirs.[47] Manny probably had possession by 1367,[48] and in 1370 his feoffees agreed to grant the manor to St. Bartholomew's hospital, London,[49] which received a release from the feoffees and Manny's widow in 1372.[50] The hospital still held the manor *c.* 1388[51] but in 1389 released it to John Sleaford, rector of Balsham, and Thomas Fotheringay, already tenants there. Fotheringay released his interest *c.* 1393 to Sleaford, who in 1399 agreed to sell Streetly to William Alington,[52] to whom Sleaford's feoffees released it in 1410.[53]

The site of the manor-house, recorded in 1260,[54] and called by *c.* 1280 Streetly Hall,[55] was presumably at Streetly Hall Farm, ½ mile west of Streetly hamlet. Its park was mentioned in 1393.[56] It had a timber-framed farm-house, enlarged eastwards in the 18th century with a three-bay brick-fronted range, which survived in 1975. The house and farm were sold *c.* 1911 to S. O. Webb,[57] whose family had been tenants there since *c.* 1800.[58] About 1912 Webb built a larger house;[59] the old farm-buildings were burnt down in 1930.[60]

In 974 King Edgar's thegn Elfhelm (d. *c.* 990) gave his wife 3 hides at Enhale on their marriage.[61] By 1066 1 hide there comprising *ENHALE*, later *YEN HALL*, manor belonged to King Edward's thegn Tochi, of whose successor William de Warenne it was held in 1086 by Lambert de Rosey.[62] From William's son William, earl of Surrey (d. 1138), lordship over Enhale passed to his younger son Reynold[63] (d. 1179), whose heirs were mesne lords under the earls of Surrey.[64] After 1209 Reynold's granddaughter Beatrice brought the mesne lordship, with the honor of Wormegay, to the Bardolfs, of whom Enhale was still held *c.* 1400.[65] Lambert de Rosey was succeeded by his son Walkelin,[66] and Ralph de Rosey (fl. 1158)[67] by his son Baldwin,[68] who went on crusade in 1189. By 1195 his land had come to Walkelin de Rosey[69] (d. 1221), who left as heir a son, Baldwin, under age.[70] Baldwin, in possession in 1242,[71] died after 1260,[72] when his lands may have passed to Walkelin de Rosey, probably his son,[73] murdered *c.* 1270,[74] or to Saher de Rosey, a ward of Earl John de Warenne *c.* 1260.[75]

By 1279 Enhale manor belonged with other Rosey estates to Sir Baldwin de Manners,[76] who was granted free warren there in 1291, was lord in 1316,[77] and died without issue in 1320. Baldwin's widow Joan sought dower in Enhale in 1321,[78] but Baldwin had in 1311 granted the reversion of other Cambridgeshire manors, and perhaps of Enhale, to Sir John Botetourt[79] (d. 1324): by 1331 Joan, widow of Botetourt's son Thomas (d. 1322), held Enhale.[80] When Joan died in 1338 Enhale descended to her son Sir John, later Lord Botetourt,[81] who held it in 1346 and 1359,[82] but had alienated it before he died in 1385.[83]

It was probably acquired by Roger Harleston, a Cambridge burgess (fl. 1359–88),[84] whose son Ives was recorded in 1390 as holding the fee and came of age in 1399.[85] Ives died in 1403 leaving a son John, aged 1,[86] whose mother Eleanor probably occupied the manor until her death in 1416.[87] John had livery in 1424.[88] In 1452–3 Enhale was briefly taken into the king's hands.[89] John died in 1457 and his son John in 1458. The latter's son and heir John, then aged 3,[90] apparently died after 1464,[91] for Enhale passed to Robert Harleston, his uncle,[92] and was forfeited upon Robert's attainder in 1471.[93] It was successively granted to Richard, duke of Gloucester, in 1471, and to Sir William Stanley in 1475.[94] The attainder was repealed in 1485,[95] and the manor presumably restored to Robert's son John (d. by 1500), who left a son Clement, aged 5.[96] In 1535 Sir Clement Harleston sold Enhale to John Wheatley of Fulbourn, whose widow Anne and son George sold it in 1549 to Sir Giles Alington (d. 1586).[97] From the 17th century the estate was erroneously

[47] B.L. Add. MS. 5823, f. 63; *D.N.B.* s.v. Manny.
[48] *Cal. Inq. p.m.* xii, pp. 128–9; B.L. Add. MS. 5823, f. 62v.
[49] *Cal. Close*, 1367–70, 415; *Cart. St. Bart.'s Hosp.* ed. N. J. M. Kerling, p. 24.
[50] B.L. Add. MS. 5823, ff. 62v., 63v.
[51] *Cal. Inq. p.m.* xvi, p. 205; ibid. p. 298 wrongly ascribes it to Manny's foundation at the London Charterhouse.
[52] B.L. Add. MS. 5823, ff. 62v.–63.
[53] Ibid. ff. 123v.–124.
[54] *Assizes at Camb. 1260*, 10.
[55] B.L. Add. MS. 5823, f. 230.
[56] Ibid. f. 99.
[57] *Kelly's Dir. Cambs.* (1912 and later edns.).
[58] Cf. C.R.O., L 60/34.
[59] Ex inf. Mr. J. D. Webb.
[60] C.U.L., Doc. 3980, box ii, Horseheath 'Village Annals', p. 42.
[61] *Cart. Sax.* ed. Birch, iii, pp. 628–31; cf. *Liber Elien.* (Camd. 3rd ser. xcii), p. 143; Dorothy Whitelock, *A.-S. Wills*, 30–1.
[62] *V.C.H. Cambs.* i. 350.
[63] Cf. *Complete Peerage*, xii (i), 49; Sanders, *Eng. Baronies*, 101.
[64] e.g. *Red Bk. Exch.* (Rolls Ser.), ii. 527; *Rot. Hund.* (Rec. Com.), ii. 429.
[65] e.g. *Liber de Bernewelle*, 253; *Bk. of Fees*, ii. 923; *Cal. Inq. p.m.* vii, p. 179; viii, p. 113; xvi, p. 309; cf. *Complete Peerage*, i. 417–21.
[66] Dugdale, *Mon.* v. 50.
[67] *Pipe R.* 1156–8 (Rec. Com.), 166.
[68] B.L. Add. Ch. 28338.
[69] *Pipe R.* 1194 (P.R.S. N.S. v), 64.
[70] *Cur. Reg. R.* x. 12, 83–4, 155.
[71] *Bk. of Fees*, ii. 923.
[72] *Close R.* 1259–61, 454.
[73] Cf. *Cal. Pat.* 1247–58, 375–6.
[74] *Close R.* 1268–72, 179; *Cal. Pat.* 1272–81, 428.
[75] *Cal. Inq. p.m.* ii, p. 195.
[76] *Rot. Hund.* (Rec. Com.), ii. 429; cf. *Bk. of Fees*, ii. 908; *Cal. Inq. p.m.* iv, p. 302.
[77] *Cal. Chart. R.* 1257–1300, 396; *Feud. Aids*, i. 155.
[78] *Complete Peerage*, viii. 379–81; C.P. 40/236 rott. 52d., 301d.
[79] C.P. 25(1)/285/29 no. 56.
[80] *Cal. Inq. p.m.* vii, p. 179; *Complete Peerage*, i. 233–5.
[81] *Cal. Inq. p.m.* viii, p. 113.
[82] *Feud. Aids*, i. 163; B.L. Add. MS. 5823, f. 85.
[83] Cf. *Cal. Inq. p.m.* xvi, pp. 77–9.
[84] Cf. Maitland, *Township and Borough*, 128–9; *Cal. Close*, 1385–9, 465.
[85] *Cal. Inq. p.m.* xvi, p. 309; C 137/19 no. 75; not son of John Harleston, as in *V.C.H. Cambs.* iii. 123.
[86] C 137/44 no. 33.
[87] *Cal. Pat.* 1402–5, 332; *Cal. Fine R.* 1413–22, 144.
[88] C 139/20 no. 47; *Cal. Close*, 1422–29, 171.
[89] *Cal. Fine R.* 1454–61, 30; Wedgwood, *Hist. Parl. 1439–1509, Biog.* 477–8; cf. *Cal. Close*, 1447–54, 431.
[90] C 139/167 no. 13.
[91] Cf. C 140/13 no. 23.
[92] Cf. *Cal. Close*, 1461–8, 406.
[93] C 145/327/5 no. 2; *Rot. Parl.* vi. 144–5.
[94] *Cal. Pat.* 1467–77, 297, 556.
[95] *Rot. Parl.* vi. 281–2.
[96] *Cal. Inq. p.m. Hen. VII*, i, pp. 377–8; ii, p. 237.
[97] B.L. Add. MS. 5823, ff. 52v., 58, 94v.

referred to as two distinct manors called Eynall and Yennolds.[98]

The manor-house, later Yen Hall, recorded by 1315,[99] stood ¾ mile north of the village, probably within a curved moat. A timber-framed farm-house, built north of the moat probably in the 17th century, was left empty from *c.* 1960 and was derelict in 1975.[1]

The yardland and the half-yardland at Wickham held in 1086 respectively by Hardwin de Scalers and by Ulveva of Richard son of Gilbert[2] presumably descended with the fees of those lords in Horseheath.[3] The Sewale family had a substantial freehold in the 14th century. John Sewale (fl. 1279–1311),[4] son of Peter Sewale (fl. *c.* 1250),[5] son of Richard,[6] son of Sewale (fl. before 1190),[7] held *c.* 30 a. under Emery Pecche in 1279, and bought much other land,[8] which passed to his son John (fl. 1303–29)[9] who held over 100 a. in 1315.[10] John's son and heir Thomas (fl. 1331–69)[11] was permitted a private oratory in 1352[12] and apparently occupied Bernhams manor in 1361.[13]

By 1484 Queens' College, Cambridge, had acquired 40 a. at West Wickham,[14] and after further purchases owned *c.* 130 a. held freely of the Alingtons in 1549.[15] At inclosure 121 a. were allotted to the college's lessee F. L. Charlton, whose underlessee farmed it from White Hall.[16] The estate comprised 146 a. when the college sold it in 1920.[17] St. John's College, Cambridge, had *c.* 1540 a close of 2 a., and after inclosure 6 a., sold in 1945.[18] Pembroke College, Cambridge, owned from *c.* 1505 18 a. attached to its Horseheath estate,[19] with which it was regularly let to the lords of Horseheath from 1748 until sold in 1877.[20]

West Wickham rectory, appropriated to Earl's Colne priory (Essex) by 1366,[21] was granted on the priory's suppression in 1536 to the priory's patron, John de Vere, earl of Oxford,[22] whose grandson Earl Edward sold it in 1592 to Edmund Stubbing, a local yeoman.[23] In 1606 Stubbing sold it to Sir Giles Alington (d. 1638), lord of the manors,[24] who by 1613 had bought out a contingent remainder made to the Crown in 1588 and granted by the Crown in 1592.[25] The rectory descended with the Alingtons' West Wickham estate[26] until William, Lord Alington (d. 1685) gave it, perhaps before 1665, to Dr. Henry Harrison, his companion on a continental tour.[27] In 1680 Harrison settled the rectory with its tithes and over 200 a. on himself with remainder to his son Alington,[28] and died in 1690.[29] Alington Harrison was succeeded in 1731 by his son Alington (d. 1733)[30] who devised the rectory absolutely to his wife Anne.[31] Anne sold it *c.* 1740 to Henry Bromley, Lord Montfort.[32] Thereafter the rectory descended with the manors, and at inclosure Lord Hardwicke was allotted 151 a. for glebe and 458 a. for tithes.[33] After the division of *c.* 1912 the estate was represented by Manor farm.[34]

ECONOMIC HISTORY. In 1086 1½ out of 2 hides, comprising land for 5 plough-teams, of Count Alan's manor lay in demesne, but he had only 1 demesne plough-team with 4 *servi* to cultivate it, while his 4 *villani* could provide 4 teams. At Streetly the abbot of Ely had only ½ hide in demesne but had 2½ teams, while his 6 *villani* had 2 teams on the remaining 1 hide. Most of the land for 3½ teams in Enhale lay in demesne, and the lord had 2 teams while 10 bordars, his only tenants, had 1½ between them. Count Alan's manor had increased in value since 1066 from £8 to £10, and Streetly from £2 to £3 5*s*., but Enhale was still worth only £5. On the land for ½ team of Hardwin de Scalers 3 bordars had succeeded 3 sokemen. Altogether the demesnes had 5½ plough-teams out of 13½ for the vill.[35]

In 1279[36] the demesnes covered at least half the parish, comprising 1,240 a. of its arable, compared with *c.* 645 a. held by free tenants and only 200 a. of villein land. The La Hayes and Bernhams demesnes, as moieties of the Vere estate, were almost exactly equal, each including 340 a. of arable, 3 a. of meadow, and 12 a. of wood. On La Hayes, however, the tenants held 253 a. freely and 73 a. by villein tenure, while on Bernhams there were only 125 a. of freehold and 22 a. of villein land. Enhale manor had 320 a. in demesne and only 110 a. of tenant land, all but 27 a. held in villeinage. At Streetly there were 240 a. of demesne,[37] 138 a. held freely, and only 22 a. of villein land. Some large freeholds belonged to landowners from neighbouring vills: William of Berardshay owned 80 a., held, under the Veres, of Hugh le Breton, whose predecessor Jordan had sold

[98] e.g. C 142/592 no. 90; C.R.O., R 70/48, deeds 1664 and later.
[99] C.U.L., Queens' Coll. Mun., 52/10.
[1] *V.C.H. Cambs.* ii. 43; local information.
[2] *V.C.H. Cambs.* i. 381, 385.
[3] See p. 74.
[4] B.L. Add. MS. 5823, f. 102; C.U.L., Queens' Coll. Mun., 52/9.
[5] B.L. Add. MS. 5823, ff. 229, 232v.
[6] Ibid. ff. 99v.; *Abbrev. Plac.* (Rec. Com.), 148.
[7] B.L. Add. MS. 5823, ff. 58, 231v.
[8] Ibid. ff. 102–3, 229–231v.; *Rot. Hund.* (Rec. Com.), ii. 569.
[9] B.L. Add. MS. 5823, ff. 94v., 102; C.U.L., Queens' Coll. Mun., 52/22.
[10] C.P. 25(1)/27/57 no. 7.
[11] C.U.L., Queens' Coll. Mun., 52/23A; B.L. Add. MS. 5823, f. 84v.
[12] *E.D.R.* (1893), 151.
[13] *Cal. Inq. p.m.* x, p. 530.
[14] C.U.L., Queens' Coll. Mun., lease 2 Ric. II.
[15] Ibid. terrier 1549; *Camb. Univ. Doc.* (1852), 220.
[16] C.U.L., Add. MS. 6081, f. 23v.; C.R.O., Q/RDc 80, p. 485.
[17] C.U.L., Maps 53(1)/92/38.
[18] *Camb. Univ. Doc.* (1852), 181; C.U.L., Add. MS. 6081, f. 14v.; C.R.O., Q/RDc 80, p. 484; C.R.O., 515/SP 1855.
[19] Pemb. Coll. Mun., Horseheath, A 3–4, 10–13; B 1–17; C.U.L., MS. Plan 337.
[20] Pemb. Coll. Mun., D 15; F 1–3.
[21] B.L. Add. MS. 5847, f. 182v.
[22] *L. & P. Hen. VIII*, xi, p. 89.
[23] C.P. 25(2)/93/856/34 Eliz. I East. no. 9.
[24] C.P. 25(2)/277/4 Jas. I Mich. no. 12.
[25] C.P. 25(2)/261/30 Eliz. I East. no. 5; E 178/3631; cf. B.L. Add. MS. 5823, f. 95.
[26] e.g. C.P. 25(2)/400/7 Chas. I Mich. no. 32.
[27] B.L. Add. MS. 5807, f. 80; *Mon. Inscr. Cambs.* 183; C.U.L., E.D.R., B 2/58. The rectory is not mentioned in Alington settlements of 1664 and later in C.R.O., R 70/48.
[28] C.P. 25(2)/634/32 Chas. II Trin. no. 12.
[29] Prob. 11/402 (P.C.C. 184 Dyke).
[30] *Alum. Cantab. to 1751*, ii. 314.
[31] Prob. 11/664 (P.C.C. 61 Ockham).
[32] B.L. Add. MS. 5807, f. 80; Add. MS. 5808, f. 173.
[33] C.R.O., Q/RDc 9, pp. 450–3.
[34] See above.
[35] *V.C.H. Cambs.* i. 365, 374, 380, 385, 408–9.
[36] The following paragraph is based on *Rot. Hund.* (Rec. Com.), ii. 429–30, 568–9; C 133/94/5 no. 3.
[37] 360 a. in 1300: C 133/94/5 no. 3.

100 a. before 1219,[38] and Geoffrey and John of Horseheath and William le Harper of Horseheath had together 100 a. Of *c.* 50 free tenants in the vill 2 occupied 40 a. each, 6 more with 15–22 a. had 115 a. in all, and 32 others with under 10 a. owned 116 a. Only 3 out of 34 customary tenants had 20 a. or more, 10 had 10 a. each, and 21, including 11 cottars holding 2 a. each of Enhale manor, had together *c.* 40 a. On both La Hayes and Bernhams manors a villein holding 20 a., besides ploughing 9 a. yearly, owed 79 week-works between Michaelmas and Lammas and 23 during harvest, and 3 carrying-services. On Enhale manor the week-work due from 20 a. was similar, and the tenant had to plough 12 a. and do 6 carrying-services. In 1300 equally heavy services of 2 works a week fell on holdings of only 10 a. at Streetly, a former monastic estate, where even a 3-a. holding owed 40 works between Michaelmas and Lammas and 14 during harvest.[39]

Although services were probably still exacted in 1300 on Streetly manor,[40] other lords exploited them for cash. In 1304 John Bernham sold his single villein, his reeve's son, with his land and descendants to a St. Albans man who probably had no other land in the parish.[41] During the 14th century the demesnes were reduced, or leased, usually to prosperous local peasants. Thus 245 a. of the Enhale demesne were alienated *c.* 1320 to 13 people,[42] and in 1338 only 180 a. remained.[43] La Hayes demesne was leased in 1366 and 1394,[44] Bernhams in 1397,[45] Streetly by 1395.[46] One manor was leased to one of the rectors, who had decamped by 1340 with his rent £120 in arrear.[47] Customary land was put to rent.[48] Under James I there were 12 to 15 tenants of the combined manors,[49] probably mostly copyholders, but by the 1790s the enlargement of the lord's holdings had reduced the copyhold land to *c.* 80 a.[50] Only *c.* 50 a. were allotted for copyhold at inclosure.[51]

In 1232 William Russell vindicated his right to run a bull and boar in the open fields and pastures of West Wickham.[52] Streetly was occasionally said in the 13th century to have fields of its own, which included Stone field,[53] later of 17 a., halfway between the village and Streetly End,[54] and *c.* 1318 the West field.[55] Surviving deeds suggest, however, that in the open fields the strips of the four main demesnes and of the tenants were intermingled throughout the vill.[56] Inclosure was already in progress in the 13th century: *c.* 1250 Sir Hugh Peverel was obtaining, partly in exchange for land, releases from his free tenants of their rights of common in his pastures, meadows, and assarts.[57] Of a 49-a. holding of Streetly manor in 1319 24 a. lay in severalty and 25 a. in common.[58]

West of the road[59] from Bartlow to West Wratting lay the West field,[60] still reckoned in 1606 to belong to Streetly,[61] and divided by 1667 into the Hither and Further West fields.[62] In 1813, with its northern neighbour Bleachman field, it covered 376 a., and Pageant Hill field[63] north of the Balsham road had 96 a. South of the road west from Streetly End lay Dodwell,[64] later Doddle, field (30 a.), east of Streetly Hall, and Down field[65] (74 a.) to the west. Between that road and the Horseheath–Balsham road lay seven named fields in the Middle Ages,[66] represented in 1813 by Tenacredean field (101 a.) near Streetly End, Causeway (formerly Chalkpit) field[67] to the west, and Stanebury Hill to the north (270 a. together). North of the village street there were in the Middle Ages four named fields,[68] of which Reading field (68½ a.) lay north-east of the village in 1813, with Willow field[69] (106 a.) to the west. North of them 238 a. of ancient inclosures then surrounded Yenhall farm. The common pasture, 60 a. in 1279 and called by 1419 the Shrub,[70] lay east of those closes. In 1813 Shrub Common covered 95 a. South-east of the village street were Little, Hall, and Stone fields[71] (114 a. together); in 1608 the tenants acknowledged the lord's customary right to keep Hall field inclosed between harvest and 1 November.[72] The land to the south and east was probably in the Middle Ages, as later, held mostly in severalty as part of the demesnes.[73] Immediately east of Streetly End Blunts field (37 a.) and Button field (20 a.) still contained arable held in strips *c.* 1450. In 1456 part of Blunts field had been newly hedged and ditched, making it several.[74]

The usual crops were grown in the open fields, the peasants perhaps sowing mostly barley.[75] A farmer in 1522 left 8 a. of wheat and 7 a. of bullymong.[76] Saffron was possibly grown before 1592.[77] The many small fields were presumably grouped into larger units in a triennial rotation, still followed on the demesne farms in the 1770s.[78] Of 795 a. under crops in 1801 there were 229 a. of wheat, 259 a. of barley, 212 a. of oats, and 66 a. of peas, but only 20 a. of turnips.[79]

In 1086 there were 266 sheep on the manors,

38 C.P. 25(1)/23/9 no. 9.
39 C 133/94/5 no. 3.
40 Ibid.
41 B.L. Add. MS. 5823, ff. 58, 102v.
42 C.P. 40/236 rott. 52d., 301d.
43 C 135/54 no. 9.
44 B.L. Add. MS. 5823, ff. 57v., 232v.
45 Ibid. f. 102v.
46 Ibid. ff. 62v., 99.
47 *E.D.R.* (1892), 704.
48 e.g. B.L. Add. MS. 5823, f. 232.
49 C.U.L., Add. MS. 6920, ff. 40, 77v.
50 Ibid. Doc. 660 no. 158.
51 C.R.O., Q/RDc 9, pp. 455–74.
52 *Cur. Reg. R.* xiv, pp. 503–4.
53 e.g. B.L. Add. MS. 5823, f. 99; C.U.L., Queens' Coll. Mun., 52/1.
54 C.R.O., Q/RDc 39.
55 B.L. Add. MS. 5823, f. 231.
56 e.g. C.U.L., Queens' Coll. Mun., 52/11–136, *passim.*
57 B.L. Add. MS. 5823, ff. 63v., 99 and v.
58 *Cal. Close*, 1323–7, 521.
59 Layout, areas, and modern names from C.R.O., Q/RDc 9, 39.
60 B.L. Add. MS. 5823, f. 231 (1318).
61 C.U.L., Add. MS. 6920, f. 40.
62 Ibid. Queens' Coll. Mun., terrier 1667.
63 C.U.L., Doc. 660 no. 158 (1783).
64 B.L. Add. MS. 5823, f. 233 (*c.* 1250).
65 C.U.L., Queens' Coll. Mun., 52/22: 'le Doune' (1329).
66 Ibid. 52/1, 9, 17, 27A, 31, 35, 81, 106, 122, 128; B.L. Add. MS. 5823, ff. 95, 99, 231 and v.
67 C.U.L., Queens' Coll. Mun., terriers 1549, 1667.
68 Ibid. 52/10, 17, 48, 110, 112, 122; B.L. Add. MS. 5823, f. 94v.
69 Cf. C.U.L., Queens' Coll. Mun., terrier 1549.
70 *Rot. Hund.* (Rec. Com.), ii. 569; C.U.L., Queens' Coll. Mun., 52/101.
71 C.U.L., Queens' Coll. Mun., 52/1, 109; ibid. terrier 1549.
72 Ibid. Add. MS. 6920, f. 78v.
73 Cf. ibid. Queens' Coll. Mun., 52/6.
74 Pemb. Coll. Mun., Horseheath, A 3–4; A 10–12; cf. C 1, terrier *temp.* Jas. I.
75 e.g. B.L. Add. MS. 5861, ff. 7, 79v., 107.
76 Ibid. f. 86.
77 Cf. C.P. 25(2)/93/856/34 Eliz. I East. no. 9.
78 C.R.O., R 55/10/44H; B.L. Add. MS. 36229, f. 186.
79 H.O. 67/9.

Enhale's flock of 146 being the largest.[80] In 1260 the Wickham shepherd was accused of taking in stolen sheep.[81] There were 4 shepherds in 1279.[82] In 1319 the lady of Streetly granted with an estate the right to run 120 sheep over all the land, several or common, where she was herself entitled to feed sheep, except for the closes around her hall.[83] In 1497 it was recalled that a Horseheath flock had pastured in the southern fields of West Wickham from the West field to Stone and Button fields in succession.[84] As the demesnes were enlarged lesser men concentrated on cattle rather than sheep.[85] Common rights were customarily measured in bullocks[86] by 1813, when claims were made for common for 59 bullocks.[87] Lord Hardwicke then claimed the sole right of sheep-walk over the common fields and wastes.[88] In 1801 his tenant at Hill farm had a flock of 160 sheep, and in 1816 one of 105 Norfolk sheep.[89]

In 1524 25 people were assessed for tax on a total sum of £86; 2 of them were assessed at £20 each, 5 others at £26 between them, and the remaining 18 at less than £2 each.[90] Those who prospered were mainly the lessees of the demesne farms: Richard Challis (d. 1616) left £200 and land in three other parishes;[91] Philip Richardson, lessee of the rectory and agent to Sir Giles Alington, bequeathed £620 in 1633 and owned land in eight neighbouring parishes.[92] About 1640 members of the Flack family held the leases of Yenhall and Streetly farms, and the Webbs that of the parsonage.[93] John Webb, whose ancestors had owned property at West Wickham since the 1470s,[94] was said to be worth £40 in 1522.[95] Richard Webb (d. 1653) provided for legacies totalling £300.[96] Those families' holdings were among the largest not absorbed into the manorial estate. In 1549, out of 215 strips abutting on Queens' College land, 97 belonged to the Alingtons, 58 to the rectory and other manors later acquired by the Alingtons, and 10 to other colleges, while only 50, including 20 owned by John Webb, were possessed by villagers. In 1667 Richard Webb had 25 and four Flacks 20 of the strips not included in the Alington estate; only 7 other landholders were named.[97]

The demesnes of the several manors were long preserved as farming units. Thus Wickham Wolves was a separate farm in 1656 as in 1524,[98] and still comprised 207 a. in 1726. The estate then also included Yennolds farm (372 a.), Wickham Lodge farm (344 a.) whose farmstead had been burnt down by *c.* 1768, Streetly Hall farm (186 a.), and three others of 260 a., 185 a., and 78 a.[99] In the 1760s Yenhall farm included 490 a. in the north part of the parish, Hill farm (505 a.) comprised most of the closes to the east, and Streetly Hall farm (260 a.) lay to the south. Former glebe and the Pembroke College land were combined in a farm of 110 a., and most of the manorial open-field land was probably divided between Parsonage farm (372 a.) and Lower House or Malting farm (300 a.), leased together from 1774. In 1775 Lord Montfort's land, including the woods and park, covered 2,390 a. Other owners had not much over 370 a., including 128 a. belonging to Queens' College and 94 a. to Richard Webb.[1]

In 1811 Lord Hardwicke, whose estate amounted in 1813 to 2,015 a. including three farms of over 400 a. and two of over 300 a.,[2] decided to inclose the parish,[3] and an Act was obtained in 1812.[4] The land was surveyed and allotted in 1813, but the award was delayed, mainly because of disputes over compensation for tithes, until 1822.[5] There were 1,688 a. of ancient inclosures and 1,328 a. of open fields and commons. Of the land allotted Lord Hardwicke received 610 a. for glebe and tithes and 395 a. for other open-field land, besides retaining 1,242 a. of old inclosures; Queens' College and its lessee received 133 a.;[6] Daniel Taylor, whose ancestor had in 1715 acquired Streetly End farm by marrying into the Allen family and who had been buying up land since 1775,[7] received 97 a.; Thomas Hayward received 62 a.; the Williamson estate at West Wratting 12 a.; and 13 others 28 a. between them, mostly for rights of common. Queens' College and Pembroke College each retained 18 a. of old inclosures, Daniel Taylor 52 a., and Stanlake Batson 206 a. once part of Horseheath park.[8]

Following the inclosure Lord Hardwicke's estate was divided into five large farms.[9] Skipper's Hall farm, probably established by 1822, covered 375 a. north and east of Burton End, and Hill farm 375 a. in the east part of the parish. Yenhall farm, varying between 425 a. and 475 a., lay north-west, and Streetly Hall farm (540 a.) south-west, with Parsonage, later Manor, farm (305 a.) between them. They survived as units into the 1950s, after their sale *c.* 1912 to the tenants.[10] In the interstices were three smaller farms: 180 a., mostly Queens' College land, were apparently farmed from the White Hart at Burton End; Streetly End farm

[80] *V.C.H. Cambs.* i. 409.
[81] *Assizes at Camb. 1260*, 11.
[82] *Rot. Hund.* (Rec. Com.), ii. 429–30, 568–9.
[83] *Cal. Close*, 1323–7, 521.
[84] B.L. Add. MS. 5823, ff. 102v., 256v.
[85] e.g. ibid. Add. MS. 5861, ff. 79v., 95v., 99 (*c.* 1520–30).
[86] e.g. C.R.O., R 55/10/44E, 44H.
[87] C.U.L., Add. MS. 6081, ff. 2v., 24v.
[88] Ibid. f. 10v.
[89] *Camb. Chron.* 3 Oct. 1801; 19 June 1816.
[90] E 179/81/134 m. 4.
[91] Prob. 11/129 (P.C.C. 22 Weldon); cf. C.U.L., Add. MS. 6920, f. 78v.
[92] Prob. 11/163 (P.C.C. 37 Seager); cf. B.L. Add. MS. 5823, f. 95.
[93] *East Anglian*, N.S. ix. 113; x. 126.
[94] C.U.L., Queens' Coll. Mun., 52/128.
[95] *L. & P. Hen. VIII*, iii (2), p. 1118.
[96] Prob. 11/238 (P.C.C. 282 Alchin).
[97] C.U.L., Queens' Coll. Mun., terriers 1549, 1667.
[98] B.L. Add. MS. 12463, f. 21v.; Add. MS. 5823, ff. 95v., 137v.
[99] C.R.O., R 70/48, 19 Jan. 1726; cf. C.U.L., Add. MS. 6082, f. 25v.
[1] C.R.O., R 70/48, 15 July 1768; B.L. Add. MS. 5807, f. 82v.; Add. MS. 36229, ff. 186, 205–6, 276–83, 295–6. The areas given include land in West Wratting, Horseheath, and Bartlow.
[2] C.U.L., Add. MS. 6081, f. 10v.
[3] Ibid. Doc. 660 nos. 3–4.
[4] 52 Geo. III, c. 59 (Private, not printed); *C.J.* lxviii. 60, 235, 384.
[5] C.U.L., Add. MS. 6082, *passim.*
[6] C.R.O., Q/RDc 9, pp. 428–90.
[7] C.R.O., R 53/4/388; R 55/10/44D, 44H; C.U.L., Doc. 660 no. 158.
[8] C.R.O., Q/RDc 9, pp. 428–90.
[9] The following paragraph is based mainly on C.R.O., L 60/34 (1822); ibid. R 52/12/14/6; ibid. 296/SP 1087 (1914); ibid. SP 173/4 (1927); H.O. 107/1761; R.G. 10/1593; *Gardner's Dir. Cambs.* (1851); *Kelly's Dir. Cambs.* (1858–1937).
[10] Cf. C.R.O., 515/SP 2185, 2220.

(120 a.), sold by Daniel Taylor in 1827,[11] descended in the Kidman and Bird families until sold again in 1899;[12] Ivy Tod farm (60 a.) was farmed until the 1880s and owned until 1914 by the Hayward family.

Most villagers continued to work on the farms during the 19th and 20th centuries. In 1821 85 families depended on agriculture and only 15 on crafts or trade.[13] In 1851, when there were 87 adult farm-labourers, the farmers employed 90 men and 19 boys.[14] In 1877 nine-tenths of the population were said to be of the labouring class.[15] In 1905 West Wickham included 2,232 a. of arable and 302 a. of grass.[16] Sugar-beet was grown on Hill farm in the 1950s.[17]

By 1700 the Allen family had a tanyard next to their farm at Streetly End, with which it descended to Daniel Taylor.[18] It was still working in 1794,[19] and probably in 1813 and 1827, but had apparently closed by the 1840s. Taylor also owned in 1827 a brick-kiln, alluded to in 1813, east of Burton End.[20] In the mid 19th century the village had up to 6 shoemakers, one or two wheelwrights, carpenters, and smiths, and in 1871 a building firm employing 9 men.[21] The village craftsmen had mostly disappeared by 1920, although there was still a building firm in the 1930s and a blacksmith's shop in 1937. The smith had retired by 1960, leaving no successor.[22]

There were two millers in 1279.[23] La Hayes manor's windmill, standing south of the village, had been demolished by 1453.[24] Bernhams manor included a windmill in 1286.[25] In the 1220s Richard of Sandford sold Streetly manor's windmill, with his villeins' suit of mill, to a Balsham man who later resold it to Sir Hugh Peverel.[26] It still belonged to Streetly manor in 1296, and apparently in 1428.[27] In 1827 Streetly End farm included a six-storey brick tower-mill, built in 1802 immediately west of the farm-house. The mill ceased working, having lost its sails, after 1895,[28] and only the base survived in 1975.

LOCAL GOVERNMENT. In 1133 Henry I confirmed to Aubrey de Vere the manor held of the honor of Richmond, with sac and soc, tol, team, and infangthief.[29] Although Bernhams manor was said in 1279 to have view of frankpledge,[30] it was to the honor court, at which in 1334 two customary tenants from Bernhams and La Hayes manors presented a defaulting ale-taster,[31] that view of frankpledge in the two manors was ascribed in 1425.[32] Each of those two manors had its own three-weekly court *c.* 1300.[33] At Streetly in the 13th century the bishop of Ely had an annual view of frankpledge with the assize of bread and of ale, gallows, and tumbrel.[34] By 1600 the Alingtons were holding a single court for their combined manors of West Wickham and Streetly. It was styled a view of frankpledge and court baron, and occasionally dealt with agricultural matters, besides transferring copyholds,[35] its only function by the 19th century. A court book survives for 1856–1937.[36]

The court elected two constables in 1606.[37] In 1705 there were two parish constables, dominated by Alington Harrison, as both lay rector and a resident J.P.[38] In the early 19th century there was usually only one churchwarden, chosen by the parishioners.[39]

Expenditure on the poor, though only *c.* £70 in 1776, had reached £255 by 1803, when there were 24 people permanently supported.[40] In 1813 the parish owned a poorhouse at Burton End,[41] and *c.* 30 people received permanent relief. The cost averaged £570,[42] and until 1833 seldom fell below £500, reaching £740 in 1818.[43] Of £538 spent in 1832 £396 went to widows, children, and the sick and aged, and only *c.* £80 on casual relief or to paupers employed by the parish.[44] From 1835 the parish was part of the Linton poor-law union,[45] and with the Linton R.D. was merged in 1934 in the South Cambridgeshire R.D.,[46] being included in 1974 in South Cambridgeshire.

The parish council established in 1894 was unusually active, nominating two constables and a pinder, keeping the pound in repair, and providing allotments.[47]

CHURCH. By *c.* 1200 West Wickham had a church,[48] which had probably belonged to the Veres before they subinfeudated their manor, for the advowson of the rectory was said in 1279 to belong to the earl of Oxford.[49] The lords of Bernhams, half the Vere fee, also claimed the advowson, which Sir William Barentyn sold with that manor to Sir Emery Pecche.[50] In 1298, however, John Bernham released the advowson to Alice, dowager countess of Oxford,

11 Ibid. R 55/10/44R; C.U.L., Maps 53/82/5.
12 C.R.O., W. Wickham ct. bk. 1856–1937, pp. 64–9, 121–4, 198–200.
13 *Census*, 1821.
14 H.O. 107/1761.
15 C.U.L., E.D.R., C 3/27.
16 Cambs. Agric. Returns, 1905.
17 C.R.O., 515/SP 2220.
18 Ibid. R 53/4/388; R 55/10/44G.
19 Vancouver, *Agric. in Cambs.* 64.
20 C.R.O., Q/RDc 9, p. 486; R 55/10/44R.
21 H.O. 107/66, 1761; R.G. 10/1593.
22 *Kelly's Dir. Cambs.* (1916–37); *Camb. Ind. Press*, 9 Sept. 1960.
23 *Rot. Hund.* (Rec. Com.), ii. 568–9.
24 C.U.L., Queens' Coll. Mun., 52/123.
25 C.P. 25(1)/26/42 no. 3.
26 B.L. Add. MS. 5823, f. 63.
27 C 133/74 no. 27; B.L. Add. MS. 5823, f. 124.
28 C.R.O., R 55/10/44R; A. C. Smith, *Windmills in Cambs.*
29 *Reg. Regum Anglo-Norm.* ii, p. 266.
30 *Rot. Hund.* (Rec. Com.), ii. 568.
31 S.C. 2/155/71 mm. 1–2.
32 *Cal. Close*, 1422–9, 234–5.
33 Cf. B.L. Add. MS. 5823, f. 102v.
34 *Rot. Hund.* ii. 430; B.L. Cott. MS. Claud. C. xi, f. 121v.
35 C.U.L., Add. MS. 6920, ff. 40–1, 77v.–78v. (ct. minutes 1606, 1608).
36 C.R.O., ct. bk. 1856–1937, uncat.
37 C.U.L., Add. MS. 6920, f. 41.
38 C.R.O., Huddleston MSS., doc. in suit 1705–6.
39 e.g. C.U.L., E.D.R., C 1/6; C 3/39.
40 *Poor Law Abstract, 1804*, 34–5.
41 C.R.O., Q/RDc 9, p. 477.
42 *Poor Law Abstract, 1818*, 28–9.
43 *Poor Rate Returns, 1816–21*, 10; *1822–4*, 37; *1825–9*, 15–16; *1830–4*, 15.
44 *Rep. Com. Poor Laws* [44], H.C., p. 257 (1834), xxviii.
45 *Poor Law Com. 1st Rep.* 249.
46 *Census*, 1931 (pt. ii).
47 C.R.O., R 54/35/1 (e.g. *sub* 1895), 3B, 3C.
48 *Val. of Norwich*, ed. Lunt, 536.
49 *Rot. Hund.* (Rec. Com.), ii. 569.
50 B.L. Add. MS. 5823, f. 84v.

with remainder to her son Earl Robert,[51] in whose heirs it descended[52] until 1361. Earl Thomas was then licensed to grant the church to his priory at Earl's Colne.[53] By 1366 the church had been appropriated to the priory.[54]

Tithe portions in West Wickham belonged to Castle Acre priory (Norf.), Linton priory, and, by the time of inclosure, to the rectors of Balsham, Horseheath, and Bartlow. Castle Acre was granted, probably *c.* 1100, the demesne tithes of Enhale by Lambert de Rosey, under-tenant of the priory's founder William de Warenne.[55] By 1290 the rector of West Wickham was collecting the tithes and paying the priory £1 2*s.* a year.[56] In 1535 Colne priory owed 2 marks a year to Castle Acre[57] for the Enhale tithes, which in 1600 the Crown granted to the bishop of Ely.[58] Linton priory was said in 1291 to be entitled to a portion of £5,[59] but in 1346 nothing had been paid for over 30 years.[60] At inclosure the rector of Horseheath claimed tithes from 56 a. of ancient closes adjoining his parish[61] which had been leased free of tithes due to West Wickham rectory in 1624.[62] The rector of Balsham claimed tithes from 37 a. of Streetly Hall farm and alleged that his predecessors had received a modus for tithes of venison from 92 a., once in Horseheath park.[63] The park itself had been sold free of tithes due to West Wickham to Stanlake Batson, whose son refused to pay the sum assessed upon it when the tithes were commuted.[64] The two rectors and the rector of Bartlow were allotted 19 a. in 1822 for their tithes.[65]

The rectory was taxed at *c.* 26 marks in 1217 and 1291 and at 30 in 1276.[66] It included 60 a. of glebe in 1279.[67] Notable early rectors included *c.* 1300 Mr. Stephen of Haslingfield, chancellor of Cambridge university,[68] and *c.* 1312 Mr. Robert of St. Albans, Dean of Arches.[69] Later the earls chose for the rich living men inadequately qualified. John Lavenham, presented in 1339, was directed to study at a university, but repeatedly broke promises to do so and in 1346 obtained leave to remain in attendance on his patron the earl.[70] His successor John Pelham, instituted in his absence in 1347, only later took major orders,[71] and received leave of absence in 1349.[72]

In 1308 John de la Rivere sought a license to endow with 30 a. a chaplain to say daily masses in a chapel at Streetly manor-house.[73] The churchwardens held 6 a. given to maintain lights and obits, which were sold by the Crown in 1550,[74] as was a former guildhall *c.* 1570.[75]

When the church was appropriated no vicarage was ordained, and the bishop authorized the prior of Colne to serve the cure by a monk of his house.[76] In 1375 the parishioners successfully sued the prior for not providing a priest.[77] There was a chaplain at West Wickham in 1379,[78] and in 1454 a parish chaplain, paid 9 marks a year in 1463, had charge of the church.[79] Curates were recorded in the early 16th century,[80] and in the 1540s were paid by the farmer of the rectory.[81] When the lay impropriators did not leave the cure deserted, as in the late 1560s,[82] they provided curates, sometimes licensed by the bishop but considered removable at pleasure.[83] In 1650 the minister had £20 a year from the lay rector's lessee.[84] Dr. Harrison, the lay rector, may have served in person from *c.* 1671, but since he held neighbouring livings such as Withersfield (Suff.) and West Wratting he employed a curate in 1682.[85] His son Alington quarrelled with the curate, Samuel Richardson, whom he had appointed *c.* 1690, and sought to eject him on his own authority. In 1705 he brought to replace him two clergymen from Cambridge, and the congregation witnessed a physical contest for the pulpit and reading-desk. Richardson won the succeeding ecclesiastical lawsuit.[86] In 1728 Harrison, having taken orders, styled himself rector of West Wickham,[87] although it does not seem that he had been admitted or instituted.

Alington Harrison the younger (d. 1733) bequeathed £30 a year charged on the rectory for the person serving as curate.[88] In the 1760s the lessees of Parsonage farm were paying the curate that sum.[89] About 1792 Lord Hardwicke increased the stipend to £50, but it was uncertain whether the cure was a donative or a perpetual curacy.[90] In 1825 Lord Hardwicke matched £1,000 received for the living by lot from Queen Anne's Bounty by settling the £50 as a permanent rent-charge,[91] and by that endowment the living became a perpetual curacy,[92] worth £88 net *c.* 1830 and in 1871.[93]

51 C.P. 25(1)/26/46 no. 15.
52 e.g. *Cal. Inq. p.m.* x, p. 520.
53 *Cal. Pat.* 1361–4, 121.
54 B.L. Add. MS. 5847, f. 182v.
55 Dugdale, *Mon.* v. 50.
56 *Tax. Eccl.* (Rec. Com.), 267.
57 Dugdale, *Mon.* v. 55.
58 B.L. Add. MS. 5817, f. 183.
59 *Tax. Eccl.* 267; *Inq. Non.* (Rec. Com.), 213.
60 *E.D.R.* (1892), 671.
61 C.U.L., Add. MS. 6081, f. 17.
62 B.L. Add. MS. 5823, f. 95v.
63 C.U.L., Add. MS. 6082, ff. 25–6; cf. ibid. Doc. 660 no. 29; MS. Plan 337.
64 C.U.L., Add. MS. 6080, pp. 48–59; Doc. 660 nos. 105–6; cf. B.L. Add. MS. 36229, f. 297.
65 C.R.O., Q/RDc 9, p. 454.
66 *Val. of Norwich*, ed. Lunt, 536, 555; *Tax. Eccl.* (Rec. Com.), 267.
67 *Rot. Hund.* (Rec. Com.), ii. 569.
68 *Vetus Liber Arch. Elien.* (C.A.S. 8vo ser. xlviii), 57; Emden, *Biog. Reg. Univ. Camb.* 292.
69 B.L. Add. MS. 5823, f. 58; Emden, *Biog. Reg. Univ. Oxon.* iii. 1623.
70 *E.D.R.* (1889), 357; (1890), 379, 449; (1892), 774.
71 Ibid. (1892), 808; (1894), 288.
72 Ibid. (1893), 73; cf. *Cal. Inq. p.m.* xii, p. 612.

73 B.L. Add. MS. 5823, f. 63v.
74 *Cal. Pat.* 1549–51, 410.
75 *Trans. C.H.A.S.* i. 400.
76 B.L. Add. MS. 5847, f. 182v.
77 Ibid. Add. MS. 5842, ff. 19, 20, 26v.
78 *East Anglian*, N.S. xiii. 191.
79 B.L. Add. MS. 5847, f. 182v.; *E.D.R.* (1906), 144.
80 e.g. B.L. Add. MS. 5861, ff. 7, 11v., 99.
81 *E.D.R.* (1912), 224; (1913), 41.
82 C.U.L., E.D.R., B 2/6.
83 e.g. ibid. B 2/8; B 2/18, f. 77; B 2/32, f. 99; B 2/40A, f. 8; B.L. Add. MS. 5823, f. 80; Gibbons, *Ely Episc. Rec.* 171.
84 Lamb. Pal. MS. 904, ff. 273–4.
85 C.U.L., E.D.R., B 2/67; cf. *Alum. Cantab. to 1751*, ii. 315.
86 C.U.L., E.D.R., B 2/72; C.R.O., Huddleston MSS., doc. in suit in consist. ct. 1705–6.
87 *Alum. Cantab. to 1751*, ii. 314; C.U.L., E.D.R., B 8/1; *Mon. Inscr. Cambs.* 183.
88 Prob. 11/664 (P.C.C. 61 Ockham).
89 B.L. Add. MS. 36229, f. 205v.
90 C.R.O., L 60/42; cf. C.U.L., E.D.R., C 1/4, 6.
91 Hodgson, *Queen Anne's Bounty*, p. cclxxxviii; C.R.O., L 60/42.
92 Cf. C.U.L., E.D.R., C 3/21.
93 *Rep. Com. Eccl. Revenues*, pp. 352–3; C.U.L., E.D.R., C 3/27.

Thomas Bromley, Lord Montfort, had chosen as curate a disreputable crony, Philip Bearcroft (d. 1776).[94] The parish was served after Bearcroft's death by John Maule, rector of Horseheath 1776–1825. In 1807 he held one Sunday service, preaching alternately in each parish, and three communions a year, attended by *c.* 10 people.[95] Lord Hardwicke offered the succeeding curate £70 a year in 1825 for performing two Sunday services, as requested by the parishioners.[96] In 1836 there were *c.* 60 communicants.[97] C. W. Lamprell, perpetual curate 1841–66 and also rector of Little Bradley (Suff.),[98] claimed an 1851 average attendance of 200, filling the available sittings.[99] From 1866 the cure was held jointly with West Wratting, where the incumbent lived, and, perhaps by association, came to be styled a vicarage. In 1877 and 1897 only one Sunday service was held. Communions every four to six weeks had small attendances.[1] In 1912 the lay rector, P. A. S. Hickey, transferred the patronage to the bishop of Ely,[2] with whom it remained in 1974. From 1973 the living was held with Horseheath rectory.[3]

The thatched 17th- or 18th-century house at Burton End, sometimes called the Old Vicarage,[4] was not a glebe house, although Lamprell probably lived there in 1851.[5]

The church of *ST. MARY*, named before the Reformation from the Assumption[6] but later simply by the Virgin's name,[7] consists of a chancel, nave with north chapel and south porch, and west tower, and is built of field stones with ashlar dressings. The tower may be 13th-century, but its west window has Decorated tracery. The chancel is 14th-century: the three south windows have curvilinear tracery and are matched by the east window, flanked by ornate contemporary niches inside and renewed after 1852,[8] while the three north windows, one blocked with a tablet to Henry Harrison (d. 1690), have simpler tracery. Glass once included the arms of England simply and the Vere arms with a label, suggesting a date before 1340.[9] The nave and porch also appear to be 14th-century, but three new windows on each side of the nave were inserted at two periods in the 15th or 16th centuries. The north chapel may have been built in the 15th century; it was walled off from the church by 1744,[10] and remained so in 1852.[11]

Three late medieval benches survive in the nave. The old rood-screen, intact in 1744,[12] was cut down and removed to the tower arch *c.* 1900.[13] The late medieval nave roof has side-posts standing on braced tie-beams, the easternmost beam being carved with vine-leaf scrolls. Following storm damage in 1579 and *c.* 1608[14] the roof was repaired in 1615.[15]

The windows were in bad repair from the mid 16th century,[16] and in 1644 William Dowsing destroyed eight superstitious pictures in the chancel,[17] which had been in decay in 1591.[18] In 1665 the impropriator was ordered to have it paved and pointed.[19] By 1783 the tiling of the nave was defective; that of the chancel was virtually all gone, so that rain poured in and services could not be held there.[20] The earls of Hardwicke had put the chancel in decent repair before 1836.[21] The whole church was thoroughly restored between 1898 and 1900, the old pews and pulpit being replaced and a new rood-screen installed.[22] An organ of 1800 brought from St. Mary's, Newmarket,[23] almost fills the north chapel.

The church had a silver chalice *c.* 1275, in the 1380s,[24] and in 1552.[25] About 1960 it had a silver beaker made at Newcastle in 1774 and a paten of 1802.[26] Of the five bells recorded in 1744 and later[27] the earliest, cast at London *c.* 1460, has a black-letter Latin inscription, as have two made by Richard Holdfield of Cambridge in 1606. The other two were cast in 1706 and 1714 by Henry Pleasant and John Thornton, both of Sudbury (Suff.).[28] The church records earlier than 1639 were all missing in 1783;[29] the surviving registers begin in 1647.[30]

NONCONFORMITY. About 1670 a Quaker from West Wickham attended the Balsham meeting[31] and there were two dissenters in 1676.[32] In 1783 two dissenting families attended the Linton meeting-house,[33] and in 1825 five Independent families, including those of two farmers, similarly worshipped elsewhere.[34] In 1836 Thomas Hopkins, the Linton Independent minister, registered a house in West Wickham for dissenting worship.[35] In 1847 James Blades registered a room and in 1849 a barn for a Primitive Methodist meeting,[36] and another building was registered for it in 1853.[37] By 1867 there was a Primitive Methodist chapel with a

[94] Palmer, *Wm. Cole*, 99–100.
[95] C.U.L., E.D.R., C 1/4; cf. *Alum. Cantab. 1752–1900*, iv. 367.
[96] C.R.O., L 60/42.
[97] C.U.L., E.D.R., C 1/6; C 3/21.
[98] *Alum. Cantab. 1752–1900*, iv. 85.
[99] H.O. 129/188/3/2/2.
[1] C.U.L., E.D.R., C 3/27, 39; *E.D.R.* (1909), 90; *Crockford* (1896 and later edns.).
[2] *Lond. Gaz.* 17 Dec. 1912, pp. 9562–3.
[3] *Crockford* (1973–4).
[4] e.g. O.S. Map 6″, Cambs. LVI. SW. (1891 edn.); C.R.O., SP 173/2 (1963).
[5] H.O. 107/1761.
[6] e.g. B.L. Add. MS. 5861, ff. 68, 90v. (1518, 1524).
[7] e.g. Ecton, *Thesaurus* (1763), 107.
[8] *Eccl. Top. Eng.* vi, no. 171.
[9] B.L. Add. MS. 5807, f. 80.
[10] Palmer, *Wm. Cole*, 115.
[11] *Eccl. Top. Eng.* vi, no. 171.
[12] Palmer, *Wm. Cole*, 115.
[13] *Proc. C.A.S.* xiii. 32, 73.
[14] C.U.L., E.D.R., D 2/10, f. 158; B 2/28, f. 178.
[15] Inscr. on beam.
[16] e.g. C.U.L., E.D.R., B 2/3, p. 86 (1549); D 2/10, f. 106 (1578).
[17] *Trans. C.H.A.S.* iii. 89.
[18] C.U.L., E.D.R., B 2/11, f. 215.
[19] Ibid. B 2/59A, f. 21.
[20] Ibid. B 7/1, p. 136.
[21] Ibid. C 3/21.
[22] *E.D.R.* (1902), 131; cf. photogs. in vestry.
[23] Inscr. on organ.
[24] *Vetus Liber Arch. Elien.* (C.A.S. 8vo ser. xlviii), 56–7.
[25] *Cambs. Ch. Goods, temp. Edw. VI*, 60.
[26] List of ch. plate *penes V.C.H.*
[27] Palmer, *Wm. Cole*, 115; *Kelly's Dir. Cambs.* (1858–1937).
[28] MS. notes by H. B. Walters (1936), *penes V.C.H.*
[29] C.U.L., E.D.R., B 7/1, p. 136.
[30] Gibbons, *Ely Episc. Rec.* 236.
[31] *Orig. Rec. of Early Nonconf.* ed. Turner, i. 41; cf. *Proc. C.A.S.* lxi. 93.
[32] Compton Census.
[33] C.U.L., E.D.R., B 7/1, p. 136.
[34] Ibid. C 1/4, 6.
[35] G.R.O. Worship Returns, Ely dioc. no. 607.
[36] Ibid. nos. 693, 708.
[37] Ibid. Worship Reg. no. 767.

minister,[38] for which a brick Gothic mission hall was built on the village street in 1870.[39] It closed between 1960 and 1974, the building being converted for a play-school.[40] The Salvation Army opened a hall near the school in 1892.[41] It drew the largest congregations in the parish in 1960,[42] and the hall was in use in 1975.[43]

EDUCATION. In 1744 the walled-off north chapel of the church was said to have been once used for a school.[44] A Sunday school, started by 1807,[45] was the only school in the parish in 1818 and 1825.[46] By 1833 it had *c.* 115 pupils, and was maintained by subscriptions.[47] The minister and his wife taught there in 1836, when it was associated with the National Society;[48] in 1846, when two masters and a mistress taught *c.* 110 children, there was still no day-school.[49] In 1861 a farm-labourer's wife was teaching a school, still open in 1871, when it had *c.* 70 children.[50] The Sunday school was still held in the church until 1877, when a schoolroom was built on land rented from Lord Hardwicke. By 1878 a National school had been opened in it, managed by a committee of the parishioners who had paid for the building. By 1883 a teacher's house had been added.[51] Average attendance was usually 45–50 from the early 1880s until after 1900.[52] After rising briefly to *c.* 60[53] it declined to the previous level.[54] In 1919 there were mixed and infants' departments.[55] Reorganization in 1937, when the older children were sent to Linton village college, halved numbers to 22. The school was closed in 1971, the younger children going to Balsham.[56]

CHARITIES FOR THE POOR. Philip Richardson, lessee of the rectory, by will proved 1634, left £10 to buy land yielding 10*s.* a year to help the parish poor.[57] If ever established, the charity had been lost by 1783.[58] In 1837 a few acres with odd names were popularly believed to be held for the benefit of the poor.[59]

[38] G.R.O. Worship Reg. no. 13421.
[39] Inscr. on bldg.; cf. *Kelly's Dir. Cambs.* (1879).
[40] *Camb. Ind. Press*, 9 Sept. 1960; *Camb. Evening News*, 12 Mar. 1974.
[41] G.R.O. Worship Reg. no. 33146.
[42] *Camb. Ind. Press*, 9 Sept. 1960.
[43] *Camb. Evening News*, 10 July, 2–4, 6 Sept. 1974.
[44] Palmer, *Wm. Cole*, 115.
[45] C.U.L., E.D.R., C 1/4.
[46] *Educ. of Poor Digest*, 66; C.U.L., E.D.R., C 1/6.
[47] *Educ. Enquiry Abstract*, 62.
[48] C.U.L., E.D.R., C 3/21.
[49] *Church School Inquiry, 1846–7*, 8–9.
[50] R.G. 9/1030; R.G. 10/1593.
[51] C.U.L., E.D.R., C 3/27; Ed. 7/5; *Kelly's Dir. Cambs.* (1879–83).
[52] e.g. *Rep. of Educ. Cttee. of Council, 1880–1* [C. 2948-I], p. 544, H.C. (1881), xxxii; *1892–3* [C. 7089-I], p. 689, H.C. (1893–4), xxvi.
[53] e.g. *Public Elem. Schs. 1907* [Cd. 3901], p. 29, H.C. (1908), lxxxiv.
[54] e.g. *Bd. of Educ., List 21, 1914* (H.M.S.O.), 29; *1932*, 18.
[55] Ibid. *1919*, 17.
[56] Ibid. *1938*, 21; Black, *Cambs. Educ. Rec.* 79.
[57] Prob. 11/165 (P.C.C. 37 Seager); cf. C.U.L., E.D.R., B 2/40A, f. 8.
[58] C.U.L., E.D.R., B 7/1, p. 136; cf. *Char. Don.* i. 88–9.
[59] *31st Rep. Com. Char.* 108.

RADFIELD HUNDRED

RADFIELD hundred lies south and east of Cambridge along the Icknield Way, which is the north-western limit of the hundred. It stretches 8 miles from its north-eastern boundary, which follows the Devil's Dyke, a post-Roman earthwork, to its south-western boundary, which follows the ancient Wool Street. Part of the south-eastern boundary of the hundred is the county boundary with Suffolk. In 1086 the hundred was composed of seven vills: Balsham, Carlton, Dullingham, Stetchworth, Weston, and Wratting were each assessed at 10 hides, and Burrough and Westley together made up a vill of 10 hides.[1] The last two were often taxed together in the Middle Ages, but developed as separate parishes. Neither Brinkley nor Willingham was mentioned in 1086, but both were presumably included in the account of Carlton. The nine parishes making up the hundred remained nearly constant, although Willingham, while failing to become a separate vill, was for a time a separate parish. By the 14th century Carlton had been divided longitudinally, Brinkley being named as a vill, to make eight vills in all. Burrough and Westley were still counted as one vill.[2]

The hundred, which remained in the king's hands, was worth 2 marks in 1260.[3] In the 13th century it was administered with Cheveley hundred by a single bailiff.[4] In the 16th century it was grouped with Cheveley, Chilford, and Whittlesford hundreds, and in the 17th century with Chilford and Whittlesford.[5] The hundred takes its name from the 'red field' in Burrough Green and Dullingham where the hundred court may have met. It has also been suggested that the court met at Mutlow hill, on the western edge of the hundred, at the junction with Staine and Flendish hundreds.[6]

Within the hundred the lord of Westley had a gallows. Five lay lords claimed view of frankpledge, the prior of Lewes had the view in Carlton, and the abbot of Warden over his tenants in Burrough and Dullingham. The bishop of Ely in Balsham and the prior of Ely in Stetchworth and West Wratting enjoyed their wider franchises. In the 14th century a tourn was held at Burrough or Newmarket for the honor of Richmond's lands in Radfield hundred.[7]

The land rises from a little over 100 ft. along the north-western edge of the hundred to over 300 ft. near the Suffolk border. It lies on the chalk, which is covered with boulder clay above *c.* 300 ft.[8] The clay was once well wooded, and extensive woodland remains in the south-east end of many parishes. All the parishes within the hundred are long and narrow, running south-eastwards from the Icknield Way. With the exception of Westley Waterless they all stretch the full width of the hundred. Balsham is the least elongated, but is still more than twice as long as it is wide. As a result each parish falls into similar sections. Following the line of the Icknield Way and passing through the north-western edge of each is the main London–Newmarket road, turnpiked in 1724.[9] The land immediately south-east of the road has little natural drainage, and until inclosure was chalk heathland. The higher open-field land lay south-east of the heath, and was inclosed between 1778 and 1822 by private agreement or act of parliament.

1 *V.C.H. Cambs.* i. 404–6.

2 *Feud. Aids*, i. 154; cf. *L. & P. Hen. VIII*, iii (2), p. 1117.

3 *Feud. Aids*, i. 154; *Assizes at Camb. 1260*, 22.

4 *Assizes at Camb. 1260*, 7, 21; J.I. 1/83 rot. 37; J.I. 1/86 rot. 56.

5 e.g. *Cal. S.P. Dom.* 1547–80, 6; ibid. 1638–9, 283.

6 *P.N. Cambs.* (E.P.N.S.), 114.

7 S.C. 2/155/71.

8 Geol. Surv. Map 1″, drift, sheet 205 (1932 edn.); ibid. solid and drift, sheet 188 (1965 edn.).

9 Stump Cross Roads Turnpike Act, 10 Geo. I, c. 12.

Most of the villages lie along the spring line, near the centre of the hundred, and are connected by a road running the length of the hundred from Linton to Newmarket. Another road between those towns can be traced further west, surviving partly as a trackway. There was considerable assarting of woodland in the Middle Ages and the land south-east of the villages tended to be inclosed early, often as demesne land.

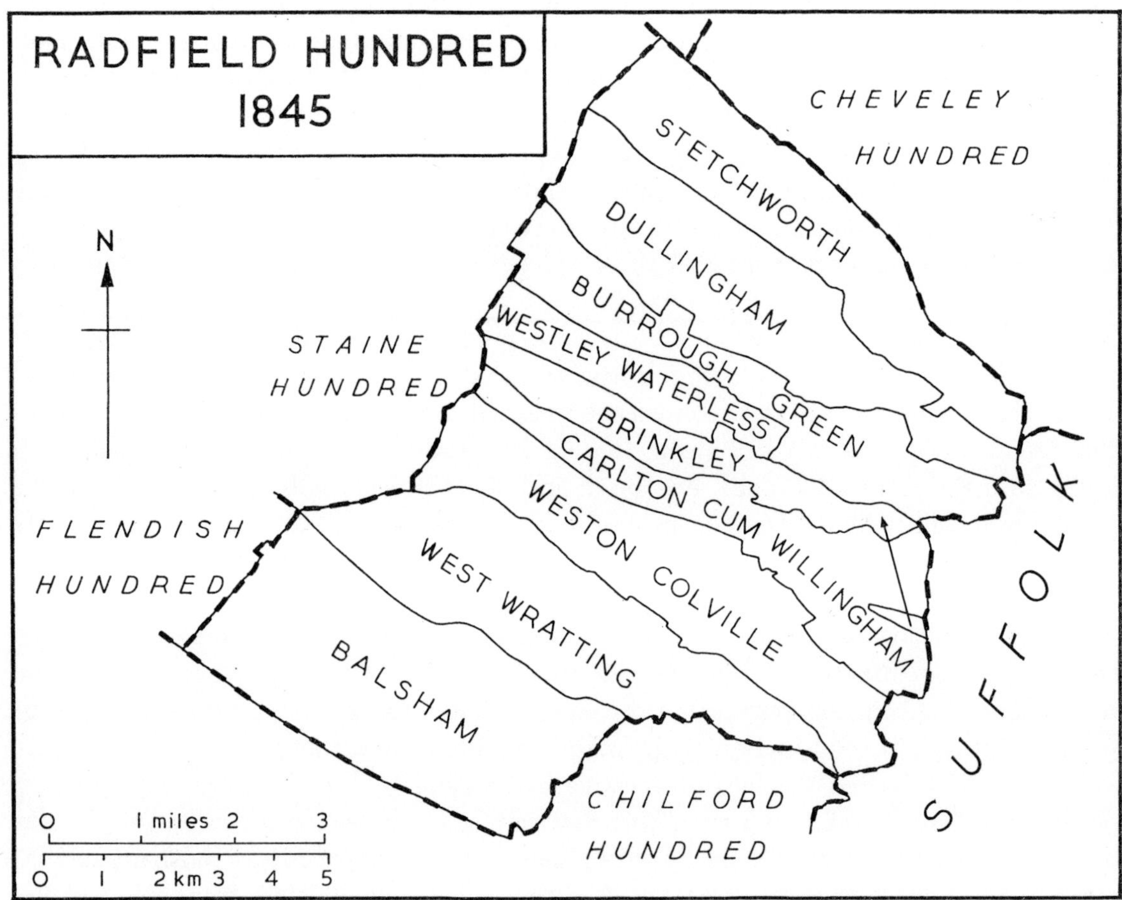

Before inclosure large flocks of sheep were folded on the heath and open fields. Barley was the chief grain crop. Since inclosure the area has been devoted to mixed farming. It is entirely agricultural; in the north-east of the hundred some farms are given over to breeding and training race-horses. In all the parishes population increased in the early 19th century, but fell after 1851 and in most places was little higher in 1971 than 150 years before. Exceptions were Balsham, which provided accommodation for Cambridge workers, and the villages near Newmarket.

BALSHAM

THE PARISH of Balsham[1] lying 9 miles south-east of Cambridge and 3 miles north-east of Linton, covers 4,550a.[2] The boundaries have long remained unchanged, following on the north-east, north-west, and south-west respectively the Fleam Dyke, an earthwork probably dating from the 7th century,[3] the Icknield Way, and Wool Street. The south-eastern boundary, between Balsham and West Wickham, is very irregular, and it has been suggested that the two parishes may have been joined at one time, and that Balsham, like West Wickham, was settled from across the Suffolk border.[4]

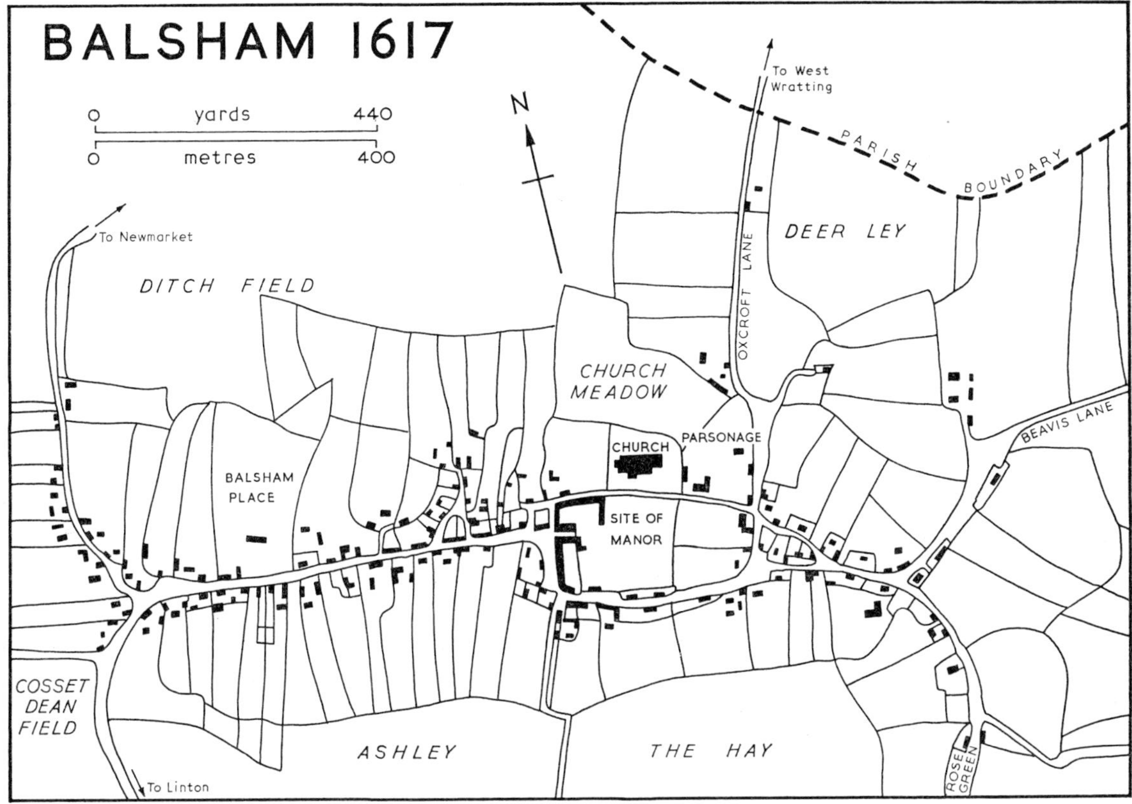

The ground rises gradually from 125 ft. at the north-western end of the parish to over 300 ft., before falling to 200 ft. to form what was once known as the Twenty Acre Valley, at the centre of the parish. It then rises to a height of 375 ft. at the eastern edge.[5] Chalk underlies the whole parish, but in the east, especially above the 300 ft. line, it is covered by boulder clay.[6] There are no streams, but on the impervious clay are many ponds; in 1974 fourteen were said to have disappeared in recent years. Wells have been sunk through the clay to the bottom of the chalk, at considerable expense. In 1908 Balsham had three such wells for public use.[7]

The chalk heathland at the north-western end of the parish once provided grazing for many sheep. Most land in the parish remained uninclosed until 1806.[8] Balsham wood (*c.* 200 a.) near the south-east end of the parish represents the remains of once extensive woodland. Charterhouse plantation, a belt of trees enclosing over 600 a. around Dotterel Hall farm in the north-west, was planted before 1885.[9] In 1951 the Fleam Dyke was designated of special interest because of its bird and plant life.[10] In 1909 there were large chalk quarries at Balsham;[11] the workings were clearly visible in 1975 *c.* 1 mile west of the village along the Fulbourn road.

Balsham village is the only centre of settlement in the parish. Reference to a church in the early 11th century points to the existence of a Saxon church,[12] probably on the site of the present church. The church, the site of the manor-house, and a small village green lie close together near the centre of a linear village, on the higher ground at the south-

1 This account was written in 1975.
2 *Census*, 1971.
3 *Camb. Region* (1938), 96–8.
4 Taylor, *Cambs. Landscape*, 89.
5 O.S. Map 1/25,000 TL 55 (1956 edn.).
6 *V.C.H. Cambs.* i. 17, 19; *Camb. Region* (1938), 108–9.
7 *Camb. Region* (1938), 108–9; *Camb. Ind. Press*, 24 Apr. 1908; *Camb. Evening News*, 22 May 1974.
8 C.R.O., Q/RDz 8.
9 O.S. Map 1/2,500, Cambs. LV. 7, 8 (1886 edn.).
10 *Nature Reserves and Sites of Special Scientific Interest* (Cambs. and Isle of Ely Planning Dept. 1965), p. 68.
11 T. McK. & M. C. Hughes, *Cambridgeshire* (1909), 61.
12 Hen. of Huntingdon, *Hist. Angl.* (Rolls Ser.), 178.

eastern end of the parish.[13] A larger open space adjacent to the small green may well be part of an originally larger green. The nucleus of the village is rectangular, with the church, manor-house, and green at the north-western corner. The high street runs along the southern and western edges and then westwards at right angles to the western edge. It stretches from the West Wickham road at the eastern end of the parish to the junction of the Fulbourn, Hildersham, and Linton roads. Most dwellings were originally along that length of road. A few others were along Fox Lane, probably the old Linton–Newmarket road which crossed the western end of the high street, or along Old House Lane, leading to Plumian or Old House Farm, which still marks the north-eastern extent of the dwellings.

In the late 19th century there was still much open ground within the village. In 1852 much of the Quadrangle, the land behind the manor-house site, bounded on two sides by the high street, was a playground for the school. At the western end of the high street there were a few houses with long closes running northwards, and next to them a meadow adjoining the grounds of Balsham Place. The southern side of the street was open, and the land opposite Balsham Place was still empty in 1886. In 1975 that part of the village still had relatively few houses, each having a large plot of land. The filling in of space within the village began between the wars. In 1926 the district council built six new houses on the Cambridge road. In 1948 it built another small estate on the West Wickham road, in an area which had been called Rose Green. In 1960 another council estate was built on the opposite side of the road, slightly nearer the centre of the village. Other infilling has been private building in small closes opening from both sides of the main street wherever there was space. By 1971 such building was said to have totalled 130 houses. In the 1960s and 1970s several estate houses were built by the Vesteys.

There are *c.* 10 surviving farm-houses of the 17th century, all with the usual three-room plan, internal chimney stack, and timber-framed and plastered walls. Most have later extensions. Most of the other older houses are smaller and of the late 18th and early 19th centuries. Balsham Manor is a small early-17th-century house greatly enlarged in the later 18th and early 19th centuries. Plumian and Lower farms were the only ones to have houses within the village in 1975. Of the outlying farms only Dungate, on the northern edge of the parish, dates from before the inclosure of 1806. It is a small 18th-century house, considerably enlarged and remodelled in the early 19th century. In 1933 Worsted Lodge, at the western corner of the parish, was described as a hamlet.[14] In 1975 besides Worsted Lodge Farm there were some 5 dwellings and a petrol station there.

In 1086 there were 12 *villani*, 12 bordars, and 2 *servi* in Balsham.[15] An increase in population brought the number of tenants to 93 in 1251, but by 1327 there were only 53 taxpayers and by 1356 the number of tenants had fallen to 50.[16] In 1377 there were 255 adults.[17] In 1563 there were 80 households, and in 1666 and 1674 101 houses were recorded.[18] In 1728 the parish contained some 670 people.[19] In the 19th century numbers rose steadily from 759 in 1811 to 1,352 in 1851, thereafter falling gradually, with a slight rally in 1911, to 650 in 1931. Afterwards the population increased, slowly at first but growing from 712 in 1961 to 1,204 in 1971.[20]

The main London–Newmarket road runs along the north-western boundary of the parish; it was turnpiked in 1724.[21] The old Newmarket–Linton road bypassed Balsham village on the west, but the road through the village and other villages to the north-east gradually became the main route. Other roads connect the village with Fulbourn, Hildersham, West Wickham, and West Wratting. From 1848 to 1851 there was a railway station 3 miles from Balsham village, on the Chesterford–Newmarket line, but after the line was closed in 1851 the nearest stations were at Six Mile Bottom and Fulbourn, 5 miles from the village.[22] In 1975 the station house at Balsham road was still standing.

In 1686 Balsham had only two guest beds and stabling for four horses.[23] The Black Bull, near the centre of the village, is said to have been a 17th-century coaching inn, and the plastered and thatched timber-framed building is of that date. It was a public house until *c.* 1940; in 1969 it was a country club, but in 1973 reverted to its former use.[24] In 1806 two public houses were noted, the Bell and the Fox and Hounds.[25] The latter, in Fox Lane, dated from the mid 17th century and was formerly called the Crown. It was a private house by 1935.[26] The Bell near the east end of the high street occurs from 1790.[27] In 1962 it was said that there had recently been eight inns in Balsham.[28] In 1975 the Queen's Head, the Bell, and the Black Bull remained.

Hugh of Balsham, bishop of Ely 1258–86 and founder of Peterhouse, was most probably born on the episcopal manor of Balsham.[29] Other clerks from the manor found places in the household of Bishop Arundel in the 14th century.[30] In the 19th century the agriculturalist Philip Howard Frere lived for some time on his father's estate, Dungate farm, the house and some of the land of which lay in Balsham. His father, William Frere, was master of Downing College and spent part of each year at Balsham.[31] The author Frederick William Rolfe ('Baron Corvo', d. 1913) was an assistant master at a private school in Balsham in the 1880s.[32]

Plough-boys used to go around the village to collect money on Plough Monday early in January, a custom which lasted in Balsham into the 20th

[13] The following description is based on O.S. Map 1/2,500, Cambs. LV. 7, 8 (1886 and later edns.); B.L. Maps, 1640 (12), (16), (17); R. Wilbraham, *J. Daniels, a Cambs. Farm Worker* (1971); *Balsham Draft Village Plan* (1972).
[14] *Kelly's Dir. Cambs.* (1933).
[15] *V.C.H. Cambs.* i. 406.
[16] B.L. Cott. MS. Claud. C. xi, 121–126v.; *Cambs. Lay Subsidy, 1327*, 15; B.L. Add. MS. 6165, f. 267.
[17] *East Anglian*, N.S. xii. 7.
[18] B.L. Harl. MS. 594, f. 199v.; see below, pp. 279, 281.
[19] C.U.L., E.D.R., B 8/1.
[20] *Census* (1811–1971).
[21] Stump Cross Rds. Turnpike Act, 10 Geo. I, c. 12.
[22] *Proc. C.A.S.* xxxi. 1–15.
[23] Ibid. xvii. 97; W.O. 30/48.
[24] M.H.L.G. list; *Camb. Evening News*, 8 Dec. 1973.
[25] C.R.O., Q/RDz 8.
[26] *Cambridge News*, 23 Sept. 1964; C.R.O., 515/SP 1402.
[27] C.R.O., R 53/5/1.
[28] *East Anglian Mag.* xxi. 317–21.
[29] *D.N.B.*
[30] Margaret Aston, *Thos. Arundel*, 251.
[31] *D.N.B.*
[32] A. J. A. Symons, *The Quest for Corvo* (1955), 57–8.

BABRAHAM HALL: the south-west front

HINXTON HALL: the south front

BALSHAM: the rectory before and after it was rebuilt *c.* 1843

DULLINGHAM HOUSE: Repton's proposals of 1801 for landscaping the garden

century. It was revived in 1972 as an annual event to raise money for local causes.[33]

MANORS AND OTHER ESTATES. Leofflaed, wife of Oswi and daughter of Beorhtnoth, by will dated 1017×1035 granted Balsham to Ely abbey. Balsham was included in Edward the Confessor's confirmation of the abbey's Cambridgeshire estates.[34] In 1086 the manor of *BALSHAM*, consisting of 9 hides, was said always to have belonged to the church of Ely.[35] On the creation of the see of Ely in 1109 the manor passed with the abbey's lands to the bishop,[36] with whom it remained when the lands were divided between bishop and monks,[37] and for the next four centuries.

In 1575 Thomas Wyborne sold his lease of the manor to Thomas Sutton.[38] In 1600 Balsham was one of the manors alienated by Bishop Heton to the Crown which a year later granted it in fee to Sutton.[39] In 1611 the manor was included in the endowment of Sutton's new foundation, the Charterhouse, which has owned it ever since.[40] A fee-farm rent in Balsham, granted by the Crown in 1601 to Sir Christopher Hatton, a cousin of the Lord Chancellor, and Francis Needham, and disputed in 1619 between Needham and Hatton's widow Alice,[41] apparently passed to Sutton, and so to his foundation.[42] In 1919 the Charterhouse sold over 1,200 a. in two lots, as Wood Hall and Dotterel farms.[43]

A manor-house in Balsham, sometimes called Balsham Hall,[44] was recorded in 1356, when its buildings were said to be ruinous. In 1357 it had a main chamber with others adjoining, chapel, room for the steward, various offices, gatehouse, stables, granary, and other farm buildings, almost all in need of repair.[45] In the 14th century Bishop Arundel visited Balsham less frequently than some other manors; his presence there is recorded only three times,[46] but it was a target for the rebels of 1381 who broke in, burned muniments, and damaged the buildings.[47] In the late 16th century Thomas Sutton lived in Balsham, and his wife died there in 1602.[48] The present Nine Chimneys house is the south wing of a large timber-framed house of the later 16th century which may have been Sutton's home. There is a tradition that it was built on the site of an older manor-house.[49] In 1617, however, the hall or manor-house was near the centre of the village, between the church and the high street,[50] on the site occupied in 1975 by the old school. In 1863 the Charterhouse gave the old manor-house for use by the National school.[51]

In 1086 Hardwin de Scalers held in Balsham from the abbot of Ely 80 a. previously occupied by three sokemen of the abbot.[52] In 1212 his descendant William de Scalers[53] held of the bishop of Ely 1½ fee in Shelford, Wratting, and Balsham.[54] The estate depended upon Caxton manor[55] with which it descended.[56] References to its land in Balsham have not been found after the early 16th century.

In 1568 William Blodwell granted Richard Killingworth an estate in Balsham,[57] which in 1590 belonged to John Killingworth, and was called *PLACE* manor,[58] later Place farm. In 1617 John Killingworth held a house on the site of what in 1975 was called Balsham Place, together with freehold and copyhold lands, an enclosure in Balsham wood, and heathland in the west part of the parish.[59] That estate may have derived from the Scalers fee. By 1618 John was dead and his son Giles held the manor of the Charterhouse.[60] A Mr. Killingworth held the estate in 1715 when it amounted to 261 a.,[61] and in 1756 it was for sale.[62] By 1790 it had descended from Henry Lagden the younger to his son, the Revd. H. A. Lagden,[63] who in 1800 shared Place farm with James Haylock. In 1806 it was divided between them and Frances Cole;[64] Haylock's son John bought Cole's share of the farm in 1819, and the rest of the estate after Lagden's death in 1833.[65] In 1884 Place farm was owned by Mrs. Annie Haylock, and in 1886 by her executors.[66] In 1904 it belonged to Hanslip Long and by 1912 to his son, also Hanslip Long.[67] On the son's death it passed to his wife Mrs. Mildred Long whose heirs offered it for sale in 1969, when it covered 490 a.[68] It was purchased by Mr. R. A. Vestey, who in 1975 was the largest landowner in the parish.[69] Balsham Place house, then separated from the land, is a plain grey brick house of *c.* 1825 standing at the western end of the village, on the north side of the high street.

In 1269 Richard de Freville, heir to half the Scalers barony, held 1½ fee in Carlton, Balsham, and Babraham, which William de Criketot, who died in that year, held of him.[70] About 1285 Criketot's heirs were said to hold in chief a tenement in

[33] *Camb. Evening News*, 9 Jan. 1973.
[34] *Liber Elien.* (Camd. 3rd ser. xcii), pp. 157, 162.
[35] *V.C.H. Cambs.* i. 364.
[36] Bentham, *Hist. Ely*, i. 130–5.
[37] *Pipe R.* 1171 (P.R.S. xvi), 116.
[38] Charterho. Mun., D 2/1–5; N. R. Shipley, 'Thos. Sutton and his landed interest in Essex', *Essex Jnl.* viii. 113–15.
[39] Bentham, *Hist. Ely*, i. 196; Charterho. Mun., Foundation of Charterho.
[40] P. Bearcroft, *Hist. Acct. of Thos. Sutton and his Foundation in Charterhouse* (1737), 63.
[41] C 2/Jas. I/H 29/24.
[42] Charterho. Mun., D 6/203; cf. ibid. D 2/14A, 14B, 15; *Cal. S.P. Dom.* 1629–31, 91.
[43] C.R.O., 515/SP 572.
[44] Charterho. Mun., MR 2/550; ibid. estate papers.
[45] B.L. Add. MS. 6165, ff. 267, 282.
[46] Margaret Aston, *Thos. Arundel*, App. 2.
[47] *Cambs. Village Doc.* 20, 24; Aston, *Arundel*, 141.
[48] Bearcroft, *Sutton*, 16.
[49] H. J. E. Burrel, *Church of the Holy Trinity, Balsham* (pamphlet 1933).
[50] Charterho. Mun., plan of Balsham, 1617.
[51] C.R.O., P 7/1/3.
[52] *V.C.H. Cambs.* i. 364. Hardwin was also said to hold the 80 a. from the king: ibid. 406; but cf. ibid. 384–5.
[53] Ibid. v. 27.
[54] *Red Bk. Exch.* (Rolls Ser.), ii. 524.
[55] C 143/362 no. 21; C.P. 25(1)/30/92 no. 14; *Cal. Pat.* 1367–70, 32; 1399–1401, 446.
[56] *V.C.H. Cambs.* v. 27–8.
[57] C.P. 25(2)/93/835/10–11 Eliz. I Mich. no. 3.
[58] C.P. 25(2)/95/854/32 Eliz. I Trin. no. 10.
[59] Charterho. Mun., plan of Balsham, 1617.
[60] C 60/479/8.
[61] Charterho. Mun., MR 2/189A.
[62] Ibid. Balsham est. papers.
[63] Ibid. MR 2/513, pp. 96–7.
[64] Ibid. p. 409; C.R.O., R 60/24/2/2.
[65] Charterho. Mun., sale partics. with plan; ibid. MR 2/515, pp. 386 sqq.
[66] C.R.O., 334/04 (1884, 1886).
[67] *Kelly's Dir. Cambs.* (1904, 1912).
[68] Camb. City Libr., Cambs. Colln. Sale Cat. 8, 1969.
[69] Ex inf. Sir John Mowbray, Bt., agent to Mr. R. A. Vestey.
[70] *Cal. Inq. p.m.* i, p. 223.

Balsham which had been John James's,[71] but in 1372 Richard de Freville's great-grandson John Freville held *JAMES'S* (later called *JACOB'S*) land in Balsham in chief together with West Wratting manor.[72] In 1302 Roger Barbedor held James's land in demesne together with ½ fee in Little Carlton of the Criketots, as did Joan Brown in 1346. Joan's heirs were holding it in 1428,[73] and John Caldbeck in 1478, but no certain reference to it has been found later.[74]

Thomas Plume (d. 1704), archdeacon of Rochester, left nearly £2,000 to build an observatory in Cambridge and found a chair of astronomy. Soon after his death the money was used to buy 235 a. in Balsham, partly copyhold but mostly freehold.[75] In 1804 34 a. were sold to meet the expenses of inclosure,[76] and in 1832 a further 14½ a. were bought. After the deaths of the original trustees the estate, known as *PLUMIAN* or *OLD HOUSE* farm, was held by successive professors of astronomy by title of their office until 1869 when it was conveyed to the university.[77]

An extensive but short-lived estate was built up in the 18th century by the Lagden family. The lands held by Henry Lagden the elder and his sister Mary Lagden passed to Henry's grandson the Revd. Henry Allen Lagden in 1786. H. A. Lagden was one of the major landholders at inclosure, but he soon moved from Balsham and the estate was being sold off before his death.[78] Besides Place farm he owned over 400 a. in the western corner of the parish, which he sold to William Bryant in 1825.[79] In 1867 George Matthews sold the estate, called *WORSTED LODGE*, to St. Bartholomew's Hospital, London, which sold it in 1920.[80]

From 1834 to 1914 21 a. in Balsham belonged to the Corporation of the Sons of the Clergy as part of its estate in West Wratting.[81]

The 40 a. in Balsham which in 1086 Almar held of Count Alan of Brittany[82] seem to have been part of Oxcroft manor in West Wratting. It may be identified with the knight's fee in Balsham held by 1355 by the earls of Oxford. By the 19th century the Oxcroft land in Balsham amounted to just over 20 a., part of Dungate farm. In 1877 that land was purchased by St. John's College, Cambridge, which sold it in 1946 to H. E. Eastwood. In 1952 it was bought by Jesus College.[83]

ECONOMIC HISTORY. There were 10 hides in Balsham in 1086. Five hides were on the demesne of the abbot of Ely, where there were 2 *servi* and 5 plough-teams, with land for 2 more teams. There were 12 *villani* with 12 teams, and 12 *bordars*, each of whom had 10 a. The 80 a. of Hardwin de Scalers and the 40 a. of Almar each had one plough-team. The 80 a. were valued at 13*s*. 4*d*. and there were 80 sheep there. The abbot's 9 hides were worth £17, an increase of £5 on the value T.R.E. His estate included woodland for 200 pigs, 12 a. of meadow, pasture worth 32*d*., and 391 sheep.[84]

In the 13th century there were five groups or classes of tenants. In 1222 7 free tenants held from 3½ to 140 a. for rents in money and kind and for ploughing and carrying services. Thirty-four yardlanders owed 3 days' work a week, at ploughing, carting, threshing, mowing, ditching, and hurdle-making, found men for haymaking and reaping, and paid witepund, a customary payment on the bishop of Ely's estates, and winesilver, a commutation of service in the vineyard at Ely. Thirteen half-yardlanders owed the same services except that between Michaelmas and Lammas they owed only 2 days' work a week. Eighteen customary tenants of holdings of varying sizes paid rent and witepund and owed services of ploughing, carrying, haymaking, and boon-works. Eighteen cottars owed 1 day's work a week between Michaelmas and Lammas, 3 for the rest of the year, and carrying services on foot. All except the free tenants had to reap an 'ale half-acre'. The manorial waste to a total of 111 a. had been divided between the tenants, 2½ a. for a yardlander, 1¼ a. for a half-yardlander, ½ a. for a cottar.

By 1251 there had been little change in the number of tenants or the services that they owed, but gersum, tallage, heriot, suit of mill, and payments for pannage were also recorded, sick-leave was regulated, and works were valued for commutation at ½*d*. each in winter and summer, 1*d*. in autumn. One yardlander gave 5*s*. 10*d*. instead of all his works. The lord could make any half-yardlander his ploughman, shepherd, overseer of the harvest, or keeper of the wood. In 1222 one customary tenant had kept the lord's wood and pigs, receiving payment in kind; in 1251 another was the village smith. The demesne arable in 1251 covered 1,028 a. and could be worked by 4 ploughs, along with the customary services. There were 7 a. of demesne meadow, 52 a. of pasture which was common from August to January, another 52 a. of permanent common pasture on the heath, and 34 a. of woodland. The demesne could support 7 cows and a bull, 42 sows and a boar, and 1,000 sheep.[85] By 1356 the number of tenants had fallen considerably. The yardlanders were represented by 27 villeins each holding 20 a., and there were 10 half-yardlanders and 9½ cotlands, owing services as in the 13th century, and 4 customary tenants called 'molmen'. Some land that appears to have been assarted before 1222 had gone out of cultivation.

Demesne farming continued in 1356. The lord had plough-horses and oxen; his ploughshares were provided by the smith in return for certain land. Of the 818 a. of demesne arable, 67 a. were leased out, along with a few acres of meadow and pasture.[86] By the mid 15th century all the demesne was

71 *Feud. Aids*, i. 139.
72 *Cal. Inq. p.m.* xiii, p. 180.
73 *Feud. Aids*, i. 142, 158, 177.
74 B.L. Add. MS. 5819, f. 132.
75 *D.N.B.*; *Rep. Com. Univ. Income* [C. 856-II], p. 23, H.C. (1873), xxxvii (3).
76 *Camb. Chron.* 23 June 1804; C.R.O., Q/RDz 8.
77 *Rep. Com. Univ. Income*, p. 23.
78 Charterho. Mun., MR 2/513, pp. 23–4; MR 2/515, p. 435; C.R.O., Q/RDz 8.
79 C.R.O., Q/RDz 8; Charterho. Mun., MR 2/175.
80 C.R.O., 296/SP 1107; ex inf. Miss N. J. Kerling, Archivist, St. Bart's.
81 C.R.O., 289/T 64; B.L. Maps, 31. c. 26.
82 *V.C.H. Cambs.* i. 379.
83 See pp. 193–4; H. F. Howard, *Finances of St. John's Coll. Camb.* (Camb. 1935), 203; ex inf. Dr. C. M. P. Johnson, Bursar of St. John's Coll.
84 *V.C.H. Cambs.* i. 364, 406.
85 B.L. Cott. MS. Tib. B. iii, ff. 127–129v.; ibid. Claud. C. xi, ff. 121–126v.
86 B.L. Add. MS. 6165, ff. 267, 282.

leased.[87] In 1617 it comprised 25 a. of pasture and enclosed meadow, 61 a. of Lammas ground, 247 a. of arable in the open fields, 2 sheep-walks for 1,000 sheep, and 143 a. of woodland.[88] A century later the demesne contained 567 a. of arable, besides pasture, heath, and Balsham wood. The largest pasture was the Yole, to the west of the wood, already inclosed in 1617.[89] By 1830 the demesne lands were divided into several farms.[90]

There is evidence of a three-course rotation in the 13th century, but the field pattern was irregular. In 1251 there were 22 fields of widely varying sizes, many of the names suggesting land recently cleared. Long ownership by the church may explain the lack of change in the pattern; many of the 13th- and 14th-century field-names survived at inclosure in the early 19th century.[91] The 13th-century crop rotation was designed to provide adequate grazing for the large number of sheep, the fields being divided into fairly compact areas of fallow and stubble.[92] The lord had the right to fold all his tenants' sheep, and in 1312 six other men had the right to fold 100 sheep in Balsham. They included the rector, Hugh Jacob, and Hugh le Despenser, earl of Winchester.[93] In 1617 seven separate heaths lay at the west end of the parish. One was common, two belonged to the demesne, two to John Killingworth, one to the rectory, and one to a William Linsdale.[94] In 1830 the owner of Oxcroft claimed sheepfold and right of sheep-walk over 67 a. of heath in Balsham for an unlimited number of sheep. The claim was based on an allotment made at inclosure acknowledging the right which had descended with the Oxcroft lands from Hugh le Despenser.[95]

In the 13th century wheat, rye, barley, oats, beans, and peas were produced on the manor. In 1356 the demesne grew wheat, barley, oats, and some peas and vetch.[96] In the 16th century there was a saffron ground in the parish.[97] In the early 17th century it was thought that large profits could be made from the sale of wood.[98] In 1794 the open fields were set with barley, oats, rye, trefoil, cinquefoil, clover, and turnips, all except the first two being sown for the extensive flock of Norfolk sheep, which grazed the 1,200 a. of heathland. No artificial manures were used, and the yield per acre was 18 bu. of wheat or barley, 14 bu. of oats or rye. The open fields covered *c.* 1,500 a. and were let at 7*s.* 6*d.* an acre; inclosures covered only *c.* 100 a. and were worth 21*s.* an acre. There were also *c.* 50 a. of meadow. Improvement of the land was thought to be possible only through inclosure.[99] Seventy years earlier Charterhouse officials had estimated that inclosure of the arable could double the value of the estate.[1] The areas inclosed before 1806 were much the same as those already in severalty in 1617: the village closes, the Yole, Balsham wood, the heath grounds, and some meadow.[2]

Of the 3,084 a. allotted at inclosure in 1806, 993 a. went to the rector, and 879 a. as demesne to the Charterhouse. In addition *c.* 650 a. of freehold were divided among 11 freeholders, in lots ranging from 10 perches to 180 a. The 900 a. of copyhold were divided among 64 people, including all the freeholders. Apart from the Charterhouse and the rector only four landowners received more than 100 a.: John Haylock 184 a., the Revd. H. A. Lagden 479 a., Thomas Symonds 106 a., and the Plumian professor 178 a. Four other estates received between 70 a. and 100 a.[3] Copyhold tenure survived in Balsham until its statutory abolition in 1925.[4]

Few farms in Balsham can be traced back to pre-inclosure times. Plumian farm, however, was leased to members of the Purkis family from 1755 until at least 1912.[5] Another exception was the 60 a. of copyhold land known as Nine Chimneys or Thomas's farm and associated with Nine Chimneys House. In the 18th and early 19th centuries it was held successively by the Burrows and Symonds families. In 1817 the ownership of the house and land were separated, and the land formed in 1975 part of Yole farm, then owned, along with Lower farm, by Kiddy and Samworth.[6] Dotterel Hall and Wood Hall farms were formed from the demesne land *c.* 1830, although there was a house at Dotterel by 1824.[7] They were at first leased separately, and were sold in 1919. Both were owned in 1975 by Mr. R. A. Vestey; Dotterel Hall farm was let, and Wood Hall was farmed along with Rectory and Place farms as one unit.[8]

After inclosure Balsham lands were farmed on an improved four-course system.[9] In 1905 there were 3,850 a. of arable.[10] In 1975 there were nine farms, together covering 4,000 a. They were divided into large arable fields farmed with a high level of mechanization.[11]

In 1811 118 families were occupied in agriculture, and 29 in trade or manufacture. In 1831 men employed by the parish received 9*s.* or 10*s.* a week; cottages cost 40*s.* to 60*s.* a year, and coal 11*s.* a bushel.[12] During the Captain Swing riots in 1830 *c.* 200 labourers assembled at Balsham to demand increased wages.[13] In 1877 the population was almost entirely poor.[14] Numbers had begun to decline

[87] S.C. 11/821.
[88] Charterho. Mun., valuation of Balsham demesne, 1617; plan of Balsham, 1617.
[89] Ibid. MR 2/550.
[90] Ibid. estate papers.
[91] *V.C.H. Cambs.* ii. 58; *Studies of Field Systems*, ed. Baker and Butlin, 294 sqq.
[92] *Studies of Field Systems*, 319.
[93] B.L. Cott. MS. Tib. B. iii, ff. 127–129v.; Charterho. Mun. MR 2/1.
[94] Charterho. Mun., plan of Balsham, 1617.
[95] C.R.O., L 86/107; Q/RDz 8.
[96] B.L. Cott. MS. Tib. B. iii, ff. 127–129v.; Add. MS. 6165, f. 267.
[97] Bodl. MS. Gough Eccl. Top. 3, f. 165; Charterho. Mun. MR 2/35.
[98] Charterho. Mun., valuation of Balsham demesne, 1617.
[99] Vancouver, *Agric. in Cambs.* 64–5.

[1] Charterho. Mun., MR 2/189A.
[2] Ibid. plan of Balsham, 1617.
[3] C.R.O., Q/RDz 8; ibid. 124/P 6.
[4] Charterho. Mun., MR 2/63.
[5] C.R.O., P 7/20/1; ibid. 334/04; *Kelly's Dir. Cambs.* (1858 and later edns.).
[6] Charterho. Mun., plan of Balsham, 1617; MR 6/17, pp. 418–19; MR 2/513, pp. 2–4; MR 2/514, pp. 370, 376; ex inf. the rector, the Revd. J. Hunter.
[7] Baker, *Map of Cambs.* (1824).
[8] Charterho. Mun., estate papers; *Kelly's Dir. Cambs.* (1847 and later edns.); ex inf. Sir John Mowbray.
[9] C.R.O., L 70/1.
[10] Cambs. Agric. Returns, 1905.
[11] Wilbraham, *J. Daniels.*
[12] *Census*, 1811; *Rep. H.L. Cttee. on Poor Laws*, H.C. 227, pp. 328–9, 332–3 (1831), viii.
[13] *Camb. Chron.* 10 Dec. 1830, p. 2.
[14] C.U.L., E.D.R., C 3/26.

as early as 1861, which was attributed to emigration.[15] When they rose again after the Second World War Balsham became primarily a commuter settlement for those working in industry or research stations outside the parish. In 1971 those employed within the parish included 24 in agriculture, 14 in the building trade, and 16 garage or agricultural engineers.[16]

In 1086 Balsham had a mill worth 4*s*., presumably a water-mill outside the parish. In 1356 a windmill in Balsham was valued at 22*s*. 8*d*. a year.[17] In 1687 there were two windmills, one in Ashley south-west of the village, and one in Button field, in the eastern part of the parish.[18] In 1753 a copyhold tenant was licensed to take down a windmill as he had two on his land and one was never used.[19] A windmill which could also be driven by steam was built in 1831 and was derelict by 1925.[20] In 1852 a mill stood behind the Black Bull near the centre of the village. In 1929 there was a steam-mill in the parish. By 1975 the mill south-west of the village had been demolished.[21]

In 1245 the bishop of Ely was granted a market on Mondays at Balsham and a fair there for three days at Holy Trinity. In 1318 the market-day was changed from Monday to Wednesday.[22] The market had been discontinued by the mid 18th century, but the fair survived in the early 19th century as a statute fair for hiring labourers. By 1851 both market and fair were said to have been long since discontinued.[23]

LOCAL GOVERNMENT. At Balsham as in his other manors the bishop of Ely enjoyed view of frankpledge, *vee de naam*, and other franchises, including cases of felony, theft, and bloodshed.[24] Court rolls and books survive from 1310 until 1935.[25] In the 14th century courts seem to have been held only three or four times a year; in the 16th and 17th centuries they were held once or twice a year; from the 18th century only once, apart from special sessions to deal with particular transactions. The court met at the manor-house; the meeting was usually called a court leet and court baron. As late as 1554 a fine for chevage is recorded. From about 1770 the presentments of the homage ceased to be concerned with leet jurisdiction and the regulation of agriculture, and became occupied solely with tenurial matters, except that the court continued to appoint a pinder and two constables, and in 1854 received a presentment of waste.

In 1825 one churchwarden was chosen by the rector and one by the parish.[26] There were usually two overseers, but in 1787 there seem to have been five, two of whom were the wives of previous overseers.[27] A parish clerk was recorded from 1665.[28] In the 18th century the overseers received rent from the town land to supplement the poor-rate, and at least once there was also a general subscription to supply the poor with coal and blankets.[29] Balsham's expenditure on the poor was consistently one of the two highest in the hundred, increasing from £141 in 1776 to £628 in 1803. The highest expenditure was £1,181 in 1825. In 1803 39 adults received permanent outside relief, and by 1814 the number had risen to 66. In 1831 there were 15 men employed by the parish and paid for from the poor-rate. There was also an allowance for large families. In 1832 £230 was spent in wages for paupers. Fuel and clothing were also distributed, but there was no land let to labourers, and few cottages had gardens.[30] Balsham became part of the Linton poor-law union in 1835, was transferred in 1934 with the rest of Linton R.D. to the South Cambridgeshire R.D.,[31] and in 1974 was included in South Cambridgeshire.

CHURCH. There was a church at Balsham by 1010.[32] A rector was mentioned between 1220 and 1225.[33] The advowson of the rectory belonged in the Middle Ages to the bishop of Ely, and the church to the bishop's peculiar jurisdiction.[34] The advowson descended with the manor, the lessees of which held it in the later 16th century. Since 1611 the Charterhouse has been patron.[35]

In 1254 the rectory was valued at 40 marks, the most valuable in Wilbraham deanery.[36] In 1291 it was in Camps deanery and, taxed at £44, was by far the wealthiest benefice there.[37] In 1535, when valued at £39 6*s*. 8*d*., it was still the wealthiest rectory in Camps deanery.[38] In 1744 Mr. Lagden of Balsham was said to have offered £316 a year for a lease of the rectory.[39] In 1835 the net value was £1,104, and in 1883 the gross value was £1,600.[40]

In 1311 the rector had the right to fold 100 sheep.[41] In the 17th century the rectory had 153 a. of arable, 8 a. of meadow, and a heath with a sheep-pen. Most tithes were paid in kind, and the rector also received tithes from lands in West Wratting and West Wickham, and a quarter of the wool-tithes of the Wickham flock.[42] At inclosure in 1806 the rector was allotted over 740 a. for tithes and over 250 a. for glebe, of which 180 a. was heathland. He was also later allotted 26½ a. in West Wratting and

15 *Census*, 1861.
16 Wilbraham, *J. Daniels*.
17 *V.C.H. Cambs.* i. 364; B.L. Add. MS. 6165, f. 267.
18 Charterho. Mun., plan of Balsham, 1617.
19 Ibid. MR 2/506.
20 *Trans. Newcomen Soc.* xxvii. 103, 114; *Proc. C.A.S.* xxxi. 25.
21 B.L. Maps 1640(17); *Kelly's Dir. Cambs.* (1929); local information.
22 *Cal. Chart. R.* 1226–57, 287; 1300–26, 393.
23 *V.C.H. Cambs.* ii. 87; *Gardner's Dir. Cambs.* (1851).
24 Cf. *V.C.H. Cambs.* v. 95; Bentham, *Hist. Ely*, i, App. V, IX; Charterho. Mun., MR 2/1, *passim.*
25 Details in the following paragraph are from Charterho. Mun., MR 2, MR 6, and estate papers.
26 C.U.L., E.D.R., C 1/6.
27 Charterho. Mun., MR 2/169B.
28 C.U.L., E.D.R., B 2/59, p. 45.
29 C.R.O., P 7/12/1; P 7/1/3.
30 *Poor Law Abstract, 1804*, 38–9; *1818*, 30–1; *Poor Rate Returns, 1816–21*, 11; *1822–4*, 38; *1825–9*, 16; *1830–4*, 16; *Rep. H.L. Cttee. on Poor Laws*, H.C. 227, pp. 332–3 (1831), viii; *Rep. Com. Poor Laws*, [44], p. 257, H.C. (1834), xxviii.
31 *Poor Law Com. 1st Rep.* 249; *Census*, 1931 (pt. ii).
32 Hen. of Huntingdon, *Hist. Angl.* (Rolls Ser.), 178.
33 B.L. Add. MS. 5807, f. 73v.; *Pat. R.* 1216–25, 588.
34 *V.C.H. Cambs.* ii. 160.
35 *Essex Jnl.* viii. 113–18; Blomefield, *Collect. Cantab.* 198.
36 *Val. of Norwich*, ed. Lunt, 215.
37 *Tax. Eccl.* (Rec. Com.), 267.
38 *Valor Eccl.* (Rec. Com.) iii. 504.
39 Palmer, *Wm. Cole*, 84.
40 *Rep. Com. Eccl. Revenues*, p. 344; C.U.L., E.D.R., C 3/36.
41 Charterho. Mun., MR 2/1.
42 C.U.L., E.D.R., H 1/1, terrier [*c.* 1665].

16½ a. in West Wickham.[43] By 1926 the glebe had been reduced to 500 a.,[44] which in 1975, still as glebe, formed Parsonage or Rat Hall farm. The farm-house had been demolished by then.

The rectory house, mentioned in 1377, was rebuilt in the 17th century.[45] In the early 1840s a large new rectory was built of brick in a simple Gothic style.[46] Another new house was built in the 1960s; in 1975 the 19th-century building, known as Sutton Hall, was occupied as a private house by Sir Frederick Catherwood.[47]

There were two guilds in Balsham in the 15th century, dedicated to the Trinity and to St. Nicholas.[48] The dates of foundation are unknown, but there were three chaplains in Balsham in 1406.[49] The chapels are said to have stood at the east end of the two aisles.[50] At least one still existed in 1521, but there was no trace of them in 1547.[51] In 1510 a chantry was founded by Geoffrey Blodwell who endowed it with an estate called Hunts, which in 1557 consisted of a messuage and 150 a.[52] In 1558 the lands were granted to Thomas Reeve and Christopher Bullit.[53] In 1553 the late incumbent of the chantry received a pension of £5.[54]

The charity of Dr. Andrew Perne (d. 1588) provided for a yearly sermon at Balsham by a fellow of Peterhouse and for catechizing the children. In 1758 10*s.* was spent on the sermon, and in 1759 3*s.* 4*d.* was distributed among the children.[55] In 1837 the money was used for the intended purposes, but by 1864 was distributed with Perne's other bequests in fuel.[56] In 1883 a Scheme devoted the money to the promotion of religious knowledge in Balsham school.[57]

Up to the 16th century the valuable rectory attracted pluralists and high officials of the church, and was used to reward service to the see of Ely or the Crown. John of Osmele (fl. 1291) was archdeacon of Ely, as was Richard Bale (fl. 1462) who also acted as the bishop's official.[58] John Blodwell (d. 1462) was administrator of the Ely temporalities; Henry Myn (fl. 1519) was steward to bishop West; William May (fl. 1540) had been the bishop's chancellor, and Andrew Perne (d. 1588) was dean of Ely.[59] Three rectors, John of Droxford, later bishop of Bath and Wells (d. 1329), Henry Snaith (fl. 1361), and John Sleaford (d. 1401), earned their preferment in the king's service. Both Sleaford and Droxford held many other benefices.[60] There are references to curates and chaplains in Balsham from the 14th century onwards.[61]

In 1550 it was found that the site of the altar had not been destroyed; otherwise there is little trace of the 16th-century religious changes.[62] William May, later archbishop-elect of York, had to resign as rector in 1554, but Andrew Perne who took the living *c.* 1556 continued to hold it under Elizabeth. He was not often resident but kept a curate in Balsham.[63] In 1644 the church was visited by William Dowsing, who broke pictures and crosses, and echoed the order of 1550 to level the chancel.[64] In 1650 the rector, Dr. Thomas Warner, was found to be a worthy, painful, and godly preacher, but in 1654 was listed as a scandalous minister.[65] From the later 17th century most rectors died in office.[66] For more than a century after 1751 they were all connected with the Charterhouse; several were ushers or readers there, and William Ramsden, 1780–1804, was master. Both he and his curate were almost strangers to the parish, and Ramsden died at the Charterhouse;[67] otherwise few complaints were recorded about the incumbents.

In 1728 there were two services on Sunday and the sacrament was administered four times a year to 20–30 communicants. In 1783 the rector regularly catechized and lectured the children.[68] In 1807 there was a sermon at evening service, and the quarterly sacraments were well attended.[69] In 1825 there were *c.* 100 communicants at Easter. By 1836 there were sermons at both Sunday services.[70] In 1851 250 attended service in the morning and 500 in the afternoon.[71] By 1877 weekly communions had been introduced but were poorly attended.[72] In 1897 there were a Mothers' Union branch, a bible class, and a boys' and young men's reading room.[73] In 1913 a church institute was built by public subscription.[74]

The church of the *HOLY TRINITY*, so called in 1518,[75] is built of field stones and brick with dressings of freestone and has a clerestoried chancel with north vestry, an aisled and clerestoried nave with south porch, and a west tower. There was a tower *c.* 1150,[76] but the surviving bell tower is of the mid to late 13th century and is the oldest part of the fabric. The chancel is of the earlier 14th century, implying a nave of considerable length by that date. The nave, with its arcades, aisles, and porch, was rebuilt in the later 14th century by John Sleaford (d. 1401). His monumental brass, and that of another rector, John Blodwell (d. 1462), both with effigies, are in the chancel. Sleaford also provided the fine set of 26 stalls in the chancel and the chancel

43 C.R.O., Q/RDz 8; C.U.L., E.D.R., H 1/7.
44 *Crockford* (1926).
45 Margaret Aston, *Thos. Arundel*, 47; M.H.L.G. List.
46 C.U.L., E.D.R., C 3/17; *Gardner's Dir. Cambs.* (1851); see above, plate facing p. 129.
47 Ex inf. the rector.
48 *Trans. C.H.A.S.* i. 384.
49 *E.D.R.* (1899), 158.
50 Blomefield, *Collect. Cantab.* 199.
51 B.L. Add. MS. 5861, f. 165.
52 *Trans. C.H.A.S.* i. 206; B.L. Harl. MS. 607, f. 134.
53 B.L. Harl. MS. 607, f. 134; *Cal. Pat.* 1557–8, p. 42.
54 *Trans. C.H.A.S.* i. 206.
55 C.R.O., P 7/25/4 and 6.
56 *31st Rep. Com. Char.* 129; *Char. Digest Cambs. 1863–4*, 2–3.
57 Cambs. Educ. Authority, *Educ. Endows.* (1908), 4–7.
58 C.R.O., P 7/28/31; B.L. Add. MS. 5807, f. 72v.; *E.D.R.* (1912), 55.
59 Burrel, *Balsham Church*; B.L. Add. MS. 5803, f. 72v.; *E.D.R.* (1912) 55.
60 *D.N.B.*; Tout, *Chapters in Admin. Hist.* iv. 163; vi. 36 sqq.; Blomefield, *Collect. Cantab.* 262.
61 e.g. *Cal. Pat.* 1350–4, p. 164; *E.D.R.* (1899), 158; (1906), 188; (1909), 128.
62 C.U.L., E.D.R., B 2/3, p. 81.
63 *D.N.B.*; Burrel, *Balsham Church*; B.L. Add. MS. 5813, f. 67; C.U.L., E.D.R., B 2/3, p. 98; B 2/6, 8, 10, 11.
64 *Trans. C.H.A.S.* iii. 90.
65 Lamb. Pal. MS. 904, f. 264; *Acts & Ords. of Interr.* ed. Firth & Rait, ii. 978.
66 List of clergy in C.R.O., P 7/28/31.
67 C.R.O., P 7/1/1; C.U.L., E.D.R., B 7/11, p. 117.
68 C.U.L., E.D.R., B 8/1; B 8/4, f. 2.
69 Ibid. C 1/4.
70 Ibid. C 1/6; C 3/21.
71 H.O. 129/188/3/3/3.
72 C.U.L., E.D.R., C 3/26.
73 Ibid. C 3/36.
74 *E.D.R.* (1913), 17–18.
75 B.L. Add. MS. 5861, p. 126.
76 Hen. of Huntingdon, *Hist. Angl.* (Rolls Ser.), 178.

screen. The rood loft is a later addition, probably of the late 15th century. It once housed the organ, and in 1840 the village band.[77] The chancel clerestory was perhaps added at about the same time as the loft. The appearance of the tower was altered in 1589 when heavy buttresses were added to the north and west sides and an octagonal brick vice to the south. The initials of Thomas Sutton are on a buttress,[78] and his arms on panelling reset in the north aisle but perhaps once forming part of a private pew. Repairs were undertaken in the earlier 19th century and included extensive renewal of the roofs and repairs to the clerestories, that of the nave being refaced with brick.[79] A vestry was completed on the north side of the chancel in 1867.[80] There was a general restoration in 1875 under the direction of William Butterfield.[81] By 1922 a chapel had been formed on the site of the old altar of the guild of St. Nicholas in the north aisle. It contains the Elizabethan altar-table and panelling from the old rectory.[82] The tower was again strengthened in 1973–4.[83] The ancient stone font has a sixteen-sided bowl and a carved wooden cover. An early coffin-lid with interlace ornament stands in the south aisle.

There were four bells and a clock bell in 1562. One of the five bells that survive is 16th-century. In 1609 two bells were recast as four, of which three survive; the treble was damaged one May Morning and was recast in 1774 by Pack and Chapman of London. In 1969 the bells could not be rung because the tower was unsafe and in 1975 remained unhung.[84]

In 1278 the church had two chalices and by 1390 there were also a silver chalice, a gilt chalice and cross, and gold ornaments.[85] In 1552 there were three silver chalices and patens.[86] By *c.* 1960 the plate included a silver cup and offering plate of 1777, and a cup and paten cover of 1838.[87] The registers start in 1559 and are virtually complete.[88]

NONCONFORMITY. About 1560 Christopher Vitels, a disciple of the Family of Love, established at Balsham a congregation which by 1574 had aroused suspicion. Six members were questioned but returned orthodox answers. They had at least five other sympathizers; there was another investigation in 1580, and some members were imprisoned.[89] In 1609 Edmund Rule and John Taylor the elder, two of the original group, were again reported to belong to the Family.[90] In 1686 John and Oliver Taylor of Balsham were named as recusants, perhaps suggesting a continuing tradition of dissent in the Taylor family.[91]

In 1669 there was a small group of Quakers in Balsham. By 1672 they had joined the meeting at Linton, but John Webb, whose name appears from the 1650s, held regular meetings at his house in Balsham.[92] In 1679 there were four Quakers in Balsham, but by 1682 some had been won back to the church by the rector, Dr. John Templar.[93]

In 1654 there were a few Baptists in Balsham, as in 1669.[94] In 1728 there were few dissenters in the parish, and in 1807 there were said to be no dissenters, chapels, or meeting-houses.[95] By 1824, however, a barn was registered for protestant worship, and a house in 1825.[96] In the same year a few Presbyterians and Methodists from Balsham were said to worship at Linton or West Wratting.[97] Meeting places in Balsham were registered in 1836 and 1840; in 1847, 1848, and 1852 Primitive Methodists were meeting in Balsham.[98] A Primitive Methodist chapel in Balsham was registered from 1859 until 1896.[99]

In 1833 a Congregational chapel was built to seat 300.[1] It may have been the chapel which was used by Baptists and Independents, and was probably also the Balsham Home Missionary chapel, a station of the Cambridgeshire County Union and Home Missionary Society, a Congregational body. That was the only nonconformist place of worship in Balsham recorded in 1851 when it was said to seat only 200, and to have been built in 1838–9.[2] In 1877 100 parishoners were chapel-goers, while another 100 attended both church and chapel. In 1897 50 out of 183 Balsham families were dissenters.[3] In 1860 the Balsham chapel had an out-station at West Wratting, and from 1905 to 1945 the two were combined. Numbers increased until 1916, but then declined. In 1954 there were only four members in Balsham, and the chapel was not mentioned after that.[4] By 1975 it had been demolished; the former manse in the high street was a private house.

In 1894 a Salvation Army barracks in Balsham already in use was registered. The registration was cancelled in 1896.[5]

EDUCATION. A schoolmaster was recorded in 1625.[6] David Appleyard, by will dated 1669, gave 1 a. in Linton to pay for teaching three poor children of Balsham. The income was devoted to educa-

[77] Pevsner, *Cambs.* 295–6; *Proc. C.A.S.* xii. 294–5; xiii. 40; Palmer, *Wm. Cole*, 84; Burrel, *Balsham Ch.*; see above, plate facing p. 112.
[78] Pevsner, *Cambs.* 294–5.
[79] C.R.O., P 7/1/3, Sept. 1818.
[80] C.R.O., P 7/8/1, 1867.
[81] Pevsner, *Cambs.* 295; C.U.L., E.D.R., C 3/26; C.R.O., P 7/6/3.
[82] Burrel, *Balsham Ch.*; *Kelly's Dir. Cambs.* (1922).
[83] Ex inf. the rector.
[84] *Cambs. Ch. Goods, temp. Edw. VI*, 73; *Cambs. Bells* (C.A.S. 8vo ser. xviii), 118–20.
[85] *Vetus Liber Arch. Elien.* (C.A.S. 8vo ser. xlviii), 60–1.
[86] *Cambs. Ch. Goods, temp. Edw. VI*, 73.
[87] List of Cambs. ch. plate *penes V.C.H.*
[88] C.R.O., P 7/1.
[89] Felicity Heal, 'Family of Love and Dioc. of Ely', *Studies in Church Hist.* ix. 215–20; Strype, *Life of Parker*, ii. 381 sqq.
[90] C.U.L., E.D.R., B 2/28, f. 18 and v.
[91] *Cal. S.P. Dom.* 1686–7, 322.
[92] *Proc. C.A.S.* lxi. 86, 93.
[93] C.U.L., E.D.R., B 2/66, f. 15; B.L. Add. MS. 5807, f. 62v.; Margaret Spufford, *Contrasting Communities*, 215–16.
[94] *Proc. C.A.S.* lxi. 86; *Orig. Rec. of Early Nonconf.* ed. Turner, i. 39.
[95] C.U.L., E.D.R., B 8/1; C 1/4.
[96] G.R.O. Worship Returns, Ely dioc. nos. 469, 488.
[97] C.U.L., E.D.R., C 1/6.
[98] G.R.O. Worship Returns, Ely dioc. nos. 601, 648, 695, 699; ibid. Cambs. no. 66.
[99] G.R.O. Worship Reg. nos. 8976, 9389.
[1] *Kelly's Dir. Cambs.* (1908).
[2] H.O. 129/188/3/3/11; *Gardner's Dir. Cambs.* (1851); *Cong. Yr. Bk.* (1894).
[3] C.U.L., E.D.R., C 3/26; C 3/36.
[4] *Cong. Yr. Bk.* (1860 and later edns.).
[5] G.R.O. Worship Reg. nos. 34227, 9392.
[6] C.U.L., E.D.R., B 2/32, f. 96v.

tional purposes by a Scheme of 1881.[7] The parish had three dame schools in 1728 and four in 1807.[8] In 1818 a lean-to schoolroom was built on the chancel of the parish church, where a National school opened with 110 children. The school was held on Sunday and Wednesday, and there was also a working school for 30 girls every weekday except Saturday.[9] An infant department with 20 boys and 40 girls was started in 1833 when 82 children attended the day-school at their parents' expense and 120 the Sunday school.[10] In 1836 both the infant and Sunday schools were taught by the curate, and supported by voluntary contributions.[11] In 1847 Balsham had two dame schools with 33 children, a village day-school with 30 boys, and the National school with an average attendance of 61 on weekdays and 168 on Sundays. The National school had only one schoolroom and no teacher's house. It was supported by a grant, school pence, and subscriptions.[12] In 1863 the Charterhouse gave the Old Hall to the National school, which in 1864 moved to new buildings there, including two schoolrooms, a classroom, and a teacher's house. The school received a state grant from 1864.[13] By 1868 evening classes were also held.[14]

The vestry levied a rate in 1877 to meet school expenses, for which in 1878 the rector agreed to be responsible, receiving *c.* £54 a year from the rates.[15] In 1884 average attendance was 148, and in 1908 142.[16] In 1930 the school became a council school, and new buildings, for 96 children, were opened on the same site in 1931. Average attendance was 103.[17] The school was reorganized between 1936 and 1938 when the seniors were transferred to Linton village college, and in 1938 average attendance was 60.[18] By 1970 building had begun on the north side of the high street for a new primary school which in 1972 served Balsham, West Wratting, Weston Colville, and West Wickham. In 1975 the old buildings remained in use, pending the erection of further classrooms on the new site.[19]

CHARITIES FOR THE POOR. The house in Balsham given before 1575 by John Woolward for the use of two poor widows named by the manorial court was presumably the alms-house recorded in 1593.[20] In 1720 and 1790 the trustees of the poor held a cottage in Balsham, probably the same building, described as an unendowed alms-house in 1728. In 1807 there were two old alms-houses, which were then vested in the parish officers and inhabited by paupers. In 1831 the double cottage for the poor was altered and improved by the Charterhouse.[21] In 1882 the vestry resolved to try to identify two cottages which had been held by trustees at inclosure; they are not mentioned thereafter.[22]

A Scheme of 1883 amalgamated and regulated the Balsham parochial charities, including Perne's, Appleyard's, Symonds's, and Wollaston's.[23] Dr. Andrew Perne, by will dated 1588, gave a rent-charge of £1 16*s.* 8*d.* of which £1 3*s.* 4*d.* was to be distributed among the poor, the residue being for sermons and catechizing.[24] In the 18th century it was said that the poor's share should be spent on white herrings in Lent.[25] In 1864 all the money was distributed in fuel, and in 1881 the poor's share was spent on calico and flannel for large families. David Appleyard, by will dated 1669, gave 14 a. in Linton for doles to the poor at Easter, a rent-charge of 15*s.* for doles on Christmas Eve, and one of 6*s.* for bread in Rogation week. Robert Symonds, by will dated 1832, gave £100 for coal for widows and orphans on Christmas Eve. In 1881 2 cwt. of coal were given to each of 50 poor widows.[26] Edward Wollaston (d. 1838), rector of Balsham, gave £200, the income to be half for the National school, and half for coal and clothing for widows and widowers.[27]

The 1883 Scheme also dealt with the income from other poor lands. In 1696 the trustees bought 4 a. with money given by various donors since 1599.[28] In 1783 the town lands yielded £5 a year, which had not been distributed or accounted for for 7 years.[29] At inclosure the trustees were allotted 5½ a. in Balsham and in 1837 distributed the rent in doles of 9*d.* per head.[30] In 1881 6*d.* was given to each of 838 poor of the parish. Distribution was then stopped, causing great ill feeling, while the Charity Commissioners considered a Scheme, by which money devoted to educational purposes continued to be so used, the distribution of coal and clothing under Symonds's and Wollaston's wills continued, and all other income was pooled. Despite the labourers' demands for the continuance of head-money two-thirds of the income was to go to poor labourers living alone, or with two children at school, to widows, and to the infirm. The other third was used to provide relief in cases of sickness, loss, or destitution. In the first year £60 was distributed. In 1974 the income of between £25 and £50 was distributed for the general benefit of the poor.[31]

By will proved 1931 Anne E. Prince left £300 for a nurse or nursing and medicaments for the poor of Balsham. In 1974 the Prince Nursing Fund had an income of £53, spent on comforts for the chronically sick, or help in sudden illness.[32]

[7] *31st Rep. Com. Char.* 130; Char. Com. files.
[8] C.U.L., E.D.R., B 8/1; C 1/4.
[9] C.R.O., P 7/1/3; *V.C.H. Cambs.* ii. 350 n.; *Educ. of Poor Digest*, 55.
[10] *Educ. Enquiry Abstract*, 50.
[11] C.U.L., E.D.R., C 3/21.
[12] *Church School Inquiry, 1846–7*, 2–3.
[13] C.R.O., P 7/1/3; Ed. 7/5; *Rep. of Educ. Cttee. of Council, 1864–5* [3533], p. 442, H.C. (1865), xlii.
[14] *Rep. of Educ. Cttee. of Council, 1868–9* [4139], p. 506, H.C. (1868–9), xx.
[15] C.R.O., P 7/8/1.
[16] *Rep. of Educ. Cttee. of Council, 1884–5* [C. 4483-I], p. 522, H.C. (1884–5), xxiii; *Public Elem. Schs. 1907* [Cd. 3901], p. 26, H.C. (1908), lxxxiv.
[17] *Bd. of Educ., List 21, 1932* (H.M.S.O.), 16.
[18] Ibid. *1938*, 19.
[19] C.R.O., E/T, 4B; Camb. City Libr., Cambs. Colln. *Balsham Review*, Dec. 1970; *Balsham Draft Village Plan* (1972); ex inf. the rector.
[20] Charterho. Mun., MR 2/35; Bodl. MS. Gough Eccl. Top. 3, f. 25.
[21] Charterho. Mun., MR 2/513, 109–10; estate papers; C.U.L., E.D.R., B 8/1; C 1/4; *Char. Don.* i. 94–5.
[22] C.R.O., P 7/8/1, 1882.
[23] Char. Com. files.
[24] C.R.O., P 7/25/6.
[25] *Char. Don.* i. 94–5; Char. Com. files.
[26] *31st Rep. Com. Char.* 101–2, 129–31; *Char. Digest. Cambs. 1863–4*, 2–3; Char. Com. files.
[27] C.R.O., P 7/25/16; P 7/25/19.
[28] C.R.O., P 7/25/6.
[29] C.U.L., E.D.R., B 7/1, p. 117.
[30] Ibid. C 1/6; C.R.O., P 7/25/10; *31st Rep. Com. Char.* 130–1.
[31] Char. Com. files; *Camb. Express*, 25 July 1883; C.R.O., P 7/8/1, 1883.
[32] Char. Com. files.

BRINKLEY

THE PARISH of Brinkley, which covers 1,303 a., lies 5 miles south-west of Newmarket and 10 miles east of Cambridge.[1] It is long and narrow, being 5 miles from north-west to south-east and less than a mile across at its widest point. Between 1816 and 1886 *c.* 33 a. to the south of the village, known as Carlton field and Spring Close, became part of Carlton parish.[2] In 1886 a detached part of Brinkley, called Norney, was also amalgamated with Carlton.[3] Much of Brinkley's north-east boundary is marked by a long break of trees which may follow the route of an ancient green way. South-east of the Dullingham road it follows a stream for some way before joining the road from Burrough Green to Great Bradley (Suff.), while the eastern end of the south-east boundary follows the river Stour from just above Sipsey Bridge. Another stream crosses the north-west end of the parish.

Like other parishes in the area Brinkley stretches from chalk heathland in the north-west to the originally wooded area of boulder clay in the east, above the 300-ft. contour. From the north-west the land rises quite steeply from *c.* 125 ft. to 300 ft., and then more gently to 375 ft. It falls slightly to 275 ft. in the south-east near the river. Brinkley wood, near the middle of the north-eastern edge of the parish, covers *c.* 20 a.

The village of Brinkley lies on high ground towards the south-east end of the parish, along what was in the 18th century the high road from Suffolk and Essex to Cambridge.[4] That road runs the length of the parish from Sipsey Bridge to Six Mile Bottom, crossed at the north-western edge of the village by the Linton–Newmarket road, and at Chalk Pit cross-roads 1½ mile north-west of the village by a minor road. Beyond the south-eastern edge of the village the high road is joined by the road from Carlton. The village was formerly grouped along a green which before inclosure in 1816 covered *c.* 25 a. The green comprised a large area on each side of the Newmarket road, a broad strip along either side of the main street up to the junction with the Carlton road, and a large triangular area at the junction. The older houses set back from the road originally stood along the edge of the green. The church, the old rectory, and Brinkley Hall lie in the angle between the main street and the Newmarket road. The Poplars or Brinkley House at the north-western end of the main street, and the Grove and the school at the south-eastern end have long marked the extent of the village. In 1919 the parish council asked that at least six new houses might be built, and in 1937 a similar request was made. After the Second World War small housing estates were built on Beechcroft Road, opposite the Hall, and along Old School Lane.[5] Houses were later built by a private developer south-west of the village, on the Weston Colville road. A village hall was built in 1920 as a war memorial at the south-east end of the main street.[6] The Fulbourn Charity Farm on the south-west side of the main street was the only farm-house left in the village after inclosure. Lower, Chalk Pit, and Hill Farms lie north-west of the village, on the road running the length of the parish, the first two being there by 1824.[7] New Farm and Cockerton's Farm lie along the same road, to the south-east of the village.

The Cambridge–Newmarket railway line crosses the northern corner of the parish; the nearest station is 4 miles from the village, at Six Mile Bottom.

In 1086 16 inhabitants were enumerated in Brinkley,[8] and 101 adults were taxed there in 1377.[9] In 1563 there were 29 households in the parish[10] and 37 houses in 1666. By 1674 the number had fallen to 34.[11] In 1728 although there were thought to be only 14 families there were *c.* 150 people.[12] In 1801 the population totalled 275. It rose gradually to 375 in 1851, and then fell over the next 100 years, to a low point of 169 in 1951. Numbers then rose to 204 in 1961 and 355 in 1971.[13]

The Red Lion, which stands at the north-western edge of the village, by the crossroads, occurs from 1709 onwards.[14] The Rose and Crown stood in 1885 at the south-east corner of the Green, on the Carlton road, and the old White Hart, offered for sale in 1944, near the centre of the village; both were private houses in 1975.[15]

MANORS AND OTHER ESTATES. Brinkley appears to be represented in the Domesday survey by the 3 hides in Carlton held by Earl Harold in 1066 and by Countess Judith in 1086. Along with Whittlesford and Kirtling they formed the marriage-portion of Judith's daughter Alice when she married Ralph de Tony.[16] Alice and Ralph's daughter Godehold married William de Mohun *c.* 1160, and her marriage-portion was the manor of *BRINKLEY*, called *MOHUN'S* in 1390, held of the de Tony barony of Kirtling.[17] In 1201 their younger son John gave 20 marks to have seisin of land in Brinkley which his brother William had given him.[18] In 1208 William's son Reynold de Mohun of Dunster (Som.) established his right to the mesne lordship of a fee in Brinkley as his grandmother's heir. John de Mohun was still in possession and Roger de Tony

[1] This account was written in 1975. Where no other reference is given the following is based on O.S. Maps 1/25,000, TL 65, TL 55 (1956 edn.); 6", Cambs. XLVIII. NE., SE., XLIX. SW. (1903 and later edns.); 1/2,500, Cambs. XLVIII. 7; XLIX. 9, 13 (1886 and later edns.).

[2] B.L. Maps 1640 (34); O.S. Map 1/2,500, Cambs. XLIX. 13 (1886 edn.).

[3] *Kelly's Dir. Cambs.* (1900); *Census*, 1891.

[4] *Camb. Chron.* 28 Mar. 1789, p. 4.

[5] C.R.O., P 16/12; R. H. Cory, *Hist. Notes on Brinkley*, 33, 39.

[6] Cory, *Brinkley*, 38; Char. Com. files.

[7] Baker, *Map of Cambs.* (1824).

[8] *V.C.H. Cambs.* i. 398.

[9] *East Anglian*, N.S. xii. 239.

[10] B.L. Harl. MS. 594, f. 199v.

[11] See pp. 279, 281.

[12] C.U.L., E.D.R., B 8/1.

[13] *Census*, 1801–1971.

[14] C.R.O., R 50/25/9.

[15] Cory, *Brinkley*, 39; C.R.O., 515/SP 1800.

[16] Farrer, *Feud. Cambs.* 48, 114; *V.C.H. Cambs.* i. 398.

[17] Farrer, *Feud. Cambs.* 50, 114; *Cal. Inq. Misc.* v. p. 299.

[18] *Rot. de Ob. et Fin.* (Rec. Com.), 136.

was the tenant in chief.[19] With the extinction of the male Tony line in 1309 the overlordship passed through Alice, sister of Robert de Tony, to the earls of Warwick, descendants of Alice's second marriage to Guy Beauchamp, earl of Warwick (d. 1315). It afterwards passed, with the barony of Kirtling, to the Norths, of whom Brinkley was held in 1521,[20] and in 1816 Francis North, earl of Guilford, received 4½ a. at inclosure for his overlordship.[21] The mesne lordship descended with the barony of Dunster,[22] which in 1375 fell into abeyance between the three daughters of John de Mohun. In 1390 Philippa, the second daughter, and her second husband Sir John Golafre, occupied 14 a. in Brinkley.[23]

William de Mohun, presumably a descendant of John de Mohun, held 3 hides in Brinkley in the 1230s. He still held land in Brinkley in 1261, and by 1285 the fee was held by Andrew de Mohun.[24] In 1390 the manor was held in demesne by Sir John Engaine and other feoffees.[25] In 1403 two-thirds of the manor passed from Thomas Engaine to Richard and Thomas Stutville and others.[26] Richard was alive in 1434,[27] and another Richard Stutville was said *c.* 1504 to have been seised of the manor in which he enfeoffed Roger Hunt of Balsham.[28] Nevertheless William Stutville (d. 1534) was succeeded in the manor by his grandson Nicholas.[29] In 1602 Thomas Stutville died holding Brinkley manor and left as heir his grandson Roger, although in 1620 Roger's mother Jane and her second husband Gilbert Rolleston held the manor in dower.[30] Roger was said to be mad in 1638.[31] He was dead by 1658 when his wife Agnes and her second husband, Richard Rich, held the manor with reversion to her son, Roger Stutville (d. 1666).[32] Roger was succeeded by a third Roger Stutville who *c.* 1689 sold Brinkley manor to Richard Godfrey.[33] Godfrey died in 1699 leaving four daughters, from whom Brinkley seems to have passed by 1711 to John Godfrey, high sheriff of Cambridgeshire in 1746.[34] The manor was conveyed in 1753 to Richard Godfrey and in 1778 to Henry Godfrey.[35] It was advertised for sale, with 686 a. of land in 1796, and by 1801 was the property of William Frost, whose father had been a tenant of the Godfreys.[36]

At inclosure in 1816 over 700 a. were allotted to Frost.[37] He died in 1818 and the manor descended to his grandson, Robert William King (d. 1869)[38] and the latter's son of the same name (d. 1920).[39] The estate next descended to Dr. Colin King whose brother Capt. Donald King occupied Brinkley Hall.[40] After Colin King's death most of the land was detached from the Hall and after several changes of ownership the house and park (*c.* 15 a.) were sold in 1952 to Col. D. R. B. Kaye who still occupied them in 1975,[41] and farmed the central area of Brinkley along with land in other parishes. Brinkley Hall incorporates parts of a small house of the 17th or 18th century, to which a new front block of brick, 5 bays long, was added *c.* 1800. There have been subsequent minor additions and internal alterations.

In the early 1230s William le Breton (d. 1261) held land in Brinkley of William de Mohun. At his death 56 a. there passed to his son John.[42] In 1286 John of Brigham released to John le Breton his right in a messuage and 1 carucate in Brinkley. In 1306 John le Breton granted Edmund le Breton 240 a. in Brinkley and other parishes.[43] In 1353 Thomas Breton leased all his lands in those parishes to Sir Thomas Walkefare. No later reference to the land in Brinkley has been found.[44]

In 1597 Thomas Stutville the younger sold to Thomas Stewkley *c.* 60 a. in Brinkley.[45] Stewkley at his death in 1639 held a messuage in Brinkley called *NAWNEY* with his manor of Great Carlton. The land formed the detached part of the parish, called the hamlet of Norney, which was transferred to Carlton in 1886.[46]

In 1449 William Spencer, Roger Philpot, and William Thomas were licensed to grant to Bateman's chantry in Burrough Green 80½ a. and a liberty of fold in Brinkley.[47] In 1548 a messuage in Brinkley called *COKYNS*, late a possession of Bateman's chantry, was granted to Gilbert Claydon, who in 1553 was licensed to grant 124 a. in Brinkley to Thomas Humfrey.[48] The Brinkley land was apparently separated from the rest of the chantry estate; Humfrey still held it on his death in 1557. In the 1580s his son John sold Cokyns to Roger Gooddaye, but Gooddaye claimed to have been misled over the number of sheep for which there was liberty of fold, and when John Humfrey died in 1597 he was still said to hold Cokyns.[49] In 1620 his son, also John, and in 1658 John's daughters and their husbands were involved in disputes with the lord of the manor over the same question.[50] Cokyns is not recorded thereafter.

In the late 12th century Ralph de Tony gave 30 a. in Brinkley to Warden abbey (Beds.). In 1390 the

19 H. C. Maxwell-Lyte, *Honour of Dunster* (Som. Rec. Soc. xxxiii), p. xiv.
20 *Complete Peerage*, s.vv. Tony, Warwick; *Cal. Close*, 1402–5, 73–4; 1405–9, 185.
21 C.R.O., Q/RDz 6.
22 *Cal. Inq. p.m.* ii, p. 593.
23 *Complete Peerage*, ix. 24; *Cal. Inq. Misc.* v, p. 299.
24 *Liber de Bernewelle*, 257–8; *Cal. Inq. p.m.* i, p. 138; ii, p. 593.
25 *Cal. Inq. Misc.* v, p. 299.
26 C.P. 25(1)/30/93 no. 19.
27 *Cal. Pat.* 1429–36, 385.
28 C 1/15 no. 93.
29 C 142/56 no. 57.
30 Prob. 11/100 (P.C.C. 45 Montague, will of Thos. Stutville); C 2/Jas. I/H 2/48.
31 C 142/572 no. 29.
32 C 5/396/153; Gibbons, *Ely Episc. Rec.* 253.
33 C.P. 25(2)/814/1 Wm. & Mary Trin. no. 10; B.L. Add. MS. 9412, f. 242.
34 C.P. 25(2)/911/7 Anne East. no. 6; C.P. 25(2)/911/10 Anne Hil. no. 10; Cory, *Brinkley*, 25.
35 C.P. 25(2)/1104/26–7 Geo. II Trin. no. 8; C.P. 25(2)/1282/19 Geo. III Mich. no. 6.
36 *Camb. Chron.* 20 Aug. 1796, p. 3; B.L. Add. MS. 9412, f. 242; ex inf. Col. D. R. B. Kaye, Brinkley Hall.
37 C.R.O., Q/RDz 6.
38 Cory, *Brinkley*, 25; ex inf. Col. Kaye.
39 *Kelly's Dir. Cambs.* (1869 and later edns.).
40 Cory, *Brinkley*, 26.
41 Ex inf. Col. Kaye.
42 *Close R.* 1231–4, 569; *Cal. Inq. p.m.* i, p. 491.
43 C.P. 25(1)/285/23 no. 38; C.P. 25(1)/26/5 no. 32.
44 *Cal. Close*, 1349–54, 598.
45 C.P. 25(2)/93/861/39 Eliz. I Trin. no. 7.
46 C 142/617 no. 45; C.U.L., MS. Dd. 8. 31, f. 52; *Kelly's Dir. Cambs.* (1900).
47 *Cal. Pat.* 1446–52, 301.
48 *Cal. Pat.* 1548–9, 84; 1553, 273; C.P. 25(2)/55/400 no. 33.
49 C 142/111 no. 17; C.P. 25(2)/94/849 27–8 Eliz. I Mich. no. 1; C 2/Eliz. I/G. 9/56; C 142/254 no. 43.
50 C 2/Jas. I/H. 2/46; C 5/396/153.

abbot of Warden claimed that he had given in fee to William Bateman and Nicholas Westerdale all his lands in Brinkley and other parishes, and that they had given them to Robert Knatchbull and John Kent.[51]

A messuage and 15 a. in Brinkley which in 1384 had been acquired by Lewes priory was held in 1551 by the heirs of Sir Thomas Elyot as of the manors of Carlton and Willingham.[52] In the 1530s Gilbert Claydon held 4 a. of pasture in Brinkley of Markyate priory (Beds.) which had received them when one of the Stutville family became a nun there.[53]

William Farmer's charity at Fulbourn was founded in 1712 with money used to buy a house and 68 a. in Brinkley. In 1816 at inclosure the charity owned a house on the main street and was allotted 40 a. for its 59 a. in the open fields.[54]

At inclosure in 1816 St. Catharine's College, Cambridge, was allotted 25½ a. from the estate of the earl of Aylesford, in exchange for land in Burrough Green. The college sold 8 a. in 1847 and the remainder in 1881 to the trustees of the Six Mile Bottom estate.[55] In 1975 all the land in the north-west part of the parish, from Chalk Pit cross-roads to Six Mile Bottom, was part of that estate, belonging to Lady Delamere.[56]

ECONOMIC HISTORY. In 1086 the demesne land amounted to half of the 3 hides presumed to have been in Brinkley, and had 2 plough-teams and 2 *servi*. There was meadow for 1 plough-team and woodland for 12 pigs. The 12 *villani* and 2 bordars shared 6 teams, the total number of teams matching the land available. In 1066 three sokemen holding 4½ a. and a man of Earl Alfgar holding 2 a. did watch and ward.[57]

By 1521 wheat, oats, barley, peas, and vetches were grown in Brinkley.[58] In that year William Stutville, son of the lord, left his wife and son 200 sheep each, and in the early 17th century the lord of the manor had sheep-walk for 480 sheep.[59] The Stutvilles were involved in frequent disputes with the tenants of Cokyns and of a piece of waste called Sprotts Hill, whose flock they succeeded in limiting to 180. They also claimed that although their tenants had a customary right to pasture cattle on Sprotts Hill any sheep were there by special permission.[60] In the late 18th century the manor had sheep-walk for 600 sheep.[61]

In the earlier 17th century land in Brinkley was divided between infields and outfields, and in 1816 the fields towards the north-west end of the parish were known as the outfields. Nearer to the village were Bramble, Mill, Kimmings, Stubble, and Little Low fields. In the south-east part of the parish lay pasture called the Lammas ground and the Shrub, and in the north-west tip was the heathland.[62] The inclosure award of 1816 dealt with *c.* 1,000 a. of open-field and common land and 372 a. of old inclosures. There were 19 allottees, but almost half the land in the parish, 718½ a., went to William Frost, lord of the manor. The rector received *c.* 235 a. for tithe and glebe, John Frost *c.* 53 a., and the Fulbourn charity *c.* 40 a. No other allotment was over 15 a.[63] During the 19th century the chief crops were wheat, beans, barley, and oats.[64] By 1905 *c.* 995 a. were devoted to arable, 168 a. to grass, and 50 a. to woodland.[65] After inclosure Lower, Chalk Pit, and Hill farms were all formed from William Frost's allotment. New farm was formed from the glebe, and in 1975 was called Glebe farm.[66]

John Frost, who in the early 19th century farmed over 100 a. in Brinkley, was a maltster.[67] There was a smith in the village in 1709, and two in the late 19th century.[68] From the mid 18th century the Hart family ran a bell-foundry in Brinkley, and in the mid 19th they became agricultural engineers. The firm closed in the 1950s on the death of the last member of the family. The workshops which stood near Charity Farm were demolished to make way for new houses.[69] There was a shop in Brinkley from the late 18th century, and throughout the 19th century the village served as a shopping centre for its neighbours. In the 1930s the Commercial Stores contained several departments,[70] but by 1975 it was a small village shop.

A windmill was recorded in Brinkley in 1600[71] and a corn windmill was offered for sale in 1815.[72] In the late 19th and early 20th centuries the mill stood north-west of the village by the Six Mile Bottom road. It seems probable that an earlier mill stood on the other side of the road, in what was called Mill field. The mill had been demolished by 1975.[73]

In 1253 William de Mohun and his heirs were granted a weekly market on Wednesdays at Brinkley and a fair there for three days at Michaelmas. No later record of the fair has been found. In 1261 the market day was changed to Tuesday.[74] A road in Burrough Green in the 17th century was called Brinkley market way. The market had ceased by 1807, but an old inhabitant then remembered the tradition of a weekly market, and that a market-cross had been standing in his childhood.[75]

[51] *Cal. Pat.* 1494–1509, 616; *Cal. Close*, 1389–92, 157.
[52] *Cal. Inq. Misc.* iv, p. 278; *Cal. Pat.* 1550–3, 42.
[53] S.C. 6/Hen. VIII/8 rot. 9; E 321/34/42.
[54] C.R.O., P 75/25/48–62; ibid. Q/RDz 6; ibid. R 60/24/2/9.
[55] C.R.O., Q/RDz 6; ex inf. Dr. S.C. Aston, Bursar, St. Cath.'s Coll.
[56] Ex inf. Messrs. Robinson and Hall, land agents.
[57] *V.C.H. Cambs.* i. 398, 405.
[58] B.L. Add. MS. 5861, p. 146.
[59] Ibid.; C 2/Jas. I/H 2/48.
[60] C 2/Eliz./G 9/56; C2/Jas. I/H 2/46.
[61] *Camb. Chron.* 2 Aug. 1796.
[62] C.U.L., E.D.R., H 1/1, terrier 1638; C.R.O., Q/RDz 6; B.L. Maps 1640 (34); *Studies of Field Systems*, ed. Baker and Butlin, 301.
[63] C.R.O., Q/RDz 6.
[64] *Kelly's Dir. Cambs.* (1869).
[65] Cambs. Agric. Returns, 1905.
[66] B.L. Maps 1640 (34).
[67] *Camb. Chron.* 25 Mar. 1809; 9 Feb. 1816; 5 July 1816; C.R.O., L 70/37.
[68] C.R.O., R 50/25/9; O.S. Map 1/2,500, Cambs. XLIX. 13 (1903 edn.).
[69] *Gardner's Dir. Cambs.* (1851); *Kelly's Dir. Cambs.* (1847 and later edns.); ex inf. Mr. R. C. Lambeth and Mr. R. H. Cory.
[70] *Town and Country Life*, xi (1), 15 Mar. 1932.
[71] Prob. 11/100 (P.C.C. 45 Montague, will of Thos. Stutville).
[72] *Camb. Chron.* 14 July 1815.
[73] O.S. Map 1/2,500, Cambs. XLIX. 9 (1886, 1903).
[74] *Cal. Pat.* 1247–58, 262; *Cal. Chart. R.* 1257–1300, 37.
[75] C.R.O., P 17/3/3; B.L. Add. MS. 9412, f. 248.

LOCAL GOVERNMENT. In 1543 Sir Edward North, lord of the honor of Kirtling, held a court leet and view of frankpledge in Brinkley.[76] By the early 17th century the Stutvilles received the profits of the court. Court minutes survive for 1673–80 and 1728. The court seems to have been held annually at those times.[77]

In the 18th century Brinkley showed opposition to direct highway rates, and continued to use indictments and conditional fines.[78] In 1776 £38 was spent on the poor. By 1803 expenditure had risen steeply to £152 but that was still the second lowest figure in the hundred. It continued to rise, reaching £360 in 1817, and later fell to £191 in 1834, being consistently the second or third lowest in the hundred. In 1803 19 adults and 7 children received regular relief, and 5*s.* was spent on materials for them to work on. By 1813 72 were being permanently relieved, but the figure fell to 57 and then 50 in the succeeding years.[79] From 1835 Brinkley was in the Newmarket poor-law union, and remained part of the Newmarket Rural District,[80] being included in 1974 in East Cambridgeshire.

CHURCH. A church was recorded at Brinkley in the late 12th century when it was among those granted by William de Mohun to the canons of Bruton (Som.).[81] In 1260, however, Roger de Tony was the patron, and although in 1305 the advowson was assigned as dower to Isabel wife of Hugh Bardolf[82] in 1315 it was held, along with the barony of Kirtling, by the earl of Warwick. It descended with Kirtling, and remained with the lords North until 1625.[83] The advowson was exercised during forfeitures and minorities by Sir John Bushy in 1399 and by the Crown in 1397, 1401, 1447, 1494, and 1505.[84] In 1626 Dudley North, Lord North, sold the advowson to Robert Sendall, the rector, and in 1672 Sendall's grandson, also Robert, sold it to Thomas Watson. In 1691 Watson, then bishop of St. David's, granted it to St. John's College, Cambridge, which still held it in 1975.[85]

The rectory was valued at 15 marks *c.* 1217, at 10 marks in 1254, and at 18 marks in 1291. In 1534 it was valued at £13 6*s.* 8*d.*[86] In 1638 the rector had a house, *c.* 12 a. of inclosed pasture, 20 a. of arable, and the great and small tithes of Brinkley, besides tithe corn from land in Carlton cum Willingham and Weston Colville that was held of Brinkley manor.[87] In 1783 the living was worth £120.[88] At inclosure in 1816 the rector was allotted 13½ a. for glebe and 201½ a. for tithe.[89] In the following year the gross income was £260, rising to £450 in 1858.[90] After the First World War Glebe or New farm was sold to a Mr. Sharpe.[91]

The parsonage house in 1783, consisting of an older part and a newer part built *c.* 1740, was too large and dilapidated to maintain, and it was recommended that at least part be pulled down.[92] The rectory was rebuilt *c.* 1825 on the site in Hall Lane where it had been in 1638.[93] In 1802 the glebe farm buildings, then near the rectory, were burned down, and later rebuilt in Common Road as New Farm. In 1937 the rectory was used as a boarding house. A new rectory house was built in High Street in 1957.[94]

A vicarage had been established by 1351 when the bishop granted it *in commendam* to the rector of Brinkley, and later record of it has not been found.[95] The parish often had non-resident rectors. In the mid 14th century William Cotesbrook was repeatedly licensed to be absent, as was Thomas Morton who in the early 15th century was also dispensed to hold two benefices.[96] In 1536 John Boner, the last prior of Anglesey, was presented to the living.[97] He employed curates in Brinkley, one of whom, Thomas Hupsely, was slow to abandon the old rites and in 1549 was ordered to minister reverently, not showing the bread to the people.[98] He was also to stop the parishioners' use of beads, and take down images. In 1552 a parishioner refused to give up a silver pyx.[99] The rector in 1561 was a royal chaplain and thus non-resident, but kept a curate.[1] In 1591 the curate was presented for serving two cures and preaching without a licence.[2] In 1650 Robert Sendall, rector since 1625, was called a good preaching minister.[3] Heigham Perne was rector for 50 years from *c.* 1663.[4] His successor, Christopher Anstey, was resident in 1728, but in 1756 also held a living in Hertfordshire and had been deaf for many years.[5] In the early 18th century Brinkley had two Sunday services and quarterly sacraments with *c.* 26 communicants.[6] In 1770 the rector held another living in Bedfordshire, and in 1775 lived in Lancashire but kept a curate at Brinkley who provided one Sunday service and three communions a year.[7] In 1807 there was again a curate and the rector lived at St. John's College, Cambridge.[8] The rector in 1817 held another living in Nottinghamshire, and by 1836 was also chaplain to Lord Scarsdale; he was non-resident in 1857.[9] In 1836

76 *L. & P. Hen. VIII*, xviii (1), p. 132.
77 Prob. 11/100 (P.C.C. 45 Montague, will of Thos. Stutville); C 5/396/153; C.R.O., R 51/25/1; R 50/17/30.
78 *V.C.H. Cambs.* ii. 84.
79 *Poor Law Abstract, 1804*, 38–9; *1818*, 30–1; *Poor Rate Returns, 1816–21*, 11; *1822–4*, 38; *1825–9*, 16; *1830–4*, 16.
80 *Poor Law Com. 2nd Rep.* 513; *Census*, 1931 (pt. ii).
81 *Cal. Doc. France*, ed. Round, p. 178.
82 C.P. 25(1)/25/30 no. 29; *Cal. Close*, 1302–7, 329.
83 *Cal. Inq. p.m.* v, p. 615; P.R.O. Inst. Bks. ser. A, iii, p. 33.
84 *E.D.R.* (1898), 72; (1902), 200; (1909), 46; *Cal. Pat.* 1396–9, 253, 579; 1399–1401, 474; 1494–1509, 429.
85 St. John's Coll. Mun. 67/61–3.
86 *Val. of Norwich*, ed. Lunt, 215, 535; *Valor Eccl.* (Rec. Com.), iii. 504.
87 C.U.L., E.D.R., H 1/1, terrier 1638.
88 Ibid. B 7/1, p. 6.
89 C.R.O., Q/RDz 6.
90 *Rep. Com. Eccl. Revenues*, pp. 344–5; *Kelly's Dir. Cambs.* (1858); *Glebe Returns*, H.C. 307, p. 36 (1887), lxiv.
91 Cory, *Brinkley*, 40.
92 C.U.L., E.D.R., C 1/1, 4, 6.
93 Ibid. H 1/1, terrier 1638; B 7/1, p. 6.
94 Cory, *Brinkley*, 5, 10; *Kelly's Dir. Cambs.* (1937).
95 C.U.L., E.D.R., G 1/1, f. 41v.
96 *E.D.R.* (1889), 357; (1890), 369, 379, 428; (1900), 178 (1901), 20; *Cal. Papal Reg.* vi. 443.
97 *V.C.H. Cambs.* ii. 234.
98 *E.D.R.* (1912), 184; B.L. Add. MS. 5861, p. 14; C.U.L., E.D.R., B 2/3, p. 47.
99 *V.C.H. Cambs.* ii. 170–1, 173.
1 B.L. Add. MS. 5813, f. 65; C.U.L., E.D.R., B 2/3, p. 101; B 2/6.
2 C.U.L., E.D.R., B 2/11.
3 Lamb. Pal. MS. 904, f. 266; cf. *Alum. Cantab. to 1751*, iv. 43.
4 Cory, *Brinkley*, 7.
5 B.L. Add. MS. 5828, f. 84; 5820, f. 92.
6 C.U.L., E.D.R., B 8/1.
7 B.L. Add. MS. 5820, f. 91v.; C.U.L., E.D.R., C 1/1.
8 C.U.L., E.D.R., C 1/4.
9 *Rep. Com. Eccl. Revenues*, pp. 344–5; C.U.L., E.D.R., C 3/21; B 1/16.

R. W. King of Brinkley Hall had complained that as there was still only one Sunday service his servants could not attend church. By 1851 there were two services: 65 people attended in the morning and 121 in the afternoon.[10] By 1897 a Bible class had been started and weekly communions introduced for *c.* 34 communicants. There had been a Sunday school from 1836.[11] By 1922 Brinkley was held with Burrough Green, and since the 1950s the rector has also held Carlton. In 1975 he lived at Brinkley.[12]

The district church of St. George at Six Mile Bottom, built in 1933 just within Brinkley parish, is annexed to the parish of Little Wilbraham whose rector serves it.[13]

The church of *ST. MARY*, so called by the 18th century,[14] is built mostly of field stones and clunch rubble with stone dressings, and has a chancel, aisled and clerestoried nave, west tower, and south porch. The much rebuilt chancel dates from the 13th century; the four-bay nave was rebuilt in the early 14th century, and the two-stage tower and the brick south porch were added in the 15th century. The pulpit and some pews survive from the 17th century; other pews are 18th-century. In 1644 William Dowsing removed two brass inscriptions and broke ten superstitious pictures.[15] In 1874–5 the church was extensively restored under the direction of Frederick Thomson. The chancel was largely rebuilt and the chancel arch enlarged; the clerestory was added to the nave, the roof renewed, the walls refaced outside and plastered inside, and the floor repaired. Green glass was put into most of the windows, but a little 14th-century stained glass survives in the chancel.[16] A chancel screen survived *c.* 1910 but has since disappeared.[17] There are 16th- and 17th-century monuments to members of the Stutville family.[18]

In the late 14th century the church had three silver chalices.[19] By the mid 16th century there were one silver chalice and paten, a copper and gilt cross, and a silver pyx.[20] The plate includes a cup and cover paten given in 1570, and a paten dated 1669 given in 1677.[21] In 1779 a faceless clock was put into the church tower. It survived in 1975 when it stood at the base of the tower.[22] There were six bells in 1975: (i) 1820, Dobson of Downham (Norf.); (ii) and (iii) 1609, John Draper; (iv) 1723, Thomas Newman; (v) 1671×1687, William Hull; (vi) 1727, Thomas Gardiner of Sudbury (Suff.).[23] The parish registers begin in 1685, but transcripts survive from 1599.[24]

NONCONFORMITY. In the 18th century the Baptist minister and hymn-writer Robert Robinson spent some time in the parish[25] but apparently exercised no influence there. In 1893 three Brinkley families regularly attended the Salvation Army meetings at Carlton.[26]

EDUCATION. In 1722 Elizabeth March of Fulbourn left land for the teaching of poor children in Brinkley and four other parishes. A year later all five had established schools.[27] In 1728 Brinkley's share of the endowment was paid to the schoolmaster of Burrough Green who taught the older children, while a mistress taught the younger ones at Brinkley. By 1775 all the teaching appears to have been done in Brinkley.[28] In 1818 the master received £22 a year besides fees from the wealthier parents.[29] In 1833 the school was attended by 11 boys and 23 girls.[30]

In 1845 a schoolroom and teacher's house were built on a site in Stubble field, at the east end of the village, given by R. W. King. It was used by the day- and Sunday schools, which by 1846 were united to the National Society.[31] The annual income of £121 in 1871 consisted of £34 from the endowment, £6 from school pence, and the remainder from contributions; any deficit was supplied by a voluntary rate. There were 41 pupils.[32] Average attendance fell to 25 in 1881, rose to 52 in 1889, and dropped to 25 again in 1919.[33] In the 1930s the school was attended by seniors from Carlton and Westley, but in 1947 all the older children were transferred to Bottisham village college. In 1959, when there were only 18 pupils, the school was closed and the children were transferred to Burrough Green. The school building was demolished in 1963 to make way for new houses in Old School Lane.[34]

Brinkley's share of the March charity was from 1914 devoted to prizes, equipment, exhibitions, and apprenticeships.[35]

CHARITIES FOR THE POOR. In 1837 the parish clerk of Brinkley held ¼ a. in Carlton for the poor of Brinkley, worth 5*s.* a year, which ceased to be recorded after 1864.[36]

In 1728 there was a stock of £40 for the benefit of the poor, and in 1775 there was also a legacy of £50, the interest to be distributed to the poor.[37] Dividends from both sums were distributed at Christmas, but by 1806 had not been claimed for some years. In 1806 the principal and dividends, totalling £61, were reinvested; the dividends were allowed to accumulate for 6 years, and then distributed, with preference given to large families. In

[10] C.U.L., E.D.R., C 3/21; H.O. 129/188/1/1/1.
[11] C.U.L., E.D.R., C 3/21; C 3/36.
[12] *Kelly's Dir. Cambs.* (1922); *Crockford* (1955 and later edns.).
[13] *Kelly's Dir. Cambs.* (1933); *Crockford* (1934 and later edns.).
[14] B.L. Add. MS. 5820, f. 92.
[15] *Trans. C.H.A.S.* iii. 84.
[16] Pevsner, *Cambs.* 308–9; Cory, *Brinkley*, 13–14; ex inf. R.C.H.M., Cambs.
[17] Camb. City Libr., Cambs. Colln. photograph index.
[18] *Mon. Inscr. Cambs.* 14–16.
[19] *Vetus Liber Arch. Elien.* (C.A.S. 8vo ser. xlviii), 53.
[20] *Cambs. Ch. Goods, temp. Edw. VI*, 70.
[21] List of ch. plate *penes V.C.H.*
[22] Cory, *Brinkley*, 9.
[23] *Cambs. Bells* (C.A.S. 8vo ser. xviii), 123.
[24] Gibbons, *Ely Episc. Rec.* 227.
[25] *D.N.B.*
[26] C.U.L., E.D.R., C 3/36.
[27] *V.C.H. Cambs.* ii. 334.
[28] C.U.L., E.D.R., B 8/1; C 1/1.
[29] *Educ. of Poor Digest*, 56.
[30] *Educ. Enquiry Abstract*, 51.
[31] Cory, *Brinkley*, 31; Ed. 7/5; *Church School Inquiry, 1846–7*, 2–3.
[32] Ed. 7/5.
[33] *Rep. of Educ. Cttee. of Council, 1880–1* [C. 2948-I], p. 542, H.C. (1881), xxxii; *1888–9* [C. 5804-I], p. 530, H.C. (1889), xxix; *Bd. of Educ., List 21, 1919* (H.M.S.O.), p. 15.
[34] Cory, *Brinkley*, 31–3.
[35] Char. Com. files; C.R.O., P 16/12.
[36] *31st Rep. Com. Char.* 133; *Char. Digest Cambs. 1863–4*, 5.
[37] C.U.L., E.D.R., B 8/1; C 1/1.

1837 the charities, called the Town Money, had a capital of £53. In 1975 the annual income was less than £2,[38] distributed amongst 3 or 4 old inhabitants.

By wills proved 1904 and 1924 Miss L. E. Maulkin and Miss M. E. Maulkin each left £50, the income to be given to the aged poor of Brinkley. In the 1960s the income thus distributed was *c.* £5 a year.[39]

BURROUGH GREEN

THE PARISH of Burrough Green, which covers 2,272 a., lies 5½ miles south of Newmarket.[1] It stretches 6 miles from north-west of the main London–Newmarket road to the Suffolk border in the south-east. There it is over 1 mile wide, but narrows to less than ½ mile in the north-west where Westley Waterless has been cut out of it. From Sipsey Bridge eastward to Plunder wood the south-east boundary follows that of the county. Parts of the north-east and south-west boundaries follow watercourses near the south-east end of the parish, and the boundary with Westley follows the road from Westley village to the main road, but elsewhere the boundaries are far less regular, sometimes not even coinciding with field boundaries, and some lands were traditionally 'interbait' with Westley. About 50 a. near Underwood Hall, in the north-western half of the parish, became part of Burrough Green under the Dullingham inclosure award in 1810.[2] The village lies in the south-eastern half of the parish along the road from Great Bradley to Dullingham and Newmarket, and roads from Brinkley and Carlton Grange cross the parish north-west of the village. The Cambridge–Newmarket railway crosses the north-western end of the parish; the nearest stations are at Six Mile Bottom and Dullingham.

The parish is well wooded, especially in the south-east; Park wood and Out wood are recorded from the early 15th century,[3] and Out wood was scheduled as of special scientific interest in 1951.[4] The land rises from 150 ft. on the north-west to 300 ft. on Cambridge Hill, and then falls a little before rising again to a plateau at 375 ft. on which the village stands. It falls again to 270 ft. in the south-east. The parish lies on the chalk, covered on the higher ground by boulder clay. The chalkpit near Underwood Hall, designated as of scientific interest, provides a section through the chalk rich in fossils.[5] The soil on the chalk is a brown or red loamy sand, and from it Redfield or Radfield in Burrough Green took the name which it gave to the hundred.[6]

There are two moated sites, one of which may be of Saxon origin, and from which Burgh, as it was originally called, took its name.[7] The name Burrough Green first occurs in the 16th century.[8] The village is grouped around a triangular green of *c.* 5 a., with the manor-house, church, and rectory on the western side, and the early-18th-century school at the northern corner. Along the north-eastern side runs the main street, with most of the older houses looking across it to the green. A number of thatched and plastered cottages survived in 1975, by when small groups of new houses and an old peoples' unit had been built on the south-western edge of the green, near the church. There was also some new building at the south-western end of the main street. In 1887 a reading room, still standing in 1975, was built next to the school by Mrs. Porcher as a memorial to her husband Charles.[9] North-west of the village lies Burrough End which, although just within Burrough parish, forms a continuation of the main street of Westley Waterless. At one time there was a hamlet at Padloe or Paddle Hole End, which lay on the track to Bushey Grove, east-south-east of the village. Only one cottage remained in 1801, and it disappeared in the course of the century.[10]

Nineteen people were enumerated in Burrough Green in 1086.[11] In 1327 there were 29 taxpayers in Burrough and Westley, and in 1377 there were 141 adults in the two parishes.[12] By the mid 16th century there were 34 households in Burrough,[13] and 54 houses a century later.[14] In 1728 there were *c.* 200 inhabitants.[15] By 1801 the number had risen to 276, though there were only *c.* 30 houses. The population rose steadily, to 529 in 1851, but then fell to 423 in 1901 and 268 in 1971.[16]

There were two inns in 1779, the White Hart and the Black Bull, which stood at each end of the north-eastern side of the green in 1837. The White Hart had a small farm attached to it,[17] and had ceased to be an inn by 1889. The timber-framed and plastered 17th-century house still stood at the eastern corner of the green in 1975,[18] when the Bull was the only inn in the parish.

MANORS AND OTHER ESTATES. In the will of Lustwine, made between 1017 and 1049, Burrough Green was left to Ely abbey, but in his son

[38] *31st Rep. Com. Char.* 133; Char. Com. files; ex inf. the rector, the Revd. R. Crowther.
[39] Char. Com. files.
[1] This account was written in 1975. The following paragraphs are based on O.S. Maps 1/25,000, TL 55 and TL 65 (1956 edn.); C.U.L., Burrough Green tithe map.
[2] C.R.O., Q/RDz 6, p. 310.
[3] C 139/8 no. 90.
[4] *Nature Reserves and Sites of Special Scientific Interest* (Cambs. and Isle of Ely Planning Dept. 1965), p. 32.
[5] Ibid. p. 92.
[6] *V.C.H. Cambs.* ii. 75; *P.N. Cambs.* (E.P.N.S.), 114.
[7] *V.C.H. Cambs.* ii. 4, 19: the earthwork north-west of the church there described as a moat is part of the 17th-century Hall garden.
[8] *P.N. Cambs.* (E.P.N.S.), 115.
[9] *Kelly's Dir. Cambs.* (1904).
[10] Lysons, *Cambs.* 95.
[11] *V.C.H. Cambs.* i. 379.
[12] *Cambs. Lay Subsidy, 1327*, 17–18; *East Anglian*, N.S. xii. 239.
[13] B.L. Harl. MS. 594, f. 199v.
[14] See p. 281.
[15] C.U.L., E.D.R., B 8/1.
[16] Ibid. C 1/4; *Census*, 1801–1971.
[17] W. M. Palmer, *Hist. of Burrough Green, Cambs.* (C.A.S. 8vo ser. liv), 135; C.U.L., E.D.R., Burrough Green tithe award.
[18] M.H.L.G. List.

Thurstan's will (1043 × 1045) it was left to Ulfketel.[19] In 1066 it belonged to Eddeva and in 1086 was held by Count Alan.[20] The manor of *BURGH* or *BURROUGH* with most of Count Alan's lands descended with the honor of Richmond, and *c.* 1166 Thomas de Burgh (d. 1199) held 4 fees of that honor.[21] In the early 13th century one of the fees was identified as Burrough. It descended in the de Burgh family for 200 years.[22] Thomas was succeeded by his sons Thomas (d. 1234) and Philip (d. 1235).[23] In 1260 Burrough was held by Philip's son Sir Thomas de Burgh, who died in 1284. His son Philip died a year later, the manor passing to Philip's son Thomas, then aged 7. Thomas was knight of the shire for Cambridgeshire in 1311, and was succeeded in 1322 by his son John.[24] Shortly before his death in 1329 John entered a religious house, and made the manor over to his brother Thomas.[25] Thomas died in 1334 leaving a son John, aged 4, and the Crown granted the custody of the manor to John de Verdon.[26] John de Burgh died in 1393 and was succeeded by his son Thomas. On Thomas's death in 1411 his estates were divided between his three half-sisters, the Cambridgeshire lands going to Elizabeth, wife of Sir John Ingoldisthorpe, who held Burrough in 1412.[27]

In 1420 Sir John was succeeded by his son Thomas Ingoldisthorpe who was still a minor when he died in 1422 leaving a son Edmund, aged one.[28] The wardship of Edmund was granted to John, Lord Tiptoft, who married Edmund to his daughter Joan.[29] Edmund died in 1456 leaving a daughter Isabel (d. 1476), who married John Neville, marquess of Montagu. On Joan's death in 1494 the Ingoldisthorpe lands were divided between Isabel's five daughters. Burrough Green went to Elizabeth, wife of Thomas, Lord Scrope of Masham, and after her death to Lucy Brown, her niece.[30] Lucy married Sir John Cutt of Childerley, who held Burrough at his death in 1521. Their son, also John, died in 1528, and his son, a third John, sold Burrough Green to Sir Anthony Cage in 1574.[31]

Cage was succeeded in 1583 by his son Anthony (d. 1603) whose son John was knighted and served as sheriff of Cambridgeshire in 1609. Sir John died in 1628. His son Sir Anthony[32] fell into great debt during the Civil Wars, and at his death in 1667 his estates were heavily mortgaged. He devised Burrough Green manor not to his sons John and William but to his daughter Anne and her husband Henry Slingsby,[33] and in 1670 Burrough Green was the Slingsbys' seat.[34] Slingsby later came under suspicion for his conduct as Master of the Mint and at his death in 1690 was much in debt. He left Burrough Green to his wife for her life with reversion to his younger son Anthony.[35] In 1696 Anthony Slingsby mortgaged the estate to Edward Russell, later earl of Orford, who eventually bought the manor, dying without issue in 1727. Burrough Green was bought by Charles Seymour, duke of Somerset, and passed to Heneage Finch, earl of Aylesford (d. 1777), through his marriage with the duke's daughter Charlotte.[36] It passed to the Finches' son Heneage, earl of Aylesford, who before he died in 1812 had begun the sale of Burrough Green to Thomas and Henry Redhead, and Henry was lord of the manor in 1815.[37] In 1837 Thomas Redhead held *c.* 800 a. in Burrough Green.[38] He died in 1839 and the manor passed to Charles Porcher of Cliffe (Dors.), who had married Thomas's daughter Elinor in 1828.[39] In 1864 she was lady of the manor, which by 1869 had passed to E. L. Kindersley, also of Cliffe. Kindersley assumed the additional name of Porcher in 1901, and died in 1907, to be followed by his son Capt. C. P. W. Kindersley (later Kindersley-Porcher),[40] who *c.* 1909 sold Burrough Green to S. A. Taylor of Newmarket. The estate was then split up, the manorial rights passing to Mrs. Gertrude Taylor, who held them in 1920 and 1939.[41] In 1913 the Hall was advertised for sale by R. J. Lacey, whose father had leased it for many years previously.[42] By 1925 it belonged to G. R. C. Foster (d. 1936) and in 1938 was bought by R. S. Way.[43] In 1958 it was sold to Sir Alan Noble, M.P., with a 37-acre stud farm, and in 1975 was owned by Miss P. K. Wolf.[44]

The earliest manor-house probably stood on the Saxon moated site in Park wood; there was a deer park in the parish in 1086. In 1330 Thomas de Burgh was licensed to impark land there.[45] Burrough Green Hall, built *c.* 1575, but possibly incorporating part of an earlier timber-framed house, stands west of the green, next to the church. It was originally much larger, having 26 hearths in 1665, and probably extended across the full width of the surviving walled forecourt.[46] The main front of brick with pedimented and pilastered surrounds to the windows has a central porch and doorway which is

[19] *Liber Elien.* (Camd. 3rd ser. xcii), p. 158; Dorothy Whitelock, *A.-S. Wills*, 81–3.
[20] *V.C.H. Cambs.* i. 379.
[21] Farrer, *Feud. Cambs.* 111.
[22] *Red Bk. Exch.* (Rolls Ser.), ii. 528; Palmer, *Burrough Green*, 4–16; for an account of the de Burgh family see *Yorks. Arch. Jnl.* xxx. 311–48.
[23] *Liber de Bernewelle*, 258.
[24] *Cat. Anct. D.* iii, D 187; *Cal. Close*, 1318–23, 236.
[25] C.P. 25(1)/27/66 no. 2.
[26] *Cal. Inq. p.m.* vii, p. 604; *Cal. Fine R.* 1327–37, 406; 1347–56, 54; *Feud. Aids*, i. 158.
[27] *Feud. Aids*, vi. 406.
[28] C 139/6 no. 46; *Cal. Close*, 1419–22, 86.
[29] *Cal. Fine R.* 1422–30, 73; *Visit. Cambs.* (Harl. Soc. xli), 124.
[30] Palmer, *Burrough Green*, 16; *Cal. Close*, 1468–76, 329; *Cal. Inq. p.m. Hen. VII*, i, p. 463; *Complete Peerage*, iv. 92–3.
[31] C 142/36 no. 17; C 142/47 no. 10; C.P. 25(2)/93/839/16 Eliz. I Hil. no. 12.
[32] Palmer, *Burrough Green*, 17–19.
[33] Prob. 11/326 (P.C.C. 44 Hare).
[34] John Evelyn, *Diary*, ed. E. S. de Beer, iii. 552–3.
[35] Palmer, *Burrough Green*, 30–3; Prob. 11/399 (P.C.C. 62 Dyke).
[36] Palmer, *Burrough Green*, 34; Lysons, *Cambs.* 96; *Complete Peerage*, s.v. Aylesford.
[37] *Camb. Chron.* 2 Aug. 1811; H.L.R.O. Private Bill, May 1815; C.R.O., R 54/10/3, f. 14v.; R 54/10/4.
[38] C.U.L., E.D.R., tithe award.
[39] C.R.O., 515/SP 444; Burke, *Land. Gent.* (1855), 964.
[40] *Kelly's Dir. Cambs.* (1864 and later edns.); C.R.O., R 59/29/2/2/4; *Kelly's Handbook to Titled Classes* (1924), 892.
[41] Palmer, *Burrough Green*, 34; C.R.O., 515/SP 444; R 54/10/3, f. 79.
[42] *Kelly's Dir. Cambs.* (1858 and later edns.); C.U.L. Maps bb. 53(1)/91/22.
[43] C.U.L. Maps 53(1)/93/85; C.R.O., 296/SP 1214; Palmer, *Burrough Green*, 35.
[44] *Camb. Evening News*, 16 Aug. 1972; Palmer, *Burrough Green*, 35.
[45] *V.C.H. Cambs.* i. 379; ii. 4, 19; *Cal. Pat.* 1327–30, 553.
[46] E 179/84/437 rot. 73; see above, plate facing p. 81.

axial to the main gateway into the forecourt and to a garden layout now largely destroyed which included a large moated enclosure some distance north-west of the house. By 1670 the house was said to be large but ruinous and in an inconvenient position.[47] It was subsequently reduced in size and in the 19th century it was remodelled as a farmhouse.

In the early 13th century Philip of Barnwell gave to Warden abbey (Beds.) land in Burrough held of Nichole and Robert de Sahoun and Hugh of Croydon.[48] In 1291 the abbey held *RAVENSHOLT* and other lands there later known as *BURGHDEN GRANGE*. There was a grange attached to each estate. About 1368 the abbey's tithe-free land in Burrough comprised 60 a. attached to Burghden Grange, 100 a. attached to Ravensholt, and woodland belonging to both.[49] In 1387 both estates were given in exchange for land in Bedfordshire to William Bateman and Nicholas Westerdale, who transferred Ravensholt to John Atwood and Burghden to Robert Knatchbull and John Kent.[50]

In 1392, however, Barnwell priory was licensed to acquire 240 a. in Burrough called Ravensholt from Bateman and Westerdale.[51] By 1534 the priory held pasture called Ravensholt which in 1541 was granted to Edward North, later Lord North.[52] Sir George Downing (d. 1684) bought from Sir Dudley North 132 a. called Ravensholt, which descended in the Downing family and formed part of the original endowment of Downing College. In the 19th century Ravensholt covered *c.* 173 a. Also known as Piper's farm, it was sold by the college in 1922 to a Mr. Vye,[53] and by 1942 formed part of the Great Thurlow Hall estate of C. F. Ryder, which was then sold to Mr. R. A. Vestey.[54]

Burghden Grange seems to have remained in lay hands after 1387. About 1501 William and Elizabeth Taylard sold it to Nicholas Hughson and others.[55] In 1567 it was held by Dorothy and Thomasin Rudston, and in the early 17th century by Sir John Cage, lord of the manor.[56] The name does not occur thereafter; the land presumably descended with the manor. The site of the grange has not been traced.

In 1231 William le Breton, a judge, was granted *c.* 8 a. in Burrough by Alice de Burgh. At his death in 1261 he held 120 a. there of the manor and 20 a. of Randal de Burgh.[57] William was succeeded by his son John who acquired further lands in the parish and in 1307 granted them to Edmund le Breton.[58] In 1353 Thomas le Breton held the land in Burrough.[59] In 1389 a tenement in Burrough called *BRETTONS* was held by Robert, a clerk, and in 1392 was granted to William Bateman to be held for rent and suit of court to the honor of Richmond.[60] In 1445 John Bateman, rector of Burrough, was licensed to found a chantry there, which Sir John Scalers and others thereupon endowed with land.[61] In the later 16th century the chantry land was known as Brettons manor or *BATEMANS CHANTRY*. In 1548 it was granted to Gilbert Claydon of Brinkley and Robert Bank, an Ipswich merchant, and in 1557 Claydon was licensed to sell it to Leonard Barrett.[62] Barrett sold the estate in 1562 to Thomas Holmes who in 1582 sold it to Anthony Cage.[63] It then descended with the manor which in the 17th century was known as Burrough cum Brettons.

The capital messuage of Brettons stood on the moated site known as the Chantry, close to the Brinkley boundary. The earthwork probably dates from the 14th century, but the house within seems to have been rebuilt in the 15th or 16th century.[64] There was apparently a chapel in the house, which was occupied by the chantry priest, and it had a bell to summon to mass.[65] It was presumably the mansion house of Leonard Barrett mentioned in 1557. The building seems to have disappeared by the early 17th century.[66]

In 1280 the prior of the Hospital of St. John of Jerusalem held 1 hide in Burrough of the honor of Richmond.[67] In 1540 Sir Richard Long was granted the reversion of land of the Hospitallers' preceptory of Shingay, including that in Burrough.[68] Later record of the land has not been found.

In the mid 15th century God's House in Cambridge acquired *GOD'S HOUSE CLOSE* in Burrough Green. In 1546 its successor Christ's College held a messuage there with 5½ a. of pasture and arable, which appears to have been sold for £28 in 1560.[69]

St. Catharine's Hall, Cambridge, held land in Burrough Green in 1586.[70] In 1816 St. Catharine's College exchanged land in the parish with the earl of Aylesford for 25 a. in Brinkley.[71]

In 1505 William Atkinson, fellow of Pembroke Hall, Cambridge, gave to the college land in Burrough Green which in 1563 amounted to *c.* 25 a. From 1741 to 1827 it was leased to the trustees of Burrough Green school.[72] In 1793 the college agreed to an exchange of land with the earl of Aylesford, and in 1925 sold *c.* 30 a. of land and a house.[73]

In 1515 James Clerk, rector of Burrough Green, gave a pightle and croft to Peterhouse, and in 1521 the college bought further land there.[74] In 1793 it

[47] Evelyn, *Diary*, iii. 552–3.
[48] *Cart. Old Wardon* (Beds. Hist. Rec. Soc. xiii), pp. 137–9.
[49] Dugdale, *Mon.* v. 370; B.L. Harl. MS. 4765, ff. 1–4.
[50] *Cal. Pat.* 1385–9, 220; *Cal. Close*, 1389–92, 157.
[51] *Cal. Pat.* 1391–6, 163; B.L. Add. MS. 5838, f. 10.
[52] *Valor Eccl.* (Rec. Com.), vi. 89; *L. & P. Hen. VIII*, xvi, p. 245.
[53] Ex inf. Dr. S. G. Fleet, Bursar, and Mr. S. French, Archivist, Downing Coll.
[54] B.L. Maps, 135. a. 64; see below, p. 151.
[55] C.P. 25(1)/30/101 no. 29; C.P. 40/958 rot. 21d.
[56] E 178/3621; B.L. Add. MS. 5838, f. 152.
[57] C.P. 25(1)/24/14 no. 25; *Cal. Inq. p.m.* i, p. 491; Foss, *Judges of Eng.* ii. 260–2.
[58] C.P. 25(1)/285/23 no. 38; C.P. 25(1)/26/47 no. 27; C.P. 25(1)/26/51 no. 3.
[59] *Cal. Close*, 1349–54, 598.
[60] C 131/37/13; B.L. Add. MS. 5838, f. 10.
[61] *Cal. Pat.* 1441–6, 329, 358.
[62] Ibid. 1548–9, 84; 1555–7, 328; cf. C 3/20/53; Req. 2/179/53.
[63] *Cal. Pat.* 1560–3, 390; C.P. 25(2)/93/833/5 Eliz. I East. no. 5; C.P. 25(2)/93/846/24 Eliz. I East. no. 7.
[64] *V.C.H. Cambs.* ii. 4, 19.
[65] E 117/1/46A.
[66] B.L. Add. MS. 5823, f. 226; Palmer, *Burrough Green*, 157–8.
[67] *Cal. Inq. p.m.* ii, p. 219.
[68] *L. & P. Hen. VIII*, xv, p. 294.
[69] *V.C.H. Cambs.* iii. 429; Palmer, *Burrough Green*, 144–5; ex inf. D. F. R. Missen, Archivist, Christ's Coll.
[70] Palmer, *Burrough Green*, 144.
[71] Ex inf. Dr. S. C. Aston, Bursar, St. Cath.'s Coll.
[72] Palmer, *Burrough Green*, 146–7.
[73] H.L.R.O. Private Bill, May 1815; C.R.O., 515/SP 803.
[74] Palmer, *Burrough Green*, 148.

exchanged *c.* 17 a. in the open fields for 11½ a. in the south-east corner of the parish.[75] Throughout the 19th century the college held between 20 a. and 30 a. in Burrough Green, which it sold in 1942.[76]

ECONOMIC HISTORY. Three of the 5 hides in Burrough in 1086 were in demesne, where there were 2 *servi* and 4 plough-teams. There was meadow for 4 oxen, and a park for hunting. The 7 *villani* and 10 bordars had 4 or 4½ plough-teams on the other 2 hides. Woodland provided pannage for the 41 pigs. The manor had been worth £10 T.R.E. and having fallen to £8 was worth £9 in 1086.[77] In 1334 there were 200 a. of demesne arable which lay in common from August to February; half was sown each year, 60 a. in winter and 40 a. in spring. The park covered 40 a. In 1422 there were still 200 a. of demesne arable, 100 a. of pasture, and 8 a. of meadow. The 80 a. of wood made no profit but there were 30 a. of underwood of which 5 a. could be sold each year. In 1334 only 20 works were owed between Lammas and Michaelmas. By 1422 there were at least 7 free tenants paying 33*s.* a year in all. The customary tenants and 10 cottars paid 40*s.* a year and all tenants gave 7 capons at Christmas.[78] Until inclosure the arable lay in up to seven open fields, divided into unequal furlongs. The largest was Outfield in the north-west part of the parish, followed by Radfield east of the village and Grove and Chalkpit fields north-west of the village. Churling, Underwood, and Stonehurst fields were much smaller.[79] In the 18th century a three-course rotation was followed.[80] Throughout the 16th and 17th centuries barley was the chief corn crop. In the mid 17th century wheat, rye, oats, peas, and a mixture of oats, peas, and beans were also grown.[81] In the late 14th century some heath was brought into cultivation, probably forming Outfield.[82] In the later 18th century more heath, previously used as grazing for sheep, was pared and burned, and then cultivated.[83] In the 17th century Sir John Cage claimed he had suffered great loss by some of his heath being taken into Hare Park at Newmarket by the king; he had to hire pasture 20 miles away, and could keep only two instead of his previous three flocks.[84] Up to the early 19th century every commoner could pasture two cows or a horse on various lands after harvest, and on the Hall meadow at Lammas. Sheep could graze Grove field at Michaelmas, Radfield at All Saints, and the glebe every third year.[85] Most of the woodland remained in the lord's hands, but in 1608 Thomas Atkinson and others owned timber in the great park and elsewhere.[86]

In the late 18th and early 19th centuries a number of copyholds were surrendered to the lord. By the late 19th century little copyhold land survived, but in 1910 the village green was sold subject to the rights of copyholders.[87] By 1793 the earl of Aylesford held most of the land in the parish, and entered into exchanges with Pembroke College, Peterhouse, the trustees of Burrough Green school and town lands, and the rectors of Burrough and Westley, to facilitate inclosure and compensate them for their surrender of common rights. No copy of any inclosure agreement survives, but in 1815 the earl's son petitioned parliament for an Act to legalize the exchanges. Although the bill was never passed the exchanges seem to have taken place.[88] In 1812, however, there was still *c.* 1,000 a. of open-field land.[89] There is no record of further inclosure, but no commonable land remained by 1837. In that year the largest estate belonged to Thomas Redhead who held *c.* 800 a. including the Hall farm, and Wick, White Hart, and Owls Hall (later Fox Hall) farms. The other large landowner was James Barker, rector of Westley, who owned Westley Lodge and Underwood Hall farms. Apart from Downing College's Ravensholt farm (170 a.) and the 62 a. of glebe, no other holding exceeded 30 a.[90] Some of Barker's land later passed to Gen. John Hall and by 1908 to A. C. Hall. As part of his Six Mile Bottom estate it was sold in 1912 to Sir Ernest Cassel, who in 1917 bought Upper Hare Park,[91] which from the 17th century had included *c.* 50 a. in Burrough Green.[92] The land later passed to Cassel's granddaughter,[93] Ruth Mary Cunningham-Reid (later Lady Delamere), who in 1975 still held the Six Mile Bottom estate. The farms which formed Redhead's estate were split up in the early 20th century.[94] Fox Hall and Ravens Hall seem to have been farmed together by 1942 when the buildings of the former were derelict. They had been demolished by 1952.[95]

In the mid 19th century the chief crops were wheat, barley, and roots.[96] In 1837 there were 1,676 a. of arable, 240 a. of grass, and 172 a. of woodland. By 1905 the figures were 1,319 a., 301 a., and 158 a. respectively.[97] In 1910 the Hall farm was run by the Lacey family as a stud: under G. R. C. Foster it was known as the Bower stud of shire horses.[98] In 1975 it was again a stud farm. By 1922 there was a market-garden in the parish, and after 1929 the rectory farm was devoted to dairying. In 1959 a large fruit farm was opened north-west of the village.[99] The woodland in the south-east part of the parish in 1975 was almost co-extensive with that of 1837. Only the 8 a. of Atkins grove had disappeared.[1] In 1910 the woodland contained oak, ash, elm, and sweet chestnut.[2] Some land in the north-west part

75 H.L.R.O. Private Bill, May 1815.
76 *Rep. Com. Univ. Income* [C. 856-II], p. 41, H.C. (1873), xxxvii (3); ex inf. Dr. R. Lovatt, Senior Tutor, Peterhouse.
77 *V.C.H. Cambs.* i. 379, 405.
78 C 135/39 no. 10; C 139/6 no. 46; C 139/8 no. 90.
79 C.R.O., R 51/25/29.
80 Ibid.
81 Palmer, *Burrough Green*, 101, 102–3.
82 B.L. Add MS. 5838, f. 10.
83 *V.C.H. Cambs.* ii. 75.
84 E 178/3621; *Proc. C.A.S.* xxiii. 72.
85 C.R.O., R 51/25/29.
86 Prob. 11/116 (P.C.C. 101 Wingfield).
87 C.R.O., R 54/10/3; ibid. 515/SP 444.
88 *L.J.* l. 47, 183, 231, 373, 384; H.L.R.O. Private Bill, May, 1815.
89 C.R.O., R 51/25/29.
90 C.U.L., E.D.R., tithe award.
91 Ibid.; *Camb. Chron.* 30 Sept. 1876; C.R.O., 296/SP 949; 296/SP 1078.
92 E 178/3621.
93 *D.N.B.*
94 C.R.O., R 59/29/2/1/1; C.U.L., Maps 53(1)/91/77.
95 B.L. Maps 135. a. 64; O.S. Map 1/25,000, TL 65 (1956 edn.).
96 *Kelly's Dir. Cambs.* (1864).
97 C.U.L., E.D.R., tithe award; Cambs. Agric. Returns, 1905.
98 C.R.O., 515/SP 444; C.U.L., Maps 53(1)/93/85.
99 *Kelly's Dir. Cambs.* (1922 and later edns.); *Camb. Ind. Press*, 6 Oct. 1961.
1 C.U.L., E.D.R. tithe award; O.S. Map 1/25,000, TL 65 (1956 edn.).
2 C.R.O., 515/SP 444.

of the parish remained as heath until the 19th century.[3]

In 1831 about two-thirds of the families in the parish were supported by agriculture.[4] There was agricultural unrest in the 1870s when a number of farm-workers joined an agricultural strike. A Mr. Jary who farmed Underwood Hall dismissed his employees who had taken part, and as a result W. H. Hall refused to renew his lease. The sale of stock before Jary's departure was used to demonstrate conservative feeling in the area.[5]

There was a forge in Burrough Green in the 17th century.[6] By the mid 19th century there were two, one in Burrough Green village and one at Burrough End. In 1864 there were also a carpenter, wheelwright, and tailor.[7]

There was a mill in Burrough in 1308.[8] The windmill there in 1334 was in bad repair and worth nothing in 1422. In the same year there was said to be a water-mill, but it was not recorded later.[9] A mill was mentioned in 1591[10] and throughout the 17th century.[11] In the late 19th century there were two windmills, one in the angle between the Brinkley and Westley roads, and one on Bungalow Hill east of the London–Newmarket road.[12] The latter, a post mill bearing the date 1766, was moved to a near-by position *c.* 1846 when the railway was built. It has been out of use since 1923, but was still standing in 1975.[13]

In 1841 a fair was held in Burrough Green for two days in June. In 1961 an old Whit-Monday fair was said to have been revived several years before.[14]

LOCAL GOVERNMENT. As Burrough Green was held of the honor of Richmond the manor owed suit at the tourns of that honor which in the 14th century were sometimes held at Burrough. Burrough was represented at the tourn by three customary tenants and three free tenants. An ale-taster and brewster were answerable to the court, which also concerned itself with the watercourses in the parish.[15] In 1299 the abbot of Warden claimed view of frankpledge over his men in Burrough.[16] A manor court for Burrough was held in 1334.[17] Court records survive for 1673–81, 1719–92, and 1795–1920. By the 17th century the courts were already concerned almost solely with tenurial matters. The appointment of one or two pinders is noted throughout the 18th century, and in 1788 two tenants were presented for taking cattle which were being impounded by the pinder. Courts were held once a year in the 17th century, but more irregularly after 1730.[18]

The amount spent on poor-relief rose from £78 in 1776 to £180 in 1803 and then, more sharply than the average, to £470 in 1813. It later fluctuated between £300 and £400 for the next 20 years, except for low points in 1816 and 1828. In 1803 8 adults and 16 children received permanent outside relief. In 1813 40 were relieved permanently, but by 1815 the number had fallen to 23.[19] In 1835 the parish joined the Newmarket poor-law union[20] and remained part of the Newmarket R.D. until 1974, being then included in East Cambridgeshire.

CHURCH. There was a church in Burrough Green in 1217.[21] The advowson of the rectory descended with the manor until the early 20th century.[22] By 1917 it belonged to James Binney and later passed to C. Binney whose brother Mr. H. Binney held it in 1975.[23] In 1570 two presentations were granted to Anthony and Richard Cutt successively, and in 1599 the second was granted to Francis Garthside, the rector.[24]

The rectory was valued at 10 marks in 1254, 20 marks in 1276, and 16 marks in 1291.[25] In 1534 it was worth £18 10*s.* and by 1650 £100.[26] By 1728 it had risen to £120, and by 1835 the gross income was £553, the second highest in the rural deanery. By 1877 it had risen to £675.[27] In 1615 there were 85 a. of glebe. The amount was given as 106 a. in 1639, but was again 85 a. in 1787.[28] In 1789 62 a. were exchanged for 30 a. of inclosed land, and in 1837 there were 73 a. of glebe. The rector was also entitled to all great and small tithes in Burrough Green and to some tithes in Stetchworth and Dullingham.[29] The rectory house, south-west of the church, was being rebuilt in 1876. Since 1958 it has been occupied as a private house, known as Brettons.[30]

There were three chantries in Burrough Green church by 1468,[31] each with a chaplain presented by the lord of the manor. Catherine de Burgh in 1407 provided for a chaplain to celebrate at the altar of the Virgin Mary in the south side of Burrough church, and by will of 1409 left vestments and other bequests to the chantry. That chantry was valued at £14 19*s.* 3*d.* in 1534,[32] and was called Dame

[3] C.U.L., E.D.R., tithe award.
[4] *Census* (1831).
[5] *Camb. Chron.* 30 Sept. 1876.
[6] E 179/244/23 rot. 68.
[7] *Kelly's Dir. Cambs.* (1864); O.S. Map 6″, Cambs. XLIX. SW. (1889 edn.).
[8] B.L. Add. MS. 5820, f. 90v.
[9] Ibid. Add. MS. 5838, f. 45; C 35/39/10; C 139/6 no. 46.
[10] Prob. 11/77 (P.C.C. 21 Sainberbe, will of Thos. Holmes).
[11] Prob. 11/143 (P.C.C. 2 Byrde, will of Fras. Cobbin); Prob. 11/294 (P.C.C. 46 Pell, will of Hen. Cobbin).
[12] O.S. Map 6″, Cambs. XLVIII. NE., XLIX. SW. (1889, 1890 edns.).
[13] *Kelly's Dir. Cambs.* (1904); *Trans. Newcomen Soc.* xxvii. 102.
[14] C.U.L., E.D.R., C 3/17; *Camb. Ind. Press*, 6 Oct. 1961.
[15] S.C. 2/155/71 mm. 1–2.
[16] *Plac. de Quo Warr.* (Rec. Com.), 99.
[17] C 135/39 no. 10.
[18] C.R.O., 515/SP 444; ibid. L 14/1–2; ibid. R 54/10/2–3.
[19] *Poor Law Abstract, 1804*, 38–9; *1818*, 30–1; *Rep. H.L. Cttee. on Poor Laws*, H.C. 227, pp. 332–3 (1831), viii; *Poor Rate Returns, 1816–21*, 11; *1822–4*, 38; *1825–9*, 16; *1830–4*, 16.
[20] *Poor Law Com. 2nd Rep.* 513; *Census*, 1931 (pt. ii).
[21] *Val. of Norwich*, ed. Lunt, 535.
[22] e.g. *Cat. Anct. D.* iii, D 187 (1260); C.P. 25 (2)/93/836/12 Eliz. I Trin. no. 5.
[23] *Crockford* (1926 and later edns.).
[24] C 2/Jas. I/C 16/14; C.R.O., P 17/2/1.
[25] *Val. of Norwich*, ed. Lunt, 535, 554.
[26] *Valor Eccl.* (Rec. Com.), iii. 504; Lamb. Pal. MS. 904, f. 267.
[27] C.U.L., E.D.R., B 8/1; ibid. C 3/26; *Rep. Com. Eccl. Revenues*, pp. 344–5.
[28] C.R.O., P 17/3/1 and 2; C.U.L., E.D.R., H 1/7, terrier 1787.
[29] H.L.R.O., Private Bill, May 1815; C.U.L., E.D.R., H 1/7, terrier 1837; C.U.L., Add. MS. 103/23.
[30] C.R.O., P 17/3/5; *Camb. Ind. Press*, 6 Oct. 1961.
[31] *E.D.R.* (1907), 136.
[32] *E.D.R.* (1898), 218; (1901), 123; Prob. 11/2A (P.C.C. 20 Marche); *Proc. C.A.S.* i. 208.

Catherine's, as was also the chantry, alternatively called the Burgh chantry, founded in 1460 under the will of Edmund Ingoldisthorpe at the same altar, for the souls of Catherine and others.[33] Bateman's chantry, founded in 1446 by John Bateman, rector of Burrough, in the chapel of the Annunciation,[34] was worth £12 in 1535.[35] In the 15th century each chantry was wealthy enough to pay a pension to a retired chaplain and support his successor.[36] In the early 16th century there was a parish guild of St. Augustine, with a guildhall for the poor.[37]

There were curates in the parish from the mid 16th century when the rector lived on his vicarage in Lancashire.[38] In 1564 the bishop reported that Thomas Holmes of Burrough Green was not conformable in religion.[39] A parishioner who appeared before the High Commission in 1640 was perhaps the one who failed to receive communion that year.[40] Thomas Wake was ejected from the rectory in 1644 on evidence of unseemly behaviour and Laudian attitudes.[41] Thomas Watson, rector from *c.* 1672, held the benefice *in commendam* when he became bishop of St. David's in 1687. After his deprivation he was charged with simony for letting Burrough rectory to another clergyman. Even before his appointment to the see he had not often resided in the parish, and in 1692 had a curate there. It was at Burrough Green that he was attacked by a mob in 1688 after being excepted from the Act of Indemnity.[42] Samuel Knight, rector 1707–46, was also a canon of Ely and Lincoln and archdeacon of Berkshire, and held three other parochial cures. He had a curate at Burrough Green, who in 1728 held two Sunday services and quarterly communions attended by *c.* 20 parishioners.[43] John Green, presented in 1746, became Regius professor of divinity at Cambridge, master of Corpus Christi College, dean of Lincoln, and vice-chancellor of Cambridge; he retained the rectory until after his promotion to the see of Lincoln in 1761, but never resided.[44] Green's successor J. F. Palmer lived in Bedfordshire in 1775 and by 1779 was insane. The cure was served by a curate who had been there under Green.[45]

Charles Wedge served as resident rector from 1801 to 1872.[46] In 1807 there was only one Sunday service, alternately morning and evening so that people could go once to Brinkley and once to Burrough Green. Only *c.* 12 attended the quarterly communions, but there was frequent catechizing in the summer. A Sunday school had been started by 1836.[47] In 1877 the rector was not yet resident but kept a curate. A third of the people attended church: there were two Sunday services and monthly communions, with once more *c.* 20 communicants, but services on other holy days had been discontinued.[48] In 1897 there were 29 regular communicants at the twice-monthly sacraments, and two-thirds of the parishioners went to at least one Sunday service.[49] From the early 20th century the rector of Burrough Green has also held Brinkley, where from the 1950s he has usually lived.[50]

The church of *ST. AUGUSTINE*, so called in 1409,[51] is built of field stones and rubble, and has a chancel, aisled nave, west tower, and south porch. The chancel, which is almost as long as the nave, dates from the 13th century. It may have been extended in the earlier 14th century. The two-stage tower and the aisles were added to the nave in the 14th century. The chancel was flanked by two chapels each stretching its full length, at least the south one being transeptal at its west end. The northern one was probably built in the early 14th century and the southern one somewhat later. The earlier windows of the chancel were blocked, and arches were opened into both chapels from the west end of the chancel and from the aisles.[52]

The south porch was added in the early 15th century when the doorway was renewed. From the mid 16th century the church began to fall into disrepair. In the early 17th century the steeple was repaired, but the Cage family refused to repair the chapels, for which they were responsible.[53] In 1644 William Dowsing broke 64 pictures and crucifixes at Burrough Green.[54] By 1665 the chancel, nave, and aisles were all in a bad condition.[55] In 1667 part of the roof had fallen in, and the church was described as a danger to the lives and health of parishioners.[56] Eventually the chapels were demolished and the arches leading to them blocked; square-headed windows were put into the chancel. Three bays of each aisle were given gables with double openings which served as a clerestory, and plain triangular-headed windows were put into the aisles. The plain octagonal font, dated 1672, was probably put in at the same time. The Cages seem to have been responsible for the work.[57] In the mid 18th century the altar stood not below the east window but against a wall running across the chancel *c.* 9 ft. from the east wall. At that date the 14th-century chancel screen was still standing.[58] It was removed between 1812 and 1877, by when the chancel arch had been demolished and two 18th-century urns placed on the responds.[59] By 1812 the nave and chancel had been given flat ceilings.[60]

[33] B.L. Add. MS. 5838, f. 120; *Cal. Pat.* 1452–61, 634; E 117/11/9.
[34] *Cal. Papal Reg.* xi. 115; *Cal. Pat.* 1441–6, 329; *E.D.R.* (1902), 181.
[35] *Valor Eccl.* (Rec. Com.), iii. 504.
[36] *E.D.R.* (1908), 120–1; (1911), 101; B.L. Add. MS. 5820, f. 90v.
[37] B.L. Add. MS. 5861, pp. 145, 163; Palmer, *Burrough Green*, 97.
[38] B.L. Add. MS. 5813, f. 65; *E.D.R.* (1913), 41; C.U.L., E.D.R., B 2/3, p. 101; B 2/6.
[39] *Camd. Misc.* ix (Camd. Soc. N.S. liii), 25.
[40] *Cal. S.P. Dom.* 1640, 401; *Cambs. Village Doc.* 59.
[41] *Walker Revised*, ed. Matthews, 87; B.L. Add. MS. 15672, ff. 54–5.
[42] *D.N.B.*; C.U.L., E.D.R., B 2/22; *MSS. of H.L.* N.S. iv. 116.
[43] *Alum. Cantab. to 1751*, iii. 29; C.U.L., E.D.R., B 8/1.
[44] *D.N.B.*
[45] Palmer, *Burrough Green*, 135; C.U.L., E.D.R., C 1/1.
[46] C.U.L., E.D.R., B 1/16.
[47] Ibid. B 8/1; C 1/4; C 3/21.
[48] Ibid. C 3/26.
[49] Ibid. C 3/36.
[50] *Crockford* (1961–2).
[51] Prob. 11/2A (P.C.C. 20 Marche, will of Cath. de Burgh).
[52] Pevsner, *Cambs.* 309–10; Palmer, *Burrough Green*, 44–53.
[53] C.U.L., E.D.R., B 2/3, p. 84; Gibbons, *Ely Episc. Rec.* 84.
[54] *Trans. C.H.A.S.* iii. 90.
[55] C.U.L., E.D.R., B 2/59, p. 49.
[56] C.R.O., P 17/6/1.
[57] Palmer, *Burrough Green*, 43, 55; Pevsner, *Cambs.* 309–10.
[58] B.L. Add. MS. 5820, ff. 88, 91.
[59] Palmer, *Burrough Green*, 44; *Arch. Jnl.* xxxiv. 122.
[60] Palmer, *Burrough Green*, 63.

The church is chiefly notable for its monuments to members of the de Burgh and Ingoldisthorpe families. One monument, a large tomb in the middle of the chancel bearing a brass of Edmund Ingoldisthorpe (d. 1456) has disappeared, probably during the 17th-century alterations. There remain six stone effigies and three canopied tombs. The three tombs all stand along the north wall of the chancel. The central one has an ogee arch which can also be traced on the outside wall of the chancel; it is in its original position. The other two have four-centred arches, and all three have canopies with crocketed mouldings in ogee curves. Since at least one of the tombs originally stood in the south chapel either of the outer two may have been moved. The effigies have been moved several times and are not well preserved. In the 18th century one of the figures under the centre canopy was on the outside chancel wall. It is impossible to identify the figures accurately. The lady and three knights in the chancel are probably all 14th-century members of the de Burgh family. The two in the north aisle may be John Ingoldisthorpe (d. 1420) and his wife Elizabeth de Burgh (d. 1421).[61] In the middle of the chancel is a large black marble monument to Anthony Cage, rector (d. 1630).

In the 13th century Burrough church had two chalices,[62] and in the mid 16th century a silver chalice and paten.[63] The plate includes a cup dated 1633 given by Samuel Knight in 1741, and a paten given by Thomas Watson in 1692.[64] In the 16th century there were three bells.[65] In 1710 Samuel Knight gave a ring of five bells cast by John Waylett. The fourth was recast in 1807, and by the 20th century the third was cracked.[66] The registers begin in 1571 and except for a break between 1637 and 1660 are complete.[67]

NONCONFORMITY. In 1807 there were a few Presbyterians in Burrough Green, and in 1825 their numbers were increasing. In 1877 *c.* 80 people attended dissenting chapels in other parishes.[68]

EDUCATION. One of the chantry chaplains seems to have acted as schoolmaster in the 15th century.[69] By will dated 1630 Dr. Anthony Cage, rector of Burrough Green, left a house and land, from which half of the rent was to go to a poor woman of the parish to teach reading, and half to be used for apprenticing. In 1794 the land was exchanged for closes and a blacksmith's shop in Burrough End. School dames were appointed from 1631, and in 1728 the school was described as a charity school for Burrough Green and Brinkley.[70]

In 1709 Thomas Watson, late bishop of St. David's, gave a messuage and pasture which helped to support another school in the school-house on the green built in the early 18th century under the will of Samuel Richardson whose date of death is not known. Samuel Knight (d. 1746), rector and Richardson's executor, also left houses and land to buy bibles for children leaving the school and to pay a master. The stone-built school is two storeys high with a central doorway above which are 2 niches with figures of a boy and a girl. Two wings were later added, one as a house for the master, the other as an alms-house.[71] By the early 19th century the educational portion of Cage's charity was usually paid to the master of Knight's school, although in 1801 the buildings were dilapidated and the master was not paid.[72]

After 1821 Cage's charity was again applied to a separate infant school.[73] In 1837 Knight's school was still badly conducted and the master unsatisfactory but by 1846 conditions had improved, and the two schools taught 62 boys and girls and 31 infants.[74] By 1877 Cage's school had ceased, and a Scheme of 1887 devoted its income to providing prizes, grants, lectures, and evening classes.[75] In 1876 Knight's school was reorganized and in 1877 reopened, attended by 15 boys and girls and 6 infants.[76] There was accommodation for 86, and numbers gradually increased, to 52 in 1884 and 98 in 1914.[77] The school received a grant from the 1880s, and in 1897 was liberally supported by Mrs. Porcher. A 1*d.* rate was also levied.[78] A new room was added in 1911.[79] Numbers fell again, to 37 in 1938, and in 1947 the seniors were transferred to Bottisham village college, moving to Linton in 1964.[80] A new building was erected in the school yard in 1975. The school was then attended by children from Burrough Green, Brinkley, and Westley Waterless. By 1975 Cage's charity was distributed in gifts for good attendance and to school leavers.[81]

CHARITY FOR THE POOR. By will dated 1719 John Jervis gave 10*s.* charged on a copyhold estate to be spent in Easter week on bread for the poor. Payment was apparently discontinued in 1820.[82]

61 Ibid. 54, 56–9; B.L. Add. MS. 5820, f. 82v.; *Mon. Inscr. Cambs.* 16, 220–1; *Arch. Jnl.* xxxiv. 121–6.
62 *Vetus Liber Arch. Elien.* (C.A.S. 8vo ser. xlviii), 52–3.
63 *Cambs. Ch. Goods, temp. Edw. VI*, 69.
64 List of ch. plate *penes V.C.H.*
65 *Cambs. Ch. Goods, temp. Edw. VI*, 69.
66 *Cambs. Bells* (C.A.S. 8vo ser. xviii), 122; MS. notes by H. B. Walters (1936), *penes V.C.H.*
67 Ex inf. the rector, the Revd. R. Crowther.
68 C.U.L., E.D.R., C 1/4; C 1/6; C 3/26.
69 Prob. 11/5 (P.C.C. 8 Godyn, will of John Bateman).
70 *31st Rep. Com. Char.* 131; C.R.O., P 17/5/1; C.U.L., E.D.R., B 8/1.
71 *31st Rep. Com. Char.* 131–2.
72 C.U.L., E.D.R., C 1/4; C.R.O., P 17/25/27.
73 *31st Rep. Com. Char.* 131.
74 Ibid. 131–2; *Church School Inquiry, 1846–7*, 2–3.
75 Char. Com. files.
76 Ed. 7/5.
77 *Rep. of Educ. Cttee. of Council, 1884–5* [C. 4483-I], p. 522, H.C. (1884–5), xxiii; *Bd. of Educ., List. 21, 1914* (H.M.S.O.), 26.
78 *Rep. of Educ. Cttee. of Council, 1880–1* [C. 2948-I], p. 542, H.C. (1881), xxxii; C.U.L., E.D.R., C 3/36.
79 *Kelly's Dir. Cambs.* (1912).
80 *Bd. of Educ., List 21, 1938* (H.M.S.O.), 19; Black, *Cambs. Educ. Rec.* 41.
81 Ex inf. the rector.
82 *31st Rep. Com. Char.* 132–3.

CARLTON CUM WILLINGHAM

THE MODERN parish of Carlton,[1] covering 2,415 a.[2] and lying 10 miles east-south-east of Cambridge, is derived from two of the three villages, hidated together in 1086, of Carlton, Willingham, and Brinkley.[3] The three were still sometimes grouped together for administrative purposes until the 14th century,[4] although they had formed independent parishes ecclesiastically before 1200. Willingham and Carlton parishes were united in the 15th century, the combination being sometimes in the 16th called Willingham with Carlton,[5] and officially until the 1950s Carlton cum Willingham.[6] The south-eastern corner, containing the demesne of Little Carlton manor, was entered in Domesday under Weston Colville,[7] with which it was occasionally linked in feudal documents until 1316.[8] The boundary with Weston Colville was slightly adjusted after 1612,[9] and when Weston was inclosed in 1778 the allotments for copyholds of Carlton manor, which paid tithes to Carlton rectory, were concentrated in Weston Brook field, south of Willingham Green, an area thenceforth reckoned as part of Carlton lordship and parish.[10] Some 60 a. of Norney farm, by the eastern boundary, remained a detached part of Brinkley lordship and parish until transferred to Carlton in 1886.[11]

The parish stretches for 5½ miles from the old Newmarket road south-eastwards, gradually widening, towards the Suffolk boundary. It lies mainly upon the chalk, overlaid in the south-eastern part by boulder clay. The ground slopes gradually upwards from *c.* 100 ft. near Six Mile Bottom at the north-western end to *c.* 370 ft. north of Willingham Green. The north-west part drains northward into Brinkley, by a water-course, which further upstream marks the Weston Colville boundary for a mile. South-eastward the land dips below 300 ft. to form the narrow valley down which the river Stour runs north-eastward into Suffolk; it then rises again to a height of over 350 ft., upon which Carlton church stands, and, after another dip, to over 375 ft. at Little Carlton.

The high ground along the eastern boundary was well wooded in the early Middle Ages. In 1086 there was woodland for 124 pigs.[12] Furthest north lay Carlton wood, where commercial felling was recorded *c.* 1580.[13] It still covered 148 a. in 1767,[14] but 19th-century clearances had reduced it by the 1880s to 25 a.[15] South of it lay a wood belonging *c.* 1225 to the lord of Brinkley,[16] with which manor it remained until purchased by the lord of Carlton in 1597, when already mostly cleared.[17] In 1767 its former area comprised the 60 a. forming the northern half of Norney farm.[18] The 60-acre wood belonging to Willingham immediately to the south had been assarted and inclosed by the early 13th century. It then adjoined the lord of Little Carlton's wood,[19] later called Lophams wood, covering 32½ a. in 1612[20] and 33½ a. in 1942.[21] Furthest south, by the boundary with Weston, was the king's wood. Henry III granted it in 1227 to the Templars,[22] who had cleared most of it by 1300, but still employed a woodward there in 1307.[23]

Settlement in the parish was confined to the south-eastern part, where scattered groups of dwellings were surrounded by ancient inclosures, probably taken in from the woodland. The north-western part was covered by heath and open fields, which remained under a triennial rotation until inclosure in 1800. The name Willingham, the dwelling of Willa's folk,[24] combined with its location on the road linking several other villages in the hundred, suggests that it may be an older settlement than Carlton. The latter, whose name might be taken to imply the dependence of its *ceorls* on another vill,[25] was first recorded in 989.[26] In 1086, however, Carlton had an enumerated population of 18, three times that of Willingham. No population was returned for what became Little Carlton.[27] Carlton and Willingham possibly contained 28 taxpayers in 1327,[28] but by 1428 there were only 4 householders at Willingham and 4 at Carlton.[29] There were still only 8 taxpayers in the parish in 1524,[30] but 22 households by 1563.[31] The population may have risen rapidly to 200 or more by 1600, thereafter fluctuating between 180 and 200 until 1700,[32] and then apparently declining. In 1676 there were 145 adults,[33] and in 1728 42 families with 180 members.[34] Numbers grew quickly from 229 in 1801 to 363 by 1821 and a peak of 469 in 1851. After 1871 the population declined steadily, falling by 1931 to 222, and although swelled to 266 in 1951 by displaced persons living in disused military hutments it numbered only *c.* 140 in the 1960s.[35]

1 This account was written in 1976.
2 *Census*, 1961.
3 *V.C.H. Cambs.* i. 405–6.
4 e.g. *Liber de Bernewelle*, 257; *Cambs. Lay Subsidy, 1327*, 17; *Inq. Non.* (Rec. Com.), 212.
5 e.g. *L. & P. Hen. VIII*, iii (2), p. 1117; inscr. on chalice, 1569.
6 *Census*, 1961.
7 *V.C.H. Cambs.* i. 384, 406.
8 e.g. *Liber de Bernewelle*, 257; *Feud. Aids*, i. 154.
9 Cf. C.U.L., MS. Plan 550R (map of Weston Colville estate 1612).
10 C.R.O., Q/RDz 1, pp. 335, 350–62; cf. ibid. L 89/15.
11 *Kelly's Dir. Cambs.* (1888); and see above, p. 136.
12 *V.C.H. Cambs.* i. 405.
13 C 2/Eliz. I/S 2/14.
14 C.R.O., R 54/21/1 (map of Carlton estate 1767, partly copied from map *c.* 1600 by Ralph Agar).
15 O.S. Map 6″, Cambs. LVI. NW. (1891 edn.); cf. B.L. Maps 135. a. 64.
16 *Lewes Chartulary, Cambs.* ed. Bullock and Palmer (C.A.S. 1938), 27.
17 C.P. 25(2)/93/861/39 Eliz. I Trin. no. 7.
18 C.R.O., R 54/71/1.
19 *Lewes Chartulary, Cambs.* 6–7, 27.
20 C.U.L., MS. Plan 550R.
21 B.L. Maps 135. a. 64.
22 *Cal. Chart. R.* 1226–57, 24; cf. C.U.L., MS. Plan 550R.
23 E 358/20 rot. 7.
24 *P.N. Cambs.* (E.P.N.S.), 117.
25 Ibid.; cf. H. P. R. Finberg, *Lucerna*, 144–60.
26 Dorothy Whitelock, *A.-S. Wills*, 32–3.
27 *V.C.H. Cambs.* i. 405–6.
28 *Cambs. Lay Subsidy, 1327*, 17.
29 *Feud. Aids*, i. 193.
30 E 179/81/134 m. 7.
31 B.L. Harl. MS. 594, f. 194v.
32 Cf. C.R.O., par. reg. TS.
33 Compton Census.
34 C.U.L., E.D.R., B 8/1.
35 *Census*, 1801–1971; cf. *Camb. Ind. Press*, 17 Nov. 1961.

In the 18th century and probably in the 17th the older houses lay in three or four small groups,[36] apart from the isolated farmsteads such as Lophams Hall and Cockshot,[37] later Cocksedge,[38] Farm. Furthest west was Willingham Green, where *c.* 8 houses stood in 1767 around a green narrowing eastward. About 1 mile to the south-east a group of cottages, *c.* 7 in 1800, lay by a lane running north from the church and rectory. At a place called in 1800 Hammonds, and later Stocks,[39] Green that lane met the road from Brinkley, curving uphill from Rayners Bridge over the Stour, recorded *c.* 1260,[40] and down again eastward towards Carlton Hall Farm. Houses and cottages, perhaps 5 *c.* 1800, stood at intervals along that road. South of the church, at Little Carlton Green, there were by 1612 *c.* 4 houses. The number of houses in the parish may have shrunk after 1700. About 50 dwellings were recorded in 1666 and 45 in 1674,[41] but only 34 houses for 44 families in 1801.[42] The later increase in population was met by subdividing existing buildings, one house being converted into three cottages and a cottage at Willingham Green into four.[43] New building, raising the number of houses to 97 by 1871, occurred especially along the road from Brinkley to Hall Farm, where there were then 28 dwellings. About 24 stood at Willingham Green, probably 16 near the church, and 17 at Little Carlton Green.[44] Thereafter the various settlements shrank, especially that at Little Carlton Green, and there were only 62 houses in 1901 and 49 in 1961.[45]

In the 19th century each settlement had its own public house. The Carpenter's Arms or Axe and Saw at Stocks Green,[46] kept by a carpenter in 1782,[47] survived until 1922,[48] and the Rose and Crown at Willingham Green until after 1961.[49] All had closed by 1975. In the mid 19th century the parish had a resident doctor.[50]

MANORS AND OTHER ESTATES. About 989 Alfhelm Poga left land at Carlton to his wife.[51] Before 1066 4 hides there belonged to Earl Alfgar and 2 at Willingham to King Edward's thegn Tochi.[52] The Carlton manor is said to have been given by the Conqueror's wife, Queen Maud, to Gundreda, wife of William de Warenne (d. 1088), to endow William's Cluniac foundation at Lewes. In 1086 the abbot of Cluny held the 4 hides of Warenne. They were included among the lands which Warenne granted to Lewes priory,[53] to which also Walter de Grandcourt gave the 2 hides at Willingham, once Tochi's, which he had held of William de Warenne in 1086.[54] The combined manors, called *GREAT CARLTON* or *CARLTON AND WILLINGHAM*, augmented by some smaller gifts of land in the 12th century,[55] and held of the Warennes in free alms,[56] remained with Lewes priory until the Dissolution.[57] About 1200 the manor was at farm for a long term to Jocelin of Walpole, whose son Henry released it to the priory.[58] In 1346 the prior leased it for 20 years at a nominal rent to Sir Walter de Crek and his brother John, a clergyman, in survivorship.[59]

After the priory's surrender in 1537[60] all its lands were granted in 1538 to Thomas Cromwell.[61] In 1540 he sold Carlton manor to Sir Thomas Elyot, to whom the Crown confirmed it after Cromwell's attainder.[62] When Elyot died in 1546 his heir was his sister Margery's son Richard Puttenham, but his widow Margaret held Carlton for life.[63] She married the lawyer James Dyer, knighted as Speaker in 1553 and chief justice of the Common Pleas 1559–82.[64] In 1552 Puttenham agreed to the settlement of Carlton upon Margaret and Dyer in survivorship, with remainder jointly to Puttenham's brother George and Margaret's brother Anthony Aborough for their lives,[65] and sold his reversionary interest to Hugh Stewkley, a lawyer from Marsh (Som.). Stewkley bought out George Puttenham's rights in 1559.[66] Margaret died in 1569,[67] but Dyer survived until 1582,[68] when Stewkley entered upon a moiety of the manor,[69] the other half being still held by Aborough (d. *c.* 1600) at Stewkley's death in 1589. Stewkley's son and heir Thomas[70] bought the 60-acre enclave of Brinkley manor, later included in Norney farm, from Thomas Stutville in 1597.[71] He was knighted in 1603.[72] He was succeeded in 1639 by his son Hugh,[73] created a baronet in 1627, who died in 1642. His son and heir Sir Hugh[74]

[36] Layout and numbers of buildings based on C.U.L., MS. Plan 550R; C.R.O., R 54/21/1; R 60/24/2/12.
[37] Cf. Essex R.O., D/DL T 19 no. 4.
[38] C.R.O., L 43/4, p. 385.
[39] H.O. 107/1761.
[40] *Lewes Chartulary, Cambs.* 8.
[41] See pp. 279, 281.
[42] *Census*, 1801. Only 25 houses in 1807: C.U.L., E.D.R., C 1/4.
[43] C.R.O., L 70/42.
[44] R.G. 10/1593.
[45] *Census*, 1901–61.
[46] H.O. 107/1761.
[47] C.R.O., L 43/4, p. 86.
[48] *Kelly's Dir. Cambs.* (1858–1922).
[49] *Camb. Ind. Press*, 17 Nov. 1961.
[50] e.g. *Kelly's Dir. Cambs.* (1858–64); R.G. 10/1593.
[51] Dorothy Whitelock, *A.-S. Wills*, 32–3.
[52] *V.C.H. Cambs.* i. 380; for Tochi's identity, cf. *Proc. C.A.S.* lxv. 36–9.
[53] *Lewes Chartulary*, i (Suss. Rec. Soc. xxxviii), 4, 10. The charters concerning those grants, though possibly not authentic, cf. *Early Yorks. Chart.* viii (Y.A.S. extra ser. vi), 59–62, seem to record genuine donations.
[54] *V.C.H. Cambs.* i. 380; *Lewes Chartulary*, i. 18, 29; cf. *Cat. Anct. D.* v, A 10988.
[55] *Cal. Doc. France*, ed. Round, p. 512; *Lewes Chartulary, Cambs.* 25.
[56] Hence not assessed in *Feud. Aids*, i: cf. *Cal. Close*, 1343–6, 525.
[57] e.g. *Liber de Bernewelle*, 257; *Cal. Pat.* 1232–47, 453; *Cal. Fine R.* 1337–47, 382; Dugdale, *Mon.* v. 19.
[58] *Lewes Chartulary, Cambs.* 11–12.
[59] *Cal. Pat.* 1345–8, 163.
[60] Dugdale, *Mon.* v. 20–1.
[61] *L. & P. Hen. VIII*, xiii (1), pp. 138–9.
[62] Ibid. xiii (1), p. 99 (possibly misplaced); xv, pp. 172, 507.
[63] C 142/74 no. 16.
[64] Foss, *Judges of Eng.* v. 479–85; L. W. Abbott, *Law-Reporting in Eng. 1485–1585*, 150–8.
[65] *Cal. Pat.* 1550–3, 42; C.U.L., Doc. 1410; cf. *D.N.B.* s.v. Puttenham, Geo.; W. Berry, *County Genealogies, Hants* (1833), 265.
[66] C.P. 25(2)/68/559 no. 2; C.U.L., Doc. 1410; cf. *Cal. Pat.* 1553–4, 427; 1558–60, 245.
[67] Not 1560, as in *D.N.B.*; R.C.H.M. *Hunts.* 251: cf. *Cal. Pat.* 1560–3, 403.
[68] Prob. 11/64 (P.C.C. 28 Tyrwhite), dating Marg.'s death.
[69] Cf. C 2/Eliz. I/S 2/14.
[70] C 142/222 no. 2; cf. Prob. 11/95 (P.C.C. 23 Wallop).
[71] C.P. 25(2)/93/861/39 Eliz. I Trin. no. 7.
[72] Nicholls, *Progresses of Jas. I*, i. 117.
[73] Wards 7/96 no. 68.
[74] Prob. 11/190 (P.C.C. 117 Campbell); G.E.C. *Baronetage*, ii. 26.

mortgaged the Carlton estate in 1668,[75] and sold it early in 1676 to Sir John James[76] (d. 1676). Sir John devised his estates to his nephew James Cane, who was to take the surname James.[77]

Sir Cane James (cr. Bt. 1682)[78] and his son John sold Carlton in 1720 to John Goodden Woolfe, who died in 1742 leaving the manor to his brother Marsh Woolfe.[79] Marsh, dying in 1748, left it to his sister Margaret's son Thomas Brand of the Hoo, in Kimpton (Herts.).[80] Brand died in 1770, leaving his lands to his son Thomas[81] (d. 1794).[82] The son had married the heiress to the barony of Dacre, to which his son Thomas succeeded in 1819. The Carlton estate descended with the barony, after Thomas's death without issue in 1851, to his brother Henry Otway Trevor (formerly Brand) (d. 1853) and the latter's sons T. C. W. Trevor (d.s.p. 1890) and H. B. W. Brand, Speaker 1872–84, created Viscount Hampden (d. 1892). Hampden's son and heir, Henry Robert Brand (d. 1906),[83] had sold Carlton Grange farm, comprising the north-western half of the parish by 1904 to A. C. Hall, with whose Six Mile Bottom estate it passed thereafter.[84] Thomas William Brand, the 3rd viscount, had by 1914 transferred Carlton Hall farm, to the south-east, to J. A. Brand,[85] and sold Church farm *c.* 1920, partly to C. F. Ryder, partly to its tenant C. L. Long.[86]

Lewes priory's manorial farmstead probably stood in the 200-ft.-square moat, the remains of which adjoin Hall Farm,[87] so named by *c.* 1600.[88] A Georgian farm-house there[89] was demolished and replaced in the 1960s.

In 1086 Durand held of Hardwin de Scalers 1 hide which had formerly belonged to Earl Alfgar's man Thurgar, and two knights of Hardwin held ½ hide previously occupied by three sokemen of Earls Alfgar and Harold. From those holdings, entered partly under Weston,[90] was derived the manor of *LITTLE CARLTON*, also called *BARBEDORS* and later *LOPHAMS*. It depended on the Scalers barony in the 13th century,[91] being held in 1269 of the Frevilles, heirs of Hardwin's son Richard;[92] a fee at Carlton was held of the Frevilles' half-barony until after 1400.[93] By 1526, however, Little Carlton was supposedly held of the Warennes' heirs.[94] William de Criketot owned land at Carlton by 1225,[95] having succeeded his father Heinfrid in 1221,[96] and died in 1235. His son William[97] held Little Carlton in demesne *c.* 1236[98] and died holding it in 1269. His son and heir William,[99] a former rebel, had had his land at Carlton granted to a royal supporter after 1265, but presumably later redeemed it.[1] He, or perhaps his father, subinfeudated the manor, and he died in 1299, leaving the mesne overlordship to his descendants,[2] four Williams in four successive generations. They died respectively in 1310, 1343, 1354, and after 1368, the last being a minor who died without issue.[3]

By 1302 the manor was held in demesne by Roger, son of William Barbedor.[4] In 1304 Roger settled over 180 a. at Little Carlton on his son William, subject to a life-interest for William Down, clerk.[5] In 1320 Robert Beverley, clerk, settled the reversion from his death on George Barbedor, presumably William's heir,[6] who died in 1335 leaving two-thirds of the manor to his young son William, not recorded later. The other third was held by a female William, probably George's mother, and her husband Robert King,[7] from whom it was successfully claimed in 1346 by Joan, widow of Roger Brown (d. by 1341). Joan declared that William de Criketot, possibly he who died in 1299, had granted it to his daughter Joan (perhaps Roger Barbedor's wife) whose son Walter was her father.[8] Joan Brown held the Criketot fee in 1346,[9] and died after 1350.[10] By 1372 Little Carlton manor had come to John Lopham,[11] still alive in 1395.[12] His successor Thomas Lopham, recorded from 1397[13] and appointed serjeant-at-law in 1415,[14] held the manor in 1412[15] and died apparently without issue in 1416.[16] In 1417 Philip Inglefield and his wife Elizabeth alienated Barbedors manor, of Elizabeth's inheritance, to Sir William Fynderne (d. 1445) and others.[17]

From the time of William's son Sir Thomas the manor remained attached to the Fynderne estate at Weston Colville for 150 years,[18] and was sold with it to John Lennard.[19] In 1613 Lennard's great-grandson Richard, Lord Dacre, sold Little Carlton

75 C.U.L., Doc. 1422.
76 C.P. 25(2)/633/27–8 Chas. II Hil. no. 8.
77 Prob. 11/353 (P.C.C. 20 Hale).
78 G.E.C. *Baronetage*, iv. 129.
79 C.P. 25(2)/1000/7 Geo. I Hil. no. 10; Prob. 11/720 (P.C.C. 287 Trenley).
80 Prob. 11/766 (P.C.C. 384 Strahan); cf. *V.C.H. Herts. Fam.* 44.
81 Prob. 11/960 (P.C.C. 320 Jenner).
82 Prob. 11/1244 (P.C.C. 123 Holman).
83 *Complete Peerage*, iv. 16–18; C.R.O., 334/08. Directories from the 1880s, e.g. *Kelly's Dir. Cambs.* (1883), describe the Brands as lords of Little Carlton, erroneously distinguishing it from Lophams.
84 C.R.O., 334/08, under 1904; cf. B.L. Maps 135.a.6.
85 C.R.O., 334/08, under 1914–23; cf. *Kelly's Dir. Cambs.* (1922).
86 C.R.O., 334/08, under 1920–1.
87 *V.C.H. Cambs.* ii. 20.
88 Cf. C.R.O., R 52/21/1.
89 Photog. in *Camb. Ind. Press*, 13 Nov. 1961.
90 *V.C.H. Cambs.* i. 384–5.
91 e.g. *Liber de Bernewelle*, 257, 262–3.
92 *Cal. Inq. p.m.* i, p. 223; cf. *V.C.H. Cambs.* v. 27–8.
93 e.g. C 143/362 no. 21; *Cal. Inq. p.m.* xiii, p. 154; *Cal. Pat.* 1399–1401, 446.
94 C 142/32 no. 32.
95 *Cur. Reg. R.* xii, p. 213; cf. *Lewes Chartulary, Cambs.* 6–7, 14–15.
96 *Cur. Reg. R.* x. 238; xiii, pp. 47–8; *Ex. e Rot. Fin.* (Rec. Com.), i. 71–2.
97 *Ex. e Rot. Fin.* i. 271–2.
98 *Liber de Bernewelle*, 257.
99 *Ex. e Rot. Fin.* ii. 485; *Cal. Inq. p.m.* i, p. 223.
1 *Rot. Selecti* (Rec. Com.), 254; cf. *Close R.* 1268–72, 98–9.
2 *Cal. Inq. p.m.* iii, pp. 409–10.
3 Ibid. iv, pp. 116–17; vii, p. 452; viii, p. 399; x, pp. 159–60; xii, p. 240; cf. Dugdale, *Baronage*, i. 771; Copinger, *Suffolk Manors*, i. 257, 274–5, 333, which wrongly inserts an extra William, d. 1307.
4 *Feud. Aids*, i. 142; cf. *Liber de Bernewelle*, 156–7.
5 C.P. 25(1)/26/49 no. 2.
6 C.P. 25(1)/27/60 no. 1.
7 *Cal. Inq. p.m.* vii, p. 452; *Cal. Close*, 1333–7, 443.
8 C.P. 40/348 rot. 311; cf. *E.D.R.* (1890), 392.
9 *Feud. Aids*, i. 158.
10 *E.D.R.* (1893), 30, 107, 120, giving 'Joan' as 'John'.
11 *Cal. Inq. p.m.* xiii, p. 154; cf. *E.D.R.* (1895), 19.
12 Cf. *Cal. Close*, 1392–6, 420.
13 Ibid. 1396–9, 223–4.
14 Ibid. 1413–19, 216.
15 *Feud. Aids*, vi. 216.
16 Prob. 11/2B (P.C.C. 31 Marche).
17 C.P. 25(1)/30/95 no. 9.
18 e.g. *Cal. Close*, 1452–61, 210–11; *Cal. Pat.* 1461–7, 521; C 142/32 no. 32; C 142/74 no. 16.
19 C.P. 25(2)/55/398 no. 15.

to Sir Stephen Soame,[20] lord mayor of London 1598–9, upon whose adjoining estate at Little Thurlow (Suff.) it depended until the 20th century.[21] Sir Stephen died in 1620 leaving Little Carlton, charged with paying £60 a year to his alms-house and school at Little Thurlow,[22] to his son William,[23] later knighted, who transferred Little Carlton and Little Thurlow in his lifetime to his son Stephen (d. 1659). Stephen devised them, subject to a life-interest for his father, to his son William,[24] created a baronet in 1685, who died in 1686. He left his lands to his uncle Bartholomew Soame,[25] who sold most of the Little Carlton demesne to various farmers and the manorial rights to William Wilkes, lord in 1704. John Abbot was named as lord in 1716.[26] The estate was afterwards recovered either by Stephen Soame (d. 1727), son of Bartholomew's brother John, or by Stephen's son Stephen,[27] who probably possessed it by 1734.[28] He died in 1764, devising Thurlow and Carlton to his elder son Henry, a clergyman until 1771.[29] Henry Soame died in 1813, having entailed the family estates on Gen. Charles Stevenson,[30] apparently the illegitimate son of Henry's younger brother Stephen Soame (d. 1771). On the general's death without lawful issue in 1828[31] the estate passed under Henry's will to a distant relative from Tobago, Stephen Jenyns Soame, who died the same year. S. J. Soame's son and heir John Frith Soame sold the western part of the Carlton property, Cocksedge farm, to John Hall of Weston Colville, and died in 1833, leaving the remainder, Lophams farm, to his mother Elizabeth Soame for life, then to his sisters Elizabeth Poole Soame and Catherine Maria Soame.[32] Mrs. Soame died probably after 1855.[33] Catherine died probably between 1874 and 1887, Elizabeth in 1889, both unmarried. The estate passed to a distant relation by marriage, Roger Bulwer Jenyns of Bottisham, who sold it *c.* 1900 to C. F. Ryder, a Leeds brewer. Ryder acquired *c.* 1920 200 a. of Church farm,[34] and died in 1942. In 1943 Lophams farm, then covering 395 a., was sold with his Thurlow lands to Mr. R. A. Vestey, who still owned it in the 1970s.[35]

Little Carlton manor-house presumably stood within the oval moat, 300 ft. across and up to 12 ft. deep, south-east of the church, by which Lophams farm-house stands.[36] The farm-house derives from a 15th-century house where Sir Thomas Fynderne probably,[37] and his son Sir William certainly, sometimes dwelt. In Sir William's time it included a chapel and parlour and was surrounded by gardens and a park,[38] the latter probably covering 78 a.[39] That house, timber-framed and comprising a hall and two cross-wings, was remodelled, probably after 1582, for use as a farm-house, one wing being demolished and the other curtailed, and additions were made on the north side in the 17th century.[40] In 1975 it was empty and under threat of demolition.[41]

In 1203 Herbert de Alençon (d. after 1238) held at Carlton, apparently in right of his wife Margaret, land[42] which was probably attached to the 1⅓ fee which he held *c.* 1236 at Swaffham Prior of the Scalers barony.[43] The yardland held at Carlton in 1086 by Wihomarc of Count Alan[44] presumably passed with Weston Moynes manor.[45]

In 1227 Henry III granted to the Knights Templars his wood at Carlton called the king's wood, kept by Roger Leverer.[46] The Templars later attached it to their manor, depending on Wilbraham preceptory, at Little Thurlow. In the king's hands from 1307, pending their suppression, it was leased from 1312 to Sir John Botetourt.[47] By 1338 it had been transferred to the Hospitallers, who then owned *c.* 180 a. in Carlton.[48] Following their dissolution in 1540 that estate, called *CARLTON AND THURLOW* manor, was sold in 1541 to Thomas Barnardiston[49] (d. by 1553). Thomas's son Sir Thomas sold 86 a. at Carlton to Sir Stephen Soame in 1594, and died in 1619. Sir Thomas's grandson and heir Sir Nathaniel Barnardiston sold the remaining 70 a. south of Lophams wood in 1626 to his brother-in-law William Soame,[50] with whose land in Little Carlton they descended thenceforth. In 1943 71 a. in Carlton were still attached to Temple End farm in Little Thurlow.[51]

In 1434 Richard Gatward owned 110 a. at Willingham,[52] which by 1452 had been acquired, as *GATWARDS* manor, by Sir Thomas Fynderne.[53] In 1516 Sir William Fynderne held it, supposedly of William Stutville, lord of Brinkley.[54] It passed with his Weston estates until 1618 when Richard Lennard, Lord Dacre, sold Gatwards farm of *c.* 85 a. to Sir Stephen Soame.[55]

ECONOMIC HISTORY. On the 12¾ ploughlands in 1086, including 7 in Great Carlton, 4 in Willingham,

[20] Essex R.O., D/DL T 19 no. 4.
[21] Cf. Copinger, *Suffolk Manors*, v. 297–9.
[22] *22nd Rep. Com. Char.* H.C. 139, pp. 198–9 (1830), xii; Char. Com. files (Little Thurlow).
[23] Wards 7/62 no. 19.
[24] Prob. 11/287 (P.C.C. 52 Pell).
[25] G.E.C. *Baronetage*, iv. 136–7; Prob. 11/385 (P.C.C. 171 Lloyd).
[26] C.R.O., R 50/19/1, ct. rolls 1704, 1716.
[27] Copinger, *Suffolk Manors*, v. 298; Prob. 11/620 (P.C.C. 63 Brook).
[28] C.R.O., L 89/6, ct. roll 1734; cf. B.L. Add. MS. 5808, f. 55.
[29] Prob. 11/905 (P.C.C. 33–4 Rushworth); B.L. Add. MS. 5808, f. 54v.; *Alum. Cantab. 1752–1900*, v. 587.
[30] Prob. 11/1544 (P.C.C. 221 Heathfield).
[31] Prob. 11/970 (P.C.C. 358 Trevor); Prob. 11/1745 (P.C.C. 504 Sutton).
[32] C.R.O., L 43/4, pp. 366–9, 382–8.
[33] Cf. *White's Dir. Suff.* (1855), 213.
[34] C.R.O., 334/08; Char. Com. files (Little Thurlow).
[35] B.L. Maps 135.a.64; Char. Com. files; cf. *Camb. Evening News*, 5 Mar. 1975.
[36] *V.C.H. Cambs.* ii. 20.
[37] Cf. *Cal. Fine R.* 1454–61, 175.
[38] Prob. 11/18 (P.C.C. 36 Holder).
[39] C.U.L., MS. Plan 550R.
[40] Ex inf. R.C.H.M., Cambs.
[41] *Camb. Evening News*, 5 Mar. 1975.
[42] *Feet of Fines* (Rec. Com.), 292–3; cf. *Cal. Pat.* 1232–47, 223.
[43] *Liber de Bernewelle*, 262–3.
[44] *V.C.H. Cambs.* i. 379.
[45] See pp. 184–5.
[46] *Cal. Chart. R.* 1226–57, 24; cf. *Rot. Hund.* (Rec. Com.), i. 52.
[47] E 358/20 rot. 7; E 358/19 rot. 32d.
[48] *Hospitallers in Eng.* (Camd. Soc. [1st ser.], lxv), 163.
[49] S.C. 6/Hen. VIII/2402 rot. 18; *L. & P. Hen. VIII*, xvi, p. 385.
[50] Copinger, *Suffolk Manors*, v. 258–9; Wards 7/62 no. 14; C.P. 25(2)/94/858/36 Eliz. I Trin. no. 12; C.P. 25(2)/400/2 Chas. I Trin. no. 9; cf. C.U.L., MS. Plan 550R.
[51] B.L. Maps 135. a. 6.
[52] C.P. 25(1)/30/97 no. 14.
[53] C 131/71/3; *Cal. Pat.* 1461–7, 77.
[54] C 142/32 no. 32.
[55] Essex R.O., D/DL T 19 no. 4.

and 1¾ in Little Carlton, there were 7¼ demesne plough-teams, while only 4 belonged to the 23 tenants, all but 6 of whom were bordars. No peasants were recorded at Little Carlton, which perhaps lay already mostly in demesne. The reported values of the manors, altogether £13 5*s.*, had not changed since 1066.[56]

The south-east part of the parish saw much clearing of woodland before 1200; the felling of Willingham wood had by then produced a 'cultura' of 60 a.[57] Although the fields thus created bore such names as Monkcroft and Woodcroft and had common boundary hedges, they contained the land of several men undivided by hedge or ditch,[58] and the assarted woodland was subject to rights of common. A grant of land there between 1225 and 1250 included pasture for cattle, pigs, and unlimited sheep wherever the grantor's own beasts could feed.[59] In the early 13th century Lewes priory bought up much freehold land in those crofts, obtaining releases of common rights and consent to its inclosing and ditching the land acquired.[60] It was consequently able to turn most of the eastern quarter of the parish into several demesne land,[61] covering *c.* 250 a.[62] South of that land lay the anciently inclosed demesne of Little Carlton manor,[63] covering in 1612 *c.* 295 a., apart from woodland.[64] North-west of Carlton Green lay some small open fields:[65] beyond the church and Pilcroft (*c.* 70 a. held in severalty by 1767) lay Carlton Crofts[66] (*c.* 35 a.); across the Stour Little Low[67] and Brook fields[68] (together *c.* 146 a.), and north of Willingham Green Kimwell,[69] later Kimmadge, and Mill fields[70] (together *c.* 35 a.) adjoining Brinkley. The names of Little Low, Kimmadge, and Mill fields matched those of adjacent larger fields in that parish,[71] suggesting that the boundary cut through what had once been an agrarian unit. Scattered among those small fields and closes were various common greens. The largest, Little Carlton Green, covered 17 a. in 1612[72] and *c.* 19 a. in 1800, when Willingham Green amounted to 6 a. One green by the southern boundary was still in 1767 intercommonable with Weston. The main open field lay to the north-west, stretching for 2 miles from Willingham Green to the lord's heath, which was held in severalty by 1767 when it covered *c.* 140 a. The great field covered almost 800 a. Although land in it was said to lie in various 'wents',[73] it contained no larger subdivisions for cultivation. It was variously styled Willingham common field,[74] Willingham Out field,[75] Carlton Out field,[76] the Heath field,[77] or the outer shift,[78] suggesting that it was not originally included in the regular rotation. In 1767 its south-eastern third was apparently reckoned to belong particularly to Willingham,[79] but the whole field was owned, cultivated, and pastured by men from the whole parish indifferently. A triennial rotation was followed in the 1790s on the inclosed Norney farm,[80] and perhaps therefore on the open fields.

Lewes priory had apparently farmed out its whole manor before 1200,[81] at a time when its free tenants were also granting long leases of their property.[82] In 1340 340 a. in Carlton, Willingham, and Brinkley were said to lie uncultivated through the impotence of the tenants.[83] On the small Temple estate the demesne, comprising in 1338 144 a. of arable and 34 a. of grass,[84] was in hand in 1307. Some 40 a. was sown each year, mainly with wheat and oats. The wheat was sold, or used with pease for liveries to the hired servants, including 2 ploughmen, the oats to feed the plough-beasts, including 3 horses and 5 oxen. A flock of *c.* 60 sheep fed also on neighbouring Temple estates. Except for ploughing-works, possibly commuted, no labour-services were recorded.[85] In 1540 the estate was on a 40-year lease to Thomas Chicheley.[86] Of the other manors, Great Carlton had *c.* 23 tenants, probably mostly copyholders, in 1642,[87] and Lophams perhaps 16 tenants in 1655,[88] whose land lay not near its demesne but in the centre of the parish.[89] At inclosure in 1800 *c.* 130 a. were allotted for copyhold of Great Carlton manor, but only 3½ a. for that of Lophams.[90]

In 1086 there were 400 sheep in two flocks at Great Carlton and Willingham.[91] A flock of 80 sheep was stolen at Little Carlton in 1344.[92] In 1447 over 1,000 fleeces were sold from the Fynderne manor there.[93] In 1625 the tenants of Lophams were ordered not to put sheep on the commons except between 1 November and 10 April, and the 7 men entitled to keep 20 cattle there were forbidden to let their stints to outsiders.[94] In the 18th century the lord of Great Carlton and his farmers were said to have the sole right of sheep-walk over the commons, but others were entitled to put cattle without stint on to the stubble after harvest, and their sheep also from 1 November.[95] In 1751 owners at Willingham might put 1 bullock for each house on Brook field.[96]

Sir William Fynderne probably had land at Little Carlton in hand at his death in 1516, for he had his

[56] *V.C.H. Cambs.* i. 405–6.
[57] *Lewes Chartulary, Cambs.* 7.
[58] e.g. ibid. 3–5, 10, 21–2, 28.
[59] Ibid. 5, 27.
[60] e.g. ibid. 3, 6–7.
[61] Ibid. *passim.*
[62] C.R.O., R 54/21/1.
[63] *Lewes Chartulary, Cambs.* 14.
[64] C.U.L., MS. Plan 550R.
[65] Layout based on C.R.O., R 54/21/1 (1767); areas calculated from C.R.O., Q/RDz 1, pp. 181–255 (1800).
[66] C.U.L., E.D.R., H 1/2, glebe terrier 1615.
[67] Ibid. 1639.
[68] C.R.O., R 55/31/5/1 (1568).
[69] C.R.O., L 89/1, ct. roll 1642.
[70] C.R.O., R 50/19/1, ct. roll 1625.
[71] See p. 138.
[72] C.U.L., MS. Plan 550R.
[73] Possibly named from adjacent field-ways: C.U.L., E.D.R., H 1/2, terrier 1615; cf. C.R.O., L 89/2, ct. rolls 1666, 1669.
[74] C.U.L., E.D.R., H 1/2, terriers 1615, 1639.
[75] C.R.O., R 55/31/5/1 (1698).
[76] Ibid. L 70/41 (1719).
[77] Ibid. R 54/21/1.
[78] Ibid. L 43/4, pp. 5–6 (1770).
[79] Ibid. R 54/21/1, note by N. bdry.
[80] Ibid. L 70/31.
[81] *Lewes Chartulary, Cambs.* 11–12.
[82] e.g. ibid. 4; *Bracton's Note Bk.* ed. Maitland, ii, pp. 510–11.
[83] *Inq. Non.* (Rec. Com.), 272.
[84] *Hospitallers in Eng.* (Camd. Soc. [1st ser.], lxv), 163.
[85] E 358/20 rott. 7, 9d.; E 358/19 rot. 32d.
[86] S.C. 6/Hen. VIII/2402 rot. 18.
[87] C.R.O., L 89/1, ct. roll 1642.
[88] Ibid. R 50/19/1, ct. roll 1655.
[89] Ibid. ct. rolls 1625, 1655.
[90] Ibid. Q/RDz 1, pp. 181–255; L 70/42.
[91] *V.C.H. Cambs.* i. 405.
[92] *Cal. Close,* 1343–6, 271.
[93] *Cat. Anct. D.* i, C 1675.
[94] C.R.O., R 50/19/1, ct. rolls 1625, 1655.
[95] Ibid. L 89/14.
[96] Ibid. L 89/13, mins. 1751.

own corn and cattle there.[97] In the 1530s the Great Carlton demesne was farmed by Gilbert Claydon, who had succeeded his father as both lessee and bailiff. He sub-let most of the arable, reserving for himself 160 a. of inclosed pasture. Both his father and he allegedly inclosed commons without licence, converted arable to pasture, and assimilated their copyhold to their freehold land. In 1541 Sir Thomas Elyot, whose purchase Claydon had tried to obstruct, turned him out.[98] By the 1590s Lophams farm, covering *c.* 200 a., was on lease to Margaret Elrington (d. 1626), grandmother of Sir Giles Alington (d. 1638). Other farms belonging to Lophams manor covered *c.* 170 a.[99] The Lennards substantially increased their rents after 1608, raising that of Lophams farm from £20 *c.* 1595 to £100 by 1618 and the total rental from £53 to almost £178.[1] About 1700 Bartholomew Soame sold from the Lophams estate two farms covering 150 a. of arable and 66 a. of pasture and heath,[2] but the estate had been reunited by 1800.[3]

By 1767 the Brand estate covered half the parish. Its 1,235 a. comprised, besides 162½ a. of wood and 137 a. of heath, 141½ a. of inclosed arable and 337 a. of inclosed pasture, with *c.* 462 a. of open field, including *c.* 320 a. in the large north-western field. It was divided among three larger farms, each with an equal share, *c.* 150 a., of open-field land, and three smaller ones, Norney farm of 125 a. being entirely inclosed. The principal farmsteads all stood among the eastern inclosures.[4] Wick Farm, recorded by 1639,[5] standing at the west end of Willingham Green, had 183 a., Church Farm 339 a., and Hall Farm *c.* 228 a. There were also *c.* 68 a. in neighbouring parishes.[6] At inclosure in 1800 Thomas Brand bought an estate including 150 a. of copyhold, of which 92 a. had passed by inheritance from the Lawsells, tenants *c.* 1730, to the Long family of Brinkley.[7] He also bought in 1801 30 a. once belonging to the Symonds family.[8] In 1833 Lord Dacre acquired *c.* 35 a. belonging at inclosure to the Frost family.[9]

An inclosure Act was obtained in 1799,[10] and the open fields had been divided and the award executed by May 1800.[11] The area involved did not include the former Weston Brook field, inclosed with Weston Colville in 1777, nor that half of Norney farm belonging to Brinkley.[12] Apart from *c.* 180 a. of woodland there were *c.* 943 a. of ancient inclosures of which Thomas Brand owned 446 a. and Henry Soame 412 a. Except for the rector's 28 a. of inclosed glebe, none of the other 19 owners had more than 10 a. of inclosures, most only 1 a. or less.[13] Of 1,055 a. of open fields and commons Thomas Brand was allotted 875 a.,[14] Soame only 4 a. Five other landowners with 12 a. or more shared *c.* 105 a., and *c.* 20 smallholders 55 a.[15]

The inclosure was at first followed by prosperity, rents rising from 6*s.* to 16*s.* an acre by 1806, and even the cottagers could profitably plough their 2-a. allotments.[16] Thomas Brand, having obtained the whole north-western field, built there a new farmstead called Carlton Grange, let in 1802 with 780 a. The first lessee, the Revd. N. C. Lane,[17] installed a flour-mill and a threshing-machine drawn by six horses, and *c.* 1806 was following a rotation of turnips, barley, tares, and barley again. In 1814 he left behind 131 a. of wheat, 208 a. of barley, 85 a. of oats, and 364 a. of grass and fallow.[18] The next lessee, John Frost, took the farm at twice the previous rent and was bankrupt by 1817.[19] The lessee of Hall farm (206 a.) owed in 1823 five years' rent.[20] By the 1830s a regular four-course rotation was followed on the Brand estate farms.[21] The number of sheep on those farms increased after inclosure from 400 to 500.[22] Five shepherds were working at Carlton in the 1860s.[23]

In 1851[24] the five large tenant-farms included *c.* 2,530 a., while three smaller farmers occupied only 48 a. Carlton Grange farm, occupied from 1817[25] until *c.* 1875 by the Nash family, covered *c.* 830 a. in 1851, but only 590 a. in 1912, having been separated from Crick's farm (237 a.) to the south-east. Both were kept in hand from 1904 until the 1930s. Hall farm (*c.* 238 a. in 1871) was leased from the 1820s to 1912 to the Nice family, and Church farm (1,040 a. in 1851) south of it was let from 1810 to William Long, with whose descendants its lease remained until C. L. Long bought 300 a. of it in 1920. Lophams farm, enlarged from 308 a. in 1871 to 395 a. by 1942, was let between 1880 and 1900 with Church farm, and subsequently managed by a farm-bailiff for C. F. Ryder.[26] Cocksedge farm covered 95 a. when bought by John Hall in 1830,[27] and 192 a. in 1912. Only *c.* 80 a. of the 1,120 a. then belonging to the Six Mile Bottom estate in Carlton was kept as permanent grass.

A brick-kiln mentioned in 1734 and 1770[28] was probably that which gave its name to Brick-kiln field near the southern boundary.[29] The village had

[97] Prob. 11/18 (P.C.C. 36 Holder).
[98] Sta. Cha. 2/10/37; cf. *L. & P. Hen. VIII*, xiii (1), p. 99.
[99] Essex R.O., D/DL E 64/1; cf. C.U.L., MS. Plan 550R; Prob. 11/152 (P.C.C. 102 Skynner).
[1] Essex R.O., D/DL E 64/1, T 19.
[2] C.R.O., R 50/19/1, ct. roll 1704.
[3] Cf. C.R.O., Q/RDz 1, pp. 283–6.
[4] C.R.O., R 54/21/1.
[5] C.U.L., E.D.R., H 1/2, terrier 1639.
[6] C.R.O., R 54/21/1.
[7] Ibid. L 43/4, pp. 16–19, 92–8, 119–24, 135–8, 155–8, 187–9; cf. ibid. Q/RDz 1, pp. 192–7.
[8] Ibid. L 43/4, pp. 164–7; cf. ibid. Q/RDz 1, pp. 181 *bis*–186 *bis*, 200.
[9] Ibid. L 43/4, pp. 229–42, 344–7; ibid. Q/RDz 1, pp. 194 *bis*–198 *ter*.
[10] *C.J.* liv. 133, 567–8, 676; Carlton cum Willingham Incl. Act, 35 Geo. III, c. 39 (Private, not printed).
[11] C.R.O., Q/RDz 1, pp. 105–291, paginated thus: 105–19, 181–200, 181–198 *bis*, 197–8 *ter*, 199–200 *bis*, 201–91.
[12] Ibid. R 60/24/2/12.
[13] Ibid. Q/RDz 1, pp. 251–85.
[14] Ibid. pp. 106, 119, 181–200, 181 *bis*–186 *bis*.
[15] Ibid. pp. 186 *bis*–250.
[16] Gooch, *Agric. of Cambs.* 35, 71.
[17] C.R.O., L 70/35; cf. *Alum. Cantab. 1752–1900*, iv. 89.
[18] Gooch, *Agric. of Cambs.* 50, 102; cf. C.R.O., L 70/36.
[19] C.R.O., L 70/24–5.
[20] Ibid. 34, 38.
[21] Ibid. 39.
[22] Gooch, *Agric. of Cambs.* 71.
[23] R.G. 9/1030; R.G. 10/1593.
[24] Paragraph based on *Gardner's Dir. Cambs.* (1851); *Kelly's Dir. Cambs.* (1858–1937); C.R.O., 334/08; B.L. Maps 135. a. 6; H.O. 107/1761; R.G. 10/1593.
[25] Cf. C.R.O., L 70/35.
[26] B.L. Maps 135. a. 64.
[27] C.R.O., L 43/4, pp. 384–8.
[28] Ibid. pp. 1–2.
[29] Ibid. Q/RDz 1, pp. 281–2.

few craftsmen, only 5 families being dependent on crafts or trade in 1811 and 8 in 1831.[30] In 1861 there were only two shoemakers, a wheelwright, and a carpenter,[31] and hardly any trades were recorded later. About 1830 there were 88 farm-labourers.[32] In 1851, when there were *c.* 80 adult labourers living at Carlton, the larger farms provided work for 111 men and 25 boys.[33] In 1871 three men were employed driving agricultural engines.[34] Except for a few farmers the whole population was said in 1897 to be farm-labourers.[35] In 1961 the only local work was on the farms, and others went to work in neighbouring towns.[36]

Mill field was presumably named after the mill near by in Brinkley. A mill conveyed with Great Carlton manor in the late 17th and 18th centuries[37] may be connected with the smock-mill attached to one farm in 1778.[38] No mill was recorded at Carlton after 1815.

LOCAL GOVERNMENT. In 1299 the prior of Lewes successfully claimed by prescription view of frankpledge, the assize of bread and of ale, and infangthief, and to be quit of suit to the county and hundred.[39] About 1540 Sir Thomas Elyot was still holding three-weekly courts baron for Great Carlton manor,[40] whose annual session in the 17th century was styled a view of frankpledge and court baron. After 1650 the recorded business was almost all concerned with copyhold transfers.[41] The court still occasionally elected constables,[42] and a pinder as late as 1740,[43] and it repeated regulations on common rights in 1751.[44] Court rolls survive, with gaps, for 1639–1766, followed by a court book for 1770–1834.[45] The court baron of Lophams manor passed and enforced rules on common rights and chose a hayward *c.* 1625, and renewed the by-laws in 1664. Court rolls survive for 1625–8, 1655, 1664, 1704, and 1716.[46]

In the late 16th and early 17th centuries the constables, churchwardens, and chief inhabitants were sometimes appointed to manage legacies for the poor.[47] In 1788 the overseers occupied half a cottage,[48] perhaps the old poorhouse.[49] The cost of poor-relief, *c.* £100 a year in the 1770s and 1780s, had doubled by 1803, when 20 people received regular payments, and again by 1813,[50] seldom thereafter falling much below £400 and occasionally, as in 1826, exceeding £500.[51] About 1830 up to ten labourers were paid from the poor-rate for work on the roads, and others were distributed among the farmers proportionately to the size of farms.[52] Although in 1832 £184, almost half the expenditure, went to widows, children, the old, and the sick, £57 was paid to paupers employed by the parish.[53] From 1835 Carlton was included in the Linton poor-law union,[54] and as part of the Linton R.D. was in 1934 incorporated in the South Cambridgeshire R.D.,[55] being included in South Cambridgeshire in 1974.

CHURCH. Carlton church was probably included in William de Warenne's endowment of Lewes priory,[56] to which Archbishop Ralph confirmed it in 1121.[57] It was possibly lost before *c.* 1200, when Fulk son of William released to Lewes all his inherited claims to Carlton church and advowson.[58] The priory usually presented rectors from *c.* 1225[59] until the early 15th century,[60] although in 1346 John, earl of Surrey, was named as patron,[61] and in 1349–50 Sir Walter and John de Crek, lessees of Carlton manor, presented.[62] In 1442, 1443, and 1445 Sir William Fynderne presented,[63] and in 1489 his grandson Sir William, claiming the Weston Colville advowson, may have obstructed presentation by the priory to Carlton, for the bishop then collated to it.[64] In 1492 Lewes leased the advowson of Carlton rectory to Sir William and his son William for their lives.[65] After the Dissolution the advowson was sold with the priory's manor to Sir Thomas Elyot,[66] and passed with it to the Stewkleys and their successors[67] until the early 19th century. The lords granted turns to present to Henry Goldsmith, who presented a kinsman in 1591,[68] to Dr. Richard Palmer, patron in 1619,[69] and to Thomas Clarke who presented himself or a namesake in 1772.[70] Between 1810 and 1830 the advowson was acquired by trustees for W. S. P. Wilder, who presented himself in 1832[71] and died in 1863. It remained until the 1950s with trustees for his family,[72] who several times appointed Wilder's kinsmen, such as Thomas Wilder Sewell,

[30] *Census*, 1811, 1831.
[31] R.G. 9/1030.
[32] *Rep. H.L. Cttee. on Poor Laws*, H.C. 227, pp. 328–9 (1831), viii.
[33] H.O. 107/1761.
[34] R.G. 10/1593.
[35] C.U.L., E.D.R., C 3/36.
[36] *Camb. Ind. Press*, 17 Nov. 1961.
[37] e.g. C.P. 25(2)/633/27–8 Chas. II Hil. no. 8; C.P. 43/752 rot. 48.
[38] *Camb. Chron.* 6 Jan. 1781.
[39] *Plac. de Quo Warr.* (Rec. Com.), 101.
[40] Sta. Cha. 2/10/37 answer.
[41] C.R.O., L 89/1–2; cf. C 142/222 no. 2.
[42] e.g. C.R.O., L 89/1, ct. rolls 1641–2; L 89/2, ct. roll 1671.
[43] e.g. ibid. L 89/6, ct. roll 1740.
[44] Ibid. L 89/13, mins. 1751.
[45] Ibid. L 89/1–8; L 43/4; also L 89/9–13, mins. 1649–1787.
[46] C.R.O., R 50/19/1.
[47] e.g. Prob. 11/69 (P.C.C. 60 Windsor, will of John Dobido); Prob. 11/152 (P.C.C. 102 Skynner, will of Marg. Elrington).
[48] C.R.O., L 43/4, p. 114.
[49] *Camb. Ind. Press*, 17 Nov. 1961.
[50] *Poor Law Abstract, 1804*, 38–9; *1818*, 30–1.
[51] *Poor Rate Returns, 1816–21*, 11; *1822–4*, 38; *1825–9*, 16; *1830–4*, 16.
[52] *Rep. H.L. Cttee. on Poor Laws*, H.C. 227, pp. 328–9 (1831), viii.
[53] *Rep. Com. Poor Laws* [44], p. 257, H.C. (1834), xxviii.
[54] *Poor Law Com. 1st Rep.* 249.
[55] *Census*, 1931 (pt. ii).
[56] Cf. *Lewes Chartulary*, i (Suss. Rec. Soc. xxxviii), 22.
[57] *Ancient Chart.* (Pipe R. Soc. x), p. 13.
[58] *Lewes Chartulary, Cambs.* 1.
[59] Ibid. 28.
[60] e.g. *E.D.R.* (1894), 329; (1898), 159.
[61] Ibid. (1892), 774.
[62] Ibid. (1893), 14, 43, 107; cf. *Cal. Pat.* 1345–8, 163.
[63] C.U.L., E.D.R., L 3/1, ff. 8, 25v.; *E.D.R.* (1904), 51.
[64] *E.D.R.* (1908), 133.
[65] *E.D.R.* (1909), 47; cf. B.L. Add. MS. 5820, f. 98v.
[66] *L. & P. Hen. VIII*, xiii (1), p. 99; xv, p. 172.
[67] e.g. C.P. 25(2)/68/557 no. 2; C 142/222 no. 2; C.P. 25(2)/633/27–8 Chas. II Hil. no. 8; C.P. 25(2)/1000/7 Geo. I Hil. no. 10; C.P. 43/752 rot. 48.
[68] Gibbons, *Ely Episc. Rec.* 485.
[69] P.R.O. Inst. Bks. ser. A, iii, p. 33.
[70] Ibid. ser. C, i (2), f. 441; cf. *Alum. Cantab. to 1751*, i. 347; *1752–1900*, ii. 55.
[71] *Rep. Com. Eccl. Revenues*, pp. 346–7; cf. C.U.L., E.D.R., C 3/21.
[72] *Gardner's Dir. Cambs.* (1851); *Kelly's Dir. Cambs.* (1858–1937); *Crockford* (1896–1952).

rector 1863–9, John Trafalgar Wilder, rector 1869–81, and P. H. E. Wilder, rector 1935–43.[73] From 1953 Carlton was combined with Burrough Green and Brinkley under a single incumbent; its patron, from 1965 Mr. R. A. Vestey, was entitled to present at every third turn.[74]

Before 1095 Walter de Grandcourt, lord of Willingham, gave Willingham church with its endowment of 1 yardland with his manor to Lewes priory,[75] which thenceforth possessed the church and its advowson. Rectors of Willingham, recorded from 1254,[76] were presented by the priory or its nominees, the last recorded presentation being in 1406.[77] Probably between 1428 and 1445[78] the two benefices were united; in 1487 Willingham church was served by an impoverished chaplain.[79] In 1489 a rector was collated to the living of Carlton with Willingham.[80] About 1540 the advowson was described as that of Carlton church with Willingham chapel annexed,[81] and rectors were thenceforth presented for a single parish.

William de Warenne's grant to Lewes priory included the tithe of his demesne at Carlton.[82] In 1225 the priory recovered from the rector the tithe of former Warenne demesne land, thereupon leasing it to him for 6*s.* a year.[83] In 1254 the priory had portions of 4 marks from Willingham and 2 marks from Carlton church,[84] not recorded after 1340.[85] Later it retained a tithe portion from the Little Carlton demesne, possibly granted by Richard de Scalers.[86] About 1225 it vindicated against the rector its right to tithes worth £2 a year from William de Criketot's demesne,[87] and *c.* 1500 was supposedly entitled to two sheaves to the rector's three from 90 a. of that demesne.[88] In practice it received a portion of 1 mark called Barbedors, which, with a pension of 14*s.* 4*d.*, remained annexed to Great Carlton manor[89] until 1800. The payments were then extinguished in return for a small reduction in the tithe-rent-charge on Carlton Hall farm.[90] The rector of Brinkley also exchanged his tithe from 48 a. in Carlton for that from 22 a. in Brinkley, previously tithing to Carlton, and a rent-charge of £7 5*s.*[91]

In 1615 the rector of Carlton's glebe comprised 25 a. of closes, including the 2 a. of Willingham chapel yard, and 28 a. of open-field land.[92] He was allotted *c.* 3 a. for glebe and *c.* 12 a. for tithes arising in Weston Colville at its inclosure in 1778,[93] and *c.* 13 a. for glebe when Carlton was inclosed in 1800.[94] His glebe amounted in 1887 to 35½ a.,[95] which he retained in 1975.[96] The tithes of Carlton were commuted at inclosure for a rent-charge of £256.[97]

Carlton rectory was taxed at 12 marks gross *c.* 1217, 20 in 1276, and 15 in 1291. Willingham was at those dates worth only 7½, 10, and 9 marks,[98] and because his income was low the rector was dispensed in 1263 to hold another cure of souls.[99] The united living was assessed at £9 in 1535,[1] and was worth £95 in 1650,[2] £140 by 1750,[3] and £287 net *c.* 1830.[4]

The rectory stood in 1615 just south of the church, in the northern corner of an 11-a. close with a 7-a. grove attached.[5] In 1750 it was surrounded by a moat,[6] of which one side survives and in which a rector was drowned in 1832.[7] Thomas Clarke, rector 1772–93, had by 1783 extensively rebuilt the old and irregular house,[8] which remained in use until *c.* 1930.[9] From 1937 the property was used as dog-kennels.[10]

Sir William Fynderne (d. 1516) provided in his will for a friar from Cambridge to assist the rector at Christmas, Easter, and Whitsun, presumably for confessions and communions, and left 25*s.* a year for masses in Willingham church every other day so long as the law allowed.[11]

Rectors were recorded at Carlton from the 1220s, including a cardinal's nephew *c.* 1225[12] and possibly a pluralist chancellor of the Exchequer *c.* 1306.[13] In 1337 the rector was absent, serving the prior of Lewes.[14] A new rector, thrice admonished to reside in 1375, resigned after three years. A chaplain was then serving in the church.[15] Another rector was licensed in 1408 to farm out the church during a three-year absence.[16] Andrew Natures, rector 1523–46, presumably related to Edmund Natures, executor of Sir William Fynderne, was a pluralist, in 1539 serving the earl of Westmorland.[17] In 1543 the church was served by a curate paid by Andrew's

73 *Alum. Cantab. 1752–1900*, v. 468; vi. 467.
74 *Crockford* (1965–6, 1973–4).
75 *Lewes Chartulary*, i (Suss. Rec. Soc. xxxviii), 18.
76 *Lewes Chartulary, Cambs.* 10; cf. *Vetus Liber Arch. Elien.* (C.A.S. 8vo ser. xlviii), 60–1.
77 e.g. *E.D.R.* (1892), 677; (1893), 14; (1897), 173; (1898), 126, 218.
78 *Feud. Aids*, i. 193; *E.D.R.* (1902), 122.
79 *E.D.R.* (1909), 128.
80 Ibid. (1908), 133.
81 *L. & P. Hen. VIII*, xiii (1), p. 99.
82 Cf. *Lewes Chartulary*, i (Suss. Rec. Soc. xxxviii), 16, 22.
83 *Lewes Chartulary, Cambs.* 12–14.
84 *Val. of Norwich*, ed. Lunt, 215; cf. *Tax. Eccl.* (Rec. Com.), 267.
85 *Inq. Non.* (Rec. Com.), 272; cf. *E.D.R.* (1891), 603; (1893), 164.
86 Cf. *Cal. Doc. France*, ed. Round, p. 512.
87 *Lewes Chartulary, Cambs.* 14–15.
88 Ibid. 14.
89 e.g. *L. & P. Hen. VIII*, xiii (1), p. 99; C.P. 25(2)/68/559 no. 2; C.P. 25(2)/386/9 Jas. I Trin. no. 3.
90 C.R.O., Q/RDz 1, pp. 254–5.
91 Ibid. pp. 250–4.
92 C.U.L., E.D.R., H 1/2, terriers 1615, 1639.
93 C.R.O., Q/RDz 1, pp. 335–6.
94 Ibid. pp. 187 *bis*–188 *bis*.
95 *Glebe Returns*, H.C. 307, p. 37 (1887), lxiv.
96 Ex inf. Messrs. Jolliffe, Andrews, & Ashwell, estate agents.
97 C.R.O., Q/RDz 1, pp. 256–89; Carlton cum Willingham Incl. Act, 39 Geo. III c. 39 (Private, not printed), pp. 8–12.
98 *Val. of Norwich*, ed. Lunt, 535, 554; *Tax. Eccl.* (Rec. Com.), 267.
99 *Cal. Papal Reg.* i. 388.
1 *Valor Eccl.* (Rec. Com.), iii. 504.
2 Lamb. Pal. MS. 904, f. 266.
3 Palmer, *Wm. Cole*, 89.
4 *Rep. Com. Eccl. Revenues*, pp. 346–7.
5 C.U.L., E.D.R., H 1/2, terrier 1615; cf. C.R.O. R 54/21/1.
6 Palmer, *Wm. Cole*, 89.
7 *Alum. Cantab. 1752–1900*, i. 310, s.v. Boldero.
8 C.U.L., E.D.R., B 7/1, pp. 4–5.
9 e.g. ibid. C 1/6; C 3/36; *Crockford* (1926).
10 *Kelly's Dir. Cambs.* (1937).
11 Prob. 11/18 (P.C.C. 36 Holder).
12 *Lewes Chartulary, Cambs.* 13–15, 28.
13 *Cal. Papal Reg.* ii. 4.
14 *E.D.R.* (1889), 344.
15 B.L. Add. MS. 5842, ff. 15, 37; cf. *E.D.R.* (1894), 339; (1895), 109.
16 *E.D.R.* (1901), 75.
17 Ibid. (1911), 70; *Faculty Office Reg. 1534–49*, ed. D. S. Chambers (1966), 196; *L. & P. Hen. VIII*, xxi (2), p. 158.

lessee.[18] Robert Kent, rector from 1561 until deprived in 1569,[19] perhaps later joined the Catholic Douai mission.[20] James Fludd, rector from 1610, was succeeded in 1619 by his brother-in-law Thomas Greek,[21] some of whose parishioners neglected the thrice-yearly communion in 1638.[22] Greek retained the living until his death in 1649.[23] His successor, Robert Sendall, son of the rector of Brinkley, was described in 1650 as an able, preaching minister,[24] and conformed after 1660, being formally presented in 1662.[25]

William Stewkley, rector 1679–1711, unrelated to the former patrons, held Carlton from 1693 in plurality with a Suffolk living, and, like his predecessor, employed a curate from the 1680s. He was briefly succeeded by his son John, rector 1711–15.[26] James Salt, rector from 1720 until he succeeded to Hildersham rectory in 1736,[27] lived at Chesterton in 1728, employing a neighbouring clergyman to perform services at Carlton twice every Sunday. There were then *c.* 20 communicants.[28] The next rector, Allen Cooper, an antiquary, also held Warboys (Hunts.), where he lived, employing the rector of Brinkley's son as curate at Carlton.[29] Thomas Clarke was resident in 1775, holding one service every Sunday, as did William Boldero, rector 1805–32, in 1807. Boldero, who usually spent half the year at his other living of Woodford (Essex), also employed a curate. There were then few communicants,[30] and only up to 16 in 1825. Many parishioners from Willingham then resorted to Brinkley and Weston Colville churches, which were nearer their homes.[31] W. S. P. Wilder from 1835 also held Great Bradley (Suff.), whose advowson also belonged to his family.[32] He was resident at Carlton in 1836, and had *c.* 20 communicants.[33] In 1851 he held two services every Sunday, and claimed an afternoon attendance of 130, besides 20 Sunday-school children.[34] In the 1890s many, after going to church, attended dissenting meetings in the evening.[35] Carlton was again held with Great Bradley from 1935 to 1952.[36]

The church of *ST. PETER*,[37] built of field stones with stone and brick dressings, comprises only a chancel and nave with south porch. The thick nave walls are probably 12th-century, part of a window reveal of that period surviving. Spirally carved shafts re-used as window-mullions may come from a Norman doorway. In the nave the south doorway and two south windows, one flat-headed with curvilinear tracery, are 14th-century. New north and west windows were inserted in the nave in the 15th century, when also a crown-post roof was built over the nave, the chancel arch and two-bay chancel were rebuilt, perhaps on a wider scale than before, and a new font was procured. The timber-framed south porch, originally 17th-century, has been much reconstructed. A 15th-century rood-screen, still in place in 1750,[38] has been re-used to form a vestry in the nave. The long communion table and the pulpit, with arcaded panelling, are early-17th-century. A brass of Sir Thomas Elyot, buried at Carlton in 1546, disappeared after 1640.[39]

The church was said to be ruinous in 1549,[40] and has had substantial buttresses added to the side-walls. There were three bells in 1552, 1750, and 1783,[41] housed, probably by 1644,[42] in a bellcot above the west gable.[43] In 1783 it was ruinous, and the rector proposed to remove it.[44] When the church was restored in 1885, with F. J. Smith as architect,[45] the west wall was entirely rebuilt, and a stone Gothic bellcot erected above it, containing as in 1975 two bells.[46] Both had black-letter inscriptions to the Virgin, and were probably cast at Bury St. Edmunds *c.* 1500.[47]

The chapel at Willingham, probably of *ALL SAINTS*,[48] stood at the west end of the green, and probably consisted only of a nave and chancel.[49] It was possibly still in use in 1552, when two chalices, perhaps for two churches, were left for the parish.[50] Sir James Dyer (d. 1582) converted it temporarily into an alms-house, providing in his will for the almsfolks' maintenance.[51] Only at the west end did the walls survive to any height in 1750;[52] the ruins were removed between 1807 and 1851.[53]

Sir William Fynderne bequeathed in 1516 to Carlton church a gilt chalice from his domestic chapel.[54] The parish has a cup and paten acquired for the town of Willingham cum Carlton in 1569, a cup and paten of 1732, and a beaker of 1798.[55] The registers, surviving as fragments for 1588-90, 1610–17, and 1711–15, are continuous only from 1726.[56]

[18] *E.D.R.* (1912), 184.
[19] C.U.L., E.D.R., B 2/3, p. 101; *E.D.R.* (1914), 327.
[20] *Alum. Cantab. to 1751*, iii. 9.
[21] Ibid. ii. 255; Gibbons, *Ely Episc. Rec.* 278–9.
[22] *Cambs. Village Doc.* 59.
[23] *Walker Revised*, ed. Matthews, 80.
[24] Lamb. Pal. MS. 904, f. 266.
[25] Cf. *Episc. Visit. Cambs. 1638–65*, 105–6; P.R.O. Inst. Bks. ser. B, i, p. 62.
[26] *Alum. Cantab. to 1751*, iv. 179; C.U.L., E.D.R., B 2/67.
[27] *Alum. Cantab. to 1751*, iv. 9.
[28] C.U.L., E.D.R., B 8/1.
[29] *Alum. Cantab. to 1751*, i. 389; Palmer, *Wm. Cole*, 89.
[30] *Alum. Cantab. 1752–1900*, i. 310; ii. 55; C.U.L., E.D.R., C 1/1, 4; B 8/4, f. 5.
[31] C.U.L., E.D.R., C 1/6.
[32] *Alum. Cantab. 1752–1900*, vi. 467; cf. *Crockford* (1896).
[33] C.U.L., E.D.R., C 3/21.
[34] H.O. 129/188/3/6/6.
[35] C.U.L., E.D.R., C 3/36.
[36] *Crockford* (1935–52).
[37] Cf. Ecton, *Thesaurus* (1763), 99. In 1516 there was an image of St. Peter: Prob. 11/18 (P.C.C. 36 Holder).
[38] B.L. Add. MS. 5820, f. 89.
[39] Cf. Prob. 11/37 (P.C.C. 14 Allen); *Mon. Inscr. Cambs.* 222.
[40] C.U.L., E.D.R., B 2/3, p. 78.
[41] *Cambs. Ch. Goods, temp. Edw. VI*, 73; Palmer, *Wm. Cole*, 89; C.U.L., E.D.R., B 7/1, pp. 4–5.
[42] *Trans. C.H.A.S.* iii. 90.
[43] B.L. Add. MS. 5820, ff. 88v.–89; cf. C.U.L., E.D.R., B 2/159A, f. 19v.
[44] C.U.L., E.D.R., B 7/1, pp. 4–5.
[45] *Proc. C.A.S.* xxxv. 82.
[46] Cf. *Kelly's Dir. Cambs.* (1883).
[47] MS. notes by H. B. Walters (1936), *penes V.C.H.*
[48] B.L. Add. MS. 5861, f. 75. The supposed dedication to St. Matthew (e.g. Ecton, *Thesaurus* (1763), 99) apparently arose from a misinterpretation of early-16th-century wills (e.g. B.L. Add. MS. 5861, ff. 25v., 66, 76, 80) which relate to Willingham in Papworth hundred.
[49] Drawing in C.R.O., R 54/21/1.
[50] *Cambs. Ch. Goods, temp. Edw. VI*, 73.
[51] Prob. 11/64 (P.C.C. 78 Tyrwhite).
[52] B.L. Add. MS. 5820, ff. 98v.–99.
[53] Lysons, *Cambs.* 160; *Gardner's Dir. Cambs.* (1851).
[54] Prob. 11/18 (P.C.C. 36 Holder).
[55] List of ch. plate *penes V.C.H.*
[56] C.R.O., par. reg. TS.; cf. C.U.L., E.D.R., C 1/6.

NONCONFORMITY. Only one family of dissenters at Carlton was recorded in 1728,[57] and one, of Presbyterians, in 1825.[58] In 1830 Thomas Hopkins, the Independent minister at Linton, registered for worship a building, probably the Independent chapel at Willingham Green, later said to have been built in 1825. It could hold 120 people in 1851, when a minister held services there on Sunday afternoons.[59] It was not recorded later. In 1848 a Weston Colville grocer registered at Carlton for the Primitive Methodists a building which in 1851 had 50 seats and standing room for 170 more. The preacher from Saffron Walden, who acted as steward, then claimed an average attendance of 120, sometimes rising to over 160.[60] The Primitive Methodist chapel may have closed by 1879,[61] although chapel services, of an unspecified denomination, were still occasionally held in a room in the parish in 1897.[62] In 1888 a man from West Wickham opened a Salvation Army hall near Carlton Green.[63] In 1897 it was attracting many people, including some church-goers,[64] but by 1923 the building was disused.[65]

EDUCATION. Although schoolmasters were licensed at Carlton *c.* 1580 and in 1617,[66] the parish had no regular school before 1800.[67] In 1818 there was one day-school with 14 pupils,[68] possibly closed by 1825.[69] In 1824 William Wright left *c.* £105, received in 1829, and yielding £3 13*s.* 6*d.* a year, to support six children at school.[70] In 1833 the money was being paid to a day-school, with 20 pupils, which was connected with the Sunday school with 40 pupils, started in 1833 and supported by the rector, Lord Dacre, and his farmers. The 22 children at two other day-schools were paid for by their parents.[71] In 1846 the Sunday school, held in the church, had *c.* 45 pupils. The Wright bequest, worth £4 a year, was then used by the rector to pay half the salary of the mistress of a dame-school with 12 pupils. It had a schoolroom and adjoining teacher's house,[72] owned by the parish, probably those still standing at the road junction at Carlton Green. In 1876 the school, by then a National school, was receiving £25 a year from a voluntary rate which continued to be paid until the 1890s, and had 42 pupils, usually taught by one mistress.[73] Attendance did not rise above the 45 recorded in 1888,[74] and after 1900 was usually just over 30,[75] falling by 1922 to 26 and, following reorganization after 1927, to 14.[76] The school was closed in 1933, the children thenceforth attending Weston Colville and Brinkley schools.[77] Wright's charity, then yielding £2 12*s.* 6*d.* a year, thus lost its object, and £71 had been accumulated by 1975 when a Scheme to benefit the village children was proposed.[78]

CHARITIES FOR THE POOR. John Dobido by will proved 1586 left £5, the interest to be distributed to the poor in Lent.[79] Margaret Elrington by will proved 1627 left £10 for doles to six poor widows on Good Friday.[80] Nothing more is known of either bequest.

Edward Briggs by will proved 1735 left 10*s.* a year charged on a house near Carlton Green for the poor. It was being paid in the 1780s, and after an interruption between *c.* 1815 and 1834 was recovered and in 1837 was being added to money subscribed for the poor at Christmas.[81] In the 20th century it was sometimes uncertain which property was charged, but the income was still being received in the 1960s and was given to one woman in 1969.[82]

DULLINGHAM

THE PARISH of Dullingham,[1] covering 3,387 a.,[2] lies 10 miles east of Cambridge and 3 south of Newmarket. It stretches, narrowing gradually south-eastwards, from north-west of the Cambridge–Newmarket road to the Suffolk boundary. The boundaries of the south-eastern part, running between ancient closes, are irregular and somewhat indented. The north-eastern boundary, dividing former open fields, is straighter. At inclosure in 1806, it was futher straightened as far south-east as the road to Stetchworth, 48 a. being ceded to Stetchworth under exchanges with landowners there. On the south-west boundary a 50-acre square ceded to the lord and rector of Burrough Green was transferred to that parish.[3]

The soil of the parish lies on the chalk, overlaid south-east of the village by boulder clay. The ground rises gradually from *c.* 150 ft. near the north-west

[57] C.U.L., E.D.R., B 8/1.
[58] Ibid. C 1/6.
[59] G.R.O. Worship Returns, Ely dioc. no. 542; H.O. 129/188/3/6/8.
[60] G.R.O. Worship Returns, Ely dioc. nos. 696, 728; H.O. 129/188/3/6/8; cf. H.O. 129/188/2/4/9.
[61] Cf. *Kelly's Dir. Cambs.* (1858–79).
[62] C.U.L., E.D.R., C 3/36.
[63] G.R.O. Worship Reg. no. 30836.
[64] C.U.L., E.D.R., C 3/36.
[65] G.R.O. Worship Reg. no. 35040.
[66] Gibbons, *Ely Episc. Rec.* 180, 184; C.U.L., E.D.R., B 2/36, f. 36v.
[67] Cf. C.U.L., E.D.R., B 8/1; C 1/4.
[68] *Educ. of Poor Digest*, 56.
[69] Cf. C.U.L., E.D.R., C 1/6.
[70] *31st Rep. Com. Char.* 133.
[71] *Educ. Enquiry Abstract*, 52; C.U.L., E.D.R., C 3/21.
[72] *Church School Inquiry, 1846–7*, 2–3.
[73] Ed. 7/5; C.U.L., E.D.R., C 3/36; cf. *Kelly's Dir. Cambs.* (1879 and later edns.).
[74] *Rep. of Educ. Cttee. of Council, 1888–9* [C. 5804-I], p. 531, H.C. (1889), xxix.
[75] e.g. *Schs. in receipt of Parl. Grants, 1900–1* [Cd. 703], p. 14, H.C. (1901), lv; *Bd. of Educ., List 21, 1914* (H.M.S.O.), 26.
[76] *Bd. of Educ., List 21, 1922* (H.M.S.O.), 15; *1932*, 16.
[77] Ibid. *1934*, 15; Black, *Cambs. Educ. Rec.* 51.
[78] Char. Com. files.
[79] Prob. 11/69 (P.C.C. 60 Windsor).
[80] Prob. 11/152 (P.C.C. 102 Skynner); cf. Essex R.O., D/DL E 64/1, f. 4v.
[81] *Char. Don.* i. 94–5; *31st Rep. Com. Char.* 133.
[82] Char. Com. files.
[1] This account was written in 1976.
[2] *Census*, 1961.
[3] C.R.O., Q/RDz 6, pp. 305–7, 310–11.

end to over 275 ft. north-west of the railway line, which shares a narrow valley at 200 ft. with a watercourse running north-east into Stetchworth. That streamlet drains a depression which rises south-eastward between two ridges, from 250 to 300 ft., and in which the village stands. Beyond its head the ground rises to over 360 ft. at Dullingham Ley, and again to over 350 ft. at the wooded south-east end of the parish.

Since the Middle Ages Dullingham has been devoted mainly to agriculture. The north-west part, except for heathland at the extremity, lay until inclosure mainly in open fields cultivated on a triennial rotation, and the south-eastern third consisted mostly of old inclosures, presumably created through clearing woodland. A wood at Dullingham was mentioned *c.* 975[4] and the main manor included in 1086 woodland for 100 pigs.[5] Its two moieties comprised *c.* 1305 140 a. of wood[6] and in 1421 360 a.[7] A grove mentioned in 1348 consisted mainly of oaks and ashes.[8] Two of the manor's principal woods, Dullingham Park recorded in 1311[9] and Ashbeds, covered in 1582 84 a. and 55 a.,[10] and at inclosure in 1806 83 a. and 52 a. They were also then, as later, called Great and Little Widgham woods.[11] The manor included another great wood, covering *c.* 1656 76 a. and also called Dullingham Park in 1644, when it was leased for felling over 8 years.[12] That was probably the parkland opposite Dullingham House, of which 38 a. remaining at inclosure[13] were still well timbered in 1976. The two Widgham woods, offered for sale in 1950,[14] were leased from 1956 to the Forestry Commission, which planted them largely with conifers, preserving a little beech.[15] White wood, established before inclosure on the north-western heath, covered 40 a. in 1898,[16] but was later reduced.

The name of Dullingham suggests that the village was an early English settlement, perhaps deriving from East Anglia.[17] In 1086 46 peasants and 4 *servi* were enumerated there,[18] and in 1347 73 tenants.[19] In 1377 115 adults paid the poll tax.[20] There were 38 taxpayers in 1524[21] and 51 households in 1563.[22] In 1676 257 adults were recorded,[23] and 86 families included 378 members in 1728.[24] The population rose from 468 in 1801 to 684 in 1831 and 809 in 1851. From a peak of 835 in 1881 it declined to *c.* 765 after 1900 and 597 in 1931, falling further to 523 in 1951 and 501 by 1971.[25]

The village stands in the middle of the parish. A road south from Newmarket towards Linton divides at the north-east boundary into two branches, which on the south-west side are linked to form a triangle by the village street, called by 1380 Stone Street[26] and from 1600 Stony Street.[27] The largest group of dwellings was around the junction with the eastern road, where stood the church, rectory, old vicarage, guildhall, dissenting chapel, and main public house. It was separated by a gap, perhaps effected to give Dullingham House a view south across the road into its park, from a smaller group near the western junction. By 1626, and probably by 1605, a smaller settlement had grown up 1 mile to the south-east around the common green called Dullingham Ley.[28] The way to it met the road south from Stetchworth village at Cross Green, perhaps named from a former market cross mentioned in 1754.[29] Under Charles II the parish contained *c.* 90 dwellings,[30] and in 1801 there were 83.[31] Two or three tall, narrow farmhouses of the 17th and 18th centuries still survive on the western part of the street, and the village contains some timber-framed and thatched cottages of that period. Many more cottages were built or remodelled in the early 19th century for the Jeaffreson estate, to which 37 belonged *c.* 1870.[32] Those are in picturesque style, the walls in brick with flint dressings, and the roofs thatched with deeply recessed dormers. Of the 54 houses recorded at inclosure in 1806 33 were in the village and 14 at Dullingham Ley. A separate farmstead, later Lordship Farm, already stood on the lord's several heath,[33] and soon afterwards another, later Hill House, was built in the former western fields. Otherwise the parish continued to be cultivated from farmsteads in the old settled areas. The number of houses grew to 147 in 1841, and 181 in 1861,[34] of which *c.* 95 were on the village street and lanes running off it, *c.* 40 at Dullingham Ley, 13 at Cross Green, and 7 at Widgham Green, near the wood in the extreme south-east.[35] Thereafter the built-up area hardly changed for 100 years, there being still 173 houses in 1951.[36] After 1951 a row of council houses was built north of Cross Green, and in the 1970s the Dullingham estate put up several houses in bright red brick near the main cross-roads.

The largest house away from the village was at Lower Hare Park, on the heathland between the Cambridge and London roads. Shortly before 1800 a training groom put up the first buildings there, later selling his lease from the Jeaffreson estate to Richard, Earl Grosvenor (d. 1802), a great racing man, who lodged there when visiting his Newmarket stud. Robert, the second earl, enlarged the place into a handsome house, where he lived during Newmarket meetings.[37] The lease passed after 1826 to Wyndham B. Portman, who lived there from *c.* 1840 until his death in 1884 and was active in parish business.[38] In 1898 the lease of the house with 120 a.

4 *Liber Elien.* (Camd. 3rd ser. xcii), p. 95.
5 *V.C.H. Cambs.* i. 371.
6 C 133/111/17 no. 3; C 134/2/19 no. 5.
7 C 138/58/43 no. 5.
8 C.R.O., 604/T 5.
9 *Cal. Inq. p.m.* vi, p. 195.
10 C.U.L., Doc. 3967, rot. 9d.
11 C.R.O., Q/RDc 14, incl. map and schedule.
12 C.U.L., Doc. 1429; C.R.O., R 58/10/18.
13 C.R.O., Q/RDc 14.
14 Ibid. 515/SP 204.
15 Ex inf. the Forestry Commission.
16 C.R.O., Q/RDc 14; ibid. R 49/3/7.
17 Cf. E. Ekwall, *Eng. Place-Names in -ing* (2nd edn.), 159–69.
18 *V.C.H. Cambs.* i. 404–5.
19 E 179/242/8 m. 7.
20 *East Anglian*, N.S. xii. 240.
21 E 179/81/134 m. 7d.
22 B.L. Harl. MS. 594, f. 199v.
23 Compton Census.
24 C.U.L., E.D.R., B 8/1.
25 *Census*, 1801–1971.
26 C.R.O., 604/T 16.
27 Prob. 11/101 (P.C.C. 16 Bolein, will of Wm. Leader).
28 C.R.O., 101/T 332, 334; cf. C.U.L., Doc. 885.
29 C.R.O., 101/T 341.
30 See pp. 279, 281.
31 *Census*, 1801.
32 C.R.O., L 89/113.
33 Ibid. Q/RDc 14.
34 *Census*, 1841–61.
35 R.G. 9/1031.
36 *Census*, 1881–1951.
37 B.L. Add. MS. 9413, f. 288; Lysons, *Cambs.* 181; cf. *Complete Peerage*, vi. 209–10.
38 H.O. 107/71; R.G. 10/1594; cf. Char. Com. files; C.R.O., L 80/111.

was acquired by Ernest de la Rue, later K.C.V.O. He designed electric starting gates and papier-mâché surgical splints and boots, whose manufacture at Dullingham he organized during the First World War. After his death in 1929[39] the house was left empty and eventually demolished, only outbuildings surviving in 1976.[40] The nearby Lordship farm, whose northern corner adjoined the old Newmarket Round Course, was occupied between 1879 and 1892 by the royal trainer, Richard Marsh, and later until the 1920s by Joseph Cannon, another trainer.[41] It was laid out in training gallops and paddocks, and was still attached in 1976 to the Egerton stud in Stetchworth. Dullingham had a resident horse-slaughterer from 1912, and a veterinary surgeon in the 1930s.[42]

The ground occupied by those properties had previously been part of Dullingham heath, over which ran a branch of the Icknield Way, later part of the London–Newmarket road. Travellers were waylaid there and murdered in 1350,[43] and in 1358 a Dullingham landowner was accused of harbouring robbers operating on Newmarket Heath.[44] The road, which was connected with the village by field-ways called in the 18th century Cambridge and Swaffham ways,[45] was turnpiked in 1724, and disturnpiked in 1871.[46] In 1846 the Newmarket–Chesterford railway began to build across the parish a line which was opened in 1848 and connected with Cambridge in 1851, when Dullingham had its own station.[47] The station, closed for goods traffic from 1964,[48] was still open for passengers in 1976.

The King's Head, the oldest public house in the parish, in use as an alehouse by 1728 and so named by 1746, is basically a 17th-century house, standing in the north-east angle of the eastern cross-roads.[49] It belonged to the parish charity until 1931,[50] and was still open in 1976. Four other beer-sellers recorded in 1851[51] probably included the Rising Sun at Dullingham Ley, closed by 1958, the Royal Oak on Stony Street, closed in 1975, and the Boot, mentioned in 1861, and still open in 1976, on the village green.[52] That green, south-east of the eastern cross-roads, covered 2 a. and was once the Camping close, used as a playground for the village youth. It belonged to the town by 1558, and was vested in the parish charity until 1931, when it was transferred to the parish council to be preserved as an open space.[53] A rent-charge of £2 a year on land owned by the parish in 1590 was used every other year, when the parish bounds were beaten, to pay for a ganging feast last held in 1832.[54] Another village feast was held at Whitsun in the 1970s.[55] In 1945 members of the Taylor family bought the former Oddfellows' hall, built near the church *c.* 1925, and gave it, as the Sidney Taylor Hall, for use as a village hall.[56]

MANORS AND OTHER ESTATES. Before 1066 6 hides at Dullingham belonged to Earl Alfgar. By 1086 that manor, later *DULLINGHAM* manor, had been granted to the Norman abbey of St. Wandrille (Seine Maritime) which held it of the king in free alms.[57] Perhaps under Henry I the manor passed, apparently by exchange, to the Somerset baron Robert Malet[58] (fl. 1130–51),[59] whose heirs later held it under the abbey free of all feudal service.[60] In the 14th century they were said to hold in free socage, rendering a nominal rent,[61] although in 1344 a jury was induced to present that Dullingham was held in chief as ¼ knight's fee.[62] In 1421 the manor was said to be held of William de la Pole, earl of Suffolk, possibly overlord of Scalers manor in Dullingham, with which there was perhaps confusion.[63]

Robert Malet's son William, steward to Henry II, held Dullingham in 1162[64] and died in 1169, leaving as heir his son Gilbert (d. 1194).[65] William had given Dullingham as dower to Ralph Picot's daughter Eugenia, whose sister Alice married Gilbert and who had herself by 1174 married Thomas son of Bernard.[66] After Thomas died in 1185[67] Eugenia held the manor under Gilbert[68] until her own death soon after 1200.[69] By 1210 it had reverted to Gilbert's son William[70] who died in rebellion in 1215, leaving daughters as coheirs.[71] Dullingham had been settled for life on William's wife Alice.[72] By 1223 she had married John Bisset,[73] who held the manor *c.* 1236 and died in 1241.[74] Alice retained it until her own death *c.* 1263,[75] after which it was equally

[39] C.R.O., R 49/3/7; *Who Was Who, 1929–40*, 349–50.
[40] Cf. *Kelly's Dir. Cambs.* (1929–37).
[41] Ibid. (1879–1925); R. Marsh, *Trainer to Two Kings* (1925), 92–3.
[42] *Kelly's Dir. Cambs.* (1912–37).
[43] *Cambs. Village Doc.* 86.
[44] C 258/13 no. 27.
[45] Clare Coll. Mun., map 1798.
[46] Stump Cross Turnpike Act, 10 Geo. I, c. 12; Annual Turnpike Acts Continuance Act, 33–4 Vic. c. 73. For the Cambridge–Newmarket turnpike, see p. 171.
[47] *Proc. C.A.S.* xxxv. 4–5; *V.C.H. Cambs.* ii. 132–3; cf. H.O. 107/1762; *Kelly's Dir. Cambs.* (1858).
[48] Clinker & Firth, *Reg. Closed Passenger Stations, 1830–1970* (1971).
[49] C.U.L., E.D.R., B 8/1; *31st Rep. Com. Char.* 133–4.
[50] Char. Com. files.
[51] *Gardner's Dir. Cambs.* (1851).
[52] H.O. 107/1762; R.G. 9/1031; C.R.O., L 80/111; ibid. 296/SP 1214; *Newmarket Jnl.* 21 Jan. 1975.
[53] B.L. Add. MS. 9412, f. 286v.; *31st Rep. Com. Char.* 134; Char. Com. files.
[54] *Char. Don.* i. 94–5; *31st Rep. Com. Char.* 134–7.
[55] *Camb. Ind. Press*, 24 Sept. 1965; *Newmarket Jnl.* 15 Jan. 1976.
[56] Char. Com. files.
[57] *V.C.H. Cambs.* i. 371; cf. *Cal. Inq. p.m.* ii, pp. 326–7.
[58] Cf. Dugdale, *Mon.* v. 143; *Cal. Inq. p.m.* ii, p. 22.
[59] *Reg. Regum Anglo-Norm.* iii, pp. 34, 100, 348; *Pipe R.* 1130 (H.M.S.O. facsimile), 5. To be distinguished from Rob. Malet, lord of Eye (Suff.): Sanders, *Eng. Baronies*, 43.
[60] e.g. *Red Bk. Exch.* (Rolls Ser.), ii. 530; *Cal. Inq. p.m.* iv, pp. 128–9.
[61] e.g. *Cal. Inq. p.m.* vii, pp. 320, 459.
[62] Ibid. p. 323.
[63] C 138/58/43 no. 6.
[64] *Pipe R.* 1162 (P.R.S. v), 48; 1167 (P.R.S. xi), 200.
[65] Ibid. 1169 (P.R.S. xiii), 160; 1170 (P.R.S. xv), 156; 1194 (P.R.S. N.S. v), 202.
[66] *Rot. de Dom.* (Pipe R. Soc. xxxv), 87; cf. *Pipe R.* 1176 (P.R.S. xxv), 207; *Rot. Cur. Reg.* (Rec. Com.), i. 389.
[67] *Pipe R.* 1185 (P.R.S. xxxiv), 106.
[68] *Rot. de Dom.* 87.
[69] Cf. *Cur. Reg. R.* i. 352.
[70] *Red Bk. Exch.* (Rolls Ser.), ii. 530; *Cur. Reg. R.* v. 62; vi. 87–8.
[71] *Rot. Litt. Pat.* (Rec. Com.), 138, 161; *Cur. Reg. R.* ix. 5.
[72] Cf. *Rot. Litt. Claus.* (Rec. Com.), i. 235.
[73] *Cur. Reg. R.* xi, pp. 44, 50.
[74] *Liber de Bernewelle*, 258; *Ex. e Rot. Fin.* (Rec. Com.), i. 353.
[75] *Close R.* 1251–3, 458; *Cal. Pat.* 1258–66, 260; *Ex. e Rot. Fin.* ii. 431.

divided between the heirs of William Malet's daughters Mabel and Helewise.

Mabel had by 1223 married Hugh de Vivonne, a Poitevin mercenary captain[76] (d. 1249). Their son William de Forz[77] (d. 1259) left four daughters as coheirs. A moiety of Dullingham was assigned to Cecily, the youngest, born *c.* 1257[78] and married by 1273 to John de Beauchamp (d. 1283), lord of Hatch Beauchamp (Som.).[79] Cecily granted the moiety, later *BEAUCHAMPS HALL*,[80] in 1288 to her younger son Robert.[81] When Robert died without issue in 1303 the moiety reverted to Cecily,[82] descending on her death, probably in 1320, to her elder son John[83] (d. 1337). It passed successively to John's son John (d. 1343) and grandson John Beauchamp,[84] of age in 1351, on whose death without issue in 1361 it was assigned to his deceased sister Eleanor's son John Meriet as coheir.[85] Shortly after coming of age in 1368 Meriet sold the moiety to Sir Aubrey de Vere,[86] who later reunited the manor by acquiring the other moiety, called *POYNTZ HALL*.

That moiety had been assigned *c.* 1265 to Nicholas Poyntz,[87] son of Helewise Malet by Hugh Poyntz (d. 1220), another Somerset landowner.[88] In 1264 and 1265 Nicholas's manor was seized and plundered by Montfortian rebels.[89] Before his death in 1273 Nicholas granted it to his eldest son Hugh[90] who by 1279 had granted it for life to Sir Henry Cockington. In 1291 Cockington returned it to Hugh[91] who died in 1308 and was succeeded by his son Nicholas.[92] The same year Nicholas (d. 1311) granted it in fee at rent to John Knight, a London merchant, but Nicholas's son and heir Hugh[93] held it in demesne at his death in 1337. Hugh's son Nicholas, of age in 1340,[94] granted the moiety, subject to a yearly rent, to his younger brother Hugh, and in 1349 sold his reversionary interest to John Wiltshire.[95] In 1353 Wiltshire conveyed his rights to John Kimble,[96] to whom Hugh Poyntz released possession of the estate in 1355.[97] Probably *c.* 1374[98] Kimble sold it to Clement Spice and others, apparently feoffees for Sir Aubrey de Vere, to whom they released Poyntz Hall in 1381.[99]

Aubrey, for whom the earldom of Oxford was restored in 1392, died holding Dullingham in 1400.[1] In 1412 his feoffees settled the manor in tail male on his younger son John, later knighted. Sir John (d.s.p. 1421) left as heir male his nephew John, earl of Oxford, who was under age. Dullingham, however, was occupied by Lewis Johan, Sir John's feoffee and second husband of his sister Alice Court. Johan, who claimed under an alleged remainder to her in the 1412 settlement,[2] retained Dullingham until *c.* 1432, when Earl John claimed it, asserting that the remainder had been forged. The earl apparently recovered Dullingham before Johan's death in 1442.[3] After the earl's execution in 1462 Dullingham was briefly taken into the king's hands,[4] and after the forfeiture of the earl's son Earl John was granted in 1471 to Richard, duke of Gloucester.[5] In 1475 it was granted to John, Lord Howard, who returned it to the Crown *c.* 1477,[6] to be restored to the earl's younger brother, Sir Thomas Vere (d.s.p. 1478), lately disattainted.[7] Dullingham was finally restored to the earl in 1485.[8] When he died in 1513 he left it for life to Margaret (d. by 1536), widow of his brother Sir George, with remainder to her son John, his heir male.[9] When John died without issue in 1526 the reversion of Dullingham descended to his sisters, Elizabeth and Ursula, and John Neville, from 1543 Lord Latimer, son of a third sister Dorothy. Elizabeth (d. 1559) was wife of Sir Anthony Wingfield (d. 1552), councillor of Henry VIII, and Ursula of Edmund Knightley.[10] In 1541 Neville entered upon a third of the third previously held by Elizabeth, widow of Earl John (d. 1513).[11] After Ursula died without issue in 1559[12] her third share was divided between Elizabeth's son Sir Robert Wingfield and Lord Latimer, each thenceforth owning a moiety.[13] Latimer died in 1577. Under a partition of 1580, his four daughters and coheirs with their husbands ceded their moiety to Sir Robert Wingfield.[14] The eldest daughter Catherine (d. 1596), wife of Henry Percy, earl of Northumberland (d. 1585), reserved, however, the woods called Dullingham Park and Ashbeds. Her son Henry[15] sold them in 1609 to Edmund Mileson, owner of Dullingham rectory,[16] with which they were eventually reunited to the main manor.[17]

76 *Rot. Litt. Claus.* (Rec. Com.), i. 303; *Ex. e Rot. Fin.* i. 109; *Cur. Reg. R.* xiv, p. 452.
77 *Close R.* 1247–52, 309; *Ex. e Rot. Fin.* ii. 61.
78 *Ex. e Rot. Fin.* ii. 301; *Cal. Inq. p.m.* i, p. 298; cf. *Close R.* 1264–8, 41–2.
79 *Cal. Inq. p.m.* ii, pp. 326–7; *Cal. Close*, 1288–96, 432; cf. *Complete Peerage*, ii. 48–50.
80 Cf. *Cal. Pat.* 1385–9, 465–6.
81 C.P. 25(1)/26/43 no. 18.
82 *Cal. Inq. p.m.* iv, pp. 128–9.
83 Ibid. vi, pp. 163–4.
84 Ibid. viii, pp. 14–15, 319–20.
85 Ibid. ix, pp. 414–15; xi, pp. 22–4.
86 *Cal. Close*, 1364–8, 435, 491.
87 *Close R.* 1264–8, 41–2; cf. *Complete Peerage*, x. 671–6.
88 *Rot. Litt. Claus.* (Rec. Com.), i. 303, 429; *Ex. e Rot. Fin.* (Rec. Com.), i. 45; *Close R.* 1231–4, 169.
89 *Rot. Selecti* (Rec. Com.), 244–6; J. 1. 1/83 rot. 20.
90 *Cal. Inq. p.m.* ii, pp. 21–2.
91 S.C. 5/Cambs. Tower ser. no. 15 rot. 1; C.P. 25(1)/26/44 no. 1.
92 *Cal. Inq. p.m.* v, pp. 13–14.
93 Ibid. vi, pp. 194–5.
94 Ibid. viii, pp. 72–3, 459; *Cal. Close*, 1339–41, 555.
95 Dorset R.O., Weld MSS. T 372.
96 C.R.O., 604/T 7.
97 *Cal. Close*, 1354–60, 188.
98 Cf. ibid. 1374–7, 78.
99 C.R.O., 604/T 18; *Cal. Close*, 1385–9, 465–6.
1 *Complete Peerage*, x. 232–4; C 137/13/52 no. 34.
2 C.R.O., 604/T 35A–B; C 138/58/43 no. 6. On Lewis Johan or John, see Wedgwood, *Hist. Parl. 1439–1509, Biog.* 503.
3 *Proc. in Chanc. Eliz. I* (Rec. Com.), i, pp. xxvii–xxix; *Cal. Inq. p.m.* (Rec. Com.), iv. 216; C.R.O. 604/T 35–42 are duplicate and partly contradictory versions of the 1412 settlement and subsequent feoffments, one set presumably not authentic.
4 *Cal. Pat.* 1461–7, 179.
5 Ibid. 1467–76, 297.
6 Ibid. 538 (giving 'Polyngham'); 1476–85, 120; cf. Dugdale, *Baronage*, ii. 266.
7 *Rot. Parl.* vi. 176–7; C 145/327/1 no. 4; cf. *Cal. Pat.* 1467–76, 317–18, 418.
8 See p. 39.
9 C 142/28 no. 123; *L. & P. Hen. VIII*, xiv (1), p. 161.
10 C 142/45 no. 7; *L. & P. Hen. VIII*, iv (2), p. 2000; iv (3), p. 2676; *Statutes of Realm*, ii. 413–15. On Wingfield, see *L. & P. Hen. VIII*, xiv (1), p. 282; xv–xx, *passim*; on Neville, *Complete Peerage*, vii. 482–4.
11 *L. & P. Hen. VIII*, xvi, pp. 277–8.
12 Cf. *Complete Peerage*, iv. 484 n.
13 *Cal. Pat.* 1560–3, 116; C.P. 25(2)/259/4 Eliz. I East. no. 23.
14 C 142/246 no. 116; cf. *Complete Peerage*, vii. 485.
15 C 142/248 no. 22.
16 Wards 7/72 no. 41.
17 See below.

Sir Robert Wingfield died in 1596. His eldest son Sir Anthony[18] (d.s.p. 1605) settled Dullingham in 1602 on Thomas, his younger brother and eventual heir.[19] Sir Thomas died in 1610, leaving as heir a son Anthony, aged three. Dullingham was included in the jointure of Sir Thomas's widow Elizabeth, who hastily married Henry Reynolds, allegedly a papist fortune-hunter, who occupied her lands *c.* 1615.[20] Her son, created a baronet in 1627,[21] died in 1638. Sir Anthony's son and heir Richard, then aged 6,[22] sold his Dullingham estate in 1656 to John Jeaffreson,[23] a pioneer settler on St. Kitts in the West Indies.[24]

Jeaffreson died in 1660, leaving his lands to his son Christopher, aged 10, who prospered as a West India planter.[25] Dying without issue in 1725 Christopher left his estates to his cousin John's eldest son, another Christopher Jeaffreson, who, the will having been found invalid, bought out his father's claims in 1728.[26] Christopher, M.P. for Cambridge 1744–9,[27] died in 1749 and his son and successor Christopher in 1788.[28] The latter's only son, Lt.-Gen. Christopher Jeaffreson, died in 1824, leaving as heir his daughter Harriet,[29] who married William Pigott in 1827 and died in 1838.[30] Pigott occupied Dullingham House almost until his death in 1875 with his son by Harriet, Christopher William,[31] born in 1836. The latter took the name of Jeaffreson in 1839 and that of Robinson, under an inheritance from his maternal grandmother, in 1857.[32] In 1870 he married Mary Marianne Marianna, daughter of John Dunn-Gardner, who had married his sister Ada.[33] Mrs. Robinson held the Dullingham estate from her husband's death in 1889[34] until she died, aged 91, in 1939. The estate then descended to her half-brother A. C. W. Dunn-Gardner's daughter Miriam, Christopher's grand-niece and wife of Harvey Leader.[35] About 1947 Mrs. Leader sold the estate to F. B. Taylor (d. 1959), whose son Mr. P. B. Taylor was the owner in 1976.[36]

Dullingham House, standing a little north of the village street, is built in red brick, and consists of a three-bay centre and two-bay wings. In the centre is a bulky doorway with Corinthian columns supporting a broken pediment. The existing house was probably constructed by Christopher Jeaffreson (d. 1749)[37] although its plan suggests that it may encase an earlier building. A third storey above the original cornice was added early in the 19th century. About 1800 it was surrounded by *c.* 30 a. of grounds, including a stable block with a central arch and wooden cupola. After inclosure the grounds were enlarged northward with a 41-acre triangle of former open field,[38] and the park was landscaped by Humphrey Repton about 1800.[39] Further alterations were made to the garden front in the 19th century.

In 1086 Hardwin de Scalers occupied $1\frac{5}{6}$ hide at Dullingham, formerly owned by sixteen sokemen, eight of whom had been Earl Alfgar's men.[40] That estate, afterwards called *CHALERS*, was later held by a cadet line of Hardwin's family under the Scalers barons of Whaddon, descended from his son Hugh.[41] In 1208 Hugh's grandson Hugh (d. *c.* 1215) vindicated against his kinsman William, lord of Caxton, his lordship over certain knights' fees, including that at Dullingham,[42] which was held in 1242 of Hugh's son Geoffrey[43] and in 1302 and 1346 of Geoffrey's descendants Thomas (d. 1341) and Thomas Scalers (d. 1364).[44] Robert de Scalers, tenant in demesne in the early 12th century, was succeeded by his son Tibbald,[45] who held $1\frac{1}{6}$ fee in 1166.[46] About 1200 Tibbald and Baldwin de Scalers granted land from their Dullingham estates to Warden abbey (Beds.).[47] In 1209 Baldwin's widow Estrange, who still held 2 hides there *c.* 1236, and her second husband Gilbert son of Walter unsuccessfully called on Tibbald, apparently as Baldwin's kinsman and lord, to warrant them against Baldwin's daughters Mary and Gillian,[48] with whom Tibbald was disputing 60 a. there in 1214.[49] The lawsuit had descended, presumably with Tibbald's lands, by 1225 to John de Scalers,[50] who was tenant in 1242,[51] and probably the sheriff of that name in 1249, 1259, and 1264.[52] A namesake held the fee in 1272 and 1279,[53] and later gave it in marriage with his daughter Maud to Andrew de Mohun of Brinkley,[54] who held it in 1302. Andrew was dead by 1309, when Maud released it to their son Andrew[55] (fl. 1322).[56]

18 C 142/246 no. 116.

19 C.P. 25(2)/94/866/44 Eliz. I Trin. no. 2; Wards 7/92 no. 124; Wards 7/30 no. 50; Prob. 11/107 (P.C.C. 7 Stafford).

20 Wards 7/43 no. 64; C 2/Jas. I/D 8/32 *passim*.

21 G.E.C. *Baronetage*, ii. 17.

22 Wards 7/91 no. 314.

23 C.P. 25(2)/539/1656 Trin. no. 7.

24 Cf. J. C. Jeaffreson, *A Young Squire of the 17th Cent.* (London, 1878).

25 Prob. 11/300 (P.C.C. 174 Nabbs); mon. in ch.

26 Prob. 11/606 (P.C.C. 254 Romney); *31st Rep. Com. Char.* 137–8.

27 *Hist. Parl., Commons, 1715–54*, ii. 172.

28 Prob. 11/767 (P.C.C. 16 Lisle); C.R.O., L 80/105.

29 C.R.O., L 80/106.

30 Ibid. L 86/65A, pedigree in case for counsel, 1839.

31 *Alum. Cantab. 1752–1900*, v. 125; cf. H.O. 107/1762; R.G. 9/1031.

32 C.R.O., R 51/25/27A; cf. Burke, *Land. Gent.* (1871), 1176–7.

33 C.R.O., L 89/113; Burke, *Land. Gent.* (1906), i. 648.

34 C.R.O., R 49/37; *Kelly's Dir. Cambs.* (1892–1937).

35 Mon. in ch.; Char. Com. files.

36 *Camb. Ind. Press*, 15 Sept. 1961; 24 Sept. 1965; local information.

37 B.L. Add. MS. 5820, f. 86; the internal arrangement *c.* 1825 is given in C.R.O., L 80/108.

38 C.R.O., Q/RDz 6, p. 302; Q/RDc 14.

39 Dorothy Stroud, *Humphrey Repton* (1962), 123–4, 169; Repton Red Bk., *penes* Mrs. R. M. Taylor, Dullingham House. See above, plate facing p. 129.

40 *V.C.H. Cambs.* i. 384, 404.

41 e.g. *Red Bk. Exch.* (Rolls Ser.), i. 369–70. For the Scalers descent, see Sanders, *Eng. Baronies*, 30–1.

42 *Cur. Reg. R.* v. 139–40.

43 *Bk. of Fees*, ii. 924.

44 *Feud. Aids*, i. 142, 159; cf. *Cal. Inq. p.m.* viii, p. 221; xi, pp. 442–3.

45 Cf. Dugdale, *Mon.* v. 143, 150.

46 *Red Bk. Exch.* i. 369–70.

47 *Cart. Old Wardon* (Beds. Hist. Rec. Soc. xiii), pp. 175–7; cf. *Pipe R.* 1199 (P.R.S. N.S. x), 147.

48 *Pleas before King's Justices*, iv (Selden Soc. lxxxiv), p. 156; *Cur. Reg. R.* vi. 5–6; *Liber de Bernewelle*, 258; cf. *Cart. Old Wardon*, p. 176.

49 *Cur. Reg. R.* vii. 162, 222–3.

50 Ibid. xii, pp. 287, 441; xiii, p. 304.

51 *Bk. of Fees*, ii. 924.

52 *Proc. C.A.S.* xxv. 93.

53 C.P. 25(1)/25/34 no. 25; S.C. 5/Cambs. Tower ser. no. 15 rot. 1. To be distinguished from John de Scalers (d.s.p. 1303) holding that family's other lands: *Cal. Inq. p.m.* iv, p. 84.

54 C.R.O., 604/T 1.

55 Ibid. T 2; *Feud. Aids*, i. 142.

56 Clare Coll. Mun., deeds 6, 16 Edw. II.

That son or a namesake held the Scalers fee in 1346 and 1355,[57] and probably another Andrew in 1380.[58] In 1383 the latter's feoffees conveyed the manor called Chalers to Sir Aubrey de Vere, to whom John de Mohun, Andrew's kinsman and heir, released it in 1386.[59] Thereafter it descended with Dullingham manor, being held in 1428 by Sir Lewis Johan, and later by the Veres and their successors, along with 80 a.[60] once owned by the local family of Baas,[61] sold by Simon Burden to Sir Aubrey in 1367.[62] Warden abbey retained the Scalers lands given to it, with other acquisitions made *c.* 1200, and amounting in 1279 to 52 a.,[63] until it sold them shortly before 1390.[64]

Soon after 1040 Thurstan son of Wini left 1 hide at Dullingham to his *cniht* Wiking,[65] probably the Wichinz who held a hide there as Earl Harold's man in 1066. By 1086 that hide and two half-hide estates, one earlier held under Eddeva the fair, were held by two knights under Count Alan of Richmond.[66] *MADFREYS* manor, later held of the honor of Richmond,[67] was presumably derived from their holdings, and perhaps belonged *c.* 1125 to Ralph son of Mafred.[68] It was probably held in succession by Henry Matfrey or Madfrey (fl. *c.* 1200) and Ralph Madfrey,[69] tenant *c.* 1236 and alive in 1260.[70] Henry Madfrey, who held 80 a. in demesne of the honor of Richmond in 1279,[71] died in 1296.[72] About 1305 75 a. at Dullingham were acquired by John Madfrey of London.[73] A John Madfrey of Dullingham, recorded *c.* 1312,[74] had 30 a. there settled on him in 1329 and died after 1339.[75] Richard Madfrey (fl. 1327–53) held land there in 1344.[76] In 1375 his former lands were sold by John Bath to Thomas Sewale of West Wratting.[77] Land called Madfreys was sold to Sir Aubrey de Vere in 1367[78] but was not included in the Vere estate later. In 1525 an estate at Dullingham called Madfreys descended from Thomas Hildersham to his son John with Patmers manor in Stetchworth,[79] with which it was sold in 1573 to Roger, Lord North, afterwards descending with the main Stetchworth estate.[80] Madfreys was presumably represented by *c.* 180 a. of old inclosures south of Dullingham Ley, which with *c.* 210 a. allotted at inclosure belonged in the 19th century to the Eaton family, owners of Stetchworth, until its sale in 1876.[81]

Under King Edgar one Oslac pledged land at Dullingham to Ethelwold, bishop of Winchester, later surrendering it to the bishop's foundation at Ely, which *c.* 1000 also acquired land there attached to an estate at Stetchworth.[82] In 1279 12 a. at Dullingham were still held of the prior of Ely.[83]

The *RECTORY* estate, appropriated to the Cluniac priory of Thetford (Norf.), was held, with other land acquired before 1200, by the priory until its dissolution.[84] In 1540 all its lands passed by exchange from the Crown to Thomas Howard, duke of Norfolk,[85] between whose attainder in 1547 and restoration in 1553 the rectory was possessed by royal lessees.[86] In 1566 it belonged to his grandson and heir, Duke Thomas,[87] and after Thomas's execution in 1572 to his eldest son Philip, earl of Arundel, with William Dix, probably again returning to the Crown upon Philip's forfeiture in 1589.[88] In 1606 James I granted the rectory to Philip's younger brother Thomas, earl of Suffolk,[89] who in 1608 sold it to Edmund Mileson of Bury St. Edmunds (Suff.). Mileson died in 1623 leaving it to his son Borrowdale Mileson[90] (d. 1678). By 1676 Borrowdale had sold it to Thomas Edgar, who had married his daughter Agatha and died in 1677. Edgar's son and heir Mileson Edgar[91] died in 1713, having just sold a third of the rectory to his uncle Devereux Edgar's son Robert.[92] About 1733 Robert sold the rectory to Christopher Jeaffreson,[93] with whose Dullingham estate it descended thereafter. At inclosure in 1806 *c.* 405 a. were allotted for the rectorial tithes.[94] The rectory farmstead then stood a little east of the eastern cross-roads.[95]

Soon after 1200 Baldwin de Scalers's daughter Gillian and others granted land at Dullingham to Anglesey priory,[96] which retained it until its dissolution. The property was sold by the Crown in 1559.[97] An estate including until *c.* 1570 200 a. with 100 a. of heath descended from William Barton (d. by 1504) successively to John, Leonard, and Stephen Barton.[98] In 1579 Stephen sold *c.* 240 a. to John

[57] *Feud. Aids*, i, 159; C.R.O., 604/T 5–6.
[58] C.R.O., 604/T 16–17.
[59] Ibid. T 21–2, 25–7.
[60] *Feud. Aids*, i. 172; C 137/13/52 no. 4; C 138/58/43 no. 6.
[61] Cf. *Proc. C.A.S.* xliv. 22; *Cal. Pat.* 1313–17, 575; *Cal. Close*, 1381–5, 125. They perhaps gave their name to Basefield wood in Stetchworth.
[62] C.R.O., 604/T 3–4, 10, 14.
[63] S.C. 5/Cambs. Tower ser. no. 15 rot. 1.
[64] *Cal. Close*, 1389–92, 157.
[65] Dorothy Whitelock, *A.-S. Wills*, 83.
[66] *V.C.H. Cambs.* i. 378, 405.
[67] e.g. *Liber de Bernewelle*, 258; *Cal. Fine R.* 1272–1307, 374.
[68] *Reg. Regum Anglo-Norm.* ii, pp. 378–9; cf. Dugdale, *Mon.* v. 151.
[69] *Cart. Old Wardon* (Beds. Hist. Rec. Soc. xiii), pp. 175–7.
[70] *Liber de Bernewelle*, 258; *Assizes at Camb. 1260*, 21.
[71] S.C. 5/Cambs. Tower ser. no. 15 rot. 1.
[72] *Cal. Fine R.* 1272–1307, 374.
[73] C.P. 25(1)/26/49 no. 14.
[74] Clare Coll. Mun., deeds 6, 16 Edw. II.
[75] C.P. 25(1)/27/65 no. 9; E 40/14510.
[76] *Cal. Inq. p.m.* viii, p. 323; *Cambs. Lay Subsidy, 1327*, 18; C.R.O., 604/T 7.
[77] *Cat. Anct. D.* vi, C 4801; B.L. Add. MS. 5819, f. 134.
[78] C.R.O., 604/T 14.
[79] C 142/56 no. 58.
[80] C.P. 25(2)/93/835/15 Eliz. I Hil. no. 7.
[81] C.U.L., MS. Plans 237R, 380; C.R.O., R 52/24/19; B.L. Maps 136. a. 4(4).
[82] *Liber Elien.* (Camd. 3rd ser. xcii), pp. 95, 139.
[83] S.C. 5/Cambs. Tower ser. no. 15 rot. 1.
[84] Dugdale, *Mon.* v. 143, 154; *Hatton's Bk. of Seals*, pp. 230–1.
[85] *L. & P. Hen. VIII*, xv, pp. 470–1.
[86] e.g. E 321/31/42.
[87] Cf. *E.D.R.* (1914), 309.
[88] Cf. Prob. 11/142 (P.C.C. 129 Swann, will of Edm. Mileson); Gibbons, *Ely Episc. Rec.* 446–7, 457.
[89] C 66/1676 no. 2.
[90] Wards 7/72 no. 41.
[91] Prob. 11/356 (P.C.C. 49 Reeves); *Alum Cantab. to 1751*, ii. 85. For the Edgars, see Burke, *Land. Gent.* (1855), 335. Their pedigree, in ibid. (1848), i. 369, is badly confused.
[92] Copinger, *Suffolk Manors*, iii. 121; C.P. 25(2)/911/12 Anne Mich. no. 3.
[93] B.L. Add. MS. 9413, f. 284v.
[94] C.R.O., Q/RDz 6, pp. 297–9.
[95] Ibid. Q/RDc 14.
[96] E 40/14469, 14500, 14501; *Cat. Anct.* D. i, B 1308.
[97] S.C. 6/Hen. VIII/264 rot. 1d.; *Cal. Pat.* 1558–60, 357–8.
[98] Clare Coll. Mun., deeds 1504, 1579; C.P. 25(2)/93/836/12 Eliz. I Hil. no. 10.

Hasyll, who resold them in 1580 to trustees for Clare College, Cambridge.[99] In 1798 the college owned 327 a., including *c.* 70 a. of heath,[1] and after inclosure *c.* 232 a.,[2] sold in 1914.[3] Queens' College, Cambridge, owned *c.* 4½ a. of wood, sold in 1948 to F. B. Taylor.[4]

ECONOMIC HISTORY. Of 6 hides belonging to the largest manor at Dullingham in 1086 half were in demesne, but there were only 3 demesne plough-teams, so that the 17 *villani* possessing 9 teams who, with 10 bordars, occupied the rest, probably did most of the demesne ploughing. The Scalers and Richmond fees each included 2 teams, but the one had 7 *villani*, the other, probably lying further east, only 2, besides 9 bordars with 1 a. each.[5]

In 1279 the parish was said to include 1,400 a. of arable, 445 a. of grassland including 300 a. of common heath, and 125 a. of manorial woodland. The demesne of the main manor, recently divided equally between two lords, comprised 340 a. of arable, 20 a. of several grass, and 120 a. of common pasture shared with six other landholders. Besides 198 a. divided among 16 free tenants, there were *c.* 330 a. of customary land, of which four villeins held 20 a. each, two *c.* 15 a., nineteen 10 a., and six 5 a., while four cottars held 1 a. each. The villeins' works were valued at 5*s.* for each 5 a. held. John de Scalers had 180 a. of arable in demesne, while 8 free tenements held of him totalled 90 a., and Henry Madfrey owned 95 a. Neither had any villein tenants. Of the land held freely by 21 people, excluding 152 a. belonging to religious houses, 254 a. belonged to six men with 20 a. or more, one holding 82 a. under six different lords, and another tenant 61 a. as ¼ knight's fee.[6] The Beauchamp and Poyntz manors each normally received *c.* 30*s.* from their free tenants,[7] of whom they had together *c.* 40 in 1347, when Beauchamps had probably 16 and Poyntz 17 customary tenants.[8] In 1307 the 12 villeins on Poyntz manor owed week-work every Monday, Wednesday, and Friday for 48 weeks of the year, amounting to 1,728 works.[9] In 1283 the 16 villeins on Beauchamps manor had been similarly burdened, owing 1,425 works over 40 weeks and 200 more, perhaps excluding boon-works, during harvest, besides ploughing altogether 72 a. a year.[10] By 1304 their obligations had been reduced by two-thirds to 480 works a year,[11] probably rendered only on Mondays, as in 1321 when, perhaps through the recent famine, there were only 7 villeins left, holding 10 a. each.[12] By 1343 the works due had been reduced again to 240 a year, and 96 in harvest,[13] and by 1361 had been entirely commuted, the money-rents having consequently risen to 10 marks a year.[14] The arable of Beauchamps had, like that of Poyntz, totalled 240 a. *c.* 1305,[15] but had fallen to 120 a. in 1321 and 1343,[16] increasing again to 400 a. by 1421 when that of Poyntz was only 100 a., and that of Scalers 60 a.[17] The Scalers demesne was usually farmed out by the mid 14th century for terms of 5 to 7 years, the lessor providing 2 oxen and 2 stots, many tools, and some seed.[18] Much copyhold survived until the 19th century. In 1655 all but £2 10*s.* of the manorial quit-rents were from copyhold,[19] and after inclosure 437 a. of the 1,000 a. not belonging immediately to the demesnes were copyhold.[20]

The ancient inclosures in the south-eastern third of the parish, covering 505 a. *c.* 1800 apart from the surviving woodland, belonged almost entirely to the demesnes.[21] The area also contained, however, *c.* 80 a. of scattered open fields, including Radfield (44 a.) adjoining Radfield in Burrough Green, and *c.* 25 a. of common pastures, including Widgham green,[22] Dullingham Ley, and the Lammas meadow. At the western end of those closes lay the moor covering 48 a., held in 1800 by the lord in severalty. The main open-field arable began with Hall field south-east of the village and Mill field further south. To the west, south of the Cambridge way, lay Rannewe field, so named by 1552 from an ancient Dullingham family, Stonehouse field, Stony hill, and Middle field by the heath. The fields south of the Cambridge way covered at inclosure *c.* 657 a., those north of it *c.* 988 a. The latter comprised, from west to east, Cropley, formerly perhaps Coplow, field, West field, Limepit field, probably connected with a lime-pit mentioned in 1713, the large Great Crouch field north of the village, and Stetchworth Mill field. The last, also called in 1783 Interbait field,[23] was until inclosure intercommonable with Stetchworth.[24] North-west of the open fields lay the heath; a Newton field adjoining it was mentioned in 1312.[25] In 1586 the tenants of the manor complained that Sir Robert Wingfield's lessee had wrongfully excluded them from common of pasture upon certain land, perhaps there.[26] By 1798 most of the 460 a. of heath was held in severalty by the lord, although Clare College retained 62½ a. of heath for itself.[27]

The arable was probably subject to a triennial rotation by 1309 when common was claimed over certain grassland throughout every third year, and yearly from Lammas to Candlemas.[28] Regular

[99] Clare Coll. Mun., deeds 1579–80; C.P. 25(2)/93/843/21–2 Eliz. I Mich. no. 3.
[1] Clare Coll. Mun., terrier 1798.
[2] C.R.O., Q/RDc 14, schedule.
[3] *Clare College, 1326–1926* (Cambridge, 1928), i. 76.
[4] C.R.O., Q/RDc 14; 515/SP 204.
[5] *V.C.H. Cambs.* i. 404–5.
[6] S.C. 5/Cambs. Tower ser. no. 15 rot. 1.
[7] e.g. C 133/2/8 no. 4; C 133/40/3 no. 2.
[8] E 179/242/8 m. 7.
[9] C 134/2/19 no. 5.
[10] C 133/40/3 no. 2.
[11] C 133/111/17 no. 3.
[12] C 134/67/3 no. 5.
[13] C 135/70/7 no. 13.
[14] C 135/157/2 no. 15.
[15] C 133/111/17 no. 3; C 134/2/19 no. 5.
[16] C 134/67/3 no. 5; C 135/70/7 no. 13.
[17] C 138/58/43 no. 6.
[18] C.R.O., 604/T 5–6.
[19] C.U.L., Doc. 1429; cf. C.R.O., R 51/25/1.
[20] C.R.O., Q/RDz 6, pp. 305–18.
[21] The following account is based for the layout of fields on Clare Coll. Mun., map attached to lease 1798; for their names, on ibid.; deeds 10 Hen. VII, 6 Edw. VI, and terriers 17th-cent. to 1798; C.U.L., E.D.R., H 1/3, glebe terriers 1615, 1713; for areas (as before the boundary changes made at inclosure) on C.R.O., Q/RDc 14.
[22] Recorded as Wodgem pasture in 1548: B.L. Add. MS. 5861, f. 34v.
[23] C.R.O., 101/T 343.
[24] Cf. ibid. Q/RDz 6, p. 305.
[25] Clare Coll. Mun., deed 6 Edw. II.
[26] *Acts of P.C.* 1586–7, 20–2.
[27] Clare Coll. Mun., map 1798.
[28] *Abbrev. Plac.* (Rec. Com.), 306.

fallows, subject to commoning, were in force on the demesne in 1343,[29] and the lessee of Scalers manor was required to fallow and sow according to the 'season' in 1348.[30] The main crops were wheat and barley, one man bequeathing 20 a. of each in 1528,[31] and each was sown in alternate years on summer-tilled land *c.* 1595.[32] A rotation in three shifts was still in use in the 1790s.[33] The crops on 1,240 a. sown in 1801 included 337 a. of wheat, 484 a. of barley, and 301 a. of oats, besides 79 a. of peas and beans, and 35 a. of rye, but only 3½ a. of turnips and potatoes.[34] Sainfoin was grown in some demesne closes in 1788.[35]

The main manor had in 1086 a flock of 68 sheep, and the Richmond fee 200.[36] To a levy of wool in 1347 Dullingham contributed 92 stone, of which the manors and monastic estates provided 34 stone, 40 freeholders 42 stone, and 33 customary tenants 16 stone.[37] Besides the fold of Dullingham manor, which was entitled *c.* 1655 to sheep-walk for 600 wethers on the common heath,[38] folds were attached to the rectory estate[39] and to Scalers manor, whose farmer was required in 1354 to maintain a grange and sheep-pen on the heath.[40] The later Clare College estate included by 1503 sheep-gate and foldage for 300 sheep.[41] One yeoman bequeathed over 60 sheep in 1495,[42] another 42 in 1594.[43] About 1,400 sheep were kept *c.* 1794, when the flock-masters were allowed to sow clover, trefoil, and rye, presumably on the fallow, for their spring feed.[44]

The sale of timber was also a source of profit and employment. When the Poyntz manor was plundered in 1264 the loss of timber felled, at 40 marks, was reckoned as heavy as that of corn,[45] and in the 14th century the sale of underwood yielded about a tenth of the manorial incomes.[46] In the 16th century Queens' College sold the crop of its 5 a. of woodland, mostly oaks, annually,[47] and Dullingham Park and Ashbeds were let in the 1580s for £35 a year.[48] The lessee could profit by sub-letting pasture rights. Ashbeds could feed 18 cattle during the summer in the 1590s.[49] In the mid 19th century the population included 8 woodmen and sawyers, mostly living at Dullingham Ley, and 7 or 8 carpenters and wheelwrights.[50]

Of the £136 assessed on the parish in 1524 three people taxed at £10 or more had £40, while ten with £3–£8 had £55, and there were 16 with £2 compared with only nine with £1.[51] The more prosperous yeoman families included those of Rannewe, recorded from 1375 until nearly 1700,[52] Breton, whose head owned over 100 a. *c.* 1500,[53] Barton,[54] and Appleyard. John Rannewe was said to be worth £60 in 1522,[55] and Robert Rannewe gave 40 a. of arable, 24 a. of grass, and 12 a. of wood to his son in 1564,[56] while Alexander Rannewe bought *c.* 52 a. between 1562 and 1564,[57] and possibly *c.* 200 a. which were sold by the Bartons *c.* 1570.[58] Thomas Appleyard, whose father Thomas (d. 1613) had bought other Barton land in 1578,[59] was lessee of Dullingham Park in 1644 and among the wealthier parishioners.[60] Having joined the royalist rising at Linton in 1648 he compounded for land worth £235, besides paying a fine of £190.[61] By the late 17th century there was perhaps a wider gap between rich and poor. Of *c.* 90 dwellings recorded in 1666, 77 had only 1 or 2 hearths and only 4 more than 4, and in 1674 more than half of those inhabitants who had only 1 hearth were excused paying tax.[62] In 1655 the Dullingham manor estate included 432 a. of arable, 116 a. of woodland, and 184 a. of heath.[63] By 1806 it had grown to include *c.* 552 a. of the 986 a. of land in severalty, while of the rest 210 a. belonged to the Stetchworth estate, and 48 a. to Clare College.[64] The only other substantial estate remaining was that of Robert King, whose father Ralph (d. 1785) had by 1781 bought the land of the Robinson family, with the beneficial lease which they had enjoyed since 1704 of the Clare College farm.[65]

An inclosure Act was obtained in 1806,[66] and an award was made in 1810. Of the land allotted, including *c.* 1,745 a. of open fields and pastures and 460 a. of heath, besides old inclosures given for exchanges, Christopher Jeaffreson received *c.* 1,275 a., Richard Eaton of Stetchworth Park *c.* 255 a., Robert King 233 a., Clare College 163 a., the vicar and neighbouring incumbents *c.* 108 a., the lord of Burrough Green 45 a., and the parish charity 38 a. Eleven lesser landowners shared *c.* 75 a., and 14 a. were allotted, mostly in blocks of 1½ rood on Dullingham Ley, for common rights attached to 27 cottages. Of the 3,390 a. left in the parish Jeaffreson emerged with *c.* 2,022 a., Eaton with 453 a., Clare College with 232 a., and King with 235 a.[67] King's property, later Heath farm, remained in his family, with the Clare College lease, until the 1870s.[68] The Eaton

[29] C 135/70/7 no. 13.
[30] C.R.O., 604/T 5.
[31] B.L. Add. MS. 5861, f. 103.
[32] Prob. 11/86 (P.C.C. 39 Scott, will of Leonard Thurnall).
[33] Vancouver, *Agric. in Cambs.* 21–2.
[34] H.O. 67/9.
[35] C.R.O., L 80/105.
[36] *V.C.H. Cambs.* i. 404–5.
[37] E 179/242/8 m. 7.
[38] C.U.L., Doc. 1429.
[39] e.g. C.P. 25(2)/277/6 Jas. I Mich. no. 29.
[40] C.R.O., 604/T 6.
[41] Clare Coll. Mun., deed 19 Hen. VII.
[42] Prob. 11/10 (P.C.C. 22 Vox, will of Wm. Breton).
[43] Prob. 11/86 (P.C.C. 39 Scott, will of Leonard Thurnall).
[44] Vancouver, *Agric. in Cambs.* 22.
[45] *Rot. Selecti* (Rec. Com.), 244.
[46] e.g. C 134/2/19 no. 5; C 135/70/7 no. 13.
[47] C.U.L., Queens' Coll. Mun., box 35, 10/49–50.
[48] C.U.L., Doc. 3967, rot. 9d.
[49] C 2/Eliz. I/O 3/1.
[50] H.O. 107/1762.
[51] E 179/81/134 m. 7d.
[52] C.R.O., 604/T 15; C.U.L., Doc. 893.
[53] Clare Coll. Mun., deed 10 Hen. VII; cf. Req. 2/8/9.
[54] See p. 162.
[55] *L. & P. Hen. VIII*, iii (2), p. 1117.
[56] C.P. 25(2)/93/833/6–7 Eliz. I Mich. no. 7.
[57] C.P. 25(2)/93/832/3 Eliz. I East. no. 7; C.P. 25(2)/93/832/4 Eliz. I East. no. 9; C.P. 25(2)/93/833/6 Eliz. I Hil. no. 4.
[58] C.P. 25(2)/93/836/12 Eliz. I Hil. no. 10.
[59] Prob. 11/122 (P.C.C. 68 Capell); C.P. 25(2)/93/842/20 Eliz. I Trin. no. 5.
[60] C.R.O., R 58/10/18; *East Anglian*, N.S. vi. 343; x. 74.
[61] *Cal. Cttee. for Compounding*, ii, p. 2750.
[62] See pp. 279, 281.
[63] C.U.L., Doc. 1429.
[64] C.R.O., Q/RDc 14, schedule (areas as before exchanges made at inclosure).
[65] C.R.O., R 60/26/5; R 51/25/2; Clare Coll. Mun., leases 1704–1813.
[66] 46 Geo. III c. 48 (Local and Personal, not printed); *C.J.* lxi. 86, 432.
[67] C.R.O., Q/RDz 6, pp. 291–329; Q/RDc 14, schedule.
[68] C.R.O., L 86/109–110; R 51/25/26D; Clare Coll. Mun., estate papers.

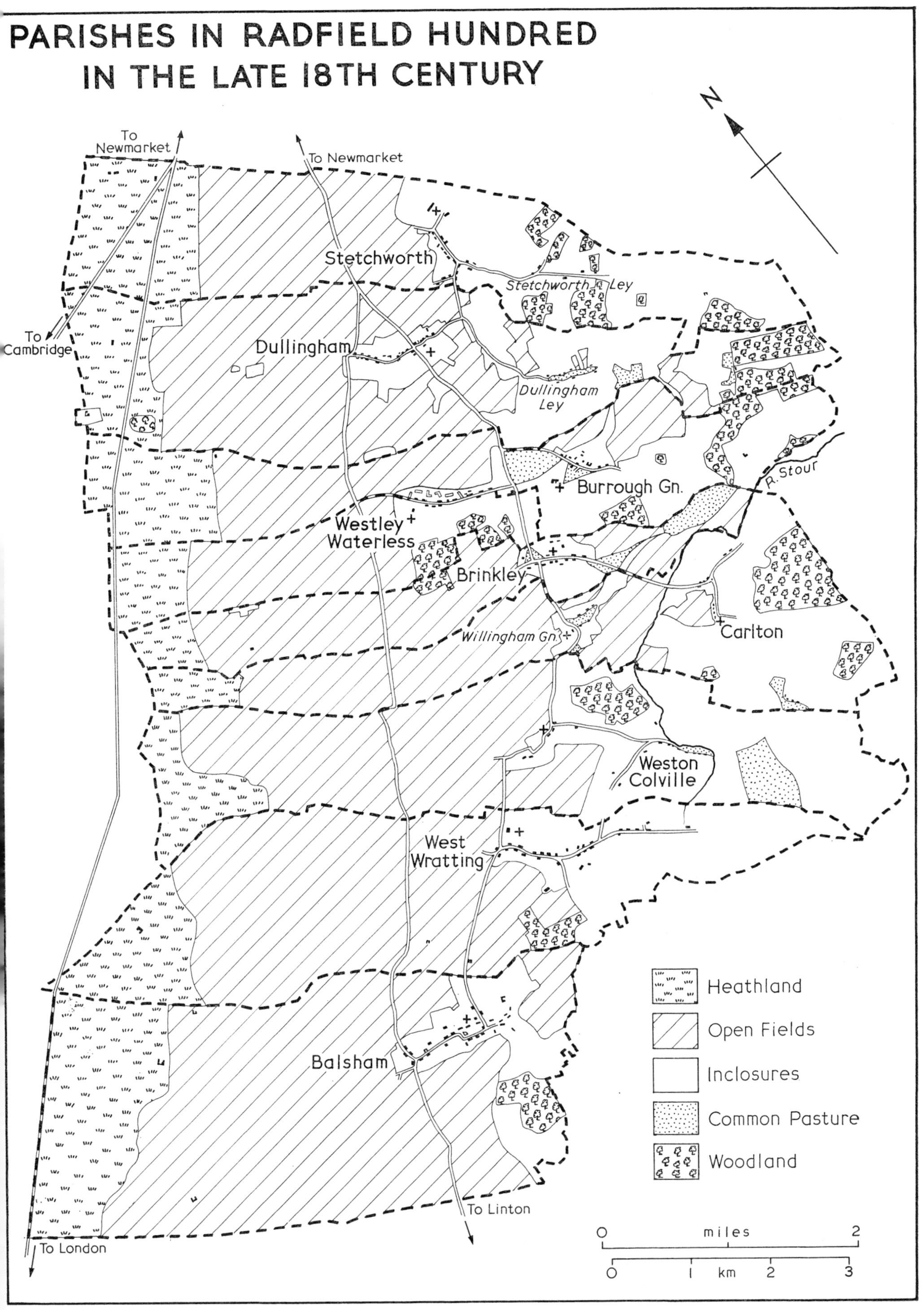

PARISHES IN RADFIELD HUNDRED
IN THE LATE 18TH CENTURY
N
To Newmarket
To Newmarket
To Cambridge
Stetchworth
Stetchworth Ley
Dullingham
Dullingham Ley
R. Stour
Burrough Gn.
Westley Waterless
Brinkley
Carlton
Willingham Gn.
Weston Colville
West Wratting
Balsham
To Linton
To London
Heathland
Open Fields
Inclosures
Common Pasture
Woodland
0
miles
2
0
1
km
2
3

land adjoining Stetchworth was usually farmed from that parish, the 180 a. in the south-east part being run from an old farm-house at Dullingham Ley.[69] On the Jeaffreson estate *c.* 1,630 a. were divided *c.* 1870 between Rectory farm of 587 a. let to Robert King, probably occupying the eastern part of the former open fields, three farms each of *c.* 240 a., Cables farm of 182 a., and Widgham Wood farm to the south-east of 133 a.[70] From 1896 Hill House farm in the north-west part of the parish was occupied by Sidney A. Taylor (d. 1937),[71] whose son F. B. Taylor later bought the manorial estate.

By 1828 the larger farms were being cultivated on a four-course rotation, including wheat, barley, clover, and turnips.[72] The presence of a water-tower on Hill House farm suggests that a steam-engine may have been used there. In the late 19th century several farmers were in difficulties. The charity farm was found to be in bad condition in 1879, its tenant having lately died insolvent.[73] On the Clare College farm the wet and heavy soil was badly overgrown with weeds, and the rent was reduced from £350 in 1871 to £184 by 1903, when the farm was let to a Newmarket butcher who fattened livestock there.[74] One small farm called Gipsy Hall was devoted in 1924 to poultry and fruit-growing.[75] Sugar-beet was grown in the parish in the 1970s, when Mr. P. B. Taylor, the principal landowner, was farming almost half of it himself.[76]

In 1831 92 labourers were employed on the farms, while there were 40 tradesmen and craftsmen.[77] There were *c.* 100 labourers in 1851, when 10 farmers provided employment for 89, and *c.* 119 in 1871.[78] In the mid 1870s up to 80 labourers were connected with the Agricultural Union, and undertook a strike.[79] In 1851 the village craftsmen had included 5 shoemakers, 2 journeymen blacksmiths, and 3 brick-layers, but such workmen had mostly disappeared by 1914.[80] A brick-works, ¾ mile south-east of the village by the road to Dullingham Ley, was working between 1883 and 1896. One large malt-house just north of the church was disused by 1903.[81] Another stood by 1885 near the railway station, and was perhaps that run by Flinn and Sons, recorded as maltsters from 1883 to 1929. In 1976 the extensive buildings were used for storing grain.[82]

A windmill, which belonged to the manor in 1279[83] and to Beauchamps moiety in 1343,[84] was perhaps that standing on an artificial mound *c.* 600 yd. south of the village, which had given its name to Mill field by 1552.[85] It belonged as copyhold to John Breton in 1683[86] and by 1795 to William Isaacson,[87] whose granddaughter Mary sold it *c.* 1850 to Elijah Moore.[88] The Moores ran it, employing three millers in 1871, almost until it closed soon after 1900.[89] Only the mound remained in 1976.

LOCAL GOVERNMENT. In 1279 and 1299 the lords of Dullingham manor claimed to hold, apparently jointly, view of frankpledge, infangthief, and the assize of bread and of ale, and to have a gallows, pillory, and tumbrel.[90] The court of that manor was still styled a view of frankpledge in the 19th century.[91] Under Elizabeth the lord was said to be 'chancellor in his own court', and claimed to provide equitable remedies there, so that counsel sometimes pleaded there.[92] An unofficial description of proceedings in 1588 shows the steward and jury putting pressure on tenants and witnesses to change their minds, even in simple cases of land transfers within a family.[93] Court minutes surviving for 1673–84 and 1823–35 are almost entirely concerned with copyhold title, as is a court book for the rectory manor for 1823–95.[94]

In 1548 money was left to the common box for distribution to the poor by the churchwardens according to the king's injunctions,[95] and in 1550 men were censured for not contributing for the poor.[96] In the 1790s the overseers paid 1*s.* to 2*s.* a week each in poor-relief to 19 people including 7 widows, besides buying fuel and footwear and helping in sickness. Their activity was supervised by occasional parish meetings.[97] By 1803 the cost had doubled since *c.* 1785 to £350. A workhouse then being built[98] with £400 raised from the parish charities had been finished by 1805, when a manager was sought. It had 19 inmates in 1813, but only 8 in 1815. In both years *c.* 30 people still received relief outside it. The total cost of relief was £609 in 1814,[99] ranging thereafter from £450 up to £900 in bad years.[1] About 1830 the parish paid 15 men from the poor-rate to work on the roads, and gave allowances for large families.[2] The workhouse, which stood by the road towards Burrough Green, was sold and converted for dwellings,[3] after the parish had been included in 1835 in the Newmarket

[69] Cf. B.L. Maps 136. a. 4(4).
[70] C.R.O., L 89/113.
[71] *Kelly's Dir. Cambs.* (1896–1937); mon. in ch.
[72] Clare Coll. Mun., survey 1828; lease 1832.
[73] Char. Com. files.
[74] Clare Coll. Mun., estate papers; surveyors' reports 1881–1914.
[75] C.R.O., 515/SP 738.
[76] *Camb. Ind. Press*, 24 Sept. 1965; local information.
[77] *Census*, 1831; *Rep. H.L. Cttee. on Poor Laws*, H.C. 227, pp. 332–3 (1831), viii.
[78] H.O. 107/1762; R.G. 10/1594.
[79] Char. Com. files, letters 11 June, 6 July 1879.
[80] H.O. 107/1762; *Kelly's Dir. Cambs.* (1858–1912).
[81] *Kelly's Dir. Cambs.* (1883–96); O.S. Map 6", Cambs. XLIX. SW. (1903 edn.).
[82] *Kelly's Dir. Cambs.* (1883–1929); local information.
[83] S.C. 5/Cambs. Tower ser. no. 15 rot. 1.
[84] C 135/70/7 no. 13.
[85] Clare Coll. Mun., deed 6 Edw. VI.
[86] C.R.O., R 51/25/1, ct. bk. iv, f. 15.
[87] Ibid. R 51/25/26B (ct. 1834), 28; Q/RDc 14; 101/T 346.
[88] Ibid. R 51/25/26K.
[89] R.G. 10/1594; *Kelly's Dir. Cambs.* (1864–1900).
[90] S.C. 5/Cambs. Tower ser. no. 15 rot. 1; *Plac. de Quo Warr.* (Rec. Com.), 99.
[91] e.g. C.P. 25(2)/260/18 Eliz. I Hil. no. 7; C.R.O., R 52/9/12N.
[92] Req. 2/192/60; C 2/Eliz. I/C 16/45.
[93] Req. 2/192/60.
[94] C.R.O., R 51/25/1; R 51/25/26B, 28.
[95] B.L. Add. MS. 5861, f. 34v.
[96] C.U.L., E.D.R., B 2/3, p. 83.
[97] Dullingham par. rec. *penes* the vicar, overseers' accts. 1790–7.
[98] *Poor Law Abstract, 1804*, 38–9.
[99] Ibid. *1818*, 30–1; *Camb. Chron.* 9 Mar. 1805.
[1] *Poor Rate Returns, 1816–21*, 11; *1822–4*, 38; *1825–9*, 16; *1830–4*, 16.
[2] *Rep. H.L. Cttee. on Poor Laws*, H.C. 227, pp. 332–3 (1831), viii.
[3] C.R.O., Q/RDc 14; Clare Coll. Mun., sale plan 1898.

poor-law union.[4] It remained in the Newmarket R.D.,[5] being included in 1974 in East Cambridgeshire.

CHURCH. In the early 12th century Robert de Scalers gave Dullingham church to the Cluniac priory of Thetford (Norf.), to which his son Tibbald and Robert Malet later confirmed it.[6] In 1277 Tibbald's heir John de Scalers confirmed the advowson to the priory.[7] By 1245, and probably by 1219, the church with 100 a. of glebe had been appropriated by the priory.[8] A vicarage was established by 1278,[9] and the advowson remained with the priory until its suppression.[10] Since the priory was an alien house the king presented in 1337 and 1349,[11] later perhaps entrusting the patronage to Mary, countess of Norfolk, who presented in 1349 and 1352.[12] In 1534 William Breton the vicar, having obtained the next turn, resigned and presented a kinsman and namesake.[13] After 1540 the advowson generally passed with the impropriate rectory,[14] Thomas, duke of Norfolk, presenting in 1566,[15] and Sir Roger Townsend and William Dix, custodians of his land, in 1589. Dix alone presented in 1591,[16] but the previous vicar disputed his nominee's title.[17] The Crown presented in 1598.[18] From 1608 the advowson passed through the Milesons, Edgars, and Jeaffresons, successively impropriators, Devereux Edgar presenting in 1707,[19] and was sold to the Taylors with the manorial estate. In 1973 it belonged to Mrs. R. M. Taylor, widow of F. B. Taylor.[20]

The vicarage was endowed, besides the small tithes,[21] with 10 combs or 1 load of wheat a year charged on the rectory, and still apparently rendered in the 19th century.[22] The vicarial glebe amounted in 1615 and 1713 to *c.* 4 a. of closes and 12 a. of open-field land.[23] At inclosure in 1806 the vicar was allotted 86 a.,[24] and his glebe subsequently comprised 87 a., which he retained in 1976.[25] Edmund Mileson (d. 1623) as impropriator bequeathed, besides 100 marks for building or buying a house for the vicar, a rent-charge on the rectory of £10 a year to make the living more attractive for a learned, preaching minister. The vicar was to forfeit 5*s.* of it for every Sunday when he provided no sermon.[26] If that bequest took effect, it was perhaps superseded when Edmund's son Borrowdale (d. 1678) left the vicar £10 a year from the rectory,[27] from which £20 a year was paid in 1786 and 1806[28] but only Borrowdale's £10 from the 1830s.[29] Under a Scheme of 1881 the money was paid thenceforth through the trustees of the parish charities.[30]

The church was said to be worth 20 marks in 1217 and 1254[31] and £20 in 1291, when the vicarage was worth only £5.[32] The latter was assessed at £12 15*s.* in 1535,[33] and yielded £40 a year in 1650[34] and £60 in 1728.[35] By 1830 it brought in £165,[36] and in 1877 £185 gross.[37]

The vicarage house originally stood just east of the rectory.[38] It was ruinous through neglect in the 16th century.[39] It was repaired *c.* 1728[40] and again *c.* 1783, when it was let to poor people, and *c.* 1807.[41] Between 1830 and 1836 S. H. Banks, vicar from 1828, built a new house on the vicarial allotment at the west end of the village street.[42] The house, a plain grey-brick block, later enlarged with Gothic detailing, was still occupied by the vicar in 1976.

Guilds of St. James and of Our Lady were receiving legacies for obits in the 1520s.[43] Land given to them for lights and obits was sold by the Crown in 1548 and 1571,[44] and a guildhall in 1563.[45] The latter was probably the long timber-framed and jettied 16th-century building standing in 1976 just north-west of the eastern cross-roads.

A priest of Dullingham was recorded *c.* 1200[46] and vicars from 1285.[47] William Breton, vicar 1488–1534, formerly master of St. Katherine's College by the Tower,[48] was son of a wealthy Dullingham yeoman,[49] and was usually resident in his parish.[50] His kinsman and successor, vicar 1534–54 and 1557–61, was also resident in the 1540s,[51] but in 1561 lived at Kelvedon rectory (Essex).[52] In his absence the churchwardens organized services.[53] His successor William Tilbrook, also a local man, caused trouble by naming his unlearned brother as parish clerk and harbouring an immoral daughter.[54]

[4] *Poor Law Com. 2nd Rep.* 513.
[5] *Census*, 1961.
[6] Dugdale, *Mon.* v. 143, 150.
[7] C.P. 25(1)/25/34 no. 28.
[8] C.P. 25(1)/24/22 no. 13; *Cur. Reg. R.* vii. 61–2; S.C. 5/Cambs. Tower ser. no. 15 rot. 1.
[9] *Vetus Liber Arch. Elien.* (C.A.S. 8vo ser. xlviii), 50.
[10] e.g. *E.D.R.* (1897), 193; (1908), 88, 121.
[11] *Cal. Pat.* 1338–40, 89; 1348–50, 341.
[12] *E.D.R.* (1893), 85, 151.
[13] B.L. Add. MS. 5820, f. 85v.
[14] See p. 162.
[15] *E.D.R.* (1914), 309.
[16] Gibbons, *Ely Episc. Rec.* 446–7.
[17] C.U.L., E.D.R., B 2/11, f. 108v.
[18] Gibbons, *Ely Episc. Rec.* 457.
[19] B.L. Add. MS. 5820, ff. 86v., 88; C.U.L., E.D.R., B 8/1.
[20] *Crockford* (1896 and later edns.).
[21] Cf. C 3/120/71.
[22] *Char. Don.* i. 94–5; Dullingham Incl. Act, 46 Geo. III, c. 48 (Local and Personal, not printed), p. 10; H.O. 129/188/1/4/4; cf. C.R.O., 515/SP 204.
[23] C.U.L., E.D.R., H 1/3, terriers 1615, 1713.
[24] C.R.O., Q/RDz 6, p. 300.
[25] *Crockford* (1926–52); ex inf. the vicar, the Revd. N. W. L. Auster.
[26] Prob. 11/142 (P.C.C. 129 Swann).
[27] Prob. 11/356 (P.C.C. 49 Reeve).
[28] *Char. Don.* i. 94–5; Dullingham Incl. Act, pp. 10–11. The £20 possibly included money from the school endowment.
[29] *31st Rep. Com. Char.* 137.
[30] Char. Com. files.
[31] *Val. of Norwich*, ed. Lunt, 215, 535.
[32] *Tax. Eccl.* (Rec. Com.), 267.
[33] *Valor Eccl.* (Rec. Com.), iii. 504.
[34] Lamb. Pal. MS. 904, f. 268.
[35] C.U.L., E.D.R., B 8/1.
[36] *Rep. Com. Eccl. Revenues*, pp. 346–7.
[37] C.U.L., E.D.R., C 3/26.
[38] C.U.L., E.D.R., H 1/3, terrier 1638; cf. C.R.O., Q/RDc 14.
[39] C.U.L., E.D.R., B 2/3, p. 83; B 2/11, f. 169.
[40] Ibid. B 8/1.
[41] Ibid. B 7/1, p. 8; C 1/4.
[42] Ibid. C 3/21.
[43] B.L. Add. MS. 5861, ff. 86, 101.
[44] *Cal. Pat.* 1548–9, 48; 1569–72, 404.
[45] Ibid. 1560–3, 556–7.
[46] *Cart. Old Wardon* (Beds. Hist. Rec. Soc. xiii), p. 176.
[47] *Assizes at Camb. 1260*, 47.
[48] Emden, *Biog. Reg. Univ. Camb.* 92.
[49] Prob. 11/10 (P.C.C. 22 Vox, will of Wm. Breton); cf. Clare Coll. Mun., deed 10 Hen. VII.
[50] e.g. B.L. Add. MS. 5861, ff. 65, 86, 93, 104.
[51] *Alum. Cantab. to 1751*, i. 212; B.L. Add. MS. 5861, ff. 18, 30v., 34v.
[52] B.L. Add. MS. 5813, ff. 64–5.
[53] C.U.L., E.D.R., B 2/3, f. 54.
[54] Ibid. D 2/10, ff. 151v.–152.

John Milward, vicar 1591–8, lived at Cambridge, visiting Dullingham to hold hasty services, sometimes reading unsurpliced and in his riding-boots.[55] John Dunch, vicar 1598–1639,[56] was faced *c.* 1610 with fierce disputes over claims to precedence in seating at church.[57] His successor Thomas Catherall, minister at Newmarket *c.* 1625, was chosen under the will of Edmund Mileson,[58] and retained the living until his death in 1658, being described in 1650 as very able.[59] A successor may have been ejected after 1660, a new vicar being instituted in 1662.[60]

Nicholas Phillips, vicar 1708–29,[61] lived on his cure, holding two services every Sunday in 1728, and had 20–30 communicants thrice a year.[62] The church then possessed a library of over 50 volumes.[63] John Symonds, vicar from 1729, also held Stetchworth from 1744 until his death in 1778.[64] By 1775 he held only one service a week.[65] The next vicar, Joseph Hall (d. 1828), from 1781 also held Bartlow rectory,[66] where he lived, serving Dullingham in 1807 through a curate also officiating at Brinkley, and in 1825 through the vicar of Stetchworth. Sunday services were in his time held alternately morning and evening, and communion four times a year, attended by *c.* 30 people.[67] S. H. Banks held Dullingham from 1828 until he died, aged 84, in 1882, with the neighbouring living of Cowlinge (Suff.).[68] In 1836 he was resident and supported a Sunday school,[69] and by 1851 held two services every Sunday, claiming to fill the church's 300 sittings on fine afternoons.[70] By 1877 there was again only one service on Sundays, and only 20 communicants.[71] Succeeding vicars held two services a week, and introduced weekly communions.[72] They included an Australian, a retired headmaster, and an ecclesiastical antiquary.[73]

The church of *ST. MARY*[74] is built mainly of field stones with ashlar dressings. It consists of a chancel, aisled and clerestoried nave with north porch and south chapel, and west tower. A blocked north window with plate tracery and a piscina show the chancel to be 13th-century. The thick-walled three-storey west tower is probably 14th-century, but was later given buttresses overlapping the aisles and new windows. The four-bay nave and aisles, with arcades having four shafts to each pier, were mainly rebuilt in the 15th century. The mouldings of the north doorway and the survival of 14th-century piscinas in the aisles suggest that earlier external walls were preserved, but all the aisle and clerestory windows, and those of the chapel, are Perpendicular. The 15th-century north porch, facing the village, has a high outer arch, side-windows on head-corbels, and a flush-work base. The south chapel, divided from the aisle by two arches once containing screens, is probably the lady chapel mentioned in 1500.[75] A south porch just west of it had vanished before 1749.[76] The chancel has a waggon-roof, ceiled over, but probably ancient, the nave a 15th-century roof on king-posts, and medieval braces survive in the roofs of the aisles and chapel. The octagonal 15th-century font received new painted royal coats of arms in 1603.[77] A medieval tomb-slab with a floriated cross lies above the altar steps,[78] and the chancel contains many monuments to members of the Jeaffreson family, including a lively rococo wall-tablet by Bottomley of Cambridge to Christopher Jeaffreson (d. 1749),[79] and one of 1778 by Richard Westmacott the elder (d. 1808), whose son Sir Richard (d. 1856) in the 1820s provided several plain neo-classical ones, and a recumbent figure of Lt.-Gen. Jeaffreson (d. 1824).[80]

In 1528 £10 was left to erect a cross for the church, perhaps that whose base survives in Dullingham Park.[81] The chancel needed repair in 1550 and 1595, and the north aisle was open to rain in 1577.[82] William Dowsing broke 30 pictured windows in 1644.[83] The whole church was repaired *c.* 1728,[84] and was in a decent state in 1783.[85] Christopher Jeaffreson (d. 1749) spent £300 on installing pews.[86] An organ was acquired in 1877. The church was restored between 1884 and 1890, the roof repaired in 1899,[87] and the tower in 1928 and 1939.[88] About 1904 a green marble pulpit was given in memory of John Dunn-Gardner.[89]

The parish owned in the 18th century 15 a. called church land, whose rent, *c.* £9, was spent on church repairs.[90] Part, 5½ a., was sold at inclosure,[91] but the town lands trustees continued to contribute towards such work sums fixed by a Scheme of 1846 at £10 a year. In 1912 that sum, with the vicar's £10, was constituted a separate ecclesiastical charity.[92]

The church had two silver chalices in 1552.[93] About 1960 the plate included a cup and paten by Samuel Head of 1699, a flagon of 1722, and a cup

[55] C.U.L., E.D.R., B 2/13, f. 88v.; Bodl. MS. Gough Eccl. Top. 3, f. 36.
[56] *Alum. Cantab. to 1751*, ii. 74.
[57] C.U.L., E.D.R., B 2/28, f. 53; Gibbons, *Ely Episc. Rec.* 41.
[58] See above.
[59] Lamb. Pal. MS. 904, f. 268; Prob. 11/285 (P.C.C. 703 Wootton).
[60] *Calamy Revised*, ed. Matthews, 361.
[61] *Alum. Cantab. to 1751*, iii. 356.
[62] C.U.L., E.D.R., B 8/1.
[63] Ibid. H 1/3, terrier 1713.
[64] *Alum. Cantab. to 1751*, iv. 77.
[65] C.U.L., E.D.R., C 1/1.
[66] *Alum. Cantab. 1752–1900*, iii. 202.
[67] C.U.L., E.D.R., C 1/4, 6.
[68] *Alum. Cantab. 1752–1900*, i. 142.
[69] C.U.L., E.D.R., C 3/21.
[70] H.O. 129/188/1/4/4.
[71] C.U.L., E.D.R., C 3/26.
[72] Ibid. C 3/37.
[73] *Crockford* (1882 and later edns.).
[74] So named by 1518: B.L. Add. MS. 5861, f. 65.
[75] Prob. 11/13 (P.C.C. 23 Blamyr, will of Hen. Rigewell).
[76] Cf. B.L. Add. MS. 5820, f. 86.
[77] Ibid. f. 88.
[78] Cf. *Mon. Inscr. Cambs.* 41.
[79] B.L. Add. MS. 5820, f. 87.
[80] Gunnis, *Dict. Brit. Sculptors*, 423, 427.
[81] B.L. Add. MS. 5861, f. 103; cf. *E.D.R.* (1898), 136.
[82] C.U.L., E.D.R., B 2/3, p. 83; D 2/10, f. 80v.; B 2/13, f. 124.
[83] *Trans. C.H.A.S.* iii. 90.
[84] C.U.L., E.D.R., B 8/1.
[85] Ibid. B 7/1, p. 8.
[86] B.L. Add. MS. 5820, f. 87.
[87] *Kelly's Dir. Cambs.* (1896, 1900); cf. *E.D.R.* (1898), 136.
[88] Char. Com. files.
[89] *Kelly's Dir. Cambs.* (1904).
[90] C.U.L., E.D.R., B 8/1; B 7/1, p. 9; Dullingham overseer's accts. 1790–7, *penes* the vicar.
[91] C.R.O., 101/T 346.
[92] *31st Rep. Com. Char.* 135; Char. Com. files.
[93] *Cambs. Ch. Goods, temp. Edw. VI*, 71.

and paten of 1840 and 1874.[94] There were four bells in 1552[95] and in 1749,[96] as in 1858 and later,[97] when they comprised one cast by John Draper in 1626–7, one by Miles Gray of 1660, one by John Bryant of Hertford in 1784, and one of 1828 by Thomas Mears of London, who also supplied the bell for a new clock installed *c.* 1830.[98] The parish registers begin in 1538,[99] and are virtually complete, including civil registers for most of the Interregnum.

NONCONFORMITY. Under Charles II five or six people were occasionally presented for not coming to church. One had left his children unbaptized and buried his servants without the rites of the church.[1] There were seven dissenters in 1676,[2] and a few, unbaptized, in 1728;[3] a house was registered for dissenting worship in 1736.[4] No dissenters were recorded thereafter until the 1820s when a few Wesleyans began to worship in a cottage.[5] In 1825 they bought land just east of the Camping close to build a chapel, opened in 1826.[6] In 1851, when there were 200 sittings, the minister claimed a congregation of 130.[7] In 1854 and 1879 the chapel was served from Mildenhall (Suff.).[8] It was still open in 1976.

Half the population were said to be dissenters in the 1870s.[9] About 1884 a Congregationalist minister from Cheveley established a mission room at the west end of Dullingham Ley, seating 130. In 1916 it had six lay preachers.[10] By 1965 membership had dwindled to 5, and it was closed *c.* 1968 and later sold.[11]

EDUCATION. An unlicensed schoolmaster teaching at Dullingham in 1578 was dismissed in 1580 for irreverence to the sacrament.[12] The parish again had a schoolmaster in 1590.[13] In 1676 Borrowdale Mileson left £5 a year to the public schoolmaster at Dullingham to teach poor boys grammar. If the vicar would teach the school, he was to have the money.[14] Between 1728 and 1825 the £5 was paid to a schoolmaster, probably usually, as in 1807, the parish clerk, to teach six poor boys. The school was kept in 1749 in the south chapel of the church, in 1807 in the vestry, probably the same place.[15] Two smaller schools were teaching reading in 1818.[16] In 1833 there were two day-schools with 30 pupils. One received the endowment money for teaching six children chosen by the vicar reading, writing, and arithmetic.[17] In 1846 two dame-schools each had *c.* 40 pupils.[18]

The vicar arranged in 1842 that his church clerk William Ingram should keep a school supported from Mileson's endowment, subscriptions, and school-pence. A Scheme of 1846 devoted half the net income of the town lands to support that school, and £10 to a Sunday school taught by Ingram who also served as postmaster and manorial bailiff. For some years he also gave evening classes for adults, but dropped them after a farmer complained that they encouraged young men to leave the parish.[19] About 75 children were receiving some schooling in 1851 and *c.* 125, including very few from Dullingham Ley, in 1871. In 1877 there were also two dame-schools.[20]

A school board, formed in 1875,[21] of which the vicar frequently served as chairman, opened a new school, with a master's house and separate rooms for infants and older children, east of the eastern cross-roads in 1878. It was taught by a master and mistress, assisted by up to four girl pupil-teachers.[22] Attendance rose from 99 in 1884 to 137 in 1903.[23] A new classroom was added in 1902.[24] Under a Scheme of 1881 the educational charity income went towards tuition fees for children under ten, prizes, premiums for pupil-teachers, and apprenticeships.[25]

Attendance fell from 106 in 1914 to 44 by 1938.[26] From 1947 the older children went to Bottisham village college,[27] but the school was still open for younger pupils in 1976. Under a Scheme of 1955 half the Educational Foundation's income of £90 a year was spent *c.* 1960 on scholarships and apprenticeships.[28]

CHARITIES FOR THE POOR. The guild of St. James *c.* 1517 was partly a benefit society, governed by an alderman and steward. It was maintained by subscriptions in money, wheat, and malt, and by the increase of the guild's livestock let out to the members, who dined together twice a week at the guildhall, poor brethren dining free of charge, while

94 List of ch. plate *penes V.C.H.*
95 *Cambs. Ch. Goods, temp. Edw. VI*, 71.
96 B.L. Add. MS. 5820, f. 86.
97 *Kelly's Dir. Cambs.* (1858–1937).
98 *Cambs. Bells* (C.A.S. 8vo ser. xviii), 140–1; *31st Rep. Com. Char.* 136–7.
99 Ex inf. the vicar; cf. C.U.L., E.D.R., C 1/6.
1 C.U.L., E.D.R., B 2/54, ff. 8, 22v.; B 2/62, f. 37v.
2 Compton Census.
3 C.U.L., E.D.R., B 8/1.
4 G.R.O. Worship Returns, Ely dioc. no. 51.
5 C.U.L., E.D.R., C 1/6.
6 Char. Com. files; G.R.O. Worship Returns, Ely dioc. no. 492; cf. *Methodist Ch. Bldg. Returns* (1940).
7 H.O. 129/188/1/4/10.
8 G.R.O. Worship Reg. no. 2076; *Bury Free Press*, 13 Dec. 1879 (from Char. Com. files).
9 Char. Com. files, letter 6 July 1879.
10 G.R.O. Worship Reg. no. 28876; *Cong. Yr. Bk.* (1895, 1916).
11 *Cong. Yr. Bk.* (1965–6, 1967–8); *Camb. Evening News*, 18 Oct. 1972.
12 C.U.L., E.D.R., D 2/10, ff. 151, 221v.
13 Ibid. B 2/11.
14 Prob. 11/356 (P.C.C. 49 Reeve).
15 C.U.L., E.D.R., B 8/1; C 1/4, 6; B.L. Add. MS. 5820, f. 86.
16 *Educ. of Poor Digest*, 58.
17 *Educ. Enquiry Abstract*, 54; cf. *31st Rep. Com. Char.* 137.
18 *Church Schools Inquiry, 1846–7*, 4–5; cf. H.O. 107/71.
19 Char. Com. files, letters 21 Feb., 30 Apr. 1878, report 1879; cf. C.U.L., E.D.R., C 3/21; C.R.O., R 51/25/26D.
20 H.O. 107/1762; R.G. 10/1594; C.U.L., E.D.R., C 3/26.
21 *Lond. Gaz.* 30 Apr. 1875, p. 2342.
22 Ed. 7/5; C.R.O., R 60/8/1, vol. i, pp. 1–40; *Rep. Educ. Cttee. of Council, 1876–7* [C. 1780-I], p. 76, H.C. (1877), xxix.
23 *Rep. Educ. Cttee. of Council, 1884–5* [C. 4483-I], p. 523, H.C. (1884–5), xxii; *Lists of Schs. under Admin. of Bd. 1903–4* [Cd. 2011], p. 16, H.C. (1904), lxxv.
24 C.R.O., R 60/8/1, vol. ii, pp. 17–20.
25 Char. Com. files.
26 *Bd. of Educ., List 21, 1914* (H.M.S.O.), 26; *1938*, 19.
27 Black, *Cambs. Educ. Rec.* 56.
28 Char. Com. files.

those bedridden received 15*d*. each.[29] The guild[30] may also have controlled the land said *c*. 1490 to belong to the town or the churchwardens, and worth ½ mark in 1524.[31] Following the guild's suppression that land was repurchased with the guildhall in 1564 and vested in feoffees to the use of the inhabitants. The guildhall may have become the town house mentioned in 1589, but was apparently later alienated. William Leader by will dated 1599 left a house and 3 a., the rent to be used to buy black frieze to clothe the parish poor, a charge still fulfilled in 1728.[32] Probably by 1775 the house, as the King's Head inn, was used as the farm-house for the town lands, with whose revenue its yield was thenceforth spent. Those lands comprised in 1786 6 a. of closes and 62 a. of field-land, yielding £24 a year, and after inclosure 56 a., all copyhold, let from 1831 for £110 a year, besides four cottages built *c*. 1815 and sold in 1875. The income was *c*. £120 *c*. 1860, but fell to £80 *c*. 1890. From 1885 12½ a. by the Camping close were let as allotments. In 1931 the public house and land, then yielding £105 a year, were sold for £2,700, invested to produce *c*. 1960 £98 a year.

In 1786 the income from the town lands went to support the rates. In the early 1830s up to £42 was distributed yearly among the poor in indiscriminate doles of 5*s*. or occasionally, as in 1831, in clothing, to honour Leader's bequest. A Scheme of 1846 directed that the balance, after paying for maintenance and £10 for church repairs, be divided equally between educational purposes and the poor, who were to receive in clothing and fuel up to £1 each. In practice, in 1878, £52 was distributed among 700 people in tickets of 2*s*. for each adult, 1*s*. for each child, valid for clothing and blankets. A new Scheme of 1881 allotted the poor's share to medical expenses, clothing, fuel, and food for needy inhabitants not on poor-relief. When, however, the trustees sought in 1883 to select really needy individuals, the parish labourers and small craftsmen successfully demanded the continuance of the previous universal and equal distribution. Between 1905 and 1910 the trustees gave out up to £38 a year in half-crown tickets for coal, clothes, and fuel to 200 adults earning under £1 a week and 130 children. A Scheme of 1912 transferring control to the parish council retained the existing trusts, most inhabitants strongly objecting to any restraint on distributions in kind. About 1960 *c*. £37 a year from that charity was available for the poor.

John Appleyard by will proved 1658 left £1 a year for the poor at Christmas,[33] a benefaction not traced later. Borrowdale Mileson by will proved 1678 left £5 a year to provide penny loaves for twelve old, poor, and sick persons every Sunday after church, the balance, £2 8*s*., being for the poor at Christmas. The charity was distributed mainly in bread in the 1780s and 1810s,[34] but payments temporarily ceased *c*. 1830. Later, because dissenters would not come to church to receive the bread, the £5 was accumulated and distributed every three years throughout the parish in flour. John Britton by will dated 1701 left 10*s*. a year for bread for the poor at Christmas. In the 1830s £2 10*s*. was given in bread every five years. The Scheme of 1881 vested both charities in the town lands charity trustees, and provided for continued distributions in bread, permitted from 1933 throughout the year. Mileson's £5 was still being received *c*. 1960; Britton's rent-charge was redeemed in 1952 for £20.

Christopher Jeaffreson by will dated 1725 gave £3 a year for the poor at Christmas. His will having been declared invalid, his heirs, though giving the £3, wrongly considered it a voluntary gift, and payment ceased after 1824. Two minor rent-charges for the poor, one given before 1590, had been lost by 1786. Ada Mariota Dunn-Gardner, niece of Mrs. Robinson, by will proved 1919 left for the parish poor £200, yielding *c*. 1960 £11 10*s*. From 1938 it was managed with the other parish charities.

STETCHWORTH

THE PARISH of Stetchworth, 3 miles south of Newmarket,[1] covers 2,891 a.[2] It stretches for 6 miles from Newmarket Heath in the north-west to the county boundary to the south-east, and is *c*. 1 mile wide. The land rises gradually from 100 ft. on the heath to 250 ft. near Lingay Hill, falls to *c*. 200 ft. where a stream crosses the parish and then rises more sharply to *c*. 325 ft., where the village lies near the centre of the parish, before levelling out in the south-eastern half. The soil overlies the chalk in the north-west, but above the 300-ft. contour the chalk is covered by boulder clay. That part of the parish was once well wooded, and the clearing of the woodland probably gave Stetchworth its name, signifying 'stump enclosure'.[3] A considerable amount of woodland remained in the south-eastern half of the parish where in the 18th and 19th centuries there were *c*. 335 a. of oak wood.[4] In that part of the parish Stetchworth Park was inclosed as a deer park in the 16th century.[5] Stetchworth was well known for its shooting in the 19th century, and in 1958 the first British Game Fair was held there.[6]

Woodland in the north-western half of the parish is composed of belts and small clumps of trees designed to provide shelter for the paddocks of the

[29] *Trans. C.H.A.S.* i. 346–8.

[30] The remainder of this section is based, unless otherwise stated, on *Char. Don.* i. 94–5; B.L. Add. MS. 9412, f. 286 and v. (for 1786); *31st Rep. Com. Char.* 134–8; *Char. Digest Cambs. 1863–4*, 16–17; Char. Com. files.

[31] E 179/81/134 m. 7d.

[32] Cf. C.U.L., E.D.R., B 8/1.

[33] Prob. 11/283 (P.C.C. 625 Wootton).

[34] *Poor Law Abstract, 1818*, 37.

[1] This account was written in 1976. Unless otherwise stated the topography is based on O.S. Maps 6″, Cambs. XLI. SE., XLII. SW., XLIX. NW., XLIX. SE. (1890 and later edns.).

[2] *Census*, 1971.

[3] *P.N. Cambs.* (E.P.N.S.), 119.

[4] Vancouver, *Agric. in Cambs.* 19.

[5] C 66/1156 m. 34; Sta. Cha. 8/120/10.

[6] B.L. Maps 136.a. 4(4); *Camb. Ind. Press*, 13 Oct. 1961.

stud farms and training stables which have characterized Stetchworth since the 19th century.[7] They are there so as to be close to the Newmarket race-courses: the July Course finishes in the northern corner of the parish. It is part of the earlier Round Course which was already marked out in the 1660s.[8] There were several stands and stables there in 1770; the present stand was rebuilt by the Jockey Club in 1935.[9] The racing establishments include the National Stud and Egerton House, and a large riding school was opened in 1959.[10]

The north-eastern boundary of the parish, between Newmarket Heath and Camois Hall in Woodditton, follows the line of the Devil's Ditch, a post-Roman defensive structure which is the largest of the Cambridgeshire dykes. In 1951 it was scheduled as a site of special scientific interest because of its plant and animal life.[11] The Two Captains tumuli lie near the dyke, south-east of the London–Newmarket road. An early, possibly pre-Roman, trackway from the direction of Linton and Balsham closely skirted the woodland edge in Stetchworth.[12] Two turnpike roads crossed the northern end of the parish: that leading from Newmarket to London was turnpiked in 1724, and that from Newmarket Heath to Cambridge in 1744. The two were linked in 1774; a toll-gate was set up at London Gap where the two separated, and other gaps in the dyke were closed.[13] The roads were disturnpiked in 1871.[14] By 1976 the junction of the two roads had been moved south-westwards to meet the road from Stetchworth, and a roundabout had been built there. North-west of the village the parish is crossed by the Dullingham–Newmarket road, which crosses the dyke at Dullingham Gap. Until inclosure two roads ran roughly parallel for most of the length of the parish between the London–Newmarket road and Stetchworth Ley, from where roads run east to Ditton Green and south-east to Stetchworth Park;[15] north-west of the village the south-western road did not survive, and south-east of the village the north-eastern road was stopped up at inclosure and survives only as a footpath.[16] Near the brook the parish is crossed by the Cambridge–Newmarket railway line, opened in 1848.[17] The nearest station is at Dullingham, 2 miles from the village.

The village of Stetchworth seems to have grown from a cluster of houses around the church and the manor-house near the north-eastern road along the parish, and spread southwards down the main street linking that road to the south-western road. Two 17th-century farm-houses stand in the northern part of the village, east of the main street. By the late 18th century there was another cluster of houses at the southern end of the street, spreading westwards from the Dullingham road along Mill Lane.[18] The village was described as large in the 18th century, but grew little between the mid 17th century and 1807, having 50–60 houses.[19] In 1770 Church Lane ran north of the church, between it and Stetchworth House;[20] by 1814 it had been diverted to run south of the church[21] as it did in 1976. Part of Camping Close, south of Church Lane, has been used as a burial ground since the early 20th century. At the junction of Church Lane and the main street is a small open space, in 1876 called the Green. There stood the May tree, used as a maypole in the 19th century.[22] Opposite it stands a group of early-19th-century houses. Up to the mid 19th century land on the east side of the main street near the southern end of the village was left open. A school was built there in the 1860s, and in 1870 H. F. Eaton built *c.* 10 houses there.[23] The extent of the village changed little, and in 1976 Stetchworth House, Aislabie Stud (earlier known as Street Farm), and the mill site still formed the northern, southern, and western limit of building. From the later 19th century there were fewer houses around the church, but spaces along the main street were filled in. Many houses were built by the local authority between 1923 and 1973: a council estate was built on Coopers Close at the south-eastern end of the village and a small private estate was built in the same area. Other new houses have been built along Mill Lane, and the Dullingham road, known as Teakettle Lane.[24] In 1948 Lady Ellesmere gave *c.* 1 a. on the west side of the main street, on which stood Watson's Barn, for a village hall as a memorial to her husband John, earl of Ellesmere. In 1956 another plot was bought, at the south-eastern edge of the village, beyond Coopers Close, and a village hall was opened there in 1963,[25] with a playing field next to it. By 1976 several new houses had been built on the first site.

Stetchworth Ley, a mile south-east of the village, was described as a hamlet in the early 19th century.[26] There were about six houses there: Stetchworth Ley, Ley Farm, and the Park farm buildings survive. Bleak House, west of Ley Farm, has disappeared. A row of cottages and the distinctive Round House have been built since 1814.[27]

From the late 19th century there have been several houses at Stetchworth Heath in the north-west end of the parish, near the junction of the Cambridge and London roads. Heath Farm had been built next to the July race-course by 1876 and Egerton House was built in 1891.[28] A row of *c.* 10 cottages was built south-east of the Newmarket road in 1897[29] and a school to the north-east in 1913. After Heath Farm was taken over by the National Stud

[7] Taylor, *Cambs. Landscape*, 186.
[8] *V.C.H. Cambs.* v. 280.
[9] Ibid.; C.U.L., MS. Plan 345.
[10] *Newmarket Jnl.* 4 July 1974.
[11] *V.C.H. Cambs.* ii. 7; *Nature Reserves and Sites of Special Scientific Interest* (Cambs. and Isle of Ely Planning Dept. 1965), p. 64. An archaeological description appears in R.C.H.M. *Cambs.* ii. 144.
[12] Fox, *Arch. Camb. Region*, 153, 157.
[13] Stump Cross Rds. Turnpike Act, 10 Geo. I, c. 12; 3 Geo. III, c. 32; Camb. Rd. Turnpike Act, 18 Geo. II, c. 23; C.R.O., T/N/AM 1.
[14] Annual Turnpike Acts Continuance Act, 33–4 Vic. c. 73; 35–6 Vic. c. 85.
[15] To be distinguished from the park adjoining Stetchworth House, sometimes called Stetchworth Park.
[16] B.L. Maps K. 8. 70; C.U.L., MS. Plan 345; C.R.O., Q/RDc 37.
[17] *V.C.H. Cambs.* ii. 132.
[18] B.L. Maps K. 8. 70.
[19] B.L. Add. MS. 5819, f. 109; E 179/84/437 rot. 73; C.U.L., E.D.R., C 1/4.
[20] C.U.L., MS. Plan 345.
[21] C.R.O., Q/RDc 37.
[22] B.L. Maps 136. a. 4(4); *Gardner's Dir. Cambs.* (1851).
[23] Inscr. on bldg.
[24] *Stetchworth Draft Village Plan* (1973).
[25] Char. Com. files.
[26] C.U.L., E.D.R., C 1/4.
[27] C.R.O., Q/RDc 37.
[28] B.L. Maps 136. a. 4(4); R. Marsh, *Trainer to Two Kings*, 92; inscr. on bldg.
[29] Inscr. on bldg.

in the 1960s some new houses and stables were built next to the race-course.

The White Horse, at the northern edge of the village opposite Church Lane by 1847, and rebuilt for the earl of Ellesmere by C. F. A. Voysey in 1905, ceased to be a public house in the 1930s.[30] From 1890 the Live and Let Live opposite the school, and from 1937 the Marquis of Granby on the corner of the main street and Teakettle Lane, were in use until 1961, but by 1973 the Marquis of Granby alone survived.[31]

Twenty-five inhabitants were recorded in Stetchworth in 1086, and 26 paid tax there in 1327, the lowest number in the hundred.[32] There were 106 adults in 1377.[33] In 1563 there were 46 householders in the parish, in 1664 62 houses were assessed for tax, but only 49 in 1674.[34] In 1685 Stetchworth had *c.* 60 families, but the number had fallen by 1728 to 53, containing *c.* 256 people.[35] By 1801 there were 342 inhabitants. The population rose sharply to 462 in 1821, and 671 in 1861, usually being fourth highest in the hundred. After a slight fall it rose to 864 in 1901, and then fell more slowly than in neighbouring parishes so that in 1921 at 659 it was the highest in the hundred. The fall continued, to 475 in 1951, but a subsequent increase brought it to 494 in 1971.[36]

MANORS AND OTHER ESTATES. In the late 10th century Oswi gave Stetchworth to Ely on his son Elfwine's entry into the abbey. In the early 11th century, however, Stetchworth was held by Oswi's daughters, Alfwenne and Alfwith, and his wife Leofflaed left the reversion to the abbey,[37] which in 1066 held 9½ hides there. One yardland was held of the abbey by Hardwin de Scalers. Half a hide of meadow there was seized by Earl Ralph, but had been restored to the abbey by 1086. One and a half yardland had been taken by Siric de Oburville and given to the abbey of St. Wandrille (Seine Maritime), presumably as part of the abbey's Dullingham lands.[38] Bishop Niel assigned the manor of *STETCHWORTH* to the monks, who vindicated their title after a lengthy dispute with Henry, son of William le Breton, in the mid 12th century.[39] The manor remained with the cathedral priory until its dissolution, and in 1541 was granted to Sir Edward North, treasurer of the Court of Augmentations, created Lord North in 1554.[40] He was succeeded in 1564 by his son Roger who in 1577 was licensed to impark 500 a. in Stetchworth and Dullingham.[41] In 1600 Roger was succeeded by his grandson Dudley North, who in 1622 sold the manor to Sir William Russell of Chippenham, treasurer of the Navy.[42] In 1667 Russell's grandson Sir John Russell sold Stetchworth to Richard Gorges, Lord Gorges (d. 1712), who devised the estate to his nephew Henry Fleming.[43] Henry was succeeded in 1713 by his nephew Richard Fleming (d. 1740) and Richard by his brother William, a lunatic.[44] After William's death in 1766 Stetchworth passed with lands in North Stoneham (Hants) to distant cousins of the Flemings, Thomas and John Willis, who adopted the name Fleming.[45]

In 1770 John Willis Fleming, John Fleming's cousin, held the manor. It was offered for sale in the 1780s and bought in 1786 by Richard Eaton,[46] who after inclosure in 1820 owned over 2,655 a., almost all the land in the parish,[47] and died in 1843. He was succeeded by his son R. J. Eaton (d. 1847) and grandson H. F. Eaton (d. 1875).[48] About 1876 the Stetchworth Park estate was bought by Sir Roger W. H. Palmer, Bt., who sold it in 1883 to Francis Egerton, earl of Ellesmere (d. 1914). Stetchworth descended with the earldom to Francis's son John (d. 1944) and grandson John who held the estate in 1976, having become duke of Sutherland in 1963.[49]

The original manor-house probably stood within the large earthwork lying south and east of the church; the moat was probably once filled with water. In the 1640s Lord Gorges built a large brick house, with 13 hearths,[50] north-west of the church. Extensive walled gardens and a summer-house, presumably built then, survived in 1976. In 1796 Richard Eaton demolished the house and built the present Stetchworth House,[51] a three-storeyed brick house with a portico on the south side and terraces to the west and north. It was enlarged to the east and a porch was added to the south side *c.* 1870. After the Second World War the eastern part, containing the service quarters, was demolished.[52]

In 1086 Count Alan held ½ hide in Stetchworth which had been held by Grim, the man of Eddeva.[53] The overlordship descended with Alan's honor of Richmond and in 1280 Philip Patmer held 1 hide in Stetchworth of that honor.[54] Philip was dead by 1324 when his widow Alice had a life-interest in *c.* 220 a. with reversion to their sons Henry and Walter.[55] On her death in 1339, however, Alice was succeeded by John, son of John Patmer, a minor.[56] In 1412 the manor of *PATMERS* was probably held by Thomas Wykes.[57] In 1438 John Coo and

[30] *Kelly's Dir. Cambs.* (1847 and later edns.); Pevsner, *Cambs.* 461; ex inf. Mr. C. Rush; see below, plate facing p. 176.
[31] *Kelly's Dir. Cambs.* (1890 and later yrs.); *Camb. Ind. Press*, 13 Oct. 1961; *Draft Village Plan* (1973).
[32] *V.C.H. Cambs.* i. 364; *Cambs. Lay Subsidy, 1327*, 18.
[33] E 179/237/7A.
[34] B.L. Harl. MS. 594, f. 199v.; E 179/84/437 rot. 73; see below, p. 281.
[35] C.U.L., E.D.R., A 6/3; B 8/1.
[36] *Census*, 1801–1971.
[37] *Liber Elien.* (Camd. 3rd ser. xcii), pp. 139, 157.
[38] *V.C.H. Cambs.* i. 352, 364, 405.
[39] *Liber Elien.* pp. 300, 405–7; *Reg. Regum Anglo-Norm.* iii, p. 95; Saltman, *Theobald, Abp. of Cant.* 146–7.
[40] *L. & P. Hen. VIII*, xvi, p. 245; *Complete Peerage*, ix. 649–51.
[41] B.L. Add. Ch. 39401; C 66/1156 m. 34.
[42] C 142/265 no. 75; C.R.O., R 56/5/98; *D.N.B.*
[43] C.P. 25(2)/633/19 Chas. II Mich. no. 22; Lysons, *Cambs.* 257; B.L. Add. MS. 5819, f. 109.
[44] B.L. Add. MS. 5819, f. 109.
[45] Ibid.; *V.C.H. Hants*, iii. 479; Burke, *Land. Gent.* (1846), i. 419–20.
[46] C.U.L., MS. Plan 345; *Camb. Chron.* 28 Feb. 1784; 23 July 1785; Lysons, *Cambs.* 257.
[47] C.R.O., Q/RDz 9, pp. 285 sqq.
[48] Burke, *Land. Gent.* (1871), i. 384.
[49] B.L. Maps 136. a. 4(4); C.R.O., L 40/6; R 53/23/32; *Kelly's Dir. Cambs.* (1869, 1875); Burke, *Peerage* (1970), 2583.
[50] E 179/244/23 rot. 66.
[51] *Camb. Ind. Press*, 13 Oct. 1961.
[52] Ex inf. Mr. D. M. Hutton, agent.
[53] *V.C.H. Cambs.* i. 378.
[54] *Cal. Inq. p.m.* ii, p. 219.
[55] C.P. 25(1)/27/62 nos. 5, 11.
[56] *Cal. Close*, 1339–41, 340.
[57] *Feud. Aids*, vi. 407.

others granted it to Ely priory, but in 1440 Coo sold the reversion of all his lands in Stetchworth, late Wykes's, to Richard Foster.[58] At his death in 1525 Thomas Hildersham held Patmers with Madfreys manor in Dullingham of the honor of Richmond.[59] Thomas was succeeded by his son John who held them in 1536.[60] In 1544 the two manors were settled on Thomas Hildersham the younger and his wife. He and his second wife Anne Pole, a niece of Cardinal Pole, were zealous Catholics, and disinherited their son Arthur, who became a puritan divine. In 1571 Thomas sold Patmers and Madfreys to James Altham.[61] Two years later Altham sold them to Roger North, Lord North, and they afterwards descended with Stetchworth manor.[62] A fee-farm rent of 3*s*. was still paid to the honor of Richmond in 1876.[63] The lands of Patmers were later known as Place farm, and in 1770 the farm-house stood at the northern end of the village, north-west of the church.[64] It had gone by 1814.

The rectory of Stetchworth was granted to Ely priory in 1191. It has since descended with Stetchworth manor. At inclosure in 1820 Richard Eaton was allotted 500 a. in the north-west end of the parish in place of the great tithes. That land afterwards formed Heath farm.[65]

ECONOMIC HISTORY. Of 10 hides in Stetchworth in 1086 3½ hides of land and ½ hide of meadow were held by Ely abbey in demesne. One yardland was held by Hardwin de Scalers, and the rest of the abbot's land was worked by 16 *villani* and by 5 bordars who had 5 a. each. There were four *servi* on the demesne, and three plough-teams although there was land enough for five. The woodland was sufficient for 260 pigs. On the rest of the land there were six teams and might have been seven. There was half a team on Count Alan's ½ hide. The Ely estate had fallen in value from £12 T.R.E. to £10 in 1086.[66]

The amount of cultivated land was considerably extended by the clearing of woodland in the south-east end of the parish, indicated by the irregular boundaries of the remaining woodland, and the smaller, irregular fields south-east of the village. Ley farm there was recorded from 1250.[67] The cleared lands and leasowes were still valued separately in the 17th century.[68] In the 16th century 500 a. at the south-east end of Stetchworth and Dullingham were imparked.[69] The whole of the south-eastern part of Stetchworth was inclosed long before the land north-west of the village.[70] In 1770 Park farm had 330 a. of inclosed land, Hall farm 295 a., and Place farm 240 a.[71]

Heathland in the extreme north-west of the parish, amounting in the 18th century to *c*. 860 a., stretched from the parish boundary to south-east of the London–Newmarket road.[72] In the 16th century the smallest of the three several heaths, belonging to the vicar, supported 200 sheep and in 1615 covered 180 a.[73] In 1770 Hall farm had 350 a. of heath, and Place farm over 300 a.[74] There were 1,200 sheep in the parish in 1806.[75] Between the heath and the village lay the open arable. In the 18th century most of it was divided between three fields: the largest, Naughts Hill, covered 390 a., Middle or Waste field covered 360 a., and Ditch field 270 a., all divided into unequal furlongs.[76] Mill field also occurs, west of the village, at one time intercommoned with Dullingham.[77] In the Middle Ages the chief crop seems to have been barley,[78] as in the 19th century. In 1801 340 a. were sown with barley, 300 a. with wheat, 200 a. with oats, and a few acres only with rye, peas, and potatoes.[79] In the early 19th century the thin chalky soil was said to produce good wheat, but the heavy wet lands needed improvement through inclosure.[80]

By the 18th century there were three large farms in the parish, Place, Hall, and Park farms. Place farm was the old manor of Patmers, which in 1438 had had 140 a. of arable, 4 a. of meadow, and 10 a. of underwood.[81] Hall farm was probably based on the demesne of Stetchworth manor; that demesne had been farmed out from the 15th century.[82] By 1770 all three farms belonged to John Fleming.[83] The parish was inclosed under an Act of 1814, and the allotment completed by 1820. By then Richard Eaton held almost all the land in the parish, having bought 10 other holdings besides Fleming's. He was allotted over 1,500 a. of the 1,730 a. of open and common land. The vicar received 130 a. and 11 others shared 22 a., none receiving more than 6 a. In all Eaton held over 2,650 a.[84] Only 4 a. of copyhold land occurred in the award, but in 1876 21 copyhold tenants were paying what were called quit-rents, worth £2 15*s*. a year. In the early 20th century the remaining copyholds were enfranchised.[85]

After inclosure the largest farm was Hall farm, formed from Eaton's allotment between the Dullingham–Newmarket and London–Newmarket roads. The farm-house had been built in the middle of the allotment by 1824. Cottages were built there by Sir Roger Palmer in the late 1870s, and a large stable block and house were added in 1887.[86] The farm

58 C 143/448 no. 21; B.L. Add. Ch. 15674.
59 C 142/56 no. 58; see above, p. 162.
60 C.P. 25(2)/4/20 no. 29.
61 C.P. 25(2)/4/22 no. 31; C.P. 25(2)/93/375/13 Eliz. I Trin. no. 4; *D.N.B.*
62 C.P. 25(2)/93/838/15 Eliz. I Hil. no. 7.
63 B.L. Maps 136. a. 4(4).
64 C.U.L., MS. Plan 345.
65 B.L. Add. MS. 5819, f. 134v.; C.R.O., Q/RDz 9, p. 316.
66 *V.C.H. Cambs.* i. 364, 378, 405.
67 Taylor, *Cambs. Landscape*, 90, 101.
68 C.U.L., Doc. 1495.
69 C 66/1156 m. 34.
70 C.U.L., MS. Plan 345; C.R.O., Q/RDc 37.
71 C.U.L., MS. Plan 345.
72 Ibid.
73 C 3/34/47; C.U.L., E.D.R., H 1/5, terrier 1615.
74 C.U.L., MS. Plan 345.
75 Vancouver, *Agric. in Cambs.* 19.
76 C.U.L., MS. Plan 345.
77 C.U.L., E.D.R., H 1/5, terrier 1615.
78 Prob. 11/9 (P.C.C. 17 Dogett, will of Thos. Kennet); Prob. 11/43 (P.C.C. 31 Mellersshe, will of Thos. Burrell).
79 H.O. 67/9.
80 Vancouver, *Agric. in Cambs.* 19.
81 C 143/448 no. 21.
82 C.U.L., Doc. 1495; C.R.O., R 59/28/1 m. 5; Prob. 11/18 (P.C.C. 10 Holder, will of John Folks); Prob. 11/142 (P.C.C. 4 Weldon, will of Oliver Bridgeman).
83 C.U.L., MS. Plan 345.
84 C.R.O., Q/RDz 9, pp. 285–323.
85 B.L. Maps 136. a. 4(4); C.R.O., R 54/2/3.
86 Baker, *Map of Cambs.* (1824); C.R.O., Q/RDc 37; inscrs. on bldgs.

covered over 900 a. in 1876, and was kept in hand by the duke of Sutherland in 1976 when the estate's other farms were leased.[87] By the 1870s Heath Farm had been built adjoining the July Course, near the junction of the London and Cambridge roads, on 240 a. allotted for tithe.[88] Park or Ditton Park farm covered *c.* 330 a. in 1876. It was leased from the Ellesmere estate until sold in 1957, when its brick-built farm-house had already been demolished.[89]

Between 1834 and 1905 the amount of arable cultivated in Stetchworth fell from *c.* 2,100 a. to 1,800 a., and the areas of grass and woodland increased from 400 a. and 270 a. to 680 a. and 519 a. respectively.[90] The changes reflect the development of stud farms and training stables. Stetchworth Park Stud was established in 1833.[91] In the 1880s Heath farm was leased to Matthew Dawson, one of a well-known northern family of trainers.[92] In the 1920s it was a stud farm, and since the 1960s has housed the National Stud.[93] In 1891 Egerton House and stables were built by the earl of Ellesmere, with profits made from the Stetchworth Park Stud. It was planned as the most up-to-date training establishment in the country; the stables, which took 2½ years to build, could accommodate up to 80 horses, and 120 a. of arable was converted to grassland, with extensive belts of trees. Egerton House was leased until 1925 to Richard Marsh who was trainer to the prince of Wales, later Edward VII, and to George V.[94] The ownership apparently passed to the earl of Ellesmere's third son, T. H. F. Egerton, who in 1925 sold it to Henry Lascelles, Viscount Lascelles, later earl of Harewood (d. 1947). Marsh was followed by W. Jarvis, also a royal trainer. In 1943 Egerton was sold to the Hon. Mrs. Macdonald-Buchanan who still owned it in 1976 when it was run as Egerton Stud.[95] Since 1903 there has also been Aislabie Stud in the village.[96]

In 1924 Egerton House alone employed 54 racing staff, and in 1973 the racing establishments and agriculture provided almost all the local employment.[97] From 1908 until 1954 there was a dairy farm at Stetchworth Ley which provided milk for the Stetchworth Dairy. The dairy, a large concern with shops in Newmarket, Cambridge, and Bury St. Edmunds, retained the name after its connexion with the parish had ceased.[98] In the 14th century there was a tailor at Stetchworth,[99] but few other non-agricultural workers occur until the 20th century. About 1950 a woodworking business was established in the village, and in 1961 had *c.* 20 employees.[1]

A windmill stood at the end of Mill Lane in the early 16th century, and was continuously recorded between 1674 and 1901.[2] By 1876 it was a wind and steam mill. It had ceased working by the late 1930s when it was converted to a private house.[3]

LOCAL GOVERNMENT. Patmers manor, for which no separate courts are recorded, owed suit to the Cambridgeshire tourn of the honor of Richmond.[4] The prior of Ely claimed liberties including view of frankpledge, the assize of bread and of ale, infangthief, and waifs and strays in Stetchworth as in his other lands.[5] Court rolls survive for Stetchworth manor for 1422–60, 1509–58, and 1626–1924 with a few gaps.[6] In the 15th and 16th centuries courts baron were held once or twice a year, combined with a view of frankpledge usually once a year. By the 17th century meetings were more irregular, with an average of one court a year which was not always a court leet, and from the mid 18th century were even less frequent. In the 15th and 16th centuries the leet dealt with cases of assault, theft, and breaking the peace, and in the 16th and 17th centuries heard charges of adultery and immorality. From the 15th century a hayward and a pinder were appointed, and from the 16th century constables and ale-tasters. The amount of agricultural regulation declined in the 18th century, and from the 1770s the court was concerned only with tenurial matters.

In 1629 the parish acquired a poorhouse, called the town house or guildhall, which probably stood at the corner of Church Lane, south of the green. It was administered and repaired by the overseers, but by 1814 it was in so bad a condition that it was demolished. A new poorhouse was built by the parish, on land given by Richard Eaton.[7] Besides cash payments to the poor, the overseers sometimes paid rent or boarding-fees and provided nursing, medicines, food, and clothing.[8] In 1813 five people were housed in the poorhouse and 24 received permanent outside relief.[9] Expenditure on poor relief rose from £85 in 1776 to £490 in 1834. Stetchworth's expenditure was usually among the lowest in the hundred, but in 1834 it was the second highest. In 1803 the number who received permanent outside relief was 26, the highest in the hundred.[10] In 1835 Stetchworth became part of the Newmarket poor-law union, remaining in the 1930s in the Newmarket R.D.[11] and in 1974 being included in East Cambridgeshire.

87 B.L. Maps 136. a. 4(4); ex inf. Mr. D. Hutton.
88 B.L. Maps 136. a. 4(4); C.R.O., Q/RDc 37.
89 B.L. Maps 136. a. 4(4); O.S. Map 1/25,000, TL 65 (1956 edn.).
90 *Rep. Com. Poor Laws* [44], p. 65, H.C. (1834), xxx; Cambs. Agric. Returns, 1905.
91 *Camb. Ind. Press*, 13 Oct. 1961.
92 C.R.O., R 54/23/34.
93 *Kelly's Dir. Cambs.* (1888 and later edns.). The National Stud was officially opened in 1967: ex inf. Mr. M. T. Bramwell, Director.
94 S. Lee, *King Edward VII*, i. 581; R. Marsh, *Trainer to Two Kings*, 92–3, 114; see below, plate facing p. 177.
95 Ex inf. Messrs. Hunters, solicitors; *Kelly's Dir. Cambs.* (1925).
96 O.S. Map 6", Cambs. XLIX. NW. (1903 edn.).
97 Marsh, *Trainer to Two Kings*, photog. facing p. 322; *Stetchworth Draft Village Plan* (1973).
98 *Camb. Chron.* 22 and 29 Aug. 1923; ex inf. Mr. D. Hutton, Mr. C. Rush.
99 *Plac. de Banco, 1327–8*, i (L. & I. xxxii), 57.
1 *Camb. Ind. Press*, 13 Oct. 1961.
2 C.R.O., R 52/5/1A rot. 3; R 59/28/2; ibid., 101/T/1148–86.
3 *Camb. Chron.* 25 Mar. 1876; ex inf. the Revd. N. W. L. Auster, vicar of Dullingham.
4 S.C. 2/155/71 mm. IV.–3.
5 *Plac. de Quo Warr.* (Rec. Com.), 104.
6 C.R.O., R 59/28/1–3; R 52/5/1A–B; R 53/18/1–6; R 59/20/1; R 54/2/1–3.
7 *31st Rep. Com. Char.* 138; C.R.O., Q/RDz 9, p. 322; Q/RDc 37.
8 C.R.O., P 145/12/1–4; R 59/20/4.
9 *Poor Law Abstract, 1818*, 30–1.
10 *Poor Law Abstract, 1804*, 38–9; *Poor Rate Returns, 1816–21*, 11; *1822–4*, 38; *1825–9*, 16; *1830–4*, 16.
11 *Poor Law Com. 2nd Rep.* 513; *Census*, 1931 (pt. ii).

CHURCH. There was a church at Stetchworth in 1191 when the rectory was annexed to Ely priory and a vicarage was ordained.[12] The advowson of the vicarage descended with Stetchworth manor. Throughout the 13th century the vicarage was valued at 20 marks. In the 14th century there was reference to its poverty, and in the 15th century, when worth £4, it was exempt from paying tenths. In 1534 it was valued at £10 12*s.* 2*d.*[13] In the early 17th century there were *c.* 46 a. of glebe in the open fields. The vicar also had a sheep-course for 200 sheep and a several heath whose boundaries had been decided by a Chancery suit in the 16th century. He received the small tithes of Stetchworth, tithe hay from certain lands in Dullingham, and a yearly pension of 23*s.* 4*d.* from Sir John North.[14] In 1658 the income was *c.* £42, and Lord Russell asked for an augmentation of £50.[15] By 1787 the vicar had ceased to receive the pension and the tithes from Dullingham, although he was awarded 6½ a. when that parish was inclosed.[16] At the inclosure of Stetchworth he was awarded 132 a., mostly on Newmarket Heath, 111 a. of which had been sold by 1892.[17] In 1835 the income of the vicarage was £174, and in 1877 £291.[18] A vicarage house with five hearths was built *c.* 1655 by Sir Francis Russell.[19] In 1728 the vicar did not live there, but boarded with a parishioner, but the house was in good repair in 1775, and until the early 18th century. In 1836 it was said to be built of lath and plaster on a timber frame.[20] The vicarage, on the west side of the main street, was probably rebuilt in the later 19th century. It was a private house by 1976.

There was a chaplain in Stetchworth in 1400, and probably in 1515,[21] and a village guild dedicated to St. Peter in 1491 and 1527.[22] In the early 16th century a parishioner refused to receive communion, and another was accused of sleeping in church.[23] The vicar in 1561 was not a graduate and was not licensed to preach.[24] In 1623 the vicar was accused of playing cards on Easter Monday instead of reading prayers.[25] Robert Poole, vicar in 1650, used the old service book. His living was sequestered in 1650 but restored in 1660, and Poole served until his death in 1675.[26] In 1662 a number of his parishioners refused to attend church.[27] In 1728 there were two Sunday services at Stetchworth, and quarterly sacraments with *c.* 20 communicants.[28] From 1743 John Symonds was vicar of Stetchworth, but lived in his other parish, Dullingham. His son, also John, served Stetchworth as curate, and from 1778 to 1808 as vicar. He was also vicar of Swaffham Bulbeck and curate of Woodditton.[29] In 1775 only one Sunday service was held, and three communions a year.[30]

In 1836 the non-resident vicar provided a curate, and in 1857 both vicar and curate were resident.[31] By 1836 two Sunday schools had been started, but only one survived in 1851 and it was poorly attended. There were then two Sunday services, attended by *c.* 100 in the morning and 150 in the afternoon.[32] By 1877 there were monthly communions. A mission was held in 1887; by 1897 there were three Sunday services, two on weekdays, and weekly communions.[33] From 1946 Stetchworth was held with Woodditton, where the vicar lived.[34] In 1976 the vicar of Dullingham was in charge of Stetchworth.

A wooden chapel was built for the Egerton stables between 1897[35] and 1901. From 1901 to 1907 it was served by its own chaplain, who also served as a hospital chaplain. After 1907 evening services were held there each Sunday by clergy from neighbouring parishes. It remained in use until after the Second World War, and in 1976 the building still stood next to Egerton Cottage.[36]

The church of *ST. PETER*, so called in the 13th century,[37] has a chancel, aisled nave, and west tower.[38] The chancel, which has lancet windows, dates from the 13th century. The chancel arch and nave of four bays were rebuilt towards the end of the 14th century, and the tower arch dates from the same period, although the tower seems to have been altered or rebuilt in the 15th century. The octagonal font is 16th-century, although its base may be older. After the mid 18th century a south porch and doorway were removed, as was the chancel screen, and the 'odd square Presbyterian' east window was replaced by one in 14th-century style, and two quatrefoil windows were inserted in each aisle. The nave and aisles were restored in 1894, when the roof was partly rebuilt, although the original tie-beams remain. In 1907 the chancel was restored, and in 1971 the tower.[39] There was a gallery in 1876, for the lord of the manor,[40] but it was probably removed during the restoration of 1894. A large monument to Henry Gorges (d. 1674), son of Lord Gorges, including his effigy in Roman dress and the demi-figures of his parents in 17th-century costume, stands in the north aisle.[41] There is also an early-15th-century brass to John and Eleanor Coo.

The church had one chalice in the 13th century,[42] and in 1552 there were two silver chalices and patens.[43] The plate includes a 16th-century silver

[12] B.L. Add. MS. 5819, f. 134v.
[13] *Val. of Norwich*, ed. Lunt, 535; *E.D.R.* (1895), 35; *E.D.R.* (1908), 42; *Valor Eccl.* (Rec. Com.), iii. 504.
[14] C 3/34/47; C.U.L., E.D.R., H 1/5, terrier 1615.
[15] *Cal. S.P. Dom.* 1658–9, 48.
[16] C.U.L., E.D.R., H 1/8, terrier 1787; C.R.O., Q/RDz 6, p. 306.
[17] C.R.O., Q/RDz 9, p. 323; *Glebe Land (Sales)*, H.C. 364, p. 455 (1892 Sess. 1), lix.
[18] *Rep. Com. Eccl. Revenues*, pp. 352–3; C.U.L., E.D.R., C 3/39.
[19] B.L. Add. MS. 5819, f. 109; E 179/84/437 rot. 73.
[20] C.U.L., E.D.R., B 7/1; B 8/1; C 1/1; C 1/4; C 3/21.
[21] *E.D.R.* (1899), 158; Prob. 11/18 (P.C.C. 10 Holder, will of John Folks).
[22] Prob. 11/9 (P.C.C. 17 Dogett, will of Thos. Kennet); *Trans. C.H.A.S.* i. 398.
[23] C.U.L., E.D.R., B 2/18, ff. 19v., 75.
[24] B.L. Add. MS. 5813, f. 64.
[25] C.U.L., E.D.R., B 2/32, f. 81v.
[26] Lamb. Pal. MS. 904, f. 248; *Walker Revised*, ed. Matthews, 86.
[27] C.U.L., E.D.R., B 2/54, f. 8v.
[28] Ibid. B 8/1.
[29] Ibid. C 1/1; B 8/4, f. 30; C 1/4; P.R.O. Inst. Bks. ser. C, i (2), f. 449v.
[30] C.U.L., E.D.R., C 1/1.
[31] Ibid. C 3/21; B 1/16.
[32] Ibid. C 1/6; C 3/21; H.O. 129/188/1/5/5.
[33] C.U.L., E.D.R., C 3/27; C 3/39.
[34] *Crockford* (1946 and later edns.).
[35] C.U.L., E.D.R., C 3/39.
[36] *Crockford* (1907); ex inf. Mr. M. Marsh and Mr. J. Waugh.
[37] B.L. Add. MS. 5819, f. 133v.
[38] The following is based on Pevsner, *Cambs.* 460–1; B.L. Add. MS. 5819, ff. 107–8v.
[39] *Kelly's Dir. Cambs.* (1900, 1912); *Camb. Ind. Press*, 15 Apr. 1971.
[40] B.L. Maps 136. a. 4(4).
[41] *Mon. Inscr. Cambs.* 155; see above, plate facing p. 65.
[42] *Vetus Liber Arch. Elien.* (C.A.S. 8vo ser. xlviii), 50–1.
[43] *Cambs. Ch. Goods, temp. Edw. VI*, 72.

chalice and paten, and also a second paten, a flagon, and an alms-dish given by Lady Gorges in 1674, 1675, and 1677.[44] In the 16th century there were four bells,[45] and in the 20th century five: (i and ii) 1608, R. Holdfield of Cambridge; (iii) *c.* 1570, probably by Richard Nicholson; (iv) 1450, made at Bury St. Edmunds; (v) 1564, Stephen Tonne.[46] The parish registers begin in 1666 and are complete.[47]

NONCONFORMITY. Some Stetchworth people who refused to attend church in the 1660s were probably protestant dissenters.[48] There were two nonconformists in 1676, and one Independent in 1728.[49] In 1807 there were two Presbyterians, and by 1825 two or three attended a Baptist meeting at Kirtling and a few others a Methodist meeting elsewhere.[50] In 1843 a house was registered for protestant worship, and a building was registered for Primitive Methodists from 1867 to 1933.[51]

In 1877 the parish had *c.* 12 dissenters.[52] In 1870 Robert Fenn and others had given land in Stetchworth for a gospel hall, with rent for its upkeep. The hall, an iron building with 400 sittings, was registered for Congregationalist use in 1885.[53] In 1897 there were *c.* 250 dissenters in the parish. By 1955 the number of Congregationalist church members had fallen to seven, but in 1967 there were eighteen.[54] By 1961 the old gospel hall had been demolished and services were being held in a local hall.[55] In 1964 a new brick-built church was opened on the site of the old hall on the eastern side of the main street.[56]

EDUCATION. There was no schoolmaster in the parish in 1636.[57] A century later there was still no school, but some children were taught to read. By 1825 there was a schoolmaster, and in 1833 three day-schools taught *c.* 50 children.[58] In the 1860s a school was built and supported by public subscription. It was altered and a classroom added in or after 1876. In 1877 *c.* 75 children attended; numbers rose and in 1892 the earl of Ellesmere enlarged the school to accommodate 150.[59] In 1897 he enlarged it further and built a new infant school.[60] Attendance reached a total of 168 in 1905–6, and then fell steadily to 33 in 1938. In 1947 the seniors were transferred to Bottisham village college.[61] In 1973 19 children attended the primary school, which was planned to be closed,[62] but the old school was still in use in 1976.

In 1913 the county council built a school in the north-west end of the parish at Stetchworth Heath; *c.* 21 attended in the first year. Numbers rose to 38 in 1919 and 1927, but had fallen to 26 by 1938. The seniors were transferred to Bottisham in 1947.[63] The junior mixed and infant school remained in 1976.

CHARITIES FOR THE POOR. In 1700 Lord Gorges and his wife established an alms-house in Stetchworth, endowed with a rent-charge of £30 on Hall farm, for two men and two women who would be given 2*s.* a week, 20*s.* a year for fuel, and a new coat or dress every two years. In 1805 Richard Eaton rebuilt the house on a different site. Payments were being made regularly in 1863.[64] The second alms-house, which stood on the west side of the main street, was a two-storeyed, thatched building, divided into two pairs of two-roomed dwellings, each with a garden. In 1952, when the alms-house was in urgent need of repair and improvement, having no piped water, drainage, sanitation, or lighting, the rent-charge was redeemed with £1,200 of treasury stock. Under a Scheme of 1954 the alms-house was sold in 1956 to Newmarket R.D.C. after the death or departure of the last occupants. The alms-house was renovated and still stood in the southern part of the village in 1976. Under another Scheme of 1960 the income from the £150 proceeds of sale and the £1,200 stock was to be used for the benefit of the poor of Stetchworth, Dullingham, and Woodditton in cases of hardship or sickness, and to help with occupational training. The income was so distributed in 1976.[65]

In 1783 there were three pieces of land of unknown origin whose rent was devoted to the poor. At inclosure trustees were allotted 1 a. which, with 5 a. of Richard Eaton's, was let to the poor as gardens. Up to 1837 the income was distributed in blankets, and in 1863 in food.[66] In 1951 the yearly income of £1 15*s.* was spent on coal. By 1965 there were no tenants for the allotments, and in 1971 the land, which lay behind the old alms-house, was sold to Newmarket R.D.C. By a Scheme of 1975 income from the £4,000 so raised was to be spent on general relief in the parish.[67]

44 List of ch. plate *penes V.C.H.*
45 *Cambs. Ch. Goods, temp. Edward VI*, 72.
46 MS. notes by H. B. Walters (1936), *penes V.C.H.*
47 C.R.O., P 145/1/1 sqq.
48 C.U.L., E.D.R., B 2/54; Palmer, *Puritans in Melbourn, 1640–88*, 24.
49 Compton Census; C.U.L., E.D.R., B 8/1.
50 C.U.L., E.D.R., C 1/4; C 1/6.
51 G.R.O. Worship Returns, Ely dioc. no. 667; G.R.O. Worship Reg. no. 18275.
52 C.U.L., E.D.R., C 3/27.
53 Char. Com. files; *Kelly's Dir. Cambs.* (1892, 1922); G.R.O. Worship Reg. no. 28878.
54 C.U.L., E.D.R., C 3/39; *Cong. Year Bk.* (1955, 1967–8).
55 *Camb. Ind. Press*, 13 Oct. 1961.
56 Ex inf. Mrs. D. Parr.
57 Bodl. MS. Gough Eccl. Top. 3, f. 76.
58 C.U.L., E.D.R., B 8/1; C 1/6; *Educ. Enquiry Abstract*, 60.
59 C.R.O., R 59/20/5, 1866; *Kelly's Dir. Cambs.* (1869, 1892); Ed. 7/5; *Rep. of Educ. Cttee. of Council, 1892–3* [C. 7089-I], p. 688, H.C. (1893–4), xxvi.
60 *Kelly's Dir. Cambs.* (1900).
61 *Public Elem. Schs. 1907* [Cd. 3901], p. 28, H.C. (1908), lxxxiv; *Bd. of Educ., List 21, 1938* (H.M.S.O.), 20; Black, *Cambs. Educ. Rec.* 73.
62 *Stetchworth Draft Village Plan* (1973).
63 Ed. 7/5; *Bd. of Educ., List 21, 1914* (H.M.S.O.), 29; *1919*, 16; *1927*, 16; *1938*, 20; Black, *Cambs. Educ. Rec.* 73.
64 *31st Rep. Com. Char.* 138; *Char. Digest Cambs. 1863–4*, 34–5; C.U.L., E.D.R., C 1/4.
65 Char. Com. files.
66 C.U.L., E.D.R., B 7/6; C.R.O., P 145/1/3; *31st Rep. Com. Char.* 138; *Char. Digest Cambs. 1863–4*, 34–5.
67 Char. Com. files; *Camb. Ind. Press*, 6 May 1971.

BABRAHAM: the school and alms-houses of 1723

STETCHWORTH: the former White Horse Inn of 1905

West Wratting: E. P. Frost at the controls of one of his flying machines

Stetchworth: a party, including the Prince of Wales and the Duke of York, at the Egerton Stud in 1896

WESTLEY WATERLESS

THE PARISH of Westley Waterless, covering *c.* 1,150 a., lies 5½ miles south-west of Newmarket.[1] The village is at the south-eastern end of the parish, on high ground, *c.* 2 miles south of Dullingham station. The land rises from 125 ft. on the chalk at Westley Bottom in the north-west to 350 ft. at the eastern end of the village. Westley appears to have been carved out of the neighbouring parish of Burrough Green with which it was assessed for tax until the late 14th century.[2] As its name implies it lies west of Dullingham Ley and Stetchworth Ley, on land cleared of the wood which once covered the boulder clay lying, in the eastern part, over the chalk.[3] There are few watercourses in the parish. A stream crosses the west corner, but one well in the village is said to have supplied the whole area with water.[4]

Burrough End, at the eastern end of the village, is in Burrough Green parish, which also juts into the part of Westley village where the school stood. Near the south-west boundary *c.* 31 a. on the Burrough Green side of the Dullingham–Brinkley road is in Westley parish. Tradition ascribes its acquisition to a trial by combat in the early 14th century between Sir John de Crek and Sir John de Burgh, when Crek won the land, known as Brinkley Common, for his manor of Westley.[5] Between the Newmarket road and the railway, both of which cross the parish in the north-west, and Westley village, the north-east boundary follows a road; the south-west boundary, fairly straight towards the Newmarket road, is less regular in the south-east, following the edge of woodland. About 25 a. of wood remain in that corner of the parish.

The village of Westley is a small group of houses along a single street that runs north-west from Burrough End, and most houses are strung out along its north-eastern side. Near the south-eastern end is a close of six council houses. On the south-west side of the road stands the rectory, and on the same side, at the north-western edge of the village, the church, Westley Hall Farm, and the site of the manor-house are grouped around a pond. A few more houses stand at the north-western end of the parish, near Westley Bottom and Six Mile Bottom, including Westley Lodge Farm. South-east of Westley Bottom is Hungry Hill, so called since at least 1426.[6] East of Hungry Hill in 1890 there stood New Farm; by 1953 it had disappeared, and there was only a sheepyard on its site. The village contained *c.* 1910 the Trace-horse public house, called the White Horse by 1937.[7] There was no public house by 1976.

The village site seems to have been occupied since the 10th century. A leaden vessel filled with tools was found there dating from 975×1066.[8] Thirteen inhabitants were recorded in 1086.[9] There were 15 households in 1563, and 14–18 in the mid 17th century.[10] In 1728 there were still only 16 families, containing *c.* 68 people, but by 1801 the population had risen to 126. Numbers continued to rise to 214 in 1851, but had fallen to 176 by 1901. There was a slight increase for the next 20 years, but the population had fallen to 134 in 1971.[11]

MANORS AND OTHER ESTATES. In 1086 Countess Judith held 3 yardlands and 10 a. in Westley which had been held by two men of Earl Harold.[12] The estate presumably descended with the rest of her lands in the barony of Kirtling, and is probably identifiable with the land of the little hall which Ralph de Tony gave to Agnes de Valognes before 1126.[13] It later passed to Agnes's granddaughter Gunnore, along with the fee which Agnes had held of the bishopric of Ely, and the two estates seem to have merged. That is presumably why, in 1617, Westley was said to be held of the manor of Kirtling.[14] The link otherwise disappears.

In 1066 the abbot of Ely held 3 hides in Westley which were later associated with lands in Fulbourn and Teversham and were possibly acquired with those lands in the late 10th century.[15] In the late 12th century Agnes de Valognes granted to Gunnore her fee in those three places, held of the bishop of Ely for the service of 2 knights. *WESTLEY* was presumably the manor, worth £15, which Agnes had held in 1185.[16] In 1212 Gunnore's second husband Robert FitzWalter (d. 1235) was lord,[17] and his descendants later held the mesne lordship, Robert FitzWalter (d. 1326) being succeeded by his son Robert (d. 1328), by that Robert's son John, later Lord FitzWalter, and by Walter, Lord FitzWalter (d. 1386).[18] By 1227 the manor had been subinfeudated to Christine, daughter of Gunnore and Robert, who held it with her second husband Raymond de Burgh.[19] Raymond died in 1230, Christine without issue in 1232, and in the mid 13th century John de Burgh, son of Raymond's uncle the justiciar Hubert de Burgh, sold the manor to Walter de Crek, whose son John, M.P. and sheriff of Cambridgeshire, held Westley in 1299 and is commemorated by a brass

1 This account was written in 1976. Where no other reference is given the topography is based on O.S. Maps 6", Cambs. XLVIII. NE., XLIX. SW., (1890 and later edns.); 1/25,000, TL 55 and TL 65 (1956 edn.).

2 *V.C.H. Cambs.* i. 405; *Cambs. Lay Subsidy, 1327*, 17; E 179/237/7A f. 239.

3 *P.N. Cambs.* (E.P.N.S.), 120.

4 *Camb. Ind. Press*, 27 May 1960.

5 C.R.O., R 59/29/2/2/3; *Camb. Evening News*, 6 Jan. 1966.

6 *P.N. Cambs.* (E.P.N.S.), 120.

7 *Camb. Ind. Press*, 27 May 1960; *Kelly's Dir. Cambs.* (1937).

8 Fox, *Arch. Camb. Region*, 300.

9 *V.C.H. Cambs.* i. 405.

10 B.L. Harl. MS. 594, f. 199v.; see below, pp. 278–81.

11 C.U.L., E.D.R., B 8/1; *Census*, 1801–1971.

12 *V.C.H. Cambs.* i. 398.

13 *Cat. Anct. D.* v, A 11090; Farrer, *Feud. Cambs.* 50.

14 *Cat. Anct. D.* ii, A 3699; B.L. Add. MS. 5838, f. 186.

15 *V.C.H. Cambs.* i. 364; Farrer, *Feud. Cambs.* 107; *Saga Bk. of Viking Soc.* iv. 113.

16 *Cat. Anct. D.* ii, A 3699; Farrer, *Feud. Cambs.* 106.

17 *Red Bk. Exch.* (Rolls Ser.), ii. 525; Saunders, *Eng. Baronies*, 129–30.

18 *Cal. Inq. p.m.* vii, p. 129; xiv, pp. 230–1; xvi, p. 141; *Complete Peerage*, v. s.v. FitzWalter.

19 *Rot. Litt. Claus.* (Rec. Com.), ii. 201; Farrer, *Feud. Cambs.* 165.

(*c.* 1325) in the church.[20] In 1353 Master John de Crek granted the manor of Westley in tail to Sir Edmund Vauncey and his wife Joan, John's niece, and Sir Edmund held it at his death in 1372.[21] His heir, also Edmund, then a minor, died in 1389 leaving his half-sister Joan as heir.[22] She and her first husband Thomas Prior held Westley in 1392 and 1412.[23] In 1422 her second husband, John Hore of Childerley, conveyed the manor to Sir Richard Waldegrave (d. 1435)[24] whose son and heir Sir Richard was succeeded *c.* 1464 by his son Sir Thomas.[25] Sir Thomas died in 1472 leaving a son William under age[26] who in 1487 sold Westley to Richard Gardiner, a London alderman (d. 1489).[27] Gardiner's lands passed to his daughter Mary, who married her father's ward, Sir Giles Alington of Horseheath (d. 1521).[28] Their eldest son, known as William Alington of Westley, died before his father, and the manor passed to William's brother Sir Giles Alington (d. 1586). Thereafter, Westley seems to have become separated from Horseheath, and passed to William (d. 1615), second son of the younger Sir Giles's second marriage, and then to William's son Giles.[29]

Giles married Anne, daughter of Robert Turner of Wratting (Suff.), and Westley apparently passed to her family, for Thomas Turner (d. 1648) left it to his son, also Thomas.[30] Thomas held the manor in 1674 but seems to have sold it to Thomas Cage, and by *c.* 1730 Westley belonged to Charles Seymour, duke of Somerset, descending with Burrough Green to Heneage Finch, earl of Aylesford (d. 1777).[31] Finch's son the 3rd earl sold it in 1811 to James Barker, rector of Westley 1836–50, who held a number of benefices and lands in Cambridgeshire.[32] In 1843 Barker sold the manor, with almost all the land in the parish, to Col. John Hall.[33] Westley descended with Hall's other lands to his nephew W. H. Bullock, who assumed the name Hall, and to Bullock's son, A. C. Hall, who sold it in 1912 as part of the Six Mile Bottom estate. It was bought by Sir Ernest Cassel (d. 1921) and passed to his granddaughter Ruth Cunningham-Reid (later Lady Delamere).[34] In 1939 Westley Hall farm was bought by Mr. A. S. Hensby who owned it in 1976.[35] Westley Lodge farm and over 600 a. in the north-western half of the parish then remained part of the Six Mile Bottom estate.[36]

Westley Hall, which was destroyed by fire in 1975, incorporated the central range and one cross-wing of a late-16th- or 17th-century house, which had 8 hearths in 1672[37] and which had been altered and partly refaced in the 18th century.

The preceptory of Shingay held some land in Westley at its dissolution. A small rent was paid from Westley to Lord Sandys, in right of Shingay manor, in the mid 18th century.[38] The prior and convent of Anglesey held land there in the late 13th century.[39] In the 16th century they had a pasture called Anglesey, which in 1557 was granted to Henry Vavasor and Thomas Warde.[40]

In 1086 two knights held 1 hide in Westley of Count Alan.[41] In 1272 Baldwin of Essex granted a messuage and 1 carucate, possibly the same estate, to Hugh of Essex.[42] In 1307 Reynold of Essex sold a messuage and *c.* 70 a. in Westley to Nicholas de Styvecle, who in 1321 conveyed to William of Hacford *c.* 80 a., still held by Reynold of Essex for life.[43] William, recorded in Westley in 1322, in 1330 renounced his rights of pasture in the Moor in Westley to William de Crek.[44] In 1369 John son of John de Styvecle quitclaimed to John son of Walter of Hacford his rights in a messuage and 48 a. in Westley.[45] Those families and that land have not been found recorded later.

Downing College, Cambridge, bought 6 a. in Westley in 1870. By 1903 it was part of Bottisham Heath farm, which the college sold in 1928.[46]

ECONOMIC HISTORY. In 1086 there were just under 5 hides in Westley. Of 3 hides belonging to Ely abbey, 1 hide and 3 yardlands were in demesne. There were two plough-teams there, and two *servi*, and there was land for three more teams. There was 4 a. of meadow. Count Alan's one hide was held by Geoffrey and another knight, and was worked by two plough-teams. It had previously been held by seven sokemen. On Countess Judith's 3 yardlands and 10 acres there was one team, and there could have been another. Hardwin de Scalers held 15 a. which had been held by two sokemen of Earl Harold's. There were 5 *villani* and 6 bordars in the vill. The Ely lands had fallen substantially in value from 100*s.* in 1066 to 10*s.* in 1086; the value of the other estates had remained unchanged.[47]

In 1086 Westley was a demesne vill of Ely abbey.[48] By 1390 the size of the demesne seems to have increased. There were 300 a. of arable, two-thirds of which appear to have been sown each year, and

[20] *Ex e Rot. Fin.* (Rec. Com.), i. 199–200, 241; *Knights of Edw. I*, i (Harl. Soc. lxxx), 160–1; *Plac. de Quo Warr.* (Rec. Com.), 106; R. K. M. Davies, *Church of Westley Waterless* (1970), 4–5.

[21] C.P. 25(1)/28/77 no. 21; *Cal. Inq. p.m.* xiv, pp. 230–1.

[22] *Cal. Inq. p.m.* xiv, pp. 230–1; C 136/64 no. 11; *V.C.H. Herts.* iii. 167.

[23] C.P. 25(1)/30/90 no. 15; *Feud. Aids*, vi. 407; *E.D.R.* (1900), 160.

[24] C.P. 25(1)/30/96 no. 1; *Cal. Fine R.* 1430–7, 216.

[25] *Cal. Fine R.* 1430–7, 237; *Cal. Pat.* 1461–7, 573.

[26] *Cal. Fine R.* 1471–85, p. 36; *Cal. Pat.* 1467–76, 338.

[27] C.P. 25(1)/30/101 no. 3.

[28] Hist. MSS. Com. 55, *Var. Coll.* ii, p. 297; *Cal. Inq. p.m. Hen. VII*, i, pp. 235–6; C.P. 25(2)/4/18 no. 30.

[29] *Visit. Cambs.* (Harl. Soc. xli), 14; *Proc. C.A.S.* xli. 50; *Cal. Pat.* 1555–7, 55–6; B.L. Add. MS. 5838, f. 186.

[30] *Visit. Cambs.* (Harl. Soc. xli), 14; Prob. 11/205 (P.C.C. 127 Essex).

[31] E 179/244/23 rot. 67v.; C.P. 25(2)/633/22 Chas. II East. no. 14; C.P. 25(2)/1102/6 & 7 Geo. II Trin. no. 16; Lysons, *Cambs.* 276.

[32] *Camb. Chron.* 2 Aug. 1811; *31st Rep. Com. Char.* 139; *Alum. Cantab. 1752–1900*, i. 152.

[33] C.R.O., L 80/203.

[34] *Kelly's Dir. Cambs.* (1858 and later edns.); Burke, *Land Gent.* (1906), i. 748; C.R.O., 296/SP 1078; *D.N.B.* s.v. Cassel.

[35] Char. Com. files.

[36] Ex inf. Messrs. Robinson & Hall, land agents.

[37] E 179/244/23 rot. 67d.

[38] *L. & P. Hen. VIII*, xv, p. 294; C.R.O., R 52/12/4/2.

[39] B.L. Add. MS. 5819, f. 154.

[40] S.C. 6/Hen. VIII/264 rot. 1; *Cal. Pat.* 1557–8, 277.

[41] *V.C.H. Cambs.* i. 379.

[42] *Cat. Anct. D.* i, A 798; C.P. 25(1)/283/17 no. 498.

[43] C.P. 25(1)/26/52 no. 8; C.P. 25(1)/27/61 no. 5.

[44] *Cal. Pat.* 1321–4, 166; B.L. Add. MS. 5819, f. 74v.

[45] Ex inf. Northumb. Co. Rec. Off., based on Alnwick Castle MS. X, II 17, Box 1C.

[46] Ex inf. Mr. S. French, Archivist, Downing College.

[47] *V.C.H. Cambs.* i. 364, 379, 384, 398, 405.

[48] Ibid. 364.

c. 15 a. of pasture.[49] In 1448 the whole manor was farmed out.[50] In the mid 13th century the glebe was sown with 2 a. of wheat, 6 a. of rye, 8 a. of oats, 1 a. of barley, and ¾ a. of vetches.[51] In the 14th century vines may have been grown in Westley and in the 16th century apples and pears were grown there.[52] In the early 19th century wheat, barley, and turnips were the chief crops, and rye was also grown. The soil was said to be mostly a good barley loam, but poorer on the heaths and near the top of hills where the chalk lies near the surface. In the early 19th century the heath at the north-west end of the parish was brought into cultivation.[53]

Much importance was attached to folding sheep on arable land.[54] The 118 sheep recorded in Westley in the 11th century were presumably the demesne flock.[55] In 1302 Sir John de Crek granted Thomas of Cambridge, a clerk, liberty of fold for 200 sheep.[56] In the 16th century tenants are recorded owning *c.* 50 sheep, and in the early 17th century the lord had sheep-walk for 300 sheep.[57] In 1793 the earl of Aylesford kept several hundred there. In 1812 the lessee of the manor owned 240 Southdown ewes, 140 Norfolk ewes, 240 half-bred lambs, and 90 Southdown wethers.[58]

In the early 17th century there were three open fields in Westley, Spaythorne, Middle, and Cambridgeway fields, apparently ranged along the length of the parish. By 1663, however, only one field, Westley field, was named. In the late 18th century it was divided into 34 furlongs, varying in size between 4 a. and 55 a.[59] In the late 18th century there were *c.* 140 a. of inclosed and *c.* 613 a. of open arable land. The latter was inclosed by the earl of Aylesford along with Burrough Green in the 1790s. Although inclosure was by private agreement the method was that of a parliamentary award, with three impartial commissioners arbitrating between the parties. No record of the allotments survives, except for the glebe.[60] As a result of inclosure rents in Westley doubled, more corn was produced, and the sheep, although fewer, were of better quality.[61]

In 1843 there were *c.* 83 a. of woodland, all in the hands of the lord of the manor, of which Hay wood and Ladies grove remained in 1975 but Park and Common woods had disappeared. In the mid 19th century land on either side of the Newmarket road was still known as the heath, although by then mostly under cultivation. At the opposite end of the parish, along the Brinkley–Dullingham road, was the Moor, mostly grassland. There were altogether 147 a. of pasture and 842 a. of arable.[62]

In the late 18th century there were seven private landowners besides the earl of Aylesford. The largest other holding soon passed to the earl. No one else's holding exceeded 50 a., and most were less than 5 a.[63] By 1843 there were only five private owners. John Hall held over 1,000 a., and the next largest holding was 31 a.[64] In the early 19th century the manorial estate was leased as two farms, being divided in 1843 into Westley Lodge farm, in the north-west part of the parish, and the Hall farm. By 1858 a farm bailiff occupied Westley Lodge, and in 1912 it was let. In the 20th century only those two farms were over 150 a.[65]

In the early 19th century most of the working population were farm labourers.[66] In 1847 the village had a wheelwright and a post office; by 1858 there was also a flour-dealer. A co-operative store had been established by 1875, when there was also a blacksmith.[67] A brick-works close to the Brinkley boundary seems to have opened by 1843 and closed *c.* 1903.[68] In 1937 there were two shops, a motor engineer, and a basket-maker in the parish.[69] There was no shop in 1976.

A pond north-west of the railway near Westley Bottom was called Mill Pond in the 19th century, the only evidence of a mill in Westley.[70]

LOCAL GOVERNMENT. In 1299 the lord of the manor claimed view of frankpledge, infangthief, tumbrel, and waif in Westley, and he had a gallows on his manor there.[71] In 1376 and 1389 his successors had a court leet there.[72] In the early 17th century a view of frankpledge was held irregularly, on average once a year. Court minutes survive for 1600–11, and record transfers of free and copyhold land, the regulation of common land and of encroachments on the highway, and the appointment of a hayward.[73]

Westley's expenditure on its poor rose from £25 11*s.* in 1776, to £84 4*s.* in 1803 and £170 19*s.* in 1818, before falling substantially to £48 10*s.* in 1834. Those sums were consistently the lowest in the hundred as befitted the smallest and least populous parish. Ten people received permanent outside relief in 1803, and twelve in 1813, while only 2 or 3 had occasional help, again among the lowest figures in the hundred.[74] In 1835 Westley joined the Newmarket poor-law union, and remained in the Newmarket R.D.,[75] being included in 1974 in East Cambridgeshire.

49 C 136/64 no. 11.
50 B.L. Add. MS. 5819, f. 74v.
51 B.L. Cott. MS. Claud. D. xiii, f. 139.
52 V. Pritchard, *Eng. Medieval Graffiti*, 62; B.L. Add. MS. 5861, p. 13.
53 Gooch, *Agric. of Cambs.* 101, 130, 133.
54 Ibid. 250.
55 *V.C.H. Cambs.* i. 405.
56 B.L. Add. MS. 5819, f. 74v.
57 B.L. Add. MS. 5861, pp. 13, 144; 5819, f. 140.
58 C.U.L., Palmer MS. B 37; *Camb. Chron.* 18 Sept. 1812.
59 C.U.L., E.D.R., H 1/6, terrier 1663; C.R.O., R 51/25/29.
60 C.R.O., R 51/25/29; C.U.L., Palmer MS. B 37; H.L.R.O. Private Bill, May 1815.
61 Gooch, *Agric. of Cambs.* 75.
62 C.U.L., E.D.R., Westley Waterless tithe award.
63 C.R.O., R 51/25/29.
64 C.U.L., E.D.R., tithe award.
65 Ibid.; *Camb. Chron.* 2 Aug. 1811; *Kelly's Dir. Cambs.* (1858 and later edns.); C.R.O., 296/SP 1078.
66 *Census*, 1801–41; *Rep. H.L. Cttee. on Poor Laws*, H.C. 227, pp. 328–9 (1831), viii.
67 *Kelly's Dir. Cambs.* (1847 and later edns.).
68 C.U.L., E.D.R., tithe award; O.S. Map 1/2,500, Cambs. XLIX. 9 (1886, 1903 edns.).
69 *Kelly's Dir. Cambs.* (1937).
70 O.S. Map 6″, Cambs. XLVIII. NE. (1890 edn.).
71 *Plac. de Quo Warr.* (Rec. Com.), 106; *Assizes at Camb. 1260*, p. vii.
72 *Cal. Inq. p.m.* xiv, pp. 230–1; C 136/64 no. 11.
73 C.U.L., Add. MS. 6920, ff. 38–46, 52, 62, 68v., 75.
74 *Poor Law Abstract, 1804*, 38–9; *1818*, 30–1; *Poor Rate Returns, 1816–21*, 11; *1822–4*, 38; *1825–9*, 16; *1830–4*, 16.
75 *Poor Law Com. 2nd Rep.* 513; *Census*, 1931 (pt. ii).

CHURCH. A church was recorded at Westley in the later 12th century when Robert de Valognes (fl. 1160), son of Agnes, gave its advowson, lands, and tithes to Binham priory (Norf.).[76] Despite the gift King John presented to the church in 1216, because the bishopric of Ely was in his hands.[77] In 1221 William de Mandeville and his wife Christine, granddaughter of Robert de Valognes, resigned to Binham any right they had in the advowson of Westley, and in 1251 the priory received papal confirmation of the gift of the church.[78] The rectory was appropriated, and from the 13th century until the late 15th the incumbents were recorded and presented as vicars; in 1480, however, the late incumbent was called rector as were nearly all his successors.[79] Moreover, although in 1233 the priory enjoyed the greater part of the endowment of the church, later in the 13th century the vicar took the whole income, paying to Binham a pension of 2*s*. In the 17th century the rector continued to pay a pension, by then 5*s*., to the patron.[80]

The advowson of the vicarage belonged to Binham priory until the Dissolution. In 1547 the Crown, and in 1599 William Campion of Camberwell (Surr.), presented a rector.[81] The advowson passed in 1615 to William's son, and in 1640 to his grandson, both William.[82] The third William Campion was patron until 1701, but Sir Henry Compton and Richard Wynne presented in 1647, and the Crown in 1690. In 1734 Mrs. Elizabeth Philips was patron, and in 1766 George Bucke.[83] From the mid 18th century to *c.* 1889 the advowson seems to have been held by successive rectors.[84] In 1892 and 1904 the patron was R. Merser, although J. Clarke was called patron in 1897. By 1908 Col. A. Merser held the advowson, and in 1912 James Mullin, probably a relative of the previous rector. Since 1918 the patron has been Mrs. D. Kelly.[85]

The church of Westley was valued at 10 marks in the earlier 13th century, at £7 in 1291, and in 1534 at £10 5*s*.[86] In 1650 it was worth £60, and £65 in the early 18th century.[87] A century later its net income was £326, and £360 in 1883.[88] In 1615 there were *c.* 38 a. of glebe and a ten-roomed rectory house, which had six or seven hearths in the mid 17th century.[89] In 1783 the house had recently been rebuilt.[90] The present building is a large, square, grey-brick and slated house of the early 19th century. In the 13th century the church of Westley had received tithes from *c.* 65 a. in Burrough Green. By 1615 the rector received tithes outside Westley from only small amounts of land there and in Brinkley.[91] The amount of glebe remained constant throughout the 17th and 18th centuries, and in the 1790s 35½ a. of open-field land was exchanged for 13 a. of inclosed land near the rectory house, the rector complaining that the exchange was unfair.[92] The glebe amounted to 17 a. in 1887,[93] the extra 4 a. probably being old inclosure.

Two 15th-century vicars of Westley were Cistercian monks, dispensed to hold a cure of souls.[94] There was a guild in the parish in 1517 and 1543.[95] Ralph Hill, rector 1559-*c.* 1599, held another cure but was resident at Westley. It was said that he was unable to preach and did not teach the children or read the scriptures, but he complained that the parishioners did not send their children to be catechized, and that the churchwardens did not present those who refused to come to church. In 1593 he refused to administer communion as only one parishioner came.[96] His successor Robert Gregory served until 1647. In the early 17th century he was troubled by William Alington, who slandered the minister, spoke against preaching and the church courts, and slept through services.[97] Gregory was followed by Thomas Ballowe, who had been ejected from a Sussex living. In 1660 he became a canon of Chichester and resigned Westley,[98] to be succeeded by Robert Sayer, a fellow of Queens' College, Cambridge, who also held a prebend in York and a rectory in Essex. Thomas Dresser, rector 1683–92, was deprived as a non-juror.[99] During his incumbency there were *c.* 45 communicants in Westley.[1] An early 18th-century incumbent who also held a cure in Kent was ordered to reside. He may have been Richard Saunders who died in 1734 having 'lived at Newmarket latterly not agreeing with his parish'.[2] By 1728 there were two Sunday services at Westley, and thrice yearly sacraments, but only eight communicants had attended at Easter.[3] William Beaty, rector 1734–66, was also president of Magdalene College, Cambridge; his successor ran a private boarding school in the village.[4] In the late 18th and early 19th centuries several rectors were non-resident, but seem always to have provided a curate. In 1775 and 1807 there was only one Sunday service, and in 1807 quarterly communions.[5]

By 1825 there were fewer communions, and only

[76] B.L. Cott. MS. Claud. D. xiii, f. 137; *V.C.H. Norf.* ii. 343.
[77] *Rot. Litt. Pat.* (Rec. Com.), 183.
[78] C.P. 25(1)/23/10 no. 7; *Cal. Papal Reg.* i. 272.
[79] B.L. Cott. MS. Claud. D. xiii, f. 138v.; *E.D.R.* (1893), 157; C.U.L., E.D.R., L 3/1, f. 33.
[80] B.L. Cott. MS. Claud. D. xiii, f. 138; C 142/357 no. 76; C 142/603 no. 84.
[81] *E.D.R.* (1913), 24; Gibbons, *Ely Episc. Rec.* 459.
[82] C 142/357 no. 76; C 142/603 no. 84.
[83] P.R.O. Inst. Bks. ser. B, iv, p. 153; ser. C, i (2), f. 451; *L.J.* x. 350.
[84] B.L. Add. MS. 5819, f. 110; C.U.L., E.D.R., B 8/4, f. 37; C 1/4; C 3/21; *Kelly's Dir. Cambs.* (1864 and later edns.).
[85] C.U.L., E.D.R., C 3/39; *Kelly's Dir. Cambs.* (1892 and later edns.); *Crockford* (1975–6).
[86] *Val. of Norwich*, ed. Lunt, 535; *Tax Eccl.* (Rec. Com.), 267; *Valor Eccl.* (Rec. Com.), iii. 504.
[87] Lamb. Pal. MS. 904, f. 268; C.U.L., E.D.R., B 8/1.
[88] *Rep. Com. Eccl. Revenues*, pp. 344–5; *Kelly's Dir. Cambs.* (1883).
[89] C.U.L., E.D.R., H 1/6, terrier 1615; E 179/84/437 rot. 76d.; E 179/244/23 rot. 67d.
[90] C.U.L., E.D.R., B 7/1, p. 7.
[91] B.L. Cott. MS. Claud. D. xiii, ff. 142v.–143; C.U.L., E.D.R., H 1/6, terrier 1615.
[92] C.U.L., Palmer MS. B 37; H.L.R.O., Private Bill, May 1815.
[93] *Glebe Returns*, H.C. 307, p. 42 (1887), lxiv.
[94] C.U.L., E.D.R., L 3/1, ff. 28, 33.
[95] Palmer, *Burrough Green*, 97; *Trans. C.H.A.S.* i. 349.
[96] C.U.L., E.D.R., B 2/3, p. 151; B 2/4, p. 131; B 2/11, ff. 119v., 125v.; B.L. Add. MS. 5813, f. 65; Bodl. MS. Gough Eccl. Top. 3, f. 15.
[97] *Reg. of Westley Waterless, 1557–1840* (Camb. 1963); C.U.L., E.D.R., B 2/28, f. 182.
[98] Lamb. Pal. MS. 904, f. 268; Palmer, *Burrough Green*, 100.
[99] B.L. Add. MS. 5819, f. 110.
[1] Ibid. 5847, f. 38.
[2] C.U.L., E.D.R., B 8/1; *Mon. Inscr. Cambs.* 126.
[3] C.U.L., E.D.R., B 8/1.
[4] B.L. Add. MS. 5819, f. 110; *Camb. Chron.* 5 Dec. 1772.
[5] C.U.L., E.D.R., C 1/1; C 1/4.

two or three communicants; the numbers attending Sunday service had also fallen.[6] J. R. Barker of Hildersham Hall, rector 1836–50, was a considerable landowner in the county, and also held the livings of All Saints Newmarket, Great Abington, and Vauxhall chapel (Surr.).[7] He was followed by E. V. Burridge who served until 1885, but in 1872 his parishioners claimed that he was unstable, frequently absent, and given to excessive drinking.[8] Even so in the 1870s there were two Sunday services and monthly communions, both well attended.[9] By 1897 fortnightly communions were attended by *c.* 24 people.[10] The rector in 1975 had served the cure, along with Weston Colville, since 1936.[11]

The church of *ST. MARY*, so called by the mid 18th century,[12] is built mainly of flint and rubble, and has a chancel, an aisled nave with a small north porch, and a small bell turret. The oldest part of the fabric was probably the round west tower, which fell in 1855.[13] The chancel dates from the early 13th century; the chancel arch and three-bay nave are 14th-century. A ceiling extends over the nave and aisles. On one of the south window surrounds is scratched, in early arabic numerals, a record of vines grown, probably for sacramental wine.[14] The north porch is built of brick. A chancel screen survived in the mid 18th century but has since been removed.[15] The 15th-century font is octagonal with traceried panels. In the south aisle is a brass to Sir John de Crek and his wife Alyne (*c.* 1325). There are 16th- and 17th-century monuments to members of the Alington family, and a black marble slab to Thomas Dalton (d. 1672), a canon of Durham.[16]

In the late 13th century Westley had two chalices, and in the mid 14th century a gold chalice was given by Sir John de Crek.[17] Mary Alington (d. 1537) left the church a silver gilt chalice, and in 1552 the church had one silver gilt chalice and a paten.[18] The plate includes a chalice and paten both dated 1569: the paten had been made from a pre-Reformation one, and the chalice may also have been altered from an earlier piece. There was also a two-handled dish dated 1661.[19] Westley had three bells in the 16th and 18th centuries and in 1837.[20] There were no bells for some time after the collapse of the tower, but a modern bell had been hung in the turret by 1936.[21] Parish registers survive from 1557, with some gaps, mostly in the 18th century, which are covered by bishops' transcripts.[22]

NONCONFORMITY. In 1807 there was one Methodist in Westley, and four in 1825. By 1877 there were seven or eight dissenters, and in 1897 there were still only about ten.[23]

EDUCATION. By 1833 Westley had two day-schools, attended by 14 and 10 children. The rector supported one of them, and also an evening school for 13 boys and a Sunday school.[24] All but the Sunday school seem to have been short-lived,[25] and in 1873 a new school was built by W. H. Hall. Westley Undenominational school opened in 1875, supported by Hall and weekly payments. It received an annual grant from the start. It was attended by 30–40 children; those at Westley Bottom went to Hall's school at Six Mile Bottom.[26] The Westley school was closed after inspection in 1896, but reopened the same year. In the interval Hall had refused to let it be used for a Church school.[27] From 1900 numbers ranged between 20 and 30. The school was transferred to the council in 1913 and reorganized as a junior and infant school in 1926. There were then 10 pupils.[28] It was closed in 1958 when the children were transferred to Burrough Green.[29] The school building on the north-eastern side of the main street was a private house in 1976.

CHARITIES FOR THE POOR. By will proved 1599 Richard Alington gave £20 for the poor of Westley, which along with £34 given by James Alington and £14 15*s.* from Robert Gregory, the rector, was used in 1617 to buy a messuage and two pightles in Westley. The estate was probably represented by the two town houses.[30] By will proved 1682 John Sayer gave £100 to buy land in trust for the poor of Westley, apparently spent on land in Huntingdon, worth £5 a year in the 18th century and £10 in 1837.[31] Some smaller benefactions were also spent on land. Seven acres in Westley, in 1775 let for £4 12*s.* a year, were in 1783 mingled with the earl of Aylesford's lands and there were fears that they would be lost.[32]

Until *c.* 1790 the £10 income from all the charity lands was distributed in beef to the poor, and the cottages were occupied rent-free by old men and widows. When he undertook inclosure Lord Aylesford promised to pay £10 rather than £5 from the Westley lands, and the fences and balks marking off the charity lands were removed. After 1811, while Aylesford's successor, Barker, was involved in a Chancery suit, the payments ceased, and all the

6 Ibid. C 1/6.
7 *Alum. Cantab. 1752–1900*, i. 152.
8 Char. Com. files.
9 C.U.L., E.D.R., C 3/27.
10 Ibid. C 3/39.
11 *Crockford* (1975–6).
12 B.L. Add. MS. 5819, f. 110.
13 C.U.L., Palmer MS. B 37.
14 V. Pritchard, *Eng. Medieval Graffiti*, 62.
15 B.L. Add. MS. 5819, f. 111.
16 *Mon. Inscr. Cambs.* 180–1, 243.
17 *Vetus Liber Arch. Elien.* (C.A.S. 8vo ser. xlviii), 52–3.
18 *Proc. C.A.S.* xli. 5; *Cambs. Ch. Goods, temp. Edw. VI*, 7–8.
19 Davies, *Ch. of Westley Waterless*, 7; list of church plate *penes V.C.H.*
20 *Cambs. Ch. Goods, temp. Edw. VI*, 8; B.L. Add. MS. 5819, f. 110; C.U.L., E.D.R., H 1/8, terrier 1837.
21 MS. notes by H. B. Walters (1936), *penes V.C.H.*
22 *Reg. of Westley Waterless, 1557–1840.*
23 C.U.L., E.D.R., C 1/4; C 1/6; C 3/27; C 3/39.
24 *Educ. Enquiry Abstract*, 62.
25 *Church School Inquiry, 1846–7*, 8–9.
26 C.U.L., E.D.R., C 3/27; Ed. 7/5; *Rep. of Educ. Cttee. of Council, 1876–7* [C. 1780-I], p. 741, H.C. (1877), xxix.
27 *Schs. in Receipt of Parl. Grants, 1896–7* [C. 8546], p. 16, H.C. (1897), lxix; C.U.L., E.D.R., C 3/139.
28 *Lists of Schs. under Admin. of Bd. 1903–4* [Cd. 2011], p. 17, H.C. (1904), lxxv; *Public Elem. Schs. 1907* [Cd. 3901], p. 29, H.C. (1908), lxxxiv; *Bd. of Educ., List 21, 1914* (H.M.S.O.), 29; *1927*, 17.
29 Black, *Cambs. Educ. Rec.* 77.
30 Prob. 11/95 (P.C.C. 2 Wallopp); *31st Rep. Com. Char.* 138–40; C.U.L., E.D.R., A 6/3; B 8/1; C 1/1; H 1/8, terrier 1837; ibid. tithe award.
31 Prob. 11/370 (P.C.C. 76 Cottle); C.U.L., E.D.R., B 8/1; C 1/1; *31st Rep. Com. Char.* 138–40.
32 C.U.L., E.D.R., C 1/1; B 7/1, p. 7; *31st Rep. Com. Char.* 138–40.

income from the Huntingdon land was used to repair the cottages. In 1837 all the income went in cash to the settled poor of the parish.[33] By 1863 the poor's land consisted of a cottage and land, yielding £21 rent, and £367 in stock bought after the sale of land to the railway company. The total income of £32 was distributed in cash.[34] In the early 20th century more land was sold to the railway. In 1952 the trustees held £837 in stock. Two of four cottages owned by the charities were sold for £800 in 1963. In 1975 the income was distributed according to a Scheme of 1906 in clothing, fuel, equipment, and medicine for the poor.[35]

WESTON COLVILLE

THE PARISH of Weston Colville,[1] 10 miles south-east of Cambridge and 6 miles south of Newmarket, forms an elongated parallelogram, covering 3,235 a.,[2] and stretching from the Suffolk boundary in the south-east almost to the Newmarket road in the north-west. The longer north-eastern and south-western boundaries mostly follow former field-boundaries, the western half of that with Carlton on the north running along an ancient field-way.[3] The parish lies upon the chalk, surrounding patches of gravel in the north-western part and overlaid by boulder clay to the south-east. The ground rises rapidly from about 150 ft. in the extreme north-west to over 300 ft. east of Chilly Hill, then more slowly to over 400 ft. It then declines gradually to fairly level ground at *c.* 350 ft., where various streamlets unite to form the head waters of the river Stour, flowing northward into Carlton.[4]

The economy of the parish has been predominantly agricultural. The western half remained open-field land, under a triennial rotation, until inclosure in 1778. To the east lay ancient closes, probably produced by clearing woodland on the heavy clay soil. In 1086 there was woodland for 300 pigs.[5] The largest surviving ancient wood lies in the centre of the parish, and belonged to Colvilles manor, whose lord was selling 15 a. of timber there for felling in 1339.[6] In 1612 it covered 67 a.[7] Later a strip of pasture divided it into Great Colvilles (later Lower) wood to the south and Little Colvilles (later Great Covens) wood to the north, covering in 1912 43 a. and 34½ a. respectively.[8] A larger demesne wood at the south-east end of the parish called Weston wood was being felled in the 1590s,[9] and had by 1612 been cleared and converted to farmland, comprising *c.* 390 a. of inclosures.[10] The demesne wood of Moynes manor, covering 24 a. in 1279, 40 a. in 1368,[11] and 29 a. in 1612, after which date it was cleared, lay by the southern boundary, as did Gazeley wood,[12] recorded until 1629.[13] Lesser estates also possessed small inclosed woods, such as St. John's College's grove of 3 a.[14] The modern wood at Hill Crofts south of the Hall, covering in 1912 24 a., dates only from the early 19th century, having been established on former open-field land, as were the narrow belts lying along the axis of the parish further west, which in 1912 came to 55 a.[15]

Settlement was recorded at Weston by 974.[16] In 1086 40 people were enumerated there,[17] and in 1327 there were 49 taxpayers.[18] In 1377 119 people paid the poll tax.[19] In 1524 28 people were assessed for the subsidy,[20] and there were 26 households in 1563.[21] Between the 1610s and 1660s the population may have risen by a third,[22] and there were 140 adults in 1676.[23] Following a slight decline there were only 130 communicants in 45 households in 1728,[24] but numbers increased again from the 1730s, probably exceeding 200 during the rest of that century and reaching 318 by 1801.[25] Thenceforward the population rose steadily to a peak of 574 in 1851 before stabilizing at *c.* 530 until the 1880s. Numbers then declined slowly, falling to 334 by 1951. By 1971 they had recovered to 385.[26]

The church and rectory stand where a road called Cambridge way by 1500[27] and running south-east from the main Newmarket road joins the Linton–Newmarket road, the two running together for ½ mile. The former site of Colvilles manor was to the north-east of the church, and Colvilles farm, the site of the modern Hall, to the west. In 1612, however, there were only six dwellings in the settlement by the church, which was linked by parallel roads called Churchway and Holeway with the larger settlement ¾ mile south-east at Weston Green. Until inclosure in 1778 the green, where there were *c.* 18 houses in 1612, covered *c.* 20 a.[28] From the green minor roads led north towards Willingham Green, south-west past Moynes Townsend and manor farm to West Wratting, and south-east past the common and Weston wood towards Withersfield (Suff.). The

33 *31st Rep. Com. Char.* 138–40.
34 *Char. Digest Cambs. 1863–4*, 38–9.
35 Char. Com. files.
1 This account was written in 1976.
2 *Census*, 1961.
3 Cf. C.U.L., MS. Plan 550R (1612).
4 O.S. Map 6″, Cambs. XLVIII. SE., XLIX. SW., LVI. SE. (1889–91 edn.).
5 *V.C.H. Cambs.* i. 380.
6 St. John's Mun. 34/99.
7 C.U.L., MS. Plan 550R.
8 e.g. C.R.O., 124/P 82 (map *c.* 1807/13); B.L. Maps 135. a. 6.
9 Essex R.O., D/DL E 63, m. 8d.
10 C.U.L., MS. Plan 550R.
11 S.C. 5/Cambs. Tower ser. no. 15 rot. 2; C 135/199 no. 2.
12 C.U.L., MS. Plan 550R.
13 St. John's Mun. 30/26.
14 Ibid. 30/29C.
15 C.R.O., 124/P 82–3; B.L. Maps 135. a. 6.
16 *Cart. Sax.* ed. Birch, iii, pp. 628–9.
17 *V.C.H. Cambs.* i. 406: excluding those on Little Carlton manor, then assessed under Weston.
18 *Cambs. Lay Subsidy, 1327*, 16–17.
19 *East Anglian*, N.S. xii. 257.
20 E 179/81/134 m. 6.
21 B.L. Harl. MS. 594, f. 199v.
22 Cf. C.R.O., par. reg. TS. (from bps'. transcripts).
23 Compton Census.
24 C.U.L., E.D.R., B 8/1.
25 C.R.O., par. reg. TS.; *Census*, 1801.
26 *Census*, 1811–1971.
27 St. John's Mun. 30/29C.
28 C.U.L., MS. Plan 550R; C.R.O., Q/RDz 1, pp. 345–9, 362–70.

old lines of the roads were mostly preserved at and after inclosure.[29]

The number of dwellings grew little between the late 17th century and the 19th, there being *c.* 45 under Charles II[30] and still only 48 in 1811.[31] Some 17th-century thatched cottages survive at Weston Green, and one or two larger timber-framed houses, such as Peacock Hall. After inclosure one farmhouse, Lark Hall, was built out in the former fields to the west, with labourers' cottages and dependent farmsteads called Spike Hall and Linnet Hall. The main farms at Weston Green, such as Pound and Street farms, received new white-brick, slated farmhouses. The Halls, lords of the manor, built a terrace of eight Tudoresque houses north of the church and later many red-brick estate cottages, and owned 57 cottages in 1912.[32] Of *c.* 115 houses in the parish *c.* 1860, some 80 were at and around the street along the former green and 20 near the church.[33] The next hundred years saw little new building, there being still only 119 houses in 1961,[34] but from the 1960s there was some infilling, council houses were built on the north-west side of the street, where most dwellings had previously stood on the south-east side, and the d'Abo estate put up a terrace north of the church.

The village's Horn fair, held in May or August, at which cattle were once sold, still flourished in the early 19th century but fell into disuse soon after 1900.[35] The Coopers Arms public house was recorded in 1778,[36] the Three Horseshoes, north of Weston Green, existed from 1800[37] until 1957,[38] and the Fox and Hounds south of the green, open by 1851 and rebuilt *c.* 1940,[39] was still open in 1975. In the 19th century the Halls, lords of the manor, gave the village a sports field, and built *c.* 1885 at the north-west end of the green as a reading-room and library a building which was later also used as a village hall.[40]

The level ground south-east of the village was requisitioned during the Second World War for a bomber airfield called Wratting Common, in use from 1943 to 1947.[41] The buildings, which for a time housed 2,000 foreign refugees, were cleared after 1952 and the land was restored to agriculture.[42]

J. R. Withers (1812–92), called the Cambridgeshire poet, a self-educated labourer whose verses were published between 1856 and 1869, was born at Weston Colville, the son of the village shoemaker, but as an adult lived at Fordham.[43] One poem describes life at Weston during his boyhood.[44]

MANORS AND OTHER ESTATES. Soon after 1000 Lustwine, husband of Ealdorman Beorhtnoth's daughter Leofwaru, devised a manor at Weston to Ely abbey.[45] The abbey did not immediately obtain possession, for Thurstan, probably Lustwine's son, held the manor when he died *c.* 1044. He then left it for life to Ethelswith, perhaps his mother's sister, and only after her death to Ely.[46] By 1066 7 hides at Weston were held under the abbey by Tochi, with whose other estates they were granted to William de Warenne (d. 1088), who held them in demesne in 1086.[47] The manor continued to be held of Warenne's descendants, the earls of Surrey,[48] as 1 knight's fee until the 14th century.[49] In 1316 John, earl of Surrey, ceded to Aymer de Valence, earl of Pembroke, the honor of Castle Acre.[50] The honor apparently included lordship over the Weston fee, which was said to be held of Aymer at his death in 1324,[51] and later, incorrectly, of his heirs.[52] By 1346 the overlordship had returned to Earl John (d. 1347),[53] and the manor continued nominally to depend on his earldom until after 1520.[54] From 1546, perhaps following inspection of Domesday Book, it was alleged to be held of the bishop of Ely.[55]

By *c.* 1150 the main Weston estate, later *COLVILLES* manor, had been subinfeudated to the Stutvilles. From Osmund de Stutville (fl. 1166)[56] it had descended by 1172 to Roger de Stutville,[57] possibly the sheriff of Northumberland 1170–85 who died *c.* 1190,[58] and from Roger to Anselm de Stutville (fl. 1194–6).[59] Anselm was dead by 1198,[60] leaving as heirs his five sisters. When his lands were divided[61] Weston was assigned to Beatrice, married by 1200 to William de Colville,[62] lord of Castle Bytham (Lincs.). William died in 1230, leaving as heir his son by Beatrice, Roger de Colville,[63] who held the manor *c.* 1236[64] and probably died *c.* 1252 when it was included in his widow Beatrice's dower.[65] She still occupied it when in 1265, her son Walter being in rebellion, the reversion was granted to Warin of Bassingbourn.[66] Walter was pardoned in 1267[67] and held the Weston manor at his death in

[29] C.R.O., Q/RDz 1, pp. 325–9.
[30] See pp. 279, 281.
[31] *Census*, 1811.
[32] Cf. B.L. Maps 135. a. 6.
[33] R.G. 9/1030.
[34] *Census*, 1961.
[35] J. R. Withers, *Poems on Various Subjects* (Camb. 1856), i. 2–4; Porter, *Cambs. Customs*, 141, 145–6.
[36] C.R.O., Q/RDz 1, p. 330.
[37] Withers, *Poems* (1856), i. 1–3.
[38] *Kelly's Dir. Cambs.* (1858–1937); local information.
[39] H.O. 107/1761; *Camb. Ind. Press*, 17 June 1960.
[40] *Kelly's Dir. Cambs.* (1892 and later edns.); C.U.L., E.D.R., C 3/39; *Camb. Ind. Press*, 17 June 1960.
[41] Ex inf. Min. of Defence, Air Hist. Branch (R.A.F.).
[42] *Camb. Ind. Press*, 17 June 1960.
[43] See J. R. Withers, *Fairy Revels and other Poems* (Camb. 1901), pp. i–xiv.
[44] Withers, *Poems* (1856), i. 1–14.
[45] *Liber Elien.* (Camd. 3rd ser. xcii), pp. 157–8.
[46] Dorothy Whitelock, *A.-S. Wills*, 80–5; cf. ibid. 190; *Liber Elien.* p. 158.
[47] *V.C.H. Cambs.* i. 380.
[48] *Complete Peerage*, xii (1), 493–514.
[49] e.g. *Pipe R.* 1156–8 (Rec. Com.), 97–8; *Bk. of Fees*, ii. 923; *Feud. Aids*, i. 141.
[50] *Cal. Pat.* 1313–17, 607; cf. *Cal. Close*, 1318–23, 254.
[51] *Cal. Inq. p.m.* vi, p. 331.
[52] e.g. ibid. p. 482; xiv, p. 87.
[53] *Feud. Aids*, i. 158; cf. *Cal. Fine R.* 1347–56, 39.
[54] e.g. *Cal. Inq. p.m.* xv, pp. 387–8; C 142/32 no. 32.
[55] e.g. C 142/74 no. 6; C 142/349 no. 158.
[56] *Red Bk. Exch.* (Rolls Ser.), i. 429; cf. *Early Yorks. Chart.* ix (Y.A.S. extra ser. vii), 27–8, and pedigree at p. 1.
[57] *Cur. Reg. R.* ii. 231; *Red Bk. Exch.* i. 53.
[58] Cf. *Pipe R.* 1170 (P.R.S. xv), 47; 1185 (P.R.S. xxxiv), 149; 1190 (P.R.S. N.S. i), 52.
[59] Ibid. 1194 (P.R.S. N.S. v), 161; *Chanc. R.* 1196 (P.R.S. N.S. vii), 176.
[60] *Pipe R.* 1198 (P.R.S. N.S. ix), 146.
[61] *Cur. Reg. R.* vi. 67, 153; *Early Yorks. Chart.* ix, 30–4.
[62] *Cur. Reg. R.* i. 471; ii. 231.
[63] *Cur. Reg. R.* xiv, pp. 144–6; *Close R.* 1227–32, 423.
[64] *Liber de Bernewelle*, 250.
[65] *Abbrev. Plac.* (Rec. Com.), 119.
[66] *Cal. Chart. R.* 1257–1300, 56; cf. *Close R.* 1264–8, 45.
[67] *Cal. Pat.* 1266–72, 146, 280–1.

1277. His son and heir Roger[68] died in 1288, leaving a new-born son Edmund[69] who came of age in 1309 and died in 1316. Edmund's son Robert, then aged 11,[70] held the manor until he died, having just survived his son Walter (d. 1367), early in 1368. His heir, Walter's son Robert,[71] died aged 5 in 1369, and the Colville inheritance passed to the descendants of Edmund's sisters Elizabeth and Alice. Weston Colville was assigned to Alice's son Sir John Gernon, who died in 1384, having settled it for life upon his widow Joan,[72] with reversion to his daughter Joan Botetourt's daughter Joan. Joan the granddaughter, who married Sir Robert Swinburne,[73] retained Weston in her own right after Robert's death in 1391.[74] She died, having survived all her sons, in 1433, and Weston passed to her daughter Margery Berners's daughter Catherine, wife of Sir Thomas Fynderne,[75] who later inherited the other Weston manors called Moynes and Leverers.[76]

Following Sir Thomas's forfeiture as a Lancastrian in 1461 his Weston properties were granted to Thomas St. Leger,[77] but by 1478 had been restored to Fynderne's son William,[78] knighted *c.* 1485.[79] Sir William was succeeded in 1516 by his son William's son Thomas,[80] upon whose death under age in 1524 the Weston estate passed, under a settlement by Sir William, to Thomas Elyot, whose mother Alice was daughter of Sir William's aunt Elizabeth.[81] Sir Thomas Elyot, diplomat and author, died without issue in 1546,[82] having settled Weston for life upon his widow Margaret,[83] who shortly married Sir James Dyer. In 1547 Elyot's nephew and heir at law Richard Puttenham sold his reversionary interest to John Lennard,[84] who obtained possession through a lease from the Dyers in 1561.[85]

Lennard died in 1591, leaving the estate to his son Sampson.[86] Sampson's son Henry inherited the barony of Dacre of the South from his mother in 1612 and Weston on Sampson's death in 1615,[87] and himself died in 1616. The Weston manors descended with the barony to his son Richard (d. 1630) and grandson Francis[88] (d. 1662). Francis's son Thomas, created earl of Sussex in 1674, sold much land to pay his debts in 1708.[89] Weston Colville was bought, probably in that year,[90] by John Carter, a London linen-draper,[91] who died in 1723, leaving it to his son John,[92] who sometimes lived in the parish and died in 1759. His son and heir John[93] after 1770 took the additional name of Pollard.[94] He died in 1806, leaving no children.[95] His sister Elizabeth had married Gen. Thomas Hall (d. 1809), whose son John (1767–1860) succeeded to Carter Pollard's estate.[96] From him it passed successively to his sons Gen. John Hall (1797–1872) and Maj. Charles Webb Hall (1802–80), and, neither son leaving issue, to his daughter Charlotte's son,[97] William Henry Bullock, who succeeded to it in 1880, taking the name of Hall. He died in 1904. His son and heir Alexander Cross Hall[98] sold his Six Mile Bottom estate, including the Weston property, in 1912[99] to the financier Sir Ernest Cassel. On Cassel's death in 1921 the estate passed to his granddaughter Ruth Mary Clarisse Ashley. She married successively Capt. A. S. Cunningham-Reid (divorced 1940), Maj. E. L. Gardine (divorced 1943), and T. P. H. Cholmondeley, Lord Delamere (divorced 1955).[1] In 1975 her estate still included the western end of the parish, but the rest had been sold, Weston Colville Hall farm having been bought *c.* 1960 for the d'Abo estate in West Wratting.[2]

The manor-house of Colvilles probably stood in a square moat ¼ mile east of the church.[3] The field to the south was in 1560 called Hall field.[4] The site was then empty, and in 1612 Colvilles demesne was cultivated from a farm-house west of the church.[5] The modern Weston Colville Hall was built at the site of the farm-house, probably by the Carters, in the early 18th century. The five-bay front has in the centre two giant Corinthian pilasters. John Carter Pollard ceased to live there in 1786,[6] and before 1806 it was used as a farm-house. John Hall (d. 1860) later remodelled it for his own residence.[7] After the 1860s his family removed to Six Mile Bottom,[8] and the Hall reverted to being a farm-house.[9]

In 1066 Godwin Child held under Eddeva the fair 1½ hide at Weston, which passed with her estates to Count Alan, of whom Wihomarc his steward held it in 1086.[10] The overlordship of that estate, later *MOYNES* manor, remained with the honor of Richmond.[11] Probably by 1130 the manor was held by Roger son of Tingry,[12] a Yorkshire landowner, living *c.* 1167,[13] whose son Richard was

68 *Cal. Inq. p.m.* ii, pp. 136–7.
69 Ibid. pp. 420–1.
70 Ibid. v, pp. 84, 375.
71 Ibid. xii, pp. 107, 195–6.
72 Ibid. pp. 324–6; B.L. Add. Ch. 22608.
73 *Cal. Inq. p.m.* xv, pp. 387–8; cf. *Cal. Fine R.* 1368–77, 365; *Collect. Topog. & Gen.* vi. 154.
74 *Cal. Close*, 1389–92, 508; *Feud. Aids*, vi. 406; cf. Prob. 11/2B (P.C.C. 54 Marche, will of Wm. Swinburne).
75 C 139/59 no. 42; *Cal. Fine R.* 1430–7, 163; cf. Morant, *Essex*, ii. 234–5.
76 See below.
77 *Rot. Parl.* v. 477–80; *Cal. Pat.* 1461–7, 77, 522.
78 *Rot. Parl.* vi. 177; cf. *Cat. Anct. D.* v, A 10788.
79 *Cal. Pat.* 1485–94, 103.
80 Prob. 11/18 (P.C.C. 36 Holder); C 142/32 no. 32.
81 C 142/42 no. 164; for Elyot's ancestry see Elyot, *Governour*, ed. Crofts, i, p. xxx; *Cal. Inq. p.m. Hen. VII*, ii, p. 64; *Topographer & Genealogist*, ed. Nichols, i. 198.
82 *D.N.B.*
83 Prob. 11/32 (P.C.C. 14 Allen).
84 C 142/74 no. 16; B.L. Add. MS. 22059, ff. 2–5v.
85 B.L. Add. MS. 22059, ff. 38v.–42v.
86 Ibid. ff. 6–9; C 142/229 no. 143.
87 C 142/349 no. 158; *Complete Peerage*, iv. 11–13.
88 C 142/359 no. 140; Wards 7/7 no. 166.
89 *Complete Peerage*, iv. 13–14.
90 C.P. 25(2)/911/6 Anne Trin. no. 7.
91 B.L. Add. MS. 5810, f. 117.
92 Prob. 11/591 (P.C.C. 93 Richmond).
93 B.L. Add. MS. 5808, ff. 43v.–44; 5810, f. 112; Prob. 11/852 (P.C.C. 8 Lynch).
94 B.L. Add. MS. 5810, f. 117.
95 Prob. 11/1502 (P.C.C. 646 Loveday); C.R.O., par. reg. TS. *sub* 1809.
96 C.R.O., R 51/8/2–5; ibid. par. reg. TS.; cf. mon. in ch.
97 C.R.O., R 51/8/9–10; mon. in ch.
98 Burke, *Land. Gent.* (1906), i. 748.
99 B.L. Maps 135. a. 6.
1 *D.N.B. 1911–21*; *New Extinct Peerage* (1972), 202; *Kelly's Dir. Cambs.* (1933–7).
2 Ex inf. Mr. M. Dobell.
3 *V.C.H. Cambs.* ii. 43.
4 C 3/72/26 replication.
5 C.U.L., MS. Plan 550R.
6 *Camb. Chron.* 7 Oct. 1786.
7 Cf. B.L. Add. MS. 9413, f. 10.
8 Cf. *Kelly's Dir. Cambs.* (1864–79).
9 Ibid. (1900–37); B.L. Maps 135. a. 6.
10 *V.C.H. Cambs.* i. 379, 406.
11 e.g. *Liber de Bernewelle*, 250; *Feud. Aids*, i. 142, 158; C 142/32 no. 32.
12 *Pipe R.* 1130 (H.M.S.O. facsimile), 46; cf. *Cal. Inq. Misc.* i, p. 168.
13 Cf. *Pipe R.* 1166 (P.R.S. ix), 49; 1167 (P.R.S. xi), 92.

recorded in 1175 and 1188.[14] Roger son of Richard[15] held $\frac{1}{4}$ knight's fee at Weston in 1212. Probably between 1216[16] and 1223 the manor was acquired by Hugh Grandin,[17] who held it *c.* 1236.[18] He died after 1245 and his widow Eleanor, tenant in 1254, was succeeded *c.* 1255 by their son William.[19] William went on crusade in 1270 and apparently did not return.[20] In 1277 $\frac{1}{3}$ of 2 carucates at Weston, the inheritance of Christine, perhaps William's daughter and coheir, was assigned by Christine's husband Roger Gobyun and John de Musters to Maud, perhaps Christine's fellow coheir, who was widow of John le Moyne (d. 1274) of Shelford.[21] Maud held the manor in 1279.[22] The next known tenant was Moyne's younger son, Sir John le Moyne, who held the $\frac{1}{4}$ fee by 1299 and died after 1316.[23] By 1346 it was held by Sir John Sutton of Wivenhoe (Essex),[24] perhaps in right of his wife Margery.[25] In 1364 the Suttons sold Moynes to John Bunting,[26] who died while indicted for robbery in 1368. His lands, then in the king's hands, were eventually restored to his widow Agnes and son John.[27] John the son held land at Weston in 1402,[28] and died after 1410.[29] In 1425 John Chamberlain and his wife Agnes, and Thomas Caley, who claimed to be kinsman and heir of John le Moyne, each released a moiety of the manor to William Alington and others,[30] probably as feoffees for Sir William Fynderne, who held Moynes in 1428[31] and died in 1445. His son and heir Sir Thomas Fynderne[32] held the manor in 1461.

Sir Thomas also owned by 1452[33] an estate called *LEVERERS*, described as a manor[34] and later said to be held of the earls of Surrey,[35] which had presumably belonged to Richard Leverer who died without surviving issue in 1428.[36] The land may previously have been held by the brothers Roger and Geoffrey Leverer of Carlton (fl. 1225–50),[37] by William Leverer (fl. 1260–90) who settled 30 a. at Weston on his son Hugh in 1289,[38] by John Leverer (fl. 1350),[39] and by Thomas Leverer, whose Weston property included 60 a. acquired in 1377 and who probably died between 1409[40] and 1412.[41]

Moynes and Leverers descended from the 1460s with the principal manor,[42] except that Richard, Lord Dacre (d. 1630), settled their lands on his younger son Thomas,[43] on whose death they returned to the main Lennard line in 1674. Moynes demesne then included 200 a. and Leverers 185 a.[44] Moynes manor-house stood in 1612 at the moat west of Weston Green where a farmstead still bears the name of Mines. The site of Leverers is probably marked by the modern Pound Farm, the field south of which was called in 1612 Leveretts Stocking.[45]

In 1249 St. Radegund's nunnery, Cambridge, acquired 12 a. at Weston.[46] At inclosure its successor, Jesus College, was allotted 2 a. adjoining West Wratting.[47] St. John's College, Cambridge, bought in 1518 from Richard Brown *c.* 45 a., with 30 a. of heath,[48] which had been assembled by the Mareys family in the early 14th century[49] and had passed by marriage to the Browns after 1364.[50] After inclosure the college had a 70-a. farm north of Weston Green,[51] which it sold in 1945.[52] The former college farm-house, a long, low, thatched house, probably of the 17th century, survived in 1975.

ECONOMIC HISTORY. In 1086 4 out of the 7 hides on the Warenne manor were in demesne, with 5 *servi* and land for 3 plough-teams, and the 19 *villani* had 12 teams between them; the value had risen from £10 to £16 a year. On the Richmond fee 2 of the 3 plough-lands were in demesne, and the 3 *villani* had only 1 team.[53] In 1203, after two of William de Colville's tenants had conveyed property by fines, his steward claimed them, unsuccessfully, as villeins.[54] In 1279 Roger de Colville's demesne included 400 a. of arable. He had 7 villeins holding 15 a. and 8 holding 10 a. each, and his 6 cottars had 20 a. together. Of over 410 a. held of him as freehold 5 tenants owned over 260 a. The rest belonged to *c.* 30 others, of whom 23 holding between them *c.* 110 a. were under-tenants of 3 substantial freeholders. On Moynes manor there were 220 a. of demesne arable, but only 3 villeins, holding respectively 15 a., 10 a., and 2 a. About 105 a. were divided among *c.* 25 freeholds, including 4 of 15 a. A smith held 3 a. by rendering 2 ploughshares yearly. Labour-services were valued but not enumerated on both manors, suggesting frequent commutation.[55]

14 Cf. ibid. 1175 (P.R.S. xxii), 5; 1188 (P.R.S. xxxviii), 51.
15 *Cal. Inq. Misc.* i, p. 169.
16 *Red Bk. Exch.* (Rolls Ser.), i. 578; cf. *Cur. Reg. R.* v. 51; vii. 223.
17 Cf. *Ex. e Rot. Fin.* (Rec. Com.), i. 117; *Cur. Reg. R.* xi, pp. 131, 506.
18 *Liber de Bernewelle*, 250.
19 *Ex. e Rot. Fin.* i. 379, 434; ii. 212; *Close R.* 1253–4, 127.
20 Cf. *Close R.* 1266–72, 440.
21 C.P. 25(1)/25/37 no. 25. Maud's husband had held no land in Weston at his death: *Cal. Inq. p.m.* ii, p. 73.
22 S.C. 5/Cambs. Tower ser. no. 15 rot. 2.
23 *Lewes Chartulary, Cambs.* ed. Bullock and Palmer (C.A.S. 1938), 12; *Feud. Aids*, i. 142; *Cal. Close*, 1288–96, 85; *Cal. Pat.* 1313–17, 350, 537.
24 *Feud. Aids*, i. 158; cf. *Cal. Pat.* 1338–40, 267.
25 C.P. 25(1)/29/79 no. 27; cf. *Cal. Papal Reg.* iii. 64.
26 C.P. 25(1)/29/81 no. 18.
27 *Cal. Inq. p.m.* xii, p. 188; *Cal. Fine R.* 1356–68, 391, 394; cf. *Cal. Inq. Misc.* iii, p. 252; *Cal. Close*, 1369–74, 49.
28 C.P. 25(1)/30/92 no. 21.
29 Cf. *Cal. Close*, 1409–13, 111.
30 C.P. 25(1)/30/96 no. 9; *Cal. Close*, 1422–9, 207.
31 *Feud. Aids*, i. 177.
32 C 139/117 no. 5.
33 C 131/71/3.
34 *Cal. Pat.* 1461–7, 177.
35 e.g. C 142/32 no. 32.
36 *Reg. Chichele* (Cant. & York Soc.), ii. 374–5; cf. brass in ch.
37 *Cal. Chart. R.* 1226–57, 24; *Lewes Chartulary, Cambs.* 2, 4–7, 10, 21; C.P. 25(1)/24/24 no. 31.
38 *Lewes Chartulary, Cambs.* 2, 8, 22; C.P. 25(1)/285/23 no. 198.
39 St. John's Mun. 34/85.
40 C.P. 25(1)/29/85 nos. 18, 28; *E.D.R.* (1901), 70; *Cal. Fine R.* 1391–9, 73, 97; *Cal. Close*, 1408–13, 77.
41 Cf. *Cal. Fine R.* 1405–13, 245, 252.
42 e.g. C 142/32 no. 32; C 142/74 no. 16; C 142/349 no. 158.
43 Wards 7/79 no. 166.
44 Essex R.O., D/DL E 68.
45 *V.C.H. Cambs.* ii. 43; C.U.L., MS. Plan 550R.
46 C.P. 25(1)/24/25 no. 12.
47 C.R.O., Q/RDz 1, p. 352.
48 St. John's Mun. 34/114–16; 36/27, 29A, 29C.
49 Ibid. 34/58–97, *passim.*
50 Ibid. 34/44–50, 66–7, 112–13.
51 C.R.O., Q/RDz 1, pp. 338–9, 373.
52 Ibid. 515/SP 1855.
53 *V.C.H. Cambs.* i. 379–80, 406.
54 *Cur. Reg. R.* ii. 133, 139, 142, 238; iii. 32, 39.
55 S.C. 5/Cambs. Tower ser. no. 15 rot. 2.

The demesne of Colvilles covered some 305 a. *c.* 1500,[56] and the arable of Moynes came to 280 a. in 1368, when no labour-services were recorded but only £4 of assised rents.[57] The combined manors had in 1598 only 6 copyholds compared with 19 freeholds,[58] and at inclosure only ¼ a. was allotted for copyhold of the Weston manors, although 32 a. were assigned for copyholds of Great Carlton manor.[59] In the 13th and 14th centuries there were 8 or 9 substantial freeholding families at Weston, including those of Robertot, Rangilun, Cobbe, and Mareys.[60] John Mareys (d. *c.* 1364) left household goods worth over £8, cattle and sheep worth £11, and crops worth over £11. His dwelling included a chamber, pantry, larder, and bakehouse.[61] His lands eventually passed to St. John's College. The other larger freeholds were eventually merged with the demesne, as was that of the Cobbes, over 36 a. *c.* 1410,[62] which by *c.* 1580 had become a demesne farm.[63]

By the 15th century at latest[64] the cultivated land was divided between open fields to the north-west and ancient inclosures to the south-east,[65] where a great assart was mentioned *c.* 1236.[66] By the north-western boundary lay *c.* 250 a. of heath, all except St. John's College's 30 a. annexed to the demesne by 1612, when 126 a. belonged to Colvilles and 96½ a. to Moynes and Leverers. South-east of the heath were the main open fields covering *c.* 1,220 a. By the 15th century there were three, which had probably absorbed smaller fields recorded *c.* 1236, some of whose names, such as Chillowe,[67] later Chilly Hill, have survived. The boundaries between them were approximately parallel to those of the parish. To the north-east was the field towards Willingham, so named by 1314,[68] also called in the 15th century Bewel field;[69] to the south-west the field towards Wratting,[70] also called before 1500 Wardlow[71] or Chalkpit field;[72] and between them Middle field, so named by 1316,[73] widening at its north-western end. By 1612 well over two-thirds of the arable in those fields belonged to the lord, over 340 a. of whose land lay in blocks of 5 a. or more. Three demesne blocks of 30 a. or more at the north-western end probably derived from encroachments on the heath: in 1214 several freeholders had sued William de Colville for depriving them of their common of pasture.[74] Further south-east, and south of the church and manor closes, was a group of smaller fields, recorded from *c.* 1300, Galisley[75] (later Gazeley), Wydewell[76] (later Woodwall), and Broadcroft[77] fields, together *c.* 160 a. North-east of them was Mill field, so called before 1500;[78] beyond it *c.* 140 a. of demesne closes surrounded Colvilles wood. Weston Brook field, *c.* 65 a., adjoined Carlton Brook field; although intercommonable with Carlton, it remained part of Weston's fields until inclosure, after which it was formally annexed to Carlton parish.[79] South-east of Weston Green, beyond *c.* 160 a. of closes belonging to Moynes and Leverers, lay Cleanley meadow[80] by the Wratting border, and further south-east was the village common. In 1279 the villagers had had 100 a. of common pasture on their green,[81] presumably the 116 a. called in 1612 the Shrub, which bordered on Weston wood. Inclosures north-west of the green, including *c.* 90 a. of demesne, had by 1450 absorbed a field called Stod field.[82]

The north-western open fields were in 1612 cultivated in three shifts.[83] The crops included wheat, barley, rye, maslin, and bullymong.[84] Saffron was being grown in closes in the 1560s.[85] There had been 535 sheep on the Warenne manor in 1086.[86] In 1347 Colvilles manor contributed 12 stone to the levy on the vill of 58 stone of wool, the rest being supplied by *c.* 60 people, only 5 of whom rendered 1 stone or more.[87] In 1674 Moynes farm had liberty of fold for 200 sheep, and Leverers for 300.[88] The St. John's estate included a sheep-gate, confirmed by the lord in 1542, for 120 sheep.[89] The tenants' rights of common were reckoned in cattle in 1598, when they were entitled, upon paying agistment to the lord, to run 53 bullocks from 1 May to 1 November on the Shrub.[90] John Webb (d. 1584) left 15 cattle and 27 mares and colts,[91] and 20 milch-cows and 20 horses were fed on two closes near Colvilles wood until they were converted to arable *c.* 1570.[92]

Of the £65 assessed on the parish in 1524 9 men with £4–6 owned £42, while another 19 had only £23 altogether.[93] The more prosperous were probably the lessees of the demesne farms, such as John Webb (d. 1584) who occupied Cobbes and Cosens on lease. He left land in neighbouring villages and *c.* £80 of legacies, besides £83 in loans.[94] In 1561 Thomas Gallant, a gentleman-farmer from Wilburton, had acquired by marriage a 40-year lease of Colvilles farm, said to include 300 a. of arable. He afterwards sublet much of the land, but incurred, as he later claimed, much trouble and expense on building

[56] *Lewes Chartulary, Cambs.* 8–10; cf. C.U.L., E.D.R., H 1/6, glebe terrier 1639.
[57] C 135/199 no. 2.
[58] Essex R.O., D/DL E 64/1.
[59] C.R.O., Q/RDz 1, pp. 350–70.
[60] St. John's Mun. 34/33–99 *passim*.
[61] Ibid. 34/66.
[62] C.P. 25(1)/30/94 nos. 5, 8; cf. Prob. 11/2B (P.C.C. 31 Marche, will of Hugh Cobbe).
[63] Cf. Essex R.O., D/DL E 64/2.
[64] Cf. St. John's Mun. 30/29A (terrier 15th cent.).
[65] Layout from C.U.L., MS. Plan 550R (map 1612); areas mostly estimated from C.R.O., Q/RDz 1, pp. 327–81; ibid. 124/P 82–3 (maps *c.* 1810).
[66] *Lewes Chartulary*, ii (Suss. Rec. Soc. xl), 122.
[67] Ibid.
[68] St. John's Mun. 34/75.
[69] *Lewes Chartulary, Cambs.* 9–10.
[70] e.g. St. John's Mun. 34/31 (1323).
[71] Ibid. 30/29A.
[72] *Lewes Chartulary, Cambs.* 8–9.
[73] St. John's Mun. 34/65.
[74] *Cur. Reg. R.* vii. 286.
[75] St. John's Mun. 34/74 (1320).
[76] Ibid. 34/30 (1301).
[77] Ibid. 34/77 (1340).
[78] Ibid. 30/29A.
[79] Cf. Weston Colville Incl. Act, 17 Geo. III, c. 123 (Priv. Act), p. 3.
[80] St. John's Mun. 34/34, 37 (before 1300).
[81] S.C. 5/Cambs. Tower ser. no. 15 rot. 2.
[82] St. John's Mun. 34/80, 100; 30/29A.
[83] C.U.L., MS. Plan 550R; cf. St. John's Mun. 30/24.
[84] St. John's Mun. 34/66; B.L. Add. MS. 5861, ff. 77v.–78; Prob. 11/278 (P.C.C. 328 Wootton, will of John Smith).
[85] C 3/70/56.
[86] *V.C.H. Cambs.* i. 406.
[87] E 179/242/8 m. 7 and d.
[88] Essex R.O., D/DL E 68.
[89] St. John's Mun. 30/24, 27; 34/118.
[90] Essex R.O., D/DL E 64/1; B.L. Add. MS. 5819, f. 141.
[91] Prob. 11/68 (P.C.C. 7 Brudenell).
[92] C 3/72/26 replication.
[93] E 179/81/134 m. 6.
[94] Prob. 11/68 (P.C.C. 7 Brudenell).

repairs and implements. After John Lennard had obtained possession of the manor, he sought to evict Gallant, alleging against him absenteeism and unlicensed tree-felling.[95] By 1598 the manor included four other substantial farms and thirteen smaller leaseholds.[96] About 1674 the demesne included, apart from Colvilles farm and Finchley farm south-east of the village, 278 a. of inclosures and 419 a. of open-field arable, divided among two large farms which together covered *c.* 365 a. and six smaller ones totalling *c.* 310 a.[97]

By the 1770s John Carter Pollard, who held the St. John's estate on lease,[98] possessed virtually the whole parish. An inclosure Act was obtained in 1777,[99] and the land was divided and the award made in 1778. The area for allotment came to 1,927 a., including 1,547 a. of open fields and *c.* 380 a. of common and heath. Pollard received, after exchanges, *c.* 1,755 a. having ceded to the rector 268 a. of old inclosures and to St. John's College 27 a. near its farmstead. The rector also obtained 40½ a. of the former fields, and other clergy, colleges, and corporations *c.* 30 a. The remainder was divided between the lord of Carlton (26½ a.), his copyholders (25 a.), and 17 smallholders.[1] Although after inclosure some farmers kept for a time to the old rotation much improvement was said to have followed. Of the 1,355 a. cropped in 1801 there were 424 a. of wheat, double the pre-inclosure area, 493 a. of barley, whose yield was doubled, and 150 a. of oats. The area under peas had declined to 100 a., but there were 178 a. of potatoes. The use of leys proved more productive than the old-fashioned fallows. Although there was less feeding grass more artificial grasses were grown, and a flock of 1,200 Norfolk ewes had replaced one of 1,000 wethers with coarser wool. The number of cows had fallen by almost half to *c.* 50, because some smallholders and cottagers had ploughed up their allotments. The annual rental of the parish had by 1805 more than doubled.[2]

In the 1790s the manorial estate included, in the anciently inclosed area to the south-east, Moynes farm of 205 a., Pound (formerly Leverers) farm of 113 a., Finchley farm near Little Carlton Green of 141 a., and two others of 131 a. and 110 a. The former open fields were divided between Hall (formerly Colvilles) farm, and the newly established Lennard (later Linnet) Hall farm.[3] In 1851 Hall farm was partly in hand, and in 1871 when it incorporated the previously separate Lark and Linnet Hall farmsteads it covered 1,300 a.; the rest of the former open fields belonged to Church End farm, reduced from 900 a. in 1851 to 400 a. by 1871. Further south-east Mines (formerly Moynes), Pound, and Finchley farms, of *c.* 250 a., 320 a., and 125 a. respectively, remained distinct until the late 1870s. Only one of seven farms in the parish was of less than 100 a.[4] In 1912 the Hall family's estate comprised *c.* 2,680 a. of the parish, including *c.* 2,240 a. of arable and only 186 a. of grass. Several of its nine farms were let to the same tenants, so that 686 a. were farmed from Lark Hall in the north-west, 707 a. from Hall farm, and 743 a. from Pound farm. Three smaller farms to the south-east covered 40 a., 160 a., and 100 a.[5] The late 19th century saw some decline in productivity in the parish especially, perhaps, on the former heath and woodland at its extremities. The Halls kept Lark Hall farm in hand for almost 25 years after 1890, and two others also from 1896 to 1905.[6] The rent of the rector's Weston Woods farm, with 364 a. on a cold and hungry clay, fell from £380 in 1878 to £80 in 1910. By 1912 112 a. of it was out of cultivation and reverting to scrub.[7] In the 1970s the parish was still devoted to arable farming, growing the traditional wheat and barley.[8]

Weston Colville seldom had much non-agricultural work, although craftsmen, such as a tailor in 1474,[9] were occasionally recorded. In 1831 82 families depended on farming, only 19 on crafts or trade.[10] Some 90 adult farm-labourers were then paid 10*s.* a week.[11] In the mid 19th century, when there were *c.* 145 labourers, including *c.* 95 adults, the farmers usually employed *c.* 100 men and 40 boys. Otherwise, there were a carpenter's shop, one or two wheelwrights and shoemakers, and two, but by 1861 only one, smiths.[12] The smithy at the west end of the green was still working in 1937.[13] In 1897 there were said to be 95 farm-labourers' families and 18 with other occupations, and many young people were leaving the parish.[14] The Hall estate was letting *c.* 14 a. as allotments for labourers in 1912.[15] In the 1960s many inhabitants worked in the neighbouring small towns or at Cambridge.[16]

By 1612 a windmill, from which a neighbouring field was named, stood on the 400-ft. ridge by the road from the church to Weston Green.[17] It was rebuilt *c.* 1830 as a smock-mill.[18] It was working throughout the 19th century, and *c.* 1880 was bought from the Livermore family by the Hall estate,[19] but closed between 1904 and 1912.[20] Only the stump, under conversion to a house, survived in 1975.[21]

LOCAL GOVERNMENT. In 1279 the lords of both Colvilles and Moynes manors claimed to have view of frankpledge and the assizes of bread and of ale, with gallows, tumbrel, and pillory.[22] In 1334 tenants from Weston Colville attended a tourn held

95 C 3/27/26; cf. Req. 2/273/20.
96 Essex R.O., D/DL E 64/1–6; cf. B.L. Add. MS. 22059, f. 12v.
97 Essex R.O., D/DL E 68, 70.
98 Cf. St. John's Mun. 110/90.
99 *C.J.* xxxvi. 66, 291, 464, 513; 17 Geo. III, c. 123 (Priv. Act).
1 C.R.O., Q/RDz 1, pp. 321–81.
2 H.O. 67/9; Gooch, *Agric. of Cambs.* 35, 57, 64.
3 C.R.O., R 51/8/2; cf. ibid. 124/P 83.
4 H.O. 107/1761; R.G. 9/1030; R.G. 10/1593; *Kelly's Dir. Cambs.* (1858–1900).
5 B.L. Maps 135. a. 6.
6 Cf. C.R.O., P 167/4/1; *Kelly's Dir. Cambs.* (1900).
7 Church Com. files.
8 Cf. C.R.O., SP 167/5.
9 *Cal. Pat.* 1467–77, 255.
10 *Census*, 1831.
11 *Rep. H.L. Cttee. on Poor Laws*, H.C. 227, pp. 328–9 (1831), viii.
12 H.O. 107/1761; R.G. 9/1030; cf. *Kelly's Dir. Cambs.* (1858–1900).
13 *Kelly's Dir. Cambs.* (1937).
14 C.U.L., E.D.R., C 3/39.
15 B.L. Maps 135. a. 6.
16 *Camb. Ind. Press*, 17 June 1960.
17 C.U.L., MS. Plan 550R.
18 A. C. Smith, *Windmills in Cambs.*
19 Cf. *Camb. Chron.* 5 May 1798; 21 Feb. 1817; C.R.O., 334/011; *Kelly's Dir. Cambs.* (1858–1904).
20 *Kelly's Dir. Cambs.* (1908); cf. B.L. Maps 135. a. 6.
21 Cf. *Proc. C.A.S.* xxxi. 28; C.R.O., SP 167/3.
22 S.C. 5/Cambs. Tower ser. no. 15 rot. 2.

for the honor of Richmond at Newmarket.[23] In the 1560s the steward took the jurors of the court baron to view the stumps of oak trees felled on the demesne without licence.[24] No court records have been traced. A constable was recorded in 1381.[25]

In the early 19th century the rector and parishioners chose the churchwardens jointly.[26] Expenditure on the poor more than doubled from £66 in 1776 to almost £140 by 1785 and again to £287 by 1803, when 21 adults received assistance.[27] By 1813 26 people were on permanent relief, and almost 40 more obtained occasional help. The cost was £695,[28] and afterwards only once fell below £300, while frequently exceeding £500.[29] Large families were receiving allowances from the rates *c.* 1830, and labourers were apportioned among the farmers according to the size of the farms.[30] In 1832 £231, almost half of the total spent, was paid to paupers working for the parish.[31] From 1834 Weston Colville was part of the Linton poor-law union,[32] and as part of the Linton R.D. was transferred in 1934 to the South Cambridgeshire R.D.,[33] being included in 1974 in South Cambridgeshire.

CHURCH. About 1044 Thurstan left land at Weston to the village church.[34] William de Warenne (d. 1088) gave Weston church with its advowson to Lewes priory,[35] to which his son Earl William (d. 1138) confirmed a grant of the church made in the 1120s by his chaplain Stephen, perhaps the incumbent.[36] Weston, however, was never appropriated. Under Henry II Osmund de Stutville presented one Reynold as parson, but his successor Anselm de Stutville released the advowson to the priory, which in 1203 vindicated its title against Anselm's sister Beatrice and her husband.[37] A claim by their son Roger de Colville in 1233 also failed,[38] and the priory remained patron until the 15th century.[39] In 1459 Sir Thomas Fynderne claimed to present. An episcopal inquest found that he was entitled to one turn, the next, to the priory's two, and, wrongly, that his predecessor Sir Robert Swinburne had presented a rector recorded *c.* 1377.[40] In the event the bishop collated by lapse,[41] as he did again, following a similar claim by Sir William Fynderne, in 1490.[42] A compromise then made, allowing the lord of the manor to name a clerk whom the prior of Lewes was to present,[43] remained in force until Sir Thomas Elyot acquired the advowson with Great Carlton manor.[44] After Elyot's estates were divided the advowson of Weston Colville was formally conveyed with Great Carlton manor until the 17th century,[45] but was apparently exercised by the lords of the Weston Colville manors,[46] conveyances of which included the advowson after 1676.[47] Turns were granted to Sir Nathaniel Curzon (d. 1758), patron in 1747, to John Dowse, patron in 1793,[48] and to Col. John Scriven, patron in 1865.[49] A. C. Hall retained the advowson after selling the estate, and it passed after his death in 1920 to his widow, and by 1930 to his son A. J. Hall, still named as patron in 1973.[50]

William de Warenne also granted to Lewes priory the tithe of his Weston demesne.[51] In 1236 the priory vindicated against the rector there its right to ⅔ of the tithes not only of Colvilles demesne but also of 20 a. of alienated demesne. It had also an ancient pension of 2*s.* 6*d.*[52] The priory's tithes, usually taxed at 5 marks, were often farmed,[53] sometimes to the rector who offered £11 13*s.* 4*d.* for them in 1328.[54] About 1500 three-fifths of the demesne tithes went to the rector and only two-fifths to the priory,[55] which, it was alleged in 1459, had in return to furnish a monk to say mass at Weston every Wednesday and Friday.[56] The priory's tithe portion, valued at £1 *c.* 1540,[57] and pension descended with Great Carlton manor.[58] At inclosure in 1778 Thomas Brand, owner of Carlton, obtained for those tithes a £28 rent-charge upon Colvilles farm.[59] Hatfield Broadoak priory (Essex) had a portion in Weston, taxed at 10*s.* in 1254 and 2 marks in 1291, which it retained in 1340.[60]

The rector, besides the remaining tithes from Weston and tithes of 7 a. in Brinkley and Willingham, had a glebe comprising in 1279 20 a.,[61] and in 1615 7 a. of closes and 51 a. of open-field arable.[62] At inclosure he was allotted 40½ a. for open-field glebe, and for the tithes received from John Carter Pollard 268 a. at the south-east end of the parish.[63] In 1832 the rector exchanged his ancient closes and glebe allotment with John Hall for 94½ a. adjoining

23 S.C. 2/155/71 mm. 1d.–2d.
24 C 3/72/26 rejoinder.
25 *Sessions of the Peace* (C.A.S. 8vo ser. lv), p. lxix.
26 C.U.L., E.D.R., C 1/6.
27 *Poor Law Abstract, 1804*, 38–9.
28 Ibid. *1818*, 30–1.
29 *Poor Rate Returns, 1816–21*, 11; *1822–4*, 35; *1825–9*, 16; *1830–4*, 16.
30 *Rep. H.L. Cttee. on Poor Laws*, H.C. 227, pp. 328–9 (1831), viii.
31 *Rep. Com. Poor Laws* [44], p. 257, H.C. (1834), xxviii.
32 *Poor Law Com. 1st Rep.* 249.
33 *Census*, 1931 (pt. ii).
34 Dorothy Whitelock, *A.-S. Wills*, 80–1.
35 *Lewes Chartulary*, i (Suss. Rec. Soc. xxxviii), 22.
36 *Early Yorks. Chart.* viii (Y.A.S. extra ser. vi), 74–5.
37 *Cur. Reg. R.* ii. 196, 218, 231.
38 Ibid. xv, p. 54.
39 e.g. *Lewes Chartulary, Cambs.* 31; *E.D.R.* (1893), 14; (1898), 56, 177; (1903), 135; C.U.L., E.D.R., L 3/1, f. 18.
40 *E.D.R.* (1904), 260.
41 Ibid. (1905), 21.
42 Ibid. (1908), 170; C.P. 40/914 rot. 239.
43 Cf. *Lewes Chartulary, Cambs.* 32; C.U.L., E.D.R., L 3/1, f. 51v.
44 *L. & P. Hen. VIII*, xiii (1), p. 99.
45 e.g. C.P. 25(2)/68/559 no. 2; C.P. 25(2)/526/3 Chas. I East. no. 4.
46 e.g. B.L. Add. MS. 5810, f. 113v.; Gibbons, *Ely Episc. Rec.* 437; P.R.O. Inst. Bks. ser. B, i, p. 81; iv, p. 153.
47 C.P. 25(2)/762/27–8 Chas. II Hil. no. 1.
48 P.R.O. Inst. Bks. ser. C, i, f. 451v.; cf. G.E.C. *Baronetage*, ii. 132.
49 List in ch.
50 *Crockford* (1916 and later edns.); *Who Was Who, 1916–28*, 452.
51 *Lewes Chartulary*, i (Suss. Rec. Soc. xxxviii), 16, 22.
52 Ibid. ii (Suss. Rec. Soc. xl), 121–2.
53 *Val. of Norwich*, ed. Lunt, 215; *Tax. Eccl.* (Rec. Com.), 267; *Rot. Parl.* i. 3.
54 *Lewes Chartulary, Cambs.* 32.
55 Ibid. 8–10.
56 *E.D.R.* (1904), 260.
57 *L. & P. Hen. VIII*, xiii (1), p. 99.
58 e.g. C.P. 25(2)/68/559 no. 2.
59 Weston Colville Incl. Act, 17 Geo. III, c. 123 (Priv. Act), pp. 2, 14–15.
60 *Val. of Norwich*, ed. Lunt, 215; *Tax. Eccl.* (Rec. Com.), 267; *Inq. Non.* (Rec. Com.), 212.
61 S.C. 5/Cambs. Tower ser. no. 15 rot. 2.
62 C.U.L., E.D.R., H 1/6, terrier 1615.
63 C.R.O., Q/RDz 1, pp. 331–5.

the tithe allotment,[64] making a holding called Weston Woods farm of 364 a. Its rent having fallen sharply, it was sold in 1912 to C. F. Ryder,[65] who owned Little Carlton farm to the north. Ryder's daughter, later Mrs. Cheshire, retained it in 1960.[66] In 1887 Anne, widow of Maj. Charles Hall, gave £6,000 to augment the rector's income.[67]

The rectory was taxed at £12 in 1217 and at £28 gross in 1276, but in 1291 at only £16 13*s.* 4*d.*[68] It was valued at £21 12*s.* 2*d.* in 1535, at £108 by 1650,[69] and in 1728 at £120, though really worth nearly £200 a year.[70] The rector's income rose from £200 *c.* 1830 to over £380 by 1851.[71]

The rectory house originally stood south-west of the churchyard.[72] Rebuilt after a fire in the mid 18th century, it was later let to poor people,[73] and although a curate lived there in 1807,[74] was described as unfit *c.* 1830.[75] In 1832 the site was exchanged with John Hall for another, across the road,[76] upon which a new house was nearly complete in 1836. The rectors lived there until the 1930s,[77] but it was let from 1951.[78]

A guildhall, converted into a town house, was sold for the Crown in 1572.[79]

About 1225 the bishop established at Weston a perpetual vicar, nominated by Eustace Fauconberg, the absentee rector, who was to receive from the living a pension of 1 mark a year.[80] The next rector, instituted by 1236, served in person, the vicarage presumably lapsing.[81] The rectors' occupations were frequently secular. One had by 1323 accumulated a debt of £400 to a knight.[82] His successor decamped *c.* 1340, having farmed the living to his brother.[83] The rector from 1348, a goldsmith from Verdun in the service of Joan of Bar, dowager countess of Surrey, was only in minor orders and was non-resident in 1352.[84] Lewes priory later presented clergy from Sussex, such as John Wodeway, rector 1401–5.[85] In 1404 he was licensed to remain absent, as was his successor in 1405.[86] Parish chaplains were recorded in 1406, 1463, and 1487,[87] the last employed by the pluralist canon lawyer Henry Rud, rector 1478–90.[88] Edmund Natures, master of Clare College (d. 1549), obtained the rectory in 1517 presumably through being executor to Sir William Fynderne.[89] He endowed an annual sermon at Weston,[90] and served the parish through curates.[91]

The rector in 1561 resided, but was thought incapable of preaching.[92] Simon Hackesup, rector 1583–1605, preached every Sunday but neglected certain prayers on weekdays.[93] Abraham Gates, rector 1605–45, acquired considerable property in the neighbourhood and left *c.* £600 among his children and grandchildren, one of whom, Ralph Garnons, was rector 1663–80.[94] Robert Haynes, presented in 1645[95] and described in 1650 as a preaching minister,[96] retained the rectory until his death in 1663.[97] In 1680 the earl of Sussex presented his former chaplain Thomas Tipping, rector until 1732, who resided on his cure and assisted his neighbours by his knowledge of law and physic. In 1728 he held two services every Sunday and had 37 communicants.[98] George Wallis, rector 1742–7, lived on his Wiltshire benefices, leaving Weston to be served by the vicar of West Wratting,[99] and Thomas Cook, rector 1747–93, lived at his other living of Semer (Suff.) in 1775, employing a curate at Weston, as did in 1807 his successor H. A. Lagden, rector 1793–1832. Lagden also held Ware (Herts.) from 1791 and later lived on his estate at Balsham. In the 18th century there were usually three or four communions a year, and one Sunday service.[1] From the 1820s there were two Sunday services, and the number of communicants rose from under 20 in 1825 to 50 by 1836, when a new rector, William Acton, who lived with his father-in-law at Wratting Park, was serving in person.[2] In 1877 37 people attended the monthly communions and up to 100 came regularly to church;[3] in 1897 the rector believed that 62 out of 113 households adhered to the church, and 15 others might attend either church or chapel.[4] From 1936 Weston was held with Westley Waterless by the Revd. R. J. Davies until he resigned, aged 92, in 1975.[5]

The church of *ST. MARY*[6] was built mainly of field stones. Its stone dressings were largely replaced by grey brick in the 1820s. It consists of a chancel with north vestry, nave with south porch, and west

[64] C.U.L., Doc. 689.

[65] Church Com. files.

[66] *Camb. Ind. Press*, 17 June 1960.

[67] Church Com. files; *Char. Digest Cambs. 1892*, H.C. 364, pp. 14–15 (1892–I), lix.

[68] *Val. of Norwich*, ed. Lunt, 535, 554; *Tax. Eccl.* (Rec. Com.), 267.

[69] *Valor Eccl.* (Rec. Com.), iii. 505; Lamb. Pal. MS. 904, f. 265.

[70] C.U.L., E.D.R., B 8/1.

[71] *Rep. Com. Eccl. Revenues*, pp. 352–3; H.O. 129/188/3/5/5.

[72] C.U.L., E.D.R., H 1/6, terrier 1615; cf. ibid. MS. Plan 550R.

[73] Ibid. E.D.R., B 7/1, p. 4.

[74] Ibid. C 1/4.

[75] *Rep. Com. Eccl. Revenues*, p. 353.

[76] C.U.L., Doc. 689.

[77] Ibid. E.D.R., C 3/21, 39; *Crockford* (1926–35).

[78] *Crockford* (1940–74); Church Com. files.

[79] *Cal. Pat.* 1567–72, p. 347.

[80] *Lewes Chartulary, Cambs.* 31.

[81] *Lewes Chartulary*, ii (Suss. Rec. Soc. xl), 122; cf. *Vetus Liber Arch. Elien.* (C.A.S. 8vo ser. xlviii), 58.

[82] C 260/35/19.

[83] *E.D.R.* (1892), 688, 704.

[84] Ibid. (1893), 14, 30, 136; *Cal. Papal Pets.* i. 287.

[85] *E.D.R.* (1898), 108, 177; cf. Prob. 11/2A (P.C.C. 9 Marche).

[86] *E.D.R.* (1900), 198; (1901), 20; Emden, *Biog. Reg. Univ. Oxon.* iii. 1412.

[87] *E.D.R.* (1899), 158; (1906), 188; (1909), 128.

[88] Ibid. (1906), 158; (1908), 170; *Cal. Papal Reg.* xiii (2), 697; Emden, *Biog. Reg. Univ. Camb.* 494.

[89] Emden, *Biog. Reg. Univ. Camb.* 419; *E.D.R.* (1910), 217; cf. Prob. 11/18 (P.C.C. 36 Holder).

[90] Cooper, *Athenae Cantab.* i. 97. Not traced later.

[91] e.g. B.L. Add. MS. 5861, ff. 14v., 85v., 108v.; *E.D.R.* (1912), 184; (1913), 41.

[92] B.L. Add. MS. 5813, f. 85.

[93] Bodl. MS. Gough. Eccl. Top. 3, f. 26; *Trans. C.H.A.S.* vi. 27.

[94] Prob. 11/193 (P.C.C. 79 Rivers); *Alum. Cantab. to 1751*, ii. 197, 200.

[95] P.R.O. Inst. Bks. ser. A, iii, p. 34.

[96] Lamb. Pal. MS. 904, ff. 205–6.

[97] Gibbons, *Ely Episc. Rec.* 372.

[98] *Mon. Inscr. Cambs.* 182; B.L. Add. MS. 5810, f. 114; C.U.L., E.D.R., B 8/1.

[99] B.L. Add. MS. 5810, ff. 112–13; *Alum. Cantab. to 1751*, iv. 351.

[1] C.U.L., E.D.R., C 1/1, 4; *Alum. Cantab. to 1751*, i. 388; *1752–1900*, iv. 75.

[2] C.U.L., E.D.R., C 1/6; C 3/21.

[3] Ibid. C 3/27.

[4] Ibid. C 3/39.

[5] *Crockford* (1936 and later edns.); Church Com. files.

[6] So named in 1419: *Cal. Papal Reg.* vii. 65.

tower. The nave, whose three south windows retained Decorated tracery in 1746,[7] was built in the early 14th century, as were the chancel arch and surviving original fragments of the chancel, where windows once contained the arms of Warenne, Colville, and Ufford.[8] The elaborately moulded south doorway and the porch, where an ogee-headed niche once contained an image of the Virgin,[9] are probably late-14th-century. A three-storey tower[10] was built in the 15th century. The north wall of the nave contains a large cusped niche, possibly once leading to the rood-stair. Money was left in 1521 for making straight the rood-loft and painting the figures above it.[11] The whole screen survived in 1746, but only its stone base by 1908.[12] Wide wall-spaces each side of the chancel arch gave room for altars. The brasses of a man, woman, and child, from the tomb of Richard Leverer (d. 1428),[13] were removed thither from the chancel, where a wall-monument with kneeling figures to Abraham Gates (d. 1645) and his wife remains.

In 1644 William Dowsing destroyed many 'superstitious pictures'.[14] Although the church was in good repair in 1728,[15] the tiled roof and the leads of the steeple were in decay by 1783,[16] and the tower collapsed in 1824. Within a year it was reconstructed,[17] mostly in grey brick; probably at the same time the chancel and the north wall of the nave were largely rebuilt, lancets with brick dressings and vertical bands of brick being inserted. The fittings are mainly early-19th-century and include a font replacing a wooden one that was still in use in 1841.[18] The late-19th-century vestry may be on the site of the Hall family vault.[19] The interior was restored in 1875.[20] In the 1880s the east window received new tracery in Perpendicular style.[21]

There was only one chalice *c.* 1277[22] and one silver chalice with a paten in 1552.[23] The existing cup and paten were given in 1635, and another paten of 1840 in 1842.[24] There were four bells in 1552,[25] and five by 1746.[26] All but one were broken when the tower fell in 1824, and the existing five bells were cast by Thomas Mears of London in 1825.[27] The surviving parish registers begin only in 1700.[28]

NONCONFORMITY. No dissenters were recorded at Weston until buildings were registered for dissenting worship in 1823 and 1826.[29] In 1843 and 1846 the village grocer had his house registered for worship,[30] and he probably promoted the building in 1847 of a Primitive Methodist chapel, called by 1854 the Rehoboth chapel.[31] The chapel had 180 sittings in 1851 when its minister claimed congregations of 250–300 at two of the three Sunday services,[32] and there was a flourishing Sunday school.[33] In 1877 50 or 60 people were said to attend the chapel, and in 1897 33 families were chapel-goers.[34] The chapel was still open in 1975, being then served from Saffron Walden.

EDUCATION. Although the curate was teaching a school at Weston in 1607,[35] the parish had no established school[36] until 1832, when a Sunday school with 42 pupils and a day-school with 20 girls, both supported by subscriptions, were started.[37] In 1868 Gen. and Miss Hall built a schoolroom and teacher's house just east of the church. The 40–50 children paid school pence in 1872.[38] The building was enlarged in 1876 and again in 1884,[39] and attendance rose from 46 in 1876 to 78 by 1889.[40] In 1897, despite £90 a year from subscriptions, the school was in financial difficulties.[41] Until the 1890s the school was kept by a master and his wife, thereafter by a mistress.[42] Attendance was 85 in 1910,[43] and the school was divided into mixed and infants' classes by 1913, when it was transferred to the county council.[44] Numbers fluctuated around 60 from 1919 until 1936, but after 1937, when the seniors were sent to Linton village college, fell to 27. The school was closed in 1971, the junior children going to Balsham.[45]

CHARITIES FOR THE POOR. Robert Cooper by will proved 1612 left the interest on £1 for yearly distribution to the poor of Weston,[46] and John Flanner by will proved 1640 left £10 as a stock.[47] Neither bequest is recorded later. Edward Briggs by will proved 1735 left a rent-charge of £1 for the poor of Weston at Christmas. That was being distributed in 1775, but the money was not received between 1807 and 1822.[48] At inclosure in 1778 1½ a. called the poor's plot was allotted in place of the right to cut fuel on the common, the rent to be distri-

[7] B.L. Add. MS. 5810, f. 111v.; cf. Add. MS. 6753, ff. 5, 7.
[8] B.L. Add. MS. 5819, f. 61; Edm. de Colville (d. 1316) married Marg. Ufford: *Complete Peerage*, iii. 324–5.
[9] *Gardner's Dir. Cambs.* (1851).
[10] Cf. B.L. Add. MS. 5810, f. 111v.
[11] Ibid. Add. MS. 5861, ff. 75v., 85v.
[12] Ibid. Add. MS. 5810, f. 116; *Proc. C.A.S.* xii. 286.
[13] *Mon. Inscr. Cambs.* 182, 243.
[14] *Trans. C.H.A.S.* iii. 90.
[15] C.U.L., E.D.R., B 8/1.
[16] Ibid. B 7/1, p. 4.
[17] Ibid. C 1/6.
[18] Ibid. C 1/6; C 3/17.
[19] Cf. *Gardner's Dir. Cambs.* (1851).
[20] C.U.L., E.D.R., C 3/39.
[21] *Kelly's Dir. Cambs.* (1883–1900).
[22] *Vetus Liber Arch. Elien.* (C.A.S. 8vo ser. xlviii), 58.
[23] *Cambs. Ch. Goods, temp. Edw. VI*, 72.
[24] List of ch. plate *penes V.C.H.*
[25] *Cambs. Ch. Goods, temp. Edw. VI*, 72.
[26] B.L. Add. MS. 5810, f. 112.
[27] *Cambs. Bells* (C.A.S. 8vo ser. xviii), 174.
[28] *Kelly's Dir. Cambs.* (1879).
[29] G.R.O. Worship Returns, Ely dioc. nos. 458, 500, 508.
[30] Ibid. nos. 670, 683.
[31] Ibid. no. 694; ibid. Worship Reg. no. 5114; *Gardner's Dir. Cambs.* (1851).
[32] H.O. 129/188/3/5/7.
[33] *Gardner's Dir. Cambs.* (1851).
[34] C.U.L., E.D.R., C 3/27, 39.
[35] C.U.L., E.D.R., B 2/23, f. 43.
[36] e.g. not in ibid. C 1/1, 4.
[37] *Educ. Enquiry Abstract*, 62; C.U.L., E.D.R., C 3/21.
[38] Ed. 7/5; cf. B.L. Maps 135. a. 6.
[39] *Kelly's Dir. Cambs.* (1879, 1888).
[40] *Rep. of Educ. Cttee. of Council, 1876–7* [C. 1780-I], p. 741, H.C. (1877), xxix; *1889–9* [C. 5804-I], p. 532, H.C. (1889), xxix.
[41] C.U.L., E.D.R., C 3/39.
[42] *Kelly's Dir. Cambs.* (1879–1904).
[43] *Bd. of Educ., List 21, 1910* (H.M.S.O.), 25.
[44] Ibid. *1914*, 29.
[45] Ibid. *1919*, 17; *1932*, 18; *1938*, 21; *Camb. Ind. Press*, 17 June 1960; Black, *Cambs. Educ. Rec.* 77.
[46] Prob. 11/119 (P.C.C. 17 Fenner).
[47] Prob. 11/183 (P.C.C. 102 Coventry).
[48] *31st Rep. Com. Char.* 140; cf. C.U.L., E.D.R., C 1/1, 4.

buted to the poor at Christmas.[49] In 1837 it was let for £1 10*s.* a year. In the 1830s that and Briggs's charity were collected every four years, and the accumulated £10 distributed indiscriminately.[50] Those charities were not recorded separately after *c.* 1880,[51] being perhaps administered with the bequest of Maj. Charles Hall's widow Anne who in 1895 gave £3,000 to found the Major Charles Hall Memorial Charity. The income was to be used for medical expenses, especially for children, or to provide fuel, clothing, or food, especially for the sick. The rector began by using the income mainly to support a coal club that he had just started, and was alleged to favour church-people. In the late 1960s the income was still spent on coal, milk, and medical expenses. Re-investment raised it from £75 in 1970 to £225 by 1973, spent mainly on milk and groceries.[52]

WEST WRATTING

WEST WRATTING parish lies 10 miles south-east of Cambridge and 7 miles south-west of Newmarket.[1] Its 3,543 a. stretch for 6 miles south-eastwards from the main London–Newmarket road to the Suffolk border. It is less than 2 miles across at its widest, and tapers to a point at the south-east end.[2] The modern boundaries resemble those of the 10th century, which on the north-west followed the highway, later the London–Newmarket road, and then ran east along a road whose course is followed by the track to Lark Hall. The boundary then ran east-south-east along the edge of woodland, and on reaching the West Wickham boundary turned west towards Yen Hall, and ran from there to the Balsham boundary, following the Fleam Dyke back to the highway.[3] There are two gaps in the dyke east of the road: Bedford Gap was cut in 1763 and Dungate is said to have been cut in the mid 19th century, although it has also been suggested that it dates from before the Conquest. The name Dungate or Denegate is recorded from the early 14th century.[4]

The land rises from *c.* 125 ft. near the main road to *c.* 350 ft. in the north-west half of the parish, and after falling slightly rises again to a plateau at *c.* 375 ft.; the village lies at the north-west edge of the plateau, with West Wratting Park to the south-east and beyond it Wratting Common and land that was part of an airfield.[5] Above the 300-ft. contour boulder clay overlies the chalk, and the higher ground was formerly wooded.[6] In 1975 there were *c.* 150 a. of woodland, mostly in the south-east end of the parish. The open fields, lying in the centre of the parish, were inclosed by an award of 1813.[7] A small brook crosses the parish in the south-east, flowing north into the river Stour. In the 17th century a watercourse ran between the heaths in the west. Another runs north from west of the village: there the lord had a fishery in the 14th century at Oxcroft farm.[8]

The parish was presumably settled from Great Wratting in Suffolk. The village is the only centre of settlement, but seems to have grown from three separate parts, spaced along the road to Withersfield (Suff.). Several houses stand at the junction of the Weston Colville, Six Mile Bottom, and Balsham roads, at the north-west end of the main street. There also stand the church, rectory and vicarage, and West Wratting Hall. A green or waste ground may once have lain between the houses on the main street and the parallel path south-west of the street. In the 19th century, however, West Wratting green lay at the south-eastern end of the village on either side of the main street near Wratting Park and Scarletts Farm, which stands on an ancient moated site. Some of the green has since been incorporated in the park, and houses standing to the south of the street have disappeared.[9] The third part of the village lies along Wratting Common. Some of the scattered houses there date from the 17th century, and it is also the site of Parys's manor-house. By the early 20th century the first two parts of the village were almost merged. Council houses were later built in a cul-de-sac near the centre of the main street and at the western edge of the village, along the Six Mile Bottom road.

At the extreme west corner of the parish stand Fleam Dyke cottages, connected with Dungate Farm. Valley Farm, near to them, was built on heathland as a racing stables, and a trial course was laid out there crossing the old Newmarket course whose seven-and eight-mile posts lay within the parish. Oxcroft was also used as a stud farm at one time.[10] The old Linton–Newmarket road crossed the parish in the west. Other modern roads in the parish probably follow their ancient courses.[11]

Thirty-three inhabitants were enumerated in West Wratting in 1086. Forty-nine people were taxed in 1327, and there were 180 adults in 1377.[12] In 1563 there were 47 households, and a century later 76 houses.[13] In 1728 the population was *c.* 250, and had risen to 541 by 1801. It rose steadily until 1831, and by 1841 had reached 912; it then fell, apparently through emigration, to 591 in 1881. A low point of 395 was reached in 1931 and numbers then rose slightly until 1951, but fell to 386 in 1971.[14]

[49] C.R.O., Q/RDz 1, pp. 330–1.
[50] *31st Rep. Com. Char.* 140.
[51] e.g. *Char. Digest. Cambs. 1863–4*, 38–9; mentioned in *Kelly's Dir. Cambs.* (1879), but not later.
[52] Char. Com. files.
[1] This account was written in 1975.
[2] O.S. Maps 1/25,000, TL 55, 64, 65 (1956 edn.).
[3] *Proc. C.A.S.* xxiv. 32.
[4] Ibid. 31–2; *Saga Bk. of Viking Soc.* iv. 111; C.U.L., Palmer MS. A 29, f. 53.
[5] O.S. Maps 1/25,000, TL 55, 64, 65 (1956 edn.); see above, p. 183.
[6] *Camb. Region* (1938), 108–9.
[7] C.U.L., Add. MS. 6058.
[8] Jesus Coll. Mun., West Wratting 2 (1658); *Cal. Pat.* 1321–4, 445.
[9] C.U.L. Add. MS. 6058, p. 5; B.L. Maps 1640 (33).
[10] Bodl. MS. Gough Maps, Suff. 13; *Camb. Chron.* 23 Oct. 1802.
[11] O.S. Maps 1/25,000, TL 55, 65 (1956 edn.); Jesus Coll. Mun., Est. 4. 10, f. 15.
[12] *V.C.H. Cambs.* i. 406; *Cambs. Lay Subsidy, 1327*, 15–16; *East Anglian*, N.S. xii. 257.
[13] B.L. Harl. MS. 594, f. 199v.; E 179/84/437 rot. 176.
[14] C.U.L., E.D.R., B 8/1; *Census*, 1801–1971.

During the 1381 revolt houses at West Wratting, including the rectory, were broken into, and the prior of Ely's court rolls burned.[15]

In 1632 three alehouses were licensed in West Wratting.[16] The Crown inn, recorded from 1788, was in 1975 called the Lamb; it lay at the west end of the village, opposite the lane to the church.[17] The Chestnut Tree, recorded in 1883, still stood in 1975 at the junction of the main street and the Bartlow road, opposite the park.[18]

MANORS AND OTHER ESTATES. In 974 King Edgar gave 2½ *mansae* at West Wratting to his thegn Elfhelm, who *c.* 990 devised the estate, except for 2 hides held by Ethelric, to Ely abbey. West Wratting was included in King Edward's confirmation of the abbey's estates, and in the early 12th century remained with the prior after the establishment of the bishopric.[19] The manor of *WEST WRATTING*, later known as *WEST WRATTING HALL*, passed in 1541 to the dean and chapter of Ely.[20] During the Interregnum it was sold, as an estate of *c.* 600 a., to George Foxcroft of London.[21] It was afterwards restored to the dean and chapter who at inclosure in 1813 were allotted *c.* 244 a. for it.[22] In 1809 the lease of the manor and Hall farm belonged to Harry Frost who eventually bought the freehold of all the Ely property in the parish. On Harry's death in 1831 the Hall estate passed to the family of his brother Edward Frost (d. 1834), and was held by Edward's grandson E. P. Frost at his death in 1922. E. P. Frost was a pioneer of aeroplane building; in the late 19th century he built a steam flying machine, and in 1908 was president of the British Aeronautical Society.[23]

By the later 19th century members of the Frost family, all descendants of Edward Frost (d. 1834), held almost all the land in the parish. Their estates were sold in the 1920s, and much of the land, including West Wratting Hall, was bought by S. A. Taylor. It was sold on his death in 1938. By 1975 most of the parish, including the Hall estate, was held by the executors of R. E. N. d'Abo, who had bought it in the early 1950s.[24] The south range of the Hall is probably the greater part of an 18th-century farm-house. Additions, with a new staircase and principal rooms, were made on the south in the early 19th century, and there were further additions, later removed, on that side in the late 19th century.

In 1086 William de Warenne held 3 yardlands which were associated with his lands in West Wickham.[25]

Hardwin de Scalers held 3 hides in 1086, previously held by 10 sokemen of the abbot of Ely, although he was also said to hold of the king. The manor, known as *SCALERS*, later corrupted to *CHARLES*, or *FREVILLES*, was later held in chief although in the 16th century the dean and chapter of Ely claimed rights of soil and waste there.[26] The manor descended in the Scalers family until *c.* 1231, when Lucy de Scalers married Baldwin de Freville, and then in the Freville family, with Caxton manor, passing from William Freville (fl. 1424) to his son William (d. 1481), and his son John.[27] In 1496 the prior of Ely claimed that John's grandfather William had enfeoffed the prior with a quarter of his manor of Wratting, which John was unjustly withholding.[28] In 1497 John and his son Robert granted the manor to Sir Gilbert Talbot. In 1524 it was held by Sir Thomas Golding, who in 1564 conveyed it to John Harrison. In 1568 Harrison conveyed it to Thomas and William Wyborowe, and in 1571 it was sold to Dr. Andrew Perne, dean of Ely.[29] Perne granted the manor, with *c.* 280 a. of land and extensive rights of common, to Peterhouse of which he was master. The master and fellows were lords there in 1591,[30] and still held the manor in 1813 when they were allotted *c.* 180 a. at inclosure.[31]

The lease of the manor was held in the early 18th century by Sir John Jacob, Bt., who built the house called West Wratting Park. His son was Hildebrand Jacob the poet (1693–1739). Sir John had sold the lease to Sir Robert Smith, Bt., by 1746, and Smith sold it to Jenison Shafto, who committed suicide in 1771, leaving the lease to his brother Robert.[32] In 1780 Robert and his son, also Robert, died and the lease was bought *c.* 1789 by Richard Taylor.[33] In 1807 it was held by Gen. Thomas Hall, and from *c.* 1813 by Sir Charles Watson (d. 1844), his son Charles (d. 1852), and grandson Charles (d. 1888).[34] The land was held in 1796 by Francis Russell, duke of Bedford, and its lease sold in 1798. From 1803 to *c.* 1837 it was held by Sir Hedworth Williamson, Bt.[35] It then passed to the Frost family, and in 1867 was held by Harry Frost's nephew W. T. Frost (d. 1870), whose estate went to his nephews E. P. and H. Frost. E. P. Frost (d. 1922) bought the freehold from Peterhouse *c.* 1909.[36] In 1935 the house and *c.* 120 a. were offered for sale by E. P. Frost's nephew and heir, E. G. G. Frost.[37] Since 1951 it has belonged to the d'Abo family. The house is a large

[15] *Cambs. Village Doc.* 35.
[16] *Proc. C.A.S.* xvii. 92.
[17] *Camb. Chron.* 5 July 1788; *Kelly's Dir. Cambs.* (1847 and later edns.).
[18] *Kelly's Dir. Cambs.* (1883).
[19] *Cart. Sax.* ed. Birch, iii, pp. 628–9; B.L. Stowe Ch. 36; *Cod. Dipl.* ed. Kemble, iv, pp. 444–7; *Liber Elien.* (Camd. 3rd ser. xcii), p. 300.
[20] *L. & P. Hen. VIII*, xvi, p. 575.
[21] C 54/3620 m. 48.
[22] C.U.L., Add. MS. 6058, pp. 19–22.
[23] C.U.L., Palmer MS. A 88; C.R.O., 289/T 60; *Kelly's Dir. Cambs.* (1908); local information; see above, plate facing p. 177.
[24] Burke, *Land. Gent.* (1937), 846; C.R.O., 289/T 57; ibid. SP 184/2; ex inf. Mr. M. Dobell, agent.
[25] *V.C.H. Cambs.* i. 380; and see above, p. 117.
[26] *V.C.H. Cambs.* i. 364, 406; C 3/202/47; C 3/58/8.
[27] *V.C.H. Cambs.* v. 27–8; C 140/80 no. 559.
[28] C.P. 40/938 rot. 314.
[29] Peterhouse Mun., E. 13, 14, 17A, 21; F. 4, 5, 10; B.L. Add. MS. 5838, f. 147v.; C.P. 25(2)/93/835/10–11 Eliz. I Mich. no. 7; C.P. 25(2)/93/837/13–14 Eliz. I Mich. no. 9; *Cal. Pat.* 1572–5, p. 337.
[30] Lysons, *Cambs.* 295; C.U.L., Palmer MS. A 29, p. 70; Peterhouse Mun., F. 30, 38.
[31] C.U.L., Add. MS. 6058, pp. 1, 54–6.
[32] Palmer, *Wm. Cole*, 115–16; *D.N.B.*; see above, plate facing p. 81.
[33] B.L. Add. MS. 5810, f. 103v.; 9412, f. 41; *Camb. Chron.* 29 July 1780; 19 June 1784; Peterhouse Mun., H. 29; Lysons, *Cambs.* 293.
[34] C.U.L., E.D.R., C 1/4; C.U.L., Maps 53/86/27; d'Abo estate papers, w. Wratting Park.
[35] Peterhouse Mun., H. 30–9; Jesus Coll. Mun., West Wratting 3 (1798); C.R.O., 289/T 80.
[36] Peterhouse Mun., G. 14, 9B; C.R.O., 289/T 58.
[37] C.R.O., 515/SP 450.

DUXFORD: the mill and mill house

WHITTLESFORD: the mill house

PAMPISFORD: the brewery *c.* 1890

DUXFORD: the chemical works of CIBA-GEIGY (UK) Ltd.

red brick building with a central block which has fronts of five bays, and is presumably the part built by Sir John Jacob, and balancing wings which appear to have been added in the late 18th century. There are extensive outbuildings of the 18th and 19th centuries.

In 1312 John of Brigham held ¼ knight's fee, called *BRIGHAMS* and later *PARYS'S* manor, of the Freville manor; the overlordship was still recorded in 1602. Brigham granted the estate to the bishop of Ely, who in turn gave it to Peterhouse without a mortmain licence so that it was taken into the king's hands on Brigham's death in 1358.[38] In that year the crown granted the land for life to John Goodrich, yeoman of the kitchen, and in 1361 the reversion to Robert Corby, another king's yeoman. Robert held the land in 1364, and was succeeded in 1365 by his son, also Robert, who in 1369 granted his lands in West Wratting and elsewhere to Robert Beverage, Thomas Sewale, and Sir Philip of Wratting.[39] In 1394 Robert Parys held a manor in West Wratting; in 1412 his granddaughter Catherine Parys held land there, and in 1449 Margery, the widow of Catherine's uncle and heir Henry Parys, held it for life. Parys's manor descended with the family's Linton and Duxford lands until 1541 when Philip Parys sold it to William Lawrence.[40] In 1561 Roland and Anne Master, who held Parys's for life with reversion to Ferdinand Parys, Philip's younger son, granted their interest to Henry Lawrence, and in 1571 released it to Ferdinand.[41] By 1587 Parys's belonged to Thomas Dalton of Hildersham, probably having passed to him with Little Abington rectory *c.* 1576.[42] Thomas died in 1602, having settled it on his son Michael (d. 1648), the author of *The Countrey Justice*. Michael had settled the reversion on his grandson, also Michael Dalton, and his wife Susan Tyrell, along with Little Abington rectory. Michael and Susan's son and grandson, both called Tyrell Dalton, inherited Parys's, the grandson holding it in 1714.[43] By the early 1720s it had been bought by the Corporation of the Sons of the Clergy, who in 1807 held over 800 a. in the parish, and at inclosure in 1813 were allotted 644 a.[44] Their West Wratting lands were divided between Grange and Randswood farms by 1821, and offered for sale as such in 1914. They were presumably bought by S. A. Taylor. Grange farm, covering 583 a., was offered for sale again in 1938, and was occupied by another Mr. S. A. Taylor in 1975 when Randswood was owned by Mr. R. J. Harrison.[45] The manor-house of Parys's was standing in 1811 and may be identified with Brook Farm House, on Wratting Common.

In 1086 Count Alan of Brittany held 1½ hide in Wratting which along with 40 a. in Balsham formed *OXCROFT* manor. It descended with the rest of his lands in the honor of Richmond, and was held of that honor in 1457. From the 15th century it was contended that Oxcroft was subordinate to Charles manor.[46] In 1086 Almar held the land of Count Alan. Between 1185 and 1190 a knight's fee in Oxcroft was held of Geoffrey Pecche, in 1235 of Hamon Pecche, and in 1271 of Hamon's son Gilbert, who in 1284 disinherited his issue by his first wife.[47] By 1355 that mesne lordship was held by the earl of Oxford, and descended with the earldom until 1632 when Robert, earl of Oxford, was seised of a knight's fee, then said to be in Balsham but usually in Balsham and Wratting.[48]

About 1185 Geoffrey Pecche's under-tenant for the fee was William, son of Aeliz, who still held it in Henry III's reign.[49] Stephen of Oxcroft forfeited the fee when he was hanged in 1234; it was granted first to William of Fordham and later to Philip Basset[50] (d. 1271). Philip's heir was his daughter Aline, wife of Roger Bigod, earl of Norfolk, but in 1280 his widow Ela, dowager countess of Warwick, held Oxcroft.[51] Aline's first husband had been Hugh le Despenser, and *c.* 1302 Oxcroft was held by their son Hugh, later earl of Winchester.[52] He was executed in 1326, and in 1327 John Aspale, king's yeoman, was granted the Balsham part of his lands.[53] Aspale interpreted the grant as conveying the whole of Oxcroft and in 1329 complained that the Wratting lands were occupied by James de Audley whom the Crown had appointed keeper. By 1341 the dispute was settled in John's favour, and he held the Oxcroft lands in Balsham and Wratting for life,[54] with reversion to James Dawtrey, king's yeoman, who succeeded on John's death in 1355.[55] In 1363 the manor passed to James's son Lionel, who in 1371 granted it for life to John Sleaford (d. 1401), rector of Balsham.[56] In 1385 Thomas Fotheringhay was granted the reversion, and in 1428 Edward Fotheringhay held the fee.[57]

In 1454 the manor was said to be late of Richard Foster. He may have been followed by another Richard, for *c.* 1480 Isabel Foster, widow, obtained custody of the land of the late Richard Foster, Oxcroft manor, and of Richard's son and heir Lawrence.[58] In 1524 Heneage de la Tour was said to hold the manor, but it was held in 1550 by Lawrence Foster, and settled in 1555 on his wife Bridget for life, with reversion to William Lawrence,[59] under whose will it passed to his younger sons, Thomas and William. In 1576 they sold the manor to Michael Heneage. Michael held it in the 1590s and on his

[38] *Cal. Inq. p.m.* v, p. 409; C 145/176 no. 20.

[39] *Cal. Pat.* 1358–61, 93–4; 1361–4, 29; *Cal. Close*, 1364–8, 86; 1369–74, 85; *Cal. Inq. p.m.* xii, p. 9.

[40] See p. 85; *E.D.R.* (1900), 74; C.U.L., Palmer MS. A 29, p. 65; C.P. 25(2)/4/21 no. 35.

[41] C.P. 25(2)/93/834/8–9 Eliz. I Mich. no. 10; C.P. 25(2)/93/837/13 Eliz. I Hil. no. 3.

[42] See p. 9; C.R.O., L 66/10.

[43] C.P. 25(2)/93/853/31 Eliz. I East. no. 11; Wards 7/26 no. 242; C.R.O., L 66/14A, 15, 21, 22; *D.N.B.*

[44] C.R.O., 289/T 68; ibid. S.P. 84/3; B.L. Add. MS. 9412, ff. 36–8; C.U.L., Add. MS. 6058, pp. 26–34.

[45] Baker, *Map of Cambs.* (1824); B.L. Maps 31. c. 26; C.R.O., SP 184/2; local information.

[46] *V.C.H. Cambs.* i. 379; C 139/165 no. 19.

[47] *V.C.H. Cambs.* i. 379; *Cat. Anct. D.* ii, A 3135; *Cal. Close*, 1234–7, 56; *Cal. Inq. p.m.* i, p. 272; Farrer, *Feud. Cambs.* 160; *Complete Peerage*, x. s.v. Pecche.

[48] *Cal. Inq. p.m.* x, pp. 227, 638; xiii, p. 125; C 142/150 no. 190; C 142/508 no. 15; Bodl. MS. Rawl. B. 319, f. 111.

[49] *Cat. Anct. D.* ii, A 3135; *Cal. Inq. Misc.* i, p. 170.

[50] *Cal. Close*, 1234–7, 56; E 40/14432.

[51] *Cal. Inq. p.m.* i, p. 272; B.L. Add. MS. 5837, f. 54.

[52] *Complete Peerage*, ix. 596; *Feud. Aids*, i. 141.

[53] *V.C.H. Bucks.* iii. 123; *Cal. Pat.* 1327–30, 26.

[54] *Cal. Fine R.* 1327–37, 84, 133; *Cal. Close*, 1327–30, 469; *Cal. Inq. Misc.* ii, pp. 262, 428.

[55] *Cal. Inq. p.m.* x, p. 227; *Cal. Pat.* 1340–3, 158–9; *Cal. Close*, 1354–60, 167.

[56] *Cal. Pat.* 1361–4, 341; 1370–4, 82.

[57] *Cal. Pat.* 1381–5, 568; *Feud. Aids*, i. 176.

[58] Bodl. MS. Rawl. B. 319, f. 111.

[59] B.L. Add. MS. 5838, f. 147v.; C.P. 25(2)/68/559 no. 22.

death in 1602 was followed by his son Thomas, who in 1641 was succeeded by his son, Sir Michael Heneage.[60] In 1760 Sir Michael's granddaughters and heirs, Elizabeth and Cecilia Heneage, sold Oxcroft to Jenison Shafto. At Shafto's death in 1771 the manor passed with his other lands to his brother Robert.[61] In 1773 Robert sold *c.* 90 a. of land and Oxcroft Hall to Richard, Lord Grosvenor, whose son Robert sold them to Lord Francis Godolphin Osborne in 1805. The remaining 350 a. were sold in parcels to Richard Taylor in 1789, to Francis Russell, duke of Bedford, in 1792, and to Sir Hedworth Williamson, Bt., in 1799. About 1816 William, Viscount Lowther, bought Osborne's share, and much of Sir Hedworth Williamson's. He sold Oxcroft in 1837 to William Purkis, who sold it in 1853 to his son-in-law Edward Frost (d. 1869).[62] The estate passed to Edward's son Harry Frost (d. 1898), and Harry's son, H. E. F. Frost, who in 1922 offered for sale Oxcroft House and *c.* 156 a. of land. It was presumably bought by G. R. C. Foster, whose executors offered it for sale in 1936.[63] Oxcroft Farm, east of the Balsham–Wratting road, with Oxcroft House opposite, stands on the site of the original manor.

In the earlier 19th century Dungate farm was detached from Oxcroft. It came to include in addition *c.* 100 a. of copyhold of West Wratting manor, and was sold in 1830 by Sir Hedworth Williamson's trustees to trustees for the Frere family, which in 1877 sold it to St. John's College, Cambridge. It then covered *c.* 530 a. It was sold in 1946 to H. E. Eastwood, who in 1952 sold *c.* 137 a. of the land to Jesus College. The farm-house stands in Balsham parish.[64]

In the early 13th century Philip Rixpand held ¼ knight's fee of Oxcroft. In 1315 Roger Rixpand held land in Wratting and John Rixpand when charged with theft in 1357 held ¼ fee which was restored to him in 1364. In 1410 John's daughter and heir Alice Maynard assigned his lands to John Moulton of West Wratting.[65] The land became known as the manor of *SCARLETTS* or *MOULTONS*, sometimes said to be held of Charles manor rather than Oxcroft because of the claim that Oxcroft was subordinate to Charles manor and because certain copyhold lands of Charles became associated with Scarletts.[66] In 1524 Scarletts was held by Sir Thomas Golding, and in 1546 by John Golding.[67] In 1568 it was conveyed with Charles manor by John Harrison to Thomas and William Wyborowe, and in 1574 Thomas sold the manor with over 300 a. of land to Dr. Andrew Perne.[68] In 1592 John Perne was succeeded in Scarletts manor and 80 a., all late John Rixpand's, by his son Andrew. By his will proved 1680 another Andrew Perne left the manor to his son John, who was succeeded in turn by his sons Chester (d. 1753) and John (d. 1770). The younger John's children, Andrew (d. 1771) and his three sisters, held land in West Wratting, but Scarletts went to John's brother Andrew (d. 1772). Andrew's son, also Andrew (d. 1807), left Scarletts to his wife for life and then to his son, John Chester Perne,[69] who held it at inclosure in 1813 and was allotted *c.* 176 a.[70] By 1851 the estate was held by Sir Charles Watson, and when sold by his son in 1863 it included what was later known as Lordship farm, presumably the portion held of Charles manor.[71] It apparently passed with Wratting Park to the Frost family, and in 1909 Scarletts farm, comprising 115 a., was among the lands of the late W. T. Frost (d. 1870) bought by his nephew E. P. Frost (d. 1922). It was offered for sale in 1922 and 1924 and bought by S. A. Taylor, being resold on his death in 1938.[72] In 1975 it was known as Scarletts Dairy and was part of the d'Abo estate. The modern Scarletts Farm is on a medieval moated site, which has been suggested, without evidence, as the site of Parys's manor-house.[73]

The reputed manor of *HAMMONDS*, recorded in the mid 16th century in association with Scarletts, was conveyed in 1576 by Thomas Wyborowe to Thomas Frenche, and in 1604 by Frenche to Michael Dalton. It was thenceforth associated with Parys's manor. In the 16th century it had *c.* 176 a. of arable and 250 a. of heath. The manor-house stood north of West Wratting green. A manor-house called Hammonds still stood near there in 1811.[74]

In the early 12th century Stephen and Gillian de Scalers gave *c.* 80 a. in West Wratting to St. Radegund's priory, Cambridge. By 1313 the priory held another 45 a. there, made up from smaller gifts. On its dissolution in 1496 the lands passed to Jesus College, Cambridge.[75] In the 17th century the estate, known as *LE GREAT NUNS* manor, included land in West Wickham and Weston Colville. At inclosure in 1813 the college was allotted 198 a. in the west part of the parish.[76] The original house, which in 1366 consisted of a hall and two chambers, had been near that of the Daltons in the village, but in the mid 18th century Jenison Shafto, the lessee, built a house and stables at the Valley for training racehorses,[77] which after inclosure became the farm-house for the college lands. In or after 1925 the buildings were replaced by a farm-house incorporating some old materials.[78]

60 C 142/150 no. 90; C.P. 25(2)/93/841/18–19 Eliz. I Mich. no. 14; C 2/Eliz. I/H 13/6; C 3/241/22; C 142/614 no. 79; C.U.L., Palmer MS. A 29, p. 71.

61 C.R.O., L 86/106; ibid. 289/T 78.

62 Lysons, *Cambs.* 296; B.L. Add. MS. 9412, ff. 41–2; C.R.O., L 86/106; ibid. 289/T 78; Burke, *Land. Gent.* (1906), i. 637.

63 C.R.O., 515/SP 633; C.U.L., Maps 53(1)/93/86.

64 C.R.O., L 86/107, 108; L 70/2; H. F. Howard, *Finances of St. John's Coll.* 203; Jesus Coll. Mun., West Wratting 4 (1952); ex inf. Dr. C. M. P. Johnson, Bursar, St. John's Coll.

65 *Liber de Bernewelle*, 257; *Cal. Inq. Misc.* iii, p. 230; *Cal. Pat.* 1354–8, 596; *Cal. Close*, 1364–8, 41; 1409–13, 77.

66 Peterhouse Mun., Misc. 5; ibid. G. 4; C 142/233 no. 16.

67 B.L. Add. MS. 5838, f. 128v.; Peterhouse Mun., Misc. 5.

68 C.P. 25(2)/93/835/10–11 Eliz. I Mich. no. 7; C.P. 25(2)/93/839/16 Eliz. I Hil. no. 9.

69 C 142/233 no. 16; Prob. 11/363 (P.C.C. 84 Bath); Prob. 11/1481 (P.C.C. 507 Ely); C.R.O., L 86/107; ibid. 289/T 9.

70 C.U.L., Add. MS. 6058, pp. 52–4.

71 C.U.L., Maps 53/86/27.

72 C.R.O., 289/T 58, 75; 515/SP 633, 726.

73 *V.C.H. Cambs.* ii. 44; C.U.L., Palmer MS. A 88.

74 C.P. 25(2)/93/840/17 Eliz. I East. no. 1; C.P. 25(2)/277/2 Jas. I Trin. no. 2; C.R.O., L 66/2–3; ibid. 289/T 68.

75 *Priory of St. Radegund* (C.A.S. 8vo ser. xxxi), 15, 44; *Cal. Chart. R.* 1300–26, 223.

76 Jesus Coll. Mun., West Wratting 2 (1625); ibid. (1757); C.U.L., Add. MS. 6058, pp. 47–9.

77 Jesus Coll. Mun., West Wratting 1 (1366); 2 (1625); 3 (1793).

78 Ibid. 3 (1859); 4 (1923), (1926).

In 1238 and 1343 the abbot of Warden (Beds.), held lands in West Wratting,[79] of which no later record has been found.[80]

West Wratting *RECTORY* was granted to the infirmary of Ely abbey in the earlier 12th century.[81] It passed in the 16th century to the dean and chapter of Ely, remaining with them until the 19th century though sold to John Skynne during the Interregnum.[82] In the 17th century the estate consisted of a house, the great tithes, *c.* 60 a. of arable, and liberty of fold and heathland for 200 sheep. At inclosure the dean and chapter were allotted 37½ a. for glebe and 642½ a. for tithes.[83] The Ecclesiastical Commissioners sold the allotment, known as Wadlow farm, to S. A. Taylor in 1919.[84]

ECONOMIC HISTORY. Of the 10 hides in West Wratting in 1086 the abbot of Ely held 4½, Hardwin de Scalers 3¼, Count Alan 1½, and William de Warrenne ¾. Seven hides were in demesne: the abbot had 3 with 2 plough-teams and land for 2 more, Hardwin had 1½ hide with 2 teams, and Alan had ¾ hide with 2 teams. There were 8 *servi* in all. Fifteen *villani* and 8 bordars had 7 plough-teams between them. There was meadow for 1 team on the abbot's estate, 4½ a. elsewhere, and woodland for 42 pigs. Hardwin's and Count Alan's estates had risen in value since 1066, but the abbot's had fallen from £5 to £4.[85]

In the early 14th century the Frevilles received 5*s.* in commutation of works from their free tenants, and 190 works worth ½*d.* each between Lammas and Michaelmas from their customary tenants, some of whom were distinguished as villeins. The lord paid for additional work on the demesne and for the services of a smith, a carpenter, and a thatcher. In 1312 two ploughmen and a shepherd were also employed.[86] In 1318 the Ely manor had nine yardlanders. They owed three works each week, ploughing, threshing and manual services, carrying service with a cart and two horses, a day's reaping by three men, fed and paid by the lord, and boon ploughing. They owed leirwite, tallage, and heriot. A yardlander's wife could succeed to the holding, but owed a fine if she remarried, when she was entitled to grain, a dwelling, and a piece of curtilage as dower. The yardlander pastured his cattle with the lord's, and paid one hen and 20 eggs, but no rent. The 8 halflanders who held 9 a. each owed two works a week from Michaelmas to Lammas, and three during harvest. They performed the same customary services, and paid a hen and 10 eggs, and 1*d.* easement. The six cottagers held 3 a. or 4 a. each, and owed two works a week between Lammas and Michaelmas and one for the rest of the year. They performed carrying services on foot. Most of the thirteen rent-paying tenants held a messuage with a few roods of land. They owed reaping services and money rents, and some owed hens at Christmas. Only one owed suit of court. The 23 freeholdings varied from ¼ a. to 16 a. The freeholders paid rent in money and kind, and some owed suit of court. There seems to have been a tradition of partible inheritance.[87] In 1347 Frevilles manor was farmed by John of Brigham.[88]

At the end of the 15th century Parys's manor had 20 tenants, and in 1680 17 copyholders and 5 others.[89] In the 16th century Charles manor had 9 copyholders and 15 freeholders, and Scarletts manor also had 15 freeholders.[90]

From the Middle Ages the arable was divided between *c.* 12 fields of varying sizes made up of unequal furlongs. Common called the Great and Little Shrub lay along the modern Wratting Common, while at the western end of the parish were Oxcroft and the Lordship heaths, the Hall sheep-walk, and Nuns or Reach Valley.[91] Domesday recorded 767 sheep in Wratting, and the heaths continued to support large flocks. In 1316 149 fleeces were sold from the Frevilles' manor. In 1317 there were 138 sheep there, and 80 about 10 years later. In 1343 the abbot of Warden owed the service of providing a sheepfold for the Frevilles' and Ely manors. In 1347 of 55 stone of wool rendered in the wool levy from West Wratting, 8 stone came from John of Brigham and 8 from John Aspale.[92]

Frevilles manor in 1312 produced 44 qr. of wheat and relatively small quantities of barley, oats, rye, dredge, and pease. A three-course rotation was followed. In the mid 14th century the Ely manor had 79 a. sown with wheat, 42 a. with maslin, besides barley, dredge, oats, and pease.[93] It also had 26½ a. of inclosed woodland, divided into five parts so that *c.* 5 a. of underwood were sold each year. There were no oaks there. In 1307 55 willows were planted on Frevilles manor. In the 16th century Ely had 16 a. of woodland called Haslye wood, and Jesus College sold its wood in the parish for £29.[94]

By the end of the 17th century *c.* 200 a. in West Wratting had been converted from arable to heath. Shortly afterwards *c.* 20 a. of the Nuns Valley, previously all grassland, was converted to arable. Half a century later part of the Valley heath was enclosed to form paddocks.[95] In the early 19th century the dean and chapter still claimed sheep-walk for 720 sheep in the parish.[96] In 1801 there were just over 1,500 a. of arable: 492 a. of barley, 383 a. of wheat, 365 a. of oats, 128 a. each of peas and turnips, 11 a. of rye, and 9 a. of beans. The yield was not high. Later in the century a four-course rotation also included cinquefoil and other green crops, and later again mustard, cole-seed, and sainfoin.[97] By

[79] *Bracton's Note Bk.* ed. Maitland, iii, pp. 270–2; B.L. Add. MS. 5837, f. 54; C.U.L., Palmer MS. A 88, f. 55.
[80] Cf. *Cal. Close*, 1389–92, 157.
[81] B.L. Harl. MS. 7046, f. 34.
[82] C 54/3665 m. 25d.
[83] C.U.L., E.D.R., H 1/6, terriers 1615, 1662; Add. MS. 6058, pp. 1, 10–11; C 54/3665 m. 25d.
[84] C.R.O., SP 184/2.
[85] *V.C.H. Cambs.* i. 364, 379–80, 385, 388, 406.
[86] C 134/30 no. 10; C.U.L., Palmer MS. A 29, pp. 1–46.
[87] C.U.L., E.D.C., 1/C/1.
[88] E 179/242/8 m. 7d.
[89] C.U.L., Palmer MS. A 29, pp. 75–7.
[90] Peterhouse Mun., F. 23.
[91] C.U.L., Palmer MS. A 29, pp. 81–3; C.R.O., 305/P 1; ibid. L 66/1–4; Jesus Coll. Mun., Est. 4. 10, ff. 15, 20.
[92] C.U.L., Palmer MS. A 29, pp. 25–30, 40–6, 55, 89; E 179/242/8 m. 7d.
[93] C.U.L., Palmer MS. A 29, pp. 6–14, 16, 30, 69, 90; ibid. B 71, p. 9 sqq.
[94] C.U.L., E.D.C., 1/C/1, f. 10; ibid. Palmer MS. A 29, pp. 1–5; Jesus Coll. Mun., West Wratting 2 (1589); S.C. 11/849.
[95] C.U.L., E.D.C., 6/1/2/11; Jesus Coll. Mun., West Wratting 2 (1707); 3 (1793).
[96] C.U.L., Palmer MS. B 71.
[97] H.O. 67/9; Jesus Coll. Mun., Est. 4. 13, p. 317; ibid. West Wratting 3 (1859).

1905 there were 2,860 a. of arable and 420 a. of grass. In 1924 the parish provided good sheep and barley land, and near the village land for wheat and beans. In 1935 77 a. of the West Wratting Park estate formed a dairy and rearing farm, and 6 a. a commercial nursery garden. In 1975 the nurseries remained and there were three dairy farms.[98] By the 18th century oak timber on the Ely estate was valued at over £50.[99] The Wadlow plantations existed by then, and Cole's wood, belonging to Jesus College, by 1802. By 1905 there were *c.* 90 a. of woodland.[1]

By the early 19th century *c.* 817 a. out of a total of *c.* 3,500 a. were inclosed. The inclosure award of 1813[2] granted land to 44 allottees, in amounts varying from ½ a. to over 1,000 a. The dean and chapter of Ely were the largest landowners, with *c.* 1,030 a.; Jesus College received 198 a., Peterhouse 180 a., and the Corporation of the Sons of the Clergy 644 a. The largest personal estate was 488 a. allotted to the trustees of Sir Hedworth Williamson; J. C. Perne received 175 a. and John Hall 102 a. The vicar was allotted 140 a. Most of the land was freehold, but 297 a. were copyhold of the Ely manor, and 40 a. copyhold of Charles manor. Because of the large holdings of corporate bodies much of the parish was farmed by leaseholders. Prominent among them was Harry Frost who was allotted only 7½ a. himself, but held over 1,000 a. from the dean and chapter. By the later 19th century members of the Frost family leased or owned most of the land in the parish.

Miscellaneous occupations outside agriculture have included a smith, a tailor, and an iron-worker.[3] In the early 19th century there were a horse-dealer and a manufacturer of drilling machines, and by the middle of the century a bricklayer, a painter and glazier, and a shoemaker. An agricultural engineer was recorded from 1900.[4]

There was a windmill on Frevilles manor in the 13th and 14th centuries. In the early 16th century Moignes mill was mentioned there, and in the 16th and 17th centuries there was also a mill on the Ely manor.[5] In the 18th century Leys mill was built on Parys's manor. It was presumably near the site of an earlier mill, and may be identified with that built in 1726, which still stood in 1975 near the boundary with Balsham and West Wickham. A smock-mill, with a low tower on a round, brick base, it was described in 1877 as a wind and steam, corn and flour mill. It ceased working in 1924.[6]

LOCAL GOVERNMENT. Courts were held for each of the three main manors in West Wratting. The court for Oxcroft, of which no rolls survive, was recorded in 1327. The manor was represented at the honor of Richmond's tourn at Newmarket, where its ale-taster was answerable.[7] In the late 16th century Peterhouse claimed that the tenants of Oxcroft owed service at the court of Charles manor, as did those of Scarletts.[8]

Fragments of court extracts for Charles manor survive for 1553 and 1591–3, court rolls from 1822 to 1887, and transcripts of lost rolls from 1273 until the mid 17th century.[9] Courts leet and baron, usually in a single session, seem to have been held no more than twice a year, even in the 13th century, and only once a year, or less, from the 16th century. By the 19th century they were held only once every two or three years. Until the 15th century the courts heard cases of robbery, assault, and bloodshed, besides dealing with the regulation of agriculture and tenurial matters. The lord had strays and the assize of ale. By 1822 the court was concerned solely with tenurial matters.

A court is recorded for the Ely manor in 1286. An extract survives from a court leet held there in 1475, and court books for 1554–7, 1589–1615, 1661–91, and 1737–1947.[10] As on his other manors the prior claimed view of frankpledge, the assize of bread and of ale, strays, and other rights. He also had a prison in West Wratting.[11] In the 17th century the lord of the manor had leet jurisdiction and the right to deodands and fugitives' and felons' goods.[12] In the 13th century at least five courts were held every year. In the 16th century they were held twice a year, and annually from the mid 18th century. There too cases of theft, bloodshed, and trespass were heard. On the election of each new prior or dean the homage owed him 29*s.* 1*d.* Besides tenurial business the court dealt with the regulation of agriculture, and in the 16th century occasionally gave permission for land to be inclosed. From the early 17th century the elections of one or two constables, a hayward or pinder, and an ale-taster were sporadically recorded. From the 18th century the business was purely tenurial. Enfranchisements of copyhold are recorded from the mid 19th century, increasing in the last years of the court up to 1947.

The dean and chapter of Ely claimed theirs as the paramount manor and at inclosure in 1813 they received the only allotment for right of soil.[13] From at least the 15th century there had been disputes between the Ely and Charles manors about the limits of their jurisdictions, and especially about rights over timber and waste.[14] In 1556 it was claimed that the lords of Parys's and Scarletts owed suit of court to Ely.[15] In the 18th century a number of land transfers were entered in the court rolls of both the Ely and Charles manors.[16]

From 1776 until 1834 West Wratting's expenditure on poor-relief was consistently one of the three

98 Cambs. Agric. Returns, 1905; C.R.O., 515/SP 726; 515/SP 1450.
99 C.U.L., E.D.C., 6/1/2/11.
1 *Camb. Chron.* 22 Nov. 1777; Jesus Coll. Mun., West Wratting, 3 (1802); Cambs. Agric. Returns, 1905.
2 C.U.L., Add. MS. 6058.
3 *Cambs. Lay Subsidy, 1327*, 15–16.
4 *Camb. Chron.* 22 Mar. 1811; 3 May 1811; *Kelly's Dir. Cambs.* (1847 and later edns.).
5 Bodl. MS. Rolls, Suff. 37; C.U.L., E.D.C., 1/C/1, f. 9; ibid. Palmer MS. A 29, p. 75–7; ibid. C.C. 109. i, f. 258–90, *passim*; C.C. bdle. 74, no. 3, f. 5.
6 C.R.O., L 66/51A; 289/T 53; *Trans. Newcomen Soc.* xxvii. 103–5; local information.
7 S.C. 6/770/2; S.C. 2/155/71.
8 Peterhouse Mun., G. 4.
9 Ibid. Misc. 7; C.R.O., R 54/10/10; C.U.L., Palmer MS. A 29, pp. 48–73.
10 Bodl. MS. Rolls, Suff. 37; Peterhouse Mun., Misc. 4; C.U.L., MS. 4463B; ibid. C.C. 109. i, iii; C.C. bdles. 74, 75.
11 *Plac. de Quo Warr.* (Rec. Com.), 104; Miller, *Abbey and Bishopric of Ely*, 204.
12 C 54/3620 m. 48.
13 B.L. Add. MS. 9412, f. 42v.; C.U.L., Add. MS. 6058, p. 15.
14 Peterhouse Mun., Misc. 4; C 3/202/47; C 3/58/8.
15 C.U.L., MS. 4463B, f. 25v.
16 e.g. C.R.O., L 66/6–9.

highest in the county. The amounts varied between £506 in 1816 and over £1,000 in 1813, 1818, and 1832. In the last year relief cost *c.* £1 7*s.* 6*d.* per head. In the early 19th century between 32 and 55 were given regular outside relief, and 300 occasional relief. By 1831 there were usually 20 unemployed. A special allowance was made from the poor-rate for large families. Besides money, coal and clothing were given to the poor.[17] In 1835 West Wratting became part of the Linton poor-law union, and in 1934 of the South Cambridgeshire R.D.,[18] being included in 1974 in South Cambridgeshire.

CHURCH. There was a church at West Wratting in the earlier 12th century when Bishop Niel granted it to the infirmary of Ely.[19] The rectory was appropriated and a vicarage had been ordained by 1217. The advowson of the vicarage, like the rectory, passed in the 16th century to the dean and chapter of Ely. In 1886 the vicarage was one of the livings assigned to be held by one of the minor canons of Ely.[20]

The vicarage was valued at 16 marks in 1217, rising to 20 marks in 1254 and 30 marks *c.* 1276.[21] In 1535 the benefice was valued at £7 17*s.* 2*d.* By 1650 it had risen to £30, and was made up to £100 during the Interregnum.[22] In the 1730s it was valued at £80, although the vicar insisted it was worth only £50.[23] The vicar received a payment out of the rectory (70*s.* in the early 16th century, £35 in the late 17th) and the small tithes for which 139 a. were allotted at inclosure in 1813. He was still entitled to the tithe of the windmill, which in 1846 was commuted for a rent-charge of 12*s.* 6*d.*[24] In 1851 the vicarage was valued at £215, and in 1886 at £250.[25]

The vicarage house, referred to in 1615 and 1662, had 6 hearths in 1672.[26] In 1783 it was a thatched house, little better than a cottage, but in reasonable repair. By 1851 a new house in the Gothic style had been built on the south-west side of the main street.[27] By 1975 that was a private house, and a new vicarage had been built opposite the church.

There were seven incumbents between 1344 and 1354. One, Peter Brown, was also chaplain of a chantry in London.[28] The vicar in 1561 also held Weston Colville, where he lived, but there was a curate at West Wratting.[29] In 1591 the vicar was denounced as unruly.[30] William Flack, vicar for over 40 years, was in 1650 said to be very insufficient for the cure.[31] His successor was not in orders when appointed in 1657, but in 1660 sought ordination and in 1661 was presented as if the living had been vacant for the last four years.[32] In 1807 the vicar, who had previously lived in his other parish in Lincolnshire, moved to West Wratting, which was by then usually held with another living.[33] In 1825 the vicar was non-resident, and his curate's health was unequal to all his duties.[34] In 1851 the vicar was living abroad, but again there was a resident curate.[35] Until 1973 the vicarage was often held with West Wickham, the incumbents living at West Wratting.[36]

There was a guild of St. Anne in the early 16th century.[37] Later in the century parents failed to send their children to be taught the catechism.[38] In 1587 two parishioners refused to attend church, and in 1595 another refused to send his daughter to communion or catechism.[39] In 1728 communion was held three times a year, with about 42 communicants. From 1807 there were two Sunday services with a sermon in the morning, and quarterly communions attended by about 30. Attendance at communion had risen to 75 by 1824.[40] In 1851 average attendance was 393 at the morning service and 626 in the afternoon. By 1897 only a third of the parishioners were church people; some attended church and chapel, but many went to neither. There was said to be religious apathy among rich and poor, although by then there were monthly communions, attended by *c.* 60 communicants.[41]

The church of *ST. ANDREW*, so called in 1556,[42] is built of rubble and has a chancel with north vestry, clerestoried nave with south porch, and west tower. Foundations said to have been discovered below the east end of the nave in the late 19th century[43] have been interpreted as the footings of a central tower; if there was such a tower it pre-dated the 13th-century chancel arch and east wall of the nave which are the oldest parts of the building. The west tower and the remainder of the nave are 14th-century, the clerestory presumably being of its later years. In the 15th century the chancel was rebuilt or remodelled and the south porch added.[44] The fabric seems to have been neglected in the 16th and 17th centuries.[45]

In 1737 the interior was remodelled at the expense of Sir John Jacob, Bt., in the classical style with ceilings and walls marked out in plaster panels and some new sash windows. A large singers' gallery was built across the west end. Fittings of the period include a pulpit, with sounding board, and

[17] *Poor Law Abstract, 1804*, 38–9; *1818*, 30–1; *Poor Rate Returns, 1816–21*, 11; *1822–4*, 38; *1825–9*, 16; *1830–4*, 16; *Rep. H.L. Cttee. on Poor Laws*, H.C. 227, pp. 328–9 (1831), viii.

[18] *Poor Law Com. 1st Rep.* 249; *Census*, 1931 (pt. ii).

[19] B.L. Harl. MS. 7046, f. 34.

[20] *Lond. Gaz.* 29 June 1886, p. 3704.

[21] *Val. of Norwich*, ed. Lunt, 535, 554.

[22] *Valor Eccl.* (Rec. Com.), iii. 504; Lamb. Pal. MS. 904, f. 265; *Proc. C.A.S.* xvi. 165–6.

[23] C.U.L., E.D.R., B 8/1.

[24] S.C. 11/849; C.U.L., E.D.C., 6/1/2/11; C.U.L., E.D.R., H 1/6, terrier 1615; C.U.L., Add. MS. 6058, pp. 12–14; 18/13679.

[25] *Gardner's Dir. Cambs.* (1851); *Lond. Gaz.* 29 June 1886, p. 3704.

[26] C.U.L., E.D.R., H 1/6, terriers 1615, 1662; C 54/3665 m. 25d.; E 179/244/23 rot. 67.

[27] C.U.L., E.D.R., B 7/1, p. 137; *Gardner's Dir. Cambs.* (1851).

[28] BL. Add. MS. 5819, f. 54v.

[29] B.L. Add. MS. 5813, ff. 65–6; C.U.L., E.D.R., B 2/3, p. 101.

[30] C.U.L., E.D.R., B 2/11, f. 146v.

[31] Lamb. Pal. MS. 904, f. 265.

[32] *Proc. C.A.S.* xvi. 165–6.

[33] C.U.L., E.D.R., C 1/4.

[34] C.U.L., E.D.R., C 1/6.

[35] H.O. 129/188/3/4/4.

[36] *Crockford* (1896 and later edns.).

[37] B.L. Add. MS. 5861, p. 177.

[38] C.U.L., E.D.R., B 2/4, p. 119.

[39] Gibbons, *Ely Episc. Rec.* 49; C.U.L., E.D.R., B 2/13, f. 143v.

[40] C.U.L., E.D.R., B 8/1; C 1/4; C 1/6.

[41] H.O. 129/188/3/4/4; C.U.L., E.D.R., C 3/39.

[42] B.L. Add. MS. 5861, f. 94.

[43] Note in church.

[44] Pevsner, *Cambs.* 480; P. G. M. Dickinson, *St. Andrew's Church, West Wratting* (1954).

[45] C.U.L., E.D.R., B 2/3, p. 84; B 2/18, f. 77v.; B 2/59A, f. 19v.; *Cambs. Episc. Visit. 1638–65*, ed. Palmer, 124.

commandment tables.[46] Almost all of the 18th-century work was removed at a restoration in 1896, mostly paid for by the Frost family, when the one surviving medieval window was reopened and the others were restored. The gallery was removed and a new ceiling built.[47] In 1922 a wrought iron screen was put into the chancel arch.[48] In the chancel are memorials to Frances (d. *c.* 1600), wife of Michael Dalton (d. 1648), and Andrew Perne (d. 1679).[49]

In the 16th century the church had a silver chalice and paten. In 1960 there were two cups dated 1846.[50] In the 16th century there were three bells, and in 1975 five, dated 1702, 1750, 1828, and two dated 1860. One of the last had originally been made by Thomas of Lenne in 1320, and was recast in 1860.[51] The registers start in 1579 and are virtually complete. The earliest contains a note that in 1579 the church was robbed and the previous register stolen.[52]

NONCONFORMITY. There were only three nonconformists in West Wratting in 1676, and few throughout the 18th century.[53] A Congregationalist meeting was founded in 1811, and in that year, 1814, and 1821 a house or cottage was licensed for worship.[54] A chapel was later said to have been built *c.* 1815.[55] In 1825 the congregation was served from Weston Colville, and came mostly from neighbouring parishes.[56] In 1851 the chapel was a station of the Cambridgeshire County Union and Home Missionary Society, attended by *c.* 30 at its one Sunday service.[57] By 1860 it was served from Balsham.[58] It was presumably the chapel named as Baptist in 1877.[59] In 1899, when the vicar reported that a third of the parish were dissenters, there were 20 Congregationalist church members.[60] The West Wratting and Balsham congregations were combined from 1905 to 1945. After that the numbers in West Wratting declined, falling to 7 in 1968 when the chapel was last listed.[61] The building, on the north side of the main street, was derelict in 1975.

EDUCATION. There was a schoolmaster in 1581, but none in 1590.[62] In 1807 there was a small day-school which in 1818 was attended by 20 children from West Wratting and 21 from other parishes. There was also another day-school, taking 24 children, 13 of whom paid.[63] By 1833 there were four day-schools, founded in 1825 (girls), 1828 (girls), 1830 (boys), and 1831 (mixed), with a combined attendance of 92.[64] By 1846 a Sunday school for 30 boys and 50 girls was held in the church and taught by a paid master, while a mistress taught 30 girls at the only day-school.[65] A new National day-school, with a schoolroom, a classroom, and a teacher's house, opened in 1861 and was attended by 60 children.[66]

In 1867 all girls of the village from 3 to 12 and all boys from 3 to 10 attended school. In addition there was a night school in the winter attended by 17 boys. For the children employed on Dungate farm, who did not necessarily go to school, the farmer had a schoolroom.[67] In the later 19th century attendance at the school fluctuated between 61 and 74, and then declined from 64 in 1914 to 28 in 1938.[68] The school was reorganized in 1926.[69] The seniors were transferred to Linton village college in 1937, and the juniors to Balsham when the West Wratting school was closed in 1971.[70] The building, on the corner of the lane leading to the church, was for sale in 1974.[71]

CHARITIES FOR THE POOR. In the early 18th century it was recorded that Thomas Symonds had left 10*s.* a year or 1 a. of land for the poor of the parish, but by 1837 there was no trace of the gift.[72] A town house probably built on the waste and regarded as a charitable endowment was by 1837 divided into four dwellings, inhabited rent-free by aged paupers. It was sold in the 1850s by order of the Poor Law Board.[73] Michael Dalton in 1636 gave an inclosure called Hunts to buy coats for 10 children. The rent was so distributed in 1775, and in 1837 the income of £2 was given in clothing to poor children. The payment was made by the tenant of Hunts at the end of the 19th century and in 1968.

Andrew Perne gave 1 a. of land in the 16th century which provided 10*s.* a year for the poor. Edward Briggs, by will proved 1735, gave £1 a year for the poor. Both sums were charged on particular allotments under the inclosure award of 1813. Before 1775 an unknown donor gave 1 a. of land to provide 6*s.* 6*d.* a year to be distributed with Perne's charity. In 1830 £18 of arrears was received by Perne's charity, which spent £12 on coals for the poor, but no further payment had been made by 1863. Neither Briggs's nor the anonymous charity had been paid for many years in 1837, but in 1895 all three had been received over the preceding 30 years and distributed to the poor, usually in coals. In 1968 the three charities, amounting with Dalton's to £3 16*s.* a year, were distributed in the parish in various charitable ways.[74]

46 Pevsner, *Cambs.* 480; Dickinson, *St. Andrew's Church*; *Proc. C.A.S.* xl. 33–4; B.L. Add. MS. 5810, f. 101.
47 Dickinson, *St. Andrew's Church*; C.U.L., E.D.R., C 3/39.
48 Dickinson, *St. Andrew's Church.*
49 B.L. Add. MS. 5810, ff. 102–4.
50 *Cambs. Ch. Goods, temp. Edw. VI*, 69; list of church plate *penes V.C.H.*
51 *Cambs. Ch. Goods, temp. Edw. VI*, 69; *Cambs. Bells* (C.A.S. 8vo ser. xviii), 180.
52 C.R.O., P 184/1.
53 Compton Census; C.U.L., E.D.R., B 8/1; B 7/1; C 1/4.
54 *Cong. Yr. Bk.* (1875); G.R.O. Worship Returns, Ely dioc. nos. 227, 283, 397.
55 H.O. 129/188/3/4/12.
56 C.U.L., E.D.R., C 1/6.
57 H.O. 129/188/3/4/12.
58 *Cong. Yr. Bk.* (1860).
59 C.U.L., E.D.R., C 3/27.
60 Ibid. C 3/39; *Cong. Yr. Bk.* (1899).
61 *Cong. Yr. Bk.* (1905 and later edns.).
62 Gibbons, *Ely Episc. Rec.* 180; C.U.L., E.D.R., B 2/11.
63 C.U.L., E.D.R., C 1/4; *Educ. of Poor Digest*, 67.
64 *Educ. Enquiry Abstract*, 62.
65 *Church School Inquiry, 1846–7*, 8–9.
66 C.R.O., 391/P 81; Ed. 7/5.
67 *1st Rep. Com. Employment in Agric.* 353, 360.
68 *Rep. of Educ. Cttee. of Council, 1868–9* [4139], p. 508, H.C. (1868–9), xx; *1880–1* [C. 2948-I], p. 544, H.C. (1881), xxxii; *Bd. of Educ., List 21, 1914* (H.M.S.O.), 29; *1938*, 21.
69 *Public Elem. Schs. 1907* [Cd. 3901], p. 29, H.C. (1908), lxxxiv; *Bd. of Educ., List 21, 1927* (H.M.S.O.), 17.
70 Black, *Cambs. Educ. Rec.* 84.
71 Camb. City Libr., Cambs. Colln. C 106c.
72 *31st Rep. Com. Char.* 140: this may have been confused with Perne's bequest mentioned below.
73 Ibid. 141; *Char. Digest Cambs. 1863–4*, 38; C.R.O., 289/T 47.
74 C.U.L., E.D.R., C 1/1; *31st Rep. Com. Char.* 140; C.R.O., R 54/34/6; Char. Com. files.

WHITTLESFORD HUNDRED

THE SMALL hundred of Whittlesford, almost due south of Cambridge, extends for about 6 miles from the river Granta in the north to the Essex boundary in the south. It consists of the same five parishes or townships in the upper valley of the Cam or Granta as in 1066, when Ickleton, Hinxton, and Duxford in the southern half each accounted for twenty of its eighty hides, while Whittlesford contributed twelve and Sawston eight.[1] In the late 10th century a moot of the county notables had met at Whittlesford[2] and the hundred court was presumably held there. It may have met near a place called by the 14th century Mutlowe moor, apparently in the northern part of that parish.[3] The hundred remained in the king's hands throughout the Middle Ages.[4] In the late 13th century it shared a bailiff with Chilford hundred, and yielded him between 2 marks and £2 of the 6 marks for which the two were farmed in the 1270s.[5] One manor in each parish and two at Duxford had view of frankpledge and the assize of bread and of ale. In addition the lords of Hinxton and Whittlesford, the prioress of Ickleton, the Earl Marshal as overlord of D'Abernons manor in Duxford, and the Templars under their general charter claimed more extensive privileges. At Ickleton suit to hundred and county was withdrawn in the mid 13th century in right of the honor of Boulogne, and other suits were withdrawn, as at Whittlesford, during the turbulent 1260s. Fees at Duxford held of the honor of Richmond did suit to that honor's court held at Babraham.[6] In the 17th century Whittlesford hundred was commonly administered with Chilford and Radfield hundreds.[7]

Whittlesford, Duxford, and Ickleton are divided from Sawston and Hinxton to the east by the Cam or Granta. Two branches of the Icknield Way run north-eastwards through the hundred. The northern branch, more used from medieval times, was turnpiked in 1769–70; a small hamlet had grown up where it crossed the river at Whittlesford. The principal village settlements all lie off that road. There was little settlement away from the main village sites until after parliamentary inclosure. Sawston has been greatly enlarged by the building of cheap cottages for its growing industrial population in the late 19th century and of new housing estates in the 20th. In the other parishes new building continued to be mostly close to the original village sites.

The hundred lies mainly upon the Lower and Middle Chalk,[8] and the ground rises steadily from the north, where parts of Sawston consist of peaty fen, to downland at over 300 ft. by the Essex border. There was extensive ancient woodland in historical times, but only modern plantations remain. Strip lynchets surviving in Ickleton may indicate that agriculture had already been introduced in the Bronze Age. From the Middle Ages the land has been devoted mainly to arable farming, and a three-course rotation was normal in open fields that persisted into the 19th century. The main corn crop was barley, much of it sold outside the neighbourhood for malting. Sheep have been widely kept, and rights of foldage and sheep-walk were important to the manorial economy. By the 13th century there were many freeholders in the villages, mostly with

[1] *V.C.H. Cambs.* i. 410–12.

[2] *Liber Elien.* (Camd. 3rd ser. xcii), p. 109.

[3] C.R.O., Huddleston MSS., deed 39 Edw. III; *P.N. Cambs.* (E.P.N.S.), 92.

[4] e.g. *Rot. Hund.* (Rec. Com.), ii. 570; *Feud. Aids,* i. 155.

[5] *Assizes at Camb. 1260,* 10, 36, 38; S.C. 5/Cambs. Chap. ho. ser. no. 1 m. 1.

[6] *Liber de Bernewelle,* 256; *Rot. Hund.* (Rec. Com.), i. 55; ii. 570; *Plac. de Quo Warr.* (Rec. Com.), 102, 107.

[7] e.g. *Cal. S.P. Dom.* 1634–5, p. 442; 1637–8, p. 133.

[8] Geol. Surv. Map 1″, drift, sheet 205 (1932 edn.).

small properties, but agriculture was dominated by the manorial demesnes, which except at Whittlesford accounted for at least half the arable in each parish. Saffron was widely grown from the late 15th to the 18th century. The two southern parishes have remained mainly agricultural. Their population declined from the mid 19th century,

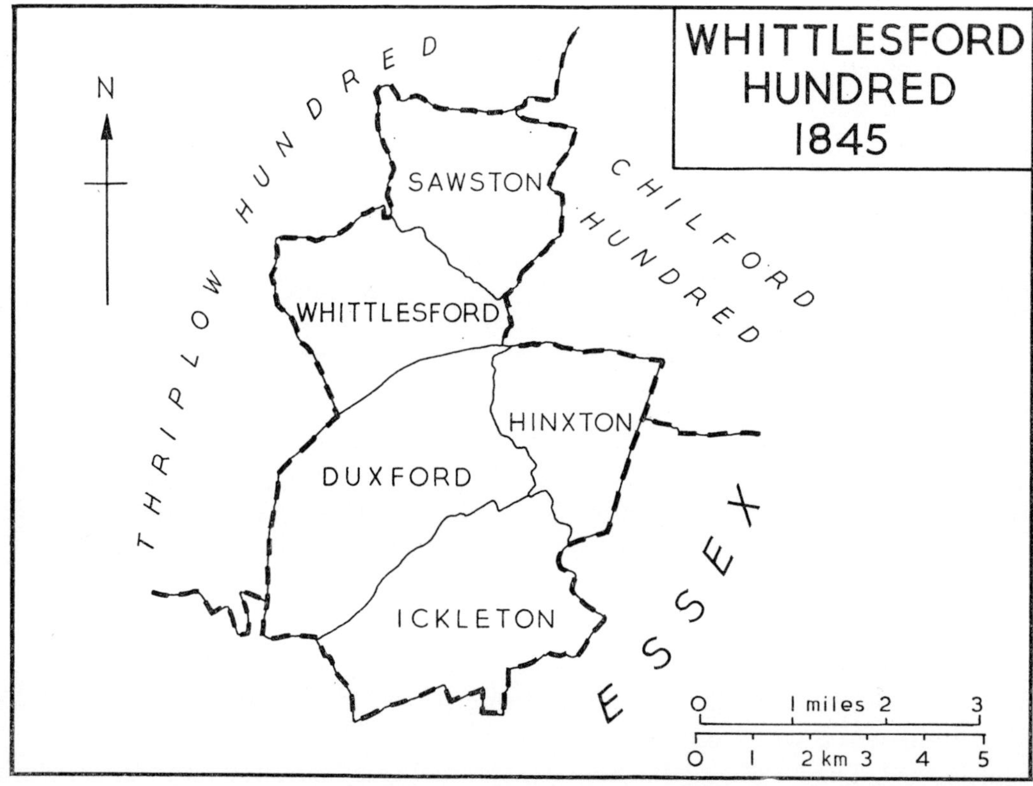

and was virtually stationary in the 20th. In the northern parishes, especially Sawston, industries developed, based originally on the river whose water-power had in the Middle Ages turned more than ten mills. The mills have been used for fulling, paper-making, oil-pressing, and bone-grinding. Other industries have included tanning, parchment-making, the processing of fertilizers and animal feeds, and the manufacture of agricultural equipment and aircraft materials. The increase in the population of the northern part of the hundred has also been encouraged, particularly since the 1950s, by the growth of commuting to Cambridge.

DUXFORD

THE VILLAGE of Duxford[1] (formerly Duxworth)[2] comprised until 1874 two ecclesiastical parishes, but is and probably always has been a single secular township. It lies about 7 miles south-east of Cambridge, a little below the point where the river Cam or Granta emerges from the uplands of north-west Essex. The parish covered 3,239 a. until 1965 when 8 ha. (20 a.) were transferred from Chrishall (Essex).[3] The parish is roughly in the shape of a trapezium, tapering to a point at its south-west corner. On the east it is bounded by the river, on the north-west by a modern road following the line of a branch of the Icknield Way;[4] on the south-east it is divided from Ickleton by old furlong boundaries running along the crest of Pepperton Hill and down the eastern side of the hill to the river. The procession balk along that boundary was mentioned in 1654.[5] The north-west part of Duxford is virtually level and lies mostly between 100 and 150 ft. above sea level. To the south-east the ground rises to over 300 ft. at the summit of Pepperton Hill. The soil of the parish, except where a strip of alluvium and gravel runs along the river, lies mostly over the chalk, which on the top of the hills is mingled with boulder clay. There was little woodland in Duxford before the 19th century. In several leases made soon after the inclosure in 1823 the landowners reserved the right to plant,[6] and two large belts of trees were later laid out across the western half of the parish, besides groves around the farmsteads there and other isolated plantations of which the largest was Chrishall Grange plantation. They served partly as windbreaks, partly to improve the shooting. In 1925 the Chrishall Grange estate was said to have some of the best partridge-shooting in the area: 515 brace had been shot in a day, besides pheasants and hares.[7] The parish was formerly devoted mainly to arable farming, being until inclosure cultivated in three fields. After 1918 much of its northern half was occupied by an R.A.F. airfield, and by 1972 three factories had been established around the village.

The village itself stands where the river approaches nearest to the road running along its left bank. On the land between road and river there stood in the Middle Ages four manor-houses. On the other side of the road two streets led westwards towards the fields. Each street had its own church, St. John's being midway along the northern street while St. Peter's stood opposite the eastern end of the southern one; the sites of the manors tithable to each church were similarly opposite, respectively, the northern and southern streets, thus producing or reflecting a certain duality of settlement in medieval times. The two streets were connected by an intricate network of lanes, and a small green lay just south of St. John's church. As late as the 1820s most of the houses in the village lay west of the main road, along those streets and lanes, where several older timber-framed, thatched houses, some with overhangs, some refronted in brick, survived in 1972. In 1823 there were, apart from Temple Farm and mill, only four houses east of the road.[8] Only after inclosure were some farmsteads built away from the village.

Duxford contained *c.* 80 houses in the 1660s,[9] and 105 inhabited dwellings in 1801. That number had increased to 133 by 1821 and to 188 by 1841, but thereafter did not grow much before the 1930s.[10] Extensive new building in the mid 20th century raised the number of houses to 284 by 1951 and 369 by 1961.[11] The new housing estates, including some council housing,[12] lay mostly north and south of the original village, which was in 1971 scheduled as a conservation area.[13]

Duxford has been one of the more populous parishes in the hundred. In 1086 37 people were enumerated there.[14] Excluding the owners of manors there were *c.* 100 landholders in 1279[15] and 44 taxpayers in 1327.[16] In 1377 104 people were assessed to the poll tax[17] and in 1525 57 persons to the subsidy.[18] In 1563 the parish contained 58 families.[19] In 1676 there were 166 adults.[20] In 1728 70 households included *c.* 240 persons.[21] There were some 87 families *c.* 1794.[22] The population increased steadily from 494 in 1801 to 670 by 1831 and 844 in 1851, reaching a peak of 881 in 1871. By 1901, when 18 houses were empty, it had fallen to 685, and after the First World War fluctuated around 740. The presence of the R.A.F. during and after the Second World War temporarily boosted the population to 1,469 in 1951, when the civil population probably amounted to 916. In 1961 it was 1,122, and in 1971 1,557.[23]

In early times Duxford lay between two branches of the Icknield Way. It was linked[24] to the southern one, passing through Ickleton, by a road called in the 17th century Walden way, whose ancient route survived the inclosure, and to Hinxton by a road which wound across the meadows and crossed the river by a ford still in use in 1972. Westwards from the village various field-ways, called in the 17th and 18th centuries, from south to north, Chrishall or Littlebush way, Crowley way, and Royston way, ran to a track along Duxford's western boundary. After inclosure they were replaced by a single

[1] This article was written in 1972.

[2] The name has no connexion with any ford: *P.N. Cambs.* (E.P.N.S.), 92.

[3] *Census*, 1971.

[4] Cf. Fox, *Arch. Camb. Region*, 144–5.

[5] C.R.O., R 58/7/1, pp. 75–6.

[6] e.g. Caius Coll. Mun. XXXV 9/a; C.R.O., R 52/9/13B.

[7] C.R.O., 296/SP 1150.

[8] Ibid. Q/RDc 44.

[9] See pp. 280–1.

[10] *Census*, 1801–1931.

[11] Ibid. 1951–61.

[12] Cf. *Camb. News*, 15 Nov. 1965; 15 Mar. 1966.

[13] *Camb. Evening News*, 15 June 1971.

[14] *V.C.H. Cambs.* i. 411–12.

[15] *Rot. Hund.* (Rec. Com.), ii. 580–4.

[16] *Cambs. Lay Subsidy, 1327*, 28.

[17] *East Anglian*, N.S. xii. 240.

[18] E 179/81/147 m. 2.

[19] B.L. Harl. MS. 594, f. 200.

[20] Compton Census.

[21] B.L. Add. MS. 5828, f. 89.

[22] Vancouver, *Agric. in Cambs.* 74.

[23] *Census*, 1801–1971.

[24] For the layout and former names of the pre-inclosure roads see Caius Coll. Mun. XXXV 1/b, c, bb; 6; 13; C.R.O., R 58/7/1; B.L. Maps, O.S.D. 146(i).

straight private road. The road along the northern boundary, called formerly London way, forms part of the main Royston–Newmarket road. It was a turnpike from 1769[25] until 1874.[26]

The main road crossed the river at Whittlesford Bridge, which probably replaced an earlier ford. By the 13th century the bridge was in the charge of the burgesses of Cambridge, who took tolls there for its repair but did not always apply the proceeds for that purpose.[27] From the 15th century the toll was farmed. It was suppressed under the turnpike Act of 1769.[28] A small hamlet, said in 1279 to be in four parishes,[29] had by the mid 13th century grown up by the bridge.[30] It centred on the hospital built south of the road in Duxford,[31] which probably provided accommodation for travellers. In the 16th century that function passed to an adjacent inn, called the White Lion until the 18th century and later the Red Lion.[32] Its original timber-framed structure has been much renovated, but is still visible on its west front. Inside there were carved medieval beams, and an elaborately carved Jacobean table was formerly shown.[33] The inn had a prosperous trade. The innkeeper John Pecke (d. 1588) left £150 to his sons.[34] A successor, John Dove, used to hire out the pasture closes around the inn to drovers bringing cattle from East Anglia towards Royston. One dissatisfied drover, who had removed his custom to the Falcon, across the road in Whittlesford, alleged in 1618 that Dove also assisted highwaymen on Newmarket Heath.[35] James I probably stopped at the Lion in 1619 on his return from a horse-race at Newmarket,[36] and in 1622 the inn was said to be very commodious for royal servants and other travellers along that road.[37] In 1686 it had 15 beds and stabling for 38.[38] Tithe audit dinners for Duxford were held there until 1902,[39] and the inn, styled since 1904 the Red Lion Hotel,[40] was still flourishing in 1972. When the Great Eastern railway line from London to Cambridge was opened in 1845[41] a station was established on the boundary with Whittlesford, west of the bridge and inn. It was still open for passenger traffic in 1972. A small settlement, 3 or 4 houses, existed near the bridge in 1675,[42] but grew little before *c.* 1900. In 1891 10 a. near the station were sold for building, in 1924 another 35 a., and by the 1920s[43] lines of fairly large houses had grown along both sides of the road between the inn and the cross-roads. In 1961 a new road, partly raised on a causeway, was completed, by-passing on the south the inn and station and the old bridge,[44] which had been rebuilt in brick replacing a wooden structure *c.* 1790.[45]

Duxford village itself contained, and contains, several public houses. The Three Horseshoes was recorded from 1786,[46] the King's Head from 1841,[47] and the Plough from 1851 when there were 6 other beer-retailers.[48] The King's Head closed after 1908, but most of the others survived in 1972.[49]

In 1279 a fair was said to have belonged to Whittlesford Bridge hospital for many years.[50] It was not recorded later. Various Maying and harvest customs were recorded at Duxford in the 19th century,[51] but later declined. A friendly society founded in 1806[52] had 71 members in 1815.[53] The village had a resident doctor from the 1840s until 1904.[54] A veterinary surgeon lived in the village between 1871 and 1879, and a dentist in 1908.[55] The Victoria Institute, founded with a parish lending library by the rector in 1887,[56] remained open until the 1930s.[57] During the Second World War it was taken over by Aero Research Ltd. for making glue and was subsequently derelict until converted into a shop in 1964.[58]

The R.A.F. airfield at Duxford was established by 1918 on land south of the main road[59] taken over from Temple and Lacy's farms. It occupied 138 a. in 1920, when four large hangars had already been erected south of the road.[60] The barracks were mostly built north of the road in Whittlesford parish. From 1920 to 1924 the airfield was used for a flying training school, and from 1924 as a fighter station, up to three squadrons being stationed there. In 1934 new headquarter buildings were constructed and in 1935 George V reviewed the R.A.F. from there. In 1940 Duxford was the centre of an R.A.F. sector, which during the Battle of Britain was especially concerned with air defence over the east coast. In 1942–3 the airfield was transferred to the U.S. Air Force, concrete runways being laid down; after its return to the R.A.F. in 1945 it continued to be used by fighters, being usually occupied by two squadrons, until its closure in 1961. The disused runways were subsequently used for gliding and for motor-racing.[61] The site, *c.* 540 a.,[62] was still owned by the Ministry of Defence in 1972. From that year the hangars were

25 Bourn Bridge Road Act, 8 & 9 Geo. III, c. 86.
26 Annual Turnpike Acts Continuance Act, 36 & 37 Vic. c. 90.
27 *Rot. Hund.* (Rec. Com.), ii. 571; *Close R.* 1242–7, 67; cf. C.R.O., Huddleston MSS., 67, ct. roll 1 Hen. V.
28 Cooper, *Annals of Camb.* i. 253; iii. 103, 288; iv. 355.
29 *Rot. Hund.* (Rec. Com.), ii. 570.
30 Caius Coll. Mun. XXXV 1/f, s, t.
31 See p. 215.
32 Barry Estate Act, 32 Geo. II, c. 36 (Priv. Act), p. 8; *Gardner's Dir. Cambs.* (1851).
33 C.R.O., R 58/5, vol. iv, pp. 60, 65.
34 Prob. 11/73 (P.C.C. 4 Leicester).
35 Sta. Cha. 8/213/5. Dove won a suit against the drover for slander.
36 Nicholls, *Progresses of Jas. I*, iii. 532.
37 *Acts of P.C.* 1621–3, 167.
38 W.O. 30/48.
39 Clare Coll. Mun., Duxford, letters 1904.
40 *Kelly's Dir. Cambs.* (1904, 1937).
41 *V.C.H. Cambs.* ii. 132.
42 Ogilby, *Britannia* (1675), 91.
43 C.R.O., 296/SP 914; ibid. SP 171/1; ibid. 515/SP 675, 779, 835, 1050; cf. O.S. Map 6″, Cambs. LIV. SE. (1950 edn.).
44 Ex inf. the County Surveyor's Dept.
45 *Camb. Chron.* 16 Jan. 1790.
46 *Camb. Chron.* 26 Aug. 1786.
47 C.U.L., Maps 53(1)/84/21.
48 *Gardner's Dir. Cambs.* (1851).
49 *Kelly's Dir. Cambs.* (1904 and later edns.).
50 *Rot. Hund.* (Rec. Com.), ii. 570, 582.
51 C.R.O., R 58/5, vol. x, pp. 277, 286.
52 Ibid. printed rules inserted at pp. 212–13.
53 *Poor Law Abstract, 1818*, 32–3.
54 *Camb. Chron.* 16 Mar. 1888; *Gardner's Dir. Cambs.* (1851); *Kelly's Dir. Cambs.* (1858–1904).
55 *Kelly's Dir. Cambs.* (1879, 1908); R.G. 10/1591.
56 *E.D.R.* (1887), 97–8; (1905), 14.
57 *Kelly's Dir. Cambs.* (1937).
58 C. A. A. Rayner, *Landmarks in Hist. of CIBA (A.R.L.) Ltd.* (1959), 20; *Camb. Ind. Press*, 3 July 1964.
59 TS. hist. of the airfield and other information supplied by the Min. of Defence, Air Hist. Branch; see also B. Collier, *Defence of the U.K.* 209, 216, 246, 443, 473; *The Aeroplane* (1959), 621–5.
60 C.U.L., Maps 53(1)/92/7.
61 *Camb. News*, 5 July 1969; *Camb. Ind. Press*, 30 July 1965; 20 Aug. 1970.
62 *Camb. Evening News*, 25 Jan. 1971.

used by the Imperial War Museum to store and display historic aircraft.[63]

MANORS AND OTHER ESTATES. Theodred, bishop of London (d. 942×951), left an estate at Duxford to the king as part of his heriot.[64] In 1066 Ulf, a thegn of King Edward, held 4½ hides there, and Herulf who owned 1¾ hide and Ingwar who owned ½ hide were also King Edward's men. Of the 13 sokemen who occupied another 4¼ hides, 11 were also commended to the king, the other two being men of Earl Alfgar and of Eddeva the fair. Eddeva herself had 6 hides, and Archbishop Stigand 3½ hides.[65]

After the Conquest Ulf's estate came to Robert de Todeni, lord of Belvoir (Leics.), of whom it was held in 1086 by Gilbert the bearded.[66] Robert's honor of Belvoir passed through two heiresses to the house of Albini Brito, whose male line expired in 1244, whereupon its heiress brought the honor to the lords Ros, ancestors of the earls, and later dukes, of Rutland.[67] Their overlordship at Duxford is not directly recorded after 1086, but the Colvilles, who were tenants by *c.* 1200 of the estate there later called *TEMPLE* manor, probably held it originally of the honor of Belvoir, as, from the 12th century, they held their Leicestershire lands at Muston and Normanton.[68] William de Colville, who probably held land in Cambridgeshire by 1177,[69] may have obtained Duxford upon his marriage[70] to Maud, the eldest daughter and eventual coheir of Ralph de Albini[71] (d. *c.* 1192),[72] who held 15 knights' fees of his brother William de Albini in 1166.[73] William de Colville died *c.* 1179 and was succeeded by his son William,[74] who was deprived of his lands by King John but was restored in 1217.[75] Having quarrelled with his eldest son Roger,[76] William before his death in 1230[77] granted much of his land to younger sons and religious houses. He gave 2 carucates and a mill at Duxford to the Knights of the Temple, and 120 a. to Tilty abbey (Essex),[78] besides endowing the hospital that he founded at Whittlesford Bridge with 1 yardland and another mill.[79] Roger and his descendants, the lords Colville,[80] retained only the overlordship of the Temple manor. In 1279 his grandson Roger was erroneously said to hold it of the honor of the counts of Aumale[81] of which his ancestors held their seat at Castle Bytham (Lincs.).[82] Under Roger the local preceptor of the Temple held in 1279 more than 4 hides in demesne.[83] The manor was taken into the king's hands in 1308 when the order was suppressed,[84] but was relinquished in 1313 for the benefit of the Knights Hospitallers.[85] Duxford, however, was claimed as an escheat by Roger's son, Edmund de Colville, who occupied it until his death in 1316, when his heir was a minor.[86] The Hospitallers secured the cancellation of such claims in 1324,[87] and were by 1333 in possession of Duxford Temple manor,[88] which became a dependency of their preceptory at Shingay.[89]

In 1540 the Crown granted the lands of the forfeited preceptory to Sir Richard Long,[90] who in 1541 settled them jointly on himself and his intended wife, Margaret Kitson.[91] He died in 1546,[92] and by 1548 Margaret had married John Bourchier, earl of Bath, with whom she held Duxford until their deaths in 1561.[93] The manor then passed to Long's son Henry,[94] who died in 1573, leaving his lands to his daughter and heir Elizabeth,[95] wife of Sir William Russell (d. 1613), Lord Deputy of Ireland 1594–7, created Lord Russell of Thornhaugh 1603.[96] Elizabeth, having quarrelled with her son Francis, died in 1609 having directed her feoffees to sell Duxford to pay certain legacies.[97] Francis paid the legacies, and in 1619 the feoffees conveyed Temple manor to him.[98] In 1627 he succeeded to the earldom of Bedford,[99] and in 1637 sold the manor to William Webb and his son William.[1]

In 1649 the Webbs conveyed Duxford to John Lamott and Maurice Abbott.[2] By 1657 Maurice Abbott the younger[3] (d. 1659), a lawyer,[4] owned the estate; he was succeeded by George Abbott, probably his brother.[5] George, who purchased Lacy's manor in 1671,[6] died between 1696 and 1698 and was succeeded by his son Maurice,[7] who owned

[63] Ibid. 24 Apr., 21 Nov. 1974; *Flight*, civ, no. 3369.
[64] Dorothy Whitelock, *A.-S. Wills*, 2.
[65] *V.C.H. Cambs.* i. 374–5, 379, 381, 385, 411–12.
[66] Ibid. 381.
[67] Sanders, *Eng. Baronies*, 12; Hist. MSS. Com. 24, *Rutland*, iv, p. 106; *Complete Peerage*, s.v.v. Ros, Rutland.
[68] Cf. Hist. MSS. Com. 24, *Rutland*, iv, p. 141; *Bk. of Fees*, ii. 953; Nichols, *Leics.* ii. 286–7; iii. 518.
[69] *Pipe R.* 1177 (P.R.S. xxvi), 185.
[70] Cf. *Ex. e Rot. Fin.* (Rec. Com.), i. 400.
[71] Cf. *Pipe R.* 1194 (P.R.S. N.S. v), 118; 1202 (P.R.S. N.S. xv), 222–3; *Feet of Fines*, 7–8 Ric. I (Pipe R. Soc. xx), pp. 99–100.
[72] *Pipe R.* 1191 & 92 (P.R.S. N.S. ii), 231.
[73] *Red Bk. Exch.* (Rolls Ser.), i. 328; cf. Hist. MSS. Com. 24, *Rutland*, iv, pp. 99–100.
[74] *Pipe R.* 1174 (P.R.S. xxi), 97; 1179 (P.R.S. xxviii), 50–1; cf. *Lincs. Eyre, 1218–19* (Selden Soc. liii), 358–9.
[75] *Rot. Litt. Claus.* (Rec. Com.), i. 323.
[76] Ibid. ii. 126; *Cur. Reg. R.* xii, p. 452.
[77] *Ex. e Rot. Fin.* (Rec. Com.), i. 199; *Cur. Reg. R.* xiv, pp. 95, 144–6.
[78] *Cur. Reg. R.* xiv, pp. 144–5.
[79] *Rot. Hund.* (Rec. Com.), ii. 582.
[80] *Complete Peerage*, ii. 374–5.
[81] *Rot. Hund.* (Rec. Com.), ii. 581.
[82] Ibid. i. 260; *Bk. of Fees*, ii. 1082; *Lincs. Eyre, 1218–19* (Selden Soc. liii), pp. liv–lvi.
[83] *Rot. Hund.* ii. 581; cf. *V.C.H. Cambs.* ii. 268.
[84] E 358/20 rot. 7d.; cf. *Essays in Med. Hist. pres. to Salter*, 155–63.
[85] *Cal. Close*, 1313–18, 29, 88–9.
[86] *Cal. Inq. p.m.* v, p. 375.
[87] *Essays pres. to Salter*, 162–3; *Cal. Close*, 1323–7, 91.
[88] *Cal. Close*, 1333–7, 124.
[89] *Hospitallers in Eng.* (Camd. Soc. [1st ser.], lxv), 165; cf. *Cal. Pat.* 1441–6, 134.
[90] *L. & P. Hen. VIII*, xv, p. 294.
[91] Ibid. xvi, p. 640.
[92] C 142/74 no. 13.
[93] *Complete Peerage*, ii. 17; C.U.L., Doc. 1096.
[94] *Cal. Pat.* 1563–6, p. 274.
[95] C 142/163 no. 6.
[96] *Complete Peerage*, xi. 237–9; Wards 7/49 no. 55.
[97] C.P. 25(2)/262/36 Eliz. I Trin. no. 2; Sta. Cha. 8/252/1; C.R.O., R 57/9/8508.
[98] B.L. Harl. Ch. 79. G. 12.
[99] *Complete Peerage*, ii. 75–9.
[1] C.P. 25(2)/400/7 Chas. I Mich. no. 30.
[2] C.P. 25(2)/538/1649 Trin. no. 12; *Visit. Surr. 1530–1623* (Harl. Soc. xliii), 90; *Visit. Lond. 1633–5* (Harl. Soc. xvii), 42, 104, 272.
[3] C.P. 43/299 rot. 173; E. Suff. R.O., HA/18/1594, Temple ct. roll 26 May 1657.
[4] Prob. 11/291 (P.C.C. 274 Pell).
[5] Ibid.; E. Suff. R.O., HA/18/1594, Temple ct. roll, 12 July 1659.
[6] See below.
[7] E. Suff. R.O., HA/18/1594, Temple ct. bk. i, ff. 28v.–29v.; *Alum. Cantab. to 1751*, i. 1.

both manors until his death in 1720.[8] Maurice's son Robert was lord there between 1722 and 1725.[9] Between 1725 and 1736 Francis Shepherd owned the manors,[10] which by 1739 had come to Nathaniel Rogers (d. 1743), who was succeeded by his sisters Lucy (d. 1746) and Elizabeth and Elizabeth's husband James Barry. The Barrys sold the manors in 1759 to Richard Crop,[11] who died in 1796 leaving them for life to his wife Mary (d. after 1806) and thereafter to his great-nephew Charles Long.[12] Long, created Lord Farnborough in 1826, died without issue in 1838[13] leaving his Duxford estate to his brother Beeston's son, William Long[14] of Hurts Hall, Saxmundham (Suff.), who died in 1875 and was succeeded by his son William Beeston Long. On W. B. Long's death without issue in 1892 his lands passed to his nephew William Evelyn Long (d. 1944). W. E. Long in 1937 retained the nominal lordship of Temple and Lacy's manors, which presumably passed to his son W. G. Long,[15] but had sold the land in Duxford attached to them in 1906 to James Binney of Pampisford Hall (d. 1935).[16] Binney offered Temple, Lacy's, and Barker's farms for sale in 1920 and Temple farm again in 1932,[17] but in 1933 still owned land in Duxford which passed to his son R. C. C. J. Binney,[18] who in 1946 sold Temple mill.[19]

The Templars' manor-house, where the preceptor dwelt, included in 1308 a hall and chamber, a chapel equipped for services, and a grange and other farm-buildings.[20] It probably stood in the area, called in 1823 Temple close,[21] around the modern Temple Farm. Traces of a rectangular moat still remain between the farm and the river.[22] The 16th-century core of the existing farm-house is probably the larger part of a medium-sized house, which was considerably extended and altered in the 18th and 20th centuries.

By 1086 5¾ hides at Duxford, formerly owned by Archbishop Stigand and Herulf, were held in chief by Eustace, count of Boulogne.[23] He was soon afterwards deprived by William II, who granted the Duxford manor to Hugh de Envermeu, who in turn exchanged it with Westminster abbey for lands in Lincolnshire. Henry I restored Duxford to Count Eustace, compensating Hugh who gave back to the abbey its former estate.[24] The overlordship of Duxford subsequently remained with the honor of Boulogne.[25] In 1086 the manor, except for ½ hide held at farm by Guy of Anjou, had been held in demesne by Count Eustace's follower, Arnulf, son of the lord of Ardres (Pas de Calais).[26] Arnulf, who had succeeded to Ardres by 1100, obtained his brother Geoffrey's share of their English lands in exchange for land in Flanders,[27] and died *c.* 1137. His eldest son Arnulf was murdered *c.* 1139 and his younger son Baldwin, lord of Ardres, died on crusade *c.* 1147 without issue.[28] Their sister and heir Adeline married Arnold of Merck,[29] on whose death *c.* 1176 the lands passed to Baldwin, count of Guisnes 1169–1206, who had married Arnold's daughter Christine.[30] In 1200 Count Baldwin exchanged manors at Duxford and Trumpington with William Marshal, earl of Pembroke, for land in Flanders. William granted the Duxford manor the same year to Roger d'Abernon in exchange for an estate at Abernon (Calvados).[31] Roger's family subsequently held the Duxford manor, thenceforth called *D'ABERNONS*, of William and his heirs.[32] The mesne lordship of D'Abernons manor may later have been included in the purparty of the coheirs of Eve Marshal, wife of William de Braose (d. 1230), for it was assigned in 1252 to her daughter Eleanor's husband Humphrey de Bohun (d. 1265).[33] By 1260 it had settled in the purparty of Roger Bigod, earl of Norfolk, son of Eve's sister Maud. Duxford was dependent on the leet of his manor at Great Chesterford (Essex), inherited from the Marshals.[34] The lordship remained with the Bigods and their successors, earls and dukes of Norfolk, until the 15th century.[35]

Roger d'Abernon, tenant from 1200, was living in 1203 and possibly in 1215.[36] He was succeeded by Walter d'Abernon, probably his brother,[37] who held Duxford when he died in 1220 leaving a minor heir[38] Ingram, who died without issue in 1234.[39] Ingram's heir Jordan, son of Walter's brother William, released his inheritance to his uncle Gilbert (d. 1236), who in return granted him D'Abernons manor to hold as ½ knight's fee.[40] Jordan still held it *c.* 1242,[41] but it passed later to the descendants of Gilbert, whose son John died after 1270.[42] John's

[8] Prob. 6/96 f. 120v.; E. Suff. R.O., HA/18/1594, Temple ct. bk. ii, p. 12.
[9] *Alum. Cantab. to 1751*, i. 1; E. Suff. R.O., HA/18/1594, Temple ct. bk. ii, pp. 15, 20.
[10] E. Suff. R.O., HA/18/1594, Temple ct. bk. ii, pp. 21–36.
[11] Ibid. pp. 39–74; iii, pp. 1–26; Barry Estate Act, 32 Geo. II, c. 36 (Priv. Act).
[12] Prob. 11/1280 (P.C.C. 494 Harris); E. Suff. R.O., HA/18/1594, Temple ct. bk. iii, pp. 101–11; Burke, *Land. Gent.* (1855), 714–15.
[13] *D.N.B.*; *Complete Peerage*, v. 257.
[14] E. Suff. R.O., HA/18/1594, abstract of title, 1859.
[15] Burke, *Land. Gent.* (1906), ii. 1041–2; (1952), 1563–4; *Kelly's Dir. Cambs.* (1937); cf. E. Suff. R.O., HA/18/1594, Temple ct. bk. v, pp. 52–122.
[16] C.U.L., Maps bb. 53(1)/92/7; *Alum. Cantab. 1752–1900*, i. 264.
[17] C.U.L., Maps bb. 53(1)/92/7; C.R.O., 296/SP 1170.
[18] Burke, *Land. Gent.* (1937), 162–3; *Kelly's Dir. Cambs.* (1933, 1937).
[19] C.R.O., SP 61/1.
[20] E 358/20 rott. 8d., 9.
[21] C.R.O., Q/RDc 44.
[22] *V.C.H. Cambs.* ii. 28.
[23] *V.C.H. Cambs.* i. 379.
[24] *Reg. Regum Anglo-Norm.* ii, p. 66.
[25] e.g. *Bk. of Fees*, i. 236; *Pat. R.* 1216–25, 131.
[26] *V.C.H. Cambs.* i. 411–12; Lambert of Ardres, *Hist. Comitum Ghisnens.* (Mon. Hist. Germ. Scriptores, xxiv), 615.
[27] Lambert, *Hist. Com. Ghisn.* 619–20; cf. Round, *Feudal Eng.* 462–4.
[28] Lambert, *Hist. Com. Ghisn.* 628–30, 634–5.
[29] Ibid. 627, 634–5.
[30] Ibid. 593–4, 600; *Pipe R.* 1168 (P.R.S. xii), 44; 1176 (P.R.S. xxv), 146; *Rot. Litt. Claus.* (Rec. Com.), i. 68.
[31] *Rot. Chart.* (Rec. Com.), i. 46, 65.
[32] e.g. *Cur. Reg. R.* v. 89–90; *Bk. of Fees*, ii. 930.
[33] *Close R.* 1251–3, 272–3; *Cal. Pat.* 1364–7, 264, 270; cf. Sanders, *Eng. Baronies*, 8, 57, 63; *Complete Peerage*, vi, s.v. Hereford.
[34] *Cal. Inq. p.m.* i, p. 240; *Plac. de Quo Warr.* (Rec. Com.), 102; cf. Sanders, *Eng. Baronies*, 111.
[35] e.g. *Cal. Inq. p.m.* iv, p. 297; xiii, p. 121; *Cal. Inq. p.m.* (Rec. Com.), iii. 267, 272; iv. 146.
[36] *Pipe R.* 1202 (P.R.S. N.S. xv), 71, 80; *Rot. Litt. Claus.* (Rec. Com.), i. 236; but cf. ibid. pp. 235, 251.
[37] Cf. *Cur. Reg. R.* i. 378; Caius Coll. Mun. XXXV 1/b.
[38] *Cur. Reg. R.* ix. 89–90.
[39] *Ex. e Rot. Fin.* (Rec. Com.), i. 270.
[40] Ibid. 272, 305; B.L. Add. Ch. 5541.
[41] *Bk. of Fees*, ii. 930.
[42] *Cal. Chart. R.* 1226–57, 434; *Close R.* 1268–72, 302.

son, Sir John d'Abernon, held Duxford in 1279[43] and in 1327 was succeeded by his son Sir John[44] (d. 1343). Despite a settlement made in 1340 on his son John's son William[45] the manor was included in the dower of the elder John's widow Alice,[46] who soon afterwards married Sir Adam Swinburne, who held the manor with her in 1346.[47] Swinburne died after 1352,[48] and Alice after 1363.[49] Meanwhile William had died in 1358, and the manor passed to Elizabeth, one of his two daughters, wife of Sir William Croyser,[50] steward to John of Gaunt,[51] who died in 1388.[52] In 1390 Elizabeth married John Grey and D'Abernons was settled on them for their lives.[53] John Grey died in 1391.[54] By 1398 Elizabeth's lands had passed to her son William Croyser (d. 1415).[55] William's heir, his daughter Alice,[56] *c.* 1434 married Sir Henry Norbury.[57] Norbury died in 1455 and Alice in 1464,[58] and their lands passed to their son Sir John Norbury,[59] who in 1485 exchanged his manor at Duxford for estates in Surrey with Sir Edmund Shaa, lord mayor of London 1482–3.[60]

Shaa died in 1488, and D'Abernons passed to his widow Gillian (d. 1494) for life[61] and then to Catherine, one of his two daughters, who married Sir William Browne[62] (d. as lord mayor of London, 1514). Their son William[63] died in 1549, leaving his land to his son Thomas[64] (d. 1567). Thomas's son John Browne was a minor,[65] and John's mother Jane, who had by 1573 married Henry Mildmay, held D'Abernons manor until 1599.[66] In 1590 John Browne had sold the reversion to Dr. Thomas Legge, master of Caius College, Cambridge,[67] who in 1599 conveyed the manor to trustees for the college.[68] From 1610[69] the college possessed the estate as part of the Frankland benefaction,[70] and still owned the manor and land, together with 212 a. bought in 1891, in 1972.[71]

D'Abernons manor-house probably stood originally in a close north of St. Peter's church, which belonged to Caius College in 1654 and 1825.[72] In 1631 the demesne included a house north of the church, from which it was presumably farmed.[73] In 1648 the college bought from Thomas Symons of Whittlesford a messuage and croft between St. John's churchyard and vicarage,[74] which remained the farmstead for all its Duxford property until after inclosure.

The 6 hides owned by Eddeva at Duxford in 1066 had, like her other lands, passed by 1086 to Count Alan of Brittany, of whom they were held by Gerard the Lorrainer.[75] That land continued to be held of the honor of Richmond,[76] under which it was held from *c.* 1200 by the Furneaux family, lords of Barham manor in Linton, and their successors there.[77] Thus in 1219 the fee at Duxford was held of Michael de Furneaux,[78] and in 1279 of Simon de Furneaux, probably his son.[79] Under those mesne lords the fee had by 1200 been divided into two parts, each held for ½ knight's fee, probably by partition between coheirs, for the two demesnes resulting were almost exactly equal.[80] One part was held *c.* 1200 by Robert of Soham, who was dead *c.* 1211 when his widow Nichole claimed dower in one carucate from his son and heir Warin[81] (d. 1235). Warin's son and heir Ralph[82] was dead by 1271 when his lands were held by Basile of Soham.[83] She soon after married Baldwin St. George, with whom she held that ½ fee in 1279, when William Mortimer, of whom Baldwin held land at Kingston, was interpolated as mesne lord under Simon de Furneaux.[84] The interest of Baldwin and Basile presumably descended in the St. George family.[85] Under them Ralph of Duxford held in 1279 2 hides in demesne for a fee-farm of 100*s.*,[86] and remained tenant until *c.* 1290. By 1294 he had been succeeded by his son Baldwin, who was tenant *c.* 1303,[87] and died after 1317.[88] Baldwin dispersed part of his land, some 30 a. of which eventually passed to Sir John d'Abernon (d. 1327) and was incorporated in D'Abernons manor.[89] In 1346 Baldwin's ½ fee was said to be occupied by Nicholas Rising (fl. 1321–46) and his

[43] *Rot. Hund.* (Rec. Com.), ii. 583.
[44] *Feud. Aids*, i. 137, 144, 155; *Cal. Fine R.* 1327–37, 69, 80; *Cal. Inq. p.m.* vii, pp. 22–3.
[45] C.P. 25(1)/287/40 no. 268. The younger John had died *c.* 1339: *Cal. Pat.* 1338–40, 138, 279.
[46] Caius Coll. Mun. XXXV 1/44A–B. Later references to a John d'Abernon probably refer to a younger brother of Wm. who took the family's Devon lands.
[47] *Feud. Aids*, i. 161; cf. ibid. i. 30; v. 125.
[48] Cf. *Cal. Pat.* 1350–4, 256.
[49] Caius Coll. Mun. XXXV 1/47; *Public Works in Med. Law*, i (Selden Soc. xxxii), 37–9.
[50] *Cal. Fine R.* 1356–68, 67–9, 84; *Cal. Inq. p.m.* x, pp. 339–40; cf. *Cal. Close*, 1354–60, 85.
[51] Somerville, *Hist. Duchy Lanc.* i. 364.
[52] Lamb. Pal. Reg. Courtenay, f. 222.
[53] C.P. 25(1)/289/56 no. 205; cf. *Cal. Close*, 1389–92, 150.
[54] C.P. 25(1)/289/56 no. 216.
[55] Caius Coll. Mun. XXXV 2/e; *Cal. Pat.* 1405–8, 134; Prob. 11/2 (P.C.C. 33 Marche); *Cal. Fine R.* 1413–22, 106.
[56] *Cal. Fine R.* 1413–22, 270–1.
[57] *Cal. Pat.* 1429–36, 380; Caius Coll. Mun. XXXV 2/h; C.P. 25(1)/292/68 no. 184 where Duxford is misspelt 'Kexford'.
[58] *Cal. Fine R.* 1452–61, 135; 1461–71, 126.
[59] Caius Coll. Mun. XXXV 2/k; *Cal. Pat.* 1461–7, 459.
[60] Caius Coll. Mun. XXXV 2/m–q.
[61] Prob. 11/8 (P.C.C. 12 Milles); *Cal. Close*, 1485–1500, pp. 234–6; Prob. 11/10 (P.C.C. 22 Vox).
[62] *Cal. Inq. p.m. Hen. VII*, i, pp. 421–2; cf. Prob. 11/8 (P.C.C. 37 Milles).
[63] Prob. 11/17 (P.C.C. 13 Fetiplace); C 142/29 no. 30.
[64] E 150/323 no. 6.
[65] E 150/334 no. 7; *Cal. Pat.* 1566–9, p. 269.
[66] Caius Coll. Mun. XXXV 5, bdle. 2, ct. rolls 10–41 Eliz. I; cf. *Visit. Essex* i (Harl. Soc. xiii), 78, 164–5, 251; *Visit. Cambs.* (Harl. Soc. xli), 15–16.
[67] C.P. 25(2)/94/856/34 Eliz. I Hil. no. 7; Caius Coll. Mun. XXXV 2/r.
[68] Venn, *Annals of Gonville & Caius* (C.A.S. 8vo ser. xl), 194–9.
[69] Caius Coll. Mun. XXXV 2/x.
[70] Venn, *Biog. Hist. Caius Coll.* iv. 41–3.
[71] Ex inf. the Domestic Bursar, Caius Coll.
[72] C.R.O., R 56/7/1, p. 86; Q/RDc 44.
[73] Caius Coll. Mun. XXXV 6, terrier, 1631.
[74] Ibid. 4/a–k.
[75] *V.C.H. Cambs.* i. 374–5.
[76] e.g. *Rot. Hund.* (Rec. Com.), ii. 580; *Cal. Inq. p.m.* ii, p. 219.
[77] For the Furneaux descent see p. 86.
[78] *Lincs. Eyre, 1218–19* (Selden Soc. liii), 230–1.
[79] *Rot. Hund.* (Rec. Com.), ii. 580.
[80] Ibid.
[81] *Cur. Reg. R.* vi. 143, 179; cf. *Pipe R.* 1209 (P.R.S. N.S. xxiv), 121; *Feet of Fines* (Rec. Com.), 338.
[82] *Ex. e Rot. Fin.* (Rec. Com.), i. 291; *Liber de Bernewelle*, 256.
[83] *Cal. Inq. p.m.* i, p. 273.
[84] *Rot. Hund.* (Rec. Com.), ii. 580; cf. C.P. 25(1)/25/39 no. 16.
[85] See *V.C.H. Cambs.* v. 107.
[86] *Rot. Hund.* (Rec. Com.), ii. 580.
[87] Caius Coll. Mun. XXXV 1/1; *Feud. Aids*, i. 137, 144.
[88] Caius Coll. Mun. XXXV 1/34–5, 37.
[89] Ibid. 1/7–14, 17–18, 21–2.

coparceners.[90] Its subsequent fate has not been traced.

The other half of the Richmond fee, later *LACY'S* manor, may have been held in John's reign by Hugh son of William of Duxford,[91] whose lands in Cambridgeshire and elsewhere were confiscated by the king in 1216 and restored in 1217. Hugh had a son named Gaudin.[92] About 1235 the ½ fee at Duxford was said to be held by Gaudin's heirs.[93] By the 1270s it had come to Sir Henry Lacy, who held 2 hides in demesne there in 1279.[94] He died after 1297.[95] His widow Alice had by 1302 married Ralph le Bret of Duxford, with whom she held *c.* 100 a. at Duxford in dower.[96] In 1307 Henry's son and heir Robert Lacy granted his brother Henry 100 a. there with the reversion of Alice's dower.[97] Robert held the manor in 1316[98] and died *c.* 1328, and his widow Maud held it in dower[99] until 1341 or later.[1] In 1350 his son Thomas sold the manor to Sir Adam Swinburne,[2] who then occupied D'Abernons manor by marriage.[3] Swinburne also acquired in 1352 a claim to the overlordship of the Duxford land held of the Scalers barony from Sir Thomas Scalers of Whaddon.[4] Lacy's manor later passed to the son of Sir Adam's brother Thomas, Sir Robert Swinburne[5] (d. 1391).[6] Sir Robert had apparently settled it on his widow Joan, and his son and heir Sir Thomas after disputing the settlement released the manor in 1397[7] and died without issue in 1412 as mayor of Bordeaux.[8]

When Joan died in 1433 the heirs to the Swinburne lands in Essex and Cambridgeshire were Sir Thomas's sisters Margery and Alice.[9] Duxford apparently came to Catherine, Margery's daughter[10] by Nicholas Berners (d. 1441).[11] Catherine had married Sir Thomas Fynderne,[12] a Lancastrian, whose lands were confiscated in 1461[13] and who was executed in 1464.[14] A grant of his lands in 1462 to Thomas St. Leger[15] did not mention Duxford, which Catherine may have retained as her inheritance until 1471 when, after her son William had fought against the Yorkists at Barnet, her property also was apparently confiscated and granted to Robert Ratcliffe.[16] William Fynderne's attainder was reversed in 1477, and his East Anglian lands were restored to him.[17] He held Lacy's manor at his death in 1516, having survived his son William, and devised its revenues for 80 years to the master of Clare College, Cambridge, subject to payments for supporting an alms-house at Little Horkesley (Essex), with remainder to the descendants of his grandson Thomas Fynderne (d.s.p. 1524), and, if they failed, to Thomas's cousin Sir Thomas Elyot (d. 1546).[18]

Clare College was accordingly occupying Lacy's in 1546.[19] In 1554 it leased the manor for 54 years to Thomas Wendy who in 1557 conveyed the lease to Thomas Bedell.[20] Thomas's father James Bedell had already in 1549 obtained the reversionary interest from Richard Puttenham, Elyot's nephew and heir.[21] Since Thomas Bedell was under age, the freehold and the lease were in practice united in the hands of James Bedell when he died, having survived Thomas, in 1575. He left Lacy's manor and other freehold lands in Duxford to his next son John.[22] By 1578 John Bedell had conveyed the manor to Dr. John Symyngs (d. 1588) and his wife Elizabeth,[23] who were styled lords until 1587[24] when they conveyed Lacy's to James Thurgar and Peter Kendall.[25] Thurgar and Kendall were perhaps acting as feoffees for Robert Taylor, who had in 1581 executed a conveyance of the manor to Symyngs and his wife,[26] and who entered upon it in 1588.[27] In 1600 Taylor sold the manor to Robert Symons the younger of Whittlesford,[28] who died in 1622 leaving it to his eldest son Thomas.[29] Thomas mortgaged it heavily between 1634 and 1654, when he sold it to James Thompson and Richard Pettit.[30] By 1659 Lacy's had come to Dr. Richard Love, master of Corpus Christi College, Cambridge, from 1632, who at his death in 1661 left the manor to his wife Grace.[31] In 1671 she and her younger son John sold the manor to George Abbott,[32] already owner of Temple manor, with which Lacy's manor subsequently descended.[33]

Lacy's manor-house probably stood originally in the moated inclosure between the river and the road, north-east of the east end of St. John's street. The

[90] *Feud. Aids*, i. 161; cf. Caius Coll. Mun. XXXV 1/39.
[91] *Cur. Reg. R.* vi. 353; x. 140.
[92] *Rot. Litt. Claus.* (Rec. Com.), i. 252, 374; *Rot. de Ob. et Fin.* (Rec. Com.), i. 587.
[93] *Liber de Bernewelle*, 256.
[94] *Rot. Hund.* (Rec. Com.), i. 55; ii. 580; Caius Coll. Mun. XXXV 1/m–g.
[95] *Knights of Edw. I*, iii (Harl. Soc. lxxxii), 5–6; cf. Caius Coll. Mun. XXXV 1/z.
[96] *Feud. Aids*, i. 144; C.P. 25(1)/25/40 no. 7; C.P. 25(1)/26/49 no. 9; cf. Caius Coll. Mun. XXXV 1/15.
[97] C.P. 25(1)/26/52 no. 24; E 40/14430.
[98] *Feud. Aids*, i. 155.
[99] C.P. 25(1)/27/64 no. 10.
[1] C.P. 25(1)/28/71 no. 11.
[2] C.P. 25(1)/28/76 no. 16; cf. *Cal. Close*, 1349–54, 273.
[3] See above.
[4] C.P. 25(1)/28/76 no. 15.
[5] For their relationship see *Cal. Close*, 1323–7, 200; *Cal. Inq. p.m.* vi, p. 424; vii, p. 319; *Cal. Pat.* 1330–4, 362; *Cal. Close*, 1346–9, 575; cf. *Hist. Northumb.* (Northumb. Cty. Cttee.), iv. 309, 324.
[6] *Archaeologia*, xlvi. 272.
[7] *Cal. Close*, 1389–92, 507–8; 1396–9, 202.
[8] Lamb. Pal. Reg. Arundel II, f. 157 and v.; *Cal. Close*, 1408–13, 366; cf. *Cal. Pat.* 1405–8, 60.
[9] C 139/59 no. 42.
[10] Ibid.; *Cal. Fine R.* 1430–7, 153, 163.
[11] *Cal. Close*, 1435–41, 98; cf. Morant, *Essex*, ii. 564.
[12] *Cal. Fine R.* 1430–7, 163; 1437–45, 300–1.
[13] *Rot. Parl.* v. 477, 479–80.
[14] Cora L. Scofield, *Edward IV*, i. 334.
[15] *Cal. Pat.* 1461–7, 77, 522.
[16] Ibid. 1467–77, 336.
[17] *Rot. Parl.* vi. 177; *Cal. Pat.* 1476–85, 191.
[18] Prob. 11/18 (P.C.C. 36 Holder); C 142/32 no. 32; C 142/42 no. 164.
[19] *Camb. Univ. Doc.* (1852), i. 273.
[20] Req. 2/65/25 answer.
[21] C.P. 25(2)/55/398 no. 55; C 142/74 no. 16.
[22] Req. 2/65/25 answer; Prob. 11/57 (P.C.C. 6 Pyckering); cf. C.P. 25(2)/93/833/6–7 Eliz. I Mich. no. 8; C.P. 25(2)/93/834/8 Eliz. I East. no. 4; C.P. 25(2)/93/834/8–9 Eliz. I Mich. no. 6.
[23] E. Suff. R.O., HA/18/1594, Lacy's ct. rolls 20, 23 Eliz. I; cf. *Alum. Oxon. 1500–1714*, p. 1541.
[24] E. Suff. R.O., HA/18/1594, Lacy's ct. rolls 24–9 Eliz. I.
[25] C.P. 25(2)/94/849/29 Eliz. I Trin. no. 6.
[26] *Cambs. Fines*, 1485–1603, ed. Palmer, 86.
[27] E. Suff. R.O., HA/18/1594, Lacy's ct. roll 30 Eliz. I.
[28] C.P. 25(2)/94/864/42–3 Eliz. I Mich. no. 16.
[29] Prob. 11/141 (P.C.C. 21 Swann).
[30] C.U.L., Doc. 1430–1; cf. C.P. 25(2)/539/1654 Mich. no. 2.
[31] Clare Coll. Mun., Duxford, petn. 1659; Prob. 11/303 (P.C.C. 26 May); cf. *Alum. Cantab. to 1751*, iii. 107.
[32] C.P. 25(2)/633/23 Chas. II Trin. no. 12.
[33] E. Suff. R.O., HA/18/1594, Lacy's ct. bks. *passim.*

surrounding close was called Lacy's in 1823,[34] and an adjoining one Dovehouse close in 1654.[35] By the 18th century the demesne was being farmed from a house north of St. John's street, built in the 16th century and later enlarged.

The fourth manor in Duxford, later called *BUSTELERS*, was derived from the 4¼ hides which Pain held in 1086 of Hardwin de Scalers, lord of Caxton.[36] The tenancy-in-chief descended in the branch of the Scalers family settled at Shelford, passing by marriage in the 13th century to the Frevilles.[37] In 1352, however, Sir Thomas Scalers of the Whaddon branch claimed to dispose of the Duxford overlordship.[38] Under the Scalers family the mesne lords of Duxford were the owners of the manor which in 1086 Pain had held of Hardwin at Boxworth,[39] later Overhall manor, Boxworth.[40] Thus in 1166 the mesne lord was probably William son of Roger.[41] About 1220 wardship of the Duxford land belonged to Henry son of William of Boxworth,[42] who was followed by his son William of Boxworth (fl. 1235–58).[43] In 1279 the manor was held of William's son Henry of Boxworth,[44] who died *c.* 1302.[45] Henry's son William held his lands in 1316,[46] and had been succeeded by 1346 by another Henry (d. by 1374),[47] who claimed wardship of Bustelers manor *c.* 1366.[48] In 1427 that manor was held of Roger Lovett, then lord at Boxworth,[49] in the 16th century of the Huttons who had succeeded to Overhall manor,[50] and in 1601 of Sir John Cutt, then owner of Overhall.[51]

The manor was by 1200 held in demesne under the lords of Boxworth by the Goiz family.[52] It may have belonged to Robert le Goiz, who had in 1166 held ½ knight's fee of Stephen and another of Hugh de Scalers.[53] He was perhaps succeeded by his son Robert le Goiz (fl. *c.* 1200).[54] After 1200 Robert's brother Andrew le Goiz,[55] a pluralist clergyman, resigned his orders and livings in order to inherit the family lands. He was dead by *c.* 1220. About 1223 the succession of his son Andrew, a ward of Henry of Boxworth, was challenged by the younger Andrew's elder brother John, born while their father was still in orders. Henry, whom John had disseised at Duxford, was then restored, and in 1227 the dispute was settled by a compromise, by which Andrew, then of age, was to hold Duxford of John as 1 knight's fee.[56] Andrew probably died between 1257 and 1259.[57] By 1272 his land had come to his son William,[58] who held more than 1 hide at Duxford in 1279[59] and died after 1287, when he granted all his land there to Mr. Robert Fileby at farm for life.[60] William had been succeeded by 1299 by his son John,[61] who held the manor in 1316[62] and died after 1327[63] without issue. John had sold the manor or its reversion to Sir William le Busteler of Hildersham, from whom his brother Andrew le Goiz unsuccessfully claimed it in 1330.[64]

Sir William was succeeded probably *c.* 1334 by his son Sir Robert le Busteler.[65] Robert died in 1366, whereupon his lands at Duxford and elsewhere passed to coheirs descended from his five sisters. One of them, John Hanchach, was then a minor. The other four coheirs sold their rights soon afterwards to Robert Parys, who successfully resisted the Crown's claim to occupy the lands because of Hanchach's minority.[66] When Robert Parys died *c.* 1377[67] Bustelers went to his elder son Nicholas Parys, who held it in 1412[68] and died in 1425.[69] It then passed to Nicholas's nephew Henry Parys (d. 1427), who also purchased from his uncle's executor the fifth of Bustelers[70] which had been forfeited by Hanchach for his part in the Peasant's Revolt in 1381 and acquired by Nicholas.[71] The reunited Bustelers manor descended in the Parys family with its lands at Linton and elsewhere[72] until the last heir male, Philip Parys, died in 1672. Under his will Bustelers passed for life to his mother Anne and her second husband Sir Joseph Colston[73] (d. 1675). It was sold in 1677 to Sir Thomas Sclater, Bt.,[74] already purchaser of the other Parys estates with which it descended eventually to Thomas Sclater King.[75] On King's insolvency it was sold by order of Chancery to Lord Montfort,[76] who by 1771 had resold the Duxford estate to Richard Trott, the lessee since *c.* 1754.[77] Trott died in 1788, leaving

[34] C.R.O., Q/RDc 44.
[35] Ibid. R 58/7/1, p. 86.
[36] *V.C.H. Cambs.* i. 385.
[37] See ibid. v. 27–8; cf. *Rot. Hund.* (Rec. Com.), ii. 582; *Cal. Inq. p.m.* xiii, p. 154.
[38] See above.
[39] Cf. *V.C.H. Cambs.* i. 388.
[40] e.g. *Cal. Inq. p.m. Hen. VII*, iii, pp. 3–7.
[41] *Red Bk. Exch.* (Rolls Ser.), i. 367.
[42] *Cur. Reg. R.* xi, p. 122.
[43] *Liber de Bernewelle*, 240; *Cal. Pat.* 1232–47, 483; *Close R.* 1253–4, 20.
[44] *Rot. Hund.* (Rec. Com.), ii. 582; cf. ibid. 478–81.
[45] *Cal. Close*, 1296–1302, 559; cf. *Feud. Aids*, i. 147.
[46] *Feud. Aids*, i. 182.
[47] Ibid. 166; cf. *Cal. Inq. p.m.* xiv, pp. 202–3.
[48] K.B. 27/440 Rex rot. 4d.
[49] C 139/29 no. 48; cf. *Feud. Aids*, i. 185.
[50] *Cal. Inq. p.m. Hen. VII*, iii, pp. 3–7; C 142/160 no. 17.
[51] C 142/265 no. 35.
[52] Also called Guiz or Gowiz: to be distinguished from the de Gouiz family which had lands in Wilts., Som., and Dors.
[53] *Red Bk. Exch.* (Rolls Ser.), i. 367, 369; cf. *Pipe R.* 1172 (P.R.S. xxvi), 185.
[54] *Rot. Cur. Reg.* (Rec. Com.), ii. 18, 113; *Cur. Reg. R.* ii. 28.
[55] Cf. *Cart. Old Wardon* (Beds. Hist. Rec. Soc. xiii), pp. 67–8.
[56] *Cur. Reg. R.* xi, p. 122; *Beds. Eyre, 1227* (Beds. Hist. Rec. Soc. iii), 46–8; C.P. 25(1)/283/9 no. 61.
[57] *Cal. Pat.* 1247–58, 540; *Close R.* 1254–6, 362; 1256–9, 385.
[58] C.P. 25(1)/25/33 no. 4; the family descent is given in C.P. 40/280 rot. 255.
[59] *Rot. Hund.* (Rec. Com.), ii. 582.
[60] *Cal. Close*, 1279–88, 493–4.
[61] Caius Coll. Mun. XXXV 1/3.
[62] *Feud. Aids*, i. 144–5.
[63] *Cambs. Lay Subsidy, 1327*, 28.
[64] C.P. 40/280 rot. 255.
[65] *Cal. Fine R.* 1327–37, 354; *Cal. Chart. R.* 1327–41, 378; *Cal. Close*, 1337–9, 114.
[66] *Cal. Inq. p.m.* xiii, pp. 7–9; *Cal. Fine R.* 1368–77, 96; *Collect. Topog. & Gen.* i. 261–2; K.B. 27/440 Rex rot. 4d.
[67] *Cal. Close*, 1377–81, 93.
[68] *Feud. Aids*, vi. 407.
[69] *Mon. Inscr. Cambs.* 231, 285.
[70] C 139/29 no. 48; Prob. 11/3 (P.C.C. 2 Luffenam).
[71] *Rot. Parl.* iii. 175; *Cal. Pat.* 1381–5, 317; *East Anglian*, N.S. vi. 245–6.
[72] For the descent see p. 85; their tenure of Duxford is recorded in Prob. 11/5 (P.C.C. 14 Godyn); C 142/126 no. 7; C 142/160 no. 17; C 142/265 no. 35; Wards 7/53 no. 276; C.P. 25(2)/401/15 Chas. I Mich. no. 22; C.R.O., L 1/102; C.P. 43/249 rot. 24d.
[73] Prob. 11/342 (P.C.C. 53 Pye).
[74] C.R.O., R 59/5/9/105, 112–14.
[75] Cf. C.P. 25(2)/988/8 Anne Trin. no. 13; C.P. 43/626 rot. 331; C.P. 25(2)/262/27 Geo. II Hil. no. 12.
[76] C.R.O., R 59/5/4/2–6.
[77] Ibid. R 59/5/9/157, 166.

that estate to Edmund Fisher, a minor, son of his daughter Sarah and Edmund Fisher, rector of Duxford St. Peter.[78] The younger Edmund, vicar of Linton 1800–44, died holding the manor in 1851,[79] and was succeeded by his son Edmund (d. 1881), also a clergyman.[80] From 1883 the estate belonged to Mrs. Fisher, presumably the last Edmund's widow,[81] in 1903 to Edmund's grandson, Capt. E. N. Fisher (d. 1909),[82] and in 1920 to Mrs. G. M. Fisher, who was said still to own the manor in 1937.[83]

The original site of Bustelers manor-house was probably inside the moat in a close just south of St. Peter's church, owned by Edmund Fisher in 1823, but by that time the demesne was being farmed from a 17th-century house near the west end of the high street, on the north side, then as later called Bustelers Farm.[84]

Robert Gernon was said in 1086 to own ½ hide at Duxford, previously owned by Alfric Campe. It had no inhabitants, and may have been attached to Gernon's neighbouring manor in Fowlmere, which Alfric had also owned.[85] The estate is not subsequently recorded under Duxford, and was presumably included in Fowlmere, where Gernon's land later passed to the Munfitchets, and through their coheirs to the Plaiz family.[86]

Warden abbey (Beds.) probably owned by 1200 land at Duxford given by Robert le Goiz, for which his grandson Andrew owed the abbey rent in 1234.[87] Its daughter house, Tilty abbey (Essex), also had land at Duxford by 1200, given by Ralph de Banks, Andrew le Goiz, and others.[88] By 1230 it had also received 120 a. from William de Colville.[89] In 1279 it held *c.* 137 a. of the Richmond fee, 70 a. of Temple manor, 50 a. of D'Abernons manor, and 34 a. of William le Goiz.[90] It retained that land as a dependency of its grange at Chrishall (Essex) until its dissolution, when it also owned a tenement and 42 a. in Duxford called Maugers, farmed separately.[91] All that property was sold by the Crown in 1544 to Edward Elrington and Humphrey Metcalfe,[92] who in 1547 sold Chrishall grange to Edward Meade.[93] Meade settled it in 1574 on his younger son Edward and died in 1577.[94] The younger Edward sold Maugers in 1592 and the grange lands, *c.* 300 a., in 1594 to Robert Taylor, then lord of Lacy's manor.[95] In 1601 Taylor sold Chrishall grange alone to Edward's kinsman Sir Thomas Meade.[96] Sir Thomas died in 1617 leaving his lands to his son John,[97] on whose death in 1638 the grange came to John's son Thomas[98] (d. 1678).[99] Thomas and his son John mortgaged it in 1676,[1] and following various assignments of those mortgages it came after 1696 to Nicholas Pollexfen, on whose marriage it was settled in 1704.[2] After further mortgages Chrishall grange had by 1717 come, perhaps through James Smith as mortgagee, to John Hanchett of Heydon (Essex). He died in 1724 and his son John in 1737.[3] John Hanchett of Chrishall grange mortgaged the estate in 1743 to Thomas Hanchett of Ickleton and died *c.* 1756, whereupon his lands were divided between his daughters. The grange went to Anne, wife of James Watson, who still held it in 1769.[4] It was later acquired by the Brand family which had held Chrishall manor with land in Duxford since 1754.[5] In 1822 the Chrishall grange estate belonged to Thomas Brand, Lord Dacre, who was allotted 303 a. in Duxford at inclosure.[6] He died without issue in 1851 and the estate descended in his family, as did Great Carlton manor, to Thomas William, Viscount Hampden,[7] who offered the Chrishall grange estate for sale in 1925.[8] Its land in Duxford then as earlier was farmed from Chrishall grange in Fowlmere.[9]

In 1279 72 a. held of D'Abernons manor belonged to the rectory of Chrishall (Essex).[10] That church had belonged since 1068 to the canons of St. Martin's-le-Grand, London,[11] by whom it had been appropriated by 1254.[12] The impropriate rectory, with other possessions of St. Martin's, was annexed by Henry VII to Westminster abbey in 1503,[13] and passed to its successors, the dean and chapter of Westminster, with whom it remained until the 19th century.[14] The rectory still owned 50 a. in Duxford in 1654 and some land in 1749,[15] but apparently nothing in 1823. In 1279 another 15 a. were held of Walden abbey (Essex), by the Templars, under whom it mostly belonged to free tenants.[16]

Whittlesford Bridge hospital, endowed with ½ yardland by William de Colville,[17] owned at its suppression 38 a., which were sold in 1548 to Thomas Tyrell of London.[18] In 1563 the land was acquired from Henry Mordaunt by Robert Twyford,[19] who in 1566 sold it to James Bedell, lord of Lacy's manor.[20] In 1590 James's son John sold it to

[78] E. Suff. R.O., HA/18/1594, Temple ct. bk. iii, pp. 72–4.
[79] *Gardner's Dir. Cambs.* (1851); for the family, see *Alum. Cantab.* 1752–1900, ii. 500.
[80] *Kelly's Dir. Cambs.* (1879).
[81] Ibid. (1883, 1892).
[82] C.R.O., 296/SP 1021.
[83] C.U.L., Maps 53(1)/91/183; *Kelly's Dir. Cambs.* (1937).
[84] C.R.O., Q/RDc 44.
[85] *V.C.H. Cambs.* i. 381, 412.
[86] Cf. ibid. v. 148; Sanders, *Eng. Baronies*, 83; *Rot. Hund.* (Rec. Com.), ii. 546–7.
[87] *Cart. Old Wardon* (Beds. Hist. Rec. Soc. xiii), pp. 67–8; C.P. 25(1)/283/10 no. 105.
[88] Dugdale, *Mon.* v. 625; *Cal. Chart. R.* 1226–57, 358–9.
[89] *Cur. Reg. R.* xiv, pp. 144–5.
[90] *Rot. Hund.* (Rec. Com.), ii. 580–4.
[91] S.C. 6/Hen. VIII/952 rot. 9d.; E 318/411/101.
[92] *L. & P. Hen. VIII*, xix, p. 278.
[93] *Cal. Pat.* 1547–8, 202.
[94] Wards 7/19 no. 76.
[95] C.P. 25(2)/94/856/34 Eliz. I Hil. no. 4; C.P. 25(2)/262/36–7 Eliz. I Mich. no. 6.
[96] C.P. 25(2)/262/43 Eliz. I Trin. no. 7; cf. *Visit. Essex*, (Harl. Soc. xiii), 448–50.
[97] C 142/371 no. 118.
[98] Wards 7/92 no. 262.
[99] Morant, *Essex*, ii. 593–4.
[1] Essex R.O., D/DB 610.
[2] Ibid. D/DB 611, 613, 615.
[3] Ibid. D/DB 625–9; Morant, *Essex*, ii. 605.
[4] Essex R.O., D/DB 637–8, 639, 641, 650.
[5] Ibid. D/DHf T 189.
[6] C.R.O., Q/RDz 10, pp. 265–6; cf. ibid. L 70/52.
[7] *Complete Peerage*, iv, vi, s.vv. Dacre of the South, Hampden; Burke, *Peerage* (1959), 1045–6.
[8] C.R.O., 296/SP 1150.
[9] Cf. Clare Coll. Mun., incl. doc.
[10] *Rot. Hund.* (Rec. Com.), ii. 583.
[11] A. J. Kempe, *Hist. Notices St. Martin's-le-Grand* (1825), 174–5, 181.
[12] *Val. of Norwich*, ed. Lunt, 351; *Tax. Eccl.* (Rec. Com.), 93.
[13] Kempe, *St. Martin's-le-Grand*, 158; *Valor Eccl.* (Rec. Com.), i. 412.
[14] *Cal. Pat.* 1558–60, 398; Morant, *Essex*, ii. 605–6.
[15] C.R.O., R 58/7/1, p. 8; Essex R.O., D/DHf T 189.
[16] *Rot. Hund.* (Rec. Com.), ii. 581.
[17] Ibid. 582.
[18] E 318/2020 m. 5; *Cal. Pat.* 1547–8, 293–4.
[19] C.P. 25(2)/93/833/6 Eliz. I Hil. no. 9.
[20] C.P. 25(2)/93/834/8–9 Eliz. I Mich. no. 3.

Robert Taylor,[21] who still held it, with Maugers land, at his death in 1609. His heir was his son Thomas.[22] The estate was later mostly merged in Lacy's manor, which included Maugers land *c.* 1670[23] and the Lion inn by the site of the hospital in 1759.[24]

At inclosure the largest non-manorial estate in Duxford was that of the Hitch family. Thomas Hitch had held at his death in 1724 over 153 a., which passed successively to his sons James and Richard.[25] When Richard died in 1753 his heir was his cousin John Hitch.[26] John's son, the Revd. James Hitch,[27] owned 369 a., by customary measure, at Duxford at his marriage in 1790, and acquired in 1793–4 another 126 a. once owned by the Amey family.[28] All was leased to his kinsman Richard Hitch (d. 1816).[29] At inclosure in 1823 James was allotted 256 a. for the former estate and 71 a. for the latter, called Jacobs farm.[30] The larger estate passed, when James died in 1824, to his daughter Alicia, who was dead by 1830, when the 71 a. were sold to James Barker. The 256 a. were sold by order of Chancery in 1842;[31] most was acquired in the 1860s by John Alfred Oslar,[32] after whose death in 1888 212 a. were sold by his widow to Caius College,[33] the owner in 1972.[34] Oslar had also acquired in 1862 James Barker's estate,[35] besides land formerly owned by the Robynet family, which had been prominent in the parish since the 15th century.[36] John Robynet, the last male of the family, died in 1809 and his representatives sold his land, for which 94 a. were allotted at inclosure, in 1864 to Thomas Scruby, a collateral relative,[37] whose heirs sold it to Oslar in 1874.[38] In 1891 Oslar's widow sold *c.* 150 a. not bought by Caius College to Rear Adm. V. A. Montagu (d. 1915),[39] who sold it in 1911.[40]

ECONOMIC HISTORY. Of about twenty ploughlands in Duxford in 1086, 9 were in the demesnes and 10¼ were occupied by 11 *villani* and 20 bordars. The *villani* had 9¼ plough-teams between them, but the demesnes were understocked, with only 5 teams. The value of the estates in the vill had fallen since 1066 from £27 6*s.* 8*d.* to £20 5*s.* On the Scalers fee the yield fell by half from £5, but on Robert de Todeni's land income had been raised from the £5 7*s.* when he received it to £7 10*s.*, almost the former value.[41]

By 1279[42] almost half of the 2,300 a. of arable recorded was included in the demesnes of the five manors. The Lacy and Duxford manors each had *c.* 246 a., the Goiz manor *c.* 146 a., D'Abernons *c.* 240 a., and the Temple manor 508 a., besides 28 a. held of other manors. Some other lords also held land of other manors. Of *c.* 1,300 a. held of the manors, *c.* 396 a. belonged to Tilty abbey and other religious houses, and the peasantry occupied under 900 a., including only 120 a. belonging to free tenants. The largest free holdings, being half-yardlands, may have been enfranchised villein tenements. Two of 15 a. were held only on life-tenure, and another on D'Abernons manor owed 7 harvest-boons. Twenty-eight cottagers shared 23 a. About 700 a. was occupied by villeins of whom 40 held half-yardlands, standard on all five manors, of 14 a. and a 1-acre messuage, and 9 others had 9-acre holdings. The nominal equality of acreage recorded in 1279 may, however, have concealed substantial variations in size. In the same year a half-yardland leased for life actually included 21 a.,[43] and in the 15th century the size of half-yardlands held of D'Abernons manor varied between 16 a. and 40 a.[44] In 1279 D'Abernons manor had the largest amount of villein land, *c.* 335 a.; Temple manor had *c.* 130 a., the Goiz manor 135 a., and the two Richmond fees only 100 a. between them, not equally divided.

The villeins' services showed much similarity on each manor; those on the Richmond fees being almost identical, while those on the Goiz and Temple manors resembled each other closely. No week-works were exacted, except on Temple manor where three a week were due from Michaelmas to Midsummer. Otherwise the villeins on each manor had to spend some, usually two, days hoeing, to mow the lord's meadow and reap 6 a. to 8 a. of his corn, to do 12 averages, and, except on the Richmond fees, to plough 3 a., harrow for 3 days, and carry 4 a. to 6 a. of corn. They also sent 3 men to do 4 or 6 harvest-boons, except on D'Abernons manor, where 2 were sent to 8 boons. The tenants of 9 a. owed services only marginally reduced. The cottagers had to attend the harvest-boons, but mainly paid rent.

The Templars' manor, in hand when it was confiscated in 1308, then employed permanently a *messor*, a carter, 6 ploughmen, a shepherd, a swineherd, and a cowboy; for the harvest it also recruited a reap-reeve, stackers, and a cook. Its villeins' services, amounting to perhaps 2,000 works a year, were still important. Only 563 of 1,510 works due over 9 months were commuted. In 1309 the principal crops sown were 80 a. of wheat, 60 a. of maslin, 50 a. of barley, 32 a. of dredge, and 41 a. of oats, but only 9 a. of peas. The wheat and the malted barley were mostly sold, while the maslin and peas provided pottage for the hired servants and acre-loaves for the harvesters. There was a flock of *c.* 110

21 C.P. 25(2)/94/854/32–3 Eliz. I Mich. no. 14.
22 Wards 7/42 no. 136.
23 C.U.L., Doc. 1529.
24 Barry Estate Act, 32 Geo. II, c. 36 (Priv. Act).
25 E. Suff. R.O., HA/18/1594, Lacy's ct. bk. ii, p. 25; Temple ct. bk. ii, pp. 20, 26.
26 Ibid. Temple ct. bk. iii, p. 2; C.R.O., R 54/31/1.
27 *Alum. Cantab. 1752–1900*, iii. 385.
28 C.R.O., R 55/28/2A–E.
29 C.R.O., 375/T 3; *Camb. Chron.* 15 Mar. 1816.
30 C.R.O., Q/RDz 10, pp. 275–7.
31 Ibid. R 55/28/4D–E; C.U.L., Maps 53(1)/83/5, 53(1)/84/21; Clare Coll. Mun., indenture 1823.
32 Cf. *Kelly's Dir. Cambs.* (1858); R.G. 9/1028; R.G. 10/1591.
33 C.R.O., R 58/5, vol. x, p. 278; Venn, *Biog. Hist. Caius Coll.* iv. 43.
34 Ex inf. the Domestic Bursar, Caius College.
35 C.R.O., R 55/28/10, 1R–Z, 1AA–CC; R 55/28/2R–U; Q/RDz 10, pp. 260–1.
36 e.g. *Cal. Close*, 1452–61, 367; E 179/81/147 m. 2; Caius Coll. Mun. XXXV 4G, rental 1578; 5, ct. rolls *passim*; C.R.O., R 58/5, vol. x, pp. 229–36.
37 C.R.O., R 55/28/4H; ibid. Q/RDz 10, pp. 292–3.
38 C.R.O., R 55/28/4*i*.
39 Ibid. 4L–M; R 55/28/2BB–CC; R 55/28/17JJ–KK; cf. Burke, *Peerage* (1931), 2095.
40 C.R.O., 296/SP 1070.
41 *V.C.H. Cambs.* i. 374–5, 379, 381, 385, 411–12.
42 Next two paragraphs based, unless otherwise stated, on *Rot. Hund.* (Rec. Com.), ii. 580–4.
43 Caius Coll. Mun. XXXV 1/bb.
44 Ibid. 4/e, rental, 20 Edw. IV.

sheep and a small herd of milking cattle.[45] In 1338 the estate was managed by a bailiff; the customers' works, valued at only £4, had perhaps been commuted.[46] D'Abernons manor was also in hand in 1337. Sir John d'Abernon (d. 1327) had actively extended his holdings at Duxford, buying up part of the Duxford manor[47] and small parcels from lesser freeholders.[48] By 1304 he was leasing Lacy's demesne.[49] He also converted some of his villein half-yardlands into life-tenancies.[50] In 1336–7, though *c.* 140 works were sold, others were still exacted. The villeins still did their three ploughings, after Michaelmas, Christmas, and Easter, besides mowing and carrying the harvest. Men were sent to a harvest-boon by 37 customary tenants. The manorial staff comprised a reeve, a *messor*, and four others. Crops included wheat and maslin, of which 22 a. and 42 a. were sown.[51]

The customary holdings were eventually converted into rent-paying copyholds. On D'Abernons manor copyholders were in 1482 paying rents, usually of 10*s.* for a half-yardland and 6*s.* 8*d.* to 10*s.* for a 9-acre 'wareland'.[52] Excluding the demesnes copyhold still greatly exceeded freehold at inclosure, when 812 a. were allotted for copyhold and only 278 a. for freehold.[53] By custom recorded in the 16th century and still nominally in force in the early 20th, copyholds were inherited by the youngest son.[54] In the 14th century the demesnes were leased to farmers, that of Bustelers by 1366[55] and the Hospitallers' by 1381, when their manor-house was attacked by a band of rioters led by John Hanchach and their farmer lost goods worth over £20. D'Abernons manor-house was also attacked, and some court rolls were burnt there.[56] Its demesne was on lease by 1387.[57]

In 1340 it was said that 240 a. were out of cultivation, and that the spring corn had perished.[58] By 1300 the arable was divided into three fields west of the village, stretching east and west.[59] The southernmost, Stock field,[60] covering by local measure *c.* 1,115 a., included the 'strong, brown, wet earth' on top of Pepperton Hill, which gave it the later name of Blackland field.[61] North of it was Middle field (*c.* 1,155 a.), and beyond that North field (*c.* 915 a.), called by the 17th century Moor field,[62] probably after the village moor, also called Duxford heath,[63] at its western end, said *c.* 1794 to contain 20 a.[64] By the 17th century *c.* 100 a. at that end of the parish were included in a separate field attached to Chrishall grange, which with Chrishall rectory owned most of the strips there.[65] In early modern times the main crops were barley, wheat, rye, peas, and oats.[66] Sown land leased by a Duxford yeoman *c.* 1595 included 80 a. of rye and 20 a. of barley, but only 5 a. of wheat.[67] Even on Temple manor, less wheat (60 a.) than barley (80 a.) was sown when it was leased in 1565.[68] About 1675 lentils were being sown with barley and rye in one field.[69] In 1714 *c.* 30 a. in the open fields had recently been inclosed and sown with sainfoin.[70] Saffron was also grown from the 15th century.[71]

The land between the river and the road through the village consisted partly of large closes around the manorial sites, partly of common meadow. In the 17th century *c.* 46 a. were included in the Midsummer and Lammas meadows.[72] The 40 a. of meadow *c.* 1794 were liable to flooding. Horses and cattle then grazed there without stint. Sheep were fed on the moor[73] and the fallow field. They had been important in the economy since 1086, when there were 429.[74] Half-yardlands let *c.* 1300 by Sir John d'Abernon had sheep-walk for 40 to 60 sheep,[75] and a farm leased in 1358 included sheep-walk for 200 sheep.[76] D'Abernons and Lacy's manors each had sheep-walk for 300 sheep in the 17th century.[77] In 1272 Sir John d'Abernon claimed that the abbot of Tilty was bound as his tenant to send 200 sheep to Sir John's fold every other night and furnish a shepherd to keep them. The abbot compromised the lawsuit by paying £10 and releasing his own right of common over d'Abernon's land.[78] The abbey's Chrishall grange possessed fold-course for 400 sheep in Duxford in the 16th and 17th centuries,[79] and was said *c.* 1794 to have sheep-walk there two days a week.[80] The abbot and other outsiders such as the prioress of Ickleton were sometimes alleged in the 15th century to be charging Duxford's commons with their sheep when they should have been by custom in severalty.[81] In 1611 a manor court prohibited taking in outsiders' cattle on the commons,[82] but no stint was recorded and most pasture regulations were concerned with restraining pigs and horses. In 1683 the parsons were directed to fulfil their ancient duty of keeping a parish bull and boar, and their common rights

[45] E 358/20 rott. 7d.–9.
[46] *Hospitallers in Eng.* (Camd. Soc. [1st ser.], lxv), 165.
[47] See above.
[48] e.g. Caius Coll. Mun. XXXV 1/n, p, u, x, y.
[49] Ibid. 1/15.
[50] e.g. ibid. 1/30, 32, 39.
[51] Ibid. 4/a, acct. 11–12 Edw. III.
[52] Ibid. 4/e, rental, 20 Edw. IV.
[53] C.R.O., Q/RDz 10, pp. 260–97.
[54] e.g. E. Suff. R.O., HA/18/1594, Lacy's ct. roll 20 Eliz. I; C.R.O., R 55/28/2cc; Prob. 11/106 (P.C.C. 61 Hayes, will of Rebecca Eyton); Prob. 11/155 (P.C.C. 6 Ridley, will of Jas. Robynet).
[55] K.B. 27/440 Rex rot. 4d.
[56] *East Anglian*, N.S. vi. 99, 168; *Cambs. Village Doc.* 27, 32.
[57] Caius Coll. Mun. XXXV 2/a; cf. ibid. 4/d(2).
[58] *Inq. Non.* (Rec. Com.), 212.
[59] For their layout see Vancouver, *Agric. in Cambs.* 73–4; C.R.O., Q/RDz 10, pp. 257–99; the areas given are calculated from C.R.O., R 58/7/1 (1654, not 1754 as dated by C.R.O. cat.).
[60] Caius Coll. Mun. XXXV 1/bb (7 Edw. I).
[61] C.R.O., R 58/7/1. In 1631 it was called South field: Caius Coll. Mun. XXXV 6.
[62] Caius Coll. Mun. XXXV 1/b (*c.* 1235), 6.
[63] Ibid. 1/12, 23 (1303, 1309); cf. *Cal. Pat.* 1557–8, 379.
[64] Vancouver, *Agric. in Cambs.* 74.
[65] C.R.O., R 58/7/1, p. 90.
[66] Cf. Vancouver, *Agric. in Cambs.* 74.
[67] C 2/Eliz. I/R 6/26.
[68] C 3/203/5.
[69] E 134/28–9 Chas. II Hil./11.
[70] Clare Coll. Mun., survey 1714.
[71] *Cambs. Local Hist. Counc. Bull.* x. 8–9; Prob. 11/194 (P.C.C. 128 River, will of Jas. Robynet).
[72] C.R.O., R 58/7/1, pp. 87–8.
[73] Vancouver, *Agric. in Cambs.* 73–4.
[74] *V.C.H. Cambs.* i. 411–12.
[75] e.g. Caius Coll. Mun. XXXV 1/bb, 2, 39, 41A.
[76] Ibid. 1/45.
[77] Ibid. 6; C.U.L., Doc. 1529.
[78] Caius Coll. Mun. XXXV 1/Ψ.
[79] e.g. C.P. 25(2)/262/36–7 Eliz. I Mich. no. 6.
[80] Vancouver, *Agric. in Cambs.* 73–4.
[81] Caius Coll. Mun. XXXV 5, bdle. 1, ct. rolls 14 Hen. IV, 18 Hen. VI.
[82] Ibid. bdle. 3, ct. roll 7 Jas. I.

were suspended until they should.[83] There were some 1,200 sheep in Duxford *c.* 1794,[84] and 2,500 in the 1830s.[85] In 1861 the parish had seven shepherds.[86]

By 1500 there had probably been some concentration of wealth and landownership among the peasantry. In 1482 the half-yardlands on D'Abernons manor were occupied by only 7 tenants, compared with 17 in 1279.[87] Of £235 of taxable wealth in the parish in 1524 £87 belonged to 5 men taxed at over £10, including 2 with £26 each, while 31 others were taxed on goods worth only from £2 to £8, and 19 men only on their wages.[88] In the early 17th century *c.* 18 yeomen owned land in the parish, 11 of whom belonged to only 5 families, those of Robynet, Rutland, King, Swan, and Rayner,[89] which flourished there from the 16th to the 18th centuries.[90] The four demesne farms continued to dominate the parish, including in 1654 *c.* 1,400 a. out of *c.* 3,000 a. by local measure, excluding the Chrishall grange field. Bustelers demesne then amounted to 198 a., that of Lacy's to 241 a., that of D'Abernons to 405 a., and Temple manor's to 515 a. Much demesne land lay in larger blocks than the single-acre strips of a peasant holding. Temple manor's was largely composed of blocks of 5 a. and more, including one of 40 a. at the west end of Moor field, adjoining a 24-acre block owned by D'Abernons manor. Of 109 a. of closes in the village 51 a. belonged to the demesnes.[91] Temple manor was said to have included 522 a. of arable in 1632,[92] D'Abernons manor 429 a. in 1631,[93] Lacy's manor 262 a. in 1650,[94] and Bustelers manor *c.* 240 a. in 1553.[95]

The demesnes were frequently let to the more substantial yeomen: John Trope, lessee of D'Abernons *c.* 1482, also held 40 a. of copyhold of it.[96] Maugers farm, 42 a. of the Tilty estate, leased from 1528 for 50 years to John Robynet,[97] was held by John's kinsman James Robynet in 1643.[98] Richard Lounde died in 1546 leaving the leases of Temple, Lacy's, and D'Abernons manors to his eldest son Richard.[99] Later the owners of some manors began to accumulate head-leases of others. James Bedell, lord of Lacy's, was from *c.* 1565 leasing Temple manor from Henry Long, and was also bailiff and perhaps lessee of D'Abernons. Bedell and his widow Elizabeth in turn sublet to local men, Lacy's by 1578 to another James Robynet, Temple in two parts.[1] About 1649 Thomas Symons of Whittlesford, a colonel in the parliament's service and owner of Lacy's, obtained somewhat informally a lease of D'Abernons from the master and fellows of Caius College shortly before their ejection. Their successors complained in 1657 that Col. Symons had paid neither his own rent nor that which he had collected as bailiff, and had let the farm buildings and land fall into ruin.[2] The college regularly let its farm after 1600 on 20-year beneficial leases.[3] By *c.* 1750 the combined Temple and Lacy's estates, *c.* 800 a., had been divided into four farms, of which Lacy's farm covered 290 a. of arable, and Temple farm *c.* 260 a.[4]

Inclosure was proposed in 1813,[5] and an Act obtained in 1822.[6] The allotment of land was apparently completed by 1823,[7] but the award was not formally executed until 1830.[8] The area allotted consisted of arable and common amounting to 2,983 a. There were also 147½ a. of ancient closes. Since the tithes were not commuted, only 56½ a. were allotted for glebe. Of the land allotted over two-thirds, 2,123 a., went to the four largest landowners. Charles Long, Lord Farnborough, received 708 a., Caius College 407½ a., and Lord Dacre 303 a. adjoining Chrishall grange in Fowlmere. For Bustelers estate, much enlarged since 1654, Edmund Fisher was allotted 704½ a., including 215 a. for copyhold. Those four estates included together 292 a. copyhold, over which the manorial lords mutually relinquished their quit-rents and incidents. Of the remaining land 520 a. was allotted for copyhold, 278 a. for freehold, out of which 328 a. went to the Hitch and 94 a. to the Robynet estate. Of the remainder J. L. Johnson received 81 a., and five local families with between 20 a. and 50 a. each shared 141 a. Five other people with 10 a. to 20 a. had 64½ a. between them, and 34 others with under 10 a. 78½ a. Just over 36 a. (included above) was allotted to 24 persons for common rights.

After the inclosure most of Duxford was included in a few large farms. Furthest west lay the Chrishall grange estate. Next came 604 a. of the Fisher estate, farmed from Duxford Grange, where a farmstead and cottages had been established by *c.* 1840, although the house is later, and then 338 a. owned by Caius College, farmed from College Farm, also built out in the fields by *c.* 1840.[9] From 1820 to after 1834 College farm was let to Edmund Fisher the younger. Beneficial leasing of it was ended in 1867, and the college divided its Duxford estate in two. Thereafter 68 a. were run from its old farmhouse in the village and 348 a. from the new farmhouse. The two were sometimes distinguished as East and West College farms.[10] East of the college land the Long estate curving west and north of the village was by 1831 divided into Temple farm, including 335 a. on the north side of the parish and the mill and 38 a. of pasture by the river, and Lacy's farm, with 42 a. of closes and 303 a. of arable west

[83] E. Suff. R.O., HA/18/1594, Temple ct. bk. i, f. 12.
[84] Vancouver, *Agric. in Cambs.* 74.
[85] Clare Coll. Mun., vicar to master of Clare, 27 Dec. 1837.
[86] R.G. 9/1028.
[87] Caius Coll. Mun. XXXV 4/e, rental 20 Edw. IV.
[88] E 179/81/147 m. 2.
[89] Cf. Caius Coll. Mun. XXXV. 6.
[90] Cf. ct. rolls and books, *passim.*
[91] C.R.O., R 58/7/1, *passim*, especially pp. 7, 86.
[92] C.P. 25(2)/400/7 Chas. I Mich. no. 30.
[93] Caius Coll. Mun. XXXV 6.
[94] C.U.L., Doc. 1430.
[95] C.P. 25(2)/55/400 no. 6.
[96] Caius Coll. Mun. XXXV 4/e, rental 20 Edw. IV.
[97] E 318/411/10 m. 2.
[98] Prob. 11/19 (P.C.C. 128 River).
[99] Prob. 11/32 (P.C.C. 27 Populwell).
[1] Req. 2/65/25; C 3/203/5; Prob. 11/57 (P.C.C. 6 Pyckering); Caius Coll. Mun. XXXV 5, bdle. 2, ct. roll 17 Eliz. I.
[2] Caius Coll. Mun. XXXV 3.
[3] Venn, *Biog. Hist. Caius Coll.* iv. 42–3.
[4] Barry Estate Act, 32 Geo. II, c. 36 (Priv. Act), pp. 7–8.
[5] Clare Coll. Mun., letter 1813.
[6] 3 Geo. IV, c. 37 (Private, not printed); *C.J.* lxxvii. 55, 176, 268.
[7] Clare Coll. Mun., bill for fencing 1823.
[8] C.R.O., Q/RDz 10, pp. 251–302; Q/RDc 44: on which the following paragraph is based.
[9] C.R.O., Q/RDc 44; C.U.L., Maps bb. 3(1)/01/41.
[10] Caius Coll. Mun. XXXV 9, leases 1820, 1834; Venn, *Biog. Hist. Caius Coll.* iv. 42.

of the village, where a farmstead but no farm-house was built; it was called Barker's after William Barker, tenant in 1831.[11] Both later lost land to the airfield.[12] The Hitch property, mostly acquired by Caius College in 1891,[13] lay south-west of the village.

In the early 19th century the population consisted mostly of the tenant-farmers and their labourers. In 1821 116 families were supported by agriculture, and only 14 by crafts or trade.[14] There were several smaller farms of under 100 a. In 1831 15 farmers employed labour and 8 worked their own plots unaided.[15] In 1851, out of 14 named farmers, 12 occupying 100 a. or less had altogether 490 a. One was also a baker, another a carrier.[16] There were 10 farmers in Duxford in 1858, 7 in 1888, 5 in 1916.[17] In 1905 the parish included 2,478 a. of arable and 207 a. of pasture.[18] There were 6 farms in 1937, Temple, Lacy's, East and West College farms, Duxford Grange, and Hills farm,[19] the former Hitch land. In 1972 arable farming predominated.

There were *c.* 100 adult labourers in 1851, and *c.* 105 in 1871, when the farms provided employment for at least 66 men and 30 boys.[20] From the mid 19th century some new occupations were becoming available, besides those of the traditional village craftsmen such as blacksmiths, carpenters, and wheelwrights. There were 7 oil-millers in 1841, 10 shoemakers in 1851, and 11 gardeners in 1871. Many women engaged in dress- and bonnet-making, and by the 1860s others went to work at the Sawston paper-mill. Several men worked on the railway,[21] and a coal-merchant traded from Whittlesford Bridge station.[22] There was a small cycle-makers' by 1904, and a threshing-machine owner from 1922.[23] A company making waterproof materials, Impervious Packages Ltd., was in the village in 1929 but had gone by 1933.[24] The village smithy was still open in 1967.[25] In the late 20th century, as the numbers required in farming declined, some residents commuted to Cambridge, or even to London, while others worked in the factories established at Duxford.[26]

There were three mills in Duxford in 1086, one on Count Eustace's manor, held at farm by Guy of Anjou, two on Robert de Todeni's.[27] Those two descended with that manor until William de Colville granted one with the manor to the Templars,[28] the other, presumably, to the hospital, which in 1279 owned a water-mill in Duxford,[29] not afterwards recorded. The Templars' mill, standing by the river east of Temple Farm, was in hand in 1307, when its miller was a hired servant and the corn from its tolls went directly into the manorial grange.[30] In 1338 it yielded 1 mark a year.[31] In 1609 the parish contained a windmill.[32] Temple manor still owned its mill from the 16th century onwards.[33] In the early 19th century it was sometimes let with Temple farm, as to William Thurnall in 1831.[34] Thurnall (d. 1842) ground on a large scale, sending much of his flour along with malt and seed to London.[35] By 1871 the mill employed three men and a boy.[36] It was working in 1937,[37] but had apparently been closed when the house and mill were sold in 1946.[38] They were later converted into a private house.[39] The existing mill buildings were put up in 1811.[40]

Near the mill in 1836 William Thurnall set up a bone-mill worked by a water-wheel, with which he produced fertilizer from the mound of bones he had accumulated 30 ft. high. The bone-milling, still conducted beside the river in the late 1840s,[41] was afterwards transferred to a new works[42] using steam power, north of the village by the Whittlesford road. In 1858 the Cambridge Manure Company, as it was styled, was managed by William's son Charles. In 1860 the business was taken over by Bird Brothers, who retained it, at first using also locally dug coprolites, until 1914. In 1900 they were producing bone-manure, gelatine, and glue, and a subsidiary, the Cambridge Chemical Co., set up by 1892, made chemicals and disinfectants. After a fire in 1914 the business was acquired in 1919 by Eastern Counties Bone Products Ltd., who still owned the factory, styled Birds Chemical Works, in 1972. They then employed ten men, and produced principally organic fertilizers and animal feeds.

The largest factory in Duxford is that of CIBA (A.R.L.) Ltd., formerly Aero Research Ltd., which produces adhesives, especially wood glues, based on synthetic resins.[43] The company was established south of the village *c.* 1934 by N. R. A. de Bruyne, a scientist from Trinity College, whose interest in designing monoplanes led to research into synthetic materials and later to making aircraft glues. 'Aerolite' cement, manufactured at Duxford from 1939, was much used in aircraft during the Second World War, when the factory had over 200 employees. After the war the firm was merged with CIBA of Basle (Switzerland), whose 'Araldite' adhesive began to be produced at Duxford in 1950 in a new factory that was enlarged in 1958 and 1965. A new factory for making 'Aeroweb' was built at Duxford in 1963, and another in 1970. Extensive laboratories were

[11] E. Suff. R.O., HA/18/1594, lease 1831; C.R.O., R 57/9/13B.
[12] C.U.L., Maps bb. 53(1)/92/7.
[13] See p. 209.
[14] *Census*, 1821.
[15] Ibid. 1831.
[16] H.O. 107/1761.
[17] *Kelly's Dir. Cambs.* (1858, 1888, 1916).
[18] Cambs. Agric. Returns, 1905.
[19] *Kelly's Dir. Cambs.* (1937).
[20] H.O. 107/1761; R.G. 10/1591.
[21] H.O. 107/76; H.O. 107/1761; R.G. 9/1028; R.G. 10/1591.
[22] *Kelly's Dir. Cambs.* (1858, 1896).
[23] Ibid. (1904, 1912).
[24] Ibid. (1929).
[25] *Camb. Ind. Press*, 28 Oct. 1960; 7 July 1967.
[26] Local information.
[27] *V.C.H. Cambs.* i. 379, 381.
[28] *Cur. Reg. R.* xiv, pp. 144–5.
[29] *Rot. Hund.* (Rec. Com.), ii. 582.
[30] E 358/20 rot. 7d.
[31] *Hospitallers in Eng.* (Camd. Soc. [1st ser.], lxv), 165.
[32] C.U.L., E.D.R., B 2/28, f. 49.
[33] e.g. C.P. 25(2)/261/29 Eliz. I Hil. no. 1; Barry Estate Act, 32 Geo. II, c. 36 (Priv. Act).
[34] E. Suff. R.O., HA/18/1594, lease 1831.
[35] C.U.L., Com. c. 812, 15.
[36] R.G. 10/1591.
[37] *Kelly's Dir. Cambs.* (1937).
[38] C.R.O., SP 61/1; see above, plate facing p. 192.
[39] *Camb. Ind. Press*, 28 Oct. 1960; 4 July 1969.
[40] C.R.O., R 58/5, vol. x, p. 274.
[41] Ibid. pp. 272–3; cf. Chas. Kingsley, *Life and Works*, i. 190–1.
[42] The following is based on *Kelly's Dir. Cambs.* (1858 and later edns.) and information supplied by Birds Chemical Works.
[43] The following is based on *Camb. Region, 1965*, 232–3; C. A. A. Rayner, *Milestones in Hist. of CIBA (A.R.L.) Ltd.* 2–29; 'Introduction to Duxford', issued by *CIBA-GEIGY*; and further information supplied by that company's Duxford office. See also above, plate facing p. 193.

also built there from 1958 onwards. In 1970 CIBA itself merged with GEIGY, also of Basle.

In 1948 de Bruyne founded another company at Duxford, Techne (Cambridge) Ltd., which in collaboration with scientists from Cambridge and elsewhere develops and manufactures precision instruments for laboratories, using particularly pneumatic control. It began its operations at Temple mill, and in 1950 bought the former rectory, its headquarters in 1972. Among its main products are laboratory water-baths, thermoregulators, gelation timers, viscometers, and fluidized baths.[44]

LOCAL GOVERNMENT. Several suits rendered to the county and hundred courts in the early 13th century[45] were later withdrawn. About 1260 the earl of Gloucester removed that owed from Andrew le Goiz's fee.[46] After *c.* 1250 the abbot of Tilty withdrew that due from his lands. Henry Lacy and Ralph of Duxford had done their suits to a court of the honor of Richmond held at Babraham, apparently since Peter of Savoy possessed the honor. One half-yardland was held of Ralph by suit to that court.[47] In the 1270s Henry Lacy conceded that an agreement about land at Duxford should be enforced by the local steward and bailiff of that honor.[48] The Templars withdrew suit owed from the Colville lands, and claimed in 1279, under their charter from Henry II, to have on their manor view of frankpledge, the assize of bread and of ale, estreats, and a tumbrel, which they had set up *c.* 1275.[49] The earl of Norfolk claimed in 1279 and 1299 to have by prescription on D'Abernons manor view of frankpledge, the assize of bread and of ale, infangthief, a gallows and tumbrel, and estreats, as appurtenances of his manor at Great Chesterford (Essex).[50] In practice he was instead paid 5*s.* at a yearly view of frankpledge held for the tenants at Duxford,[51] and attempts by the earl's officers to distrain for his dues there were sometimes violently resisted.[52] In 1334 brewers and ale-tasters from Duxford were still being amerced by a court of the honor of Richmond held at Linton.[53]

The court of D'Abernons manor was regularly styled only a court baron in the 15th and 16th centuries, and confined itself to tenurial business and to regulating agricultural practice. Court rolls survive for 1401–17, 1439, 1495–1502, 1536–7, and 1550, and from 1558 to 1648, followed by court books extending to 1910.[54] Temple manor's court should have had leet jurisdiction, and was normally styled a view of frankpledge in conveyances from the 17th century,[55] as was that of Lacy's from *c.* 1600.[56] In practice, however, neither attempted to exercise leet jurisdiction, and concerned themselves mainly with rules about commoning and admissions to copyholds. Court rolls for Lacy's are extant for 1563 to 1602, and court books for both manors from 1671 to the 1920s.[57] Bustelers court baron can be traced only in surviving copyhold title-deeds.[58]

In 1596 Lacy's court elected two constables and a hayward.[59] In 1683 two constables were chosen at Temple manor court,[60] and in 1722 two others at Lacy's, as was also for several years a hayward. One constable was said then and in 1766 to be for St. John's, the other for St. Peter's parish,[61] but in general the administration does not seem to have been divided on parochial lines. The two churches may have had separate churchwardens, perhaps until the early 19th century,[62] but for all secular purposes Duxford was governed as a single unit. A single poor- and church-rate was levied,[63] and in 1834 a single vestry was administering the whole village. It consisted of the churchwardens, overseers, and assembled parishioners.[64] In 1724 the overseers bought a cow and a hog to support two widows.[65] The poor-rates increased from £57 in 1776 to £138 *c.* 1785 and £408 in 1803, when *c.* 30 were on permanent relief,[66] as in 1815, when their support cost £589.[67] Such expenditure, though reduced for a year or two to under £400, had again reached £550 in 1818, and except in the mid 1820s was until 1834 usually well over £500.[68] In 1830 the parish had only six men out of work, and was selling coal to the poor at a cheap rate.[69] From 1835 it was part of the Linton poor-law union,[70] in 1934 passed from the Linton to the South Cambridgeshire R.D.,[71] and in 1974 was included in South Cambridgeshire.

CHURCH. Duxford is an instance[72] of a single township anomalously containing two parish churches, each with its own incumbent. The duplication probably arose from the separate foundation before *c.* 1200[73] of churches at the northern and southern ends of the village by the lords of the two manors to which the two advowsons were at first annexed, that of St. John's belonging to Lacy's manor, that of St. Peter's to Bustelers. To which church inhabitants were liable to pay tithe was determined principally by tenure. St. John's received tithe from the lords and tenants of Lacy's and Temple manors, whose chief messuages stood

[44] *Camb. Region, 1965*, 236–7.
[45] Cf. *Liber de Bernewelle*, 256.
[46] *Assizes at Camb. 1260*, 38.
[47] *Rot. Hund.* (Rec. Com.), i. 55; ii. 581.
[48] Caius Coll. Mun. XXXV 1/s.
[49] *Rot. Hund.* i. 55; ii. 570; cf. *Plac. de Quo Warr.* (Rec. Com.), 107, where Bukesworth is probably a mistake for Dukesworth.
[50] *Rot. Hund.* ii. 570; *Plac. de Quo Warr.* 102.
[51] *Cal. Inq. p.m.* i, p. 240; iv, p. 297; xiii, p. 121.
[52] e.g. *Cal. Pat.* 1317–21, 174.
[53] S.C. 2/155/71 m. 2.
[54] Caius Coll. Mun. XXXV 5, ct. rolls.
[55] e.g. C.P. 25(2)/400/7 Chas. II Mich. no. 30.
[56] e.g. C.P. 25(2)/94/864/42–3 Eliz. I Mich. no. 16; cf. E. Suff. R.O., HA/18/1594, Lacy's ct. roll 38 Eliz. I. In a ct. roll of 32 Eliz. I it was styled a court baron.
[57] E. Suff. R.O., HA/18/1594, ct. rolls and bks.
[58] e.g. C.R.O., R 54/31/1; R 55/28/3A–L.
[59] E. Suff. R.O., HA/18/1594, Lacy's ct. roll 38 Eliz. I.
[60] Ibid. Temple ct. bk. i, f. 12.
[61] Ibid. Lacy's ct. bk. ii, pp. 16 sqq.; iii, p. 5.
[62] Cf. Prob. 11/57 (P.C.C. 6 Pyckering, will of Jas. Bedell); C.U.L., E.D.R., C 1/6.
[63] Cf. Clare Coll. Mun., corr. 1852; *Gardner's Dir. Cambs.* (1851); C.U.L., E.D.R., C 3/21.
[64] *Rep. Com. Poor Laws* [44], p. 53, H.C. (1834), xxxii.
[65] Hampson, *Poverty in Cambs.* 185.
[66] *Poor Law Abstract, 1804*, 40–1.
[67] Ibid. *1818*, 32–3.
[68] *Poor Rate Returns, 1816–21*, 12; *1822–4*, 39; *1825–9*, 15–16; *1830–4*, 15.
[69] *Rep. H.L. Cttee. on Poor Laws*, H.C. 227, pp. 328–31 (1831), viii.
[70] *Poor Law Com. 1st Rep.* 249.
[71] *Census*, 1931 (pt. ii).
[72] Cf. Swaffham Prior.
[73] *Val. of Norwich*, ed. Lunt, 536.

opposite the east end of St. John's Street, St. Peter's from those of Bustelers and D'Abernons, whose manor-houses once stood on each side of St. Peter's church.[74] There is no record of any formal territorial division of the cure of souls. Parishioners seem usually to have attended whichever church was nearest to their own dwelling, and in modern times to have worshipped in both at different hours, until St. John's church became disused after the benefices were united in 1874.

The advowson of St. John's church belonged by 1279 to Sir Henry Lacy,[75] and descended with Lacy's manor in his family until the 1340s. A plan to appropriate the church to Ipswich priory (Suff.) in 1344[76] fell through, and in 1346 Sir Thomas Lacy sold the advowson to Elizabeth de Burgh,[77] who was licensed in the same year to appropriate the church to her new foundation of Clare College.[78] A vicarage was established; the college was given the patronage and presented regularly, except in 1690 when the bishop of St. Asaph presented on behalf of the Crown through lapse.[79] The advowson of St. Peter's was owned in 1279 by William le Goiz,[80] and passed with Bustelers manor through the Bustelers to Robert Parys and his descendants.[81] The Crown's claim to present in 1370 by right of wardship was successfully resisted.[82] Although recusants the Paryses continued to present for a time after the Reformation. In 1602 Bishop Heton of Ely requested Philip Parys to present one of his chaplains.[83] The Crown presented in 1596,[84] and again by lapse in 1616 following Philip Parys's death. Charles Parys's guardian, Sir John Cutt, presented in 1618.[85] Although an Act of 1605 transferred recusants' patronage to the universities, it was not until 1642 that Cambridge University was able to present its own nominee.[86] Meanwhile in 1638 Parys had granted the advowson to George Carleton.[87] In 1665 Francis Westrope presented for that turn.[88] In 1686 George Flack acquired the advowson from Thomas Smith, Robert Flack, and John Rayner and their wives,[89] and in 1688 it was conveyed by Dr. Humphrey Ridley, his wife Sarah, and Thomas Buckworth to Thomas Harris,[90] whom Sarah Harris presented later that year.[91] In 1704 Harris sold the advowson to Thomas Tenison, archbishop of Canterbury,[92] who upon his death in 1715 bequeathed it to Corpus Christi College, Cambridge, directing that the rectory be given to a master or fellow of that college.[93] The college sold the advowson in 1868 to Clare College,[94] which retained the patronage of the united benefices until *c.* 1966, when it was exchanged with the bishop of Ely.[95]

In 1279 St. John's church possessed a messuage and glebe of *c.* 60 a.[96] On the appropriation Clare College took the great tithes and *c.* 22 a. of glebe, while the vicar received *c.* 40 a. of glebe with a house, the small tithes including those of hay, and a pension of 40*s.* charged on the rectory.[97] The rector of St. Peter's had in 1279 a glebe of 1 yardland,[98] said in 1638 to amount to *c.* 16 a.[99] He retained his full share of all the tithes, great and small, of Duxford.

From the 16th century Clare College normally leased St. John's rectory and great tithes on a beneficial lease for £8 a year,[1] at first to local farmers such as the Rutlands, tenants from 1577 to 1610.[2] By 1645 the lease had come to Dr. Richard Love, later lord of Lacy's manor;[3] in 1674 and 1681 it belonged to Love's widow Grace, and in 1714 to his son-in-law Archbishop Tenison.[4] After Tenison's death Clare College bought the lessees' interest and annexed it to Blythe's benefaction,[5] trustees for which sublet to local farmers. From 1770 to 1793 Edmund Fisher, rector of St. Peter's, was undertenant.[6]

Although the tithes were earlier divided between the two churches according to which manor a piece of land was held of, by the 17th century the great tithes were sometimes paid in cash at 4*s.* to 6*s.* an acre, and when taken in kind might be gathered promiscuously and later divided by the bushel between the rector of St. Peter's and the impropriator, presumably equally,[7] so that the ancient distinction of the parishes was being forgotten. In 1654 a survey made by order of Chancery determined to which manor each plot of land belonged and to which church it was consequently tithable; the tithe of land not known to belong to a manor was to be divided equally between the two churches.[8] Thenceforth each parson could collect the tithes due to him in kind independently, as was apparently being done in 1674 and 1714.[9] About 1795 the tithe of corn was being commuted at 2*s.* 6*d.* an acre.[10] During the Napoleonic wars the village farmers leased from Clare College its great tithes for £290 a year.[11]

[74] Clare Coll. Mun., copies of 1654 decree.
[75] *Rot. Hund.* (Rec. Com.), ii. 580.
[76] *Cal. Pat.* 1343–5, 268.
[77] C.P. 25(1)/78/74 no. 14.
[78] *Cal. Pat.* 1345–8, 135–6; cf. *Cal. Papal. Reg.* iii. 253.
[79] *E.D.R.* (1899), 32; (1903), 20; *Camb. Univ. Doc.* (1852), i. 272; P.R.O. Inst. Bks. *passim.*
[80] *Rot. Hund.* (Rec. Com.), ii. 582.
[81] e.g. *E.D.R.* (1905), 254; (1909), 87; (1914), 295, 309.
[82] *Cal. Pat.* 1370–4, 9; C.U.L., MS. Mm. 1. 39, p. 183; *E.D.R.* (1898), 90.
[83] Hist. MSS. Com. 4, *5th Rep.* p. 487.
[84] Gibbons, *Ely Episc. Rec.* 454.
[85] P.R.O. Inst. Bks. ser. A, iii, p. 30.
[86] Ibid.; Presentation of Benefices Act, 3 Jas. I, c. 5; C.U.L., MS. Mm. 1. 44, p. 225.
[87] C.P. 25(2)/401/14 Chas. I Mich. no. 11.
[88] P.R.O. Inst. Bks. ser. B, i, p. 64.
[89] C.P. 25(2)/771/1–2 Jas. II Hil. no. 10.
[90] C.P. 25(2)/771/3–4 Jas. II Hil. no. 9.
[91] P.R.O. Inst. Bks. ser. B, iv, p. 136.
[92] C.P. 25(2)/910/2 Anne Mich. no. 1.
[93] Masters, *Hist. Corpus Christi*, ed. Lamb, 437.
[94] Clare Coll. Mun., conveyance 1868.
[95] *Crockford* (1896, 1961–2, 1969–70); ex inf. the rector, and the Domestic Bursary, Clare Coll.
[96] *Rot. Hund.* (Rec. Com.), ii. 580; cf. *Cal. Pat.* 1343–5, 268.
[97] C.U.L., E.D.R., H 1/3, terrier 1638; ibid. C 3/21; Clare Coll. Mun., leases 1681 (abstract), 1751; survey 1714; tithe agreements 1839.
[98] *Rot. Hund.* (Rec. Com.), ii. 582.
[99] C.U.L., E.D.R., H 1/3, terrier 1638.
[1] e.g. Clare Coll. Mun., lease 1751.
[2] C.U.L., E.D.R., D 2/10, f. 60; B 2/18, f. 75v.; B 2/30A, f. 6.
[3] Cf. *Trans. C.H.A.S.* iii. 89.
[4] E 134/28–9 Chas. II Hil./11; Clare Coll. Mun., lease 1681 (abstract); survey 1714.
[5] Ibid. order 1716.
[6] Ibid. leases 1751–1830.
[7] E 134/28–9 Chas. II Hil./11.
[8] Clare Coll. Mun., copies of 1654 decree; C.R.O., R 58/7/1 is a copy of the survey.
[9] E 134/28–9 Chas. II Hil./11; Clare Coll. Mun., survey 1714.
[10] Vancouver, *Agric. in Cambs.* 74.
[11] Clare Coll. Mun., correspondence *c.* 1820.

Under the inclosure Act of 1822 each allotment was divided for tithes in the same proportion as the property for which it was allotted had previously owed tithe to the two churches.[12] St. John's church thereby received tithe from 1,462 a., St. Peter's from 1,424 a.[13] Following the inclosure Clare College's collection of tithes in kind caused sharp disputes.[14] The tithes were finally commuted in 1839, those of each church being valued at £500 a year. Of St. John's tithe-rent-charge £354 was assigned to Clare College, £146 to the vicar.[15]

At inclosure Clare College was allotted *c.* 11 a. for glebe, the vicar of St. John's 35 a., and the rector of St. Peter's *c.* 11 a.[16] The vicarial glebe was sold in 1919, and that of St. Peter's between 1944 and 1960.[17]

Clare College possessed no farmstead in Duxford, but only a tithe-barn which stood a little east of St. John's vicarage.[18] The latter, probably on the original site of the parsonage, stands a little south of St. John's church. In 1783 it was a thatched house in good repair,[19] but by the 1830s was described as an old lath-and-plaster building, occupied only by interloping paupers. It was demolished *c.* 1844, and the vicar, John Clark, built a new brick house with a loan from Queen Anne's Bounty.[20] After the benefices were united the vicarage was let until its sale in 1919,[21] and the rector lived at St. Peter's rectory. That had in 1638 comprised a house, barn, stable, and other farm-buildings.[22] The house stood near the edge of the village, south-west of St. Peter's church. It was said in 1783 to have been occupied for the last 100 years by poor families, although then in tolerable repair.[23] By *c.* 1822 W. H. Markby, rector 1819–66, had rebuilt it as a square grey-brick house in Regency style, with the help of the patron.[24] The new house was sold in 1950,[25] and in 1972 the rector lived in a house in Moorfields Road.[26]

St. John's rectory was taxed at 15 marks in 1217, 16 marks in 1254, and 25 marks in 1291.[27] After the appropriation the vicarage was worth £13 3*s.* 4*d.* in 1535[28] and £20 in 1650 and 1728.[29] In 1812 Queen Anne's Bounty gave £300 and John Clark, the new vicar, £200 to augment the living.[30] About 1830 it was worth *c.* £170 a year.[31] Clark claimed in 1837 that he had raised the income to £195.[32] Shortly before the union of the benefices the vicarage brought in £180 net.[33]

St. Peter's church was taxed at 20 marks in 1217, 18 marks in 1254, and £25 6*s.* 8*d.* in 1276.[34] In 1535 it was worth £21 6*s.* 8*d.*,[35] in 1650 £90, and in 1728 £110.[36] About 1830 it yielded *c.* £430, in 1851 £511, and *c.* 1870 £404 net.[37]

The free chapel or hospital of St. John the Baptist[38] at Whittlesford Bridge, founded by William de Colville (d. 1230),[39] survived until the Reformation. Its patronage was vested in the bishops of Ely,[40] although in 1397 the Crown claimed to present, following the attainder of Thomas, duke of Gloucester.[41] The office of master, rector, or warden was by the 14th century a sinecure, sometimes held in plurality.[42] At the hospital's suppression, *c.* 1548, it was said that the tiled chapel was in decay and no services had been held there for over 7 years. There was then no dwelling-house.[43] The chapel, built of field stones with dressings of freestone, has an undivided chancel and nave. Only a few fragments of walling survive from the 13th-century structure, which was rebuilt in the early 14th century. The western end may have been designed for domestic occupation. For many years the chapel was used as a barn for the adjoining Red Lion inn.[44] Between 1947 and 1954 it was restored by the Ministry of Works, which rebuilt its west end, for preservation as an ancient monument.[45]

William de Colville charged Temple manor with 5 marks a year for a chaplain, still being paid in 1339.[46] Some 21 a. or 35 a. in Duxford, given for obits, was confiscated under Edward VI and sold in 1548 and 1550.[47] The village contained in the early 16th century two guilds, of St. John and St. Peter, the latter recorded in 1489. One was presumably attached to each church.[48] Robert Stythe, vicar of St. John's (d. 1552), left money for a drinking at his burial 'after the custom and manner of the town'.[49] St. John's guildhall stood on a site given before 1536 by Thomas Farnham to the churchwardens,[50] who retained it after the guilds were suppressed until 1583 when it was taken into the lord's hands because they could produce no title-deeds.[51]

[12] Ibid. correspondence 1821–2; Masters, *Hist. Corpus Christi*, 438; 3 Geo. IV, c. 37 (Private, not printed), p. 16; C.R.O., Q/RDc 44.

[13] Masters, *Hist. Corpus Christi*, 435; Clare Coll. Mun., tithe agreement 1839.

[14] Clare Coll. Mun., corr. and cases for counsel *c.* 1825.

[15] Ibid. tithe agreement 1839; H.O. 129/188/1/5/5.

[16] C.R.O., Q/RDz 10, pp. 257–61.

[17] C.U.L., Maps 53(1)/91/183; ex inf. the Church Com.

[18] Clare Coll. Mun., leases 1770 sqq.; map in case for counsel *c.* 1825.

[19] C.U.L., E.D.R., B 7/1, p. 121.

[20] Clare Coll. Mun., corr., vicar to master of Clare 1837–44.

[21] *Kelly's Dir. Cambs.* (1892 and later edns.); C.U.L., Maps 53(1)/91/183.

[22] C.U.L., E.D.R., H 1/3, terrier 1638.

[23] Ibid. B 7/1, p. 121.

[24] Masters, *Hist. Corpus Christi*, 437.

[25] Ex inf. the Church Com.

[26] Ex inf. the rector, the Revd. D. A. Lyon.

[27] *Val. of Norwich*, ed. Lunt, 226, 536, 555; *Tax. Eccl.* (Rec. Com.), 267.

[28] *Valor Eccl.* (Rec. Com.), iii. 504.

[29] Lamb. Pal. MS. 904, f. 263; B.L. Add. MS. 5828, f. 90.

[30] Hodgson, *Queen Anne's Bounty*, 310.

[31] *Rep. Com. Eccl. Revenues*, pp. 346–7.

[32] Clare Coll. Mun., letters 1837; cf. letter 1844.

[33] Ibid. file on reunion 1867–72.

[34] *Val. of Norwich*, ed. Lunt, 226, 536, 555.

[35] *Valor Eccl.* (Rec. Com.), iii. 504.

[36] Lamb. Pal. MS. 904, f. 262; B.L. Add. MS. 5828, f. 90.

[37] *Rep. Com. Eccl. Revenues*, pp. 346–7; H.O. 129/188/1/5/5; Clare Coll. Mun., file on reunion 1867–72.

[38] Cf. *E.D.R.* (1909), 13.

[39] See above.

[40] *Rot. Hund.* (Rec. Com.), ii. 582.

[41] *Cal. Pat.* 1396–9, 251; the reference may be to the chapel in Hinxton.

[42] e.g. *Cal. Papal Reg.* vii. 42, 471. For a list of masters, see *E.D.R.* (1899), 73; cf. *Proc. C.A.S.* x. 380–1.

[43] E 318/2020 m. 5; *Cal. Pat.* 1547–8, 293–4.

[44] e.g. Lysons, *Cambs.* 182.

[45] *Proc. C.A.S.* lii, p. xii; *Arch. Jnl.* cxxiv. 229–30; *Camb. Ind. Press*, 28 Oct. 1960.

[46] *Hospitallers in Eng.* (Camd. Soc. [1st ser.], lxv), 165.

[47] *Cal. Pat.* 1548–9, 48; 1549–51, 410.

[48] Prob. 11/8 (P.C.C. 24 Milles, will of Thos. Swan); B.L. Add. MS. 5861, f. 70.

[49] *Cambs. Local Hist. Counc. Bull.* x. 8–9.

[50] Caius Coll. Mun. XXXV 5, bdle. 1, ct. roll 27 Hen. VIII.

[51] Ibid. bdle. 2, ct. roll 25 Eliz. I.

The incumbents of both livings[52] were apparently resident in the parish in the early 13th century.[53] In the 1270s Walter Barbedor, presumably of the family with land at Hinxton and Ickleton, held St. John's.[54] His successor John Lacy was involved in 1309 in a riot and robbery at Ickleton.[55] John Hinxton, the last rector at St. John's, aided an attack by the earl of Oxford on John Segrave's park at Great Chesterford (Essex).[56] His contemporary at St. Peter's sometimes acted as a royal purveyor.[57] Robert Candlesby, rector there from 1400, obtained a licence for three years' absence,[58] perhaps for study. Few incumbents of either church, however, had attended university before the late 15th century, when St. Peter's began to be held by absentee graduates.[59] John Ward, formerly master of the bridge hospital, held that rectory from 1500 in plurality with Snailwell, where he died in 1526, and paid a parish priest to do the duty at Duxford.[60] Ward's successor, William Capon, master of Jesus College 1516–46, was also a pluralist and non-resident, employing a priest at Duxford.[61] On the poorer living of St. John's Thomas Wentworth, vicar 1446–89,[62] studied canon law while incumbent, and later served as official to the archdeacon of Colchester.[63] The vicars may have been usually resident.[64]

From 1564 to 1567 the two livings were held together by George Chatburn, vicar since 1561,[65] but the joint incumbency was not continued. For many years the better living, St. Peter's, was usually, as before, held by non-residents. Fulk Lloyd, rector 1567–96, a pluralist although no graduate, lived in Wales, leaving Duxford to a curate,[66] as did the later rectors Robert Tinley, 1606–16, archdeacon of Ely, and Henry Smith, 1618–42, master of Magdalene College.[67] The vicars of St. John's were more probably resident. John Lambert, 1572–1621, who from 1588 also held Weeting (Norf.), built up a small estate in Duxford and left £13 for the poor there.[68] His successor William Archer, fellow of Clare College since 1606, was approved by the puritans in 1650, and despite his age retained his living through the Interregnum until his death in 1665.[69] George Chamberlain, presented to St. Peter's rectory by Cambridge University in 1642, was captured by Waller at the siege of Hereford, and had suffered sequestration by 1646.[70] By 1650 he had been replaced by Samuel Mills, considered an able preaching minister.[71] Mills joined the Cambridge Presbyterian classis in 1658[72] but accepted episcopal ordination in 1660.[73]

The union of the two benefices had been suggested in 1650.[74] In 1659 an inquiry promoted by the parishioners of St. Peter's resulted in an order that the two parishes be united,[75] with St. Peter's as the parish church. The patrons and parishioners of St. John's resisted the union on the grounds that neither church could by itself contain all the village's inhabitants and that whereas St. John's stood in the more inhabited part of the town and had the larger churchyard St. Peter's was smaller, was much out of repair, and stood on the outskirts.[76] The parish registers support the implication that St. John's had then the larger congregation.[77] The planned union was forestalled by the Restoration, but rivalry between the congregations apparently persisted. In 1675, after disputes between them, the bishop directed that Henry Wastell, a new vicar who was apparently serving both churches, should alternately read the service and preach in one church on Sunday morning and in the other in the afternoon, since the parishioners could easily attend either.[78]

Thomas Harris, presented to St. Peter's in 1688 and to St. John's also in 1690, held both livings until his death in 1738.[79] After Harris's death Corpus Christi College regularly presented its members as rectors, and Clare began to appoint to the vicarage its own fellows or members, who were usually non-resident.[80] The vicarage was served by the rectors of St. Peter's, who were often formally appointed as curates and usually lived, as Harris had in 1728, in the vicarage.[81] In 1775 Edmund Fisher, rector 1761–1819, normally held services in St. Peter's on Sunday morning and in St. John's in the afternoon for an identical congregation.[82] In 1807 the curate acting for Fisher, then resident at Linton, did the same. At communion, held four times a year in each church, the number of communicants had recently increased to 35.[83] John Clark, vicar 1811–52, was at first resident, but in 1825 was assisting the sick vicar of Hinxton, while the rector served both Duxford churches, which then had 30 to 50 communicants.[84] Clark later withdrew to a Suffolk curacy, leaving Duxford to his colleague, whom he paid as his curate there.[85]

52 For lists see *E.D.R.* (1899), 32, 51.
53 e.g. Caius Coll. Mun. XXXV 1/a, b, f.
54 Ibid. 1/n.
55 *Cal. Pat.* 1307–13, 240.
56 Ibid. 1340–3, 96–7; cf. *Sessions of the Peace* (C.A.S. 8vo ser. lv), 13–14.
57 *Sessions of the Peace*, p. xvi.
58 *E.D.R.* (1898), 90; (1900), 178.
59 e.g. John Williams, 1471–84; John Edmonton d. 1500: Emden, *Biog. Reg. Univ. Camb.* 205, 640.
60 Ibid. 616; Prob. 11/22 (P.C.C. 8 Porch).
61 *Alum. Cantab. to 1751*, i. 290; *E.D.R.* (1912), 184, 244.
62 *E.D.R.* (1902), 141; (1908), 149.
63 Emden, *Biog. Reg. Univ. Camb.* 628.
64 e.g. B.L. Add. MS. 5861, ff. 18v., 22, 25, 70, 101.
65 *E.D.R.* (1914), 295, 309; C.U.L., E.D.R., B 2/3, p. 98; B 2/4, p. 22.
66 C.U.L., E.D.R., B 2/6; D 2/10, f. 153; Bodl. MS. Gough Eccl. Top. 3, f. 50.
67 *Alum. Oxon. 1500–1714*, 1489; *Alum. Cantab. to 1751*, iv. 99; C.U.L., E.D.R., B 2/18, f. 75; B 2/25, f. 10v.; B 2/32, f. 97; *Cambs. Village Doc.* 61.
68 *Alum. Cantab. to 1751*, iii. 37; Prob. 11/138 (P.C.C. 88 Dale).
69 *Alum. Cantab. to 1751*, i. 39; Lamb. Pal. MS. 904, f. 263.
70 *Walker Revised*, ed. Matthews, 78.
71 Lamb. Pal. MS. 904, f. 262.
72 *Bury Classis*, ii (Chetham Soc. N.S. xlii), 190, 202.
73 C.U.L., E.D.R., B 2/58; P.R.O. Inst. Bks. ser. B, i, p. 64.
74 Lamb. Pal. MS. 904, f. 248.
75 Ibid. Comm. xii. c. 1, ff. 93v., 94; xii. c. 2, p. 564.
76 Ibid. iv. 11, p. 246; Clare Coll. Mun., petn. to trustees 1659.
77 C.R.O., TS. copy of bps.' transcripts, 1599–1686.
78 *E.D.R.* (1913), 103; cf. P.R.O. Inst. Bks. ser. B, i, p. 64.
79 See above; *E.D.R.* (1899), 32, 51.
80 See *E.D.R.* (1899), 32, 51; *Alum. Cantab. to 1751*, *1752–1900*, under their names.
81 B.L. Add. MS. 5828, f. 90.
82 C.U.L., E.D.R., C 1/1.
83 Ibid. C 1/4.
84 Ibid. C 1/6.
85 Ibid. C 3/21; cf. Clare Coll. Mun., corr. vicar to master of Clare.

From *c.* 1845 the bishop began to insist that both incumbents reside,[86] and St. John's had its own curate by 1851, when services were still held for the whole village alternately in each church. Morning congregations might amount to 75, afternoon ones to 150, besides 100 Sunday-school children.[87] After Clark's death a new proposal of 1852 to unite the two livings was abandoned because the inhabitants opposed the intended demolition of St. John's church.[88] The proposal was revived in 1867, and Corpus Christi sold its advowson to Clare in 1868. Bitter opposition by the majority of the parishioners, led or instigated as in 1852 by William Long, the principal landowner, prolonged the debate[89] until the union was finally made in 1874.[90] H. J. Carter, vicar since 1865, was presented to the rectory also.[91] In 1877 he had a regular congregation of 550, and many chapel-goers also attended church occasionally. He held three services on Sundays at St. Peter's and communion every six weeks, obtaining an average attendance of 40.[92] In 1897 there were 98 communicants, and Carter thought that about two-thirds of the inhabitants were church-goers.[93] Former members of Clare College continued to be presented as rectors until the 1940s.[94] In the 1960s the size of the congregation was said to be keeping pace with the growth of the village's population.[95]

The church of *ST. JOHN THE BAPTIST*, so called by *c.* 1260,[96] consists of a chancel with north chapel, central tower, and nave with north aisle and south porch. It is built of field stones and clunch. The original fabric of the chancel, nave, and lower part of the tower is 12th-century. The tower is divided from the chancel and nave by Norman arches, of which that to the nave has to the west triple shafts and a billet moulding. The original walls retain internally traces of early medieval painted decoration. The south doorway has also a round arch, but the tympanum under it contains a cross with stepped arms recalling early Anglo-Saxon design.[97] In the 13th century the tower was raised, and a lancet inserted in the south wall of the chancel, which was probably extended eastwards soon after. The east window, probably of the mid 14th century, retained until *c.* 1640 glass with the arms of Clare, de Burgh, and Mortimer, associated with Elizabeth de Burgh, and in the lower lights the kneeling figures of a lady and a knight bearing the arms of Lacy countercharged.[98] The north chapel with its Decorated windows was probably built in the 14th century, perhaps by the man buried under a slab with an inset for the brass of a knight.[99] The north aisle, with the arch from it to the tower, was built in the 15th century, when also the windows of the nave and the south tower window were inserted. The much-repaired south porch was also erected in that period. Stone screens dividing the tower from chancel and nave survived at chest-height in 1742.[1] The nave roof was once covered with wainscot on which painted figures of saints were still visible in 1742.[2] Some early-16th-century pews survive under the tower, and in the 1920s the north chapel still contained other stalls with carved and panelled heads, perhaps once part of a screen.[3]

The chancel windows were out of repair in 1577.[4] In the 17th century the chancel east window was replaced with one of four lights, with straight mullions and no tracery. In 1644 William Dowsing destroyed several inscriptions and 50 pictures.[5] The pulpit was probably 17th-century. It formerly stood near the tower on the north side,[6] but in 1972 was lying upside-down in the nave. The chancel floor formerly contained inscribed brasses to two vicars, Thomas Wentworth (d. 1489) and John Lambert (d. 1621).[7] From the mid 17th century to *c.* 1847 the north chapel was boarded off from the chancel to form a schoolroom. A door was broken through the north wall and a brick chimney built up through the east window.[8] In 1685 the chancel was found to be dangerously cracked, and the communion rails were ordered to be restored,[9] but although the present rails with twisted balusters are of that period, they were not recorded in 1742.[10] In 1783 the chancel windows had recently been cleared of plaster and reglazed.[11] A west gallery inserted probably in the 18th century survived in 1916.[12] The church was very dilapidated in the 1860s,[13] and after the union of benefices it was soon disused except for funerals, and became increasingly derelict.[14] In 1959–64 the north aisle and chapel received a new roof and stone floor.[15] The leaded wooden spire on the tower has a curve, popularly ascribed to an attempt to attach to it a flagstaff for the Diamond Jubilee of 1897.[16]

In the 13th century the church was reasonably equipped with books and ornaments.[17] In 1552 it had two chalices. The tower then contained three bells[18] and six in 1742 and 1783.[19] There were said to be five in the late 19th century,[20] but six remained in 1916 in an old frame designed to hold only three.[21] They included one of 1564 with a black-letter inscription, one by Miles Gray of 1632, one of 1699, and three of 1777 by Edward Arnold of St. Neots.[22] In 1949 they were removed to St. Peter's church.[23] In 1575 James Bedell left £2 to buy a clock for

86 Clare Coll. Mun., file on reunion 1867–72.
87 H.O. 129/188/1/5/5.
88 Clare Coll. Mun., correspondence 1852–3.
89 Ibid. file on reunion 1867–72.
90 *Lond. Gaz.* 15 May 1874, pp. 2566–7.
91 *Crockford* (1896).
92 C.U.L., E.D.R., C 3/26.
93 Ibid. C 3/37.
94 Cf. *Crockford* (1907 and later edns.).
95 Ex inf. the rector.
96 Cf. Caius Coll. Mun. XXXV 1/f.
97 *Proc. C.A.S.* xxx. 63–77.
98 B.L. Add. MS. 5819, f. 57.
99 *Mon. Inscr. Cambs.* 41–2.
1 Palmer, *Wm. Cole*, 93–4.
2 Ibid.
3 Clare Coll. Mun., report from S.P.A.B. 1916; photog. in *Country Life*, 23 Dec. 1922.
4 C.U.L., E.D.R., D 2/10, f. 60.
5 *Trans. C.H.A.S.* iii. 89.
6 Palmer, *Wm. Cole*, 93–4.
7 *Mon. Inscr. Cambs.* 42.
8 Palmer, *Wm. Cole*, 93–4.
9 C.U.L., E.D.R., B 2/59A, f. 20.
10 Palmer, *Wm. Cole*, 93–4.
11 C.U.L., E.D.R., B 7/1, p. 121.
12 Clare Coll. Mun., report 1916.
13 Ibid. file on reunion.
14 Cf. *Kelly's Dir. Cambs.* (1900); Clare Coll. Mun., rep. and corr. 1916; *Country Life*, 23 Dec. 1922.
15 *Camb. Daily News*, 30 Apr. 1959; 21 July 1960; *Camb. News*, 20 Dec. 1963. See above, plate facing p. 112.
16 *Camb. News*. 20, 27, 30 Dec. 1963.
17 *Vetus Liber Arch. Elien.* (C.A.S. 8vo ser. xlviii), 68–9.
18 *Cambs. Ch. Goods, temp. Edw. VI*, 4.
19 Palmer, *Wm. Cole*, 93; C.U.L., E.D.R., B 7/1, p. 121.
20 e.g. *Kelly's Dir. Cambs.* (1858 and later edns.).
21 Clare Coll. Mun., report 1916.
22 *Cambs. Bells* (C.A.S. 8vo ser. xviii), 141.
23 *Camb. Ind. Press*, 28 Oct. 1960.

St. John's church, to strike on its great bell.[24] In 1783 St. John's was said to have registers starting in 1538,[25] but in 1825,[26] as in 1972, none were extant before 1684.

The church of *ST. PETER*, so called by 1275,[27] consists of a chancel, aisled and clerestoried nave, and west tower. It is built of flint and field stones with ashlar dressings. The tower is 12th-century and has two round-arched belfry-windows in each face. It opens to the nave by a wide, low arch. The chancel retains one 12th-century window in the north wall. Later a lancet window was inserted there. About 1310 new work on the south side of the church was begun by Robert Gose, a local farmer; the parishioners agreed to complete and maintain it.[28] It may perhaps be linked with a 14th-century window in the chancel. The three-bay nave was rebuilt in the late 14th or 15th century, its arcades and windows and the chancel arch being Perpendicular in style. The font is probably 12th-century. The nave retained in 1852 a late medieval roof, much defaced.[29] The chancel had before 1742 contained eight stalls on each side, by then removed in favour of pews, and was divided from the nave by a painted screen, since removed.[30] The partly defaced canopied niches on each side of the east window of each aisle perhaps once contained the images of the Virgin, St. Peter, St. Catherine, and St. Margaret mentioned in early-16th-century wills.[31] There were formerly monuments to Richard King (d. 1646), founder of the village school, and Thomas Harris, rector 1688–1738.[32]

The church was in decent repair in 1593,[33] but was alleged by the parishioners of St. John's to be out of repair in 1659.[34] In 1665 the east window was ordered to be cleared of plaster and reglazed,[35] and in 1685 the chancel was cracked.[36] In 1728 the tower was partly repaired in brick. A tall spire was removed because of its weight and the present short one substituted.[37] In 1783, although the fabric was sound, some windows were again blocked with plaster, and much seating was broken.[38] In 1852 some windows lacked mullions.[39] The church had 250 sittings in 1851,[40] but was in little better state than St. John's *c.* 1870.[41] After the benefices were united it was chosen as the sole parish church, and was very thoroughly restored between 1884 and 1891 under the direction of Ewan Christian. The stonework was largely renewed, a small vestry built north of the chancel, the internal fittings mostly replaced, and the sanctuary decorated with marble and mosaic by Powell of White Friars.[42] In 1968–70 the tower was partitioned off as a vestry, and a new organ installed.[43]

The church was well supplied with books in the 13th century.[44] It had two chalices in 1552; the plate includes a cup and paten of 1808. There were 4 bells and a sanctus bell in 1552 and in 1742,[45] but in the 19th and 20th centuries the tower contained only one bell, from the set cast by Edward Arnold in 1777,[46] until the bells from St. John's were installed in 1949.[47] The registers were said in 1783 to begin in 1558,[48] but in 1828[49] and 1972 only those from 1684 survived. Bishops' transcripts for both parishes date from 1599.[50] Both churchyards were closed in 1879, and a new cemetery north of St. John's Road was given by the rector.[51]

NONCONFORMITY. Duxford had few dissenters before the late 18th century. Only one was recorded in 1676.[52]

In 1783 the three or four protestant dissenters in the parish went to a meeting at Fowlmere.[53] The Congregational church at Duxford[54] owes its origin to the labours of John Berridge,[55] who preached there frequently between 1760 and his death in 1793. It is said that Thomas Brown, a shepherd, had preached even earlier. Itinerant preachers sent by Berridge were supported by such Duxford farmers as John Rayner of Temple Farm. About 1792 Berridge's Duxford followers, disappointed in the absentee rector's choice of curate, seceded from the parish church. They were backed by several of the more substantial farmers, such as Rayner, James Robynet, and Richard Hitch; and one, James Teversham, offered for their meetings a barn in Mill Lane which was licensed in 1792.[56] Weekly lectures by neighbouring ministers were begun at once. The new congregation soon called as minister Benjamin Pyne, who bought a site on the main street on which a chapel was built, and licensed in 1794.[57] Pyne remained minister until 1831 and died in 1833. His congregation was drawn partly from such neighbouring villages as Hinxton, Ickleton, and Whittlesford.[58] A continuous series of ministers succeeded him, there being twelve between 1832 and 1922, and a manse was built in St. Peter's Street between 1848 and 1854. In 1859 a schoolroom and vestry were

24 Prob. 11/57 (P.C.C. 6 Pyckering).
25 C.U.L., E.D.R., B 7/1, p. 123.
26 Ibid. C 1/6.
27 Cf. Caius Coll. Mun. XXXV 1/aa.
28 *Vetus Liber Arch. Elien.* (C.A.S. 8vo ser. xlviii), 68–9.
29 *Eccl. Top. Eng.* vi. 154.
30 Palmer, *Wm. Cole*, 93.
31 e.g. B.L. Add. MS. 5861, ff. 76, 81v.
32 *Mon. Inscr. Cambs.* 42.
33 Bodl. MS. Gough Eccl. Top. 3, f. 50.
34 Clare Coll. Mun., petn. 1659.
35 C.U.L., E.D.R., B 2/59, p. 32.
36 Ibid. B 2/59A, f. 21.
37 Palmer, *Wm. Cole*, 93.
38 C.U.L., E.D.R., B 7/1, p. 121.
39 *Eccl. Top. Eng.* vi. 154.
40 H.O. 129/188/1/5/5.
41 Clare Coll. Mun., file on reunion.
42 *Proc. C.A.S.* xxxv. 83; *Kelly's Dir. Cambs.* (1900); *E.D.R.* (1905), 246.
43 Ex inf. the rector.
44 *Vetus Liber Arch. Elien.* (C.A.S. 8vo ser. xlviii), 68–9.
45 *Cambs. Ch. Goods, temp. Edw. VI*, 5; list of ch. plate *penes V.C.H.*; Palmer, *Wm. Cole*, 93.
46 *Kelly's Dir. Cambs.* (1888, 1900, 1937); *Cambs. Bells* (C.A.S. 8vo ser. xviii), 141.
47 See above.
48 C.U.L., E.D.R., B 7/1, p. 123.
49 Ibid. C 1/6.
50 TS. copy in C.R.O. There are gaps in the 1640s.
51 *Lond. Gaz.* 3 Dec. 1878, p. 6911; 10 Jan. 1879, p. 118; *Kelly's Dir. Cambs.* (1883); C.U.L., E.D.R., C 3/26.
52 Compton Census.
53 C.U.L., E.D.R., B 7/1, p. 123.
54 The following account is based, unless otherwise stated, on cuttings from *Haverhill Mag.* (Feb. 1882), in C.R.O., R 58/5, vol. x, pp. 214–16; *Duxford Cong. Church, a short hist.* (1924), pp. 7–20.
55 Cf. *D.N.B.*
56 C.U.L., E.D.R., B 4/1, f. 19v.
57 Ibid. f. 20.
58 Ibid. C 1/4, 6; *Cong. Yr. Bk.* (1860).

built in front of the chapel.[59] Pyne House, built by Pyne next to the chapel, was also bought *c.* 1888.

In 1851 the chapel, with 480 sittings, had a congregation of 350, besides 80 Sunday-school children.[60] In 1877 its congregation averaged 250, some of whom also went to church.[61] About a third of the population were said to be dissenters in 1897, but not all assiduously attended the chapel,[62] which in 1899 had only 75 full members. There were then 10 teachers and 7 lay preachers. Membership fell from 89 in 1905 to 59 in 1925, including Hinxton and Ickleton, and afterwards fluctuated between 40 and 50. In 1967–8 Duxford chapel had 46 members.[63]

EDUCATION. Schoolmasters were recorded at Duxford in 1581 and 1596.[64] Richard King, vicar of Wasenham (Norf.) a native of Duxford,[65] by will proved 1646 bequeathed £300 to endow a school there, and from 1648 his son Robert's executors paid £16 a year for a schoolmaster. Agreements to pay the £300 or settle land worth £17 a year on trustees for the school and other charitable purposes were confirmed in 1657;[66] later it was said that only £120 was actually paid, with which 24 a. at Duxford was bought.[67] By 1659 a schoolroom had been established in St. John's church. The schoolmaster's salary was then £16 a year.[68] John Stallan, schoolmaster in 1679, was alleged to neglect teaching according to King's bequest[69] but died in office in 1701.[70] In 1728 16 children were being taught at the school, whose income was £6 or £7 a year.[71]

In 1783 a decent schoolmaster had, besides £9 from the land, money allowed him by the principal inhabitants.[72] In 1818 he received £27 a year and was teaching 35 children.[73] At inclosure in 1823 King's charity was allotted 19 a.,[74] which yielded in 1837 £26 a year; the master, in office since 1815, was said to be efficient, and was teaching *c.* 35 boys, still in St. John's church. All but 12 very poor pupils paid money for heating to encourage regular attendance. Children from other parishes were admitted on payment.[75] In 1833, however, the school had had only 20 pupils, while 3 other day-schools had between them 36 pupils, paid for by their parents.[76]

In 1837 the schoolmaster also taught a church Sunday school[77] which was started in 1796 and had *c.* 60 pupils in 1825. In 1847 there were 70 pupils and the school was associated with the National Society.[78] In that year a new National day-school was built with the aid of grants on ground east of St. John's church given by Clare College. It included separate schoolrooms for girls and boys, and a master's house;[79] £20 a year was to come from King's endowment, £45 from school-pence.[80] In 1860 there was a certificated teacher with 2 apprentices. The school received four more building grants between 1860 and 1876,[81] and was supposed to have accommodation for 169 pupils from 1880.[82] By 1914 it was divided into mixed and infants' departments.[83] Attendance averaged 76 *c.* 1852, fell to 54 in 1868, but rose to 143 in 1897.[84] Thereafter it fell steadily, except between 1914 and 1918, to 90 in 1927.[85] From 1930 the older children went to Sawston village college.[86] Attendance in 1938 was only 38.[87] In 1960 a new school was opened further west along the street.[88] In 1971 Duxford school was still a Church of England maintained school.[89]

A dissenting Sunday school had *c.* 80 pupils in 1833 and 1851.[90] Some dissenters' children from Duxford may have attended the British school at Ickleton:[91] in 1877 20 children went to schools outside the parish. There was then a night-school in Duxford attended by some 40 young men and boys.[92]

A private boarding school was kept at Duxford in the 1780s,[93] and another in 1833[94] may have been that which was recorded in 1841 and 1861.[95]

CHARITIES FOR THE POOR. In 1562 Lettice Martin of Chrishall (Essex) left lands whose income was to be divided among certain parishes in north-west Essex and south-east Cambridgeshire, including Duxford, whose share was to be 6*s.* 8*d.*[96] Following disputes and lawsuits over the administration of the charity in the 18th century[97] the amount distributed among the parishes was increased. In 1775 Duxford received 13*s.* 4*d.*, distributed to the poor on Lady day,[98] and in 1815[99] and 1837 £1 6*s.*, given to the poor and aged. Later the charity was normally administered with Bedell's charity, mentioned below. When the land was sold in 1901 and

59 *Kelly's Dir. Cambs.* (1900).
60 H.O. 129/188/1/5/12.
61 C.U.L., E.D.R., C 3/26.
62 Ibid. C 3/37.
63 *Cong. Yr. Bk.* (1899 and later edns.).
64 Gibbons, *Ely Episc. Rec.* 180; *V.C.H. Cambs.* ii. 338.
65 *Mon. Inscr. Cambs.* 42.
66 C 93/24/17.
67 Ibid.; B.L. Add. MS. 5819, f. 48v.
68 Clare Coll. Mun., petn. 1659.
69 C.U.L., E.D.R., B 2/66, f. 15v.
70 C.R.O., R 58/5, vol. x, p. 229.
71 B.L. Add. MS. 5828, f. 90.
72 C.U.L., E.D.R., B 7/1, p. 123.
73 *Educ. of Poor Digest*, 58.
74 C.R.O., Q/RDz 10, p. 295.
75 *31st Rep. Com. Char.* 200–1.
76 *Educ. Enquiry Abstract*, 54.
77 *31st Rep. Com. Char.* 201.
78 C.U.L., E.D.R., C 1/6; *Church School Inquiry, 1846–7*, 4–5.
79 *E.D.R.* (1897), 209; C.R.O., 391/P 28.
80 *Church School Inquiry*, *1846–7*, 4–5; Ed. 7/5.
81 *Rep. of Educ. Cttee. of Council, 1860–1* [2828], pp. 125, 529, H.C. (1861), xlix; *1868–9* [4139], p. 507, H.C. (1868–9), xx; *1872–3* [C. 812], p. 385, H.C. (1873), xxiv; *1876–7* [C. 1780-I], p. 740, H.C. (1877), xxix.
82 Ibid. *1880–1* [C. 2948-I], p. 543, H.C. (1881), xxxii.
83 *Bd. of Educ., List 21, 1914* (H.M.S.O.), 26.
84 *Rep. of Educ. Cttee. of Council, 1852–3* [1624], p. 319, H.C. (1852–3), lxxx; *1868–9* [4139], p. 507, H.C. (1868–9), xx; *Schs. in receipt of Parl. Grants, 1896–7* [C. 8546], p. 14, H.C. (1897), lxix.
85 *Bd. of Educ., List 21, 1919* (H.M.S.O.), 15; ibid. *1927*, 15.
86 Black, *Cambs. Educ. Rec.*, 56.
87 *Bd. of Educ., List 21, 1938* (H.M.S.O.), 19.
88 *Camb. News*, 13 Mar. 1964.
89 Ex inf. the headmaster.
90 *Educ. Enquiry Abstract*, 54; H.O. 129/188/1/5/12; cf. *Camb. News*, 27 Dec. 1963.
91 Cf. Ed. 7/5.
92 C.U.L., E.D.R., C 3/26.
93 *Camb. Chron.* 22 Dec. 1787; 17 Apr. 1790.
94 *Educ. Enquiry Abstract*, 54.
95 H.O. 107/76; R.G. 9/1028; R.G. 10/1591; cf. *Gardner's Dir. Cambs.* (1851).
96 Except where otherwise stated, this account is based on *31st Rep. Com. Char.* 200–1; Char. Com. files.
97 For details see *32nd Rep. Com. Char.* H.C. 108, pp. 877–82 (1837–8), xxv.
98 C.U.L., E.D.R., C 1/1; cf. *Char. Don.* i. 100–1.
99 *Poor Law Abstract, 1818*, 33.

stock bought, £52 17*s.* of it was allotted to Duxford, where £1 6*s.* was still being distributed in doles in the 1940s.

James Bedell by will proved 1574 charged his copyhold lands with supplying red and white herrings to the poor of both Duxford parishes during Lent. He also directed that £4, of which £3 should be for St. Peter's parish, be put out as loans for 3-year periods, in the same way as money already supplied by Clare College for St. John's parish.[1] That loan charity was lost but the herring charity survived, and had by the 18th century been changed into a £3 rent-charge, used to buy 1,000 red and 500 white herrings which in 1775 and 1807 were distributed to the poor on Good Friday.[2] In 1837 the distribution was made in November. About 1860 the churchwardens abandoned the vexatious task of handing out herrings piecemeal to the village poor, and distribution ceased until, under a Scheme of 1867, the rent-charge was vested in trustees to provide needy and deserving inhabitants with food, clothing, or other assistance. In the 1940s the £3 was given out in 2*s.* doles. Subsequently distribution became less regular.

Richard King's will of 1646, besides endowing the school, also provided 10*s.* a year for the poor of St. Peter's on Ash Wednesday and 10*s.* for a commemoration sermon. It also directed that the schoolmaster pay £1 a year each to two poor widows.[3] Those charities had lapsed by 1837, but the revival of the latter was recommended. Payments were accordingly being made to poor widows *c.* 1900 in cash or credit at the village shop. In 1904, after the school charity had come under the Board of Education, the payment of £2 was constituted a separate eleemosynary charity, but it continued to be managed by the educational trustees, who supposed that the £2 was charged only on the letting of shooting rights over the charity land. When the shooting was no longer let distribution also ceased until 1949 and afterwards occurred at irregular intervals.

HINXTON

THE PARISH of Hinxton[1] lies on the east bank of the river Cam or Granta, 9 miles south-south-east of Cambridge and 5 miles north-west of Saffron Walden (Essex). The village, which is the only settlement in the parish, stands where the road from Cambridge to Saffron Walden running beside the river meets the edge of the chalk upland. The southern and eastern boundaries of the parish, which are also part of the county boundary, follow one branch of the ancient Icknield Way, and the northern boundary follows the other branch for about ½ mile before diverging to run due east along field boundaries.[2] The river forms the western boundary of the parish for most of its length. Hinxton parish is compact and triangular in shape; its area was 1,503 a. until 1886, when 61 a. west of the river were transferred from Ickleton to Hinxton.[3]

Apart from the river valley, the whole parish lies on the Middle Chalk.[4] The soil is therefore well drained, brown, and chalky, becoming thinner towards the south-east; only in the north-west part of the parish is there a large area of alluvium and gravel, although the land by the river has always been liable to flooding.[5] The western half of Hinxton is flat and low-lying, except for the slight rise on which the village stands, but in the eastern half it slopes gently from 100 to 200 ft., and the eastern boundary stands at the foot of a steeper ascent. The parish has long been agricultural, and its farming is typical of its region in being predominantly arable. In the 19th century Hinxton was also known as good sporting country; it was described in 1884 as one of the best partridge manors in the eastern counties, and one of the fields was called Partridge Hill.[6]

Neolithic, Bronze Age, and Iron Age finds in the valley of the Cam or Granta indicate its use very early as a route from the south into Cambridgeshire.[7] Notwithstanding stray finds from earlier times, however, there is no firm evidence of settlement at Hinxton before the Saxon period, from which its name derives.[8] By 1086 the village was certainly well established, and Domesday Book mentions 38 inhabitants there.[9] Some expansion had taken place by 1279, when one of the two manors had at least 35 tenants, but population had probably fallen by 1377 when 115 people paid the poll tax in the parish.[10] Population appears to have changed little by the 16th century, when 46 inhabitants of Hinxton were taxed in 1525 and there were 43 householders in 1563.[11] Total population probably remained at *c.* 200 throughout the 16th and 17th centuries; there were 111 adults in 1676.[12] The number of inhabitants rose to 230 in 1728 and 269 in 1779,[13] and the 19th century saw a steady increase until Hinxton's population reached its highest point at 465 in 1851.[14] The decline after that date, which was attributed partly to emigration, continued until 1901 by which year the total had fallen to 266. Population in the 20th century has fluctuated between that figure and 325, until 1971 when it was 260.[15]

The village grew along the valley road, and is long but narrow, consisting of one main street 700 yd.

[1] Prob. 11/57 (P.C.C. 6 Pyckering); cf. B.L. Add. MS. 5861, f. 118.
[2] C.U.L., E.D.R., C 1/1; B 7/1, p. 122; C 1/4.
[3] C 93/24/17.

[1] This account was written in 1971.
[2] Fox, *Arch. Camb. Region*, 144–5.
[3] *Census*, 1891.
[4] *Camb. Region* (1938), 9.
[5] *Camb. Region, 1965*, 84; O.S. Map 6″, Cambs. LIV. SE. (1903 edn.).
[6] C.U.L., Maps bb. 53(1)/88/12.
[7] Fox, *Arch. Camb. Region*, 7–8, 24, 30, 112, Map V.
[8] *P.N. Cambs.* (E.P.N.S.), 94.
[9] *V.C.H. Cambs.* i. 361, 363, 385, 392.
[10] *Rot. Hund.* (Rec. Com.), ii. 584–5; *East Anglian*, N.S. xii. 241.
[11] E 179/81/147 mm. 2–3 (the return of the first assessment of the subsidy, in 1524, is incomplete for Hinxton); B.L. Harl. MS. 594, f. 200.
[12] See pp. 280–1; Compton Census.
[13] C.U.L., E.D.R., B 8/1, f. 18; ibid. Add. MS. 5821, f. 5.
[14] *Census*, 1831, 1851.
[15] Ibid. 1861–1971.

long, with lanes running off it on both sides. Towards the northern end of the high street the Duxford road runs west to the river and crosses it at a ford. A similar road south of the village crosses to Ickleton by the only bridge in the parish. The high street once continued *c.* 200 yd. further south, to a point just south of Hinxton Hall, but, when the park around the Hall was made between 1833 and 1886, the street was cut short outside its gates and the Ickleton road was diverted to run round the north-west edge of the grounds. At the same time New Road, from the Hall gates east to the main road, was built.[16] The position of the village street, parallel to and *c.* 250 yd. west of the main road from Cambridge to Saffron Walden, suggests that the main road once ran through the village but has been moved. North of the village its line may be traced from old field boundaries as a continuation of the high street, while to the south an extension of the street and the probable course of the original road formed the boundary of early inclosures.[17] The village street and the main road were separate by 1615.[18] The main road was turnpiked in 1724, under the same Act as the road from Stump Cross to Newmarket, and both were disturnpiked by an Act of 1870.[19] The Royston–Newmarket road, which forms part of Hinxton's northern boundary, was a turnpike from 1769 to 1874, and a turnpike-house was built at Whittlesford Bridge.[20]

Sixteenth-century tax-lists show at least three substantial farmers in Hinxton,[21] and the Old Manor, Lordship Farm, Hall Farm, and Oak House all date from that period. The Red Lion is a 17th-century building, and has been used as a public house since at least 1841; there was an inn at Hinxton by 1744,[22] and the Red Lion's unusual plan suggests that it may have been built for that purpose. The narrow frontages of most of the houses of the 17th century and earlier suggest that the street was continuously built up. The many gaps between them may be partly due to serious fires: in 1665 or 1666 a fire damaged 'almost half the town' and the number of hearths taxed fell from 131 in 1664 to 99 in 1666;[23] major fires were also recorded in 1740 and 1744,[24] but there was apparently little rebuilding. The only substantial house of the 18th century is Hinxton Hall, originally of modest size, at the southern end of the high street.

The population increase of the 19th century led to further building. For the first time Hinxton had resident landlords, and the Green family at the Hall took a philanthropic interest in the village. Four cottages opposite the Red Lion date from *c.* 1820, and six more were built east of the high street and further south before 1886.[25] The 19th century also saw the building of the Congregational chapel in 1871, a new school in 1872, and the only houses away from the village when Hinxton Grange was erected *c.* 1835.

The village continued to grow in the early 20th century. By 1904 there was a reading room, which was converted into a village hall in 1968.[26] A row of council houses was built in North End Road before the Second World War, and a motor filling-station flourished briefly *c.* 1933.[27] A few houses east of the street were built in the 1950s, and in the 1960s bungalows were built in Church Green and houses opposite in the high street. In spite of this infilling, however, the village was losing population and facilities. The King William IV public house, open by 1841, was closed *c.* 1950, as were both the chapel and school by 1961; all three were used as private houses in 1971.[28]

The main railway line from London to Cambridge, which follows the Cam or Granta valley and crosses the parish boundary several times, was opened in 1845. A branch line from Great Chesterford (Essex) to Newmarket was opened in 1848, but on the completion in 1851 of the line from Cambridge to Six Mile Bottom, the section between Chesterford and Six Mile Bottom was closed.[29] Its course, close to the road from Stump Cross to Newmarket, was still visible in 1971.

MANORS AND OTHER ESTATES. By 1086 Picot the sheriff had received for two manors 15½ hides in Hinxton once held by 20 sokemen, mostly King Edward's men.[30] They passed with the rest of his property to the Peverel family. The estate, held originally as 1 knight's fee, descended to Asceline de Waterville, a sister and coheir of William Peverel (d. after 1147), and was eventually divided between her two daughters.[31]

One moiety of *HINXTON* manor was assigned to her daughter Asceline, whose son Roger Torpel inherited her lands in 1220.[32] On his death in 1225 the manor descended to his son Roger (d. 1229) whose son William died under age in 1242. The estate then passed to Roger's daughter Asceline,[33] later married to Ralph de Camoys (d. 1259). It was next held by their son Ralph (d. 1277), who was succeeded by his son John,[34] who held it as ½ fee in 1284. By 1289 he had sold the manor to Sir John Lovetot,[35] who re-sold it in 1290 to Walter Stourton (d. by 1302) and his wife Gillian who possessed it in 1302 and 1316.[36] Their son John inherited the manor *c.* 1325, and settled it in 1326 on himself and his wife Alice.[37] He was dead by 1346, but the manor remained with Alice until her death in 1374 when

[16] C.R.O., Q/RDc 47; O.S. Map 1/2,500, Cambs. LIX. 4 (1886 edn.).
[17] C.R.O., Q/RDc 47.
[18] C.U.L., E.D.R. H 1/4, terrier 1615.
[19] Stump Cross Roads Turnpike Act, 10 Geo. I, c. 12; Annual Turnpike Acts Continuance Act 1870, 33 & 34 Vic. c. 73.
[20] Bourn Bridge Road Turnpike Act, 8 & 9 Geo. III, c. 86; Annual Turnpike Acts Continuance Act 1873, 36 & 37 Vic. c. 90; C.U.L. Add. MS. 5821, f. 71.
[21] e.g. E 179/81/147 mm. 2–3; E 179/82/214 m. 1.
[22] H.O. 107/76; C.U.L., Add. MS. 5821, f. 54v.
[23] W. A. Bewes, *Church Briefs*, 280; E 179/84/437 rot. 105d.; see below, p. 280.
[24] Bewes, *Church Briefs*, 319; Palmer, *Wm. Cole*, 98.
[25] O.S. Map 1/2,500, Cambs. LIX. 4 (1886 edn.).
[26] *Kelly's Dir. Cambs.* (1904); *Camb. News*, 1 Aug. 1968.
[27] Ex inf. S. Cambs. R.D.C.; *Kelly's Dir. Cambs.* (1933).
[28] H.O. 107/76; local information; *Camb. Ind. Press*, 19 May 1961.
[29] *V.C.H. Cambs.* ii. 132–3.
[30] *V.C.H. Cambs.* i. 392.
[31] Ibid. v. 6; cf. *Liber de Bernewelle*, 255–6.
[32] *Ex. e Rot. Fin.* (Rec. Com.), i. 46.
[33] Ibid. 133, 137; *Cal. Pat.* 1232–47, 301.
[34] *Ex. e Rot. Fin.* ii. 303–4; *Cal. Inq. p.m.* ii, pp. 129–30.
[35] *Feud. Aids*, i. 137; *Cal. Inq. p.m.* ii, p. 437.
[36] *Cal. Chart. R.* 1257–1300, 356; *Feud. Aids*, i. 144, 155.
[37] *Cal. Close*, 1323–7, 523; *Cal. Pat.* 1324–7, 270.

she was buried in Hinxton church. Alice's daughter and heir Gillian Talmage had already *c.* 1371 granted the reversion of the manor to Sir William Clopton and his feoffees.[38] When Sir William died in 1378 it passed to his son,[39] Sir William Clopton the younger, who granted Hinxton in 1382 to Sir Thomas Skelton, later a chief steward of the duchy of Lancaster.[40] Before his death in 1416 Skelton had acquired the other purparties of the manor, being said to hold a whole fee in 1401, as were his successors in 1428.[41]

On the division of the manor in the 12th century the other moiety, also called *HINXTON*, was assigned to Asceline de Waterville's daughter Maud who married William de Dive. On her death in 1228 it was divided between her three granddaughters, whose descendants each held $\frac{1}{6}$ knight's fee.[42]

The first granddaughter was Maud (d. 1275), wife of Saher St. Andrew, who gave her third in 1268 to her younger son Laurence (d.s.p.).[43] On Maud's death, therefore, the lands passed to her grandson Roger St. Andrew, son of her elder son Robert.[44] Roger came of age *c.* 1281 and settled his third of the manor in 1307 upon his son Richard St. Andrew.[45] The land descended from Richard (d. 1330) to his son Sir John (d. 1360), whose son John died in 1368 and was succeeded by his brother Edmund.[46] Probably Edmund St. Andrew granted the property in Hinxton to Sir Thomas Skelton, to whom Robert St. Andrew, another son of Sir John, and Sir John's widow Gillian confirmed the grant in 1384.[47]

The second of Maud de Dive's three granddaughters, Alice, married Richard de Mucegros. She and her husband were both living in 1243. In 1279 their third of the manor was held of the heirs of Richard's son Robert de Mucegros (d. 1254)[48] by Walter of Glemsford, vicar of Hinxton from *c.* 1259 (d. 1299), whose heir was Thomas of Glemsford, son of Walter's kinsman Richard.[49] In 1323 Thomas settled the estate on his daughter Margery and her husband Robert Reyner. On Margery's death in 1374 it passed to their son Stephen, a cleric.[50]

The third granddaughter of Maud de Dive was Asceline, who married Richard de Mucegros's brother Simon. Both were still living in 1243.[51] Their son and heir John died in 1266 leaving his sisters Alice and Agatha as heirs to that third.[52] Alice, who married Ralph de Dive, tenant in 1279, died in 1305 and her purparty passed to Agatha's son John Ratingden.[53] He granted it in 1318 to Thomas Stevene (d. by 1335), whose son Andrew was succeeded in 1349 by his sister Maud Oky.[54] When she died in 1361 her heir was her cousin Ives (or Eudes) atte Ash who was succeeded in 1368 by his son John,[55] who came of age in 1385. By 1401 both those thirds had presumably been acquired by Sir Thomas Skelton.[56]

The reunited manors were granted by Sir Thomas in 1416 to Richard Vere, earl of Oxford, and his wife Alice.[57] Alice, who later married Nicholas Thorley (d. 1442), held them from the earl's death in 1417 to her own death in 1452.[58] Both Alice's son John and her grandson John, earls of Oxford, forfeited their lands to the Crown as Lancastrians and the land was granted in 1471 to Richard, duke of Gloucester, who as king granted it in 1483 to John Howard, duke of Norfolk.[59] The manors were restored in 1485 to John, 13th earl of Oxford (d. 1513), who granted them in 1494 to Earl's Colne priory (Essex).[60] Upon its dissolution in 1536 its site and property were immediately regranted to the earl of Oxford.[61] The Veres remained lords of the manor at Hinxton, until in 1588 Edward, the 17th earl, was forced by his debts to sell it to John Machell of Hackney (Mdx.). Machell, being himself indebted to Sir James Deane, a London alderman and draper, was induced to sell the manor in 1597 to Sir James's brother Richard;[62] Machell's family was still trying to recover the estate in 1641.[63] On Richard Deane's death in 1601 his property passed to Sir James, who died in 1608 without issue, devising his estate in Hinxton to be divided equally between five of his nephews, Richard and James Holdip and Walter, John, and James Chamberlain.[64] Two-fifths were immediately purchased from the Holdips by Edward Dod, a former fellow of Jesus College, Cambridge, resident in Hinxton.[65] He died in 1616 leaving it to his son Thomas[66] (d. 1670). Thomas devised those two-fifths of the manor to his son Edward,[67] from whom they were bought in 1676 by Robert Flack, an attorney of Linton.[68]

The remaining three-fifths were held in 1624 by John and James Chamberlain, whose descendants sold them to Robert Flack and his son John in 1697.[69]

38 *Feud. Aids*, i. 161; *Cal. Inq. p.m.* xiv, p. 208–9; *Mon. Inscr. Cambs.* 229.
39 *Cal. Inq. p.m.* xv, p. 8; *Cal. Pat.* 1370–4, 117; 1374–7, 246.
40 *Cal. Pat.* 1381–5, 183; Somerville, *Hist. Duchy Lancaster*, i. 367, 427.
41 *Mon. Inscr. Cambs.* 82; *Feud. Aids*, i. 175, 180.
42 *V.C.H. Cambs.* v. 141, 180; *Rot. Hund.* (Rec. Com.), ii. 584–5.
43 *Cal. Inq. p.m.* ii, p. 75.
44 Ibid.; not Maud's nephew as suggested in *Cal. Fine R.* 1272–1307, 115.
45 *Cal. Inq. p.m.* ii, p. 195; *Cal. Pat.* 1301–7, 535; *Cal. Close*, 1313–18, 259.
46 *Cal. Inq. p.m.* vii, p. 235; x, p. 467; xii, p. 273.
47 *Cal. Close*, 1381–5, 448–9; cf. *Feud. Aids*, i. 175.
48 K.B. 26/126 rot. 12; *Rot. Hund.* (Rec. Com.), ii. 584–5; *Cal. Inq. p.m.* ii, p. 195. Rob. de Mucegros was said to hold the manor *c.* 1285: *Feud. Aids*, i. 137; but Alice's son Rob. and her great-grandson Rob. were dead by 1281: F. T. S. Houghton, 'The Family of Muchgros', *Trans. Birm. Arch. Soc.* xlvii. 24, 26.
49 *Cal. Inq. p.m.* iii, p. 389.
50 *Cal. Pat.* 1321–4, 292; *Cal. Inq. p.m.* xiv, p. 29.
51 K.B. 26/126 rot. 12.
52 *Cal. Inq. p.m.* i, p. 199.
53 *Feud. Aids*, i. 144; *Rot. Hund.* (Rec. Com.), ii. 585; *Cal. Inq. p.m.* iv, p. 187.
54 *Cal. Pat.* 1317–21, 142; 1334–8, 187; *Cal. Inq. p.m.* ix, p. 253.
55 *Cal. Inq. p.m.* xi, p. 148; xii, p. 426.
56 Ibid. xvi, pp. 34–5; *Feud. Aids*, i. 175.
57 *Cal. Pat.* 1416–22, 6, 54.
58 *Cal. Close*, 1413–19, 418; 1422–9, 144; 1441–7, 112; 1447–54, 310; *Feud. Aids*, i. 180.
59 *Cal. Pat.* 1461–7, 193; 1467–77, 297; 1476–85, 359.
60 *Cal. Close*, 1485–1500, p. 226.
61 *L. & P. Hen. VIII*, xi, p. 89.
62 C 3/267/9.
63 C 2/Jas. I/C 21/23; Hist. MSS. Com. 3, *4th Rep., H.L.*, 76.
64 *V.C.H. Hants* iv. 134; Prob. 11/111 (P.C.C. 52 Windebanck).
65 C.P. 25(2)/277/8 Jas. I Trin. no. 5; *Alum. Cantab. to 1751*, ii. 150.
66 Prob. 11/150 (P.C.C. 136 Hele, will of Edw. Dodd).
67 Prob. 11/332 (P.C.C. 18 Penn).
68 C.P. 25(2)/633/28 Chas. II Trin. no. 10.
69 C 2/Jas. I/C 21/23; C.P. 25(2)/815/9 Wm. III Trin. no. 4.

Nevertheless the Flacks claimed to hold only four-fifths in 1698, when the manor was settled on Anne Barrington on her marriage to John Flack.[70] Six years later, however, Robert devised the four-fifths to his own wife Anne, who died soon after him, for life and then to trustees for his infant grandson Barrington Flack, the child of John and Anne.[71] After 1704 the manor was regarded as undivided.

Anne Flack married as her second husband Sutton John Cony, and they and Barrington Flack were lords of the manor in 1725.[72] After Cony's death in 1748 Anne retained part of the lordship until her own death, probably in 1755.[73] Barrington Flack died in 1749, having devised his estate to his wife Susanna for life and then to her brother Fitzwilliams Barrington.[74] Susanna Flack was still in sole possession of the manor in 1775, but by 1781 it had passed to her brother,[75] who sold it to Ebenezer Hollick of Whittlesford (d. 1792).[76] Ebenezer left the manor to his nephew William Hollick. On William's death in 1817 it passed to his daughter Anne and her husband Wedd William Nash, a Royston solicitor who had for many years acted as William Hollick's steward at Hinxton.[77] Nash's heir, his grandson Charles Nash, lord by 1858, was succeeded in 1869 by his son Charles Herbert Nash.[78] All Nash's lands and rights at Hinxton were sold in 1884 to Major E. H. Green de Freville (formerly Green) of Hinxton Hall.[79] The lordship and lands passed by sale *c.* 1899 to P. L. Hudson, who resold them in 1900.[80] By 1904 the manor was held by R. B. Wilkinson (d. 1931), who gave it to trustees between 1916 and 1922. His brother-in-law, C. L. P. Robinson, was described as squire of Hinxton at his death in 1936.[81]

Two hides in Hinxton, held before 1066 by Siward from Earl Harold, became after the Conquest part of the bishop of Lincoln's fee, and were held in 1086 by Robert.[82] By *c.* 1235 that land was held as ½ knight's fee by William Barbedor (I), after whose family it was named *BARBEDORS* manor.[83] Probably by 1279 the manor was held by William's younger son Roger, the elder son, William (II), having entered a religious order.[84] Both Roger and his son William (III) were living in 1303–4. In 1335 George Barbedor died possessed of the manor, which passed to his infant son William (IV).[85] Sir Philip Limbury had probably acquired it by 1360. On his death at Constantinople in 1367 his lands passed to his wife Joan[86] (d. 1388), and next to his daughter Elizabeth, wife of Sir Thomas Trivet (d. 1388).[87] By 1391 Elizabeth was probably remarried to Sir Thomas Swinburne. In 1408 they sold the manor to Sir Thomas Skelton.[88] Skelton apparently held it at his death in 1416, but in 1428, with the two manors which Skelton had granted to Richard, earl of Oxford, in 1416, it was held by Alice, formerly the earl's wife.[89] Thereafter it descended with the other Hinxton manors.

Each of the Hinxton manors had at least one house attached to it in the late 13th or early 14th century.[90] That of the St. Andrew manor was described as ruinous in 1330, but two years later part of it was assigned as dower.[91]

There was a single manor-house by *c.* 1600, when the manor court was held in its courtyard.[92] The house was said in 1698 to adjoin Dovehouse Close, an area west of the high street at the southern end of the village,[93] and may possibly be identified with the house known in the 20th century as the Old Manor. The house appears to have been built *c.* 1500 as a court-house and to have been converted for occupation as a manor-house about 100 years later. It was extensively restored in the 1960s. Lordship Farm was the manor farm by 1802, and was later occupied by the lord's steward.[94] Its site close to the mill, and the existence of a moat partly surrounding it, suggest that an earlier manor-house may have stood there. At least one wing of the present house is of the 16th century, but it was remodelled and extended in the earlier 19th century.

As both lord of the manor and farmer of the rectory, Wedd William Nash was able at inclosure in 1833, by exchanging parcels between the manorial and rectorial allotments, to consolidate his holding so that it covered almost all the northern half of the parish; *c.* 1835 he built a house, Hinxton Grange, on his new estate,[95] and also a lodge on the road from Cambridge to Saffron Walden, a farmstead later known as New Farm, and three cottages.[96] The lodge had been pulled down by 1971. The Nash family lived at the Grange until *c.* 1875 when they left Hinxton.[97] Their whole estate of over 1,000 a., including Hinxton Grange, New farm, Lordship farm, and 15 cottages in the village, was purchased in 1884 by the de Frevilles, and thereafter passed with the de Freville estate.[98]

Barnwell priory, besides the impropriate rectory, which was leased to William Barbedor (I) in the mid 13th century,[99] apparently owned other small plots

[70] C.R.O., R 57/24/1/12.
[71] Prob. 11/491 (P.C.C. 254 Eedes).
[72] C.R.O., Linton par. reg. TS.; R 57/24/1/54A.
[73] Ibid. R 59/5/13/1; Linton par. reg. TS., if Anne Flack (d. 1755) was the same person as Anne Cony.
[74] Prob. 11/773 (P.C.C. 281 Lisle).
[75] C.R.O., R 57/24/1/25; R 57/24/1/54F.
[76] Prob. 11/1223 (P.C.C. 496 Fountain, will of Fitzwilliams Barrington); C.R.O., R 58/5/10, p. 304. The churchwardens who stated in 1795 that William Vachell was lord of the manor appear to have confused ownership of Hinxton Hall with the lordship: C.U.L., E.D.R., B 7/11.
[77] Prob. 11/1220 (P.C.C. 337 Fountain); Prob. 11/1596 (P.C.C. 481 Effingham).
[78] *Kelly's Dir. Cambs.* (1858, 1875).
[79] C.U.L., Maps bb. 53(1)/88/12; *Kelly's Dir. Cambs.* (1888).
[80] C.R.O., R 57/24/1/50–1.
[81] *Kelly's Dir. Cambs.* (1904 and later edns.); C.R.O., 331/Z 6, 1931, July, p. 62; 331/Z 7, 1936, Nov. p. 88.
[82] *V.C.H. Cambs.* i. 363.
[83] *Liber de Bernewelle*, 255; C.P. 25(1)/30/94 no. 6.
[84] *Rot. Hund.* (Rec. Com.), ii. 584–5; *Feud. Aids*, i. 137; *Liber de Bernewelle*, 156.
[85] C.P. 25(1)/26/49 no. 2; *Cal. Inq. p.m.* vii, p. 452.
[86] *Cal. Inq. p.m.* xii, p. 129; *Cal. Close*, 1364–8, 350.
[87] *Cal. Inq. p.m.* xvi, pp. 205, 297–8.
[88] C.P. 25(1)/289/56 no. 222; C.P. 25(1)/30/94 no. 6.
[89] Prob. 11/2B (P.C.C. 34 Marche, will of Sir Thos. Skelton); *Feud. Aids*, i. 181.
[90] C 133/16 no. 9; C 133/116 no. 21; *Cal. Inq. p.m.* iii, p. 389.
[91] C 135/25 no. 1; C 135/34 no. 9.
[92] Sta. Cha. 8/127/16.
[93] C.R.O., R 57/24/1/12; R 57/24/1/47.
[94] C.U.L., Add. MS. 5821, f. 49; *Gardner's Dir. Cambs.* (1851).
[95] C.R.O., Q/RDz 10; ibid. 296/P 18.
[96] Ibid. R 57/24/1/51.
[97] *Kelly's Dir. Cambs.* (1879 and later edns.).
[98] C.U.L., Maps bb. 53(1)/88/12; C.R.O., R 57/24/11/2.
[99] *Liber de Bernewelle*, 156–7.

partly leased after its dissolution with the rectory;[1] other former Barnwell property was sold in 1570–2.[2]

The rectory estate, belonging to the bishop of Ely from 1562, consisted of tithes of corn and hay and a farm with *c.* 80 a. dispersed in Church, Middle, and Bridge fields, which was let on long leases for years or lives.[3] From 1535 to *c.* 1577 the lessee was John Baker, who was succeeded by his stepson Thomas Norton of Hinxton.[4] Although the Crown granted leases to Francis Neale, the bishop's auditor, in 1590 and 1593 while the bishopric was vacant,[5] Thomas Norton still occupied the farm, presumably as undertenant, in 1595 and was succeeded by his daughter Mary.[6] The head-lease was granted to Sir Thomas Smith, clerk of the Parliaments and the Privy Council, and his family in 1601, 1604, and 1608,[7] under whom the farmer from 1610 until his death in 1633 was Sir Edward Hinde, who had married Mary Norton.[8] Sir Edward's second wife, Barbara, retained possession until at least 1648 and probably until her death in 1667, having obtained in 1640 a lease to Sir Thomas Dayrell, her son by a previous marriage.[9] Thereafter the Dayrells held the rectory for several generations, though after *c.* 1660 they lived at Castle Camps and Shudy Camps and not at Hinxton.[10] In 1664 and 1666 Sir Thomas possessed an 11-hearth house, the largest in the village, occupied in 1674 by William Nunn.[11] William Hollick purchased the lease from Marmaduke Dayrell in 1811 and devised it in 1817 to his daughter,[12] whose husband Wedd William Nash was lessee in 1820 and 1836.[13] In 1833 the rectory farm-house stood west and south of the churchyard, but the site was empty by 1884. At inclosure in 1833 42 a. were allotted to the impropriator for glebe and 193 a. for tithes. The exchanges made by Nash with the bishop's consent between rectorial and manorial land meant that the former manor-house became part of the rectory estate; in 1884, however, it was included in the sale of the Nash family's lands in Hinxton.[14]

In 1506 the Cambridge college of Michaelhouse was licensed to acquire land in mortmain in Hinxton.[15] Soon afterwards the college owned *c.* 75 a. in the three fields and a tenement in the village.[16] The whole estate was surrendered to the Crown in 1546 to be immediately regranted to Trinity College as part of its original endowment.[17] The college was allotted 14 a. at inclosure, and held 17½ a. in 1873, which was sold in 1902–3 to R. B. Wilkinson.[18]

The first substantial house on the site of Hinxton Hall was built, probably after 1737, by Joseph Richardson of Horseheath, who owned it from 1748. Richardson's friend William Cole described it as 'a pretty neat box'.[19] The property was sold in 1748 to Thomas Brown of Ickleton, whose nephew Richard Holden settled it on his daughter Mary.[20] Mary's first husband, John Bromwell Jones, pulled down Richardson's house and built Hinxton Hall between 1748 and 1756.[21] Mary outlived her second husband John Younghusband and in 1775 surrendered her estate to her daughter Mary and son-in-law William Vachell, who were already resident at the Hall.[22] Each owner had added to the property, and Vachell continued to acquire land until in 1798 he sold an estate of 130 a. to Edward Green.[23] Green died in 1804, directing that his estate should be sold; the purchaser, Jonathan Miles, mortgaged it back to Green's family which continued to live at the Hall.[24] In 1806 Miles sold the Hall with 139 a.;[25] it was re-sold in 1832,[26] and was occupied by Charles Newberry in 1833.[27] Edward Humphrys Green, the son of Edward Green, was resident and probably owned the Hall from *c.* 1834.[28] The park had grown to 13½ a. by 1860.[29] Both Green and his cousin Edward Henry Green, who succeeded him in 1868, took the name de Freville.[30] The Hall, sold with the rest of their estate *c.* 1899, and again in 1900,[31] was subsequently owned by R. B. Wilkinson and then by his trustees, and was occupied from *c.* 1917 to 1953 by the Robinson family.[32] By 1953 it belonged to Col. R. P. W. Adeane of Babraham, who in that year sold it with the surrounding park to Tube Investments Ltd. for use as research laboratories.

Hinxton Hall is a substantial red-brick house. The central portion, which has principal fronts of five bays, and is of two storeys with an attic, was built in the mid 18th century, and partly remodelled, inside and out, in the late 18th or early 19th century. Those alterations coincided with the enlargement of the house by the addition of two-storeyed projecting wings. The principal, north-eastern, room in the new work was decorated with wall-paintings in the Pompeian style.[33] The house was further enlarged to the south in the early 20th century. New buildings in the grounds for laboratories and staff facilities were erected by Tube Investments between 1954 and 1958,[34] although the 19th-century stables and

1 *Trans. C.H.A.S.* i. 371.

2 *Cal. Pat.* 1569–72, pp. 345, 347, 370, 402; cf. *East Anglian*, N.S. vi. 223.

3 C.U.L., E.D.R., H 1/4, terrier 1639; Lamb. Pal. MS. 908, f. 74.

4 S.C. 6/Hen. VIII/7286 rot. 7d.; C.U.L., E.D.R., B 2/10, f. 36; Prob. 11/67 (P.C.C. 32 Watson, will of John Baker).

5 *Cal. S.P. Dom.* 1581–90, 676; C 66/1400 m. 34.

6 C 66/1429 m. 24; C.U.L., E.D.R., B 2/18, f. 31.

7 B.L. Add. MS. 5847, f. 16.

8 C.U.L., E.D.R., B 2/30A, f 6v.; B 2/40A, f. 6; *Visit. Cambs.* (Harl. Soc. xli), 67.

9 *Cambs. Village Doc.* 65; Lamb. Pal. MS. 908, ff. 74–5; *Mon. Inscr. Cambs.* 81.

10 B.L. Add. MS. 9412, f. 76; see above, pp. 40, 51.

11 E 179/84/437 rot. 105d.; E 179/244/22 f. 91; E 179/244/23 rot. 87d.

12 C.U.L., Add. MS. 5821, f. 20; Prob. 11/1596 (P.C.C. 481 Effingham).

13 Hinxton Incl. Act, 60 Geo. III & 1 Geo. IV, c. 3 (Private, not printed); C.U.L., E.D.R., C 3/21.

14 C.R.O., Q/RDz 10; C.U.L., Maps 53(1)/88/4.

15 *Cal. Inq. p.m. Hen. VII*, iii, p. 600.

16 S.C. 11/7.

17 *L. & P. Hen. VIII*, xxi (2), pp. 147, 343.

18 C.R.O., Q/RDz 10; *Rep. Com. Univ. Income* [C. 856-II], p. 431, H.C. (1873), xxxvii (3); Trin. Coll. Mun., college accts. 1903.

19 C.R.O., R 57/24/1/47; Palmer, *Wm. Cole*, 98.

20 C.R.O., R 57/24/1/47; inscr. to Mary Vachell in Hinxton church.

21 Palmer, *Wm. Cole*, 98; see above, plate facing p. 128.

22 C.R.O., R 57/24/1/25; Palmer, *Wm. Cole*, 98.

23 C.R.O., R 57/24/1/28.

24 Ibid. R 57/24/13A/5; R 57/24/1/47.

25 C.R.O., R 57/24/1/52.

26 *Camb. Chron.* 11 May 1832.

27 C.R.O., Q/RDz 10.

28 Ibid. R 57/24/13D/3.

29 Ibid. R 57/24/13D/8.

30 Ibid. R 57/24/13D/7; R 57/24/24/6.

31 Ibid. R 57/24/1/50–1.

32 *Kelly's Dir. Cambs.* (1904 and later edns.); local information.

33 See above, plate facing p. 113.

34 Ex. inf. Tube Investments Ltd.

much of the setting of lawns and trees have been preserved.

An early addition to the Hall estate was a copyhold farm centred on a house now in New Road. In the 16th and 17th centuries it belonged to the Howsdens, a prominent yeoman family of Hinxton, and was acquired from them by Henry Meriton, rector of Oxburgh (Norf.), who sold the farm-house and 13 a. in 1681 to Arthur Joscelyn of Babraham. Arthur's son and namesake succeeded in 1699.[35] Joscelyn's daughter married William Greaves, vicar of Little Abington, who inherited her large fortune and estate.[36] The house and 73 a. were sold to William Vachell by Greaves in 1771, and bought by Edward Green in 1798.[37]

Ameys farm, which grew from 79 a. of freehold in the 18th century to 219 a. of freehold and copyhold by 1803, was named from the Amey family whose first member in Hinxton was apparently Roger, John Machell's steward of the manor in 1588.[38] The estate descended in the family until 1742, when it passed on the foreclosure of a mortgage to John Hanchett of Ickleton, who sold it in 1752 to George Saville of Horseheath. Thomas Saville, George's cousin, inherited the farm in 1757. In 1758 Thomas's daughter Ellen Pettit sold it to Charles Amey, whose daughter Martha Claydon held it until 1803,[39] when it was purchased by Edward Green.[40]

ECONOMIC HISTORY.

The largest estate in Hinxton in 1086 was that of Picot the sheriff. Seven hides and 3 yardlands were in his demesne, which was large enough for 4 plough-teams although only one was kept. There were 12 bordars, each holding 1 a., and 20 *villani* with 9 ploughs between them had replaced the 20 sokemen there before the Conquest. The other small estates contained arable for 5 plough-teams; of the 4 which were there, 3 belonged to the 9 *villani*. There were also 5 bordars, of whom 2 held 1 a. each, and 2 *servi*. The livestock recorded included 268 sheep. The number of pigs[41] suggests the presence of woodland.

The manor held by Ralph de Camoys until 1277 was then said to include 160 a. of demesne arable, 4 a. of meadow, and a little pasture. His 13 villeins owed services worth £4 1*s.* 7½*d.*, and 14 cottars services worth 25*s.* 5*d.* The rents of free tenants yielded 11*s.* 10*d.* a year.[42]

The other moiety was divided into three in 1279, the respective demesnes including altogether 78 a., 49 a., and 35 a., while *c.* 330 a. were held of them by free and villein tenants. Of its 16 freeholders with *c.* 150 a. John Herdleston and Roger Barbedor had substantial holdings of 62 a. and 61 a., and one man 9 a., but no others held more than 3½ a., and some had only one-acre crofts. Barbedor paid only nominal quit-rents. The rates of money rent paid by the other free tenants varied widely from ½*d.* to 6*s.* an acre. Of the 14 villein tenants 11 held 15 a. each, and were bound to plough 7½ a., mow and carry the lord's hay, reap and gather stubble for 5 days, and send 2 men to 4 harvest-boons. Three others and four cottagers held only 1 a. each, rendering 14*d.* and 3 harvest-boons each.[43] By 1305 at least 3 cottagers and 2 villeins paid only money rents.[44]

In 1332 the open fields included South field, Bridge field, Northcroft, Middle field (also called Foxhole field), and Burgh field, and the permanent grassland included Short meadow.[45] The pattern was basically the same in the 16th and 17th centuries.[46] South field then lay south and south-east of the village; Church field east of it extended to the north-east corner of the parish; Middle field lay north and north-east of the village; and Bridge, or Whittlesford Bridge, field covered the north-west portion of the parish.[47] Sheep moor and Cow moor in the north-west part of the parish provided common grazing: there was a common herdsman in 1674.[48] The land by the river, too wet for cultivation, was inclosed at an early date and used for pasture. Some small parcels of land west and south of the village, the largest being Bardhouse close of *c.* 40 a., had been inclosed by 1698,[49] but ancient inclosures amounted to only 141 a. in the whole parish in 1833.[50]

The manorial demesne in 1698 consisted of 565 a. of arable, 56½ a. of inclosures, and 48 a. of meadow, all of which was leased.[51] Other holdings too had grown since the Middle Ages, and a group of small yeoman farmers had emerged;[52] estates of 100 a. or more were rare before the 19th century.

Crops grown in the parish from the 16th century included rye and barley.[53] Much of the barley grown in southern Cambridgeshire was used for malting,[54] and some of the wealthiest men at Hinxton in the 17th and 18th centuries were maltsters.[55] Other crops grown in the 18th and 19th centuries were wheat, oats, rye, peas, rape, and potatoes; turnips were tried without success.[56] In 1792 the parish was following a three-course rotation: first wheat and rye, then barley, peas, and oats, and in the third year fallow. Some farmers also sowed sainfoin and other grasses for livestock.[57] A less common crop was saffron, which was grown in small plots and gardens in the 16th and 17th centuries and was tithed at 2*s.* a rood in 1692.[58] A dealer in saffron lived at Hinxton in 1772, and its cultivation there apparently died out only in the early 19th century.[59]

35 C.R.O., R 57/24/1/16; R 57/24/1/4.
36 Ibid. R 57/24/1/47; Palmer, *Wm. Cole*, 80.
37 C.R.O., R 57/24/1/28.
38 Ibid. R 57/24/1/31–2; C 2/Eliz. I/H 5/40.
39 C.R.O., R 57/24/1/32.
40 Ibid. R 57/24/1/31.
41 *V.C.H. Cambs.* i. 361, 411.
42 C 133/16 no. 9.
43 *Rot. Hund.* (Rec. Com.), ii. 584–5. The descriptions of John de Camoys's and Roger Barbedor's manors in 1279 have not survived.
44 C 133/116 no. 21.
45 C 135/34 no. 9.
46 B.L. Add. MS. 5861, p. 126; S.C. 11/7.
47 C.R.O., Q/RDc 47.
48 C.U.L., E.D.R., H 1/4, terrier 1639; E 179/244/23 rot. 87d.
49 C.R.O., R 57/24/1/12.
50 Ibid. Q/RDz 10.
51 Ibid. R 57/24/1/12.
52 e.g. E 179/81/147 mm. 2–3 (1525); E 179/83/358 m. 1 (1611).
53 Req. 2/8/189; B.L. Add. MS. 5861, pp. 126, 188.
54 Defoe, *Tour*, ed. Cole, i. 78; *Jnl. Royal Agric. Soc.* vii. 48.
55 e.g. Christopher Cooper: C.R.O., R 57/24/1/47; John North: ibid. R 57/24/1/14; Jas. Moore: ibid. R 57/24/1/53T.
56 Vancouver, *Agric. in Cambs.* 69; H.O. 67/9.
57 C.R.O., R 57/24/1/26.
58 B.L. Add. MS. 5861, pp. 27, 80, 91; C.U.L., E.D.R., H 1/4, terrier 1692.
59 C.R.O., R 51/29/12/5; *E.D.R.* (1890), 500–1.

By custom three flocks of sheep were kept in the parish. Amounting to 450 or 500 animals[60] they belonged respectively to the lord of the manor, Ameys farm, and the cottagers with rights of common. The cottagers' flock was turned into the fallow field in spring with the manorial flock, until William Spencer, tenant of the manor farm *c.* 1780, refused to allow any but his own and the other farm's sheep to graze there. The cottagers were obliged to sell their sheep, and to give up raising turkeys each autumn in the common fields, formerly 'a great benefit to the poorer sort'.[61]

Inclosure of the parish, although advocated in the late 18th century, was opposed by William Hollick as lord of the manor.[62] An inclosure Act was obtained only in 1820, and the award was neither signed nor put into effect until 1833.[63] The allotment of the 1,365 a. of newly inclosed land and 141 a. of ancient inclosure increased the dominance of a few large landowners. Wedd William Nash received 982 a., nearly two-thirds of the parish, as lord of the manor and lay rector. Edward Green, who later settled at Hinxton Hall, received 124 a., and one farmer 107 a. The vicar, Trinity College, and three other owners were allotted between 9 a. and 65 a. each, but none of the remaining 20 landholders and commoners received more than 4 a.[64] Within two years of inclosure most of the copyhold land in the parish had been enfranchised, although some small plots were omitted accidentally and a few tenements remained unenfranchised in 1884.[65] In spite of the greater efficiency made possible by inclosure, and the widespread adoption of a four-course rotation,[66] agriculture was depressed in the late 1840s, and farmers at Hinxton were among those unable to pay their rents in 1849.[67] The rest of the community also suffered, for there was little alternative employment: in 1851 92 men, out of 107 householders, were agricultural labourers. Many women worked as domestic servants, charwomen, laundresses, and dressmakers.[68]

In 1888, under the Allotments Act of 1887[69] and on the initiative of the vicar, a Hinxton Village Dairy Association was formed to protect local cowkeepers with less than 20 a. of land, and to promote the supply of milk and free butter to the cottagers.[70] Cows continued to graze on the road-side verges, but land was specially acquired for allotment gardens for the poor. The area south of Church Green, formerly the site of the rectory farm and presumably given by Nash, was already used for the purpose by 1884, and remained in use until bungalows were built there in the 1960s;[71] in 1889, again on the vicar's initiative, more land was given for allotments, probably in the area east of the village assigned to the vicar at inclosure.[72]

Three large farms and one smallholding occupied all the agricultural land in the parish in 1861 and 1900, and all but *c.* 220 a. was under arable cultivation.[73] The three farms—Hinxton Hall farm, New farm at Hinxton Grange, and Lordship farm—were in 1971 growing mainly wheat, barley, and sugar-beet, with some cattle and sheep at New farm. They employed only a few local people, and most of the inhabitants worked at Duxford, Sawston, or Cambridge.[74] Tube Investments Ltd. at Hinxton Hall were the largest employers in the parish, but their work-force was drawn mainly from Cambridge, Saffron Walden, and Haverhill (Suff.).[75]

Apart from domestic rural crafts such as shoemaking, no industry has ever been practised at Hinxton, though in the 18th century some villagers combined agriculture with spinning for a Colchester clothier and baize-exporter.[76]

There has been a corn-mill on the river at Hinxton since at least 1086, when three mills, worth 21*s.*, 8*s.*, and 4*d.* a year, were enumerated.[77] A water-mill was shared between the manors in and after 1279.[78] By 1698 the mill was on its present site close to Lordship Farm,[79] where it may well have stood since the 11th century. The wheel drove three pairs of stones in 1884.[80] The mill was closed *c.* 1950.[81] A plot known as Fulling Mill croft in South field in the 18th century[82] derived its name from the Great Chesterford fulling mill near by, not from any Hinxton mill.

LOCAL GOVERNMENT. In 1279 John de Camoys and his coparceners claimed view of frankpledge, the assize of bread and of ale, and estreats at Hinxton.[83] A court leet was being held for the manor of the St. Andrew family by 1332.[84] Courts were held at least once a year by Earl's Colne priory and by the earl of Oxford in the early 16th century.[85] Edward Hinde, as lessee of the manor from John Machell, held courts at the end of the 16th century in the courtyard of the manor-house.[86] All the lords of the manor from 1698 or earlier held courts baron for their tenants, probably combined with view of frankpledge.[87] The manor-house was still the meeting-place of the court in 1804.[88] No manorial records for Hinxton are known to have survived, although court rolls were extant in 1792.[89]

By 1552 there were two churchwardens,[90] and there were two or more constables by 1661.[91] The

60 Vancouver, *Agric. in Cambs.* 68; C.U.L., Add. MS. 5821, f. 4.
61 C.R.O., R 57/24/1/26; C.U.L., Add. MS. 5821, f. 2.
62 Vancouver, *Agric. in Cambs.* 69; C.R.O., R 57/24/1/31.
63 Hinxton Incl. Act, 60 Geo. III & 1 Geo. IV, c. 3 (Private, not printed); C.R.O., Q/RDz 10.
64 C.R.O., Q/RDz 10.
65 Ibid. R 57/24/13D/6B; C.U.L., Maps bb. 53(1)/88/12.
66 *Jnl. Royal Agric. Soc.* vii. 40.
67 C.R.O., R 57/24/13D/5.
68 H.O. 107/1761.
69 50 & 51 Vic. c. 48.
70 Porter, *Cambs. Customs*, 399.
71 C.U.L., Maps bb. 53(1)/88/4; C.R.O., air photograph no. 202763.
72 C.R.O., air photograph no. 202763; *E.D.R.* (1889), 253; (1890), 368.
73 R.G. 9/1028; C.R.O., R 57/24/1/51; Cambs. Agric. Returns, 1905.
7 Local information.
75 Ex inf. Tube Investments Ltd.
76 *East Anglian Studies*, ed. L. M. Munby, 148.
77 *V.C.H. Cambs.* i. 363, 392.
78 e.g. *Rot. Hund.* (Rec. Com.), ii. 584–5; *Cal. Inq. p.m.* i, p. 199; xii, p. 273; *Cal. Close*, 1447–54, 310.
79 C.R.O., R 57/24/1/12.
80 C.U.L., Maps bb. 53(1)/88/12.
81 Local information.
82 C.R.O., R 57/24/1/54A; R 57/24/1/54C.
83 *Rot. Hund.* (Rec. Com.), ii. 570.
84 C 135/34 no. 9.
85 Req. 2/8/189.
86 Sta. Cha. 8/127/16.
87 e.g. C.R.O., R 57/24/1/14–15; R 57/24/1/54C; R 57/24/1/54F.
88 Ibid. R 57/24/1/33.
89 Ibid. R 57/24/1/26.
90 *Cambs. Ch. Goods, temp. Edw. VI*, 2.
91 C.R.O., Q/S. 01, p. 14. It is not clear whether the constables were parochial or manorial officials.

churchwardens may have been the only overseers of the poor during the 17th century, for in 1671 an order concerning the poorhouse was addressed to them.[92] There were, however, separate overseers of the poor by 1833, as well as surveyors of highways.[93]

A small plot of ground in the village was leased to the churchwardens and parishioners in 1656 to build a house for the poor.[94] Known as the town house or guildhall, it stood east of the high street and north of Ameys Farm.[95] Until the late 18th century parish resources were adequate to deal with poverty; poor widows were housed in the town house, the poor-rate averaged *c.* £28, and paupers without settlement were removed from the parish only when they became chargeable.[96] From 1777 the poor-rate rose rapidly to £627 in 1801, and later it was always over £200.[97] By 1802 there were three town houses, comprising eight tenements, and Edward Green owned four tenements known as the widows' cottage.[98] Twelve people lived on permanent relief in 1815.[99] Poor-relief in and out of the poorhouse was farmed in 1833 to two Essex sack-makers, who also undertook to repair the unturnpiked roads in Hinxton.[1] The parish was included in the Linton poor-law union in 1835, and was transferred with the rest of Linton R.D. to the South Cambridgeshire R.D. in 1934,[2] becoming part of South Cambridgeshire in 1974.

One of the town houses listed in 1802 on Church Green may have been the 'engine house' on the green in 1833.[3] Sarah Stutter, daughter of a lessee of the manor farm, had in 1830 left £100 to the parish to buy a fire-engine,[4] which was actually used at a fire in 1882.[5] The building on Church Green, still standing in 1886, was described as the fire-engine house in 1903.[6] It had disappeared by 1971, although the fire-engine itself was still extant in a collection at Ickleton.[7]

At inclosure one rood was allotted to the church clerk for land apparently belonging to his office.[8] From 1920 the rent was paid to the parish council. The land was sold for development in 1963, and the proceeds invested in trust for the council.[9]

CHURCH. A church at Hinxton existed by 1092, when Picot the sheriff granted it to his newly founded house of canons in Cambridge, later Barnwell priory.[10] In 1229 the prior was referred to as parson of Hinxton, which may indicate that the benefice was already appropriated to Barnwell, and a vicarage had been ordained by 1259 when Walter of Glemsford was vicar.[11] The priory continued to own the rectory and advowson until its dissolution.[12] The crown granted the rectory to the bishop of Ely in 1562 in an exchange of property.[13] A presentation to the vicarage in 1539 was probably made under a previous grant by Barnwell.[14] In 1558 the advowson was given at the request of Bishop Thirlby to Jesus College, Cambridge.[15] The Crown presented in 1716, and the bishop in 1725 by lapse, but the advowson still belonged to Jesus College in 1971. In 1930 the vicarage was united with that of Ickleton, with alternate presentations by the college and the Lord Chancellor; the union was greatly resented in Hinxton, and in 1955 it was dissolved and a separate vicar presented, with the help of a legacy to the Church Commissioners from a parishioner.[16] Since that date Hinxton and Ickleton have been held as distinct benefices.

The earliest known valuation of the vicarage, in 1535, estimated it to yield £8 5*s.* 2½*d.* a year.[17] The vicar also received £2 a year from Barnwell priory, a payment continued by lessees of the rectory after the Dissolution.[18] The vicarage was worth *c.* £37 in 1685 and had been recently augmented under the will of Bishop Gunning.[19] About 1830 its average annual value was £150 gross, and it remained at that figure until 1862 when it was augmented with £192 a year from the Proby Fund by Jesus College.[20] The college augmented the living again five years later, and the Ecclesiastical Commission added £30 a year in 1882.[21]

The vicar's tithes on garden-produce, with the exception of saffron, were commuted for a money payment in 1524 after a long dispute between the vicar and the parishioners. Married couples were to pay 2*d.*, other householders 1*d.*, and other communicants ½*d.* twice a year, while all parishioners paid ½*d.* to the vicar four times a year, to cover mortuaries and oblations as well as garden tithes.[22] The vicar received 64 a. in place of his tithes at inclosure in 1833.[23]

The vicarial glebe was said in 1615, 1663, and 1692 to consist only of the 1½ a. around the vicarage house,[24] and at inclosure 1½ a. was allotted to the vicar for glebe.[25] Part of the 65½ a. owned from 1833 was sold in 1863 for the Newmarket and Chesterford railway, and the remainder was later sold to the de Freville family. In 1955 the only glebe remaining to the united benefices of Hinxton and Ickleton, a piece of land in Ickleton village, was allotted to Hinxton as the poorer living.[26]

In the 17th century the vicarage was a thatched

[92] Ibid. p. 173.
[93] C.U.L., Doc. 93.
[94] C.R.O., R 57/24/1/3.
[95] Ibid. R 57/24/1/32.
[96] C.U.L., Add. MS. 5821, ff. 77v.–78; Hampson, *Poverty in Cambs.* 138 n.
[97] C.U.L., Add. MS. 5821, f. 78; e.g. *Poor Law Abstract, 1818*, 32–3; *Poor Rate Returns, 1830–4*, 17.
[98] C.U.L., Add. MS. 5821, ff. 23, 56, 61, 65.
[99] *Poor Law Abstract, 1818*, 32–3.
[1] C.U.L., Doc. 93.
[2] *Poor Law Com. 1st Rep.* 249; *Census*, 1931 (pt. ii).
[3] C.R.O., Q/RDz 10.
[4] Inscr. in Hinxton church; Prob. 11/1779 (P.C.C. 725 Beard).
[5] C.R.O., R 58/5, vol. x, p. 317.
[6] O.S. Maps 1/2,500, Cambs. LIX. 4 (1886 and 1903 edns.).
[7] *Camb. News*, 3 Apr. 1964.
[8] C.R.O., Q/RDz 10.
[9] Char. Com. files.
[10] *V.C.H. Cambs.* ii. 142.
[11] *Cal. Pat.* 1225–32, 300; see above, p. 222.
[12] C 1/745 no. 23.
[13] *Cal. Pat.* 1560–3, 224–6.
[14] C 1/745 no. 23.
[15] *Cal. Pat.* 1557–8, 40.
[16] Ex inf. the Jesus Coll. Archivist; *Lond. Gaz.* 16 May 1930, pp. 3049–50; and see below, p. 242.
[17] *Valor Eccl.* (Rec. Com.), iii. 504.
[18] S.C. 6/Hen. VIII/7286 rot. 7d.; *Cal. Pat.* 1560–3, 224–6.
[19] C.U.L., E.D.R., A 6/3; H 1/8, terrier 1837; *Proc. C.A.S.* lv. 51.
[20] *Rep. Com. Eccl. Revenues*, pp. 348–9; *Rep. Com. Univ. Income* [C. 856-II], p. 294, H.C. (1873), xxxvii (3).
[21] Ex inf. the Jesus Coll. Archivist; *Lond. Gaz.* 3 Feb. 1882, p. 433.
[22] *E.D.R.* (1911), 167, 186.
[23] C.R.O., Q/RDz 10.
[24] C.U.L., E.D.R., H 1/4, terriers 1615, 1663, 1692.
[25] C.R.O., Q/RDz 10.
[26] Ex inf. the Jesus Coll. Archivist.

house east of the churchyard, with a hall, parlour, small kitchen, and two little chambers.[27] By 1800, however, it stood south of the churchyard;[28] described in 1851 as a handsome new building,[29] it remained the vicar's residence until its sale in 1930.[30] A new house east of the churchyard was built in 1959.[31]

Wills of 1518, 1522, and 1525 mentioned a guild of St. Mary.[32] At the Hinxton end of Whittlesford Bridge there was by 1401 a chapel dedicated to St. Anne and served by a hermit.[33] The vicar of Hinxton celebrated mass once a year in the chapel, while the hermit was required to assist in the parish church on Christmas Day and to pay the vicar £2 a year.[34] A house and 2 a. formerly held by the hermit were occupied by the parson in 1585, when they were alleged to be concealed lands.[35]

Lay interest in the church *c.* 1300 is suggested by the gift of a chasuble by Gillian Stourton.[36] Some early-16th-century vicars seem to have been ill educated or non-resident: Thomas Palmer, 1522–4, was required to submit himself for further examination on the Bible, and William Grant, 1524–5, was prior of the Cambridge convent of Austin friars and suffragan bishop of Panada to the bishop of Ely.[37] In the later 16th century the incumbents were frequently fellows of Jesus or other Cambridge colleges, who consequently lived elsewhere and neglected the parish.[38] The first resident vicar, John Conway, 1617–57, escaped ejectment, and during the Interregnum was licensed as the registrar for civil marriages.[39] During the 16th century the living had occasionally been held by sequestrators, appointed to serve the cure and receive the vicar's revenues without being instituted, and from the later 17th century the device was used more frequently. Between 1747 and 1805 no vicar was appointed.[40] The sequestrators were all members of Cambridge colleges, and they included some distinguished men; among them were the antiquary James Nasmith, *c.* 1763 to 1773, who served for many years as chairman of the county quarter sessions,[41] and an amateur playwright, James Plumptre, 1797–1805, whose activities included the vaccination of parishioners.[42] Vicars presented after 1805 were either resident or provided a curate, and in the later 19th century took an active interest in the social welfare of their parishioners.[43] There were morning and afternoon services on Sundays throughout the 19th century, and monthly communions from at least 1877.[44] Attendance at services reached a peak of 230 in 1897, nearly as many people as the church would hold; numbers of communicants were also at their highest in 1897 at *c.* 42, having been estimated at between 20 and 30 since 1825.[45]

The church of *ST. MARY AND ST. JOHN THE EVANGELIST* has borne that name since the later 19th century, before which it was dedicated only to St. Mary.[46] The church is built of rubble with ashlar dressings and has a chancel with transeptal south chapel, nave with south aisle and porch, and west tower with a lead-covered spire. Parts of the nave and west tower survive from a late-12th-century building, and the chancel was probably rebuilt in the earlier 14th century when the south chapel was added. The chapel incorporates an east window of 13th-century design, completely restored in the 19th century, which may have been reset from the earlier chancel. The nave was refurbished later in the 14th century, when its north windows and roof were renewed and the south porch was added. The south aisle, which occupies the space between the porch and the chapel, was built under a bequest of Sir Thomas Skelton (d. 1416),[47] whose brass lies in the chapel flanked by those of his two wives. All three may also be commemorated on the corbels to the aisle arches. Later in the 15th century the west tower was remodelled, new windows were put into the chancel and the south wall of the nave and chapel, and a new south doorway was made for the nave. The chapel was also provided with a new roof and diagonal buttresses. Part of the 15th-century rood-screen survives, and there was a loft approached by a stair in the north wall of the nave.

During the 16th and early 17th century the chancel was reported as ruinous,[48] and when it was repaired, possibly by Sir Edward Hinde (d. 1633), it may have been shortened, the original 14th-century buttresses being reset against a thin east wall. The chancel roof probably dates from that period of repair. The chancel contains many monuments to members of the Dayrell family between 1669 and 1729. More extensive repairs were carried out from the mid 19th century onwards. Much of the ashlar was renewed, and it is not certain that the east window or the stonework followed the medieval patterns.

In the 16th century there were three large bells, and a sanctus bell in the steeple[49] which survived in 1971. Two were replaced in 1665 and 1667 with bells by Miles Gray,[50] but the third was sold *c.* 1785 after it had cracked.[51] An annual gift of 7½*d.* from Great Chesterford church to Hinxton church, established in the 17th century for bell-ropes, was normally deducted from the payment to Great Chesterford under Anne Howsden's charity.[52] The church plate in 1552 included three silver chalices.[53] A silver paten and remade cup given by the Revd.

27 C.U.L., E.D.R., H 1/4, terrier 1663.
28 C.U.L., Add. MS. 5821, f. 56 (loose plan).
29 *Gardner's Dir. Cambs.* (1851).
30 C.U.L., E.D.R., C 3/26; C 3/37.
31 Ex inf. the Jesus Coll. archivist.
32 B.L. Add. MS. 5861, pp. 126, 168, 180.
33 *Proc. C.A.S.* x. 377–8.
34 Ibid.; *E.D.R.* (1911), 186.
35 *East Anglian*, N.S. vi. 223.
36 *Vetus Liber Arch. Elien.* (C.A.S. 8vo ser. xlviii), 70–1.
37 *E.D.R.* (1911), 56, 88; Emden, *Biog. Reg. Univ. Camb.*, 268; Knowles, *Religious Orders in Eng.* iii. 494.
38 C.U.L., E.D.R., B 2/4, p. 127; B 2/36, f. 95.
39 B.L. Add. MS. 5808, f. 115.
40 Gibbons, *Ely Episc. Rec.* 155–6, 163; B.L. Add. MS. 5808, f. 114v.; C.U.L., E.D.R., B 8/4, f. 18.
41 *Alum. Cantab. 1752–1900*, iv. 515.
42 *D.N.B.*; *Alum. Cantab. 1752–1900*, v. 141; *Clare College 1326–1926*, ed. M. D. Forbes, 254–6.
43 *E.D.R.* (1888), 138; (1890), 368.
44 C.U.L., E.D.R., C 1/1; C 1/4; C 3/26; C 3/37.
45 Ibid. C 3/37; C 1/6.
46 *Eccl. Top. Eng.* vi. 156; *E.D.R.* (1888), 120.
47 Prob. 11/2B (P.C.C. 34 Marche); see below, plate facing p. 241.
48 C.U.L., E.D.R., B 2/3, pp. 28, 146; B 2/10, f. 160; B 2/25, f. 9.
49 *Cambs. Ch. Goods, temp. Edw. VI*, 2.
50 *Cambs. Bells* (C.A.S. 8vo ser. xviii), 151.
51 C.U.L., E.D.R., B 7/1, p. 125; B 7/2, p. 29.
52 *31st Rep. Com. Char.* 201; see below.
53 *Cambs. Ch. Goods, temp. Edw. VI*, 2.

James Plumptre in 1805 and a pewter flagon and plate were in 1837 the only vessels.[54] A paten and wafer box have been added since 1900. The registers begin in 1538 and are complete.

NONCONFORMITY. A Hinxton woman, probably a Catholic, was imprisoned and fined £260 for refusal to attend church in 1598, and another was presented as a recusant in 1622 and 1638.[55] Catholic recusancy at Hinxton was, however, confined to individuals, and there were no recusants in 1676.[56]

Only one protestant dissenter was reported at Hinxton in 1676,[57] although 18 people had been presented in the previous year for refusing to receive communion.[58] In 1704 a house there was licensed for nonconformist worship,[59] but the number of dissenters remained low throughout the 18th century: there were six Presbyterians and two Anabaptists in 1728,[60] one Presbyterian family in 1779, and in 1799 about six families described as Methodists, although they were more likely Congregationalists.[61] With the building of the Congregational chapel at Duxford in 1794, the number of dissenters in neighbouring parishes began to increase.[62] A house in Hinxton was licensed as a meeting-house in 1826.[63] Nonconformity at Hinxton received much encouragement from the Nashes, lords of the manor 1817–84, who were themselves dissenters. Wedd William Nash, lessee of the rectory, refused to pay the parish clerk's wages,[64] and the family declined to donate land for a Church school.[65] Having acquired the rectory farmstead at inclosure, Wedd William Nash conveyed part of it in 1836 to trustees, for nonconformist preaching and education. A barn was repaired for use as a meeting-house with 170 sittings, and from *c.* 1844 the British school was held in the same building.[66] In 1871 a Congregational chapel was built on the site of the barn, west of the churchyard, but the congregation continued to be served by the minister from Duxford.[67] Average attendance in 1851 was 130, and the vicar reported in 1877 that most families in the parish regularly attended both church and chapel.[68] By 1897, however, the number of dissenters in Hinxton was estimated at only forty.[69] The chapel had been unused for some years in 1949; it was sold in 1950 and converted into a private house.[70]

EDUCATION. A schoolmaster licensed at Hinxton in 1580 had gone by 1593,[71] and education was evidently only intermittently provided there until the late 18th century. Thomas Billett, a nonconformist, was by 1798 running an evening school in Hinxton, assisted by the nonconformist teacher at Duxford, and Billett's wife kept a day-school.[72] Another school was taught by the parish clerk.[73] A day-school with *c.* 30 children flourished throughout the earlier 19th century, supported by subscriptions and payments from the parents, though its numbers had fallen to 15 by 1847.[74] There was also a Sunday school, held from at least 1807 in the church and attended by almost 60 children in 1847.[75] In 1833 a nonconformist Sunday school with 44 pupils was recorded.[76] A schoolmaster and schoolmistress were recorded in 1841, and from *c.* 1844 there was a British school at Hinxton,[77] held in the barn which also served as the Congregational chapel: it had been set up by Wedd William or Charles Nash.[78] School-pence were paid according to the parents' means, and there was an average attendance of 50 children.[79]

A new school for 75 pupils was built on the west side of the high street in 1872, with the aid of a government grant, to replace the British school.[80] The incumbents of Hinxton provided religious teaching in the new school under the terms of its trust deed, and some vicars also held a night-school.[81] The day-school had 60 pupils in 1877 and 59 in 1897, but average attendance remained between 40 and 50.[82] The Church school building was renovated and redecorated in 1904, most of the expense being borne by R. B. Wilkinson.[83] The school was closed in 1960, since when the children of Hinxton have attended schools at Duxford and Sawston.[84]

CHARITIES FOR THE POOR. Hinxton was one of the parishes to benefit under the charity of Lettice Martin.[85] The parish received 13*s.* 4*d.* a year in the later 18th century.[86] In 1837 26*s.* was distributed in small sums among widows, the aged, and large families. Only £1 was received in 1900;[87] in 1957 £1 1*s.* was paid to each of 6 recipients, and gifts of 2*s.* 6*d.* were made to 12 others.

Anne Howsden, by indenture dated 1631, gave a messuage and 49 a. at Moggerhanger, in Blunham (Beds.), to provide £15 a year for the poor of Hinxton. Another £2 each was to be paid yearly to the churches of Hinxton and Great Chesterford, and the trustees might spend £1 on an annual feast. In

54 C.U.L., E.D.R., H 1/8, terrier 1837; list of ch. plate, *penes V.C.H.*
55 *Recusant Rolls, 1594–6* (Cath. Rec. Soc. lxi), 135; Bodl. MS. Gough Eccl. Top. 3, f. 127; *Cambs. Village Doc.* 65.
56 Compton Census.
57 Ibid.
58 C.U.L., E.D.R., B 2/63A, f. 7v.
59 C.R.O., Q/S. 01, p. 51.
60 C.U.L., E.D.R., B 8/1.
61 Ibid. Add. MS. 5821, f. 77.
62 Ibid. E.D.R., C 1/6.
63 Ibid. B 4/1, f. 79v.
64 Ibid. C 3/21.
65 Ed. 7/5.
66 Ibid.; *Gardner's Dir. Cambs.* (1851).
67 Anon. *Duxford Cong. Church, a short hist.* 18; *Cong. Yr. Bk.* (1860 and later edns.).
68 H.O. 129/188/1/7/13; C.U.L., E.D.R., C 3/26.
69 C.U.L., E.D.R., C 3/37.
70 Char. Com. files; *Camb. Ind. Press*, 19 May 1961.
71 Gibbons, *Ely Episc. Rec.* 178; Bodl. MS. Gough Eccl. Top. 3, f. 31.
72 C.R.O., R 57/24/13B/3; C.U.L., Add. MS. 5821, f. 34.
73 C.U.L., Add. MS. 5821, f. 24.
74 e.g. *Educ. of Poor Digest*, 60; *Educ. Enquiry Abstract*, 57; *Church School Inquiry, 1846–7*, 4–5.
75 C.U.L., E.D.R., C 1/4; C 3/21; *Church School Inquiry, 1846–7*, 4–5.
76 *Educ. Enquiry Abstract*, 57.
77 H.O. 107/76; Ed. 7/5.
78 *Church School Inquiry, 1846–7*, 4–5; H.O. 129/188/1/7/13.
79 Ed. 7/5.
80 Ibid.; *Kelly's Dir. Cambs.* (1883).
81 C.U.L., E.D.R., C 3/37; C 3/26.
82 Ibid.; *Kelly's Dir. Cambs.* (1883 and later edns.).
83 *E.D.R.* (1904), 228.
84 *Camb. Ind. Press*, 19 May 1961.
85 See p. 219. Unless otherwise stated, this section is based on *31st Rep. Com. Char.* 201–2; Char. Com. files.
86 C.U.L., E.D.R., C 1/1; *Char. Don.* i. 100–1.
87 *Kelly's Dir. Cambs.* (1900).

1775 the sexton was paid 4*s.* for tending the graves of the Howsden family, and the trustees held their dinner after the annual distribution on 12 November.[88] At the inclosure of Blunham in 1796 the trustees were allotted 33½ a. Income had risen to £60 a year by 1867,[89] and in the 1890s it was distributed in coal and cash to the aged. The charity was regulated by a Scheme of 1896 confirmed in 1966; separate charities were formed in 1896 for the payments to Hinxton and Great Chesterford churches, which continued in 1969, and for poor-relief. A memorial in Hinxton churchyard to Anne Howsden was set up in 1903. In 1969 the charity received from the land and investments *c.* £110 mostly disbursed in coal.

By will proved *c.* 1877 a Miss Clarkson of Hinxton left £200 from which 1 guinea was to be given every Christmas to each of 6 poor people, preferably widows. The charity continued in 1962, when its income was *c.* £6 10*s.*

ICKLETON

ICKLETON, most southerly parish in Whittlesford hundred, lies on the west bank of the river Cam or Granta, 11 miles south of Cambridge.[1] The southern branch of the pre-Roman Icknield Way ran through the parish, and the village evolved close to the point at which the road crossed the river. The parish is roughly rectangular, and extends westwards from the river, which forms most of its eastern boundary, for 2 miles. Its northern and southern sides follow field boundaries, and the western boundary lies on the course of a disused road from Cambridge via Thriplow to Elmdon (Essex), extant in the 18th century.[2] The western, southern, and most of the eastern boundaries of Ickleton form part of the county boundary, marked by a procession balk in 1545.[3] The parish covered an area of 2,700 a. from 1886, when 61 a. were transferred to Hinxton.[4] In 1965 2 ha. from Chrishall (Essex) and 9 ha. from Great Chesterford (Essex) were transferred to Ickleton, which covered 1,080 ha. (2,669 a.) in 1971.[5]

The land, low-lying and fairly flat by the river, slopes gently to *c.* 250 ft. in the west. A stream runs from west to east down the middle of the parish, eventually joining the river; north and south of it the land rises more steeply to hills of *c.* 330 ft., the parish boundaries lying along the crests. In the south-east corner of the parish by the road from Strethall a massive series of terraced banks lies along the western side of Coploe Hill. Several small late-19th-century plantations are the only woodland in the parish, which is otherwise open and has probably been so since prehistoric times.[6] Ickleton lies on the Middle Chalk, and the soil on the hills to north and south is thin, dry, and chalky. A chalk-pit on Coploe Hill, open by 1542, has since 1957 been protected as a nature reserve.[7] Towards the centre of the parish the ground becomes wetter and heavier, and by the river is damp and unsuitable for tillage.[8] The area north of the village was sometimes called Clay field, and in 1738 the lord of the manor's tenants were said to have the right to dig clay from the lord's claypits to repair copyhold tenements.[9] Sheep have been kept successfully on the chalkland and cattle fattened in the valley, but the farming of the parish has been mainly arable. There were three open fields until 1810 when the parish was inclosed.

The conjunction of the Icknield Way and the river has encouraged settlement at Ickleton since early times, the evidence including a Neolithic axe-head, a barrow close to the probable course of the Icknield Way,[10] a Bronze Age spear-head, gold bracelet, and torque,[11] the banks on Coploe Hill, which may represent Bronze Age agriculture,[12] a Roman building west of the Great Chesterford road,[13] built after A.D. 117 and probably a villa or farm-house associated with Great Chesterford,[14] and possibly re-used Roman material in the arcade of Ickleton parish church.[15]

The village existed in its own right in Saxon times, when it received its present name meaning Icel's farm,[16] and by 1086 there were 43 tenants in the parish.[17] Their numbers had risen sharply to *c.* 115 by 1279.[18] Eighty-six people were assessed to the subsidy in 1524,[19] showing a decline since the 13th century, and 68 households were counted in 1563, when it was the largest village of the five in the hundred.[20] The numbers of houses varied between 65 in 1662 and 98 in 1666.[21] There were 251 adults in the parish in 1676.[22] The late 17th century and the 18th saw renewed growth, and in 1707 Ickleton was a large village with more than 120 families, many of them poor.[23] In 1801 it was again the most populous village in the hundred, with 121 families comprising 493 people. Population grew steadily to a peak of 813 in 1851, remaining entirely dependent on agriculture.[24] The resulting

[88] C.U.L., E.D.R., C 1/1.
[89] *Char. Digest Cambs. 1863–4*, 394.
[1] This account was written in 1972.
[2] C.U.L., Maps bb. 53(1)/93/52.
[3] C.R.O., R 63/D.D.B. 1115.
[4] *Census*, 1891.
[5] *Census*, 1971.
[6] Fox, *Arch. Camb. Region*, Map III.
[7] Trin. Coll. Mun., Box 21, IIa, ct. roll 34 Hen. VIII; *Camb. Region, 1965*, 58.
[8] *Camb. Region* (1938), 9; Vancouver, *Agric. in Cambs.* 69.
[9] C.R.O., R 51/29/12/38; R 51/29/1H.
[10] *Camb. Region, 1965*, 117; O.S. Map 6″, Cambs. LIX. SE. (1891 edn.).
[11] *V.C.H. Cambs.* i. 273 n.; *Antiq. Jnl.* lii. 358–63.
[12] Fox, *Arch. Camb. Region*, 306; see above, plate facing p. 80.
[13] *Arch. Jnl.* vi. 15 sqq.; *Camb. Region, 1965*, 128–9.
[14] Fox, *Arch. Camb. Region*, 183–4. For Great Chesterford, see *V.C.H. Essex*, ii. 72–88.
[15] *Proc. C.A.S.* xi. 183–5.
[16] The name does not, as has been suggested, share a common root with that of the Icknield Way: *P.N. Cambs.* (E.P.N.S.), 95; *Place-Names of Cambs.* (C.A.S. 8vo ser. xxxvi), 18.
[17] *V.C.H. Cambs.* i. 411.
[18] *Rot. Hund.* (Rec. Com.), ii. 585–9.
[19] E 179/81/132 mm. 1–2.
[20] B.L. Harl. MS. 594, f. 200.
[21] See pp. 278, 280.
[22] Compton Census.
[23] C.U.L., E.D.R., A 4/2.
[24] *Census*, 1801–51.

poverty drove young men to emigrate, and many settled in Queensland, encouraged by the lord of the manor, Sir Robert Herbert, the colony's first premier.[25] After 1851 the population fell gradually to 598 in 1911, and 543 in 1921, after which there was for a time a slow increase. In 1971, however, there were 526 inhabitants.[26]

Two roads cross the river from the east into Ickleton, both part of the parallel series of tracks which once formed the Icknield Way.[27] The northern route crosses from Hinxton, and runs only a short distance before turning south to the east end of the village. The road formerly ran west to the Duxford road, and continued across the parish before turning north-west to meet the surviving stretch of the Icknield Way at the north-west corner of the parish. West of the Duxford road this route was known as Delway, and formed the boundary between Hill and Middle fields.[28]

The other river-crossing with its road, *c.* 700 yd. further south, has been the more important. The church was built close to it *c.* 1100, and the section of the road between the church and the Duxford–Strethall road forms the main village street. Coming from Stump Cross, the road crossed the main western branch of the river by a bridge, which had been replaced by a ford and footbridge by 1867.[29] The construction of the railway line across the road in 1845 cut off the route to the east, in spite of a level-crossing, and the section east of the railway was an overgrown track in 1972. West of the village the road was called Royston way and ran slightly north of the present east–west road across the parish, turning north-west to join the Thriplow–Elmdon road. Traces of that road or Delway were visible in the late 18th century.[30] Ickleton Old Grange was built by the last stretch of Royston way, and the road's subsequent change of direction explains the angle of the Grange to the present road.[31] Three roads run south from the parish: one to Elmdon, one to Strethall, known as Portway[32] (later Coploe Road), and one from the east end of the village by the river to Great Chesterford.

The area north of the village and close to the northern east–west road was known as Brookhampton; the surviving part of the road is called Brookhampton Street, the bridge was Brookhampton Bridge, Brookhampton closes lay north of the stream, and the road running west was called the highway from Brookhampton.[33] The application of the name suggests that a separate settlement may once have existed there, although no documentary evidence of such a settlement has been found.

The settlement of Ickleton began near the river, and extended north, south, east, and west along the four streets. The road from the river was called the fulling-mill street (later Mill Lane) by 1432,[34] and Brookhampton Street was so called by 1528.[35] The south street (later Paddock Street, afterwards Frog Street) was mentioned in 1335,[36] and the west street (later Abbey Street) in 1518.[37] The name Green Street was applied to the road south of the church by the village green in 1431–2;[38] the road north of the church, however, was not named as Hill Street (later Butcher's Hill) until the 18th century, and may not have been in early use.[39]

The parish was dominated in the later Middle Ages by Ickleton priory, founded in the mid 12th century. In spite of the prioress's close control of village life and the smallness of the population in the 15th and 16th centuries Ickleton was prosperous, and five of its inhabitants were required to contribute to the loan of 1522.[40] James Russell, an early-15th-century tax-commissioner for the county, lived at Ickleton,[41] and Joan, widow of Sir Baldwin St. George, settled there in the 1430s.[42] A smith and a husbandman of Ickleton were both trading with Londoners in the later 15th century,[43] and the parish was on the edge of the north Essex cloth-producing area.[44] Several of the larger medieval houses survive: parts of Hovells, Norman Hall, Frog Hall, the Mowbrays, and several cottages contain 15th-century work. Most are timber-framed and plastered, and some are decorated with pargetting.

The wealthiest residents of the village in the 16th and 17th centuries were farmers, and most of the buildings surviving from that period are farm-houses or cottages. There were many middling but no large houses at Ickleton in the later 17th century, and in 1674 3 houses were taxed on 5 hearths and 11 on 4 hearths.[45] Durhams farm-house dates from the 16th century, and Priory Farm was built in the 17th. The Grange (later the Old Grange), the only pre-inclosure house away from the village, had been built by 1685, Brookhampton Hall was a farm-house of the late 17th or early 18th century, and in the late 17th century Abbey Farm replaced the decaying buildings of Ickleton priory. From the later 18th century the village had resident lords of the manor, and Caldrees Manor, enlarged from a 17th-century farm-house, became the largest house.

Several cottages, small houses, and out-buildings in Abbey Street were destroyed by a fire in 1789, but they were quickly rebuilt,[46] and the building of small houses continued throughout the 19th century to house the expanding population. The amenities of the village gradually improved, with the opening of the two nonconformist chapels in 1842 and 1852, of the school in 1871, and of a reading room in a barn behind Brookhampton Hall by 1886.[47] Most of the building outside the village also dates from the 19th century; Rectory farmstead, with two cottages, was built between 1818 and 1825, and Vallance Farm and a lodge of two cottages in 1824. A block of 6 cottages west of Coploe Road had been

[25] Ibid. 1861; *D.N.B.* 1901–11, s.v. Sir Rob. Herbert.
[26] *Census*, 1851–1971.
[27] Fox, *Arch. Camb. Region*, 143.
[28] C.R.O., R 63/D.D.B. 1116; ibid. Q/RDc 20; Trin. Coll. Mun., Box 21, I, 20 July 5 Hen. VII.
[29] C.R.O., Q/Rdz 7; ibid. R 51/29/12/38.
[30] *Ancient Cambs.* ii (C.A.S. 8vo ser. xx), 56.
[31] C.U.L., Maps bb. 53(1)/93/52.
[32] C.R.O., R 63/D.D.B. 1119.
[33] Ibid. R 63/D.D.B. 1120.
[34] Trin. Coll. Mun., Box 21, IIa, ct. roll 10 Hen. VI.
[35] B.L. Add. MS. 5861, p. 219.
[36] Trin. Coll. Mun., Box 21, I, 30 June 9 Edw. III.
[37] B.L. Add. MS. 5861, p. 126.
[38] Trin. Coll. Mun., Box 21, IIa, ct. roll 10 Hen. VI.
[39] C.R.O., R 51/29/9/5.
[40] *L. & P. Hen. VIII*, iii (2), p. 1118.
[41] *Cal. Fine R.* 1413–22, 221, 300, 415; 1422–30, 5, 214.
[42] *Cal. Pat.* 1429–36, 435.
[43] Ibid. 1452–61, 264; 1461–7, 297; 1476–85, 294.
[44] *V.C.H. Essex*, ii. 385.
[45] See p. 281.
[46] C.R.O., R 51/29/2c, pp. 104–6.
[47] O.S. Map 1/2,500, Cambs. LIX. 8 (1886 edn.).

put up by 1886,[48] and the New Grange close to the Old Grange dates from the 1890s. Piecemeal infilling has taken place in the 20th century, but the area of the village has not increased. Mr. and Mrs. G. W. H. Bowen in 1927 built the Gertrude Homes in Frog Street, and in 1937 a large red-brick house in Brookhampton Street known as the Place. Nine pairs of semi-detached council houses were built around Birds Close, east of Coploe Road, in 1929 and 1948–54.[49] The hillside north of the churchyard was filled for the first time in 1965, when four new houses were built there. A few old cottages in Abbey Street have also been replaced by new houses, but most of the older buildings have been carefully preserved, and Ickleton won the competition for the best-kept village in Cambridgeshire in 1964.[50]

In the 16th century there was an inn perhaps called the Rose,[51] and a messuage called the Bell was mentioned in 1592.[52] A house called the White Lion, south of the village green and burned down shortly before 1699,[53] was succeeded on the same site by the Chequer, mentioned in 1778,[54] and then by the Duke of Wellington, open under that name by 1847, which closed *c.* 1957 and became a private house.[55] The Lion in Abbey Street in 1728[56] was perhaps the Red Lion, used as an inn by 1800 and still open in 1972.[57] The other public house then open was the New Inn, in Brookhampton Street, mentioned in 1884.[58] The Greyhound, a public house at the south-east tip of Ickleton parish on the outskirts of Great Chesterford, was open by 1851 and survived in 1972.[59]

The main railway line from London to Cambridge, constructed in 1845, runs along the eastern edge of the parish by the river.[60] A cottage was built in Mill Lane for the level-crossing gate-keeper; the crossing was closed in 1969.[61]

Ickleton priory was attacked at least twice at times of strong popular anti-clerical feeling. Landholders and their tenants dispossessed after the battle of Evesham attacked the priory *c.* 1266,[62] and in 1381, during the Peasants' Revolt, James Hog forced his way into the house and burnt its muniments.[63] In 1309 a band of local men assaulted the servants of Pain de Tiptoft at Ickleton and carried away his goods.[64]

MANORS AND OTHER ESTATES. One hide at Ickleton was devised in the late 10th or early 11th century by Elfhelm of Wratting, a thegn of King Edgar, to his kinsman Elfhelm.[65] That hide was probably merged by 1066 in the large manor, comprising 19½ of the 20 hides in Ickleton, held from King Edward by Alsi Squitrebil. The remaining ½ hide in Ickleton, held T.R.E. by Estred from Earl Alfgar, was given after the Conquest to Hardwin de Scalers, from whom it was held by Durand. That small estate has not been traced further and was probably absorbed in the main manor.[66]

Ickleton was given by William I with many other lands to Eustace, count of Boulogne, after their reconciliation following Eustace's treason in 1067. By 1082 Eustace had been succeeded by his son of the same name, who in 1086 held 19½ hides in Ickleton,[67] and the land thereafter formed part of the honor of Boulogne. Eustace's daughter Maud married King Stephen, who controlled the honor until her death in 1152.[68] In 1141 the king gave Ickleton to Geoffrey de Mandeville,[69] but presumably resumed it after Geoffrey's downfall in 1143. About 1150 Stephen and Maud gave the manor to Eufeme, second wife of Aubrey, earl of Oxford, on her marriage. About 1153 she gave £5 worth of land there to Colne priory (Essex), and died without issue soon after,[70] whereon the rest presumably reverted to the honor of Boulogne. After the death of Stephen's son Count William in 1159 Henry II took possession of the honor. The demesne in Ickleton was later divided, being partly held in fee-farm.[71] By *c.* 1183 the largest portion of Ickleton was held by Roger de Lucy,[72] who was named as tenant, probably in error, in 1217.[73] He may have been the predecessor of Richard de Lucy, who succeeded to land in Cambridgeshire *c.* 1200 and in 1212 held 1 knight's fee there of the honor of Boulogne.[74] Richard's father Reynold (d. 1199) was a kinsman of the justiciar Richard de Lucy,[75] and the tenure may well have been connected with King Stephen's grants to the justiciar of lands from the honor of Boulogne.[76] Richard's descendants remained mesne lords of the honor's estates in Ickleton until the mid 14th century. Richard died in 1213;[77] his widow Ada married Thomas de Multon, lord of Egremont (Cumb.), and Richard's two daughters married Thomas's two sons by a former marriage.[78] The elder daughter, Amabel, married Lambert de Multon (d. 1246), and their son and heir, Thomas de Multon, was mesne lord of the Ickleton lands of the honor of Boulogne in 1279.[79] Thomas was succeeded in 1294 by his grandson Thomas de Multon (d. 1322),[80] whose son John died without issue in 1334. His large estates included ½ knight's fee at Ickleton, which was given to his widow Alice in dower.[81] John's three sisters succeeded to his lands;

48 O.S. Map 1/2,500, Cambs. LIX. 7 (1886 edn.).
49 Ex inf. S. Cambs. R.D.C.
50 *Camb. Ind. Press*, 24 July 1964.
51 E 134/31–2 Eliz. I Mich./27; E 179/82/191 m. 8.
52 C.U.L., E.D.R., B 2/11, f. 42v.; Trin. Coll. Mun., Box 21, IIa, ct. roll 34 Eliz.
53 Clare Coll. Mun., Ickleton, MSS. re Pytches estate.
54 C.R.O., R 60/20/8/3.
55 *Kelly's Dir. Cambs.* (1847); local information.
56 C.R.O., R 51/29/2A.
57 Ibid. L 69/30.
58 Ibid. R 58/5, vol. x, p. 508.
59 *Gardner's Dir. Cambs.* (1851).
60 *V.C.H. Cambs.* ii. 132.
61 *Illustrated Lond. News*, July–Dec. 1845, p. 73, shows the keeper's cottage as 'Ickleton station'.
62 *V.C.H. Cambs.* ii. 393.
63 *Cambs. Village Doc.* 29.
64 *Cal. Pat.* 1307–13, 240.
65 *A.-S. Wills*, ed. Dorothy Whitelock, 32–3.
66 *V.C.H. Cambs.* i. 385, 411.
67 Ibid. 411; Freeman, *Norman Conquest*, iv. 745–7.
68 *Trans. Essex Arch. Soc.* N.S. vii. 144.
69 *Reg. Regum Anglo-Norm.* iii, pp. 102–3.
70 Ibid. p. 87; *Complete Peerage*, x. 202 n., 205.
71 J. H. Round, *Studies in Peerage and Fam. Hist.* 172; *Rot. Hund.* (Rec. Com.), ii. 588.
72 *Bk. of Fees*, i. 239.
73 Ibid. 243.
74 *Rot. de Ob. et Fin.* (Rec. Com.), 45; *Red Bk. Exch.* (Rolls Ser.), ii. 529.
75 *Complete Peerage*, viii. 247; cf. *Genealogist*, N.S. xv. 129–33.
76 *Trans. Essex Arch. Soc.* N.S. vii. 144.
77 *Complete Peerage*, viii. 248.
78 Ibid. 248–9.
79 Ibid. ix. 401–2; *Rot. Hund.* (Rec. Com.), ii. 587–9.
80 *Complete Peerage*, ix. 403; *Feud. Aids*, i. 144.
81 *Cal. Inq. p.m.* vii, p. 431; *Cal. Close*, 1333–7, 375.

Ickleton passed to the youngest, Margaret, who had married Thomas de Lucy, the great-grandson of Richard de Lucy's younger daughter Alice, whose descendants had taken the name of Lucy.[82] Thomas died in 1365; his son Anthony de Lucy, lord of Ickleton in 1367,[83] died in 1368 without male heirs.[84] No reference to the mesne lordship after that date has been found. By the early 13th century the Lucys had given part of their land to religious houses and had subinfeudated the rest.

Ickleton priory was founded in the mid 12th century for Benedictine nuns, probably by a member of the Valognes family.[85] The estate which it held at Ickleton by the 1180s was possibly derived in part by exchange or otherwise from that of Colne priory, for in 1279 it was apparently said to have been given by a count of Boulogne and his wife Eufeme.[86] *PRIORY* or *NUNS* manor, which produced most of the priory's income in 1535,[87] comprised 714 a. in 1536,[88] and was known as the chief manor of Ickleton, being the largest single estate in the parish.[89] The priory was dissolved in 1536, and the Crown granted its manor to the bishop of Ely in 1538, together with the Ickleton lands of the dissolved abbeys of West Dereham, Calder, and Tilty, in exchange for the manor of Hatfield (Herts.).[90]

Hamon Walter, whose mother was of the Valognes family, held an estate in Ickleton which his brothers Hubert Walter, archbishop of Canterbury, and Tibbald had by 1199 granted to the Premonstratensian abbey of West Dereham (Norf.), founded by Hubert in 1188.[91] The estate, later called *DURHAMS* manor, was assessed at 1 hide, *c.* 1235.[92] In 1279 the abbey held *c.* 52 a. mostly of Robert son of Reynold the knight, and possibly 68 a. of Ickleton priory.[93]

The Cistercian abbey of Calder (Cumb.) received lands in Ickleton before 1213 from Richard de Lucy, from whose successors they were held as ¼ knight's fee. In 1231 Henry III confirmed to the abbey land in Ickleton and Brookhampton and part of a mill in Brookhampton given by Roger son of William, and half a mill in Ickleton given by Richard de Lucy.[94] The abbey's lands in the parish, known as *CALDREES* manor, were held in 1279 from Thomas de Multon as of the honor of Boulogne, and the abbot owed suit of court twice a year for them at St. Martin's-le-Grand, London.[95]

By 1183 Ralph Brito (d. by 1194) held land at Ickleton of the honor of Boulogne.[96] The daughter of his successor Thomas Brito, tenant *c.* 1218, was given in marriage to Robert Hovel, who held the estate by 1221 and to whom William Brito, presumably Thomas's heir male, released a carucate at Ickleton in 1222.[97] Probably by 1251 the estate had been given to the Cistercian abbey of Tilty (Essex), to which Ralph Hovel confirmed 140 a. in 1253.[98] The abbey's manor, known as *HOVELLS*, covered *c.* 190 a. in 1279, and was mostly held from Robert Hovel who held of the honor of Boulogne.[99]

The manors of Priory, Durhams, Caldrees, and Hovells descended together from 1538, although they retained their distinct names and lands. Bishop Goodrich granted the reversion of a Crown lease of the Priory manor to his kinsman Thomas Goodrich, and after a series of assignments the lease came into the hands of John Wood of Hinxton.[1] Wood (d. 1590) and his brother Edward of Fulbourn (d. 1599)[2] both had an interest in the lands in the 1580s and 1590s.[3] Edward was succeeded by his son John.[4] In 1600 Bishop Heton on his appointment to the see surrendered the four episcopal manors at Ickleton to the Crown,[5] and John Wood bought the manors two years later.[6]

Wood sold the whole estate in 1623 to William Holgate, a member of the corporation of Saffron Walden, and his son Edmund[7] (d. 1626). William settled the manors in 1628 on his youngest son John Holgate, a lawyer of Saffron Walden, who held them until his death in 1673. John's heir, his grandson John Holgate, had by 1700 been succeeded by his younger brother William. On William's death in 1717 the manors passed to his son John (d. 1738), a London druggist,[8] who had by 1719 conveyed them to Henry O'Brien, earl of Thomond.[9]

The earl died childless in 1741, and his estates were inherited by Percy Wyndham, son of his wife's sister Catherine. Wyndham, who attained his majority *c.* 1744, had assumed the name O'Brien in 1741, and was created earl of Thomond in 1756.[10] He was an M.P. 1745–74, lord of the Treasury 1755–6, and treasurer and cofferer of the Household 1757–65.[11] When he died unmarried in 1774 his estate at Ickleton passed first to his nephew George O'Brien, earl of Egremont, and then by gift before 1784 to George's younger brother, Percy Charles

[82] *Complete Peerage*, viii. 249–53; ix. 405.
[83] Ibid. viii. 253; *Cal. Inq. p.m.* xii, p. 128.
[84] *Complete Peerage*, viii. 253.
[85] *V.C.H. Cambs.* ii. 223.
[86] *Bk. of Fees*, i. 239, 243; *Rot. Hund.* (Rec. Com.), ii. 585 (entry incomplete).
[87] *Valor Eccl.* (Rec. Com.), iii. 505.
[88] S.C. 6/Hen. VIII/264 rot. 4d.
[89] e.g. C.R.O., R 63/D.D.B. 1115.
[90] *V.C.H. Cambs.* ii. 225–6; *L. & P. Hen. VIII*, xiii (2), p. 377; S.C. 6/Hen. VIII/2632; cf. *V.C.H. Cumb.* ii. 177; *V.C.H. Essex*, ii. 136.
[91] *V.C.H. Norf.* ii. 414; C. R. Cheney, *Hubert Walter*, 29; *Rot. Chart.* (Rec. Com.), i. 21.
[92] *Liber de Bernewelle*, 256.
[93] *Rot. Hund.* (Rec. Com.), ii. 588–9.
[94] *V.C.H. Cumb.* ii. 176; Dugdale, *Mon.* v. 340–1.
[95] *Rot. Hund.* (Rec. Com.), ii. 589.
[96] *Bk. of Fees*, i. 239; *Pipe R.* 1194 (P.R.S. N.S. v), 22.
[97] *Bk. of Fees*, i. 243; ii. 1431; *Cur. Reg. R.* x. 134; C.P. 25(1)/23/10 no. 13.
[98] *Cal. Chart. R.* 1226–57, 359; C.P. 25(1)/25/28 no. 6.
[99] *Rot. Hund.* (Rec. Com.), ii. 588.
[1] S.C. 6/Hen. VIII/264 rot. 4d.; C 2/Eliz. I/A 3/55.
[2] C 3/223/46; for their dates of death see Prob. 11/76 (P.C.C. 72 Drury); Gibbons, *Ely Episc. Rec.* 302.
[3] e.g. C 2/Eliz. I/F 5/23; see below.
[4] C 142/262 no. 104. Sir John Wood of Ickleton (kt. May 1603, d. 1634) should be distinguished from Sir John Wood, clerk of the signet (kt. July 1603, d. 1610): Nichols, *Progresses of Jas. I*, i. 156, 210; Thoresby, *Ducatus Leodiensis* (2nd edn. 1816), 206; Prob. 11/117 (P.C.C. 1 Wood); Morant, *Essex*, i. 177. The two are confused in *Alum. Cantab. to 1751*, iv. 452; Shaw, *Knights of Eng.* ii. 109, 116.
[5] Bentham, *Hist. Ely*, 196: the Priory manor is omitted from the list in n. 1, but was transferred with the other three.
[6] Windsor, St. George's Chap. MS. XVI. 4. 5; C 66/1581 mm. 14–16.
[7] C 2/Jas. I/H 5/28. Wood retired to Beeston (Yorks. W.R.) and continued his litigious career: Thoresby, *Ducatus Leodiensis*, 206; J. T. Cliffe, *Yorks. Gentry from Ref. to Civil War*, 119–20; cf. below, p. 237.
[8] C.R.O., R 51/29/3; for the Holgates see *Misc. Gen. et Her.* 2nd ser. v. 161–2; *Visit. Essex*, ii (Harl. Soc. xiv), 666–7; Morant, *Essex*, ii. 212.
[9] C.R.O., R 51/29/2B.
[10] Ibid.; ibid. R 51/29/1H, ct. roll 1741; *Complete Peerage*, xii (1), 712–13.
[11] *Hist. Parl., Commons*, 1754–90, iii. 667.

Wyndham.[12] Wyndham too was an M.P. 1782–4 and 1790–6,[13] and he converted and took up residence at Caldrees Manor in Ickleton.[14] On his death in 1833 the manors passed to his nephew Algernon Herbert, son of the earl of Carnarvon, author of works on folklore and history.[15] His widow Marianne held the estate from 1855 until her death in 1870, and was succeeded by their only son, Sir Robert George Wyndham Herbert (kt. 1882).[16] Sir Robert, whose childhood was spent at Ickleton, was colonial secretary and the first premier of Queensland, Australia, 1859–66, and permanent under-secretary of state for the colonies, 1871–92.[17] He died unmarried at Ickleton in 1905, and was apparently succeeded as lord of the manors by George Frederick Herbert, a grandson of his uncle William Herbert, dean of Manchester.[18] By 1909 the lady of the manor was G. F. Herbert's sister, Beatrice Mary Herbert (d. 1948). Percy Charles Dryden Mundy, a great-grandson of William Herbert, held the manors from that year until his death in 1959.[19]

Although the lordships of Priory, Durhams, Caldrees, and Hovells manors descended together from 1538, the lands belonging to them were soon divided. The site of the priory, known as Abbey Farm, was leased with *c.* 400 a. from 1644,[20] and in 1804 the tenant farmed 447 a.[21] Before 1776 the farm was owned by William Parker, whose nephew William Parker Hamond claimed 380 a. and received 261½ a. at inclosure for that and another farm.[22] Hamond and his heirs remained in possession until in 1893 Lt.-Col. R. T. Hamond of Pampisford Hall sold Abbey farm with 388 a.[23] It was farmed from 1892 until 1933, and owned by 1900, by James Welch.[24]

The priory and its farm-buildings, once extensive, gradually collapsed through fire, demolition, and neglect.[25] In the later 17th century a new house was built on the site, incorporating pieces of the medieval structure. The house has been extended and modernized at various times in the 19th and 20th centuries.

Hovells farm, consisting of the manor-house and 150 a., also owned by William Parker and his grandson before 1776 and in 1810,[26] later ceased to be a separate farm. The house stands on the west side of Frog Street and although extensively remodelled may be a late medieval hall-house.

The Grange (later Ickleton Old Grange) was built at the extreme west end of the parish, 2 miles from the village, between 1618 and 1685.[27] It may have been built before 1623 by Sir John Wood, who moved a barn from the priory to a site a mile away:[28] a list of Cambridgeshire gentry mentions 'Wood of Ickleton Grange'.[29] By 1685 a large estate in the western half of the parish was farmed from the Grange,[30] comprising 364 a. in 1810.[31] At inclosure P. C. Wyndham received his allotment of 314 a. around the Grange, though he lived in Caldrees Manor in the village.[32] The 17th-century house was refronted in the 18th century. Some blocks of limestone in a barn at the back of the house may have come from the priory.

Ickleton New Grange was built between 1885 and 1901 close to the Old Grange.[33] Its owner until 1937 was G. W. H. Bowen, whose father, Sir George Bowen (1821–99), had served, as the first governor of Queensland, with Sir Robert Herbert.[34] The New Grange was later the home in retirement of Sir Claude Frankau (d. 1967), an eminent surgeon.[35]

The house called Caldrees Manor, at the east end of Abbey Street, was created by P. C. Wyndham in the late 18th century from a 17th-century farm-house. He also purchased land north and east of the house and laid out pleasure grounds and a park, which in 1812 covered 7 a.[36] Sir Robert Herbert extended the grounds by exchanging land with Clare Hall in 1870 and 1884, and diverted a stream to make ornamental ponds.[37] Sir Robert left the house to W. F. Beddoes and G. W. H. Bowen,[38] and Beddoes, whose wife was Sir Robert's niece, lived there until his death in 1929.[39] Mrs. Beddoes left Caldrees Manor in 1933 to P. C. D. Mundy,[40] who lived in the house until his death in 1959. It was sold in 1960 and again in 1971.[41]

The lands of Durhams remained with the lords of the manor, being farmed as a separate estate by the late 17th century.[42] Sir Robert Herbert devised the farm in 1905 with Caldrees Manor.[43] The 17th-century farm-house, which stands north of Butcher's Hill, was sold without any land in 1971.[44]

By 1162 Henry II had confirmed a grant by Count William's steward of an estate at Ickleton to the hospital of Montmorillon (Vienne).[45] In 1279 Thomas the deacon held *c.* 100 a. of demesne for life from the hospital.[46] In 1300 the hospital was licensed to convey its estate to Aymer de Valence, earl of

[12] *Complete Peerage*, xii (1), 713; *Cat. of Petworth Ho. Archives*, ed. F. W. Steer and N. H. Osborne, i, p. xvi (pedigree); C.R.O., R 51/29/2C.
[13] *Hist. Parl., Commons*, 1754–90, iii. 667.
[14] C.U.L., E.D.R., C 1/4; Mary Bristowe, *Short Guide to Ickleton*, 11.
[15] *D.N.B.*; C.R.O., R 51/29/2C.
[16] C.R.O., R 51/29/2C; Walford, *County Families of U.K.* (1888), 506.
[17] *D.N.B.* 1901–11.
[18] C.R.O., R 51/29/2E, p. 266.
[19] Ibid.; tomb in churchyard.
[20] C 5/29/235.
[21] St. George's Chap. MS. C.C. 120151.
[22] Parker Hamond Estates Act, 42 Geo. III, c. 53 (Private and Personal, not printed); C.U.L., Doc. 640, nos. 2, 32; C.R.O., Q/RDz 7.
[23] C.R.O., 296/SP 947; for the Hamonds see above, pp. 106–7.
[24] C.R.O., 296/SP 947; *Kelly's Dir. Cambs.* (1900 and later edns.).
[25] C.R.O., R 63/D.D.B. 1119 (cover); E 134/4 Jas. I Mich./25.
[26] Parker Hamond Estates Act; C.U.L., Doc. 640, no. 32.
[27] It is mentioned in Trin. Coll. Mun., Box 21, IIe, terrier 1685, but not in ibid. Box 21, IIc, terrier 1618.
[28] St. George's Chap. MS. XVI.4.5.
[29] Bodl. MS. Gough Cambs. 68.
[30] Trin. Coll. Mun., Box 21, IIe, terrier 1685; C.U.L., Maps bb. 53(1)/93/52.
[31] C.U.L., Doc. 640, no. 60.
[32] C.R.O., Q/RDz 7; ibid. R 60/21.
[33] O.S. Maps 6″, Cambs. LIX. SW. (1891, 1903 edns.); ex inf. Mrs. R. L. Bristowe, Brookhampton Hall, Ickleton.
[34] *Kelly's Dir. Cambs.* (1896 and later edns.); *D.N.B.* (1st suppl.); C.R.O., 331/Z 7, 1936, Dec. p. 97; 1937, Sept. p. 70.
[35] *The Times*, 1 July 1967.
[36] C.R.O., R 60/21.
[37] Clare Coll. Mun., Ickleton.
[38] C.R.O., R 51/29/8/32.
[39] Ibid. 331/Z 6, 1929, Jan. p. 2.
[40] *Kelly's Dir. Cambs.* (1933).
[41] C.R.O., R 60/20/7/3; local information.
[42] C.R.O., R 51/29/12/22.
[43] Ibid. R 51/29/8/32.
[44] Ibid. SP 96/1.
[45] *Cal. Pat.* 1247–58, 382; *Early Yorks. Chart.* viii. (Y.A.S. extra ser. vi), 17–18; M. L. Rédet, *Dict. Topog. du Département de la Vienne* (Paris, 1881), 275.
[46] *Rot. Hund.* (Rec. Com.), ii. 587.

Pembroke, to whom Thomas released his rights in 1305.[47] Aymer granted *VALENCE* manor for life to Sir John Wollaston.[48] After Aymer's death in 1324 the reversion was assigned to one of his three heirs, Elizabeth Comyn, younger daughter of his sister Joan.[49] Elizabeth married Richard Talbot,[50] with whom she leased the manor to Richard's brother John for life in 1330. Two years later John surrendered his life-interest,[51] and Richard and Elizabeth immediately conveyed the manor to Richard of Barking, a London merchant.[52] In 1333 Barking sold the Ickleton estate to William le Waleys, Queen Isabel's tailor, who sold it a year later to Thomas of Lavenham and Ralph Mendham, rector of Hargham (Norf.).[53] In 1344 Ralph conveyed the manor to John Illegh, rector of Icklingham (Suff.), and Thomas Keningham, a fellow and later master of Michaelhouse, Cambridge.[54] Illegh granted Valence manor in 1345 to Michaelhouse, for his earlier foundation of two poor scholars and a chantry priest.[55]

When Michaelhouse was surrendered in 1546 its lands at Ickleton were immediately granted to Trinity College, Cambridge.[56] In 1612 the manor was extended at 307 a.,[57] and at inclosure in 1814 the college received a compact allotment of 243 a. south of the Elmdon road.[58] Trinity's farm at Ickleton, consisting of 340 a., was sold in 1946 to Mrs. E. M. Scales and J. B. Wamsley.[59] In 1972 it was owned by Mrs. E. M. Wamsley.

Valence manor had a manor-house by 1324.[60] The manor-house in 1612, probably the same as in 1324, 1461, and 1508,[61] stood on the south side of Mill Lane, and was a tiled building with six rooms on the ground floor and two solars above, and a thatched range of out-buildings including a gatehouse.[62] The same house was in use in 1685 and 1726.[63] By 1810 there was no house with the manor,[64] and in 1824 Trinity built a new farm-house and farmstead known as Vallance Farm on the land that it had acquired at inclosure.[65]

An estate including *c.* 60 a. of demesne was held in 1279 by Roger de Neville under Thomas de Multon of the honor of Boulogne, with Mr. William Boys as life-tenant. Another 127 a. held of Neville by Roger Barbedor presumably descended with Barbedors manor in Hinxton.[66] In 1302 ¼ knight's fee in Ickleton was held by Philip de Neville; by 1316 it had passed to Sir John Limbury,[67] and acquired the name of *LIMBURYS* manor. Sir John held 100 a. in Ickleton of the Multons in 1335, when he was sheriff of Cambridgeshire, and his widow Gillian was in possession by 1343.[68] Between 1346 and 1367 she was succeeded by Sir Philip Limbury, perhaps her son, who died at Constantinople in 1367.[69] His widow Joan, who afterwards married Sir John Clinton, held the manor[70] until her death in 1388, when it passed to her daughter Elizabeth, wife of Sir Thomas Trivet (d. 1388).[71] In 1391 it was settled on Elizabeth and her second husband Sir Thomas Swinburne who still held lands in Ickleton at his death in 1412.[72] Elizabeth died in 1433. In 1456 Limburys was sold with *c.* 80 a. to Clare Hall, Cambridge, by her executor Nicholas Wimbish,[73] a Chancery clerk.[74] Clare Hall held the manor in 1546,[75] and had 123 a. in Ickleton in 1810, receiving at inclosure 77½ a., mostly close to the village.[76] In 1819 it bought the lands and farm-house of Mowbrays manor, *c.* 160 a., of which 30 a. were to endow scholarships.[77] It bought another 9 a. in Ickleton in 1876, and 30 a. from the executors of H. F. Beales, the tenant, in 1927.[78] Clare College still owned Mowbrays Farm and its land in 1972.

Limburys manor had a messuage attached to it by 1279.[79] In 1388 and 1389 the estate included two messuages;[80] the site of one was perhaps the close called Old Limburys, north-west of Caldrees Manor.[81] In 1545 the farmstead stood on the west side of Frog Street, close to its junction with Abbey Street.[82] The same site contained only farm-buildings, without a house, in 1704.[83] From 1819 the tenants of Clare Hall's farm occupied the Mowbrays.[84]

The later manor of *MOWBRAYS* was derived from 30 a. held in 1279 of Dereham abbey by the heirs of William de Beauchamp of Bedford, which descended through a female heir to the Mowbrays.[85] John Mowbray of Axholme (Lincs.) held 30 a. at Ickleton of the honor of Boulogne at his death in 1368. His eldest son John[86] died under age in 1383 and was succeeded by his younger brother Thomas,[87] later duke of Norfolk, who died in banishment in

[47] *Cal. Pat.* 1292–1301, 513; *Cat. Anct. D.* v, A 10793.
[48] *Cal. Inq. p.m.* vi, p. 320.
[49] Ibid. p. 339; *Cal. Fine R.* 1319–27, 338.
[50] *Complete Peerage*, xii (1), 613–14.
[51] Trin. Coll. Mun., Box 21, I, 1 Nov. 4 Edw. III; 6 July 6 Edw. III.
[52] *Cal. Pat.* 1330–4, 310; 1343–5, 481–2.
[53] Trin. Coll. Mun., Box 21, I, 3 May 7 Edw. III; 2 Oct. 8 Edw. III.
[54] Ibid. 11 Jan. 17 Edw. III; Emden, *Biog. Reg. Univ. Camb.* 344.
[55] Trin. Coll. Mun., Box 21, I, 11 Mar. 20 Edw. III; Emden, *Biog. Reg. Univ. Camb.* 326.
[56] *Camb. Univ. Doc.* (1852), i. 125; *L. & P. Hen. VIII*, xxi (2), pp. 147, 342.
[57] Trin. Coll. Mun., Box 21, IIc, terrier 1612.
[58] C.R.O., Q/RDz 7.
[59] Ex inf. the Senior Bursar, Trinity Coll.
[60] *Cal. Inq. p.m.* vi, p. 320.
[61] Trin. Coll. Mun., Box 21, I, 1 Edw. IV, lease to John Fuller; Box 21, III, 23 Hen. VII, lease to John Fraunceys.
[62] Ibid. Box 21, IIc, terrier 1612.
[63] Ibid. Box 21, IIe, terrier 1685; C.R.O., R 63/D.D.B. 1121.
[64] C.U.L., Doc. 640, no. 90.
[65] Trin. Coll. Mun., Box 21, VII, builders' bills.
[66] *Rot. Hund.* (Rec. Com.), ii. 587; cf. Emden, *Biog. Reg. Univ. Oxon.* i. 238–9.
[67] *Feud. Aids*, i. 144, 155, 161.
[68] *Cal. Inq. p.m.* vii, p. 431; P.R.O. *List of Sheriffs*; *E.D.R.* (1890), 404.
[69] *Feud. Aids*, i. 161; *Cal. Inq. p.m.* xii, pp. 128–9.
[70] *Cal. Close*, 1364–8, 350; *Complete Peerage*, iii. 314.
[71] *Cal. Inq. p.m.* xvi, pp. 205–6, 297–9; *V.C.H. Beds.* ii. 360.
[72] *Feud. Aids*, vi. 406; C.P. 25(1)/289/56 no. 222.
[73] *Reg. Chichele* (Cant. & York Soc.), ii. 495–7; *Clare Coll. 1326–1926*, ed. M. D. Forbes, 74.
[74] Emden, *Biog. Reg. Univ. Oxon.* iii. 2120–1.
[75] *Camb. Univ. Doc.* (1852), i. 271.
[76] C.U.L., Doc. 640, no. 10; C.R.O., Q/RDz 7.
[77] W. J. Harrison, *Notes on Masters etc. of Clare Coll. Camb.*, 86–7; see below.
[78] Clare Coll. Mun., Estates Bk., s.v. Ickleton.
[79] *Rot. Hund.* (Rec. Com.), ii. 587.
[80] *Cal. Inq. p.m.* xvi, pp. 205–6.
[81] C.R.O., R 60/21.
[82] Ibid. R 63/D.D.B. 1115.
[83] Ibid.; Clare Coll. Mun., terrier 1704.
[84] See below.
[85] *Rot. Hund.* (Rec. Com.), ii. 588; for the descent see Sanders, *Eng. Baronies*, 10–11; *Complete Peerage*, ix. 375–85.
[86] *Cal. Inq. p.m.* xii, p. 380.
[87] *Complete Peerage*, ix. 384, 601.

1399. Thomas had settled his estate at Ickleton on his eldest son Thomas's marriage to Constance Holland.[88] His widow Elizabeth was granted dower in the lands in 1399,[89] but the estate reverted after her death in 1425 to Constance, whose husband had been executed in 1405.[90] On Constance's death in 1437 the manor passed to her husband's nephew, John, duke of Norfolk, who was succeeded in 1461 by his son John.[91] In 1469 John and his wife Elizabeth conveyed Mowbrays with many other lands to feoffees,[92] including Thomas Hoo (d.s.p. 1486). Thomas was possibly succeeded by the four daughters of his half-brother Thomas, Lord Hoo,[93] including Anne, the younger of two daughters of that name and wife of Roger Copley. A William Copley died in 1490 leaving his brother Lionel heir to a manor in Ickleton held of the earls of Oxford,[94] perhaps that called Copleys *c.* 1530.[95] In 1540 William Copley and his wife conveyed Mowbrays manor to John Hinde, who presumably sold it soon afterwards, for in 1547 George Rolle conveyed it to John Crudd.[96]

Eleanor, another daughter of Lord Hoo, married secondly James Carewe,[97] and Richard Carewe of Ickleton (d. *c.* 1510), who was later said to have held Mowbrays,[98] may have been her descendant. Richard's daughter and heir Margaret, wife of William Morris, sold part of the estate in 1544 to John Crudd,[99] who had bought the rest in 1543 from George Rolle and his wife.[1]

Crudd, one of a large and prosperous yeoman family of Ickleton, considerably enlarged the manor.[2] He or his son of the same name died in 1607, shortly after enfeoffing a younger son Daniel of his lands.[3] In 1646 Daniel conveyed Mowbrays to his kinsman John Crudd.[4] John, accused of raising forces for an anti-parliamentarian rising at Linton in 1648, died *c.* 1652 before the case was completed.[5] Mowbrays remained in the Crudd family until 1714, when Thomas Crudd died unmarried,[6] having devised Mowbrays and Brays manors to his sister Anne Hanchett (d. 1721) for life, and then to his nephew Thomas Hanchett, eldest son of his sister Joan.[7]

Thomas Hanchett was succeeded *c.* 1744[8] by his son John (d. by 1759), who by his first wife had two daughters, Rachel and Susanna. Half Mowbrays manor was settled on Rachel, on her marriage to William Warner, and the other half on Susanna, who in 1765 married Zachary Brooke, vicar of Ickleton (d. 1788). William Warner, who apparently survived his wife, conveyed his moiety in 1789 to Susanna Brooke, and by will proved 1792 released all his rights to Susanna's three children.[9] Mrs. Brooke (d. 1812) owned over 280 a. in Ickleton in 1810, and her children were alloted 160 a. lying south of the village at inclosure in 1814.[10] The whole estate was sold by the Brookes in 1819 to Clare Hall, Cambridge, and still belonged to the college in 1972.

In the 14th century there was apparently no manor-house, but in 1438 there was a site of 3 a. and probably a house.[11] The present house, the Mowbrays, just outside the south-west wall of the churchyard, was built in the 15th century, when it had a central hall and two cross-wings. In the later 17th century the hall was raised to two storeys and another wing was added on the west. Extensive improvements and repairs were made in 1819 and 1912.[12]

William Brito, son and heir of Robert Brito (d. by 1199), who had held an estate at Ickleton,[13] still held the land of the king at farm in 1230 and 1242.[14] In 1279 land in Ickleton was held by John le Bray,[15] possibly a descendant of William Brito whose name was also written le Breton or le Bret.[16] John le Bray held *BRAYS* manor of the honor of Boulogne in 1302; it had passed to John Sawston by 1346,[17] and in 1428 was divided between John Pauly and Thomas Andrew.[18] The descent of the manor is unclear from that date until 1523, when Richard Bendyshe of Steeple Bumpstead (Essex) died leaving Brays to his only son John, a minor.[19] In 1540 John conveyed the manor to his father-in-law Thomas Crawley.[20] The manor later came to John Trigge, whose son John, a yeoman of Ickleton, succeeded him.[21] Much of the land was claimed by a John Crudd, to whom in 1604 five members of the Trigge family sold Brays.[22] Crudd was possibly not the John Crudd who held Mowbrays in 1607,[23] but by 1704 the two manors were held together by Thomas Crudd, who devised both of them to Anne and then Thomas Hanchett.[24] Brays descended from John Hanchett (d. *c.* 1759) to his son by his second marriage, John,[25] and was sold in 1778 to Henry

[88] *Complete Peerage*, ix. 603–4; *Cal. Inq. Misc.* vi, p. 233; *Cal. Close*, 1399–1402, 142.
[89] *Cal. Pat.* 1399–1401, 294.
[90] *Cal. Close*, 1405–9, 5; *Complete Peerage*, ix. 604–5.
[91] C 139/89 no. 60; *Cal. Inq. p.m.* (Rec. Com.), iv. 314.
[92] *Essex Fines* (Essex Rec. Soc.), iv. 65–6. The manor was therefore not involved in the division of the Mowbray estates after 1481, and the statement in Lysons, *Cambs.* 218 that it passed to Wm., marquess of Berkeley, is incorrect; cf. *Cal. Close*, 1476–85, pp. 399–400.
[93] *Cal. Inq. p.m. Hen. VII*, i, p. 74; *Complete Peerage*, vi. 564.
[94] *Complete Peerage*, vi. 565; *Cal. Inq. p.m. Hen. VII*, i, p. 258.
[95] C 1/620 no. 23.
[96] C.P. 25(2)/4/21 no. 24; C.P. 25(2)/55/398 no. 21.
[97] *Complete Peerage*, vi. 565.
[98] C 142/298 no. 67.
[99] Prob. 11/17 (P.C.C. 23 Fetiplace); C 1/542 no. 8; C.P. 25(2)/4/22 no. 21.
[1] C 142/298 no. 67; C.P. 25(2)/4/21 no. 78.
[2] For another acquisition see *Cambs. Fines, 1485–1603*, ed. Palmer, 53.
[3] C 142/298 no. 67; C 2/Jas. I/C 12/32.
[4] C 3/399/176; C.P. 25(2)/401/22 Chas. I Trin. no. 7.
[5] *Cal. Cttee. for Money*, ii. 1145–7; C.R.O., R 51/29/1B, ct. roll 1653.
[6] *Mon. Inscr. Cambs.* 86.
[7] Ibid.; Essex R.O., D/DB 866.
[8] C.R.O., R 51/29/1*i*, ct. roll 1745.
[9] Clare Coll. Mun., abstract of title of Brooke family 1819.
[10] C.U.L., Doc. 640, no. 16; C.R.O., Q/RDz 7.
[11] *Cal. Inq. p.m.* xii, p. 380; *Cal. Inq. Misc.* vi, p. 233; C 139/89 no. 60.
[12] Clare Coll. Mun., Ickleton.
[13] *Pipe R.* 1197 (P.R.S. N.S. viii), 81–2; 1199 (P.R.S. N.S. x), 155.
[14] Ibid. 1230 (P.R.S. N.S. iv), 144; 1242 (ed. H. L. Cannon), 217.
[15] *Rot. Hund.* (Rec. Com.), ii. 588.
[16] e.g. *Essex Fines* (Essex Rec. Soc.), i. 97.
[17] *Feud. Aids*, i. 144, 161.
[18] Ibid. 180.
[19] C 142/42 no. 158.
[20] Morant, *Essex*, ii. 350–1; C.P. 25(2)/4/21 no. 30.
[21] C 3/175/6.
[22] Ibid.; C.P. 25(2)/277/2 Jas. I Mich. no. 7.
[23] C 142/298 no. 67; see above.
[24] Clare Coll. Mun., terrier 1704.
[25] C.R.O., R 51/29/11/5.

Hanchett of Ickleton (d. 1795), who left it to his son Samuel.[26] At inclosure in 1814 Samuel was allotted 106 a. close to the village,[27] which by will proved 1835 he devised to his nephew John Hanchett. John died intestate in 1848, leaving two daughters, on whose behalf the property was sold in 1867. Part was bought by Sir Robert Herbert,[28] but much was again for sale in 1873 with an arable farm of 112 a. formerly held by William Hanchett,[29] and the farm, with 8 cottages and 28 a. of arable, was sold yet again in 1877.[30]

John le Bray held a messuage with his land in 1279.[31] By 1545, however, the site of the manor of Brays was a pasture full of bushes with a stream running through it, in the south-east angle of Brookhampton Street.[32] The farm-house attached to the estate from at least 1730 was the Little Farm, east of the churchyard.[33] By 1867 the farm-house had been amalgamated with an adjoining tenement to form Norman Hall.[34] After its sale in that year the house was no longer used as a farm-house. The oldest part of the house is a late medieval hall and cross-wing. It was extended and remodelled in the 16th century and again in the 18th.

Ickleton rectory was appropriated to the priory, probably from the priory's foundation, and passed to the Crown in 1536. The priory's lands thereafter were treated as a single manorial estate, and the rectory therefore consisted only of tithes. By a composition of 1516 the prioress received both great and small tithes,[35] as did later lay rectors.[36] In 1547 the Crown granted the rectory to the dean and canons of St. George's Chapel, Windsor,[37] who held it until 1867 when their estates were vested in the Ecclesiastical Commissioners.[38]

In the later 16th century a dispute developed between the dean and canons and their farmers, and members of the Wood family, lessees of the former priory demesne.[39] In 1579 John and Edward Wood refused to pay tithes from the demesne. A long series of lawsuits and appeals ensued. Edward's son John, eventually lord of Priory manor, was still opposing the dean and canons in 1620. The courts consistently upheld the rectors.[40] By the later 18th century tithes had apparently been commuted for money payments, for a proposal in 1776 to collect tithes in kind raised 'no small stir' in the parish.[41]

The dean and canons' lessees in the 16th and earlier 17th centuries tended to be eminent men without local connexions, although Sir William Byrd, dean of the Arches, who held the rectory 1615–24, was the son of a gentleman of Saffron Walden.[42] His widow Jane married Sir William Acton, Bt., to whom the lease was transferred in 1630. The lessee from 1660 was John Bennett of Abington, who was succeeded by his widow Elizabeth by 1668 and his son John in 1675. In 1698 Bennett sold the lease to William Russell of London, and two years later it was transferred to Edward Evans of London, who held it until 1718.[43] John Hanchett of Chrishall Grange, whose wife was Evans's niece, was the dean and canons' farmer at Ickleton from 1718 until his death in 1737; his son-in-law and executor, Thomas Fuller the elder, held the lease from then until 1747, when it passed to Hanchett's son John.[44] Thomas Wolfe was lessee 1763–77, and the rectory was leased to Thomas Fuller from 1777 to *c.* 1826.[45]

At inclosure in 1814 the dean and canons of Windsor received 640½ a. in lieu of tithes. By far the largest allotment in Ickleton, it lay in four pieces with the largest covering 438 a. north of Grange Road.[46] Thomas Fuller devised his lease to two trustees, one of whom, James Raymond, held it from *c.* 1826 to 1840. His nephew and heir W. F. Raymond, archdeacon of Northumberland, was lessee from 1840 until his death in 1860, and his nephew, Lt.-Gen. William Inglis, later of Hildersham Hall, held the property 1861–82. He was succeeded at Ickleton by George Jonas, whose father Samuel Jonas of Chrishall Grange had farmed the land from Lt.-Gen. Inglis.[47] The Ecclesiastical Commissioners sold the farm in 1920 to H. F. Beales, whose executors offered it for sale again with 612 a. in 1927.[48]

Between 1818 and 1825 Thomas Fuller, as the dean and canons' lessee, built a farmstead on the large allotment north of Grange Road, but his undertenant was still required to live in Fuller's own farmhouse in the village over a mile away.[49] The rectory's farmstead was known first as Ickleton Farm, and later as Rectory Farm.[50]

ECONOMIC HISTORY. The small estate of Hardwin de Scalers could be cultivated with half a plough-team. It had been worth 5*s*. T.R.E., and 12*d*. when given to Hardwin, and was worth 32*d*. by 1086.[51] The rest of Ickleton, held in 1086 by Count Eustace, comprised 19½ hides, of which 9 hides were in demesne. There were 3 plough-teams on the demesne, and there was land for 1 more. The meadow was sufficient for 3 teams. Three *servi*

[26] Ibid. R 51/29/12/37; for the date of Henry Hanchett's death, see inscr. in church.
[27] C.R.O., Q/RDz 7.
[28] Ibid. R 51/29/12/37–9.
[29] C.U.L., Maps 53(1)/87/34.
[30] Ibid. Maps 53(1)/87/92.
[31] *Rot. Hund.* (Rec. Com.), ii. 588.
[32] C.R.O., R 63/D.D.B. 1120.
[33] Trin. Coll. Mun., Box 21, IIe, meadow survey bk. 1730, p. 14; C.R.O., R 51/29/11/5.
[34] C.R.O., R 51/29/12/38.
[35] *E.D.R.* (1911), 150.
[36] E 321/33/24.
[37] *Cal. Pat.* 1547–8, 149–50.
[38] *MSS. St. George's Chapel, Windsor Castle*, ed. Dalton, p. ii.
[39] The following account is based on: Req. 2/101/20; Req. 2/34/30; Req. 2/91/45; C 2/Eliz. I/F 5/23; E 134/31–2 Eliz. I Mich./27; E 134/4 Jas. I Mich./25; St. George's Chap. MS. XVI. 4. 5.
[40] By 31 Henry VIII, c. 13, s. 21 only monastic land which had been tithe-free before the Dissolution was to be exempt thereafter.
[41] St. George's Chap. MS. XVI.4.5.
[42] *MSS. St. George's Chapel*, 431–2; Morant, *Essex*, ii. 596.
[43] *MSS. St. George's Chapel*, 431–2; *Chapter Acts of D. & C. Windsor, 1430–1672*, ed. Bond, 90, 111, 124, 142, 180, 276.
[44] *MSS. St. George's Chapel*, 432; Essex R.O., D/DB 1076; D/DB 867.
[45] St. George's Chap. MS. typed index of leases; C.U.L., Doc. 640, no. 90.
[46] C.R.O., Q/RDz 7.
[47] St. George's Chap. MS. typed index of leases; ibid. XVII.28.2; *Kelly's Dir. Cambs.* (1858 and later edns.).
[48] C.U.L., Maps 53(1)/92/131.
[49] St. George's Chap. MS. C.C. 120151, survey 1818; ibid. XVII.28.2.
[50] O.S. Map 6″, Cambs. LIX. SE. (1891 and 1903 edns.).
[51] *V.C.H. Cambs.* i. 385, 411.

worked on the estate, and there were also 10 bordars. The 30 *villani* had 16 plough-teams, with land for 4 more. Eleven of them held ½ hide each, one held 1 yardland, and one held 1 hide. Count Eustace's estate had been worth £24 T.R.E. and when he received it, but by 1086 it was worth £20.[52]

In 1279 the vill included *c.* 790 a. of demesne land, over 225 a. of freeholdings, and *c.* 900 a. held in villeinage. The largest demesne, that of Ickleton priory, covered *c.* 300 a.; Tilty, West Dereham, and Calder abbeys possessed respectively 112 a., 110 a., and 48 a., and Montmorillon hospital *c.* 100 a., farmed for 10 marks a year. Of the two lay fees Roger de Neville held in demesne 61 a., also farmed, and John de Bray 48 a. Of the 27 freeholders recorded with field land only two, with 55 a. together, owned over 15 a., and more than 12 others had only their messuages. Of the villein land 4 men on the later Valence manor held 30 a. each and 3 on the Neville fee 20 a. each, but the normal tenement was a half-yardland of 15 a., of which there were probably 40, including 17 on Valence manor. Another 8 half-yardlands were divided into fractions of between 3 and 9 a., held by *c.* 20 tenants. There were also *c.* 30 cottagers occupying *c.* 18 a. Three half-yardlands on the Tilty manor yielding substantial rents had probably been recently enfranchised. Most customary tenements owed small money-rents and renders of hens and eggs. The labour-services required were relatively light. Apart from 2 divided half-yardlands on Ickleton priory's manor, whose tenants owed week-work between Michaelmas and Lammas and had to reap altogether 28 a. in harvest, the villeins were required, probably only once a year, to harrow, weed, thresh, carry corn, and build haystacks. Some had to thresh 30 sheaves of barley and 12 of wheat. On the priory manor all villeins, down to the cottagers, had also to do 4 boon-works for every 15 a. or less, on the Neville and Montmorillon fees 5 a year. No details of work were recorded on the other estates, and the low values set on them, from 4*d.* to 7*d.* a holding, suggest an ancient commutation.[53]

In 1279 the land under cultivation covered more than 1,900 a. of the 2,700 a. in the parish. The arable had contracted by 1341, when 2 plough-lands lay uncultivated because of the poverty of their tenants.[54] The three main open fields, Middle, Heath, and South fields, were all established by 1432.[55] The name West field, also in use, was probably then as later an alternative name for Middle field.[56] The fields stretched from east to west along the contours of the valley west of the village, and cultivation probably began in the bottom of the valley and later extended up the slopes to north and south. Middle field, by far the largest, reached from the west boundary of the parish to the Duxford road, including all the land north of Grange Road. Heath field lay south of Middle field, from the western boundary nearly as far east as the Strethall road. South field, the smallest, took in a strip of land along part of the southern boundary, another strip west of the Strethall road, and all the land south of the village between the Strethall and Chesterford roads.[57] Brookhampton field, or Clay field, north of the village, was mentioned from 1432, but was never listed in terriers as one of the three main fields.[58]

Distinct areas within the three fields were sometimes given field-names of their own. Warren field was part of South field in the south-east corner of the parish.[59] North of Middle field, along the boundary with Duxford, was an area known as the Hills; Windmill hill, Stony hill, Skipping hill, and 'Horenhyll' were mentioned in 1432, and Gallow hill, Calf hill, Tutt hill, Stocking, Highdown, and the Rows in 1545.[60] Stocking field, Highdown, and the Rows were marked in 1814 as distinct areas along the parish boundary, with a long narrow Hill field lying south of them,[61] and in 1794 the arable was said to lie in five distinct open fields, presumably including Brookhampton and Hill fields;[62] the invariable division of estates between three main fields in terriers,[63] however, suggests that cultivation, at least, was organized on a three-field basis.

Sheep-farming was widely practised at Ickleton by the 15th century.[64] Richard Carewe (d. *c.* 1510) kept sheep for their wool,[65] but later farmers fattened sheep for the London market.[66] A sheepcote had been built on Valence manor by 1508,[67] and in 1545 the bishop's Penpiece of 46 a. in Heath field contained a sheep-pen.[68] The priory estate produced *c.* 400 lambs in a year in the later 16th century,[69] and there were *c.* 1,400 sheep in the parish in 1794.[70]

The chief crops grown in the 15th and 16th centuries, as in 1279, were barley and wheat,[71] with a smaller amount of rye.[72] In 1655 the tenant of Abbey farm had 193 a. under cultivation, growing wheat, barley, rye, peas, lentils, oats, and vetch.[73] Several of the prominent farmers in the 16th and 17th centuries were also maltsters.[74] By the 18th century little barley was malted locally, and the malting-house and kiln at Durhams Farm had fallen into disrepair by 1750.[75]

Saffron was first mentioned at Ickleton in the late 15th century; the disputes over tithes on saffron

[52] *V.C.H. Cambs.* i. 411.
[53] *Rot. Hund.* (Rec. Com.), ii. 585–9.
[54] *Inq. Non.* (Rec. Com.), 215.
[55] Trin. Coll. Mun., Box 21, IIa, ct. roll 10 Hen. VI.
[56] e.g. C.R.O., R 63/D.D.B. 1126.
[57] Ibid. Q/RDc 20.
[58] e.g. ibid. R 63/D.D.B. 1120, where the land is listed with the meadows.
[59] Ibid. R 63/D.D.B. 1115.
[60] Ibid. R 63/D.D.B. 1116.
[61] Ibid. Q/RDc 20.
[62] Vancouver, *Agric. in Cambs.* 69.
[63] e.g. C.R.O., R 63/D.D.B. 1115–17, 1119 (1545); Trin. Coll. Mun., Box 21, IIc, terrier (1612); C.U.L., E.D.R., H 1/4, terriers 1615, 1633; Trin. Coll. Mun., Box 21, IIe, survey bks. (1730).
[64] C.R.O., R 60/20/1, *passim*; B.L. Add. MS. 5861, pp. 19, 126, 145, 194.
[65] Prob. 11/17 (P.C.C. 23 Fetiplace).
[66] *Jnl. Royal Agric. Soc.* vii. 38.
[67] Trin. Coll. Mun., Box 21, III, lease 27 July 23 Hen. VII.
[68] C.R.O., R 63/D.D.B. 1119.
[69] Windsor, St. George's Chap. MS. XVI.4.5.
[70] Vancouver, *Agric. in Cambs.* 70.
[71] *Rot. Hund.* (Rec. Com.), ii. 585–9; B.L. Add. MS. 5861, pp. 19, 145; Prob. 11/9 (P.C.C. 28 Dogett, will of John Fulston the elder); Prob. 11/22 (P.C.C. 32 Porche, will of Ric. Crudd).
[72] Req. 2/91/45; Prob. 11/35 (P.C.C. 31 Powell, will of Rob. Clerke).
[73] C 5/29/235.
[74] e.g. John Smith: Req. 2/101/20; Wm. White: Essex R.O., D/DB 856; Ric. Edwards: Trin. Coll. Mun., Box 21, IIb.
[75] C.R.O., R 51/29/1*i*.

before 1516 suggest that it was then a new crop there.[76] It was planted in small gardens and plots: parts of the Priory demesne were inclosed before 1536 and leased for growing saffron.[77] It was grown in the parish throughout the 17th century,[78] but was not mentioned later.

The only inclosed land in the parish before 1814 lay round the village and close to the river, where wetness and flooding made cultivation difficult. The closes and meadows were attached to the various demesnes, and little was common. There was a common near the river called the Goosehome,[79] Olive or Oly mead, part of Valence, was several until Lammas and then common,[80] and Great Nyardes, pasture south of the village, was divided among the lordships in fixed proportions until Whitsun week and then became common.[81] The only land permanently available to the parish as common was the heath, an uncultivated area in the middle of Heath field. The few animals kept, besides sheep, were mainly cows and pigs.[82]

In 1545 all three fields contained large parcels of 'leys which be seldom eared or sown'.[83] Nearly a third of the priory estate in 1536 was leys,[84] and in 1627 75½ a. were leys out of Valence's 110 a. in South field.[85] Some of the leys in Heath field had been recently ploughed up in 1545, and Valence's remaining 20 a. of leys *c.* 1680 were let for cultivation by the acre.[86] Ley-farming was not mentioned at Ickleton in the 18th century. Pressure on land in the 16th and 17th centuries led to a gradual extension of cultivation. The tenant of Abbey farm in the later 16th century was not to convert land to tillage without permission.[87] John Wood claimed to have improved the estate by increasing the area under cultivation, but Wood's opponents said that although he had ploughed some sheep-walks he had left an equal area of demesne unsown.[88] Tenants were fined in the 1640s and 1650s for ploughing the balks between strips.[89] By 1730 2,236 a. in the parish were arable land.[90]

On all the manors copyholds descended by borough-English to the youngest son, youngest daughter, or youngest sister of the tenant.[91] The heir succeeded as a matter of course on paying an entry-fine, and a tenant might sell, assign, or devise his land.[92] In 1623 a group of villagers sued Sir John Wood who as lord refused to admit their nominees to a copyhold.[93] Some copyholds were enfranchised by individual agreements in the early 18th century, and there was further enfranchisement after inclosure, when more than 400 a. was allotted as copyhold.[94]

In the early 16th century the priory's demesne, with 3 or 4 ploughs,[95] had a bailiff, a hogherd, and a shepherd, besides labourers, who were probably drawn from the large class of wage-earners, a third of the taxpayers at Ickleton in 1524.[96] Later holders of the priory lands leased out parcels of the demesne,[97] and the large estates tended to be divided between several tenants. Valence was farmed as one estate in 1508, but by 1610 was divided between two members of the Swan family, and was held in four parts in 1636.[98] In the 18th century it was generally leased as two farms, each of *c.* 140 a.[99] The two farms derived from the priory estate were larger: in 1726 the Grange had 378 a. of land, and Abbey farm had 380 a.[1] The Limburys estate was also divided into two farms, one freehold and one copyhold. The copyhold farm, held from 1699 by the Westropp family, descended to Mary Pytches in 1747.[2] In 1810 Mrs. Pytches claimed 175 a. in her own right and 123 a. leased from Clare Hall, both estates being farmed by Samuel Hanchett.[3]

Two-thirds of Ickleton's tax in 1524 was paid by the 14 men with goods worth more than £5.[4] The wealthiest inhabitants were Richard and John Crudd, assessed at £48 and £46 respectively, whose family remained prominent until the 18th century, when their property passed to the Hanchetts. By the 18th century John Hanchett, lessee of the tithes, occupied 226½ a.: 140 a. were leased from Trinity College as half of Valence, and the remainder was added by purchase and exchange.[5] He later acquired also the Little Farm and its 100 a. In 1726 there were four large farms, based on the Grange, Abbey Farm, Valence, and Chrishall Grange in Fowlmere parish.[6] Of the 22 main occupiers of land in Ickleton in the 18th century, only 9 farmed more than 50 a. William Simonds occupied 493 a. in the three fields, probably as tenant of either Abbey farm or the Grange. John Hanchett had 360 a., and there were other farms of 298 a., 252 a., 184½ a., and 167 a.[7] The distribution of land had changed little by 1804, when only 11 out of 31 occupiers farmed more than 50 a. Abbey farm was the largest with 447 a., and John and Samuel Hanchett between them had 465 a. There were 6 other holdings of more than 100 a.[8]

76 Prob. 11/7 (P.C.C. 8 Logg, will of Stephen Crudd); *E.D.R.* (1911), 150.
77 *Proc. C.A.S.* xi. 192; E 134/31–2 Eliz. I. Mich./27.
78 P. C. D. Mundy, *Memorials of Ickleton*, 5; *Proc. C.A.S.* xvi. 161.
79 C.U.L., E.D.R., H 1/4, terrier 1615.
80 C.R.O., R 63/D.D.B. 1120.
81 Ibid.; Trin. Coll. Mun., Box 21, IIe, meadow survey bk. 1730.
82 B.L. Add. MS. 5861, p. 194; C.R.O., R 51/29/1a.
83 C.R.O., R 63/D.D.B. 1115, 1116, 1119; Trin. Coll. Mun., Box 21, IIc, terriers 1612, 1627.
84 S.C. 6/Hen. VIII/264.
85 Trin. Coll. Mun., Box 21, IIc, terrier 1627.
86 C.R.O., R 63/D.D.B. 1119; Trin. Coll. Mun., Box 21, IIe, terrier 1685.
87 C.R.O., R 63/D.D.B. 1119 (cover).
88 St. George's Chap. MS. XVI.4.5.
89 C.R.O., R 51/29/1A–B.
90 Trin. Coll. Mun., Box 21, IIe, South field survey bk. 1730.
91 C 3/226/37. Priory, Caldrees, Hovells, and Durhams: C.R.O., R 51/29/1B; Limburys: ibid. R 51/29/8/14; Mowbrays: C 3/34/57; Brays: C 3/175/6; Valence: *31st Rep. Com. Char.* 202.
92 C.R.O., R 51/29/1A–I; R 60/20/1, transcr. of wills of Wm. Simonds and Barnabas Carder; Trin. Coll. Mun., Box 21, IIa, ct. rolls *passim*; Req. 2/6/187.
93 C 3/385/14.
94 C.R.O., R 51/29/2B; ibid. Q/RDz 7.
95 E 134/31–2 Eliz. I Mich./27.
96 E 134/4 Jas. I Mich./25; E 179/81/132 mm. 1–2.
97 E 134/4 Jas. I Mich./25.
98 Trin. Coll. Mun., Box 21, III, lease to John Fraunceys; Box 21, III, lease to Francis Swan; Box 21, III, lease to Wm. Swan.
99 Trin. Coll. Mun., Tower, corner press North, drawer 16; C.R.O., R 63/D.D.B. 1126.
1 C.R.O., R 63/D.D.B. 1121.
2 Clare Coll. Mun., Pytches estate.
3 C.U.L., Doc. 640, nos. 10, 47–8.
4 E 179/81/132 mm. 1–2.
5 C.R.O., R 63/D.D.B. 1121; Essex R.O., D/DB 878.
6 C.R.O., R 63/D.D.B. 1121.
7 Ibid. R 63/D.D.B. 1125.
8 St. George's Chap. MS. C.C. 120151.

All the large pre-inclosure farms had rights of sheep-walk and foldage for large flocks in the common fields. Mowbrays had rights for 400 sheep, and Abbey farm and the Grange for 360 each;[9] the Limburys sheep-walk for 180 was divided in 1790 between Clare Hall and Mrs. Pytches,[10] and Valence also had rights for 180 which were apparently leased in units of 30 with pieces of land in the 16th century.[11] The Grange flock alone could be fed and folded in Stocking and Hill fields, when they were fallow, between Lady day and Ickleton fair (22 July), though the Valence flocks could feed then in Stocking field during the day.[12] It was said in 1794 that the sheep were healthy, but that no improvement in the stock was possible until the parish was inclosed.[13]

The growth of large farms at the expense of small ones was accentuated by inclosure. Some proprietors favoured inclosure in 1803, and three unsuccessful bills were drawn up;[14] the Act was passed in 1810,[15] and the award covering 2,672 a. was made in 1814. An estate covering 640½ a. in place of tithes was awarded to the dean and canons of Windsor. Allotments of 314 a., 261½ a., 243 a., 160 a., and 106 a. were made to the owners of the Grange, Abbey farm, Valence, Mowbrays, and Brays. There were 5 allotments of between 50 a. and 100 a., 5 between 20 a. and 50 a., and 9 between 5 a. and 20 a. Forty people received less than 5 a., many of them ½ a. for rights of common.[16]

The largest parcels were immediately divided to allow the rotation of crops. One of Clare Hall's parcels was divided into four *c.* 1825, and the other into two,[17] and the rectory estate was similarly divided.[18] Clare Hall's tenant pursued a complicated rotation, including wheat, barley, rye, turnips, clover, oats, peas, and seeds, using the turnips and clover to maintain a flock of sheep.[19] In 1843 the same farm had 65½ a. of barley, 41 a. of seeds, 40 a. of wheat, 19 a. of peas, and 34 a. lying fallow.[20] Trinity College's tenant in 1824 was growing mainly barley and oats, with some spring wheat and vetches, and small areas of turnips, potatoes, clover, rye, and peas.[21] Samuel Jonas, an Ickleton farmer whose prize essay on Cambridgeshire farming was published in 1846, recommended the cultivation of turnips and mangolds to feed the sheep, and large flocks were fattened in that way on Clare Hall's farm.[22]

After inclosure the number of farms gradually fell. The tenant of Mowbrays allegedly made a loss in every year from 1818 to 1821,[23] and the dean and canons' lessee reported that some of their allotment was poor land on the hills, as their agent had preferred quantity to quality at inclosure.[24] There were 12 occupiers of land at Ickleton in 1831, and 9 farmers in 1883.[25] Their numbers fell gradually to 8 by 1888, 7 by 1896, 6 by 1912, and 5 by 1937.[26] The decline resulted not from land going out of cultivation, for almost 2,500 a. remained arable in 1905,[27] but from the amalgamation of small farms with large.[28] In 1972 there were 8 farms; most were mainly arable, growing corn and sugar-beet, with some potatoes, but sheep and pigs were also kept. Durhams was used for grazing, and there was a milking herd at the New Grange. Pigs and poultry were also raised on two smallholdings.[29]

The land of Durhams farm was leased to butchers in the 18th and 19th centuries,[30] and by 1905 Durhams was a dairy farm, with its land at the east end of the parish in the river valley.[31] Mowbrays and Valence farms also kept small herds of cows in the 19th century, as well as pigs and poultry,[32] and there were a cattle-dealer and a cow-keeper at Ickleton in 1879 and 1888.[33] Market-gardening was established in the parish in the early 20th century, but did not apparently survive after 1940.[34]

Eighty of the 133 families in Ickleton in 1831 were supported by agriculture, and the lack of alternative employment, as the farms came to employ fewer men, caused much hardship in the later 19th century.[35] Other occupations were principally those supporting the farmers, such as carpenters, blacksmiths, wheelwrights, and saddlers.[36] The village had its own shoemakers, butchers, and bakers, and there was generally a grocer;[37] the only unusual craftsman was a watch-maker, established by 1865.[38] Developments in farm machinery were exploited by William Godfrey, who by 1873 was manufacturing and selling agricultural implements, machines, and engines, while acting also as an ironmonger, wheelwright, smith, and coach-builder.[39] By 1900 the business had extended to contracting and building, as well as making agricultural implements,[40] and it survived in 1972 as a family concern.

In 1865 there were only four shops in the village,[41] but when professional people began to settle there local trade grew, with a newsagent and a hairdresser by 1933 and a café by 1937.[42] A surgeon lived there in 1864 but soon moved to Duxford; Ickleton had a veterinary surgeon by 1883 and a physician by 1922, and an optician and four physicians in 1937.[43] It has continued to attract professional people,

[9] C.U.L., Doc. 640, nos. 16, 32, 60.
[10] Ibid. Doc. 640, no. 10; Clare Coll. Mun., terrier 1790.
[11] C.U.L., Doc. 640, no. 90; Trin. Coll. Mun., Box 21, IIa, ct. rolls 31 Hen. VIII, 28 Eliz. I.
[12] C.U.L., Doc. 640, no. 60.
[13] Vancouver, *Agric. in Cambs.* 70.
[14] *C.J.* lviii. 174; lix. 109; lx. 99.
[15] Ickleton Incl. Act, 50 Geo. III, c. 67 (Local and Personal, not printed).
[16] C.R.O., Q/RDz 7.
[17] Clare Coll. Mun., Dr. Webb's improvements 1823–8.
[18] St. George's Chap. MS. C.C. 120151, survey 1832.
[19] Clare Coll. Mun., Dr. Webb's improvements 1823–8.
[20] Ibid. farm report 1843.
[21] Trin. Coll. Mun., Box 21, VII.
[22] Clare Coll. Mun., valuations 1889, 1897; *Jnl. Royal Agric. Soc.* vii. 35–72.
[23] Clare Coll. Mun., letter from tenant 1821.
[24] St. George's Chap. MS. XVII. 28. 2.
[25] *Census*, 1831; *Kelly's Dir. Cambs.* (1883).
[26] *Kelly's Dir. Cambs.* (1888 and later edns.).
[27] Cambs. Agric. Returns, 1905.
[28] e.g. C.R.O., 296/SP 947; 296/SP 999; 296/SP 932.
[29] Ex inf. Mrs. R. L. Bristowe.
[30] C.R.O., R 51/29/12/22; R 51/29/12/29.
[31] Ibid. R 51/29/8/32; *Kelly's Dir. Cambs.* (1916 and later edns.).
[32] Clare Coll. Mun., list of stock sold 1828; Trin. Coll. Mun., Box 21, VII.
[33] *Kelly's Dir. Cambs.* (1879, 1888).
[34] Ibid. (1908 and later edns.).
[35] *Census*, 1831; C.U.L., E.D.R., C 3/38.
[36] *Kelly's Dir. Cambs.* (1847 and later edns.).
[37] Ibid.; Trin. Coll. Mun., Box 21, IVa, IVb.
[38] *Kelly's Dir. Cambs.* (1865).
[39] *Harrod's Dir. Cambs.* (1873).
[40] *Kelly's Dir. Cambs.* (1900).
[41] Ibid. (1865).
[42] Ibid. (1933, 1937).
[43] Ibid. (1864 and later edns.).

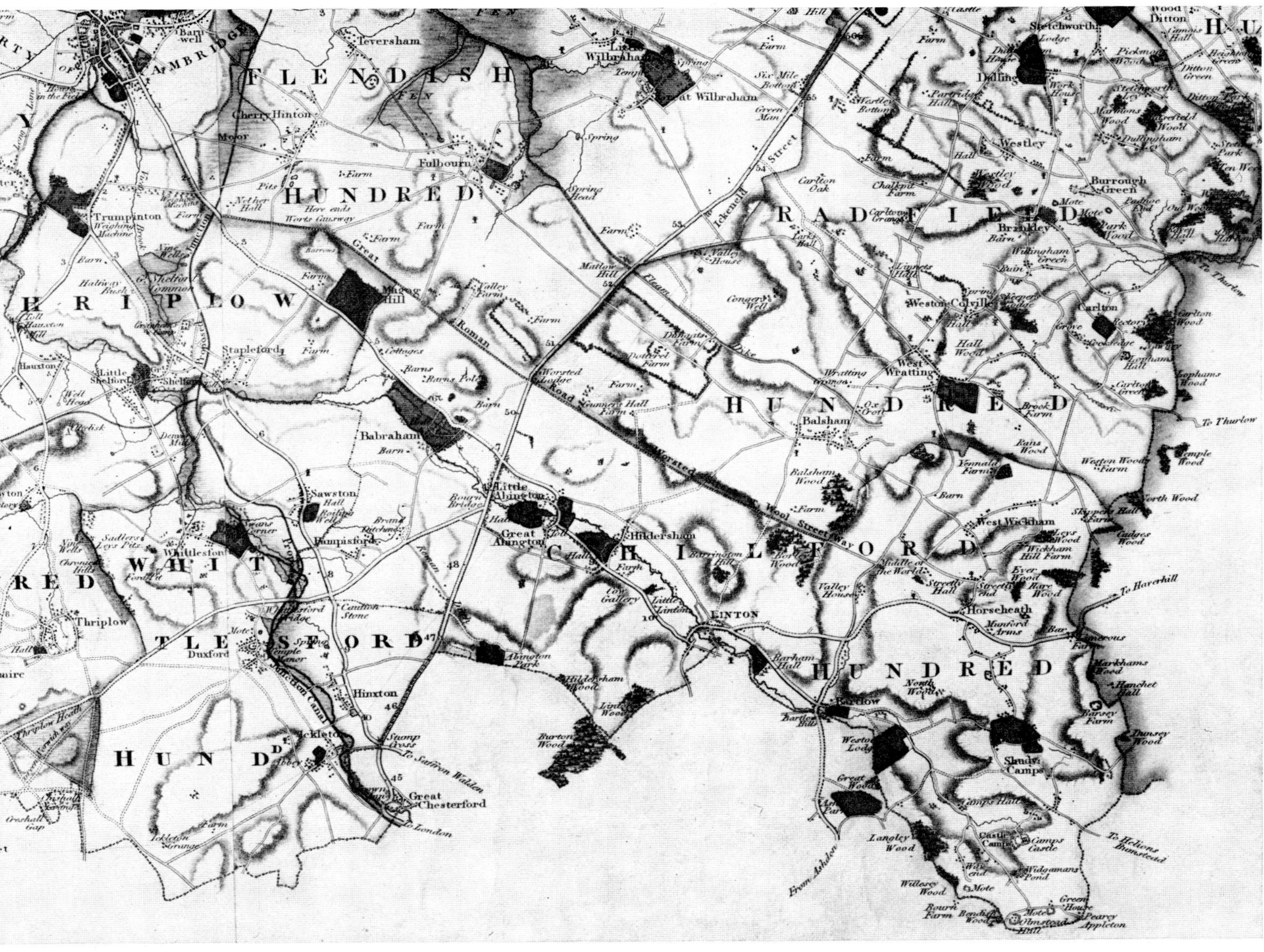

Chilford, Radfield, and Whittlesford hundreds as shown on Baker's Map of Cambridgeshire, 1824

Hinxton Church: the south chapel and aisle built by Sir Thomas Skelton (d. 1416) whose brass is on the floor

Ickleton Church: the south arcade

many of whom commute to Cambridge or London. Most inhabitants work at Duxford and Sawston, and there is little employment in the parish.

Cloth-making at Ickleton was probably on a very small scale. The surname Fuller occurred locally in the later Middle Ages,[44] and there were weavers there in the 16th century.[45] Cloth-finishing was carried on at the Great Chesterford fulling-mill close to Ickleton.[46] A wool-comber was recorded in the 18th century.[47] There were tailors at Ickleton throughout the 18th and 19th centuries,[48] but the manufacture of cloth had probably ceased there by *c.* 1700.

There were two mills at Ickleton worth 30*s.* in 1086.[49] One was perhaps the water-mill at Brookhampton, part of which belonged to Calder abbey in 1231, and part to Valence manor in 1279.[50] The Valence estate included a third of a mill in 1324, and Brookhampton mill was mentioned in 1338,[51] but by the 16th century Valence had no mill and there was none in the Brookhampton area.[52]

The other mill in 1086 was probably the water-mill in Ickleton, of which Calder abbey owned half in 1231 and 1279, and Tilty abbey the other half in 1279.[53] It had gone by 1545, when a former mill of Hovells and Caldrees manors south of the village was mentioned.[54]

The name Windmill hill, in use by 1432, suggests that there was then a windmill at Ickleton.[55] In 1545 the windmill stood on or very close to its later site, west of the Duxford road, with the old Brookhampton highway north of it.[56] It continued in use throughout the 19th century,[57] but closed soon after 1900, and by 1925 its shell had been converted into a house.[58]

In 1818 a water-mill was built on the river at Camping close, west of the church and south of Mill Lane.[59] It was sold with the Hanchett estate in 1867,[60] and closed in 1927 when the last miller was killed in the water-wheel.[61]

A windmill by Great Chesterford village stood just inside Ickleton parish, west of the railway, by 1872; it was still there in 1903,[62] but had been demolished by 1910.[63]

A market on Thursdays at Ickleton was granted to the prioress in 1222 and 1227, possibly in confirmation of an earlier grant by King Stephen[64] although in the 14th century the prioress claimed it by grant of Henry III.[65] No further evidence of the market has been found. The prioress also held an annual fair at Ickleton, which she claimed by a charter of King Stephen.[66] It was held in July in 1287.[67] The profits of the fair were leased with the site and lands of the priory in 1536 and 1557.[68] In the later 16th century the fair was held for five days around the feast of St. Mary Magdalen (22 July), the patron saint of the priory, in the great barnyard of the former convent,[69] where wooden stalls were set up.[70] It was still held on 22 July in the 18th and early 19th centuries,[71] when horses and cheese were the main commodities.[72] In 1872 it was owned by Joseph Heydon of Abbey Farm, and was probably still held on its original site. Under the Fairs Act, 1871, Ickleton fair was abolished from 1872,[73] but it may have lingered until 1875.[74]

The bishop of Ely was in 1556 granted a Friday market at Ickleton and a fair on 14–16 February;[75] no evidence has been found that either was ever held.

LOCAL GOVERNMENT. As part of the honor of Boulogne, Ickleton was said *c.* 1235 to owe 2*s.* a year as wardpenny to the sheriff, but not to owe suit to his court.[76] In 1260, however, the suit formerly made by the vill to the county and the hundred had been withdrawn for the last five years by the keeper of the honor.[77] Ickleton was one of the three places in Cambridgeshire where the honorial court of Boulogne was held in 1333.[78]

The prioress in 1299 claimed view of frankpledge in the parish by prescription. She also had infangthief and the assize of bread and of ale, with a tumbrel, pillory, and gallows;[79] the site of the gallows was probably Gallow hill, west of the Duxford road.[80] All the other manors except possibly Brays held courts baron for their tenants.[81] The court of Priory manor was still after 1536 the only one with view of frankpledge; its court rolls, surviving for most years in the periods 1644–59 and 1710–57, show it making orders about commoning and the maintenance of balks, and presenting

[44] *Inq. Non.* (Rec. Com.), 215; Trin. Coll. Mun., Box 21, IIc, rental 9 Hen. IV.
[45] B.L. Add. MS. 5861, p. 136.
[46] Cf. C.R.O., R 51/29/12/38.
[47] C.R.O., R 51/29/1H.
[48] Essex R.O., D/DB 859; Mundy, *Memorials of Ickleton*, 6; *Kelly's Dir. Cambs.* (1847 and later edns.).
[49] *V.C.H. Cambs.* i. 411.
[50] Dugdale, *Mon.* v. 340; *Rot. Hund.* (Rec. Com.), ii. 587.
[51] C 134/83 no. 32C; Trin. Coll. Mun., Box 21, I, 16 Apr. 12 Edw. III.
[52] Trin. Coll. Mun., Box 21, III, leases 27 July 23 Hen. VII, 1 Dec. 8 Jas. I; C.R.O., R 63/D.D.B. 1120.
[53] Dugdale, *Mon.* v. 340–1; *Rot. Hund.* (Rec. Com.), ii. 588–9.
[54] C.R.O., R 63/D.D.B. 1115.
[55] Trin. Coll. Mun., Box 21, IIa, ct. roll 10 Hen. VI.
[56] C.R.O., R 63/D.D.B. 1120.
[57] Ibid. Q/RDc 20; *Kelly's Dir. Cambs.* (1892).
[58] *Kelly's Dir. Cambs.* (1900, 1904); *Trans. Newcomen Soc.* xxvii. 104.
[59] C.R.O., R 51/29/12/38; Bristowe, *Short Guide to Ickleton*, 13. The lane was named from a fulling-mill in Great Chesterford.
[60] C.R.O., R 60/20/7/1; R 51/29/12/38.
[61] *Camb. News*, 3 Apr. 1964; local information.
[62] Electoral reg. 1872 (P.R.O. Census Room); O.S. Map 6″, Cambs. LIX. SE. (1903 edn.).
[63] *Trans. Newcomen Soc.* xxvii. 118.
[64] *Rot. Litt. Claus.* (Rec. Com.), 508; *Cal. Chart R.* 1226–57, 30; *Rot. Hund.* (Rec. Com.), ii. 570.
[65] *Plac. de Quo Warr.* (Rec. Com.), 102.
[66] *Rot. Hund.* (Rec. Com.), ii. 570.
[67] *Proc. C.A.S.* xxvi. 86.
[68] S.C. 6/Hen. VIII/264; C 2/Eliz. I/A 3/55.
[69] C.R.O., R 63/D.D.B. 1119 (cover).
[70] *Proc. C.A.S.* xi. 192.
[71] Carter, *Hist. Cambs.* 210; *Camb. Chron.* 5 July 1788; B.L. Add. MS. 9412, f. 24; *Gardner's Dir. Cambs.* (1851).
[72] C.R.O., R 58/5, vol. x, p. 496; Bristowe, *Short Guide to Ickleton*, 5.
[73] *Lond. Gaz.* 11 June 1872, p. 2713.
[74] C.R.O., R 58/5, vol. x, p. 496; *Kelly's Dir. Cambs.* (1883).
[75] *Cal. Pat.* 1555–7, 68–9.
[76] *Liber de Bernewelle*, 256.
[77] *Assizes at Camb. 1260*, 38.
[78] S.C. 2/155/46.
[79] *Plac. de Quo Warr.* (Rec. Com.), 102; *Rot. Hund.* (Rec. Com.), ii. 570.
[80] C.R.O., R 63/D.D.B. 1116.
[81] Mowbrays: C 139/89 no. 60; Limburys: C.R.O., R 51/29/8; Valence: *Cal. Inq. p.m.* vi, p. 320; Caldrees, Hovells, and Durhams: C.R.O., R 51/29/1A.

encroachments.[82] The last manorial court was apparently held in 1882, though admissions to copyholds continued until the 1920s.[83]

Ickleton had at least one constable by 1285,[84] and more than one in 1388.[85] The Priory court appointed constables, probably for the whole parish, in the 17th and 18th centuries, and in some years a hayward and one or two pinders.[86]

In 1524 the 'town stock' was valued at 40*s*.[87] It had been supplemented by 1545 by the town lands, 23 a. of which were held by 1569 by trustees for the payment of taxes.[88] In 1779 the 23 a. were held with the other town lands, the income being applied to poor-relief.[89] By 1658 seventeen cottages had been given for the poor; all the endowments were administered by the overseers, and were normally sufficient for the relief of all Ickleton's poor.[90] In the 18th century expenditure on the poor rose sharply from £107 in 1776 to £223 *c.* 1784, and reached £358 in 1803. In that year 41 people received permanent relief.[91] Expenditure fell to £181 in 1814, but averaged over £400 in the 1820s.[92] In 1831 unemployed labourers with large families were given task work, and the poor-rate had risen to £644.[93] Ickleton became part of the Linton poor-law union in 1835, was transferred to the South Cambridgeshire R.D. in 1934,[94] and was included in South Cambridgeshire in 1974.

Three acres allotted at inclosure for land held by the parish clerk 'since time immemorial'[95] were let for £2 8*s*. 6*d*. in 1835, and for *c.* £5 in 1865, paid to the clerk.[96] The clerk's land was in 1966 a registered charity, the income going to the church clerk.[97]

CHURCH. Ickleton church has not been found in records before the 14th century, but its architecture shows it to date from *c.* 1100. The church was appropriated to Ickleton priory, probably in the mid 12th century as part of the original endowment of that house.[98] The parish church has been said to be the priory church, but in fact the nuns had their own church at the priory, described after the Dissolution as a pretty church with a steeple and three bells, and employed a chaplain to serve it.[99] The parish church was served in 1341 by a vicar presented by the prioress.[1] Several vicars in the 14th and 15th centuries were former chaplains of the priory, but the two offices were always held separately.[2]

In 1536 the advowson of the vicarage passed to the Crown, which, apparently by an oversight, included the advowson both in the grant of monastic lands to the bishop of Ely in 1538 and in the grant of the rectory to the dean and canons of Windsor in 1547.[3] It is not known who made the next presentation, between 1552 and 1561, but in 1588 the dean and canons presented.[4] When Bishop Heton returned his Ickleton lands to the Crown in 1600 the advowson was expressly reserved to him.[5] In 1612 both parties claimed the patronage, which was apparently awarded to the bishop.[6] Vicars were collated in 1618, 1641, and 1660 by the bishop,[7] but in 1678 the dean and canons re-asserted their claim, their presentee being also collated by the bishop. On the next vacancy, in 1684, the bishop collated his domestic chaplain as vicar.[8] The bishop granted the next presentation to the bishop of London, who exercised his right in 1689, but all the 18th-century vicars were collated by the bishop of Ely, the dean and canons of Windsor having abandoned their claim.[9] The patronage of the vicarage was transferred in 1852 to the bishop of Peterborough, and from him in 1874 to the Lord Chancellor.[10] The vicarage of Ickleton was held jointly with that of Hinxton from 1930, with alternate presentation by Jesus College, Cambridge, and the Lord Chancellor, but the two benefices were separated again in 1955 and the Lord Chancellor still held the patronage of Ickleton in 1972.[11]

The vicarage was valued at £8 6*s*. 8*d*. in 1535, and was worth only £47 a year in 1707.[12] It was augmented by Queen Anne's Bounty in 1803, and by a parliamentary grant in 1816; in 1864 the living was so poor that the bishop of Peterborough had great difficulty in finding an incumbent.[13] In 1877 the vicar estimated his gross income at £123, but by 1897 it was £288, most of it given by the Ecclesiastical Commissioners.[14]

In the Middle Ages the vicar was entitled to the small tithes, while the prioress, as appropriator, collected the great tithes of corn and hay.[15] In 1516 the vicar complained that his income was too small; by a later arrangement the prioress received all tithes, both great and small, and paid the vicar £8 6*s*. 8*d*. a year, besides all charges on the church

82 C.R.O., R 51/29/1A–I.
83 Ibid. R 51/29/2D–E.
84 *Assizes at Camb. 1260*, 48.
85 *Cal. Close*, 1385–9, 533–4.
86 C.R.O., R 51/29/1A, 1F.
87 E 179/81/132 mm. 1–2.
88 C.R.O., R 63/D.D.B. 1116; C 3/385/14. Francis Swan was a trustee, not the donor of the lands; cf. *31st Rep. Com. Char.* 203.
89 *31st Rep. Com. Char.* 203; for the town lands see below, p. 245.
90 Hampson, *Poverty in Cambs.* 44.
91 *Poor Law Abstract, 1804*, 40–1.
92 *Poor Law Abstract, 1818*, 32–3; *Poor Rate Returns, 1822–4*, 39; *Poor Rate Returns, 1825–9*, 17.
93 *Rep. H.L. Cttee. on Poor Laws*, H.C. 227, pp. 328–9 (1831), viii.
94 *Poor Law Com. 1st Rep.* 249; *Census*, 1931 (pt. ii).
95 C.R.O., Q/RDz 7; *31st Rep. Com. Char.* 204.
96 *31st Rep. Com. Char.* 204; C.U.L., E.D.R., H 1/8, terrier 1865.
97 Char. Com. files.
98 *V.C.H. Cambs.* ii. 223.
99 E 134/4 Jas. I Mich./25.
1 *Inq. Non.* (Rec. Com.), 215.
2 e.g. John Quaille: *Cal. Close*, 1354–60, 330; *V.C.H. Cambs.* ii. 224; Rob. Burton: *E.D.R.* (1909), 61.
3 *L. & P. Hen. VIII*, xiii (2), p. 377; *Cal. Pat.* 1547–8, 149–50.
4 Gibbons, *Ely Episc. Rec.* 443.
5 B.L. Add. MS. 5846, p. 152.
6 *Chapter Acts of D. & C. Windsor, 1430–1672*, ed. Bond, 79; C.U.L., MS. Mm. 1. 39, p. 131.
7 P.R.O. Inst. Bks. ser. A, iii, p. 32; B, i, f. 69.
8 B.L. Add. MS. 5846, p. 83. P.R.O. Inst. Bks. ser. B, iv, p. 141 records, apparently in error, a second presentation in 1684.
9 P.R.O. Inst. Bks. ser. B, iv, p. 141; C, i, f. 443v.; B.L. Add. MS. 5846, p. 83.
10 *Lond. Gaz.* 4 June 1852, p. 1584; 10 July 1874, pp. 3438–9.
11 C.U.L., E.D.R., G 3/23B, p. 162; *Ely Diocesan Dir.* (1971–2).
12 *Valor Eccl.* (Rec. Com.), iii. 504; C.U.L., E.D.R., A 4/2.
13 C. Hodgson, *Queen Anne's Bounty*, 200, 311; Windsor, St. George's Chap. MS. XVII.19.6.
14 C.U.L., E.D.R., C 3/27; C 3/38.
15 E 321/33/24; B.L. Add. MS. 5842, p. 34.

and the vicarage.[16] In 1547 the Crown raised the vicar's stipend to £10, which was still being paid by the dean and canons' farmers in 1650.[17] In 1660 it was raised to £30, and by 1707 it was £35 a year.[18]

In the 16th and 17th centuries the vicar owned *c.* 29 a. of glebe.[19] He claimed 29 a. in 1810, and was awarded 15 a. at inclosure in 1814.[20] The glebe consisted in 1887 of 17 a., let for £16 a year.[21] From 1955, when the remaining glebe was allotted to Hinxton on the separation of that living from Ickleton, the vicarage of Ickleton had no glebe.[22]

A reference to a close called 'the old vicarage' in 1485 suggests that a new house had been built; in 1527 the vicarage was a good house with a well-furnished hall.[23] In 1615 the house stood south of the green near the river, and had a large hall, a parlour, kitchen, four small chambers and a large one, a buttery and a milkhouse, and a study recently added. There were also farm-buildings, and a gate-house with a chamber over it.[24] The vicarage was taxed on 3 hearths in 1664 and 1666, but in 1678 it was a substantial house with 10 rooms.[25] In 1705 a fire destroyed much of the house and in 1783 it was described as a mere cottage.[26] It was unfit for residence by the incumbent throughout the earlier 19th century, and by 1841 part of it had fallen down.[27] A new vicarage was built in 1846 north of Butcher's Hill.[28] The old vicarage was demolished *c.* 1870.[29]

Two small pieces of meadow south of the village, belonging to Ickleton church but not part of the vicar's glebe, had probably been given by the priory, and were traditionally used to provide rushes for the church. The land, known as the church plot or platt, was still used for that purpose in 1730.[30] In the open fields were several small pieces of land which paid Maundy money, mentioned in 1545,[31] but payment had ceased by *c.* 1550.[32]

Before the Reformation there were two guilds in Ickleton, in honour of the Holy Trinity and Corpus Christi. A chalice was given in the earlier 14th century to the Trinity guild,[33] which had an altar in the church in 1510, and owned £7 worth of goods in 1524.[34] The Corpus Christi guild had a light in the church in 1520, and goods in 1524 worth £3.[35] Both guilds owned small amounts of land. In 1553 18 a. of guild land was sold by the Crown, and in 1572 two more small parcels.[36] The guildhall in Ickleton, sold as concealed land in 1571, was bought in 1575 by John Paxton of Great Chesterford.[37]

By will dated 1510, Richard Carewe of Ickleton left at least 10 a. for an obit and a chantry priest.[38] The land was sold in 1572, and eventually bought by John Paxton.[39] Two chantry chapels in the church, north of the chancel, dating probably from the 15th century, were demolished in the 18th century.[40]

Several 15th-century vicars were Cambridge graduates.[41] Robert Burton, vicar 1496–1527, left money to the priest who helped him in the parish and to 'my poor scholar'.[42] Robert Davy, 1527–*c.* 1553, chaplain to Lord Mountjoy,[43] probably lived in Ickleton, and later-16th-century vicars were resident. Neither Robert Procter, *c.* 1553–88, nor Michael Coule, 1588–1612, was a graduate, but both were said to be learned and good preachers.[44] Preaching was popular in the parish, and a parishioner in 1602 left money for four sermons a year.[45] The vicar in 1650, Arthur Lund, described as 'a man mean of life and conversation',[46] was replaced by Augustine Rolfe, 1660–78, who was also curate of Hinxton 1662–76 and possessed books worth £12 at his death.[47]

After 1678 the standard of pastoral care declined, as most incumbents held other benefices, and the condition of the vicarage and the poverty of the living did not encourage residence. Thomas Sayes, 1689–1744, lived a mile away at Chesterford, where his father-in-law was vicar.[48] Zachary Brooke, vicar 1744–88, became a royal chaplain in 1758 and Lady Margaret professor of divinity in 1765.[49] In 1775 he lived at Cambridge, and shared his duties at Ickleton with a 'gentleman of the university'.[50] The curate in 1788, James Buck, was headmaster of Newport grammar school in Essex, and a lecturer in Greek and Hebrew at Cambridge.[51] George Hewitt, vicar 1789–91, was described as 'a scandalous old reprobate'.[52] Zachary Brooke the younger, 1793–1802, son of the former vicar, was also domestic chaplain to the prince of Wales.[53] Both the Brookes were joint holders of Mowbrays manor.[54] Nicholas Bull held Ickleton with Saffron Walden 1803–44, employing his son as curate. Although both lived

[16] *E.D.R.* (1911), 150; E 321/33/24.
[17] *Cal. Pat.* 1547–8, 149–50; Lamb. Pal. MS. 917, f. 207.
[18] *MSS. St. George's Chapel, Windsor Castle*, ed. Dalton, 432; C.U.L., E.D.R., A 4/2,
[19] C.R.O., R 63/D.D.B. 1115–16, 1119–20, *passim*; C.U.L., E.D.R., H 1/4, terrier 1615; Lamb. Pal. MS. 917, f. 208.
[20] C.U.L., Doc. 640, no. 3; C.R.O., Q/RDz 7.
[21] *Glebe Returns*, H.C. 307, p. 39 (1887), lxiv.
[22] See p. 227.
[23] Trin. Coll. Mun., Box 21, IIc, rental 1 Hen. VII; *Proc. C.A.S.* xi. 191.
[24] C.U.L., E.D.R., H 1/4, terrier 1615.
[25] E 179/84/437 rot. 104d.; E 179/244/22 ff. 91v.–92v.; *Proc. C.A.S.* xvi. 161.
[26] C.U.L., E.D.R., A 4/2; B 7/1, p. 127.
[27] Ibid. C 1/6; C 3/21; C 3/17.
[28] Trin. Coll. Mun., Box 21, VII, letters between vicar and coll. 1845.
[29] Mundy, *Memorials of Ickleton*, 4.
[30] C.R.O., R 63/D.D.B. 1120; Trin. Coll. Mun., Box 21, IIe, meadow survey bk. 1730.
[31] C.R.O., R 63/D.D.B. 1116.
[32] C.U.L., E.D.R., D 5/17.
[33] *Vetus Liber Arch. Elien.* (C.A.S. 8vo ser. xlviii), 70.
[34] Prob. 11/17 (P.C.C. 23 Fetiplace, will of Ric. Carewe); E 179/81/132 mm. 1–2.
[35] B.L. Add. MS. 5861, p. 136; E 179/81/132 mm. 1–2.
[36] *Cal. Pat.* 1553, 43–4; 1569–72, p. 341, 347.
[37] E 178/2885; *Cal. Pat.* 1569–72, p. 370; C.R.O., R 52/18/17.
[38] Prob. 11/17 (P.C.C. 23 Fetiplace, will of Ric. Carewe); C 1/542 no. 9.
[39] E 178/2885; *Cal. Pat.* 1569–72, p. 334; C.R.O., R 52/18/17.
[40] *Proc. C.A.S.* xxx. 32–4, 40–4.
[41] e.g. Paul Green, 1438–45, and John Stenyour, from 1445: Emden, *Biog. Reg. Univ. Camb.* 269, 553.
[42] *Proc. C.A.S.* xi. 191.
[43] *Faculty Office Reg.* 1534–49, ed. Chambers, 175.
[44] B.L. Add. MS. 5813, f. 67; Bodl. MS. Gough Eccl. Top. 3, f. 46.
[45] Prob. 11/105 (P.C.C. 39 Hayes, will of Ric. Thurlowe).
[46] Lamb. Pal. MS. 904, f. 261.
[47] *Alum. Cantab. to 1751*, iii. 482; B.L. Add. MS. 5846, p. 83; *Proc. C.A.S.* xvi. 161.
[48] C.U.L., E.D.R., B 8/1; Essex R.O., D/DB 865.
[49] *D.N.B.*; *Alum. Cantab. to 1751*, i. 228.
[50] C.U.L., E.D.R., C 1/1.
[51] *Alum. Cantab. 1752–1900*, i. 429.
[52] Ibid. iii. 349.
[53] Ibid. i. 395.
[54] See p. 236.

at Saffron Walden where they kept a school, two services with sermons were held on Sundays.[55] A later curate lived at Duxford.[56] Bull established a Sunday school, and encouraged his wealthier parishioners to augment the church plate.[57]

His successor W. J. Clayton built a new vicarage, and from that date all incumbents were resident. He also employed a curate, who lived in the village.[58] Even so, less than half of the seats in the church were filled at each service on Census Sunday in 1851.[59] Clayton maintained a day-school, and collected money to replace the old high pews in the church.[60] John Amps, vicar 1864–1907, raised the number of communion services from four to twelve a year; during his incumbency the chancel was entirely rebuilt.[61]

The churchyard, no longer sufficient by 1877,[62] was closed in 1883, to be replaced by a cemetery with a small chapel west of the Hinxton road;[63] a burial board administered the cemetery in 1888, the parish council by 1896.[64]

A room in a cottage on the New Grange estate was used in the early 20th century as a chapel, known as St. Barnabas. Services were held there on Sundays until 1937 by G. W. H. Bowen for his tenants, with monthly visits by the vicar.[65]

The church of *ST. MARY MAGDALEN* was originally dedicated to the Virgin Mary,[66] but by the mid 18th century it had adopted the dedication of Ickleton priory.[67] The church, at the east end of the village north of the village green, is of field stones and rubble with ashlar dressings, and has a chancel, crossing tower with north vestry and south transept, and aisled and clerestoried nave with south porch.[68] The cruciform plan is largely determined by the surviving parts of the early-12th-century church, which was a substantial building with an aisled nave of four bays, in which two piers in each arcade are thought to be re-used monolithic columns from a Roman building. In the 14th century the south transept was rebuilt and the aisle widened to align with it; the porch was added, the clerestory heightened and a new roof put over the nave, the transept arches were rebuilt, and a spire was placed over the tower. The chancel was rebuilt and provided with a north chapel and a vestry in the mid 15th century, which was probably the occasion of the church's rededication in 1452.[69] In the same century new west windows were put into the nave and north aisle, and there were new pews, stalls, and a rood-screen. Although not always in good repair, the building survived largely unaltered until the 18th century, when, before 1791, the ruinous north transept, chapel, and vestry were taken down.[70] The chancel was rebuilt in 1882,[71] some of the 15th-century features being re-used though not all in their original positions.

There were four bells and a sanctus bell in 1552, one of which was probably the great bell mentioned in 1521.[72] In 1742 the six bells included a saints' bell; there were then two sanctus bells on the outside of the steeple,[73] but only one by the later 19th century, when it was used as a curfew or fire bell,[74] and later as an hour-bell for the church clock.[75] The six bells, all made or recast in the 18th century, were restored in 1907.[76] By 1927 the largest was broken, having fallen when the frame collapsed, and in that year the remaining bells were recast and three more were added.[77] In 1972 there were eight bells, besides the sanctus bell: (i) 1927, Gillett & Johnston; (ii) 1927; (iii) 1927, Lester & Pack; (iv) 1729, Thomas Newman of Norwich; (v) 1781, William Chapman of London; (vi) 1755, Lester & Pack; (vii) 1729, Newman of Norwich; (viii) 1751, Thomas Lester of London.

Ickleton church was unusually rich in plate in the Middle Ages, having four chalices, one gilded, an ivory pyx, and three processional crosses.[78] In 1552 there were a chalice, censers, a ship, a cross, two candlesticks, a pyx, and a pax with a crucifix, all containing silver.[79] A silver cup and a pewter chalice, the only vessels in 1771,[80] had by 1835 been augmented by two pewter flagons and a pewter plate, with a recently presented silver flagon and paten.[81] A silver chalice was given in 1950. The registers begin in 1558 and are virtually complete.

NONCONFORMITY. Three or four women in Ickleton, thought to be Quakers, were said in 1669 to attend conventicles in other places,[82] and two men were presented for the same practice in 1677. Six people were presented in 1675 for refusing to receive the sacrament,[83] and in 1676 there were seven adult nonconformists in Ickleton.[84] By 1690 the congregation was large enough to invite two Cambridge ministers to preach in Ickleton every third Sunday.[85] A house in the village, licensed for nonconformist worship in 1715, may have been the barn where fortnightly meetings were held in 1728. Described as the meeting-house in 1740 and the meeting barn in 1790, it was licensed again in 1801[86] but had been pulled down by 1861.[87] Numbers remained low throughout the 18th century, and the

[55] C.U.L., E.D.R., C 1/4; St. George's Chap. MS. XVII.28.2.
[56] C.U.L., E.D.R., C 1/6.
[57] Ibid. C 1/4; St. George's Chap. MS. XVII.28.2.
[58] *Kelly's Dir. Cambs.* (1858, 1864).
[59] H.O. 129/188/1/6/7.
[60] St. George's Chap. MS. XVII.19.6.
[61] C.U.L., E.D.R., C 3/27.
[62] Ibid.
[63] *Lond. Gaz.* 24 July 1883, pp. 3711–12; 13 Nov. 1883, p. 5374; *Kelly's Dir. Cambs.* (1888).
[64] *Kelly's Dir. Cambs.* (1888, 1896).
[65] C.R.O., 331/Z 7, 1936, Dec., p. 97; ex inf. Mrs. R. L. Bristowe.
[66] Prob. 11/9 (P.C.C. 22 Dogett, will of John Pyry).
[67] Ecton, *Thesaurus* (1763), 100.
[68] For a plan, see *Arch. Jnl.* cxxiv. 229; see above, plate facing p. 241.
[69] *Proc. C.A.S.* xi. 186.
[70] Ibid. xxx. 40–1.
[71] Ibid. 31.
[72] *Cambs. Ch. Goods, temp. Edw. VI*, 1; B.L. Add. MS. 5861, p. 145.
[73] Palmer, *Wm. Cole*, 100.
[74] C.R.O., R 58/5, vol. x, p. 421.
[75] A. R. Flitton, *Bells of Ickleton.*
[76] Ibid.
[77] *Proc. C.A.S.* xxx. 30 n.
[78] *Vetus Liber Arch. Elien.* (C.A.S. 8vo ser. xlviii), 70.
[79] *Cambs. Ch. Goods, temp. Edw. VI*, 1.
[80] C.U.L., E.D.R., H 1/8, terrier 1771.
[81] St. George's Chap. MS. XVII. 28. 2.
[82] *Orig. Rec. of Early Nonconf.* ed. Turner, i. 40.
[83] C.U.L., E.D.R., B 2/62, f. 15v.; B 2/63A, f. 18.
[84] Compton Census.
[85] *Freedom after Ejection*, ed. Gordon, 13.
[86] C.R.O., Q/SO 3, p. 208; C.U.L., E.D.R., B 8/1; C.R.O., R 51/29/1H, ct. roll 1740; Clare Coll. Mun., Ickleton, terrier 1790; C.U.L., E.D.R., B 4/1, f. 23.
[87] C.R.O., R 51/29/2D, p. 199.

congregation was served by ministers from Cambridge, Linton, and Saffron Walden, while some Independents and Baptists attended meetings at Saffron Walden.[88]

In 1842 a Congregational chapel was built on the east side of Frog Street.[89] It was twice enlarged between 1876 and 1896, when it had 200 sittings,[90] and was served by the minister from Duxford once a fortnight.[91] It was closed *c.* 1954,[92] and the building, sold in 1956,[93] was derelict in 1972.

Two houses, one near the Red Lion and the other in Frog Street, were licensed for worship in 1824 and used by Methodists.[94] Martha Ridding who occupied both houses was their teacher, and they were known as the Old Wesleyan church people.[95] By 1851 Ickleton was a station of the Cambridge Primitive Methodist connexion, served by a minister from Saffron Walden; it had no chapel, but on Census Sunday 80 people attended the evening service.[96] A brick chapel on the north side of Abbey Street was built in 1852, with seating for 160 people.[97] The congregation numbered 95 in 1877.[98] In 1972 the chapel was served by a minister from Saffron Walden.

There was a Salvation Army hall in Ickleton between 1899 and 1903.[99]

EDUCATION. Ickleton schoolmasters were licensed in 1601 and 1625,[1] and a school was held in part of the church in 1638 and in 1678.[2] There was, however, no other school when the vicar, Nicholas Bull, started a Sunday school *c.* 1804,[3] which had more than 60 pupils in 1807 and *c.* 100 by 1818.[4] The schoolroom in the church, probably part of the tower, was rebuilt in 1824.

There was one day-school by 1825, and two by 1833, with 34 and 25 pupils respectively.[5] They may have been the two dame-schools, of which one was held near the green and the other in one of the town houses.[6]

The British school at Ickleton was established in 1846, in the Congregational chapel and schoolroom built in 1842 in Frog Street. The children paid 1*d.*, 2*d.*, or 3*d.* a week according to their age and the size of the family. Average attendance in 1870 was 80,[7] said by the vicar to be mostly children from other parishes.[8] The building was enlarged after 1876.[9] The British school was still open in 1888[10] but has not been traced later.

There was no Church day-school until the vicar, W. J. Clayton, established one *c.* 1848.[11] It was held in a room on the south side of Mill Lane, which was sold in 1867 as part of the Hanchett estate.[12] In 1871 a new school and teacher's house were built in Church Street. Each child paid school pence; in 1872 the average number of pupils was 57.[13] Attendance rose rapidly to 97 in 1877 and 103 in 1888, and the school was enlarged in 1884.[14] The vicar also held evening-classes, but they were poorly attended.[15] The school closed in 1961, and the village children were transferred to schools at Duxford and Sawston.[16] The building was bought by the village and converted into a village hall.[17]

CHARITIES FOR THE POOR. Ickleton was one of the parishes to benefit under the charity of Lettice Martin.[18] In 1783 the income of 13*s.* 4*d.* a year was distributed to the poor every three years,[19] and by 1836 26*s.* a year was received from the charity.

By will proved 1659[20] Richard Swan left 1¼ a. to the churchwardens for poor widows. The land, known as the Widow's Acre, yielded 8*s.* 9*d.* in 1783.[21] At inclosure the charity was allotted 1 a., yielding by 1865 £1 16*s.* a year, which was distributed among poor widows.[22]

The town lands amounted to 40 a. by 1545, and in the 16th and 17th centuries were leased to farmers, the income being devoted to poor-relief.[23] The rural dean in 1783 accused the trustees, all substantial farmers, of occupying the lands themselves instead of allotting 3 a. to each poor family at a low rent, while the income was no longer distributed among the needy.[24] The trustees were allotted 50 a. at inclosure, and in 1825 the town lands were let for £41 which was distributed to the poor at Easter.[25] Town houses were also given in the 17th and 18th centuries; by 1837 there were ten cottages let for £15, and the number had grown to seventeen by 1851.[26] The town lands and houses were administered together in the 19th century, and the income, amounting to £148 in 1900, was distributed in food, clothing, and money.[27]

In 1911 the charities of Lettice Martin, Richard Swan, and the town lands and houses were amalgamated as the Ickleton United Charities. As early as 1835 expenditure on the upkeep of the town houses had exceeded that on doles, and the houses were gradually sold by the trustees. By 1959 five

88 C.U.L., E.D.R., B 8/1; B 7/1; C 1/4.
89 Ed. 7/5.
90 *Duxford Cong. Church: a short hist.* 18; *Cong. Yr. Bk.* (1896).
91 *Cong. Yr. Bk.* (1860); *Duxford Cong. Church,* 18.
92 *Cong. Yr. Bk.* (1953).
93 Char. Com. files.
94 C.U.L., E.D.R., B 4/1, ff. 74v., 77.
95 Ibid. C 1/6.
96 H.O. 129/188/1/6/9.
97 Inscr. on bldg.; *Methodist Ch. Bldg. Ret.* (1940).
98 C.U.L., E.D.R., C 3/27.
99 G.R.O. Worship Reg. no. 37233.
1 C.U.L., E.D.R., B 2/18, f. 78; B 2/32, f. 97v.
2 *Cambs. Village Doc.* 66; C.U.L., E.D.R., B 2/59A.
3 B.L. Add. MS. 9412, f. 24; C.U.L., E.D.R., C 1/4.
4 C.U.L., E.D.R., C 1/4; *Educ. of Poor Digest,* 61.
5 C.U.L., E.D.R., C 1/6; *Educ. Enquiry Abstract,* 57.
6 Mundy, *Memorials of Ickleton,* 9.
7 Ed. 7/5.
8 C.U.L., E.D.R., C 3/27.
9 *Duxford Cong. Church,* 18.
10 *Kelly's Dir. Cambs.* (1888).
11 *Church School Inquiry, 1846–7,* 6–7; Windsor, St. George's Chap. MS. XVII.19.6.
12 C.R.O., R 60/20/7/1; R 51/29/12/38; R.G. 9/1028.
13 Ed. 7/5.
14 C.U.L., E.D.R., C 3/27; *Kelly's Dir. Cambs.* (1883 and later edns.).
15 C.U.L., E.D.R., C 3/38.
16 Bristowe, *Short Guide to Ickleton,* 5.
17 *Camb. Ind. Press,* 13 May 1963.
18 See p. 219. Except where otherwise stated, this section is based on *31st Rep. Com. Char.* 202–4; Char. Com. files.
19 C.U.L., E.D.R., B 7/1, p. 128.
20 Prob. 11/288 (P.C.C. 117 Pell).
21 C.U.L., E.D.R., B 7/1, p. 128.
22 C.R.O., Q/RDz 7; C.U.L., E.D.R., H 1/8, terrier 1865.
23 C.R.O., R 63/D.D.B. 1116; Hampson, *Poverty in Cambs.* 44.
24 C.U.L., E.D.R., B 7/1, pp. 127–8.
25 C.R.O., Q/RDz 7; C.U.L., E.D.R., C 1/6.
26 *Gardner's Dir. Cambs.* (1851).
27 *Kelly's Dir. Cambs.* (1900); *Char. Digest Cambs. 1863–4,* 24–5.

cottages, let at low rents to the needy, remained to the charity, two of which were sold in 1962. The income of the Ickleton United Charities in 1961 was *c.* £200, which was spent partly on rates and repairs to the town houses and partly on gifts of coal.

Ann, widow of Samuel Jonas, founded a clothing club for the poor; members' weekly subscriptions were augmented by contributions from wealthier parishioners, and the fund was distributed in clothing to the members. In 1882, after Ann's death, her children purchased £350 stock in memory of their parents, to be held in trust by the vicar and churchwardens. Payments from the fund were made in clothing until the 1960s. In 1927 Mr. and Mrs. G. W. H. Bowen built and endowed three bungalows in Frog Street for elderly parishioners, with a preference for their former servants. Mrs. Bowen (d. 1967) left £1,000 to the alms-houses, known as the Gertrude Homes, which were modernized in 1971. A Scheme of 1970 joined the Jonas and Bowen charities with the Ickleton United Charities.

SAWSTON

SAWSTON lies 7 miles south of Cambridge, and is notable as one of the very few industrial villages in the county. The parish covers 1,898 a., and is compact but irregular in shape; its western boundary follows the former course of the river Cam or Granta and part of its northern boundary follows the river Granta, called the Old River or Stapleford River in 1802.[1] The rest of the northern and eastern boundaries follow old field boundaries and trackways and a stream. Apart from Huckeridge Hill north of the village, the whole parish lies below 100 ft.

Sawston's streams and rivers have been beneficial as a source of fish,[2] and as the means of driving mills used by the paper industry; the high lime content of the streams encouraged the development of the leather and parchment industry.[3] The wet land by the rivers has, however, been of restricted use. It is drained by ditches, which required regular scouring, a responsibility assumed by the parish in the 16th century.[4] Peat and sedge were cut there in the Middle Ages, but livestock pastured on the commons by the river frequently suffered from disease.[5] Dernford Fen, 73 a. of undrained fen in the north-west part of the parish, was scheduled as a site of special scientific interest in 1951, and is the home of several rare plants, especially mosses, and birds.[6] The Hall Meadow, 17 a. of rough peaty pasture, once part of a much larger peat fen south-east of Sawston Hall, is also a protected site.[7] Since the construction of the railway embankment near the Cam or Granta in 1845, severe floods have from time to time affected the houses west of the village.[8]

The southern half of the parish lies on the Middle Chalk, and the northern on the Lower Chalk. The soil is generally light and chalky, becoming heavier and wetter towards the north.[9] There was a gravel-pit on Huckeridge Hill in the 19th century.[10] The parish was predominantly agricultural from the 11th to the mid 19th century, when the paper and leather industries already established there began a rapid expansion. There were six open fields until inclosure in 1802. In 1972 the land north and east of the village was still agricultural, although new housing estates were constantly encroaching upon it.

Thirty-eight tenants were mentioned at Sawston in 1086, and *c.* 125 in 1279,[11] but population probably fell as a result of the Black Death in 1348–9 when many deaths were reported.[12] It had apparently recovered by 1525, when 80 people were assessed for the subsidy.[13] Although only 64 households were recorded there in 1563, there were 76 houses in the village in 1580, and *c.* 80 under Charles II.[14] In 1676 there were 209 adults, and *c.* 300 people in 1728.[15] In 1801 Sawston contained 466 people, and from then on the village grew steadily, overtaking all the surrounding parishes. In 1831 771 people were returned, but the vicar believed the true figure to be *c.* 1,000, paupers without legal settlement having been omitted.[16] Unlike most rural villages Sawston grew rapidly in the decade 1851–61 because of the success of its paper and leather industries, its population rising from 1,124 to 1,363. Expansion continued steadily until 1891, when the population was 1,882, but industrial depression and emigration led to a decline in the next three decades. Numbers rose gradually from 1,530 in 1921 to 1,684 in 1931. Since the Second World War the population has risen sharply to 2,133 in 1951, 3,377 in 1961, and 5,597 in 1971, as employment opportunities increased.[17]

The village grew up on the east bank of the Cam or Granta along the road from Cambridge to Saffron Walden, which may follow a prehistoric trackway. The Ashwell or Street way may be another prehistoric route traversing the parish, crossing the river at Whittlesford mill and following

[1] C.R.O., P 136/26/1, p. 11. This article was written in 1972.

[2] T. F. Teversham, *Hist. of Village of Sawston* (Sawston, 1942–7), ii. 89. Mr. Teversham, a Sawston inhabitant of long standing, wrote a two-volume history of the village and other works on its past, which despite a few inaccuracies are most valuable. His work was largely based on the Huddleston MSS., now in C.R.O.; as the collection was uncatalogued in 1972, reference has been made to Teversham in preference to the MSS.

[3] W. R. Davidge, *Cambs. Regional Planning Rep.* (1934), 23.

[4] Teversham, *Hist. Sawston*, ii. 63, 65–7, 91.

[5] Vancouver, *Agric. in Cambs.* 65–6.

[6] *Nature Reserves and Sites of Special Scientific Interest* (Cambs. and Isle of Ely Planning Dept. 1965), p. 48.

[7] Ibid. p. 56.

[8] Teversham, *Hist. Sawston*, ii. 262–3; *E.D.R.* (1903), 154; *Camb. Evening News*, 30 May 1972.

[9] *Camb. Region.* (1938), 9, 27; Vancouver, *Agric. in Cambs.* 65.

[10] Teversham, *Hist. Sawston*, i. 8; C.R.O., P 136/26/1, p. 16.

[11] *V.C.H. Cambs.* i. 410–11; *Rot. Hund.* (Rec. Com.), ii. 575–80.

[12] Teversham, *Hist. Sawston*, i. 32, 44–5.

[13] E 179/81/147 mm. 4–5.

[14] B.L. Harl. MS. 594, f. 200; Teversham, *Hist. Sawston*, ii. 48; see below, pp. 280, 282.

[15] Compton Census; C.U.L., E.D.R., B 8/1, f. 26v.

[16] *Census*, 1801–31; C.U.L., E.D.R., C 3/21.

[17] *Census*, 1851–1971.

footpaths and Church Lane in a north-easterly direction to Copley Hill (in Babraham) and Fleam Dyke.[18] The north–south road, which became High Street, remained the focus of settlement, and as late as 1872 the village was described as mostly one long rather tortuous street, with lanes branching off towards the fields.[19] From the east side of High Street, Church Lane leads past the church but peters out into a track which joins Babraham Road, the only other road leading east from Sawston. To the west New Road (formerly Borough Mill Road) and Mill Lane join to become Mill Road, which crosses the river at the paper-mill (formerly Borough Mill) and probably once continued to Newton. Further south, Common Lane (formerly Water Lane)[20] led over the commons to the river until it was cut off by the construction of the railway. Between the roads alleys and lanes led into the fields.[21] The main road through Sawston was turnpiked in 1724 and disturnpiked in 1870,[22] a toll-house being built at the north end of the parish by Stapleford Bridge.[23] A new road bypassing the village on the west was opened in 1968.[24]

Finds from the Bronze Age and later, including a Saxon grave on Huckeridge Hill, were apparently associated with the road,[25] and the village was probably established by the Saxons.[26] Dernford Mill in the north part of the parish may have existed by the 10th century,[27] and the manor-site close to it suggests that a separate settlement may once have stood there. Borough or Burgh Mill may also have been the centre of a small settlement in the Middle Ages, when it was mentioned as the name of a hamlet.[28] The position of the early-12th-century church suggests that settlement began near the south end of the present village, as does the siting of the village cross at the junction of Church Lane and High Street; in the 16th century the cross was a tiled building like a market-cross, although no market is recorded at Sawston. The building was sold in 1815 so that only the stump of a cross remained; its top was renewed in the 1880s, and in 1919 it was further modified to become the village war memorial.[29]

Substantial 15th- and 16th-century houses confirm the evidence of 16th-century subsidy assessments that Sawston had some prosperous inhabitants.[30] The Old Vicarage, demolished in 1948, was a 15th-century house, as is the Queen's Head. In 1580 houses extended from the Brook, flowing westwards through the parish *c.* 500 yd. south of the church, to just south of Babraham Road in the north, where there was a stone cross. The extremities were known as Brook End and Cambridge Town's End.[31] A few cottages were built on the roads leading off High Street,[32] but settlement was concentrated along the road, and apart from a small southern extension the area of the village remained much the same until the late 19th century. The Huddleston family, lords of two and eventually all of the manors, settled in Sawston in the early 16th century, and the family and their house, Sawston Hall, dominated the parish until modern times; several members of the family, especially in the 18th century, took a close personal interest in all aspects of parish life, perhaps encouraged by their Catholicism which barred them from other administrative and political activities.

Sawston also contained a number of prosperous yeoman farmers. Several houses had six, five, or four hearths in the later 17th century,[33] and more were built in the 18th century.[34] The village lacked professional or independent people, perhaps because of Sawston's lack of visual charm,[35] and only four professional people lived there in 1831.[36]

The industrial growth of the 19th century brought a great expansion in the working-class population without a corresponding increase in the middle and upper classes, enabling the small group of large employers to dominate the village. Most notorious was Thomas Sutton Evans, owner of the Old Yard leather and parchment works from 1850 to 1882, who in 1871 employed *c.* 250 people.[37] Evans carried on bitter feuds with the local doctor, baker, and manufacturer of mineral water, and to all three he established rivals in Sawston whom his employees were obliged to patronize. He set up a brewery at his skinyard and owned four public houses where his workmen had to receive part of their pay in beer, and after the Education Act of 1870 made elementary education compulsory he allowed boys from the skinyard to attend school only after a heavy morning's work. Evans opposed the co-operative movement in Sawston, and in competition with Edward Towgood, the owner of the paper-mill, he bought a mill in Wales which contributed to his financial downfall. After eloping with the vicar's daughter Evans obtained some control of church affairs, especially after his brother-in-law, Edwin Swann Daniel, became vicar in 1855. Eventually, however, he quarrelled with the ministers of both church and chapel, and forbade his employees to attend either. In 1853 he purchased some land at the southern tip of the parish and built a beerhouse and rows of cottages in South Terrace and along the main road for his workmen, who called the area the Spike, after the Irish penal settlement.

The other main employer in Sawston was Edward Towgood (d. 1889), who in 1871 employed nearly 400 people at the paper-mill.[38] In 1866 he rebuilt the National school, and after his purchase of the

[18] Fox, *Arch. Camb. Region*, 148–9.
[19] *Daily News*, 5 Apr. 1872 (Camb. Public Libr., scrapbk. p. 143).
[20] Teversham, *Hist. Sawston*, ii. 65.
[21] G. Challis, *Sawston in the Late Sixties and Early Seventies* (Sawston, n.d.), 8–9.
[22] Stump Cross Roads Turnpike Act, 10 Geo. I, c. 12; Annual Turnpike Acts Continuance Act, 1870, 33 & 34 Vic. c. 73.
[23] Challis, *Sawston*, 8.
[24] *Camb. News*, 22 Sept. 1967.
[25] *Archaeologia*, xviii. 341; Fox, *Arch. Camb. Region*, 259–60, 323; *V.C.H. Cambs.* i. 267 n., 279, 316, 328.
[26] *P.N. Cambs.* (E.P.N.S.), 96–7.
[27] Hart, *Early Charters of E. Eng.* pp. 40–1.
[28] Teversham, *Hist. Sawston*, i. 78–9; ii. 7.
[29] Ibid. ii. 54, 260–1; Challis, *Sawston*, 7.
[30] *L. & P. Hen. VIII*, iii (2), p. 1118; E 179/81/147 mm. 4–5.
[31] Teversham, *Hist. Sawston*, i. 6; ii. 53.
[32] C.R.O., P 136/26/1.
[33] See pp. 278, 280, 282.
[34] Teversham, *Hist. Sawston*, ii. 124.
[35] Challis, *Sawston*, 10; *Daily News*, 5 Apr. 1872.
[36] *Census*, 1831; Char. Com. files.
[37] R.G. 10/1591. For Evans, see Teversham, *Hist. Sawston*, ii. 257–8, 260, 266–9, 272, 282; Challis, *Sawston*, 7, 11–12; T. F. Teversham, *Story of a Country Printing House* (Sawston, 1962), 13–17; C.R.O., 331/Z 6, 1932, Jan., p. 7; *Cambs. Local Hist. Counc. Bull.* xxvi (1971), 19–23; *Camb. Ind. Press*, 5 Feb. 1960.
[38] R.G. 10/1591.

advowson in 1879 he and his brother Hamer were generous patrons of the church. Like Evans, Towgood built houses for his workmen, including five rows of brick terrace houses in New Road in 1878.[39] John Crampton (d. 1910), the proprietor of a general store, a printing-works, and a mineral-water factory, was the third leader of Sawston society in the later 19th century. He built Crampton Terrace, north of Mill Lane, in 1882;[40] Prince's Terrace, another private development, was built by Frederick Prince, village doctor from 1844 to 1889.[41] The tradition of the benevolent employer was continued in the 20th century by H. G. Spicer (d. 1944), who bought the paper-mill in 1917. He and his wife gave land for the village college in 1930, and in 1932 built a theatre, later converted to a cinema and closed in 1963.[42] His wife helped to found the Sawston maternity and infant welfare centre in 1918, to which H. G. Spicer left £1,000.[43] By 1961 the firm of Spicers owned more than 100 houses in the area, and in 1971 it held two blocks of flats and money in trust for necessitous former employees and their dependents.[44]

The physical development of Sawston was closely connected with economic fluctuations in its industries. In the early 1870s high rents, which only skilled workmen could pay, created a demand for cheap housing, and rapid building continued to fill the gaps in the medieval village plan: 40 or 50 villas and cottages were built in a few years before 1883, and more building was then in progress.[45] Discontent and poverty, however, led to emigration and strikes of agricultural labourers in 1872 and paper-workers *c.* 1890.[46] The Old Yard declined after T. S. Evans's death in 1882, and by 1895 30 cottages stood empty and there was no longer a demand for building land.[47] Another depression affected the leather industry in the 1920s and 1930s, but building continued. The first council houses were built in 1921 and by 1972 there were over 750 council houses in Sawston.[48] By 1950 much of Mill Lane and New Road was built up, and development had begun in Church Field where there had been no houses in 1933.[49] Building on the Church Field estate continued throughout the 1950s and by 1963 *c.* 40 of the 55 a. available were built over,[50] with further development by 1969. The 1960s also saw the creation of new housing estates north of Babraham Road, between New Road and Mill Lane, along Common Lane, and west of the main road between the Brook and the Spike. Much of the development was undertaken by private companies and consisted of mixed houses and bungalows, such as the Deal Grove estate,[51] and land and house prices were high. Further expansion of the village was planned in the 1970s with the intention that Sawston should be independent of Cambridge and become a centre for the surrounding area.[52] After the Second World War light industry was encouraged by the county council to settle in Sawston instead of Cambridge, and an industrial estate was built north-east of the village.[53]

A gas supply was provided in 1867, and the main street was first lit in 1882,[54] but the company was wound up in 1898.[55] By 1901 the church was lit with acetylene gas, which by 1904 had been extended to the rest of the village.[56] Main sewerage was provided *c.* 1878, when a drain was built along High Street with settling beds in Common Lane.[57] A new sewage works built in 1962 was already overloaded by 1972, and development in the village was discouraged until it had been extended.[58]

Several outbreaks of smallpox occurred in the 1870s, derived from infected rags used at the paper-mill. Typhoid also broke out periodically, because of impure water supplies: many cottages up to the Second World War had only surface wells or used a parish pump.[59] Piped water was introduced in 1937. Electricity was brought to the village in 1926.

Sawston had a public library, maintained by subscriptions, in 1884.[60] After 1930 the village college became the centre of social, educational, and cultural life for the neighbouring villages. The parish council acquired a fire engine in 1896,[61] and a new fire station was built in 1971.[62] A health centre was opened in 1969.

A co-operative society was founded in the village in 1867 by a group of craftsmen from the leather works and elsewhere, who built a shop. In spite of opposition from T. S. Evans the society flourished, though in 1872 it was said that labourers could not use the shop because they were paid fortnightly and needed credit.[63] A lodge of the Oddfellows was recorded in 1883, and a court of the Foresters, recorded in 1890,[64] survived in 1972; a women's friendly society, founded *c.* 1892, had 44 members in 1900; the friendly society movement in Sawston was closely linked with the church.[65]

The London–Cambridge railway line, opened in 1845, runs through the parish on an embankment beside the Cam or Granta. The nearest stations were at Whittlesford and Great Shelford, both over a mile away, and a suggested station at the paper-mill was opposed by Edward Towgood.[66] A branch line from Shelford to Haverhill (Suff.), built in 1865, crossed

39 Teversham, *Country Printing Ho.* 28.
40 Ibid. *passim.*
41 Teversham, *Hist. Sawston*, i. 7.
42 *Camb. Ind. Press*, 5 Feb. 1960; *Camb. News*, 4 Sept. 1963; *Kelly's Dir. Cambs.* (1937).
43 Char. Com. files.
44 Ibid.; *The Times*, 26 Oct. 1961, suppl.
45 *Daily News*, 5 Apr. 1872; *Kelly's Dir. Cambs.* (1883).
46 *Daily News*, 5 Apr. 1872; Challis, *Sawston*, 14; Teversham, *Hist. Sawston*, ii. 269.
47 Char. Com. files.
48 *Sawston and Pampisford Festival of Britain Week Programme*; ex inf. S. Cambs. R.D.C.
49 *Camb. Chron.* 15 Mar. 1933; C.R.O., airphotographs, 1946, 1949, 1953, 1962, and 1969.
50 *Introduction to Sawston* (Sawston Par. Council [1963]).
51 C.R.O., SP 136/2A.
52 *Town Map no. 3 for Sawston* (Cambs. and Isle of Ely Planning Dept. 1965).
53 *Town and Country Planning*, xxii. 423–4.
54 Challis, *Sawston*, 28–9; *Kelly's Dir. Cambs.* (1883).
55 Teversham, *Country Printing Ho.* 22.
56 *E.D.R.* (1901), 17; *Kelly's Dir. Cambs.* (1904).
57 Challis, *Sawston*, 29–30; Teversham, *Hist. Sawston*, ii. 65.
58 *Camb. Ind. Press*, 15 June 1962; *Camb. Evening News*, 27 July 1972.
59 Teversham, *Hist. Sawston*, ii. 275; Challis, *Sawston*, 18; C.R.O., 515/SP 449; 515/SP 1473.
60 C.R.O., R 58/5, vol. x, p. 127.
61 *Camb. Ind. Press*, 2 Oct. 1896; 13 Nov. 1896; *Kelly's Dir. Cambs.* (1904).
62 *Camb. Evening News*, 30 Sept. 1971.
63 Teversham, *Country Printing Ho.* 14, 16–17; *Daily News*, 5 Apr. 1872.
64 C.R.O., R 58/5, vol. x, pp. 127, 141.
65 *E.D.R.* (1892), 739; (1891), 588; (1900), 51.
66 Challis, *Sawston*, 30.

the northern part of the parish. It was closed in 1967, and the tracks had been removed by 1972.

Sawston's position on a main road fostered the establishment of inns and public houses, and an inn called the Saracen's Head was mentioned in the 15th century.[67] Early inns included the White Horse, mentioned in 1633,[68] and the Green Man, open in 1711.[69] The Black Bull, open in 1687, was probably replaced by the Vine, mentioned in 1711 and renamed the Black Bull before 1755.[70] In 1872 there were 14 public houses and beer-retailers, and 13 in 1900.[71] Public houses and inns open in Sawston in 1972 were the White Horse and the Black Bull, mentioned above, the White Lion, open by 1757, the Queen's Head, open *c.* 1810,[72] the Greyhound and the King's Head, both open by 1847,[73] the University Arms at the Spike, built by T. S. Evans in the 1850s, and the Cross Keys and the Woolpack, recorded in 1937.[74]

The village feast was traditionally held on Easter Monday.[75] By the later 19th century an amusement fair was held around the cross in Easter week, lasting three days *c.* 1870 and a week by the 1890s,[76] and parishioners were resisting attempts by the county council to abolish the event.[77] Other feasts were held in the 18th century by the Huddlestons for their tenants, the sainfoin feast in December and the wood feast and the coal supper when the Hall's winter fuel was delivered.[78] The beating of the parish bounds on Gang Monday was another occasion of feasting and drinking.[79] The custom was observed in 1624 and 1725, but probably died out at inclosure.[80] On Plough Monday a plough was dragged through the village, and on Shrove Tuesday there were children's games in Camping Close, a custom which later developed into an annual amusement fair.[81] The picking of the Town Peas is described below.[82]

MANORS AND OTHER ESTATES. Two of the 8 hides in Sawston were held freely in 1066 by Orgar from King Harold. After the Conquest William I granted the land, later called the manor of *DERNFORD*, to his half-brother Robert, count of Mortain, who gave it before 1086 to his father Herluin's Benedictine foundation at Grestain (Eure).[83] The abbey's estate at Sawston, which covered 332 a. in 1279,[84] was administered in the 13th century by Grestain's cell at Wilmington (Suss.).[85] In 1348 the abbey needed money for its patron's ransom,[86] and Dernford was demised on a 1,000-year lease to Tideman de Lymbergh, who by 1354 had conveyed the manor to Michael de la Pole and his brothers Thomas (d. 1361) and Edmund.[87] Michael, later earl of Suffolk, apparently released his rights in Dernford to Edmund, who had sole possession in 1356 and settled the manor on himself and his second wife Maud in 1373. Sir Edmund lived at Sawston,[88] where he was granted free warren in 1383.[89] Dernford thereafter descended with Pyratts manor, as described below. Dernford manor-house, recorded in 1279,[90] burnt down shortly before 1580, when the site was empty.[91] Dernford Farm was built on the same site north-west of the village before 1662,[92] and was rebuilt in the 19th century.

The main estate in Sawston at Domesday, comprising 4 hides, was held before the Conquest by three unfree sokemen from Alfric Campe. William I gave the land to Eudes the steward,[93] and it presumably became part of his honor, though no overlord was mentioned after 1086, and by 1236 the terre tenant held the estate in chief.[94] In 1086 it was held from Eudes by Pirot, and it became known as *PYRATTS* or *SAWSTON* manor. By *c.* 1210 it was held by Ralph Pirot,[95] presumably by direct descent from Pirot. Ralph died in 1222 and his son and heir Richard between 1224 and 1227.[96] The Sawston manor remained for her life with Ralph's widow Joan, who held 2 fees there with her second husband Richard Attaneston *c.* 1235, and died after 1256.[97] Richard Pirot's brother Ralph was lord over Pyratts manor in 1236 and 1242.[98] After Ralph's death in 1252 his son Ralph succeeded to the manor, which comprised 397 a. in 1279.[99] Shortly before he died in 1305 Ralph Pirot conveyed his land at Sawston to his younger son Simon;[1] Simon was alive in 1327, but by 1329 his widow Elizabeth was in possession as joint tenant.[2] She held it with her second husband, William Warde, until his death in 1357, and then alone until she died in 1375.[3] The reversion had been divided between Simon Pirot's two sisters, Catherine (d. by 1375), wife of Henry Wardedieu, and Emma, wife of Robert Deddam. Emma and

67 Teversham, *Hist. Sawston*, ii. 6; C 1/48 nos. 539–40.
68 C.R.O., R 51/17/2D.
69 *Proc. C.A.S.* xvi. 190.
70 C.R.O., Huddleston MSS., list of copyholds 1637–1725; ibid. R 53/12/29; R 53/12/40.
71 *Daily News*, 5 Apr. 1872; *Kelly's Dir. Cambs.* (1900).
72 C.U.L., Doc. 651, nos. 197, 199, 207; Teversham, *Hist. Sawston*, ii. 169.
73 *Kelly's Dir. Cambs.* (1847).
74 Ibid. (1937).
75 Carter, *Hist. Cambs.* 252; *Eng. Topog.* (Gent. Mag. Libr.), ii. 66.
76 Challis, *Sawston*, 20–1; C.R.O., R 58/5, vol. x, p. 44; Teversham, *Hist. Sawston*, ii. 278–9.
77 *Camb. Ind. Press*, 2 Oct. 1896.
78 Teversham, *Hist. Sawston*, ii. 148–9.
79 *Eng. Topog.* (Gent. Mag. Libr.), ii. 70 n.
80 Prob. 11/148 (P.C.C. 13 Hele, will of John Jefferie); Teversham, *Hist. Sawston*, ii. 149; C.R.O., 331/Z 6, 1930, Mar. p. 21.
81 Challis, *Sawston*, 20; Teversham, *Hist. Sawston*, 254.
82 See pp. 262–3.
83 *V.C.H. Cambs.* i. 372, 411; *V.C.H. Suss.* ii. 122.
84 *Rot. Hund.* (Rec. Com.), ii. 579.
85 *V.C.H. Suss.* ii. 122.
86 D. Matthew, *Norman Mons. and their Eng. Possessions*, 142 n.
87 *Cal. Pat.* 1348–50, 221; 1354–8, 158.
88 Ibid. 1370–4, 285; *Complete Peerage*, xii (1), 437–40; *Proc. C.A.S.* xxxvi. 19–22; Teversham, *Hist. Sawston*, i. 45.
89 *Cal. Chart. R.* 1341–1417, 287.
90 *Rot. Hund.* (Rec. Com.), ii. 579.
91 Teversham, *Hist. Sawston*, i. 22.
92 E 179/84/436 rot. 44.
93 *V.C.H. Cambs.* i. 384, 410.
94 Farrer, *Honors and Knights' Fees*, iii. 168–9, 219.
95 *Red Bk. Exch.* (Rolls Ser.), ii. 528.
96 For the Pirot descent from 1086, see *Complete Peerage*, x. 473–5.
97 Ibid. 475 n.; *Liber de Bernewelle*, 256; *Close R.* 1234–7, 342.
98 *Bk. of Fees*, i. 582; ii. 923, 927.
99 *Cal. Inq. p.m.* i, p. 60; *Rot. Hund.* (Rec. Com.), ii. 575.
1 *Cal. Chanc. Wts.* i. 236; *Cal. Inq. p.m.* iv, p. 222.
2 *Cambs. Lay Subsidy, 1327*, 27–8; *Cal. Pat.* 1327–30, 375.
3 *Cal. Inq. p.m.* x, p. 297; xiv, p. 235.

Robert granted their interest to William Warde, who settled it on his daughter Margery and her husband Richard of Kelshall, a judge of the Common Pleas, after whose deaths without issue their heirs sold it in 1361 to Sir Robert Thorpe (d. 1372). Robert's brother and heir William conveyed the manor in 1376, subject to Henry Wardedieu's life-interest in one moiety, to Sir Edmund de la Pole, his wife Maud, and their son Walter,[4] who already held Dernford manor.[5]

Sir Edmund died in 1419,[6] and his son Sir Walter in 1434. The manors were thereupon settled for life on his second wife Margaret, who occupied them in 1466.[7] The heir, Sir Edmund Ingoldisthorpe of Burrough Green, son of Margaret, Sir Walter's daughter by his first wife Elizabeth,[8] had died in 1456; his daughter and heir Isabel[9] in 1457 married John Neville, later marquess of Montagu.[10] The Sawston estate, however, was held in 1473 by Sir Edmund's widow Joan, and on her death in 1494 probably passed to creditors for 6½ years, then descending to Isabel Neville, one of Isabel's five daughters.[11]

Isabel Neville married William, a younger son of the family of Huddleston of Millom (Cumb.), and her descendants were lords of the manor in Sawston from the 16th to the 20th century.[12] Isabel was succeeded in 1516 by her son John (d. 1530), whose widow Elizabeth held the manor until her son John came of age in 1539.[13] Sir John Huddleston (kt. 1553), a J.P. and sheriff of Cambridgeshire under Edward VI, supported Queen Mary in the early days of her reign and by 1554 had been made vice-chamberlain, a privy councillor, and captain of King Philip's guard in England.[14] He was succeeded in 1557 by his widow Bridget and son Sir Edmund (d. 1606),[15] who purchased the other two manors in Sawston in 1576.

Sir Edmund's son and heir Henry, a Catholic, was involved in the Gunpowder Plot and amassed large debts, also forfeiting his Essex estates.[16] Despite extensive land transactions to pay debts and recusancy fines in the 17th century, the family retained the lordship of the four Sawston manors,[17] except that Huntingdons was sold in 1635 to John Byatt, descended in 1650 to his eight granddaughters of whom two died in 1658,[18] and had been reunited in the Huddlestons' possession by the early 18th century.[19] Henry Huddleston died in 1657 and his eldest son Sir Robert, who had kept the game for Charles I at Newmarket,[20] in the same year without surviving issue. Robert's brother and heir Henry, who had fought for the king and compounded,[21] was succeeded in 1665 by his son Henry (d. 1713),[22] whose son Richard (d. 1717) borrowed money abroad and improved the family's financial position. The estates were managed by a bailiff until the majority in 1735 of Richard's son Richard (d. 1760),[23] who was succeeded by his son Ferdinand (d. 1808). After inclosure in 1802 the family estate covered all of the parish east of the main road and a few plots to the west.[24] Ferdinand's son Richard died unmarried in 1847 and the manors passed to his brother Edward (d. 1852) and Edward's son Ferdinand. Under a settlement made by Ferdinand the estate descended in 1890 to his sister Isabella's son Denys Alexander Lawlor,[25] and then in 1921 to William Reginald Herbert (d. 1929), another of Ferdinand's nephews, each of whom added the name of Huddleston to their own.[26] In 1922 W. R. Herbert-Huddleston sold 1,045 a. in Sawston, leaving his successor Capt. R. F. Eyre-Huddleston, grandson of Ferdinand's sister Jane, only the Hall and grounds, a field of 11 a., and the lordship of the manors.[27] Capt. Eyre-Huddleston was succeeded in 1970 by his nephew, Major A. C. Eyre.

The early manor-house of Pyratts, built by 1279, stood near the church on a moated site close to the present house, where foundations are sometimes visible in dry weather.[28] In the mid 15th century it included a hall, two cross chambers, 30 other chambers, numerous outhouses, a gatehouse, two barns, two stables, and a dovecot. Sir Walter's widow Margaret de la Pole was alleged to have let the buildings deteriorate, but the house was inhabited by the Huddlestons in the early 16th century.[29]

The story of Queen Mary's flight to Sawston in 1553 and the subsequent destruction of the manor-house has been embellished by its narrators, but is based on fact.[30] Mary certainly spent the night before or after the death of Edward VI on 6 July 1553 at the house, on her way to Norfolk to escape from the duke of Northumberland.[31] Tradition relates that she escaped the next morning in disguise, riding

[4] *Cal. Inq. p.m.* xiii, p. 189; xiv, pp. 235–6; C.P. 25 (1)/29/80 no. 7; *Cal. Pat.* 1374–7, 188; *Cal. Close*, 1374–7, 532; 1419–22, 142–3; Foss, *Judges of Eng.* iii. 450.

[5] See above.

[6] C 138/41 no. 63.

[7] C 139/64 no. 33; *Cal. Close*, 1429–35, 340–1; *Cal. Pat.* 1461–7, 525.

[8] C 139/64 no. 33; Teversham, *Hist. Sawston*, i. 34. Eliz. was buried in Sawston church in 1423/4: Teversham, *Hist. Sawston*, ii. 23–4.

[9] C 139/165 no. 20.

[10] *Complete Peerage*, ix. 92–3.

[11] *Cal. Inq. p.m. Hen. VII*, i, pp. 463–4; *Cal. Close*, 1468–76, pp. 329–30; *Complete Peerage*, ix. 93–4 n.

[12] *Visit. Cambs.* (Harl. Soc. xli), 27.

[13] C 142/32 no. 69; C 142/52 no. 5; Teversham, *Hist. Sawston*, ii. 38. Teversham elsewhere mistakes John's age: *Hist. Sawston*, i. 35.

[14] See below. For Sir John Huddleston's career, see *Hist. Parl., Commons*, 1509–58, forthcoming.

[15] C 142/111 no. 15; Teversham, *Hist. Sawston*, i. 36.

[16] Teversham, *Hist. Sawston*, ii. 100.

[17] Ibid. 102; e.g. C.P. 25(2)/277/6 Jas. I East. no. 24; C.P. 25(2)/538/1650 Hil. no. 13; C.P. 25(2)/910/4 Anne Hil. no. 1.

[18] Teversham, *Hist. Sawston*, i. 54; ii. 103, 105.

[19] C.P. 25(2)/910/4 Anne Hil. no. 1.

[20] *Genealogist*, iii. 300; B.L. Add. MS. 5819, f. 147v.; Burke, *Land. Gent.* (1855), 587, which however dates Hen.'s death incorrectly.

[21] Burke, *Land. Gent.* (1855), 587; *Cal. Cttee. for Compounding*, iii. 2236.

[22] Teversham, *Hist. Sawston*, ii. 106–7, 110; cf. Burke, *Land. Gent.* (1855), 587, and B.L. Add. MS. 5798B, p. 331, both of which give an incorrect descent for the later 17th cent.

[23] Teversham, *Hist. Sawston*, ii. 133–5.

[24] Ibid. i. 41–2; ii. 211; C.R.O., P 136/26/1.

[25] Teversham, *Hist. Sawston*, i. 42–3; Burke, *Land. Gent.* (1906), 866–7.

[26] Burke, *Land. Gent.* (1952), 1307; *Cath. Rec. Soc.* xxvii. 219 n.

[27] C.U.L., Maps 53(1)/92/33; Teversham, *Hist. Sawston*, ii. 297; Burke, *Land. Gent.* (1952), 1307.

[28] *Rot. Hund.* (Rec. Com.), ii. 575; Teversham, *Hist. Sawston*, i. 20.

[29] C 1/48 no. 540.

[30] For the traditional version, see *D.N.B.* s.v. Mary I; Fuller, *Hist. of Worthies of Eng.* (1840 edn.), i. 258; J. Foley, *Recs. of Eng. Province of Soc. of Jesus*, v. 584 n.

[31] *Hist. Parl., Commons*, 1509–58, forthcoming, s.v. John Huddleston.

pillion behind John Huddleston or one of his servants, and that a Protestant mob from Cambridge set fire to the house behind her. The most likely culprit, however, was the duke of Northumberland himself, who left London for Cambridge on 14 July and began pillaging and burning the houses of Mary's supporters;[32] a mass-book and grail used by her were taken from Sawston, and by 18 July one of Huddleston's tenants was spreading the news that 'the tyrant hath burned good Master Huddleston's house and spoiled his goods'.[33] In addition to his knighthood, offices, and the manor of Great Wilbraham,[34] John Huddleston received from Queen Mary a grant of stone from Cambridge castle with which to rebuild his house.[35]

Date-stones of 1557 and 1584 may mark the beginning and end of the rebuilding of Sawston Hall. Some 15th- and early-16th-century architectural features in the hall range suggest that the house had not been totally destroyed in 1553 and that its remains were incorporated in the new building. The courtyard plan, with the hall on the north, service rooms on the west, and parlour on the east, could also be of medieval origin, although the principal elevations are contrived to be nearly symmetrical, the hall occupies only the ground floor, and there is a characteristically late-16th-century long gallery on the first floor of the south range. Much 16th- and 17th-century panelling and a contemporary priest's hole remain inside. The house was taxed on 17 hearths in 1662 and 1674;[36] there was some internal refitting in the 18th century but much of the older work survived and was consolidated in a general restoration of 1850.[37] In 1580 there was a 'large court being quadrant',[38] presumably before the north front, but there is no evidence that the house had a park of any size and much of the existing planting appears to be of the mid or late 19th century. The terraces and formal rose gardens are of recent origin.

The manor of *DALE*, held from the lords of Pyratts by service of sending a mounted serjeant with the lord to the king's host,[39] may be named from William de Dal who in 1197 held 8 a. from Master Benet of Sawston.[40] About 1236 John son of William of Sawston held $\frac{1}{8}$ of Ralph Pirot's 2 knights' fees.[41] John of Sawston purchased a messuage, a mill, and 30 a., held of Ralph Pirot, from Alice le Child in 1270.[42] By 1279 John had been succeeded by his son William, who then held 1 hide.[43] Sir William of Sawston died holding $\frac{1}{4}$ knight's fee in Sawston in 1308 and his lands passed to his son John (d. after 1366).[44] By 1376 the manor belonged to Thomas Sawston,[45] who by will dated 1392 devised it to his eldest son Ralph.[46] Ralph Sawston was alive in 1434,[47] but his widow Thomasina held the manor in 1435. Ralph's son John, lord in 1460,[48] was followed by 1483 by Thomas Sawston. Thomas died in 1513 leaving Dale manor to his son William,[49] whose lands were valued at £20 a year in 1525.[50] Ralph Sawston, William's son and heir, died *c.* 1542, and the manor was divided between his five sisters and coheirs.[51] Two of the fifths were bought in 1552 by Thomas Potto, a Sawston butcher,[52] and another was sold in 1554 to Thomas Rand.[53] Part of Dale manor was held *c.* 1570 by Ferdinand Parys of Linton, who sold the lordship to Sir Edmund Huddleston in 1576,[54] since when it has descended with the manors described above.

A sheep-walk and *c.* 60 a., formerly part of the manor, were bought by Dean Lloyd and settled by him before 1581 on Pembroke Hall, Cambridge.[55] The college leased the land to the Huddlestons from 1698, and in 1799 Ferdinand Huddleston purchased the estate, for which his son was allotted 71½ a. at inclosure.[56]

The manor-house of Dale, recorded in 1279,[57] stood on a moated site later covered by Deal Grove, east of the road from Cambridge. It was leased with its dovecot and orchard in 1580 and 1592,[58] but had apparently disappeared by 1766.[59] Deal Farm was built beside the road near the grove after 1922.

The remaining 2 hides in Sawston, later *HUNTINGDONS* or *SOMERYS* manor, were held freely before the Conquest by Sigar, steward of Ansgar the staller.[60] By 1086 Roger de Somery held the land from Geoffrey de Mandeville,[61] whose grandson Geoffrey became earl of Essex in 1140.[62] Until the 15th century the estate and a court leet were held from the earls of Essex, passing with the earldom to Henry de Bohun, husband of Maud de Mandeville (d. 1236),[63] and descending to their heirs. Earl Humphrey de Bohun died in 1373 leaving two young daughters as coheirs, and the view of frankpledge was released to the elder, Eleanor, on her marriage in 1380 to Thomas, earl of Buckingham[64] (d. 1397). After Eleanor's death in 1399 her rights at Sawston were assigned to her elder daughter Anne, wife of Edmund, earl of Stafford[65] (d. 1403), and were held by Anne until 1421,[66] when

32 *Cal. S.P. Spanish*, 1553, 107.
33 Foxe, *Bk. of Martyrs*, viii. 591; *Archaeologia*, xxiii. 41.
34 *Cal. Pat.* 1553–4, 4.
35 J. Caius, *Hist. Cantabrigiensis Academiae . . .* (Lond. 1574), 8; E 178/3612.
36 See below, pp. 278, 282.
37 *Ecclesiologist* (1861), 404–5; see below, plate facing p. 256.
38 Teversham, *Hist. Sawston*, i. 21.
39 *Rot. Hund.* (Rec. Com.), ii. 577.
40 *Feet of Fines* (Rec. Com.), 262–3.
41 *Bk. of Fees*, i. 582.
42 Teversham, *Hist. Sawston*, i. 47.
43 Ibid. 48; *Rot. Hund.* (Rec. Com.), ii. 577.
44 *Kts. of Edw. I*, iv (Harl. Soc. lxxxiii), 215; *Cal. Inq. p.m.* v, pp. 48–9; xiii, p. 64.
45 *Cal. Close*, 1374–7, 532.
46 Teversham, *Hist. Sawston*, i. 49.
47 *Cal. Pat.* 1429–36, 385–6.
48 Teversham, *Hist. Sawston*, i. 49.
49 Ibid.; C 142/28 no. 125.
50 E 179/81/147 mm. 4–5.
51 Teversham, *Hist. Sawston*, i. 50; C.P. 40/1150 rot. 321.
52 C.P. 40/1152 rot. 217; for his occupation, see *E.D.R.* (1913), 104.
53 *Cambs. Fines*, 1485–1603, ed. Palmer, 59.
54 Teversham, *Hist. Sawston*, i. 50; ii. 89; C.P. 25(2) 93/841/18 Eliz. Trin. no. 2.
55 B.L. Add. MS. 9412, f. 272.
56 Teversham, *Hist. Sawston*, ii. 75, 126–7; C.R.O., P 136/26/1, p. 42; ibid. Huddleston MSS., terrier of Pembroke Hall estate 1592.
57 *Rot. Hund.* (Rec. Com.), ii. 577.
58 Teversham, *Hist. Sawston*, i. 23–4; ii. 76, 99.
59 C.R.O., Huddleston MSS., terrier of Hall estate 1766.
60 *V.C.H. Cambs.* i. 411; 'Esgar' should read 'Ansgar': Farrer, *Feud. Cambs.* 263; cf. *V.C.H. Cambs.* v. 229.
61 *V.C.H. Cambs.* i. 411.
62 *Complete Peerage*, v. 113–15.
63 Ibid. 134.
64 *Cal. Inq. p.m.* xiii, pp. 130, 133; *Cal. Close*, 1377–81, 390–1.
65 *Cal. Close*, 1396–9, 183; 1399–1402, 162–3; *Cal. Inq. p.m.* (Rec. Com.), iii. 263.
66 *Cal. Close*, 1402–5, 226, 253.

the Bohun inheritance was divided between her and Henry V, as son and heir of Mary, Eleanor's younger sister; the view of frankpledge at Sawston fell to the king,[67] and was granted to Queen Catherine in dower in 1422.[68]

The mesne lordship over that manor descended from Roger de Somery to the Somery family who were lords of Haslingfield,[69] descending from Roger de Somery (d. *c.* 1198) to his son Miles. One third of a fee at Sawston held of Roger passed from Ralph de Somerville to his daughter Cecily, whose eldest son Hugh Archer ceded it before 1190 to Philip de Somery but recovered it from him in 1201. In 1204 Hugh's son Ralph ceded it for life to Juette,[70] perhaps the Juette de Somery whose grandson Robert claimed land at Sawston in 1225 and held ⅔ of 2 fees *c.* 1235.[71] The estate was probably held *c.* 1246 by Walter de Somery.[72] By 1279 the manor, covering 249 a., was held as 1 knight's fee by Robert Bayard of Robert de Monteny, a grandson and coheir of Miles, under the earl of Essex.[73] Robert Bayard granted two-thirds of the manor in 1288 to Ralph of Coggeshall for 11 years.[74] In 1302 Robert's son John granted the estate, of which the other third was then held in dower by Hawise, wife of Reynold de Durenne, to Ralph Huntingdon and his wife Denise.[75] After Ralph's death Denise married before 1317 Geoffrey of Haverhill, who was the wealthiest man in Sawston in 1327. Both were living in 1335.[76] Ralph Huntingdon's son Hugh, the next lord, was succeeded *c.* 1360 by his brother Ralph.[77] Ralph's son John followed his father before 1390, and was succeeded between 1403 and 1412 by his son Walter Huntingdon (d. 1443).[78] Walter devised the manor to his mother Elizabeth for life, and then to his eldest son Thomas,[79] whose elder daughter Margaret, wife of John Parys, succeeded him in 1498.[80] In 1517 Margaret settled Huntingdons manor on her son Philip Parys,[81] who in 1542 settled it on John Huntingdon, probably the son of Robert, younger son of Walter (d. 1443), and on John's wife Joyce.[82] John died without issue in 1554, and Joyce married secondly Thomas Moore. By 1558 the manor had reverted to Sir Philip Parys (d. 1558), who settled it on his younger son Ferdinand.[83] Huntingdons was sold with Dale manor to Sir Edmund Huddleston in 1576.[84]

The original manor-house of Huntingdons, recorded in 1279, probably stood on the moated site just west of the present farm-house.[85] In 1580 the house was a tiled timber building with a hall, two parlours, a kitchen, and other chambers, and stood on one side of a courtyard with a gatehouse and extensive farm-buildings.[86] Huntingdons Farm in 1972 was a 17th-century house of hall and cross-wing form, extensively remodelled in the 19th century.

The preceptory of the Hospitallers of St. John of Jerusalem at Shingay had appropriated Sawston church by *c.* 1278.[87] In 1540 the preceptory's property was granted by the Crown to Sir Richard Long.[88] For the next 90 years the rectory estate, consisting in 1580 of 35½ a. in Sawston with land in Babraham and Pampisford[89] and the great tithes worth £100 a year in 1685,[90] descended in the Long and Russell families like Temple manor in Duxford.[91] In 1631 it was conveyed by Francis, earl of Bedford, to Robert Balam, son-in-law of John Byatt who had farmed the rectory since at least 1625.[92] The rectory was apparently in Byatt's possession at his death in 1650, for it passed to his eight granddaughters, reduced to six by the deaths of Alice and Jane Balam in 1658, and thereafter descended in six parts.[93]

One part was sold in 1661 by Paul and Susan Calton to Arthur Stock, whose son Arthur sold it in 1689 to William Greenell.[94] Several of the other sixths were bought in 1662 and 1664 by John Greenell, perhaps the John Greenell, or Greenhalgh, of Harston who was impropriator in 1685 as guardian of his nephew.[95] William Greenell conveyed one-sixth in 1693 to agents for Henry Huddleston,[96] who was said to own the great tithes in 1707.[97] James Bostock, Henry's brother-in-law and probably acting for Henry's son, sold five-sixths in 1716 to Stephen Corby, a Sawston farmer, and his son John (d. 1723). Stephen died in 1727, leaving the rectory to his two daughters, who married Samuel Jaggard and William Clarke. Their children and heirs, Sarah Jaggard and John Clarke, sold their shares of the estate in 1790 to John Gosling, a wealthy farmer and tanner. In 1800 Gosling, who lived in the rectory farm-house and farmed its land, agreed to sell to Ferdinand Huddleston two more sixths, thus bringing the latter's portion up to half the rectory.[98] At inclosure Gosling received 130½ a. for glebe and tithes, and Huddleston 182½ a.[99] Both estates thereafter became merged with their owners' other lands. The rectory farm-house, known later as Goslings, stands east of the main road at the southern end of

[67] *Rot. Parl.* iv. 136.
[68] Ibid. 187.
[69] For their descent, see *V.C.H. Cambs.* v. 229–30.
[70] *Cur. Reg. R.* i. 447; *Cal. Inq. p.m.* xiii, p. 137; *Feet of Fines* (Rec. Com.), 283, 310.
[71] *Cur. Reg. R.* xii, p. 59; *Liber de Bernewelle*, 256.
[72] *Cambs. Fines*, 1196–1485 (C.A.S. 8vo ser. xxvi), 28.
[73] *Rot. Hund.* (Rec. Com.), i. 55; ii. 570, 578; *V.C.H. Cambs.* v. 230.
[74] C.P. 25(1)/26/43 no. 17.
[75] C.P. 25(1)/26/48 no. 16.
[76] *Cal. Pat.* 1313–17, 699; 1330–4, 403; *Cambs. Lay Subsidy, 1327*, 27; *Cambs. Fines*, 1196–1485, 100–1.
[77] Teversham, *Hist. Sawston*, i. 52. References to Hugh in 1373 and 1380 appear to be retrospective: *Cal. Inq. p.m.* xiii, p. 137; *Cal. Close*, 1377–81, 392–3.
[78] Teversham, *Hist. Sawston*, i. 52–3; *Cal. Close*, 1402–5, 226, 253.
[79] Teversham, *Hist. Sawston*, i. 53.
[80] *Cal. Inq. p.m. Hen. VII*, ii, pp. 278–9.
[81] Teversham, *Hist. Sawston*, ii. 94.
[82] Ibid. i. 53; *Cambs. Fines*, 1485–1603, ed. Palmer, 48.
[83] Teversham, *Hist. Sawston*, i. 53–4; C.P. 25(2)/68/558 no. 43; *Misc. Gen. et Her.* (5th ser.), ii. 124–5.
[84] C.P. 25(2)/93/841/18 Eliz. I. Trin. no. 2
[85] *Rot. Hund.* (Rec. Com.), ii. 578; *V.C.H. Cambs.* ii. 38.
[86] Teversham, *Hist. Sawston*, i. 25–6.
[87] *Vetus Liber Arch. Elien.* (C.A.S. 8vo ser. xlviii), 72–3.
[88] *L. & P. Hen. VIII*, xv, p. 294.
[89] Teversham, *Hist. Sawston*, ii. 251.
[90] Ibid. i. 140.
[91] See p. 203.
[92] C.P. 25(2)/400/7 Chas. I Trin. no. 7.
[93] Teversham, *Hist. Sawston*, ii. 105.
[94] C.P. 25(2)/632/13 Chas. II Mich. no. 16; C.P. 25(2)/814/1 Wm. & Mary East. no. 6.
[95] C.P. 25(2)/632/14 Chas. II Mich. no. 16; C.P. 25(2)/632/16 Chas. II East. no. 1; Teversham, *Hist. Sawston*, ii. 252. See also Prob. 11/356 (P.C.C. 13 Reeve, will of John Greenhill).
[96] C.P. 25(2)/814/5 Wm. & Mary East. no. 4 (not 1692 as stated in Teversham, *Hist. Sawston*, ii. 110, 252).
[97] Teversham, *Hist. Sawston*, ii. 252.
[98] Ibid. 252–4; C.U.L., Doc. 651 no. 156.
[99] C.R.O., P 136/26/1.

the village and is a symmetrically fronted red-brick house, probably of the mid 18th century.[1]

ECONOMIC HISTORY. In 1086 Pirot's estate at Sawston was worth £8, Dernford £6, and Huntingdons £5, all three having maintained their value since before the Conquest. On Pirot's there were 2 demesne plough-teams, with 1 *servus*, and on Dernford 1 team; the 2 teams on Huntingdons were possibly demesne ones, and there was 1 *servus* there. In all 23 *villani* and 13 bordars, the largest group of each being on Pirot's estate, had 5 or 7 plough-teams between them.[2] Of *c.* 1,425 a. recorded in 1279 87 a. lay in closes and crofts. Of *c.* 105 a. of several meadow and pasture *c.* 70 a. belonged to the demesnes, as did *c.* 600 a. of the 1,240 a. of arable. Ralph Pirot held 165 a. of arable, and his vassal William of Sawston 128 a. Huntingdons included 140 a. and Grestain abbey had 160 a. Sawtry abbey (Hunts.) and Sir Roger Walsham each held 60 a. freely of Pirot, and two other freeholders 26 a. each. Of *c.* 55 other freeholders occupying *c.* 185 a. of arable no others possessed over 20 a., while 27 with 5 a. or less had only 42 a. altogether, and nine more only their messuages. Grestain abbey had no free tenants, but only 12 villeins and 13 cottagers. Of the other manors Pyratts included 26 villein tenements, but Huntingdons only 4, besides 14 cottagers. The villein holdings were also mostly small. Of *c.* 240 a. divided among 23 covering 5 a. or more, only five, including four held of Dernford, comprised even 20 a. each, and there were one of 15 a. and seven of 10 a. each. Of *c.* 55 other tenants in villeinage and cottagers 44, including 5 of 7 holding of William of Sawston, had only their homesteads and 1–2 a., with barely 15 a. of arable between them.

Like the free tenants the villeins all owed money-rents which were heaviest on Dernford manor. Almost all, even the cottagers, were bound to send two or three men to two or three boon-works a year, and to do one or two days' mowing. On Dernford manor those doing boon-work were entitled to have bread, cheese, and herrings from the lord. On Pyratts nine of those holding 5 a. or more owed only such services, but five others also owed 40 works for every 5 a., and had to reap 4 a. at harvest. Several tenants on Huntingdons, especially cottagers, had to help lift the hay, and some on Dernford also had to cart the lord's corn.[3]

Tenants defaulting on their obligations to provide labour were fined in 1349, 1351,[4] and 1406, and in 1445 a copyholder was required to do one boon-work in harvest, and to help at the lord's hay-making.[5] Grain was supplied in 1453 to tenants of Pyratts for their boon-works.[6] The manors also employed permanent specialized labour: each estate was managed in the 14th century by a bailiff, and in 1364 Pyratts employed 2 carters, 3 ploughmen, 3 drivers, 1 dairyman, and 2 boys.[7] In 1352 there was also a shepherd, and in 1358 a hayward who held a copyhold tenement by virtue of his office.[8]

The chief crops grown in the 14th and 15th centuries were wheat and barley, with smaller amounts of oats. Other crops mentioned were beans, peas, vetches, and the mixed crops maslin and dredge.[9] The demesne of Pyratts produced 140 qr. of wheat, 34 qr. of maslin, and 5 qr. of peas in 1363–4, and 63 qr. of wheat and maslin, 74 qr. of barley, and 10 qr. of peas in 1389–90.[10]

Field-names recorded in the 13th and 14th centuries included Cambridge, Church, 'Crokelhel', Holme, Howcrouch, West, and White fields.[11] By 1515 there were at least four open fields, called Howe, Breach, Church, and Holme fields,[12] and in 1580 these and Great White field and Little White field were listed.[13] The division of the arable into six fields, probably then already long established, lasted until inclosure. The largest, Howe field, of 369 a. in 1580, covered the north-west part of the parish. East of it was Holme field of 180 a. Church field of 142 a., with another 91½ a. inclosed by 1580, extended northwards from Church Lane. Great White field of 206 a., Little White field of 65 a., and Breach field (or the Brach) of 76 a., all west of the main road and north of New Road,[14] were reckoned to be the best arable land in the parish.[15]

The position of the parish between two rivers ensured that there was much meadow for cattle. One-quarter of the Dale estate in 1308 was meadow,[16] although other manors had smaller amounts. In 1314 Pyratts manor's meadow was valued at 2*s.* an acre while each arable acre was worth only 6*d.*[17] A tenant rented 15 of the lord's cows in 1349. In 1453 Pyratts demesne livestock included a bull, 4 bullocks, 5 cows, and 4 calves.[18] Pigs and geese as well as cattle were kept on the meadows, which provided hay for winter feed.[19] Cows remained the most numerous animals apart from sheep: many Sawston farmers in the later 17th century had dairies, with implements for making cheese, and Henry Huddleston had a small dairy-herd at his death in 1713.[20] In 1719 common rights were recognized for 123 cows, 20 bullocks, and 3 bulls, in addition to 3 cows and a bullock for each cottager.[21]

Sheep were the most important livestock kept in 1086 and remained important in Sawston's economy until inclosure. The Pyratts flock contained 120 sheep in 1352 and 74 a century later, and Dernford manor had 176 sheep in 1390.[22] Henry Huddleston sold

[1] Illus. in A. E. Richardson and H. D. Eberlein, *Smaller Eng. House of the later Renaissance*, 11.

[2] *V.C.H. Cambs.* i. 372, 384, 410–11.

[3] *Rot. Hund.* (Rec. Com.), ii. 575–80. For Pyratts in the 13th century, see also *Cal. Inq. p.m.* i, p. 60.

[4] T. F. Teversham, *Dernford Manor Sawston: Court Rolls 1337–60* (Sawston, 1965), 16–17, 36–7.

[5] Teversham, *Hist. Sawston*, ii. 3, 5.

[6] Ibid. 13.

[7] T. F. Teversham, *Sawston Estate Accts. of 14th cent.* (Sawston, 1959), 7.

[8] Teversham, *Dernford Ct. Rolls*, 42–3; T. F. Teversham, *Huddleston Doc. of Sawston Hall* (Sawston, 1970), 11.

[9] Teversham, *Dernford Ct. Rolls*, 6–7; Teversham, *Estate Accts.* 8; Teversham, *Hist. Sawston*, ii. 10, 13–14.

[10] Teversham, *Estate Accts.* 25, 44.

[11] Teversham, *Hist. Sawston*, i. 14–15.

[12] Teversham, *Dernford Ct. Rolls*, p. xxiii.

[13] Teversham, *Hist. Sawston*, ii. 60.

[14] Ibid. 61; C.R.O., P 136/26/1.

[15] C.U.L., Doc. 651 no. 214.

[16] *Cal. Inq. p.m.* v, pp. 48–9.

[17] B.L. Add. MS. 5837, f. 85.

[18] Teversham, *Hist. Sawston*, i. 87; ii. 15.

[19] Teversham, *Hist. Sawston*, i. 89, 97.

[20] C.U.L., Ely Probate Rec., consist. ct. inventories 1660–1700 *passim*; Teversham, *Hist. Sawston*, ii. 128.

[21] C.R.O., Huddleston MSS., ct. roll 1719.

[22] Teversham, *Hist. Sawston*, i. 88, 98; ii. 15.

352 sheep in 1607,[23] and George Greenell, a wealthy farmer, had 173 couples of ewes and lambs and 76 dry sheep at his death in 1683.[24] There were *c.* 460 sheep at Sawston in 1792.[25] The lord's right of sheepfold was jealously guarded, and tenants were frequently fined in the 14th century for folding their sheep elsewhere.[26] Each of the four manors had a sheep-walk with foldage rights, although by 1581 that of Dale manor was owned by Pembroke College. The sheep-walks were leased in 1607 to the Huddlestons' steward, who could keep 400 sheep in the parish, with the feed of certain closes from All Saints' Day until 10 May. Henry Huddleston (d. 1713) became under-tenant of the Pembroke College sheep-walk for 200 sheep in 1685, undertaking to fold sheep on 20 a. of the tenant's land each year.[27] By 1802 Ferdinand Huddleston possessed all the rights of sheep-walk in the parish, except for half the sheep-walk for 60 ewes and a ram belonging to Brook farm. His own rights were without stint, said to be sufficient for *c.* 500 sheep, and were divided between the tenants of Home, Flowers, and Dernford farms.[28]

The frequency with which tenants were presented for encroaching on the commons in the Middle Ages and later suggests a shortage of pasture. The lord of Dale manor was presented in 1581 for pasturing cattle on Dale Moor before the town herd was put there.[29] Rights of common were restricted to householders, and later to ratepayers, with an exception for the poor who hired cows from the lord.[30] Although those rights were sometimes said to be unstinted, stints were occasionally fixed, usually allowing 3 or 4 cows and a horse to each commoner.[31] In 1580 there were at least 120 a. of common pasture, and there were *c.* 500 a. in 1802; some of the land was virtually unusable, such as Dernford Fen, but some was fertile though liable to flooding. Another 160 a. in 1802 were common mowing meadows, of which most belonged to Ferdinand Huddleston and became common after the hay harvest.[32] The town cattle were allowed on the stubble before the sheep, and there was pasture intercommonable with Babraham in the north-east corner of the parish.[33]

The land by the rivers, suitable only for meadow and pasture, was probably inclosed from the date of Sawston's settlement. By the 14th century land at Sunderlands, east of Church field, was also inclosed by the lords of Pyratts manor, who had 70 a. of inclosed arable there in 1390, besides some pasture.[34] Further inclosure at Sunderlands may have taken place shortly before 1580, when Edmund Huddleston had 92 a. of arable there.[35] About 50 a. of closes lay round Sawston Hall in 1581.[36] By 1802 the southern half of the parish contained 408 a. of inclosed land, of which four-fifths belonged to Ferdinand Huddleston.[37]

Saffron, the most important of several new crops introduced to the parish in the 16th century, was mentioned in 1525, and was apparently well established by the 1540s.[38] Its cultivation continued throughout the 17th century, but died out after *c.* 1735.[39] Hops were also grown in 1580–1.[40] Lentils were mentioned from 1662,[41] and turnips had been introduced by 1719.[42] Shortly before 1718 Henry Huddleston divided the inclosures at Sunderlands into strips and leased them for growing sainfoin.[43]

The concentration of the land and wealth of the parish in the hands of the Huddlestons discouraged the emergence of any other large landowner at Sawston. In 1525 John Huddleston and John Huntingdon between them paid more than half the village's contribution to the subsidy, and about half the taxpayers were assessed as wage-earners.[44] Dernford manor in 1581 had 20 copyholders but no free tenants, but Pyratts had 11 free tenants, as well as 10 tenants at will whose holdings later developed into Home, Huntingdon, and Dernford farms which were tenanted on long leases.[45] After the Huddlestons bought Dale manor in 1576, the demesnes were divided among about 10 leading inhabitants, but many of them had most of their land outside the parish and no new group of landowners arose. In 1707 33 people occupied land in Sawston: only four, the tenants of Huntingdon, Home, and two other farms, farmed more than 90 a., and 22 held less than 10 a.[46] Ferdinand Huddleston was owner or tenant of 9 farms in 1802, when there were *c.* 38 freeholders and copyholders in the parish, only 7 or 8 of them substantial.[47]

Copyhold tenure survived well into the 19th century at Sawston, though many copyholders enfranchised their property at inclosure. Copyholds descended to the eldest son or to daughters jointly, and could be sold or let for not more than 3 years, subject to entry fines.[48] Most copyhold properties were also subject to heriots: 20 out of Dernford's 22 copyhold tenements in 1581 were heriotable, and 8 of the 9 in Pyratts.[49] Heriots were frequently recorded in the Middle Ages, and in the 16th century the lord took a tenant's best animal or a piece of pewter.[50] A feather bed was taken as a heriot in 1755. A copyholder resisted a claim to a cow in 1757, and as late as 1803 the bailiff was authorized to seize one of a deceased tenant's best goods.[51]

The parish was inclosed under an Act of 1802,

[23] Teversham, *Hist. Sawston*, ii. 101.
[24] C.U.L., Ely Probate Rec., consist. ct. inventory 1683.
[25] Vancouver, *Agric. in Cambs.* 66.
[26] Teversham, *Dernford Ct. Rolls*, 4–5, 44–5, 66–7.
[27] Teversham, *Hist. Sawston*, ii. 80, 101–2.
[28] C.U.L., Doc. 651 nos. 36, 53; C.R.O., Huddleston MSS., farm valuation 1798.
[29] Teversham, *Hist. Sawston*, ii. 70.
[30] C.R.O., Huddleston MSS., ct. orders 1763.
[31] C.U.L., Doc. 651 nos. 53, 204; cf. Teversham, *Hist. Sawston*, ii. 77; C.R.O., Huddleston MSS., ct. roll 1719.
[32] C.U.L., Doc. 651 no. 53.
[33] Teversham, *Hist. Sawston*, ii. 153; Teversham, *Estate Accts.* 54.
[34] Teversham, *Hist. Sawston*, i. 95; Teversham, *Estate Accts.* 56.
[35] Teversham, *Hist. Sawston*, i. 120; ii. 72.
[36] Ibid. ii. 72.
[37] C.R.O., P 136/26/1, p. 11; C.U.L., Doc. 651 no. 53.
[38] B.L. Add. MS. 5861, pp. 15, 56, 62, 65–6, 181, 218–19.
[39] Teversham, *Hist. Sawston*, ii. 91, 118, 126; C.U.L., Ely Probate Rec., consist. ct. inventories 1700–40 *passim*.
[40] Teversham, *Hist. Sawston*, ii. 47, 72.
[41] C.U.L., Ely Probate Rec., consist. ct. inventories 1660–1700 *passim*.
[42] Teversham, *Hist. Sawston*, ii. 148, 258.
[43] Ibid. 73, 126, 135–6.
[44] E 179/81/147 mm. 4–5.
[45] Teversham, *Hist. Sawston*, ii. 74, 78–9, 82–4.
[46] Ibid. 75, 128.
[47] C.U.L., Doc. 651 nos. 36, 53.
[48] Teversham, *Hist. Sawston*, ii. 80; C 3/242/9.
[49] Teversham, *Hist. Sawston*, ii. 77, 82–3.
[50] Ibid. i. 84; ii. 77–8.
[51] C.R.O., Huddleston MSS., heriots 1755–9; instructions to counsel 1757; bailiff's authorization 1803.

before any other parish in Whittlesford hundred, though the neighbouring parishes of Little Shelford and Pampisford preceded it by a few years. The decision was made by Ferdinand Huddleston alone, with the sometimes reluctant consent of the major farmers.[52] The process of allotment was virtually complete by 1803, though the award was not enrolled until 1811.[53] The award related to 1,408½ a. of open field and common. A proposal to leave some common pasture for cottagers was rejected, and separate allotments were given instead.[54] Just over half the parish, 972 a. including 274 a. of old inclosure, was awarded to Ferdinand Huddleston,[55] whose son paid almost £3,000 as his share of inclosure expenses.[56] Charles Martindale received 148 a. around Borough Mill, which he owned, and John Gosling was awarded 153 a. in scattered parcels, mostly for his half-share of the great tithes. The vicar received 82½ a. for tithes and rights of common. Apart from one farmer and the trustees of Huntingdon's charity, no other proprietor obtained more than 50 a.; three received between 10 and 25 a., seven between 5 and 10 a., and all the other 34 landholders less than 5 a., 16 of them receiving 1 a. or less.

The Huddleston allotment was immediately divided between the various farms on the estate and leased as it had been in the 18th century. North Farm, the only new farm-house, was built by Ferdinand Huddleston (d. 1808) after 1803 in the north-east part of the parish.[57] Only in 1922, with the sale of the Huddleston estate, did Huntingdon's, Church, Dernford, and North farms pass into separate ownership.[58] Gosling's Farm in High Street with 120 a. was sold in 1913, much of it for building.[59] The tenants of the farms in the later 19th century were often the owners of Sawston's industrial concerns; Edward Towgood employed 10 men and boys in farming 186 a. at Mill farm in 1871, and T. S. Evans farmed 488 a. with 30 employees at Church farm, on a lease later taken over by John Crampton who already farmed over 300 a. at Huntingdon's farm.[60]

Pasture farming declined at Sawston after inclosure, and by 1905 1,036 a. were arable and only 284 a. were permanent grassland.[61] Cattle and breeding flocks of sheep continued to be kept on a small scale. Poultry-farming was carried on in the 1930s, and pig-farming in the 1970s.[62] The demand for labour on enlarged arable farms was at first sufficient to absorb the 19th-century increase in population, but in 1823 agricultural labourers rioted at Sawston for higher wages.[63] The development of industry in the village created competition between farm-workers and artisans for cottages, rents soared, and in 1872 the agricultural labourers again demanded higher wages.[64] In 1831 equal numbers of families were supported by agriculture and by trade and industry, and Sawston became steadily less agricultural; by 1963 fewer than 40 men worked on the land.[65] In 1972 there were four working farms in the parish, growing mainly wheat, barley, and oats, and raising pigs and cattle.

A windmill stood by the Babraham road in 1811. It was still working in 1892, but had been demolished by 1930.[66] The estate of Roger de Somery, later Huntingdons manor, included a mill in 1086, and in 1279 there was a water-mill near Borough Mill, but no later references to a mill attached to Huntingdons manor have been found.[67] Pirot held two mills in 1086, which were granted by Alice le Child in the late 13th century to John of Sawston as part of the estate which became Dale manor,[68] and Borough Mill or Mills, so called by 1300, descended with the lordship.[69] The mill was later owned by the Ellis, Rand, and Symons families of Whittlesford.[70] Borough Mill was a grist-mill in 1719, held by Gilbert Cockerton and later by his son.[71] From *c.* 1753 it became a paper-mill, as described below.

The other medieval mill at Sawston belonged to Dernford manor. It may have been the mill at 'Dereforda' given with the vill of Stapleford by King Eadred to Ely abbey *c.* 955,[72] and a mill was part of the manor in 1086, though it was not recorded in 1279.[73] Dernford Mill was grinding corn in the mid 14th century.[74] The surname Fuller occurred at Sawston from *c.* 1310, borne by at least one Dernford man, and in 1433 Dernford Mill was used for fulling.[75] It was a fulling-mill in 1525 and 1581,[76] and probably so continued until *c.* 1665. Tenter meadow was close to Dernford Mill in the north-east tip of the parish.[77] No other evidence of a cloth industry at Sawston has been found, except for references to a weaver in 1619 and a shearman in 1659.[78]

The manufacture of paper at Sawston probably dates from 1664 or 1665, when Richard Allen, a paper-maker, became the tenant of Dernford Mill, which was described as a fulling-mill lately occupied by a clothworker.[79] Another paper-maker, Joseph Carby, took the mill on a long lease in 1695 and left stocks of paper and rags there at his death in 1719.[80] William Tassell and John Sparke made paper at

52 *Proc. C.A.S.* xl. 78–9; *C.J.* lvii. 77–8, 187, 354; Sawston Incl. Act, 42 Geo. III, c. 29 (Private and Personal, not printed).
53 C.U.L., Add. MS. 6065, f. 12.
54 C.R.O., P 136/26/1, pp. 10–11.
55 Ibid. pp. 41–8. The measurements of allotments in Teversham, *Hist. Sawston*, ii. 210–14 contain many errors.
56 C.U.L., Doc. 651 no. 222.
57 Teversham, *Hist. Sawston*, ii. 204, 221–2.
58 C.U.L., Maps 53(1)/92/33.
59 Ibid. Maps 53(1)/91/96.
60 R.G. 10/1591; Teversham, *Country Printing Ho.* 9, 18.
61 Cambs. Agric. Returns, 1905.
62 *Kelly's Dir. Cambs.* (1929, 1933, 1937); *Camb. Evening News*, 30 May 1972.
63 *V.C.H. Cambs.* ii. 117.
64 *Daily News*, 5 Apr. 1872.
65 *Census*, 1831; *Intro. to Sawston* (Sawston Par. Council).
66 C.R.O., P 136/26/1, p. 12; *Kelly's Dir. Cambs.* (1892); *Proc. C.A.S.* xxxi. 25 sqq.
67 *V.C.H. Cambs.* i. 411; *Rot. Hund.* (Rec. Com.), ii. 578; Teversham, *Hist. Sawston*, i. 78–9.
68 *V.C.H. Cambs.* i. 410; Teversham, *Hist. Sawston*, i. 47, 78–9.
69 *Cal. Inq. p.m.* v, pp. 48–9; Teversham, *Hist. Sawston*, i. 49.
70 C.P. 25(2)/68/558 no. 11; Teversham, *Hist. Sawston*, ii. 115.
71 Teversham, *Hist. Sawston*, ii. 137.
72 *Liber Elien.* (Camd. 3rd ser. xcii), pp. 102, 262, 300, 304; Hart, *Early Charters of E. Eng.* pp. 40–1.
73 *V.C.H. Cambs.* i. 411; *Rot. Hund.* (Rec. Com.), ii. 579–80.
74 Teversham, *Dernford Ct. Rolls*, 14–15, 22–3.
75 Teversham, *Hist. Sawston*, i. 52, 83, 89; ii. 10.
76 Ibid. ii. 82; E 179/81/147 mm. 4–5.
77 C.R.O., P 136/26/1, p. 68.
78 Teversham, *Hist. Sawston*, ii. 115; Prob. 11/289 (P.C.C. 187 Pell, will of Ric. Hagger).
79 Teversham, *Hist. Sawston*, i. 46; ii. 142.
80 Ibid. ii. 137; C.U.L., Ely Probate Rec., consist. ct. inventories 1719.

Dernford Mill in the 18th century, but it was in poor repair in 1771 and was inconveniently situated.[81] By 1786 the tenant was Charles Martindale, who in 1791 bought Borough Mill and from *c.* 1796 ceased to manufacture paper at Dernford.[82] In 1806 James Nutter, a corn-merchant, took over Martindale's lease of Dernford Mill, which was described as a flour mill in 1851,[83] though sometimes also used as an oil mill for the tanning industry.[84] The mill eventually became ruinous and was demolished in 1927.[85]

Paper had been made at Borough Mill since *c.* 1753, when the mill was bought by Joseph Keir, a paper-maker, and William Fairchild.[86] They built a new mill adjoining the old one and insured both in 1760 and 1778, although only one was recorded thereafter. Fairchild went bankrupt in 1779, and in 1784 Borough Mill was bought by Joseph Vowell, a London stationer, whose heir sold it in 1791 to Charles Martindale.[87] The mill had two vats in 1778 and 1791.[88] The Fourdrinier family, inventors of paper-making machines, were associated with the mill by 1780, and some of the earliest machinery in England was installed there.[89] By 1835 Martindale's widow Elizabeth had leased Borough Mill to Edward Towgood, a paper-maker of St. Neots (Hunts.), who in that year transferred his lease to his brother Matthew.[90] The mill was owned and worked for the rest of the 19th century by Edward's sons, Edward and Hamer Towgood,[91] and it became the largest industrial concern in Sawston, employing nearly 400 people in 1871.[92] Steam-power was introduced, and a new factory was built in 1851.[93] Many women, and children over 12, were employed in the mill, where the work was generally cleaner and more regular, though less well paid, than in the leather industry.[94] About 1890 falling wages caused an unsuccessful strike.[95] In 1917 after the death of Hamer Towgood the business was sold to Spicer Bros. Ltd., and continued as Edward Towgood & Sons Ltd. to produce high quality paper, employing 160 people in 1972.[96] In 1963 the mill had recently been modernized and reconstructed to produce top-grade stationery paper and processed paper with a plastic base.[97] A large paper-conversion factory, built near the railway by Spicers in 1925 and considerably enlarged in 1964, produced items such as envelopes, waxed wrappings, and account books. In 1972 it employed 600 people, and like Towgoods was part of the Reed International Group.[98] A subsidiary of the Spicers group, Dufay-Chromex Ltd., was established at Sawston in the 1920s to develop the manufacture of non-inflammable colour film, and continued production there until 1951.[99]

The leather industry probably settled at Sawston because running water with a high lime content and local supplies of sheepskins were available.[1] There may have been leather-workers in the parish in the Middle Ages, and in the mid 17th century the Goole family had a tanyard north of the Brook, later the site of the Old Yard.[2] William Priest, the Gooles' successor, had stocks of bark, a barkmill, and hides and backs worth £150 at his death in 1681.[3] Priest was succeeded by William Harris and his two sons, by Henry Guiver, and by Stephen and Thomas Adams in the 18th century, all of whom worked in the tanyard on the Brook.[4]

Parchment-making was introduced in the early 19th century, and by 1841 there were 13 parchment-makers in Sawston besides 5 skinners and 7 fellmongers.[5] The chief employer was Thomas Evans, a Welsh leather-worker who bought the tanyard in 1844. His son Thomas Sutton Evans succeeded him in 1850 and greatly expanded the business. Steam-power was introduced,[6] and in 1871 Evans employed 186 men, 4 women, and 54 boys at the Old Yard, mostly as fellmongers, skinners, parchment-makers, leather-dressers, glove-cutters, and makers of chamois leather, a manufacture which he introduced to Sawston.[7] The main destination of parchment and leather from Sawston was the United States, where a slump in the later 1870s caused a depression in the leather industry[8] when Evans was already in financial difficulties. Thomas Frederick Evans inherited the business from his father in 1882 but was unable to revive its fortunes, and in 1884 the firm became a limited liability company.[9] Another decline in the 1930s was blamed on foreign competition.[10] After several changes of ownership, a controlling interest in the company was bought in 1938 by Charles Bowers, formerly the manager, whose son was the director in 1972.[11] As T. S. Evans & Son the firm specialized in making high quality chamois leather and in 1972 employed *c.* 40 people.[12]

The Eastern Counties Leather Co. Ltd., set up in 1879 by a group including John Crampton, Frederick Prince, and the Congregational minister J. McC. Uffen, to provide employment for workers dismissed by T. S. Evans, built a new tannery known as the New Yard at Langford Arch, just over the parish boundary in Pampisford.[13] The venture suffered at

[81] Teversham, *Hist. Sawston*, ii. 142–3.
[82] A. H. Shorter, *Paper Mills and Paper Makers in Eng. 1495–1800*, 148.
[83] C.U.L., Doc. 651 no. 194; Teversham, *Hist. Sawston*, ii. 143; H.O. 107/1761.
[84] B.L. Add. MS. 9412, f. 94; Challis, *Sawston*, 12; Teversham, *Hist. Sawston*, i. 22.
[85] *Intro. to Sawston* (Sawston Par. Council); Teversham, *Dernford Ct. Rolls*, p. xxii.
[86] Teversham, *Hist. Sawston*, ii. 143.
[87] Ibid. 145–6; Shorter, *Paper Mills*, 148.
[88] Shorter, *Paper Mills*, 406; Teversham, *Hist. Sawston*, ii. 145–6.
[89] Teversham, *Hist. Sawston*, ii. 145; *D.N.B.* s.v. Henry Fourdrinier; *Camb. Region* (1938), 160.
[90] C.R.O., R 49/14/19.
[91] Teversham, *Hist. Sawston*, ii. 247.
[92] R.G. 10/1591.
[93] Teversham, *Hist. Sawston*, ii. 264; H.O. 107/1761.
[94] H.O. 107/1761; Challis, *Sawston*, 13.
[95] Teversham, *Hist. Sawston*, ii. 269.
[96] *Camb. Region* (1938), 160. The mill was closed in 1974: *Camb. Evening News*, 4 Mar. 1974.
[97] *Intro. to Sawston* (Sawston Par. Council).
[98] *The Times*, 26 Oct. 1961, suppl.; ex inf. Spicers Ltd.
[99] *Camb. Region* (1938), 161; ex inf. Spicers Ltd.
[1] W. R. Davidge, *Cambs. Regional Planning Rep.* (1934), 23; cf. *Ag. H.R.* xiv. 38 n.
[2] Teversham, *Hist. Sawston*, i. 99; ii. 141.
[3] C.U.L., Ely Probate Rec., consist. ct. inventories 1681.
[4] Teversham, *Hist. Sawston*, i. 67, 108; ii. 141.
[5] H.O. 107/76.
[6] *Cambs. Local Hist. Counc. Bull.* xxvi (1971), 19.
[7] R.G. 10/1591; Challis, *Sawston*, 12; Teversham, *Hist. Sawston*, ii. 266.
[8] Teversham, *Hist. Sawston*, ii. 265, 269; *Camb. Ind. Press*, 5 Feb. 1960.
[9] Teversham, *Hist. Sawston*, ii. 267–9.
[10] Davidge, *Cambs. Regional Planning Rep.* (1934), 23.
[11] *S. Cambs. R.D.: Official Guide* (1960), 70.
[12] The processes in the manufacture of chamois leather are described in T. McK. and M. C. Hughes, *Cambs.* 103–6.
[13] Teversham, *Country Printing Ho.* 17.

Castle Camps Castle in the 18th century

Sawston Hall from the south-west

Linton Church in the early 19th century

Great Abington Church in the late 18th century

Bartlow Church in the early 19th century

Little Abington Church in the late 18th century

first from competition with the Old Yard, but by 1972 it was employing *c.* 100 people making sheepskin coats, hats, and rugs, and chamois leather.[14] The New Yard also produced gloves, which became a local speciality, and at least three other firms were making gloves and chamois leather in the parish in 1963.[15] In 1966 the South of England Hide Market Ltd. built a tannery in Sawston, to export hides and serve as a depot.[16]

John Crampton took over a local printing-works in 1860, opened the Sawston Emporium, a post office and general store, in 1861, and by 1863 owned a factory for bottling mineral-water. The printing business moved to a new factory in 1900. The depression of the 1920s forced the mineral-water plant to close in 1928, but Crampton's printing-works were still active in 1972. T. S. Evans opened a rival mineral-water factory, the Sawston Aerated Water Co., in 1878. That company became insolvent after 1939 and its premises were taken over by J. N. Baldry, the proprietor of another mineral-water company, for use as a depot which was later closed.[17]

Rope-making was mentioned in 1766 and 1807.[18] Seven rope-makers were recorded at Sawston in 1841, and three in 1871,[19] but the trade apparently died out in the later 19th century. Catley's Walk, a short track at the southern end of the village, derives its name from a rope-maker who used it as a rope-walk for over 20 years.[20]

Bricklayers were mentioned in 1576, 1662, and 1766,[21] and in 1847 there were four builders active.[22] Among firms settled at Sawston in 1972 were Camtiles Ltd., on the Babraham Road industrial site, which employed *c.* 100 people making roofing tiles and concrete pipes, and another company making prefabricated houses.[23] One of the larger firms was Simplex of Cambridge Ltd., employing *c.* 500 people in the manufacture of advanced farming equipment.[24] British Home Stores had their largest warehouse at Sawston in 1972.[25] About a quarter of the employed population worked in manufacturing in 1972, and firms inside the parish provided employment for almost half of the working population of Sawston.[26]

LOCAL GOVERNMENT. In 1279 the earl of Essex claimed view of frankpledge and tumbrel in Sawston, and the view was held by the tenant of Huntingdons manor.[27] It descended with the overlordship of Huntingdons, and payments for holding courts leet at Sawston were occasionally recorded on the court rolls of the honor of Mandeville in the 14th and 15th centuries.[28] The lords of Huntingdons manor afterwards held the view of frankpledge as tenants of the honor.[29] Court rolls of the Huntingdons court leet, which from the 14th century until *c.* 1550 was held on the morrow (10 June) of St. Barnabas, survive for 1412, 1414–15, 1452, 1456–8, and for most years between 1520 and 1576.[30] Besides making agricultural orders, the court elected ale-tasters in the 16th century.[31] Court rolls of Pyratts manor survive for 1336, most years between 1345 and 1362, between 1386 and 1407, and 1435–7, 1455, and spasmodically from 1512.[32] Dernford manor's court rolls cover most years in the periods 1349–73, 1390–1407, and for the same years as Pyratts from 1435.[33] In 1466 Edward IV granted leet jurisdiction then belonging to the Crown, presumably that acquired by Henry V, to Margaret de la Pole, with remainder to her heirs the lords of Pyratts and Dernford.[34] By 1455 courts for those two manors were usually held on the same day and recorded on the same roll.[35] In the 16th century courts with view of frankpledge were held at Sawston Hall at irregular intervals, sometimes as often as four times a year, for Pyratts and Dernford.[36] The lords of Dale manor held a court baron, whose records survive for 1406–7, 1435, 1460, 1517, and 1572–3, before it was absorbed into the Huddleston estate.[37] In the 17th and 18th centuries courts baron were held for all four manors, and courts leet for Pyratts, Dernford, and Huntingdons. Court rolls for all the courts, which were entered together, survive for most years between 1576 and 1731 with a few of later date.[38]

A hayward had been elected in 1349 by the Pyratts court,[39] which continued to appoint the hayward in the 16th century and later, probably for the whole parish.[40] Similarly the election of one or two constables, mentioned in 1316 and 1407, was gradually assumed for the whole parish by Pyratts.[41] Other officers were a herdsman, 2 drivers of the commons, 2 pinders, and in 1608 2 *testatores* whose function is not clear.[42] Agricultural orders by the Pyratts court, such as prohibition of ploughing up balks, took substantially the same form from the 16th to the 18th century.

The relief of the poor was financed for many years by John Huntingdon's charity, as described below; rates for the poor were collected only in years when the charity's income was insufficient, and became regular only from 1695.[43] Part of the overseers' expenditure was on rents for the poor, and in 1742

[14] Teversham, *Hist. Sawston*, ii. 270; *Camb. Ind. Press*, 25 Aug. 1967.
[15] *Intro. to Sawston* (Sawston Par. Council); *S. Cambs. R.D.: Official Guide* (1960), 71–2.
[16] *Camb. News*, 27 Aug. 1969.
[17] For Crampton's enterprises, see Teversham, *Country Printing Ho.*; *Cambs., Hunts., and Peterborough Life*, Feb. 1971, pp. 45–6; Teversham, *Hist. Sawston*, ii. 265–6.
[18] Teversham, *Hist. Sawston*, ii. 169–70; C.R.O., C/CT/E 1/1.
[19] H.O. 107/76; R.G. 10/1591.
[20] Challis, *Sawston*, 9.
[21] C 3/121/15; C.U.L., Ely Probate Rec., consist. ct. inventories 1662; Teversham, *Hist. Sawston*, ii. 169.
[22] *Kelly's Dir. Cambs.* (1847).
[23] *Camb. News*, 22 Feb. 1966.
[24] *Intro. to Sawston* (Sawston Par. Council).
[25] *Cambs., Hunts., and Peterborough Life*, Mar. 1972, p. 21.
[26] Cambs. Coll. of Arts and Tech., Village Survey 1972.
[27] *Rot. Hund.* (Rec. Com.), ii. 570.
[28] e.g. D.L. 30/64/805; D.L. 30/67/839; D.L. 30/70/866.
[29] D.L. 30/72/893.
[30] For a full list, see Teversham, *Hist. Sawston*, i. 60–3.
[31] Teversham, *Huddleston Doc.* 20; C.R.O., Huddleston MSS., Huntingdons ct. roll 1521.
[32] For a full list, see Teversham, *Hist. Sawston*, i. 59–63.
[33] Ibid.
[34] *Cal. Pat.* 1461–7, 525.
[35] Teversham, *Hist. Sawston*, ii. 5–6.
[36] C.R.O., Huddleston MSS., 16th-cent. ct. rolls *passim*; C 3/121/15.
[37] Teversham, *Hist. Sawston*, i. 59–63.
[38] Ibid. 63–8 for a full list of the ct. rolls in the Huddleston MSS., now in C.R.O.; see also C.R.O., R 51/17/2B; R 51/17/2D; R 59/14/25/1, 1A, 1B.
[39] Teversham, *Hist. Sawston*, i. 86.
[40] Ibid. ii. 88.
[41] Ibid. 3, 88, 115; *Cambs. Village Doc.* 9; C.R.O., Huddleston MSS., ct. rolls 1608, 1617.
[42] Teversham, *Hist. Sawston*, ii. 114–15, 117.
[43] Ibid. 161, 163; for the charity, see below, p. 262.

the charity trustees bought a house in Mill Lane as a town house.[44] Some light work such as spinning was provided, but many of the inmates were classed as impotent poor.[45] Able-bodied paupers were employed outside the town house on tasks such as digging gravel or cutting willows. In 1792 the parish adopted the roundsman system, but the overseers often had to supplement wages.[46]

Numbers of paupers and the expense of poor-relief increased at Sawston in the late 18th century, but the parish was probably better off than its neighbours because of the employment provided by industry. By 1804, however, 22 families were receiving outdoor relief, and there were 30 or 40 paupers in the town house and other parish workhouses in Mill Lane.[47] Paupers were vaccinated in 1817 and 1826.[48] The old town house was not used after 1811, and was eventually demolished and replaced by the Huntingdon's charity alms-houses.[49] The cost of poor-relief continued to rise in the 1830s, from £518 in 1829 to almost £900 in 1832.[50] Sawston became part of the Linton poor-law union in 1835, and was transferred with the rest of Linton R.D. to the South Cambridgeshire R.D. in 1934,[51] and included in South Cambridgeshire in 1974.

CHURCH. Sawston church was probably founded by the Pirot family. Ralph Pirot (fl. 1166–95) was said to have pledged it to the Hospitallers' preceptory of Shingay, as security for a loan of barley, which he failed to repay, and the church, with a messuage and 1 yardland, passed to Shingay.[52] By *c.* 1278 the church was appropriated to the preceptory and a vicarage had been ordained.[53] Master Benet of Sawston, mentioned in 1197, may have been an incumbent, and several chaplains and deacons witnessed deeds in the early 13th century.[54]

Apart from one instance in 1383 when Richard Maisterman successfully claimed the patronage and the vicar resigned and was presented anew,[55] all known presentations to the vicarage before 1540 were made by the prior of Shingay. The advowson thereafter descended with the rectory as described above. The Crown presented to the living in 1580,[56] Henry Long in 1570, and Sir Charles Morrison, who had married Long's widow Elizabeth, and his wife Dorothy in 1587.[57] Elizabeth Balam and her father John Byatt were patrons for one turn in 1639, and as Elizabeth Blundell she presented with Arthur Stock and John Greenell in 1664. In 1671 and 1674 George Greenell held the advowson, and John Greenell presented in 1683.[58] For much of the 18th century Sawston was held by sequestrators appointed by the bishop.[59] In 1836 the Crown presented by lapse, and John Gosling, the joint owner of the advowson, presented in 1855, Ferdinand Huddleston being a papist.[60] Gosling's son James and Ferdinand Huddleston sold the advowson in 1877 and the Revd. R. B. Kingsford presented in 1878.[61] In the following year the advowson was bought by Edward Towgood, the owner of the paper-mill,[62] whose brother and heir Hamer Towgood (d. 1914) devised the advowson to trustees, who still held it in 1972. The archbishop of Canterbury presented in 1931 by lapse.[63]

Sawston vicarage was assessed at 7 marks in 1276 and £5 in 1291.[64] After disputes with the parishioners, the vicar agreed in 1471 to receive offerings on All Saints' Day in place of mortuary fees.[65] The vicarage was valued at £13 10*s.* 2*d.* in 1535, £20 in 1650, and £15 in 1685.[66] Its income remained low throughout the 18th century, and the incumbent was nominated as one of the diocese's ten 'poor vicars' in 1792.[67] Income rose sharply after inclosure when the vicar received 81 a. for the small tithes; by 1806 the value was said to have more than doubled, and *c.* 1830 it was £118 net, part of which came from a parliamentary augmentation of 1816.[68] Gross income in 1877 had recently increased from £170 to £214.[69] The living was augmented again under the will of Edward Towgood (d. 1889), and was worth £245 net in 1897.[70]

Before inclosure the vicar had no glebe.[71] The value of the small tithes had fallen by 1685 through the loss of those of saffron, although that crop was still grown in the parish.[72] By 1756 there was a modus for the small tithes.[73] The vicar in 1802 claimed tithes on all produce except corn and hay, including lambs' wool.[74]

At inclosure in 1802 the vicar received 82½ a. for tithes and rights of common.[75] With the proceeds of 3 a. sold to the railway company in 1845 25 a. in Little Shelford were bought for the living. That land and 56 a. at Dernford were sold in 1921, and in 1947 21 a. of glebe remained,[76] reduced to 16½ a. by 1972.[77]

There was no vicarage house at Sawston in the 17th century,[78] and none had been mentioned during the Middle Ages. Elizabeth Wakelin, by will proved 1637, left her house in High Street near the church and 1½ a. to the incumbent, provided that he lived

[44] Teversham, *Hist. Sawston*, i. 8.
[45] Ibid. ii. 187; Hampson, *Poverty in Cambs.* 95–6.
[46] Hampson, *Poverty in Cambs.* 187, 190–1.
[47] Teversham, *Hist. Sawston*, ii. 178, 191–2.
[48] Ibid. 195, 197.
[49] Ibid. 177; *31st Rep. Com. Char.* 206.
[50] Teversham, *Hist. Sawston*, ii. 199.
[51] *Poor Law Com. 1st Rep.* 249; *Census*, 1931 (pt. ii).
[52] *Rot. Hund.* (Rec. Com.), ii. 575; *Complete Peerage*, x. 474; *V.C.H. Cambs.* ii. 267, where the size of the rectory estate is incorrectly given.
[53] *Vetus Liber Arch. Elien.* (C.A.S. 8vo ser. xlviii), 72–3.
[54] *Proc. C.A.S.* xlii. 42.
[55] *E.D.R.* (1895), 182.
[56] Ibid. (1914), 379.
[57] Ibid. 327; Gibbons, *Ely Episc. Rec.* 442.
[58] P.R.O. Inst. Bks. ser. A, iii, p. 34; ser. B, i, f. 78; iv, p. 150; C.R.O., R 58/5, vol. x, p. 115.
[59] *Proc. C.A.S.* xlii. 57–62. C.U.L., E.D.R., B 8/4, f. 32, records that Stephen Corby presented in 1785, but he had died in 1727.
[60] *Proc. C.A.S.* xlii. 64.
[61] *Cambs. Local Hist. Counc. Bull.* xxvi (1971), 20.
[62] *E.D.R.* (1889), 265.
[63] *Proc. C.A.S.* xlii. 65–6; *Ely Dioc. Dir.* (1972–3).
[64] *Val. of Norwich*, ed. Lunt, 555; *Tax. Eccl.* (Rec. Com.), 267.
[65] *E.D.R.* (1907), 153.
[66] *Valor Eccl.* (Rec. Com.), iii. 505; Lamb. Pal. MS. 904, f. 263; Teversham, *Hist. Sawston*, i. 140.
[67] C.U.L., E.D.R., B 8/4, f. 57v.
[68] Gooch, *Agric. of Cambs.* 75; *Rep. Com. Eccl. Revenues*, pp. 350–1; C. Hodgson, *Queen Anne's Bounty*, 311.
[69] C.U.L., E.D.R., C 3/27.
[70] *E.D.R.* (1889), 265; C.U.L., E.D.R., C 3/39.
[71] C.U.L., E.D.R., H 1/5, terrier 1615.
[72] Teversham, *Hist. Sawston*, i. 140.
[73] Ibid. ii. 258; *Proc. C.A.S.* xlii. 63.
[74] C.U.L., Doc. 651 no. 14.
[75] C.R.O., P 136/26/1, pp. 18, 20–2.
[76] Teversham, *Hist. Sawston*, ii. 211, 245–6, 254.
[77] Ex inf. the vicar, the Revd. Canon R. Bircham.
[78] C.U.L., E.D.R., H 1/5, terrier 1615.

in the parish, preached an annual sermon, and paid certain sums to the poor.[79] Few vicars chose to live in the house, which was used as an alehouse in 1685 and was described by the vicar in 1836 as a miserable wretched cottage.[80] Between 1828 and 1836 the churchwardens managed the property, after the vicar had refused to fulfil the conditions of the bequest. Resident 19th-century incumbents lived in lodgings or in their own houses until 1882, when a new vicarage was built on land in Church Lane given by Ferdinand Huddleston, much of the cost being borne by Edward Towgood.[81] Elizabeth Wakelin's house partly collapsed in 1935 and was demolished in 1948.[82]

The church estate or Ward's charity, a house and *c.* 35 a. in Sawston, Babraham, and Pampisford, was given for the upkeep of the church in the 16th century, probably by John Ward, rector of St. Peter's, Duxford (d. 1526), an uncle of John Huntingdon.[83] Income was £21 a year in 1783, which may have been misapplied, for the church was then in disrepair.[84] By 1860 the income was £90, making church rates in the parish unnecessary.[85] At inclosure in 1802 the trustees received 19 a., a small part of which was sold in 1896 and the rest in 1925.[86] The income of the charity was in 1972 still used for church repairs. The house, standing east of the High Street, is a 16th-century timber-framed and plastered building with 17th-century additions, much restored in the 19th century.

There were three guilds at Sawston in 1389, in honour of the Invention of the Holy Cross and the Nativities of St. John the Baptist and of the Blessed Virgin. All three had been recently founded to assist the repair of the church.[87] Two guilds of St. Mary and St. Margaret were mentioned in the early 16th century.[88] A cottage called the guildhall, sold by the Crown in 1549 and again in 1571, and probably included in another grant of 1592,[89] was demolished in the 17th century.[90] Land in Sawston given for obits was granted by the Crown to the earl of Warwick in 1550.[91] John Huntingdon, who had also bought obit lands from the king, devised them in 1554 to the owners of Huntingdons manor after the death of his wife, with the obligation to plant peas for the poor,[92] and the land subsequently descended with the manor.

Chaplains and curates attended manorial courts far more often than the vicars in the Middle Ages, and many incumbents were probably non-resident.[93] Few were graduates, and the more learned vicars in the 15th and 16th centuries held Sawston in plurality with other livings.[94] William Marshall was presented in 1526 on condition that he be examined by the bishop after two years of study. His successor, Richard Marshall, employed a stipendiary curate in 1543–4.[95] Two men charged with strange heretical opinions in 1540 may have misunderstood protestant ideas.[96] John Huntingdon, lord of Huntingdons manor, made a strongly protestant will in 1554.[97] Robert Baker, vicar 1560–70, and Anthony Fletcher, vicar 1571–9, both also held the vicarage of Pampisford, but served the cure themselves.[98] William Bromstead, vicar 1580–7, was a drunkard.[99] Seventeenth-century incumbents were mostly graduates, but many held more than one living, and the church was allowed to fall into disrepair.[1] Most of the twenty men who served the cure in the 18th century were fellows of Cambridge colleges and lived in Cambridge, where they performed some Sawston marriages in college chapels.[2] None retained the living for more than ten years, except Thomas Cautley, vicar 1786–1835, whose father-in-law Francis Henson and brother-in-law of the same name had both served the cure.[3]

All the incumbents after Cautley were resident and grappled with the problems arising from Sawston's rapid growth. Edwin Daniel, vicar 1836–55, kept a Sunday school and held a second service on Sunday afternoons, attended by 320 people on Census Sunday in 1851.[4] To help to support his large family, he kept a school for gentlemen's sons in his house.[5] The next vicar, his son Edwin Swann Daniel, 1855–77, began the restoration of the church.[6] Edward Towgood, who gave many new furnishings for the church, in 1887 built the church institute for the recreation of male members of the congregation.[7] By his will he left money for the institute and for the surpliced choir introduced *c.* 1885.[8] Edward's brother Hamer made further gifts, including a cricket ground for the church institute, which still flourished in 1972,[9] and an extension of the graveyard, consecrated in 1898; the old churchyard had been closed in 1880, and a cemetery north of the village with a small brick chapel was opened in its place.[10]

C. E. Crump, vicar 1886–1904, a follower of the Oxford Movement, continued the renovation of the church. Bible-teaching was restored to the curriculum of the village schools,[11] and Church and Chapel maintained keen rivalry for members. By 1897 communion services were held six times a month, and

[79] Teversham, *Hist. Sawston*, ii. 244–5.
[80] *Proc. C.A.S.* xlii. 57; C.U.L., E.D.R., C 3/21.
[81] Teversham, *Hist. Sawston*, ii. 245, 247.
[82] Char. Com. files; *Proc. C.A.S.* xlii. 53, pl. facing p. 66.
[83] Teversham, *Hist. Sawston*, ii. 241; Emden, *Biog. Reg. Univ. Camb.* 616.
[84] C.U.L., E.D.R., B 7/1, pp. 132–3.
[85] Char. Com. files.
[86] Teversham, *Hist. Sawston*, ii. 212.
[87] C 47/38/29.
[88] E 179/81/147 mm. 4–5; B.L. Add. MS. 5861, pp. 146, 174.
[89] *Cal. Pat.* 1549–51, 91; 1569–72, p. 404; C 66/1382 mm. 21–47.
[90] Teversham, *Hist. Sawston*, i. 128.
[91] *Cal. Pat.* 1549–51, 374.
[92] Teversham, *Hist. Sawston*, i. 110.
[93] *Proc. C.A.S.* xlii. 43–5.
[94] e.g. Ric. Nelson, 1476–82?, and Edw. Sheffeld, 1521–5: Emden, *Biog. Reg. Univ. Camb.* 420, 521.
[95] *E.D.R.* (1911), 88; (1912), 184, 224.
[96] *E.D.R.* (1913), 104.
[97] Teversham, *Hist. Sawston*, i. 110.
[98] B.L. Add. MS. 5813, ff. 66–7; C.U.L., E.D.R., B 2/10, f. 153v.
[99] *Proc. C.A.S.* xlii. 52.
[1] Ibid. 54–7.
[2] Ibid. xlii. 57–62; xlv. 14–19, 22–3.
[3] *Alum. Cantab. 1752–1900*, i. 542.
[4] C.U.L., E.D.R., C 3/21; H.O. 129/188/1/3/3.
[5] H.O. 107/76; H.O. 107/1761; *D.N.B.* 1901–11, s.v. Sir Rob. Herbert.
[6] Teversham, *Hist. Sawston*, i. 150.
[7] *E.D.R.* (1889), 265; C.R.O., 331/Z 7, 1933, Oct., p. 83.
[8] *E.D.R.* (1889), 265; (1885), 29.
[9] Teversham, *Hist. Sawston*, ii. 248; *Camb. Ind. Press*, 27 Jan. 1972.
[10] *E.D.R.* (1898), 69; *Lond. Gaz.* 2 Mar. 1880, p. 1789.
[11] *E.D.R.* (1887), 5.

there were then 240 communicants in the parish.[12] Two hundred communicants attended a Christmas service in 1904.[13] Church life in the parish has maintained its vigour in the 20th century, although church membership has not kept pace with the increase in population.

The church of *ST. MARY THE VIRGIN*, so called by 1521,[14] is of rubble with ashlar dressings and has a chancel with north chapel, an aisled and clerestoried nave of five bays with a north porch, and a west tower with south vestry. Its earliest architectural feature is the head of an early-12th-century doorway, reset in the chancel in the 13th century, suggesting an earlier chancel occupying the area that became the eastern end of the nave. An aisled nave of three bays was built on to the chancel late in the 12th century. Further enlargement of the church took place in the earlier 13th century: the nave and aisles were extended two bays eastwards, and a new chancel was built beyond them. The south chapel was built to replace the east end of the south aisle in the earlier 14th century, and at about the same time the western part of the aisle was rebuilt, its predecessor having presumably been narrower, and the west tower was added, possibly on earlier footings. Later in the 14th century the whole of the north aisle was rebuilt and the north porch was added. Other work of the 15th and early 16th centuries included the west window, new windows in the chancel, two chapels north of the chancel, the clerestory, the chancel arch and screen, and parclose screens in the aisles.

From the mid 16th century onwards the structural history of the church is largely a record of repeated decay and repairs. One north chapel was pulled down *c.* 1760,[15] and a west gallery was put in soon after 1815 and removed in 1878.[16] Most of the old fittings including the chancel screen and chapel screens were removed in 1870.[17] The church was restored in 1890, 1892, and 1900, and the vestry against the tower was added in 1899.[18]

There were four bells and a sanctus bell in 1552, five bells in 1757, and six in 1815.[19] Two new bells by Mears and Stainbank were added in 1885, and all the bells were rehung in 1891.[20] Of the six older bells, one of 1678 was by John and Christopher Hodson, one of 1755 was probably by Joseph Eayre, and four of 1774–5 were by Edward Arnold of St. Neots.[21]

The parish had only two chalices *c.* 1278.[22] The number had increased to three by 1552, including one recently given by Richard Godding.[23] The plate in 1972 included a silver chalice and paten of 1661.[24] The registers begin in 1641, but bishop's transcripts exist from 1599.[25]

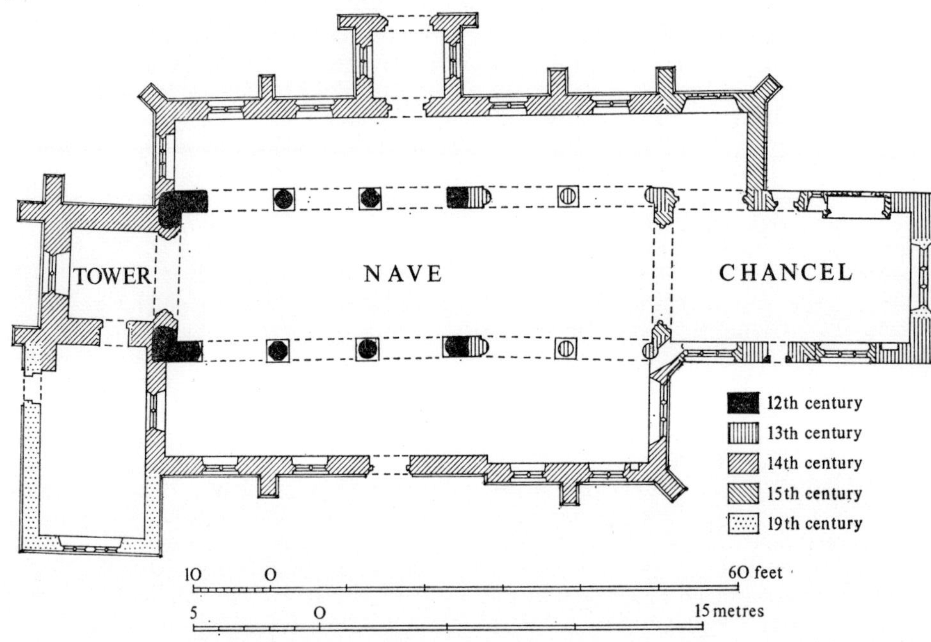

THE CHURCH OF ST. MARY THE VIRGIN, SAWSTON

ROMAN CATHOLICISM. The Huddlestons were one of the most prominent Catholic families in Cambridgeshire. Henry Huddleston (d. 1657) was converted by the Jesuit John Gerard *c.* 1593, and always kept at least one Catholic priest in his household.[26] The best-known priest's hole at Sawston Hall, said to have been constructed by Nicholas

[12] C.U.L., E.D.R., C 3/39.
[13] *E.D.R.* (1904), 291.
[14] B.L. Add. MS. 5861, p. 146.
[15] Palmer, *Wm. Cole*, 108–9.
[16] *Eng. Topog.* (Gent. Mag. Libr.), ii. 68 and n.; Teversham, *Hist. Sawston*, i. 150.
[17] Teversham, *Hist. Sawston*, i. 150.
[18] Ibid. 151–3.
[19] *Cambs. Ch. Goods, temp. Edw. VI*, 5–6; Palmer, *Wm. Cole*, 108; *Eng. Topog.* (Gent. Mag. Libr.), ii. 67.
[20] T. F. Teversham, *Parish Church of St. Mary the Virgin, Sawston* (Sawston [1954]), 33.
[21] *East Anglian* [1st ser.], iii. 134.
[22] *Vetus Liber Arch. Elien.* (C.A.S. 8vo ser. xlviii), 72–3.
[23] *Cambs. Ch. Goods, temp. Edw. VI*, 5–6; B.L. Add. MS. 5861, p. 186.
[24] Teversham, *Parish Ch.* 32.
[25] Transcript in C.R.O.
[26] *John Gerard*, ed. P. Caraman, 33.

Owen, dates from the late 16th century, and there are two other hiding-places of a later date.[27] The Hall contained a private chapel, described in 1757 as 'a gloomy garret and no ways ornamented',[28] and in the late 18th century a room at the east end of the south range was converted into a more permanent chapel. Jesuit priests lived at the Hall as chaplains throughout the 18th century, and some were buried in Sawston parish church.[29]

Apart from the Huddleston family, one man was presented for recusancy in 1577, one woman in 1582 and 1622, and four women in 1638.[30] In 1619 a recusant's grave was dug secretly in the churchyard at night,[31] and a Catholic was accused in 1624 of converting two women in Sawston.[32] Three people who refused to receive the sacrament in 1675 were probably the same as the three papists reported in 1676.[33] The Huddlestons were the only Catholic family in the district in 1783.[34] Their private chapel, registered for public worship in 1791, was opened to the public whenever services were held,[35] and congregations on Census Sunday in 1851 numbered 20 in the morning and 30 in the afternoon, drawn from a wide area.[36]

Industrial development in the 20th century attracted Polish, Italian, and Irish immigrants to Sawston, and the Catholic congregation eventually outgrew the chapel in the Hall.[37] In 1958 the church of Our Lady of Lourdes was built on a site given by Capt. Eyre-Huddleston, and it became the parish church for a large area in southern Cambridgeshire.[38]

PROTESTANT NONCONFORMITY. There were no protestant nonconformists at Sawston in 1676,[39] but in 1728 twelve families of Independents lived there and attended their licensed meeting-house about once a year.[40] Their numbers had fallen to two or three families in 1783.[41] A building was licensed in 1798 for Baptist worship; its congregation was described as Anabaptist by the vicar in 1807,[42] and may have been the same as the Congregational group which until 1810 met in a barn in Common Lane.[43]

The first Congregational chapel, a small plain red-brick building, was built in 1811. Its membership soon included nonconformists from other villages who had previously attended the chapel at Duxford, and was described by the minister in 1837 as 'Calvinistic of the old school'.[44] By 1851 the chapel was attracting congregations of 200, mainly poor agricultural labourers, at the afternoon service.[45] The vicars of Sawston from 1836 to 1877, Edwin and E. S. Daniel, who shared the Congregational minister's strong anti-Catholic feelings, sometimes attended the chapel. From 1886, however, when a High Church vicar was appointed, strife between Church and Chapel divided the village. The most notable Congregational minister was James McClune Uffen, 1867–84, who attacked T. S. Evans's use of the drink trade, was the first chairman of the school board, and was instrumental in opening the new non-denominational cemetery in 1881.[46] During Uffen's ministry at Sawston a new Congregational chapel was built in 1879, a large red-brick building with stone dressings, in an early Gothic style, designed by J. Sulman, standing between High Street and the old chapel, which was converted into a lecture hall and later a reading room.[47] There were 216 church members in 1899, 147 in 1916, 70 in 1945, and 56 in 1967–8.[48]

Houses licensed for dissenting worship in 1822 and 1834 may have been used by Methodists,[49] who in the 1830s probably met in the building that later became the National school.[50] A Primitive Methodist chapel, of brick with a slate roof, was built in 1861.[51] Miss Jane Wakefield, who kept one of the village shops, by will proved 1916 left money in trust to the chapel,[52] which had 19 members in 1964, but was closed by 1972.

There was a Salvation Army barracks at Sawston between 1887 and 1904.[53]

EDUCATION. In 1561 Mr. Dale taught boys Latin privately in Sawston, though he was unlicensed and accused of recusancy.[54] Joyce Moore (d. 1564), formerly wife of John Huntingdon, gave 40*s*. a year for a clerk to teach school in Sawston,[55] and there was a schoolmaster in 1596, from 1601 to 1610,[56] and for 7½ years before 1650.[57] About 1728 Mr. Alcock taught 16 children at their parents' expense.[58]

There was no school in the parish in 1818,[59] but one had been established by 1825, perhaps kept by the parish clerk, a shoemaker.[60] In 1833 six day-schools with 97 children probably included a school for tradesmen's sons.[61] A nonconformist Sunday school had 40 pupils, and the Church Sunday school,

27 *Country Life*, 22 Mar. 1962, p. 662.
28 Palmer, *Wm. Cole*, 108. A small chalice and paten of *c*. 1660 from the chapel, on loan to the Victoria and Albert Museum, was illustrated in *Country Life*, 24 June 1954, p. 2095.
29 Teversham, *Hist. Sawston*, ii. 157, 227; *Cath. Rec. Soc.* xxv. 134, 162; *Camb. Ind. Press*, 8, 22 Nov. 1963.
30 *Cath. Rec. Soc.* xxii. 79; liii. 3; Bodl. MS. Gough Eccl. Top. 3, f. 107; *Cambs. Village Doc.* 69.
31 C.U.L., E.D.R., B 2/37, f. 76.
32 *V.C.H. Cambs.* ii. 176.
33 C.U.L., E.D.R., B 2/63A, f. 10v.; Compton Census.
34 C.U.L., E.D.R., B 7/1, p. 132.
35 G.R.O. Worship Returns, Cambs. no. 38.
36 H.O. 129/188/1/3/14.
37 *Camb. Ind. Press*, 5 Feb. 1960.
38 *Camb. Daily News*, 18 Dec. 1958; *Camb. News*, 19 Apr. 1966.
39 Compton Census.
40 C.U.L., E.D.R., B 8/1, f. 26v.
41 Ibid. B 7/1, p. 132.
42 Ibid. B 4/1, f. 20v.; C 1/4.
43 R. Ball, *Hist. Sawston Cong. Church* (1947), 3.
44 Ibid. 4–5, 8.
45 H.O. 129/188/1/3/10.
46 Teversham, *Hist. Sawston*, ii. 271–3.
47 Ball, *Hist. Sawston Cong. Ch.* 10, 14.
48 *Cong. Yr. Bk.* (1899 and later edns.).
49 C.U.L., E.D.R., B 4/1, f. 70; G.R.O. Worship Returns, Ely dioc. nos. 441, 576.
50 Teversham, *Hist. Sawston*, ii. 271, 279–80.
51 Ed. 7/5.
52 Char. Com. files; not the Congregational chapel as suggested by Teversham, *Hist. Sawston*, ii. 248–9, which received a separate bequest from Miss Wakefield.
53 G.R.O. Worship Reg. nos. 30574, 35782; *Kelly's Dir. Cambs.* (1892, 1896, 1904).
54 C.U.L., E.D.R., B 2/3, p. 147.
55 Teversham, *Hist. Sawston*, i. 128–9.
56 C.U.L., E.D.R., B 2/18, f. 75v.; B 2/23, ff. 13v., 42v.; B 2/30A, f. 7v.; *V.C.H. Cambs.* ii. 338 n.
57 Teversham, *Hist. Sawston*, i. 128–9.
58 C.U.L., E.D.R., B 8/1, f. 26v.
59 *Educ. of Poor Digest*, 64.
60 C.U.L., E.D.R., C 1/6; Teversham, *Hist. Sawston*, ii. 279.
61 *Educ. Enquiry Abstract*, 59; Challis, *Sawston*, 22.

founded in 1832, had over 100.[62] There was also a British school, taught by the postmaster and held in a barn in Mill Lane and from 1861 in the new Primitive Methodist chapel. By 1861 64 children attended the British school, where numbers were increasing rapidly and the master held an evening school three days a week.[63]

The first Church day-school was opened in 1841, when the vicars of Sawston, Pampisford, and Babraham purchased a double cottage, formerly a meeting-house, with the help of a grant from the National Society. Children who also attended the Church Sunday school paid 1*d.* a week and others 2*d.*, and by 1844 there was an average attendance of 28 boys and 16 girls.[64] The low-church teaching of the vicar kept numbers low, and Richard Huddleston (d. 1847) founded a private Catholic school at the Hall.[65] The National school was apparently closed by 1862, perhaps for lack of suitable accommodation, leaving the parish ill provided.[66]

The National school was revived in 1866 when it was rebuilt by Edward Towgood for 250 children.[67] A school board for Sawston was formed in 1872; it built a new school in 1875 for boys and rented the National school building for girls.[68] Pupils paid between 2*d.* and 6*d.* a week according to their parents' means, and in 1877 120 boys, 97 girls, and 96 infants attended the schools.[69] An infants' school was built in 1882.[70] Numbers at the three schools reached almost 400 *c.* 1896, and a night school, discontinued before 1877, was restarted in 1893, and was still held in the winter in 1913.[71]

The first village college in Cambridgeshire was built at Sawston in 1930, on a site of 4 a., later enlarged to 26 a., given by H. G. Spicer.[72] Senior pupils from the schools in Sawston and nine surrounding villages were transferred to the village college in that year, and in 1972 there were 793 children aged 11–16 at the college. The old infants' school, renamed the John Falkner County Infants' School after the boys' schoolmaster 1893–1926, accommodated 265 children aged 5–7 in 1972. In 1963 a new primary school was opened, renamed the John Paxton County Primary School in 1972 after a 16th-century steward of the manors, and by 1972 it had 350 pupils. The Icknield County Primary School was opened in 1972 with 52 children aged 5–11 from the Babraham Road estates.[73]

CHARITIES FOR THE POOR. By will proved 1555 John Huntingdon left the reversion of three estates for the poor of Sawston, with doles of £8 at Christmas and Easter; in 1590 Sawston's lands, Swets's lands, and Pott's lands amounted to 96½ a.[74] From 1622 the income, amounting to £28 in 1615, was given to the parish overseers after payment of the doles, and the charity became entangled with parish poor-relief. Under a Scheme made at the request of the inhabitants in 1738 the overseers became the trustees, until a dispute in 1765 led to the appointment of new trustees. In the earlier 18th century the income was spent on rents, medical aid, and gifts of fuel and money; after the lawsuit in the 1760s the charity was in debt for many years.[75]

The trustees were awarded 66 a. in Sawston at inclosure in 1802,[76] besides land in Pampisford and Babraham. In 1835 28 a. were let to the poor as allotments.[77] In 1927 33 a. were sold and another 13½ a. in 1943. In 1972 the trustees held *c.* 30 a. in Sawston and 12 a. in Pampisford and Babraham.[78] The income, over £100 a year in the 19th century, was usually spent on coal, which was sold cheaply to the settled poor in 1835.[79] Coal was distributed to 229 people in 1892, 276 in 1904, and 127 in 1939.[80] Over £100 was spent on coal in 1965, and in 1970 the charity had assets of over £2,500, besides the land. Four alms-houses of red brick with slate roofs were built by the trustees in 1819 to replace the former town house.[81] In 1847 they were occupied by eight people who received coal and a weekly allowance, but by 1862 sixteen people lived in them, two to a room.[82] By 1939 the alms-houses were occupied rent-free as eight one-room tenements. The building was condemned and demolished in 1966. Two acres of charity land were sold to the county council in 1972 for an old people's home.[83]

Huntingdon's charity was administered in the 19th century by the handful of landowners and manufacturers who managed every other aspect of parish life, and since tradesmen were unwilling to incur unpopularity by becoming trustees, it was the trustees who occupied most of the charity lands.[84] In the 1870s T. S. Evans was accused of confining the distribution of charity coal to his own employees.[85] The charity was regulated by Schemes of 1917 and 1972.

The Town Peas charity was also founded under John Huntingdon's will, which provided that 2 a. should be sown each year with white peas for the poor of Sawston.[86] Each year a day in July was appointed for the picking, described in 1835 as 'a complete scene of scramble and confusion, attended with occasional conflicts'.[87] The vicar in 1862 wanted to abolish the custom, but between 200 and 500 people took part and it was greatly valued in Sawston. The obligation to grow the peas was a condition of the sale of Huntingdons farm in

[62] *Educ. Enquiry Abstract*, 59; *Church School Inquiry, 1846–7*, 6–7.
[63] Challis, *Sawston*, 22; Ed. 7/5.
[64] Teversham, *Hist. Sawston*, ii. 256, 279–80.
[65] Ibid. 256–7; *Church School Inquiry, 1846–7*, 6–7.
[66] Char. Com. files.
[67] Teversham, *Hist. Sawston*, ii. 280.
[68] Ibid. 282; *Lond. Gaz.* 15 Mar. 1872, p. 1453.
[69] Ed. 7/5; C.U.L., E.D.R., C 3/27.
[70] Teversham, *Hist. Sawston*, ii. 282.
[71] *Kelly's Dir. Cambs.* (1896); C.U.L., E.D.R., C 3/27; C.R.O., R 60/8/1/32, p. 206; ibid. 331/Z 1, 1913, Oct.
[72] *Camb. Ind. Press*, 5 Feb. 1960. For village colleges, see *V.C.H. Cambs.* ii. 353; *Camb. Region, 1965*, 194–7.
[73] Ex inf. County Educ. Dept.
[74] Prob. 11/37 (P.C.C. 19 More); Teversham, *Hist. Sawston*, i. 113, 116, 118; C 3/60/9.
[75] Teversham, *Hist. Sawston*, i. 126–7; ii. 160, 162, 164–71.
[76] C.R.O., P 136/26/1, pp. 60, 68.
[77] *31st Rep. Com. Char.* 206.
[78] Char. Com. files.
[79] *31st Rep. Com. Char.* 206.
[80] Char. Com. files; *E.D.R.* (1892), 651, 840; C.R.O., 331/Z 1, 1904, Dec.
[81] Char. Com. files.
[82] Ibid.; *Kelly's Dir. Cambs.* (1847).
[83] Char. Com. files; *Camb. Evening News*, 12 July 1967; 26 July 1972.
[84] Char. Com. files.
[85] *Cambs. Local Hist. Counc. Bull.* xxvi (1971), 20.
[86] Teversham, *Hist. Sawston*, i. 112.
[87] Ibid. ii. 183; *31st Rep. Com. Char.* 206.

1922.[88] The town pea-picking was still held in 1972, although since the early 20th century it has no longer been confined to the poor.

By will proved 1636 John Jefferie charged his lands in Sawston and neighbouring parishes with the yearly distribution to the poor of 4 bushels of rye and 4 of barley on St. Thomas's day and of 6*s.* in twopenny bread on Gang Monday.[89] The charity apparently lapsed between *c.* 1787 and 1800.[90]

Elizabeth Wakelin by will dated 1637 charged the house left for the vicar with annual payments of 40*s.* to the poor and 6*s.* in bread to poor children.[91] In 1835 the 40*s.* was distributed among 20 poor parishioners,[92] and in 1862 among 27 widows. Sixty-two penny loaves were given away in 1862, and the gift of bread to poor children continued until the 1880s, when the 6*s.* was added to the 40*s.* for general distribution.[93] The charity was regulated by Schemes of 1884 and 1921, and in 1970 the income was given in coal to two people.

Alexandrina, widow of D. Lawlor Huddleston, by will proved 1936 gave £500 for the sick and poor of Sawston aged over 60. The first distribution was made in 1938, and in 1961 the charity's income was *c.* £15.[94]

WHITTLESFORD

THE VILLAGE of Whittlesford stands by the river Cam or Granta, 7 miles south of Cambridge. The parish, roughly rectangular in shape and 1,976 a. in extent,[1] is bounded on the south by the Royston–Newmarket road, formerly a branch of the Icknield Way, and on part of the west by a brook rising at a place called Nine Wells. The eastern boundary follows various branches and former channels of the river. The northern boundary with Little Shelford was undefined until inclosure, the land being partly intercommonable.[2] The parish lies mostly between 50 and 125 ft. above sea level, and has little sharp relief. The subsoil is mostly chalk, with alluvium along the river, but there is a gravel rise near Stanmoor Hall in the north-west quarter of the parish, and south of the village, where gravel lies over the chalk, the ground also swells gently to over 100 ft. The level northern part of the parish is drained by small streams and water-courses mostly leading north-east into the river.

The parish was cultivated until its inclosure *c.* 1810 on a traditional three-field system, and was thereafter mainly devoted to mixed arable farming. Large areas of common pasture and meadow remained until inclosure along its northern and eastern edges. There was also some woodland, mostly between the Cambridge road and the river.[3] The manor in, probably, the 17th century contained £400 worth of timber,[4] and in the 19th the Whittlesford estate included from *c.* 65 a. to 100 a. of wood.[5] In the late 19th century low-lying and boggy land west of the village called Middlemoor, used as pasture until inclosure, was left to be overgrown with trees, and a belt of trees was established along the western boundary with Thriplow.[6]

Whittlesford had 33 inhabitants recorded in 1086,[7] there were *c.* 105 tenants in 1279,[8] and 33 persons paid tax there in 1327.[9] In 1377 142 adults paid the poll tax.[10] In 1477 there were *c.* 75 men over 12 in the village, sharing 43 surnames.[11] In 1525 49 persons paid the subsidy,[12] and there were 49 families in 1563.[13] There were 73 households taxed in 1664 and 88 in 1674,[14] and in 1676 there were said to be 200 conformists.[15] In 1728 58 families comprised 244 people, besides 5 dissenting families.[16] In 1801 the population was 416, and it grew steadily throughout the 19th century, reaching 579 in 1841 and 875 in 1891. The growth was sustained by the establishment of small-scale industries in Whittlesford and Sawston. By 1901 numbers had begun to fall, and *c.* 1920 the civilian population was only *c.* 720. Between 1931 and 1951 there were *c.* 800 inhabitants in the village, but the population had risen to 1,012 by 1961[17] and 1,190 by 1971.[18]

The village stands almost in the centre of the parish, along two sides of a triangle of roads. The north-east side is formed by a road running from Cambridge to Duxford and beyond, roughly parallel with the river. To the north-east, amid river-meadows and former manorial closes, the church and the moated side of the former manor-house stand slightly detached from the village. A lane west from them crosses the Cambridge road to become the main village street, the south-east side of the triangle, which runs along the northern edge of the gravel rise. It was formerly called South Street[19] but in 1973 High Street, continuing after a bend to West End. Half-way along West End, near the former parsonage, it once widened into a small green.[20] Before inclosure most of the dwellings in the village lay along that street, where many timber-framed and thatched cottages, not all in good repair,

88 C.U.L., Maps 53(1)/92/33.
89 Prob. 11/148 (P.C.C. 13 Hele).
90 *Char. Don.* i. 102–3; *31st Rep. Com. Char.* 208.
91 Teversham, *Hist. Sawston*, ii. 244–5.
92 *31st Rep. Com. Char.* 207.
93 Char. Com. files; Teversham, *Hist. Sawston*, ii. 247.
94 Char. Com. files; C.R.O., 331/Z 7, 1937, Jan., pp. 6–7; 331/Z 8, 1938, Jan., p. 8.
1 This account was written in 1973.
2 C.R.O., P 171/26/1, pp. 4, 44.
3 Ibid. P 171/26/2.
4 C.U.L., Doc. 1529.
5 C.R.O., R 58/5, vol. ix, pp. 245–67; 296/SP 1108; County Council Rec. T 279.
6 O.S. Map 6", Cambs. LIV. SW. (1890 and later edns.).
7 *V.C.H. Cambs.* i. 410.
8 *Rot. Hund.* (Rec. Com.), ii. 571–5.
9 *Cambs. Lay Subsidy, 1327*, 28–9.
10 *East Anglian*, N.S. xii. 257.
11 C.R.O., Huddleston MSS., tithing roll 17 Edw. IV.
12 E 179/81/147 m. 1.
13 B.L. Harl. MS. 594, f. 200.
14 E 179/84/437 rot. 103 and d.; E 179/244/23 rot. 86 and d.
15 Compton Census.
16 C.U.L., E.D.R., B 8/1.
17 *Census*, 1801–1961.
18 Ibid. 1971.
19 H.O. 107/76.
20 C.R.O., P 171/26/2.

survived in 1973. Among the larger old houses were Markings Farm, an L-shaped 17th-century house, and one red-brick Georgian house with segmental-headed windows and a classical doorcase. Along the Cambridge road north-west of the cross-roads, formerly called North Street, there were in 1810 a few scattered cottages. Its south-western side, however, was mainly occupied by large farmsteads,[21] as at the Grove, formerly Grove House Farm, where a Georgian front block has been added to a 16th-century timber-framed house, and Rayners Farm at the north end, an L-shaped house of *c.* 1500 with prominent chimney-stacks, which retains two original timber-mullioned windows and fireplaces, perhaps 17th-century, with shafts supporting rude pediments.[22] By 1810 a few houses, including one cottage with a bulky stepped chimney-breast, stood at the junction with the Cambridge road of Whippletree Lane, later Middlemoor Road, which led to West End, but along most of that road there were no buildings then or later.[23] Under Charles II the village contained *c.* 80 dwellings,[24] but in 1801 only about 60 houses. By 1831 there were 113 dwellings and in 1851 135,[25] of which *c.* 60 were in South Street and *c.* 30 in North Street.[26] Building later progressed more slowly, so that there were by 1900 only *c.* 180 houses compared with 160 in 1861. Except for farmsteads built after inclosure at Wells, Stanmoor Hall, and Hill farms, settlement was still largely confined to the old village site. Later there was ribbon development along the road south to Whittlesford station and Duxford. Almost 40 houses were built between 1921 and 1931 and over 80 between 1951 and 1961.[27] Council houses were built at the north-western and south-western corners of the village, and a larger council estate was laid out between Church Lane and Mill Lane. In 1962 there were *c.* 90 council houses.[28]

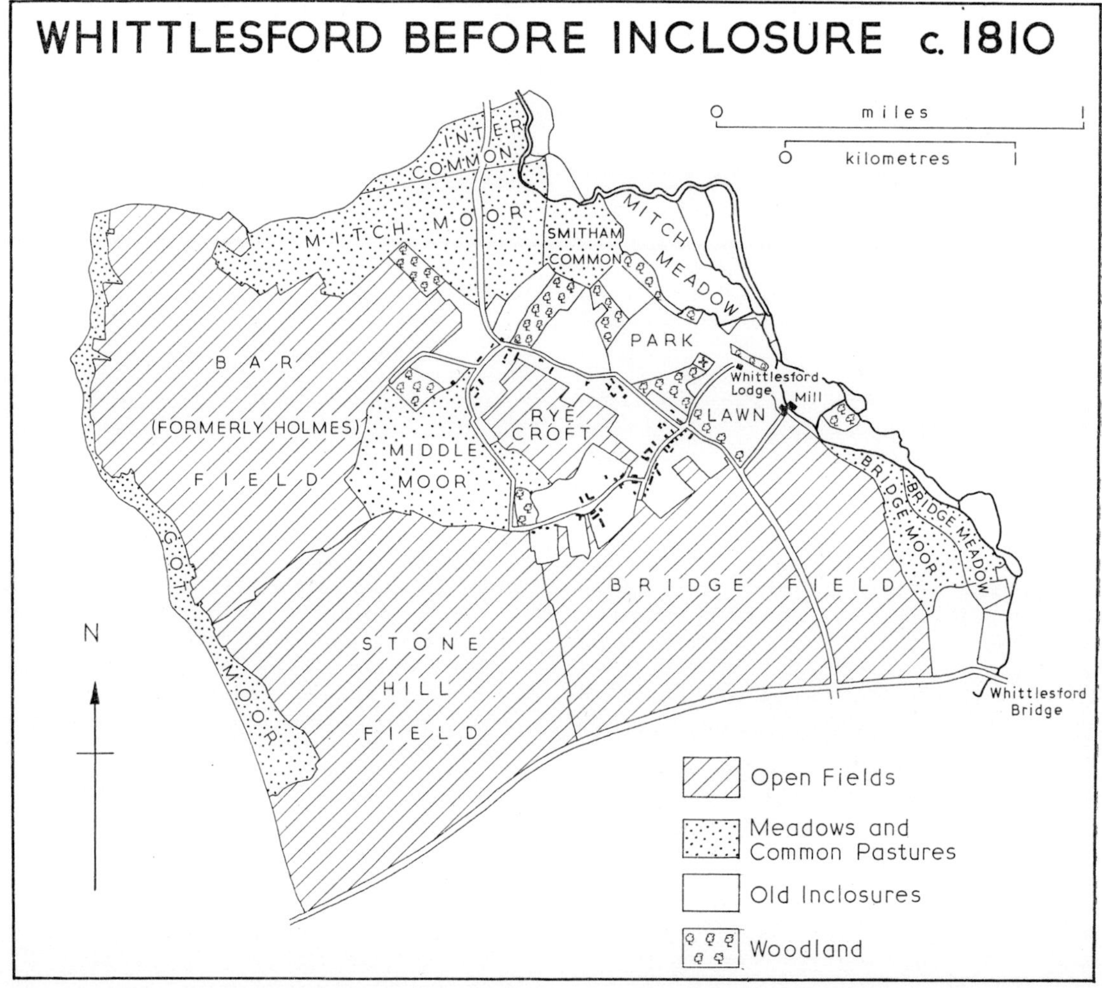

The village formerly contained several public houses, the oldest and most prominent being the Waggon and Horses, recorded from 1810 to 1937. In 1851 there were five other beer-retailers, in 1904 seven, and in 1937 six named public houses.[29] The inns at Whittlesford Bridge are mentioned above under Duxford.

Like most neighbouring villages, Whittlesford lay off the main routes of the area, standing about a mile from the Royston–Newmarket road, a turnpike from

[21] H.O. 107/76; C.R.O., P 171/26/2.
[22] M.H.L.G. List.
[23] C.R.O., P 171/26/2.
[24] E 179/244/22 f. 89.
[25] *Census*, 1801–51.
[26] H.O. 107/1761.
[27] *Census*, 1861–1961.
[28] *Camb. Daily News*, 27 Sept. 1962; *Camb. News*, 12 Nov. 1962.
[29] C.R.O., P 171/26/1, p. 2; *Gardner's Dir. Cambs.* (1851); *Kelly's Dir. Cambs.* (1858–1937).

1770 to 1874,[30] to which it was connected by the road south from Cambridge. A minor road leading west from the village towards Thriplow was stopped at inclosure; another towards Newton was straightened.[31] The London–Cambridge railway, completed in 1845, crosses the south-east corner of the parish. Whittlesford station, opened in 1845 and rebuilt between 1877 and 1890,[32] was still in use for passengers in 1973.

Robert Maynard, an agricultural tool-maker, founded in 1866 a Working Man's Institute, furnished with a lecture hall and reading and bagatelle rooms.[33] It closed between 1922 and 1925, to be replaced by 1929 with a new village institute, to which H. G. Spicer of Sawston added *c.* 1930 a reading room and library.[34] The Whittlesford Co-operative and Industrial Society, established *c.* 1891, merged between 1922 and 1929 with the Sawston Co-operative Society.[35] Its shop had closed by 1973. During the First World War a hospital for the wounded, taking up to 1,000 patients, was set up at Whittlesford and remained in use until 1919.[36] Barracks for Duxford airfield, under construction in 1918, remained in use until 1961.[37]

The village feast was held in the 18th and 19th centuries on St. Barnabas's day.[38] It was revived as a neo-Victorian festivity in 1971.[39] Traditional ceremonies on Plough Monday, Shrove Tuesday, and Mayday were still being celebrated by the youth of the village in the mid 19th century.[40] Camping close, opposite the Victorian vicarage, is said to have been used for the game of camping, a rough kind of football common in East Anglia.[41]

MANORS AND OTHER ESTATES. Before the Conquest Earl Gurth, King Harold's brother, owned the manor comprising almost all the township. By 1086 it had been given to the Countess Judith, the Conqueror's niece and Earl Waltheof's widow.[42] Part of her Cambridgeshire lands, called the barony of Kirtling, and including *WHITTLESFORD* manor, passed to her younger daughter Alice (or Adelize) who married Ralph de Tony[43] (d. 1126). Alice's heir was their son Roger de Tony (d. by 1162). The overlordship of the manor, which by the late 12th century had been subinfeudated to a junior branch of the Tony family, descended with that barony in its main line to Robert de Tony (d.s.p. 1309). Robert's sister and heir Alice[44] married Guy de Beauchamp, earl of Warwick,[45] and Kirtling manor with its dependencies descended with the earldom of Warwick until its forfeiture in 1499.[46] In 1500 Whittlesford was said to be held of the Crown as of the barony of Kirtling,[47] and after 1534[48] of the lords North, owners of Kirtling manor.[49]

Like the barony of which it was held,[50] Whittlesford manor was not held by knight service, but nominally in free socage, although its tenure approximated to a military serjeanty. Its tenants were obliged to attend the lord of Kirtling when he went to the wars in the king's company.[51] In 1279 that service was due to Ralph de Tony (d. *c.* 1295) from Hugh fitz Otes, who had been interpolated as mesne lord between Ralph and Sir John de Akeny, tenant in demesne, who was said to hold of Hugh for $\frac{1}{20}$ knight's fee.[52] By 1400 the military duty had been changed into the yearly render of a sparrow-hawk or 2*s.* to the earls of Warwick,[53] which was still due in the 16th century.[54] Occasionally in the 15th century, however, Whittlesford was said to be held as $\frac{1}{4}$ knight's fee.[55]

Whittlesford was probably among the lands given by Roger de Tony (d. by 1162) to his younger son Roger (d. by 1185) whose son Baldwin de Tony[56] held it in 1206.[57] Baldwin died after 1215,[58] and by 1228, perhaps by 1217, all his lands had come to Roger de Akeny,[59] who held Whittlesford *c.* 1235 and died *c.* 1240.[60] Although Roger left daughters as his heirs,[61] all his East Anglian lands, including Whittlesford, had passed by 1241 to Baldwin de Akeny,[62] who in 1267 received a grant of free warren in Whittlesford, and survived until 1272.[63] In 1279 Whittlesford was held by Baldwin's son Sir John de Akeny,[64] who was dead by 1293 when his widow Alice apparently held the manor. She died after 1300,[65] and was followed by their son Baldwin de Akeny (fl. 1311).[66] He is said to have married Joan, whose second husband William Howard[67] held Whittlesford, presumably in right of her dower, in 1316 and 1327[68] and died in 1328.[69] In 1331 Baldwin's son John de Akeny sold the manor to Roger

[30] Bourn Bridge Road Act, 8 & 9 Geo. III, c. 86; Annual Turnpike Acts Continuance Act, 36 & 37 Vic. c. 90.
[31] C.R.O., P 171/26/1, pp. 6–11; B.L. Maps, O.S.D. 235.
[32] *V.C.H. Cambs.* ii. 132; C.R.O., R 58/5, vol. vii, p. 103.
[33] *Kelly's Dir. Cambs.* (1879).
[34] Ibid. (1922, 1925, 1929); C.R.O., 331/Z 6, 1928, Jan., p. 4; Nov., p. 93; 1929, Jan., p. 6; 1931, Nov., p. 87.
[35] *E.D.R.* (1892), 772; *Kelly's Dir. Cambs.* (1892, 1922, 1929).
[36] C.R.O., 331/Z 5, 1916, Aug.; 1919, June; *Camb. Ind. Press*, 30 June 1961.
[37] C.R.O., 331/Z 5, 1918, May.
[38] B.L. Add. MS. 9412, f. 252; *E.D.R.* (1905), 188.
[39] *Camb. Evening News*, 10 June 1971.
[40] C.R.O., R 58/5, vol. vii, pp. 6–7, 119–20, 125.
[41] Ibid. pp. 7–9.
[42] *V.C.H. Cambs.* i. 398.
[43] Farrer, *Feud. Cambs.* 48.
[44] *Complete Peerage*, xii (1), 761–74.
[45] Ibid. xii (2), 371–2; cf. *Cal. Inq. p.m.* v, p. 400.
[46] *Complete Peerage*, xii (2), 372–97; cf. C 139/178/55 no. 11.
[47] *Cal. Inq. p.m. Hen. VII*, ii, p. 279.
[48] Cf. North Estate Act, 28 Hen. VIII, c. 40.
[49] e.g. E 150/102 no. 7; Wards 7/69 no. 68.
[50] Cf. *Feud. Aids*, i. 139; Sanders, *Eng. Baronies*, 117–18.
[51] *Liber de Bernewelle*, 256.
[52] *Rot. Hund.* (Rec. Com.), ii. 571.
[53] C.R.O., Huddleston MSS., bailiff's acct. [1–2 Hen. IV]; cf. C 139/178/55 no. 11.
[54] E 150/102 no. 7.
[55] e.g. *Cal. Close*, 1405–8, 185; *Cal. Inq. p.m. Hen. VII*, ii, p. 279.
[56] *Rot. de Dom.* (Pipe R. Soc. xxxv), 51; *Cur. Reg. R.* iv. 122; cf. *Complete Peerage*, xii (1), 764 n.; *V.C.H. Oxon.* v. 137–8.
[57] *Rot. Litt. Claus.* (Rec. Com.), i. 74.
[58] Ibid. 238.
[59] Ibid. 323; *Cur. Reg. R.* xiii, pp. 142, 266.
[60] *Liber de Bernewelle*, 256; *Ex. e Rot. Fin.* (Rec. Com.), i. 334, 345.
[61] *Cal. Pat.* 1232–47, 283.
[62] *Close R.* 1237–42, 260.
[63] C.P. 25(1)/25/34 nos. 36–7; *Cal. Chart. R.* 1257–1300, 73–4.
[64] *Rot. Hund.* (Rec. Com.), ii. 571; cf. Blomefield, *Norf.* ix. 233.
[65] C.P. 25(1)/26/44 no. 17; *Cal. Close*, 1296–1302, 70, 387.
[66] *Cal. Chanc. Wts.* i. 335.
[67] Burke, *Peerage* (1949), 1492.
[68] *Feud. Aids*, i. 155; *Cambs. Lay Subsidy, 1327*, 28.
[69] *Cal. Fine R.* 1327–37, 99, 104.

Wateville and his wife Margery.[70] Roger probably died the next year,[71] and Margery was occupying the manor-house in 1346.[72] A John Wateville was living at Whittlesford *c.* 1340.[73]

By 1358 the manor probably belonged to William Muschet of Fen Ditton, who died after 1362.[74] In 1365 and 1368 it was held by Sir Richard Muschet[75] (d. after 1371),[76] and in 1374 by Sir John Muschet.[77] In 1378 it was settled on Sir George Muschet.[78] Probably *c.* 1394 Sir George sold it to Joan, widow of Roger, Lord Scales (d. 1388),[79] and her second husband, Sir Edmund Thorp, who held it in her right in 1401.[80] Joan died in 1415, having devised it for life to her husband, killed in France in 1418. The manor had been entailed by Joan's will successively on her grandson, Robert, Lord Scales (d.s.p. 1419), and her two daughters by Thorp, Joan, wife of Sir John Clifton (d. 1447), and Isabel (d. 1436), who married Philip Tilney (d. 1453).[81] Joan Clifton probably held Whittlesford until she died without issue in 1450.[82] Philip Tilney, who had taken orders by 1444, may have arranged that it should pass to his younger son Robert,[83] whose title was apparently disputed by Thomas, Lord Scales (d. 1460), Robert Scales's brother. In 1451 Thomas entailed the manor on Robert Tilney,[84] who held it until his death in 1500. His son and heir Robert, aged 9 at his father's death,[85] died in 1542. After a dispute 120 a. of the demesne was assigned as dower to his second wife Audrey,[86] who held them with her second husband William Johnson until *c.* 1590.[87] Robert Tilney's son and heir John, being much indebted,[88] sold the manor in 1552 to William Hawtrey.[89] Sir John Huddleston of Sawston used his influence at court to oblige Hawtrey to sell it to him in 1555.[90] Huddleston died holding the manor in 1557,[91] and it descended with the Sawston estate in the Huddleston family[92] until the early 18th century. Its income was sometimes assigned to junior members of the family.[93] In 1735 the court of Whittlesford was held in the name of Henry Howard, Lord Morpeth (later earl of Carlisle),[94] probably as trustee for Richard Huddleston (d. 1760), who is said to have sold the manor[95] to John Stevenson of Newton, to whom the earl conveyed it in 1745.[96] Stevenson's son Robert sold it in 1765 to Ebenezer Hollick,[97] a prosperous miller.[98] Hollick, who died in 1792, entailed the estate, which he had enlarged to over 700 a., on his brother William's son Ebenezer,[99] who after further purchases of *c.* 300 a. owned over half the parish after inclosure.[1] He went bankrupt in 1825[2] and died in 1828. His heir was his daughter Ann Blunkett Hollick, who died unmarried in 1864 leaving her land to her half-sister Caroline's son, Joseph Hollick Tickell, a lawyer.[3] Tickell sold almost all the Whittlesford estate in 1877 to Major Christopher Pemberton,[4] but retained the lordship of the manor which he left on his death in 1883 to his son Joseph Harkness Tickell.[5] The latter died in 1915 and his son Capt. J. A. Tickell in 1941. Capt. Tickell's son, J. H. de la T. Tickell,[6] kept the Tickell Arms, the principal village inn, in 1973.[7]

Major Pemberton was dead by 1885.[8] In 1888 most of his Whittlesford land passed by foreclosure of a mortgage to W. R. C. Farquhar (d. 1901), and was sold by Alfred Farquhar in 1909 to G. R. C. Foster.[9] When Foster sold the remaining 820 a. in 1919 the estate was broken up: the Cambridgeshire county council bought *c.* 440 a.,[10] and H. G. Spicer *c.* 90 a., including land called the Lawn and the Park, which he still owned in 1937.[11] By 1960 the Lawn had been acquired by the South Cambridgeshire R.D.C., which built many council houses there in the 1960s.[12]

The medieval manor-house presumably stood within the rectangular moat which remained, overgrown with trees, in 1972, south-east of the church.[13] The house, in decay in 1514,[14] was repaired or rebuilt by Robert Tilney (d. 1542). Its windows once contained glass with the arms of Howard impaling Tilney.[15] In the late 18th century it was demolished, and a new house, called Whittlesford Lodge, was built, probably *c.* 1785, by the younger Ebenezer Hollick[16] by the south-west side of the moat. It was of red brick, three bays by five, in the Georgian style. Irregular rooms at the back, on a different level, were said to derive from the older house. A range of stables stood near by.[17] The Lodge, empty

[70] C.P. 25(1)/28/67 no. 16.
[71] Last recorded in *Cal. Pat.* 1330–4, 293.
[72] *E.D.R.* (1892), 790.
[73] *Inq. Non.* (Rec. Com.), 213.
[74] *Cal. Close*, 1354–60, 496–7; *Cal. Pat.* 1361–4, 216.
[75] C.R.O., Huddleston MSS., deeds 39, 42 Edw. III.
[76] *Cal. Fine R.* 1368–77, 126.
[77] *E.D.R.* (1894), 329.
[78] C.P. 25(1)/29/86 no. 5.
[79] C.R.O., Huddleston MSS., ct. roll 17 Ric. II; cf. *Complete Peerage*, xi. 503–4.
[80] C.P. 25(1)/30/92 no. 12; *Cal. Close*, 1405–8, 185.
[81] *Testamenta Vetusta*, ed. Nicolas, i. 183–5; *Reg. Chichele* (Cant. & York Soc.), ii. 143–9, 679; *Complete Peerage*, iii. 308; Blomefield, *Norf.* v. 148–51.
[82] *Cal. Fine R.* 1445–52, 177; cf. Blomefield, *Norf.* i. 376–7; Req. 2/3/76, answer.
[83] *Visit. Norf.* (Harl. Soc. xxxii), 287.
[84] C.P. 25(1)/30/99 no. 6; C 139/78/55 no. 11.
[85] *Cal. Inq. p.m. Hen. VII*, ii, p. 279.
[86] Req. 2/3/76, bill; *E.D.R.* (1912), 91; C.R.O., Huddleston MSS., list of dower lands.
[87] C.R.O., Huddleston MSS., ct. rolls 1 Mary, 33 Eliz. I.
[88] Cf. Req. 2/3/76.
[89] C.P. 25(2)/55/399 nos. 29, 36; C.R.O., Huddleston MSS., schedule of deeds, 1555.
[90] C 3/93/68.
[91] E 150/102 no. 7.
[92] See p. 250.
[93] e.g. C.R.O., Huddleston MSS., deeds 1627, 1637.
[94] C.R.O., R 58/5, vol. ix, p. 146.
[95] Ibid. p. 179.
[96] B.L. Add. MS. 9412, f. 252; C.P. 43/648 rott. 30–1.
[97] C.P. 25(2)/1281/5 Geo. III Trin. no. 10; cf. C.R.O., R 58/5, vol. ix, p. 150.
[98] C.R.O., R 58/5, vol. ix, pp. 153, 179; see also pp. 167, 205–7.
[99] Prob. 11/1220 (P.C.C. 337 Fountain); C.R.O., P 171/26/1, pp. 42–50.
[1] C.R.O., P 171/26/1, pp. 22–42.
[2] C.R.O., R 58/5, vol. ix, pp. 210, 276.
[3] Ibid. pp. 182, 189–96.
[4] Ibid. pp. 218, 278; C.U.L., Maps 53/87/9.
[5] C.R.O., R 58/5, vol. ix, pp. 270, 301.
[6] C.R.O., 331/Z 4, 1915, May; Z 8, 1941, Feb., p. 20.
[7] *Camb. Ind. Press*, 3 Sept. 1965; *Camb. Evening News*, 24 Aug. 1972; *Guardian*, 14 Oct. 1970.
[8] C.R.O., 296/SP 860.
[9] C.R.O., County Council Rec. T 279; 296/SP 1037, 1052.
[10] C.R.O., 296/SP 1108.
[11] Ibid.; *Kelly's Dir. Cambs.* (1937).
[12] Cf. *Camb. News*, 12 Apr. 1962.
[13] Cf. *V.C.H. Cambs.* ii. 44.
[14] C.R.O., Huddleston MSS., rental 1514.
[15] *Mon. Inscr. Cambs.* 193, 244. Thos. Howard, duke of Norfolk (d. 1524), married successively two of Rob. Tilney's cousins: *Complete Peerage*, ix. 614–15.
[16] B.L. Add. MS. 9412, f. 252.
[17] C.R.O., R 58/5, vol. ix, pp. 167–8, 173.

since 1828, was demolished in 1858.[18] The Tickells only occasionally lived in the village, in converted cottages.[19]

In 1086 Girard, Count Alan's tenant at Duxford, held ½ yardland and the soke of another 1¼ yardland at Whittlesford of the count, and Hardwin de Scalers had another yardland previously held by a man of Earl Gurth.[20] No more is recorded of those properties.

In the early 13th century Barnwell priory owned 120 a. there, held of Whittlesford manor, of which Prior Lawrence (1213–51) enfeoffed Stephen le Cheyney for 20*s.* fee farm. Stephen's son William divided the land among many under-tenants, who were holding of Adam le Cheyney in 1279, and from whom the priory had difficulty in recovering the service due in 1290.[21] Another 120 a. had been granted before 1233 by John le Cheyney, tenant under the Akenys, for life to Baldwin de Freville,[22] who still held that carucate in 1250, when William le Cheyney claimed to be his lord.[23] In 1272 William conveyed 115 a. to Maud Devereux, who in 1276 conveyed a carucate in Whittlesford to Thomas de Sollers.[24] In 1278 Thomas and Simon de Sollers granted it to Adam and Henry of Kirkcudbright,[25] who in 1279 held of Simon as tenant of Adam le Cheyney 122 a. in demesne and *c.* 105 a. occupied by free tenants.[26] The later descent has not been traced, but the estate may have included the 92 a., called a carucate, held in the 15th century by five generations of the Gedding family.[27]

In 1279 Ickleton priory owned 34 a. at Whittlesford.[28] In 1505 Pembroke College, Cambridge, acquired from the executors of John Ward *c.* 35 a. which Ward had acquired or possessed since 1472,[29] and in 1547 bought from Robert Lockton *c.* 55 a. called Bewlies which Thomas Lockton had acquired in and after 1448 and which his son and heir Walter had released to his younger brother Thomas in 1472.[30] For the combined estate of 90 a. the college received at inclosure 57 a. It still held 60 a. in 1873.[31]

Before John Tilney sold the manor he had already in 1546–7 sold Whittlesford mill and *c.* 100 a. to Henry Veysey who in 1557 conveyed the 100 a. to the brothers Richard and Robert Symons.[32] Robert was later said to have acquired half the demesne, having in or after 1578 bought out John Rogers, purchaser of another part[33] and died in 1611 possessed, besides the lease of the impropriate rectory, of *c.* 230 a. which passed to his son Robert[34] (d. 1622). The younger Robert's son and heir Thomas[35] occupied that estate *c.* 1630,[36] but apparently disposed of it between 1644 and 1654.[37]

The impropriate rectory, held by St. Mary's college, Warwick,[38] included, besides the great tithes, *c.* 31 a. of land.[39] In 1552 the Crown granted a lease in reversion from 1563,[40] which was acquired by Roger Ascham, Queen Elizabeth's tutor. His wife Margaret was probably daughter of Thomas Howe, lessee of half the rectory since 1551, and two of his sons were born at Whittlesford. Ascham died in 1568.[41] Margaret, who later married Thomas Rempston, and her sons Giles and Thomas Ascham received a fresh lease in 1579.[42] By 1599 Giles and Thomas had under-let the rectory for 60 years to Robert Symons (d. 1611).[43] In 1608 Thomas Ascham assigned half his interest under a fresh Crown lease, granted in 1600, to Symons,[44] on whose behalf the freehold of the rectory, sold by the Crown in fee farm, was bought in 1610.[45] Symons's son Robert sold all his interest in 1622 to Thomas Ventris,[46] who purchased the other half-share of the head-lease in 1624, so re-uniting the rectory.[47] The fee-farm rent, equal to the old reserved rent, was bought from the Crown by Heneage Finch, earl of Nottingham (d. 1682), to endow an alms-house at Ravenstone (Bucks.),[48] to which it was still paid in the 19th century.[49]

Thomas Ventris settled half the rectory on his daughter Mathew, who in 1630 married Thomas Dod, to whom Ventris, when he died in 1637, left the other half, subject to the life-interest of his second wife Ellen,[50] whom Dod bought out in 1646.[51] Before Dod died in 1670[52] he had settled the rectory on his younger son Thomas, who dying without issue in 1667 left it to his elder brother Edward[53] (d. 1678). Edward's son and heir Thomas[54] sold the estate in 1707.[55] By 1711 it had come to Felix Calvert[56] (d. 1713), whose heir was his son Peter (d. 1772). Peter's son Peter Calvert, dean of Arches, died without issue in 1788, and the estate was sold[57] in 1789 to Thomas Thurnall whose

18 Ibid. pp. 168, 183, 273–4; cf. H.O. 107/76.
19 C.R.O., R 58/5, vol. ix, pp. 272, 275.
20 *V.C.H. Cambs.* i. 374, 388.
21 *Liber de Bernewelle*, 312–17; cf. *Rot. Hund.* (Rec. Com.), ii. 571–4.
22 *Cur. Reg. R.* xv, p. 152.
23 C.P. 25(1)/24/25 no. 6.
24 C.P. 25(1)/25/33 no. 3; C.P. 25(1)/284/20 no. 6; cf. Sanders, *Eng. Baronies*, 87.
25 C.P. 25(1)/25/37 no. 24.
26 *Rot. Hund.* ii. 572–3.
27 C.P. 25(1)/30/94 no. 4; *Cal. Close*, 1405–8, 361; *Cal. Inq. p.m. Hen. VII*, ii, p. 280.
28 *Rot. Hund.* ii. 571–4.
29 Pemb. Coll. Mun., Whittlesford, A 1–9; B 1–9.
30 Ibid. D 10–11; E 1–4; F 1–4; G 1–2; H 1–5; I 1–2.
31 C.R.O., P 171/26/1, pp. 79–80; *Rep. Com. Univ. Income* [C. 856-II], p. 98, H.C. (1873), xxxvii.
32 C.P. 25(2)/4/22 no. 69; C.P. 25(2)/55/398 no. 5; C.P. 25(2)/55/399 no. 32.
33 B.L. Add. MS. 5819, f. 54; C.R.O., Huddleston MSS., survey 1578, f. 4.
34 Wards 7/69 no. 68; and see below.
35 Prob. 11/141 (P.C.C. 21 Swan).
36 B.L. Add. MS. 5819, f. 54.
37 Gibbons, *Ely Episc. Rec.* 378; C.U.L., Doc. 1430–1.
38 See p. 272.
39 B.L. Add. Ch. 15875; C.U.L., Doc. 469.
40 *Acts. of P.C.* 1552–4, 89–90.
41 *D.N.B.*; C.R.O., R 58/5, vol. ii, p. 153; ibid. Huddleston MSS., deed 1551.
42 E 310/9/13 no. 28; cf. C.R.O., R 58/5, vol. ix, p. 100.
43 *Proc. C.A.S.* xxxii. 48; cf. C.R.O., R 58/5, vol. ix, p. 100.
44 *Proc. C.A.S.* xxxii. 49; C.U.L., Doc. 444, 447.
45 C.U.L., Doc. 450; B.L. Add. Ch. 15875; cf. C.R.O., R 58/5, vol. ii, p. 41.
46 C.P. 25(2)/278/20 Jas. I Mich. no. 10.
47 C.P. 25(2)/278/22 Jas. I Mich. no. 25; C.U.L., Doc. 453.
48 *27th Rep. Com. Char.* H.C. 225, pp. 179–82 (1834), xxi.
49 C.U.L., Doc. 463; C.R.O., 296/SP 860, 1002.
50 Prob. 11/173 (P.C.C. 43 Goare); C 3/400/101.
51 C.P. 25(2)/401/22 Chas. I Mich. no. 8.
52 Prob. 11/332 (P.C.C. 18 Penn).
53 C.P. 43/332 rot. 54; C.U.L., Doc. 462; Gibbons, *Ely Episc. Rec.* 379.
54 Prob. 11/336 (P.C.C. 31 Reeves); cf. *Genealogist*, iii. 242–3.
55 C.R.O., R 58/5, vol. ii, p. 41; C.U.L., Doc. 463; C.P. 25(2)/910/5 Anne Hil. no. 5.
56 C.U.L., Doc. 464–6.
57 Ibid. 467–8; *V.C.H. Herts. Fam.* 462–4; C.R.O., R 58/5, vol. ii, pp. 41–2.

family had leased it since 1723.[58] At inclosure Thurnall was allotted 18 a. for glebe and c. 275 a. for the rectorial tithes, until then received in kind.[59] He was succeeded in 1818 by his son Henry John Thurnall (d. 1866).[60] The estate was sold in 1872 to Robert Maynard and Allen White, who divided it, White taking 146 a., sold again in 1885, and Maynard 139 a.,[61] including the old parsonage farm-house, where the Dods had lived in the 17th century. It was a three-bay building, brick-fronted to the high street, timber-framed with three gables behind. Maynard demolished it in 1872, and built a new house there, later called Ascham House.[62] After Maynard's death in 1883 four of his children sold his land to the fifth, Albert (d. 1915), whose son R. J. Maynard sold it in 1920 to the Cambridgeshire county council.[63] The council was thereafter the largest landowner in Whittlesford, owning *c.* 765 a. in 1973.[64]

ECONOMIC HISTORY. Almost the whole township, 11¼ hides out of 12, was in 1066 and 1086 included in a single manor. Five hides lay in demesne, and 13 *villani* and 15 bordars shared the rest. There were also 5 thralls. The demesne had only 2 plough-teams, and the *villani* with 9 teams evidently did most of its ploughing. Whittlesford's yearly value increased slightly after the Conquest, from £15 to £16 in 1086.[65]

By 1279 only just over 2 hides remained in demesne, the tenants occupying allegedly 9⅛ hides, of which *c.* 750 a., besides 55 a. of glebe, was held freely and *c.* 305 a. in villeinage. The arrangement of the free holdings was complex, with tenancies and subtenancies sometimes on two or three levels. Of the five major tenants immediately under Sir John de Akeny, Barnwell priory held *c.* 130 a., mostly held under it by Adam le Cheyney. Henry Lacy held *c.* 70 a., Baldwin de Romilly *c.* 75 a., and John Gopil 40 a. Each of those larger holdings, like the 22 or so remaining free holdings, also directly held of Akeny, were split up into small parcels whose actual occupiers combined them with holdings of other fees. The outcome was that, besides 1 large holding of 122 a., 11 of 20–60 a. amounted to *c.* 360 a., 10 of 10–15 a. covered 116 a., and 45 of under 10 a. contained only *c.* 150 a. between them. The rents paid, mostly between 1*d.* and 4*d.* an acre, but reaching up to 12*d.*, had evidently been fixed over a long period. Few freeholders owed boon-work.

The villein tenements were more regularly arranged. Eight half-yardlanders had 15 a. each, and 24 other villeins 9 a. each. The former owed 76 works a year, and sent 4 men to 4 harvest-boons, the latter only 32 works, and 4 harvest-boons with 2 men. Both classes also performed three averages, and had to mow, carry the hay, reap, and cart manure. The 9 cottagers were to send 1 man to the harvest, and help to stack the lord's hay, cover his house, and make his pond. All the customary tenants were said then to be the lord's neifs.[66] By the late 14th century only one family of bondmen, subject to such dues as leirwite, remained in the village, though others paying chevage lived in the neighbourhood.[67] The customary land had by 1400 been farmed to its tenants at rents then amounting to £23 7*s.* 6*d.* a year.[68] Later the standard rate was 1*s.* an acre.[69] Entry fines were nominally uncertain,[70] but in the 16th century were in practice twice the yearly rent.[71] In the 1390s the lord employed 4 carters and ploughmen and a thresher,[72] and a shepherd in 1400. Even for the harvest tenant-labour was not called on. In 1400 the lord hired 32 men with 16 carts to clear his crops in one day. They were paid by the acre besides receiving a substantial harvest supper. That year *c.* 198 a. of the demesne had been sown, including some closes near the manor-house. The crops included *c.* 100 a. of dredge and 32 a. of barley, but only *c.* 20 a. of wheat and 15 a. of oats. The lord used only part of his several meadow and pasture, and farmed the herbage of the rest, also selling 12 ricks of hay. He had in 1400 only 6 sheep but *c.* 40 pigs.[73] The demesne, already once leased *c.* 1396 to a Cambridge burgess, was by 1407 at farm to its former bailiff.[74] It was usually farmed thereafter.[75] By 1463 almost 200 a. of the demesne had been leased to 22 tenants in parcels of up to 20 a., mostly for 1*s.* an acre, and two villagers were jointly farming the remainder. Only a few orchards and meadows remained in hand.[76]

Meanwhile the copyholders' properties grew larger as their numbers fell. Of *c.* 500 a. held in copyhold in 1488 one man, a former farmer of the demesne, occupied *c.* 80 a. and 7 others with more than 30 a. each another 250 a. Ten smaller tenants with 10–20 a. had *c.* 140 a. In 1514 *c.* 21 copyholders, who also possessed several of the 27 free tenements, occupied 416 a., and most of 183 a. of leased demesne land.[77] In 1525 28 men were taxed on land and goods, and only 21 on wages, but of £140 of movables in the parish £94 was owned by only 9 men.[78] Among the most prosperous families were those of Symons and Rande. In 1462 five members of the Symons family together held over 70 a. and leases of *c.* 50 a. of demesne.[79] In 1525 Robert and Richard Symons together had goods taxed at £36.[80] That family later acquired part of the demesne and the lease of the rectory.[81] William Rande, lessee of the rectory in the 1520s when he lost 600 quarters of corn in a fire in the barn,[82] left 160 a. of arable at his death

[58] C.R.O., R 58/5, vol. ii, pp. 41–2, 150–1.
[59] Ibid. P 171/26/1, pp. 17–19; cf. Vancouver, *Agric. in Cambs.* 76.
[60] C.R.O., R 58/5, vol. ii, p. 151.
[61] C.U.L., Maps 53(1)/87/55; C.R.O., 296/SP 860, 1002.
[62] C.R.O., R 58/5, vol. ii, pp. 148–50; P 171/26/2; cf. E 179/84/437 rot. 103.
[63] C.R.O., County Council Rec. T 280.
[64] Ex inf. the County Land Agent.
[65] *V.C.H. Cambs.* i. 398.
[66] *Rot. Hund.* (Rec. Com.), ii. 571–5.
[67] C.R.O., Huddleston MSS., ct. rolls 15, 19 Ric. II, 1–2 Hen. IV.
[68] Ibid. bailiff's accts. [1–2 Hen. IV], 2–3 Edw. IV.
[69] Ibid. ct. roll 1 Edw. IV; rental 1488.
[70] Ibid. survey 1578.
[71] e.g. ibid. ct. roll 16 Eliz. I.
[72] Ibid. ct. roll 16 Ric. II.
[73] Ibid. bailiff's acct. [1–2 Hen. IV].
[74] Ibid.; ibid. ct. rolls 20 Ric. II, 8 Hen. IV.
[75] e.g. ibid. ct. roll 2 Hen. V; C 1/3 no. 152.
[76] C.R.O., Huddleston MSS., bailiff's accts. 2–3, 17–18 Edw. IV; rental 1488.
[77] Ibid. rentals 1488, 1514.
[78] E 179/81/147 m. 1.
[79] C.R.O., Huddleston MSS., bailiff's acct. 2–3 Edw. IV.
[80] E 179/81/147 m. 1.
[81] See above.
[82] C 1/440 no. 49.

in 1552.[83] In 1578 there were 48, mostly small, free tenements, but only 20 copyholders.[84] At inclosure *c.* 200 a. were allotted for copyhold.[85]

From the 13th century the arable lay in three main fields,[86] Bridge field in the south-east, Stonehill field in the south-west, and Holmes field, called in the 18th century Bar field,[87] in the north-west. In the angle between the high street and the Cambridge road was a smaller field called Ryecroft, some 43 a. In 1809 the open fields were said to include *c.* 1,500 a. out of 2,470 a. in the parish,[88] but the local acre was a three-rood acre.[89] In the 14th century a triennial rotation was followed. In 1341 it was alleged that the whole lenten crop had perished,[90] and the winter field and the lent field, presumably including the barley field and pease field, were frequently mentioned in court records from the 14th to the 16th century.[91] The predominant crop was apparently barley rather than wheat. One man in 1631 had 55 a. of barley growing compared with 26 a. of wheat and rye.[92] Saffron was also grown from the 16th century to the late 18th.[93]

The lords of the manor had extensive closes around the manor-house, used either for arable, as in 1400 when 32 a. were sown,[94] or for grass. The village had much meadow and pasture, amounting in 1809 to 600 a., by local measure, besides 70 a. of Lammas meadow. The meadows lay mostly beside the river, and the largest block of permanent common adjoined the northern border.[95] Some of the commons were held in severalty by the lord for part of the year.[96] The commons were extensive, and although in the 15th century the number of beasts that could be commoned for each tenement was restricted,[97] no fresh stints were laid down in the 16th century or later. Inhabitants were forbidden to set up by-herds of their own, and a common herdsman was employed.[98] The lord was to keep a free bull and boar.[99] In the 18th century sheep were not allowed on any common until cattle had had some days feeding there.[1]

Of the lord's right to fold 400 sheep, half passed with the land sold in 1551 to the Symonses,[2] whose successors still enjoyed it in 1578, when another fold for 100 sheep was attached to the former Chesterford chantry lands. The lord's fold took the copyholders' sheep;[3] those of the freeholders were folded by turns on the land of the four principal freeholders, who for that right paid a rent to the lord and the shepherd's wages.[4] Of the sheepwalks for 880 sheep 740 belonged *c.* 1800 to the lord, whose tenant actually kept in 1802 734 sheep, which yielded 609 lambs.[5] There were altogether some 840 sheep *c.* 1795,[6] and some 700 Leicester sheep on one of Hollick's farms in 1808.[7]

The manor farm, which *c.* 1550 probably did not exceed 240 a.,[8] was later enlarged. A holding that was apparently the demesne included, probably *c.* 1670, 300 a. of arable and 60 a. of pasture, forming a single farm, besides 80 a. let in parcels, and sheepwalk for 400 sheep.[9] In the late 18th century Ebenezer Hollick and his nephew and namesake substantially enlarged the estate, swallowing many smaller farms and leaving the farmsteads derelict.[10] In 1809 the nephew claimed to own 178 a. of closes and over half the arable, and only *c.* 15 other landowners were left including Pembroke College and its lessee William Blow, the last two each having *c.* 100 a. The land was not consolidated: a farm of 155 a. lay in 158 places.[11] The traditional rotation was still largely followed on the 1,000 a. (by national measure) of open fields. The 941 a. sown in 1801 (presumably local measure) included 426 a. of barley, 200 a. of wheat, 122 a. of pease, and 90 a. of rye, but only 32 a. of turnips and 2 a. of potatoes. In the 1790s, however, cinquefoil was being sown on the thinner soil to improve the yield of grass for mowing.[12]

An inclosure Act was obtained in 1809,[13] not without opposition from the impropriator and Hollick's former tenant Blow,[14] and the land was probably divided and inclosed the same year.[15] The award was executed in 1815.[16] Of the 1,969 a. of the parish, the open fields and commons covered 1,617 a. and old closes 302 a.[17] Over half the land allotted, *c.* 885 a., went to Ebenezer Hollick. The lay rector received *c.* 300 a., and the vicar 72 a. Pembroke College obtained 57 a. and the chantry estate *c.* 45 a. Blow had 69 a., Story Barns 52 a., and two others 77 a. together. The remaining 20 allottees had barely 80 a. between them.[18]

The 19th century saw a considerable concentration of both ownership and occupation. In 1812 out of 71 persons rated ten, including Hollick and Thurnall, were farming almost the whole parish. The smaller farmers usually combined land from

[83] Prob. 11/37 (P.C.C. 5 Moore); C 3/151/62.
[84] C.R.O., Huddleston MSS., survey 1578.
[85] Ibid. P 171/26/1, *passim*.
[86] For the layout, ibid. P 171/26/2 (incl. map); names from *Liber de Bernewelle*, 313–16.
[87] C 114/33, terrier 1767; C.U.L., Doc. 470.
[88] C.R.O., R 58/5, vol. vii, p. 379.
[89] Char. Com. files.
[90] *Inq. Non.* (Rec. Com.), 213.
[91] e.g. C.R.O., Huddleston MSS., ct. rolls 18, 20 Ric. II; 4 Hen. IV; 2 Hen. V; 13 Edw. IV; 9 Hen. VIII.
[92] C.U.L., Doc. 726. Barley is mentioned in early wills, wheat is not: e.g. B.L. Add. MS. 5861, f. 12v.; Prob. 11/37 (P.C.C. 25 Moore, will of John Campion); Prob. 11/44 (P.C.C. 10 Loftes, will of John Sadler); C 47/38/37.
[93] B.L. Add. MS. 5861, f. 24; C.R.O., R 58/5, vol. iv, p. 70.
[94] C.R.O., Huddleston MSS., bailiff's acct. [1–2 Hen. IV].
[95] C.R.O., R 58/5, vol. vii, p. 379; cf. P 171/26/2.
[96] Ibid. Huddleston MSS., survey 1578.
[97] Ibid. ct. roll 2 Hen. V; cf. ct. roll 1 Mary.
[98] Ibid. ct. rolls 23 Eliz. I; 1616, 1618.
[99] Teversham, *Hist. Sawston*, ii. 27.

[1] C.U.L., Doc. 470; cf. C.R.O., Huddleston MSS., ct. roll 15 Eliz. I.
[2] C.P. 25(2)/55/398 no. 5; C.P. 25(2)/55/399 no. 32.
[3] C.R.O., Huddleston MSS., survey 1578; cf. Wards 7/60 no. 62; also below, p. 272.
[4] C 2/Jas. I/W 4/55; cf. C.R.O., Huddleston MSS., ct. roll 2 & 3 Phil. & Mary.
[5] C.R.O., R 58/5, vol. ii, p. 193; vol. vii, p. 379.
[6] Vancouver, *Agric. in Cambs.* 75–6.
[7] *Camb. Chron.* 12 Mar. 1808.
[8] C.R.O., Huddleston MSS., ct. roll 1 Mary; deed 1550.
[9] C.U.L., Doc. 1529.
[10] C.R.O., R 58/5, vol. vii, pp. 193–6.
[11] Ibid. p. 379.
[12] Vancouver, *Agric. in Cambs.* 75–6; H.O. 67/9; cf. C.R.O., R 58/5, vol. iii, p. 168.
[13] Whittlesford Incl. Act, 49 Geo. III c. 99 (Private, not printed); *C.J.* lxiv. 24, 305.
[14] C.R.O., R 58/5, vol. vii, p. 380. For Blow see *Camb. Chron.* 19, 26 Sept., 3 Oct. 1807; 15 Mar., 14 June 1816.
[15] C.R.O., P 171/26/1, p. 6.
[16] Ibid. p. 99.
[17] Ibid. p. 3.
[18] Ibid. pp. 17–100.

several smaller landowners.[19] The Hollick estate was usually divided into two or three large farms. Thus *c.* 1850 Stanmoor Hall farm included *c.* 600 a., West or Marking's farm 128 a., and John Rayner's farm 114 a.[20] The last two were combined by 1877 to cover *c.* 220 a.[21] In 1919 the manorial estate, *c.* 515 a., excluding only Rayner's farm, was let to a single tenant.[22] Meanwhile Robert Maynard, besides purchasing half Parsonage farm,[23] had bought *c.* 120 a. of the lesser allotments made in 1815, and William Blow's land and other property amounting to 104 a. had been acquired by the Cambridge banker Ebenezer Foster (d. 1875).[24]

Most inhabitants made their living by farming in the early 19th century. About 1830 there were 110 farm-labourers and 14 farmers, of whom only 2 employed no labour.[25] In 1851 out of 10 farmers 4 with a total of *c.* 350 a. employed 62 men, and the 6 with *c.* 325 a. another 21.[26] Farming was and remains mainly of a standard mixed arable type. About 1900 Hill farm was described as mainly a sheep farm.[27] Numbers of turkeys were also reared for the London market and driven up before Christmas in flocks of 800–900.[28] The village contained usually 6–8 farms in the late 19th century,[29] but 10–12 from the 1920s[30] after the county council had purchased 815 a. for letting to smallholders. In 1973 its property was divided into 10 larger and 3 part-time holdings.[31]

In 1206 Baldwin de Tony was granted a weekly market on Tuesdays in his manor at Whittlesford.[32] In 1242 his successor Baldwin de Akeny complained that the bailiffs of Cambridge were taking toll at Whittlesford Bridge which should rather belong to him in right of his market.[33] By a compromise the lords of Whittlesford later collected the bridge tolls on Tuesdays, a practice still followed in 1578 and 1770,[34] long after the market had expired. In 1267 Baldwin de Akeny was granted a market on Mondays and a three-day fair from 23 to 25 August,[35] but by 1460 the market, said to be on Tuesday, the fair, at Trinity, and its pie-powder court were all yielding nothing, although the bridge tolls produced 12*d.* a year,[36] and renders were still due from some tenements for admission to the market green.[37] In 1800 the village was still said to have been a market-town.[38]

Three mills belonged to the manor in 1086,[39] but in 1279 there was only one.[40] Besides the corn-mill, to which suit from the tenants was still exacted *c.* 1420,[41] a fulling-mill was in use in the 1390s but not in 1400.[42] The corn-mill, recorded in 1462, was in decay in 1514.[43] John Tilney alienated it to Henry Veysey in 1546, but in 1553 William Hawtrey re-united it to the manor,[44] with which it descended until *c.* 1700.[45] By 1760 Ebenezer Hollick had bought it from a Mrs. Creek and converted it to produce oil from linseed, rape, and mustard. Cattle-cake was made as a by-product.[46] After the younger Ebenezer Hollick died in 1828 Charles Thurnall (d. 1889) carried on the business until the 1880s, employing 20 workmen in 1851. In 1861 the mill was producing linseed-oil, oil-cake, and artificial manure.[47] It later reverted to being a corn-mill, managed from the 1890s by Wisbey & Son, and from 1922 until after 1937 by Fred. Smart & Co.[48] The mill and mill-house belonged in 1968 to Sir Hamilton Kerr, who in 1970 gave it to be used after his death by the Fitzwilliam Museum.[49] The mill-house was evidently built by Ebenezer Hollick in 1763.[50] It has a five-bay front in red brick with segmental headed windows and prominent voussoirs. The front of the former oil-mill across the river is disguised with large ogee-headed windows.

Two large maltings built by Richard Blow in 1773 survived until 1852.[51] Charles Thurnall kept a brewery in 1851,[52] and there were four breweries in 1888.[53] Among tradesmen out of the ordinary were a watch-maker from 1858 and a timber-merchant *c.* 1900.[54] The main sources of non-agricultural employment at that period, however, were the Sawston paper-mill,[55] where 24 Whittlesford people, mostly women, worked in 1841 and 91 in 1861,[56] and the works established by Robert Maynard in 1834, near the centre of the high street, to produce agricultural implements.[57] In 1861 he employed 30 men.[58] After Maynard's death in 1883 the business was carried on by his son Robert and later his grandson R. J. Maynard. By 1904 an iron-foundry was attached to the works.[59] In the mid 1950s, after R. J. Maynard's death, the works were closed, and in 1959 the buildings were sold to Phoenix Tinsel Products Ltd., which in 1973 made artificial Christmas trees,

[19] Ibid. R 58/5, vol. vii, pp. 116 sqq.; cf. ibid. p. 193.
[20] Ibid. vol. ix, pp. 245–67; cf. H.O. 107/1761.
[21] C.R.O., County Council Rec. T 279.
[22] Ibid. 296/SP 1108. [23] See above.
[24] C.R.O., 296/SP 49,860; C.U.L., Maps 53/87/9; Maps 53(1)/93/50.
[25] *Census*, 1831; *Rep. H.L. Cttee. on Poor Laws*, H.C. 227, pp. 328–31 (1831), viii. [26] H.O. 107/1761.
[27] C.R.O., 296/SP 1002.
[28] Ibid. R 58/5, vol. vii, pp. 21–2.
[29] *Kelly's Dir. Cambs.* (1864, 1879, 1900).
[30] Ibid. (1922, 1937).
[31] Ex inf. the County Land Agent.
[32] *Rot. Litt. Claus.* (Rec. Com.), i. 74.
[33] *Close R.* 1242–7, 6–7.
[34] C.R.O., Huddleston MSS., survey 1578; Cooper, *Annals of Camb.* iv. 355. For a tariff see Teversham, *Hist. Sawston*, ii. 26.
[35] *Cal. Chart. R.* 1257–1300, 73–4.
[36] C 139/178/55 no. 11.
[37] e.g. C.R.O., Huddleston MSS., rental 1488 m. 3.
[38] Lysons, *Cambs.* 279.
[39] *V.C.H. Cambs.* i. 398.
[40] *Rot. Hund.* (Rec. Com.), ii. 571.
[41] C.R.O., Huddleston MSS., ct. roll 9 Hen. V.
[42] Ibid. ct. roll 15 Ric. II; bailiff's acct. [1–2 Hen. IV].
[43] Ibid. bailiff's acct. 2–3 Edw. IV; rental 1514.
[44] C.P. 25(2)/4/22 no. 69; C 3/96/68.
[45] Last conveyed with the manor in C.P. 25(2)/815/13 Wm. III Hil. no. 8.
[46] C.R.O., R 58/5, vol. iii, p. 193; vol. ix, pp. 153–4, 175–8; B.L. Add. MS. 9412, f. 94; C.U.L., MS. Plan 174/27.
[47] H.O. 107/1761; R.G. 9/1028; *Gardner's Dir. Cambs.* (1851); *Kelly's Dir. Cambs.* (1864, 1879); C.R.O., R 58/5, vol. ii, p. 239.
[48] *Kelly's Dir. Cambs.* (1896, 1916, 1937); cf. C.R.O., 515/SP 490.
[49] *Camb. Ind. Press*, 1 Nov. 1968; *Camb. Evening News*, 12 Oct. 1972; 20 Aug. 1974.
[50] Inscr. on bldg. See above, plate facing p. 192.
[51] C.R.O., R 58/5, vol. vii, p. 21.
[52] *Gardner's Dir. Cambs.* (1851).
[53] *Kelly's Dir. Cambs.* (1888).
[54] Ibid. (1858, 1888, 1892, 1900).
[55] Cf. C.U.L., E.D.R., C 3/39.
[56] H.O. 107/76; R.G. 9/1028.
[57] *Kelly's Dir. Cambs.* (1858, 1879); C.R.O., R 58/5, vol. ii, p. 248; vol. vii, p. 164; *Jnl. Royal Agric. Soc.* vii. 46; cf. C.R.O., R 58/5, vol. vii, pp. 165, 299–300.
[58] R.G. 9/1028.
[59] C.R.O., County Council Rec. T 280; O.S. Map 6″, Cambs. LIV. SW. (1885 edn.); *Kelly's Dir. Cambs.* (1904–37); cf. *Camb. Region* (1938), 157.

decorative lighting, and display goods there.[60] St. George's works, possibly another agricultural tool factory, was recorded in the 1930s.[61] From 1929 the village contained a small artificial fertilizer factory, owned by Packard & Fison of Ipswich.[62] By 1970 part of Hill farm was occupied by CIBA Agrochemicals Ltd., and a large building was being erected in 1972 as the headquarters for their marketing and technical development.[63] The largest employer of labour from the parish in the 1960s was still the Sawston paper-mill.[64]

LOCAL GOVERNMENT. Under Edward I the lord of Whittlesford claimed view of frankpledge, the assize of bread and of ale, estreats, a pillory, tumbrel, and gallows, but by what warrant was unknown. Suit owed from the township to the county court and sheriff's tourn had been withdrawn since 1265.[65] In 1488 ½ a. was held by serving as hangman.[66] Court rolls survive, with gaps, for 1391–1422, 1461–82, 1514–23, and 1553–1618.[67]

In the late 14th century and the 15th an annual court leet was held on Trinity Monday, and a separate court baron in the autumn or winter. From the mid 16th century courts leet and baron combined were usually held only once a year, sometimes at longer intervals.[68] In 1391 it was declared that only villeins by birth, not customary tenants, owed suit to the court baron.[69] The combined court conducted the usual business of minor jurisdiction, agricultural regulation, and transfer of copyhold land. Its by-laws were said to be made with the assent of the whole vill, or of the lord and all free and customary tenants, but in practice business was conducted oligarchically.[70] In 1564 a man was amerced for revealing the secrets of the chief pledges and homage.[71] The election of constables,[72] ale-tasters,[73] and haywards[74] was occasionally recorded. In 1519 the court prohibited dice, cards, and other unlawful games on weekdays,[75] and in 1574 forbade householders to lodge outsiders as inmates.[76] It was still making orders about common rights in 1766.[77]

The churchwardens were occasionally mentioned from 1479.[78] By 1578 they were cutting and lopping willows growing on common land for the benefit of the whole township.[79] In the late 17th century the parish was apparently managed by a small vestry of five or six, including the churchwardens and constables, who themselves nominated the overseers.[80] In the 1720s the parish employed a book-keeper to record expenditure on its property.[81] In the early 19th century the parishioners elected both churchwardens.[82]

A poor-box had been placed in the chancel, as prescribed by recent legislation, by 1548.[83] By *c.* 1600 the former guildhall was being used as a poorhouse or workhouse, to which a superintendent was appointed in 1635. Its able-bodied inmates were set to spinning, and wool was also distributed to poor people to spin into yarn at home.[84] Putting the poor to work had ceased by 1652, when the overseers were distributing cash to several poor people occasionally throughout the year.[85] At first the town lands produced enough revenue to support those applying for relief, and rates were needed only to pay for apprenticeships, but by 1680 rates were being regularly levied to meet expenditure that rose from *c.* £10 a year in the 1660s to *c.* £40 about 1700, and occasionally almost to £70.[86] In 1724 the parish bought turf in large quantities, presumably as fuel for the poor. The poor were still sometimes employed in the 18th century, as in 1764 on moving stones.[87] The guildhall was again in use as a workhouse by 1776, when it had 40 inmates[88] who cost *c.* £50. By 1784 expenditure on the poor had reached almost £130.[89] In 1803 37 people were on permanent relief: the 19 in the workhouse, then being farmed, cost £206, and 18 outside, with, presumably, 18 others occasionally relieved, cost £156. Those outside the workhouse earned *c.* £5.[90] The parish also sold rye to the poor at reduced prices, and augmented wages.[91] By 1813 only 5 or 6 people were in the workhouse and 38 on permanent outside relief, but the cost had risen to £766 because 120 others received occasional support. That number had been cut to 15 by 1815, but expenditure was still almost £520.[92] Of some £350 spent *c.* 1830 almost half, £172, went to the sick and aged and widows and children, and *c.* £60 for occasional relief, while *c.* £85 was paid to paupers working for the parish.[93] In 1829 12 unemployed men and boys were doing roadwork.[94] In 1835 the parish was merged in the Linton poor-law union,[95] and in 1934 was transferred with the rest of Linton R.D. to the South Cambridgeshire R.D.,[96] being included in South Cambridgeshire in 1974.

CHURCH. The church at Whittlesford, recorded

[60] Ex inf. the Secretary, Phoenix Tinsel Products Ltd.; cf. *Camb. Ind. Press*, 1 Nov. 1968.
[61] *Kelly's Dir. Cambs.* (1933, 1937).
[62] Ibid. (1929, 1937).
[63] Ex inf. the Head of Administration, Agrochemical Division, CIBA-GEIGY (U.K.) Ltd.; cf. *Camb. News*, 26 Sept. 1969.
[64] *Camb. Ind. Press*, 30 June 1961.
[65] *Rot. Hund.* (Rec. Com.), i. 55; ii. 570.
[66] C.R.O., Huddleston MSS., rental 1488.
[67] Ibid. ct. rolls. From *c.* 1560 mostly drafts alone survive.
[68] C.R.O., Huddleston MSS., ct. rolls, *passim*; cf. Teversham, *Hist. Sawston*, ii. 26.
[69] C.R.O., Huddleston MSS., ct. roll 15 Ric. II.
[70] Ibid. 15 Ric. II; 2 Hen. V.
[71] Ibid. 6 Eliz. I.
[72] Ibid. 2 Hen. V.
[73] Ibid. 18 Edw. IV.
[74] Ibid. 5 Eliz. I.
[75] Ibid. 11 Hen. VIII.
[76] Ibid. 16 Eliz. I.
[77] C.U.L., Doc. 470.
[78] C.R.O., Huddleston MSS., ct. roll 18 Edw. IV.
[79] Ibid. survey 1578.
[80] Ibid. R 58/5, vol. ii, pp. 2–62.
[81] Ibid. pp. 108–11, 268–72.
[82] C.U.L., E.D.R., C 1/6.
[83] B.L. Add. MS. 5861, f. 35v.
[84] Hampson, *Poverty in Cambs.* 3, 43.
[85] C.R.O., R 58/5, vol. iii, pp. 274–5.
[86] Ibid. pp. 2–62.
[87] Hampson, *Poverty in Cambs.* 184, 187.
[88] Ibid. 100.
[89] *Poor Rate Returns, 1787*, Parl. Papers, 1st ser. vol. ix, pp. 309, 562–3.
[90] *Poor Law Abstract, 1804*, 40–1.
[91] Hampson, *Poverty in Cambs.* 211, 213, 217.
[92] *Poor Law Abstract, 1818*, 32–3.
[93] *Rep. Com. Poor Laws*, [44], p. 257, H.C. (1834), xxviii.
[94] *Rep. H.L. Cttee. on Poor Laws*, H.C. 227, pp. 328–31 (1831), viii.
[95] *Poor Law Com. 1st Rep.* 249.
[96] *Census*, 1931 (pt. ii).

by 1217,[97] had evidently been founded before the manor was subinfeudated, by one of the main line of the Tonys, with whose manor of Kirtling the advowson descended until the late 14th century.[98] The church, though a rectory *c.* 1275,[99] had previously been sometimes served by vicars, one of whom left land at Sawston to his son's mother.[1] By grant of Thomas, earl of Warwick (d. 1401) in 1385[2] and a papal bull of 1390 the church was appropriated in 1392–3 to St. Mary's college, Warwick. A vicarage was ordained, the advowson being assigned to the college,[3] which retained it until its dissolution in 1544.[4] The Crown then exercised the patronage[5] until 1558 when at the instance of Bishop Thirlby the Crown granted the advowson to Jesus College, Cambridge,[6] which retained it in 1972.[7]

The rector had 40 a. of glebe in 1279,[8] and his church was valued at 25 to 30 marks in the earlier 13th century[9] and 40 marks in 1276 and 1291.[10] In 1393 the vicar had 12 a. of glebe and the small tithes and offerings, with plough-alms (*elemosina sulcorum*) and 'a devotion called certeynes', besides the tithe of the water-mills.[11] Later he obtained a pension of 2 marks charged on the rectory, which had also to pay 26*s.* 8*d.* to a deacon (later confused with a dean) to serve in the church.[12] The vicar was charged in 1392–3 with repairing the chancel,[13] but by the 17th century that burden had been transferred to the impropriator.[14]

The vicar received *c.* 1800 £30 a year for his small tithes under an ancient modus.[15] He also had 13*s.* 4*d.* from Whittlesford mill. At inclosure he was allotted 65 a. for tithes and 7 a. for glebe.[16] The vicarage had 76½ a. in 1887,[17] and still retained 78½ a. in 1972.[18]

In 1393 the vicar was assigned a hall and chamber in the rectory house, apparently near the church, and a grange and dovecot nearby.[19] The vicarage house was said in 1728 to be very small and indifferent,[20] and vicars did not usually live there in the later 18th century.[21] In 1836 it was called a mere cottage.[22] By 1851 it had been sold and by 1894 demolished. A new house in North Street[23] was built in the 1870s.[24]

The vicarage was worth £10 in 1535,[25] £23 in 1650,[26] and *c.* £27 in 1728.[27] From 1813 Jesus College substantially increased the income by paying rent for land at Willingham, whose proceeds went to the vicar,[28] so that he received £170 a year *c.* 1830.[29] Further contributions by the college of £200 a year, granted in 1867 and 1872,[30] raised his income to *c.* £350 by 1877,[31] but the glebe brought in only £82 in 1887 and 1897.[32] When the college's support ceased soon after 1900, the income fell to *c.* £207.[33]

In 1351 Henry Cyprian granted land worth 5 marks a year for a chaplain to sing mass at the Virgin Mary's altar in Whittlesford church. Three successive chaplains held that chantry until 1393, when, because no licence in mortmain had been obtained, it was supposedly forfeited to the Crown.[34] The township apparently recovered the land, which was held in 1432 by feoffees and, having been converted to other purposes, escaped confiscation at the Reformation.[35] Some 110 a. in Whittlesford called chantry land *c.* 1540 belonged not to Cyprians but to a chantry at Great Chesterford (Essex), suppressed by 1549.[36] In 1279 3½ a. were held of the church by providing bread and wine for the Easter Sunday mass.[37] In 1520 assized rents of *c.* 5*s.* were due from of old for the sepulchre light.[38] In 1500 John Newton left 12 a. to the church for an obit.[39]

A guild in honour of St. John the Baptist was founded shortly before 1389, when it raised 50*s.* to repair the church.[40] The south chapel was called St. John the Baptist's *c.* 1500.[41] In 1525 the village guild had a stock of £3.[42] After the Reformation the parish retained possession of its guildhall, using it as a workhouse, poorhouse, or schoolroom. The building, standing north-east of the cross-roads, is a timber-framed early-16th-century building, having a jettied upper storey with brackets and a carved bressumer and one medieval doorway. In 1966 the parish council sold the building,[43] which was being renovated in 1972.

Rectors were occasionally recorded from the mid 13th century. Edmund of London, rector 1296–1316 or later, was a pluralist and in the king's service.[44] Thomas Machye, vicar 1496–1508, had been a fellow of King's and headmaster of Eton, and his successor

97 *Val. of Norwich*, ed. Lunt, 536.
98 *Rot. Hund.* (Rec. Com.), ii. 571; *Cal. Inq. p.m.* v, p. 400; xii, p. 305.
99 *Vetus Liber Arch. Elien.* (C.A.S. 8vo ser. xlviii), 66.
1 C.R.O., Huddleston MSS., early-13th-cent. deed.
2 *Cal. Pat.* 1381–5, 580.
3 E 164/22 ff. 79–96v.
4 e.g. *E.D.R.* (1897), 193; (1912), 18; cf. *V.C.H. Warws.* ii. 81.
5 e.g. *Cal. Pat.* 1555–7, 501.
6 Ibid. 1557–8, 40.
7 *Crockford* (1971–2).
8 *Rot. Hund.* ii. 571.
9 *Val. of Norwich*, ed. Lunt, 226, 536.
10 Ibid. 555; *Tax. Eccl.* (Rec. Com.), 267.
11 E 164/22 f. 97; cf. C.U.L., E.D.R., H 1/6, terrier 1615.
12 S.C. 6/Hen. VIII/3751 rot. 14; L.R. 2/181 ff. 205v., 208; B.L. Add. Ch. 15875.
13 E 164/22 ff. 97, 99 and v.
14 C.U.L., E.D.R., B 2/59A, f. 21v.; cf. C.U.L., Maps 53(1)/87/55.
15 C.R.O., R 58/5, vol. ii, pp. 193–4; vol. vii, p. 380.
16 Whittlesford Incl. Act, 49 Geo. III c. 99 (Private, not printed), pp. 15–16; C.R.O., P 171/26/1, pp. 18, 20.
17 *Glebe Returns*, H.C. 307, p. 43 (1887), lxiv.
18 Ex inf. the vicar, the Revd. C. J. L. Jones.
19 E 164/22 f. 97.
20 C.U.L., E.D.R., B 8/1.
21 e.g. C.U.L., E.D.R., C 1/1; B 7/1, p. 134; C 1/6.
22 Ibid. C 3/21.
23 C.R.O., R 58/5, vol. ii, p. 79.
24 C.U.L., E.D.R., C 3/27.
25 *Valor Eccl.* (Rec. Com.), iii. 504.
26 Lamb. Pal. MS. 904, f. 259.
27 C.U.L., E.D.R., B 8/1.
28 Ex inf. the Archivist, Jesus Coll.; cf. C.U.L., E.D.R., C 3/25.
29 *Rep. Com. Eccl. Revenues*, pp. 354–5.
30 *Rep. Com. Univ. Income* [C. 856-II], p. 294, H.C. (1873), xxxvii (3).
31 C.U.L., E.D.R., C 3/27.
32 *Glebe Returns*, H.C. 307, p. 43 (1887), lxiv; C.U.L., E.D.R., C 3/39.
33 *Crockford* (1896, 1907).
34 *Cal. Inq. Misc.* vi, pp. 19–20.
35 C.R.O., R 58/5, vol. iii, pp. 163–5; see below, p. 275.
36 C.R.O., Huddleston MSS., assignment of dower; *Cal. Pat.* 1548–9, 388–9; Wards 7/60 no. 62.
37 *Rot. Hund.* (Rec. Com.), ii. 571.
38 C.R.O., Huddleston MSS., rental 1520.
39 Ibid. R 58/5, vol. ii, pp. 49–50.
40 C 47/38/37.
41 Prob. 11/12 (P.C.C. 13 Moore, will of Rob. Tilney).
42 E 179/81/147 m. 1.
43 *Camb. News*, 19 May, 22 Oct. 1966.
44 *Cal. Papal Reg.* ii. 92; *Cal. Pat.* 1313–17, 508; cf. *E.D.R.* (1891), 627.

had a degree in civil law:[45] in the early 16th century the church was probably served by the curates who witnessed parishioners' wills.[46] Although Jesus College became patron in 1558, it did not begin to appoint ex-fellows as vicars regularly until 1597.[47] Between 1600 and 1640 the vicars usually served through curates, one of whom remained in office for over 10 years after being charged with fathering an illegitimate child.[48] Robert Symons (d. 1622) left a rent-charge of £10 a year from Borough mill, Sawston, for a sermon at Whittlesford every other Sunday.[49] By the 18th century the vicar had appropriated the money as part of his stipend.[50]

Robert Clarkson, vicar from 1638 and a fellow of Jesus, was ejected in 1644.[51] His successor John Swan, not a Jesus man, said to be a good preacher in 1650,[52] retained the living, in plurality with Sawston, until his death in 1671.[53] Thereafter until 1807 only two vicars were instituted,[54] and the living was usually held by sequestration,[55] perhaps on account of its poverty. In 1792 the incumbent was reckoned as one of the diocese's ten poorest vicars.[56] In the late 17th century and again from *c.* 1780 to 1806 the ministers were frequently styled curates. Except from 1771 to 1807 they were usually Jesus men, and frequently fellows.[57] When one fellow was legally prevented *c.* 1728 from holding the living, a nominal vicar was instituted, under whom he served the cure.[58] The sequestrators often did the duty by deputy. Over 20 clergymen signed the register as curates between 1725 and 1747.[59] Later the ministers usually lived in college, and went out on Sundays to read the service. In 1728 there were two Sunday services, and *c.* 35 attended the three communion services. In 1775 and 1807 the minister performed only one service, alternately morning and evening, and only *c.* 20 came to communion in 1807.[60]

Fellows of Jesus continued to hold the vicarage until 1844, and were still non-resident, occasionally employing curates and not holding more than one service a week until after 1840. In 1825 a congregation of ten at communion was thought unusually large, and some parishioners refused to pay church rates. The prevalence of dissent meant that many did not go to church. In 1836 the congregation seldom exceeded 200;[61] on Census Sunday 1851, when there were again two services, the afternoon service was attended by 142, besides 78 school children.[62] The vicars went on living at Cambridge until the 1870s. In 1873 245 people were said to go to church, and the monthly communions had up to 22.[63] A. C. Jennings, vicar 1877–86, quarrelled sharply with his most prominent parishioners, especially the Maynards, and would not act with them on parish matters. He also alienated Edward Towgood, owner of Sawston paper-mill, who had previously brought his workmen to Whittlesford, but thereupon led them back to Sawston church.[64] In 1897, although there were *c.* 60 communicants, only a third of the inhabitants were considered steady church people.[65] In 1937 it was said that fewer than 250 inhabitants attended church.[66] E. C. Sherwood, vicar 1933–45, who had served 27 years as a headmaster, turned the large Victorian vicarage house into a training house for ordinands styled St. Andrew's Theological College. Some of its students helped as curates. Sherwood moved the college briefly to Pampisford *c.* 1946.[67]

The church of *ST. ANDREW*, so called in the later Middle Ages,[68] received the additional name of *ST. MARY*, patron of the chantry, after the 16th century.[69] In the late 19th century it was thought to bear the name of St. Barnabas, on whose day the village feast was held.[70] The church consists of a chancel with south chapel, central tower, and nave with south aisle and porch, and is built of field stones with ashlar dressings. Until stripped *c.* 1910 the walls were plastered externally.[71] The Norman church comprised only a nave, central tower, and chancel. The thick north wall of the nave survives, with one round-headed window, and the lower stage of the tower, with four such windows. The south window is surrounded by linear carvings of grotesque creatures. In the 13th century the chancel was rebuilt, with a row of lancets, mostly later blocked, in its north wall; a south aisle, divided from the nave by a three-bay arcade, was added alongside the nave and tower. The nave walls were heightened, and its roof raised, bringing a tower window inside the church. Square openings over the nave arcade may represent clerestory windows of that period. In 1352 the high altar was reconsecrated,[72] probably after further remodelling, in which two Decorated windows were inserted in the north wall of the nave. The west window, of the same period, formerly contained the arms of Wateville.[73] The porch was built by Henry Cyprian (fl. 1350).[74] About 1390 the church, especially its roof, was said to be ruinous.[75] In the early 15th century new windows were inserted in the south aisle, and the tower was given new arches to the nave and chancel and a taller belfry stage. The

[45] *E.D.R.* (1898), 61; C.U.L., E.D.R., L 3/1, f. 57; Emden, *Biog. Reg. Univ. Camb.* 384.
[46] e.g. B.L. Add. MS. 5861, ff. 69v., 74v., 87v.–88.
[47] *Alum. Cantab. to 1751*, iv. 351, s.v. Watts, Boniface; and *passim*.
[48] C.U.L., E.D.R., B 2/18, f. 40v.; B 2/32, ff. 7, 31, 99; B 2/47A, f. 5.
[49] Prob. 11/141 (P.C.C. 21 Swann).
[50] Whittlesford Incl. Act, p. 15; cf. C.U.L., E.D.R., B 7/1, p. 135. For an abortive sermon charity under the will of John Sadler (1560) see Prob. 11/44 (P.C.C. 10 Loftes); C.U.L., E.D.R., D 2/10, f. 64.
[51] *Walker Revised*, ed. Matthews, 78.
[52] Lamb. Pal. MS. 904, f. 260.
[53] *Alum. Cantab. to 1751*, iv. 190; *Proc. C.A.S.* xlii. 54.
[54] P.R.O., Inst. Bks. ser. B, iv, p. 153; ser. C, i, f. 451 and v.
[55] Cf. Bacon, *Thesaurus* (1786), 232; C.R.O., R 58/5, vol. vii, p. 380.
[56] C.U.L., E.D.R., B 8/4, f. 57v.
[57] Ibid. B 2/67, 72; *Alum. Cantab. to 1751, 1752–1900.*
[58] C.U.L., E.D.R., B 8/1.
[59] C.R.O., R 58/5, vol. ii, p. 304.
[60] C.U.L., E.D.R., B 8/1; C 1/1, 4.
[61] Ibid. C 1/6, 17, 21.
[62] H.O. 129/188/1/4/4.
[63] C.U.L., E.D.R., B 1/16; C 3/25.
[64] C.R.O., R 58/5, vol. vii, pp. 67–72, 75–6; Char. Com. files.
[65] C.U.L., E.D.R., C 3/39.
[66] C.R.O., 331/Z 7, 1937, Nov.
[67] Ibid. 1936, Sept., 1937, Nov.; *Crockford* (1935, 1940, 1947).
[68] e.g. B.L. Add. MS. 5861, ff. 33, 66, 88.
[69] Cf. Ecton, *Thesaurus* (1763), 100.
[70] *Gardner's Dir. Cambs.* (1851); *E.D.R.* (1905), 188.
[71] Palmer, *Wm. Cole*, 117; *E.D.R.* (1910), 213.
[72] *E.D.R.* (1894), 192.
[73] *Mon. Inscr. Cambs.* 192.
[74] Palmer, *Wm. Cole*, 118.
[75] C 47/38/37.

tower bore the arms of Scales and, allegedly, Beauchamp.[76] Its new belfry windows cut off the tops of earlier ones. It is surmounted by a short leaded spire, which was missing in the early 19th century.[77] By 1500 a two-bay chapel had been built south of the chancel;[78] the original screens between chancel and chapel survive.[79] The east windows are probably early-16th-century, that of the chancel once containing the arms of Tilney impaling Playters.[80] Bequests for glazing the church were made in 1521.[81]

The plain square font is 13th-century. There are remains of medieval decorative painting in the blocked lancets in the chancel. Fifteenth-century seating, with carved fronts and bench-ends, remains in the nave, and a contemporary desk with poppy-heads in the chancel. Fragments of one or more alabaster retables were found in 1876, walled up in the south chapel.[82] Insets in the nave formerly contained brasses to John Newton (d. 1500) and his two wives.[83] There are wall-tablets to Mary (d. 1690), wife of Thomas Dod, and William Westley (d. 1723) who endowed the village school.

After the Reformation the south chapel, called *c.* 1665 the lord's chapel, fell into disrepair. In 1638 the church was overcrowded with prominent parishioners' pews.[84] In 1783 many windows were decaying and blocked with plaster, their mullions gone.[85] In 1873 the church contained reserved pews for 87, benches for 117, and a large pew for 90 children at the west end.[86] The high pews, except for the manorial pew under the tower which survived until 1913, were swept away when the interior was cleaned and restored between 1875 and 1882.[87] The roofs and external fabric were thoroughly restored between 1905 and 1922.[88]

The church was well equipped with vessels and vestments in the early 14th century. One vestment had been given by the countess of Warwick, the patron's wife.[89] In 1552 both chalices and patens were silver gilt.[90] The plate is of the 19th and 20th centuries.[91] There were four bells and a sanctus bell in 1552.[92] There were five bells in 1742 and in the 19th century,[93] cast in 1631 (by Miles Gray), 1672, 1708, 1730, and 1793.[94] They were rehung in 1905, and after 1922 there were said to be six.[95] The registers begin in 1559 and are virtually complete.[96]

NONCONFORMITY. In 1728 there were 5 dissenting families[97] in Whittlesford, and in 1783 2 or 3 dissenters who worshipped at Fowlmere.[98] Dissent increased after Ebenezer Hollick (d. 1792) bought the manor. He was a trustee of a Baptist chapel in Cambridge, and allowed the Baptist congregations of Cambridge and Saffron Walden to use the river at Whittlesford for adult baptism. In 1767 *c.* 40 people, in the white gowns that Hollick kept for the purpose, were dipped near the mill by Andrew Gifford.[99] The Hollicks remained Baptists and declined to be buried in the churchyard, building a family monument just outside it.[1] They probably worshipped at Cambridge,[2] but their principal tenant, William Blow, had his house licensed for dissenting worship in 1800, and in 1809 a building owned by Ebenezer Hollick was similarly licensed.[3] In 1825 over half the population were Baptists, most of them born and bred in that sect.[4]

They had then no regular teacher,[5] and after Hollick died in 1828 they came under the influence of the Duxford Independent church. In 1851 its minister was serving a chapel at Whittlesford, where he reported a congregation of 250 at his evening services.[6] Whittlesford was a preaching station of Duxford in 1860, when an Independent chapel was registered at Whittlesford.[7] By 1872[8] the Duxford minister was holding monthly communion services in a barn. About 112 people probably attended in 1873, and 250 were chapel-goers in 1877.[9] About 1875 a congregation, with its own lay pastor, independent of that at Duxford, was established, and a new chapel had been built by 1878.[10]

Religious dissent was encouraged by the Maynards,[11] the principal employers in the parish, and in 1897 two-thirds of the inhabitants were dissenters.[12] In 1903 the congregation had a new red-brick chapel with 325 sittings built by the Duxford road. The old one was used as a Sunday school until it was burnt down in 1918.[13] The chapel had 80 members and 115 children in its Sunday school in 1905.[14] Its membership later declined from 96 in 1916 to 41 in 1955, but recovered, as population grew, to 58 in 1968.[15] By 1970 it was sharing a minister with Sawston and Little Shelford.[16]

There were a few Methodists in the parish in

76 Palmer, *Wm. Cole*, 118; *Kelly's Dir. Cambs.* (1922).
77 C.R.O., R 58/5, vol. ii, p. 197.
78 Prob. 11/12 (P.C.C. 13 Moore, will of Rob. Tilney).
79 *Proc. C.A.S.* xiii. 72.
80 *Mon. Inscr. Cambs.* 244. A John Tilney married Mary, daughter of Wm. Playters (d. 1512): *Visit. Suff. 1561–1612*, ed. W. C. Metcalf (Exeter, 1882), 57; cf. *Genealogist*, N.S. i. 173–4, 246–7.
81 B.L. Add. MS. 5861, f. 80.
82 *Proc. C.A.S.* vii. 106–11, and plates xxx–xxxiii.
83 *Mon. Inscr. Cambs.* 244; cf. C.R.O., R 58/5, vol. ii, pp. 49–51.
84 Gibbons, *Ely Episc. Rec.* 88; *Cambs. Village Doc.* 74; C.U.L., E.D.R., B 2/59; B 2/59A, ff. 12v., 21v.
85 C.U.L., E.D.R., B 7/1, p. 134; cf. C.R.O., R 58/5, vol. ii, pp. 9, 80–1.
86 C.U.L., E.D.R., C 3/25.
87 C.R.O., R 58/5, vol. ii, p. 81; *Kelly's Dir. Cambs.* (1888, 1900); C.R.O., 331/Z 4, 1913, Oct.
88 *E.D.R.* (1905), 143, 249; (1910), 213; (1912), 221; (1913), 171; *Kelly's Dir. Cambs.* (1922). See above, frontispiece.
89 *Vetus Liber Arch. Elien.* (C.A.S. 8vo ser. xlviii), 66.
90 *Cambs. Ch. Goods, temp. Edw. VI*, 3.
91 List of ch. plate, *penes V.C.H.*
92 *Cambs. Ch. Goods, temp. Edw. VI*, 4.
93 Palmer, *Wm. Cole*, 118; *Kelly's Dir. Cambs.* (1864, 1900).
94 *Eng. Topog.* (Gent. Mag. Libr.), ii. 95.
95 *Kelly's Dir. Cambs.* (1908, 1922, 1933).
96 Gibbons, *Ely. Episc. Rec.* 236.
97 C.U.L., E.D.R., B 8/1.
98 Ibid. B 7/1, p. 134.
99 Rob. Robinson, *Hist. Baptism* (1790), 541–3; St. Andrew's Baptist Ch., Camb., 250th anniversary pamphlet, pp. 8–9; C.R.O., R 58/5, vol. ix, pp. 205–7.
1 C.R.O., R 58/5, vol. ix, pp. 179–80, 187.
2 Ibid. pp. 173–4, 191.
3 Ibid. p. 183; C.U.L., E.D.R., B 4/1, ff. 22v., 31.
4 C.U.L., E.D.R., C 1/6.
5 Ibid.
6 H.O. 129/188/1/4/11.
7 *Cong. Yr. Bk.* (1860); G.R.O. Worship Reg. no. 10365.
8 For what follows, until 1934, the main source is E. W. Howes, *These Sixty Years* [1934].
9 C.U.L., E.D.R., C 3/25, 27.
10 *Kelly's Dir. Cambs.* (1879).
11 C.R.O., R 58/5, vol. ix, pp. 67–72.
12 C.U.L., E.D.R., C 3/39.
13 *Kelly's Dir. Cambs.* (1904); G.R.O. Worship Reg. no. 40318; *Cong. Yr. Bk.* (1916).
14 *Cong. Yr. Bk.* (1905).
15 Ibid. (1916, 1955, 1968).
16 *Camb. Evening News*, 19 Jan. 1970.

1807.[17] George Barker, who bought the old vicarage, built on the site a Primitive Methodist chapel, which still existed in 1873[18] and may have been used by the Independent congregation in the 1870s.[19]

EDUCATION. About 1601 the curate was acting as schoolmaster.[20] A schoolmaster recorded in 1605 was called a card-player and a fencer, who would not go to church.[21] The parish had no established school until the 18th century, when William Westley, a Cambridge butcher born at Whittlesford, left by will proved 1723 *c.* 66 a. at Hempstead (Essex) in reversion to endow a C. of E. school at Whittlesford for 30 boys and 15 girls from poor families, from Duxford and Sawston if there were too few in Whittlesford.[22] A master was to teach the boys reading, writing, and accounting, and a mistress to teach the girls reading, sewing, and knitting. The surplus income was for apprenticing, books, and clothing the children.

After Westley's widow died in 1737 the land was conveyed in 1741 to trustees, who hired the guildhall as a schoolroom; no Scheme was approved until the 1760s, when the last surviving trustee's heirs tried to appropriate the income. Ebenezer Hollick (d. 1792) had recovered the estate in Chancery by 1768, and in 1771 a Scheme in accordance with Westley's will was made. The endowment produced *c.* £45 a year in 1771, and £70 in 1825,[23] including the hire of a schoolroom, the guildhall having been converted by 1770 into a poorhouse. In the early 19th century the boys' and girls' schools were usually held in separate cottages.[24] In 1854 the boys' schoolroom was in a ruinous shed, once a blacksmith's shop.[25] About 1810 the master was a bad-tempered one-armed ex-marine,[26] and the veteran in office in 1854 was thought unlikely to merit a certificate.[27] In 1825 the boys were taught reading, writing, and arithmetic, the girls sewing and knitting.[28] Numbers rose from 30 boys and 30 girls in 1818[29] to 40 and 42 in 1846.[30] In 1833 the parish contained two other schools, with 24 pupils paid for by their parents, and one evening school with 10 pupils.[31]

P. C. M. Haskin, vicar from 1844, wished to reform the charity school, but was long frustrated by the aged trustee, Ebenezer Hollick, 'an old infidel chartist'. About 1854 Haskin sought a Scheme by which the management of the school, freed from the detailed prescriptions in Westley's will, was transferred to the churchwardens, and subscribers. Under the Scheme funds from Westley's endowment, later supplemented by a parliamentary grant, were used to buy a site and build a school-house, completed in 1859, in which a National school, including an infants' department, was then opened.[32] In 1860 its staff of four included one certificated teacher.[33] In 1873 there were *c.* 90 boys and girls, besides 47 infants. The endowment probably yielded £50 of the cost, the remainder being raised from subscriptions and school-pence.[34] Financial difficulties *c.* 1888 were met by a voluntary rate,[35] but that resource had failed by 1897, when the endowment produced only £15 and subscriptions £56.[36] Attendance at the school, including the infants, declined steadily from a peak of 174 in 1884 to 105 *c.* 1904, and 75 *c.* 1927.[37] The school estate was sold in 1922 for £875, the interest being usually spent thereafter on building repairs.[38] The school was re-organized in 1930 into junior mixed and infants' departments, the older children being sent to Sawston village college.[39] Whittlesford school, still C. of E., was moved in 1972 from its old site on the high street to new buildings off Mill Lane, accommodating 300.[40]

In 1873 an adult evening class was attended by *c.* 20 pupils.[41] A girls' boarding school was set up *c.* 1808, and one was kept between *c.* 1892 and 1904 at the Grove.[42]

CHARITIES FOR THE POOR. Whittlesford's principal charity[43] was formed by combining Cyprian's lands and Swallow's charity. Cyprian's lands, formerly the endowment of a chantry, amounted in 1517 to *c.* 70 a.[44] It is not known how the endowment escaped confiscation or was used before 1625, when it was agreed that the money should no longer be used to pay taxes or the king's carriage, but should meet the common charges of the inhabitants.[45]

Nicholas Swallow, by will proved 1557, left his house and croft, after his widow's death, for the common charges of the town and 20 a. for a dole to the poor at Christmas and Easter.[46] The trustees entered on 22 a. in 1558. From 1591 to *c.* 1608, by agreement, they received only a £2 rent-charge for the land, but vindicated their proper title in 1624.

In 1649 Cyprian's and Swallow's lands were settled on the same trustees. In the late 17th century they yielded together *c.* £6 a year, usually distributed by the overseers.[47] The combined lands, called the town or poor land, amounted to 94 a. in 1767 and

[17] C.U.L., E.D.R., C 1/4.
[18] Ibid. C 3/25; C.R.O., R 58/5, vol. ii, p. 79.
[19] *Camb. Ind. Press*, 30 June 1961.
[20] C.U.L., E.D.R., B 2/18, f. 75v.
[21] Ibid. B 2/25, f. 10v.
[22] The following passage up to 1837 is based mainly on *31st Rep. Com. Char.* 208–12.
[23] C.U.L., E.D.R., C 1/6.
[24] *Church School Inquiry, 1846–7*, 8–9.
[25] Char. Com. files.
[26] C.R.O., R 58/5, vol. ii, p. 255.
[27] Char. Com. files.
[28] C.U.L., E.D.R., C 1/6.
[29] *Educ. of Poor Digest*, 67.
[30] *Church School Inquiry, 1846–7*, 8–9.
[31] *Educ. Enquiry Abstract*, 62.
[32] Ed. 49/544; cf. C.R.O., 391/P 70.
[33] *Rep. of Educ. Cttee. of Council, 1860–1* [2828], p. 125, H.C. (1861), xlix.
[34] C.U.L., E.D.R., C 3/25, 27, 39; cf. Ed. 49/544.
[35] *E.D.R.* (1888), 105.
[36] C.U.L., E.D.R., C 3/39.
[37] *Rep. of Educ. Cttee. of Council, 1884–5* [C. 4483-I], p. 524, H.C. (1884–5), xxiii; *List of Schs. under Admin. of Bd. 1903–4* [Cd. 2011], p. 17, H.C. (1904), lxxv; *Bd. of Educ., List 21, 1927* (H.M.S.O.), 17.
[38] Ed 49/544.
[39] Black, *Cambs. Educ. Rec.* 78; cf. *Bd. of Educ., List 21, 1932* (H.M.S.O.), 18.
[40] Cf. *Camb. Evening News*, 10 Feb. 1970; 11 Apr. 1972; ex inf. the vicar.
[41] C.U.L., E.D.R., C 3/25.
[42] *Camb. Chron.* 3 Dec. 1808; *Kelly's Dir. Cambs.* (1892, 1900, 1904).
[43] This section is based, unless otherwise stated, on *31st Rep. Com. Char.* 212–14; Char. Com. files.
[44] C.R.O., R 58/5, vol. iii, pp. 129–36, 163–5.
[45] *Eng. Topog.* (Gent. Mag. Libr.), ii. 98.
[46] C 114/186, copy of will.
[47] C.R.O., R 58/5, vol. iii, pp. 2–42.

were let for *c.* £35,[48] of which £7 was in the 1780s given in cash to the poor at Christmas and Easter, and the remainder used for poor-relief.[49] In 1815 35 a. were allotted to the charity for general purposes, and 10 a. for the poor's distribution.[50]

In 1837, when the income was no longer used to relieve the poor-rates, £16 was indiscriminately distributed in cash doles, 2 guineas subscribed to Addenbrooke's Hospital, Cambridge, and the rest mainly used for selling coal at reduced prices. In the 1850s up to £20 a year was given in cash among *c.* 140 families[51] in proportion to the number of their children. In 1880 122 families, about two-thirds of the population, each received 1¼ cwt. of cheap coal and up to 3*s.* in money. The charity farm was let from 1789 until *c.* 1892 to members of the Maynard family,[52] to which several trustees belonged. In 1880 the vicar complained of favouritism and nepotism, and a Scheme imposed in 1881 made tenants and suppliers ineligible as trustees. In 1900 £9 out of £100 income was spent in doles and £50–60 in selling coal at half-price to *c.* 100 people.

A Scheme of 1911 combined the other parish charities with the town lands charity, the income to be spent partly on such public purposes as building cottages and lighting roads, partly in subscriptions to hospitals and provident societies and on apprenticeships, limiting the amount to be spent on doles to the aged poor to £30 a year. In 1925 two cottages were built on the Charity land, and over £40 a year was subscribed to the local coal club. In 1960 the yearly income was *c.* £180, of which £73 was spent on charitable purposes. After 1968 the old charity farm-house and other cottages were sold, and the proceeds went towards building 15 houses, mostly bungalows, completed in 1971, in Swallow's Close, to be let to young married couples and pensioners. Of £240 yielded by the land in 1970 *c.* £75 was used for charity, the balance paying mortgages on the new houses.

John Tharbye, by will proved 1617, left a rent-charge of £2 a year for the poor. The charity was known as Scutches after the property charged.[53] In 1783 it was distributed at Christmas and Easter,[54] and in 1837 with Swallow's money. Whittlesford also benefited from Lettice Martin's dole,[55] receiving in 1786 13*s.* 4*d.*[56] and in 1837 £1 6*s.*, distributed to poor widows, and holding £52 17*s.* worth of stock in 1911, when Scutches and Martin's charities were merged with the town land charity. Scutches rent-charge was redeemed for £30 in 1970.

Land allotted for common rights attached to the guildhall, called the town house in 1837 when it was considered to be a charity, was then let by the parish officers who applied the rent in relief of the rates. Land called Askams, owned by the Huddlestons, then rendered to the township 1 qr. of malt in place of its aftermath. The beer made from the malt was drunk by those beating the bounds of the parish on Ganging Monday. Payment ceased *c.* 1850.[57]

[48] C 114/33, terrier 1767; C.U.L., E.D.R., B 8/1.
[49] *Char. Don.* i. 102; C.U.L., E.D.R., B 7/1, pp. 134–5.
[50] C.R.O., P 171/26/1, p. 94.
[51] Ibid. R 58/5, vol. iii, pp. 167–8.
[52] Ibid. p. 159.
[53] Prob. 11/130 (P.C.C. 96 Walden).
[54] C.U.L., E.D.R., B 7/1, p. 135.
[55] Cf. p. 219.
[56] *Char. Don.* i. 102.
[57] C.R.O., R 58/5, vol. iii, p. 253; vii, pp. 137–8, 143.

ANALYSIS OF CAMBRIDGESHIRE HEARTH TAX ASSESSMENTS, CHILFORD, RADFIELD, AND WHITTLESFORD HUNDREDS, 1662, 1666, AND 1674

Introductory Note

THE following analyses have been prepared from the Cambridgeshire Hearth Tax Assessments preserved in the Public Record Office for 1662 Michaelmas [E 179/84/436], 1666 Lady Day [E 179/244/22], and 1674 Lady Day [E 179/244/23]. In addition, the 1664 Michaelmas Assessment [E 179/84/437], which was a revision of that of 1662 Michaelmas, has been used for recovering the details of hearths in some defective entries. The assessments have been fully described, and the nature of the tax and value of its records have been briefly discussed, in *V.C.H. Cambs.* iii. 500 and iv. 272. The 1662 lists were prepared by petty constables in June and early July 1662 and were designed to be simply lists of taxpayers, though during the next eighteen months many persons in the lists secured exemption. The 1666 lists were made out in the summer of 1666, after collection had taken place, by the officers of George Wilmot, the sub-farmer, and are drawn up under the headings of 'Paid' and 'Unpaid'; many of the persons with one or two hearths included under the latter heading may have been entitled to exemption, but the lists do not indicate them since they were included as taxpayers in default. The lists for 1674 were made out by the sub-collectors of Edward Miller, the receiver, with the assistance of parish officials, during the spring and summer of 1674, after collection had been made. They are divided into taxpayers and those legally exempt by certificate. The exemption certificates themselves, made out during the winter of 1673–4, survive incomplete and heavily damaged [E 179/326/10]. Among the taxpayers the owners of empty or recently destroyed houses or hearths and the occupiers of houses recently built or with new hearths in them are distinguished. The exempt may include paupers, even though they did not need to be certified.

The three documents have been analysed on the same principle. Against each place is given, in separate columns, the total of entries recording persons as occupiers of from one to ten hearths and a further column gives the occupiers of houses with eleven or more hearths: final columns give the total number of entries and hearths in each place. For 1662 only one line is needed for each place. For 1666 three lines are needed: for those recorded as 'Paid'; for the 'Unpaid'; and for the combined total of the two categories. For 1674 up to four lines may be needed: for the taxpayers; for those among the taxpayers with empty houses, etc.; for the exempt; and for the combined total of those categories. No exempt are recorded for seven out of the twenty-five places in the three hundreds. Certificates also survive which were made out in 1672 or early in 1673 and apparently served for the three collections from Lady Day 1672 to Lady Day 1673 [E 179/84/440]. They include certificates for all the seven places without exempt in 1674, all save one of which were in Chilford hundred. The probable reason why no exempt were recorded for those places in 1674 was that the certificates did not reach the clerk of the peace in time for enrolment. It has therefore been thought useful to give the number of persons in the certificates of 1672 in footnotes to each hundred in the table for 1674. The number is in some cases less than the number of names originally entered in the certificate because in a few certificates some names were cancelled before, or when, the justices of the peace countersigned them. In general, attention is also drawn in footnotes to a few special entries, chiefly of alms-houses or town houses; and to differences, through faulty addition and chiefly in 1674, between the total number of hearths in the recorded entries and the total given in the documents.

In conclusion, a word may be said about the relative comprehensiveness of the assessments. It may be understood that in all lists a person may occur more than once when as a landlord he or she is entered for the hearths in a tenant's house, but in general the number of entries represents the number of households. There is little difference between the totals of entries for 1666 and 1674, which are slightly higher for 1666. The difference is one of five or less, either way, for all but one place in Chilford, two in Radfield, and three in Whittlesford hundreds. In the remaining six places the total is higher for 1666 in four—Ickleton (6), Stetchworth (6), Great Abington (8), and Whittlesford (10)—and for 1674 in two—Burrough Green (7) and Hinxton (8). In Chilford hundred the 1666 lists have the most entries for eight places, the 1674 lists for two places, and in the other they are equal; six of the eight places, however, for which the 1674 lists have fewer entries have no exempt, and if the exempt in those places were about the same as those certified in 1672 the balance would be much more even. In Radfield hundred the 1666 lists have the most entries for six places, the 1674 lists for one, and in the other two they are equal. In Whittlesford hundred the 1666 lists have the most entries for three places and the 1674 lists the most for the other two. The 1662 lists were intended to include only taxpayers. In most other districts in the county they have, however, generally supplied a list for one place which has solely, or jointly with one of the other assessments, the highest number of entries. In these three hundreds they do not do so; their number of entries is the lowest for all places and, in total, the lowest for each hundred. Their totals are also substantially lower than the totals of those chargeable in 1674, but since far more details of the 1662 assessments survive for the country as a whole than from any other date, those lists are the most useful for comparative studies of England and Wales generally.

ANALYSIS OF CAMBRIDGESHIRE HEARTH TAX: CHILFORD, RADFIELD, AND WHITTLESFORD HUNDREDS

1662 Michaelmas

	Totals of entries, with hearths											Totals	
	1	*2*	*3*	*4*	*5*	*6*	*7*	*8*	*9*	*10*	*over 10*	*Entries*	*Hearths*
CHILFORD HUNDRED													
Great Abington	16	7	3	1	..	..	..	..	..	..	1 of 24	28	67
Little Abington	4	6	4	1	..	..	..	..	1	..	..	16	41
Babraham	3	5	4	..	2	..	..	1	1	..	1 of 43	17	95
Bartlow	..	3	3	1	..	1	..	..	1	..	..	9	34
Castle Camps	18	11	8	2	1	1	..	..	..	1	1 of 20 1 of 15	44	128
Shudy Camps	10	6	3	4	4	2	2	..	..	..	..	31	93
Hildersham	2	6	4	..	..	..	4	1	..	..	..	17	62
Horseheath	12	8	3	3	2	1	3	..	..	..	..	32	86
Linton	65	42	24	12	4	..	5	2	1	1	1 of 19 1 of 14	158	392
Pampisford	9	8	4	2	1	1	..	..	1	..	..	26	65
West Wickham	6	7	5	3	3	1	..	..	..	..	1 of 11	26	79
Total	145	109	65	29	17	7	14	4	5	2	7 (with 146)	404	1,142
RADFIELD HUNDRED													
Balsham	17	27	6	2	..	..	..	1	..	1	1 of 12	55	127
Brinkley	9	5	3	3	3	2	..	1	..	..	..	26	75
Burrough Green	25	4	2	..	..	..	1	..	..	..	1 of 26	33	72
Carlton cum Willingham	17	8	2	2	..	..	..	..	1	..	..	30	56
Dullingham	26	8	8	5	1	1	1	..	..	..	..	50	104
Stetchworth	15	10	5	1	1	1	..	..	..	..	..	33	65
Westley Waterless	7	3	2	..	..	1	..	1	..	..	..	14	33
Weston Colville	20	10	2	..	2	..	..	..	1	..	..	35	65
West Wratting	18	21	6	5	1	1	..	..	1	..	..	53	118
Total	154	96	36	18	8	6	2	3	3	1	2 (with 38)	329	715
WHITTLESFORD HUNDRED													
Duxford	31	22	3	6	..	..	1	..	..	..	1 of 12	64	127
Hinxton[a]	8	10	7	8	4	..	..	..	..	..	1 of 11	38	112
Ickleton[b]	33	17	4	9	2	..	..	..	..	..	..	65	125
Sawston	16	12	8	4	1	1	..	..	1	..	1 of 17	44	117
Whittlesford	16	16	12	4	..	..	3	1	1	1	..	54	148
Total	104	77	34	31	7	1	4	1	2	1	3 (with 40)	265	629

[a] Two details of hearths recovered from the 1662 copy in the 1664 Michaelmas assessment.
[b] Eight details of hearths similarly recovered.

1666 Lady Day

	Totals of entries, with hearths											Totals	
	1	*2*	*3*	*4*	*5*	*6*	*7*	*8*	*9*	*10*	*over 10*	*Entries*	*Hearths*
CHILFORD HUNDRED													
Great Abington, paid	21	10	3	1	..	..	..	..	..	..	1 of 14	36	68
unpaid	5	..	2	2	..	..	..	..	..	..	..	9	19
total	26	10	5	3	..	..	..	..	..	..	1	45	87
Little Abington, paid	4	6	1	5	..	..	..	..	..	..	..	16	39
unpaid	2	2	1	..	..	..	..	..	..	..	..	5	9
total	6	8	2	5	..	..	..	..	..	..	..	21	48
Babraham, paid	7	3	5	1	1	..	..	..	1	..	1 of 40	19	86
unpaid	5	..	..	..	1	..	..	..	..	..	..	6	10
total	12	3	5	1	2	..	..	..	1	..	1	25	96
Bartlow, paid	6	1	1	3	1	1	..	..	..	..	..	13	34
unpaid	1	1	..	..	..	..	..	..	..	..	..	2	3
total	7	2	1	3	1	1	..	..	..	..	..	15	37
Castle Camps, paid	32	11	3	3	1	..	..	..	..	2	1 of 20	53	120
unpaid	10	3	1	1	..	1	..	..	..	..	..	16	29
total	42	14	4	4	1	1	..	..	..	2	1	69	149
Shudy Camps, paid	14	10	7	3	2	..	..	..	..	..	..	36	77
unpaid	2	1	2	1	..	..	..	..	..	..	..	6	14
total	16	11	9	4	2	..	..	..	..	..	..	42	91
Hildersham, paid	7	4	4	2	..	1	2	..	..	..	..	20	55
unpaid	2	..	..	2	..	..	..	..	..	..	..	4	10
total	9	4	4	4	..	1	2	..	..	..	..	24	65
Horseheath, paid	19	9	4	3	1	1	..	..	..	..	1 of 16	38	88
unpaid	4	2	2	2	..	..	..	..	..	..	..	10	22
total	23	11	6	5	1	1	..	..	..	..	1	48	110
Linton, paid	72	41	21	14	2	1	2	2	..	..	1 of 18	156	337[a]
unpaid	15	2	3	6	2	1	..	..	..	..	..	29	68
total	87	43	24	20	4	2	2	2	..	..	1	185	405
Pampisford, paid	15	10	5	2	..	1	..	..	..	..	..	33	64
unpaid	2	..	1	1	..	..	..	..	..	..	..	4	9
total	17	10	6	3	..	1	..	..	..	..	..	37	73
West Wickham, paid	24	7	2	3	2	1	..	..	..	1	..	40	82
unpaid	7	2	..	1	..	..	..	..	..	..	..	10	15
total	31	9	2	4	2	1	..	..	..	1	..	50	97
Total, paid	221	112	56	40	10	6	4	2	1	3	5 (with 108)	460	1,050
unpaid	55	13	12	16	3	2	..	..	..	..	..	101	208
combined	276	125	68	56	13	8	4	2	1	3	5	561	1,258
RADFIELD HUNDRED													
Balsham, paid	31	24	8	4	1	1	..	..	..	1	..	70	140
unpaid	19[b]	9	2	1	..	..	..	..	..	..	..	31	47
total	50	33	10	5	1	1	..	..	..	1	..	101	187
Brinkley, paid	15	5	5	2	2	1	..	1	..	..	..	31	72
unpaid	2	2	1	..	1	..	..	..	..	..	..	6	14
total	17	7	6	2	3	1	..	1	..	..	..	37	86
Burrough Green, paid	27	7	1	1	..	..	1	..	..	..	1 of 20	38	75
unpaid	5	4	1	1	..	..	..	..	..	..	..	11	20
total	32	11	2	2	..	..	1	..	..	..	1	49	95
Carlton cum Willingham, paid	32	2	3	2	..	..	1	..	..	..	..	40	60
unpaid	5	3	1	1	..	..	..	..	..	..	..	10	18
total	37	5	4	3	..	..	1	..	..	..	..	50	78
Dullingham, paid	52	11	7	3	1	2	..	..	..	..	..	76	124
unpaid	11	3	..	..	..	1	..	..	..	..	..	15	23
total	63	14	7	3	1	3	..	..	..	..	..	91	147
Stetchworth, paid	20	8	6	2	2	..	1	..	..	..	..	39	79
unpaid	11	4	1	..	..	..	..	..	..	..	..	16	22
total	31	12	7	2	2	..	1	..	..	..	..	55	101
Westley Waterless, paid	11	3	..	1	..	..	1	..	..	..	..	16	28
unpaid	1	..	1	..	..	..	..	..	..	..	..	2	4
total	12	3	1	1	..	..	1	..	..	..	..	18	32
Weston Colville, paid	19	11	3	2	..	..	1	..	..	..	1 of 12	37	77
unpaid	3	2	1	1	..	..	..	..	..	..	..	7	14
total	22	13	4	3	..	..	1	..	..	..	1	44	91

[a] The total in the book is given wrongly as 336, owing to the entries on p. 13 of the book being wrongly totted as 58 hearths instead of 59.

[b] One of the entries is for *Two Townehouses*.

1666 Lady Day (cont.)

	Totals of entries, with hearths											Totals	
	1	*2*	*3*	*4*	*5*	*6*	*7*	*8*	*9*	*10*	*over 10*	*Entries*	*Hearths*
RADFIELD HUNDRED (*cont.*)													
West Wratting, paid	30	14	3	4	..	4[c]	..	..	..	..	..	55	107
unpaid	8	2	3	1	..	..	..	..	..	..	..	14	25
total	38	16	6	5	..	4	..	..	..	..	..	69	132
Total, paid	237	85	36	21	6	8	5	1	..	1	2 (with 32)	402	762
unpaid	65	29	11	5	1	1	..	..	..	..	..	112	187
combined	302	114	47	26	7	9	5	1	..	1	2	514	949
WHITTLESFORD HUNDRED													
Duxford, paid	25	19	12	6	1	1	1	..	..	1	..	66	151
unpaid	9	2	1	3	..	..	..	..	..	..	..	15	28
total	34	21	13	9	1	1	1	..	..	1	..	81	179
Hinxton, paid	16	6	6	4	2	..	..	..	..	..	1 of 11	35	83
unpaid	6	1	..	2	..	..	..	..	..	..	..	9	16
total	22	7	6	6	2	..	..	..	..	..	1	44	99
Ickleton, paid	52	26	6	4	..	..	..	..	..	..	..	88	138
unpaid	4	1	2	2	1	..	..	..	..	..	..	10	25
total	56	27	8	6	1	..	..	..	..	..	..	98	163
Sawston, paid	25	19	11	7	1	2	..	..	..	..	1 of 12	66	153
unpaid	4	3[d]	2	2	1	..	..	..	..	..	..	12	29
total	29	22	13	9	2	2	..	..	..	..	1	78	182
Whittlesford, paid	44	13	8	4	..	1	..	1	1	1	..	73	143
unpaid	2	3	1	1	1	1	..	..	..	..	..	9	26
total	46	16	9	5	1	2	..	1	1	1	..	82	169
Total, paid	162	83	43	25	4	4	1	1	1	2	2 (with 23)	328	668
unpaid	25	10	6	10	3	1	..	..	..	..	..	55	124
combined	187	93	49	35	7	5	1	1	1	2	2	383	792

[c] One of the entries is noted as for two houses.
[d] One of the entries has two names against it.

1674 Lady Day

	Totals of entries, with hearths											Totals	
	1	*2*	*3*	*4*	*5*	*6*	*7*	*8*	*9*	*10*	*over 10*	*Entries*	*Hearths*
CHILFORD HUNDRED[a]													
Great Abington, charged	18	12	3	3	..	..	..	..	..	..	1 of 24	37	87
Little Abington, charged	2	7	2	4	..	..	..	..	1	..	..	16	47
Babraham, charged	8	1	7	..	2	..	..	..	2	..	1 of 40	21	99
Bartlow, charged	3	2	2	1	1	1	..	..	1	..	..	11	37
Castle Camps, charged	16	15	7	4	1	1	..	..	..	1	1 of 20 1 of 15	47	139
exempt	26	..	..	..	..	..	..	..	..	..	..	26	26
total	42	15	7	4	1	1	..	..	..	1	2	73	165
Shudy Camps, charged	13	7	7	6	2	2	..	..	..	..	..	37	94
exempt	8	..	..	..	..	..	..	..	..	..	..	8	8
total	21	7	7	6	2	2	..	..	..	..	..	45	102
Hildersham, charged	4	6	4	1	..	1	3	1	..	..	..	20	67
Horseheath, charged	17	8	6	3	3	1	2	..	..	..	1 of 26	41	124
exempt	6	..	..	..	..	..	..	..	..	..	..	6	6
total	23	8	6	3	3	1	2	..	..	..	1	47	130
Linton, charged	47	42	23	16	10	3	5	1	..	2	1 of 19	150	414[b]
exempt	29	2	..	..	..	..	..	..	..	..	..	31	33
total	76	44	23	16	10	3	5	1	..	2	1	181	447
Pampisford, charged	12	14	4	2	1	..	..	..	1	..	..	34	74

[a] The numbers of persons in the 1672 exemption certificates for Chilford hundred were: Great Abington 7; Little Abington 2; Babraham 6; Bartlow 3; Castle Camps 26; Shudy Camps 7; Hildersham 2; Horseheath 10; Linton 28; Pampisford 3; West Wickham 16. Fragmentary 1674 certificates survive for Castle Camps, Horseheath, Linton, and West Wickham.
[b] Wrongly given as 411 in the roll.

1674 Lady Day (cont.)

	Totals of entries, with hearths											*Totals*	
	1	*2*	*3*	*4*	*5*	*6*	*7*	*8*	*9*	*10*	*over 10*	*Entries*	*Hearths*
CHILFORD HUNDRED (*cont.*)													
West Wickham, charged	8	9	6	3	3	1	..	..	..	..	1 of 11	31	88[c]
exempt	19	..	..	..	..	..	..	..	..	..	..	19	19
total	27	9	6	3	3	1	..	..	..	..	1	50	107
Total, charged	148	123	71	43	23	10	10	2	5	3	7 (with 155)	445	1,270
exempt	88	2	..	..	..	..	..	..	..	..	..	90	92
combined	235	125	71	43	23	10	10	2	5	3	7	535	1,362
RADFIELD HUNDRED[d]													
Balsham, charged	27	26	12	6	3	1	..	1	..	..	1 of 13	77	181
empty	1	..	..	..	..	..	..	..	..	..	..	1	1
newly erected	1	..	..	..	..	..	..	..	..	..	..	1	1
exempt	22	..	..	..	..	..	..	..	..	..	..	22	22
total	51	26	12	6	3	1	..	1	..	..	1	101	205
Brinkley, charged	7	6	3	4	2	4	..	1	..	..	..	27	86
exempt	7	..	..	..	..	..	..	..	..	..	..	7	7
total	14	6	3	4	2	4	..	1	..	..	..	34	93
Burrough Green, charged	19	6	2	..	..	1	..	..	..	..	1 of 22	29	65
newly erected[e]	2	..	..	..	..	..	..	..	..	..	..	..	2
exempt	25	..	..	..	..	..	..	..	..	..	..	25	25
total	46	6	2	..	..	1	..	..	..	..	1	54	92
Carlton cum Willingham, charged	27	4	3	3	..	..	..	..	..	..	1 of 11	38	67
exempt	7	..	..	..	..	..	..	..	..	..	..	7	7
total	34	4	3	3	..	..	..	..	..	..	1	45	74
Dullingham, charged	32	14	10	3	2	1	1	..	..	..	..	53	125
empty	..	1	..	..	..	..	..	..	..	..	..	1	2
exempt	34	..	..	..	..	..	..	..	..	..	..	34	34
total	66	15	10	3	2	1	1	..	..	..	..	88	161
Stetchworth, charged	17	12	8	3	3	..	..	..	..	..	1 of 13	44	105[f]
exempt	5	..	..	..	..	..	..	..	..	..	..	5	5
total	22	12	8	3	3	..	..	..	..	..	1	49	120
Westley Waterless, charged	9	4	..	..	1	..	1	1	..	..	..	16	37
Weston Colville, charged	14	11	7	1	1	..	1	..	..	..	1 of 11	36	84
exempt	8	..	..	..	..	..	..	..	..	..	..	8	8
total	22	11	7	1	1	..	1	..	..	..	1	44	92
West Wratting, charged	22	21	6	4	1	3	..	..	1	..	..	58	130
exempt	9	..	..	..	..	..	..	..	..	..	..	9	9
total	31	21	6	4	1	3	..	..	1	..	..	67	139
Total, charged	174	104	51	24	13	10	3	3	1	..	5 (with 70)	388	880
empty	1	1	..	..	..	..	..	..	..	..	..	2	3
newly erected	3	..	..	..	..	..	..	..	..	..	..	1	3
exempt	117	..	..	..	..	..	..	..	..	..	..	117	117
combined	295	105	51	24	13	10	3	3	1	..	5	508	1,003
WHITTLESFORD HUNDRED[g]													
Duxford, charged	16	23	10	9	2	..	2	..	..	..	1 of 13	65	165
exempt	15	..	..	..	..	..	..	..	..	..	..	15	15
total	31	23	10	9	2	..	2	..	..	..	1	78	180
Hinxton, charged	9	10[h]	8	7	5	..	..	..	..	..	1 of 11	40	117
exempt	12	..	..	..	..	..	..	..	..	..	..	12	12
total	21	10	8	7	5	..	..	..	..	..	1	52	129
Ickleton, charged	32	27	5	11	3	..	..	..	..	..	..	78	160
exempt	14	..	..	..	..	..	..	..	..	..	..	14	14
total	36	27	5	11	3	..	..	..	..	..	..	92	174

[c] Wrongly given as 81 in the roll.

[d] The numbers of persons in the 1672 exemption certificates for Radfield hundred were: Balsham 15, 5 of whom were receiving alms; Burrough Green 24; Dullingham 35, 5 of whom were living in town houses; Stetchworth 17; Westley 6; Weston Colville 7. Damaged 1674 certificates survive for Balsham, Brinkley, Burrough Green, Carlton cum Willingham, Dullingham, Stetchworth, Weston Colville, and West Wratting.

[e] Both the newly erected hearths were in existing houses and are therefore not reckoned in the totals of entries.

[f] Wrongly given as 96 in the roll.

[g] The numbers of persons in the 1672 exemption certificates for Whittlesford hundred were: Duxford 23, of whom 4 were marked paid; Hinxton 9; Ickleton 16; Sawston 15, of whom 8 were marked paid; Whittlesford 9.

[h] One of these entries—*Tho Clarke for the vicarage*—is marginated *Arrear 1 yeare*, but is not said to be empty.

1674 Lady Day (cont.)

	Totals of entries, with hearths											Totals	
	1	*2*	*3*	*4*	*5*	*6*	*7*	*8*	*9*	*10*	*over 10*	*Entries*	*Hearths*
WHITTLESFORD HUNDRED (*cont.*)													
Sawston, charged	22	17[i]	12	7	1	3	..	..	..	..	1 of 17	63	160
empty	..	..	..	1	..	..	..	..	..	..	..	1	4
exempt	17	..	..	..	..	..	..	..	..	..	..	17	17
total	39	17	12	8	1	3	..	..	..	..	1	81	181
Whittlesford, charged	17	19	11	6	..	..	1	1	1	1	..	57	146
empty	..	..	..	..	..	..	..	..	1	..	..	1	9
exempt	14	..	..	..	..	..	..	..	..	..	..	14	14
total	31	19	11	6	..	..	1	1	2	1	..	72	169
Total, charged	96	96	46	40	11	3	3	1	1	1	3 (with 41)	301	746
empty	..	..	..	1	..	..	..	..	1	..	..	2	13
exempt	72	..	..	..	..	..	..	..	..	..	..	72	72
combined	168	96	46	41	11	3	3	1	2	1	3	375	831

[i] One of these is marked *Arrear 1 yeare*, but is not said to be empty.

INDEX

NOTE. An italic page-number denotes an illustration on that page or facing it. The pages containing the substantive history of a parish are indicated by bold-face type. A page-number followed by *n* is a reference only to the footnotes on that page.

Among the abbreviations used in the index the following may require elucidation: adv., advowson; agric., agriculture; Alex., Alexander; And., Andrew; Ant., Antony; abp., archbishop; archit., architect; Bart., Bartholomew; Benj., Benjamin; bp., bishop; b., born; Camb., Cambridge; Cath., Catherine; chant., chantry(-ies); char., charity(-ies); Chas., Charles; Chris., Christopher; ch., church(es); Coll., College; ctss., countess; ct(s)., court(s); Dan., Daniel; dau., daughter; d., died; dom. archit., domestic architecture; Edm., Edmund; Edw., Edward; Eliz., Elizabeth; fam., family; fl., flourished; Fred., Frederick; Geof., Geoffrey; Geo., George; Gilb., Gilbert; Hen., Henry; ho., house(s); Humph., Humphrey; inc., inclosure; ind., industry; Jas., James; Jos., Joseph; Kath., Katherine; ld., lord; man., manor(s); Marg., Margaret; mkt., market; m., married; Mat., Matthew; Mic., Michael; Nat., Nathaniel; Nic., Nicholas; nonconf., nonconformity; par., parish; pk., park; Phil., Philip; pop., population; prehist., prehistoric; prot., protestant; rly., railway; rem., remain(s); Ric., Richard; Rob., Robert; Rog., Roger; Rom., Roman; R.D., Rural District; Sam., Samuel; sch., school(s); Sim., Simon; s., son; sta., station; Steph., Stephen; Thos., Thomas; vct., viscount; Wal., Walter; w., wife; Wm., William.

CORRIGENDA

See also corrigenda printed in *Index* to Volumes I–IV and in *V.C.H. Cambs.* v. 337.

Vol. II, page 21, line 7, *for* 'NE.' *read* 'SW.'
,, ,, 21, line 8, *for* 'NW.' *read* 'SE.'
,, ,, 21, line 26, *for* 'NW.' *read* 'SE.'
,, ,, 21, plan, *reverse orientation*
,, ,, 35, *s.v.* Melbourn, *the two moats at Sheene Farm should be under Meldreth*
,, ,, 132, note 18, *for* 'And' *read* 'An'
,, ,, 133, line 8, *for* '2 October 1850' *read* '21 October 1850'
,, ,, 133, line 9, *for* '3 August 1851' *read* '1 August 1851'
,, ,, 133, line 13, *for* '1 August 1862' *read* 'Passengers 7 July 1862 Goods 1 August 1862'
,, ,, 267*a*, line 8, *delete* '50 acres'
Vol. IV, page 105*a*, line 4 from end, *for* 'Worsley' *read* 'Scrimshire'
,, ,, 105*a*, line 3 from end, *for* 'was still' *read* ', apparently, was'
,, ,, 105, note 58, *for* 'ii (2)' *read* 'ii (1)'
Index vol., page 60, *between* 'Scrimshaw' *and* 'Scrope' *insert* 'Scrimshire, Malbon, iv. 105'
,, ,, 75, *s.v.* Worsley, *delete* 'Malton, iv. 105;'
Vol. V, page xvi, line 34, *for* 'H.C. 294 (1820), xii' *read* 'H.C. 82 (1818), xix'
,, ,, 149*a*, line 8, *for* '(1273–1324)' *read* '(1273–1334)'
,, ,, 235*b*, line 38, *for* 'lease of 1523' *read* 'lease of 1520'
,, ,, 255*a*, line 14 from end, *for* 'Norton' *read* 'Nocton'
,, ,, 255*a*, lines 14–13 from end, *for* '1420' *read* '1423' *and for* 'Margaret' *read* 'Margery'
,, ,, 255, note 15, *for* '78.' *read* '78, which gives Norton in error for Nocton.'
,, ,, 284*a*, line 4, *for* 'Prince's' *read* 'Marsh's'
,, ,, 284, note 52, *for* 'T. H. Cook' *read* 'T. A. Cook'
,, ,, 308*b*, *s.v.* Blyton, *for* 'Marg., m. John Wimbish' *read* 'Margery, m. John Wimbish'
,, ,, 314*c*, *s.v.* Dowsing, *for* '24' *read* '25'
,, ,, 323*b*, *s.v.* Lincolnshire, *for* 'Norton' *read* 'Nocton'
,, ,, 326*b*, *between* 'Nixon' *and* 'Noel' *insert* 'Nocton (Lincs.), 255'
,, ,, 326*c*, *s.v.* Norton (Lincs.), *delete entry*
,, ,, 335*c*, *s.v.* Wimbish, *for* 'Marg.' *read* 'Margery'